Incomplete Information: Rough Set Analysis

Studies in Fuzziness and Soft Computing

Editor-in-chief
Prof. Janusz Kacprzyk
Systems Research Institute
Polish Academy of Sciences
u. Newelska 6
01-447 Warsaw, Poland
E-mail: kacprzyk@ibspan.waw.pl

Vol. 1. J. Kacprzyk and M. Fedrizzi (Eds.)
Fuzzy Regression Analysis, 1992
ISBN 3-7908-0591-2 (ISBN 83-85262-07-5)

Vol. 2. A.M. Delgado et al. (Eds.)
Fuzzy Optimization, 1994
ISBN 3-7908-0749-4

Vol. 3. A. Geyer-Schulz
Fuzzy Rule-Based Expert Systems and Genetic Machine Learning, 2nd ed. 1996
ISBN 3-7908-0964-0

Vol. 4. T. Onisawa and J. Kacprzyk (Eds.)
Reliability and Safety Analyses under Fuzziness, 1995
ISBN 3-7908-0837-7

Vol. 5. P. Bosc and J. Kacprzyk (Eds.)
Fuzziness in Database Management Systems, 1995
ISBN 3-7908-0858-X

Vol. 6. E.S. Lee and Q. Zhu
Fuzzy and Evidence Reasoning, 1995
ISBN 3-7908-0880-6

Vol. 7. B.A. Juliano and W. Bandler
Tracing Chains-of-Thought, 1996
ISBN 3-7908-0922-5

Vol. 8. F. Herrera and J.L. Verdegay (Eds.)
Genetic Algorithms and Soft Computing, 1996
ISBN 3-7908-0956-X

Vol. 9. M. Sato et al.
Fuzzy Clustering Models and Applications, 1997
ISBN 3-7908-1026-6

Vol. 10. L.C. Jain (Ed.)
Soft Computing Techniques in Knowledge-based Intelligent Engineering Systems, 1997
ISBN 3-7908-1035-5

Vol. 11. W. Mielczarski (Ed.)
Fuzzy Logic Techniques in Power Systems, 1998
ISBN 3-7908-1044-4

Vol. 12. B. Bouchon-Meunier (Ed.)
Aggregation and Fusion of Imperfect Information, 1998
ISBN 3-7908-1048-7

Ewa Orłowska (Ed.)

Incomplete Information: Rough Set Analysis

With 54 Figures
and 23 Tables

Physica-Verlag
A Springer-Verlag Company

Prof. Dr. Ewa Orłowska
Institute of Telecommunications
ul. Szachowa 1
PL-04-894 Warsaw, Poland

ISBN 978-3-7908-2457-5 e-ISBN 978-3-7908-1888-8

Library of Congress Cataloging-in-Publication Data
Die Deutsche Bibliothek – CIP-Einheitsaufnahme
Incomplete information: rough set analysis; with 23 tables / Ewa Orłowska (ed.). – Heidelberg; New York: Physica-Verl., 1998
(Studies in fuzziness and soft computing; Vol. 13)

Printed in Germany

Hardcover Design: Erich Kirchner, Heidelberg

88/2202-5 4 3 2 1 0 – Printed on acid-free paper

Foreword

In 1982, Professor Pawlak published his seminal paper on what he called "rough sets" - a work which opened a new direction in the development of theories of incomplete information. Today, a decade and a half later, the theory of rough sets has evolved into a far-reaching methodology for dealing with a wide variety of issues centering on incompleteness and imprecision of information - issues which play a key role in the conception and design of intelligent information systems.

"Incomplete Information: Rough Set Analysis" - or RSA for short - presents an up-to-date and highly authoritative account of the current status of the basic theory, its many extensions and wide-ranging applications. Edited by Professor Ewa Orłowska, one of the leading contributors to the theory of rough sets, RSA is a collection of nineteen well-integrated chapters authored by experts in rough set theory and related fields. A common thread that runs through these chapters ties the concept of incompleteness of information to those of indiscernibility and similarity.

Some time ago when I became aware of Professor Pawlak's work on rough sets, a question that naturally arouse in my mind was: What is the connection, if any, between the concepts of rough sets and fuzzy sets? I realized that the similarity of the terms "rough sets" and "fuzzy sets" tends to create a misunderstanding. More specifically, a fuzzy set is a class with unsharp boundaries whereas a rough set is a crisp set which is coarsely described. There is a close connection, however, between the concept of a rough set and that of a fuzzy graph. Thus, a fuzzy graph is a disjunction of granules which collectively approximate to a function or a relation, with a granule being a clump of points which are drawn together by indiscernibility, similarity or functionality. In the case of rough sets, the granules are equivalence classes which are the elements of a partition. When the concept of equivalence is generalized to that of similarity, as was done in some of the recent extensions of the theory of rough sets, the concept of a rough set and that of fuzzy graph become very close in meaning and use.

Although there is this point of contact between the theories of rough sets and fuzzy sets, the theories evolved in different directions and, today, are largely complementary rather than competitive. However, the recent extensions of the theory of rough sets in which the focus moves away from indiscernibility - a crisp concept - to similarity, which is a fuzzy concept, bring the two theories close together.

What is more fundamental is that both theories address, each in its own way, the basic issue of information granulation, with the theory of rough sets focused on crisp information granulation and the theory of fuzzy sets focused on fuzzy information granulation. What is true of both theories is that information granulation plays a central role in most of their applications.

The theory of rough sets provides an effective and broadly applicable tool for the analysis and design of information systems. By providing an authoritative and up-to-date account of the theory of rough sets, RSA serves an important function. Clearly, it is a must reading for anyone who has a serious interest in information processing and knowledge-based systems. Professor Pawlak, the father of the theory of rough sets, the editor, Professor Ewa Orłowska and the contributors to RSA deserve our deep thanks and warm congratulations.

Berkeley, CA, Spring 1997

Lotfi A. Zadeh

Table of Contents

Preface

After nearly 15 years of research on the rough set theory methods of modelling and processing incomplete information this book provides an exhaustive survey of what we have got and where we have arrived. Over all these years the technical and foundational development of the field have been very fast. We accumulated a vast amount of sophisticated formalisms and applicable methods.

The problems of incompleteness of information and processing incomplete information may be placed in the sphere of artificial intelligence, even though many of them have a longer genealogy going back to the methodology of science, cognitive science and logic. The term 'reasoning with incomplete information' in the narrow sense means the way of representing a partial information that is available to a user about a fragment of reality, and the way of processing such an information. But a broader interpretation of that term has become common in recent years. It is used to denote the interdisciplinary sphere of research concerned with the search for methods of modelling uncertain knowledge acquired from partial and imprecise information and of using such a knowledge. Those methods can refer to any application domain and any level of knowledge: one seeks ways of representing both object-level knowledge and meta-level knowledge, the latter being the knowledge about the former. In this broader sense, reasoning with incomplete information is a subfield of the area of knowledge representation and cognitive science.

The modelling of uncertain knowledge that is acquired from incomplete information is a very important topic of research in Artificial Intelligence. The increasing number of applications relying on software that processes incomplete information makes it necessary to develop formal theories for modelling such systems as well as methods, techniques and tools to ensure the correctness of the modelled systems. In theoretical issues uncertainty of knowledge and incompleteness of information are strongly connected to algebra and logic, and inherit many classical concepts developed in those established fields of science. However, the analysis of practical issues considerably interacts with the classical theories, bringing new problems and new insights.

Incompleteness of information is manifested in various ways: Information might be fuzzy, interval based, probabilistic, possibilistic etc. In this book we concentrate on the rough set theory approach to incompleteness. The methods of reasoning with incomplete information presented here and the methods offered by probability theory and fuzzy set theory are not contending, but complementing formalisms that model different aspects of human cognition.

Usually, our primary concern about a given domain is semantic in character. Our views of the respective part of the real word are formed in abstraction from language. The term domain is understood here both generally and broadly. In object-level knowledge, we are interested in a given sphere of applications, for instance, in medical system, in patients, and certain data about them. In meta-level knowledge, the domain consists of the knowledge at the former level. We can continue this sequence of domains through an arbitrary number of levels. Hence, the first step in the development of a method of representation and handling uncertain knowledge should be a definition of the conceptual primitives specific to the knowledge level. Thus the object-level primitives should characterise the domain of applications, and the meta-level primitive concepts should accordingly describe the characteristics of the object-level knowledge in question. Next, the relationships between these concepts are to be established. The second step is to provide the linguistic counterpart of the conceptual model adopted in the first step. The point here is to define a formal language to be used in expressing information about those domains, to which a given conceptual model pertains. There must be a strict correspondence between the model and the language connected with it. The primitive concepts included in the model should have their linguistic counterparts at the level of atomic expressions. Furthermore, compound expressions should be constructed from the atomic ones with the use of operators selected according to the type of the domain. The third step is to provide the methods for handling and processing the knowledge represented by means of the language introduced within the second component of the method. The working out of such a method consists in formulating logical principles to be used and the methods of inference that are in the agreement with those principles.

The methods presented in this book cover all the three aspects of representation listed above. They provide a deep insight into the concept of incompleteness of information, and allow for explicit articulation of a type of incompleteness and its consequences for knowledge representation and acquisition. The paradigms of incompleteness treated in this book appear under the names 'indiscernibility-type incompleteness' and 'similarity-type incompleteness'. The adoption of a domain the information about which is to be represented and processed includes, among others, the listing of objects of the domain and their properties. It may occur that two different objects possess the same properties in the given domain. This means that those objects are indiscernible (or indistinguishable) in terms of the given set of properties, and this fact is the manifestation of indiscernibility-type incompleteness of information about the objects. In this setting indiscernibility of entities is related to lack of discriminative resources. This phenomenon appears in various forms and is addressed in different ways in computer science. The problem of identity and indiscernibility is a central issue in every theory of knowledge and the Leibnitzian principle of 'indiscernibility of identical's' is a cornerstone of many of them. Also the natural interpretation of indiscernibility as being relative to properties that are attributed to objects is crucial in many areas. All the theories and methods presented in the book have in their background this view of indiscernibility.

Indiscernibility-type incompleteness of information has far reaching consequences for knowledge discovery methods. From incomplete information we can only get lower and upper approximations of concepts, not the crisp concepts. The approximations are obtained in the process of qualitative analysis of given information and the basic component of that analysis is indiscernibility. Similarly, the objects can share some properties but differ with respect to the others. This fact is interpreted as the manifestation of similarity-type incompleteness of information. In both cases information about objects available from the data about the domain under consideration is not sufficient to characterise these objects uniquely, exactly and precisely. We are only able to describe them with a tolerance, up to indiscernibility or up to similarity. In fact, possibilities and our abilities of discrimination are never perfect, and discriminative resources in application domains are never total. As a consequence, these two types of incompleteness of information are inseparably connected to our lingual and practical handling of objects, and they constitute the epistemological source of uncertainty of knowledge. Methods of analysis and discovery of knowledge from indiscernibility-type incomplete information are collectively named as rough set theory.

The major goal of the book is to provide readers with a comprehensive perspective on developments related to rough set modelling and handling of incomplete information and uncertain knowledge discovered from that information. The book provides an overview of the current research and applications concerned with specification and reasoning with incomplete information that takes into account indiscernibility and/or similarity induced by that information. The book aims at unifying theory and practice by demonstrating how concepts developed on the theoretical level apply to various areas of AI, in particular to machine learning and dependency theory. The material included in the book provides an environment for the study of mathematical theory of indiscernibility/similarity-based incompleteness of information, as well as the means of specification and design of systems that handle incomplete information.

Collected together in this book are the articles which contain an up to date discussion of the state-of-the-art in rough set-based models and methods of reasoning with incomplete information. Each article is written specifically for this volume.

In the introductory chapter the fundamentals of rough set theory are surveyed in a general setting that creates an environment for both studying the classical theory and for development of its various extensions.

Papers in Part I are concerned with learning decision rules. In Chapter 2 a method of generating descriptions of structured objects is presented and discussed taking into account indiscernibility. Based on this method, an algorithm is presented for the automatic extraction of relevant features in a system for hand-written digit recognition. The two papers in Chapter 3 and 4 are concerned with machine learning and the analysis of learning algorithms. In both these papers learning from examples is discussed. The basic assumption is that input data are presented in the form of a decision table, where examples are characterised by attributes and categorised by a decision value. The first of these papers describes a theoretical basis for learning from inconsistent examples. A new tool, called a lower boundary and based on rough set theory, is introduced. The lower boundary may be used for efficient testing whether a subset of the set of all attributes is a covering. The concept of lower boundary may be used not only for inconsistent decision tables but also for consistent decision tables, thus becoming a universal tool. The second paper presents results of experiments on two machine learning algorithms: LEM1 and LEM2. At the beginning of the LERS building process (Learning from Examples based on Rough Sets) at the University of Kansas, the fundamental question was which versions of two basic algorithms, namely a global algorithm LEM1 or a local algorithm LEM2 should be used. In LEM1, two different methods of computing coverings were compared: a direct method based on comparing partitions on the set of all examples and a method based on lower boundaries, introduced in the former paper. The conclusion drawn from experiments is that the lower boundary method is more efficient computationally. Also, a number of different ways of performing local computations in the LEM2 algorithm were experimentally compared. The final conclusion is that in computing local coverings the best sequence of criteria is: the maximum intersection first, then the maximum conditional probability.

In the papers of Part II, rough set modelling paradigms and model analysis techniques are presented for specification of and reasoning with incomplete information, with an emphasis on their broad applicability.

The papers in Part III provide an exhaustive, self-contained survey of algebraic systems and methods that can be a common framework for modelling incomplete information structures.

Part IV is concerned with the methods of specification and reasoning about constraints in information systems.

In Part V an analysis of indiscernibility-type incompleteness of information is presented from various methodological points of view. Methods of reasoning in the presence of indiscernibility are developed, and their applications are discussed.

In Part VI similarity-type incompleteness of information is discussed, and various manifestations of similarity are analysed. Deduction systems for similarity-based reasoning are presented and investigated.

In Part VII a generalisation of the deduction methods presented in Part V and Part VI is investigated that allows for direct representation of both sets of objects and sets of their properties that lead to indiscernibility and/or similarity. Next, first order extensions of indiscernibility-based formalisms are presented and discussed.

It is worthwhile to stress that the methods of reasoning presented in the book do not require any auxiliary assumptions about data, like probability or membership function values. They are suitable to direct processing of the data given in the form of a list of objects and their properties.

The material presented in the book provides a deep insight into the methods of algebra, logic and proof theory that can be used to rigorously synthesise, specify, verify, model and process incomplete information. We emphasise and reinforce the point that formal methods can and should be used in practical constructions of high quality, reliable knowledge-based systems. We focus on declarative programming paradigm of computational logic augmented with the means of detecting incompleteness of information, and making some of its manifestations an explicit component of this information. The book creates an environment both for the study of the theory of uncertainty of knowledge and the design of knowledge-based systems.

The book is intended for the readers involved in the theory and practice of AI systems and in cognitive science, in particular for the researchers and practitioners interested in development and application of tools for specification, verification, analysis and construction of knowledge based systems. The book presents original advances in these fields, both theoretical and practical. The material presented in the book can also be a basis for a graduate course on formal methods in computer science.

Chapter 1

Introduction: What You Always Wanted to Know about Rough Sets

Ewa Orłowska

Institute of Telecommunications

Szachowa 1, 04–894 Warsaw, Poland

E–mail: orlowska@itl.waw.pl

Abstract: In this chapter the major principles and the methodology of the rough set–style analysis of data are presented and discussed. A survey of various formalisms that provide the tools of this analysis is given. We discuss the aspects of incompleteness of information that can be handled in the presented formalisms. The formalisms are related to the methods and/or structures presented in this volume, in each case we point out a relevant link and we give the reference to the respective chapter.

1 Principles of Rough Set Analysis

In this chapter we attempt to identify the elementary components of the rough set–style analysis of data. First, we discuss a type of data that the rough set analysis applies to. Second, we show how in the successive steps of the analysis we derive and discover new knowledge from the given data. We identify the basic 'building blocks' of that knowledge and we show how each of them can be derived from the given data. Third, we present formal models of the structures built with those elementary components of knowledge and we suggest a methodology for investigation of these models. It includes investigation of the typical methodological problems well established and recognised in logic and universal algebra, but moreover, it poses some new problems that emerge in connection with the rough set analysis.

Rough set analysis applies to data that have the form of descriptions of some entities, referred to as objects, in terms of their properties. Consider, for example, a file containing information about the degrees of some persons P1,...,P6 and the languages that these persons speak:

	Lan	Deg
P1	F, D	BS, MS, PhD
P2	H, R	BS
P3	F, D, S	BS, MS
P4	F	BS, MS
P5	F, D	BS
P6	R	BS

In that file we are given a set OB={P1,...,P6} of objects. Properties of these objects are of the form 'having some degree' and 'speaking some language'. 'Degree' and 'Language' play the role of attributes, they determine these properties in that each of the properties can be expressed by an attribute and a value of this attribute. Hence, we have the set AT={Degree (Deg), Language (Lan)} of attributes, and the sets VAL_{Deg}={BS, MS, PhD}, VAL_{Lan}={D, F, H, R, S} of values of these attributes. According to information given in our file object P2 possesses properties {H, R} of speaking Hungarian and Romanian, object P3 does not possess those properties. Formally, the attributes can be treated as mappings a: $OB \rightarrow P(VAL_a)$ from the set of objects into the family of subsets of their values. So, for example, Lan(P2)={H, R}. Any collection of data specified in the form of a structure (OB, AT, $\{VAL_a: a \in AT\}$) such that OB is a nonempty set (of objects), AT is a nonempty set of functions (attributes) a: $OB \rightarrow P(VAL_a)$, and $\{VAL_a: a \in AT\}$ is an indexed family of sets (of values of the attributes) is referred to as an information system. It should be stressed that an information system contains always a partial information that is available at a given moment of time. Any set a(x) where $a \in AT$, $x \in OB$ is referred to as the set of a–properties of object x, and its complement $VAL_a - a(x)$ is referred to as the set of negative a–properties of x. In our example {H, R} is the set of Lan–properties of P2 and the negative Lan–properties of P3. Rough set analysis applies to data that can be presented in the form of an information system. A discussion of this kind of data can also be found in chapters 11 and 16.

The two major principles of rough set analysis are:

(1) In the course of the analysis only the given data are processed. These data constitute an explicit information provided by a user. No external parameters outside these data (e.g. degrees of certainty) are needed. Any presuppositions about a character of data (e.g. that they are numerical) are avoided.

(2) The main tool of the analysis are relationships among data items derived from the explicit information. These relationships are an implicit information that should be disclosed in the course of the analysis.

In the following sections we present a survey of the formal methods of the rough set–style analysis that constitute a practical realisation of the principles (1) and (2).

2 Information Relations Derived from Information Systems

Let an information system (OB, AT, $\{VAL_a: a\in AT\}$) be given. Relationships among the objects from set OB are determined by their properties. Typically, the relationships have the form of binary relations. These relations are referred to as information relations. There are two major groups of information relations: the relations that reflect various forms of indistinguishability of objects in terms of their properties and the relations that indicate distinguishability of the objects. Below we present a list of the classes of atomic relations that generate the whole family of information relations. To each of these classes we assign a name that suggests an aspect of incompleteness of information that the underlying relations reflect.

We admit the usual notation from the calculus of sets: $\cup$, $\cap$, $-$, $\subseteq$ are union, intersection complement and inclusion of sets, respectively; $\emptyset$ is the empty set.

Indistinguishability relations:

- Strong (weak) indiscernibility: $(x,y)\in ind(A)$ $(wind(A))$ iff $a(x)=a(y)$ for all (some) $a\in A$,
- Strong (weak) similarity: $(x,y)\in sim(A)$ $(wsim(A))$ iff $a(x)\cap a(y)\neq\emptyset$ for all (some) $a\in A$,
- Strong (weak) forward inclusion: $(x,y)\in fin$ $(wfin(A))$ iff $a(x)\subseteq a(y)$ for all (some) $a\in A$,
- Strong (weak) backward inclusion: $(x,y)\in bin$ $(wbin(A))$ iff $a(y)\subseteq a(x)$ for all (some) $a\in A$,
- Strong (weak) negative similarity: $(x,y)\in nim(A)$ $(wnim(A))$ iff $-a(x)\cap -a(y)\neq\emptyset$ for all (some) $a\in A$,
- Strong (weak) incomplementarity: $(x,y)\in icom(A)$ $(wicom(A))$ iff $a(x)\neq -a(y)$ for all (some) $a\in A$,

  where $-$ is the complement with respect to set VAL_a.

Observe that if A is a singleton set, then the respective strong and weak relations coincide. Intuitively, two objects are A–indiscernible whenever their sets of a–properties determined by the attributes $a\in A$ are the same. In other words, up to discriminative resources provided by properties determined by A these objects are the same. For example, in the file given in section 1 objects P3 and P4 are Deg–indiscernible since we have Deg(P3)=Deg(P4). Objects are weakly A–indiscernible whenever some of the sets of their properties determined by members of A are the same. Objects are A–similar (weakly similar) whenever all (some) the sets of their properties determined by the attributes from A are not disjoint, in other words the objects share some properties. For example, $(P1, P3)\in sim(Lan)$. A similar intuitive interpretation can be given to all the remaining information relations. We have, for example, $(P2, P5)\in icom(Lan)$ which means that, up to our present knowledge, P2 and P5 are not 'completely' distinct with respect to the attribute Lan, because the set of Lan–properties of P2 does not equal to the set of negative Lan–properties of P5.

Since the file contains only a partial information, one cannot exclude that they both speak Swedish, although at the present moment of the analysis this fact is not known.

All the relations defined above reflect various kinds of indistinguishability–type incompleteness of information which is given in the form of an information system. Indiscernibility relations derived from information systems were introduced in Konrad et al. (1981). Similarity and forward inclusion were introduced in Orłowska (1985). Negative similarity was introduced in Vakarelov (1991).

Distinguishability relations:

- Strong (weak) diversity: $(x,y) \in div(A)$ $(wdiv(A))$ iff $a(x) \neq a(y)$ for all (some) $a \in A$,
- Strong (weak) right orthogonality: $(x,y) \in rort(A)$ $(wrort(A))$ iff $a(x) \subseteq -a(y)$ for all (some) $a \in A$,
- Strong (weak) left orthogonality: $(x,y) \in lort(A)$ $(wlort(A))$ iff $-a(x) \subseteq a(y)$ for all (some) $a \in A$,
- Strong (weak) right negative similarity: $(x,y) \in rnim(A)$ $(wrnim(A))$ iff $a(x) \cap -a(y) \neq \emptyset$ for all (some) $a \in A$,
- Strong (weak) left negative similarity: $(x,y) \in lnim(A)$ $(wlnim(A))$ iff $-a(x) \cap a(y) \neq \emptyset$ for all (some) $a \in A$,
- Strong (weak) complementarity: $(x,y) \in com(A)$ $(wcom(A))$ iff $a(x) = -a(y)$ for all (some) $a \in A$,

  where $-$ is the complement with respect to set VAL_a.

Objects are A–orthogonal (weakly orthogonal) whenever all (some) of their sets of properties (or negative properties) determined by attributes from A are disjoint, and they are A–diverse (weakly diverse) if all (some) of their sets of properties determined by members of A are different. Objects are A–complementary if their respective sets of properties are complements of each other. In our example we have $Lan(P3) = -Lan(P2)$, hence $(P3, P2) \in com(Lan)$; $Lan(P3) \subseteq -Lan(P6)$, so $(P3, P6) \in rort(Lan)$.

For any information system the information relations derived from the system are defined according to a certain common pattern. It leads to a closure property on the set of relations generated by the information relations with the standard operations of union, intersection, complement, and converse of relations. This closure property is expressed in the form of derivability in a certain logical system related to syllogistic (Wedberg 1948, Shepherdson 1956). The details can be found in Orłowska (1996). The discussion of methods of construction of 'full' classes of information relations (in some precisely defined sense) can also be found in chapter 16.

Relational systems consisting of a family of relations on a set are often referred to as frames. By a frame derived from an information system $S=(OB, AT, \{VAL_a: a \in AT\})$ we mean a relational system $K_{S,R}=(OB, \{R(A): A \subseteq AT\})$, where $\{R(A): A \subseteq AT\}$ is any of the families of information relations defined above except for forward and backward inclusions, and right and left negative similarities. For these families it is more natural to define derived frames of the form $K_{S,R,Q}$=(OB, {R(A):A ⊆AT},{Q(A):A⊆AT}), where R=fin, (wfin) and Q=bin (wbin) or R=rnim (wrnim) and Q=lnim (wlnim), respectively. Observe that relations in these frames depend on subsets of set AT. These subsets play the role of indices (or parameters), that is we deal with families of relations indexed with subsets of a set. Frames with parameterised relations are introduced in Orłowska (1988) and investigated, among others, in Konikowska (1987, 1997) and in the chapters 15 and 17 of this volume. Usually, we are interested in studying relationships between information relations that belong to different families. Hence, it is also natural to consider frames with families of relations of different types. A great variety of such frames is studied in the literature, see for example chapters 11, 15, 16, 17, Balbiani (1997), Demri and Orłowska (1996a), Konikowska (1987, 1997), Orłowska (1984, 1989), Vakarelov (1989, 1991a). However, most of them include the relations from the indistinguishability group. Till now the theories of distinguishability relations have not been developed. An elaboration of the logics for the frames with distinguishability relations and the algebraic structures with the operators determined by these relations might be a direction for further work. In chapter 13 a generalisation of the inclusion frames is discussed and an analogy to mereological treatment of the relation of 'being a part' is pointed out. A many–valued extension of information relations obtained by admitting fuzzy attributes is suggested in Orłowska (1997).

3 Information Frames

One of the directions in rough set analysis is the investigation of information frames derived from information systems. An important step in these investigations is an abstract characterisation of various classes of frames: those defined in section 2, their extensions (e.g. obtained by imposing an algebraic structure on the underlying family of relations), and some of their special cases (e.g. obtained by restricting the class of relations to the relations indexed by singleton sets of parameters). This characterisation is provided in the form of a construction of classes of frames where the relevant properties of the relations in a frame are postulated, and not any direct definitions of the relations. Each class should correspond uniquely to the respective class of frames derived from an information system. The formal models obtained in this way provide a foundation for development of the algorithms for processing both the explicit data and the relationships among them.

The following properties of relations are used in the characterisation of the frames defined in section 2. A binary relation R on a set U is:

- Reflexive: for all x∈U, (x,x)∈R (I⊆R), where I is the identity on U
- Weakly reflexive: for all x,y∈U, if (x,y)∈R, then (x.x)∈R (I∩(R;1)⊆R),
- Irreflexive: for all x∈U, (x,x)∉R (I⊆−R).
- Symmetric: for all x,y∈U, if (x,y)∈R, then (y,x)∈R ($R \subseteq R^{-1}$).
- Transitive: for all x,y,z∈U, if (x,y)∈R and (y,z)∈R, then (x,z)∈R (R;R⊆R).

- Intransitive: for all $x,y,z \in U$, if $(x,y) \in R$ and $(y,z) \in R$, then $(x,z) \notin R$ ($R;R \subseteq -R$).

where $1=U\times U$, ; is the composition of relations, and $^{-1}$ is the converse of a relation.

We introduce some generalisations of reflexivity, irreflexivity and transitivity that are needed for the characterisation of some information relations. Let R be a binary relation on U and $n \geq 1$. By an R,n–path from x to y we mean a sequence $x, x_1, \ldots, x_{n-1}, y$ such that $(x,x_1) \in R$, $(x_{n-1},y) \in R$ and for all $i=1,\ldots,n-2$ $(x_i,x_{i+1}) \in R$. Informally, an R,n–path consists of n arrows and n–1 intermediate points between x and y. We define the following properties of relation R:

- n–reflexive: for every $x \in U$ there is an R,n–path from x to x ($I \subseteq R;\ldots;R$ n–times).
- n–irreflexive: for every $x \in U$ there is no an R,n–path from x to x ($I \subseteq -R;\ldots;-R$ n–times).
- n–transitive: for all $x,y \in U$, if there is an R,n–path from x to y, then there is the R,1–path from x to y (n–times $R;\ldots;R \subseteq R$).

In particular, R is reflexive (irreflexive) iff R is 1–reflexive (1–irreflexive), R is transitive iff R is 2–transitive, and R is 3–transitive if for all $x,y,z,t \in U$, if $(x,y) \in R$, $(y,z) \in R$ and $(z,t) \in R$, then $(x,t) \in R$. In a similar way one can generalise several other properties of binary relations.

Let $K=(U, \{R(P):P \subseteq A\})$ be a relational system such that U and A are nonempty sets, and $R: P(A) \rightarrow P(U\times U)$ is a mapping that assigns binary relations on U to the subsets of set A. Elements of set A are referred to as parameters and mapping R is referred to as a type of relations (Orłowska 1988).

- K is an information frame with strong relations (FS) if for every $P,Q \subseteq A$ the relations from K satisfy the following conditions:
  $R(P\cup Q)=R(P)\cap R(Q)$
  $R(\varnothing)=U\times U$.

- K is an information frame with weak relations (FW) if for every $P,Q \subseteq A$ the relations from K satisfy the following conditions:
  $R(P\cup Q)=R(P)\cup R(Q)$
  $R(\varnothing)=\varnothing$

We define more specific classes of frames postulating some conditions that the relations are assumed to satisfy.

Information frames with indistinguishability relations:

- Indiscernibility frame (IND): an information frame with strong equivalence relations.
- Similarity frame (SIM): strong tolerance relations.
- Negative similarity frame (NIM): strong, weakly reflexive and symmetric relations.

- Incomplementarity frame (ICOM): strong symmetric relations such that for all $a \in A$, $-R(\{a\})$ is 3–transitive and n–irreflexive for every odd n.
- Inclusion frame (IN): frame of the form $(U, \{R(P):P \subseteq A\}, \{Q(P):P \subseteq A\})$ with two families of strong relations such that all relations R(P) and Q(P) are reflexive, transitive, and for all $P \subseteq A$, $R(P)=S(P)^{-1}$.
- Weak indiscernibility frame (WIND): weak tolerance relations and $R(\{a\})$ is transitive for all $a \in A$.
- Weak similarity frame (WSIM): weak tolerance relations.
- Weak negative similarity frame (WNIM): weak, symmetric relations.
- Weak incomplementarity frame (WICOM): weak symmetric relations whose complements are 3–transitive and n–irreflexive for every odd n.
- Weak inclusion frame (WIN): frame with two families of relations $(U, \{R(P):P \subseteq A\}, \{Q(P):P \subseteq A\})$ such that all relations R(P) and Q(P) are weak, reflexive relations, $R(\{a\})$ and $Q(\{a\})$ are transitive for all $a \in A$, and for all $P \subseteq A$, $R(P)= S(P)^{-1}$.

<u>Information frames with distinguishability relations:</u>

- Diversity frame (DIV): strong relations whose complements are tolerance relations and $-R(\{a\})$ is transitive for all $a \in A$.
- Right orthogonality fame (RORT): strong relations whose complements are tolerance relations.
- Left orthogonality frame (LORT): strong relations whose complements are weakly reflexive and symmetric.
- Complementarity frame (COM): strong, symmetric, 3–transitive relations that are n–irreflexive for every odd n .

  This characterisation of complementarity relations has been proposed by S. Demri (1996), the characterisation of incomplementarity, weak complementarity and weak incomplementarity relations is its consequence (see also Demri and Orłowska 1996b, 1996c).
- Right–left negative similarity frame (RLNIM): frame of the form $(U,\{R(P):P \subseteq A\},\{Q(P):P \subseteq A\})$ with two families of strong symmetric relations whose complements are reflexive , $-R(\{a\})$ and $-Q(\{a\})$ are transitive for all $a \in A$, and for all $P \subseteq A$, $-R(P)=-S(P)^{-1}$.
- Weak diversity frame (WDIV): weak relations whose complements are equivalence relations.
- Weak right orthogonality frame (WRORT): weak relations whose complements are tolerance relations.
- Weak left orthogonality frame (WLORT): weak relations whose complements are symmetric.
- Weak complementarity frame (WCOM): weak, symmetric, and for all $a \in A$, $R(\{a\})$ is 3–transitive and n–irreflexive for every odd n.
- Weak right–left negative similarity frame (WRLNIM): frame of the form $(U, \{R(P):P \subseteq A\}, \{Q(P):P \subseteq A\})$ with two families of weak symmetric relations such

that complements of relations R(P) and Q(P) are reflexive and transitive, and for all $P \subseteq A$, $-R(P)=-S(P)^{-1}$.

It is easy to see that for any information system S we have:
$K_{S,ind} \in IND$, $K_{S,sim} \in SIM$, $K_{S,nim} \in NIM$, $K_{S,icom} \in ICOM$, $K_{S,fin,bin} \in IN$,
and the analogous conditions hold for the respective frames with weak relations.

Similarly, for any information system S:
$K_{S,div} \in DIV$, $K_{S,rort} \in RORT$, $K_{S,lort} \in LORT$, $K_{S,com} \in COM$, $K_{S,rlnim} \in RLNIM$,
and the analogous conditions hold for the respective frames with weak relations.

Hence, the formal models of our concrete frames reflect all the essential distinguishing features of the respective relations derived from information systems. A natural question arises whether these concrete frames are the typical examples in the respective classes of abstract frames. To formulate this problem in a precise way we introduce the notion of informational representability of frames. Let C be a class of frames. Intuitively, a frame K from C is informationally representable if there is an information system S and a frame K_S derived form this system such that K_S is in the class C and, moreover, K is similar (e.g. isomorphic, modally equivalent etc.) to K_S. In Demri and Orłowska (1996b) the notion of informational representability of frames is introduced in a formal way, a method of proving representability is given and representability results are proved for various classes of frames. An inspiration for these results was a result of that kind for logic NIL of nondeterministic information given in Vakarelov (1987).

4 Information Operators

The next step in the rough set analysis of data is to disclose an interaction between the information relations and subsets of objects. This interaction is expressed by means of operators acting on sets of objects. Each of the operators is determined by an information relation. Let $S=(OB, AT, \{VAL_a: a \in AT\})$ be an information system and let $\{R(A): A \subseteq AT\}$ be a family of information relations derived from S. There are four major groups of operators.

<u>Information operators:</u>

[] $[R(A)]X=\{x \in OB: \text{for all } y, \text{ if } (x,y) \in R(A) \text{ then } y \in X\}$
<> $\langle R(A)\rangle X=\{x \in OB: \text{there is } y \in X \text{ such that } (x,y) \in R(A)\}$
[[]] $[[R(A)]]X=\{x \in OB: \text{for all } y, \text{ if } y \in X \text{ then } (x,y) \in R(A)\}$
<<>> $\langle\langle R(A)\rangle\rangle X=\{x \in OB: \text{there is } y \notin X \text{ such that } (x,y) \notin R(A)\}$.

Let $R(A)x=\{y \in OB: (x,y) \in R(A)\}$ be the set of all the R(A)–successors of object x. We clearly have the following:
(1) $x \in [R(A)]X$ iff $R(A)x \subseteq X$,
(2) $x \in \langle R(A)\rangle X$ iff $R(A)x \cap X \neq \emptyset$,

(3) $x \in [[R(A)]]X$ iff $(-R(A))x \subseteq -X$,

(4) $x \in \langle\langle R(A)\rangle\rangle X$ iff $(-R(A))x \cap -X \neq \emptyset$,

where the complement $-$ is taken with respect to the relevant universes, that is $-R(A)$ is an abbreviation of $OB \times OB - R(A)$ and $-X$ is to be understood as $OB-X$.

We say that operator f is dual to operator g if $f(R)X=-g(R)-X$ for any set X and any relation R. It is easy to see that we have the following pairs of dual operators:

$\langle\rangle$ $[\,]$

$\langle\langle\rangle\rangle$ $[[\,]]$

Operators f and g are said to be conjugated if $f(R)X=g(-R)-X$ for any X and R. The following are the conjugated pairs of operators:

$\langle\rangle$ $\langle\langle\rangle\rangle$

$[\,]$ $[[\,]]$

From these relationships between the operators one can deduce relationships between the respective sets of objects defined with these operators.

Several instances of the information operators are extensively studied in the literature. The classical rough set analysis employs the indiscernibility relations. It is easy to see that, in view of (1) and (2), if R(A) is an indiscernibility relation determined by a set A of attributes, then $[R(A)]X$ and $\langle R(A)\rangle X$ are the A–lower and the A–upper approximation of X, respectively. For a detailed discussion of the operators $[]$ and $\langle\rangle$ determined by the indiscernibility relations and their application to the analysis of vagueness of concepts see chapter 11, Reed (1994 – chapter 7), Orłowska (1988a). An application of these operators to learning concepts can be found in chapters 3 and 4. A philosophically oriented discussion of relationships between the indiscernibility and the identity as well as a proposal for some other information operators that can play the role of approximation operators can be found in chapter 12.

Clearly, if R(A) is an indiscernibility relation, then $x \in [[R(A)]]X$ iff X is included in the equivalence class of R(A) generated by object x, and $x \in [R(A)]X$ iff the equivalence class of R(A) generated by object x is included in X. Hence, these operators enable us to express strong definability of sets considered in chapter 11.

Operators of the form $[[R]]$ lead to various kinds of complement operations. If R(A) is a diversity relation, then the structure $(P(OB), -, \cup, \cap, \{[[R(A)]]: A \subseteq AT\})$ is a Brouwer–Zadeh lattice, where the information operators $[[R(A)]]$ play the role of (multiple) intuitionistic–like orthocomplementations (Cattaneo 1997). The intuitive interpretation of set $[[R(A)]]X$ in this case is that any object x in this set is different (in the sense of diversity relation) from all the objects in the set X. The similar operators are investigated in the context of quantum logics (Cattaneo and Nistico 1989, Cattaneo et al. 1993, Goldblatt 1993 – chapter 2).

In general, observe that for any relation R on a set U, the operators defined as superpositions $[[R]][[R^{-1}]]$ and $[[R^{-1}]][[R]]$, are closure operations on P(U). If R is symmetric, then clearly the operations $[[R]]$ and $[[R^{-1}]]$ coincide. Let R be a symmetric relation, and consider the set of closed elements of P(U), that is the elements that satisfy $X=[[R]][[R]]X$. It forms a complete lattice and, moreover, $[[R]]$

is de Morgan negation in this lattice. If, in addition, R is irreflexive, then [[R]] is the Boolean complement.

Any information system $S=(OB, AT, \{VAL_a: a\in AT\})$ determines derived algebras with information operators in the following way. Let $(P(OB), -,\cup,\cap,OB,\emptyset)$ be the Boolean algebra of the subsets of the set OB of objects. Each set $A\subseteq AT$ determines a family of information relations defined as in section 2, and these relations in turn determine the respective information operators. Adjoining these operators to this Boolean algebra we form the following algebras. Let R be any type of information relations from {ind, sim, fin, bin, nim, icom, div, rort, lort, rnim, lnim, com}, and let wR be the type of the respective weak relation. Then we define:

<u>Information algebras derived from an information system:</u>

- $B_{S,\langle R\rangle}=(P(OB), -,\cup,\cap,OB,\emptyset,\{\langle R(A)\rangle: A\subseteq AT\})$
- $B_{S,\langle wR\rangle}=(P(OB), -,\cup,\cap,OB,\emptyset,\{\langle wR(A)\rangle: A\subseteq AT\})$
- $B_{S,\langle\langle R\rangle\rangle}=(P(OB), -,\cup,\cap,OB,\emptyset,\{\langle\langle R(A)\rangle\rangle: A\subseteq AT\})$
- $B_{S,\langle\langle wR\rangle\rangle}=(P(OB), -,\cup,\cap,OB,\emptyset,\{\langle\langle wR(A)\rangle\rangle: A\subseteq AT\})$.

Algebras $B_{S,\langle R\rangle}$ and $B_{S,\langle wR\rangle}$ resemble the normal Boolean algebras with operators introduced in Jonsson and Tarski (1951, 1952). A normal Boolean algebra with operators (normal BAO) is an algebra $(B, \{f_i: i\in I\})$ such that B is a Boolean algebra and each f_i is an operation of some finite rank that is additive in each of its arguments, and normal, that is it takes on the value 0 whenever one of the arguments is 0. Algebras $B_{S,\langle R\rangle}$ and $B_{S,\langle wR\rangle}$ satisfy these conditions. However, in these algebras the family of operators adjoined to the Boolean algebra is indexed with subsets, and not with elements of a set. It is needed for modeling adequately the information operators which are parameterised with subsets of attributes. The remaining algebras apparently do not belong to BAO: the $\langle\langle\rangle\rangle$ operators are neither normal nor additive. Observe that within the family of the normal BAO's we cannot distinguish between operators determined by strong and weak relations. In the following section we present the abstract families of algebraic systems that capture all the relevant features of the algebras derived from information systems (Orłowska 1995). These formal models of information algebras derived from information systems provide the calculi for computing the effects of actions of information operators (in particular the classical approximation operators) on sets of objects. They enable us development of a theory of uncertainty where a variety of aspects of vagueness of concepts is taken into account, not only the indiscernibility, as it is the case in the classical rough set analysis.

5 Information Algebras

Information algebras are extensions of complete atomic Boolean algebras obtained by adjoining families of unary parameterised operators and by postulating some additional axioms. We define four classes of information algebras.

Let $\Delta=(B, (f(P): P\subseteq A\})$ be an algebraic system such that B is a complete and atomic Boolean algebra $(B,-,+,\cdot,1,0)$, A is a nonempty finite set, and each f(P) is an unary operator in B.

- Δ is an <u>information algebra with strong normal operators</u> (SN) if for all P,Q $\subseteq A$ and $x,y\in B$ the following conditions are satisfied:
  $f(P)0=0$
  $f(P)(x+y)=f(P)x+f(P)y$
  If $x\neq 0$, then $f(\emptyset)x=1$
  If x is an atom of B, then $f(P\cup Q)x=f(P)x\cdot f(Q)x$

- Δ is an <u>information algebra with weak normal operators</u> (WN) if for all P,Q $\subseteq A$ and $x,y\in B$ the following conditions are satisfied:
  $f(P)0=0$
  $f(P)(x+y)=f(P)x+f(P)y$
  $f(\emptyset)x=0$
  $f(P\cup Q)x=f(P)x+f(Q)x$

- Δ is an <u>information algebra with strong conormal operators</u> (SCN) iff for all $P,Q\subseteq A$ and $x,y\in B$ the following conditions are satisfied:
  $f(P)1=0$
  $f(P)(x\cdot y)=f(P)x+f(P)y$
  $f(\emptyset)x=0$
  $f(P\cup Q)x=f(P)x+f(Q)x$

- Δ is an <u>information algebra with weak conormal operators</u> (WCN) iff for all $P,Q\subseteq A$ and $x,y\in B$ the following conditions are satisfied:
  $f(P)1=0$
  $f(P)(x\cdot y)=f(P)x+f(P)y$
  If $x\neq 1$, then $f(\emptyset)x=1$
  If x is a coatom of B, then $f(P\cup Q)x=f(P)x\cdot f(Q)x$

It is clear that for any information system S and for any relation types R and wR we have:

- $B_{S,<R>}\in SN$, $B_{S,<wR>}\in WN$, $B_{S,<<R>>}\in SCN$, and $B_{S,<<wR>>}\in WCN$.

The classes defined above enable us to distinguish between weak and strong operators and between normal and conormal operators. To model the operators determined by information relations from a particular class, we need more specific classes of algebras. Till now the following classes have been proposed (Orłowska 1995):

- An indiscernibility algebra (IND) is an algebra from class SN such that the following conditions are satisfied for all $P \subseteq A$:
  $x \leq f(P)x$
  $f(P)(x \cdot f(P)y) = f(P)x \cdot f(P)y$.

- A weak indiscernibility algebra (WIND) is an algebra from class WN such that the following conditions are satisfied for all $P \subseteq A$:
  $x \leq f(P)x$
  $x \cdot f(P)y = 0$ iff $y \cdot f(P)x = 0$.
  $f(a)(x \cdot f(a)y) = f(a)x \cdot f(a)y$, where $a \in A$

- A similarity (weak similarity) algebra (SIM, WSIM, respectively) is an algebra from class SN (WN) such that the following conditions are satisfied for all $P \subseteq A$:
  $x \leq f(P)x$
  $x \cdot f(P)y = 0$ iff $y \cdot f(P)x = 0$.

- A right orthogonality (weak right orthogonality) algebra (RORT, WRORT, respectively) is an algebra from class SCN (WCN) such that the following conditions are satisfied for all $P \subseteq A$:
  $x \leq f(P)(-x)$
  $x \cdot f(P)y = 0$ iff $y + f(P)x = 1$.

- A diversity algebra (DIV) is an algebra from class SCN such that the following conditions are satisfied for all $P \subseteq A$:
  $x \leq f(P)(-x)$
  $x \cdot f(P)y = 0$ iff $y + f(P)x = 1$.
  $f(a)(x + -f(a)y) = f(a)x \cdot f(a)y$, where $a \in A$

- A weak diversity algebra of type A (WDIV) is an algebra from class WCN such that the following conditions are satisfied for all $P \subseteq A$:
  $x \leq f(P)(-x)$
  $f(P)(x + -f(P)y) = f(P)x \cdot f(P)y$

For any information system S the information algebras derived from S satisfy the following conditions:

- $B_{S,\langle ind \rangle} \in IND$, $B_{S,\langle wind \rangle} \in WIND$, $B_{S,\langle sim \rangle} \in SIM$, $B_{S,\langle wsim \rangle} \in WSIM$,
- $B_{S,\langle\langle rort \rangle\rangle} \in RORT$, $B_{S,\langle\langle wrort \rangle\rangle} \in WRORT$, $B_{S,\langle\langle div \rangle\rangle} \in DIV$, $B_{S,\langle\langle wdiv \rangle\rangle} \in WDIV$.

These facts show that the abstract characterisation of the algebraic structures derived from information systems captures all the relevant features of these structures.

Algebraic systems related to indiscernibility algebras were originated in Iwiński (1987). The classes of algebras introduced by Iwiński have been an inspiration for the studies of algebras derived from the indiscernibility frames determined by information systems. Indiscernibility algebras in a slightly different form have been introduced and investigated in Comer (1991). The intended interpretation of these algebras was that the set A represented a set of attributes, and operators f(P) were the algebraic versions of the operators <ind(P)>. An attempt to define similarity algebras has been made in Pomykała (1993). A further development is needed of the classes of abstract information algebras that would be the counterparts of the algebras derived from information systems with the operators determined by the information relations of type R=fin, bin, nim, icom, lort, rnim, lnim, com, and the respective types of the form wR.

The abstract structures are adequate models of the concrete structures provided that they are informationally representable. We say that an algebra Δ from a class C of information algebras is informationally representable iff there is an information system S and an algebra $B_S \in C$ such that Δ is isomorphic with B_S. Some results of that kind can be found in SanJuan (1996). Similarly, an important issue is a relationship between information frames and information algebras. An extension of the Jonsson–Tarski duality theory (Jonsson and Tarski 1951, 1952) for the information frames and the information algebras, suggested in Orłowska (1995), has been developed in SanJuan (1996).

A number of other algebraic structures derived from information systems have been identified and characterised in an abstract way. Some results in this direction are presented in chapters 5, 6 and in Banerjee and Wasilewska (1995), Düntsch (1992), Pomykała and Pomykała (1988), SanJuan (1996), Wasilewska (1997), Wasilewska and Vigneron (1995, 1996, 1997).

6 Information Logics

Information operators defined in section 4 are also used as propositional operations in logical systems designed for reasoning about data given in the form of an information system. These logics are referred to as information logics. Most often information logics are modal logics whose semantics is defined in terms of information frames. From the logical perspective operators [ ] and <> are necessity and possibility operators, respectively, and [[ ]], <<>> are sufficiency operators (Gargov et al. 1987).

Let a modal language be given such that its formulas are built from propositional variables taken from an infinite denumerable set VARPROP with the classical propositional connectives of negation ($\neg$), disjunction ($\vee$), conjunction ($\wedge$), implication ($\rightarrow$), equivalence ($\leftrightarrow$), and information operators $\langle\rangle$, $[\,]$, $\langle\langle\rangle\rangle$, $[[\,]]$ that play the role of modal operators. As usual, each modal operator is determined by a binary relation, so in the modal language we admit constants that denote these relations. For the sake of simplicity we denote these constants with the same symbols as the relations in the respective models, and we write $\langle R(P)\rangle$, $[R(P)]$, $\langle\langle R(P)\rangle\rangle$, $[[R(P)]]$ in the formulas. Let $K=(U, \{R(P):P\subseteq A\})$ be an information frame. A model based on the frame K is any system of the form $M=(K, m)$ such that m is a meaning function that assigns subsets of U to propositional variables and relations R(P) to the respective relational constants. In the usual way we define satisfiability of formulas by objects from U:

M,x sat p iff $x\in m(p)$ for $p\in$ VARPROP,
M,x sat $\neg F$ iff not M,x sat F,
M,x sat $F\vee G$ iff M,x sat F or M,x sat G,
M,x sat $F\wedge G$ iff M,x sat F and M,x sat G,
M,x sat $F\rightarrow G$ iff M,x sat $\neg F\vee G$,
M,x sat $F\leftrightarrow G$ iff M,x sat $(F\rightarrow G)\wedge(G\rightarrow F)$,
M,x sat $[R(P)]F$ iff for all $y\in U$, $(x,y)\in R(P)$ implies M,y sat F,
M,x sat $\langle R(P)\rangle F$ iff there is $y\in U$ such that $(x,y)\in R(P)$ and M,y sat F,
M,x sat $[[R(P)]]F$ iff for all $y\in U$, M,y sat F implies $(x,y)\in R(P)$,
M,x sat $\langle\langle R(P)\rangle\rangle F$ iff there is $y\in U$ such that not M,y sat F and $(x,y)\notin R(P)$.

A formula F is true in model $M=(U, \{R(P):P\subseteq A\}, m)$ ($\models_M F$) iff M,x sat F for all $x\in U$. Formula F is true in frame $K=(U, \{R(P):P\subseteq A\})$ ($\models_K F$) iff $\models_M F$ for every model M based on K. Formula F is true in a class C of frames iff $\models_K F$ for every frame $K\in C$. By a logic L(C) of class C of frames we mean the set of formulas that are true in C. We say that F is valid in L(C) ($L(C)\models F$) iff F is true in C. In any modal language by 'true' and 'false' we denote formulas of the form $F\vee\neg F$ and $F\wedge\neg F$, respectively.

Modal formulas described properties of relations. Below we give a list of formulas that correspond to properties of relations from the information frames considered in this paper. The list should be read as follows: for each pair formula–property, the formula is true in a frame iff the underlying relation from the frame possesses the property.

$K=(U, \{R(P):P\subseteq A\})$ is a frame with strong relations iff for all $P,Q\subseteq A$ the following formulas are true in K:

(s1) $\langle\langle R(P\cup Q)\rangle\rangle\mathrm{false}\leftrightarrow\langle\langle R(P)\rangle\rangle\mathrm{false}\vee\langle\langle R(Q)\rangle\rangle\mathrm{false}$
(s2) $\neg\langle\langle R(\emptyset)\rangle\rangle\mathrm{false}$.

$K=(U, \{R(P):P\subseteq A\})$ is a frame with weak relations iff for all $P,Q\subseteq A$ the following formulas are true in K:

(w1) $\langle R(P\cup Q)\rangle\mathrm{true}\leftrightarrow\langle R(P)\rangle\mathrm{true}\vee\langle R(Q)\rangle\mathrm{true}$

(w2) $\neg<R(\emptyset)>true$.

For the sake of brevity, in what follows we drop the symbol P and we write R instead of R(P).

(ref)	$F\rightarrow<R>F$	R reflexive
(wref)	$<R> true \rightarrow(F\rightarrow<R>F)$	R weakly reflexive
(n–ref)	$F\rightarrow<R>\ldots<R>F$, n operators $<R>$	R n–reflexive
(irref)	$F\rightarrow<<R>>\neg F$	R irreflexive
(n–irref)	$F\rightarrow<<R>>\ldots<<R>>\neg F$ (n operators $<<R>>$ in the consequent of the implication)	R n–irreflexive
(sym)	$<R>\neg<R>F\rightarrow F$	R symmetric
(tran)	$<R><R>F\rightarrow<R>F$	R transitive
(n–tran)	$<R>\ldots<R>F\rightarrow<R>F$ (n operators $<R>$ in the antecedent of the implication)	R n–transitive
(intran)	$<R><R>F\rightarrow<<R>>\neg F$	R intransitive
(inv)	$F\rightarrow\neg<R>\neg<Q>F$	$R^{-1}\subseteq Q$

The above formulas provide a basis for the axiomatisation of the information logics for the classes of frames presented in section 3. The details can be found in Orłowska (1996). In the literature one can find a great variety of information logics. All of them refer to some collections of the information relations presented in section 3. A representative sample of these results can be found in the present volume. In chapters 11, 15, 16, 17, 18, 19 various classes of information logics are presented and investigated. In chapter 14 a comparative study of fuzzy set–based reasoning and rough set–based reasoning is presented. Some other information logics are presented in Düntsch (1997), Rasiowa (1988, 1991), Rasiowa and Skowron (1985).

Among the methodological problems considered in connection with the information logics are the standard problems of complete axiomatisation, decidability, complexity. Some recent results in this direction can be found in Demri (1996a,b, 1997), Demri and Orłowska (1996, 1996a). However, a close connection of information logics to information systems suggests a new methodological problem that has not been considered so far in theories of logical systems, namely, the problem of informational representability. In general, information logics have two kinds of models: general models based on the abstract information frames, and standard models based on the frames derived from information systems. Applicability of a logic to practical reasoning should always be justified by informational representability of its frames. If the models of an information logic are based on the frames that are informationally representable, then the deduction system of the logic provides adequate tools for processing information given in an information system.

7 Reduction of Data and Dependencies among Data

An important issue in the rough set analysis is a reduction of data. The reduction must preserve the information content of data. From a perspective of information frames, the reduction is understood as a process of finding, for each relation type R and each subset P of properties, a minimal subset Q of P such that R(P)=R(Q). The methods of reduction of that kind developed in the rough set theory are usually presented in terms of some instances of the following notions.

Let K=(U, {R(P):P$\subseteq$A}) be an information frame and let P be a subset of set A. We say that the parameter p$\in$P is R–indispensable in P whenever R(P)$\neq$R(P–{p}). A set P is said to be R–independent whenever each of its elements is R–indispensable in P, otherwise P is R–dependent. By the R–core of a set P we mean the set of all the R–indispensable elements of P. A subset Q of P is an R–reduct of P whenever R(Q)=R(P) and Q is R–independent.

Till now the systems for computing reducts and cores are developed in the classical case only, that is for R being the indiscernibility type. Given an information system (OB, AT, {VAL_a: a$\in$AT}), an essential component of the method of reduction of sets of attributes is an algorithm for computing, for any two objects x and y from OB, the sets c(x,y)={a$\in$AT: (x,y)$\in$dis(a)} of the attributes that enable us to discern between x and y in terms of the respective properties admitted in the system.

In a general setting, given an information frame K=(U, {R(P):P$\subseteq$A}) and x,y$\in$U, we define c_R(x,y)= {a$\in$A: (x,y)$\in$R(a)}. The algorithms for computing R–reducts and R–cores, analogous to those presented in Rauszer and Skowron (1992) that employ the diversity relation, can be developed based on an analysis of sets c_R(x,y).

A formal structure that enables us, among others, reasoning about reduction of data is what is called dependence space. A dependence space is a system of the form (A, K), where A is a finite nonempty set and K is a congruence on the semilattice (P(A), $\cup$) of the subsets of A. In particular, such a congruence can be determined by a relation type R: (P, Q)$\in K_R$ iff R(P)=R(Q). A theory of dependence spaces is presented in chapters 7 and 8.

In chapters 9 and 10 the classical theories of dependencies in information systems. Most of this dependecies can be expressed in terms of indiscernibility relations derived from the information systems. A generalisation of these theories to dependencies in the other information frames is an open problem. Such a generalisation should be based on a formulation of dependencies for an arbitrary relation type R. Let an information frame K=(U, {R(P):P$\subseteq$A}) be given. We define a dependence relation $\rightarrow_R$ in the family of subsets of set A as follows: P$\rightarrow_R$Q iff R(P)$\subseteq$R(Q). It is a generalisation of the functional dependency. Clearly, all the dependencies discussed in chapters 9 and 10 can be generalised in a similar way.

8 Conclusion

This chapter provides an outline of the atomic steps of the rough set analysis of data. In any process of this analysis the derivation of information relations and information operators constitutes the preliminary step, and all the subsequent steps make use of its outcome. We presented the two types of formalisms, namely logical and algebraic, that provide a means of reasoning about data in the course of the rough set analysis.

In recent years a number of experiments with data sets from various fields of application have been carried out within the framework of rough set theory. The results of some of those experiments can be found in Czyżewski (1995), Czogała et al. (1995), Düntsch and Gediga (1995, 1997a), Grzymała–Busse (1988, 1992), Kostek (1996), Krysiński (1995), Nowicki et al. (1992), Pawlak (1991), Słowiński (1992), Woolery (1994), and in the proceedings of the rough set workshops: Ziarko (1993), Lin and Wildberger (1994), Tsumoto et al. (1996). These experiments show that the rough set analysis is useful for a pre–processing of data. It should precede a fuzzy set analysis, or a Demster–Shaefer analysis or a statistical analysis. As a result of the rough set analysis one can obtain directly from the data the grades of membership (see e.g. Pawlak, Z. and Skowron, A. 1994), or the probability distributions (see e.g. Düntsch and Gediga 1997a), or the values of the belief functions (see chapter 2 section 2.2, and Skowron, A. and Grzymała–Busse, J. 1994) that might be needed in the further processing steps.

The rough set–based models of incomplete information structures discussed in this chapter can be extended in different ways. Some proposals for extensions can be found in chapters 12, 13, and in Bryniarski and Wybraniec–Skardowska (1997), Katzberg and Ziarko (1996), Orłowska (1997), Ziarko (1993).

References

[B] Balbiani, Ph. (1997) A modal logic for data analysis. Proceedings of the 21st International Symposium on Mathematical Foundations of Computer Science, Krakow, Poland, September 1996. Lecture Notes in Computer Science 1113, Springer, 167–179.

[BW] Baneerje, M. and Wasilewska, A. (1995) Rough sets and topological quasi–Boolean algebras. Proceedings of CSC'95 Workshop on Rough Sets and Database Mining, Nashville, Tennessee, USA, 54–59.

[BWS] Bryniarski, E. and Wybraniec–Skardowska, U. (1997) Calculus of contextual rough sets in contextual spaces. Journal of Applied Non–Classical Logics, to appear.

[C] Cattaneo, G. (1997) Generalized rough sets. Preclusivity fuzzy–intuitionistic (BZ) lattices. Studia Logica 58, 47–77.

[CN] Cattaneo, G. and Nistico, G. (1989) Brouver–Zadeh posets and three–valued Lukasiewicz posets. Fuzzy Sets and Systems 33, 165–190.

[CDG] Cattaneo, G., Dalla Chiara, M. L. and Giuntini, R. (1993) Fuzzy–intuitionistic quantum logics. Studia Logica 52, 1–24.

[Co] Comer, S. (1991) An algebraic approach to the approximation of information. Fundamenta Informaticae 14, 492–502.

[CMP] Czogała, E., Mrózek, A. and Pawlak, Z. (1995) The idea of rough–fuzzy controler. International Journal of Fuzzy Sets and Systems 72, 61–63.

[Cz] Czyżewski, A. (1997) Speaker–independent recognition of digits – experiments with neural networks, fuzzy logic and rough sets. Journal of the Intelligent Automation and Soft Computing, to appear.

[D1] Demri, S. (1996) Private communication.

[D2] Demri, S. (1996a) The validity problem for logic DALLA is decidable. Bulletin of the PAS, Mathematics, vol. 44, No 1, 79–86.

[D3] Demri, S. (1996b) A class of information logics with a decidable validity problem. Proceedings of the 21st International Symposium on Mathematical Foundations of Computer Science, Krakow, Poland, September 1996. Lecture Notes in Computer Science 1113, Springer, 291–302

[D4] Demri, S. (1997) A completeness proof for a logic with an alternative necessity operator. Studia Logica 58, No 1, 99–112.

[DO1] Demri, S. and Orłowska, E. (1996) Every finitely reducible logic has the finite model property with respect the class of ◇–formulae. ICS Research Report 10/96, Warsaw University of Technology.

[DO2] Demri, S. and Orłowska, E. (1996a) Logical analysis of indiscernibility. ICS Research Report 11/96, Warsaw University of Technology. Also in this volume.

[DO3] Demri, S. and Orłowska, E. (1996b) Informational representability of models for information logics. ICS Research Report 9/96, Warsaw University of Technology. Extended abstract in: Proceedings of the First Online Workshop on Soft Computing, Nagoya, Japan, 1996, 139–144.

[DO4] Demri, S. and Orłowska, E. (1996c) Informational representability of complementary relations. Manuscript.

[Du1] Düntsch, I. (1994) Rough relation algebras. Fundamenta Informaticae 21, 321–331.

[Du2] Düntsch, I. (1997) A logic for rough sets. Theoretical Computer Science, to appear.

[DG1] Düntsch, I. and Gediga, G. (1995) Rough set dependency analysis in evaluation studies: An application in the study of repeated heart attacks. Informatics Research Reports 10, University of Ulster, 25–30.

[DG2] Düntsch, I. and Gediga, G. (1997) Algebraic aspects of attribute dependencies in information systems. Fundamenta Informaticae 29, 119–133.

[DG3] Düntsch, I. and Gediga, G. (1997a) Statistical evaluation of rough set dependency analysis. International Journal of Human–Computer Studies, to appear.

[FO] Fariñas del Cerro, L. and Orłowska, E. (1985) DAL–a logic for data analysis. Theoretical Computer Science 36, 251–264. Corrigendum: ibidem 47, 1986, 345.

[G] Gargov, G. (1986) Two completeness theorems in the logic for data analysis. ICS PAS Report 581, Warsaw.

[GPT] Gargov, G., Passy, S. and Tinchev, T. (1987) Modal environment for Boolean speculations. In: Skordev, D. (ed) Mathematical Logic and Applications. Plenum Press, New York, 253–263.

[Go] Goldblatt, R. (1993) Mathematics of Modality. CSLI Publications, Lecture Notes No. 43, Stanford, California, USA.

[Gr1] Grzymała–Busse, J. (1988) Knowledge acquisition under uncertainty – a rough set approach. Journal of Intelligent and Robotic Systems 1, 3–16.

[Gr2] Grzymała–Busse, J. (1992) LERS–a system for learning from examples based on rough sets. In [Sl], 3–18.

[I] Iwiński, T. (1987) Algebraic approach to rough sets. Bulletin of the PAS, Mathematics, vol 35, 673 –683.

[JT1] Jonsson, B. and Tarski, A. (1951) Boolean algebras with operators. Part I. American Journal of Mathematics 73, 891–939.

[JT2] Jonsson, B. and Tarski, A. (1952) Boolean algebras with operators. Part II. American Journal of Mathematics 74, 127–162.

[KZ] Katzberg, J. and Ziarko, W. (1996) Variable precision extension of rough sets. Fundamenta Informaticae 27, 155–168.

[K1] Konikowska, B. (1987) A formal language for reasoning about indiscernibility. Bulletin of the PAS, Mathematics, vol 35, 239–249.

[K2] Konikowska, B. (1997a) A logic for reasoning about relative similarity. Studia Logica 58, 185–226.

[KOP] Konrad, E., Orłowska, E. and Pawlak, Z. (1981) Knowledge representation systems. ICS PAS Report 433.

[Ko] Kostek, B. (1997) Rough set and fuzzy set methods applied to acoustical analyses. Journal of the Intelligent Automation and Soft Computing, to appear.

[Kr] Krysiński, J. (1995) Rough sets in the analysis of the structure–activity relationships of antifungal imidazolium compounds. Journal of Pharmaceutical Sciences 84, 243–247.

[LW] Lin, T. Y. and Wildberger, A. M. (eds) (1994) Proceedings of the 3rd International Workshop on Rough Sets and Soft Computing, San Jose, USA, November 1994.

[NSS] Nowicki, R., Słowiński, R. and Stefanowski, S. (1992) Rough set analysis of diagnostic capacity of vibroacoustic symptoms. Journal of Computers and Mathematics with Applications 24, 109–123.

[O1] Orłowska, E. (1983) Semantics of vague concepts. In: Dorn, G. and Weingartner, P. (eds) Foundations of Logic and Linguistics. Problems and Solutions. Selected contributions to the 7th International Congress of Logic, Methodology, and Philosophy of Science, Salzburg 1983. London–New York, Plenum Press, 465–482.

[O2] Orłowska, E. (1984) Logic of indiscernibility relations. Lecture Notes in Computer Science 208, Springer, Berlin–Heidelberg–New York, 177–186.

[O3] Orłowska, E. (1985) Logic of nondeterministic information. Studia Logica XLIV, 93–102.

[O4] Orłowska, E. (1987) Logic for reasoning about knowledge. Bulletin of the Section of Logic 16, No 1, 26–38. Also in the Zeitschrift für Mathematische Logik und Grundlagen der Mathematik 35, 1989, 559–572.

[O5] Orłowska, E. (1988) Kripke models with relative accessibility and their application to inferences from incomplete information. In: Mirkowska, G. and Rasiowa, H. (eds) Mathematical Problems in Computation Theory. Banach Center Publications 21, 329–339.

[O6] Orłowska, E. (1988a) Logical aspects of learning concepts. Journal of Approximate Reasoning 2, 349–364.

[O7] Orłowska, E. (1995) Information algebras. Proceedings of the AMAST'95, Montreal. Lecture Notes in Computer Science 639, Springer, Berlin–Heidelberg–New York, 50–65.

[O8] Orłowska, E. (1996) Studying incompleteness of information: A class of information logics. ICS Research Report 27/96, Warsaw University of Technology. To appear in: Kijania–Placek, K. and Woleński, J. (eds) The Lvov–Warsaw School and Contemporary Philosophy. Kluwer.

[O9] Orłowska, E. (1997) Many–valuedness and uncertainty. Proceedings of the 27th International Symposium on Multiple–Valued Logic, Antigonish, Canada, May 1997.

[Pa] Pawlak, Z. (1994) Rough Sets. Kluwer, Dordrecht.

[PS] Pawlak, Z. and Skowron, A. (1994) Rough membership functions. In: Yaeger, R. R., Fedrizzi, M. and Kacprzyk, J. (eds) Advances in the Dempster–Shaefer Theory of Evidence, John Wiley & Sons, New York, 251–271.

[P1] Pomykała, J. A. (1987) Approximation operations in approximation space. Bulletin of the PAS, Mathematics, vol 35, 653–662.

[P2] Pomykała, J. A. (1988) On definability in the nondeterministic information system. Bulletin of the PAS, Mathematics, vol 36, 193–210.

[P3] Pomykała, J. A. (1993) Approximation, similarity and rough constructions. ILLC Prepublication Series, University of Amsterdam, CT–93–07.

[PP] Pomykała, J. A. and Pomykała, J. M. (1988) The Stone algebra of rough sets. Bulletin of the PAS, Mathematics, vol 36, 495–508.

[R1] Rasiowa, H. (1988) Logic of approximation reasoning. Lecture Notes in Computer Science 239, Springer, Berlin–Heidelberg–New York, 188–210.

[R2] Rasiowa, H. (1991) On approximation logics, a survey. Jahrbuch 1990, Kurt Goedel Gesellschaft, Vienna 1990, 63–87.

[RO] Rasiowa, H. and Orłowska, E. (eds) (1997) Reasoning with Incomplete Information. Studia Logica 58, No 1. Special Issue.

[RS] Rasiowa, H. and Skowron, A. (1985) Approximation logic. In: Bibel, W. and Jantke, K. P. (eds) Mathematical Methods of Synthesis and Specification of Software Systems. Mathematical Research 31, Akademie Verlag, Berlin, 123–139.

[RaS] Rauszer, C. and Skowron, A. (1992) The discernibility matrices and functions in information systems. In: [Sl], 331–362.

[Re] Read, S. (1994) Thinking about Logic. Oxford University Press, Oxford, UK.

[SJ] SanJuan, E. (1996) Information frames and algebras. Manuscript, Pierre Mendes France University, Grenoble.

[S] Shepherdson, J. C. (1956) On the interpretation of Aristotelian syllogistic. Journal of Symbolic Logic 21, 137–147.

[SB] Skowron, A. and Grzymała–Busse, J. (1994) From rough set theory to evidence theory. In: Yaeger, R. R., Fedrizzi, M. and Kacprzyk, J. (eds) Advances in the Dempster–Shaefer Theory of Evidence, John Wiley & Sons, New York, 193–236.

[Sl] Słowiński, R. (ed) (1992) Intelligent Decision Support. Handbook of Applications and Advances in the Rough Set Theory. Kluwer, Dordrecht.

[T] Tsumoto, S., Kobayashi, S., Yokomori, T., Tanaka, H. and Nakamura, A. (eds) (1996) Proceedings of the 4th International Workshop on Rough Sets, Fuzzy Sets and Machine Discovery, Tokyo, Japan, November 1996.

[V1] Vakarelov, D. (1987) Abstract characterization of some knowledge representation systems and the logic NIL of nondeterministic information. In: Jorrand, Ph. and Sgurev, V. (eds) Artificial Intelligence II, Methodology, Systems, Applications. North Holland, Amsterdam, 255–260.

[V2] Vakarelov, D. (1989) Modal logics for knowledge representation systems. Lecture Notes in Computer Science 363, Springer, Berlin–Heidelberg–New York, 257–277. Also in Theoretical Computer Science 90, 1991, 433–456.

[V3] Vakarelov, D. (1991a) Logical analysis of positive and negative similarity relations in property systems. Proceedings of the First World Conference on the Fundamentals of Artificial Intelligence, Paris, France, 1991, 491–500.

[V4] Vakarelov, D. (1991b) A modal logic for similarity relations in Pawlak knowledge representation systems. Fundamenta Informaticae 15, 61–79.

[W] Wasilewska, A. (1997) Topological rough algebras. In: Lin, T. Y. (ed) Rough Sets and Database Mining, Kluwer, Theory and Decision Library, Dordrecht. Chapter 21, 411–425.

[WV1] Wasilewska, A. and Vigneron, L. (1995) Rough equality algebras. Proceedings of the Annual Joint Conference on Information Sciences, Wrightsville Beach, North Carolina, USA, 26–30.

[WV2] Wasilewska, A. and Vigneron, L. (1996) Rough and modal algebras. Proceedings of CESA'96 IMACS Multiconference: Computational Engineering in Systems Applications, Lille, France. Vol. I, 123–130.

[WV3] Wasilewska, A. and Vigneron, L. (1997) Rough R4 and R5 algebras. International Journal of Information Sciences, to appear.

[We] Wedberg, A. (1948) The Aristotelian theory of classes. Ajatus, vol. 15, 299–314.

[WG] Woolery, L. K. and Grzymała–Busse, J. (1994) Machine learning for an expert system to predict preterm birth risk. Journal of the American Medical Informatics Association 1, 439–446.

[Z1] Ziarko, W. (1993) Variable–precision rough set model. Journal of Computer and System Sciences 40, 39–59.

[Z2] Ziarko, W. (ed) (1993) Rough Sets, Fuzzy Sets and Knowledge Discovery. Proceedings of the 2nd International Workshop on Rough Sets and Knowledge Discovery, Banff, Canada, October 1993. Springer, Berlin.

I

ROUGH SETS AND DECISION RULES

Chapter 2

Synthesis of Decision Rules for Object Classification

Jan G.Bazan[1], *Hung Son Nguyen*[2], *Tuan Trung Nguyen*[3],
Andrzej Skowron[2], *Jaroslaw Stepaniuk*[4*]

1 Institute of Mathematics, Pedagogical University, Rejtana 16A, 35-310 Rzeszów, Poland
2 Institute of Mathematics, University of Warsaw, Banacha 2, 02-097 Warsaw, Poland
3 Institute of Computer Science, University of Warsaw, Banacha 2,02-097 Warsaw, Poland
4 Institute of Computer Science, Technical University of Białystok, Wiejska 45A, 15-351 Białystok

Abstract: We discuss two applications of logic to the problem of object classification. The first is related to an application of multi-modal logics to the automatic feature extraction. The second is concerned with inductive reasoning for discovering an optimal feature set with respect to the precision of classification and for improving the performance of decision algorithms. We also present an exemplary system for recognizing handwritten digits based on Boolean reasoning, rough set methods and feature discovery by applying multi-modal logic.

1 Introduction

In this paper we present a general system for classifying objects. The aim of the system is to generate, on the basis of training object samples, a set of decision rules for correct classification of objects, in particular new ones, different from those in the training set. We assume that this system operates on a set of objects that have been classified by an expert. In this system the set of attributes (for an object) is not predefined, by the designers, as in the traditional classification systems, but the appropriate set of attributes is automatically selected from a general set of attributes specified by the designer. Attributes in the system are represented by multi-modal formulae that express the structural properties of the classified objects. Objects are represented by labeled graphs from a Kripke model. In any such model, the problem of searching for relevant attributes can be regarded as finding multi-modal formulae

* This work was partially supported by the grant T11C01011 from State Committee for Scientific Research (Komitet Badan Naukowych).

distinguishing the states of the Kripke model. The system has been designed so that the user can decide what type of labeled graphs are to be used for the representation of objects. This makes the system very flexible in the inductive reasoning method of searching for relevant attributes.

In our exemplary system each object is represented by a knowledge representation graph. The nodes and edges in such a graph are labeled by some pairs of the form (formula, logical value) or by triples (formula, logical value, pointer). In the latter case the pointer is given from the formula to a sub-graph (or a partial order of sub-graphs in more complicated cases) defining a model in which the formula is evaluated. The pairs (formula, logical value), where the formula is a multi-modal formula, represent attributes. One of the simplest examples of a knowledge representation graph can be constructed by splitting raster images representing objects into sections; the nodes of the graph are labeled with atomic formulae (and their corresponding logical values) representing patterns contained in the sections, and the edges are labeled with information about the interconnection between adjacent sections.

Our method is based on a logical approach and uses some ideas known in the knowledge representation literature [BL85].

Two nodes labeled with the same (formula, value) pair can be distinguished by their positions in the knowledge representation graph. This is the idea underlying procedures for searching for attributes of an object which approximate the classification of the object given by an expert. These attributes are called *classifiers* ([SS91a]). Our method can be regarded as a formal approach to constructive induction ([KM90]). The searching process can either be interactive or automated.

One of the most important steps in searching for the appropriate set of attributes is the strategy for selecting the best attributes from those constructed in the preceding step [AD91], [BSS94], [BS94], [FU92], [K86], [KTM93], [MMS91], [ZS93]. Rough set methods [Pa91] provide possible strategies. One of them is based on the idea of reducts [Pa91] calculated from the original set of attributes. However, the accuracy of the classification induced by a randomly chosen reduct is not satisfactory for unseen objects. In [BSS94] a new method of calculating dynamic reducts has been presented. This method enables us extracting the most promising attributes by indicating the most frequent reducts found on subsets of the training set of objects.

The problem of decision rules synthesis for object classification has been intensively studied (see e.g. [KM90], [MCM83], [MCM86], [MT94], [SL90], [GB92], [GB93], [PS93], [S93a,b], [Dr92]). We apply the so-called *Boolean reasoning* [Br90] and *rough set* methods for synthesis of decision rules.

We discuss the problem of the optimal synthesis of decision rules. Decision rules have the following form: $\tau \rightarrow \tau'$ where τ and τ' are Boolean combinations of descriptors (i.e. pairs $a=v$ where a is an attribute and v is its value) built from conditional attributes and a decision approximating the expert decision [SG94], respectively. The decision rules are generated with some numerical factors expressed in terms of basic functions of evidence theory (basic probability assignments, belief and plausibility functions) and rough membership functions computable from a given decision table. These factors can be used in the decision making. Our approach of rule synthesis is based on construction of some boolean functions from modified discernibility matrices [SR91]. Two kinds of optimal decision rules are considered: rules with minimal number of conditions and rules with minimal number of descriptors [PS93], [S93a,b].

To determine the efficiency of the system we implement three searching methods, namely automatic attribute generation, relevant feature extraction (using dynamic reducts) and inductive reasoning methods. We apply these methods in pattern recognition, in particular, optical character recognition (OCR) (see e.g. [IOO92], [PR93]). Our aim is to illustrate how the system can be used to solve problems in OCR, among others the problem of the handwritten character recognition.

OCR is probably the most rapidly growing area of *artificial intelligence* research over the past few years. The idea of using printing and handwriting as a computer interface has received an attention of many industrial companies as well as leading research centers all over the world. While the problem of recognizing machine-printed characters has virtually been solved resulting in the development of high perfomance recognition systems, the problem of recognizing handwritten characters has not been completely solved yet.

There are two main approaches to the problem of handwritten pattern recognition: the statistical/decision theoretic approach and the syntactic/linguistic/grammatical/structural approach. Each of them has their own merits and demerits. Statistical techniques do not handle satisfactorily the information about interconnections in complex patterns. On the other hand, syntactic-formal language theories exihibit some serious drawbacks in dealing with recognition of handwritten patterns, where class variations are practically infinite and do not always obey strict rules imposed by formal mathematical models. The only reasonable solution is a hybrid method combining ideas from both approaches. The majority of recent publications have been dedicated to different models and solutions of static analyzers which are specific to some subclass of the problem. Only very few attempts have been made in the field of automated design of universal and flexible recognizers. In this paper we propose an approach to the problem of handwritten character recognition based on the rough set method [Pa91, S93c]. We have attempted to develop an integrated system for interactive generation of recognition engines using modern tools such as modal logic and rough set methods. Our system is not only a new approach to the traditional OCR problem but it also provided a convincing illustration of the major role that logic and rough set theory play in the fields of artificial intelligence and pattern recognition.

The paper is structured as follows:

In Section 2 we recall basic notions concerning rough sets and modal logic, in particular to decision tables, set approximations, and the syntax and semantics of multi-modal logics. In Section 3 various types of decision rules are recalled including the rules with minimal number of conditions or descriptors on the left hand side [PS93], [S93a,b] as well as the rules with certainty coefficients [S93a,b], and some examples of the inductive inference method are given. In Section 4 we present a thorough description of the methods implemented in the system; we briefly describe the problem of approximating the expert's decision using decision tables and dynamically constructed attribute sets; we explain the nature of attribute classes used in the system, namely mask, topological and modal attributes. In Section 5 we describe the main modules of the system - feature extraction and optimization. The feature extraction module allows for creating various attributes that meet the preferences of a designer; the optimization model uses optimal decision rules (discussed in Section 3) to reduce the created sets of attributes with minimal loss of the approximation precision. We describe how the algorithm for searching formulae distinguishing objects is implemented in the system, as well as how dynamic reducts [BSS94] are computed and used for the extraction relevant features.

In Section 6 the results of computer tests determining the efficiency of the system are presented and discussed, in particular, we discuss the influence of modal attributes on the classification accuracy.

Section 7 concludes with some proposals concerning further work.

The general scheme of the system is represented in Figure 1:

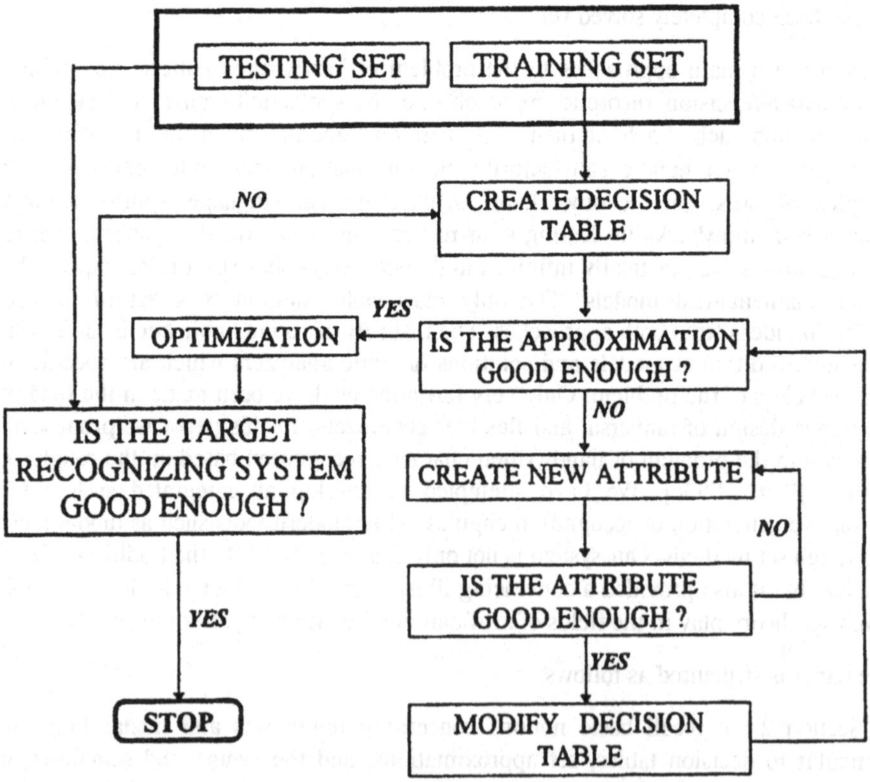

Figure 1.

2 Basic Notions

2.1 Rough Set Preliminaries

2.1.1 Basic Definitions

Information systems [Pa91] (sometimes called data tables, attribute-value systems, condition-action tables, knowledge representation systems etc.) are used for representing knowledge.

Rough sets have been introduced as a tool to deal with inexact, uncertain or vague knowledge in artificial intelligence applications.

In this section we recall some basic notions related to information systems and rough sets.

An *information system* is a pair $\mathbf{A}=(U,A)$, where U is a non-empty, finite set called the *universe* and A - a non-empty, finite set of *attributes*, i.e. $a\colon U\to V_a$ for $a\in A$, where V_a is called *the value set of a*.

Elements of U are called *objects* and interpreted as, e.g. cases, states, processes, patients, observations. Attributes are interpreted as features, variables, characteristic conditions etc.

Every information system $\mathbf{A}=(U,A)$ and a non-empty set $B\subseteq A$ define *a B-information function*

$$Inf_B : U \to \mathrm{P}\left(B\times\bigcup_{a\in B} V_a\right)$$

defined by $Inf_B(x)=\{(a,a(x))\colon a\in B\}$. The set $\{Inf_A(x)\colon x\in U\}$ is called the *A-information set* and it is denoted by $INF(\mathbf{A})$.

We consider a special case of information systems called decision tables. A *decision table* is any information system of the form $\mathbf{A}=(U,A\cup\{d\})$, where $d\notin A$ is a distinguished attribute called *decision*. The elements of A are called *conditions*.

One can interpret a decision attribute as a kind of classification of the universe of objects given by an expert decision-maker, operator, physician, etc. Decision tables are called sets of examples in machine learning [KM90].

The cardinality $|d(U)|$ of the image $d(U) = \{v\colon d(x)=v \text{ for some } x\in U\}$ is called the *rank* of d and is denoted by $r(d)$. We assume that the set V_d of values of the decision d is equal to $\{1,\dots,r(d)\}$.

The decision d determines the partition $CLASS_{\mathbf{A}}(d)=\{X_1,\dots,X_{r(d)}\}$ of the universe U, where $X_k=\{x\in U\colon d(x)=k\}$ for $1\le k\le r(d)$. The set X_i is called the *i-th decision class of* $\mathbf{A}$.

Let **A**=(U, A) be an information system. With every subset of attributes $B \subseteq A$, an equivalence relation, denoted by $IND_{\mathbf{A}}(B)$ (or, $IND(B)$, in short) called the *B-indiscernibility relation*, is associated and defined as follows:

$$IND(B)=\{(s,s')\in U^2 : \text{for every } a\in B,\ a(s)=a(s')\}$$

Objects s,s' satisfying relation IND(B) are indiscernible by attributes from B.

Minimal subsets $B \subseteq A$ satisfying $IND(B)=IND(A)$ are called *reducts* of **A**. The set of all reducts of **A** is denoted by $RED(\mathbf{A})$.

Let **A** be an information system with n objects. By M(**A**) [SR91] we denote an n×n matrix (c_{ij}), called the *discernibility matrix* of **A** such that

$$c_{ij} = \{a\in A:\ a(x_i)\neq a(x_j)\} \text{ for } i,j=1,\dots,n.$$

A discernibility function $f_{\mathbf{A}}$ for an information system **A** is a Boolean function of m Boolean variables $a_1^*,\dots,a_m^*$ corresponding to the attributes $a_1,\dots,a_m$ respectively, and defined by

$$f_{\mathbf{A}}(a_1^*,\dots,a_m^*) =_{df} \bigwedge\{\bigvee c_{ij}^* : 1\leq j<i\leq n,\ c_{ij}\neq\emptyset\}$$

where $c_{ij}^*=\{a^* : a\in c_{ij}\}$.

It has been shown [SR91] that the set of all *prime implicants* of f_A determines the set $RED(\mathbf{A})$ of all reducts of **A**.

If **A**=(U,A) is an information system, $B\subseteq A$ is a set of attributes and $X\subseteq U$ is a set of objects then the sets

$$\{s\in U : [s]_B\subseteq X\} \text{ and } \{s\in U : [s]_B\cap X\neq\emptyset\}$$

are called *B-lower* and *B-upper approximation* of X in **A**, and they are denoted by $\underline{B}X$ and $\overline{B}X$, respectively.

The set $BN_B(X)= \overline{B}X-\underline{B}X$ is called the *B-boundary* of X. When $B=A$ we write also $BN_{\mathbf{A}}(X)$ instead of $BN_A(X)$.

Sets which are unions of some classes of the indiscernibility relation $IND(B)$ are called *definable* by B in **A**. Some subsets (categories) of objects in an information system cannot be expressed exactly by employing available attributes but they can be roughly defined. The set X is *B-definable* if $\overline{B}X=\underline{B}X$.

The set $\underline{B}X$ is the set of all elements of U which can be classified with certainty as elements of X, given the knowledge represented by attributes from B; $\overline{B}X$ is the set of elements of U which can be possibly classified as elements of X, in view of knowledge represented by attributes from B; $BN_B(X)$ is the set of elements which can be classified neither to X nor to -X, given knowledge represented by B.

If $X_1,\dots,X_{r(d)}$ are decision classes of A then the set

$$\underline{B}X_1 \cup \ldots \cup \underline{B}X_{r(d)}$$

is called the *B-positive region of* **A** and is denoted by $POS_B(d)$.

If $\mathbf{A}=(U,A\cup\{d\})$ is a decision table then we define a function

$$\partial_A\colon U \rightarrow P(\{1,..,r(d)\})$$

called the *generalized decision* in **A**, by

$$\partial_A(x) = \{i{:}\exists x' \in U \; x' IND(A) x \text{ and } d(x)=i\} = d([x]_{IND(A)})$$

A decision table **A** is called *consistent* (*deterministic*) if $|\partial_A(x)|=1$ for any $x \in U$, otherwise **A** is *inconsistent* (*non-deterministic*).

A subset B of the set A of attributes of decision table $\mathbf{A}=(U,A\cup\{d\})$ *is a relative reduct of* **A** iff B is a minimal set with respect to the following property: $\partial_B=\partial_A$. The set of all relative reducts in **A** is denoted by $RED(\mathbf{A},d)$. If $B \in RED(\mathbf{A},d)$ then the set $\{(Inf_B(x),d(x))\colon x \in U\}$ is called the *trace of B in* **A** and is denoted by $Trace_{\mathbf{A}}(B)$.

2.1.2 Dynamic Reducts

Dynamic reducts [BSS94] have been introduced as a tool for extraction of the most relevant features for the given set of features. In this subsection we recall some basic definitions related to dynamic reducts.

If $\mathbf{A}=(U,A\cup\{d\})$ is a decision table then any system $\mathbf{B}=(U',A\cup\{d\})$ such that $U' \subseteq U$ is called a *subtable* of **A**.

Let $\mathbf{A}=(U,A\cup\{d\})$ be a decision table and $\boldsymbol{F}$ be a family of subtables of **A**. By $DR(\mathbf{A},\boldsymbol{F})$ we denote the set

$$RED(\mathbf{A},d) \cap \bigcap_{\mathbf{B}\in \boldsymbol{F}} RED(\mathbf{B},d)$$

Any element from $DR(\mathbf{A},\boldsymbol{F})$ is called a ***F****- dynamic reduct* of **A**.

It follows that a relative reduct of **A** is dynamic if it is also a reduct of all subtables from a given family $\boldsymbol{F}$. This notion can be sometimes too much restrictive so we apply also a more general notion of dynamic reducts. They are called $(\boldsymbol{F},\varepsilon)$*-dynamic reduct*. The set $DR_\varepsilon(\mathbf{A},\boldsymbol{F})$ of all $(\boldsymbol{F},\varepsilon)$-dynamic reducts is defined by

$$DR_\varepsilon(\mathbf{A},\boldsymbol{F}) = \{C \in RED(\mathbf{A},d)\colon \frac{|\{\mathbf{B} \in \boldsymbol{F}\colon C \in RED(\mathbf{B},d)\}|}{|\boldsymbol{F}|} \geq 1-\varepsilon\}$$

Proposition 2.1

1. If $\boldsymbol{F}=\{\mathbf{A}\}$ then $DR(\mathbf{A},\boldsymbol{F}) = RED(\mathbf{A},d)$.
2. If $\boldsymbol{F} \subseteq \boldsymbol{F}'$ then $DR(\mathbf{A},\boldsymbol{F}') \subseteq DR(\mathbf{A},\boldsymbol{F})$, for any families of subtables of **A**.
3. If $\varepsilon \leq \varepsilon'$ then $DR_\varepsilon(\mathbf{A},\boldsymbol{F}) \subseteq DR_{\varepsilon'}(\mathbf{A},\boldsymbol{F})$,

4. $DR_\varepsilon(\mathbf{A},\mathcal{F}) \supseteq DR(\mathbf{A},\mathcal{F})$, for any $\varepsilon \geq 0$.

5. $\mathrm{DR}_0(\mathbf{A},\mathcal{F}) = \mathrm{DR}(\mathbf{A},\mathcal{F})$.

The number $\frac{|\{\mathbf{B} \in \mathcal{F}: C \in RED(\mathbf{B},d)\}|}{|\mathcal{F}|}$ is called the *stability coefficient* of $C \in RED(\mathbf{A},d)$.

The methods based on calculation of all reducts enable us to compute the description of all decision classes of a given consistent decision table **A** in the form of decision rules (which are exact in **A** as well as complete and minimal with respect to descriptors [PS93], [S93a,b]). Unfortunately, the decision rules calculated by this method might not be appropriate to classify new objects. We suggest that the rules computed by means of dynamic reducts are predisposed better to classify new objects. The idea of their construction comes from the intuitive observation that reducts frequently appearing in different subtables have greater chance to contain relevant attributes than those rarely appearing in subtables. This hypothesis has been supported by various experiments [BSS94] as well as by our experiment with handwritten digit recognition. This method can be extended to construct so-called *dynamic decision rules* [BSS94], [SP97].

2.1.3 Reduction of Attributes

In this section we propose the attribute reduction method based on the notion of the dynamic reduct. This reduction is intended to extract from a given set A of attributes the most relevant ones with respect to recognition of new objects.

Let $\mathbf{A}=(U,A)$ be an information system and $DR_\varepsilon(\mathbf{A},\mathcal{F})$ the set of all the $(\mathcal{F},\varepsilon)$-dynamic reducts of system **A**. By $DRA_\varepsilon(\mathbf{A},\mathcal{F})$ we denote the set:

$$\bigcup DR(\mathbf{A},\mathcal{F}) = \{a \in A\colon a \in R \textit{ for some } R \in DR(\mathbf{A},\mathcal{F})\}.$$

The set $DRA_\varepsilon(\mathbf{A},\mathcal{F})$ is called the $(\mathcal{F},\varepsilon)$*-dynamic core* of **A**. It is a set of all attributes contained in $(\mathcal{F},\varepsilon)$ dynamic reducts, i.e. attributes intuitively relevant for classification. One can apply the constructed above $\mathcal{F}$-dynamic core of **A** to predict the decision for new objects. Another method allows to predict the decision on a new object as a result of a competition between the family of decision rule sets corresponding to reducts from $DR(\mathbf{A},\mathcal{F})$. These ideas have been verified in numerous practical applications [BSS94]. The results of our experiments are presented in Section 5.

2.2 Evidence Theory Preliminaries and Relationships Between Evidence Theory and Rough Set Theory

The classification problems are central for the rough set approach [Pa91] as well as for the evidence theoretic approach [Sh76].

The fundamental assumption in the rough set approach is the following one: the objects from the universe are perceived only through the accessible information about them, i.e. the values of attributes which can be evaluated on these objects. Objects with the same information are indiscernible. As a consequence the classification of objects is based on the accessible information about them, not on the objects themselves.

Together with information about objects from a finite set of objects the classification of them delivered by an expert is given. The classification problem in this case is related to the question to what extent it is possible to reflect the classification done by an expert by the available conditions.

In evidence theory [Sh76] the information about sets creating a given partition is embedded directly in some numerical functions called the *basic probability assignment, belief function and plausibility function,* whereas in the case of the rough set approach the information about classified sets and objects is included in a decision table.

The evidence theory approach is based on the idea of asssigning a number from the interval [0,1], given, e.g. by an expert, to indicate a degree of belief for a given proposition on the basis of a given evidence.

It is possible to compute the basic functions of evidence theory from a given decision table [SG94]. First, we recall some basic notions of evidence theory .

A *frame of discernment* Θ is a finite non-empty set.

The basic probability assignment (bpa) on Θ is any function $m : \mathbf{P}(\Theta)\rightarrow\mathbf{R}_+$, where $\mathbf{R}_+$ is the set of non-negative reals, satisfying the following two conditions:

$$m(\varnothing)=0 \text{ and } \sum_{\Delta\subseteq\Theta} m(\Delta) = 1$$

For a given bpa m two functions are defined.

A function Bel: $\mathbf{P}(\Theta)\rightarrow\mathbf{R}_+$ is called *the belief function over* Θ (generated by m) iff for any $\theta\subseteq\Theta$

$$Bel(\theta) = \sum_{\Delta\subseteq\Theta} m(\Delta)$$

A function Pl: $\mathbf{P}(\Theta)\rightarrow\mathbf{R}_+$ is called *the plausibility function over* Θ (generated by m) iff for any $\theta\subseteq\Theta$

$$Pl(\theta) = \sum_{\Delta\subseteq\theta} m(\Delta)$$

A function $Q : \mathbf{P}(\Theta) \to \mathbf{R}_+$ is called *the commonality function* iff for any $\theta \subseteq \Theta$

$$Q(\theta) = \sum_{\Delta \subseteq \theta} m(\Delta)$$

Let us observe that the inequality $Bel(\theta)+Bel(\Theta-\theta) \leq 1$ can not be in general reduced to the equality $Bel(\theta)+Bel(\Theta-\theta)=1$ ($P(\theta)+P(\Theta-\theta)=1$ for any probability function on $\mathbf{P}(\Theta)$). This enables us to take into account ignorance, e.g. if we have no evidence at all, for or against θ, then $Bel(\theta) = Bel(\Theta-\theta) = 0$.

The plausibility function Pl is definable by the belief function, namely:

$$Pl(\theta)=1-Bel(\Theta-\theta) \text{ for any } \theta \subseteq \Theta.$$

Now we describe how decision tables determine these functions.

A decision d from the decision table $\mathbf{A}=(U, A \cup \{d\})$ defines a set $\Theta_{\mathbf{A}}=\{1,\ldots,r(d)\}$ called the *frame of discernment defined by d in* **A**. The frame of discernment Θ is called *compatible with* **A** if $r(d)=|\Theta|$. In the sequel, to simplify notation, we assume $\Theta=V_d=\Theta_{\mathbf{A}}=\{1,\ldots,k\}$, where $k=r(d)$ for considered decision tables and frames of discernment.

The objects from the universe U of **A** can be classified using the knowledge represented by conditions from A. This enables us to decide that either an object belongs to the lower approximation of a given set $X \subseteq U$ or it is in the complement of the upper approximation of X or belongs to the boundary region corresponding to X. However, one can classify the objects from the boundary regions in a more adequate way. This is based on the following observation [SG94]:

Proposition 2.2 Let $\mathbf{A}=(U, A \cup \{d\})$ be a decision table. The family of all non-empty sets from

$$\{\underline{A}X_1,\ldots,\underline{A}X_{r(d)}\} \cup \{Bd_{\mathbf{A}}(\theta) : \theta \subseteq \Theta_{\mathbf{A}} \text{ and } |\theta| > 1\}$$

(where $Bd_{\mathbf{A}}(\theta) = \bigcap_{i \in \theta} BN_A(X_i) \cap \bigcap_{i \notin \theta} -BN_A(X_i)$) is a partition of the universe U.

Moreover, the following equality holds:

$$\bigcup_{i \in \theta} \underline{A}X_i \cup \bigcup_{\Delta \subseteq \theta, |\Delta|>1} Bd_A(\Delta) = \underline{A} \bigcup_{i \in \theta} X_i \text{ for } \theta \subseteq \Theta_{\mathbf{A}} \text{ with } |\theta|>1.$$

□

The classification (partition) of the universe U described in Proposition 2.2 is called the *standard classification of U approximating in* **A** *the classification* $CLASS_{\mathbf{A}}(d)$ (given by an expert).

By $APP\_CLASS_{\mathbf{A}}(d)$ we denote the family:

$$\{\underline{A}X_1,\ldots,\underline{A}X_{r(d)}\} \cup \{Bd_{\mathbf{A}}(\theta) : \theta \subseteq \Theta_{\mathbf{A}} \text{ and } |\theta| > 1\}$$

We have a clear interpretation of the new classification. An object from the universe U of **A** is represented by an information (from $INF(\mathbf{A})$) described in the rows of **A**. The object can be classified exactly on the basis of that information only if the category (i.e. the equivalence class of the indiscernibility relation $IND_{\mathbf{A}}(A)$) corresponding to that information) is included in X_i for some i. Otherwise, that category is included in a boundary region of the form $Bd_{\mathbf{A}}(\theta)$, for some θ. Then the considered object from U (represented by a given information) belongs to the boundary region of all sets X_i, where $i \in \theta$ and do not belong to sets X_j, where $j \notin \theta$ (i.e. it is in the union $\bigcup_{i \in \theta} X_i$ but we do not have enough information to decide in which of the sets X_i).

There is a natural correspondence between subsets of Θ and elements of APP_CLASS (d), which can be expressed by the following function:

$$F_A(\theta) = \begin{cases} \underline{A}X_i & \text{if } \theta = \{i\} \text{ for some } i \; (1 \le i \le r(d) \\ \varnothing & \text{if } \theta = \varnothing \\ Bd\,(\theta) & \text{if } |\theta| > 1 \end{cases}$$

It is easy to observe that the generalized decision ∂_A has the following property: $\partial_A(x)$ is the unique subset θ of Θ such that $x \in F_{\mathbf{A}}(\theta)$ for any $x \in U$.

The function $m_{\mathbf{A}}$: $\mathbf{P}(\Theta) \rightarrow \mathbf{R}_+$, called *the standard basic probability assignment of* **A** is defined by

$$m_A(\theta) = \frac{|F_A(\theta)|}{|U|}, \text{ for any } \theta \subseteq \Theta.$$

Proposition 2.3 ([SG94]) The function $m_{\mathbf{A}}$ defined above is a basic probability assignment (in the sense of evidence theory).

□

The above definition has a clear interpretation. If $\theta = \{i\}$ then $m(\theta)$ is the ratio of the number of all objects from the universe U (of **A**) certainly classified by attributes from A as being in X_i to the number of all objects in U. If $|\theta| > 1$ then $m_{\mathbf{A}}(\theta)$ is the ratio of the number of all objects from the universe U (of **A**) certainly classified by attributes from A as being in the boundary region $Bd_{\mathbf{A}}(\theta)$ to the number of all objects in U.

The belief function Bel of **A** is defined by

$$Bel_{\mathbf{A}}(\theta) = \sum_{\Delta \subseteq \theta} m_A(\Delta)$$

where $\theta \subseteq \Theta$ and $m_{\mathbf{A}}$ is the standard probability assignment of **A**.
The interpretation of the above definition follows from the following theorem [SG94]:

Theorem 2.4 Let **A**=$(U, A \cup \{d\})$ be a decision table. For arbitrary $\theta \subseteq \Theta$ the following equality holds:

$$Bel_{\mathbf{A}}(\theta) = \frac{\left| \underline{A} \bigcup_{i \in \theta} X_i \right|}{|U|}$$

□

The belief function $Bel_{\mathbf{A}}$ is Bayesian iff all decision classes of **A** are definable by the set A of conditions. In particular, the belief function $Bel_{\mathbf{B'}}$ where **B'**=$(U, A \cup \{\delta_{\mathbf{A}}\})$, is Bayesian.

Corollary 2.5

Let **A**=$(U, A \cup \{d\})$ be a decision table. For arbitrary $\theta \subseteq \Theta$ the following equality holds:

$$Pl_{\mathbf{A}}(\theta) = \frac{\left| \overline{A} \bigcup_{i \in \theta} X_i \right|}{|U|}$$

□

The value $Bel_{\mathbf{A}}(\theta)$ ($Pl_{\mathbf{A}}(\theta)$) is the ratio of the number of objects from U certainly (possibly) classified into the union $\bigcup_{i \in \theta} X_i$ to the number of all elements in the universe U.

The *commonality function of* **A** is defined by

$$Q_{\mathbf{A}}(\theta) = \sum_{\Delta \subseteq \theta} m_A(\Delta)$$

where $\theta \subseteq \Theta$.

2.3 Modal Logic Preliminaries

In this section we present some applications of modal logics, which for the last 20 years have been investigated in Computer Science (see [Sti92]).

Besides the classical proposition connectives the modal logic has special functors called *modal connectives* (or modal operators) expressing natural notions such as: "it's possible that ...", " it's necessary, that ...". Only one of these two notions is needed as a basic term, because each them can be defined by the other:

"It's possible that A" is equivalent to "It's not necessary, that not A"

Modal logic is intensional, because logical values of its compound formulae depend not only on logical values of component formulae.

Modal logics, whose formulae contain more than one type of modalities are called *multi-modal*. The syntax of the propositional multi-modal logic is presented below:

1. The language of multi-modal propositional logic takes as primitive symbols the following ones:

i) A denumerable infinite set V of propositional variables, which we write as p, q, r...(with or without numerical subscripts).

ii) A set of classical propositional connectives: $\neg$, $\wedge$, $\vee$, $\rightarrow$, $\leftrightarrow$;

iii) The family of modal connectives: $\{\Box_m, \Diamond_m\}_{m\in M}$, where M is a finite set of actions or modality labels.

2. *Well-formed formulae* of multi-modal propositional logic are defined as follows:

i) Any propositional variable is a formula.

ii) If φ and ψ are formulae, then $\neg\varphi$, $\varphi\wedge\psi$, $\varphi\vee\psi$, $\varphi\rightarrow\psi$, $\varphi\leftrightarrow\psi$, $\Box_m\varphi$, $\Diamond_m\varphi$ are formulae.

iii) Every formula is either a propositional variable or is constructed from propositional variables (or from already constructed formulae) by applying the rule ii) a finite number of times.

Some connectives are definable by means of the others:

$\varphi\wedge\psi =_{Df} \neg(\neg\varphi\vee\neg\psi)$, $\varphi\rightarrow\psi =_{Df} \neg\varphi\vee\psi$, $\varphi\leftrightarrow\psi =_{Df} (\varphi\rightarrow\psi)\wedge(\psi\rightarrow\varphi)$,

$\Diamond_m\varphi =_{Df} \neg\Box_m\neg\varphi$.

Let φ be a formula of a multi-modal propositional logic. The *depth* $|\varphi|$ of a formula φ is defined inductively by:

i) $|\varphi| = 0$ for $\varphi\in V$;

ii) $|\neg\varphi| = |\varphi|$;

iii) $|\varphi\wedge\psi| = |\varphi\vee\psi| = |\varphi\rightarrow\psi| = |\varphi\leftrightarrow\psi| = \max(|\varphi|, |\psi|)$;

iv) $|\Box_m\varphi| = |\Diamond_m\varphi| = |\varphi| + 1$.

S.Kripke [K59], [K63] defined the so-called possible world semantics for modal formulae. His work is regarded as a major breakthrough in this field, because it brought not only a highly suggestive and intuitive, but also well-defined semantics.

A Kripke model is any triple $\mathcal{K} = \langle W, \{R_m\}_{m\in M}, val\rangle$ where

- W is a non-empty set (set of possible worlds, set of states);

- $\{R_m \subseteq W\times W, m\in M\}$is a family of binary (accessibility) relations over W;

- A valuation function $val : V\times W \to \{0,1\}$ assigns a logical value to any propositional variable in a given world.

For a given Kripke model $\mathcal{K}$, the logical value of any compound modal formula φ in a world $w\in W$ is determined by the so-called *satisfiability relation* $\mathcal{K}, w \models \varphi$ defined as follow:

i) for $p\in V$ $\mathcal{K}, w \models p$ if and only if $val(p,w) = 1$

ii) $\mathcal{K}, w \models \varphi\vee\psi$ if and only if $\mathcal{K}, w \models \varphi$ or $\mathcal{K}, w \models \psi$

iii) $\mathcal{K}, w \models \neg\varphi$ if and only if it is not true, that $\mathcal{K}, w \models \varphi$

iv) $\mathcal{K}, w \models \Box_m \varphi$ if and only if $\mathcal{K}, w' \models \varphi$ for any $w'\in W$ such that $(w,w')\in R_m$

v) $\mathcal{K}, w \models \Diamond_m\varphi$ if and only if there is some $w'\in W$ such that $(w,w')\in R_m$ and

$\mathcal{K}, w' \models \varphi$

In the sequel we show how modal formulae and Kripke models can be applied to the feature extraction.

3 Decision Rules

In this section we recall the definition of decision rules and some methods based on Boolean reasoning for their synthesis.

Let $\mathbf{A}=(U, A\cup\{d\})$ be a decision table and let

$$V = \bigcup_{a\in A} V_a \cup V_d$$

The atomic formulae over $B\subseteq A\cup\{d\}$ and V are the expressions of the form $a=v$, called *descriptors over B and V*, where $a\in B$ and $v\in V_a$. The set $\mathbf{F}(B,V)$ of formulae over B and V is the least set containing descriptors over B and V and closed with respect to the classical propositional connectives $\vee$ (disjunction) and $\wedge$ (conjunction).

Let $\tau\in\mathbf{F}(B,V)$. Then by $\tau_{\mathbf{A}}$ we denote the meaning of τ in the decision table $\mathbf{A}$, i.e. the set of all objects from U with the property τ, defined inductively as follows:

- if τ is of the form $a=v$ then $\tau_{\mathbf{A}} = \{x\in U: a(x)=v\}$.

- $(\tau\wedge\tau')_{\mathbf{A}}=\tau_{\mathbf{A}}\cap\tau'_{\mathbf{A}}$; $(\tau\vee\tau')_{\mathbf{A}}=\tau_{\mathbf{A}}\cup\tau'_{\mathbf{A}}$.

We do not use the negation connective because in the case of information systems the complement of any definable set is definable by union and intersection.

The set $\mathbf{F}(A,V)$ is called the *set of conditional formulae* of **A** and is denoted by $\mathbf{C}(A,V)$.

A *decision rule* for **A** is any expression of the form

$$\tau\Rightarrow d=i \text{ where } \tau\in\mathbf{C}(A,V) \text{ and } i\in V_d.$$

The decision rule $\tau\Rightarrow d=i$ for **A** is *true in* **A** iff $\tau_{\mathbf{A}}\subseteq(d=i)_{\mathbf{A}}$; if $\tau_{\mathbf{A}}=(d=i)_{\mathbf{A}}$ then we say that the rule is **A**-*exact*.

In the following sections we present a method for the synthesis of different forms of decision rules. The method is based on Boolean reasoning, the discernibility matrices and their modifications.

3.1 Decision Rules for Consistent Decision Tables

In this section we assume that considered the tables under consideration are consistent. We present two methods for the synthesis of decision rules.

The first method enables us to obtain the exact decision rules, i.e. the description of all decision classes in the form of decision rules. The description of decision classes is minimal in the following sense: it is not possible to describe all decision classes by any proper subset of the set of conditions occurring on the left hand side of any rule.

The second method also enables us to obtain the description of all decision classes in the form of decision rules. The left hand side of a rule is a disjunction of descriptor conjunctions. The description of the decision classes is minimal in the following sense: a conjunction of descriptors occurring on the left hand side of the rule is minimal, i.e. the rule will not remain valid if one eliminates any descriptor from that conjunction. Some versions of the methods presented here are discussed in [S93a-c].

3.1.1 Decision Rules with Minimal Number of Conditions

The method which we are going to present consists of two steps. In the first step we show how to modify the notion of discernibility matrix to compute the set $RED(\mathbf{A},d)$ of all relative reducts of **A**. In the second step we show how any relative reduct $B\in RED(\mathbf{A},d)$ enables us to obtain directly the description of each decision class in the form of a decision rule. On the left hand side of every decision rule only the attributes from B occur. The description of the decision classes is minimal in the following sense: it is not possible to obtain a description of all decision classes by means of attributes from any proper subset of B.

Let $\mathbf{A}=(U,A\cup\{d\})$ be a consistent decision table and let $M(\mathbf{A})=(c_{ij})$ be its discernibility matrix. We construct a new matrix $M'(\mathbf{A})=(c'_{ij})$ assuming $c'_{ij}=\emptyset$ if

$d(x_j)=d(x_j)$ and $c'_{ij}=c_{ij}-\{d\}$, otherwise. The matrix $M'(\mathbf{A})$ is called the *relative discernibility matrix* of **A**. Now one can construct the *relative discernibility function* $f_{M'(\mathbf{A})}$ *of* $M'(\mathbf{A})$ in the same way as the discernibility function was constructed from the discernibility matrix (see Section 2). One can show that the following proposition is true:

Proposition 3.1 For any $B \subseteq A$ the following conditions are equivalent:

(*i*) $B \in RED(\mathbf{A}, d)$

(*ii*) $\wedge B$ is a prime implicant of $f_{M'(\mathbf{A})}$.

□

Let us recall that in the condition (ii) elements of B are treated as Boolean variables corresponding to attributes. Proposition 3.1 allows to compute the set of all relative reducts by computing the set of all prime implicant of $f_{M'(\mathbf{A})}$.

Now, for any $B \in RED(\mathbf{A}, d)$ we construct the set $Trace_{\mathbf{A}}(B)=\{(\mathrm{Inf}_B(x), d(x)) : x \in U\}$.

To obtain the decision rule corresponding to the i-th decision it is sufficient to take all pairs from $Trace_{\mathbf{A}}(B)$ with the second element equal to $d=i$ and create the disjunction α_i of all conjunctions of descriptors occurring on the first position in those pairs. The constructed decision rule has the form

$$\alpha_i \Rightarrow d=i$$

We have the following:

Proposition 3.2 Let $\mathbf{A}=(U, A \cup \{d\})$ be a consistent decision table and let $B \in RED(\mathbf{A}, d)$. The decision rules $\alpha_i \Rightarrow d=i$ where $i=1,\dots,r(d)$ are exact in **A** and the descriptions of decision classes defined by them are minimal, i.e. for any $B' \subset B$ there are no formulae β_i, for $i=1,\dots,r(d)$, in $\mathbf{C}(B', V)$ such that the decision rules $\beta_i \Rightarrow d=i$ are exact in **A** for $i=1,\dots,r(d)$.

□

3.1.2 Decision Rules with Minimal Number of Descriptors

First, we show how to construct a description of the decision classes by decision rules that are exact in **A**

$$\alpha_i \Rightarrow d=i$$

where $\alpha_i \in \mathbf{C}(A, V)$ is a disjunction $\vee \wedge \gamma_i$ of conjunctions $\wedge \gamma_i$ of minimal sets γ_i of descriptors for i=1,...,$r(d)$. The set γ_i defines a non-empty set of objects in **A**, i.e. $(\gamma_i)_{\mathbf{A}} \neq \emptyset$ and it is minimal in the following sense: the decision rule

$$\wedge \gamma'_i \Rightarrow d=\mathrm{i}$$

is no longer valid in **A** for any $\gamma'_i \subset \gamma_i$ satisfying $(\wedge\gamma'_i)_{\mathbf{A}} \neq \emptyset$. The decision rule with the above property is called *minimal with respect to the descriptors in* **A**.

The method enables us to generate decision rules with one more property, namely if

$$\vee\wedge\gamma_i \Rightarrow d=i$$

is any of the constructed decision rules for **A**, and γ is a set of descriptors such that

$$\wedge\gamma \Rightarrow d=i$$

is valid in A and $(\wedge\gamma)_{\mathbf{A}} \neq \emptyset$, then $\gamma_i \subseteq \gamma$ for some i. The decision rules with the above property are called *complete with respect to the descriptors in* **A**.

Now we recall a method ([S93a-c]) of computing, for a given consistent decision table **A**, the description of all decision classes of **A** in the form of decision rules exact in **A** which are complete and minimal with respect to descriptors.

Let **A**= $(U,A\cup\{d\})$ be a consistent decision table and $M'(\mathbf{A})=(c'_{ij})$ be its relative discernibility matrix. We construct new matrices (columns of relative discernibility matrix)

$$M(\mathbf{A},k)=(c^k_{ij}) \text{ for any } x_k \in U$$

assuming $c^k_{ij} = c'_{ij}$ if $d(x_i) \neq d(x_j)$ and $(i=k \vee j=k)$, otherwise $c^k_{ij} = \emptyset$. The matrix $M(\mathbf{A},k)$ is called the *k-relative discernibility matrix of* **A**. Now one can construct *the k-relative discernibility function* $f_{M(\mathbf{A},k)}$ *of* $M(\mathbf{A},k)$ in the same way as the discernibility function was constructed from the discernibility matrix [SR92].

Let $Atr(\gamma)$ denote the set of all attributes corresponding to propositional variables occurring in the prime implicant γ of $f_{M(\mathbf{A},k)}$ and let $Trace(\mathbf{A},k)$ be the following set of descriptor conjunctions:

$$\{\bigwedge\{a=a(x_k): a \in Atr(\gamma)\}: \gamma \text{ is a prime implicant of } f_{M(\mathbf{A},k)}\}.$$

Now let α_i for any $i \in \{1,\ldots,r(d)\}$) be a disjunction of all formulae from the set

$$\bigcup_k \{Trace(\mathrm{A},k): d(x_k)=i\}.$$

Proposition 3.3 [S93a-c] Let $\mathbf{A}=(U,A\cup\{d\})$ be a consistent decision table. The decision rules:

$$\alpha_i \Rightarrow d=i \text{ where } i \in \{1,\ldots,r(d)\}$$

are complete and minimal with respect to descriptors in **A**.

□

Similarities of these rules to those discussed for AQ algorithms are discussed in [St94].

3.2 Decision Rules for Inconsistent Decision Tables

In this section we consider inconsistent decision tables. One can transform an arbitrary inconsistent decision table $\mathbf{A}=(U,A\cup\{d\})$ into a consistent decision table $\mathbf{A}_\partial=(U,A\cup\{\partial_\mathbf{A}\})$ where $\partial_\mathbf{A}$: $U\rightarrow\mathbf{P}(\Theta)$ is the generalized decision of $\mathbf{A}$ defined in Section 2.1 and $\Theta=\{1,...,r(d)\}$ (see also [St94] for more details). It is easy to see that $\mathbf{A}_\partial$ is a consistent decision table. Hence, one can apply to $\mathbf{A}$ the methods presented in the previous section. As a result one obtains, for any $\theta\subseteq\Theta$ with $(\delta_\mathbf{A}=\theta)_{\mathbf{A}_\delta}\neq\emptyset$, the decision rules of the form:

$$\alpha_\theta\Rightarrow\partial_\mathbf{A}=\theta$$

We have the following proposition relating these rules with the standard basic probability assignment of $\mathbf{A}$:

Proposition 3.4 If $\alpha_\theta\Rightarrow\partial_\mathbf{A}=\theta$ is a decision rule obtained by applying to $\mathbf{A}_\partial$ any method presented in Section 3.1 and $(\partial_\mathbf{A}=\theta)_{\mathbf{A}_\partial}\neq\emptyset$ then

(i) $\{x\in U:\partial_\mathbf{A}(x)=\theta\}=(\alpha_\theta)_\mathbf{A}=(\partial_\mathbf{A}=\theta)_{\mathbf{A}_\partial}$

(ii) $m_\mathbf{A}(\theta)=\dfrac{|\{x\in U:\partial_\mathbf{A}(x)=\theta\}|}{|U|}$.

□

In a similar way one can construct the rules corresponding to the lower approximation of the union of decision classes X_i, where $i\in\theta$. The cardinality of this set is related to the value $Bel_\mathbf{A}(\theta)$ (see Section 2.2). It is sufficient to construct a decision table

$$\mathbf{B}_\theta=(U,A\cup\{b_\theta\})$$

where $b_\theta(x)=1$ if $\partial_\mathbf{A}(x)\subseteq\theta$ and $b_\theta(x)=0$, otherwise.

It is easy to observe that $\mathbf{B}_\theta$ is a consistent decision table. Hence applying the methods presented in Section 3.1 we have:

Proposition 3.5 If $\beta_\theta \Rightarrow b_\theta=1$ is a decision rule obtained by applying to $\mathbf{B}_\theta$ any method presented in Section 3.1 and $(\partial_{\mathbf{A}} = \theta)_{\mathbf{A}_\partial} \neq \emptyset$ then

(*i*) $\{x \in U : \partial_{\mathbf{A}}(x) \subseteq \theta\} = (\beta_\theta)_{\mathbf{A}} = (b_\theta = 1)_{\mathbf{B}_\theta}$

(*ii*) $$Bel_{\mathbf{A}}(\theta) = \frac{|\{x \in U : \partial_{\mathbf{A}}(x) = \theta\}|}{|U|}$$

□

In a similar way one can construct the rules corresponding to the upper approximation of the union of decision classes X_i, where $i \in \theta$. The cardinality of this set is related to the value $Pl_{\mathbf{A}}(\theta)$ (see Section 2.2). It is sufficient to construct a decision table

$$\mathbf{P}_\theta=(U, A \cup \{p_\theta\})$$

where $p_\theta(x)=1$ if $\partial_{\mathbf{A}}(x) \cap \theta \neq \emptyset$ and $p_\theta(x)=0$, otherwise.

It is easy to observe that $\mathbf{P}_\theta$ is a consistent decision table. Hence, applying the methods presented in Section 3.1 we have:

Proposition 3.6. If $\gamma_\theta \Rightarrow p_\theta=1$ is a decision rule obtained by applying to p_θ any method presented in Section 3.1 and $(b_\theta = 1)_{\mathbf{B}_\theta} \neq \emptyset$ then

(i) $\{x \in U : \partial_{\mathbf{A}}(x) \cap \theta \neq \emptyset\} = (\gamma_\theta)_{\mathbf{A}} = (p_\theta = 1)_{\mathbf{P}_\theta}$

(ii) $$Pl_{\mathbf{A}}(\theta) = \frac{|\{x \in U : \partial_{\mathbf{A}}(x) \cap \theta \neq \emptyset\}|}{|U|}$$

□

One can apply the same method for the generation of decision rules related to the commonality function.

4 Two Main Concepts: Feature Extraction and Classification of New Objects

4.1 Feature Extraction

The vast majority of pattern-recognition systems developed in the past 20 years contains systems that have been designed to deal with a specific problem or a set of objects (postal address, numerals, etc.). In each system the recognizing concepts and techniques are pre-defined and remain unchanged during the development of the system. Such systems may exhibit excellent performances in dedicated applications, but they are usually inadequate for other environments or other sets of objects. Our research has been focused on a meta-system which can be used as a high level tool to develop various recognition engines that meet user's needs. The approach used in our system is based on the *Rough Set theory* and target recognition systems are built using a *machine-learning* process. In our example each recognition system is based on a decision table that has the digit image database as its object space. The decision attribute contains information about the recognition results (expert decision) of the digits. At the beginning, all the digits in the table are totally indiscernible because the attribute set is empty. During the learning process the user will successively create new attributes for the object set and add them to the decision table. Each new attribute brings a new information into the decision table that may divide existing boundary sets into smaller ones. This will mean that the approximation of expert's classification is improved.

Therefore, with the attributes being added to the decision table, the recognition of objects becomes more accurate. The user continues the process until all digits in the base are properly classified. He may then test his new system on a set of digits not belonging to the database to see how it performs on new objects. During the attribute creation process he will be able to see the effects of his actions on the classifying results and therefore can make the best choice concerning the next step. The process of building a target recognition table is also referred to as *training* or *information acquisition*. The difference between our meta-system and the other dedicated recognizers lies in the flexibility of the attribute set. While dedicated systems have fixed attribute sets specific to the concepts employed, our meta-system gives the user the possibility of modifying his attribute set in order to produce the target recognizer that is best suited to his needs. This unique feature of the system allows the users to create various kinds of recognizers using one common high-level tool.

From the pattern recognition point of view, attributes are used to extract the patterns specific to each class of objects. The system scans for these patterns in new test objects to determine to which class they belong. Therefore the final performance of the target systems relies completely on the chosen attribute set. Attributes used to create recognition systems can be classified as statistical or syntactic-structural. Statistical attributes are usually used to extract the common numerical and discrete patterns contained in the objects from the training set, while syntactic-structural are intended to reflect the structural patterns (e.g., strokes or shapes in digit images) and the interconnections between them. Depending on the nature of the object set, one kind of attributes may be better than the other and vice versa, but the best performance is usually gained by combining the two approaches.

Attributes are used as a means to distinguish classes of objects from each other. In terms of *Rough Set theory* it meant splitting the boundary sets into smaller ones. In the process of building target recognizers in the meta-system, the decision whose boundary set is to be split should be made by the user, and therefore he should have a tool to divide any boundary set of his choice. In our system we have created such a tool using modal concepts described in Section 2. The main idea is to find characteristic modal formulae that have different values for objects belonging to different classes. It allows for distinguishing them from each other. An algorithm for finding such formulae has been developed. This new kind of attribute has proved to be powerful in splitting classes which are very hard to divide by the other traditional attributes and it is one of the unique features of our system.

4.1.1 Implementation of the Modal Concept

The states (worlds) $u,w \in W$ are called *distinguished by a formula* φ if only

$$\mathcal{K},u \models \varphi \text{ and } \mathcal{K},w \models \neg\varphi$$

For a given Kripke model $\mathcal{K} = \langle W,\{R_m\}_{m\in M}, val\rangle$ we define a family of binary relations $\{D_n, n\in \mathbf{N}\}$ in W assuming: $(u,w)\in D_n$ if and only if u and w can be distinguished by a formula whose depth is not greater than n.

It's obvious that $D_n \subseteq D_k$ if $n \le k$, where $n,k \in \mathbf{N}$.

For each label $m\in M$ and each state $w\in W$ we define $R_m(w)$ as the set of states $u\in W$ such that $(w,u)\in R_m$.

Remarks

We can assume that if states u and w are distinguished by formula φ, then φ has one of the following forms: $\Box_m\psi$ or $\neg\Box_m\psi$ or p or $\neg p$, where $p\in V$. This fact is easy to prove by induction with respect to the structure of formula φ. Indeed, if formula φ distinguishes states u and w and φ is e.g. of the form $\varphi=\varphi_1\vee\varphi_2$ then we have

$$\mathcal{K},u \models \varphi_1\vee\varphi_2 \text{ and } \mathcal{K},w \models \neg(\varphi_1\vee\varphi_2), \text{ so}$$

$$(\mathcal{K},u \models \varphi_1 \text{ or } \mathcal{K},u \models \varphi_2) \text{ and } (\mathcal{K},w \models \neg\varphi_1 \text{ and } \mathcal{K},w \models \neg\varphi_2)$$

i.e. either φ_1 or φ_2 distinguishes u from w.

Lemma 4.1 If $D_n = D_{n+1}$ for some $n\in\mathbf{N}$ then $D_n = D_{n+t}$ for any $t\in\mathbf{N}$.

Proof We shall prove this lemma by induction with respect to t. The case $t = 1$ is obvious. Let us suppose that $D_n = D_{n+1}$ and $D_n = D_{n+t} \neq D_{n+t+1}$ for some $t,n\in\mathbf{N}$.
Since $D_{n+t} \subset D_{n+t+1}$, there exists a pair $(u,w)\in D_{n+t+1}$ such that $(u,w)\notin D_{n+t}$. Hence, there exists a formula φ with depth $n+t+1$ which distinguishes u from w i.e.

$$\mathcal{K},u \models \varphi \text{ and } \mathcal{K},w \models \neg\varphi$$

Let us notice that without losing the generality we can assume that $\varphi = \Box_m\psi$ for some $m\in M$, then we have $\neg\varphi \Leftrightarrow \neg(\neg\Diamond_m\neg\psi) \Leftrightarrow \Diamond_m\neg\psi$ and $|\psi| = n+t$.

Let $R_m(u) = \{u_1,..,u_i\} \subseteq W$ and $R_m(w) = \{w_1,..,w_j\} \subseteq W$. We have

$$\mathcal{K},u \models \varphi \text{ iff } \forall k\in\{1,..,i\}\ \mathcal{K},u_k \models \psi \qquad (1)$$

$$\mathcal{K},w \models \neg\varphi \text{ iff } \exists l\in\{1,..,j\}\ \mathcal{K},w_l \models \neg\psi \quad (2)$$

We can assume that $i\geq 1$, because if $R_m(u)=\emptyset$ then $(u,w)\in D_1$. From (1) and (2) it follows that formula ψ distinguishes states $u_1,..,u_i$ from state w_l. Then $\{(u_1,w_l),..,(u_i,w_l)\}\subseteq D_{n+t}=D_n$. It means that there exist formulae $\psi_1,..,\psi_i$ with depth not greater than n such that formula ψ_k distinguishes u_k from w_l for any $k\in\{1,..,i\}$ i.e. $\mathcal{K},u_k \models \psi_k$ and $\mathcal{K},w_l \models \neg\psi_k$.

Let $\eta = \psi_1 \vee \psi_2 \vee .. \vee \psi_i$ and $\phi = \Box_m \eta$, then

$$|\phi| = |\eta| + 1 \leq \max(|\psi_1|,|\psi_2|,..,|\psi_i|) + 1 \leq n+1.$$

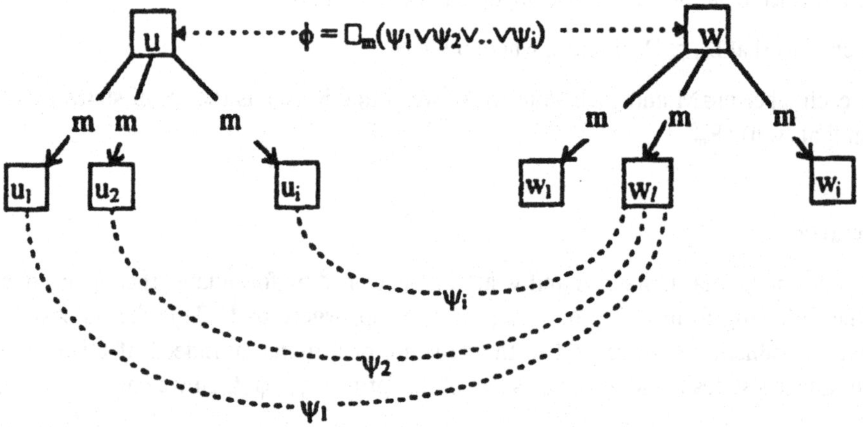

Figure 2.

For any $k\in\{1,..,i\}$ $\mathcal{K},u_k \models \eta$ and $\mathcal{K},w_l \models \neg\eta$, so $\mathcal{K},u \models \phi$ and $\mathcal{K},w \models \neg\phi$ i.e. u can be distinguished from w by formula ϕ with depth not greater than n+1, therefore $(u,w) \in D_{n+1} = D_n = D_{n+t}$, a contradiction.

□

The idea of the lemma is illustrated on Figure 2.

Now we can construct an algorithm generating all the pairs that are distinguishable. The algorithm has the following structure:

Algorithm 4.2

Procedure Analysis

begin
Compute (D_0);
n := 0;
repeat
    n := n+1;
    Compute (D_n)
until $D_n = D_{n-1}$
end.

Application

Using procedure **Analysis** one can easily solve the following problems:

- **Problem 1:** For a given Kripke model $\mathcal{K} = \langle W, \{R_m\}_{m\in M}, val\rangle$ and states $u,w\in W$ check if there exists a formula which distinguishes u from w.

- **Problem 2:** For a given Kripke model $\mathcal{K} = \langle W, \{R_m\}_{m\in M}, val\rangle$ find the set of all pairs $(u,w) \in W\times W$ of distinguishable states .

- **Problem 3:** For a given Kripke model $\mathcal{K} = \langle W, \{R_m\}_{m\in M}, val\rangle$, subsets $S, S' \subseteq W$ check if "S $dist_{\mathcal{K}}$ S' " i.e. if there exists a formula φ such that $\mathcal{K},s \models \varphi$ and $\mathcal{K},s' \models \neg\varphi$ for any $s\in S$ and $s'\in S'$.

The method presented above may be used in searching for partition of a given set of states in order to split them into "*classes of discernibility*" such that two states belonging to different classes are always distinguishable .We will apply this method to the machine learning process used in handwritten digit recognition .

4.2 Classification of New Objects

The main purpose of every recognition system is a correct recognition of objects which it has been designed to deal with. Once we have obtained a decision system with properly classified examples, there are many ways to classify new objects. The simplest way is to compare the attribute value vector of a new object with the value vectors of every object in the decision table in order to find an exact match. If there is such a match, the new object is stated to belong to the same class as its matched counterpart. If the table contains no object with the same value vector, the new object is said to be rejected.

There are two kinds of errors in the process of recognition of new objects: one is rejection and the other is a wrong classification i.e. the new object is assigned a class to which it actually does not belong. Wrong classification and rejection are usually two sides of a medal: If the decision system easily accepts new objects, the wrong classification rate can be high and vice versa. This is because rejection is the result of information overloading in the decision table, while a wrong classification is due to information shortage. Many methods have been developed to improve correct recognition rate as well as to reduce rejection rate (see e.g. [KM90], [MCM83,86], [MT94]). In our system we investigate some such methods by applying rough set tools. One of them is to compute *reducts* and *decision rules* corresponding to these reducts in order to decrease the information overloading with classification structure remaining intact. Another approach is to use special classification function that examines the similarity of new objects to already classified objects, instead of their identical matching. Such functions are usually referred to as *distances measures*, because they are based on some similarities (expressed often in terms of distances) of new objects to those present in the decision table. They can greatly reduce the rejection rate but must be chosen with special care to assure the correctness of the classification.

In our experiments, instead of exact value vectors matching, we used a method based on matching with decision rules. From the original decision table **A** a set of decision rules with minimal number of descriptors is created. For each value vector v of an unseen object the rule set is scanned to find all the rules $\alpha \Rightarrow d=i$, whose left hand side α matches the value vector v, i.e. $v \in \alpha_{\mathbf{A}}$. The new object with the value vector v is assigned a decision i by a number $n_i(v)$ of rules matching v with i. We have different strategies of choosing v, the final decision is computed from the set of numbers $n_i(v)$. The simplest one applied in our system is so-called *majority voting*, i.e. the final decision is the one with the greatest number $n_i(v)$, more precisely, it is chosen randomly from the set

$$\{j: n_j(v) = \max_i n_i(v)\}.$$

In our system we have also implemented some other general strategies for classifying new objects. Among them there is the following one.

From the original decision table **A** a set of subtables is created. Any subtable corresponds to a dynamic reduct (with the stability coefficient greater than a given threshold). Next, we generate a family of sets of decision rules for these subtables with minimal number of descriptors. The final decision of a new object is the result of a competition between the decisions proposed by sets of decision rules from that family.

5 Description of the System

As an illustration of application of pattern recognition concepts discussed in Section 2 we have implemented a meta-system in which a user can create systems recognizing hand-written numerals. We use a database of 800 scanned handwritten digits for learning purposes and a set of 400 other digits for testing. The system can be divided in two modules: The Attribute Module enables a user to create his own attributes of different kinds. They can be used later in the Learning Module to create user-defined recognition system. The Database used in the system is a part of the huge handwritten character database maintained by the National Institute of Standards and Technologies of the United States. It is called "NIST Special Database" and serves as a valuable source of data for many researchers all over the world. The data have been collected with scanners and different pointing devices to extract characters and digits from the special forms written by many people in the US. All digits in our database have one normalized format of 32x32 and are black-white. Information about a digit is stored in a file containing its binary image, which has the size of 128 bytes and its character identification (i.e. what is the type of the digit stored in the file).There are 1200 files of digits from 0 to 9 written by 18 different persons.

5.1 Feature Extraction

The attributes used to create decision tables are of three different kinds: Mask Attributes, Modal Formula Attributes and Topological Attributes. Below is the detailed description of them:

5.1.1 The Mask Attribute Concept

Each mask attribute contains a special bitmap image called a *mask*. A mask is a table of 32x32 pixels which can have values of 1 or 0. Therefore a mask is a bitmap image with the same format as digit's binary representation.

When we compare such a mask with a binary image of a digit, we will find that on some positions the two images have the same pixel's value, on other positions the values are different. Each position at which the values are identical is considered as a match. For every pair of a mask and a digit image we have a unique number of matches ranging from 0 to 1024 (so this number can be treated as the *Hamming distance* between the mask and the digit). If two digits are similar, there is a great chance that in the comparison with the same mask the numbers of matches will not differ very much from each other. Therefore, the number of matches can be used as a characteristic of digit classes. We can then use this number to produce attributes that distinguish digit classes from each other.

The basic concept of mask attributes can be evaluated and improved in order to create better distinguishing attributes. We can, for example, specify explicitly some regions in the mask as relevant. Then in the comparison process only the pixels from these regions will be taken into account instead of all the pixels of the mask. We can also use different functions that transform the number of matches into the attribute value, in order to improve the tolerance and flexibility of the attribute. In our system the user has the ability to edit, save the mask to the disk as well as load a previously saved mask. He will also be able to select the acceptance level as a parameter for the attribute's value assigning function: $f\colon \mathbf{D}\rightarrow\{0,1\}$ where $\mathbf{D}$ is the set of digits

$$f(d) = \begin{cases} 1 \text{ iff percentage of the number of matches in the comparison of d with the mask over the total number of pixels specified is greater than the acceptance level} \\ 0 \text{ if otherwise} \end{cases}$$

We also allow the user to use a special kind of masks, i.e. masks loaded from digit image. By selecting a proper acceptance level, the user can create an attribute that selects all the digits similar to the digit served as a mask.

5.1.2 Modal Formulae as an Attribute Concept

This concept is derived from the modal logic theory described in Section 2. We describe here the implementation of the algorithm presented in Section 4.2.

Let us suppose that $W=\{w_1,w_2,..,w_k\}$. We code the set W as the set $\{1,2,..,k\}$. We define a global array

Result : **Array** [1..k,1..k] **of** Key

```
where  Key = record
               minus : Boolean;
               next  :  {0,..,k};
               label  :  M;
             end;
```

Result [i.j] $\neq$ **nil** if w_i and w_j are distinguished and found (at the current step of the algorithm). Then information containd in "Key" can be used to find a formula distinguishing w_i from w_j. We have some conditions to determine if $(u,w) \in D_n$:

- there exists a propositional variable $p \in V$ such that $val(p,u) \neq val(p,w)$, then $(u,w) \in D_0$ and Result[u,w].next =0. The formula which distinguishes u from w has the form $\varphi = p$.

- there exists a label $m \in M$ such that $R_m(u)=\emptyset$ and $R_m(w)\neq\emptyset$, then $(u,w)\in D_1$, Result[u,w] = [False, w', m], where $w' \in R_m(w)$, and the formula which distinguishes u from w has the form $\varphi = \Box_m \psi$ where $\psi = p$ if $val\ (p,w') = 1$ and $\psi = \neg p$ otherwise, for any p from V.

- there exist a label $m \in M$ such that $R_m(u)\neq\emptyset$ and there exists a state $w' \in R_m(w)$ such that $\forall u' \in R_m(u)$, $(u',w') \in D_{n-1}$ then Result[u,w] = [True,w',m] and Result[w,u] = [False,w',m] and the formula which distinguishes u from w has the form $\varphi=\Box_m(\psi_1 \vee .. \vee \psi_l)$ if $R_m(u) = \{u_1,..,u_l\}$ and ψ_I distinguishes u_i from w' for i=1,..l.

- $(w,u)\in D_n$ and Result[w,u].minus = False, then the formula which distinguishes u from w has the form $\varphi = \neg\psi$ where ψ distinguishes w from u.

Now we present a procedure Compute(i: Integer) which computes the binary relation D_i, assuming that array Result contains all pairs of D_{i-1}.

```
Procedure Compute ( i :Integer);

{we assume that i ≥ 2 and the array Result contains all the pairs of D_{i-1} }

begin

D_i := D_{i-1};

1. for j:=1 to k do
   begin
      S := { s∈W : Result[j,s] is not empty};
      { S is a set of states s∈W such that (j,s)∈D_{i-1}}
      for each m∈M do
      begin
            X := { u ∈W : R_m(u) ⊆ S };
            Y := { w ∈W : j ∈ R_m(w) };
            D_i := D_i ∪ (X × Y) ;
      end
   end
2. Update array Result with information corresponding to those pairs that belong to
   the set (D_i \ D_{i-1})
end;
```

Below we present the detailed description of the procedure Find (i,j : W) which produces a formula distinguishing state w_i from w_j (if such a formula exists) [TS93].

```
Procedure Find ( i,j : W);

{recursive procedure }

begin
if Result[i,j].next = 0 then
      Find a variable p∈ V such that val(p,i) ≠ val(p,j)
      if val(p,i)=1 then write(v)
      else write(¬v)
else
      if Result [i,j].minus then
      begin
            write('-');
            Find(j,i);
      end
      else
      begin
            m:= Result[i,j].label;
            s := Result[i,j].next;
            write('□_m');
            if R_m(i) = ∅ then
            {let p ∈ V }
                  if val(p,s) = 1 then   write(p)
```

```
                else  write (¬p)
          else
          begin
                write('(');
                for each r∈Rm(i)  do
                begin
                      write('v');
                      Find(r,s);
                end;
                write(')');
          end
     end
end;
```

Remarks [TS93]:

- If |M|=n and |V|=e, then the procedure Analysis can find all distinguishable pairs in $O(n*k^4 + e*k^2)$ time, where k is a number of states in the Kripke model.

- Given the array Result, it is possible to find a formula (if such a formula exists) distinguishing given states with time complexity of order $O(k^2*n*e)$.

The main idea is to build an oriented, labeled graph which provides a representation of each digit image from the database. Then we will use the algorithm 4.2 to find a modal formula that has different values for the graph representation of digits belonging to different classes. The values of such a formula calculated for all the digits in the database can be used as a distinguishing attribute for the decision table. In order to apply this algorithm, we will combine graphs of two digits for which we want to find a distinguishing formula into one graph and apply the algorithm for special initial nodes that are specific to the graph type.

The modal formula concept is very flexible and is proved to be resistant to the noise in the digit images. The graph representation can reflect both local and non-local features of the digit image and allows for producing very universal attributes. Its weak spot may be the time required to find the formula, due to the high complexity cost of the algorithm.

We use three graph types in our system to implement the modal logic concept described above. In the first graph type each digit image from the database is divided into 32 rows. In each row we consider sequences of neighbouring black pixels as nodes. Each node has one attribute, the value of which depends on the length of the black sequence. If this length is greater than 8, the node will be attributed as "Long", otherwise it will have value "¬Long".

The edges of the graph are established in accordance with the following rules:

Two nodes in the graph are connected iff:

- They correspond to two black sequences in two adjacent rows and

- Their corresponding black sequences have a vertically adjacent part, i.e. there is at least one pixel in one sequence lying directly below or above another pixel in the second sequence.

The labels of the edges are defined as follows:

Assume that *e* is an edge leading from a node n_1 in the row r_1 to a node n_2 in the row r_2 and c_1 and c_2 are the horizontal coordinates of the middle points of the corresponding black sequences. Then the edge *e* is labeled as:

- "LDown" iff $(r_1 < r_2)$ and $(c_1\text{-}2 > c_2)$
- "Down" iff $(r_1 < r_2)$ and $(c_1\text{-}2 \leq c_2 \leq c_1+2)$
- "RDown" iff $(r_1 < r_2)$ and $(c_1+2 < c_2)$
- "LUp" iff $(r_1 > r_2)$ and $(c_1\text{-}2 > c_2)$
- "Up" iff $(r_1 > r_2)$ and $(c_1\text{-}2 \leq c_2 \leq c_1+2)$
- "RUp" iff $(r_1 > r_2)$ and $(c_1+2 < c_2)$

This graph type is intended to reflect the local connectivity of black strokes in the image. For example, the topmost node of the digit "0" will probably have two lower neighbours, while the similar node of the digit "1" will probably not.

The second graph type is a bit more flexible and is described as follows: Each binary image is divided into rectangular regions of size m×n, where $1 \leq m,n \leq 32$ are parameters specified by a user. Each such a rectangle is considered as a node of the graph. The user can choose some attributes for all nodes in the graph from a set of six pre-defined attributes:

- The first attribute has value 1 iff all the pixels in the rectangle are white.
- The second attribute is 1 iff all the pixels in the rectangle are black.
- The third through sixth attribute is 1 iff the number of black pixels exceeds 20%, 40%, 60%, 80% of the total number of pixels in the rectangle.

The user will also be able to choose a set of pre-defined labels to be used in the graph. They reflect a simple information about adjacency of nodes concerned, i.e. if e is the edge leading from n_1 to n_2, then the label of e tells us whether n_2 is in the North, South, East, West, NE, SE, SW, NW of n_1. The second graph type enables us to store both local and non-local information about the digit image in the graph. The user can adjust the ratio between two types of information by selecting various rectangular sizes and attribute sets.

We have also decided to include a third graph type as an interesting variation of the second type. In this type, instead of eight different label types we have only one denoting the neighbouring relation between rectangles. The user has only to mention the attribute types that are to be included in the graph.

5.1.3 The Topological Attribute Concept

The idea of using topological features of the digit images is to simulate human way of digits recognition. The digit image is scanned in order to extract information about special shapes or curves. It is very easy to see that each type of digits has its own characteristic shapes and strokes that the other types might not have. The topological features can then be very effective tools to produce powerful distinguishing attributes. They can withstand heavy noise in the digit images because is does not depend very much on local features in the image. The main disadvantage of this concept is the trade-off between the efficiency and the complexity of the algorithm used to extract topological information.

Our topological attributes are created as follow: Every white pixel in the digit image is scanned in four directions: North, East, South, West for black pixels. The white pixels may be then surrounded by 0, 1, 2, 3, or 4 black pixels.

We are particularly interested in the following bay configurations:

Enclosed Bay: The white pixels are surrounded by black pixels in all four directions.

North Open Bay :The pixels are surrounded in three directions except the North.

Analogously for **East, South, West, NE, SE, SW** and **NW Open Bays**.

The user can specify what types of bay he is interested in. He will also choose a type in the acceptance level similar to the one for mask attributes. If percentage of the number of pixels that have the specified bay configuration exceeds the acceptance level, the digit will have an attribute value 1. Otherwise, this value will be 0.

Topological attributes allow us to produce distinguishing attributes very quickly. For example, to separate digits type "0" from "5", one can simply create an attribute searching for an Enclosed Bay.

5.2 Optimization of Target Systems

Once a decision table has reached the full approximation of the expert's decision, it can be regarded as a knowledge base for the classification of new digits. However, systems constructed by the interactive process of creating and adding various kinds of attributes usually contain noise and much more information than is actually needed to recognize new digits. This leads to high rejection and confusion rates of classification of new objects and therefore to a low performance of the generated systems. In order to improve efficiency of target systems, we must eliminate the information overloading in the final decision table so that to exclude as many redundancy as possible. In this system we compute the decision rules [BSS94] for each generated system on the basis of the dynamic reducts. Then new digits are classified using these decision rules.

5.3 Remarks on the Implementation

The system has been implemented on IBM PC as a Windows application using the C++ programming language. All Windows graphics interfaces have been designed and implemented using Resource Workshop and Object Windows library from Borland C++ 4.52 Frameworks. Extensive works are being conducted to port the system to UNIX platforms.

6 Experiments with the System

In the experimental system we have implemented two concepts of recognizing new digits. The first one uses a simple identity relation for classification and the second uses dynamic rules calculated for the decision table generated during the learning process. The results of the tests showed the superiority of the second method over the first. Using 800 objects for training and 400 of the others for testing, the system has properly recognized 34% of new digits by the first method and 87% by the second.

Another problem of the recognition process is the variation of the input data which can be illustrated in handwriting by different writing styles of different persons. The variation in writing styles has been proved to be infinite and unpredictable. This fact has tremendous effects on the quality of the recognizers. If a collection of new digits is written by an author whose style is not recorded in the learning database, one can expect a rapid decrease of the recognition efficiency. The problem is widely known and, unfortunately, no satisfactory solution has been found so far, except for using extremely large sets of data for the learning process. This, however, causes many difficulties to and reduces seriously the efficiency and flexibility of the produced systems.

In our experiments we have chosen for testing a more difficult data configuration in order to demonstrate the abilities of the concepts implemented in our system. As a learning data base we have taken 800 digits samples from about 20 writers and for testing purposes we used 400 digit samples from completely different persons. In addition, the testing set has been chosen a specially to contain strangely looking digits which may cause problems even for a human being. The attribute set has been produced during a short learning process. We simply took ten mask attributes based on ten digits written by the first author with acceptance levels around 70 percent, a set of nine topological attributes with acceptance levels 1 (reflecting only the presence of corresponding topological feature). A few modal attributes have been added in the final phase to improve the classification quality within the decision table. We have noticed that the learning time and the classification will be better if we use mask attributes as the first to be included in the decision table. The topological and modal attributes perform much better on boundary sets and classification classes produced by mask attributes. The attribute type that we recommend to add in the next step is the topological type. With wisely chosen acceptance levels they can do the majority of the job needed to classify the digits in the learning database. The modal attributes are especially useful in the final phase to split ambiguous classes that remained.

We also present a study of how each attribute type affects the rejection and confusion rates. From the experiences with the system we have drawn the following conclusion about the efficiency of attribute categories:

i) Mask attributes:

These are very simple and can be quickly computed. Their classification power is not as high as topological attributes but they do not cause many reject cases. The efficiency of mask attributes increases rapidly on data which come from similar sources i.e. written by the same person.

ii) Topological attributes:

Very powerful and flexible. They can greatly increase the recognition quality and keep rejection rates in low level. Their main drawback is the high computing cost.

iii) Modal attributes:

Very efficient in eliminating ambiguities but may cause high rejection rates. They produce information overloading in the values generated for classes that did not require splitting operation. It may cause unnecessary rejection while recognizing new objects. The modal attributes are intended to split a set of indiscernible objects into two smaller sets with a better classification, this they do extremely well. But this operation also has a side effect. Part from the classes it splits, the modal attribute assigns to every other class in the decision tables a value which is more or less inadequate for them. This "gifted" information occasionally may help to improve the classification, but in most cases they rather increase an information redundancy, as they do not necessarily reflect the real features of the objects they are attached to. Although the classification results are not affected by this information overloading, modal attributes may raise the rejection rate during the process of classifying new objects.

We have done some experiments to illustrate the effectiveness of inductive reasoning and dynamic reduction methods introduced in Section 2. We have created a decision table over a set of 800 objects with 80 attributes, of which 18 are topological, 46 are masks and 16 are modal logic attributes. The classification rate was 100% i.e. all 800 training objects were properly recognized (learned). Then we performed two tests of classification on 400 new objects. Two approaches to the classification of new objects have been employed. The first one was based on the identity comparison, while the second used the procedures for calculating dynamic rules. The first approach gave a very poor classification rate. The second method has been realized in two attempts. In the first attempt we grouped the attributes by 5, thus creating a decision table with 18 attributes. For that table we calculated a set of reducts and used reduct majority voting to classify new objects. With this method a recognition rate of 87 % has been achieved. In the second attempt the attributes have been grouped by 2 resulting in a table with 40 attributes. From this attribute set 83 reducts have been extracted. Moreover, we have found three dynamic reducts, each consisting of 26 grouped attributes. The rules produced by these reducts allowed to achieve a new object recognition rate of 86%, thus comparable with the results obtained by the static rules.

Moreover, the rules computed from one of these three reducts allowed to achieve a new object recognition rate of 84%, which is also comparable with the result obtained by the static rules.

By applying the reduct approximations and local dynamic reducts [BS94] we have managed to increase the classification rate up to over 92%.

7 Conclusions

Two main aspects of the problem of object classification have been discussed: feature extraction and decision rule synthesis.

In our system we have implemented several different methods for feature synthesis. We have employed an automated mechanism for feature searching as well as an interactive tool for defining features explicitly by a user. In the former case we proposed an algorithm for searching for feature from a set of multi-modal formulae while the later case involves designing topological and mask attributes.

In addition to some standard methods of decision rule synthesis, we have implemented some new methods for improving the quality of the classification of new objects. One of them is related to dynamic reducts and allows to extract relevant features used in the process of decision rule synthesis. The other is intended to resolve conflicts arising in the process of the classification of new objects induced by a given set of decision rules.

The performed experiments have shown the effectiveness of the proposed methods. We are working on an extension of the system by implementing new algorithms for searching for formulae that can help in distinguishing two collections of objects (current implementation allows for searching for a formula distinguishing pairs of isolated objects only), as well as employing more advanced tools for designing non-structural attributes, namely tolerance relations and attribute quantization. We work also on inductive reasoning methods for improving the quality of new object classification. We are under a process of porting the software to more powerful UNIX platform, and conducting experiments with a much larger data base (about 230.000 digit samples).

This work was partially supported by the grant T11C01011 from State Committee for Scientific Research (Komitet Badan Naukowych).

References

[AD92] Almuallim H., Dietterich T.G., Efficient algorithms for identifying relevant features, Proc. of the Ninth Canadian Conference on Artifitial Intelligence, University of British Columbia 1992, Vancouver, British Columbia, 38-45.

[BSS94] Bazan J., Skowron A., Synak P., Dynamic Reducts as a tool for extracting laws from decision tables, In: Proc. of the International Symposium on Methodologies for Intelligent Systems, October 16-19, 1994, Charlotte, NC, Lecture Notes in Artificial Intelligence No.869, (eds.) M. Zemankova, Z. Ras, Springer-Verlag, Berlin, 1994, 346-355.

[BS94] Bazan J., Skowron A., Synak P., Discovery of decision rules from experimental data, Proceedings of the Third International Workshop on Rough Sets and Soft Computing (RSSC'94), November 10-12, 1994, San Jose State University 1994, 526-533.

[BK86] Bhatnager R.K., Kanal, L.N.: Handling uncertain information: A review of numeric and non-numeric methods. In: Uncertainty in Artificial Intelligence, (eds.) L.N. Kanal. and J.F. Lemmer, North - Holland, Amsterdam 1986.

[BL85] Brachman R.J., Levesque H.J.: Readings in Knowledge Representation, Morgan Kaufmann 1985.

[Br90] Brown F.M. Boolean Reasoning, Kluwer, Dordrecht 1990.

[D92] Downton, A., C., Tregidgo, R.,W., S., Leedham, C., G., Hendrawan, Recorgnition of handwritten British postal addresses. From Pixels to Features III. Frontiers in Handwriting Recorgnition, (eds.) S. Impedovo and J.C .Simon, North-Holland 1992, 129-144.

[Dr92] De Raedt L., Interactive Theory Revision. An Inductive Logic Programming Approach, Academic Press, 1992.

[DP80] Dubois D., Prade H.: Fuzzy Sets and Systems: Theory and Applications, Academic Press, 1980.

[FU92] Fawcett T.E., Utgoff P.E.: Automatic feature generation for problem solving systems, In: Proc. of Ninth International Workshop on Machine Learning (ML92) (ed.) D. Sleeman, Morgan Kaufmann, San Mateo, 1992, 144-153.

[GB92] Grzymała-Busse J.W.: LERS- A System for learning from examples based on rough sets, In: Intelligent Decision Support. Handbook of Applications and Advances of the Rough Sets Theory (ed.) R. Słowiński, Kluwer, Dordrecht 1992, 3-18.

[GB93] Grzymała-Busse D.M., Grzymała-Busse J.W.: Comparison of machine learning and knowledge acquisition methods of rule induction based on rough sets, Proc. of the International Workshop on Rough Sets and Knowledge Discovery RSKD'93, Banff, Canada, October 12-15, 1993, 297-306.

[HC84] Hughes G.E., Cresswell M.J.: A Companion to Modal Logic, Methuen London & New York 1984.

[IOO92] Impedovo S., Occhinegro S., Ottaviano L., A new method for automatic reading of typed/handwritten numerals. In: From Pixels to Features III. Frontiers in Handwriting Recognition, (eds.) S. Impedovo and J.C.Simon, North-Holland 1992, 163-169.

[K59] Kripke S.: A completeness proof in modal logic, J. Symbolic Logic 24, 1-14-1959.

[K63] Kripke S.: Semantical analysis of modal logic I: normal propositional calculi, Zeitschrift für Mathematische Logic und Grundlagen der Mathematik 9, 67-96, 1963.

[K86] Kittler J.: Feature selection and extraction, In: Handbook of pattern recognition and image processing, (eds.)Young and Fu, Academic Press, New York 1986

[KM90] Kodratoff Y., Michalski R.: Machine learning: An Artificial Intelligence approach, vol.3, Morgan Kaufmann, San Mateo, 1990.

[KTM93] Kane R., Tchoumachenko I., Milgram M.: Extraction of knowledge from data using constrained neural networks, Proc. ECML'93, Lecture Notes in Artificial Intelligence vol.667, Springer Verlag, Berlin, 1993.

[MMS91] McMillan C., Mozer M.C., Smolensky P.: The connectionist science game: Rule extraction and refinement in neural network, Proc. of the 13-th Annual Conference on the Cognitive Science Society, Hilsdale, NJ (also as CU-CS-530-91, University of Colorado) 1991.

[MCM83] Michalski R., Carbonell J, Mitchell T.: Machine learning: An Artificial Intelligence approach, vol.1, Tioga, Palo Alto, 1983

[MCM86] Michalski R., Carbonell J, Mitchell T.: Machine learning: An Artificial Intelligence approach, vol.2, Morgan Kaufmann, Los Altos, 1986

[MT94] Michalski R.,Tecuci G.: Machine learning: A Multistrategy approach, vol.4, Morgan Kaufmann, San Mateo, 1994

[Mu92] Muggelton S. (ed.): Inductive logic programming, Academic Press 1992

[PR93] Pattern Recognition Vol.26 Number 3. Handwriting Processing and Recognition, Pergamon Press, March 1993

[Pa82] Pawlak Z.: Rough sets, International Journal of Information and Computer Science 11(1982) 344-356.

[Pa91] Pawlak Z.: Rough sets: Theoretical aspects of reasoning about data, Kluwer, Dordrecht 1991.

[PS93] Pawlak Z., Skowron A.: A rough set approach for decision rules generation. ICS Research Report 23/93, Warsaw University of Technology, also In: Proc. of the IJCAI'93 Workshop W12: The management of Uncertaining in AI, France 1993.

[SD90] Shavlik J.W., Dietterich T.: Readings in Machine Learning, Morgan Kaufmann, San Mateo, 1990.

[Sh76] Shafer G.: Mathematical Theory of Evidence, Princeton University Press 1976.

[SP90] Shafer G., Pearl J., Readings in Uncertain Reasoning, Morgan Kaufmann, San Mateo, California, 1990.

[SL90] Shrager J, Langley P, Computational methods of scientific discovery and theory formation, Morgan Kaufman, San Mateo, 1990.

[SG94] Skowron A., Grzymala-Busse J.W.: From rough set theory to evidence theory. In: Advances in the Dempster-Shafer Theory of Evidence, (eds.) R.R.Yager, M. Fedrizzi and J. Kacprzyk, John Wiley and Sons, New York 1994, 193-236.

[Sk90] Skowron A.: The rough sets theory and evidence theory. Fundamenta Informaticae 13,(1990), 245-262.

[S93a] Skowron A.: Boolean reasoning for decision rule generation, In: Proceedings of the 7-th International Symposium ISMIS'93, Trondheim, Norway 1993, (eds.): J. Komorowski and Z. Ras Lecture Notes in Artificial Intelligence, vol.689, Springer-Verlag, Berlin, 1993, 295-305.

[S93b] Skowron A.: A Synthesis of Decision Rules: Applications of Discernibility Matrices, Proceedings of the Conference on Intelligent Information Systems, Augustow, Poland, June 7-11, 1993.

[S95] Skowron A.: Synthesis of decision systems from experimental data, In: Proc. SCAI-95 Fifth Scandinavian Conference on Artificial Intelligence, (eds) A.Aamodt, J. Komorowski, IOS Press 1995, 220-238.

[SP97] Skowron A., Polkowski L.: Synthesis od decision systems from data tables, In: Rough Sets and Data Mining: Analysis of Imprecise Data, (eds.) T.Y. Lin and N. Cecerone, Kluwer 1997, 259-300.

[SS91] Skowron A., Stepaniuk J.: Towards an approximation theory of discrete problems, Fundamenta Informaticae vol.15(2) 1991, 187-208.

[SS91a] Skowron A., Stepaniuk J.: Searching for Classifiers In:, Proceedings of the First World Conference on Foundations of Artificial Intelligence (eds.) M. de Glas, D. Gabbay, Paris, July 1-5 1991, 447-460.

[SS93] Skowron A., Stepaniuk J.: Intelligent Systems Based on Rough Set Approach, Foundations of Computing and Decision Sciences, vol.18(3-4), 1993, 343-360.

[St94] Stepaniuk J.: Decision Rules for Decision Tables, Bulletin of the Polish Academy of Sciences, Technical Sciences, Vol.42, No. 3, 1994, 457-469.

[Sti92] Stirling C.: Modal and temporal logics, In: Handbook of Logic in Computer Science vol.2, (eds.) S. Abramsky, D.M. Dabbay and T.S. Maibaum, Clarendon Press, Oxford 1992, 478-563.

[TS93] Trung N.T., Son N.H.: An Approach to the Handwriting Digit Recognition Problem Based on Modal Logic, ICS Research Report 44/93, Warsaw University of Technology, 1-58.

[ZS93] Ziarko W., Shan N.: An incremental learning algorithm for constructing decision rules, Proc. of the International Workshop on Rough Sets and Knowledge Discovery, Banff 1993, 335-346.

Chapter 3

On the Lower Boundaries in Learning Rules from Examples

Chien-Chung Chan[1] and Jerzy W. Grzymala-Busse[2]

[1] Department of Mathematical Sciences,
University of Akron, Akron, OH 44325

[2] Department of Electrical Engineering and Computer Science
University of Kansas
Lawrence, KS 66045

Abstract: The paper studies multi-concept learning from inconsistent examples. The main assumption is that knowledge is acquired in the form of production rules, while induced rules represent minimal discriminant description. The paper presents an approach to the elimination of irrelevant attributes in the concept description, or, to be more specific, a new method for determining coverings, the minimal sets of relevant attributes. This method is based on a new tool created within rough set theory. In the presented approach to learning rules from examples, methods of rough set theory are used twice: first, in defining lower boundaries, and then, to deal with inconsistencies. Inconsistent representation of examples is a kind of uncertainty in input data, resulting from gathering information from inconsistent experts or lack of sufficient number of attributes to describe input data.

1 Introduction

Learning rules from examples is one of the most popular methods of machine learning. In this paper, learning the minimal discriminant description of a concept is considered. Discriminant description is defined as complete and consistent. All notations and definitions, used but not explained here can be found in [8]. A preliminary version of this paper, written in different terminology and without proofs, was presented as [1]. This paper includes additional results, not given in [1].

In the process of learning *examples* are given (in other works also called *objects* or *instances*). The set of all examples is called an *universe* and denoted U. Each example is described by n attributes $A_1, A_2,..., A_n$. An attribute A_i may take a value from the finite set V_i of attribute values, where $i = 1, 2,..., n$. For any two different attributes their value sets may or may be not exclusive. An example E is represented by a vector of the length n of pairs (A_i, v_i), where v_i is the value of attribute A_i for example E. Two different examples may be represented by the same vector $((A_1, v_1), (A_2, v_2),..., (A_n, v_n))$. A nonempty subset of the universe is called a *concept* to be learned. In other works the concept is also called a *class*. Members of the concept are called *positive examples*, while all remaining members of the universe are called *negative examples.* In the process of learning, a *representation* of the concept is sought. In this paper, like in the most of other approaches to learning from examples, a set of production rules is such a representation. This paper discusses multiple-concept learning, i.e. learning k concepts $C_1, C_2, \ldots, C_k$. It is assumed that concepts are mutually exclusive and that their union is equal to the universe U. In other words, $\{C_1, C_2, \ldots, C_k\}$ is a partition on U. Note that any concept C_i is a set of positive examples, while $U - C_i$ is the set of negative examples for C_i, where $i = 1, 2, \ldots, k$.

The assumption that concepts $C_1, C_2, \ldots, C_k$ are mutually exclusive does not exclude *inconsistent representation of examples*, i.e., overlapping of sets of vectors of the length n of pairs (attribute, value) corresponding to $C_1, C_2, \ldots, C_k$. Thus learning systems under consideration must handle this kind of uncertainty, caused by, e.g., gathering information from inconsistent experts, or lack of sufficient number of attributes to describe examples. The latter may happen when more than n attributes are required for exact description of examples, but only n attributes are accessible. When such sets of vectors of (attribute, value) pairs are mutually disjoint, the corresponding learning under consideration is called *learning from consistent representation of examples*, otherwise it is called *learning from inconsistent representation of examples.*

Let A denote the set $\{A_1, A_2, \ldots, A_n\}$ of all attributes. Let B be a subset of A, containing l attributes. Two examples, E_1 and E_2, represented by the same vector of length l of pairs (attribute, value), where each attribute is a member of B, are called *B-indiscernible*, and denoted $E_1 \underset{B}{\sim} E_2$. Obviously, $\underset{B}{\sim}$ is an equivalence relation on the universe U. This relation induces a partition on U, denoted B*. Such a partition B* is the set of all equivalence classes of $\underset{B}{\sim}$, called *blocks* of B*.

Conversely, every partition on universe U defines an attribute. Thus we may think about new attributes, different from all attributes from the set A, and corresponding to the partitions $\{C_1, C_2, \ldots, C_k\}$ and $\{C_i, U - C_i\}$, where $i = 1, 2, \ldots, k$. Thus, the new attribute, corresponding to the partition $\{C_1, C_2, \ldots, C_k\}$ will be called a *multi-conceptual variable.* The new attribute, corresponding to $\{C_i, U - C_i\}$, will be called *conceptual variable.*

In many papers on machine learning from examples the importance of using relevant attributes in representation of the concept has been observed [1 - 3, 5, 6]. Nevertheless, very few methods for the selection of relevant attributes were given [1, 5]. The problem of selection of relevant attributes is the main problem of this paper. First of all, the formal definition of relevant attribute is needed. The following definition of dependency is borrowed from relational databases, where it is known under the name of functional dependency [11, p. 213]. Here, the name of functional dependency is abbreviated to dependency because it is the only kind of attribute dependency which is discussed. Let B and D be two subsets of the set of all attributes A. Set D *depends on* set B, denoted $B \to D$, if and only if $B^* \leq D^*$, where $B^* \leq D^*$ means that for each block b of B* there exists a block d of D* such that $b \subseteq d$.

Concept C_i *depends on* a subset B of set A, denoted $B \rightarrow C_i$, if and only if $B^* \leq C_i,^*$, where $C_i,^*$ is equal to the partition $\{C_i, U - C_i\}$ on U.

Practically, concept C_i depends on a subset B of the set A of all attributes if and only if the description of positive examples by attributes from B is sufficient to recognize the concept C_i. In other words, the set of all positive examples is the union of some blocks of B^* (and then, as a consequence, the set of all negative examples is also the union of some blocks of B^*). In production rules describing concept C_i, which depends on B, if-parts may contain attributes only from subset B, instead of attributes from the entire set A. Hence such rules are simpler.

Obviously, the most interesting case is when the size of the set B is the smallest possible. Thus, a new definition is needed: a subset B of the set A of all attributes is called a *covering* of the set D if and only if D depends on B and B is minimal. This is equivalent to the following: B is a *covering* of D if and only if D depends on B and no proper subset B' of B exists such that D depends on B'. The notion of a covering B of the set D, for $D^* = A^*$, is analogous to that of a key of relation scheme [11, p. 217]. In the special case of D equal to a single attribute and D^* equal to $C_i,^*$, B is called a *covering of the concept* C_i.

An algorithm for learning rules from examples with consistent representation, and another algorithm for learning rules from examples with inconsistent representation and based on lower and upper approximations [4], were implemented as programs LEM1 [2] and LERS1 [7], respectively. Both programs are written in Franz Lisp and are running on VAX 11/780. A descendant of LERS1, an improved version, called LERS1.1, was implemented on VAX11/780 in 1989. A newer program, called LERS_LB (Learning from Examples based on Rough Sets - Lower Boundaries), was recently implemented on VAX11/780.

2 Rough Sets

The notion of a rough set was first introduced by Pawlak [9], see also [10, 12]. The fundamental idea of rough set theory is the notion of *approximation space*, which is an ordered pair (U, α), where U is a nonempty set, called the *universe*, and α is an equivalence relation on U, called an *indiscernibility relation*. Equivalence classes of α are called *elementary sets*. We assume that the empty set is elementary. Another notion is the definability of subsets of the universe in terms of elementary sets in an approximation space. A *definable set* is any finite union of elementary sets. For each subset X in U, X is characterized by a pair of sets, the lower and upper approximation of X. For $x \in U$, let $[x]_\alpha$ denote the equivalence class of α containing x. Then, the *lower approximation of X* is defined as:

$$\underline{\alpha} X = \{x \in U \mid [x]_\alpha \subseteq X\}.$$

The *upper approximation of X* is defined as:

$$\overline{\alpha} X = \{ x \in U \mid [x]_\alpha \cap X \neq \emptyset \}.$$

A subset X of U is definable if and only if $\underline{\alpha} X = \overline{},\alpha X$. A *rough set* is the family of all subsets of U having the same lower and upper approximations. The lower approximation of X is the greatest definable set contained in X. The upper approximation of X is the least definable set containing X.

Thus, for a nonempty subset B of the set A of all attributes, an ordered pair $(U, \underset{B}{\sim})$ is an approximation space. For convenience, for any $X \subseteq U$, the lower approximation of X and the upper approximation of X will be called *B-lower approximation of X* and *B-upper approximation of X*, and will be denoted by $\underline{B}X$ and $\overline{B}X$, respectively. A definable set X will be called *B-definable*. Thus, X is B-definable if and only if $\underline{B}X = \overline{B}X$, and X is *B-undefinable* if and only if $\underline{B}X \neq \overline{B}X$. Similarly, a partition χ of U will be called *B-definable* if and only if every block b of χ is B-definable.

3 Rough Definability of Sets and Partitions

In order to test whether a subset X of U is B-definable, it is sufficient to compute B-lower or the B-upper approximation of X, as follows from the following proposition.

Proposition 1. (Definability of Sets) *Let* $X \subseteq U$ *and let* $B \subseteq A$. *Then the following statements are equivalent.*
(1) X *is* B-*definable,*
(2) $\underline{B}X = X$,
(3) $\overline{B}X = X$.

Proof is straightforward. ■

The extension of the above result to the definability of a partition χ on U is obvious. It is given in the following proposition.

Proposition 2. (Definability of Partitions) *Let* $\chi = \{X_1, X_2, ..., X_n\}$ *be a partition on* U *and let* $B \subseteq A$. *Then the following statements are equivalent.*
(1) *The partition* χ *is* B-*definable,*
(2) *For each* X_i *in* χ, $\underline{B}X_i = X_i$,
(3) *For each* X_i *in* χ, $\overline{B}X_i = X_i$.

Proof is straightforward. ■

Proposition 3. *Let* B *and* D *be two subsets of* A. *The following conditions are equivalent.*
(1) $B \rightarrow D$,
(2) *For each* $X \subseteq U$, $\underline{D}X \subseteq \underline{B}X$,

(3) *For each* $X \subseteq U$, $\overline{B}X \subseteq \overline{D}X$.

Proof. (1) $\Rightarrow$(2) is obvious.

(2) $\Rightarrow$ (1). Suppose that for each $X \subseteq U$, $\underline{D}X \subseteq \underline{B}X$, and $B^* \not\leq D^*$. Then there exists $b \in B^*$ such that for all $d \in D^*$, $b \not\subseteq d$. Thus there exists $a \in D^*$, $a \cap b \neq \emptyset$, and $b \not\subseteq a$. Furthermore, $\underline{D}a = a$ and $\underline{B}a$ is a proper subset of a. But then $\underline{D}a \not\subseteq \underline{B}a$, a contradiction.

The proof for (1) $\Leftrightarrow$ (3) is analogous. ■

Corollary 4. *Let* $X \subseteq U$ *and let* B *and* D *be two subsets of* A. *Then* $\underline{B}X \cup \underline{D}X \subseteq \underline{B \cup D}X$ *and* $\overline{B \cup D} \subseteq \overline{B}X \cap \overline{D}X$.

Proof. First, $\underline{B}X \subseteq \underline{B \cup D}X$ because $(B \cup D)^* \leq B^*$ and Proposition 3. Similarly, $\underline{D}X \subseteq \underline{B \cup D}X$. Thus $\underline{B}X \cup \underline{D}X \subseteq \underline{B \cup D}X$.

On the other hand, $\overline{B \cup D}X \subseteq \overline{B}X$ because $(B \cup D)^* \leq B^*$ and Proposition 3. Similarly, $\overline{B \cup D}X \subseteq \overline{D}X$. Thus $\overline{B \cup D}X \subseteq \overline{B}X \cap \overline{D}X$. ■

Example. An illustration of the above notions is given by the following example, see Table 1. The universe U is equal to $\{E_1, E_2, E_3, E_4, E_5, E_6\}$. Let B = {Pressure, Temperature} and D = {Speed}. Then

$$B^* = \{\{E_1\}, \{E_2\}, \{E_3\}, \{E_4\}, \{E_5\}, \{E_6\}\},$$
$$D^* = \{\{E_1, E_2\}, \{E_3, E_5, E_6\}, \{E_4\}\}.$$

Thus, $B \to D$, because $B^* \leq D^*$. Moreover, B = {Pressure, Temperature} is a covering of D = {Speed}. Another covering of {Speed} is {Temperature, Noise}. Observe that {Pressure, Noise} is not a covering of {Speed}.

Table 1

Attributes	Multi-Conceptual Variable			
	Pressure	Temperature	Noise	Speed
E_1	Low	Low	High	Decrease
E_2	Normal	Low	High	Decrease
E_3	Low	Medium	High	Increase
E_4	Normal	Medium	Normal	Normal
E_5	Low	High	Normal	Increase
E_6	Normal	High	Normal	Increase

4 Lower and Upper Boundaries

The major computation in finding coverings is associated with checking the attribute dependency. Let B and D be two sets of attributes. One way to verify that D depends on B is to check whether $B^* \leq D^*$. Another way to verify that D depends on B is by testing whether each block in D^* is B-definable. Notions of lower and upper boundaries, introduced below, will speed up the process of checking whether D depends on B.

Let $X \subseteq U$ and let $B \subseteq A$. The set $X - \underline{B}X$, denoted $\underline{\Delta}_B(X)$, will be called a *B-lower boundary of X*. Similarly, the set $\overline{B}X - X$, denoted $\overline{\Delta}_B(X)$, will be called a *B-upper boundary of X*.

From the above definition, when $X = \emptyset$ or $X = U$, for every nonempty subset B of A, we have $\underline{\Delta}_B(X) = \emptyset$ and $\overline{\Delta}_B(X) = \emptyset$. This corresponds to the fact that both $\emptyset$ and U are always definable. Intuitively, a smaller lower or upper boundary indicates a better approximation of a set of objects. For set B of attributes, a B-lower boundary of X represents those objects in X that are not certainly belonging to X, on the basis of the information provided by the set B. Therefore, the empty B-lower boundary of X means that all objects either certainly belong to X or they certainly do not, on the basis of the information provided by the set B. Similarly, a B-upper boundary of X represents those objects in the universe U that possibly do not belong to X, on the basis of information provided by the set B. Thus, the empty B-upper boundary of X means, again, that all objects either certainly belong to X or they certainly do not, on the basis of the information provided by the set B. Hence, either lower or upper boundaries may be used to test the definability of sets. This is stated in the following proposition.

Proposition 5. *Let* $X \subseteq U$ *and let* $B \subseteq A$. *Then the following statements are equivalent.*

(1) X *is* B-*definable,*

(2) $\underline{\Delta}_B(X) = \emptyset$,

(3) $\overline{\Delta}_B(X) = \emptyset$.

Proof is straightforward. ■

When we try to describe an undefinable set of objects by using more attributes, the important question is when the new, bigger set of attributes is sufficient to define a set. A sufficient condition for determining that the union of two sets of attributes is good enough to define a set is given in the following proposition.

Proposition 6. *Let* $X \subseteq U$ *and let* B *and* D *be two subsets of* A.
(1) *If* $\underline{\Delta}_B(X) \cap \underline{\Delta}_D(X) = \emptyset$ *then set* X *is* (B∪D)*-definable,*
(2) *If* $\overline{\Delta}_B(X) \cap \overline{\Delta}_D(X) = \emptyset$ *then set* X *is* (B∪D)*-definable.*

Proof. (1) $\underline{\Delta}_B(X) \cap \underline{\Delta}_D(X) = (X - \underline{B}X) \cap (X - \underline{D}X) = X - (\underline{B}X \cup \underline{D}X) \supseteq X - \underline{B \cup D}\,X = \underline{\Delta}_{B\cup D}(X)$, by Corollary 4. Thus if $\underline{\Delta}_B(X) \cap \underline{\Delta}_D(X) = \emptyset$ then $\underline{\Delta}_{B\cup D}(X) = \emptyset$, and set X is (B∪D)-definable by (1) of Proposition 5.

(2) $\overline{\Delta}_B(X) \cap \overline{\Delta}_D(X) = (\overline{B}X - X) \cap (\overline{D}X - X) = \overline{B}X \cap \overline{D}X - X \supseteq \overline{B \cup D}\,X - X = \overline{\Delta}_{B\cup D}(X)$, by Corollary 4. Thus if $\overline{\Delta}_B(X) \cap \overline{\Delta}_D(X) = \emptyset$ then $\overline{\Delta}_{B\cup D}(X) = \emptyset$, and set X is (B∪D)-definable by (2) of Proposition 5. ■

The following proposition gives a characterization of (B∪D) - definability.

Proposition 7. *Let* $X \subseteq U$ *and let* B *and* D *be two subsets of* A. *Then the following statements are equivalent.*
(1) X *is* (B∪D)*-definable,*
(2) $\underline{\Delta}_{B\cup D}(X) = \emptyset$,
(3) *For all* $x \in \underline{\Delta}_B(X) \cap \underline{\Delta}_D(X)$, $[x]_B \cap [x]_D \subseteq X$,
(4) $\overline{\Delta}_{B\cup D}(X) = \emptyset$,
(5) *For all* $x \in \overline{\Delta}_B(X) \cap \overline{\Delta}_D(X)$, $[x]_B \cap [x]_D \subseteq \overline{\Delta}_B(X) \cap \overline{\Delta}_D(X)$.

Proof. (1) ⇔ (2). A set X is (B∪D)-definable ⇔ $X = \underline{B \cup D}\,X \Leftrightarrow X - \underline{B \cup D}\,X = \emptyset$ ⇔ $\underline{\Delta}_{B\cup D}(X) = \emptyset$.
Proof that (1) ⇒ (3) is obvious.
(3) ⇒ (1). Let $x \in X$. Then either $x \in \underline{B}X \cup \underline{D}X$ or $x \in X - (\underline{B}X \cup \underline{D}X)$. Suppose that $x \in \underline{B}X \cup \underline{D}X$. Say that $x \in \underline{B}X$. Then $[x]_B \subseteq X$, and $[x]_{B\cup D} = [x]_B \cap [x]_D \subseteq [x]_B \subseteq X$. Suppose that $x \in X - (\underline{B}X \cup \underline{D}X)$. Then $[x]_{B\cup D} = [x]_B \cap [x]_D \subseteq X$ by (3). Therefore, X is (B∪D)-definable.
Proof that (1) ⇔ (4) is analogous to the proof that (1) ⇔ (2).
Proof that (1) ⇒ (5) is obvious.
(5) ⇒ (1). Suppose that (5) holds and X is not (B∪D)-definable. Then there exists $x \in X$ such that $[x]_{B\cup D} \not\subseteq X$. Say that $y \in [x]_{B\cup D}$ and $y \notin X$. Furthermore, $[x]_{B\cup D} \subseteq \overline{B \cup D}\,X$ by the definition of upper approximation, and $\overline{B \cup D}\,X \subseteq \overline{B}X \cap \overline{D}X$, by Corollary 4. Thus, $[x]_{B\cup D} \subseteq \overline{B}X \cap \overline{D}X$, and $y \in (\overline{B}X \cap \overline{D}X) - X$, because $y \in [x]_{B\cup D}$ and $y \notin X$. By (5), $[y]_{B\cup D} \subseteq \overline{\Delta}_B(X) \cap \overline{\Delta}_D(X) = (\overline{B}X - X) \cap (\overline{D}X - X) = (\overline{B}X \cap \overline{D}X) - X$. Moreover, $[x]_{B\cup D} \subseteq (\overline{B}X \cap \overline{D}X) - X$, since $[x]_{B\cup D} = [y]_{B\cup D}$. Therefore, $[x]_{B\cup D} \cap X = \emptyset$, hence $x \notin X$, a contradiction. ■

Example (continued). For Table 1, let $X = \{E_1, E_2\}$ be a concept (it is the set of all examples characterized by the value 'Decrease' of the multi-conceptual variable Speed). Then

$$\underline{\Delta}\,B\{\text{Pressure}\}(X) = X - \underline{\{\text{Pressure}\}}\,(X) = \{E_1, E_2\} - \emptyset = \{E_1, E_2\}.$$

Thus, X is not {Pressure}-definable, or, X is not definable by the attribute {Pressure}.

On the other hand,

$$\underline{\Delta}\,B\{\text{Temperature}\}(X) = X - \underline{\{\text{Temperature}\}}\,(X) = \{E_1, E_2\} - \{E_1, E_2\} = \emptyset.$$

Thus, X is {Temperature}-definable, or, X is definable by the attribute {Temperature}.

In order to find rules for a concept C_i depending on as a small number of attributes as possible it is necessary to find coverings of C_i.

In Table 2, the set of examples from Table 1 is presented, where the multi-conceptual variable Speed is replaced by three conceptual variables: $Speed_{Decrease}$, $Speed_{Normal}$, and $Speed_{Increase}$. The partition, corresponding to the conceptual variable $Speed_{Decrease}$, is $\{Speed_{Decrease}\}^* = \{\{E_1, E_2\}, \{E_3, E_4, E_5, E_6\}\}$, where positive examples are E_1 and E_2, negative examples are E_3, E_4, E_5, E_6, and {Temperature} is the only covering of the concept $\{E_1, E_2\}$. The following rule is induced from the covering {Temperature}:

(Temperature, Low) $\rightarrow$ (Speed, Decrease).

Similarly, $\{Speed_{Normal}\}^* = \{\{E_1, E_2, E_3, E_5, E_6\}, \{E_4\}\}$. Here, the only positive example is E_4, all remaining examples are negative. There are two coverings of the concept $\{E_4\}$: {Pressure, Temperature} and {Temperature, Noise}. From the coverings {Pressure, Temperature} and {Temperature, Noise} the following rules may be induced, respectively:

(Pressure, Normal) $\wedge$ (Temperature, Medium) $\rightarrow$ (Speed, Normal),

(Temperature, Medium) $\wedge$ (Noise, Normal) $\rightarrow$ (Speed, Normal).

Finally, $\{Speed_{Increase}\}^* = \{\{E_1, E_2, E_4\}, \{E_3, E_5, E_6\}\}$, the positive examples are E_3, E_5, E_6, and negative examples are E_1, E_2, E_4. Again, there are two coverings of the concept $\{E_3, E_5, E_6\}$: {Pressure, Temperature} and {Temperature, Noise}. From the covering {Pressure, Temperature} the following rules may be induced, after dropping conditions [6]:

(Pressure, Low) $\wedge$ (Temperature, Medium) $\rightarrow$ (Speed, Increase),

(Temperature, High) $\rightarrow$ (Speed, Increase),

and from the covering {Temperature, Noise}, after dropping conditions, the following rules may be induced:

(Temperature, Medium) $\wedge$ (Noise, High) $\rightarrow$ (Speed, Increase),

(Temperature, High) $\rightarrow$ (Speed, Increase).

Table 2

Attributes	Conceptual Variables					
	Pressure	Temperature	Noise	$Speed_{Decrease}$	$Speed_{Normal}$	$Speed_{Increase}$
E_1	Low	Low	High	yes	no	no
E_2	Normal	Low	High	yes	no	no
E_3	Low	Medium	High	no	no	yes
E_4	Normal	Medium	Normal	no	yes	no
E_5	Low	High	Normal	no	no	yes
E_6	Normal	High	Normal	no	no	yes

5 Certain and Possible Rules

In learning rules from an inconsistent representation of examples, the produced rules are categorized into certain and possible [2, 4]. For a concept C_i, certain rules are induced by the A-lower approximation $\underline{A}\, C_i$ of the set H_i as the set of positive examples, and by $U - \underline{A}\, C_i$ as the set of negative examples. Possible rules are induced by the A-upper approximation $\overline{A}\, C_i$ as the set of positive examples, and by $U - \overline{A}\, C_i$ as the set of negative examples. A multi-conceptual variable is replaced by 2k new conceptual variables. The first k of them will be called *lower conceptual variables.* The remaining k, will be called *upper conceptual variables*. Here again, in order to find certain rules for a concept C_i depending on as a small number of attributes as possible it is necessary to find coverings of the set $\underline{A}\, C_i$. Similarly, in order to find possible rules depending on as a small number of attributes as possible it is necessary to find coverings of the set $\overline{A}\, C_i$. The following results will be helpful for that purpose.

Proposition 8. *Let* $B \subseteq A$, *let* $Y \subseteq X \subseteq U$, *and let* X *be* B-*definable. Then* Y *is* B-*definable if and only if* $X - Y$ *is* B-*definable*.

Proof of the necessary condition is obvious. For the proof of the sufficient condition, suppose that Y is B-undefinable. Then there exists $x \in Y$ such that $[x]_B \not\subseteq Y$, i.e., there exists $y \in [x]_B$ with $y \notin Y$. Furthermore, $[x]_B \subseteq X$ since X is B-definable, by definition. Thus $y \in X - Y$, or $[y]_B \subseteq X - Y$. Moreover, $\underline{B}(X - Y) = X - Y$, since $X - Y$ is B-definable and Proposition 1. Thus $[y]_B \subseteq \underline{B}(X - Y)$. However, $[x]_B = [y]_B$, hence $x \in [x]_B \subseteq \underline{B}(X - Y) = X - Y$, and $x \in X - Y$, i.e. $x \notin Y$, a contradiction. ■

Proposition 9. *Let* $\mathcal{X} = \{X, U - X\}$ *be a two-block partition of* U *and let* $B \subseteq A$. *Then the following statements are equivalent.*
(1) X *is* B-*definable*,
(2) U − X *is* B-*definable*,
(3) {X, U − X} *is* B-*definable*.

Proof. This proposition follows from Proposition 8. ■

The relationship between the lower and upper boundaries of a subset X is given in the following proposition.

Proposition 10. *Let* $X \subseteq U$ *and let* $B \subseteq A$. *Then* $\underline{\Delta}_B(X) = \overline{\Delta}_B(U - X)$ *and* $\overline{\Delta}_B(X) = \underline{\Delta}_B(U - X)$.

Proof. $\underline{\Delta}_B(X) = X - \underline{B}X = (U - \underline{B}X) - (U - X) = \overline{B}(U - X) - (U - X) = \overline{\Delta}_B(U - X)$. Moreover, $\overline{\Delta}_B(X) = \overline{B}X - X = (U - X) - (U - \overline{B}X) = (U - X) - \underline{B}(U - X) = \underline{\Delta}_B(U - X)$. ■

Table 3

Attributes				Multi-conceptual variable
	Pressure	Temperature	Noise	Speed
E_1	Low	Low	High	Decrease
E_2	Normal	Low	High	Decrease
E_3	Low	Medium	High	Increase
E_4	Normal	Medium	Normal	Normal
E_5	Low	High	Normal	Increase
E_6	Normal	High	Normal	Increase
E_7	Normal	Medium	Normal	Increase
E_8	Low	High	Normal	Normal

Example (continued). The following illustrates how to induce minimal certain and possible rules from examples. Table 3 presents a new set of examples, obtained from Table 1 by adding two new examples, E_7 and E_8. Note that examples E_4 and E_7 have the same values for all attributes yet they belong to different concepts. Thus, E_4 and E_7 represent inconsistent examples. Another inconsistency is represented by examples E_5 and E_8.

Table 4

	E_1	E_2	E_3	E_4	E_5	E_6	E_7	E_8
$Speed_{Decrease}$	yes	yes	no	no	no	no	no	no
$\underline{A}\ Speed_{Decrease}$	yes	yes	no	no	no	no	no	no
$\overline{A}\ Speed_{Decrease}$	yes	yes	no	no	no	no	no	no
$Speed_{Normal}$	no	no	no	yes	no	no	no	yes
$\underline{A}\ Speed_{Normal}$	no	no	no	no	no	no	no	no
$\overline{A}\ Speed_{Normal}$	no	no	no	yes	yes	no	yes	yes
$Speed_{Increase}$	no	no	yes	no	yes	yes	yes	no
$\underline{A}\ Speed_{Increase}$	no	no	yes	no	no	yes	no	no
$\overline{A}\ Speed_{Increase}$	no	no	yes	yes	yes	yes	yes	yes

Table 4 presents all conceptual variables and their lower and upper approximations for the set of examples from Table 3.

Table 5

Conceptual Variable	Coverings of concepts corresponding to conceptual variables
$Speed_{Decrease}$	{Temperature}
$\underline{A}Speed_{Decrease}$	{Temperature}
$\overline{A}\ Speed_{Decrease}$	{Temperature}
$Speed_{Normal}$	Ø
$\underline{A}\ Speed_{Normal}$	Ø
$\overline{A}\ Speed_{Normal}$	{Pressure, Temperature}
$Speed_{Increase}$	Ø
$\underline{A}\ Speed_{Increase}$	{Pressure, Temperature}
$\overline{A}\ Speed_{Increase}$	{Temperature}

In Table 5 coverings for all concepts, related to conceptual variables and their lower and upper approximations are given. The corresponding certain rules are

$$(\text{Temperature, Low}) \rightarrow (\text{Speed, Decrease}),$$
$$(\text{Pressure, Low}) \wedge (\text{Temperature, Medium}) \rightarrow (\text{Speed, Increase}),$$
$$(\text{Pressure, Normal}) \wedge (\text{Temperature, High}) \rightarrow (\text{Speed, Increase}),$$

and the corresponding possible rules are

$$(\text{Temperature, Low}) \rightarrow (\text{Speed, Decrease}),$$
$$(\text{Pressure, Normal}) \wedge (\text{Temperature, Medium}) \rightarrow (\text{Speed, Normal}),$$

(Pressure, Low) ∧ (Temperature, High) → (Speed, Normal),
(Temperature, Medium) → (Speed, Increase),
(Temperature, High) → (Speed, Increase).

6 Algorithms for Learning Rules from Consistent Examples

In the algorithm presented below, minimal rules are produced from coverings of concepts. In this section, we present a procedure for finding all such coverings by using lower boundaries.

Let $C_1, C_2,..., C_k$ be the set of all concepts. When examples are consistent, the partition $\{C_i, U - C_i\}$ is A-definable. By Proposition 9, the condition that the partition $\{C_i, U - C_i\}$ is A-definable may be replaced by the condition that the set C_i is A-definable. Therefore, the task of finding all coverings for all C_i is reduced to finding all minimal subsets B of A such that C_i is B-definable. This is done by the following procedure CONSISTENT.

Input: Concepts $C_1, C_2,..., C_k$.

Output: All coverings of all concepts $C_1, C_2,..., C_k$.

Procedure CONSISTENT (concepts $C_1, C_2,..., C_k$);

{CONSISTENT produces all coverings of all concepts $C_1, C_2,..., C_k$}

begin

for each a in A **do**

Compute the partition $\{a\}^*$ of U generated by a;

for each C_i , i = 1, 2, ..., k **do**

begin

for each a in A **do**

begin

Compute the {a}-lower approximation $\underline{\{a\}}C_i$;

Compute the {a}-lower boundary $\underline{\Delta}_{\{a\}}(C_i)$;

end;

if the A-lower boundary of C_i is not empty **then** no covering for C_i exists

else FIND_ALL_COVERINGS (C_i);

{Procedure FIND_ALL_COVERINGS (C_i) generates all minimal subsets B of C such that C_i is B-definable.}

end;

end; {CONSISTENT}

The A-lower boundary of C_i can be computed due to Proposition 7. The time complexity for finding all coverings of concept is exponential with respect to the number of attributes. However, it takes only polynomial time to find one covering of a concept in the set of all condition attributes.

All coverings of C_i are found on the basis of positive examples represented by set C_i by the following procedure FIND_All_COVERINGS.

Procedure FIND_All_COVERINGS (C_i: a subset of U);
{The input, set C_i, to this procedure represents the set of positive examples of a concept that is C-definable. Attributes are represented by positive numbers i, where i = 1, 2, ..., |C| = n. A nonempty subset B = $\{a_{i_1}, a_{i_2}, ..., a_{i_k}\}$ of A is represented by a subset $\{i_1, i_2, ..., i_k\}$ of the set of positive numbers {1, 2, ..., n}, and the empty set Ø is represented by {0}.}

begin

COVERINGS := {0};

B := {0}; {Initially, B is set to be empty set. }

ROOT := GEN_CHILDREN (B);

{A child B' of B is superset of B such that |B'| = |B| + 1.

ROOT is a set of subsets B' of A such that B' is a child of B.

Procedure FIND_All_COVERINGS produces a tree with the empty set, {0}, as its root, and each member of ROOT is used as the root of a subtree.}

repeat

PRUNING_SET := {0};

for each B in ROOT **do**

if $\underline{\Delta}_B(C_i)$ = {0} **then**

begin

Add B to COVERINGS;

Add B to PRUNING_SET;

end;

ROOT := ROOT – PRUNING_SET;

if ROOT ≠ {0}

```
        then for each B in ROOT do
                begin
                    TEMP_ROOT:= {0};
                    NEW_ROOT := GEN_CHILDREN (B);
                    for each B' in NEW_ROOT do
                        if for all B" in PRUNING_SET, B' is not a superset of B"
                        then Add B' to TEMP_ROOT;
                end;
                ROOT := TEMP_ROOT;
    until ROOT = {0};
end; {FIND_ALL_COVERINGS}
```

In the procedure FIND_All_COVERINGS, supersets of B are generated by using the following procedure.

```
Procedure GEN_CHILDREN (B: a subset of A);
                {This procedure generates a set GEN_CHILDREN (B) of subsets B'
                of A  such that B' is a superset of B and |B'| = |B| + 1.}
begin
    GEN_CHILDREN (B):= {0};
    M := MAX (B);      {Function MAX (B) returns the maximum number in B.}
    for i = M + 1 to |C| = n do
        begin
            B' := B ∪ {i};
            Add B' to GEN_CHILDREN (B);
        end;
end; {GEN_CHILDREN}
```

7 Algorithms for Learning Certain and Possible Rules from Inconsistent Examples

As mentioned in Section 5, minimal certain and possible rules are produced from coverings of lower and upper approximations of concepts. The procedure for finding these coverings is presented below. Since $\underline{A}\, C_i$ and $\overline{A}\, C_i$ are both A-definable, the processes of finding coverings for lower and upper approximations of concepts are identical. Therefore, this can be accomplished by one procedure, and the difference lies only in inputs to the procedure. The procedure CONSISTENT given in Section 6 can be extended to a general procedure GENERAL for finding all coverings of lower and upper approximations.

Input: Concepts $C_1, C_2, \ldots, C_k$.
Output: All coverings of $\underline{A}\, C_i$ and $\overline{A}\, C_i$, $i = 1, 2, \ldots, k$.

Procedure GENERAL (concepts $C_1, C_2, \ldots, C_k$);

begin

for each a in A **do**

Compute the partition $\{a\}^*$ on U;

for each C_i, $i = 1, 2, \ldots, k$ **do**

begin

for each a in A **do**

begin

Compute the {a}-lower approximation $\underline{\{a\}}\, C_i$ of C_i;

Compute the {a}-lower boundary $\underline{\Delta}_{\{a\}}(C_i)$ of C_i;

end;

if the A-lower boundary of C_i is not empty

then

begin

{Find all coverings for lower and upper approximations.}

Compute the {a}-lower approximation $\underline{\{a\}}\, (U - C_i)$ of $U - C_i$;

Compute the {a}-lower boundary $\underline{\Delta}_{\{a\}}(U - C_i)$ of $U - C_i$;

$\underline{A}\, C_i := C_i - \underline{\Delta}_A(C_i)$;

```
            Ā Cᵢ := U − Δ_A(U − Cᵢ);
            for each a in A do
              begin
                Compute the {a}-lower approximation {a} A̲ Cᵢ of
                A̲ Cᵢ;
                Compute the {a}-lower approximation {a} Ā Cᵢ of
                Ā Cᵢ;
              end;
            FIND_All_COVERINGS (A̲ Cᵢ);
            FIND_All_COVERINGS (Ā Cᵢ);
          end;
      else FIND_All_COVERINGS (Cᵢ);
   end;
end; {GENERAL}
```

8 Conclusions

The paper presents new notions of lower and upper boundaries. Results of the paper, establishing properties of these new ideas, justify two new algorithms: for learning rules from consistent representation of examples and for learning rules from inconsistent representation of examples. In the case of inconsistent examples, learned rules are categorized into certain and possible, following the idea presented for the first time in [4]. The main advantage of that approach is the possibility of parallel processing. For example, when certain and possible rules are applied in expert systems, two different inference engines may be utilized, both based on classical logic. The first engine is looking for a certain solution using certain rules. Concurrently, the second engine is searching for a possible solution using possible rules. Program LERS_LB, recently implemented in the Department of Computer Science of University of Kansas is much more efficient than previous versions of LERS family members, due to fact that lower boundaries, used in the algorithms of LERS_LB, are smaller sets than lower approximations. Thus the computational complexity is further reduced. Finally, lower boundaries are used as a basic tool for both algorithms for learning rules from consistent and inconsistent examples. Hence these algorithms are simpler.

References

[1] C.-C. Chan, J. W. Grzymala-Busse. Rough-set boundaries as a tool for learning rules from examples. *Proc. 4th Int. Symp. on Methodologies for Intelligent Systems, Oct. 12 - 14, 1989, Charlotte, NC,* 281 - 288

[2] J. S. Dean, J. W. Grzymala-Busse. An overview of the learning from examples module LEM1. *Report TR-88-2, Department of Computer Science, University of Kansas,* 1988

[3] D. H. Fisher, J. C. Schlimmer. Concept simplification and prediction accuracy. *Proc. 5th Conf. on Machine Learning, University of Michigan, Ann Arbor, MI, June 12 - 14, 1988,* 22 - 28

[4] J. W. Grzymala-Busse. Knowledge acquisition under uncertainty: a rough set approach. *Journal of Intelligent and Robotic Systems* 1, 1988, 3 - 16

[5] J. W. Grzymala-Busse. On the learning of minimal discriminant rules from examples. *Report TR-89-3, Department of Computer Science, University of Kansas,* 1989

[6] J. W. Grzymala-Busse. Learning minimal discriminant rules from examples with inconsistencies - a rough set approach. *Report TR-89-4, Department of Computer Science, University of Kansas,* 1989

[7] J. W. Grzymala-Busse, D. J. Sikora. LERS1 - a system for learning from examples based on rough set theory. *Report TR-88-3, Department of Computer Science, University of Kansas,* 1988

[8] R. S. Michalski. A theory and methodology of inductive learning. In *Machine Learning. R. S. Michalski, J. G. Carbonell, T. M. Mitchell (eds.),* Tioga Publ. Co., 1983, 83 - 134

[9] Z. Pawlak. Rough sets. Basic notions. Institute Comp. Sci. Polish Acad. Sci. Rep. #431, Warsaw, 1981. Also in *Int. J. Computer and Information Sci.* 11, 1982, 341-356

[10] Z. Pawlak. Rough classification. *Int. J. Man-Machine Studies* 20, 1984, 469-483

[11] J. D. Ullman. Principles of Database Systems. Computer Science Press, 1982

[12] A. Wasilewska. Definable sets in knowledge representation systems. *Bull. Polish Acad. Sci., Math.* 35, 1987, 629 - 635

Chapter 4

On the Best Search Method in the LEM1 and LEM2 Algorithms

*Jerzy W. Grzymala-Busse and Paolo Werbrouck**

Department of Electrical Engineering and Computer Science
University of Kansas
Lawrence, KS 66045

Abstract: This report presents results of experiments on two algorithms of machine learning: LEM1 and LEM2. Both algorithms belong to the LEM (Learning from Examples Module) family developed at the Department of Computer Science, University of Kansas.
For LEM1, two different approaches to test attribute dependence were compared: partition and lower boundaries. The two different versions of the algorithm were developed and their run times on a set of test files were compared.
For LEM2 a number of experiments were made to find the best search method of the description space. Some heuristics used within the algorithm to pick the "best" attribute-value pairs for the generation of rules were selected and tested. The quality of different methods has been compared on the basis of the total number of conditions, the total number of rules, and the average length of rules.

1 Introduction

Learning from examples forms the background of the research work presented in this paper, and is part of a larger area of research referred to as *machine learning*. The development of computer systems with the capability of learning, i.e., acquiring or discovering new knowledge or developing skills without the intervention of a programmer has been a primary research goal in artificial intelligence (AI).

The focus of learning from examples is the process of generating valid generalizations or detecting patterns from a collection of facts. The practical importance of developments in this area is immediately clear when we consider its application to the knowledge acquisition phase in expert system construction, although the applications are not limited to building a knowledge-basis for expert systems.

The key concept in learning from examples is the application of certain inference rules to obtain general assertions that describe the given set of examples. Examples are vectors of symbolic values corresponding to *attributes* and *decision*. Objects or

---

* Currently: Andersen Consulting, 20121 Milano, Italy

examples are described by attributes and classified by decisions. The outcome of the process consists of inductive statements that seek to describe the decisions in terms of the attributes. The set of the examples is referred to as the *decision table*. We shall note the set of examples as U and the set of all attributes as A. A *concept* is any non-empty subset of U. The examples belonging to a concept are called *positive examples*, whereas members of the complement U – C of the concept are called *negative examples.* A typical concept is the subset of U for which a decision has the same value. A decision table is said to be *consistent* if for each concept C, as defined above, and example $e \in C$, a vector of attribute values describing e does not also describe any example from U – C. We shall introduce an approach based on *rough set theory* to handle such inconsistencies [1], [4].

Given a set B of attributes ($B \subseteq A$), two examples e_1 and e_2 represented by the same vector of attribute values corresponding to the set B are said to be B-*indiscernible*, denoted $e_1 \underset{B}{\sim} e_2$. Naturally, $\underset{B}{\sim}$ is an equivalence relation on the set U of all examples. The relation induces a partition on U, denoted as B*. The partition B*, *generated by* B, is the set of all equivalence classes of $\underset{B}{\sim}$, or simply classes of B*. Of particular interest is the partition {d}* generated by the decision. The outcome of the learning process is a set of induced hypothesis to describe the classes of {d}* or concepts. The decision {d} is then said to *depend on* the set of attributes B, denoted $B \to \{d\}$, iff

$$B^* \leq \{d\}^*,$$

that is, for every class X of B* there exists a class Y of {d}* such that

$$X \subseteq Y.$$

Let t denote the pair (q, v), where q is an attribute and v is its value, and T a set of such pairs. The *block* of t is the set of examples $[t] \subseteq U$ for which attribute q has value v. The partition {d}* is the set of all [(d, w)] for all possible values w of the decision d. The set T of attribute-value pairs is *compatible* if it contains no more than one pair (q, v) for each attribute $q \in A$. If T is compatible then the block of T, denoted [T], is defined by

$$[T] = \bigcap_{t \in T} [t].$$

The knowledge generated by the learning process is represented in the form of production rules. Production rules are used in the knowledge-base of production systems. Production systems operate on the principle of an *inference engine* matching facts contained in a data-base with production rules to generate new facts or decisions. The programming language OPS83 works on such a principle as do certain expert systems. Production rules are expressions in the form:

if <conditions> then <action>.

The rules that are generated by the learning programs discussed in this paper are, more exactly, in the form:

$$C_1 \wedge C_2 \wedge C_3 \wedge \ldots \wedge C_n \to A$$

a conjunction of conditions that imply an action (d, w). The conditions are attribute-value pairs of the form (q, v), as seen above. In order for rules generated to be "correct and valid" descriptions of a concept, as sought, they must satisfy the following two conditions [5]: completeness and consistency.

Let C be a concept, e an example belonging to C, and D, D' concept descriptions. Completeness states that:

$$\forall(e \in C)\ \exists D, \text{e is described by D},$$

that is, all examples in the concept must be described by the rules.
Consistency states that:

$$\forall(e \in C), \text{e is not described by two different descriptions D and D'},$$

that is, every example is characterized by at most one concept description.

Section 2 introduces the LEM2 Single Local Covering algorithm and discusses the enhancement and developments that were brought to it as the main focus of the research work. It introduces the general approach of the algorithm, discusses its possible limitation and the rationale behind the introduction of the enhancements. Some results and comparisons between the production rules obtained by varying parameters within the algorithm are discussed.

Section 3 introduces the LEM1 Single Global Covering algorithm and discusses the two possible methods that can be employed to test for attribute dependency, namely lower boundaries and partitions. Some of the theoretical background is discussed in that regard and the results of comparing the two are presented and discussed.

Section 4 discusses the conclusions. Recommendations are made as to how the results of the research work should be incorporated in a larger project. It also discusses briefly how the issue of attribute priority could be further developed in future work.

2 LEM2 (Single Local Covering)

The following section introduces the LEM2 algorithm for learning *minimal rules* from examples. The rules generated are said to be minimal because they do not include unnecessary conditions, i.e., if any of the conditions are excluded (dropped) from a minimal rule the rule will no longer be consistent with the concept it describes. The algorithm is based on the definition of *dependency* for attribute-value pairs, which states that the concept C depends on the set T of attribute-value pairs,

$$T \rightarrow C \text{ iff } [T] \subseteq C \text{ and } [T] \neq \emptyset.$$

A *minimal complex* of C is then defined as the set T such that C depends on T and T is minimal. If $\mathbf{T}$ is a set of such minimal complexes of C, $\mathbf{T}$ is said to be a *local covering* of C iff

$$\bigcup_{T \in \mathbf{T}} [T] = C$$

and $\mathbf{T}$ is minimal.

Such a local covering consists of a single set of rules for a *minimal discriminant description* of the concept, i.e., a set of rules that are sufficient to distinguish examples belonging to the concept from those belonging to the concepts complement. These rules do satisfy the consistency and completeness requirements [1], [2], [3], [4].

The strategy of constructing a local covering consists of computing minimal complexes to cover the examples in the concept until all examples are covered. Because a single minimal complex may not be sufficient, at each new iteration the procedure seeks a new minimal complex to cover the members of the concept that have not been included by the previous complexes, until the whole concept is covered. Figure 1 describes the algorithm to find a single local covering of a concept.

The procedure for finding a minimal complex for a set G of examples is similarly simple. First all the attribute-value pairs relevant to the examples in G are collected

```
Procedure:      Find_Single_Local_Covering
Input:          Concept C
Output:    Covering 𝐓 of C

start
           G = C { goal = concept }
           𝐓 = ∅
           do
                T = Find_Minimal_Complex(C,G)
                𝐓 = 𝐓 ∪ {T}
                G = C −   ⋃   [T]       { update G }
                         T∈𝐓
           until G = ∅
           { minimize 𝐓 }
           do ∀T ∈ 𝐓
                if (   ⋃     [S]) = C  then 𝐓 = 𝐓 − {T}
                    S∈𝐓−{T}
           enddo
stop
```

Figure 1. Find_Single_Local_Covering

in a set which shall be denoted T(G), defined as:

$$T(G) = \{t \mid [t] \cap G \neq \emptyset\}.$$

Next the "best" pairs are selected from T(G) and combined into a minimal complex T until the condition that C depends on T, $[T] \subseteq C$, is achieved. Set T is then minimized by attempting to drop redundant attribute-value pairs before returning the result as a minimal complex. The pairs are removed in the order of selection.

The selection of the best attribute value pair is based on the maximum intersection of its block with the concept: $[(q, v)] \cap C$. If this first test generates ties between several attribute-value pairs, the criterion of maximum conditional probability is applied to break the tie. Probability can only be approximated in this context by relative frequency. Thus the conditional probability P (C | [(q, v)]) is approximated by the formula:

$$\mathbf{P}(C \mid [(q,v)]) = \frac{|C \cap [(q,v)]|}{|[(q,v)]|} .$$

If two attribute-value pairs have intersections of same cardinality with the concept, then the second criterion corresponds to choosing the pair with the smallest block. If this second criterion also leads to ties an arbitrary selection is made. Figure 2 presents the algorithm to find a minimal complex of a set G of examples within a concept C.

```
Procedure:      Find_Minimal_Complex
Input:          Concept (C) and goal (G), G ⊆ C
Output:         A minimal complex of C

start
        found = false
        T = Ø
        T(G) = { t | [t] ∩G ≠ Ø}
        do
        select a pair t ∈ T(G) such that |[t]∩G| is
                    maximum; break ties by selecting t
with                smallest  [t];  if  further  ties,
select first;

            T1 = { t'∈ T(G) | [t'] ∩G = [t] ∩G }
            T = T ∪ T1
            if [T] ⊆ C then found = true
                else
                    G = [t] ∩G
                    T(G) = { t | [t] ∩ G ≠ Ø }
                    T(G) = T(G) - T1
                endif
        until found
        do ∀t ∈ T   { minimize T}
            if [T- {t}] ⊆ C then T = T - {t}
        enddo
        return T            { T is a minimal complex }
stop
```

Figure 2. Find_Minimal_Complex

We can make the following observations and comments:

• The algorithm terminates as soon as the completeness condition is satisfied for the local covering: all the examples in C are covered by at least one complex.

• Each minimal complex satisfies the consistency condition. Set T is returned as a valid complex only if [T] includes only members of the concept to be covered.

• The complexes are determined by two factors:

a) The selection of the "best" attribute-value pair,

b) The order in which the complex T is minimized.

Because the algorithm is seeking a **single** local covering of a concept, there may be many more undiscovered rules describing the same concepts. It is, therefore, important to ask whether we can obtain different sets of rules with different characteristics using the same general approach. This is particularly true because the next best solution is to generate **all** the rules from the table which is an exponential problem.

The remainder of this section focuses on the procedure to generate minimal complexes. Some alternative approaches to the selection of the best (q, v) pair are proposed and discussed. The possibility of altering the order in which the selection criteria are applied is also discussed. Finally comparisons of the local coverings produced by the different approaches are presented.

Find_Minimal_Complex

The procedure Find_Minimal_Complex is centered on the selection of the "best" attribute-value pair out of the set T(G) of the pairs relevant to the goal G to be covered. In the original algorithm this selection is determined by the two criteria of maximum intersection and conditional probability of the pair's block [(q, v)] with respect to the concept C. We shall first introduce three alternative approaches and discuss the relative rationales of all five.

The (q, v) Pair Selection Criteria

The following alternative criteria for pair selection were used:

A. Maximum Intersection,

B. Maximum Conditional Probability,

C. Attribute Priority,

D. Attribute-Value Pair Priority,

E. Random.

Criteria A and B were used in the original algorithm, while criteria C, D and E have been introduced as part of this study. In criterion C we create a mapping from set A of all attributes to the positive numbers, representing the priority for each attribute in A. In selecting a pair (q, v) from T(G) we will choose those corresponding to the attribute q with the highest assigned priority. In criterion D each individual pair (q, v) is assigned a positive priority, which is then used to choose the "best" pair. In criterion E all relevant pairs (q, v) are equally likely to be picked as the "best". All of the original and the new criteria have a different rationale.

The criterion of *maximum intersection* is based on the idea that to generate the shortest complexes in local coverings, the best attribute-value pairs are the ones that describes the most examples in the concept. This translates into selecting the pair for which $|[(q, v)] \cap C|$ is maximum.

The criterion of *maximum conditional* probability,

$$\text{Max} (\mathbf{P} (C \mid (q, v)) = \frac{|C \cap [(q,v)]|}{|[(q,v)]|}$$

seeks to maximize the probability that the pair (q, v) implies the concept C. In fact, the higher the conditional probability the more the pair (q, v) discriminates the concept C from its complement U – C. Because the algorithm seeks a minimal discriminant description of C, the criterion is intuitively reasonable.

The criterion of *attribute priority* is very different from the previous two in that it does not rely on the distribution of values in the decision table. Instead it is based on decisions, made by the user of the learning system, about the concepts in the table. These decisions may be based on prior knowledge or preference that the user wishes to apply to the learning process. Naturally this involves a user knowledgeable about the subject matter of the decision table.

The priority that is assigned to the attributes, before starting LEM2, may be dictated by any number of characteristics of the application problem. There are many possible scenarios. The user of the system may be an expert in his/her own right and may wish to verify that the attributes that he/she considers most relevant are in fact the best to describe the table. The values for certain attributes may be hard to find, unreliable, typically unknown or, expensive to obtain and, therefore, the user prefers to obtain minimal descriptive rules that do not make use of those values, except where absolutely necessary. The user may also obtain different sets of rules, by varying the attribute-priorities, which he/she can then combine into a more extensive knowledge-base than what can be obtained by a single local covering.

The *attribute-value pair priority* criterion is based on the same notion that an expert user of the learning system may be interested in focusing the learning process on some specific characteristics of the problem. In the case of (q, v) priorities, the user is asked to identify particular values for attributes that carry more weight or significance than others. Such would be considered critical values in the context of the decision table's application area. The two approaches based on priorities, listed as sequences C and D, also involve a small change in the minimization stage of the algorithm. The pairs in T are first sorted in order of increasing priority. This is necessary so that when T is minimized, pairs of lower priority are the first to be tested for deletion.

The rationale of the *random* criterion may be disputed. Many would argue against a non-deterministic component in any kind of machine learning algorithm. Yet, because all the pairs in T(G) are relevant and can be used to express minimal complexes a random criterion gives if not the "best", then a valid (q, v) choice. The random criterion could be used to test whether criteria A and B **do** pick the better than average pairs out of the set T(G). It could be used to make the arbitrary choice of a pair when ties persist after the main criteria are applied.

The last two criteria are of little practical value. They will be more or less ignored in the rest of this study.

Given the three (five) criteria for selecting a pair the question of which ordering of the criteria yields the best results is natural. We built a modification of the LEM2 algorithm in which each criterion is applied independently of the other and the criteria can be applied in any order.

Testing Rule Induction

We experimented with the following sequences of attribute-value selection sequences:
A. Maximum Conditional Probability, Maximum Intersection,
B. Maximum Intersection, Maximum Conditional Probability,
C. Attribute Priority, Maximum Conditional Probability,
D. Attribute Priority, Maximum Intersection,
E. Maximum Intersection, Random.

	Number of Conditions		Number of Rules		Average Number of Conditions per Rule	
Data Set	A	B	A	B	A	B
Soybean (Large)	186	155	55	39	3.38	3.97
Soybean (Small)	7	6	5	4	1.40	1.50
Nursing	94	107	31	29	3.03	3.69
Iris	51	52	39	38	1.31	1.37
Rain (5%)	586	525	179	147	3.27	3.57
House (Consistent)	111	100	28	26	3.96	3.85
House (Original)	110	107	27	26	4.07	4.12
Hepatitis	95	97	78	32	1.22	3.03
Hepatitis (Clustered)	109	102	55	28	1.98	3.64

A: Maximum Conditional Probability, Maximum Intersection,

B: Maximum Intersection, Maximum Conditional Probability

Table 1

Different parameters may be used to quantify the *quality of the rules* generated: number of rules, total number of conditions, average number of conditions per rule, shortest and longest rule. Of these the most relevant are the total number of rules and the total number of conditions because they directly relate to the storage required to hold the rules generated as part of, say, a knowledge-based system.

We focused on the comparison in the quality of rules generated by applying the criteria sequences A and B. The reason for this is that the sequence B is in the original form of the algorithm and A is its natural alternative. The A sequence, in fact, resembles the criterion used by the PRISM learning algorithm. Sequences A and B represent true generalized concept acquisition in LEM2. Following is a comparison of the results obtained.

The test was run on a series of decision tables that varied widely in the number of examples, attributes and concepts. We focused on the quality of the rules generated. Computational time was disregarded in this experiment for a number of reasons. Machine learning time is typically an irrelevant factor in the development of knowledge-based systems because it only affects the early construction of the knowledge-base, and is only done once.

The measures of the quality of rules generated by the LEM2 algorithm is the total number of conditions in the rules for all the concepts, the number of rules and the average number of conditions per rule. Table 1 displays the result of the tests.

The graphs in the next pages better display the relative performance of the A and B sequence in each of the 3 categories for rule quality. The graph in Figure 3 displays the comparison of the total number of conditions in the set of all rules for every data set.

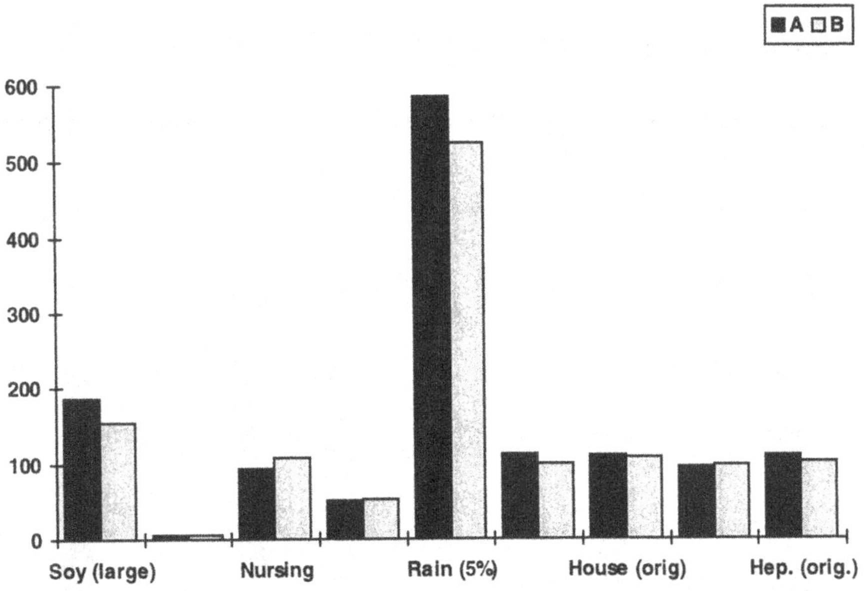

Figure 3. Total Number of Conditions

The next measure of the quality of the rules generated is the total number of rules. The following diagram (Figure 4) shows the performance of A and B for the same series of experiments.

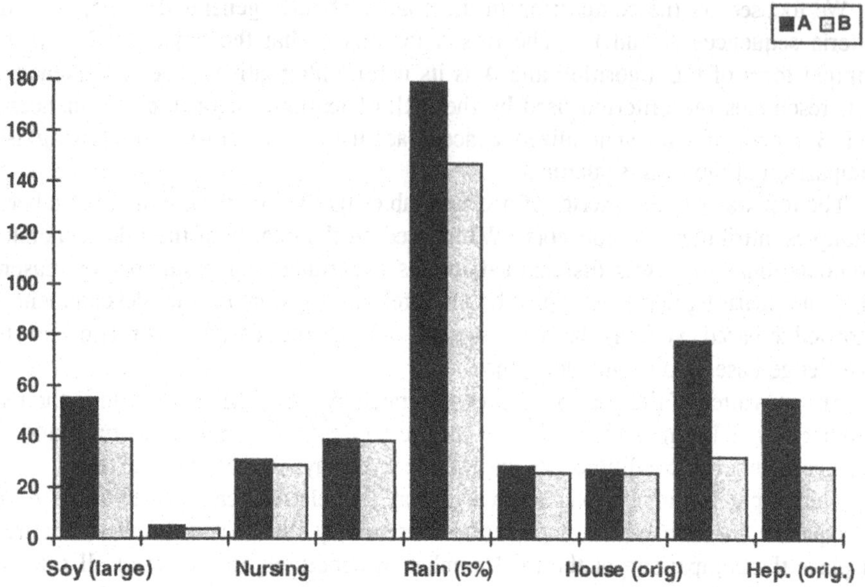

Figure 4. Total Number of Rules

Finally, Figure 5 shows the same analysis for the average number of conditions per rule for sequences A and B.

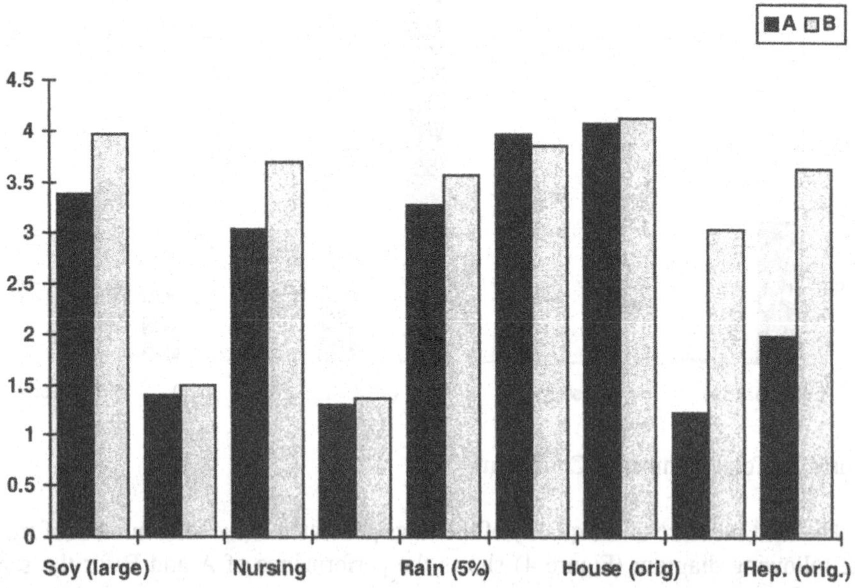

Figure 5. Average Number of Conditions per Rule

The Wilcoxon matched-pairs signed rank test, applied for data of Table 1, gives the following conclusions:

• Both sequences, A and B, of pair selection criteria does not differ significantly on the *total number of conditions* in the induced rules (a two-tailed test at the 10% significance level),

• The sequence B of pair selection criteria induces a smaller *total number of rules* than sequence A (a one-tailed test at the 0.5% significance level),

• The sequence A has favorable effect on the *average length of a rule* (i.e., an average number of conditions per rule) when compared with sequence B (a one-tailed test at the 2.5% significance level).

Data: Soybean (Large)

	# of Calls
MAXIMUM INTERSECTION	482
MAXIMUM CONDITIONAL PROBABILITY	472
Ties	11
Total	965

Table 2

Concerning the selection sequences C and D involving the use of attribute priority a limited set of experiments was performed. It is necessary in order to properly test this criterion to have expert knowledge of the subject area of the decision table. Lacking this knowledge it is only possible to test using randomly assigned priorities to the attributes. The results we obtained were far inferior to those resulting from applying sequences A or B. There was little difference between sequences C and D. In order to better understand how the individual selection criteria affect the calculation of minimal complexes we introduced a variable in the algorithm which counts the number of times that each criterion is invoked to resolve a tie between attribute-value pairs in T(G). In one experiment the count had the values presented in Table 2. This means that during that particular test there was a total of 965 calls to the procedure to select the "best" pair. In 482 (49.95%) cases the first criterion (MAXIMUM INTERSECTION) identified a single pair; in 472 (48.91%) cases the second criterion (MAXIMUM CONDITIONAL PROBABILITY) resolved the tie, and in 11 (1.7%) cases an unresolved tie was generated by the two criteria. Yet the second criterion was only invoked to resolve 483 (472 + 11) ties, of which it broke 472 or 97.7%. In the run parallel to this one MAXIMUM CONDITIONAL PROBABILITY was called to break 893 ties of which it resolved 869 or 97.0%. In general throughout the different experiments the MAXIMUM CONDITIONAL PROBABILITY criterion resolves a high percentage (80% - 90%) of the ties, whereas MAXIMUM INTERSECTION only averages about half of the ties. This difference in the individual criteria of the LEM2 algorithm may suggest some further alternatives to constructing minimal complexes.

3 LEM1 (Single Global Covering)

The following section introduces an algorithm for learning from examples based on the notion of attribute dependency (global approach). In the global approach we seek a subset B of the set of all attributes A, such that the set {d}, or the decision d, *depends* on B. From the set B we can then produce the set of production rules that describe the classes of d. We will run some experiments in our learning system to compare two different approaches to test for dependency.

The definition of dependency is naturally different from the one used in the local approach. Let B and D be two subsets of A. Set D depends on B, $B \rightarrow D$, iff $B^* \leq D^*$, or for each class b of B* there exists a class d of D* such that $b \subseteq d$. Because the algorithm seeks a set B to describe a concept C, we will denote $B \rightarrow C$, iff $B^* \leq C^*$, where C* is the partition on U into positive and negative examples of C, i.e.,

$$C^* = \{ C, U - C \}.$$

The set B is said to be a *global covering* of C if $B \rightarrow C$ and B is minimal, or no proper subset B' of B exists such that $B' \rightarrow C$. The LEM1 single global covering algorithm calculates a global covering and generates rules from it for each concept in the decision table. The rules generated may include many redundant conditions and the redundant conditions can be dropped from the rules in a second stage.

The algorithm to compute a single global covering for a concept C is very simple (see Figure 6).

```
Procedure:        Find_Single_Global_Covering
Input:            Concept C
Output:     Global_Covering B of C

start
            B = A {let B start as all attributes}
            do ∀q ∈ A
                  if (B - {q}) →C then B = B - {q}
            enddo
stop
```

Figure 6. Find_Single_Global_Covering

The procedure traverses the set A deleting the attributes that are not necessary to cover concept C. Those that cannot be deleted form the global covering B.

The most intuitive way of testing the dependency, $B \rightarrow C$, is to compute the partition B* and test whether $B^* \leq C^*$. This is equivalent to testing that:

$$\forall (b \in B^*), b \subseteq C \text{ or } b \subseteq (U - C)$$

or

$$b \subseteq C \text{ or } (b \cap C) = \emptyset.$$

The time complexity of calculating B* is of order $O(n^2)$, where n = |U| is the number of examples in the table. A second approach based on rough set theory has been developed and it is the goal of this second part of this report to compare it with calculating partitions.

Lower Boundaries in Testing Attribute Dependency

In [2] a second approach to testing attribute dependency was introduced. This second approach is based on *rough set theory* [6] which was first introduced by Z. Pawlak. The idea of rough sets is based on the notion of *approximation space*, an ordered pair (U, α) where U is the universe set, in our case the set of examples, and α an indiscernibility relation on U, whose classes we called *elementary sets*. Any finite union of elementary sets is said to be α-definable. Not all subsets of U are definable. A subset X of U is, therefore, characterized by a pair of definable sets, the lower and upper approximation of X. The lower approximation is defined as:

$$\underline{\alpha}B = \{ x \in U \mid [x]_\alpha \subseteq X \},$$

whereas the upper approximation is defined as:

$$\overline{\alpha}B = \{ x \in U \mid [x]_\alpha \cap X \neq \emptyset \}.$$

Set X is definable if the its lower and upper approximations are the same.

The pair (U, $\underset{B}{\sim}$), where B is a subset of all the attributes A, is an approximation space. Within the approximation space a subset X of U, is said to be *B-definable* if $\underline{B}X = \overline{B}X = X$. A second way to test if a set D depends on B is to check that each class of D* is B-definable. For a concept C it is sufficient to verify that C itself is B-definable.

Unfortunately this does not represent a gain because to verify that concept C is B-definable it is necessary to compute B*.

The B-definability criterion can be read as:

X is B-definable if

$$X - \underline{B}X = \emptyset$$

or

$$\underline{\Delta}_B (X) = \emptyset. \qquad \text{(Condition A)}$$

The *lower boundary* of X in the approximation space (U, $\underset{B}{\sim}$), indicated by the symbol $\underline{\Delta}_B$ (X), is the difference between X and its lower approximation $\underline{B}X$. Taking advantage of the properties of lower boundaries [1, 2] we can show that for X to be B-definable it is *sufficient* that:

$$\bigcap_{q \in B} \underline{\Delta}_{\{q\}} (X) = \emptyset \qquad \text{(Condition B)}$$

or that the intersection of the lower boundaries of X with respect to the single attributes in B is empty. That idea was implemented in LERS_LB 2.5 [1]. The lower boundaries for all $q \in B$ are first computed and whenever attribute dependency is tested this first test is performed, based on the pre-calculated set of lower boundaries $\underline{\Delta}_{\{q\}}$(X), and if it fails then the condition for the lower boundary of X in B, $\underline{\Delta}_B(X) = \emptyset$, is verified. The second condition involves computing B* and is computationally equivalent to the partition method, discussed in the previous section. Whenever the sufficient condition is satisfied the algorithm avoids the expensive, $O(n^2)$, calculation of B*.

Partitions vs. Lower Boundaries

We ran some experiments with our learning system to verify our expectation that with the condition B applied before testing condition A the learning process is faster. We also monitored via a counting variable how many times the first test was successful in determining dependency. Following are the results of a typical experiment, see Table 3.

Data: Soybean (Large)

266 Examples

35 Attributes

15 Decisions

	Partitions	Lower Boundaries
CPU Time	2m 10s	1m 40s
GC	59	32
Dependency Test	525 = 152 + 373	

Table 3

With lower boundaries condition B was satisfied 152 out of 525 times. The ratio between the total CPU times approximately correspond to this difference. The algorithm that used partitions took 30% more time (100s vs. 130s) than the one using lower boundaries which terminated its dependency tests with condition B about 30% of the time (152 / 525 = .2895).

A majority of the decision tables tested showed the condition B never or very seldom terminated the dependency test. In such cases the lower boundary version showed a slightly higher total CPU time, probably due to the overhead of computing the initial set of lower boundaries for all the attributes in A. Certain characteristics of the decision table obviously determine the effectiveness of the scheme, and, yet since the two approaches are in the worst case identical, there is a clear advantage in using lower boundaries vs. partitions in testing for attribute dependency.

The overhead of calculating the initial lower boundaries for the single attributes may be ignored if the partitions {q}* for each single attribute are also computed initially to be combined when calculating the partitions of larger subsets of A. The lower boundaries can then be directly calculated for each concept from the partitions of the single attributes.

4 Conclusions

LEM2 (Local Approach)

The LEM2 Single Local Covering Algorithm for the generation of local coverings of classes or concepts from tables of examples was originally created with an intuitive understanding of learning from examples process. The rules it generates are valid minimal descriptions of the concepts in U (set of examples). Through experimentation and comparison with some alternatives we were able to confirm the original intuitive notions that were build into the learning procedures and add a useful feature that will make the system more flexible.

The following conclusions were drawn from this work.

In computing minimal complexes and local coverings the key element is the selection of the "best" attribute-value pair (q, v) from the set T(G) of pairs relevant to the goal of the complex. Two different approaches to the selection of (q, v), based on two simple criteria, were compared:

A. Maximum Conditional Probability, Maximum Intersection,

B. Maximum Intersection, Maximum Conditional Probability.

The first corresponds to the principle applied in PRISM, a popular learning from examples algorithm. The second, the obvious alternative to the first, corresponds to the original intuitive notion applied in the LEM2 algorithm.

Based on the tests performed through our LEM2 learning system on data from real world applications, collected from different public domain sources we have drawn the following conclusions and recommendations:

a. The best results are generated by the B sequence: Maximum Intersection then Maximum Conditional Probability when the measure of quality for the production rules is the total number of rules.

b. The alternative, sequence A of criteria, yields more rules, but the average length of the rules is smaller. A preference on the part of the user of the learning system for shorter rules could be addressed by using this alternative sequence.

On the issue of the use of attribute priority in the calculation of minimal complexes we feel that it is useful to include such a possibility in the learning system. A knowledgeable user could gain much insight from a comparison of the results obtained from the algorithm learning with or without attribute priority. When priorities are used the pairs with highest priorities should be picked from T(G) and when this generates ties in the selection, such ties should be resolved by the criteria of the basic LEM2 approach.

In the course of the development of the learning system the approach was suggested of pre-processing the decision table so that the attributes would be read in the order of their relative priorities. In such a way the first attributes in the table would be the most frequently used in selection. This is clearly not sufficient because the ordering of the attributes would only affect the selection of (q, v) when a tie would persist after the first two selection criteria were applied. The priority of attributes is only useful is if applied as the first independent selection criteria.

LEM1 Global: Partitions vs. Lower Boundaries

A second approach to learning from examples is developed by the LEM1 Single Global Covering algorithm. The idea is to seek a subset of all the attributes in the decision table such that the decision or concept depends on it. In the LEM1 single global covering algorithm only one such subset is computed, although more may exists. Each attribute in A is in turn deleted from A if attribute dependency condition holds.

The focus of this second set of experiments was to determine which was the most efficient way to test for attribute dependency. The two methods for testing attribute dependency are:

A. Partitions,

B. Lower Boundaries.

Both are based on the same definition of attribute dependency. The lower boundaries approach, though, results in a *sufficient* condition for dependency that may be tested more efficiently than the *necessary* condition. The necessary condition for dependency, in fact, involves the same type of computation for both of the two methods. In both cases the partitions of U over the set of attributes B to be tested needs to be computed.

In the tests we compared the performance of the lower boundaries approach against that of the partitions approach. We also monitored whether the *sufficient* condition was satisfied in computations with lower boundaries. We have drawn the following conclusions, which are intuitively true and have found experimental confirmation:

A. For a number of test cases the sufficient condition was never satisfied. In such cases the partitions approach was faster by 2 to 3 seconds of CPU time.

B. Whenever, for a test file, the sufficient condition was satisfied in the lower boundaries approach, this approach proved to be immediately more efficient than partitions. The difference in the total CPU time between the two approaches appears, in such cases, to be proportional to the relative number of times that the sufficient condition was satisfied.

From these observations we shall conclude that the lower boundary approach is to be preferred to partition in testing for attribute dependency. Intuitively, the two perform equally when lower boundary test operates under less favorable conditions. In such cases there is no real advantage to use partitions, whereas with lower boundaries it is possible to have a much better performance. The advantage of using lower boundaries over partitions also applies to the version on LEM1 algorithm that seeks *all* possible global coverings of a concepts. In the all-covering version the number of attribute dependency test is exponential instead of linear in the number of attributes.

References

[1] A. Budihardjo, J. W. Grzymala-Busse, An overview of the learning program LERS_LB 2.5. *Report TR-90-4, Department of Computer Science, University of Kansas*, 1990

[2] C.- C. Chan, J. W. Grzymala-Busse, Rough-set boundaries as a tool for learning rules from examples. *Proc. of the ISMIS–89, 4th International Symposium on Methodologies for Intelligent Systems, Charlotte, North Carolina, October 12–14*, 1989, 281–288

[3] C.- C. Chan, J. W. Grzymala-Busse, On the Attribute Redundancy and the Learning Programs ID3, PRISM, and LEM2. *Report TR-91–14, Department of Computer Science, University of Kansas*, 1991

[4] J. W. Grzymala-Busse, L. Yue, The Machine Learning Programs LEM2 and LERS_LB2 based on Single Coverings and Blocks. *Report TR-90-3, Department of Computer Science, University of Kansas*, 1990

[5] R. S. Michalski, A theory and methodology of inductive learning, In *Machine Learning. R. S. Michalski, J. G. Carbonell, T. M. Mitchell (eds.), Tioga Publ. Co.* 1983

[6] Z. Pawlak, Rough sets. Basic notions, *Institute Comp. Sci. Polish Academy Sci. Rep. #431, Warsaw*, 1981

II

ALGEBRAIC STRUCTURE OF ROUGH SET SYSTEMS

Chapter 5

Rough Sets and Algebras of Relations

Ivo Düntsch

School of Information and Software Engineering
University of Ulster at Jordanstown, Newtownabbey, BT 37 0QB, N.Ireland
I.Duentsch@ulst.ac.uk

Abstract: A survey of results is presented on relationships between the algebraic systems derived from the approximation spaces induced by information systems and various classes of algebras of relations. Rough relation algebras are presented and it is shown that they form a discriminator variety. A characterisation of the class of representable rough relation algebras is given. The family of closure operators derived from an approximation space is abstractly characterised as certain type of Boolean algebra with operators. A representation theorem is given which says that every such an algebra is isomorphic with a similar algebra that is derived from an information system.

1 Notation and definitions

The history and the impact of rough sets as a means of modelling incomplete information are considered elsewhere in this Volume, so we shall be content to just state the basic notions. Let U be a set and θ an equivalence relation on U. The pair $\langle U, \theta\rangle$ will be called an *approximation space.* For $A \subseteq U$, $A_u = \bigcup\{\theta x : x \in A\}$ is the *upper approximation of* A, and $A \subseteq U$, $A_d = \bigcup\{\theta x : \theta x \subseteq A\}$ is its *lower approximation.* A *rough subset of* U with respect to θ is a pair $\langle X_d, X_u\rangle$ with $X \subseteq U$. The collection of all rough subsets of U with respect to θ is denoted by $Sb_r^\theta(U)$, and will sometimes be called a *full algebra of rough sets.* If θ is understood, we shall just write $Sb_r(U)$

2 Rough Sets and Regular Double Stone Algebras

An algebraic approach to rough sets was first proposed in [Iw1]. Iwinski's aim – later extended by [PP1] – was to endow the rough subsets of U with a natural algebraic structure. It turns out that regular double Stone algebras are the proper setting.

A double Stone algebra (DSA) $\langle L, +, \cdot, {}^*, {}^+, 0, 1\rangle$ is an algebra of type $\langle 2, 2, 1, 1, 0, 0\rangle$ such that

1. $\langle L, +, \cdot, 0, 1\rangle$ is a bounded distributive lattice,

2. x^* is the pseudocomplement of x, i.e. $y \leq x^* \Leftrightarrow y \cdot x = 0$,
3. x^+ is the dual pseudocomplement of x, i.e. $y \geq x^+ \Leftrightarrow y + x = 1$,
4. $x^* + x^{**} = 1$, $x^+ \cdot x^{++} = 0$.

Conditions 2. and 3. are equivalent to the equations

$$\begin{array}{ll} x \cdot (x \cdot y)^* = x \cdot y^*, & x + (x + y)^+ = x + y^+ \\ x \cdot 0^* = x, & x + 1^+ = x \\ 0^{**} = 0, & 1^{++} = 1 \end{array}$$

so that DSA is an equational class. L is called *regular*, if it additionally satisfies the equation $x \cdot x^+ \leq y + y^*$. This is equivalent to $x^+ = y^+$ and $x^* = y^*$ imply $x = y$.

The *center* $B(L) = \{x^* : x \in L\}$ of L is a subalgebra of L and a Boolean algebra, in which * and $^+$ coincide with the Boolean complement which we denote by $-$. An element of the centre of L will also be called a *Boolean element.* The *dense set* $\{x \in L : x^* = 0\}$ of L is denoted by $D(L)$, or simply D, if L is understood. For any $M \subseteq L$, M^+ is the set $\{x^+ : x \in M\}$.

A construction of regular double Stone algebras which is important for our purposes is given by

Lemma 1. *[Ka1] Let $\langle B, +, \cdot, -, 0, 1\rangle$ be a Boolean algebra and F be a not necessarily proper filter on B. Set*

$$\langle B, F\rangle = \{\langle a, b\rangle \in B \times B : a \leq b \text{ and } -b + a \in F\} .$$

Then, $L = \langle B, F\rangle$ is a 0,1 – sublattice of $B \times B$, and it becomes a regular double Stone algebra by setting

$$\langle a, b\rangle^* = \langle -b, -b\rangle, \ \langle a, b\rangle^+ = \langle -a, -a\rangle .$$

Furthermore, $B(L) \cong B$ as Boolean algebras, and $D(L) \cong F$ as lattices. Note that

$$B(L) = \{\langle a, a\rangle : a \in B\}, \ D(L) = \{\langle a, 1\rangle : a \in F\} .$$

Conversely, if M is a regular double Stone algebra, $B = B(M)$, $F = D(M)^{++}$, then the mapping which assigns to each $x \in M$ the pair $\langle x^{++}, x^{**}\rangle$ is an isomorphism between M and $\langle B, F\rangle$.

If $F = B$, then $\langle B, F\rangle$ is also denoted by $B^{[2]}$.

In view of things to come it is useful to note that by Lemma 1 each element x of a regular double Stone algebra is uniquely described by the greatest Boolean element below x and the smallest Boolean element above x.

Now, suppose that $\langle U, \theta\rangle$ is an approximation space. We can view the classes of θ as atoms of a complete subalgebra of the Boolean algebra $Sb(U)$. Conversely, any atomic complete subalgebra B of $Sb(U)$ gives rise to an equivalence relation θ on U, and this correspondence is bijective. The elements of B are $\emptyset$ and the unions of classes of its associated equivalence relation. If $\{a\} \in B$, then, for every $X \subseteq U$ we have

If $a \in X_u$, then $a \in X$, and the rough sets of the corresponding approximation space are the elements of the regular double Stone algebra $\langle B, F \rangle$, where F is the filter of B which is generated by the union of singleton elements of B^1. Note that, if θ is the identity on U, then $F = \{U\}$, and we see that the full algebra of rough sets on U need not be of the form $B^{[2]}$. At any rate, we have

Proposition 2. *[Iw1, PP1, Co2] Suppose that $\langle U, \theta \rangle$ is an approximation space. Then, $Sb^{\theta}_{r}(U)$ is a regular double Stone algebra with the operations of Lemma 1.*

Steve Comer has shown that a converse also holds:

Proposition 3. *[Co1, Co2] Let L be a regular double Stone algebra. Then, there is an approximation space $\langle U, \theta \rangle$ such that L is isomorphic to a subalgebra of $Sb(U)^{[2]}$*

Proof. Every Stone algebra can be embedded into an algebra of the form $B^{[2]}$, where B is a complete and atomic Boolean algebra, see [BG1]. As remarked above, each such algebra is isomorphic to a full algebra of rough sets. □

3 Rough Relation Algebras

Pawlak's original approach to model incomplete information was to take sets as the basic entity. However, sets can themselves have an underlying structure or a special form. Subsequently, [Co2] proposed to look at the case where the underlying sets are binary relations, and how incomplete information about these can be modelled.

If we are given a set U, then the subsets of U can be thought of as truth sets of unary predicates, and appropriate operations on subsets of U are the usual Boolean ones which, in the case of rough sets, lead to certain regular double Stone algebras. If we look at binary relations we have additional natural operations, namely, relational composition $\circ$, relational converse $^{-1}$, and the identity relation $1'$ as a new constant: Here,

$$\begin{aligned} R \circ S &= \{\langle a, c \rangle \in U \times U : \text{ There is some } b \in U \text{ such that } R(a,b) \text{ and } S(b,c)\}, \\ R^{-1} &= \{\langle b, a \rangle : R(a,b)\}, \\ 1' &= \{\langle a, a \rangle : a \in U\}. \end{aligned}$$

With these operations we can view the set of all binary relations on U as an algebra

$$Rel(U) = \langle Sb(U^2), \cup, \cap, -, \emptyset, U \times U, ^{*}, ^{-1}, 1' \rangle \ ,$$

called the *full algebra of binary relations on U.* Any subalgebra of $Rel(U)$ is called an *algebra of binary relations (BRA) on U.*

Tarski has introduced a class of algebras which generalizes the notion of BRA: A relation algebra (RA) $\langle A, +, \cdot, -, 0, 1, \circ, ^{-1}, 1' \rangle$ is a structure of type $\langle 2, 2, 1, 0, 0, 2, 1, 0 \rangle$ which satisfies

[1] I should like to thank Piero Pagliani for pointing this out.

1. $\langle A, +, \cdot, -, 0, 1\rangle$ is a Boolean algebra.
2. $\langle A, \circ, ^{-1}, 1'\rangle$ is an involuted monoid.
3. For all a, b, c the following conditions are equivalent:

$$(a \circ b) \cdot c = 0,\ (a^{-1} \circ c) \cdot b = 0,\ (c \circ b^{-1}) \cdot a = 0\ .$$

It can be shown that the class of RAs is equational. For the background and the relevant facts of RAs the reader is invited to consult [Jo2] or [TG1].

A relation algebra A is called *representable*, if it is a subalgebra of a product of full algebras of binary relations.

Now, we shall generalize RAs to rough structures [Co2]: Let $\langle U, \theta\rangle$ be an approximation space, and set $V = U \times U$. θ defines in a canonical way an equivalence ${}^2\theta$ on V by

$$\langle x, y\rangle \equiv_{^2\theta} \langle u, v\rangle \text{ iff } x \equiv_\theta u \text{ and } y \equiv_\theta v\ ,$$

and $\langle V,\ {}^2\theta\rangle$ is an approximation space.

A *rough relation on* $\langle U, \theta\rangle$ is a rough subset of $\langle V,\ {}^2\theta\rangle$. In other words, a rough relation on $\langle U, \theta\rangle$ is a pair $\langle S_d, S_u\rangle$, where $S \subseteq V$ and for all $\langle a, b\rangle \in V$

$$\langle a, b\rangle \in S_d \Leftrightarrow {}^2\theta\langle a, b\rangle \subseteq S,$$
$$\langle a, b\rangle \in S_u \Leftrightarrow {}^2\theta\langle a, b\rangle \cap S \neq \emptyset\ .$$

(Recall that ${}^2\theta\langle a, b\rangle$ is the equivalence class of $\langle a, b\rangle$ with respect to ${}^2\theta$.)

$Sb_r^{^2\theta}(V)$ is a regular double Stone algebra by the results of the preceding section. We define the additional relational operators on $Sb_r^{^2\theta}(V)$ as follows:

$$\langle T_d, T_u\rangle \circ \langle S_d, S_u\rangle = \langle T_d \circ S_d, T_u \circ S_u\rangle\ ,$$
$$\langle S_d, S_u\rangle^{-1} = \langle S_d^{-1}, S_u^{-1}\rangle\ ,$$
$$1' = \langle \theta, \theta\rangle\ .$$

The structure $\langle Sb_r^{^2\theta}(V), \cup, \cap,\ ^*,\ ^+, \emptyset, V, \circ,\ ^{-1}, \langle\theta,\theta\rangle\rangle$ is called the *full algebra of rough relations over* $\langle U, \theta\rangle$. Subalgebras of $Sb_r^{^2\theta}(V)$ are called *algebras of rough relations*.

Rough relation algebras are a generalization of relation algebras, where the Boolean part is replaced by a regular double Stone algebra, and the following set of axioms was proposed by [Co2]:

A rough relation algebra (R^2A) is an algebra

$$\langle L, +, \cdot,\ ^*,\ ^+, 0, 1, ;,\ ^{-1}, 1'\rangle$$

such that

1. $\langle L, +, \cdot,\ ^*,\ ^+, 0, 1\rangle$ is a regular double Stone algebra,
2. $(x; y); z = x; (y; z)$,
3. $(x + y); z = x; z + y; z$,
4. $x; 1' = 1'; x = x$,
5. $(x^{-1})^{-1} = x$,

6. $(x+y)^{-1} = x^{-1} + y^{-1}$,
7. $(x;y)^{-1} = y^{-1};x^{-1}$,
8. $(x^{-1};(x;y)^*) \cdot y = 0$,
9. $(x;y) \cdot z \leq x;x^{-1};z$,
10. $(x^*;y^*)^{**} = x^*;y^*$,
11. $(1')^{**} = 1'$.

If B is a relation algebra, then $B^{[2]}$ becomes a rough relation algebra if ; and $^{-1}$ are defined componentwise. We shall denote this algebra by $B_r^{[2]}$.

It is clear that every full algebra of rough relations is an R²A. A rough relation algebra is representable, if it is a subalgebra of a product of full algebras of rough relations.

Many equations which hold in RAs also hold in R²As. Some properties specific to rough relation algebras are given in

Proposition 4. *[Co2, Du1] Let L be an R^2A. Then,*

1. *$B(L)$ is closed under ; and $^{-1}$, and $1' \in B(L)$.*
2. *$B(L)$ is a relation algebra and a subalgebra of L.*
3. *If $L \cong Sb_r^{2\theta}(V)$ for some approximation space, then $B(L) \cong Rel(U/\theta)$.*
4. *$D(L)$ is closed under ; and $^{-1}$.*
5. *$(x;y)^{**} = x^{**};y^{**}$ for all $x, y \in L$.*

Proof. 1. The closure of $B(L)$ under ; and $1'$ are just axioms (x) and (xi). Since $^{-1}$ distributes over *, and $(a^{-1})^{-1} = a$, we have

$$a^* \cdot a = 0 \Rightarrow (a^*)^{-1} \cdot a^{-1} = 0 \Rightarrow (a^*)^{-1} \leq (a^{-1})^* \ ,$$

and conversely,

$$a^{-1} \cdot (a^{-1})^* = 0 \Rightarrow a \cdot ((a^{-1})^*)^{-1} = 0 \Rightarrow ((a^{-1})^*)^{-1} \leq a^* \Rightarrow (a^{-1})^* \leq (a^*)^{-1} \ .$$

2. To show that L satisfies condition 3. for RAs, one can use 2.1. of [CT1] which goes through unchanged. Clearly, $B(L)$ is a subalgebra of L.

3. This follows immediately from the definition of $B(L)$.

4. Let $x, y \in D(L)$. Then,

$$1 = x^{**} = y^{**} = x^{**};y^{**} = (x;y)^{**} \ ,$$

and therefore $(x;y)^* = 0$.

5. Clearly, $x \leq x^{**}$ and $y \leq y^{**}$ imply

$$(x;y)^{**} \leq (x^{**};y^{**})^{**} = x^{**};y^{**} \ .$$

For the converse assume that $(x;y)^{**} < x^{**};y^{**}$. Then, $(x^{**};y^{**})\cdot(x;y)^* > 0$, and

$$\begin{aligned}((x^{-1})^{**};(x;y)^*)\cdot y^{**} &> 0\ ,\\ ((x^{-1})^{**};(x;y)^*)\cdot y &> 0\\ (x^{**};y)\cdot(x;y)^* &> 0\\ ((x;y)^*\cdot y^{-1})\cdot x^{**} &> 0\\ ((x;y)^*\cdot y^{-1})\cdot x &> 0\\ (x;y)\cdot(x;y)^* &> 0\ ,\end{aligned}$$

a contradiction. □

Just like relation algebras, R^{2}As have very strong structural properties: An algebra A is a *discriminator algebra* if there is some term operation f in the language of A such that

$$f(a,b,c) = \begin{cases} c, & \text{if } a = b,\\ a, & \text{otherwise.}\end{cases}$$

A variety $\mathbf{V}$ is called a *discriminator variety* if it is generated by a class K of algebras such that some term operation f in the language of $\mathbf{V}$ represents the discriminator term as above on each member of K. Discriminator algebras have, among others, the following pleasant properties, see [JAN1]:

Proposition 5. *Let* $\mathbf{V}$ *be a discriminator variety. Then,*

1. $\mathbf{V}$ *is congruence permutable, congruence distributive, congruence extensile, and semisimple.*
2. *For every non trivial algebra* A *in* $\mathbf{V}$ *the following are equivalent:*
   (a) A *is simple.*
   (b) A *is subdirectly irreducible.*
   (c) A *is directly indecomposable.*
3. *There is an effective way of associating with each open Horn formula* φ *in the language of* $\mathbf{V}$ *an equation* σ_φ *in this language such that* φ *and* σ_φ *have the same truth set in every simple member of* $\mathbf{V}$.

To show that R^{2}A is a discriminator variety we first state

Lemma 6. *[Du1] Let* L *be an* R^2A *and* $\psi \in Con(B(L))$. *Then,*

1. $\psi_L \in Con(L)$.
2. $Con(L) \cong Con(B(L))$.

We now have

Proposition 7. *[Du1] The variety of* R^2A*s is a discriminator variety.*

Proof. It is enough to show that a simple $\mathrm{R}^2\mathrm{A}$ L is a discriminator algebra. For $a, b \in B(L)$ we denote the symmetric difference by $a \otimes b$; recall that $a = b \Leftrightarrow a \otimes b = 0$. Set

$$\tau(a,b) = 1; (a^{**} \otimes b^{**} + a^{++} \otimes b^{++}); 1.$$

Then,

$$\tau(a,b) = \begin{cases} 1, \text{ if } a \neq b, \\ 0, \text{ otherwise.} \end{cases}$$

Let $a = b$; then, since L is regular, $a^{**} = b^{**}$ and $a^{++} = b^{++}$, and thus $a^{**} \otimes b^{**} = a^{++} \otimes b^{++} = 0$. It follows that

$$[1; (a^{**} \otimes b^{**}); 1] + [1; (a^{++} \otimes b^{++}); 1] = 1; [(a^{**} \otimes b^{**})) + (a^{++} \otimes b^{++})] = \tau(a,b) = 0.$$

Conversely, let $a \neq b$. Then, $a^{**} \neq b^{**}$ or $a^{++} \neq b^{++}$. Since L is simple, so is $B(L)$ by Lemma 6. We know from [Jo1] that for a relation algebra A and $x \in A$,

$$x \neq 0 \Leftrightarrow 1; x; 1 = 1.$$

Therefore,

$$1; (a^{**} \otimes b^{**}); 1 = 1 \text{ or } 1; (a^{++} * b^{++}); 1 = 1,$$

since $a^{**}, b^{**}, a^{++}, b^{++}$ are Boolean. Consequently,

$$1 = [1; (a^{**} \otimes b^{**}); 1] + [1; (a^{++} \otimes b^{++}); 1] = \tau(a,b).$$

Now, set

$$\sigma(a,b,c) = \tau(a,b) \cdot a + \tau(a,b)^* \cdot c.$$

If $a = b$, then $\tau(a,b) = 0$, and hence $\sigma(a,b,c) = \tau(a,b)^* \cdot c = c$. If $a \neq b$, then $\tau(a,b) = 1$, and therefore $\sigma(a,b,c) = \tau(a,b) \cdot a = a$. □

Finally, the representable $\mathrm{R}^2\mathrm{A}$s can be characterized as follows:

Proposition 8. *[Du1] Suppose that $L = \langle B, F \rangle$ is an R^2A. Then, L is representable if and only if $B(L)$ is a representable relation algebra and L satisfies the equation $(x;y)^{++} = x^{++}; y^{++}$.*

Proof. Call an $\mathrm{R}^2\mathrm{A}$ *canonical* which satisfies the equation. To show the result, we first prove some auxiliary results which seem interesting in their own right. Our first claim explains why we call these algebras canonical:

Claim 1 *L is canonical if and only if*

$$\langle a, b \rangle; \langle c, d \rangle = \langle a; c, b; d \rangle$$

for all $\langle a, b \rangle, \langle c, d \rangle \in \langle B, F \rangle$.

Proof. "⇒": Suppose L is canonical, and let $\langle a,b\rangle, \langle c,d\rangle \in \langle B,F\rangle$. Then, there are $x,y \in L$ such that $a = x^{++}, b = x^{**}, c = y^{++}, d = y^{**}$, and

$$\begin{aligned}\langle x++, x**\rangle;\langle y++, y**\rangle &= x;y\\ &= \langle (x;y)++, (x;y)**\rangle\\ &= \langle x++;y++, x**;y**\rangle\ .\end{aligned}$$

"⇐": Let $\langle a,b\rangle, \langle c,d\rangle \in \langle B,F\rangle$. Then,

$$(\langle a,b\rangle;\langle c,d\rangle)^{++} = \langle a;c,b;d\rangle^{++} = \langle a;c,a;c\rangle = \langle a,a\rangle;\langle c,c\rangle = \langle a,b\rangle^{++};\langle c,d\rangle^{++},$$

which proves the claim. □

Claim 2 *For any* L, $B(L)_r^{[2]}$ *is canonical and, if* L *is canonical, then it is a subalgebra of* $B(L)_r^{[2]}$.

Proof. This follows immediately from the definition of $B_r^{[2]}$ and Claim 1. □

Claim 3 *If* C *is (isomorphic to) a full relation algebra* $Rel(U)$, *then* $C_r^{[2]}$ *is isomorphic to a full algebra of rough relations.*

Proof. Let $U' = \{x' : x \in U\}$ be disjoint from U, and set $V = U \cup U'$. Define an equivalence relation θ on V by identifying x and x', so that $\theta x = \{x, x'\}$. Then, $B(R_V)$ and C are isomorphic as relation algebras. Let $\langle R_d, R_d\rangle \in B(R_V)$, and define

$$S = R \cup \{\langle x,y\rangle : x,y \in U, \theta x \times \theta y \subseteq -R_d\}\,.$$

Then, $S_d = R_d$, $S_u = 1$, and thus $\langle R_d, 1\rangle \in D(R_V)$ for each $R \in C$. Now, the mapping defined by $\langle R_d, R_d\rangle \mapsto \langle R_d, 1\rangle$ is a lattice isomorphism, and hence $B(R_V) \cong D(R_V)$. It follows that $R_V = B(R_V)_r^{[2]} \cong C_r^{[2]}$. □

Now we can prove the Proposition:

"⇒": It is enough to show that every full algebra R_U of rough relations is canonical. Let $L = R_U$ be the full algebra of rough relations over $\langle U, \theta\rangle$. Then, $B(L) \cong Rel(U/\theta)$, and thus $B(L)$ is a representable relation algebra.

Next, let $\langle R_d, R_u\rangle$, $\langle S_d, S_u\rangle \in R_U$. Then,

$$\begin{aligned}(\langle R_d, R_u\rangle, \langle S_d, S_u\rangle)^{++} &= (\langle R_d; S_d, R_u, S_u\rangle)^{++},\\ &= \langle R_d; S_d, R_d, S_d\rangle,\\ &= \langle R_d; R_d\rangle;\langle S_d, S_d\rangle,\\ &= \langle R_d; R_u\rangle^{++};\langle S_d, S_u\rangle^{++}.\end{aligned}$$

"⇐": Suppose that $L = \langle B,F\rangle$ is canonical, and that B is a representable relation algebra. Since $L \leq B_r^{[2]}$ by Claim 2, we can assume that $L = B_r^{[2]}$; furthermore, we may assume by 7 and 5 that L is simple. Then, B is simple by 6, and, since it is representable, there is some set U such that $B \leq Rel(U)$. It follows that $L = B_r^{[2]} \leq Rel(U)_r^{[2]}$, which is representable by Claim 3. □

In particular, the representable rough relation algebras form an equational class.

Relation algebras are a special case of the more general concept of Boolean algebras with operators. Motivated by rough relation algebras, Steve [Co3] has investigated the theory of regular double Stone algebras with operators.

4 Information Systems

In the previous sections we have looked at the algebraic structure arising from one given approximation space, and we have considered the special case when the underlying carrier set was the universal binary relation on some other set. In this section we shall describe the algebraic structure of a set of approximation spaces derived from an information system. It turns out that there is a close connection between the resulting structures and cylindric algebras and their derivatives. The standard reference for cylindric algebras are the books [HMT1, HMT2] and we shall refer to these for definitions and results on these algebras. All results in this section are due to Steve Comer.

An information system $S = \langle U, \Omega, V, f \rangle$ as discussed e.g. in [Pa1, Pa2], consists of

1. A set U of objects,
2. A finite set Ω of attributes,
3. A set V of attribute values,
4. An information function $f : U \times \Omega \to V$.

We think of $f(u, x)$ as the value which object u takes at the attribute x. With each $Q \subseteq \Omega$ we can associate an equivalence relation θ_Q on U by setting

$$a \equiv_{\theta_Q} b \stackrel{\text{def}}{\Longleftrightarrow} f(a, x) = f(b, x) \text{ for all } x \in Q,$$

so that $\langle U, \theta_Q \rangle$ is an approximation space.

Intuitively, $a \equiv_{\theta_Q} b$ if the objects a and b are indiscernible with respect to the values of their attributes from Q. Given $A \subseteq U$, we denote its upper approximation with respect to θ_Q by $\overline{Q}A$, and its lower approximation by $\underline{Q}A$. Clearly, $\overline{Q}$ is a closure operator on $\langle Sb(U), \subseteq \rangle$, and $\underline{Q}$ is an interior operator. A set $A \subseteq U$ is called *definable with knowledge* $Q \subseteq \Omega$, if A is a union of equivalence classes of θ_Q; equivalently, A is definable from Q, iff $\overline{Q}A = \underline{Q}A$.

As an example – which uses rough relations – let us consider the following scenario: Suppose that U is a set of car brands, Ω a set of attributes associated with cars, e.g. *colour, price, reliability* etc, V a set of appropriate attributes, and f an information function. Let R be a binary relation on U which was obtained by presenting to a subject two car models, and asking her to decide which she likes better. In order to find out what were the decisive factors in her choice, we can now use rough set methods: Let, as a simple example, θ be the equivalence on U which identifies cars by their colour. If ${}^{\theta}\langle a, b \rangle \in R$ and, say, a is red and b is green, we can infer that there is some evidence that she generally prefers green cars over red ones, and if $R = {}^{2}\underline{\{\text{colour}\}R}$, then she is never inconsistent in her choices with respect to colour.

The *knowledge approximation algebra* $\mathfrak{B}_S$ associated with S is the structure

$$\langle Sb(U), \cup, \cap, -, \emptyset, U, \overline{Q} \rangle_{Q \subseteq \Omega} .$$

We note that $\mathfrak{B}_S$ is a complete and atomic Boolean algebra with the additional closure operators $\overline{Q}$, $Q \subseteq \Omega$. If $Q \subseteq \Omega$, the reduct $\langle Sb(U), \cup, \cap, -, \emptyset, U, \overline{Q} \rangle$ of $\mathfrak{B}_S$ is denoted by $Rd_Q\mathfrak{B}_S$, and it is called an *approximation closure algebra.*

[Col] has proposed the following axioms for a class of algebras which are intended to capture the knowledge approximation algebras associated with information systems: An algebra $\mathfrak{B} = \langle B, +, \cdot, -, 0, 1, \kappa_P \rangle_{P \subseteq \Omega}$ is a *knowledge approximation algebra of type* Ω – called a KA_Ω – if each κ_P is a unary operator on B, and

1. $\langle B, +, \cdot, -, 0, 1 \rangle$ is a complete atomic Boolean algebra,
2. $\kappa_P 0 = 0$,
3. $x \leq \kappa_P x$,
4. $\kappa_P(x \cdot \kappa_P y) = \kappa_P x \cdot \kappa_P y$,
5. If $x \neq 0$, then $\kappa_\emptyset x = 1$,
6. $\kappa_{P \cup Q} x = \kappa_P x \cdot \kappa_Q x$, if x is an atom of B,

for all $x, y \in B$ and $P, Q \subseteq \Omega$. The class of all knowledge approximation algebras of type Ω is denoted by $\mathbf{KA}_\Omega$. We note that axioms A1 – A4 tell us that for each $P \subseteq \Omega$, the reduct $Rd_P\mathfrak{B}_S = \langle B, +, \cdot, -, 0, 1, \kappa_P \rangle$ of $\mathfrak{B}$ is a cylindric algebra of dimension 1 ($\mathbf{CA}_1$) in the sense of [HMT1]. Thus, we can regard the operators κ_P as (in general non - commuting) cylindrifications, and it follows from the corresponding properties of cylindric algebras that the properties given below hold:

Proposition 9. *[Col] Let* $\mathfrak{B} = \langle B, +, \cdot, -, 0, 1, \kappa_P \rangle_{P \subseteq \Omega}$ *be an approximation algebra. Then,*

1. *If* $x \leq y$, *then* $\kappa_P x \leq \kappa_P y$.
2. $\kappa_P \kappa_P x = \kappa_P x$.
3. $\sum_i \kappa_P x_i = \kappa_P(\sum_i x_i)$
4. $\kappa_P(\prod_i \kappa_P x_i) = \prod_i(\kappa_P x_i)$.

The next result shows that the algebra associated with an information system is a $\mathbf{KA}_\Omega$:

Proposition 10. *[Col] Let* $S = \langle U, \Omega, V, f \rangle$ *be an information system, and* $\mathfrak{B}_S$ *be its associated knowledge approximation algebra. Then,*

1. $\mathfrak{B}_\in \mathbf{KA}_\Omega$,
2. *Each* $Rd_Q\mathfrak{B}_S$ *is a cylindric algebra of dimension one.*

Proof. 1. $\mathfrak{B}_S$ is a complete and atomic Boolean algebra, and the operations $\overline{Q}$ are closure operators. This implies A1, A2, and A3. For A4 we need to show that $\overline{Q}(C \cap \overline{Q}D) = \overline{Q}C \cap \overline{Q}D$ for all $C, D \subseteq \Omega$:

"$\subseteq$": Let $x \in \overline{Q}(C \cap \overline{Q}D)$. Then, there is some $y \in C \cap \overline{Q}D$ such that $x \equiv_{\theta_Q} y$. Hence, $x \in \overline{Q}C$, and, since $\overline{Q}D$ is a union of θ_Q classes, we also have $x \in \overline{Q}D$.
"$\supseteq$": Let $x \in \overline{Q}C \cap \overline{Q}D$. Then, there are $y \in C,\ z \in D$ such that $x \equiv_{\theta_Q} y$ and $x \equiv_{\theta_Q} z$. Since D is a union of θ_Q classes, we have in fact $y \in \overline{Q}D$, which shows that $x \in \overline{Q}(C \cap \overline{Q}D)$.

A5 follows from the fact that $\theta_\Omega = {}^2U$. To show A6, let $P, Q \subseteq \Omega$. Because of A5, we can suppose that both P and Q are not empty. Let $x, y \in U$; then,

$$\begin{aligned} y \in \overline{P \cup Q}\{x\} &\Leftrightarrow y \equiv_{P \cup Q} x, \\ &\Leftrightarrow f(y,z) = f(x,z) \text{ for all } z \in P \cup Q, \\ &\Leftrightarrow f(y,z) = f(x,z) \text{ for all } z \in P \\ &\qquad \text{and } f(y,z) = f(x,z) \text{ for all } z \in Q, \\ &\Leftrightarrow y\theta_P x \text{ and } y\theta_Q x, \\ &\Leftrightarrow y \in \overline{P}\{x\} \cap \overline{Q}\{x\}. \end{aligned}$$

2. follows immediately from the definition. □

In order to show that the converse also holds, i.e. that the models of the algebras in $\mathbf{KA}_\Omega$ are as expected, we require some preparation. The definition of $\mathbf{KA}_\Omega$ and Proposition 9 show that each element of $\mathbf{KA}_\Omega$ is a completely atomic normal Boolean algebra with operators, i.e. a completely atomic Boolean algebra whose extra operators distribute over arbitrary joins, and do not move 0.

The completeness of the algebra and the operators imply that each κ_P is already determined by its values on the atoms of the Boolean part $\mathbf{B}$ of $\mathfrak{B}$. The *atomic structure* $\mathbf{At(B)}$ of $\mathfrak{B}$ is $\langle At(B), T_P \rangle_{P \subseteq \Omega}$, where $At(B)$ is the set of atoms of $\mathbf{B}$, and for each $P \subseteq \Omega$, T_P is the relation

$$\{\langle x, y \rangle \in At(B) \times At(B) : y \leq \kappa_P x\} .$$

Proposition 11. *[Co1] Let S be an information system and $\mathfrak{B}_S$ be its associated $\mathbf{KA}_\Omega$ with atomic structure $\mathbf{At(B_S)}$. Then, for all $P, Q \subseteq \Omega$,*

1. *T_P is an equivalence relation,*
2. *$T_\emptyset = {}^2At(B_S)$,*
3. *$T_P \cap T_Q = T_{P \cup Q}$.*

In particular, $\mathbf{At(B_S)}$ is a $\cap$ - subsemilattice of the partition lattice $\Pi(At(B_S))$.

Proof. 1. We show that $xT_Py \Leftrightarrow \kappa_P x = \kappa_P y$, from which the claim follows: Let $y \leq \kappa_P x$, and assume that $x \not\leq \kappa_P y$. Then, since x is an atom of B, we have $x \cap \kappa_P y = \emptyset$, and A2 and A4 imply that $\kappa_P x \cap \kappa_P y = \emptyset$. This contradicts $y \leq \kappa_P x$. The other direction is obvious.

2. is an immediate consequence of A5.

3. "$\subseteq$": Let $\langle x, y\rangle \in T_P \cap T_Q$, i.e. $\kappa_P x = \kappa_P y$ and $\kappa_Q x = \kappa_Q y$. Since x and y are atoms and using A4 we obtain

$$\kappa_{P\cup Q} x = \kappa_P x \cap \kappa_Q x = \kappa_P y \cap \kappa_Q y = \kappa_{P\cup Q} y.$$

"$\supseteq$": Let $\langle x, y\rangle \in T_{P\cup Q}$. Then, using A6,

$$x \leq \kappa_{P\cup Q} x = \kappa_{P\cup Q} y \leq \kappa_P y \cap \kappa_Q y$$

shows that $xT_P y$ and $xT_Q y$. □

A relational structure $L = \langle U, T_P\rangle_{P\subseteq \Omega}$ is called a *knowledge approximation atom structure*, if for all $P, Q \subseteq \Omega$,

1. T_P is an equivalence relation on U,
2. $T_\emptyset = {}^2U$,
3. $T_P \cap T_Q = T_{P\cup Q}$.

If Ω is finite and not empty, we can associate with each such structure an information system $S(L)$ in the following way: For each $x \in \Omega$ let $V(x)$ be the set of blocks of $T_{\{x\}}$, and set $V = \bigcup_{x\in\Omega}$. Then, define the knowledge function $f : U \times \Omega \to V$ by

$$f(u, x) = \text{ The block of } T_{\{x\}} \text{ containing } u.$$

It is easy to see that $S(L) = \langle U, \Omega, V, f\rangle$ is an information system. Furthermore,

Proposition 12. *[Co1] Let $\mathfrak{B}$ be a KA_Ω, Ω finite, and $L =$ $\mathbf{At(B)}$ be its atomic structure. Then, $\mathfrak{B} \cong \mathfrak{B}_{S(L)}$.*

Proof. The carrier set $B_{S(L)}$ of $\mathfrak{B}_{S(L)}$ is the power set of $At(B)$. Thus, the mapping $g : B \to B_{S(L)}$ defined by $g(b) = \{x \in At(B) : x \leq b\}$ is a Boolean isomorphism.

Now, let $x \in B$, and $P \subseteq \Omega$. We need to show that

$$g(\kappa_P^{\mathfrak{B}} x) = \kappa_P^{\mathfrak{B}_{S(L)}} g(x) \ . \tag{1}$$

This is clearly true if $P = \emptyset$, so that we can suppose that $P \neq \emptyset$; indeed, by A6 we may assume that P is an atom of $Sb(\Omega)$, say, $P = \{a\}$. Furthermore, by the additivity of g and κ_P, we may suppose that x is an atom of B.

Let y be an atom of B. Then,

$$\begin{aligned} y \in g(\kappa_P^{\mathfrak{B}} x) &\Leftrightarrow y \leq \kappa_P^{\mathfrak{B}} x \\ &\Leftrightarrow y T_P x \\ &\Leftrightarrow T_P y = T_P x \\ &\Leftrightarrow f(x, a) = f(y, a) \\ &\Leftrightarrow y \theta_P x \\ &\Leftrightarrow y \in \theta_P x = \kappa_P^{\mathfrak{B}_{S(L)}} x = \kappa_P^{\mathfrak{B}_{S(L)}} g(x), \end{aligned}$$

and we are done. □

This shows that the axioms for knowledge approximation algebras are complete for the intended models. A converse for the second part of 10 is given by

Proposition 13. *[Co1]*

1. *Every complete atomic* $\mathbf{CA}_1$ *is isomorphic to an approximation closure algebra.*
2. *Every* $\mathbf{CA}_1$ *is embeddable into an approximation closure algebra.*

Proof. 1. Let $\langle B, c_0 \rangle$ be a complete and atomic $\mathbf{CA}_1$, and Ω be a nonempty finite set. For each non empty $P \subseteq \Omega$ let $\kappa_P x = c_0 x$; also, let $\kappa_\emptyset x = 0$ if $x = 0$, and $\kappa_\emptyset x = 1$ if $x > 0$. Then, $\langle B, \kappa_P \rangle_{P \subseteq \Omega}$ is an approximation algebra, and the rest follows from 12

2. By 2.7.20 of [HMT1], each $\mathbf{CA}_1$ is embeddable into a complete and atomic one. □

The situation regarding the decidability of the first order theory of $\mathbf{KA}_\Omega$ is rather disappointing, though not altogether unexpected:

Proposition 14. *[Co1]*

1. *If* $|\Omega| = 1$*, then the theory of* $\mathbf{KA}_\Omega$ *is decidable.*
2. *If* $2 \leq |\Omega| < \omega$ *then the theory of* $\mathbf{KA}_\Omega$ *is undecidable and finitely inseparable.*

Proof. 1. Let $|\Omega| = 1$. Then, the algebras in $\mathbf{KA}_\Omega$ are of the form $\langle B, \kappa_\emptyset, \kappa_\Omega \rangle$, where $\langle B, \kappa_\Omega \rangle$ is a completely atomic $\mathbf{CA}_1$, and κ_Ω is definable in the Boolean part. It was shown in [HMT1] that the theory of complete atomic $\mathbf{CA}_1$'s is the same as the theory of finite $\mathbf{CA}_1$'s, and that it is decidable.

2. Let $\mathbf{Eq}$ be the theory of two equivalence relations; it is known that $\mathbf{Eq}$ is finitely inseparable, see [Mo1]. There it is also shown that to prove that a theory T is finitely inseparable, it is enough to show

> There are formulas θv_0, $\overline{R} v_0 v_1$, $\overline{S} v_0 v_1$ in the language of T such that for every finite model $\mathbf{A} = \langle X, R, S \rangle$ of $\mathbf{Eq}$ there is a finite model $\mathbf{B}$ of T such that $\langle \theta^{\mathbf{B}}, \overline{R}^{\mathbf{B}}, \overline{S}^{\mathbf{B}} \rangle \cong \mathbf{A}$.

Let $r, s \in \Omega$, $r \neq s$. We first give a translation of $\mathbf{Eq}$ into the language of $\mathbf{KA}_\Omega$:

$$\theta v_0 : v_0 \text{ is an atom.}$$

$$\overline{R} v_0 v_1 : \theta v_0 \wedge \theta v_1 \wedge \kappa_{\{r\}} v_0 = \kappa_{\{r\}} v_1.$$

$$\overline{S} v_0 v_1 : \theta v_0 \wedge \theta v_1 \wedge \kappa_{\{s\}} v_0 = \kappa_{\{s\}} v_1.$$

If we apply the translation to some $\mathfrak{B} \in \mathbf{KA}_\Omega$, it follows from Proposition 11 that $\langle At(B), \overline{R}^{\mathfrak{B}}, \overline{S}^{\mathfrak{B}} \rangle$ is a model of $\mathbf{Eq}$.

Finally, let $\mathbf{A} = \langle X, R, S \rangle$ be a finite model of $\mathbf{Eq}$. We obtain a knowledge approximation atom structure $L = \langle X, T_P \rangle_{P \subseteq \Omega}$ by setting

1. $T_{\{r\}} = R$, $T_{\{s\}} = S$, $T_{\emptyset} = T_{\{i\}} = {}^2X$ for all $i \in \Omega, i \notin \{r, s\}$.
2. $T_P = \bigcap\{T_{\{i\}} : i \in P\}$, for all $P \subseteq \Omega$ with $|P| \geq 2$.

If **A** is finite, so is $\mathfrak{B}_{S(L)}$, and it is straightforward to show that $\langle At(B), \overline{R}^{\mathfrak{B}}, \overline{S}^{\mathfrak{B}} \rangle$ is isomorphic to **A**.

In [Co2] a close connection of knowledge approximation algebras to a variant of diagonal free cylindric algebras was established. Since a discussion of these results would require an unproportional amount of new definitions and notation, we refer the reader to Comer's paper.

References

[BG1] Balbes, R. & Grätzer, G.: Injective and projective Stone algebras. Duke Math. J., **38**, (1971), 339–347

[CT1] Chin, L. & Tarski, A.: Distributive and modular laws in the arithmetic of relation algebras. University of California Publications, **1**, (1951), 341–384

[Co1] Comer, S.: An algebraic approach to the approximation of information. Fund. Inform., **14**, (1991), 492–502

[Co2] Comer, S.: On connections between information systems, rough sets, and algebraic logic. In: Algebraic Methods in Logic and Computer Science, Banach Center Publications, **28**, (1993), 117–124

[Co3] Comer, S.: Perfect extensions of regular double Stone algebras. Algebra Universalis, **34**, (1995), 96–109

[Du1] Düntsch, I.: Rough relation algebras. Fund. Inform., **21**, (1994), 321–331

[HMT1] Henkin, L., Monk, J.D. & Tarski, A.: Cylindric Algebras. Part I, North Holland, Amsterdam, (1971)

[HMT2] Henkin, L., Monk, J.D. & Tarski, A.: Cylindric Algebras. Part II, North Holland, Amsterdam, (1985)

[Iw1] Iwinski, T.B.: Algebraic approach to rough sets. Bull. Polish Acad. Sci. Math., **35**, (1987), 673–683

[Jo1] Jónsson, B.: Varieties of relation algebras. Algebra Universalis, **15**, (1982), 273–298

[Jo2] Jónsson, B.: The theory of binary relations. In: Algebraic Logic, edited by Andréka, H., Monk, J.D. & Németi, I.: volume 54 of Colloquia Mathematica Societatis János Bolyai, North Holland, Amsterdam, (1991), 245–292

[JAN1] Jónsson, B., Andréka, H. & Németi, I.: Free algebras in discriminator varieties. Algebra Univ, **28**, (1991), 401–447

[Ka1] Katriňák, T.: Construction of regular double p–algebras. Bull. Soc. Roy. Sci. Liège, **43**, (1974), 294–301

[Mo1] Monk, J.D.: Mathematical Logic. Springer, (1976)

[Pa1] Pawlak, Z.: Information systems, theoretical foundations. Information Systems, **6**, (1981), 205–218

[Pa2] Pawlak, Z.: Rough sets. Internat. J. Comput. Inform. Sci., **11**, (1982), 341–356

[PP1] Pomykala, J. & Pomykala, J.A.: The Stone algebra of rough sets. Bull. Polish Acad. Sci. Math., **36**, (1988), 495–508

[TG1] Tarski, A. & Givant, S.: A Formalization of Set Theory without Variables. Volume 41 of Colloquium Publications, Amer. Math. Soc., Providence, (1987)

Chapter 6

Rough Set Theory and Logic-Algebraic Structures

Piero Pagliani

Research Group on Knowledge and Communication Models
Via Imperia 6, 00165 Roma, Italy

Abstract: Any Rough Set System induced by an Approximation Space can be given several logic-algebraic interpretations related to the intuitive reading of the notion of Rough Set. In this paper Rough Set Systems are investigated, first, within the framework of Nelson algebras and the structure of the resulting subclass is inherently described using the properties of Approximation Spaces. In particular, the logic-algebraic structure given to a Rough Set System, *understood as* a Nelson algebra is equipped with a weak negation and a strong negation and, since it is a finite distributive lattice, it can also be regarded as a Heyting algebra equipped with its own pseudo-complementation. The double weak negation and the double pseudo-complementation are shown to be projection operations connected to the notion of definability in Approximation Spaces. From this analysis we obtain an interpretation of Rough Sets Systems connected to three-valued Łukasiewicz algebras where the roles of projections operators are played by the two endomorphisms of these algebras. Finally, continuing to explore the point of view of Multi-Valued Logics suggested by the latter interpretation we achieve in a quite "natural" way an interpretation based on the notion of Chain Based Lattice. Here the projection operators are provided by the pseudo-supplementation and dual pseudo-supplementation.

1 Introduction

Concept forming in the presence of incomplete information is a main topic in Artificial Intelligence. Following essentially a definition originating in Aristotle's work, we assume that "when you learn a concept, you learn how to treat different things as instances of the same category. Without this classification procedure, thinking would be impossible because each event or entity would be unique" [J-L1].

In the fields of mathematics and mathematical logic, since the beginning of the eighties several approaches to Knowledge Representation have emerged based on the notion of indiscernibility of objects or of decidability of the extension of properties. In particular, two algebraic approaches occupy a central position: the theory of *Concept Lattices* [Wil] based on the polarity $\langle$*intension*, *extension*$\rangle$

and the theory of *Approximation Spaces* [Paw1] and [Paw5] based on the pair $\langle property, classification\rangle$. In this Introduction we recall basic features of the theory of Approximation Spaces in order to provide the reader with an intuitive background for our logic-algebraic analysis.

We assume the reader to have just a basic acquaintance with distributive lattices. All the other algebraic notions needed in the paper are provided in the text. The theory of Approximation Spaces takes primarily into account systems of information about a universe of discourse U (like in the theory of Concept Lattices), called *Information Systems* and represented by a quadruple $\mathbf{C} = (U, At, V, v)$.

Any Information System $\mathbf{C}$ makes it possible to compute the extension $[[D_i]]$ on the *universe* U of a *basic deterministic property* D_i. A deterministic property is a set $D_i = \{\langle att, val\rangle\}$, where *att* ranges over the *set of parameters* At, *val* ranges over the *set of values* V and if $\langle att, val_1\rangle \in D_i$ and $\langle att, val_2\rangle \in D_i$, then $val_1 = val_2$. We call such a property: **C**-*property*, since it can be formulated using the linguistic material from $\mathbf{C}$. The extension $[[D_i]]$ is then determined by the *information function* v.

Here we are not concerned with problems of dependency among subsets of At with respect to the same description capability, so we assume that any property D_i is given by a total function $d_i : At \longmapsto V$. If $g \in U$ and the diagram of the parameterized function $v_g : At \longmapsto V$ equals D_i, then $g \in [[D_i]]$. So $g, g' \in [[D_i]]$ iff $v_g = v_{g'}$, that is if the diagrams of the two parameterized functions coincide.

Thus **C**-properties allow the classification of the objects from U in different disjoint equivalence classes: the objects that are in the same class are *indiscernible* by means of our system of information $\mathbf{C}$.

Moreover, since $\forall g \in U, v_g$ is a **C**-property, every object from U will belong to the extension of some **C**-property. So we get the first important characteristic for our analysis:

1.1 *The set* $Ind(\mathbf{C}) = \{[[D_i]] : D_i \text{ is a } \mathbf{C} - property\}$ *is a partition of* U *and can be seen as the family of the equivalence classes of an equivalence relation* R.

These classes, or blocks, are the atoms of more complex conceptual constructions. In Rough Set Theory, they are called "elementary" or "basic" "classes" or "categories" and we adopt this use. In particular, the theory of Approximation Spaces takes into account *disjunctions* of properties (contrary to the Concept Lattices, based on the theory of Galois connections, where the disjunction is not taken into account).

To any disjunction of basic properties there corresponds a union of elementary classes. The *Approximation Space* $\mathbf{AS}(\mathbf{C})$ induced by $\mathbf{C}$, represents in fact these linguistic descriptions of concepts.

This explains intuitively why we can define an Approximation Space $\mathbf{AS}(\mathbf{C})$ as the partially ordered set of all the unions of elementary classes plus the emptyset $\emptyset$ (an arbitrary **C**-property could have an empty extension).

We assume from now on that U and At are finite.

Thus, from an algebraic point of view, we have:

1.2 *For any Information System* **C**, *the Approximation Space* **AS**(**C**) *is the finite Boolean algebra of sets for which* Ind(**C**) *is the set of atoms.*

Of course we do not usually have full information about U: the opposite hypothesis is neither likely nor interesting from a mathematical point of view. Thus, if we assume that the extension of a generic "concept", virtually definable on U, is a generic subset of elements of U (associated by the links described by that concept), then we have immediately that the granularity of the knowledge represented by our properties does not allow the exact representation of arbitrary concepts.

This restriction is algebraically reflected by the following fact:

1.3 *For any Information System* **C**, *the Approximation Space* **AS**(**C**) *is a subalgebra of the Boolean algebra* **B**(U) *of all the subsets of the universe* U.

Thus, if X is a subset of U, then in general it will not belong to **AS**(**C**).

Anyway we can imagine that every concept is described by means of the material at our disposal, even if only in a vague, approximate way.

In Pawlak's theory of Rough Sets, the solution for by-passing this information gap is to associate to any subset X of U the greatest element of **AS**(**C**) that is contained in X, what is called *lower approximation* of X, $(lR)(X)$, and the least element of **AS**(**C**) that contains X, what is called *upper approximation* of X, $(uR)(X)$. The relation R of 1.1 appears in the notation since these approximations depend strictly on it.

Thus, any concept X is replaced by a pair $\langle (uR)(X), (lR)(X) \rangle$ of concepts that are describable in the Approximation Space **AS**(**C**). If a concept is exactly definable in **C**, then $X = (lR)(X) = (uR)(X)$. Such a set is said to be a *definable set* in **C**.

This approach induces the notion of *rough set:*

1.4 *A* rough set *is an equivalence class of extensions of concepts modulo the equality of the upper approximations and of the lower ones.*

It follows that a Rough Set is naturally representable by a pair $\langle X_1, X_2 \rangle$ of elements of **AS**(**C**).

If we now consider the (by now informal) set

1.5 $RS(\mathbf{C}) = \{\langle X_1, X_2 \rangle \in \mathbf{AS}(\mathbf{C}) \times \mathbf{AS}(\mathbf{C})\colon \langle X_1, X_2 \rangle$ *is a Rough Set in* $\mathbf{C}\}$

we immediately have the problem of its formal characterization. A first subproblem is:

1.6 *For any Approximation Space* **AS**(**C**), *determine the* internal characteristics *that must be satisfied by the elements of the pairs representing a rough set.*

The answer depends on the intuitive motivations that drive our reading of the nature of rough sets.

A first, and in a sense the most immediate and "naive", solution is considering pairs of the form $\langle (lR)(X), (uR)(X) \rangle$ (see [Iw1]). An immaterial modification is taking into account the pairs of the form $\langle X_1, X_2 \rangle$ such that the first element, X_1 is to represent the upper approximation and the second element, X_2, is to represent the lower approximation that describes the equivalence class in question. That is, the rough set of a set $X \in \mathbb{P}(U)$ is represented by $\langle (uR)(X), (lR)(X) \rangle$.

From this point of view the "internal property" of a pair $\langle X_1, X_2 \rangle$ is necessarily:

$$X_2 \subseteq X_1 \ . \tag{1}$$

Thereafter we call such a representation: *decreasing representation* of a rough set, which we prefer to adopt instead of the symmetric one since, in a precise sense, this reading is linked to the notion of *refinement of an approximation* as it is interpreted within the framework of *multi-valued logics* (see for instance [Ra2], [ER1], [Tr1]).

A second reading, probably less "naive" but still intuitive, is suggested by the application of Rough Set Theory to some semantics for Logics of Knowledge and Learning (see for instance: [Paw4], [Or2], [Or3], [RZ1]) and is connected to the following intuition: any rough set represents what we know definitely as belonging to a concept and what we know definitely as not belonging to it. Between the two areas there is a *doubtful region* that is due to the finiteness of our knowledge.

In a more logical setting, the upper approximation $(uR)(X)$ corresponds to the modal application $\mathbf{M}(X)$ -"it is *possible* that X"- and the lower approximation $(lR)(X)$ corresponds to the modal application $\mathbf{L}(X)$ -"it is *necessary* that X"- by interpreting the pair $(U, \mathbf{AS}(\mathbf{C}))$ as an S5 modal space structured by the equivalence relation R. Thereafter $\neg\mathbf{M}(X)$ will mean "it is *impossible* that X".

Hence, $\mathbf{L}(X)$ and $\neg\mathbf{M}(X)$ are the only statements expressing "certainty". Thus, a definite knowledge about a specific phenomenon will be expressed by a pair

$$\langle \mathbf{L}(X), \neg\mathbf{M}(X) \rangle$$

(we will not deal any further with this modal interpretation, but we will use in the paper the "topological" part of it).

In order to make rough sets reflecting the above intuitions, one must represent a rough set as a pair $\langle (lR)(X), -(uR)(X) \rangle$, that we call *disjoint representation* of a rough set.

Thereafter from this point of view the "internal property" of a pair $\langle X_1, X_2 \rangle$ is necessarily:

$$X_1 \cap X_2 = \emptyset \ . \tag{2}$$

A second sub-problem is:

1.7 *For any Approximation Space* $\mathbf{AS}(\mathbf{C})$, *determine the* global characteristics *of the ordered pairs representing a Rough Set System (independently of the "internal representation").*

More precisely, if we assume the decreasing representation we have to notice that not all the pairs of elements with the property (1) are legal. In other terms, (1) is a necessary but not sufficient condition for a pair in order to represent a rough set of an Information System $\mathbf{C}$.

This fact depends on the cardinality of the elementary classes of $\mathbf{AS}(\mathbf{C})$: if an elementary class E is a singleton then for any $X \subseteq U$, E belongs to $(lR)(X)$ whenever E belongs to $(uR)(X)$, hence, for instance, the pair $\langle E, \emptyset\rangle$ fulfils property (1) but it is not a legal one, while $\langle E, E\rangle$ is.

In the same case, if we assume the disjoint representation, we would have to discard, for instance, the pair $\langle \emptyset, \emptyset\rangle$: indeed it enjoys property (2) but it is clear that the singleton E must necessarily be included either in X_1 or in X_2, for any pair $\langle X_1, X_2\rangle$. Again (2) is only a necessary condition.

The problem becomes thereafter:

1.8 *For any Approximation Space* $\mathbf{AS}(\mathbf{C})$ *characterize the set* $RS(\mathbf{C})$ *within the Cartesian product* $\mathbf{AS}(\mathbf{C}) \times \mathbf{AS}(\mathbf{C})$.

Finally, a related problem is:

1.9 *Determine if there is any logic-algebraic structure behind Rough Set Systems.*

Now, it is well known that the set $\mathbf{B}^{[n]} = \{\langle a_1, ..., a_{n-1}\rangle \in \mathbf{B}^{n-1} : a_i \geq a_j \text{ for } i \leq j\}$, where $\mathbf{B}$ is a Boolean algebra, is an example of n-valued Łukasiewicz algebra (see [BFGR1]).

Thus $\mathbf{AS}(\mathbf{C})^{[3]}$ is a three-valued Łukasiewicz algebra.

From this consideration it follows that $RS(\mathbf{C})$ is a *substructure* of $\mathbf{AS}(\mathbf{C})^{[3]}$ if we assume the decreasing representation.

On the side of the disjoint representation, if $\mathbf{D}$ is a finite distributive lattice with least element $\bot$, then the set $\mathbf{K}(\mathbf{D}) = \{\langle a_1, a_2\rangle \in \mathbf{D}^2 : a_1 \wedge a_2 = \bot\}$ is an example of DeMorgan algebra. In particular if $\mathbf{D}$ is a finite Boolean algebra, then $\mathbf{K}(\mathbf{D})$ is a Post algebra of order three. Since $\mathbf{AS}(\mathbf{C})$ is a Boolean algebra, it follows from the above considerations that if we assume the disjoint representation, then $RS(\mathbf{C})$ is a *substructure* of the Post algebra $\mathbf{K}(\mathbf{AS}(\mathbf{C}))$ of order three.

The above problem can now be restated in the following way:

1.10 *For any Approximation Space* $\mathbf{AS}(\mathbf{C})$, *characterize within* $\mathbf{AS}(\mathbf{C})^{[3]}$ *and* $\mathbf{K}(\mathbf{D})$ *the substructure* $RS(\mathbf{C})$ *using only parameters depending on* $\mathbf{AS}(\mathbf{C})$.

In Section 3 we start answering these questions by representing $RS(\mathbf{C})$ as a *semi-simple Nelson algebra.* We decide to start from this interpretation since the duality theory of Nelson algebras provides us with the mathematical machinery that is needed for exhibiting a rigorous characterization of $RS(\mathbf{C})$. The main result of the section is that for any Approximation Space $\mathbf{AS}(\mathbf{C})$ the Rough Sets System $RS(\mathbf{C})$ is a finite semi-simple Nelson algebra, precisely definable by means of a parameter S depending on $\mathbf{AS}(\mathbf{C})$. The reverse result, i.e. any finite semi-simple Nelson algebra is isomorphic to the rough set system induced by an Approximation Space $\mathbf{AS}(\mathbf{C})$, is presented at the end of this paper together with a logic-algebraic decomposition of the structure of a Rough Set System. These Nelson algebras are trivially proved to be also Heyting algebras and a deeper insight from this point of view makes it possible to see that the characteristic

Heyting algebras operation of relative pseudo-complementation can be defined by means of the operations of weak and strong negation provided by the Nelson algebra structure. In this way we are able to recover the fact (see [PP1]) that Rough Set Systems can be given the structure of *double Stone algebras.* This perspective is more deeply analyzed in this volume by I. Düntsch in chapter 5.

Particular attention is given to the logic-algebraic characterization of definable sets. It is shown that it is possible to define, by means of the weak negation and the pseudo-complementation, two operators that project any rough set X onto particular exact elements, that is elements $\langle X_1, X_2 \rangle$ such that $X_1 \cup X_2 = U$ (assuming X to be in disjoint representation).

In Section 4 we exploit the well-known relationships between the class of semi-simple Nelson algebras and the class of *three-valued Łukasiewicz algebras* in order to move from the point of view of disjoint representation to the standpoint of Multi-Valued Logics. In that Section we prove that for any Approximation Space $\mathbf{AS}(\mathbf{C})$ the Rough Set System $RS(\mathbf{C})$ is a finite three-valued Łukasiewicz algebra. In this framework the projection operators correspond to the two endomorphisms of these algebras.
The point of view of Multi-Valued Logics is fully assumed in Subsection 4.2 and in Subection 4.3. In Subsection 4.2 we discuss an "ideal case" in wich $RS(\mathbf{C})$ can be interpreted as a *Post algebra of order three.* But in order to achieve a full generality we have to exploit the generalization of Post algebras called *Chain Based Lattices* (see [EH2]). In particular, in Subsection 4.3 we will see that for any Approximation Space $\mathbf{AS}(\mathbf{C})$ the Rough Set System $RS(\mathbf{C})$ is a $P_2-lattice$ that can be characterized by means of the same parameter S used in Section 3. Moreover, it is shown that the pseudo-supplementation and the dual pseudo-supplementation definable in P_2-lattices play the role of projection operators.

Throughout the paper, these logic-algebraic interpretations enabling us recovering of some typical mechanism of Rough Set Theory are taken into account. Many examples will help a non-specialist reader in understanding the text.

In particular, in Section 2 we recall some basic notions concerning orders and lattices and elementary concepts of topology; moreover, we present the basic duality results for finite Heyting and Boolean algebras. The same is done for Nelson algebras in Section 3. This is necessary since in view of our introductory discussion it is clear that a most intuitive "mathematical environment" for our analysis is "topology" and we will also support some algebraic results by means of their counterpart in dual spaces. In Section 3 we will prove a general theorem directly connecting Nelson spaces to the representation of Nelson algebras required by our problem.

Now we would like to account for the title of the paper. The term "logic-algebraic" is intended here in a broader sense. Actually the adjective "logic" refers to the fact that these structures are models of some logical systems. We will not deal here with these systems themselves. Anyway we have decided to keep the qualification "logic" for two reasons. The first is historical: these structures, from Boolean algebras up to P_2-lattices have been developed in strict connection with logical problems and logical systems. The second reason is to the author's refusal of considering as "logical" only what deals with syntax and "algebraic" or "set-theoretical" what deals with semantics.

As soon as a structure provides us with operations that have conceptual-linguistic meanings, the author thinks that the term "logic" is appropriate. Also in everyday language a "Boolean gate" continues to be considered a "logical gate".

But there is also a third reason: modern logic, computer sciences, cognitive sciences, knowledge-based systems and so forth, tend in fact to break down the distinction between syntax and semantics. Gabbay's "Labeled Deductive Systems" may be considered as an example (see [Ga1]) and Orłowska's investigations on Relational Logics as well (see [Or4]).

Eventually, the Rough Set Theory is to be considered within this trend. And in fact this is the perspective that we assume throughout this study.

Acknowledgments. This research is a part of the study of the application of logic-algebraic models to various systems of partial information. The author is grateful to Professor Z. Pawlak of the Technical University of Warsaw, Professor A. Skowron of the University of Warsaw and Professor R. Wille of the Technische Hochschule of Darmstadt, for the possibilities given to him for discussing his theses in Warsaw, in Rome and in Darmstadt. Special thanks to Professor E. Orłowska of the Polish Academy of Sciences for her valuable encouragement to accomplish this work. The content of the paper is, however, entirely the author's responsibility.

2 Basic Concepts

2.1 Notation

Throughout the paper, we shall use the following conventions:

1. Sets are denoted by strings prefixed by capital italic Latin letters (A, At, B, ...);
2. Structures and functors are denoted by capital bold Latin letters (**A, B, N, H,...**); usually, if **A** is a structure, then A will denote its carrier.
3. If f is a function, then $\mathbf{Im}f$ denotes the image of f; Id will denote the identity map;
4. given a set S, by $\mathbb{P}(S)$ we denote the powerset of S;
5. If X is a set, then $card(X)$ will denote the cardinality of X;
6. If **S** is any structure with carrier S, in order to denote the membership of x to the carrier S we will use in general the notation $x \in S$ while we will use the notation $x \in \mathbf{S}$ if we want to underline the particular structure of **S**;
7. If R is an equivalence relation, then lower case greek letters (possibly indexed by a set of indeces) will denote generic equivalence classes modulo R.

Now we need a few preliminary definitions. The following subsections may be skipped by the reader familiar with the basic notions related to orders, lattices, topology and on the most elementary logic-algebraic structures. The reader is anyhow invited to consider the notations used in the text.

2.2 Lattices and Orders

Definition 1. Let S be a set and $R \subseteq S \times S$. Let us consider the following properties that may be satisfied by R:

1. transitivity: $\forall a, b, c \in S$, if $\langle a, b\rangle \in R$ and $\langle b, c\rangle \in R$, then $\langle a, c\rangle \in R$;
2. reflexivity: $\forall a \in S, \langle a, a\rangle \in R$;
3. antisymmetry: $\forall a, b \in S$, if $\langle a, b\rangle \in R$ and $\langle b, a\rangle \in R$, then $a = b$;
4. symmetry: $\forall a, b \in S$ if $\langle a, b\rangle \in R$, then $\langle b, a\rangle \in R$;
5. if R enjoys 1 and 2, then R is a *pre-order* and it will be denoted by $\preceq$, while $\mathbf{P} = (P, R)$ is a *pre-ordered set*;
6. if R fulfils 1, 2 and 3, then R is a *partial order* and it will be denoted by "$\leq$", while $\mathbf{P} = (P, R)$ is a *partially ordered set* (poset);
7. if R enjoys 4,2 and 1, then R is an *equivalence relation* and will be denoted by "$\equiv$";
8. if $\mathbf{P} = (P, R)$ is such that $\forall x, y, \langle x, y\rangle \in R$ iff $x = y$, then R is a *discrete ordering*.

We shall also use the infixed notation "aRb" instead of the prefixed one.

Definition 2. If $\mathbf{P} = (P, R)$ is at least a preordered set, then given $P' \subseteq P$, we have the following notable subsets of P:

1. the close interval $[x, y] = \{z : xRzRy\}$;
2. the *order ideal generated by* (or *down-set of*) P': $\downarrow P' = \{p \in P : \exists p' \in P' \wedge pRp'\}$; if $P' = \{p\}$, then we denote $\downarrow \{p\}$ also by $\downarrow p$;
3. dually we have the *order filter* (or *up-set*) of P': $\uparrow P' = \{p \in P : \exists p' \in P' \wedge p'Rp\}$; if $P' = \{p\}$, then we denote $\uparrow \{p\}$ also by $\uparrow p$;
4. the set of order filters of $\mathbf{P}$ will be denoted by $\Omega_A(\mathbf{P})$ (the *Alexandrov completion* of $\mathbf{P}$);
5. the set of *minimal elements* of P': $\mathbf{min}(P') = \{x \in P' : \forall x' \in P'$, if $x'Rx$, then $xRx'\}$;
6. the set of *maximal elements* of P': $\mathbf{max}(P') = \{x \in P' : \forall x' \in P'$, if xRx', then $x'Rx\}$.
   Clearly, if R is a partial ordering "$\leq$", then the above definitions amount to saying:
   $\mathbf{min}(P') = \{x \in P' : \forall x' \in P'$, if $x' \leq x$, then $x' = x\}$ and $\mathbf{max}(P') = \{x \in P' : \forall x' \in P'$, if $x \leq x'$, then $x' = x\}$;
7. if $\mathbf{min}(P') = \{x\}$ ($\mathbf{max}(P') = \{x\}$), then the element x will be denoted by $\mathbf{lst}(P')$ (by $\mathbf{grt}(P')$), the least (greatest) element of P'. Clearly, these elements may not exist (also in finite ordered structures);

If $x, y \in P$ and neither xRy nor yRx, then we say that x and y are *parallel*: $x \parallel y$.

Proposition 3. *Let $(X, \preceq)$ be a pre-ordered set. Consider the equivalence relation "$\equiv$" defined by: $\forall x, y \in X, x \equiv b$ iff $x \preceq y$ and $y \preceq x$. Then the quotient structure $(X/_{\equiv}, \leq)$ where $\leq$ is naturally induced by $\preceq$, is a poset.*

Definition 4. Let $\mathbf{P} = (P, \leq)$ and $\mathbf{P}' = (P', \leq')$ be two posets and $f : P \longmapsto P'$. Then

1. if $P = P'$ and for all $x, y \in P$, $x \leq y$ iff $y' \leq x'$, then $\mathbf{P}'$ is called the *dual* of $\mathbf{P}$;
2. f is *order preserving* if for all $x, y \in P$, $x \leq y$ implies $f(x) \leq' f(y)$;
3. f is an *order embedding* if $x \leq y$ iff $f(x) \leq' f(y)$. In this case f is injective;
4. f is an *order isomorphism* if f is a surjective order embedding. In this case we write $\mathbf{P} \cong_P \mathbf{P}'$. If $\mathbf{P}'$ is the dual of $\mathbf{P}$, then f is a *dual-order automorphism* on $\mathbf{P}$;
5. if $\mathbf{P} = \mathbf{P}'$ and $f(f(x)) = x, \forall x \in P$, then f is called an *involution* and if $\forall x \in P, f(x) \leq x$ or $x \leq f(x)$ then f is said to be *linear*.
6. if $\mathbf{X} = (\mathbf{P}, g)$ and $\mathbf{X}' = (\mathbf{P}', g')$ are posets equipped with the involutions g and g', respectively, such that f is an order isomorphism between $\mathbf{P}$ and $\mathbf{P}'$ and $\forall x \in P, f(g(x)) = g'(f(x))$ then we say that $\mathbf{X}$ and $\mathbf{X}'$ are *PI-isomorphic* and we write $\mathbf{P} \cong_{PI} \mathbf{P}'$.

For our purposes we shall deal only with finite structures. In particular we will concentrate on finite distributive lattices.

Definition 5. A finite lattice will be denoted by $\mathbf{L} = (L, \wedge, \vee, 0, 1)$. We assume $\mathbf{L}$ to be equipped by the usual partial order $\leq$: $a \leq b$ iff $a \wedge b = a$ iff $a \vee b = b$. Given a finite lattice $\mathbf{L}$, we have:

1. $\mathbf{lst}(L) = 0 = \bigvee \emptyset$; $\mathbf{grt}(L) = 1 = \bigwedge \emptyset$;
2. the set of atoms of $\mathbf{L}$, $Atom(\mathbf{L}) = \mathbf{min}(L - \{0\})$.
3. the set of *co-prime elements* of $\mathbf{L}$: $\mathcal{CP}(\mathbf{L}) = \{p \in L : \forall L' \subseteq L,$ *if* $\bigvee L' \geq p$, *then* $\exists x \in L', x \geq p\}$.
4. The set of *join irreducible elements* $\mathcal{J}(\mathbf{L}) = \{p \in L : \forall L' \subseteq L,$ *if* $\bigvee L' = p$, *then* $\exists x \in L', x = p\}$. In finite distributive lattices $\mathcal{CP}(\mathbf{L}) = \mathcal{J}(\mathbf{L})$. Notice that since $0 = \bigvee \emptyset$, $0 \notin \mathcal{J}(\mathbf{L})$;
5. A subset $F \subset L$ is called a *proper filter* of $\mathbf{L}$ if F is an up-set that is closed with respect to $\wedge$. If, moreover, $a \in F$ or $b \in F$ whenever $a \vee b \in F$ then F is said to be a *prime filter*. If F has the form $\uparrow x$ for $x \in L$, then F is *principal filter*. In finite distributive lattices any filter is principal, thus a filter is prime if it has the form $\uparrow p$ for $p \in \mathcal{J}(\mathbf{L})$.
6. By $\mathbf{X}(\mathbf{L})$ we shall denote the poset $(\mathcal{J}(\mathbf{L}), \leq)$ with the order induced by the set-theoretic ordering among the prime filters generated by its elements (that is the dual of the ordering induced by $\mathbf{L}$).
7. Given a lattice $\mathbf{L}$ and an equivalence relation $\equiv$ on it, $\equiv$ is called a congruence on $\mathbf{L}$ if for all $a, b, c, d \in L$, $a \equiv b$ and $c \equiv d$ imply $a \vee c \equiv b \vee d$ and $a \wedge c \equiv b \wedge d$.

Remark. Notice that in our finite case, the choice of the direction of the ordering $\leq$ for the set $\mathcal{J}(\mathbf{L})$ would not be essential. We adopt the above definition in view of the usual preference of logicians for thinking in terms of "truth" and "maximal consistent sets of formulas". The algebraic companions of these notions are those of "filter" and "maximal proper filters"; hence, the order induced by filters is the suitable one and we will see below that the ordering "$\leq$" on $\mathcal{J}(\mathbf{L})$ allows for the construction of the concrete models of a logic-algebraic structure, in terms of order-filters.

Definition 6. Let $\mathbf{L} = (L, \vee, \wedge, 0, 1)$ and $\mathbf{L}' = (L', \vee', \wedge', 0', 1')$ be two bounded lattices and let f be the application $f : L \longmapsto L'$. Then

1. f is an *L-homomorphism* if it preserves the binary operations: $f(a \vee b) = f(a) \vee' f(b)$, $f(a \wedge b) = f(a) \wedge' f(b)$. Moreover, if f preserves also the nullary operations, that is $f(0) = 0', f(1) = 1'$, then f is a *0-1 homomorphism.* If $\mathbf{L} = \mathbf{L}'$, then f is called an *endomorphism*;
2. f is an *L-monomorphism* if it is an injective homomorphism;
3. f is an *L-isomorphism* if it is a surjective monomorphism. In this case we write $\mathbf{L} \cong_L \mathbf{L}'$. If $\mathbf{L} = \mathbf{L}'$, then f is called an *L-automorphism.*

Proposition 7. *If* $\mathbf{L}$ *and* $\mathbf{L}'$ *are two lattices, then* $\mathbf{L} \cong_L \mathbf{L}'$ *iff* $\mathbf{L} \cong_P \mathbf{L}'$.

2.3 Topology

Definition 8. A *topological space* $(X, \Omega(X))$ is a set X and a family $\Omega(X)$ of privileged elements of $\mathbb{P}(X)$, called the *frame of the open subsets*, such that:

1. $\emptyset \in \Omega(X)$ and $X \in \Omega(X)$;
2. if $X, Y \in \Omega(X)$ then $X \cap Y \in \Omega(X)$;
3. $\bigcup_{i \in I}\{O_i : O_i \in \Omega(X)\} \in \Omega(X)$ for any I.

Definition 9. Given a topological space $\tau = (X, \Omega(X))$,

1. a set $Z \subseteq X$ is called *closed* in τ if Z is the complement of an open set of $\Omega(X)$;
2. a set $Z \subseteq X$ in is called *clopen* in τ if Z is both open and closed in τ;

Sometimes it is suitable to define a topology by starting from a particular subset of the frame of the open sets:

Definition 10. Given a topological space $\tau = (X, \Omega(X))$ and a set $B \subseteq \mathbb{P}(X)$:

1. if $\Omega(X)$ equals the set of all arbitrary unions of elements of B, then B is called a *basis* for τ;
2. if $\Omega(X)$ equals the set of all arbitrary unions of finite intersections of elements of B, then B is called a *subbasis* for τ;
3. τ is called *0-dimensional* if it has a basis of clopen subsets;
4. given a set X, the 0-dimensional topological space $(X, \mathbb{P}(X))$ is called *discrete topology* on X.

The classification of topological spaces is fundamental with respect to their separation capabilities, that is with respect to a possibility that two distinct points of the set X could be distinguished by means of the elements of $\Omega(X)$. In particular, this characteristic is important in the "spatial" intuitions of Approximation Spaces and Rough Sets, as we will see in the next Subsections.

Definition 11. Let $\tau = (X, \Omega(X))$ be a topological space and let x, y be two arbitrary elements of X such that $x \neq y$, then τ is said to be

1. T_0*–space* if either there is a $O \in \Omega(X)$ such that $x \in O$ and $y \notin O$ or there is a $O' \in \Omega(X)$ such that $x \notin O'$ and $y \in O'$;
2. T_1*–space* if there is a $O \in \Omega(X)$ such that $x \in O$ and $y \notin O$ and there is a $O' \in \Omega(X)$ such that $x \notin O'$ and $y \in O'$;
3. T_2*–space* (or *Hausdorff space*) if there are $O, O' \in \Omega(X)$ such that $O \cap O' = \emptyset$ and $x \in O$, $y \in O'$;
4. let $\tau_1 = (X, \Omega(X))$, $\tau_2 = (X, \Omega'(X))$ be two topological spaces on a set X; then τ_1 is said to be *finer* then τ_2 (or τ_2 is said to be *coarser* then τ_1) if $\forall Z \subseteq X$, if $Z \in \Omega'(X)$ then $Z \in \Omega(X)$. This relation is a partial order on the set of the topologies definable on a set X.

Proposition 12. *Let X be a set and let τ_0, τ_1, τ_2 be topologies defined on X of type T_0, T_1 and T_2, respectively. Then τ_0 is coarser then τ_1 and τ_1 is coarser then τ_2.*

Proposition 13. *Let X be a finite set and $\tau = (X, \Omega(X))$ be a topology on X. Then τ is a T_2 space iff τ is the discrete topology on X, that is $\Omega(X) = \mathbb{P}(X)$.*

We recall also that for any topological space $(X, \Omega(X))$

Definition 14. The relation "$\ll$" defined $\forall x, y \in X$, by

$$x \ll y \text{ iff } \forall O \in \Omega(X),\ (x \in O) \text{ implies } (y \in O)$$

is called *specialization preorder*; if $x \ll y$, then x is said to be *specialized* by y.

Remark. The relation $\ll$ is a partial order on X only if $\Omega(X)$ is at least T_0. It is then provable that, given a poset $(X, \leq)$, $\Omega_A(X)$ is the strongest topology for which the specialization preorder $(X, \ll)$ coincides with $(X, \leq)$.

Moreover, Proposition 3 tells us how to transform a topological space $(X, \Omega(X))$ into a T_0-space $(X, \Omega'(X))$ such that $\Omega(X) \cong_L \Omega'(X)$. This transformation is called T_0*–ification.*

Definition 15. Let $\tau = (X, \Omega(X))$ be a topological space and let $\Gamma(X) = \{Z \subseteq X : Z \text{ is closed in } \Omega(X)\}$. Then define the following operator on $\mathbb{P}(X)$:

$$\mathcal{C}_\tau(Z) = \bigcap \{B \in \Gamma(X) : Z \subseteq B\} \ .$$

$\mathcal{C}_\tau$ is called the *topological closure operator* induced by τ and it satisfies the following properties, $\forall Z, Y \in \mathbb{P}(X)$:

1. $\mathcal{C}_\tau(\emptyset) = \emptyset$;
2. $Z \subseteq Y$ implies $\mathcal{C}_\tau(Z) \subseteq \mathcal{C}_\tau(Y)$;
3. $\mathcal{C}_\tau \mathcal{C}_\tau(Z) = \mathcal{C}_\tau(Z)$;
4. $\mathcal{C}_\tau(Z \cup Y) = \mathcal{C}_\tau(Z) \cup \mathcal{C}_\tau(Y)$.
5. $Z \subseteq \mathcal{C}_\tau(Z)$.

Vice-versa, given an operator $\mathcal{C}$ on $\mathbb{P}(X)$ satisfying the properties $1-5$ above, the family

$$\Gamma_{\mathcal{C}}(X) = \{Z \subseteq X : Z = \mathcal{C}(Z)\}$$

is the set of closed subsets of a topological space on X.

Dually, we can define the *interior* operator on $\mathbb{P}(X)$:

Definition 16. Let $\tau = (X, \Omega(X))$ be a topological space. The following operator on $\mathbb{P}(X)$:

$$\mathcal{I}_\tau(Z) = \bigcup\{O \in \Omega(X) : O \subseteq Z\} \ .$$

is called the *topological interior operator* induced by τ and it satisfies the following properties, $\forall Z, Y \in \mathbb{P}(X)$:

1. $\mathcal{I}_\tau(X) = X$;
2. $Z \subseteq Y$ implies $\mathcal{I}_\tau(Z) \subseteq \mathcal{I}_\tau(Y)$;
3. $\mathcal{I}_\tau\mathcal{I}_\tau(Z) = \mathcal{I}_\tau(Z)$;
4. $\mathcal{I}_\tau(Z \cap Y) = \mathcal{I}_\tau(Z) \cap \mathcal{I}_\tau(Y)$.
5. $\mathcal{I}_\tau(Z) \subseteq Z$.

Vice-versa, given an operator $\mathcal{I}$ on $\mathbb{P}(X)$ satisfying the properties $1-5$ above, the family

$$\Omega_{\mathcal{I}}(X) = \{Z \subseteq X : Z = \mathcal{I}(Z)\}$$

is the frame of the open subsets of a topological space on X.

We will adopt also the usual notion of "boundary" and the notion of "external":

Definition 17. Let $\tau = (X, \Omega(X))$ be a topological space and let $\mathcal{I}$ and $\mathcal{C}$ be the induced interior and closure operators, respectively. Then for any $Z \subseteq X$

1. the set $\mathcal{E}(Z) = X \cap -\mathcal{C}(Z)$ is the *external* of Z (in τ);
2. the set $\mathcal{B}(Z) = \mathcal{C}(Z) \cap -\mathcal{I}(Z)$ is the *boundary* of Z (in τ).

Obviously for any $Z \subseteq X$, $\mathcal{E}(X) \in \Omega(X)$. Moreover, the following additional fact will be useful in our context:

Proposition 18. *Let $\tau = (X, \Omega(X))$ be a 0-dimensional topological space on a finite set X, then $\forall Z \subseteq X, \mathcal{B}(Z) \in \Omega(X)$.*

Definition 19. Given a topological space $(X, \Omega(X))$,

1. a set $Z \subseteq X$ is called *dense* in $\Omega(X)$ iff $\mathcal{I}(-Z) = \emptyset$ iff $-\mathcal{I}(-Z) = X$ iff $\mathcal{I}\mathcal{C}(Z) = X$;
2. a set $Z \subseteq X$ is called *regular* iff $\mathcal{I} - \mathcal{I}(-Z) = Z$ iff $\mathcal{I}\mathcal{C}(Z) = Z$.

2.4 Basic logic-algebraic structures

Definition 20. Let $\mathbf{L} = (L, \vee, \wedge, 1, 0)$ be a distributive lattice, then

1. $\mathbf{L}$ is a *pseudo-complemented lattice* if $\forall x \in L$ there is an element x^* such that $\forall y \in L$,
$$x \wedge y = 0 \text{ iff } y \leq x^* \ .$$
The element x^* is termed *pseudo-complement* of x.
2. If for $x \in \mathbf{L}$ there is an element x' such that
$$x \wedge x' = 0 \text{ and } x \vee x' = 1$$
then x is called *complemented* and x' is the *complement* of x.
3. the set $\mathcal{CTR}(\mathbf{L}) = \{x \in L : x \text{ is complemented}\}$, is called the *centre* of $\mathbf{L}$.

Definition 21. A structure $\mathbf{H} = (H, \vee, \wedge, \Longrightarrow, \neg, 1, 0)$ is a *Heyting algebra* if

1. $(H, \vee, \wedge, 1, 0)$ is a distributive lattice;
2. the operations $\wedge$ and $\Longrightarrow$ fulfil the following *adjunction property*:
$$\forall a, b, c \in H, a \wedge c \leq b \text{ iff } c \leq a \Longrightarrow b;$$
3. $\neg x = x \Longrightarrow 0$.

(Heyting algebras are named *Pseudo Boolean algebras* in [Ral]).

The operation "$\Longrightarrow$" is called *relative pseudo-complementation.* It follows from Definition 21.3 and Definition 20.1, that the operation "$\neg$" is a pseudo-complementation.

Definition 22. Let x be an element of a Heyting algebra $\mathbf{H}$, then

1. x is *dense* iff $\neg x = 0$ iff $\neg\neg x = 1$.
2. x is *regular* iff $\neg\neg x = x$.

Proposition 23. *Any finite distributive lattice is a Heyting algebra, in fact we can put:*
$$a \Longrightarrow b = \bigvee\{x : x \wedge a \leq b\} \ .$$

Definition 24. A *Boolean algebra* is a Heyting algebra $\mathbf{A}$ such that $\forall a \in A$,
$$a \vee \neg a = 1$$

Proposition 25. *Given a set S, $\mathbf{B}(S) = (\mathbb{P}(S), \cap, \cup, -, \Longrightarrow, \emptyset, S)$ is a Boolean algebra of sets. Here for $A, B \in \mathbb{P}(S)$, $A \Longrightarrow B =_{def} -A \cup B$.*

$\mathbf{B}(S)$ is called the *Boolean* of S.

Definition 26. Let $\mathbf{H} = (H, \vee, \wedge, \neg, \Longrightarrow, 0, 1)$ and $\mathbf{H}' = (H', \vee', \wedge', \neg', \Longrightarrow', 0', 1')$ be two Heyting algebras and $f : H \longmapsto H'$. Then f is a *H-homomorphism* (0-1 H-homomorphism, H-monomorphism, H-isomorphism) if f is an L-homomorphism (0-1 L-homomorphism, L-monomorphism, L-isomorphism) such that, moreover, the relative pseudo-complementation is preserved: $f(a \Longrightarrow b) = f(a) \Longrightarrow' f(b)$.

If f is a H-isomorphism we write $\mathbf{H} \cong_H \mathbf{H}'$ and if they are Boolean algebras, we write also $\mathbf{H} \cong_B \mathbf{H}'$.

From Proposition 23 we have immediately:

Proposition 27. *Let* $\mathbf{H}$ *and* $\mathbf{H}'$ *be two finite Heyting algebras, then* $\mathbf{H} \cong_H \mathbf{H}'$ *iff* $\mathbf{H} \cong_L \mathbf{H}'$.

Duality results for a class of algebraic structures provide representation theorems that allow for representing any algebra from the class as a "concrete" structure. Typically this "concrete model" is an algebra of sets isomorphic to the original (abstract) structure. The construction of the model uses the notion of a "dual space", typically an ordered structure possibly equipped with some additional features, and a particular topological manipulation of this space provides the resulting isomorphic structure.

Since we will deal only with finite structures, the duality results which we are going to use follow from Birkhoff's results for finite distributive lattices. In particular, if $\mathbf{PS}(\mathbf{A}) = (X_A, \tau, \leq)$ is the Priestley Space of an algebra $\mathbf{A}$ (see [Pr1], [DP1], we do not define this notion here), then in the finite case the topological property of totally order disconnectedness of $\mathbf{PS}(\mathbf{A})$ (see the quoted works) is immaterial in identifying the isomorphic image of $\mathbf{A}$ in $\mathbf{PS}(\mathbf{A})$. Since in this case $\mathbf{PS}(\mathbf{A})$ is a discrete space, all the subsets are clopen and the relevant information information for identifying the isomorphic image of $\mathbf{A}$ in $\mathbf{PS}(\mathbf{A})$ is supplied by the ordering of the dual space.

Nevertheless, in order to make the comparison with general results from the literature and in order to justify some terminology borrowed from topology, one may adopt the following strategy: let $\mathbf{X} = (X, \leq)$ be a preordered set; we have that $(X, \Omega_A(X))$ is a topological space with the Alexandrov topology of X, where $\Omega_A(X)$ is the frame of open subsets (see Definition 2.4). $\mathcal{I}_A$ and $\mathcal{C}_A$ will denote the interior and, respectively, closure operators induced by $\Omega_A(X)$ (see definitions 15 and 16). $\forall Z \subseteq X$ we have: $\mathcal{C}_A(Z) = \downarrow Z$, $\mathcal{I}_A(Z) = - \downarrow -Z$.

2.5 Birkhoff's duality results

Definition 28. A finite *Heyting space* is a poset $\mathbf{P} = (P, \leq)$. Given a finite Heyting space $\mathbf{P}$ we can define its dual Heyting algebra $\mathbf{H}(\mathbf{P})$ in the following way: $\mathbf{H}(\mathbf{P}) = (\Omega_A(P), \wedge, \vee, \Longrightarrow, \neg, 0, 1)$, where for $A, B \in \Omega_A(P)$:

1. $A \Longrightarrow B = - \downarrow (A \cap -B)$;
2. $\neg A = A \Longrightarrow \emptyset = - \downarrow (A)$;
3. $A \wedge B = A \cap B$;

4. $A \vee B = A \cup B$;
5. $1 = P$;
6. $0 = \emptyset$.

Vice-versa, given a finite Heyting algebra $\mathbf{A} = (A, \wedge, \vee, \Longrightarrow, \neg, 0, 1)$ we can get its dual Heyting space $\mathbf{HS}(\mathbf{A})$ setting $\mathbf{HS}(\mathbf{A}) = \mathbf{X}(\mathbf{A})$ (i.e. $\mathbf{HS}(\mathbf{A}) = (\mathcal{J}(\mathbf{A}), \leq)$, see Definition 5.6).

We have that if $\mathbf{A}$ is a finite Heyting algebra and $\mathbf{X}$ is a finite Heyting space, then:

$$\mathbf{A} \cong_H \mathbf{H}(\mathbf{HS}(\mathbf{A})) \text{ and } \mathbf{X} \cong_P \mathbf{HS}(\mathbf{H}(\mathbf{X})) \ ,$$

In particular, the mapping:

2.1 $h : A \longmapsto \mathbb{P}(\mathcal{J}(\mathbf{A}))$: $h(a) = \{j \in \mathcal{J}(\mathbf{A}) : j \leq a\} = \{j \in \mathcal{J}(\mathbf{A}) : a \in \uparrow j\}$,

provides the first isomorphism (clearly, for any a, $h(a)$ is an up-set in $\mathcal{J}(\mathbf{A})$).

Remark. In view of Definitions 19 we can justify the terms "dense" and "regular" adopted in Definition 22: an element x in a Heyting algebra $\mathbf{A}$ is dense only if $\neg x = 0$, so the element $h(x)$ of the dual algebra $\mathbf{H}(\mathbf{HS}(\mathbf{A}))$ is dense only if $- \downarrow h(x) = \emptyset$ only if $-\mathcal{C}_A(h(x)) = \emptyset$ only if $\mathcal{I}_A(-h(x)) = \emptyset$ only if $\mathcal{I}_A\mathcal{C}_A(h(x)) = \mathcal{J}(A)$.

Similarly, taking into account that $\neg h(x) = -\mathcal{C}_A(h(x)) = \mathcal{I}_A(-h(x))$, we have the justification of the term "regular" in Definition 22.2.

Example 1. Throughout this Section we will develop some examples based on the Heyting algebra $\mathbf{H}$ that is presented in Fig. 1.

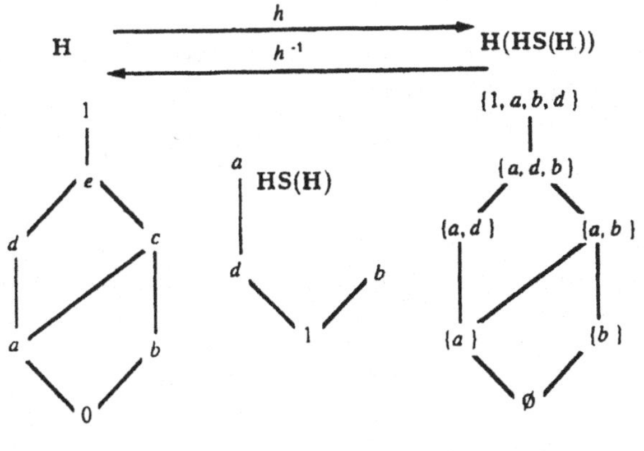

Fig. 1.

Let us compute, for instance, on the dual algebra $\mathbf{H}(\mathbf{HS}(\mathbf{H}))$ $\{b\} \Longrightarrow \{a\}$ using Definition 28 above: $\{b\} \Longrightarrow \{a\} = - \downarrow (\{b\} \cap -\{a\}) = - \downarrow (\{b\} \cap \{d, 1, b\}) = - \downarrow \{b\} = -\{b, 1\} = \{a, d\}$. Here one can easily see that $\neg c = 0$

in **H**. But $h(c) = \{a, b\}$ that is dense in $\mathbf{H}(\mathbf{HS}(\mathbf{H}))$ *understood as* a topological space (the density of a subset Z of $\mathbf{HS}(\mathbf{H})$ is pictorially suggested by the fact that Z contains all the maximal elements of $\mathbf{HS}(\mathbf{H})$). One can also verify that $\neg\neg d = d$ and $h(d) = \{a, d\}$ that is regular in $\mathbf{H}(\mathbf{HS}(\mathbf{H}))$

Proposition 29. *If* $\mathbf{A}$ *is a finite Boolean algebra, then* $\mathcal{J}(\mathbf{A}) = Atom(\mathbf{A})$. *The order on* $Atom(\mathbf{A})$ *is a discrete order and the dual algebra* $\mathbf{H}(\mathbf{HS}(\mathbf{A}))$ *is the Boolean algebra of sets* $\mathbf{B}(Atom(\mathbf{A}))$. *Hence,* $\mathbf{H}(\mathbf{HS}(\mathbf{A}))$ *is the discrete topology on* $\mathbf{HS}(\mathbf{A})$.

Definition 30. Let S be a family of pairwise disjoint sets. By $\mathbf{B}^S$ we mean the frame of clopen subsets for which S is a subbasis. $\mathbf{B}^S$ is intended as a Boolean algebra of sets, with $0 = \emptyset$ and $1 = \bigcup S$. Clearly $\mathbf{HS}(\mathbf{B}^S) = S$

2.6 Information Systems and Approximation Spaces

Definition 31. Let **C**= (U, At, V, v) be a structure such that U, At and V are finite non-empty sets, $v : U \times At \longmapsto V$ an (information) function and $card(V) = n$; then **C** is said to be an n-valued context in the sense of [Wil], or an Information System in the sense of [Pawl].

By fixing the first component of the domain of v, we obtain a family $\{v_x : At \longmapsto V\}_{x \in U}$ of functions described by: $v_x(a) = v(< x, a >)$. Now we are going to see how to collect in this way the objects that are not discernible with respect to the available information function.

Let $\mathbf{C} = \langle U, At, V, v\rangle$ be an arbitrary Information System; we shall consider the following equivalence classes

Definition 32. $[x]_C = \{x' : v_{x'} = v_x\}$.

Thus these classes are determined by an *equivalence relation* eq_v on U given by the following characteristic function:

$$eq_v(\langle x, y\rangle) = \begin{cases} 1 \text{ if } \forall m \in At, v_x(m) = v_y(m) \\ 0 \text{ otherwise} \end{cases}$$

Thus for $x \in U$, $[x]_C$ is the equivalence class of x modulo eq_v. The notation $[x]_C$ shows the dependence of the equivalence relation, both on the function v and on the set At.

Definition 33. By $Ind(\mathbf{C})$ we denote the set of classes $\{[x]_C : x \in U\}$. The elements of $Ind(\mathbf{C})$ are termed *elementary* (or *basic*) *sets* (or *concepts* or *categories*) of **C**.

It is obvious that $Ind(\mathbf{C}) = U/_{eq_v}$.

Definition 34. Let $\mathbf{AS}(\mathbf{C}) = (A, \cap, \cup, \emptyset, U) = \mathbf{B}^{Ind(\mathbf{C})}$ (see Definition 30) be the lattice of clopen subsets of U for which the family $Ind(\mathbf{C})$ is a subbasis. Then $\mathbf{AS}(\mathbf{C})$ is called the *Approximation Space* induced by **C**.

Definition 35. By $\mathbf{AS}([\mathbf{C}])$ we denote the lattice $\mathbf{B}(Ind(\mathbf{C}))$.

From Proposition 29 we immediately have:

Lemma 36. *For any Information System* $\mathbf{C}$,

1. $\mathbf{AS}(\mathbf{C})$ *is a Boolean algebra;*
2. $\mathbf{AS}(\mathbf{C})$ *is a subalgebra of* $\mathbf{B}(U)$*;*
3. $Ind(\mathbf{C}) = Atom(\mathbf{AS}(\mathbf{C})) = \mathbf{HS}(\mathbf{AS}(\mathbf{C}))$*;*
4. $\mathbf{AS}([\mathbf{C}]) = \mathbf{H}(\mathbf{HS}(\mathbf{AS}(\mathbf{C}))) \cong_B \mathbf{AS}(\mathbf{C})$*;*
5. $Atom(\mathbf{AS}([\mathbf{C}])) = \{\{\alpha\} : \alpha \in eq_v\}$*;*

Throughout the paper $\mathbf{C} = (U, At, V, v)$ will stand for a generic Information System and $\mathbf{AS}(\mathbf{C}) = (A, \cap, \cup, -, \Longrightarrow, \emptyset, A)$ will denote the Approximation Space induced by $\mathbf{C}$. While speaking about Approximation Spaces the set A will denote the carrier of $\mathbf{AS}(\mathbf{C})$.

In view of the above definitions it is clear that the diagram of any v_x is a set of descriptors of the form $\langle attribute, value\rangle$ (such a set is a "property" in the terminology used in the Introduction). These sets aggregate the objects into the basic categories. Thus, any arbitrary element of $\mathbf{AS}(\mathbf{C})$ which is a union of the categories is determined by a disjunction of properties.

Example 2. Consider the Information System $\mathbf{C} = (U = \{a, b, c, d, e\}, At = \{A_1, A_2\}, V = \{1, 0, 2\}, v)$, where the information function v is given by the table:

v	A_1	A_2
a	1	0
b	1	0
c	1	2
d	1	2
e	2	2

then $\mathbf{B}(U)$ is the 5-cube with atoms $\{a\}, \{b\}, \ldots, \{e\}$ while $\mathbf{AS}(\mathbf{C})$ and $\mathbf{AS}([\mathbf{C}])$ are the 3-cubes illustrated by the Hasse diagrams given in Fig. 2.

Remark. It is clear that the best description is achieved when $\mathbf{AS}(\mathbf{C})$ is the discrete topology on U: in fact this topology is the finest that we can define on U and it provides the best separation properties (see Subsection 2.3). But, usually, our systems of data are not that well-informed. In topological terms this is explained by the fact that the specialization preorder induced by $\mathbf{AS}(\mathbf{C})$ is not a partial order: in the above example we have, for instance, $a \ll b$ and $b \ll a$ but $a \neq b$; thus, generally, $\mathbf{AS}(\mathbf{C})$ is not even T_0. We know how to perform the T_0-ification of $\mathbf{AS}(\mathbf{C})$ (see Proposition 3); the factorized universe that we get is the domain of the so-called "representation" of the Information System $\mathbf{C}$ (see Definition 77). At this point let us remark that in the finite case this operation coincides with the operation of *soberification* (see [Jo1]): "discarding

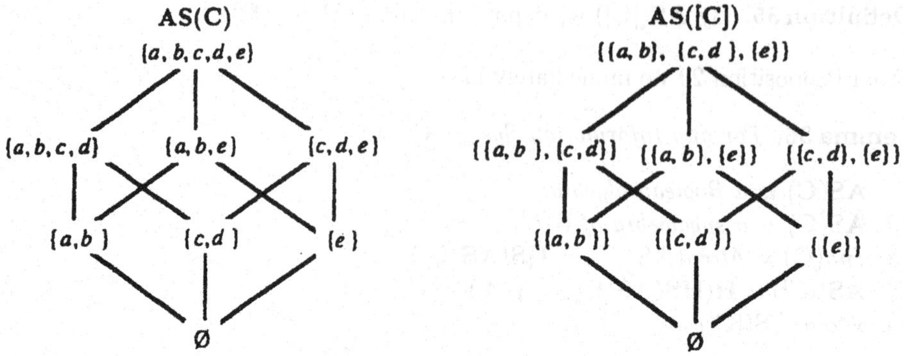

Fig. 2.

the superfluous elements", that is the elements redundant in "distinguishing the open sets".

Now, Approximation Spaces *understood as* topological spaces, are not generally sober. This is the very reason that we speak of "approximation": if we think of the open sets as (abstract) "properties" (and this is the starting point also for denotational semantics for programming languages and for pointless topology), then the properties definable in our systems of information are too "rough" with respect to the given universe of discourse. In other terms, generally we do not have enough properties for distinguishing the points. On the contrary, if some property is sharp, then there will be a unique element of the universe of discourse distinguishing it (and vice-versa). We will see that such properties are the "filtering" features describing the different logical behaviors of Rough Set Systems.

Now we are ready to approximate any arbitrary subset of U in terms of the information provided by $\mathbf{AS}(\mathbf{C})$.

2.7 Rough Sets

From now on, by $\mathcal{C}$ and $\mathcal{I}$ we shall mean the *closure* and *interior* operators, respectively, with respect to $\mathbf{AS}(\mathbf{C})$ *understood as* a 0-dimensional topological space.

Definition 37. Given an Information System $\mathbf{C}$ and two sets $X, Y \in \mathbb{P}(U)$:

1. $\mathcal{I}(X)$ is called *lower approximation* of X;
2. $\mathcal{C}(X)$ is called the *upper approximation* of X;
3. X, Y are said to be *rough top equal*, $X \eqsim Y$, iff $\mathcal{C}(X) = \mathcal{C}(Y)$.
4. X, Y are said to be *rough bottom equal*, $X \simeq Y$, iff $\mathcal{I}(X) = \mathcal{I}(Y)$.
5. X, Y are said to be *rough equal*, $X \approx Y$, iff $X \simeq Y$ and $X \eqsim Y$.
6. $X \in \mathbb{P}(U)$ is said to be *definable* iff $X = \mathcal{C}(X) = \mathcal{I}(X)$.

The above definitions are justified by comparing the usual definitions of lower and upper approximations and Definitions 16 and 15. We immediately have:

Lemma 38. *A subset* $X \in \mathbb{P}(U)$ *is definable iff* $X \in \mathbf{AS}(\mathbf{C})$.

Definition 39. Given an Information System **C**, a *rough set* in **C** is an ordered pair $\langle I, B\rangle$ such that

1. $I, B \subseteq U$;
2. $I, B \in \mathbf{AS}(\mathbf{C})$;
3. $I \cap B = \emptyset$;
4. $\forall x \in B, \exists y \in B$ such that $x \neq y$ and $y \in [x]_C$.

Let $Z \subseteq \mathbb{P}(U) \times \mathbb{P}(U)$ be the set of the pairs fulfilling conditions 1-4 of Definition 39.

Consider the map:

2.2 $r_1 : \mathbb{P}(U) \longmapsto \mathbb{P}(U) \times \mathbb{P}(U) : r_1(X) = \langle \mathcal{I}(X), \mathcal{B}(X)\rangle$.

Then

Lemma 40. *For any Approximation Space* $\mathbf{AS}(\mathbf{C})$, $r_1^{-1}(\mathbf{Im}r_1) = r_1^{-1}(Z) = \mathbb{P}(U)/_{\approx}$.

Proof. see [Iw1] and [PP1].

Definition 41. For any Approximation Space $\mathbf{AS}(\mathbf{C})$, by $RS(\mathbf{C})$ we will denote the system of the rough sets induced by $\mathbf{AS}(\mathbf{C})$.

3 Rough Sets and Nelson Algebras

Motivations and the plan of the section

Given an Information System $\mathbf{C} = (U, At, V, v)$, we transform the representation of rough sets guarateed by Lemma 40, into a new representation function r such that $\forall X \subseteq U$, $r(X)$ equals $K(At)(X)$ where $K(At)$ is the epistemic operator introduced in [Or2], [Or3]: "the cognitive agent *At*, knows ... ".

Here any cognitive agent is identified with its own information about the universe of discourse U. This information is assumed to be objective. Given a concept X and an object x, if $K(At)(X) = \langle X_1, X_2\rangle$ then if $x \in X_1$ we have that *At* knows that *necessarily* x *belongs* to the concept X; if $x \in X_2$ we have that *At* knows that *necesarily* x *does not belong* to X, while $\mathcal{B}(X)$ is the *doubtful* region of X for the cognitive agent *At*. For an epistemological and semantical discussion about $K(At)$ we refer to the quoted works. Anyway, this intuitive approach suggests the disjoint representation for rough sets. The family of rough sets of an Approximation Space $\mathbf{AS}(\mathbf{C})$ represented in this way will be denoted by $RS_r(\mathbf{C})$

Under this representation, Rough Set Systems can be investigated as finite semi-simple Nelson algebras. Thus, it is shown that for any Information System

$\mathbf{C} = (U, At, V, v)$ and its Approximation Space $\mathbf{AS}(\mathbf{C})$, the family $RS_r(\mathbf{C})$ can be given the structure $\mathbf{N}_\Theta(\mathbf{AS}(\mathbf{C}))$, where $\mathbf{N}_\Theta$ is the application of Sendlewksi's functor $\mathbf{N}_\Theta$ (which we introduce in Lemma 53) to the Boolean algebra $\mathbf{AS}(\mathbf{C})$ and the congruence Θ on the Boolean algebra $\mathbf{AS}(\mathbf{C})$ depends on the class of the sharp elementary sets definable in the Information System. If all the elementary sets of $\mathbf{AS}(\mathbf{C})$ are singletons, then Θ is minimal and the algebraic structure of $RS_r(\mathbf{C})$ is given by Sendlewksi's functor $\overleftarrow{\mathbf{N}}$. If no elementary set of $\mathbf{AS}(\mathbf{C})$ is a singleton, then Θ is maximal and the algebraic structure of $RS_r(\mathbf{C})$ is given by Sendlewksi's functor $\overrightarrow{\mathbf{N}}$. In the former case the logical properties of $RS_r(\mathbf{C})$, change drastically: in fact, they are represented by a Boolean algebra isomorphic to the centre of $\overrightarrow{\mathbf{N}}(\mathbf{AS}(\mathbf{C}))$. In the latter case $RS_r(\mathbf{C})$ is a Post algebra of order three and it will be investigated in Section 4.2. It follows that semi-simple Nelson algebras are able to describe the intermediate cases, that is, the general situations.

Moreover, since $RS_r(\mathbf{C})$ is a finite distributive lattice, it is a Heyting algebra. We will show that in our case the typical operation of $RS_r(\mathbf{C})$ *understood as* a Heyting algebra, that is the "relative pseudo-complementation", is definable with the operations provided by $RS_r(\mathbf{C})$ *understood as* a Nelson algebra.

As a Heyting algebra, $RS_r(\mathbf{C})$ is revealed to be a double Stone algebra in which the dual pseudo-complementation coincides with the weak negation provided by Nelson algebras. Properties of double Stone algebras are exploited in order to define two projection operators projecting rough sets onto the family of the r−images of the definable sets.

Remark. It follows from Subsection 2.6 that what we really need in order to obtain a Rough Set Structure from an Approximation Space stays in the realm of the manipulations of Boolean algebras. In any case these transformations are specific cases of more general techniques that have been applied to Heyting algebras. Since a Boolean algebra is a Heyting algebra, this fact is not surprising. Indeed, we prefer to introduce the needed techniques in a more general context. First, we present a general theory and then the differences with the particular Boolean case are illustrated within of the conceptual framework provided by Rough Set Theory.

Moreover, we think that as soon as we deal (in another paper) with nondeterministic Information Systems ([OP1]) the broader framework will be shown to be of central interest.

3.1 Nelson algebras

Definition 42. An algebra $\mathbf{N} = (N, \wedge, \vee, \rightarrow, \neg, \sim, 0, 1)$ is a *Nelson algebra* if

1. $(N, \wedge, \vee, 0, 1)$ is a bounded distributive lattice and for any $a, b \in N$:
2. $\sim\sim a = a$;
3. $\sim (a \vee b) = \sim a \wedge \sim b$;
4. $a \wedge \sim a \leq b \vee \sim b$;
5. $a \wedge x \leq (\sim a \vee b)$ iff $x \leq a \rightarrow b$;

6. $a \to (b \to c) = (a \wedge b) \to c$;
7. $\neg a = a \to \sim a = a \to 0$;

We recall briefly the following definition

Definition 43. An algebra A is called *semi-simple* if it is a subdirect product of simple algebras.

Proposition 44. *A Nelson algebra* $\mathbf{N}$ *is* semi-simple *if* $\forall a \in N,\ a \vee \neg a = 1$.

(Nelson algebras are named *Quasi-Pseudo Boolean algebras* in [Ra1]. The importance of the notion of semi-simplicity will become clear when we will decompose a Rough Set System in its logical components).

The operation "$\sim$" is called *strong* (or *constructive*) *negation*; "$\neg$" is the *weak* (or *intuitionistic*) *negation* and "$\to$" is the *weak implication.*

Analytically, axioms 1, 2 and 3 say that $(N, \wedge, \vee, \sim, 0, 1)$ is a DeMorgan algebra; axiom 4 is the *regularity principle* specifying that this DeMorgan algebra is a Kleene algebra and axioms 5 and 6 state the specific features of Nelson algebras: axiom 5 claims that $x \to y$ is the largest element c such that $c \wedge x$ is less or equal to the classic implication $\sim x \vee y$ - in other terms $x \to y$ is the *pseudo-complement* of x *relative* to $(\sim x \vee y)$- while axiom 6 specifies that this relative pseudo-complementation fulfils the so called *Currying* property (transforming one two-argument function in two one-argument functions). Axiom 7 says that $\neg a$ is a the pseudo-complement of a relative to its strong negation.

Definition 45. Let $\mathbf{N}$ and $\mathbf{N}'$ be two Nelson algebras and let $f : N \longmapsto N'$ be an L-isomorphism such that $\forall x \in N, f(\sim x) = \sim' f(x)$. Then $\mathbf{N}$ and $\mathbf{N}'$ are isomorphic and we write $\mathbf{N} \cong_N \mathbf{N}'$.

The above definition will be justified later.

In a Nelson algebra it is possible to define also the following additional implication

3.1 *For any* $x, y \in N : x \Rightarrow y =_{def} (x \to y) \wedge (\sim y \to \sim x)$.

The operation $\Rightarrow$ is called the *strong* (or *contrappositional* or *extensional*) *implication.*

Lemma 46. *For any Nelson algebra* $\mathbf{N}$ *the following holds:*

1. $\sim (a \to b) \longleftrightarrow a \wedge \sim b = 1$, *(where* $a \longleftrightarrow b =_{def} a \to b \wedge b \to a$*)*;
2. $a \wedge \sim a \longleftrightarrow 0 = 1$;
3. *the relation* $\preceq$ *defined by:* $a \preceq b$ iff $a \to b = 1$, *is a preorder on* N;
4. *the relation* $\leq$ *defined by:* $a \leq b$ *iff* $a \Rightarrow b$, *is the lattice order on* N;
5. *the relation* $\equiv$ *defined by:* $a \equiv b$ *iff* $a \longleftrightarrow b = 1$, *is a congruence on* $(N, \wedge, \vee, \to, \neg, 0, 1)$;
6. $\mathbf{N}/_{\equiv}$ *is a Heyting algebra;*
7. $\mathbf{N}$ *is* semi-simple *iff* $\mathbf{N}/_{\equiv}$ *is a Boolean algebra;*
8. *if* $\mathbf{N}$ *is semi-simple then* $\mathbf{N}/_{\equiv} \cong_B \mathcal{CTR}(\mathbf{N})$.

3.2 Duality results for Nelson Algebras (finite case)

Definition 47. A finite Nelson space is a pair $\mathbf{X} = (\mathbf{P}, g)$ such that $\mathbf{P}$ is a poset, g is an involutive linear dual-order automorphism (see Definition 4) fulfilling, in addition, the following interpolation property (see [Mon1] and [Ci4]):
(IN) if $x \geq g(x), y \geq g(x), x \geq g(y), y \geq g(y))$, then $\exists c \in X$ such that $c \leq x, c \leq y, g(x) \leq c, g(y) \leq c$.
Given a Nelson space $\mathbf{X} = (\mathbf{P}, g)$ we can define its dual Nelson algebra $\mathbf{N}(\mathbf{X})$ in the following way:

$$\mathbf{N}(\mathbf{X}) = (\Omega_A(\mathbf{P}), \wedge, \vee, \rightarrow, \sim, \neg, 0, 1) \ ,$$

where for any $A, B \in \Omega_A(\mathbf{P})$ the operations are defined by:

1. $1 = P$;
2. $0 = \emptyset$;
3. $A \wedge B = A \cap B$;
4. $A \vee B = A \cup B$;
5. $\sim A = -g(A)$;
6. $A \rightarrow B = - \downarrow (A \cap g(A) \cap -B)$;
7. $\neg A = - \downarrow (A \cap g(A))$.

On the other hand, given a finite Nelson algebra $\mathbf{A} = (A, \wedge, \vee, \rightarrow, \neg, \sim, 0, 1)$ we can recover its dual Nelson space $\mathbf{NS}(\mathbf{A})$ setting $\mathbf{NS}(\mathbf{A}) = (\mathbf{X}(\mathbf{A}), g)$, where for any $x \in \mathbf{X}(\mathbf{A})$ the involution g is given by $g(x) = \mathbf{lst}(\mathbf{X}(\mathbf{A}) \cap -\{\sim b : b \in \uparrow x\})$ and both "**lst**" and "$\uparrow$" are defined with respect to the ordering on $\mathbf{A}$.

We have that if $\mathbf{A}$ is a finite Nelson algebra and $\mathbf{X}$ is a finite Nelson space, then:

$$\mathbf{A} \cong_N \mathbf{N}(\mathbf{NS}(\mathbf{A})) \text{ and } \mathbf{X} \cong_{PI} \mathbf{NS}(\mathbf{N}(\mathbf{X})) \ .$$

We recall from 5 of Lemma 46, that given a Nelson space $\mathbf{X}$, in $\mathbf{N}(\mathbf{X})$ the equivalence relation $\equiv$ is a congruence for $\cap, \cup, \rightarrow$ and $\neg$ and $\mathbf{N}(\mathbf{X})/_{\equiv}$ is a Heyting algebra that we will denote by $\mathbf{H}^{\equiv}(\mathbf{N}(\mathbf{X}))$.

Definition 48. For any Nelson space $\mathbf{X} = (\mathbf{P}, g)$,

1. $X^+ = \{x \in \mathbf{P} : x \leq g(x)\}$;
2. $\mathbf{X}^+ = (X^+, \leq|_{X^+})$.

It is easy to see that the following holds for all $A, B \in \mathbf{N}(\mathbf{X})$,

3.2 $A \rightarrow B = 1$ *iff* $A \cap X^+ \subseteq B \cap X^+$.

Then $A \equiv B = 1$ iff $A \cap X^+ = B \cap X^+$. Thus, from point 5 of Lemma 46, we have that $\mathbf{H}(\mathbf{X}^+)$ is isomorphic to $\mathbf{H}^{\equiv}(\mathbf{N}(\mathbf{X}))$.

Henceforth this observation suggests a way to single out, up to isomorphism, all the Nelson algebras $\mathbf{N}_i$ such that $\mathbf{N}_i/_{\equiv}$ is isomorphic to a given Heyting algebra $\mathbf{H}$, that is all the Nelson algebras $\mathbf{N}_i$ constructible from the given Heyting algebra $\mathbf{H}$: they will be the algebras such that the set $\mathbf{NS}(\mathbf{N}_i)^+$ is isomorphic to the dual space of $\mathbf{H}$. It is precisely the mechanism of constructing these Nelson algebras that will provide the refinement of Kalman's functor that we need.

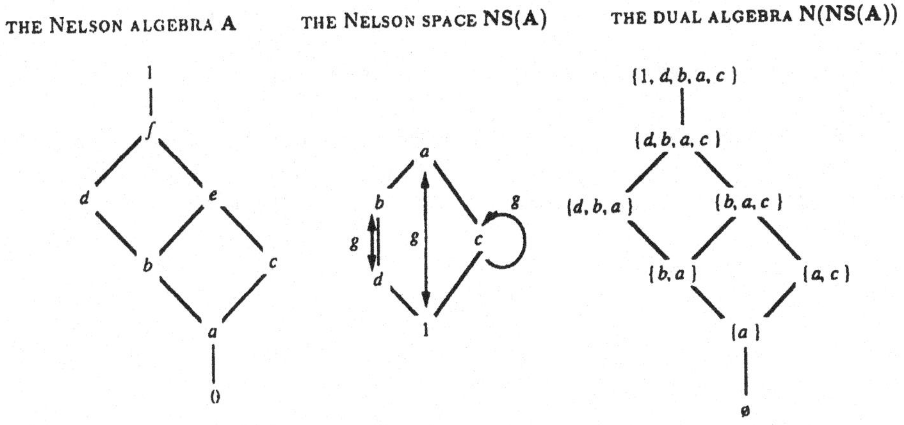

Fig. 3.

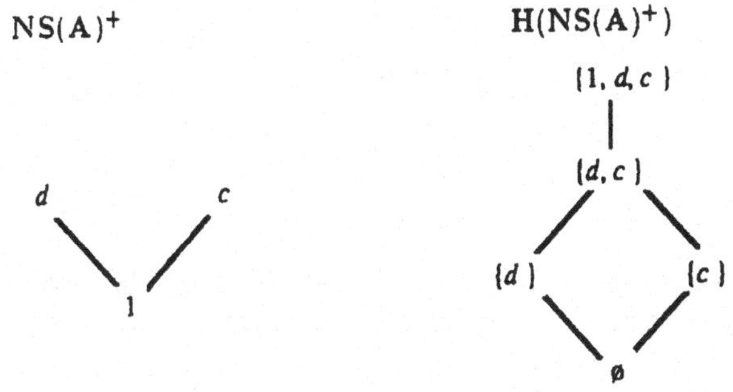

Fig. 4.

Example 3. Let us examine the shape of the space $\mathbf{NS}(\mathbf{A})^+$ and of its dual Heyting algebra:

Let us compute, for instance, $g(b)$:

$$\begin{aligned} g(b) &= \mathbf{lst}(\mathbf{X}(\mathbf{A}) \cap -\{\sim x : x \in \uparrow b\}) = \mathbf{lst}(\mathbf{X}(\mathbf{A}) \cap -\{\sim x : x \in \{b, e, d, f, 1\}\}) \\ &= \mathbf{lst}(\mathbf{X}(\mathbf{A}) \cap -\{e, b, c, a, 0\}) = \mathbf{lst}(\mathbf{X}(\mathbf{A}) \cap \{d, f, 1\}) = \mathbf{lst}(\{d, 1\}) = d. \end{aligned}$$

Now we calculate, for instance, $\{b, a, c\} \longrightarrow \{b, a\}$, $\{b, a, c\} \longrightarrow \{a, c\}$ and $\sim \{b, a, c\}$:

$$\begin{aligned} \{b, a, c\} \longrightarrow \{b, a\} &= - \downarrow (\{b, a, c\} \cap g(\{b, a, c\}) \cap -\{b, a\}) \\ &= - \downarrow (\{b, a, c\} \cap \{d, 1, c\} \cap \{d, 1, c\}) \\ &= - \downarrow \{c\} = -\{c, 1\} = \{d, b, a\}. \end{aligned}$$

$$\begin{aligned} \{b, a, c\} \longrightarrow \{a, c\} &= - \downarrow (\{b, a, c\} \cap g(\{b, a, c\} \cap -\{a, c\}) \\ &= - \downarrow (\{b, a, c\} \cap \{d, 1, c\} \cap \{1, d, b\}) = - \downarrow \emptyset = \{1, d, b, a, c\}. \end{aligned}$$

$$\sim \{b,a,c\} = -g(\{b,a,c\}) = -\{d,1,c\} = \{b,a\}.$$

Similar easy computations show that $(\{b,a,c\} \longleftrightarrow \{a,c\}) = (\emptyset \longleftrightarrow \{a\} \longleftrightarrow \{b,a\}) = 1$.

Thus, the equivalence relation $\equiv$ has the following classes: $\alpha = \{\{a\},\{b,a\},\emptyset\}$, $\beta = \{\{b,a,c\},\{a,c\}\}, \gamma = \{\{d,b,a\}\}, \delta = \{\{d,b,a,c\}\}, \epsilon = \{\{1,d,b,a,c\}\}$ and $\mathbf{H}^{\equiv}(\mathbf{NS}(\mathbf{A}))$ has the following form (isomorphic to $\mathbf{H}(\mathbf{NS}(\mathbf{A})^{+})$):

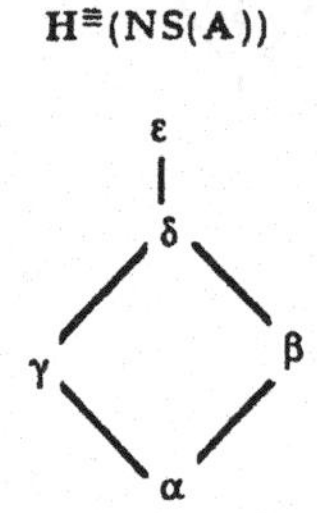

Fig. 5.

Sendlewski's topological construction of Nelson algebras (finite case)
Let $\mathbf{H}$ be a finite Heyting algebra and $\mathcal{J}(\mathbf{H})$ be the set of coprime elements of $\mathbf{H}$. Remember that $\mathbf{HS}(\mathbf{H}) = (\mathcal{J}(\mathbf{H}), \leq)$.

Let us consider a primed disjoint copy, $\mathcal{J}(\mathbf{H})'$, of $\mathcal{J}(\mathbf{H})$ i.e. $\mathcal{J}(\mathbf{H})' = \{a' : a \in \mathcal{J}(\mathbf{H})\}$.

Let us equip $\mathcal{J}(\mathbf{H})'$ with the dual ordering, $\leq'$ of $\mathbf{HS}(\mathbf{H})$. Thus, we get the poset $\mathbf{HS}(\mathbf{H})' = (\mathcal{J}(\mathbf{H})', \leq')$. The maps: $f : \mathcal{J}(\mathbf{H}) \longmapsto \mathcal{J}(\mathbf{H})' : f(a) = a'$ and $f' : \mathcal{J}(\mathbf{H})' \longmapsto \mathcal{J}(\mathbf{H}) : f'(a') = a$, establish two dual order isomorphisms between $\mathbf{HS}(\mathbf{H})$ and $\mathbf{HS}(\mathbf{H})'$ such that $f'(f(a)) = a$ and $f(f'(a')) = a'$.

Let $S \subseteq \mathbf{max}(\mathbf{HS}(\mathbf{H}))$ and let $P = \mathbf{max}(\mathbf{HS}(\mathbf{H})) \cap -S$.

Consider the set $\mathcal{J}(\mathbf{H}(S)) = \mathcal{J}(\mathbf{H}) \cup f(\mathcal{J}(\mathbf{H}) \cap -S)$. On $\mathcal{J}(\mathbf{H}(S))$ we define an involution g_S and a partial order $\leq$ in the following manner:

3.3 $$g_S(x) = \begin{cases} f(x) & \textit{if } x \in \mathcal{J}(\mathbf{H}) \textit{ and } x \notin S \\ x & \textit{if } x \in \mathcal{J}(\mathbf{H}) \textit{ and } x \in S \\ f'(x) & \textit{otherwise} \end{cases} \qquad \forall x, y \in \mathcal{J}(\mathbf{H}(S)).$$

3.4 *$\leq$ is the transitive closure of the relation* $\{\langle a,b\rangle, a,b \in \mathcal{J}(\mathbf{H}), a \leq b\} \cup \{\langle a',b'\rangle : a',b' \in f(\mathcal{J}(\mathbf{H}) \cap -S), a' \leq' b\} \cup \{\langle p, g_S(p)\rangle : p \in P\} \cup \{\langle a,b'\rangle : a \in S, b' \in \mathcal{J}(\mathbf{H})', a' \leq' b'\}$.

Definition 49. 1. $\mathbf{X}(\mathbf{H}(S))$ will denote the poset $(\mathcal{J}(\mathbf{H}(S)), \leq)$;
2. $\mathbf{X}(\mathbf{H} \nearrow S)$ will denote the space $(\mathbf{X}(\mathbf{H}(S)), g_S)$

Obviously, from Definition 48 we have:

3.5 $\mathbf{X}(\mathbf{H} \nearrow S)^+ = \mathbf{HS}(\mathbf{H})$.

Example 4. Let us consider the Heyting algebra $\mathbf{H}$ of example 1. In this algebra, $\mathbf{max}(\mathbf{HS}(\mathbf{H})) = \{a, b\}$. Consider for instance the set $S = \{a\} \subseteq \mathbf{max}(\mathbf{HS}(\mathbf{H}))$. We obtain thereafter the following space:

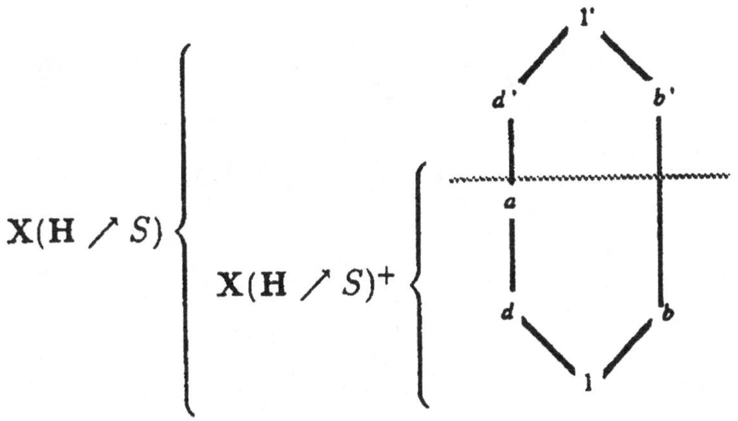

Fig. 6.

Definition 50. By $\mathbf{N}_S(\mathbf{HS}(\mathbf{H}))$ we will denote the algebraic structure

$$(\Omega_A(\mathbf{X}(\mathbf{H}(S))), \cap, \cup, \rightarrow, \neg, \sim, \mathcal{J}(\mathbf{H}(S)), \emptyset)$$

with the operations defined in Definition 47.

Lemma 51. *For any Heyting algebra* $\mathbf{H}$*:*

1. $\mathbf{X}(\mathbf{H} \nearrow S)$ *is a Nelson space and* $\mathbf{N}_S(\mathbf{HS}(\mathbf{H}))$ *is a Nelson algebra.*
2. $\mathbf{N}_S(\mathbf{HS}(\mathbf{H}))/_{\equiv} \cong_H \mathbf{H}$.

Proof. See [Se2]. □

Example 5. Let us consider the space $\mathbf{X}(\mathbf{H} \nearrow S)$ of example 4; then applying $\mathbf{N}_S$ to this space we obtain the Nelson algebra illustrated by the diagram in Fig. 7. In this diagram the double arrows link (using transitivity) the elements that are equivalent modulo the equivalence relation $\equiv$.

Given the algebra $\mathbf{N}_S(\mathbf{HS}(\mathbf{H}))$, we introduce another method to represent its elements yielding an isomorphic algebra $\mathbf{N}_S^K(\mathbf{HS}(\mathbf{H}))$ (the exponent "K" stays for "Kalman". Let us notice that the following result is a specialization of the "Polarity Theorem" of [Du1]):

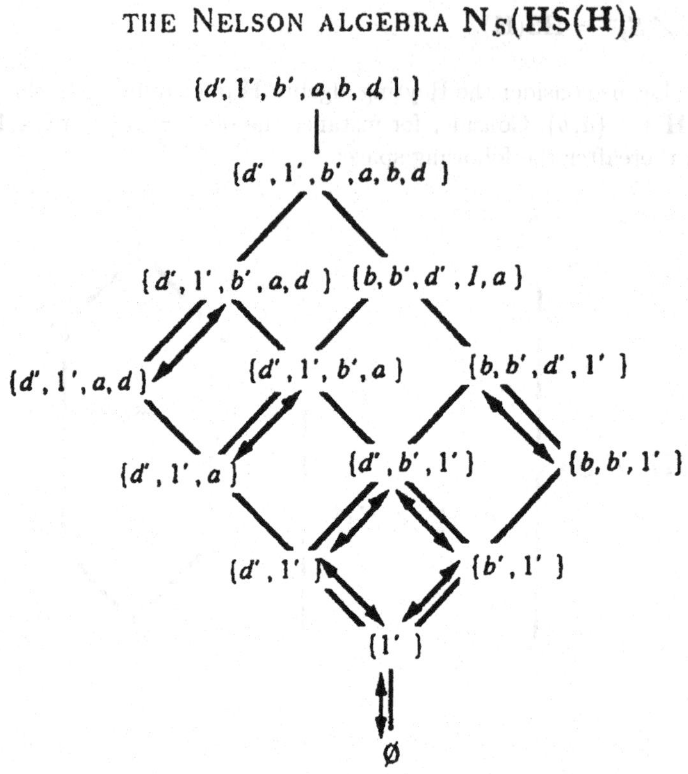

Fig. 7.

Proposition 52. *Let* $\mathbf{N}_S(\mathbf{HS}(\mathbf{H}))$ *be a Nelson algebra as in the Lemma 51. Let us define the following map:*

$$\kappa : \Omega_A(\mathbf{X}(\mathbf{H}(S))) \longmapsto \Omega_A(\mathbf{HS}(\mathbf{H})) \times \Omega_A(\mathbf{HS}(\mathbf{H})) \ ;$$

$$\kappa(A) = \langle A \cap \mathcal{J}(\mathbf{H}), \mathcal{J}(\mathbf{H}) \cap -g_S(A) \rangle \ .$$

The image of κ, **Im**κ, *will be denoted by* $N_S^K(\mathbf{HS}(\mathbf{H}))$. *Consider the algebraic structure*

$$\mathbf{N}_S^K(\mathbf{HS}(\mathbf{H})) = (N_S^K(\mathbf{HS}(\mathbf{H})), \wedge, \vee, \rightarrow, \neg, \sim, 0, 1)$$

with the following operations:

1. $1 = \langle \mathcal{J}(\mathbf{H}), \emptyset \rangle$;
2. $0 = \langle \emptyset, \mathcal{J}(\mathbf{H}) \rangle$;
3. $\langle A_1, A_2 \rangle \vee \langle B_1, B_2 \rangle = \langle A_1 \cup B_1, A_2 \cap B_2 \rangle$;
4. $\langle A_1, A_2 \rangle \wedge \langle B_1, B_2 \rangle = \langle A_1 \cap B_1, A_2 \cup B_2 \rangle$;
5. $\langle A_1, A_2 \rangle \rightarrow \langle B_1, B_2 \rangle = \langle A_1 \Longrightarrow B_1, A_1 \cap B_2 \rangle$;
6. $\sim \langle A_1, A_2 \rangle = \langle A_2, A_1 \rangle$;
7. $\neg \langle A_1, A_2 \rangle = \langle \neg A_1, A_1 \rangle$,

where $\cap, \cup, \Longrightarrow$ *and* $\neg$ *applied inside the ordered pairs are the operations of the Heyting algebra* $\mathbf{H}(\mathbf{HS}(\mathbf{H}))$.

Then $\mathbf{N}_S^K(\mathbf{HS}(\mathbf{H}))$ *is a Nelson algebra isomorphic to* $\mathbf{N}_S(\mathbf{HS}(\mathbf{H}))$.

Proof. **(a)** From Definition 49, if A is an up-set in $\mathbf{X}(\mathbf{H} \nearrow S)$ then $A \cap \mathcal{J}(\mathbf{H})$ is an up-set in $\mathbf{HS}(\mathbf{H})$. Moreover, since g_S is order-reversing, $g_S(A)$ is a down-set and $-g_S(A)$ an up-set in $\mathbf{X}(\mathbf{H} \nearrow S)$. Hence, $\mathcal{J}(\mathbf{H}) \cap -g_S(A)$ is an up-set in $\mathbf{HS}(\mathbf{H})$.

(b) the map κ is 1-1 and onto: from the definition of κ and the fact that g_S is 1-1.
$\pi(\langle A_1, A_2\rangle) = A_1 \cup g_S(-A_2)$ is 1-1 and corresponds to κ^{-1};

(c) $\kappa(\sim A) = \sim \kappa(A)$:

$$\begin{aligned}\kappa(\sim A) &= \kappa(-g_S(A)) = \langle \mathcal{J}(\mathbf{H}) \cap -g_S(A), \mathcal{J}(\mathbf{H}) \cap -g_S(-g_S(A))\rangle \\ &= \langle \mathcal{J}(\mathbf{H}) \cap -g_S(A), A \cap \mathcal{J}(\mathbf{H})\rangle = \sim \kappa(A) \ .\end{aligned}$$

since $-g_S - (x) = g_S(x)$ and g_S is an involution.

(d) $A \leq B$ in $\mathbf{N}_S(\mathbf{HS}(\mathbf{H}))$ iff $\kappa(A) \leq \kappa(B)$ in $\mathbf{N}_S^K(\mathbf{HS}(\mathbf{H}))$:

$$\begin{aligned}A \leq B \text{ iff } & A \rightarrow B = \sim B \rightarrow \sim A = 1 \\ \text{iff } & A \cap \mathcal{J}(\mathbf{H}) \subseteq B \cap \mathcal{J}(\mathbf{H}) \text{ and } \sim B \cap \mathcal{J}(\mathbf{H}) \subseteq \sim A \cap \mathcal{J}(\mathbf{H}) \\ \text{iff } & A \cap \mathcal{J}(\mathbf{H}) \subseteq B \cap \mathcal{J}(\mathbf{H}) \\ & \quad \text{and } (-g_S(B)) \cap \mathcal{J}(\mathbf{H}) \subseteq (-g_S(A)) \cap \mathcal{J}(\mathbf{H}) \\ \text{iff } & A_1 \subseteq B_1 \text{ and } B_2 \subseteq A_2 \\ \text{iff } & \kappa(A) \rightarrow \kappa(B) = \kappa(\sim B) \rightarrow \kappa(\sim A) = 1 \\ \text{iff } & \kappa(A) \leq \kappa(B).\end{aligned}$$

(e) $\kappa(A \cup B) = \kappa(A) \vee \kappa(B)$:

$$\begin{aligned}\kappa(A \cup B) &= \langle (A \cup B) \cap \mathcal{J}(\mathbf{H}), \mathcal{J}(\mathbf{H}) \cap -g_S(A \cup B)\rangle \\ &= \langle (A \cap \mathcal{J}(\mathbf{H})) \cup (B \cap \mathcal{J}(\mathbf{H})), \mathcal{J}(\mathbf{H}) \cap -(g_S(A) \cup g_S(B))\rangle \\ &= \langle (A \cap \mathcal{J}(\mathbf{H})) \cup (B \cap (\mathbf{H})), \mathcal{J}(\mathbf{H}) \cap -g_S(A) \cap -g_S(B)\rangle \\ &= \langle A_1 \cup B_1, A_2 \cap B_2\rangle \\ &= \kappa(A) \vee \kappa(B);\end{aligned}$$

In view of 2. and 3. of Definition 42, we can prove:

(f) $\kappa(A \cap B) = \kappa(A) \wedge \kappa(B)$.
In view of axioms 5. and 6. of Definition 42, using (c), (d) and (e) above, we can prove:

(g) $\kappa(A \rightarrow B) = \kappa(A) \rightarrow \kappa(B)$.

□

Example 6. Continuing the previous examples, we apply the functor $\mathbf{N}_S^K$ to the Heyting space $\mathbf{HS}(\mathbf{H})$. First, let us see an application of the map k to an element of $\mathbf{N}_S(\mathbf{HS}(\mathbf{H}))$ (remember that $\mathcal{J}(\mathbf{H}) = \{1, a, d, b\}$):

$$\begin{aligned} k(\{b, b', d', 1', a\}) &= \langle \{b, b', d', 1', a\} \cap \mathcal{J}(\mathbf{H}), \mathcal{J}(\mathbf{H}) \cap -gs(\{b, b', d', 1', a\}) \rangle \\ &= \langle \{a, b\}, \mathcal{J}(\mathbf{H}) \cap -\{b, b', d, a, 1\} \rangle = \langle \{a, b\}, \mathcal{J}(\mathbf{H}) \cap \{d'1'\} \rangle \\ &= \langle \{a, b\}, \emptyset \rangle \end{aligned}$$

In this way we obtain the lattice presented in Fig. 8.

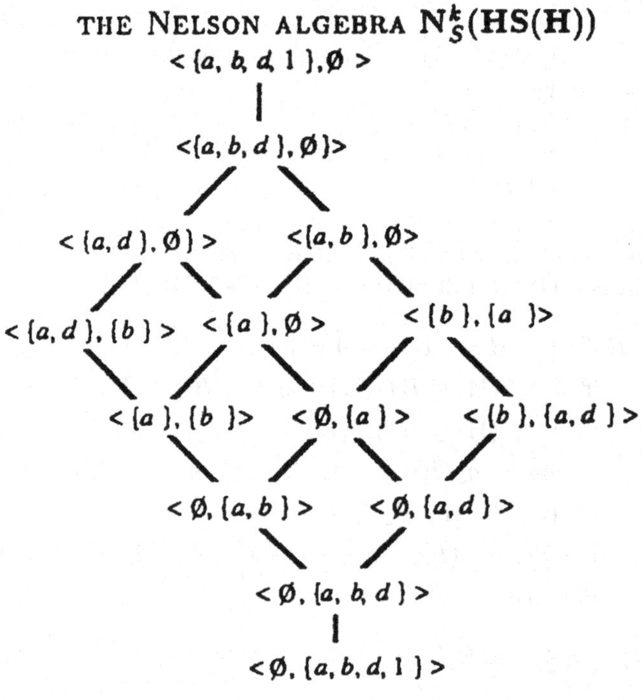

Fig. 8.

Now we shall see that Nelson algebras that are images of $\mathbf{N}_S^K$ correspond, by Heyting algebra duality, to Sendlewski's construction of Nelson algebras from Heyting ones. More precisely, let $\mathbf{H}$ be a Heyting algebra, then via the isomorphism h of Point 2.1, the map

3.6 $h^* : N_S^K(\mathbf{HS}(\mathbf{H})) \longmapsto H \times H : h^*(\langle A_1, A_2 \rangle) = \langle h^{-1}(A_1), h^{-1}(A_2) \rangle$

determines an isomorphic Nelson algebra of ordered pairs of elements of $\mathbf{H}$.

Example 7. Continuing the previous examples, let us compute an instance of the application of the map h^* to some element of $\mathbf{N}_S^k(\mathbf{HS}(\mathbf{H}))$ (remember how the isomorphism h acts in example 1):

$$h^*(\langle \{a, b\}, \emptyset \rangle) = \langle h^{-1}(\{a, b\}), h^{-1}(\emptyset) \rangle = \langle c, 0 \rangle \ ;$$

$$h^*(\langle\{a,d\},\{b\}\rangle) = \langle h^{-1}(\{a,d\}), h^{-1}(\{b\})\rangle = \langle d,b\rangle \ .$$

Applying h^* to $k(\Omega_A(\mathbf{X}(\mathbf{H}(S))))$ we obtain the Nelson algebra illustrated in Fig. 9 in which we have grouped the elements that are equivalent modulo the equivalence relation $\equiv$:

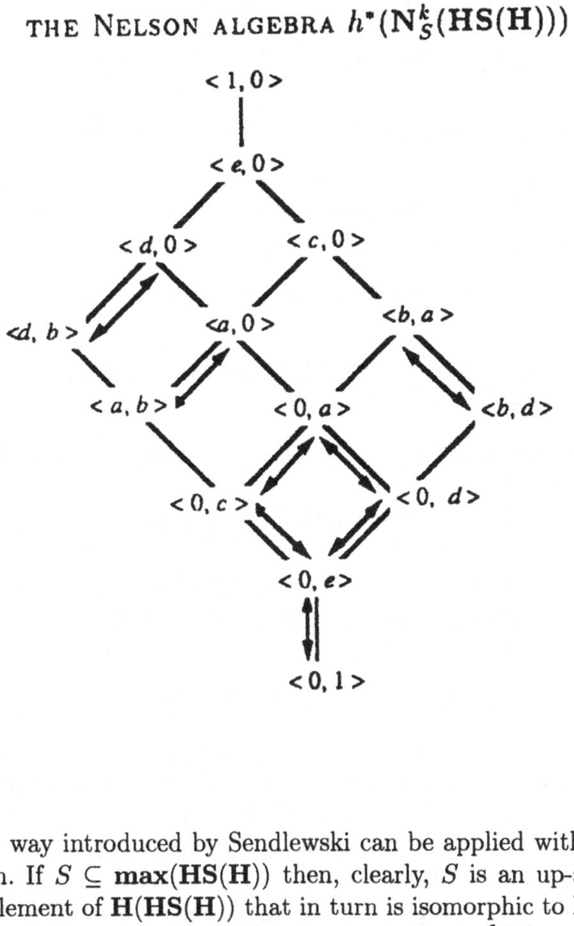

Fig. 9.

The direct way introduced by Sendlewski can be applied with the following basic intuition. If $S \subseteq \mathbf{max}(\mathbf{HS}(\mathbf{H}))$ then, clearly, S is an up-set in $\mathbf{HS}(\mathbf{H})$, thus it is an element of $\mathbf{H}(\mathbf{HS}(\mathbf{H}))$ that in turn is isomorphic to $\mathbf{H}$ by means of the application h. Let us then consider the pre-image $h^{-1}(S) = s$. Hence s will be an element of $\mathbf{H}$ and $\uparrow s$ is thus a (principal) filter on $\mathbf{H}$.

Hence it induces a congruence relation Θ on $\mathbf{H}$ in the usual way:

3.7

$$a\Theta b \textit{ iff } \exists c \in\uparrow s \textit{ such that } a \wedge c = c \wedge b \ .$$

Since $\uparrow s$ contains all the dense elements of $\mathbf{H}, \mathbf{H}/_\Theta$ is a Boolean algebra. In other words Θ is a Boolean congruence on $\mathbf{H}$. So we are able to recover the following

Sendlewski's algebraic construction of Nelson algebras (finite case)

Lemma 53. *Let* $\mathbf{H} = (H, \wedge, \vee, \neg, \Longrightarrow, 0, 1)$ *be a Heyting algebra and* Θ *a Boolean congruence on it. Consider the following set:*

$$N_\Theta(H) = \{\langle a_1, a_2\rangle \in H \times H : a_1 \wedge a_2 = 0 \text{ and } (a_1 \vee a_2)\Theta 1\} \ ,$$

with $\wedge, \vee, 0, 1$ *with respect to* $\mathbf{H}$. *Then the structure:*

$$\mathbf{N}_\Theta(\mathbf{H}) = (N_\Theta(H), \wedge, \vee, \rightarrow, \neg, \sim, \langle 0, 1\rangle, \langle 1, 0\rangle)$$

with the operations:

1. $\langle a_1, a_2\rangle \wedge \langle b_1, b_2\rangle = \langle a_1 \wedge b_1, a_2 \vee b_2\rangle$;
2. $\langle a_1, a_2\rangle \vee \langle b_1, b_2\rangle = \langle a_1 \vee b_1, a_2 \wedge b_2\rangle$;
3. $\langle a_1, a_2\rangle \rightarrow \langle b_1, b_2\rangle = \langle a_1 \Longrightarrow b_1, a_1 \wedge b_2\rangle$;
4. $\sim \langle a_1, a_2\rangle = \langle a_2, a_1\rangle$;
5. $\neg\langle a_1, a_2\rangle = \langle \neg a_1, a_1\rangle$,

where $\wedge, \vee, \Longrightarrow$ *and* $\neg$ *when applied inside the ordered pairs are the operations of* $\mathbf{H}$, *is a Nelson algebra called N-Lattice.*

By Heyting algebra duality, $\mathbf{N}_\Theta(\mathbf{H}) \cong_N \mathbf{N}^K_S(\mathbf{HS}(\mathbf{H}))$ and $\mathbf{N}_\Theta(\mathbf{H})/_\equiv \cong_H \mathbf{N}^K_S(\mathbf{HS}(\mathbf{H}))/_\equiv \cong_H \mathbf{H}$.

Clearly, also $\uparrow S$ itself is a filter on $\mathbf{H}(\mathbf{HS}(\mathbf{H}))$ inducing a congruence relation Θ^*.

Obviously $\mathbf{N}_{\Theta^*}(\mathbf{H}(\mathbf{HS}(\mathbf{H}))) = \mathbf{N}^K_S(\mathbf{HS}(\mathbf{H}))$. If $\mathbf{H}$ is not trivial, then we have two limit situations given, for the functor $\mathbf{N}^K_S$, by $S = \emptyset$ and $S = \mathbf{max}(\mathbf{HS}(\mathbf{H}))$ and, for the functor $\mathbf{N}_\Theta$, by the top and bottom elements in the lattice of the Boolean congruences of $\mathbf{H}$. They yield the functors $\overrightarrow{\mathbf{N}}$ and $\overleftarrow{\mathbf{N}}$, respectively.

Example 8. Let us take into account the Heyting algebra $\mathbf{H}$ of the previous examples and the subset $S = \{a\}$ of the set of the maximal elements of $\mathbf{X}(\mathbf{H})$. Then $h^{-1}(S) = a$ and $\uparrow a = \{a, c, d, e, 1\}$. We can easily verify that the set of the elements that are dense in $\mathbf{H}$, that is $\{e, 1\}$, is included in $\uparrow a$. So taking into account the congruence relation Θ induced by $\uparrow a$ we have that $\mathbf{H}/_\Theta$ is a Boolean algebra. In this example $\mathbf{H}/_\Theta$ is a two element chain. The same considerations apply to the congruence Θ^* induced on $\mathbf{H}(\mathbf{HS}(\mathbf{H}))$ by $\uparrow S$.

Now it is easy to verify that, for instance, $b \wedge 0 = 0$ but $b \vee 0 = b \notin [1]_\Theta$; thus $\langle b, 0\rangle$ and (by the commutativity of $\vee$) $\langle 0, b\rangle$ are not admissible pairs in $\mathbf{N}_\Theta(\mathbf{H})$. With an analogous reasoning it can be immediately verified that $\langle\{b\}, \emptyset\rangle$ and $\langle\emptyset, \{b\}\rangle$ are not admissible in $\mathbf{N}_{\Theta^*}(\mathbf{H}(\mathbf{HS}(\mathbf{H}))) = \mathbf{N}^K_S(\mathbf{HS}(\mathbf{H}))$.

In the diagrams below the double arrows link the elements in the same equivalence class modulo the congruences Θ and Θ^*:

In particular if $S^+ = \{a, b\} = \mathbf{max}(\mathbf{HS}(\mathbf{H}))$ then $h^{-1}(S^+) = c$ and $\uparrow c = \{c, e, 1\}$ that is the set of all and only the dense elements in $\mathbf{H}$. We denote the induced congruence by Θ^+. In this case it is well-known that $\mathbf{H}/_{\Theta^+}$ is isomorphic to the Boolean algebra $\mathbf{REG}(\mathbf{H})$ of the regular elements of $\mathbf{H}$ (see Definition

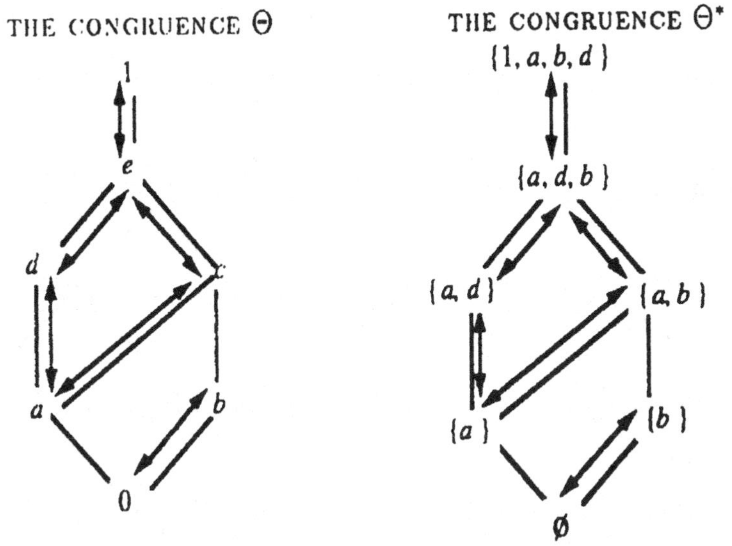

Fig. 10.

22.2): this case is an extreme one and induces the application of the functor $\overleftarrow{\mathbf{N}}$. The following example illustrates the situation. In the resulting lattice we have drawn by dotted lines the subset of $\mathbf{N}_\Theta(\mathbf{H})$ which we lose by making b and b' collapsing, that is by assuming $S = \{a, b\}$ (see Fig 11).

The other extreme case is represented by $S^- = \emptyset$. We denote the congruence relation induced by $h^{-1}(S)$ by Θ^-. In this case the Boolean congruence is trivial and $\mathbf{H}/_{\Theta^-}$ is a degenerate one point Boolean algebra and we get an application of the functor $\overrightarrow{\mathbf{N}}$.

In the diagram illustrating the resulting Nelson algebra, we have drawn by a dotted line the part of the lattice that we gain with respect to $\mathbf{N}_\Theta(\mathbf{H})$ by relaxing the constraint $a = a'$, that is by assuming $S = \emptyset$; let us note, moreover, that now there is a symmetric element, $\langle 0, 0\rangle$, that is an element x such that $\sim x = x$. This element is sometimes called *center* (see Fig 12).

Let us end this Subsection with a deeper insight into the Heyting algebra $\mathbf{N}_\Theta(\mathbf{H})/_\equiv$:

Definition 54. An element of the form $\sim \neg a$ (i.e. $\langle a_1, \neg a_1\rangle$) is denoted by a^*.

Lemma 55. *Let* $\mathbf{H}$ *be a Heyting algebra and* $\equiv$ *be the equivalence relation on* $\mathbf{N}_\Theta(\mathbf{H})$ *defined in Lemma 46. Then for any* $a \in N_\Theta(H)$: $a^* = \mathbf{lst}\{a' \in [a]_\equiv\}$.

Proposition 56. (Corollary)

Take the elements of the form a^* *as canonical representatives of the equivalence classes modulo* $\equiv$*; hence the algebra:*

$$\mathbf{N}_\Theta(\mathbf{H})^* = (\{a^* : a \in N_\Theta(H)\}, \wedge^*, \vee, \sim^*, \neg^*, \rightarrow^*, 0, 1)$$

THE CONGRUENCE Θ^+

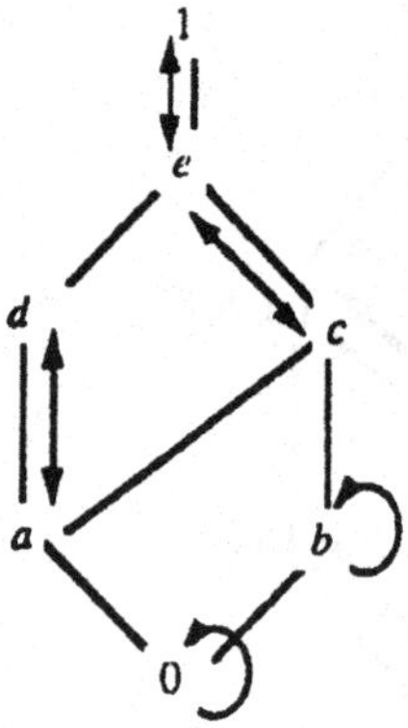

THE NELSON ALGEBRA $N^+(H)$

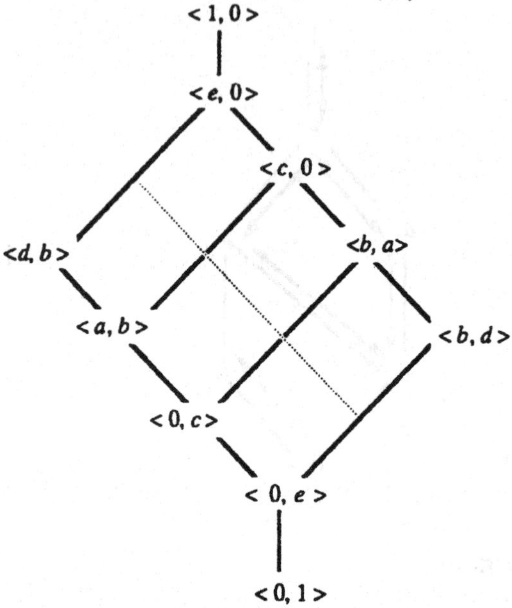

Fig. 11.

THE CONGRUENCE Θ^-

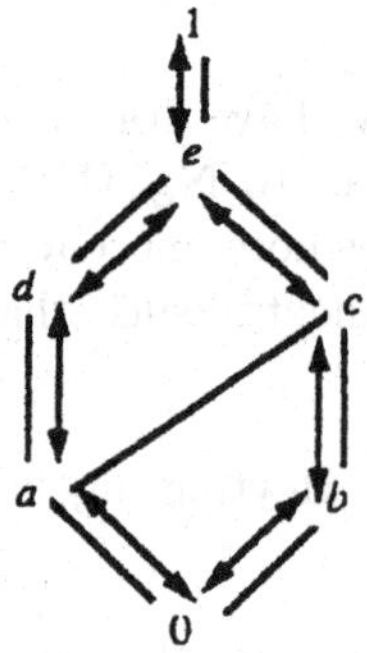

THE NELSON ALGEBRA $N^-(H)$

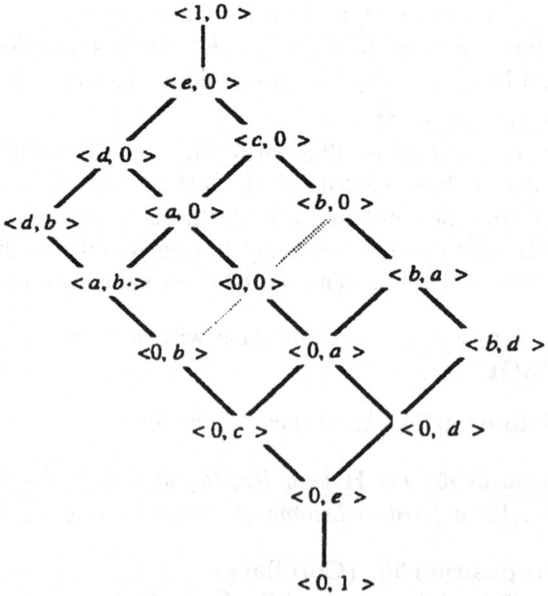

Fig. 12.

where $a \wedge^* b =\sim \neg(a \wedge b)$*;* $\sim^* a =\sim \neg \sim a$*;* $\neg^* a =\sim \neg\neg a$*;* $a \rightarrow^* b =\sim \neg(a \rightarrow b)$*, is isomorphic to* $\mathbf{N}_\Theta(\mathbf{H})/_\equiv$ *and to* $\mathbf{H}$*.*

Proof. : See [Se2] and [Pal]. □

What is worth noticing here is that the isomorphism is given by the first projection π_1 of a^*. On the side of dual spaces we have the function f^* given by $f^*([A]_\equiv) = A \cap \mathcal{J}(\mathbf{H})$.

Example 9. Consider the Nelson algebra depicted in example 7, then, for instance, it is not difficult to see that $\alpha = \{\langle d, b\rangle, \langle d, 0\rangle\}$ is a class of the equivalence relation $\equiv$.

Now $\sim \neg\langle d, 0\rangle =\sim \langle b, d\rangle = \langle d, b\rangle =\sim \neg\langle d, b\rangle$. Thus $\langle d, b\rangle = \mathbf{lst}(\{x : x \in \alpha\})$. Similarly, we get the other representatives: $\langle 0, 1\rangle, \langle d, b\rangle, \langle a, b\rangle, \langle c, 0\rangle, \langle e, 0\rangle$ and $\langle 1, 0\rangle$. It is easy to verify that the lattice of these elements is isomorphic to $\mathbf{H}$. Notice, moreover, that $\mathbf{N}_\Theta(\mathbf{H})^*$ is not a sublattice of $\mathbf{N}_\Theta(\mathbf{H})$: for instance, $\langle d, b\rangle \wedge \langle b, d\rangle = \langle 0, e\rangle \in [\langle 0, 1\rangle]_\equiv$. To get the right representative we must use the operation $\wedge^*$: $\sim \neg(\langle d, b\rangle \wedge \langle b, d\rangle) =\sim \neg\langle 0, e\rangle = \langle 0, 1\rangle$.

Again, $\sim \langle c, 0\rangle = \langle 0, c\rangle \in [\langle 0, 1\rangle]_\equiv$ and $\sim \neg \sim \langle c, 0\rangle = \langle 0, 1\rangle$.

Finally $\langle c, 0\rangle \rightarrow \langle b, d\rangle = \langle b, a\rangle \in [\langle b, d\rangle]_\equiv$ and again we must "normalize" the result using the operator $\sim \neg$ (in the same way we could verify that $\sim \langle a, b\rangle = \langle b, a\rangle = \neg\langle a, b\rangle$ whereas $\sim \neg\langle b, a\rangle = \langle b, d\rangle$). Notice that $\sim \neg(x \vee y) =\sim \neg x \vee \sim \neg y$.

Observe that if $\mathbf{H}$ is a Boolean algebra, we no longer need the "normalization" step except for the operation "$\sim$". The reader is invited to compare this discussion with the results of lemmata 97 and 111.

3.3 Disjoint representation of Rough Sets

Now we are ready for an algebraic analysis of Rough Set Systems. In view of Definition 17 let us introduce the following map r :

Definition 57. (THE "ROUGH SET" APPLICATION). Given an Approximation Space $\mathbf{AS}(\mathbf{C})$,

$$r : \mathbb{P}(U) \longmapsto A \times A : r(X) = \langle \mathcal{I}(X), \mathcal{E}(X)\rangle \ .$$

For any $X \in \mathbb{P}(U)$, the ordered pair $r(X)$ is said to be a *disjoint representation* of the rough set of X in $\mathbf{C}$.

The above definition is legitimated by the following Lemma:

Lemma 58. *For any* $X, Y \in \mathbb{P}(U), X \approx Y$ *iff* $r(X) = r(Y)$*.*

Proof. The map

$$\begin{aligned} h(r_1(X)) &= \langle \mathcal{I}(X), -\mathcal{B}(X) \cap -\mathcal{I}(X)\rangle = \langle \mathcal{I}(X), -(\mathcal{C}(X) \cap -\mathcal{I}(X)) \cap -\mathcal{I}(X)\rangle = \\ &= \langle \mathcal{I}(X), (-\mathcal{C}(X) \cap I(X)) \cap -\mathcal{I}(X)\rangle = \langle \mathcal{I}(X), -\mathcal{C}(X)\rangle \\ &= \langle \mathcal{I}(X), \mathcal{I}(-X))\rangle \end{aligned}$$

supplies the obvious bijection between r and the function r_1 defined in 2.2. □

Definition 59. By $RS_r(\mathbf{C})$ we mean the image **Imr** of $\mathbb{P}(U)$ by r.

It is trivial that $\mathcal{E}(X) \cap I(X) = \emptyset$.

Thus, if we are going to find a logic-algebraic structure reflecting the properties of Rough Set Systems, a first attempt should be to use the Kalman's functor **K** (see [Kal]):

3.8 *Given a distributive lattice* $\mathbf{D} = (D, \wedge, \vee, 0, 1)$,

$$\mathbf{K}(D) = \{\langle d_1, d_2\rangle : d_1, d_2 \in D \text{ and } d_1 \wedge d_2 = 0\} \ .$$

However, by applying **K** to the Boolean algebra **AS**(**C**) we will not get our goal.

To deal with the problems related to the cardinality of the elementary classes (reflected in definition 39 by condition 4) we need a more refined functor. Since Kalman's functor is used in order to construct DeMorgan lattices, the required logic-algebraic structures will also be refined DeMorgan lattices: as a matter of fact they will be shown to be Nelson algebras.

Let us see how we may grasp their shapes.

From the discussion in the Introduction we know that **Imr** is a rather peculiar subset of the Cartesian product $A \times A$. In fact, what we have said in the Introduction about the elementary classes that are singletons, can now be restated in the following way: any rough set is a pair $\langle X, Y\rangle$ of subsets of elements of A such that $X \cap Y = \emptyset$; but not any such a pair represents a rough set of **AS**(**C**).

Indeed, if an elementary class E has cardinality 1, then $E \subseteq \mathcal{I}(X)$ whenever $E \subseteq \mathcal{C}(X)$. Since $\mathcal{I}(X) \subseteq \mathcal{C}(X)$, the latter statement amounts to saying that for any elementary class α such that $card(\alpha) = 1$ the following relation holds:

$$\alpha \subseteq \mathcal{I}(X) \text{ iff } \alpha \subseteq \mathcal{C}(X) \ .$$

Hence, we can have the following situations:

a) $\alpha \subseteq \mathcal{I}(X)$ iff $\alpha \not\subseteq \mathcal{E}(X)$
b) $\alpha \not\subseteq \mathcal{I}(X)$ iff $\alpha \subseteq \mathcal{E}(X)$.

It follows that any arbitrary singleton elementary class either is included in $\mathcal{I}(X)$ or is included in $\mathcal{E}(X)$. Hence, the union

3.9 $S = \bigcup\{\alpha \in Atom(\mathbf{AS}(\mathbf{C})) : card(\alpha) = 1\}$

must be partitioned between $\mathcal{I}(X)$ and $\mathcal{E}(X)$, for any $X \in \mathbb{P}(U)$. Thus, we have:

Lemma 60. *For any Approximation Space* **AS**(**C**), *the pair* $\langle X_1, X_2\rangle$ *is a disjoint representation of a rough set in* **C** *iff* $X_1, X_2 \in A$, $X_1 \cap X_2 = \emptyset$ *and* $X_1 \cup X_2 \supseteq S$.

Let us give an algebraic interpretation of these requirements.

By definition of **AS**(**C**), $S \in A$, since it is a union of the elementary classes.

Let us consider the principal filter $\uparrow S$ generated by S in **AS**(**C**) (see Definition 5).

The following relation Θ is a congruence on **AS**(**C**) (see point 3.7):

Definition 61. $\forall X, Y \in A$, $X\Theta Y$ iff $\exists Z \in\uparrow S$ such that $X \cap Z = Z \cap Y$.

From the definition of Θ we easily have:

Lemma 62. *For any Approximation Space* $\mathbf{AS}(\mathbf{C}), \forall X \in A$,

$$X\Theta U \textit{ iff } X \supseteq S \ .$$

In other words, an element X of the Approximation Space $\mathbf{AS}(\mathbf{C})$ is in the same Θ-congruence class as the top element U of $\mathbf{AS}(\mathbf{C})$ *iff* the set S is included in it.

Now we can exploit this fact in order to single out all the legal ordered pairs of elements of A representing rough sets of $\mathbf{AS}(\mathbf{C})$.

We will actually use two kinds of verification for a pair $\langle X, Y\rangle \in A \times A$:

i) first, we have to verify if $X \cap Y = \emptyset$
ii) then we verify if $(X \cup Y)\Theta U$.

If this is the case, then $X \cup Y \supseteq S$. We can then deduce that S is partitioned between X and Y, as required.

This discussion leads to the following application:

Definition 63. $N_\Theta(A) = \{\langle X_1, X_2\rangle \in A^2\colon X_1 \cap X_2 = \emptyset \text{ and } (X_1 \cup X_2)\Theta U\}$

We can prove:

Proposition 64. *Let* $\mathbf{AS}(\mathbf{C})$ *be an Approximation Space and let* Θ *be defined as in Definition 61, then:*

$$N_\Theta(A) = RS_r(\mathbf{C}) \ .$$

The proof can be easily obtained from the presented discussion.

It happens that $N_\Theta(A)$ can be given a well defined logic-algebraic structure.

Indeed, since any Approximation Space $\mathbf{AS}(\mathbf{C})$ is a Boolean algebra, we have the following immediate corollary.

Proposition 65. (FIRST THEOREM OF REPRESENTATION OF ROUGH SET SYSTEMS)

For any Approximation Space $\mathbf{AS}(\mathbf{C})$, *the Rough Set System* $RS_r(\mathbf{C})$ *equipped with the following operations:*

1. $1 = \langle U, \emptyset\rangle$;
2. $0 = \langle \emptyset, U\rangle$;
3. $\langle X_1, X_2\rangle \wedge \langle Y_1, Y_2\rangle = \langle X_1 \cap Y_1, X_2 \cup Y_2\rangle$;
4. $\langle X_1, X_2\rangle \vee \langle Y_1, Y_2\rangle = \langle X_1 \cup Y_1, X_2 \cap Y_2\rangle$;
5. $\langle X_1, X_2\rangle \rightarrow \langle Y_1, Y_2\rangle = \langle X_1 \Longrightarrow Y_1, X_1 \cap Y_2\rangle$;
6. $\sim \langle X_1, X_2\rangle = \langle X_2, X_1\rangle$;
7. $\neg\langle X_1, X_2\rangle = \langle -X_1, X_1\rangle = \langle X_1, X_2\rangle \rightarrow \langle \emptyset, U\rangle$;

(where $U, \emptyset, \cap, \cup, -$ *and* $\Longrightarrow$ *applied inside the ordered pairs are the operations of* $\mathbf{AS}(\mathbf{C})$*), is a semi-simple Nelson algebra.*

Proof. From Proposition 64, $RS_r(\mathbf{C}) = N_\Theta(A)$. Thus, from the results of Lemma 53, we get the required condition. □

Notice how the characteristic property of semi-simple Nelson algebras (see Proposition 44) is verifiable in virtue of the fact that $\mathbf{AS}(\mathbf{C})$ is a Boolean algebra and "$-$" is a complementation: $\langle X_1, X_2\rangle \vee \neg\langle X_1, X_2\rangle = \langle X_1 \cup -X_1, X_1 \cap X_2\rangle = \langle U, \emptyset\rangle$.

Moreover, we have to notice that since $\mathbf{AS}(\mathbf{C})$ is a Boolean algebra, definition of $\rightarrow$ in point 5 above becomes

5': $\langle X_1, X_2\rangle \rightarrow \langle Y_1, Y_2\rangle = \langle -X_1 \cup Y_1, X_1 \cap Y_2\rangle = \neg\langle X_1, X_2\rangle \vee \langle Y_1, Y_2\rangle$.

Definition 66. For any Approximation Space $\mathbf{AS}(\mathbf{C})$, $\mathbf{N}(\mathbf{AS}(\mathbf{C}))$ will denote the Nelson algebra $(RS_r(\mathbf{C}), \wedge, \vee, \sim, \neg, \rightarrow, 1, 0)$ with the operations defined in Proposition 65.

Proposition 67. *For any Approximation Space* $\mathbf{AS}(\mathbf{C})$*, let* Θ *be defined as in Definition 61, then*

$$\mathbf{N}(\mathbf{AS}(\mathbf{C})) = \mathbf{N}_\Theta(\mathbf{AS}(\mathbf{C})) \; ,$$

where $\mathbf{N}_\Theta$ *is Sendlewski's functor described in Lemma 53.*

Example 10. Let us consider the Information System of example 2 and its induced Approximation Space $\mathbf{AS}(\mathbf{C})$. In Fig. 13 the Rough Set System $\mathbf{N}(\mathbf{AS}(\mathbf{C}))$ is presented.

In the boxes we have grouped the subsets of the universe U belonging to the same equivalence class modulo $\approx$.

The arrows illustrate the *rough application* r, that is they map any element of such a class to the corresponding rough set in disjoint representation.

Notice that the eight elements of the center are situated at the outmost edges of the diagram and they are characterized by the fact that they are the images of the singleton equivalence classes. For instance $\langle\{a, b, e\}, \{c, d\}\rangle \in \mathcal{CTR}(\mathbf{N}(\mathbf{AS}(\mathbf{C})))$. This property will be re-examined in Subsection 3.4.

3.4 An intuitive dual construction

Now we show how to construct a suitable Nelson space (see Subsection 47) on the ground of the intuitive meaning of rough sets. The basic point is an alternative reading of the proof of the preceding constructions: any elementary class α_i may be included in the interior $\mathcal{I}(X)$ and/or in the closure $\mathcal{C}(X)$ of a set $X \in \mathbb{P}(U)$. But from elementary topology:

3.10 *If* $\alpha_i \subseteq \mathcal{I}(X)$ *then* $\alpha_i \subseteq \mathcal{C}(X)$.

and from the discussion at the beginning of the last Subsection:

3.11 *If* $card(\alpha_i) = 1$*, then* $\alpha_i \subseteq \mathcal{C}(X)$ *iff* $\alpha_i \subseteq \mathcal{I}(X)$.

THE ROUGH SETS SYSTEM N(AS(C)) AND THE ROUGH APPLICATION r:

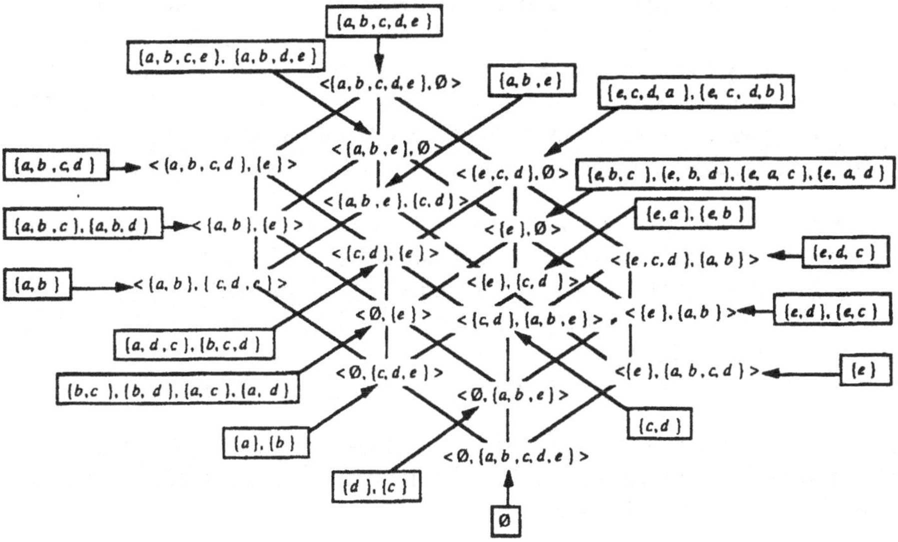

Fig. 13.

Moreover we can think that this Nelson space has to represent "*what happens when, in view of Rough Set Theory, we assign elementary classes for forming the upper approximation (the closure) and the lower approximation (the interior) of a set* $X \in \mathbb{P}(U)$". So it should be organized as follows. First, we distinguish the roles played by any elementary class $\alpha_i \in Ind(\mathbf{C})$ by duplicating them by means of an assignment of two labels: the label $\mathcal{C}$ for marking that α_i can be "used" for forming a closure and the label $\mathcal{I}$ for marking that α_i can be used for forming an interior. Clearly, constraint 3.11 makes the two "uses" collapsing for any elementary set that is a singleton. In this case we decide to assign the label $\mathcal{I}$. Now we have to take into account if there is some precedence in "spending" the elementary classes. As a matter of fact, constraint 3.10 states that an elementary class cannot be assigned to the "interior" of a set X if this class has not been already assigned to its "closure": to enter the house one must enter the front garden (obviously the opposite is not required). Thus we have to order $\alpha_i^{\mathcal{C}}$ and $\alpha_i^{\mathcal{I}}$ in such a way that the order could induce the respect of this priority in our construction. In order to fit the preference of logicians for "truth" and thus for "filters" recalled in the Remark after Definition 5, we assign the lower level to $\alpha_i^{\mathcal{I}}$ and the upper level to $\alpha_i^{\mathcal{C}}$ and we repeat this structure for all the elementary classes but the singletons. In this way, as we are going to see, any legal access to the various levels is guaranteed to be an up-set.

We will see that the definition of the dual space suggested by this intuitive construction of the lower and upper approximations, leads to a Nelson algebra, $\mathbf{N}_{\Theta^*}(\mathbf{AS}([\mathbf{C}]))$, which is defined on pairs of disjoint subsets of elementary classes, that is, pairs of disjoint elements of $\mathbf{AS}([\mathbf{C}])$ (sets of sets); in fact we are working using the "encapsulated" elementary classes as basic material and the family of these "encapsulated" classes is $Atom(\mathbf{AS}([\mathbf{C}]))$. Nevertheless, we have an isomorphism $h : \mathbf{AS}(\mathbf{C}) \longmapsto \mathbf{AS}([\mathbf{C}])$ that assigns an element $X \in A$ to the set Y of elementary classes s. t. $X = \bigcup Y$ (see Point 2.1). Thus, by applying h^* to both the elements of any pair of $\mathbf{AS}([\mathbf{C}])$, we get back the algebra $\mathbf{N}_\Theta(\mathbf{AS}(\mathbf{C}))$ of ordered pairs of disjoint elements of $\mathbf{AS}(\mathbf{C})$ (see Point 3.6).

To explain more rigorously these intuitions, we proceed as follows:

Definition 68. 1. Any $\alpha_i \in Ind(\mathbf{C})$ shall be denoted also by $\alpha_i^{\mathcal{I}}$ and throughout this Subsection $Ind(\mathbf{C})$ will be denoted also by $Ind(\mathbf{C})^{\mathcal{I}}$.
2. $Ind(\mathbf{C})^{\mathcal{C}}$ denotes the set $\{\alpha_i^{\mathcal{C}} : \alpha_i^{\mathcal{I}} \in Ind(\mathbf{C})^{\mathcal{I}}$ and $card(\alpha_i) \geq 2\}$.
3. $S^* = \{\alpha_i^{\mathcal{I}} \in Ind(\mathbf{C})^{\mathcal{I}} : card(\alpha_i) = 1\}$;
4. $T = Ind(\mathbf{C})^{\mathcal{I}} \cup Ind(\mathbf{C})^{\mathcal{C}}$.
5. $\mathbf{T} = (T, \leq)$, where $\langle x, y\rangle \in \leq$ iff $x = y$ or $x = \alpha_i^{\mathcal{I}}$ and $y = \alpha_i^{\mathcal{C}}$.

(Notice that S^* is a member of $\mathbf{AS}([\mathbf{C}])$). In a sense, for any $X \subseteq U$ we are going to analyse the interior and the closure of X in terms of elementary constituents. Thus let us define the following maps:

Definition 69. 1. $h^1 : \mathbb{P}(U) \longmapsto \mathbb{P}(Ind(\mathbf{C})^{\mathcal{I}}) : h^1(X) = \{\alpha_i^{\mathcal{I}} : \alpha_i \subseteq \mathcal{I}(X)\}$;
2. $h^2 : \mathbb{P}(U) \longmapsto \mathbb{P}(Ind(\mathbf{C})^{\mathcal{C}} \cup S^*) : h^2(X) = \{\alpha_i^{\mathcal{C}} : \alpha_i \subseteq \mathcal{C}(X)\} \cup \{\alpha_i^{\mathcal{I}} \in S^* : \alpha_i \subseteq \mathcal{C}(X)\}$;
3. $h^3 : \mathbb{P}(U) \longmapsto T : h^3(X) = h^1(X) \cup h^2(X)$.

Notice that $\bigcup h^1(X) = \mathcal{I}(X)$, $\bigcup h^2(X) = \mathcal{C}(X)$. Moreover, since $\forall X \subseteq U$, $\mathcal{I}(X) \subseteq \mathcal{C}(X)$, then $h^3(X)$ is an up-set in $\mathbf{T}$ and it is not difficult to show:

Lemma 70. $\Omega_A(\mathbf{T}) = \mathbf{Im}h^3$.

(For the definition of Ω_A see point 4 in Definition 2). Now let us set:

Definition 71. 1. $f : Ind(\mathbf{C})^{\mathcal{I}} \longmapsto Ind(\mathbf{C})^{\mathcal{C}} \cup S^* : f(\alpha_i^{\mathcal{I}}) = \begin{cases} \alpha_i^{\mathcal{C}} \text{ if } \alpha_i \notin S^* \\ \alpha_i^{\mathcal{I}} \text{ if } \alpha_i \in S^* \end{cases}$
2. $f' : Ind(\mathbf{C})^{\mathcal{C}} \longmapsto Ind(\mathbf{C})^{\mathcal{I}} : f'(\alpha_i^{\mathcal{C}}) = \alpha_i^{\mathcal{I}}$;
3. $g_{S^*} : T \longmapsto T : g_{S^*}(x) = \begin{cases} f(x) \text{ if } x \in Ind(\mathbf{C})^{\mathcal{I}} \\ f'(x) \text{ otherwise} \end{cases}$
4. $\forall X, Y \in \mathbf{AS}([\mathbf{C}]), X\Theta^*Y$ iff $\exists Z \in \uparrow S^*$ such that $X \wedge Z = Z \wedge Y$.

Since $Ind(\mathbf{C})^{\mathcal{I}}$ is discretely ordered, then $\mathbf{max}(Ind(\mathbf{C})^{\mathcal{I}}) = Ind(\mathbf{C})^{\mathcal{I}}$ and $S^* \subseteq \mathbf{max}(Ind(\mathbf{C})^{\mathcal{I}})$. Moreover, the dual space, $\mathcal{J}(\mathbf{AS}(\mathbf{C}))$, of $\mathbf{AS}(\mathbf{C})$ is $Ind(\mathbf{C})^{\mathcal{I}}$ itself. Thereafter *Mutatis mutandis* we are in the situation described in Subsubsection 3.2. So $\mathbf{T} = \mathbf{X}(\mathbf{AS}(\mathbf{C})(S^*))$ and the map g_{S^*} is an involutory dual order-automorphism on $\mathbf{T}$, fulfilling trivially the interpolation clause of Monteiro introduced in Definition 47 of Subsection 3.1. We have trivially:

Lemma 72. $T^+ = \{t \in T : t \leq g_{S^*}(t)\} = Ind(\mathbf{C})^{\mathcal{I}}$.

From the above construction of the dual space and the results of Subsection 3.2, we have:

Lemma 73. *1.* $\mathbf{T}^+ = (T^+, =) = \mathbf{HS}(\mathbf{AS}(\mathbf{C}))$;
2. $(\mathbf{T}, g_{S^*})$ *is a Nelson space;*
3. $\mathbf{N}_{S^*}(\mathbf{HS}(\mathbf{AS}(\mathbf{C})))$ *is a Nelson algebra;*
4. $\mathbf{N}_{S^*}(\mathbf{HS}(\mathbf{AS}(\mathbf{C})))/_{\equiv}$ *is isomorphic to* $\mathbf{AS}([\mathbf{C}])$.

Vice-versa, since $\mathbf{AS}(\mathbf{C})$ is a Boolean algebra, hence a Heyting algebra, by identifying $\alpha_i^{\mathcal{C}}$ with α_i' in the construction of Sendlewski space given in Subsection 3.2, we have: $(\mathbf{T}, g_{S^*}) = \mathbf{X}(\mathbf{AS}(\mathbf{C}) \nearrow S^*)$. Hence the construction described in that Subsection can be applied and it yields $\mathbf{N}_{S^*}(\mathbf{HS}(\mathbf{AS}(\mathbf{C})))$.

Now, if we apply the map κ of Proposition 52 to $\mathbf{Im}h^3$, we get that for any $X \in \mathbf{Im}h^3$,

$$\kappa(X) = \langle T^+ \cap X, T^+ \cap -g_{S^*}(X)\rangle = \langle\{\alpha_j^{\mathcal{I}} \in X\}, T^+ \cap -g_{S^*}(\{\alpha_i^{\mathcal{C}} \in X\})\rangle \ .$$

Hence, $\kappa(\mathbf{Im}h^3) = N_{\Theta^*}(\mathbb{P}(Ind(\mathbf{C})^{\mathcal{I}}))$ and, recalling that from Definition 35 $\mathbb{P}(Ind(\mathbf{C})^{\mathcal{I}})$ is the carrier of $\mathbf{AS}([\mathbf{C}])$, we find that κ determines an isomorphism between $\mathbf{N}_{S^*}(\mathbf{HS}(\mathbf{AS}(\mathbf{C})))$ and $\mathbf{N}_{\Theta^*}(\mathbf{AS}([\mathbf{C}]))$. The map h^* of Point 3.6 of Subsection 3.2 gives then the set

3.12 $h^*(\kappa(\mathbf{Im}h^3)) = \{\langle\bigcup A_1, \bigcup A_2\rangle : \langle A_1, A_2\rangle \in \kappa(\mathbf{Im}h^3)\}$.

and determines an isomorphism between $\mathbf{N}_{\Theta^*}(\mathbf{AS}([\mathbf{C}]))$ and $\mathbf{N}_{\Theta}(\mathbf{AS}(\mathbf{C}))$.

But from Proposition 67 $\mathbf{N}_{\Theta}(\mathbf{AS}(\mathbf{C})) = \mathbf{N}(\mathbf{AS}(\mathbf{C}))$.

Example 11. Let us consider the Approximation Space of example 2.

Below we have constructed the Nelson space $\mathbf{X}(\mathbf{AS}(\mathbf{C}) \nearrow S^*)$:

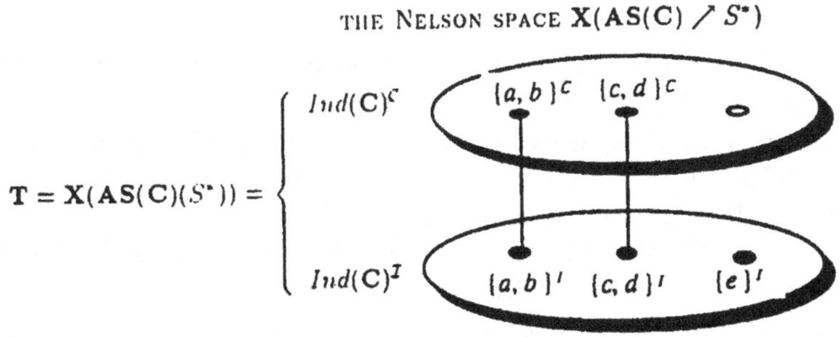

Fig. 14.

The resulting Nelson algebra $\mathbf{N}_{S^*}(\mathbf{HS}(\mathbf{AS}(\mathbf{C})))$ is presented in Fig. 14. It is worth noticing that the elements of the center of this algebra are characterized by the fact that they contain for any $\alpha_i^{\mathcal{C}}$ the corresponding $\mathcal{I}$-element $\alpha_i^{\mathcal{I}}$ (for instance, $\{\{a,b\}^{\mathcal{C}}, \{a,b\}^{\mathcal{I}}, \{e\}^{\mathcal{I}}\}$). This means that they are images of subsets of U that have no boundary in $\mathbf{AS}(\mathbf{C})$.

To end this subsection we sum-up the above discussion in the following

THE NELSON ALGEBRA $\mathbf{N}_{S^*}(\mathbf{HS}(\mathbf{AS}(\mathbf{C})))$

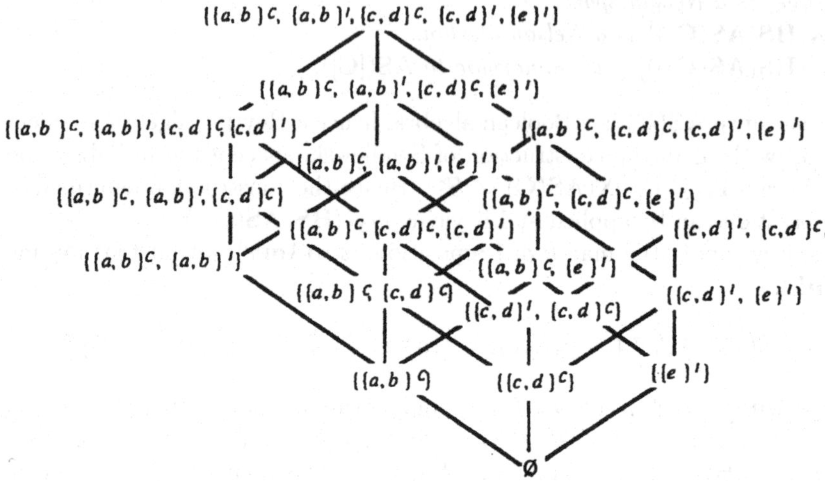

Fig. 15.

Proposition 74. *Let* $\mathbf{C}$ *be an Information System and* S^* *and* Θ^* *be defined as in Definitions 68 and 71. Let* $S = h^{-1}(S^*)$ *and let* Θ *be the congruence induced by* S *on* $\mathbf{AS}(\mathbf{C})$. *Then*

$$\mathbf{N}^K_{S^*}(\mathbf{HS}(\mathbf{AS}(\mathbf{C}))) = \mathbf{N}_{\Theta^*}(\mathbf{AS}([\mathbf{C}])) \cong_N \mathbf{N}_\Theta(\mathbf{AS}(\mathbf{C})) = \mathbf{N}(\mathbf{AS}(\mathbf{C})) \ .$$

We can now ask if there is a space $\mathbf{X}$ and a set S such that

3.13 $\mathbf{N}(\mathbf{AS}(\mathbf{C})) = \mathbf{N}^K_S(\mathbf{X})$.

In other words, we would like to get a deeper insight into the structure of $\mathbf{AS}(\mathbf{C})$ looking for a space X such that $\mathbf{AS}(\mathbf{C})$ itself is its dual algebra. Actually $\mathbf{AS}(\mathbf{C})$ is a topological space, subalgebra of $\mathbf{B}(U)$. If we analyse its specialization preorder (see Definition 14 in Subsection 2.3) we see that $a \ll b$ iff $b \ll a$ iff $a \in [b]_C$ (compare with Remark after Example 2).

We denote by $\mathbf{SP}$ the ordered set $\langle U, \ll \rangle$. Then it follows immediately that $\mathbf{AS}(\mathbf{C}) = \mathbf{H}(\mathbf{SP})$. Thus, a solution of the equation 3.13 above is $X = \mathbf{SP}$ and $S = \{x : \nexists y \neq x \text{ such that } x \ll y\}$.

Let us now consider two extreme cases:

Case 1: no elementary class from $Ind(\mathbf{C})$ is a singleton: $S^* = \emptyset$. Hence $h^{-1}(S^*) = S = \bigcup \emptyset = \emptyset$.

Case 2: every elementary class is a singleton: $S^* = Ind(\mathbf{C})$. Hence $h^{-1}(S^*) = S = \bigcup Ind(\mathbf{C}) = U$

From the point of view of the congruence induced by $\uparrow S$, we have:

Case 1: $\uparrow S = \uparrow \emptyset = \mathbf{AS}(\mathbf{C})$. This means that every element of $\mathbf{AS}(\mathbf{C})$ is trivially Θ-congruent with the top element U. Thereafter we get the set:

3.14 $\vec{N}(A) = \{\langle X_1, X_2 \rangle \in A^2 : X_1 \cap X_2 = \emptyset\}$.

Case 2: $\uparrow S = \uparrow U = U$. This means that the only element Θ-congruent with the top element U is U itself. We obtain the set:

3.15 $\overleftarrow{N}(A) = \{\langle X_1, X_2\rangle \in A^2 \colon X_1 \cap X_2 = \emptyset \textit{ and } X_1 \cup X_2 = U\}$.

Remark. In view of the discussion after Lemma 53 $\uparrow S$ is the filter of all and only the dense elements of $\mathbf{AS}(\mathbf{C})$ - in this case just the top element; hence we are making a filtration with respect to the classical tautologies. The following conclusions are then natural from a logical point of view.

It is clear that the constraint for forming the set $\overleftarrow{N}(A)$ yields the following

Lemma 75. *For any Approximation Space* $\mathbf{AS}(\mathbf{C})$, *for any* $\langle X_1, X_2\rangle \in A \times A$,

$$\langle X_1, X_2\rangle \in \overleftarrow{N}(A) \textit{ iff } X_2 = -X_1 \ .$$

In fact $X_1 \cup X_2 \Theta U$ iff $X_1 \cup X_2 = U$ and since $X_1 \cap X_2 = \emptyset$, X_1 must be the complement of X_2. Moreover, it is straightforward to prove the following lemma:

Lemma 76. *For any Approximation Space* $\mathbf{AS}(\mathbf{C})$, *for any congruence* Θ *on* $\mathbf{AS}(\mathbf{C})$, $\overleftarrow{\mathbf{N}}(\mathbf{AS}(\mathbf{C})) = \mathcal{CTR}(N_\Theta(\mathbf{AS}(\mathbf{C}))) \cong_N \mathbf{N}_\Theta(\mathbf{AS}(\mathbf{C}))/_\equiv \cong_B \mathbf{AS}(\mathbf{C})$.

Definition 77. Let $\mathbf{C} = \langle U, At, V, v\rangle$ be an Information System, and U^* a set of representatives of U/eq_v, then $\mathbf{C}^* = \langle U^*, At, V, v|U^*\rangle$ is said to be a *representation* of $\mathbf{C}$.

Lemma 78. *For any Information System* $\mathbf{C}$ *let* S^* *be defined as in Definition 68; then*

$$N_{S^*}(\mathbf{HS}(\mathbf{AS}(\mathbf{C}^*))) \cong_N \overleftarrow{\mathbf{N}}(\mathbf{AS}(\mathbf{C}^*)) \cong_N \mathbf{AS}(\mathbf{C}^*) \cong_B \mathbf{AS}(\mathbf{C}) \ .$$

Applying the above discussion we easily get a classic result on Approximation Spaces:

Proposition 79. (Corollary) *Let* $\mathbf{C}^*$ *be a representation of an Information System* $\mathbf{C}$, *then*

$$\mathbf{AS}(\mathbf{C}) \cong_B \mathbf{N}(\mathbf{AS}(\mathbf{C}^*)) \ .$$

The other related ways to get this result will be discussed in the next Sections.

So far we have established that $\overleftarrow{\mathbf{N}}$ and $\overrightarrow{\mathbf{N}}$ are two limit cases between which we find the general situations.

Remark. Notice that a representation $\mathbf{C}^*$ of an Information System $\mathbf{C}$ induces a T_0-ification of $\mathbf{AS}(\mathbf{C})$. In fact $\mathbf{AS}(\mathbf{C}^*)$ is a discrete topology on U^*. This is the topological content of the above Corollary. Continuing our discussion in the introduction of this Section, we can say that $\overleftarrow{\mathbf{N}}$ is related to the possibility of a cognitive agent to decide, for any object x, if x belongs to the extension of a concept, that is to a subset X of U.

In particular, the ability of reducing elementary categories in an Information System seems to be dependent on the cognitive agent's ability of exact classification (conceptualization) of any datum (of any set of cognitive objects). In the intermediate cases this could be expressed by saying that if $\alpha_i \in S^*$, then the information about α_i is strong enough to approximate sufficiently an exact classification: $\forall X \subseteq U$, α_i is either included in the positive part of $K(At)(X)$ or it is included in its negative part; thus, when $\bigcup S^* \subseteq X$ or $\bigcup S^* \subseteq -X$, we can also have the "special" cases $K(At)(X) = \langle M, \emptyset\rangle$ and $K(At)(X) = \langle \emptyset, M\rangle$ for some $M \supseteq S$ and respectively. In particular, we have $\langle S, \emptyset\rangle$ and $\langle \emptyset, S\rangle$. They are "limit elements" since $\uparrow \langle S, \emptyset\rangle = \{\langle X, \emptyset\rangle : X \in A\}$ and $\downarrow \langle \emptyset, S\rangle = \{\langle \emptyset, X\rangle : X \in A\}$

The logical interpretation of this fact is that the elementary classes that are singletons have a "Boolean behaviour". Finally, $\overrightarrow{\mathbf{N}}$ reflects the other extreme situation: no elementary category represents an exact classification, so every pair of disjoint elements of **AS(C)** must be taken into account in the Rough Set System $RS_r(\mathbf{C})$. If $S^* = \emptyset$, then we also have that $K(At)(X)$ may equal the "special" element $\langle \emptyset, \emptyset\rangle$, that represents from a logical point of view the intermediate value "unknown". Nelson algebras with such an element, that is the "center" (see example 8), are called *Special Nelson lattices* (see [Val]).

Observe that in our case a central element exists only if $S^* = \emptyset$. In other words, the value "unknown" is admissible only if no elementary class has a "Boolean behaviour" (see also the Remark after point 3.15). This, in turn, depends on the fact that no elementary class is given by a sharp, or exact, classification of the objects from U.

Post algebras of order three are the suitable framework for studying this particular case as we will see in Subsection 4.2.

3.5 Rough Set Systems as Heyting algebras

In what follows, given an Approximation Space **AS(C)**, by $a, b, \ldots, 1, 0$ we shall denote the ordered pairs, belonging to $N_\Theta(A)$, $\langle A_1, A_2\rangle$, $\langle B_1, B_2\rangle$, ..., $\langle U, \emptyset\rangle$ and $\langle \emptyset, U\rangle$, respectively (with A_1, A_2, B_1, B_2, U and $\emptyset$, belonging to $A \subseteq \mathbb{P}(U)$).

Let us note that neither the operation $\rightarrow$ nor $\Rightarrow$ fulfil the adjunction property of point 2 of Definition 21 for arbitrary $a, b \in RS_r(\mathbf{C})$. This can be interpreted by saying that $\rightarrow$ and $\Rightarrow$ are not defined by means of the lattice order $\leq$.

Example 12. Consider the Nelson algebra of example 10: $\langle\{e\}, \{a, b\}\rangle \rightarrow \langle\{a, b\}, \{c, d, e\}\rangle = \langle\{a, b, c, d\}, \{e\}\rangle$, but $\langle\{e\}, \{a, b\}\rangle \wedge \langle\{a, b, c, d\}, \{e\}\rangle = \langle\emptyset, \{a, b, e\}\rangle \not\leq \langle\{a, b\}, \{c, d, e\}\rangle$.

Similarly, $\langle\{e\}, \{a, b\}\rangle \rightarrow \langle\emptyset, \{a, b, c, d, e\}\rangle = \neg\langle\{e\}, \{a, b\}\rangle = \langle\{a, b, c, d\}, \{e\}\rangle$.

But $\langle\{e\}, \{a, b\}\rangle \wedge \langle\{a, b, c, d\}, \{e\}\rangle = \langle\emptyset, \{a, b, e\}\rangle \neq \langle\emptyset, \{a, b, c, d, e\}\rangle$.

Let us define an operation $\supset$ fulfilling the quoted adjunction property for any a, b belonging to $N_\Theta(A)$. That is: for all $c \in N_\Theta(A)$,

3.16 $a \wedge c \leq b$ *iff* $c \leq a \supset b$.

First, we show that searching for such an operation is not a hopeless effort.

Lemma 80. (EXISTENCE OF THE ELEMENT $a \supset b$)
For any Approximation Space $\mathbf{AS}(\mathbf{C})$, $\forall a, b \in RS_r(\mathbf{C})$, *the element* $a \supset b$ *is always defined.*

Proof. Since $(N_\Theta(A), \cap, \cup, 0, 1)$ is a distributive finite lattice, it follows from Proposition 23 that the relative pseudo-complementation is always defined. □

Since we established that the element $a \supset b$ is always defined, we can try to characterize it.

Proposition 81. (CHARACTERIZATION OF THE ELEMENT $a \supset b$)
For any Approximation Space $\mathbf{AS}(\mathbf{C})$, $\forall a, b \in RS_r(\mathbf{C})$:

$$a \supset b = (\neg a \wedge \neg \sim b) \vee \sim \neg \sim a \vee b \ .$$

Proof. In order to fulfil the adjunction property, $a \supset b$ must be an element $\langle C_1, C_2 \rangle$ such that

(a) C_2 is the $\subseteq$-least element X of A such that $X \cup A_2 \supseteq B_2$, while
(b) C_1 must be the $\subseteq$-greatest element Y of A such that $Y \cap A_1 \subseteq B_1$, and $X \cap Y = \emptyset$.

We claim that $C_2 = B_2 \cap -A_2$. In view of the first requirement, $B_2 \cap -A_2$ is the least element X such that $X \cup A_2 \supseteq B_2$. Now, in view of the disjunction condition and the requirement of maximality of C_1 , $B_2 \cap -A_2$ is the best solution for C_2. Now, the greatest element Y of A such that $Y \cap A_1 \subseteq B_1$ is $-A_1 \cup B_1$ but in order to get the condition of disjointedness we have to subtract C_2 from it obtaining $(-A_1 \cup B_1) \cap -(B_2 \cap -A_2)$. Let us then develop this Boolean polynomial:

$$\begin{aligned}(-A_1 \cup B_1) \cap -(B_2 \cap -A_2) &= (-A_1 \cup B_1) \cap (-B_2 \cup A_2)\\ &= (-A_1 \cap (-B_2 \cup A_2)) \cup (B_1 \cap (-B_2 \cup A_2))\\ &= (-A_1 \cap -B_2) \cup (-A_1 \cap A_2) \cup (B_1 \cap -B_2)\\ &\quad \cup (B_1 \cap A_2)\\ &= (-A_1 \cap -B_2) \cup A_2 \cup B_1 \cup (B_1 \cap A_2)\end{aligned}$$

but since $(A_2 \cup B_1) \supseteq (B_1 \cap A_2)$ the last expression reduces to $(-A_1 \cap -B_2) \cup A_2 \cup B_1$.

Hence, we have:

(*) $C_1 = (-A_1 \cap -B_2) \cup (A_2 \cup B_1)$;
(**) $C_2 = B_2 \cap -A_2$.

It follows that $\langle C_1, C_2 \rangle$ is the disjunction in $\mathbf{N}(\mathbf{AS}(\mathbf{C}))$ of two elements d and e such that $D_1 \cup E_1 = (-A_1 \cap -B_2) \cup (A_2 \cup B_1)$ and $D_2 \cap E_2 = B_2 \cap -A_2$. Again, d is the conjunction in $\mathbf{N}(\mathbf{AS}(\mathbf{C}))$ of two elements d' and d'' such that $D'_1 \cap D''_1 = -A_1 \cap -B_2$ and $(D'_2 \cup D''_2) \cap E_2 = D_2 \cap E_2 = B_2 \cap -A_2$, while

e is the disjunction of two elements e' and e'' such that $E_1' \cup E_1'' = A_2 \cup B_1$ and $(E_2' \cap E_2'') \cap (D_2' \cup D_2'') = (E_2' \cap E_2'') \cap D_2 = D_2 \cap E_2 = B_2 \cap -A_2$.
We are going to find a solution with minimal structural complexity.
We claim that $d' = \neg\langle A_1, A_2\rangle, d'' = \neg \sim \langle B_1, B_2\rangle$, $e' = \sim \neg \sim \langle A_1, A_2\rangle$ and $e'' = \langle B_1, B_2\rangle$.
On the one hand we have: $\neg\langle A_1, A_2\rangle \wedge \neg \sim \langle B_1, B_2\rangle = \langle -A_1, A_1\rangle \wedge \neg \sim \langle -B_2, B_2\rangle = \langle -A_1 \cap -B_2, A_1 \cup B_2\rangle$.
On the other hand: $\sim \neg \sim \langle A_1, A_2\rangle \vee \langle B_1, B_2\rangle = \langle A_2, -A_2\rangle \vee \langle B_1, B_2\rangle = \langle A_2 \cup B_1, B_2 \cap -A_2\rangle$.
But $\langle -A_1 \cap -B_2, A_1 \cup B_2\rangle \vee \langle A_2 \cup B_1, B_2 \cap -A_2\rangle$ equals
(***) $\langle(-A_1 \cap -B_2) \cup (A_2 \cup B_1), (A_1 \cup B_2) \cap (B_2 \cap -A_2)\rangle$.
Since $(A_1 \cup B_2) \geq B_2 \leq (B_2 \cap -A_2)$, we have $(A_1 \cup B_2) \cap (B_2 \cap -A_2) = (B_2 \cap -A_2)$.

Hence (***) becomes $\langle(-A_1 \cap -B_2) \cup (A_2 \cup B_1), B_2 \cap -A_2\rangle$ as required by (*) and (**). □

Proposition 82. (Corollary) *For any Approximation Space* **AS(C)**, $\forall a \in RS_r(\mathbf{C})$,

$$a \supset 0 = \sim \neg \sim a \ .$$

Definition 83. We shall denote the sequence $\sim \neg \sim$ by the symbol $\div$.

It follows from the above discussion that $\supset$ is the relative-pseudo complementation and $\div$ the pseudo complementation in the lattice $RS_r(\mathbf{C})$ *understood as* a Heyting algebra.

Now we shall show that the operation $\div$ has a central role in the algebraic analysis of Rough Set Systems. As a matter of fact in the following Section we shall study the role of the operations $\div$ and $\neg$ in characterizing definable sets, rough top and rough bottom equalities.

3.6 Negations, Projections and Definability in Rough Set Systems

In the following, given r and an element $a \in N_\Theta(A)$, if $a = r(X)$ for a uniquely determined $X \in \mathbb{P}(U)$, then by $r^{-1}(a)$ we shall denote X itself. Let us analyse more closely the algebraic properties of $\mathbf{N}(\mathbf{AS}(\mathbf{C}))$. First, some definitions are needed.

Definition 84. A distributive lattice $\mathbf{L} = (L, \vee, \wedge, ^+, 1, 0)$ is a *dual pseudo-complemented lattice* if $\forall x \in L$, $\exists x^+ \in L$ such that for any $y \in L$,

$$x \vee y = 1 \text{ iff } x^+ \leq y \ .$$

The element x^+ is termed *dual pseudo-complement* of x.

Definition 85. A distributive lattice $\mathbf{L}$ is a *double pseudo-complemented lattice* if it is both a pseudo-complemented and a dual pseudo-complemented lattice.

Definition 86. A pseudo-complemented lattice $\mathbf{L} = (L, \wedge, \vee, *, 0, 1)$ is a *Stone algebra* if $\forall x \in L$,

$$x^* \vee x^{**} = 1 \ .$$

Definition 87. A dual pseudo-complemented lattice $\mathbf{L} = (L, \wedge, \vee, ^+, 0, 1)$ is a *dual Stone algebra* if $\forall x \in L$,

$$x^+ \wedge x^{++} = 0 \ .$$

Definition 88. A distributive lattice $\mathbf{L}$ is a *double Stone algebra* if it is both a Stone and a dual Stone algebra.

Definition 89. A double Stone algebra L is *regular* if $\forall x, y \in L$, $x \wedge x^+ \leq y \vee y^*$.

We can recover in our setting a result stated in [PP1], [Iw2], and enhanced by Ivo Düntsch in chapter 5.

Proposition 90. *For any Approximation Space* $\mathbf{AS(C)}$, $\mathbf{N(AS(C))}$ *is a regular double Stone algebra with respect to the pseudo-complementation* $\div$, *and the dual pseudo-complementation* $\neg$.

Proof. We have seen that for any Approximation Space $\mathbf{AS(C)}\div$ is the pseudo-complementation in $\mathbf{N(AS(C))}$. Moreover, from the definition of $\div$, if $a \in \mathbf{N(AS(C))}$ then $\div \div a = \langle -A_2, A_2 \rangle$ and $\div a = \langle A_2, -A_2 \rangle$.

Thus $\div \div a \vee \div a = \langle -A_2 \cup A_2, A_2 \cap -A_2 \rangle = \langle U, \emptyset \rangle = 1$. Hence, $\mathbf{N(AS(C))}$ is a Stone algebra with respect to the operation $\div$.

In order to see that $\neg a$ is the dual pseudo-complementation of $\mathbf{N(AS(C))}$ it is sufficient to notice that $\neg a = \langle -A_1, A_1 \rangle$ and $\neg\neg a = \langle A_1, -A_1 \rangle$. Hence, $\neg$ fulfils the same properties with respect to the dual ordering of $\leq$ as $\div$ does with respect to the ordering $\leq$. □

The regularity condition comes from the definition of $\neg$ and $\sim$ (or, if we interpret $\mathbf{N(AS(C))}$ as a Łukasiewicz algebra, from cosiderations connected to the "determination principle" discussed, for instance, in [BFGR1]).

Definition 91. Let $\mathbf{P} = (P, \leq)$ be a partially ordered set and $g : P \longmapsto P$ an order preserving map, that is $\forall a, b \in P$, $a \leq b$ implies $g(a) \leq g(b)$; then,

1. g is a *projection operator* if $\forall a \in P$, $g(g(a)) = g(a)$;
2. g is a *closure operator* if g is a projection and $\forall a \in P$, $a \leq g(a)$;
3. g is a *kernel operator* if g is a projection and $\forall a \in P$, $g(a) \leq a$.

(Notice that the last two notions are generalizations of the topological ones - see definitions 15 and 16).

Lemma 92. *Consider the lattice* $\mathbf{N(AS(C))}$ *and the lattice ordering* $\leq$. *Then,*

1. *The operator* $\neg\neg$ *is an operator of kernel.*
2. *The operator* $\div\div$ *is an operator of closure.*

Proof. This is a standard result for double pseudo and dual pseudo-complementations (see [BD1]). However, we give here a proof based on our representation by ordered pairs.

1: if $a \leq b$ then $A_1 \subseteq B_1$ and $B_2 \subseteq A_2$. Hence $\neg\neg a \leq \neg\neg b$: in fact $\neg\neg a = \langle A_1, -A_1\rangle$ and $\neg\neg b = \langle B_1, -B_1\rangle$, therefore from the hypothesis it follows that $-B_1 \subseteq -A_1$. Moreover, by an easy verification we have that $\neg\neg\neg\neg a = \neg\neg a$. Thus, $\neg\neg$ is a projection. Finally, since $A_2 \subseteq -A_1$, we get that $\neg\neg a \leq a$.

2: A dual reasoning yields the second part of the proof. In fact it is sufficient to notice that since $\div\div a = \langle -A_2, A_2\rangle$ and $A_1 \subseteq -A_2$, then $a \leq \div\div a$. □

Now we are going to see how the above notions are related to the central concept of "definable subset" in Approximations Spaces.

Definition 93. We say that an element $a \in \mathbf{N}(\mathbf{AS}(\mathbf{C}))$ is *exact* iff $A_1 \cup A_2 = U$.

Lemma 94. *For any Approximation Space* $\mathbf{AS}(\mathbf{C})$, $\forall a \in RS_r(\mathbf{C})$,

1. *a is exact iff $a \vee \sim a = 1$;*
2. *$\div a$ is exact;*
3. *$\neg a$ is exact;*
4. *a is exact iff $\sim a$ is exact;*
5. *If a is exact then $r^{-1}(a)$ is a definable subset of U.*

Proof. 1-4: follow trivially from Definition 93 and the following equations (since $A_i \vee -A_i = U$ for $1 \leq i \leq 2$): $\div a = \sim\neg\sim\langle A_1, A_2\rangle = \langle A_2, -A_2\rangle; \neg\langle A_1, A_2\rangle = \langle -A_1, A_1\rangle$.

5: follows from 1. and point 6 of Definition 37. □

Proposition 95. *The set of all the exact elements of* $\mathbf{N}(\mathbf{AS}(\mathbf{C}))$ *is the center* $\mathcal{CTR}(\mathbf{N}(\mathbf{AS}(\mathbf{C})))$.

Proof. From Lemma 94, an element a of $\mathbf{N}(\mathbf{AS}(\mathbf{C}))$ is exact if $A_1 = -A_2$. It follows immediately that $\sim a \vee a = 1$ and $\sim a \wedge a = 0$. □

It is easy to see that if $a \in \mathcal{CTR}(\mathbf{N}(\mathbf{AS}(\mathbf{C})))$, then $\sim a = \neg a = \div a$.

Let us now define four equivalence relations by means of the operators $\div\div$ and $\neg\neg$ and the strong negation $\sim$.

Definition 96. For any Approximation Space $\mathbf{AS}(\mathbf{C})$, $\forall a, b \in RS_r(\mathbf{C})$,

1. By $[a]_{\eqsim}$ we denote the equivalence class of a modulo the relation: $a \eqsim b$ iff $\div\div a = \div\div b$.
2. By $[a]_{\simeq}$ we denote the equivalence class of a modulo the relation: $a \simeq b$ iff $\neg\neg a = \neg\neg b$.
3. By $[a]_{\sim\eqsim}$ we denote the equivalence class of a modulo the relation: $a \sim\eqsim b$ iff $\sim a \eqsim \sim b$.
4. By $[a]_{\sim\simeq}$ we denote the equivalence class of a modulo the relation: $a \sim\simeq b$ iff $\sim a \simeq \sim b$.

In the following Lemma, we present the operators constructed by means of various complementations. In fact, what we want to show are the relationships between the two operators $(\div\div)$ and $(\neg\neg)$ and how pushing the strong negation $\sim$ in innermost or outermost positions transforms one operator into the other. Observe the analogy with the properties of the set theoretic complement "$-$" of mutually changing the closure operator $\mathcal{C}$ and the interior operator $\mathcal{I}$ in a topological space. This analogy is not accidental; on the contrary, we will see in the next Subsection that $(\div\div)$ and $(\neg\neg)$ are related to the closure and interior operator, respectively, induced by an Approximation Space $\mathbf{AS}(\mathbf{C})$ *understood as* a topological space on U. We will exploit this relationship in order to get the characterization of rough top and rough bottom equalities.

Lemma 97. *For any Approximation Space* $\mathbf{AS}(\mathbf{C})$, $\forall a \in RS_{\Gamma}(\mathbf{C})$,

1. $a = b$ *iff* $\sim a = \sim b$.
2. $\sim(\div)a = (\neg)\sim a = \div\div a$.
3. $\sim(\neg)a = (\div)\sim a = \neg\neg a$.
4. $\sim(\div\div)a = (\neg\neg)\sim a = \div a$.
5. $\sim(\neg\neg)a = (\div\div)\sim a = \neg a$.
6. $a \simeq b$ *iff* $\neg a = \neg b$.
7. $a \eqsim b$ *iff* $\div a = \div b$.
8. $a \eqsim b$ *iff* $a \sim\simeq b$.
9. $a \simeq b$ *iff* $a \sim\eqsim b$.
10. $\div\div a$ *is the greatest element of* $\mathbf{N}(\mathbf{AS}(\mathbf{C}))$ *in the class* $[a]_{\eqsim}$.
11. $\neg\neg a$ *is the least element of* $\mathbf{N}(\mathbf{AS}(\mathbf{C}))$ *in the class* $[a]_{\simeq}$.
12. $a \simeq b$ *iff* $a \to b = b \to a = 1$.
13. $a \eqsim b$ *iff* $\sim a \to\sim b = \sim b \to\sim a = 1$.

Proof. 1: trivially from Lemma 46;

2-5: by easy calculation.

6: $a \simeq b$ iff $\neg\neg a = \neg\neg b$ (by Definition 96.2) iff $\sim\neg\neg a = \sim\neg\neg b$ (by 1.) iff $\neg a = \neg b$ (from 5).

7: Similar.

8: $a \eqsim b$ iff $\div a = \div b$ (from 7.) iff $\sim\div a = \sim\div b$ (from 1.) iff $\neg\sim a = \neg\sim b$ (by 1.) iff $\sim a \simeq \sim b$ (from 5.) iff $a \sim\simeq b$ (by 4).

9: Similar.

10: trivial from the shape of $\div\div a$ and the definition of the ordering $\leq$.

11: Similar.

12: $a \simeq b$ iff $\neg\neg a = \neg\neg b$ iff $\langle A_1, -A_1\rangle = \langle B_1, -B_1\rangle$ iff $A_1 = B_1$ (iff $-A_1 = -B_1$).

13: Similar. □

Proposition 98. *For any Approximation Space* $\mathbf{AS}(\mathbf{C})$, $\forall X \subseteq U$ *such that* $r(X) = a$ *for* $a \in RS_{\Gamma}(\mathbf{C})$,

1. $r^{-1}(\neg a)$ *is the greatest definable set* Y *such that* $\mathcal{I}(X) \cap Y = \emptyset$.
2. $r^{-1}(\neg\neg a)$ *is the greatest definable set* Y *such that* $Y \subseteq X$.

3. $r^{-1}(\div a)$ *is the greatest definable set* Y *such that* $\mathcal{C}(X) \cap Y = \emptyset$.
4. $r^{-1}(\div\div a)$ *is the least definable set* Y *such that* $X \subseteq Y$.

Proof. 1: by Lemma 94.3, $\neg a$ is an exact element of $\mathbf{N}(\mathbf{AS}(\mathbf{C}))$.
Moreover, $\neg a = \langle -\mathcal{I}(X), \mathcal{I}(X)\rangle$. Hence if $Y = r^{-1}(\neg a)$ then $\mathcal{I}(Y) = -\mathcal{I}(X)$. But from Lemma 94.5, Y is definable, thus $Y = \mathcal{I}(Y) = -\mathcal{I}(X)$.

2: by 94.3, $\neg\neg a$ is an exact element in $\mathbf{N}(\mathbf{AS}(\mathbf{C}))$. By points 10 and 11 of Lemma 97, $r^{-1}(\neg\neg a)$ is a subset Y such that $\mathcal{I}(X) = \mathcal{I}(Y)$. Since Y is definable, we have $\mathcal{I}(X) = \mathcal{I}(Y) = Y$ and the result follows immediately.

3: by 94.2, $\div a$ is an exact element in $\mathbf{N}(\mathbf{AS}(\mathbf{C}))$. $\div a = \langle \mathcal{E}(X), \mathcal{C}(X)\rangle$. It follows that if $Y = r^{-1}(\div a)$ then $\mathcal{I}(Y) = \mathcal{E}(X) = -\mathcal{C}(X)$. Since Y is definable, $\mathcal{I}(Y) = -\mathcal{C}(X)$.

4: from points 9 and 12 of Lemma 97, $r^{-1}(\div\div a)$ is a subset Y such that $-\mathcal{C}(X) = -\mathcal{C}(Y)$. Then $\mathcal{C}(X) = \mathcal{C}(Y)$ and since Y is definable, from 94.5 we have $\mathcal{C}(X) = \mathcal{C}(Y) = Y$ and the result follows. □

Proposition 99. (Corollary) *For any Approximation Space* $\mathbf{AS}(\mathbf{C})$, $\forall X \subseteq U$,

1. $r(\mathcal{I}(X)) = \sim\neg r(X)$;
2. $r(\mathcal{C}(X)) = \neg\sim r(X)$;
3. $r^{-1}(\sim\neg r(X)) = \mathcal{I}(X)$;
4. $r^{-1}(\neg\sim r(X)) = \mathcal{C}(X)$;

It is worth noticing the duality of the pairs $\langle \eqsim, \sim\eqsim\rangle$ and $\langle \simeq, \sim\simeq\rangle$ in terms of closure/interior and in the pair $\langle \eqsim, \simeq\rangle$ in terms of greatest/least. This duality reflects faithfully, from an algebraic point of view, the duality expressed in [NP2].

Thus, the two operators "$\div\div$" and "$\neg\neg$" project (both intuitively and algebraically) any rough set x onto a specific exact element, representing a definable set.

Observe the similarity between these operators of projection and the analogous notions that one can find in the semantical investigations of *Quantum Logic*. More precisely, we think that a comparison between our approach and Brouwer-Zadeh Lattices introduced in [CN1] (see also [Gi1]) may be of interest both for Quantum Logic and Rough Set Theory.

Now in order to show how it is possible to apply the present algebraic interpretation to analysing the general properties of Rough Set Systems, let us study some mechanisms and features related to rough top and rough bottom equalities, (see [Pa2]).

3.7 Nelson algebra operations and Rough Set operations

Now we want to see how the operations of Nelson algebras act on rough sets. First, let us define the map:

Definition 100. For any Approximation Space $\mathbf{AS}(\mathbf{C})$,

$$k^3 : RS_{\Gamma}(\mathbf{C}) \longmapsto A \times A : k^3(\langle A_1, A_2\rangle) = \langle A_1, -A_2\rangle \ .$$

Lemma 101. $\mathbf{Im}k^3$ *is the Rough Approximation Space of [Iw1] discussed in the Introduction.*

Proof. From 57 and the definition of k^3, $\mathbf{Im}k^3 = \{\langle \mathcal{I}(X), \mathcal{C}(X)\rangle : X \subseteq U\}$.

We denote the elements of $\mathbf{Im}k^3$ by pairs of the form $a^* = \langle A_1^*, A_2^*\rangle$. The following algebraic structure (see [PP1]) has been defined on $\mathbf{Im}k^3$:

Definition 102.

1. $\mathbf{RAS}(\mathbf{C}) = (\mathbf{Im}k^3, \wedge, \vee, \langle \emptyset, \emptyset\rangle, \langle U, U\rangle)$, where $\forall a^*, b^* \in \mathbf{Im}k^3$:
2. $\langle A_1^*, A_2^*\rangle \wedge \langle B_1^*, B_2^*\rangle = \langle A_1^* \cap B_1^*, A_2^* \cap B_2^*\rangle$;
3. $\langle A_1^*, A_2^*\rangle \vee \langle B_1^*, B_2^*\rangle = \langle A_1^* \cup B_1^*, A_2^* \cup B_2^*\rangle$.

$\mathbf{RAS}(\mathbf{C})$ is a complete lattice and it is immediate that it is isomorphic to the same fragment of $\mathbf{N}(\mathbf{AS}(\mathbf{C}))$. Thus, in the latter structure $\vee$ and $\wedge$ relate to rough sets in the same manner as $\vee$ and $\wedge$ in $\mathbf{RAS}(\mathbf{C})$. □

As for the disjunction, we can just say that $r(X) \vee r(Y) = r(Z)$ for $Z \in \mathbf{min}(\{X' \vee Y' : X' \in [X]_{\approx}$ and $Y' \in [Y]_{\approx}\})$. A dual condition holds for $\wedge$.

Things are more uniform when we deal with complements. As a matter of facts, on $\mathbf{Im}k^3$ the following kinds of complements are definable (see [PP1]):

3.17 *For any* $\langle A_1^*, A_2^*\rangle \in \mathbf{Im}k^3$*:*

1. $\overline{r}\langle A_1^*, A_2^*\rangle =_{def} \langle -A_2^*, -A_1^*\rangle$ *(*rough complement*);*
2. $\overline{i}\langle A_1^*, A_2^*\rangle =_{def} \langle -A_1^*, -A_1^*\rangle$ *(*internal complement*);*
3. $\overline{p}\langle A_1^*, A_2^*\rangle =_{def} \langle -A_2^*, -A_2^*\rangle$ *(*pseudo-complement*).*

Now we immediately see that:

Lemma 103. *For any Approximation Space* $\mathbf{AS}(\mathbf{C})$,

1. $(k^3)^{-1}(\overline{r}\langle A_1^*, A_2^*\rangle) = (k^3)^{-1}(\langle -A_2^*, -A_1^*\rangle) = \langle A_2, A_1\rangle =\sim (k^3)^{-1}(\langle A_1^*, A_2^*\rangle)$;
2. $(k^3)^{-1}(\overline{i}\langle A_1^*, A_2^*\rangle) = (k^3)^{-1}(\langle -A_1^*, -A_1^*\rangle) = \langle -A_1, A_1\rangle = \neg(k^3)^{-1}(\langle A_1^*, A_2^*\rangle)$;
3. $\overline{rir}\langle A_1^*, A_2^*\rangle = \overline{ri}\langle -A_2^*, -A_1^*\rangle = \overline{r}\langle A_2^*, A_2^*\rangle = \langle -A_2^*, -A_2^*\rangle = \overline{p}\langle A_1^*, A_2^*\rangle$.

Proof. Since $RS_r(\mathbf{C}) = N_{\Theta}(A)$ for some congruence Θ, and since $\mathbf{AS}(\mathbf{C})$ is a Boolean algebra, the set-theoretic complement "$-$" coincides with its pseudo-complementation. □

From the above results we have the following Lemma for which we give also a direct proof:

Lemma 104. $(k^3)^{-1}(\overline{p}\langle A_1^*, A_2^*\rangle) = \div(k^3)^{-1}(\langle A_1^*, A_2^*\rangle)$

Proof. $(k^3)^{-1}(\overline{p}\langle A_1^*, A_2^*\rangle) = (k^3)^{-1}(\langle -A_2^*, -A_2^*\rangle) = (k^3)^{-1}(\langle A_2, A_2\rangle) = \langle A_2, -A_2\rangle = \div\langle A_1, A_2\rangle = \div(k^3)^{-1}(\langle A_1^*, A_2^*\rangle)$. □

3.8 Applications

Now we propose two applications of the logic-algebraic intrepretations introduced in this Section. The first deals with a typical mathematical problem in the theory of Rough Sets itself, while the second is concerned with an application of Rough Set Theory to Machine Learning.

First, let us see how the logic-algebraic operators studied so far provide a method for recognizing if two subsets of U are rough top equal or rough bottom equal.

Proposition 105. (LOGIC-ALGEBRAIC CHARACTERIZATION OF ROUGH TOP EQUALITY)

For any Approximation Space $\mathbf{AS}(\mathbf{C})$ *on a universe* $U : \forall X, Y \subseteq U$ *, the following statements are equivalent:*

1. $X \overline{\simeq} Y$.
2. $\div\div r(X) = \div\div r(Y)$.
3. $\neg\div r(X) = \neg\div r(Y)$.
4. $\neg\sim r(X) = \neg\sim r(Y)$.
5. $\sim\div r(X) = \sim\div r(Y)$.
6. $\div r(X) = \div r(Y)$.

Proposition 106. (LOGIC-ALGEBRAIC CHARACTERIZATION OF ROUGH BOTTOM EQUALITY)

For any Approximation Space $\mathbf{AS}(\mathbf{C})$ *on a universe* $U : \forall X, Y \subseteq U$ *the following statements are equivalent:*

1. $X \simeq Y$.
2. $\neg\neg r(X) = \neg\neg r(Y)$.
3. $\sim\neg r(X) = \sim\neg r(Y)$.
4. $\neg r(X) = \neg r(Y)$.

Now we shall derive from the above results the well-known properties of rough top and rough bottom equalities (see [NP2], [NP3]). The reader is also referred to chapter 7 of this volume. The problem is how to recognize that an equivalence relation of $\mathbb{P}(U)$ is a rough top equality, a rough bottom equality or none of them.

Lemma 107. *For any Approximation Space* $\mathbf{AS}(\mathbf{C})$ *on an universe* U*:*

1. $\div\div r$ *is a* $0-1$ *homomorphism from the semilattice* $(\mathbb{P}(U), \cup)$ *to the semilattice* $(RS_\Gamma(\mathbf{C}), \vee)$.
2. $\neg\neg r$ *is a* $0-1$ *homomorphism from the semilattice* $(\mathbb{P}(U), \cap)$ *to the semilattice* $(RS_\Gamma(\mathbf{C}), \wedge)$.

Proof. **(1)** **(a)** $\div\div r(\emptyset) = \div\div\langle\emptyset, U\rangle = \langle\emptyset, U\rangle$;
(b) $\div\div r(U) = \div\div\langle U, \emptyset\rangle = \langle U, \emptyset\rangle$;

(c) $\div\div r(X \cup Y) = \div\div\langle \mathcal{I}(X \cup Y), -\mathcal{C}(X \cup Y)\rangle = \langle \mathcal{C}(X \cup Y), -\mathcal{C}(X \cup Y)\rangle = \langle \mathcal{C}(X) \cup \mathcal{C}(Y), -\mathcal{C}(X) \cap -\mathcal{C}(Y)\rangle = \langle \mathcal{C}(X), -\mathcal{C}(X)\rangle \vee \langle \mathcal{C}(Y), -\mathcal{C}(Y)\rangle = \div\div\langle \mathcal{I}(X), -\mathcal{C}(X)\rangle \vee \div\div\langle \mathcal{I}(Y), -\mathcal{C}(Y)\rangle = \div\div r(X) \vee \div\div r(Y)$.

(2) by dual reasoning.

□

Lemma 108. *For any Approximation Space* $\mathbf{AS}(\mathbf{C})$ *on a universe* U*:*

1. $\forall X, Y \in \mathbb{P}(U)$, *if* $X \subseteq Y$ *then* $r(X) \leq r(Y)$ *in* $\mathbf{N}(\mathbf{AS}(\mathbf{C}))$.
2. $\forall a, b \in \mathbf{N}(\mathbf{AS}(\mathbf{C}))$, *if* b *is exact and* $a \leq b$, *then* $r^{-1}(a) \leq r^{-1}(b)$.

Proof. **(1)** immediate from the definition of r (or from the above Lemma and Lemma 46.4).

(2) Let $a = r(X), b = r(Y)$. If $a \leq b$ then $\mathcal{I}(X) \subseteq \mathcal{I}(Y)$ and $-\mathcal{C}(Y) \subseteq -\mathcal{C}(X)$; thus $\mathcal{C}(X) \subseteq \mathcal{C}(Y)$. Either $\mathcal{I}(X) \subset X \subset \mathcal{C}(X)$ or X is definable: $\mathcal{I}(X) = X = \mathcal{C}(X)$. In both cases $X \subseteq \mathcal{C}(Y)$ and since Y is definable, we get $X \subseteq \mathcal{C}(Y) = Y$.

□

Lemma 109. *For any Approximation Space* $\mathbf{AS}(\mathbf{C})$ *on a universe* U*, the mapping:*

$$r^{-1} \div \div r : \mathbb{P}(U) \longmapsto \mathbb{P}(U)$$

(equivalently, $r^{-1}\neg\div r$ *or* $r^{-1}\neg \sim r$ *or* $r^{-1} \sim \div r$*) is a topological closure operator on* $\mathbb{P}(U)$.

Proof. The algebraic proof is the following: from Lemma 92.2, $\div\div$ is a closure operator in $\mathbf{N}(\mathbf{AS}(\mathbf{C}))$. Moreover, since $\div\div x$ is exact for all $x \in RS_{\Gamma}(\mathbf{C})$, in view of the above Lemma we have that $r^{-1} \div \div r$ is a closure operator on $(\mathbb{P}(U), \subseteq)$.

From Lemma 107.1, $r^{-1} \div \div r$ is also topological (alternatively, Corollary 99 says that $r^{-1} \div \div r$ – in the form $r^{-1}\neg \sim r$ – coincides with the closure operator of $\mathbf{AS}(\mathbf{C})$). □

Lemma 110. *For any Approximation Space* $\mathbf{AS}(\mathbf{C})$ *on a universe* U *the mapping*

$$r^{-1}\neg\neg r : \mathbb{P}(U) \longmapsto \mathbb{P}(U)$$

(equivalently, $r^{-1} \sim \neg r$ *or* $r^{-1}\neg \div r$*) is a topological interior operator on* $\mathbb{P}(U)$.

Proof. From Lemma 92.1, $\neg\neg$ is an interior operator in $\mathbf{N}(\mathbf{AS}(\mathbf{C}))$. Thus from Lemma 107.2 we get the result (again Corollary 99 says that $r^{-1}\neg\neg r$ -in the form $r^{-1} \sim \neg r$ – coincides with the interior operator of $\mathbf{AS}(\mathbf{C})$). □

The above results must not be confused with the following interesting properties of $\div\div$ and $\neg\neg$.

Lemma 111. $\div\div$ *and* $\neg\neg$ *are endomorphisms in the lattice* $\mathbf{N}(\mathbf{AS}(\mathbf{C}))$*:*

1. $\div\div$ *distributes over* $\vee$;

2. $\div\div$ *distributes over* $\wedge$;
3. $\neg\neg$ *distributes over* $\vee$;
4. $\neg\neg$ *distributes over* $\wedge$.

Proof. (1) we have to prove that $\div\div(a \vee b) = \div\div a \vee \div\div b$: $\div\div(a \vee b) = \langle -(A_2 \cap B_2), A_2 \cap B_2 \rangle = \langle -A_2 \cup -B_2, A_2 \cap B_2 \rangle = \langle -A_2, A_2 \rangle \vee \langle -B_2, B_2 \rangle$.
(2) similar;
(3) from 2 and the duality principle of the proof of Lemma 108.
(4) from 1 and the duality principle of the proof of Lemma 108.
(Notice that (2) and (3) are standard results for double pseudo-complementations and dual pseudo-complementations, while (1) and (4) are characteristic for double Stone algebras (see [BD1]). Here we showed how these facts are proved within our specific representation). □

Proposition 112. *Let* **AS**(**C**) *be an Approximation Space on a universe* U. *Then,*

1. *the equivalence relation* $\approx$ *on* $\mathbb{P}(U)$ *is a congruence on the semilattice* $(\mathbb{P}(U), \cup)$;
2. *the equivalence relation* $\simeq$ *on* $\mathbb{P}(U)$ *is a congruence on the semilattice* $(\mathbb{P}(U), \cap)$.

Proof. Consider the pre-images $\Gamma(a) = (\div\div r)^{-1}(a)$ and $\Delta(a) = (\neg\neg r)^{-1}(a)$ of the homomorphisms $\div\div r$ and $\neg\neg r$ of Lemma 107. $\Gamma(a), \Delta(a) \subseteq \mathbb{P}(U)$ and they differ from $\emptyset$ iff a is an exact element in $\mathbf{N}(\mathbf{AS}(\mathbf{C}))$. By standard results in lattice theory we have that for any $a \in RS_{\Gamma}(\mathbf{C})$, $\Gamma(a)$ is a congruence class with respect to the operation $\cup$ and $\Delta(a)$ is a congruence class with respect to the operation $\cap$. □

Thus, the first requirement for an equivalence relation R on $\mathbb{P}(U)$ to be a rough top (resp. rough bottom) equality is being a $\cup$-semilattice congruence (resp. a $\cap$-semilattice congruence).

This is not sufficient, as the following example from Novotný's paper illustrates:

Example 13. Consider a universe $U = \{a, b, c\}$. In the diagram of the Fig. 16 elements linked by a double arrow belong to the same equivalence class of a relation R on the powerset $\mathbb{P}(U)$

One can verify that R is indeed an $\cup$-congruence. Nevertheless, if the subsets $\{b\}$ and $\{a, b\}$ had the same upper approximation, namely $\{a, b\}$, then $a \in C(\{b\})$. But any element of **AS**(**C**) is clopen, thus $b \in C(\{a\})$. It would follow that $\{a, b\}$ is also the upper approximation of $\{a\}$. But $\{a\}$ is not R-congruent to $\{a, b\}$.

If K is a congruence relation on the semilattice $(\mathbb{P}(U), \cup)$ (on the semilattice $(\mathbb{P}(U), \cap)$), then by $C^{\cup}(K)$ we shall understand the set $\{\bigcup X : X \in K\}$ (by $C^{\cap}(K)$ we shall understand the set $\{\bigcap X : X \in K\}$). As a matter of facts, there is another characteristic property of rough top (rough bottom) equalities linked to these notions. We recall it briefly (see [NP2] and chapter 7):

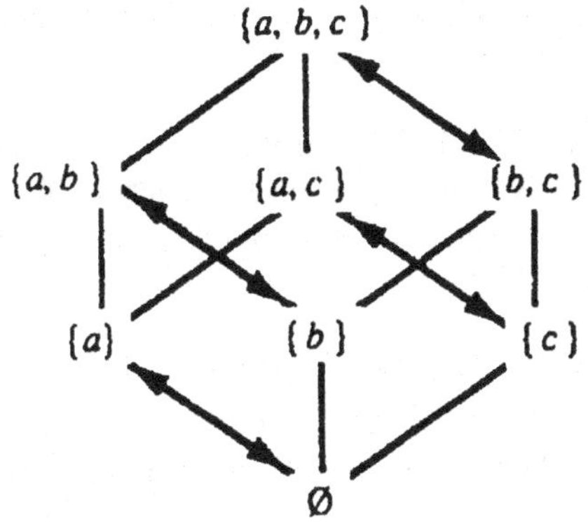

Fig. 16.

Proposition 113. *The following are equivalent statements for a congruence relation K on the semilattice $(\mathbb{P}(U), \cup)$ (on the semilattice $(\mathbb{P}(U), \cap)$):*

(i) *K is a rough top equality (is a rough bottom equality);*
(ii) *$(C^{\cup}(K), \cap, \cup, -, \emptyset, U)$ $((C^{\cap}(K), \cap, \cup, -, \emptyset, U))$ is a (Boolean) subalgebra of* $\mathbf{B}(U)$.

It can immediately be seen that the $\cup$-semilattice congruence in the preceding example fails to be a rough top equality because it lacks this property.

The last part of the Section is devoted to recovering the proof of the characteristic property stated in the Proposition above by pure algebraic arguments, exploiting the algebraic features of our logic-algebraic interpretation. At this aim we report the following result from Subsection 3.1:

Lemma 114. *Let $\mathbf{H}$ be a Heyting algebra, Θ a Boolean congruence on it and $\mathbf{N}_{\Theta}(\mathbf{H})$ be a Nelson algebra of ordered pairs of disjoint elements of $\mathbf{H}$. Let $\equiv$ be the equivalence relation on $\mathbf{N}_{\Theta}(\mathbf{H})$ defined in point 5 of Lemma 46. Then the quotient structure*

$$\mathbf{N}_{\Theta}(\mathbf{H})/_{\equiv} = (\{[x]_{\equiv} : x \in N_{\Theta}(H)\}, \vee, \wedge, \longrightarrow, \neg, 0, 1)$$

is a Heyting algebra, isomorphic to $\mathbf{H}$.

Proposition 115. *Let $\mathbf{AS}(\mathbf{C})$ be an Approximation Space on a universe U.
Let us set $G(A) = \{r^{-1}\neg\neg r(X) : X \in \mathbb{P}(U)\}$.
Then $\mathbf{G}(A) = (G(A), \cap, \cup, -, \emptyset, U)$ is a (Boolean) subalgebra of $\mathbf{B}(U)$.*

Proof. Since $\mathbf{N}(\mathbf{AS}(\mathbf{C}))$ is a Nelson algebra, we can define on it the equivalence relation $\equiv$. Hence, from the preceding Lemma we find that the quotient structure $\mathbf{N}(\mathbf{AS}(\mathbf{C}))/_{\equiv}$ is a Boolean algebra isomorphic to $\mathbf{AS}(\mathbf{C})$. Since by Lemma 97.12 $a \equiv b$ iff $a \simeq b$, from Lemma 97.11 we find immediately: $a \equiv b$ iff $\neg\neg a = \neg\neg b$. Thus we can take $\neg\neg a$ as the representative of $[a]_{\equiv}$.

Hence $\mathbf{N}(\mathbf{AS}(\mathbf{C}))/_{\equiv} \cong \mathbf{G}(\mathbf{A})) \cong \mathbf{AS}(\mathbf{C})$. Moreover, considering the pre-image $r^{-1}\neg\neg a$ we find that $\mathbf{G}(\mathbf{A})$ is $\mathbf{AS}(\mathbf{C})$ itself. □

We can get the same result by considering that since $C = \{\neg\neg x : x \in RS_r(\mathbf{C})\}$ is the centre of $\mathbf{N}(\mathbf{AS}(\mathbf{C}))$ (from Proposition 95 and Lemma 94), then r maps bijectively A on C (from a different point of view, we can consider $r^{-1}\neg\neg r$ as a retraction of A in $\mathbb{P}(U)$).

Proposition 116. *Let* $\mathbf{AS}(\mathbf{C})$ *be an Approximation Space on a universe* U.
Let us denote by $F(A) = \{r^{-1} \div \div r(X) : X \in \mathbb{P}(U)\}$.
Then $\mathbf{F}(A) = (F(A), \cup, \cap, -, \emptyset, U)$ *is a (Boolean) subalgebra of* $\mathbf{B}(U)$.

Proof. Consider the following equivalence: $a \sim\equiv b$ iff $\sim a \rightarrow\sim b \wedge \sim b \rightarrow\sim a = 1$. Since by Lemma 97.13 $a \sim\equiv b$ iff $a \approx b$, from Lemma 97.10 we find that $a \sim\equiv b$ iff $\div\div a = \div\div b$.

So we can use the equivalence relation $\sim\equiv$ instead of $\equiv$ and repeat the same reasoning of the preceding Lemma. □

With a proof analogous to that of [NP2] we can obtain the reverse implications. Noticing that in view of Proposition 112 $G(A) = C^{\cup}(\cong)$ and $F(A) = C^{\cap}(\cong)$, we have the well-known characterization of rough top equalities and rough bottom equalities stated in the aforementioned paper.

Example 14. Let us consider the Approximation Space $\mathbf{AS}(\mathbf{C})$ on the universe U of example 13, with the following family of elementary classes: $\{\{c\}, \{a, b\}\}$. Fig. 17 shows the Rough Set Systems $\mathbf{N}(\mathbf{AS}(\mathbf{C}))$, the rough set application r and the application of the operator $\neg\neg$. It is easy to see, for instance, that pulling back $\neg\neg r(\langle\{c\}, \{a, b\}\rangle)$ we obtain $\{\{c\}, \{a, c\}, \{b, c\}\}$ that is a $\cap$-sublattice of $\mathbf{B}(U)$. $r^{-1}(\langle\{c\}, \{a, b\}\rangle) = \{c\} = \bigcap(\neg\neg r)^{-1}(\langle\{c\}, \{a, b\}\rangle)$.

In order to sketch the second application, let us now notice that Proposition 64 tells us what we get when we add or delete objects from an Information System $\mathbf{C}$. In fact, using Proposition 64, we can algebraically treat the case of an unreliable teacher within a learning by examples application of Approximation Spaces (see [Ku1]): if we add one example to an Information System $\mathbf{C}$ such that $RS_r(\mathbf{C}) = N_{\Theta}(A)$ for Θ induced by $k^{-1}(S^*) = \bigcup S^*$, $S^* \subseteq Ind(\mathbf{C})$, then we have the map *add* defined in the following way:

3.18 $add(\mathbf{N}(\mathbf{AS}(\mathbf{C}))) = \mathbf{N}(\mathbf{AS}(\mathbf{C}^+) = \mathbf{N}_{\Theta_+}(\mathbf{AS}(\mathbf{C}^+))$ *where*

1. *if we have a new elementary set* α:
   (a) $Ind(\mathbf{C}^+) = Ind(\mathbf{C}) \cup \alpha$;
   (b) Θ_+ *is induced by* $k^{-1}(S^*) \cup \alpha$.
2. *if some* $\alpha \in S$ *increases its cardinality:*
   (a) $Ind(\mathbf{C}^+) = Ind(\mathbf{C})$;
   (b) Θ_+ *is induced by* $k^{-1}(S^*) \cap -\alpha$.
3. *We have no changes, otherwise*

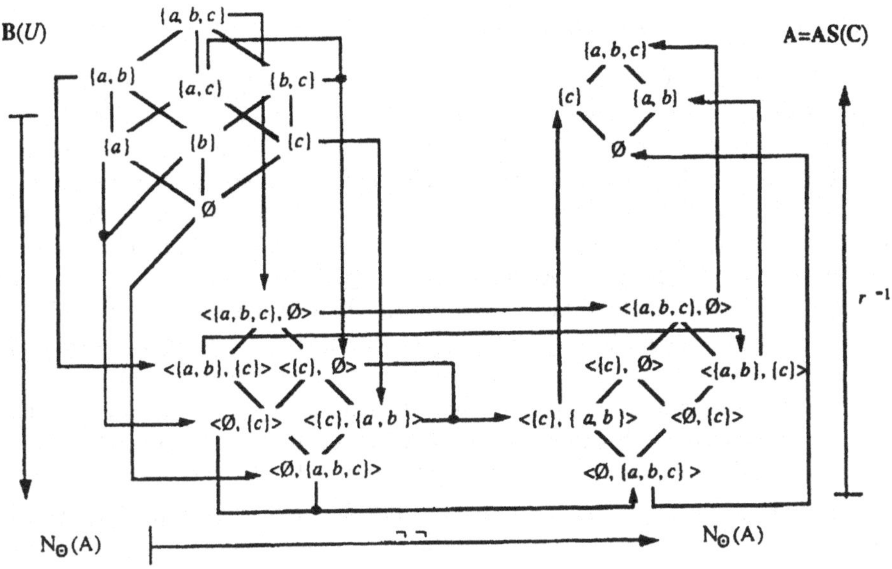

Fig. 17.

If we delete one example, we have the map *del*:

3.19 $del(\mathbf{N}(\mathbf{AS}(\mathbf{C}))) = \mathbf{N}(\mathbf{AS}(\mathbf{C}^-)) = \mathbf{N}_{\Theta_-}(\mathbf{AS}(\mathbf{C}^-))$ *defined dually: either*

1. *we lose an elementary set* α, *or*
2. *now* $card(a) = 1$ *for some* $\alpha \in S^*$.

4 Rough Sets and Multiple-Valued Logics

Motivations and plan

Let us now consider the ordering induced by the Nelson lattice structure of the Rough Set System $RS_r(\mathbf{C})$. We have that $\forall X, Y \subseteq U, r(X) \leq r(Y)$ iff $\mathcal{I}(X) \subseteq \mathcal{I}(Y)$ and $\mathcal{E}(Y) \subseteq \mathcal{E}(X)$.

Notice that we can have X and Y such that $\mathcal{I}(X) \subset \mathcal{I}(Y)$ but $\mathcal{E}(Y) \not\subseteq \mathcal{E}(X)$ or even $\mathcal{E}(Y) \parallel \mathcal{E}(X)$.

Nevertheless, we have $\forall X, Y \subseteq U$:

4.1

$$\textit{if } X \subseteq Y \textit{ then } r(X) \leq r(Y) \ .$$

Then we have the following $\leq$-limit possibilities in the evaluation of $X \subseteq U$ via function r:

1. $\top = \langle \mathcal{I}(X) = U, \mathcal{E}(X) = \emptyset \rangle$;
2. $\delta = \langle \mathcal{I}(X) = \emptyset, \mathcal{E}(X) = \emptyset \rangle$;

3. $\bot = \langle \mathcal{I}(X) = \emptyset, \mathcal{E}(X) = U \rangle$.

Thus, since for any X we have $\bot \leq r(X) \leq \top$, **Imr** is likely to be a model for a three valued logic (see [MP1] for an early approach in this direction. For a more general discussion observe that De Morgan lattices fulfilling the regularity property of axiom 4 of Definition 42, enjoy the 3-valued homomorphism separation property). In any case, we have seen in the REMARK after Lemma 78 that the possibility for a pair $\langle X_1, X_2 \rangle$ to have the empty set as one of the elements is *sub judice*: $X_i = \emptyset$ only if $S \subseteq X_j$ for $1 \leq i \neq j \leq 2$.

So if $S \neq \emptyset$ we cannot have a real intermediate value between $\top$ and $\bot$. Actually, in three-valued Łukasiewicz algebras we have not three real values but only two endomorphisms that operate "on behalf" of the three values.

Nevertheless in the framework of Chain Based Lattices (Subsection 4.3) the elements of the form $\langle S, \emptyset \rangle$ will be able to play the role of "third" value also in the case of $S \neq \emptyset$. Specific algebraic results on three-valued Łukasiewicz algebras and lattices of the form $\overrightarrow{\mathbf{N}}\,(\mathbf{A})$, for a Boolean algebra **A**, are discussed in [Va1] and in [Ci4]. Some general connections between the class of semi-simple Nelson algebras and the class of three-valued Łukasiewicz algebras are presented in [BD1] and exploited in the present context. Anyway the main results will be directly proved in the framework of the representation $RS_{r^*}(\mathbf{C})$ by pairs of decreasing elements of an Approximation Space $\mathbf{AS}(\mathbf{C})$.

4.1 Rough Set Systems and Three-valued Łukasiewicz algebras

Let us now introduce the axioms of Traczyk for Łukasiewicz algebras (see [BD1]):

Definition 117. A Łukasiewicz algebra of order $n \geq 2$, is an algebra

$$\mathbf{L} = (L, +, \bullet, -, D_1, D_2, ..., D_{n-1}, 0, 1) \ ,$$

where $+$ and $\bullet$ are binary operations, $-, D_1, D_2, ..., D_{n-1}$, are unary operations and $0, 1$ are nullary operations satisfying the following properties:

1. $(L, +, \bullet, -, 0, 1)$ is a deMorgan algebra.
2. $D_i(x + y) = D_i(x) + D_i(y)$; $D_i(x \bullet y) = D_i(x) \bullet D_i(y)$, $1 \leq i \leq n - 1$.
3. $D_i(x) \bullet D_j(x) = D_j(x)$, $1 \leq i \leq j \leq n - 1$.
4. $D_i(x) + -D_i(x) = 1$; $D_i(x) \bullet -D_i(x) = 0$, $1 \leq i \leq n - 1$.
5. $D_i(-x) = -D_{n-i}(x)$, $1 \leq i \leq n - 1$.
6. $D_i(D_j(x)) = D_j(x)$, $1 \leq i, j \leq n - 1$.
7. $x + D_1(x) = D_1(x)$; $x \bullet D_{n-1}(x) = D_{n-1}(x)$.
8. $D_i(0) = 0$; $D_i(1) = 1$, $1 \leq i \leq n - 1$.
9. $-x \bullet D_{n-1}(x) = 0$; $-x + D_1(x) = 1$.
10. $y \bullet (x + -D_i(x) + D_{i+1}(y)) = y$, $1 \leq i \leq n - 2$.

(These axioms are not independent; for instance for the class of three-valued Łukasiewicz algebras more compact systems of axioms are presented in [BFGR1]. Notice that in the axiomatisation that we adopt here, we have a chain $D_1(x) \geq$

$D_2(x) \geq ... \geq D_{n-2}(x) \geq D_{n-1}(x)$ for any element $x \in L$ while in [BFGR1] the chain $\phi_1(x) \leq \phi_2(x) \leq ... \leq \phi_{n-2}(x) \leq \phi_{n-1}(x))$ is taken into account.

From axiom 4 we have that $\forall x \in L, D_i(x) \in \mathcal{CTR}(\mathbf{L})$.

Now it is well known that in the case of $n = 3$, $D_1(x)$ is the least element of $\mathcal{CTR}(\mathbf{L})$ greater or equal to x (see [Ci3]).

Similarly, given an Approximation Space $\mathbf{AS(C)}$, the endomorphism $\div\div$ maps any element $x \in \mathbf{N}(\mathbf{AS(C)})$ to the least exact element x' such that $x' \geq x$. Moreover, in Łukasiewicz algebras of order three $D_2(x) = -D_1(-x)$ from axiom 5.

By duality, $D_2(x)$ is to be the greatest element x' of $\mathcal{CTR}(\mathbf{L})$ such that $x' \leq x$. Similarly, the endomorphism $\neg\neg$ maps any element $x \in \mathbf{N}(\mathbf{AS(C)})$ to the greatest exact element x' such that $x' \leq x$. Moreover, it is clear from the preceding Section that a set $X \subseteq U$ is definable only if $r(X) \in \mathcal{CTR}(\mathbf{N}(\mathbf{AS(C)}))$.

These remarks suggest that it is reasonable to interpret rough set structures as three-valued Łukasiewicz algebras.

As a matter of fact we are going to see that the operators $\div\div$ and $\neg\neg$ in $RS_r(\mathbf{C})$ considered as a Nelson algebra coincide with D_1 and D_2, respectively, in $RS_r(\mathbf{C})$ considered as a Łukasiewicz algebra.

Let us start from a more general point of view. Given an n-valued Łukasiewicz algebra, let us consider the endomorphisms D_1 and D_{n-1}. From axiom 5 of Definition 117 we get easily:

Lemma 118. *Let* $\mathbf{L}$ *be a Łukasiewicz algebra of order* n, *then* $\forall x \in \mathbf{L}$:

1. $D_1(x) = -D_1(-D_1(x))$
2. $D_{n-1}(x) = -D_{n-1}(-D_{n-1}(x))$
3. $-D_1(x) = -D_{n-1}(-x)$.

Proof. **1** $D_1(x) = D_{n-(n-1)}(D_1(x)) = D_{n-(n-1)}(- - D_1(x)) = -D_1(-D_1(x))$, from axioms 6, 1, 5.

2 $D_{n-1}(x) = D_1(- - D_{n-1}(x)) = -D_{n-1}(-D_{n-1}(x))$, from axioms 1, 6, 5.

3 $-D_1(x) = D_{n-1}(-x) = - - D_{n-1}(-x)$, from axiom 5 and point 1 of 117.

□

Now we prove that in any Łukasiewicz algebra $\mathbf{L}$ of order three, $\forall a \in L$, $-a = \sim a, -D_1(a) = \div a$ and $-D_{n-1}(a) = \neg a$:

Lemma 119. *Let* $\mathbf{B} = (B, \vee, \wedge, \neg, 0, 1)$ *be a Boolean algebra and* Θ *a congruence relation on* $\mathbf{B}$. *Set* $D_1 = \div\div$ *and* $D_2 = \neg\neg$, *then*

$$\text{Ł}(\mathbf{B}) = (N_\Theta(B), \vee, \wedge, \sim, D_1, D_2, \langle 0, 1\rangle, \langle 1, 0\rangle)$$

is a Łukasiewicz algebra of order three.

Proof. 1 From the definition of Nelson algebras, $(N_\Theta(B), \vee, \wedge, \sim, \langle 0, 1\rangle, \langle 1, 0\rangle)$ is a DeMorgan lattice. Let us now verify the remaining conditions:

2 from Lemma 111

3 $D_i(x) \wedge D_j(x) = D_j(x)$, $(1 \leq i, j \leq 3 - 1)$, from Lemma 92.

4 $D_i(x)\vee \sim D_i(x) = 1; D_i(x)\wedge \sim D_i(x) = 0$, $(1 \le i \le 3-1)$, from Proposition 90.
5 $D_i(\sim x) =\sim D_{n-i}(x)$, $(1 \le i \le 3-1)$, from points 4 and 5 of Lemma 97.
6 $D_i(D_j(x)) = D_j(x)$, $(1 \le i, j \le 3-1)$, from Proposition 90 and Proposition 95.
7 $x \vee D_1(x) = D_1(x); x \wedge D_2(x) = D_2(x)$, from Lemma 92.
8 $D_i(0) = 0; D_i(1) = 1$, $(1 \le i \le n-1)$, from lemma 109 and lemma 110.
9 $\sim x \wedge D_2(x) = 0; \sim x \vee D_1(x) = 1$, from 2 and 3 of Lemma 97 and the fact that $\neg$ is a Boolean complement.
10 $y \wedge (x \vee \sim D_1(x) \vee D_2(y)) = y$, by verification.

□

So 3 of Lemma 118 corresponds to 4 of Lemma 97 and using 5 of Lemma 97 we easily have:

Lemma 120. *Let* **B** *be a Boolean algebra and* Θ *a congruence on it. Let* $\sim, \neg$ *and* D_1, D_2 *be defined by definitions 6 and 7 of Proposition 65 and in Lemma 119, respectively, then* $\forall a \in N_\Theta(B)$,

1. $-D_1(a) =\sim \div \div a = \div a$;
2. $-D_2(a) =\sim \neg\neg a = \neg a$.

Proof. From Lemma 118. □

On the other side, given a three-valued Łukasiewicz algebra **L**, we can introduce two new operations $\neg$ and $\rightarrow$ in such a way that the resulting structure $\mathbf{L}^+ = (L, \vee, \wedge, -, \neg, \rightarrow, 0, 1)$ is a semi-simple Nelson algebra:

Lemma 121. *Let* **L** *be a three-valued Łukasiewicz algebra and* D_1, D_2 *its two endomorphisms. Define* $\forall a, b \in L$ *the following two new operations:*

1. $\neg a = -D_2(a)$;
2. $a \rightarrow b = -D_2(a) \vee b$.

Then the structure $\mathbf{L}^+$ *is a semi-simple Nelson algebra.*

Proof. By an easy verification of the axioms of semi-simple Nelson algebras or exploiting the relation between D_2 and the centre of **L**. □

So we have proved:

Proposition 122. (Second Theorem of Representation of Rough Set Systems)
For any Approximation Space **AS(C)**, *the structure*

$$\mathbf{Ł}(\mathbf{AS(C)}) = (RS_{\Gamma}(\mathbf{C}), \vee, \wedge, \sim, D_1, D_2, \langle \emptyset, U \rangle, \langle U, \emptyset \rangle)$$

with D_1 *and* D_2 *defined like in Proposition 119, is a Łukasiewicz algebra of order three.*

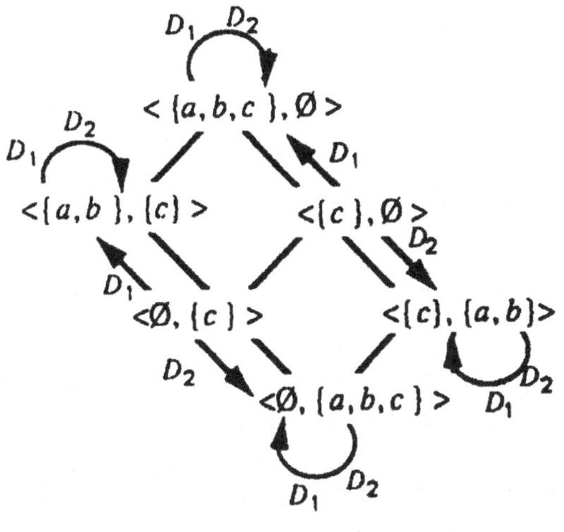

Fig. 18.

Example 15. Consider the Approximation Space of example 14. Fig. 18 shows the lattice $RS_{\Gamma}(\mathbf{C})$ from the point of view of the theory of Łukasiewicz algebras:

Now it can be noticed that if we are given the Łukasiewicz three-valued algebra $\mathbf{Ł}(\mathbf{AS}(\mathbf{C}))$ we could recover the relative pseudo-complementation "$\supset$" exploiting Moisil's definition of the residuation operation on n-valued Łukasiewicz algebra for the case $n = 3$ (see [Mo2], [Mo3], [Mon4]):

Definition 123. Let $\mathbf{L}$ be a three-valued Łukasiewicz algebra, then the following operation:

$$a \sqsupset b = b \vee -D_1(a) \vee (-D_2(a) \wedge D_1(b))$$

is called Moisil's residuation.

Lemma 124. *Let* $\mathbf{L}$ *be a three valued Łukasiewicz algebra. Then* $\forall a, b \in L$,

$$a \sqsupset b = a \supset b \ .$$

Proof. Using Lemma 120, the above Proposition and 2 of Lemma 97, by easy calculation: $a \sqsupset b = b \vee \sim \div \div a \vee (\sim \neg\neg a \wedge \div \div b) = b \vee \div a \vee (\neg a \wedge \neg \sim b)$. □

We end this Subsection by listing some relationships among the various operations in semi-simple Nelson algebra interpretations and in three-valued Łukasiewicz algebra interpretations of Rough Set Systems, allowing, for instance, to single out some minimal complete sets of operations on $RS_{\Gamma}(\mathbf{C})$.

4.2 *1.* $a \to b = \neg a \vee b$;
2. $a \to b = a \supset (\sim a \vee b)$;
3. $a \Rightarrow b = (a \supset b) \vee \sim a$;
4. $\sim a = \div a \vee (a \wedge \neg a)$;

5. $\sim a = a \Rightarrow \bot$
6. $\neg a = a \rightarrow \bot$;
7. $\neg a = a \rightarrow\sim a$;
8. $\neg a = a \Rightarrow\sim a$;
9. $\div a = a \supset \bot$;
10. $-D_1(a) = \div a$;
11. $-D_2(a) = \neg a$;
12. $D_1(a) = \div \div a$;
13. $D_2(a) = \neg\neg(a)$.

4.2 Rough Set Systems and Post algebras

The relationships between the class of Łukasiewicz algebras and that of Post algebras have been widely studied in algebraic literature (see [BD1], [BFGR1], [Ci2], [Ci4]). We will exploit them in order to complete our analysis of the relationships between Rough Set Systems and Multi-Valued Logics. From a categorial point of view, if we denote by $\mathcal{P}_n$ and $\mathcal{L}_n$ the categories of Post algebras andŁukasiewicz algebras of order n, respectively, then for $n \geq 2$, $\mathcal{P}_n$ is a full reflective subcategory of $\mathcal{L}_n$ and the injective objects of $\mathcal{L}_n$ are the complete objects of $\mathcal{P}_n$. We recall from the discussion after example 8 that a Nelson (Łukasiewicz) algebra $\mathbf{N}$ such that there exists an element c satisfying the equation $\sim c = c$, is called *centered* and c will be called the *symmetric element* (or center) of $\mathbf{N}$. In particular, if $n = 3$, we have the following relationships among semi-simple Nelson algebras, $\mathcal{L}_3$ and $\mathcal{P}_3$ (see [Mon2], [Mon3], [Ci2], [Ci4]):

Lemma 125. *The following statements are equivalent:*

1. $\mathbf{A}$ *is a semi-simple centered Nelson algebra.*
2. $\mathbf{A}$ *is a Post algebra of order three.*
3. $\mathbf{A}$ *is a centered Łukasiewicz three-valued algebra.*

Notice that the above results concern the systems with symmetric elements, hence they can be used in the analysis of Approximation Spaces in which no elementary class is a singleton. Only in this case the induced Rough Set Systems may be interpreted as centered semi-simple Nelson algebras, and hence as centered three-valued Łukasiewicz algebras, and as Post algebras of order three. If we admit arbitrary Approximation Spaces, then we have to weaken the theory of Post algebras and use the concept of Chain Based Lattices.

At the basis of our constructions there will be the fact that we can represent rough sets from an Approximation Space $\mathbf{AS(C)}$ as a pair of *decreasing* elements of A instead of a pair of disjoint elements of A.

The algebraic construction The following are Rousseau's axioms for Post algebras of order n (see [Ra1]):

Definition 126. A Post algebra of order $n \geq 2$, is an algebra

$$\mathbf{P} = (P, +, \bullet, -, \Longrightarrow, D_1, D_2, ..., D_{n-1}, 0 = e_0, ..., e_{n-1} = 1) \ ,$$

where $+, \bullet, \Longrightarrow$ are binary operations, $-, D_1, D_2, ..., D_{n-1}$, are unary operations and $e_0, ..., e_{n-1}$ are nullary operations satisfying the following properties:

1. $(P, +, \bullet, -, \Longrightarrow, 0, 1)$ is a Heyting algebra.
2. $D_i(x+y) = D_i(x) + D_i(y)$; $D_i(x \bullet y) = D_i(x) \bullet D_i(y)$, $1 \leq i \leq n-1$.
3. $D_1(x) + -D_1(x) = 1$.
4. $D_i(-x) = -D_1(x)$, $1 \leq i \leq n-1$.
5. $D_i(D_j(x)) = D_j(x)$, $1 \leq i, j \leq n-1$.
6. $$x = \sum_{i=1}^{n-1} (D_i(x) \bullet e_i).$$
7. $$D_i(x \Longrightarrow y) = \prod_{j=1}^{i} (D_j(x) \Longrightarrow D_j(y)).$$
8. $D_i(e_j) = \begin{cases} 1 \text{ for } 1 \leq i \leq j \leq n-1 \\ 0 \text{ for } n-1 \geq i \rangle j \geq 0 \end{cases}$

Equation 6. is called *monotonic representation of* x.

Since $D_i(x) + -D_i(x) = D_1(D_i(x)) + -D_1(D_i(x)) = 1$, from axioms 5 and 3, we have at once that $\forall x \in P, D_i(x) \in \mathcal{CTR}(\mathbf{P})$. Now, under the condition that there are no elementary sets $\alpha \in Atom(\mathbf{AS}(\mathbf{C}))$ such that $card(\alpha) = 1$, the interpretation of the Approximation Space $\mathbf{AS}(\mathbf{C})$ as a Post algebra is a corollary of the following

Lemma 127. *Let* $\mathbf{B} = (B, \vee, \wedge, -, 0, 1)$ *be a Boolean algebra,* $D_1 = \div\div$ *and* $D_{n-1} = \neg\neg$*; then*

$$\mathbf{P}^{\#}(\mathbf{B}) = (\vec{N}\ (B), \vee, \wedge, \div, \supset, D_1, D_2, 0 = e_0, e_1, e_2 = 1) \ ,$$

with the operation defined in Proposition 65, Proposition 81 and Corollary 82 and $e_1 = \langle 0, 0 \rangle$, *is a Post algebra of order three.*

Proof. The translation of an n-valued Łukasiewicz algebra $\mathbf{L}$ which can exhibit a chain of constants $e_0, \ldots, e_{n-1}$ such that axiom 8 of Definition 126 holds, in a Post algebra of order n, is a well-known topic in the literature (see for instance [BD1]): the Post operation "$-$" is defined by means of the Łukasiewicz operation "$-D_1$". Thus we have simply to check that the three-valued Łukasiewicz algebra $\mathbf{Ł}(\mathbf{B}) = (\vec{N}\ (B), \vee, \wedge, \sim, D_1, D_2, 0, 1)$ defined in Proposition 119 has a chain $\langle e_0, \ldots, e_2 \rangle$ of constants satisfying axiom 8 of 126.

Recall that e_1 is the symmetric element that is present in $\overrightarrow{N}(B)$ because the functor $\overrightarrow{N}$ uses the trivial congruence on $\mathbf{B}$; hence, any ordered pair of disjoint elements of $\mathbf{B}$ is allowed.

Let us verify that $\div$ and $\supset$ have been suitably chosen (the verification of axiom 8 is straightforward):

2 from Lemma 111.
3 $D_1(x) \vee \div D_1(x) = 1$: from Definition 86 and Proposition 90.
4 $D_i(\div x) = D_i(\sim D_1(x)) =\sim D_{n-1}(D_1(x)) =\sim D_1(x) =\sim \div\div x = \div x = \div\div\div x = \div D_1(x)$, from 4 of Lemma 97, axiom 5 of Definition 117 and Lemma 4.2 (in other words, since $\div x$ is an exact element, $D_i(\div x) = \div x$)).
7 $D_1(x \supset y) = D_1(x) \supset D_1(y)$ follows from the fact that $\div$ and $\supset$ are the pseudo-complement and the relative pseudo-complement of a Heyting algebra; respectively, in particular $D_1(x \supset y) = \div x \vee \div\div y$. $D_2(x \supset y) = \neg\neg(x \supset y) = \neg\neg((\neg x \wedge \neg \sim y) \vee \sim \neg \sim x \vee y) = (\neg x \wedge \neg \sim y) \vee \neg\neg \sim x \vee \neg\neg y)$. But since $\neg \sim y \leq \neg\neg y$, we have $D_2(x \supset y) = \neg\neg \sim x \vee \neg\neg y = \div x \vee \neg\neg y$. $D_2(x) \supset D_2(y) = \neg\neg x \supset \neg\neg y = (\neg x \wedge \neg\neg y) \vee (\neg x \vee \neg\neg y) = \neg x \vee \neg\neg y$. Thus

$$D_1(x) \supset D_1(y) \wedge D_2(x) \supset D_2(y) = (\div x \vee \div\div y) \wedge (\neg x \vee \neg\neg y) =$$
$$= (\div x \wedge (\neg x \vee \neg\neg y)) \vee (\div\div y \wedge (\neg x \vee \neg\neg y)) =$$
$$= \div x \vee (\div x \wedge \neg\neg y) \vee (\div\div y \wedge \neg x) \vee \neg\neg y =$$
$$= \div x \vee (\div\div y \wedge \neg x) \vee \neg\neg y = \div x \vee \neg\neg y = D_2(x \supset y)$$

□

Now it is worth analysing, as in Subsection 3.4, a more "concrete" representation of rough sets as Post algebras of order three. Actually the construction of the Nelson space $\mathbf{X}(\mathbf{AS}(\mathbf{C}) \nearrow \emptyset)$ related to the application r, illustrated in Section 3.1, is a candidate for a Post space.

Indeed, that this Nelson space is the dual space of a Post algebra comes immediately from duality theory: a Post algebra of order n is the coproduct $\mathbf{B} \coprod \mathbf{n}$ of a Boolean algebra $\mathbf{B}$ and a chain $\mathbf{n}$ (see [BD2], we do not define here the notion of "coproduct"). Thus its dual space is $\mathbf{HS}(\mathbf{B}) \times \mathbf{HS}(\mathbf{n}) = \mathbf{HS}(\mathbf{B}) \times \mathbf{n-1}$ (see [Pr1]). But if $\mathbf{AS}(\mathbf{C})$ does not have any singleton elementary class, then $S = \bigcup S^* = \emptyset$; therefore the Nelson space dual of $\mathbf{N}(\mathbf{AS}(\mathbf{C}))$ is $\mathbf{X}(\mathbf{AS}(\mathbf{C}) \nearrow \emptyset)$ that in turn happens to correspond exactly to $\mathbf{HS}(\mathbf{AS}(\mathbf{C})) \times (\{\mathcal{I}, \mathcal{C}\}, \mathcal{I} \leq \mathcal{C})$.

However, in order to exhibit more directly the Post algebra of rough sets we shall follow the construction of Post algebras by means of Post field of sets (see [Ra1], [Tr1], [Dw1]).

The topological construction

Definition 128. A topological space $(X, \Omega(X))$ is said to be a *Post space* of order $n \geq 2$ if

1. $X = \bigcup\{X_1, \dots, X_{n-1} : X_i \cap X_j = \emptyset, \text{ for } 1 \leq i, j \leq n-1\}$;

2. there exists a Boolean algebra $\mathbf{B}$ with dual space $\mathbf{HS}(\mathbf{B})$ and homeomorphisms $g_i : X_i \longmapsto \mathbf{HS}(\mathbf{B})$ of X_i onto $\mathbf{HS}(\mathbf{B})$, $1 \leq i \leq n-1$,
3. the family $B(X) = \{\bigcup_{i=1}^{n-1} g_i^{-1}(C)$: C is a clopen subset of $\mathbf{HS}(\mathbf{B})\}$ is a basis for $(X, \Omega(X))$.

This Post space is denoted by $\mathbf{X} = (\{X_i, g_i\}_{1\leq i \leq n-1}, B(X))$.

Intuitively, to use a geological metaphor, a Post space $\mathbf{X}$ is a *regular stratification* of disjoint homeomorphic Boolean spaces. Any element of $B(X)$ is the *core*, drilled throughout all the strata, by a drilling ring with the section equal to a clopen set of $\mathbf{B}$.

We recall that :

4.3 *1. For any Post space* $\mathbf{X}$, $\mathbf{B}^*(X) = (B(X), \cap, \cup, -, \Longrightarrow, \emptyset, X)$ *is the field of all simultaneously open and closed subsets of* $\mathbf{X}$.

2. $e_0 = \emptyset, e_1 = X_1, e_2 = X_1 \cup X_2, \ldots, e_{n-1} = X$, *is a chain;*

3. by $P(X)$ *we mean the class of all subsets of* X *of the form* $Y = Y_1 \cap e_1 \cup \ldots \cup Y_{n-1} \cap e_{n-1}$ *where* $Y_i \in B(X)$ *for* $1 \leq i \leq n-1$.

4. there exist operations $D_i : P(X) \longmapsto B(X)$, *for* $1 \leq i \leq n-1$, *which with every* $Y \in P(X)$ *associate uniquely determined coefficients* $D_i(X) \in B(X)$ *such that any* $Y \in P(X)$ *has a unique monotonic representation* $Y = D_1(Y) \cap e_1 \cup \ldots \cup D_{n-1}(Y) \cup e_{n-1}$, *where* $D_1(Y) \supseteq D_2(Y) \supseteq \ldots \supseteq D_{n-1}(Y)$.

5. condition 8 of Definition 126 holds.

Continuing our "geological explanation", e_i is the *accumulation* of the strata up to the ith*–level* (counting from the surface), while any element Y is a *cumulative* set of *samples of various strata* such that any sample of the ith stratum is greater or equal to the sample of the $i+1^{th}$ stratum. Finally $D_i(Y)$ is the call for a *core drilling* with the section of the same dimension as the ith sample forming the element Y.

We have the following Representation Theorem (see [Dw1], [Ra1], [Tr1]):

Lemma 129. *Every Post algebra* $\mathbf{P} = (P, +, \bullet, -, \Longrightarrow, D_1, D_2, \ldots, D_{n-1}, 0 = e_0, \ldots, e_{n-1} = 1)$ *is isomorphic to a Post field* $\mathbf{P}(X) = (P(X), \cup, \cap, \div, \supset, D_1, D_2, \ldots, D_{n-1}, 0 = e_0, \ldots, e_{n-1} = 1)$ *of subsets of a Post space* $\mathbf{X} = (\{X_i, g_i\}_{1\leq i\leq n-1}, B(X))$, *where, for all* $Z, Y \in P(X)$*:*

1. $C(Y) = X \cap -D_1(Y)$.

2. $Z \supset Y = (CD_1(Z) \cup D_1(Y)) \cap e_1 \cup ((CD_1(Z) \cup D_1(Y)) \cap (CD_2(Z) \cup D_2(Y))) \cap e_2 \cup \ldots \cup ((CD_1(Z) \cup D_1(Y)) \cap \ldots \cap (CD_{n-1}(Z) \cup D_{n-1}(Y))) \cap e_{n-1}$.

3. $\div Z = {}'Z \supset 0$.

Now, suppose we are given an Approximation Space $\mathbf{AS}(\mathbf{C})$, such that $Atom(\mathbf{AS}(\mathbf{C})) = \{\alpha_1, \ldots, \alpha_m\}$ and $\forall \alpha_i, card(\alpha_i) \geq 2$. Let us set $X_1 = \{\alpha_1^{\mathcal{C}}, \ldots, \alpha_m^{\mathcal{C}}\}$ and $X_2 = \{\alpha_1^{\mathcal{I}}, \ldots, \alpha_m^{\mathcal{I}}\}$. Remember that as in Definition 68 we identify $\alpha_1^{\mathcal{I}}$ and α_i; so $X_2 = Ind(\mathbf{C}) = Atom(\mathbf{AS}(\mathbf{C}))$.

Let us consider the Nelson space $(\mathbf{T}, g_\emptyset)$ built in exactly the same manner as in Subsection 3.4.

In this case $S^* = \emptyset$. Thus $card(Ind(\mathbf{C})^{\mathcal{I}}) = card(Ind(\mathbf{C})^{\mathcal{C}})$.

So $T = X_1 \cup X_2$ and $(\mathbf{T}, \emptyset) = \mathbf{X}(\mathbf{AS}(\mathbf{C}) \nearrow \emptyset)$, as it is defined in Definition 68 (we recall that $\mathbf{T} = (T, \leq)$). Clearly $X_1 \cap X_2 = \emptyset$. Moreover, $\tau_1 = (X_1, \mathbb{P}(X_1)), \tau_2 = (X_2, \mathbb{P}(X_2))$ and $\tau = (Atom(\mathbf{AS}(\mathbf{C})), \mathbb{P}(Atom(\mathbf{AS}(\mathbf{C}))))$ are three (discrete) topological spaces such that τ is the dual space of the Boolean algebra $\mathbf{AS}(\mathbf{C})$ (where τ_2 is a dummy copy of τ).

Then consider the following maps:

4.4 *1.* $g_1 : X_1 \longmapsto Atom(\mathbf{AS}(\mathbf{C})) : g_1(\alpha_i^{\mathcal{C}}) = \alpha_i$, *for* $1 \leq i \leq m$*;*
2. $g_2 : X_2 \longmapsto Atom(\mathbf{AS}(\mathbf{C})) : g_2(\alpha_i^{\mathcal{I}}) = \alpha_i$, *for* $1 \leq i \leq m$*;*

The maps g_1 and g_2 are two homeomorphisms from τ_1 and τ_2 to τ, respectively.

The family $B(T)$ of the complemented sets is

$$\{\{\alpha_i^{\mathcal{C}}, \ldots, \alpha_j^{\mathcal{C}}, \alpha_i^{\mathcal{I}}, \ldots, \alpha_j^{\mathcal{I}}\}_{0 \leq i \leq j \leq m}\} \ .$$

Clearly, both $\emptyset = \{\alpha_0^{\mathcal{C}}, \alpha_0^{\mathcal{I}}\}$ and $T = \{\alpha_1^{\mathcal{C}}, \ldots, \alpha_m^{\mathcal{C}}, \alpha_1^{\mathcal{I}}, \ldots, \alpha_m^{\mathcal{I}}\}$ are elements of $B(T)$. Moreover, since for any $X \in B(T)$ the indices of the $\mathcal{I}$-part and the indices of the $\mathcal{C}$-part are the same, we have that the following maps are isomorphisms:

4.5 $f^* : \mathbf{B}^*(T) \longmapsto \mathbf{AS}([\mathbf{C}]) : f^*(x) = X_2 \cap x.$

4.6 $f : \mathbf{B}^*(T) \longmapsto \mathbf{AS}(\mathbf{C}) : f(x) = \bigcup f^*(x),$

Indeed, in view of 2. of 4.3 let us set $e_0 = \emptyset, e_1 = X_1, e_2 = T$.

We have that the relations $e_0 \subset e_1 \subset e_2$ hold. Hence $\mathbf{X}(\mathbf{C}) = (\{X_1, X_2\}, B(T))$ is a Post space. It follows that the Post field of sets $\mathbf{P}(T)$ is isomorphic to $(\Omega_A(\mathbf{T}), \cap, \cup, \div, \supset, D_1 = \div\div, D_2 = \neg\neg, e_0, e_1, e_2)$ via the identity map.

But the monotonic representation of Definition 126 of the elements of $P(T)$ suggests another one determined by ordered pairs. In what follows we need a map pj, projecting any element from $X_1 \cup X_2$ onto its natural companion in $Ind(\mathbf{C})$ (differently from the case of the disjoint representation where the identification of $Ind(\mathbf{C})$ and $Ind(\mathbf{C})^{\mathcal{I}}$ was suitable and sufficient since we used to filter any element of the dual algebra by the $\mathcal{I}$-level):

4.7 $pj : T \longmapsto Atom(\mathbf{AS}(\mathbf{C})) : pj(x) = \begin{cases} g_1(x) \text{ if } x \in X_1 \\ g_2(x) \text{ if } x \in X_2 \end{cases}$

Now, for all $Z = (b_1 \cap e_1) \cup (b_2 \cap e_2)$ with $b_1 \supseteq b_2$ and $b_1, b_2 \in \mathcal{CTR}(\mathbf{P}(T))$, we set:

4.8 $Z' = \langle b_1 \cap e_1, b_2 \cap e_2 \rangle$ *and* $Z^* = \langle \bigcup pj(b_1 \cap e_1), \bigcup pj(b_2 \cap e_2) \rangle$.

Definition 130. Given an Approximation Space $\mathbf{AS}(\mathbf{C})$,

$$RS_{r^*}(\mathbf{C}) = \{Z^* : Z \in P(T) \text{ and } Z \text{ is in monotonic representation}\} \ .$$

Hence, we obtain:

Proposition 131. *Given an Approximation space* $\mathbf{AS}(\mathbf{C})$ *such that* $\forall\alpha \in Ind(\mathbf{C})$, $card(\alpha) \geq 2$, *the algebraic structure*

$$(RS_{r^*}(\mathbf{C}), \wedge, \vee, \supset, \div, D_1, D_2, e_0, e_1, e_2)$$

where

1. $e_0 = \langle\emptyset, \emptyset\rangle, e_1 = \langle U, \emptyset\rangle, e_2 = \langle U, U\rangle$;
2. $a \vee b = \langle A_1 \cup B_1, A_2 \cup B_2\rangle$;
3. $a \wedge b = \langle A_1 \cap B_1, A_2 \cap B_2\rangle$;
4. $a \supset b = \langle A_1 \Longrightarrow B_1, (A_1 \Longrightarrow B_1) \cap (A_2 \Longrightarrow B_2)\rangle$;
5. $\div a = \langle \neg A_1, \neg A_1\rangle$;
6. $D_i(a) = \langle A_i, A_i\rangle$, *for* $1 \leq i \leq 2$,

and the operations inside the ordered pairs are the operations of $\mathbf{AS}(\mathbf{C})$, *is a Post field of decreasing 2-element sequences of elements of* A.

Proof. The proof is a corollary of the above construction and the results from [Ra1] and [Tr3]. □

So we get the following representation of rough sets which, as we will see, corresponds to the representation as approximating (decreasing) sequences of definable elements from an Approximation Space $\mathbf{AS}(\mathbf{C})$:

Proposition 132. (THIRD THEOREM OF REPRESENTATION OF ROUGH SET SYSTEMS)

Let $\mathbf{AS}(\mathbf{C})$ *be an approximation Space such that for any elementary set* α *belonging to* $Atom(\mathbf{AS}(\mathbf{C}))$, $card(\alpha) \geq 2$. *Then the structure*

$$\mathbf{P}(\mathbf{AS}(\mathbf{C})) = (RS_{r^*}(\mathbf{C}), \wedge, \vee, \supset, \div, D_1 = \div\div, D_2 = \neg\neg, e_0, e_1, e_2)$$

with the operations defined in 131, is a Post field of decreasing 2-elements sequences of elements of A *and the following map is a Post isomorphism:*

$$k : \mathbf{P}^{\#}(\mathbf{AS}(\mathbf{C})) \longmapsto \mathbf{P}(\mathbf{AS}(\mathbf{C})) : k(\langle A_1, A_2\rangle) = \langle -A_2, A_1\rangle \ .$$

Proof. Let us only verify that $k(a \supset b) = k(a) \supset k(b)$:

$$\begin{aligned} k(a) \supset k(b) &= \langle -A_2, A_1\rangle \supset \langle -B_2, B_1\rangle \\ &= \langle -A_2 \Longrightarrow -B_2, (-A_2 \Longrightarrow -B_2) \cap (A_1 \Longrightarrow B_1)\rangle \\ &= \langle - - A_2 \cup -B_2, (- - A_2 \cup -B_2) \cap (-A_1 \cup B_1)\rangle \\ &= \langle A_2 \cup -B_2, (A_2 \cup -B_2) \cap (-A_1 \cup B_1)\rangle; \end{aligned}$$

but

$$\begin{aligned} (A_2 \cup -B_2) \cap (-A_1 \cup B_1) &= ((A_2 \cup -B_2) \cap -A_1) \cup ((A_2 \cup -B_2) \cap B_1) \\ &= (A_2 \cap -A_1) \cup (-B_2 \cap -A_1) \cup (A_2 \cap B_1) \\ &\quad \cup (-B_2 \cap B_1) \\ &= (-B_2 \cap -A_1) \cup (A_2 \cup B_1). \end{aligned}$$

Thus we have $k(a) \supset k(b) = \langle A_2 \cup -B_2, (-B_2 \cap -A_1) \cup (A_2 \cup B_1)\rangle$.

$$k(a \supset b) = k((\neg a \wedge \neg \sim b) \vee \sim \neg \sim a \vee b) = k(\langle((-A_1 \cap -B_2) \cup A_2 \cup B_1), -A_2 \cap B_2\rangle$$
$$= \langle A_2 \cup -B_2, (-B_2 \cap -A_1) \cup (A_2 \cup B_1)\rangle.$$

In particular: $k(\div a) = k(\sim \neg \sim A) = k(\langle A_2, -A_2\rangle) = \langle A_2, A_2\rangle = \div k(a)$. □

Moreover, if we are given the monotonic representation of the elements of a Post algebra **Pn** of order n, we can define a strong negation $\sim$ in the following way:

Definition 133. For all $a \in \mathbf{Pn}$ such that $a = (d_1 \cap e_1) \cup \ldots \cup (d_{n-1} \cap e_{n-1})$ we set

$$\sim a = (-d_{n-1} \cap e_1) \cup \ldots \cup (-d_1 \cap e_{n-1}) \ .$$

Hence in the case of a Post algebra of decreasing sequences of order $n-1$ we have:

4.9 $\sim a = \sim \langle a_1, \ldots, a_{n-1}\rangle = \langle -a_{n-1}, \ldots, -a_1\rangle$.

Now we define an "inner" weak negation $\neg$ by means of the equation:

4.10 $\neg a = \neg\langle a_1, \ldots, a_{n-1}\rangle = \langle -a_{n-1}, \ldots, -a_{n-1}\rangle$.

So we can define a weak implication $\rightarrow$ by means of the equation:

4.11 $a \rightarrow b = \neg a \vee b$;

(We recall that from Lemma 129, $\div a = \div\langle a_1, \ldots, a_{n-1}\rangle = \langle -a_1, \ldots, -a_1\rangle$)). We then have:

Lemma 134. *The map k of Proposition 132 defines a Nelson isomorphism between* $\overrightarrow{\mathbf{N}}$ $(\mathbf{AS}(\mathbf{C}))$ *and the algebra* $(RS_{r^*}(\mathbf{C}), \wedge, \vee, \rightarrow, \neg, \sim, \langle U, U\rangle, \langle \emptyset, \emptyset\rangle)$.

Proof. Let us first verify that the characteristic equation $\div a = \sim \neg \sim a$ holds in general: $\sim a = \langle -a_{n-1}, \ldots, -a_1\rangle; \neg \sim a = \langle -a_1, \ldots, - -a_1\rangle$; $\sim \neg \sim a = \langle -a_1, \ldots, -a_1\rangle = \langle -a_1, \ldots, -a_1\rangle = \div a$. We could also consider the fact that from 5. of Lemma 97 we can set $\neg a = -D_{n-1}(a)$; so:

$$\sim \neg \sim a = \sim -D_{n-1}(\langle -a_{n-1}, \ldots, -a_1\rangle) = \sim -\langle -a_1, \ldots, -a_1\rangle = \sim \langle a_1, \ldots, a_1\rangle$$
$$= \langle -a_1, \ldots, -a_1\rangle = \div a.$$

Let us prove the case of the weak implication for $n = 3$:

$$k(a \rightarrow b) = k(\langle -a_1 \vee b_1, a_1 \wedge b_2\rangle)$$
$$= \langle -a_1 \vee -b_2, -a_1 \vee b_1\rangle = \langle -a_1, -a_1\rangle \vee \langle -b_2, b_1\rangle$$
$$= \neg\langle -a_2, a_1\rangle \vee \langle -b_2, b_1\rangle = \langle -a_2, a_1\rangle \rightarrow \langle -b_2, b_1\rangle = k(a) \rightarrow k(b).$$

□

Example 16. $\mathbf{C} = (U = \{a,b,c,d\}, A = \{A_1, A_2\}, V = \{0,1,2\}, v)$, where I is given by:

v	A_1	A_2
a	1	0
b	1	0
c	1	2
d	1	2

Then we have the following Approximation Space $\mathbf{AS}(\mathbf{C})$ and the following induced Post space $\mathbf{X}(\mathbf{C})$ (Fig. 19):

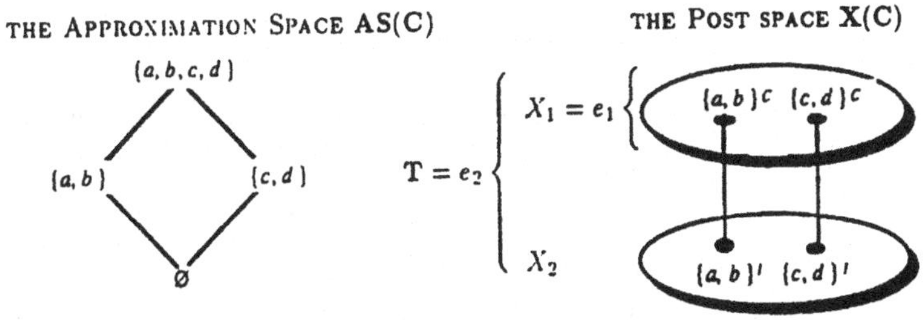

Fig. 19.

$B(X) = \{b = \emptyset, b_1 = \{\{a,b\}^{\mathcal{I}}, \{a,b\}^{\mathcal{C}}\}, b_2 = \{\{c,d\}^{\mathcal{I}}, \{c,d\}^{\mathcal{C}}\}, b_3 = X_1 \cup X_2\}$. $e_0 = \emptyset, e_1 = X_1, e_2 = X_1 \cup X_2$ The set $Y = \{\{a,b\}^{\mathcal{I}}, \{a,b\}^{\mathcal{C}}, \{c,d\}^{\mathcal{C}}\}$ has the monotonic representation $b_3 \cap e_1 \cup b_1 \cap e_2$; thus: $Y' = \langle b_3 \cap e_1, b_1 \cap e_2 \rangle = \langle \{\{a,b\}^{\mathcal{C}}, \{c,d\}^{\mathcal{C}}\}, \{\{a,b\}^{\mathcal{I}}, \{a,b\}^{\mathcal{C}}\} \rangle$;

$$\begin{aligned} Y^* &= \langle \bigcup pj(\{\{a,b\}^{\mathcal{C}}, \{c,d\}^{\mathcal{C}}\}), \bigcup pj(\{\{a,b\}^{\mathcal{I}}, \{a,b\}^{\mathcal{C}}\}) \rangle \\ &= \langle \bigcup \{\{a,b\}, \{c,d\}\}, \bigcup \{\{a,b\}\} \rangle \\ &= \langle \{a,b,c,d\}, \{a,b\} \rangle. \end{aligned}$$

We get the following Post algebras:

Let us notice that the interpretation provided by Proposition 132 is allowed only in the case when in the Approximation Space $\mathbf{AS}(\mathbf{C})$ there are no elementary sets reduced to singletons. If we want to interpret a rough set structure as a chain based lattice also in the presence of elementary sets of cardinality 1, we must refer to the generalizations of Post algebras proposed by Traczyk and developed by Epstein and Horn.

4.3 Rough Set Systems and Chain Based Lattices

Definition 135. 1. A P_0*-lattice* is a bounded distributive lattice $\mathbf{A} = (A, +, \bullet, 0, 1)$ such that A is generated by $\mathbf{B} \cup \{0 = e_0 \leq \ldots \leq e_{n-1} = 1\}$, where $\mathbf{B}$ is a Boolean subalgebra of $\mathcal{CTR}(\mathbf{A})$.
The finite sequence $0 = e_0 \leq \ldots \leq e_{n-1} = 1$ is called a *chain base* of $\mathbf{A}$.

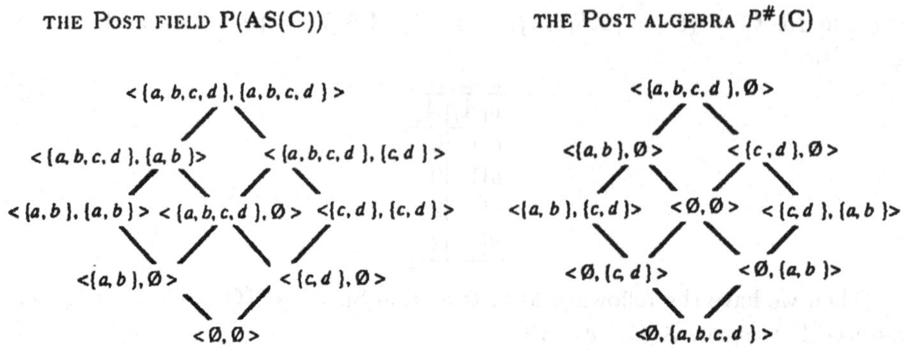

Fig. 20.

2. In any P_0-lattice, $\mathbf{A}$, every element $x \in A$ is representable in the form:

$$\sum_{i=1}^{n-1}(b_i \bullet e_i), \text{ where } b_i \in \mathbf{B} \ .$$

3. If $b_i \geq b_{i+1}$ for all $0 \leq i \leq n-1$, then 2. is called a *monotonic representation* of x.
4. If $b_i \bullet b_j = 0$ for $i \neq j$, then *2* is called a *disjoint representation* of x.
5. A P_0-lattice $\mathbf{A}$ is said to be of *order* n if n is the smallest integer such that $\mathbf{A}$ has a chain base with n terms.
6. If $\mathbf{A} = (A, +, \bullet, \neg, \rightarrow, 0 = e_0 \leq \ldots \leq e_{n-1} = 1)$ is a P_0-lattice of order n such that $(A, +, \bullet, \neg, \rightarrow, 0, 1)$ is a Heyting algebra and $e_{i+1} \rightarrow e_i = e_i$, then $\mathbf{A}$ is called a P_1 *– lattice* of order n.
7. In any P_1-lattice: $e_i \rightarrow e_j = \begin{cases} e_j \text{ for } i\rangle j \\ 1 \text{ for } i \leq j \end{cases}$

(Notice that here "disjoint representation" does not have the same meaning as we ascribed to it in the preceding Sections in the term "disjoint representation of rough sets". The examples at the end of this Section will clarify the present meaning).

We recall from 1 of Definition 22 that in a pseudo-complemented lattice (thus in a Heyting algebra) with pseudo-complementation $\neg$, an element x is said to be dense if $\neg x = 0$.

Let us quote the following results from [EH1]

Lemma 136. *If* $\mathbf{A} = (A, +, \bullet, \neg, 0 = e_0 \leq \ldots \leq e_{n-1} = 1)$ *is a pseudo-complemented* P_0*-lattice, then* $\mathbf{A}$ *has a chain base* $f_0 \leq f_1 \leq \ldots \leq f_{n-1}$ *such that* f_1 *is the smallest dense element of* $\mathbf{A}$.

Lemma 137. *If* $\mathbf{A} = (A, +, \bullet, \neg, \rightarrow, 0 = e_0 \leq \ldots \leq e_{n-1} = 1)$ *is a* P_0*-lattice and* $(A, +, \bullet, \neg, \rightarrow, 0, 1)$ *is a Heyting algebra,then there exists a chain base* $0 = f_0 \leq f_1 \leq \ldots \leq f_{n-1} = 1$ *such that* $(A, +, \bullet, \neg, \rightarrow, 0 = f_0 \leq f_1 \leq \ldots \leq f_{n-1} = 1)$ *is a* P_1*-lattice.*

In order to get the required chain base one can refer to the previous Lemma 136, taking for f_1 the first dense element of $\mathbf{A}$, and inductively for f_{n+1} the smallest dense element of the convex interval $[f_n, 1]$.

In a bounded distributive lattice $\mathbf{A}$ with center $\mathcal{CTR}(\mathbf{A})$ (hence in P_0 and P_1 lattices) it is possible to define the following two operations:

4.12 *1.* relative pseudo-supplementation*:* $x \overset{c}{\Rightarrow} y$*:* $x \bullet b \leq y$ *iff* $b \leq x \overset{c}{\Rightarrow} y$ *for* $b \in \mathcal{CTR}(\mathbf{A})$*;*

2. pseudo-supplementation*:* $!x : 1 \overset{c}{\Rightarrow} x$*.*

Definition 138. Given a distributive lattice $\mathbf{A}$, if for any $x, y \in A$, $x \overset{c}{\Rightarrow} y$ exists, then $\mathbf{A}$ is called a *B-algebra*.

Definition 139. A P_2 – *lattice* is a P_1-lattice $\mathbf{A} = \langle A, +, \bullet, \neg, \rightarrow, 0 = e_0 \leq \ldots \leq e_{n-1} = 1 \rangle$ such that $!e_i$ exists, all i.

Lemma 140. *[EH1] If* $\mathbf{A} = \langle A, +, \bullet, \neg, \rightarrow, 0 = e_0 \leq \ldots \leq e_{n-1} = 1 \rangle$ *is a* P_0*-lattice and* $\langle A, +, \bullet, \neg, \rightarrow, 0, 1 \rangle$ *is a B-algebra, then there exists a unique chain* $f_0 \leq \ldots \leq f_{n-1}$ *such that* $\langle A, +, \bullet, \neg, \rightarrow, 0 = f_0 \leq \ldots \leq f_{n-1} = 1 \rangle$ *is a* P_2*-lattice.*

Now we shall prove:

Proposition 141. (FOURTH THEOREM OF REPRESENTATION OF ROUGH SET SYSTEMS)

Let $\mathbf{AS}(\mathbf{C})$ *be an Approximation Space, then there are a map* p*:* $\overrightarrow{N}(A) \longmapsto RS_{r^*}(\mathbf{C})$ *and three elements* e_0, e_1, e_2 *such that:*

$$\mathbf{P2}(\mathbf{AS}(\mathbf{C})) = \langle RS_{r^*}(\mathbf{C}), \wedge, \vee, \supset, \div, p(e_0) \leq p(e_1) \leq p(e_2) \rangle$$

with the operations defined in 131, is a P_2*-lattice of order three.*

Proof. We could directly prove that $RS_{r^*}(\mathbf{C})$ can be made into a P_0-lattice. Then using the fact that $RS_{r^*}(\mathbf{C})$ is finite, we could use Theorem 4.11 of [EH1] and get the result. □

But in order to highlight some mechanisms related to rough sets, here we prefer to use the following fact (see [EH1]):

Lemma 142. *Every* P_2*-lattice is a principal ideal in a Post algebra.*

Now we show how to characterize a Rough Set System within the De Morgan Lattice $\mathbf{K}(\mathbf{AS}(\mathbf{C}))$, which in this case is the Post algebra $\overrightarrow{N}(\mathbf{AS}(\mathbf{C}))$, by means of the same parameter S that we used for Nelson algebras.

In fact, in view of the above Lemma we shall obtain the proof of Proposition 141 using exactly the same parameter S that we used for Nelson algebras.

First, we recall that $S = h^{-1}(S^*)$ and $S^* = \{\alpha \in Ind(\mathbf{C}) : card(\alpha) = 1\}$ and that Θ is the Boolean congruence on $\mathbf{AS}(\mathbf{C})$ induced by the principal filter $\uparrow S$.

Now since $(RS_{r^*}(\mathbf{C}), \cup, \cap) \cong (RS_r(\mathbf{C}), \cup, \cap) = (N_\Theta(A), \cup, \cap)$ we will work on $N_\Theta(A)$, that is a sublattice of the Post algebra $\mathbf{P}^\#(\mathbf{AS}(\mathbf{C}))$ defined in Lemma 127 (the map k of Proposition 132 guarantees that $\mathbf{P}^\#(\mathbf{AS}(\mathbf{C}))$ is isomorphic to a Post field of 2-elements decreasing sequences of elements of A).

Let g be the largest element of $\vec{N}(A)$ such that $G_1 \cup G_2$ disjoint to S: $g = \langle U \cap -S, \emptyset \rangle$. The down set $\downarrow g$ is a principal ideal (see Subsection 2.2) in the Post algebra $\mathbf{P}^\#(\mathbf{AS}(\mathbf{C}))$.

More precisely, we show that under the above assumptions the following holds:

Lemma 143. *$\downarrow g$ is order isomorphic to* $\mathbf{N}_\Theta(\mathbf{AS}(\mathbf{C}))$.

Proof. Let p be the following map:

$$p : \vec{N}(A) \longmapsto N_\Theta(A) : p(x) = \mathbf{lst}\{y \in N_\Theta(A) \text{ such that } y \geq x \text{ in } \vec{N}(A)\} .$$

We prove that p determines an order isomorphism between $\downarrow g$ and $N_\Theta(A)$: now, if $x \in N_\Theta(A)$ then $p(x) = x$; hence, if $x \neq y$ then $p(x) \neq p(y)$. Otherwise $p(x) = \langle X_1 \cup Z_x, X_2 \rangle$ where $Z_x = S \cap -X_1 \cap -X_2$. It follows that since Z_x is uniquely determined by the constant S and by x, if $x \neq y$ then $p(x) \neq p(y)$.

Similarly, we can prove that p is order preserving and onto.

It follows from Lemma 142 that $\mathbf{N}_\Theta(\mathbf{AS}(\mathbf{C}))$ is a P_2-lattice of order three.

In particular $f_0 = p(e_0) = e_0, f_1 = p(e_1)$ and $f_2 = p(g) = e_2$. □

Let us notice that the element $\langle \emptyset, \emptyset \rangle$ – that is the element e_1 of $\mathbf{P}^\#(\mathbf{AS}(\mathbf{C}))$ – does not belong to $N_\Theta(A)$ if Θ is not trivial.

The map p provides the way to recover a new element f_1 according to the results of Lemma 136 and Lemma 137: $p(e_1) = \langle \emptyset \cup S, \emptyset \rangle = \langle S, \emptyset \rangle$ that is the least dense element in the interval $[\langle \emptyset, U \rangle, \langle U, \emptyset \rangle]$ of $N_\Theta(A)$.

It must be noticed that here "dense" must be understood with respect to the operation "$\div$", that is the pseudo-complementation of $\mathbf{P2}(\mathbf{AS}(\mathbf{C}))$ (see Proposition 141).

Thus the element $\langle S, \emptyset \rangle$ plays the role of intermediate value, that is the same role played by the symmetric element $\langle \emptyset, \emptyset \rangle$ in the case of $\mathbf{P}^\#(\mathbf{AS}(\mathbf{C}))$.

Observe that we can have a "symmetric" proof of the above Proposition, by applying duality theory.

First, notice that $\Omega_A(\mathbf{T})$ (see Definition 68) is (clopen) decreasing in the dual Priestley space of $\mathbf{AS}(\mathbf{C}) \coprod \mathbf{3}$, thus it is the dual of a P_2-lattice $\mathbf{L2}$ (see [Pr1]). So we have our result at a glance.

But we can go somewhat further in characterizing this lattice within the Post algebra $\mathbf{AS}(\mathbf{C}) \coprod \mathbf{3}$: $\mathbf{L2}$ must correspond by duality to a quotient of $\mathbf{AS}(\mathbf{C}) \coprod \mathbf{3}$ modulo a principal filter F. As a matter of fact it is possible to prove that $F = \uparrow g$.

In the congruence relation Φ induced by $\uparrow g$ on $\mathbf{AS}(\mathbf{C}) \coprod \mathbf{3}$, $g\Phi 1, e_1 \Phi f_1$, $\sim g\Phi \langle S, g_1 \rangle = \sim (!g)$.

Example 17. Consider example 14 from the point of view of Chain Based Lattices: the lattice $\mathbf{P0} = (RS_{r^*}(\mathbf{C}), \wedge, \vee, \supset, \div, e_0 = \langle \emptyset, \emptyset \rangle, e_1 = \langle \{a, b\}, \emptyset \rangle, e_2 =$

$\langle\{a,b,c\},\{a,b,c\}\rangle)$ is a P_0-lattice but not a P_1-lattice. It can be made into a P_1-lattice (hence in this case, into a P_2-lattice) if we substitute e_1 by $f_1 = \langle\{a,b,c\},\{c\}\rangle$ (see [Tr3]).

THE LATTICE **P1**

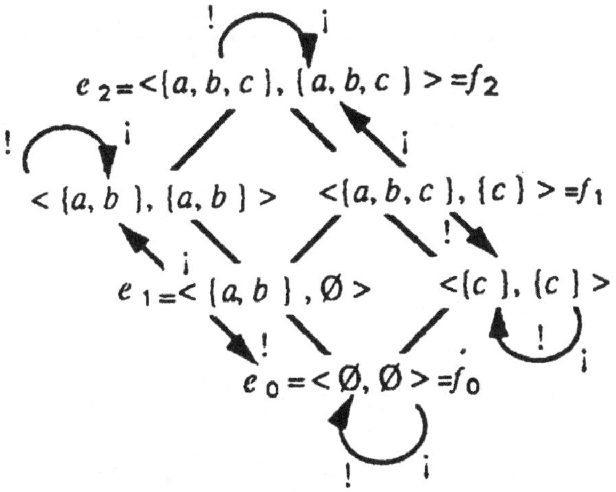

Fig. 21.

For a more complete example let us come back to the Approximation Space of example 2. Here $S^* = \{\{e\}\}$. In the following diagram the Post algebra $\mathbf{P}^{\#}(\mathbf{AS}(\mathbf{C}))$ is shown (only the relevant elements are explicit).

The lattice $N_\Theta(A)$ equals the carrier of $\mathbf{P}^{\#}(\mathbf{AS}(\mathbf{C}))$, $\vec{N}\,(A)$, minus the plane drawn in dotted lines.

The congruence relation Θ on the Boolean algebra $\mathbf{AS}(\mathbf{C})$ is induced by the filter $\uparrow \{e\}$.

The double arrows show the congruence relation Φ on $\mathbf{P}^{\#}(\mathbf{AS}(\mathbf{C}))$ induced by $\uparrow g = \uparrow \langle U \cap -\{e\}, \emptyset\rangle$.

The ideal $\downarrow g$ is isomorphic to $N_\Theta(A)$:

Notice that $p(e_1) = p(\langle\emptyset,\emptyset\rangle) = \langle\{e\},\emptyset\rangle = f_1$ is the least dense element in the interval $[f_0, f_2]$. To see this from a topological point of view (see example 1), it suffices to notice that $\langle\{e\},\emptyset\rangle = \langle\bigcup\{e\},\bigcup\emptyset\rangle = h^*(\langle S^*,\emptyset\rangle) = k(\{\{e\}^{\mathcal{I}}, \{c,d\}^{\mathcal{C}}, \{a,b\}^{\mathcal{C}}\})$. The latter element is dense in the Alexandrov topology $\Omega_A(\mathbf{X}(\mathbf{AS}(\mathbf{C}) \nearrow S^*))$; in fact we have:

- $-\{\{e\}^{\mathcal{I}}, \{c,d\}^{\mathcal{C}}, \{a,b\}^{\mathcal{C}}\} = \{\{a,b\}^{\mathcal{I}}, \{c,d\}^{\mathcal{I}}\}$; thus
- $\mathcal{I}(-\{\{e\}^{\mathcal{I}}, \{c,d\}^{\mathcal{C}}, \{a,b\}^{\mathcal{C}}\}) = \emptyset$ and
- $\mathcal{IC}(\{\{e\}^{\mathcal{I}}, \{c,d\}^{\mathcal{C}}, \{a,b\}^{\mathcal{C}}\}) = \mathbf{X}(\mathbf{AS}(\mathbf{C}) \nearrow S^*)$.

(It is worth noticing that since any P_2-lattice (of order n) is a Stone lattice (of order n), we get immediately the first part of the results of Subsection 3.4).

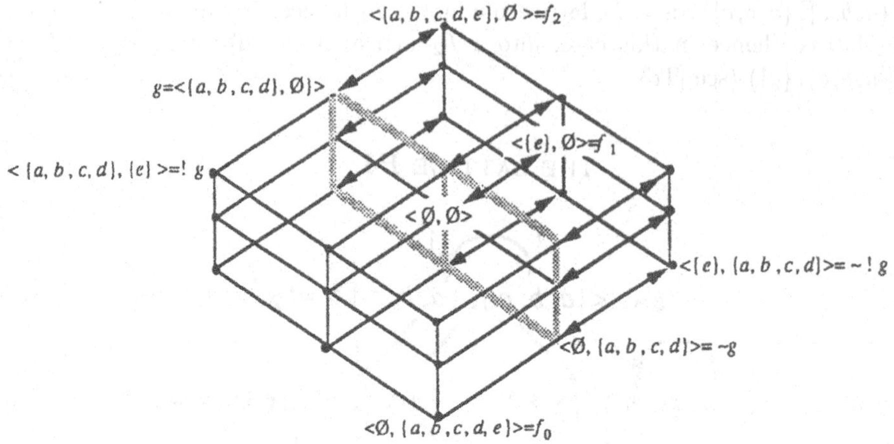

Fig. 22.

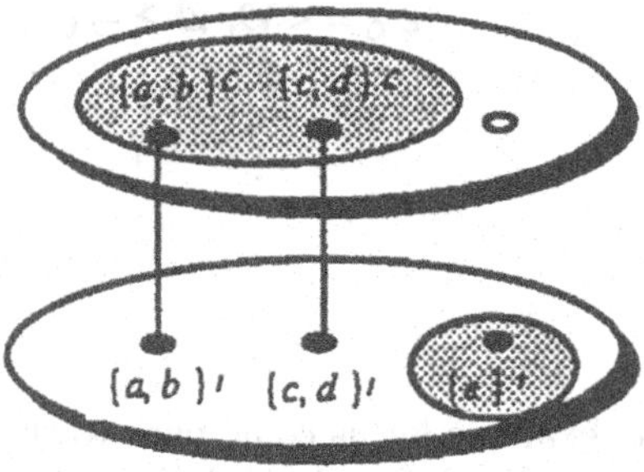

Fig. 23.

This interpretation for Rough Set Systems leads to natural operations connected to definability. We need some definitions:

Definition 144. 1. a Heyting algebra $\mathbf{A} = (A, \wedge, \vee, \neg, \Longrightarrow, 0, 1)$ is called an *L-algebra* if for all $x, y \in A$,

$$(x \Longrightarrow y) \vee (y \Longrightarrow x) = 1 \ .$$

2. a *B*-algebra $\mathbf{A} = (A, \wedge, \vee, \neg, \overset{c}{\Rightarrow}, 0, 1)$ is called a *BL-algebra* if for all $x, y \in A$,

$$(x \overset{c}{\Rightarrow} y) \vee (y \overset{c}{\Rightarrow} x) = 1 \ .$$

3. A bounded distributive lattice $\mathbf{A}$ such that both $\mathbf{A}$ and its dual $\mathbf{A}^d$ are L-algebras and BL-algebras is called a *P-lattice*.

We recall the following fact that one can recover from the results in [EH1] and [EH2]

Lemma 145. *Let* **A** *be a finite distributive lattice: then* **A** *is a P-algebra iff* **A** *is a* P_0*-lattice.*

Lemma 146. *If* **A** *is a* P_0*-lattice then* ! *is an interior operator satisfying* $!(x \vee y) = !x \vee !y$ *and* $!(x \wedge y) = !x \wedge !y$.

This result and the dual that one can state after the next definition, must be directly related to Lemma 111. Since for a P-algebra **A**, both **A** and $\mathbf{A}^d$ (the dual of **A**) are Heyting algebras and B-algebras, the following operations are always defined in **A**:

4.13

1. dual relative pseudo-complementation: $x \leftarrow y : x \vee z \geq y$ *iff* $z \geq x \leftarrow y$.
2. dual pseudo-complementation: $\star x : x \leftarrow 1$.
3. dual relative pseudo-supplementation: $x \overset{\mathcal{C}}{\Leftarrow} y : x \vee z \geq y$ *iff* $z \geq x \overset{\mathcal{C}}{\Leftarrow} y$ *for* $z \in \mathcal{CTR}(\mathbf{A})$.
4. dual pseudo-supplementation: ¡x: $0 \overset{\mathcal{C}}{\Leftarrow} x$.

From this definitions we have that

Lemma 147. *In any P-algebras*

1. *$!x$ is the greatest element in $\mathcal{CTR}(\mathbf{A})$ less or equal to x.*
2. *¡x is the least element in $\mathcal{CTR}(\mathbf{A})$ greater or equal to x.*

The following table illustrates the correspondences among the interpretations of Rough Set Systems introduced till now:

semi-simple Nelson algebras	*3-valued Lukasiewicz algebra*	P_2 *− algebras*
$\div\div$	D_1	¡
$\neg\neg$	D_2	!

In order to understand which representation of rough sets is defined by the above constructions, consider the following map:

4.14 $r^* : \mathbb{P}(U) \longmapsto \mathbb{P}(U) \times \mathbb{P}(U) : r^*(X) = \langle \mathcal{C}(X), \mathcal{I}(X) \rangle$

From the construction of the Post field $\mathbf{P}(\mathrm{T})$ and Definition 130 it follows that $RS_{\mathrm{r}^*}(\mathbf{C}) = \mathrm{r}^*(\mathbb{P}(U))$

Let $r^*(X) = x$ and let $(d_1 \wedge e_1) \vee (d_2 \wedge e_2)$ be the monotonic representation of the element $x \in r^*(\mathbb{P}(U))$.

The monotonic representation reflects the intuitive fact that e_1 evaluates the closure and e_2 the interior of X. Thus e_0 evaluates the boundary of X (the 0-th layer).

More precisely, consider the map:

$$\textbf{4.15}\ c_X : U \longmapsto \{e_0, e_1, e_2\} : c_X(a) = \begin{cases} e_2 \textit{ if } a \in I(X) \\ e_1 \textit{ if } a \in C(X) \\ e_0 \textit{ if } a \in \mathcal{B}(X) \end{cases}$$

(c_X is not a function: $c_X^{-1}(e_1) \cap c_X^{-1}(e_0) \supseteq \emptyset$)

Clearly $c_X^{-1}(e_i)$ is a definable subset of U. Hence

$$r^*(c_X^{-1}(e_i)) \in \mathcal{CTR}(\mathbf{P}(\mathbf{AS}(\mathbf{C}))) \ .$$

Then if $d_1 = r^*(c_X^{-1}(e_1))$ and $d_2 = r^*(c_X^{-1}(e_2))$ we have:

$$d_1 \supseteq d_2 \text{ and } r^*(X) = (d_1 \wedge e_1) \vee (d_2 \wedge e_2)$$

(monotonic representation)

If we set $d_0 = r^*(c_X^{-1}(e_0))$ we will have:

$$d_0 \wedge d_2 = \emptyset \text{ and } r^*(X) = (d_0 \wedge e_1) \vee (d_2 \wedge e_2)$$

(disjoint representation).

In general we obtain the following representations of rough sets:

4.16 *1.* $r(X) = \langle c_X^{-1}(e_2), -c_X^{-1}(e_1)\rangle = \langle \mathcal{I}(X), \mathcal{E}(X)\rangle$;
2. $r^*(X) = \langle c_X^{-1}(e_1), c_X^{-1}(e_2)\rangle = \langle \mathcal{C}(X), \mathcal{I}(X)\rangle$;
3. $r_2(X) = \langle c_X^{-1}(e_1), c_X^{-1}(e_0)\rangle = \langle \mathcal{C}(X), \mathcal{B}(X)\rangle$;
4. $r_1(X) = \langle c_X^{-1}(e_2), c_X^{-1}(e_0)\rangle = \langle \mathcal{I}(X), \mathcal{B}(X)\rangle$.

Lemma 148. *The maps r, r^*, r_1 and r_2 from $\mathbb{P}(U)$ to $\mathbb{P}(U) \times \mathbb{P}(U)$, are bijections from the quotient set $\mathbb{P}(U)/_{\equiv}$ onto the set $Z \subseteq \mathbb{P}(U) \times \mathbb{P}(U)$ whose elements satisfy conditions (i)-(iv) of Definition 39*

(see [PP1], [Iw1], [Pa2]).

The algebraic operations definable on $r(\mathbb{P}(U))$ and $r^*(\mathbb{P}(U))$ have a more intuitive evidence and more elementary definitions.

Example 18. Let us consider the Post algebra of example 16 and the subset $Z = \{a, b, c\}$ of U. Then let us verify 4.15: $c_Z^{-1}(e_2) = \{a, b\}$, $c_Z^{-1}(e_1) = \{a, b, c, d\}$, $c_Z^{-1}(e_0) = \{c, d\}$.

Thus $d_0 = r^*(c_Z^{-1}(e_0)) = \langle\{c, d\}, \{c, d\}\rangle = \langle \bigcup pj(\{c, d\}^{\mathcal{I}}, \{c, d\}^{\mathcal{C}}), \bigcup pj(\{c, d\}^{\mathcal{I}}, \{c, d\}^{\mathcal{C}})\rangle = b_2^*$; $d_1 = r^*(c_Z^{-1}(e_1)) = \langle\{a, b, c, d\}, \{a, b, c, d\}\rangle = b_3^*$; $d_2 = r^*(c_Z^{-1}(e_2)) = \langle\{a, b\}, \{a, b\}\rangle = b_1^*$.

Hence, we can verify that if we use the monotonic representation then we have:

$$\begin{aligned} Y^* &= (b_3^* \wedge e_1^*) \vee (b_1^* \wedge e_2^*) \\ &= (d_1 \wedge \langle\{a, b, c, d\}, \emptyset\rangle) \vee (d_2 \wedge \langle\{a, b, c, d\}, \{a, b, c, d\}\rangle) \\ &= \langle\{a, b, c, d\}, \emptyset\rangle \vee \langle\{a, b\}, \{a, b\}\rangle = \langle\{a, b, c, d\}, \{a, b\}\rangle. \end{aligned}$$

If we use the disjoint representation then we obtain:

$$\begin{aligned} Y^* &= (b_2^* \wedge e_1^*) \vee (b_1^* \wedge e_2^*) \\ &= (d_0 \wedge \langle\{a, b, c, d\}, \emptyset\rangle) \vee (d_2 \wedge \langle\{a, b, c, d\}, \{a, b, c, d\}\rangle) \\ &= \langle\{c, d\}, \emptyset\rangle \vee \langle\{a, b\}, \{a, b\}\rangle = \langle\{a, b, c, d\}, \{a, b\}\rangle. \end{aligned}$$

We can also obtain $r^*(\mathbb{P}(U))$ by means of a generalization of the ideal function construction proposed in [Ra2] (see also [ER1]).

Definition 149.

1. Let $\mathbf{T}$ be the poset $(\{\mathcal{C},\mathcal{I}\},\mathcal{C}\leq\mathcal{I})$.
2. Let $LT(\mathbf{T}) = \{I : I \text{ is an order ideal of } \mathbf{T}\}$. Thus $LT(\mathbf{T}) = \{0=\emptyset, 1=\{\mathcal{C}\}, 2=\{\mathcal{C},\mathcal{I}\}\}$.
3. Let ELT be the ordered set of Post constants $(e_0 \leq e_1 \leq e_2)$; the order of ELT is clearly induced, via the indices, by the subset ordering of $LT(\mathbf{T})$.

Then the structure:

4.17 $\mathbf{P}(\mathbf{T}) = (LT(T), \cup, \cap, \langle d_t\rangle_{t\in T}, ELT)$ *with the following operation:*

$$d_t : LT(\mathbf{T}) \longmapsto \{e_0, e_2\} : d_t(I) = \begin{cases} e_2 \ \textit{if}\ t\in I \\ e_0 \ \textit{otherwise} \end{cases}$$

$I \in LT(\mathbf{T})$, $t\in\mathbf{T}$ *is said to be a* basic (semi) Post algebra.

Now consider the field $\mathbf{B} = \Omega_A(Atom(\mathbf{AS}(\mathbf{C})))$ – that is the Boolean algebra of $\mathbb{P}(Atom(\mathbf{AS}(\mathbf{C})))$ – and the set $\mathbf{F}_T(Atom(\mathbf{AS}(\mathbf{C})))$ of all functions $f : Atom(\mathbf{AS}(\mathbf{C})) \longmapsto LT(\mathbf{T})$.

Assign to every $f \in \mathbf{F}_T(Atom(\mathbf{AS}(\mathbf{C})))$ a function $d_t f(\alpha)$. It follows from the definition of d_t that

Lemma 150. $d_t f(\alpha) = \begin{cases} e_2 \ \textit{if}\ t\in f(\alpha) \\ e_0 \ \textit{otherwise} \end{cases}$

Intuitively, $f(\alpha)=1$ means that α is a subset of the closure, $f(\alpha)=2$ means that α is included in the interior and $f(\alpha)=0$ means that α is included in the external. Clearly:

4.18 *if* $t\leq s$ *then* $d_t f(\alpha)\geq d_s f(\alpha)$.

Thus $d_{\mathcal{C}} f(\alpha) \geq d_{\mathcal{I}} f(\alpha)$. And this means precisely that the interior is included in the closure.

Let us define subsets of $Atom(\mathbf{AS}(\mathbf{C}))$ for each $t\in T$ in the following way:

$$\mathcal{S}(d_t f) = \{\alpha \in Atom(\mathbf{AS}(\mathbf{C})) : d_t f(\alpha) = e_2\} \ .$$

Finally, let us consider the sequences of type

$$\langle \mathcal{S}(d_t f)_{t\in T}\rangle \text{ for } f\in \mathbf{F}_T(Atom(\mathbf{AS}(\mathbf{C})))$$

and their projections on A:

$$\langle \bigcup \mathcal{S}(d_t f)_{t\in T}\rangle \ .$$

From 4.18 these sequences are (2-elements) decreasing sequences. This is the classical construction. But $\mathbf{P}(\mathbf{AS}(\mathbf{C}))$ is a sublattice of the lattice $(\{\langle\bigcup \mathcal{S}(d_t f)_{t\in T}\rangle : f\in\mathbf{F}_T(Atom(\mathbf{A}))\}, \subseteq)$.

Indeed, we have to discard some sequence in order to get exactly $\mathbf{P}(\mathbf{AS}(\mathbf{C}))$. If S^* is the set of elementary sets α such that $card(\alpha) = 1$, our intuition about rough sets suggests consideration of the following subset $\mathbf{F}_T(S^*)$ of $\mathbf{F}_T(Atom(\mathbf{AS}(\mathbf{C})))$:

$$\{f \in \mathbf{F}_T(Atom(\mathbf{AS}(\mathbf{C}))) : \forall \alpha \in S^*, (f(\alpha) \neq 0 \Longrightarrow f(\alpha) = 2)\} \ .$$

As a matter of fact saying that $f(\alpha) = e_2$ means that α is a subset both of the interior and of the closure of a set and this is precisely what is expected to happen for any elementary set reduced to a singleton. Thus we have

4.19

$$\{\langle \bigcup \mathcal{S}(d_t f)_{t \in T}\rangle : f \in \mathbf{F}_T(S)\} = RS^*_r(\mathbf{C}) \ .$$

Example 19. Using lattice **P1** of example 17, we can illustrate an instance of this functional construction: let us, first, notice that $r^*(\{c, b\}) = r^*(\{c, a\}) = \langle\{a, b, c\}, \{c\}\rangle \in r^*(\mathbb{P}(U))$. Now the element $\langle\{a, b, c\}, \{c\}\rangle$ is defined by the following function f: $f(\{a, b\}) = 1$, $f(\{c\}) = 2$.

Since $f(\{c\}) = 2$, $f \in \mathbf{F}_T(S^*)$ for $S^* = \{\{c\}\}$. So f is a legal function.

Then $\mathcal{S}(d_C f) = \{\{a, b\}, \{c\}\}, \mathcal{S}(d_{\mathcal{I}} f) = \{\{c\}\}$.

Hence $\langle \bigcup \mathcal{S}(d_t f)_{t \in \{C \leq \mathcal{I}\}}\rangle = \langle \bigcup\{\{a, b\}, \{c\}\}, \bigcup\{\{c\}\}\rangle = \langle\{a, b, c\}, \{c\}\rangle$.

5 Representation of Finite Semi-Simple Nelson Algebras by Rough Set Systems

We end the paper by showing that Rough Set Systems are, in a sense, inherent to finite semi-simple Nelson algebras (and therefore to finite three-valued Łukasiewicz algebras). We will support this claim by proving a representation theorem for finite semi-simple Nelson algebras in terms of Rough Set Systems.

First, we would like to sum up the discussion of the first four Sections by proving a result that is a sort of "anatomic analysis" of Rough Set Systems.

We recall that given a Heyting algebra $\mathbf{H} = (H, \vee, \wedge, \Longrightarrow, \neg, 0, 1)$ and an Approximation Space $\mathbf{AS}(\mathbf{C})$:

1. Θ^- is the greatest Boolean congruence on $\mathbf{H}$;
2. Θ^+ is the least Boolean congruence on $\mathbf{H}$;
3. Θ^- is induced by the non-proper filter H;
4. Θ^+ is induced by the filter of all and only the dense elements of $\mathbf{H}$ (an element $x \in \mathbf{H}$ is dense iff $\neg\neg x = 1$);
5. $\overrightarrow{\mathbf{N}}(\mathbf{H})$ is the Nelson algebra with carrier $\overrightarrow{N}(\mathbf{H}) = \{\langle a_1, a_2\rangle \in \mathbf{H}^2 : a_1 \wedge a_2 = 0, (a_1 \vee a_2)\Theta^- 1\}$; hence $\overrightarrow{N}(\mathbf{H}) = \{\langle a_1, a_2\rangle \in \mathbf{H}^2 : a_1 \wedge a_2 = 0\}$;
6. $\overleftarrow{\mathbf{N}}(\mathbf{H})$ is the Nelson algebra with carrier $\overleftarrow{N}(\mathbf{H}) = \{\langle a_1, a_2\rangle \in \mathbf{H}^2 : a_1 \wedge a_2 = 0, (a_1 \vee a_2)\Theta^+ 1\}$;
7. $S^* = \{\alpha \in Ind(\mathbf{C}) : card(\alpha) = 1\}$;
8. $P^* = Ind(\mathbf{C}) \cap -S^*$.

9. $\mathbf{N}(\mathbf{AS}(\mathbf{C})) = \mathbf{N}_\Theta(\mathbf{AS}(\mathbf{C}))$, where Θ is induced by $\uparrow \bigcup S^*$.

Then

Proposition 151. *Given an Approximation Space* $\mathbf{AS}(\mathbf{C})$,

1. $\mathbf{AS}(\mathbf{C}) \cong_B \mathbf{B}^{P^*} \times \mathbf{B}^{S^*}$, *where given a set* X, $\mathbf{B}^X$ *is defined in 30;*
2. $\mathbf{N}(\mathbf{AS}(\mathbf{C})) \cong_N \overrightarrow{\mathbf{N}}(\mathbf{B}^{P^*}) \times \overleftarrow{\mathbf{N}}(\mathbf{B}^{S^*})$.

We have seen that $\overleftarrow{\mathbf{N}}(\mathbf{B}^{S^*})$ is a Boolean algebra: in fact for all $\langle A_1, A_2\rangle \in \overleftarrow{N}(\mathbf{B}^{S^*})$, $A_2 = -A_1$.

On the contrary, $\overrightarrow{\mathbf{N}}(\mathbf{B}^{P^*})$ is a "centered" semi-simple Nelson algebra with "central element" $\langle\emptyset,\emptyset\rangle$; thus it can be made into a Post algebra of order three taking as Post chain: $(0 = \langle\emptyset, \bigcup P^*\rangle, \langle\emptyset,\emptyset\rangle, \langle\bigcup P^*, \emptyset\rangle = 1)$.

Proof. The proof uses the following general result (see [DD1]). In what follows, given a (Nelson, Heyting) space $\mathbf{X}$, by $\mathbf{O}(\mathbf{X})$ we mean the generic operation of taking the dual (Nelson, Heyting) algebra:

Lemma 152. *Let* $\mathbf{X}$ *and* $\mathbf{X}'$ *be two spaces, then*

$$\mathbf{O}(\mathbf{X} \oplus \mathbf{X}') = \mathbf{O}(\mathbf{X}) \times \mathbf{O}(\mathbf{X}')$$

where $\oplus$ *is the ordinal sum (juxtaposition) of the two spaces.*

So, since $\mathbf{X}(\mathbf{AS}(\mathbf{C})) = \mathbf{HS}(\mathbf{AS}(\mathbf{C})) = Ind(\mathbf{C})$ we can partition $\mathbf{X}(\mathbf{AS}(\mathbf{C}))$ in the two subspaces S^* and P^*. Clearly $S^* \oplus P^* = \mathbf{X}(\mathbf{AS}(\mathbf{C}))$, $P^* = \mathbf{X}(\mathbf{B}^{P^*})$ and $S^* = \mathbf{X}(\mathbf{B}^{S^*})$. Thus: $\mathbf{AS}(\mathbf{C}) \cong_B \mathbf{O}(\mathbf{X}(\mathbf{AS}(\mathbf{C}))) \cong_B \mathbf{O}(\mathbf{X}(\mathbf{B}^{P^*}) \oplus \mathbf{X}(\mathbf{B}^{S^*})) \cong_B \mathbf{O}(\mathbf{X}(\mathbf{B}^{P^*})) \times \mathbf{O}(\mathbf{X}(\mathbf{B}^{S^*})) \cong_B \mathbf{B}^{P^*} \times \mathbf{B}^{S^*}$.

For the second part we apply the above Lemma and the following one (see [BD1]):

Lemma 153. *Let* $\mathbf{L} \in \mathcal{L}_n$. *Then any prime ideal of* $\mathbf{L}$ *is contained in exacly one maximal chain of at most* $n-1$ *prime ideals.*

Since the class of semi-simple Nelson algebras and the class $\mathcal{L}_3$ coincide, by reasoning on prime filters instead of prime ideals and substituting prime filters by coprime elements (since we are in the finite case), we find that the dual space of $\mathbf{N}_\Theta(\mathbf{AS}(\mathbf{C}))$ can be split in two parts: $\mathbf{NS}(\mathbf{N}_\Theta(\mathbf{AS}(\mathbf{C})))^{P^*} = \{\alpha : \alpha$ is a chain of exactly two coprime elements$\}$ and $\mathbf{NS}(\mathbf{N}_\Theta(\mathbf{AS}(\mathbf{C})))^{S^*} = \{\alpha : \alpha$ is the singleton of a coprime element$\}$.

Now it is easy to see that $\mathbf{NS}(\mathbf{N}_\Theta(\mathbf{AS}(\mathbf{C})))^{S^*} \cong_{PI} \mathbf{X}(\mathbf{B}^{S^*} \nearrow S^*)$ and $\mathbf{NS}(\mathbf{N}_\Theta(\mathbf{AS}(\mathbf{C})))^{P^*} \cong_{PI} \mathbf{X}(\mathbf{B}^{P^*} \nearrow \emptyset)$. Hence $\mathbf{N}(\mathbf{NS}(\mathbf{N}_\Theta(\mathbf{AS}(\mathbf{C})))^{S^*}) \cong_N \overleftarrow{\mathbf{N}}(\mathbf{B}^{S^*})$ while $\mathbf{N}(\mathbf{NS}(\mathbf{N}_\Theta(\mathbf{AS}(\mathbf{C})))^{P^*}) \cong_N \overrightarrow{\mathbf{N}}(\mathbf{B}^{P^*})$.

But $\mathbf{NS}(\mathbf{N}_\Theta(\mathbf{AS}(\mathbf{C})))^{P^*} \oplus \mathbf{NS}(\mathbf{N}_\Theta(\mathbf{AS}(\mathbf{C})))^{S^*} = \mathbf{NS}(\mathbf{N}_\Theta(\mathbf{AS}(\mathbf{C})))$. Thus $\mathbf{N}(\mathbf{AS}(\mathbf{C})) = \mathbf{N}_\Theta(\mathbf{AS}(\mathbf{C})) \cong_N \mathbf{N}(\mathbf{NS}(\mathbf{N}_\Theta(\mathbf{AS}(\mathbf{C})))) \cong_N \overleftarrow{\mathbf{N}}(\mathbf{B}^{S^*}) \times \overrightarrow{\mathbf{N}}(\mathbf{B}^{P^*})$.

□

Proposition 154. *1. For any Approximation Space* $\mathbf{AS(C)}$, $RS(\mathbf{C})$ *can be made into a finite semi-simple Nelson algebra* $\mathbf{N(AS(C))}$ *(into a finite three-valued Łukasiewicz algebra* $\mathbf{Ł(AS(C))}$*);*
2. any finite semi-simple Nelson algebra (finite three-valued Łukasiewicz algebra) is isomorphic to such an algebra.

Proof. The first part has been proved in the previous Sections. Now we prove the second part, that is given a finite semi-simple Nelson algebra $\mathbf{A}$, we show how to recover an Approximation Space $\mathbf{AS(A)}$ such that $\mathbf{N(AS(A))} \cong_N \mathbf{A}$.

Since $\mathbf{A}$ is semi-simple we have seen that $\mathbf{NS(A)}$ is formed of chains of coprime elements of at most length 2. Thus we have:

(i) $\forall y \in \mathbf{NS(A)}, y \in [g(x), x]$ or $y \in [x, g(x)]$ implies $y = x$ or $y = g(x)$.
Let us then consider the sets:
(ii) $[x]_g = \{x, g(x)\}$ and
(iii) $I(\mathbf{A}) = \{[x]_g : x \in \mathcal{J}(\mathbf{A})\}$

From the linearity of g and from the fact that g is totally defined, $I(\mathbf{A})$ is a partition of $\mathcal{J}(\mathbf{A})$. Let us set $\mathbf{AS(A)} = \mathbf{B}^{I(\mathbf{A})}$. Then $\mathbf{AS(A)}$ is a subalgebra of $\mathbf{B}(\mathcal{J}(\mathbf{A}))$.

Let us show that $\mathbf{N(AS(A))} \cong_N \mathbf{A}$.

If $S^* = \{[x]_g \in I(\mathbf{A}) : card([x]_g) = 1\}$, $S = \bigcup S^*$ and Θ is the congruence induced by the filter $\uparrow S$, we know from the first part of this Proposition that $\mathbf{N(AS(A))} = N_\Theta(\mathbf{AS(A)})$.

Consider the space $\mathbf{X}(\mathbf{AS(A)} \nearrow S^*)$ defined with the construction referred to in the first part of this proof.

We know that $\mathbf{N}(\mathbf{X}(\mathbf{AS(A)} \nearrow S^*)) \cong_N \mathbf{N}^K_{S^*}(\mathbf{HS}(\mathbf{AS(A)})) = \mathbf{N}_\Theta(\mathbf{AS(A)})$, and this means that $\mathbf{X}(\mathbf{AS(A)} \nearrow S^*)$ and $\mathbf{X}(\mathbf{N}_\Theta(\mathbf{AS(A)}))$ are PI-isomorphic.

Consider the map:

$$h : \mathbf{X}(\mathbf{AS(A)} \nearrow S^*) \longmapsto \mathbf{NS(A)} : h(W) = \begin{cases} \mathbf{min}(W) & \text{if } W \le g_{S^*}(W) \\ \mathbf{max}(W) & \text{if } g_{S^*}(W) \le W \end{cases}$$

The definition is correct since if $g_{S^*}(W) = W$ then $card(W) = 1$ and $\mathbf{max}(W) = \mathbf{min}(W)$.

(a) h is order preserving:
if $W \le Z$ then $Z = g_{S^*}(W) \ge W$; hence $h(W) = \mathbf{min}(W) \le \mathbf{max}(W) = h(Z)$.

(b) h is an order embedding:
if $h(W_1) = h(W_2)$ then either $\mathbf{min}(W_1) = \mathbf{min}(W_2)$ or $\mathbf{max}(W_1) = \mathbf{max}(W_2)$. Since $I(\mathbf{A})$ is a partition of $\mathcal{J}(\mathbf{A})$, $W_1 \ne W_2$ implies $W_1 \cap W_2 = \emptyset$, thus in both cases, we have $W_1 = W_2$. Hence, if $W_1 \ne W_2$, then $h(W_1) \ne h(W_2)$.

(c) h is an epimorphism, hence an order isomorphism:
we have to prove that $\forall x \in \mathcal{J}(\mathbf{A}), \exists a \in \mathbf{X}(\mathbf{AS(A)} \nearrow S^*)$, such that $x = h(a)$. So let $x \in \mathcal{J}(\mathbf{A})$ and consider the elements $[x]_g$ and $[x]'_g$ belonging to $\mathbf{X}(\mathbf{AS(A)} \nearrow S^*)$: since $[x]_g \le [x]'_g$, $[x]_g \le g_{S^*}([x]_g) = [x]'_g$ and $[x]_g =$

$g_{S^*}([x]'_g) \leq [x]'_g$. If $\forall y \in [x]_g, x \leq y$, then $x = \mathbf{min}([x]_g) = h([x]_g)$. Dually, if $x \geq y$, then $x = \mathbf{max}([x]_g) = h([x]'_g)$ (obviously, if $[x]_g = [x]'_g$, then $\forall y \in [x]_g, x = y$; thus $[x]_g = g_{S^*}([x]'_g) = g_{S^*}([x]_g) = [x]'_g$ and $h([x]_g) = h([x]'_g)$).

Therefore:

a) both $\mathbf{X}(\mathbf{AS}(\mathbf{A}) \nearrow S^*)$ and $\mathbf{NS}(\mathbf{A})$ are partitioned in chains of length at most 2.
b) g_{S^*} is an involutive order reversing automorphism on $\mathbf{X}(\mathbf{AS}(\mathbf{A}) \nearrow S^*)$,
c) g is an involutive order reversing automorphism on $\mathbf{NS}(\mathbf{A})$ and
d) h is an order-isomorphism between $\mathbf{X}(\mathbf{AS}(\mathbf{A}) \nearrow S^*)$ and $\mathbf{NS}(\mathbf{A})$. It follows that $g(h(x)) = h(g_{S^*}(x)), \forall x \in \mathbf{X}(\mathbf{AS}(\mathbf{A}) \nearrow S^*)$, that is, the two structures are PI-isomorphic.

Thus $\mathbf{A} \cong_N \mathbf{N}(\mathbf{NS}(\mathbf{A})) \cong_N \mathbf{N}(\mathbf{X}(\mathbf{AS}) \nearrow S^*) \cong_N \mathbf{N}(\mathbf{AS}(\mathbf{A}))$. □

Observe that due to their very general algebraic meaning these results are related to the decomposition and representation results of Moisil and Cignoli (see [Mo1] and [Ci1]). Our contribution consists in proving that given a finite semi-simple Nelson algebra **A** (a finite Łukasiewicz algebra), the decomposition process of **A** may be suspended at a well determined moment, namely when we get the point corresponding to the P^*/S^*-decomposition of the atoms of $\mathbf{AS}(\mathbf{A})$, thus exhibiting the "logical core" of the analyzed structure.

References

[BD1] Balbes, R., Dwinger, Ph.: Distributive Lattices. University of Missouri Press, (1974)

[BD2] Balbes, R. & Dwinger, Ph.: Coproducts of Boolean algebras with applications to Post algebras. Colloq. Math., **24**, 1, (1971), 15–25

[BFGR1] Boicescu, V., Filipoiu, A., Georgescu, G. & Rudeanu, S.: Łukasiewicz-Moisil Algebras. North-Holland, Amsterdam-New York-Oxford-Tokio, (1991)

[CN1] Cattaneo, G. & Nisticó, G.: Brouwer-Zadeh posets and three-valued Łukasiewicz posets. Jour. of Fuzzy Sets and Systems, **25**, (1988), 165–190

[Ci1] Cignoli, R.: Algebras de Moisil de orden n. Ph. D. Thesis, Univ. Nacional del Sur, Bahia Blanca, (1969)

[Ci2] Cignoli, R.: Representation of Łukasiewicz and Post algebras by continuous functions. Colloq. Math., **24**, 2, (1972), 127–138

[Ci3] Cignoli, R.: Coproducts in the category of Kleene and three-valued Łukasiewicz algebras. Studia Logica, **38**, (1979), 237-245

[Ci4] Cignoli, R.: The class of Kleene algebras satisfying an interpolation property and Nelson algebras. Algebra Universalis, **23**, (1986), 262–292

[Co1] Comer, S.: On connections between information systems, rough sets and algebraic logic. In: Algebraic Methods in Logic and Computer Science. Banach Center Publ. **28**, (1993)

[CF1] Cornish, W.H. & Fowler, P.R.: Coproducts of Kleene algebras. Journ. Austral. Math. Soc., **27**, (1979), 209–220

[DP1] Davey, B.A. & Priestly, H.A.: An Introduction to Lattices and Order. Oxford Univ. Press

[DD1] Davey: B.A. & Duffus, D.: Exponentiation and duality. In [Riv1], 43–95

[Du1] Dunn, J.M.: The Algebra of Intensional Logics. Ph.D. Dissertation, University of Pittsburg, (1966)

[Dw1] Dwinger, Ph.: Notes on Post algebras I and II. Indag. Math., **28**, (1966), 462–478

[EH1] Epstein, G. & Horn, A.: P-algebras, an abstraction from Post algebras. Algebra Universalis, **4**, (1974), 195–206. Reprinted in [Ri1], 108–120

[EH2] Epstein, G. & Horn, A.: Chain based lattices. Journal of Mathematics, **55**, 1, (1974), 65–84. Reprinted in [Ri1], 58–76

[ER1] Epstein, G. & Rasiowa, H.: Approximation reasoning and Scott's information systems. Proc. 2nd Int. Symp. on Methodol. for Intelligent Systems, North-Holland, (1987)

[GHKLMS1] Gierz, G., Hofmann, K.H., Keimel, K., Lawson, J.D., Mislove, M. & Scott, D.: A Compendium of Continuous Lattices. Springer Verlag, (1980)

[Ga1] Gabbay, D.M.: LDS - labelled deductive systems. Dept. of Computing, Imperial College of Science, Technology & Medicine, (1992)

[Gi1] Giuntini, R.: A Semantical Investigation on Brouwer-Zadeh logic. Jour. of Phil. Logic, **20**, (1991), 411–433

[Iw1] Iwinski, T.B.: Algebraic approach to rough sets. Bull. Pol. Acad. of Sciences, Math., **35**, 3-4, (1987), 673–683

[Iw2] Iwinski, T.B.: Rough orders and rough concepts. Bull. Polish Acad. of Sciences, Math., **37**, 3-4, (1988), 187–192

[J-L1] Johnson-Laird, P.N.: The Computer and the Mind. Harvard University Press, (1988)

[Jo1] Johnston, P.T.: Stone Spaces. Cambridge University Press, (1982)

[Ku1] Kubat, M.: Conceptual inductive learning: the case of unreliable teachers. Artificial Intell., **52**, (1991), 168–182

[Ka1] Kalman, J.: Lattices with involution. Trans. Amer. Math. Soc., **87**, (1958), 485–491

[LW1] Loksch, P. & Wille, R.: A mathematical model for Conceptual Knowledge Systems. Tech. Hochschule Darmstadt, Preprint Nr. 1325, (1988)

[MP1] Marek, W. & Pawlak, Z.: Rough sets and information systems. Fundamenta Informaticae, **VII**, 1, (1984), 105–115

[MMOU1] Miglioli, P.A., Moscato, U., Ornaghi, M. and Usberti, U.: A constructivism based on classical truth. Notre Dame Jour. of Formal Logic, **30**, 1, (1990), 67–90

[Mo1] Moisil, Gr.C.: Notes sur les logiques non-crysippiennes. Ann. Sc. Univ. Jassy, **26**, (1949)

[Mo2] Moisil, Gr.C.: Les logiques non-chrisyppiennes et leurs applications. Acta Phil. Fennica, **16**, (1963), 137–152

[Mo3] Moisil, Gr.C.: Old and new Essays on Non-Classical Logics. (in Rumanian) Stintifiča, Bucarest, (1965)

[Mon1] Monteiro, A.: Construction des algébres de Nelson finies. Bull. Pol. Acad. of Sciences, Math., **11**, (1963), 359–362

[Mon2] Monteiro, A.: Algebras de Nelson semi-simples (abstract). Rev. Union Mat. Argentina, **21**, (1963), 145–146

[Mon3] Monteiro, A.: Construction des algébres de Łukasiewicz trivalentes dans les algébres de Boole monadiques, I. Math. Japonicae, **12**, (1967), 1–23

[Mon4] Monteiro, A.: Sur les algébres de Heyting symmetriques. Portugaliae, Math., **39**, (1980), 1–237

[NP1] Novotný, M. & Pawlak, Z.: On representation of rough sets by means of information systems. Fundamenta Informaticae, **6**, (1983), 189–296

[NP2] Novotný, M. & Pawlak, Z.: Characterization of rough top equalities and rough bottom equalities. Bull. Polish Acad. of Sciences, Math., **33**, 1-2, (1985), 91–97

[NP3] Novotný, M. & Pawlak, Z.: On rough equalities. Bull. Polish Acad. of Sciences, Math., **33**, 1-2, (1985), 99–104

[NP4] Novotný, M. & Pawlak, Z.: Black box analysis and rough top equalities. Bull. Polish Acad. of Science., Math., **33**, 1-2, (1985), 105–113

[NP5] Novotný, M. & Pawlak, Z.: Algebraic theory of independence in information systems. Fundamenta Informaticae, **14**, (1991), 454–476

[Ob1] Obtułowicz, A.: Rough sets and Heyting algebra valued sets. Bull. Pol. Acad. of Sciences, Math., **35**, 9-10, (1987), 667–671

[Or1] Orłowska, E.: Logic approach to information systems. Fundamenta Informaticae, **VIII**, 3-4, (1985), 359–378

[Or2] Orłowska, E.: Semantics of knowledge operators. Bull. Pol. Acad. of Sciences, Math., **35**, 5-6, (1987), 643–652

[Or3] Orłowska, E.: Logic for reasoning about knowledge. Zeitschr. f. Math. Log. und Grund. d. Math., **35**, (1989), 559–572

[Or4] Orłowska, E.: Relational interpretation of modal logics. In: Andreka, H., Monk, J.D. & Nemeti, I. (eds.): Algebraic Logic, North-Holland, (1991)

[OP1] Orłowska, E. & Pawlak, Z.: Representation of nondeterministic information. Theoretical Computer Science, **29**, (1984), 27–39

[Pa1] Pagliani, P.: Some remarks on special lattices and related constructive logics with strong negation. Notre Dame Jour. of Formal Logic, **31**, 4, (1990), 515–528

[Pa2] Pagliani, P.: A pure logic-algebraic analysis on rough top and rough bottom equalities. In: Ziarko W. (ed.) Proc. of Rough Sets and Knowledge Discovery'93, Banff, October 1993. Springer, 1994, 227–236

[Pa3] Pagliani, P.: Towards a logic of rough set systems. In: Lin, T.Y. & Wildberg, A.M. (eds) Soft Computing, The Society for Comp. Simulation, (1995), 59–62

[Pa4] Pagliani, P.: Rough sets and Nelson algebras. Fundamenta Informaticae, **27**, 2-3, (1996), 205–219

[Paw1] Pawlak, Z.: Rough sets. ICS PAS Reports, **431**, (1981)

[Paw2] Pawlak, Z.: Rough sets. Algebraic and topological approach. Intern. Journ. of Inf. and Comp. Sciences, **11**, (1982), 341–366

[Paw3] Pawlak, Z.: Rough sets and fuzzy sets. Fuzzy Sets and Systems, **17**, (1985), 99–102

[Paw4] Pawlak, Z.: On learning – A rough set approach. In [Sk1], 197–227

[Paw5] Pawlak, Z.: Rough Sets: A Theoretical Approach to Reasoning about Data. Kluwer, Dordrecht-Boston, (1991)

[PP1] Pomykała, J. & Pomykała, J.A.: The Stone algebra of rough sets. Bull. Polish Acad. of Sciences, Math., **36**, 7-8, (1988), 495–508

[Pr1] Priestly, H.A.: Ordered sets and duality for distributive lattices. In: Pouzet, M. & Richard, D. (eds.) Orders: description and roles (Annales of Discrete Mathematics 23), North Holland, (1984), 39–60

[RZ1] Ras, Z.W. & Zemankova, M.: Learning in knowledge based systems, a possibilistic approach. Proc. of 1986 CISS, Princeton, Math., **34**, 3-4, (1986), 844–847

[Ra1] Rasiowa, H.: An Algebraic Approach to Non Classical Logics. North-Holland, (1974)

[Ra2] Rasiowa, H.: Logic approximating sequences of sets. Proc. Int. School and Sympos. on Math. Logic, Drushba, (1987), 167–186

[RS1] Rasiowa, H. & Skowron, A.: Rough concept logic. In: [Sk1], 288–297

[Rau1] Rauszer, C.M.: An equivalence between indiscernibility relations in information systems and a fragment of intuitionistic logic. In: [Sk1], 298–317

[Ri1] Rine, D.C.: Computer Science and Multiple-Valued Logic. Theory and Applications. North-Holland, (1991)

[Riv1] Rival I.: (ed.), Ordered sets. NATO ASI Series 83, Reidel, (1982)

[Se1] Sendlewski, A.: Some investigations of varieties of N-lattices. Studia Logica, **XLIII**, (1984), 258–280

[Se2] Sendlewski, A.: Nelson algebras through Heyting ones: I. Studia Logica, **49**, 1, (1990), 105–126

[Sk1] Skowron, A.: (ed.) Proc. 5th Symp. on Computation Theory. LNCS, 208, Springer-Verlag, (1984)

[Tr1] Traczyk, T.: Axioms and some properties of Post algebras. Colloq. Math., **10**, (1963), 193–210

[Tr2] Traczyk, T.: Lattices with greatest (least) chain base. Bull. Pol. Acad. Sciences, Math., **23**, (1975)

[Tr3] Traczyk, T.: Post algebras through P_0 and P_1 lattices. In: [Ri1], 121–142

[Va1] Vakarelov, D.: Notes on N-lattices and constructive logics with strong negation. Studia Logica, **36**, (1977), 109–125

[Wi1] Wille, R.: Restructuring lattice theory. In: [Riv1], 445–470

III

DEPENDENCE SPACES

Chapter 7

Dependence Spaces of Information Systems

Miroslav Novotný

Masaryk University,
Botanická 68a, Brno, Czech Republic

Abstract: A general model is introduced and investigated of a great variety of finite structures studied in computer science. The model is referred to as dependence space. The main feature of the model is that it enables us to deal with the indiscernibility-type incompleteness of information that a modelled structure might be burdened with. The model provides a general framework for expressing the concept of independence of a set and the concept of dependency between sets with respect to a dependence space. It is shown that these concepts lay the foundation on which many applied structures rest. The theory of dependence spaces is developed aimed at providing tools for studying the problems relevant for the modelled structures.

1 Motivation of the Study of Dependence Spaces

Information systems in Pawlak's sense have many applications (see [Pa7]). These applications are based on a theory of information systems that is developed in the quoted book by Pawlak and in further publications. When studying this theory we meet with an interesting fact: there exist different problems concerning information systems whose solutions are similar but not identical. We quote some examples of such problems: (1) looking for a minimal subtest of a test; (2) cancelling superfluous conditions in a decision table; (3) cancelling superfluous values of conditions in a decision table. This situation leads us to assume that there is a structure and a problem concerning this structure of which the above mentioned problems are special cases.

This structure is called a dependence space in this text. It may be defined to be a finite closure space, but in the text we prefer another formulation of the definition. The aim of this text is to present the theory of dependence spaces (Chapter 7) and its applications to information systems (Chapter 8).

Dependence plays an important role in mathematics and was investigated many times from various points of view. We may quote, e.g., Marczewski ([Ma1]) or Głazek ([Gl1]) for overviews of this matter. The term dependence space appears in the literature also in a different meaning ([HNP1]). Our study of dependence spaces is directed purely to information systems and starts with some results from lattice theory ([Bi1], [BB1], [Sz1]). We investigate particularly finite semilattices, their homomorphisms and congruences. An important role is played by the semilattice of all subsets of a finite nonempty set provided with the operation of union; if a congruence of this semilattice is given, then a dependence space is defined. The set of all subsets of a finite nonempty set provided by rough top equality is presented as an illustration of a dependence space. Complete characterization of rough top equalities is formulated. The results can be transferred to rough bottom equalities. These investigations are completed by a survey of fundamental properties of rough equalities.

For any subset of a dependence space its reducts, subreducts, and superreducts can be defined. Particularly, an algorithm for finding a reduct and an algorithm for finding all reducts of a subset of a dependence space is in the center of our interest. Then, dependence between two subsets of a dependence space is introduced and some problems concerning dependence are solved by means of reducts.

These results are applied to contexts (cf. [Wi1]); to any context, its dependence space is assigned and the problem of generating a concept in an economical way is solved using reducts of subsets of the dependence space. Then all contexts with a prescribed dependence space are constructed. Relational systems may be considered to be contexts of a particular form; thus, any relational system defines a dependence space and all relational systems with a prescribed dependence space can be constructed. The most important relational systems are those whose relations are equivalences; they are called classificatory systems. Classificatory systems are very close to information systems; a dependence space of an information system is defined to be the dependence space of the corresponding classificatory system.

A set of attributes in an information system may be considered to be a test. Natural problems concerning tests are solved, e.g., looking for a subtest of a test such that both provide the same results. This is solved by means of reducts in the corresponding dependence space. Another dependence space is assigned to an information system if studying the so called descriptors. These results are used in the so called consistent decision tables which are particular cases of information systems. Superfluous conditions and superfluous values of conditions in such tables may be found and cancelled using reducts in suitable dependence spaces.

Then, all classificatory systems with a prescribed dependence space are constructed. This means that also the construction of all information systems with a prescribed dependence space is known. In any information system partial dependence is introduced and a distance function on the dependence space is defined using the partial dependence.

In this way, the theory of dependence spaces has become a part of the semilattice theory. This approach enables us to solve various problems concerning information systems by means of modifications of one algorithm. Furthermore, the theory offers some possibilities to study further structures, e.g., Wille's contexts, and enables us to find some relationships between contexts and information systems. Finally, it provides many results concerning information systems that are proved in a different way in the literature.

The author is very grateful to E. Orlowska and Z. Pawlak for the kind invitation to present his results in this form and for fruitful discussions concerning the matter. J. Novotný read a preliminary version of the text and contributed to its improvement, further improvements are due to the referee. I. Hollanová and J. Pelikán helped to prepare the final version of the manuscript. The author would like to express his sincere thanks to all these collaborators.

2 Preliminaries

In what follows we use standard terminology and notation. For the reader's convenience we repeat fundamental definitions and symbols.

We start with sets. The symbol $\emptyset$ denotes the empty set. The operations of union, intersection, difference, and Cartesian product are denoted by $\cup$, $\cap, -$, and $\times$, respectively. If $\mathbf{A}$ is a system of sets, we write $\bigcup\{A; A \in \mathbf{A}\}$ for the union and $\bigcap\{A; A \in \mathbf{A}\}$ for the intersection of these sets. Furthermore, inclusion of sets is denoted by $\subseteq$. For any set A, $\mathbf{B}(A)$ is the system of all subsets of A. If A is a finite set, the number of its elements is denoted by $|A|$.

If A, B are sets and $r \subseteq A \times B$, then r is said to be a correspondence from A to B; if $A = B$, r is called a relation on A. The fact $(x, y) \in r$ is often symbolized by xry. The most important relations have certain particular properties: A relation r on a set A is said to be reflexive if $(x, x) \in r$ for any $x \in A$; it is called transitive if for any elements x, y, z in A the conditions $(x, y) \in r$, $(y, z) \in r$ imply that $(x, z) \in r$. If $(x, y) \in r$ implies that $(y, x) \in r$ for any elements x, y in A, the relation r is said to be symmetric; if $(x, y) \in r$, $(y, x) \in r$ imply that $x = y$, the relation r is called antisymmetric. If r is a relation on A, we put $r^{-1} = \{(y, x) \in A \times A;\ (x, y) \in r\}$. A reflexive and transitive relation is said to be a preordering.

A symmetric preordering r on a set A is called an equivalence on A. If $a \in A$ is arbitrary, then all elements $x \in A$ with $(a, x) \in r$ form a set that is called the block (or equivalence class) of r. The set of all blocks is denoted by A/r; this set is a decomposition (or partition) of the set A, i.e., any two different elements in A/r have empty intersection and the union of all elements in A/r equals A. An important role is played by the equivalence $\mathrm{id}_A = \{(x, x) \in A \times A;\ x \in A\}$.

An antisymmetric preordering on a set is called an ordering. A set with an ordering is said to be an ordered set. Let $\leq$ be an ordering on a set A and $B \subseteq A$. Then $\leq \cap (B \times B)$ is an ordering on B called the restriction of $\leq$ to B that is usually denoted also by $\leq$. We mention that $a < x$ means $a \leq x$, $a \neq x$.

Let $\leq$ be an ordering on a set A, $a \in A$ an element. Then a is said to be the greatest (least) element of A if $x \leq a$ ($a \leq x$) holds for any $x \in A$. An element $a \in A$ is called maximal (minimal) if for any $x \in A$ the condition $a \leq x$ ($x \leq a$) implies $x = a$. If A is a finite set with an ordering $\leq$, then for any $a \in A$ there exists an element $b \in A$ such that $a \leq b$ ($b \leq a$) and that b is maximal (minimal) in A.

These notions enable further constructions. Let A be a set with an ordering $\leq$. Suppose $X \subseteq A$, $a \in A$. Then a is said to be an upper (lower) bound of X if

$x \le a$ ($a \le x$) holds for any $x \in X$. If the set Y of all upper (lower) bounds of X has a least (greatest) element, then it is called the least upper (greatest lower) bound of X and is denoted by $\sup X$ ($\inf X$). If $\sup\emptyset$ exists, it is the least element of the ordered set. More about ordering relations may be found in the books [Bi1], [BB1], [Sz1].

An ordering $\le$ on a set A is said to be linear if for any elements $x \in A$, $y \in A$ either $x \le y$ or $y \le x$ holds.

Finite ordered sets may be represented by their Hasse diagrams in a usual way. In particular, in many of our examples, we shall consider the set $\mathbf{B}(A)$ ordered by inclusion where $A = \{a, b, c\}$. For the sake of brevity, we put $\emptyset = 0, \{a\} = 1, \{b\} = 2, \{c\} = 3, \{a, b\} = 12, \{a, c\} = 13, \{b, c\} = 23,\ A = 123$. The Hasse diagram of $\mathbf{B}(A)$ is represented in Fig. 1.

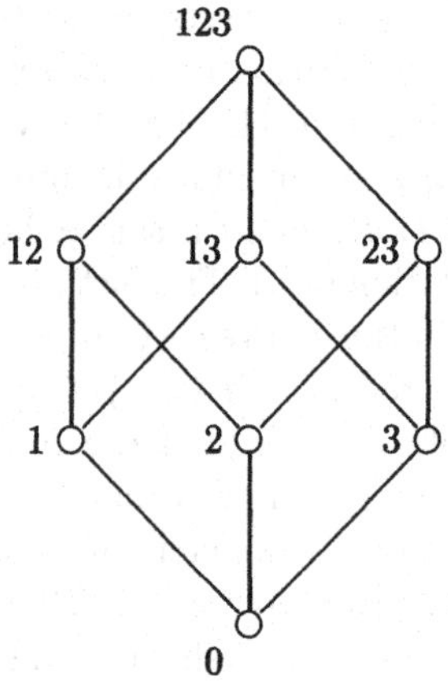

Figure 1

Besides sets provided with relations also algebras will play an important role in our text. We confine ourselves to algebras with binary, unary, and nullary operations.

A binary operation on a set A is a mapping of $A^2 = A \times A$ into A; similarly, a unary operation on A is a mapping of $A^1 = A$ into A. Thus, a nullary operation is a mapping of A^0 into A; since A^0 has exactly one element (sequence of length 0), a nullary operation on A being a mapping of A^0 into A is given by a fixed element in A (a constant).

An algebra is a set called carrier with a system of operations on this set. Our text offers, as example, a semilattice $(S, \bullet)$ where S is a set and $\bullet$ is a binary operation on S meeting some conditions; as usually, we write $x \bullet y$ for $\bullet(x, y)$. Another example of an algebra is the Boolean algebra $(\mathbf{B}(A), \cup, \cap, Co, \emptyset, A)$ where $\cup$, $\cap$ are binary operations of union and intersection, respectively, $Co\ X = A - X$ is the unary operation of complementation with respect to A, and $\emptyset$, A are nullary operations.

Another example of a Boolean algebra appearing in our considerations is the free Boolean algebra $(\mathbf{FR}(P), \vee, \wedge, ^-, 0, 1)$ over the set P that is supposed to be finite and nonempty. Elements in P are regarded as variables, $\vee, \wedge$ are binary, $^-$ unary, and 0, 1 nullary operations. Elements in $\mathbf{FR}(P)$ are Boolean expressions that are defined inductively as follows: (1) Any variable and 0, 1 are Boolean expressions. (2) If α, β are Boolean expressions, then $\alpha \vee \beta$, $\alpha \wedge \beta$, $\bar{\alpha}$ are Boolean expressions. (3) Boolean expressions are only expressions defined by (1) and (2). — If the set of all Boolean expressions is defined, then an equality among them must be introduced. Two Boolean expressions α, β are equal if one of them may be transformed into the other in a finite number of steps using an equation satisfied in Boolean algebras in every step; we shall not quote these equations, they may be found in the above cited monographs. Hence elements in $\mathbf{FR}(P)$ are blocks of equal expressions; any of these expressions may be considered to represent the block. Thus, we shall consider $\mathbf{FR}(P)$ to be the set of all Boolean expressions defined above, but we shall identify the equal expressions.

An algebra is said to be finite if so is its carrier.

The notion of homomorphism of algebras will appear only in particular situations in the following text: We shall need homomorphisms for some particular cases of Boolean algebras and homomorphisms of semilattices. While the latter will be explained in Section 4, the former may be presented here.

If $(\mathbf{FR}(P), \vee, \wedge, ^-, 0, 1)$ and $(\mathbf{B}(A), \cup, \cap, Co, \emptyset, A)$ are Boolean algebras as above and h is a mapping of $\mathbf{FR}(P)$ into $\mathbf{B}(A)$, then it is called a homomorphism of the first algebra into the second if it respects all operations which means: $h(0) = \emptyset$, $h(1) = A$ and for any α, $\beta \in \mathbf{FR}(P)$ the following conditions are satisfied: $h(\alpha \vee \beta) = h(\alpha) \cup h(\beta)$, $h(\alpha \wedge \beta) = h(\alpha) \cap h(\beta)$, $h(\bar{\alpha}) = Co(h(\alpha))$.

Similarly, we shall need the notion of congruence only for semilattices which will be introduced and investigated in Section 4.

3 Semilattices

Semilattices are in the center of our interest now, but we start with a more general algebra because it will appear in Section 7 of Chapter 8.

A *groupoid* is a nonempty set S provided with a binary operation $\bullet$; we shall denote it by $(S, \bullet)$.

Example 1. Let $\mathbf{N}$ be the set of all nonnegative integers, + the operation of addition, . the operation of multiplication. Then $(\mathbf{N},+)$, $(\mathbf{N},.)$ are groupoids.

Example 2. Let U be a finite nonempty set. We denote by $\mathbf{DI}(U)$ the set whose elements are all disjoint systems of nonempty subsets of the set U; a system of sets is said to be *disjoint* if any two different sets of the system have empty intersection. We now define an operation $*$ on the set $\mathbf{DI}(U)$ as follows: For any P, $Q \in \mathbf{DI}(U)$, we put $P * Q = \{p \in P;$ there exists $q \in Q$ with $p \subseteq q\}$. Clearly, $P * Q \in \mathbf{DI}(U)$. Hence, $(\mathbf{DI}(U), *)$ is a groupoid. It will be studied later.

Let $(S, \bullet)$ be a groupoid and $X \subseteq S$, $Y \subseteq S$ be sets. We put $X \circ Y = \{x \bullet y;\ x \in X,\ y \in Y\}$. Thus, $(\mathbf{B}(S), \circ)$ is a groupoid. The operation $\circ$ enables us to define the set of all products obtained from a given finite sequence of elements in S. If $n \geq 1$ is an integer and $a_1, \ldots, a_n$ are elements in S, we denote by $P(a_1, \ldots, a_n)$ the set of products of the finite sequence $(a_1, \ldots, a_n)$; it is a subset of S and is defined inductively as follows.

(i) $P(a) = \{a\}$.
(ii) $P(a_1, \ldots, a_n) = \bigcup\{P(a_1, \ldots, a_i) \circ P(a_{i+1}, \ldots, a_n); 1 \leq i < n\}$.

Usually, we write $\bullet$ for $\circ$. More about groupoids can be found in the monograph [Bo1].

A *semilattice* is a groupoid $(S, \bullet)$ such that the following conditions are satisfied.

(1) If $x \in S$, then $x \bullet x = x$ (law of idempotence).
(2) If $x,\ y \in S$, then $x \bullet y = y \bullet x$ (law of commutativity).
(3) If $x,\ y,\ z \in S$, then $(x \bullet y) \bullet z = x \bullet (y \bullet z)$ (law of associativity).

Example 3. If A is a finite nonempty set, then $(\mathbf{B}(A), \cup), (\mathbf{B}(A), \cap)$ are semilattices. Such semilattices will often appear in what follows. We need to know their properties. Theory of semilattices enables us to prove some theorems and apply them to $(\mathbf{B}(A), \cup)$ so as to $(\mathbf{B}(A), \cap)$.

Due to associativity of the operation in a semilattice the following well-known result holds.

Theorem 1. *If $(S, \bullet)$ is a semilattice, $n \geq 1$ an integer and $a_1, \ldots, a_n$ elements in S, then $P(a_1, \ldots, a_n)$ has exactly one element.*

Thus if $P(a_1, \ldots, a_n) = \{a\}$, we write $a_1 \bullet \ldots \bullet a_n = a$.

The operation on a semilattice enables to define an ordering.

Theorem 2. *Let $(S, \bullet)$ be a semilattice. For any $x,\ y \in S$ put $x \leq y$ if and only if $x \bullet y = y$. Then $\leq$ is an ordering on the set S and for any integer $n \geq 1$ and any elements $a_1, \ldots, a_n$ in S the condition $\sup\{a_1, \ldots, a_n\} = a_1 \bullet \ldots \bullet a_n$ is satisfied. Particularly, $\sup\{x, y\} = x \bullet y$ holds for any $x,\ y$ in S.*

Proof. Condition (1) implies reflexivity, condition (2) antisymmetry. If $x \leq y$ and $y \leq z$ hold, then $x \bullet y = y$, $y \bullet z = z$ which implies that $x \bullet z = x \bullet (y \bullet z) = (x \bullet y) \bullet z = y \bullet z = z$ by condition (3). Thus $x \leq z$ and the relation $\leq$ is transitive. Hence, $\leq$ is an ordering.

If $n \geq 1$ is an integer and $a_1, \ldots, a_n$ are elements in S, put $p = a_1 \bullet \ldots \bullet a_n$. Let us have $i \in \{1, \ldots, n\}$. Using (1), (2), (3), we prove easily that $a_i \bullet p = a_i \bullet a_1 \bullet \ldots \bullet a_n = a_1 \bullet \ldots \bullet a_n = p$, i.e., $a_i \leq p$ for any $i \in \{1, \ldots, n\}$ which means that p is an upper bound of the set $\{a_1, \ldots, a_n\}$. If $q \in S$ is an upper bound of this set, then $a_i \bullet q = q$ for any $i \in \{1, \ldots, n\}$. Put $t = q \bullet \ldots \bullet q$ where q appears n times. Using (2), (3), we obtain that $p \bullet t = a_1 \bullet \ldots \bullet a_n \bullet t = t$. By (1), we obtain $t = q$. Thus, $p \bullet q = q$ and, therefore, $p \leq q$. We have proved that $\sup\{a_1, \ldots, a_n\} = p = a_1 \bullet \ldots \bullet a_n$. □

Example 4. If we construct the ordering in the semilattice $(\mathbf{B}(A), \cup)$, we obtain the inclusion $\subseteq$; if we do the same for the semilattice $(\mathbf{B}(A), \cap)$, we obtain the relation $\supseteq$.

We agree that a semilattice $(S, \bullet)$ will be always regarded as an ordered set with the ordering constructed in Theorem 2. This ordering will be said to be *derived* from the operation $\bullet$ if it is necessary to mention this fact.

Corollary 3. *If $(S, \bullet)$ is a finite semilattice with a least element, then any subset of S has a least upper bound and a greatest lower bound.*

Proof. The existence of least upper bounds has been proved. For any $X \subseteq S$ let Y be the set of all its lower bounds; it is easy to prove that $\sup Y = \inf X$. □

Let $(S, \bullet)$ be a semilattice, $B \subseteq S$ a set. The set B is said to *generate* $(S, \bullet)$ if for any $a \in S$ there exists a subset $B(a)$ (possibly empty) of B such that $a = \sup B(a)$. Clearly, S generates $(S, \bullet)$. We are interested in small subsets of S generating $(S, \bullet)$. To this aim, we introduce the following.

Let $(S, \bullet)$ be a finite semilattice with a least element, $a \in S$ an element. The element a is said to be *totally irreducible*, if for any set $X \subseteq S$ with the property $a = \sup X$ the condition $a \in X$ holds.

We give a criterion for recognizing totally irreducible elements.

Theorem 4. *Let $(S, \bullet)$ be a finite semilattice with a least element, $a \in S$ an element. Then a is totally irreducible if and only if* $\sup\{x \in S; x < a\} < a$.

Proof. Clearly, $\sup\{x \in S; x < a\} \leq a$.

If $\sup\{x \in S; x < a\} = a$, the element a is not totally irreducible, by definition.

If a is not totally irreducible, there exists a set $B(a)$ such that $a = \sup B(a)$, $a \notin B(a)$. The last condition implies that $B(a) \subseteq \{x \in S; x < a\}$ and, therefore $a = \sup B(a) \leq \sup\{x \in S; x < a\} \leq a$ and, thus, $\sup\{x \in S; x < a\} = a$.

Hence, a is not totally irreducible if and only if $\sup\{x \in S; x < a\} = a$. This implies the assertion immediately. □

Example 5. The totally irreducible elements in the semilattice $(\mathbf{B}(A), \cup)$ considered in Example 3 are precisely all one-element subsets of A.

Theorem 5. *Let $(S, \bullet)$ be a finite semilattice with a least element. Then for any $a \in S$ there exists a set $B(a)$ of totally irreducible elements such that* $\sup B(a) = a$.

Proof. Let $V(x)$ be the following property of elements $x \in S$: x is the least upper bound of a set of totally irreducible elements.

If o is the least element in S and $a = o$, we put $B(a) = \emptyset$ and $V(o)$ holds.

Suppose that $a \neq o$ and that for any $x \in S$ with the property $x < a$ the assertion $V(x)$ holds, i.e., there exists a set $B(x)$ of totally irreducible elements such that $x = \sup B(x)$. If a is totally irreducible, we put $B(a) = \{a\}$ and $V(a)$

holds. If a is not totally irreducible, we set $B(a) = \bigcup\{B(x); x < a\}$. By Theorem 4, we obtain $a = \sup\{x \in S; x < a\} = \sup\{\sup B(x); x < a\} = \sup\{\bigcup\{B(x); x < a\}\} = \sup B(a) \leq a$ and, therefore, $a = \sup B(a)$ where $B(a)$ is a set of totally irreducible elements. Thus $V(a)$ holds.

We have proved that $V(o)$ holds and that for any a with $o < a$ the validity of $V(x)$ for any $x < a$ implies the validity of $V(a)$. Since S is finite, $V(a)$ holds for any $a \in S$. □

Corollary 6. *If $(S, \bullet)$ is a finite semilattice with a least element, the set of all its irreducible elements is the least subset of S with respect to inclusion that generates $(S, \bullet)$.*

Proof. By Theorem 5, the set of all totally irreducible elements in $(S, \bullet)$ generates $(S, \bullet)$. Let B be an arbitrary set generating $(S, \bullet)$ and a a totally irreducible element. Then there exists a set $B(a) \subseteq B$ such that $a = \sup B(a)$. Since a is totally irreducible, we obtain $a \in B(a) \subseteq B$. Thus B contains all totally irreducible elements. □

Example 6. If A is a finite nonempty set, then the system of all one-element subsets of A generates the semilattice $(\mathbf{B}(A), \cup)$.

4 Homomorphisms and Congruences of Semilattices

Section 3 includes fundamental facts concerning a semilattice. In this Section we shall consider possible structural relationships between two semilattices. This leads to the study of homomorphisms and congruences. It is convenient to start with more general concepts, hence, we go back to groupoids.

Let $(S, \bullet)$, $(T, *)$ be groupoids, h a mapping of the set S into the set T such that $h(x \bullet y) = h(x) * h(y)$ holds for any elements x, y in S. Then h is said to be a *homomorphism* of the groupoid $(S, \bullet)$ into the groupoid $(T, *)$.

Suppose that $(S, \bullet)$ is a groupoid and E an equivalence on the set S. Then E is said to be a *congruence* on $(S, \bullet)$ whenever it satisfies the following condition: If x, x', y, y', are in S and $(x, x') \in E$, $(y, y') \in E$ hold, then $(x \bullet y, x' \bullet y') \in E$.

For any groupoid $(S, \bullet)$ and its congruence E we define a groupoid $(S, \bullet)/E = (S/E, \circ)$ where the operation $\circ$ is defined as follows: For any $X \in S/E$ and any $Y \in S/E$, there exists exactly one $Z \in S/E$ such that $X \bullet Y \subseteq Z$ which follows from the definition of congruence; we put $X \circ Y = Z$. Then $(S/E, \circ)$ is said to be the *quotient groupoid* of $(S, \bullet)$ by E.

If $(S, \bullet)$ is a groupoid, E a congruence on $(S, \bullet)$, and h a mapping assigning to any $x \in S$ the block $B \in S/E$ such that $x \in B$, then h will be called the *natural surjection* of S onto S/E.

The following is well-known.

Theorem 7. *Let $(S, \bullet)$ be a groupoid, E a congruence on $(S, \bullet)$, h the natural surjection of S onto S/E. Then h is a surjective homomorphism of $(S, \bullet)$ onto $(S, \bullet)/E$.*

Proof. Clearly, the mapping h is surjective. If $x,\ y \in S$ are arbitrary, and $X,\ Y$ are blocks of E such that $h(x) = X,\ h(y) = Y$, then $x \in X,\ y \in Y$ which implies that $x \bullet y \in X \circ Y$. Thus $h(x \bullet y) = X \circ Y = h(x) \circ h(y)$. We have proved that h is a homomorphism. □

We now specialize our considerations to semilattices. If $(S, \bullet)$, $(T, *)$ are semilattices and h is a homomorphism of $(S, \bullet)$ into $(T, *)$, then the condition $h(x \bullet y) = h(x) * h(y)$ may be expressed, due to Theorem 2, in the form $h(\sup\{x, y\}) = \sup\{h(x), h(y)\}$ which can be extended, by induction. Thus, if X is a finite nonempty subset of S, we have $h(\sup X) = \sup\{h(x); x \in X\}$.

Lemma 8. *Let $(S, \bullet)$, $(T, *)$ be finite semilattices with least elements, h a surjective homomorphism of $(S, \bullet)$ onto $(T, *)$. Then $h(\sup X) = \sup\{h(x); x \in X\}$ holds for any subset X of S.*

Proof. Since S is finite, the equation holds for any nonempty X, as we have seen. If $X = \emptyset$, then $\sup X = o$ where o is the least element in $(S, \bullet)$ and $\sup\{h(x); x \in X\} = \sup\emptyset = o'$ where o' is the least element in $(T, *)$. Put $a' = h(o)$; since h is surjective, there exists an element $a \in S$ such that $h(a) = o'$. Since $a = \sup\{o, a\}$, we obtain $o' = h(a) = h(\sup\{o, a\}) = \sup\{h(o), h(a)\} = \sup\{a', o'\} = a'$. Thus $h(o) = o'$ which means that the equation holds also for $X = \emptyset$. □

Lemma 9. *Let $(S, \bullet)$, $(T, *)$ be finite semilattices with least elements, h a surjective homomorphism of $(S, \bullet)$ onto $(T, *)$. If B is a subset of S generating $(S, \bullet)$, then $\{h(x); x \in B\}$ generates $(T, *)$.*

Proof. Let $x' \in T$ be arbitrary. Then there exists $x \in S$ such that $h(x) = x'$. Furthermore, there exists $B(x) \subseteq B$ such that $x = \sup B(x)$. By Lemma 8, we obtain $x' = h(x) = h(\sup B(x)) = \sup\{h(t); t \in B(x)\}$ where $\{h(t); t \in B(x)\} \subseteq \{h(t); t \in B\}$. □

Corollary 10. *Let $(S, \bullet)$, $(T, *)$ be finite semilattices with least elements, h a surjective homomorphism of $(S, \bullet)$ onto $(T, *)$. If $a' \in T$ is totally irreducible, then there exists $a \in S$ such that a is totally irreducible and $h(a) = a'$.*

Proof. Let B, B' denote the sets of totally irreducible elements in $(S, \bullet)$, $(T, *)$, respectively. Then B generates $(S, \bullet)$ by Corollary 6 which implies that the set $\{h(x); x \in B\}$ generates $(T, *)$, by Lemma 9. By Corollary 6, we obtain $B' \subseteq \{h(x); x \in B\}$ which implies the assertion immediately. □

Example 7. Let A, A' be finite nonempty sets, h a surjective homomorphism of the semilattice $(\mathbf{B}(A), \cup)$ onto $(\mathbf{B}(A'), \cup)$. Using Example 5 and Corollary 10, we obtain that for any $x' \in A'$, there exists $x \in A$ such that $h(\{x\}) = \{x'\}$.

Lemma 11. *Let $(S, \bullet)$ be a semilattice with a least element o, $(T, *)$ a semilattice, h a surjective homomorphism of $(S, \bullet)$ onto $(T, *)$. Then $h(o)$ is the least element in $(T, *)$.*

Indeed, if $x' \in T$ is arbitrary, there exists $x \in S$ with $h(x) = x'$. It follows that $h(o) * x' = h(o) * h(x) = h(o \bullet x) = h(x) = x'$ which implies that $h(o) \leq x'$.

We now give a simple criterion for recognizing congruences of semilattices.

Theorem 12. *Let $(S, \bullet)$ be a semilattice, E an equivalence on the set S. Then the following conditions are equivalent.*

(i) E is a congruence on $(S, \bullet)$.

(ii) For any x, x', y in S the condition $(x, x') \in E$ implies that $(x \bullet y, x' \bullet y) \in E$.

Proof. Clearly, *(i)* implies *(ii)*. If *(ii)* holds and $(x, x') \in E$, $(y, y') \in E$, then $(x \bullet y, x' \bullet y) \in E$, $(y \bullet x', y' \bullet x') \in E$ hold. Since the operation $\bullet$ is commutative, we obtain $(x' \bullet y, x' \bullet y') \in E$. The transitivity of E implies that $(x \bullet y, x' \bullet y') \in E$. Thus *(ii)* implies *(i)*. □

If $(S, \bullet)$ is a semilattice and E a congruence on $(S, \bullet)$, then $(S, \bullet)/E$ is a groupoid, by definition; but it is a semilattice as it follows from the next theorem.

Theorem 13. *Let $(S, \bullet)$ be a semilattice, E a congruence on $(S, \bullet)$. Then $(S, \bullet)/E$ is a semilattice.*

Proof. If $X \in S/E$ is arbitrary and $x \in X$, then $X \circ X$ is the block of E containing $x \bullet x = x$, i.e. X. Similarly, if X, Y are in S/E and $x \in X$, $y \in Y$, then $X \circ Y$ is the block of E containing $x \bullet y$ and $Y \circ X$ is the block containing $y \bullet x$. Since $x \bullet y = y \bullet x$, these blocks coincide and we obtain $X \circ Y = Y \circ X$ which is the commutativity of the operation $\circ$. The proof of its associativity is similar. □

Corollary 14. *Let $(S, \bullet)$ be a finite semilattice with a least element, E a congruence on $(S, \bullet)$, h the natural surjection of S onto S/E. If $X \in S/E$ is totally irreducible in the semilattice $(S, \bullet)/E$, then there exists $x \in X$ that is totally irreducible in $(S, \bullet)$.*

Proof. By Theorem 13, $(S, \bullet)/E$ is a finite semilattice, by Lemma 11, it has a least element. By Corollary 10, if $X \in S/E$ is totally irreducible, there exists $x \in S$ such that x is totally irreducible and $h(x) = X$, i.e., $x \in X$. □

Example 8. Let $A = \{a, b, c\}$ and $\mathbf{B}(A)$ be presented similarly as in Section 2. (Cf. Fig. 2 and Fig. 3).

Suppose that the equivalence E on $\mathbf{B}(A)$ has the following blocks: $\{0\}$, $\{1, 2, 12\}$, $\{3\}$, $\{13, 23, 123\}$. It is easy to see that E is a congruence on the semilattice $(\mathbf{B}(A), \cup)$. Thus $(\mathbf{B}(A), \cup)/E$ is a semilattice with a least element whose totally irreducible elements are $\{1, 2, 12\}$, $\{3\}$. Let h be the natural surjection of $\mathbf{B}(A)$ onto $\mathbf{B}(A)/E$. Then 1, 3 are irreducible elements in $(\mathbf{B}(A), \cup)$ such that $h(1) = \{1, 2, 12\}$, $h(3) = \{3\}$.

Theorem 15. *Let $(S, \bullet)$ be a finite semilattice, E a congruence on $(S, \bullet)$. Then the following assertions hold.*

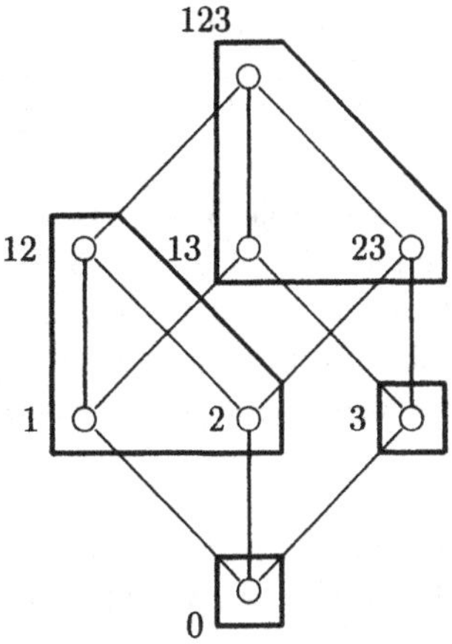

Figure 2

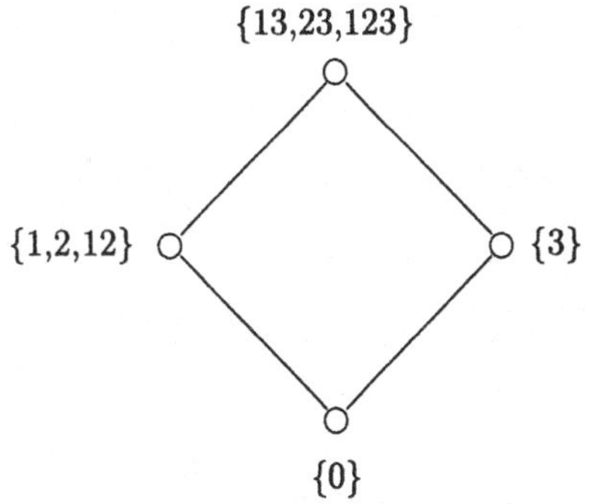

Figure 3

(i) *If $p \geq 1$ is an integer and $x_1, \ldots, x_p$, $y_1, \ldots, y_p$ elements in S such that $(x_1, y_1) \in E, \ldots, (x_p, y_p) \in E$, then $(x_1 \bullet \ldots \bullet x_p, y_1 \bullet \ldots \bullet y_p) \in E$ holds.*
(ii) *Any block of E has a greatest element.*
(iii) *If B is a block of E and x, y, z are elements in S such that x, z are in B and $x \leq y \leq z$ holds, then $y \in B$.*

(Cf. [NP6].)

Proof. *(i)* follows from the definition of a congruence by an easy induction. Let $B = \{x_1, \ldots, x_p\}$ be a block of E. Then $(x_1, x_i) \in E$ for any i with $1 \leq i \leq p$ which implies that $(x_1 \bullet \ldots \bullet x_1, x_1 \bullet \ldots \bullet x_p) \in E$, by *(i)*, where x_1 appears p times in the first member of the ordered pair. But this first member equals x_1 and the second is the least upper bound of B by Theorem 2. Hence the least upper bound of B is contained in B and it is its greatest element. Therefore *(ii)* holds.

If x, $z \in B$, then $(x, z) \in E$. Furthermore, $x \leq y, y \leq z$ may be expressed in the form $x \bullet y = y$, $y \bullet z = z$. It follows that $(x \bullet y, z \bullet y) \in E$ which means $(y, z) \in E$. Thus $y \in B$ and *(iii)* holds. □

Congruences on semilattices may be defined by means of subsets and by means of closure operators. We describe these constructions.

Theorem 16. *Let $(S, \bullet)$ be a semilattice, G a nonempty subset of S. We put* $\mathbf{T}(G) = \{(x, y) \in S \times S;$ for any $g \in G$ the conditions $x \leq g$ and $y \leq g$ are equivalent$\}$. *Then $\mathbf{T}(G)$ is a congruence on $(S, \bullet)$.*

Proof. Clearly, $\mathbf{T}(G)$ is an equivalence on S. Let x, x', y be in S and suppose that $(x, x') \in \mathbf{T}(G)$. Let $g \in G$ be arbitrary and suppose $\sup\{x, y\} \leq g$. Then $x \leq g$, $y \leq g$ and, therefore, $x' \leq g$. Thus $\sup\{x', y\} \leq g$. Similarly, $\sup\{x', y\} \leq$

g implies that $\sup\{x,y\} \leq g$. Since $\sup\{x,y\} = x \bullet y$, $\sup\{x',y\} = x' \bullet y$, we obtain that $(x \bullet y, x' \bullet y) \in \mathbf{T}(G)$. By Theorem 12, $\mathbf{T}(G)$ is a congruence on $(S, \bullet)$. □

Example 9. Let $(\mathbf{B}(A), \cup)$ be the semilattice of Example 8. Put $\mathbf{G} = \{3,\ 12\}$. Then 0 is the only element in $\mathbf{B}(A)$ such that $0 \subseteq 3$, $0 \subseteq 12$; 3 is the only element in $\mathbf{B}(A)$ with $3 \subseteq 3$, $3 \not\subseteq 12$; 1, 2, 12 are the elements that are included in 12 but are not included in 3; finally, 13, 23, 123 are the elements that are included neither in 12 nor in 3. Thus $\mathbf{T}(\mathbf{G})$ coincides with the congruence from Example 8.

Let $(S, \bullet)$ be a semilattice, $\leq$ the ordering derived from its operation, C a mapping of S into itself. Then C is said to be a *closure operator* if it satisfies the following conditions.

(i) $x \leq C(x)$ for any $x \in S$ (law of extensivity).
(ii) If x, y are in S and $x \leq y$, then $C(x) \leq C(y)$ (law of monotony).
(iii) $C(C(x)) = C(x)$ holds for any $x \in S$ (law of idempotence).

Let $(S, \bullet)$ be a finite semilattice, E a congruence on $(S, \bullet)$. For any $x \in S$ there exists exactly one block B of E such that $x \in B$; this block has a greatest element by Theorem 15; we denote it by $\mathbf{C}(E)(x)$. Thus, $\mathbf{C}(E)$ is a mapping of S into itself.

Theorem 17. *Let $(S, \bullet)$ be a finite semilattice, E a congruence on $(S, \bullet)$. Then $\mathbf{C}(E)$ is a closure operator on $(S, \bullet)$.*

Proof. Since $\mathbf{C}(E)(x)$ is the greatest element in the block of E containing x, we have (i). If x, $y \in S$ and $x \leq y$, then $(\mathbf{C}(E)(x), x) \in E$, $(\mathbf{C}(E)(y), y) \in E$ imply that $(\mathbf{C}(E)(x) \bullet \mathbf{C}(E)(y), y) = (\mathbf{C}(E)(x) \bullet \mathbf{C}(E)(y), x \bullet y) \in E$. By definition of $\mathbf{C}(E)(y)$ we obtain $\mathbf{C}(E)(x) \leq \sup\{\mathbf{C}(E)(x), \mathbf{C}(E)(y)\} = \mathbf{C}(E)(x) \bullet \mathbf{C}(E)(y) \leq \mathbf{C}(E)(y)$ using Theorem 2 which is (ii). By (i), we have $x \leq \mathbf{C}(E)(x)$ which entails $\mathbf{C}(E)(x) \leq \mathbf{C}(E)(\mathbf{C}(E)(x))$ by (ii), for any $x \in S$. Since $(\mathbf{C}(E)(\mathbf{C}(E)(x)), \mathbf{C}(E)(x)) \in E$, $(\mathbf{C}(E)(x), x) \in E$, we obtain $(\mathbf{C}(E)(\mathbf{C}(E)(x)), x) \in E$ by transitivity of E and, therefore, $\mathbf{C}(E)(\mathbf{C}(E)(x)) \leq \mathbf{C}(E)(x)$ by definition of $\mathbf{C}(E)(x)$. From these results, it follows that (iii) holds. □

Example 10. If we continue Example 8, we obtain $\mathbf{C}(E)(0) = 0$, $\mathbf{C}(E)(1) = \mathbf{C}(E)(2) = \mathbf{C}(E)(12) = 12$, $\mathbf{C}(E)(3) = 3$, $\mathbf{C}(E)(13) = \mathbf{C}(E)(23) = \mathbf{C}(E)(123) = 123$.

A congruence on a semilattice may be defined by means of a closure operator. More exactly

Theorem 18. *Let C be a closure operator on a semilattice $(S, \bullet)$. Put $\mathbf{K}(C) = \{(x,y) \in S \times S;\ C(x) = C(y)\}$. Then $\mathbf{K}(C)$ is a congruence on the semilattice $(S, \bullet)$.*

Proof. If x, x', y are elements in S such that $(x, x') \in \mathbf{K}(C)$, then $C(x) = C(x')$. By Theorem 2, we have $x' \leq \sup\{x', y\} = x' \bullet y$ which implies that $x \leq C(x) = C(x') \leq C(x' \bullet y)$. Furthermore, $y \leq \sup\{x', y\} = x' \bullet y$ entails $y \leq C(y) \leq C(x' \bullet y)$. Thus, $C(x' \bullet y)$ is an upper bound of the set $\{x, y\}$ and, therefore, $x \bullet y = \sup\{x, y\} \leq C(x' \bullet y)$. It follows that $C(x \bullet y) \leq C(C(x' \bullet y)) = C(x' \bullet y)$. Similarly we obtain $C(x' \bullet y) \leq C(x \bullet y)$. Thus, $C(x \bullet y) = C(x' \bullet y)$ and we have $(x \bullet y, x' \bullet y) \in \mathbf{K}(C)$. By Theorem 12, $\mathbf{K}(C)$ is a congruence on $(S, \bullet)$. □

Example 11. If we continue Example 10, we obtain that the blocks of $\mathbf{K}(\mathbf{C}(E))$ are the following: $\{0\}$, $\{1, 2, 12\}$, $\{3\}$, $\{13, 23, 123\}$. Thus, $\mathbf{K}(\mathbf{C}(E)) = E$.

This is no accidental result as it follows from the following

Theorem 19. *Let $(S, \bullet)$ be a finite semilattice. Then the following assertions hold.*

(i) *If K is a congruence on $(S, \bullet)$, then $\mathbf{K}(\mathbf{C}(K)) = K$.*
(ii) *If C is a closure operator on $(S, \bullet)$, then $\mathbf{C}(\mathbf{K}(C)) = C$.*

Proof. If K is a congruence on $(S, \bullet)$, then for any x, $y \in S$ the condition $(x, y) \in \mathbf{K}(\mathbf{C}(K))$ means $\mathbf{C}(K)(x) = \mathbf{C}(K)(y)$ which is equivalent to $(x, y) \in K$. Thus, *(i)* holds.

If C is a closure operator on $(S, \bullet)$ and $x \in S$ is arbitrary, then $\mathbf{C}(\mathbf{K}(C))(x)$ is the greatest element $y \in S$ with $(y, x) \in \mathbf{K}(C)$. If $(y, x) \in \mathbf{K}(C)$, then $y \leq C(y) = C(x)$. Since $C(C(x)) = C(x)$, we have $(C(x), x) \in \mathbf{K}(C)$ and $C(x)$ is the greatest element $y \in S$ with $(y, x) \in \mathbf{K}(C)$. Thus, $\mathbf{C}(\mathbf{K}(C))(x) = C(x)$ for any $x \in S$ which implies that *(ii)* holds. □

Let $(S, \bullet)$ be a semilattice, C a closure operator on $(S, \bullet)$. An element $x \in S$ is said to be *C-closed* if $C(x) = x$. We give a simple characterization of C-closed elements.

Theorem 20. *Let $(S, \bullet)$ be a semilattice, C a closure operator on $(S, \bullet)$. Then the set of all C-closed elements in $(S, \bullet)$ coincides with the set $\{C(x); x \in S\}$.*

Proof. Put $A = \{C(x); x \in S\}$. If $x \in S$ is C-closed, then $x = C(x) \in A$. If $x \in A$, there exists $y \in S$ such that $x = C(y)$ and, therefore, $C(x) = C(C(y)) = C(y) = x$ which means that x is C-closed. □

The operators $\mathbf{T}$ and $\mathbf{K}$ are in a close connection.

Theorem 21. *Let $(S, \bullet)$ be a semilattice, C a closure operator on $(S, \bullet)$, G the set of all C-closed elements in $(S, \bullet)$. Then $\mathbf{T}(G) = \mathbf{K}(C)$.*

Proof. Suppose $(x, y) \in S \times S$.

If $(x, y) \in \mathbf{T}(G)$, then for any $g \in G$ the conditions $x \leq g$, $y \leq g$ are equivalent. Since $C(x) \in G$ by Theorem 20 and $x \leq C(x)$, we have $y \leq C(x)$ which implies that $C(y) \leq C(C(x)) = C(x)$. Similarly, $C(x) \leq C(y)$ holds. We have $C(x) = C(y)$ and, therefore, $(x, y) \in \mathbf{K}(C)$.

Suppose that $(x, y) \in \mathbf{K}(C)$ holds. Then $C(x) = C(y)$. If $g \in G$ is such that $x \leq g$, then $y \leq C(y) = C(x) \leq C(g) = g$. Similarly, if $g \in G$ and $y \leq g$ holds, then we obtain $x \leq g$. Hence, $(x, y) \in \mathbf{T}(G)$. □

Example 12. Consider the same semilattice $(\mathbf{B}(A), \cup)$ as in Example 8, let C be a closure operator on $(\mathbf{B}(A), \cup)$ where $C(0) = 0$, $C(1) = C(2) = C(12) = 12$, $C(3) = 3$, $C(13) = C(23) = C(123) = 123$. Then the set of C-closed elements is $\mathbf{G} = \{0, 12, 3, 123\}$. Therefore, 0 is the only element in $\mathbf{B}(A)$ that is included in all sets from $\mathbf{G}$; $1, 2, 12$ are included in $12, 123$ and are not included in 0 and 3; 3 is included in 3 and 123 but is not included in 0 and 12; finally $13, 23, 123$ are included in 123 and are not included in other sets from $\mathbf{G}$. Thus $\mathbf{T}(\mathbf{G})$ coincides with the congruence E from Example 8. Furthermore, C coincides with $\mathbf{C}(E)$ from Example 10. Thus, $\mathbf{K}(C) = \mathbf{K}(\mathbf{C}(E)) = E$ which was demonstrated in Example 11 directly.

Let $(S, \bullet)$ be a finite semilattice with a least element. By Corollary 3 we know that $\sup X$ and $\inf X$ exist for any $X \subseteq S$. The following definition is based on this fact.

Let $(S, \bullet)$ be a finite semilattice with a least element, G a nonempty subset of S. We define $[G]$ to be the least subset of S with respect to inclusion such that it has the following properties.

(a) $G \subseteq [G]$.
(b) The greatest element of S is in $[G]$.
(c) If $x \in [G]$, $y \in [G]$, then $\inf\{x, y\} \in [G]$.

We now have

Lemma 22. *Let $(S, \bullet)$ be a finite semilattice with a least element, G a nonempty subset of S. Then the following assertions hold.*

(i) $\mathbf{C}(\mathbf{T}(G))(x) = \inf\{g \in G; x \leq g\}$ *for any* $x \in S$.
(ii) The set of all $\mathbf{C}(\mathbf{T}(G))$*-closed elements coincides with* $[G]$.

Proof. Let $x \in S$ be arbitrary. Denote by e the greatest element in S, i.e., $e = \sup S$.

If there exists no $g \in G$ such that $x \leq g$, then $e \leq g$ holds for no $g \in G$ which implies that $(x, e) \in \mathbf{T}(G)$; clearly, e is the greatest element in the block of $\mathbf{T}(G)$ that contains x. Thus, $\mathbf{C}(\mathbf{T}(G))(x) = e = \inf\emptyset = \inf\{g \in G; x \leq g\}$.

If there is at least one $g \in G$ with $x \leq g$, put $y = \inf\{g \in G; x \leq g\}$. It is easy to see that $(x, y) \in \mathbf{T}(G)$. If $(x, z) \in \mathbf{T}(G)$, then $z \leq g$ for any $g \in G$ with the property $x \leq g$. Thus, z is a lower bound for the set $\{g \in G; x \leq g\}$ which implies $z \leq y$. Thus, y is the greatest element in the block of $\mathbf{T}(G)$ that contains x; hence $\mathbf{C}(\mathbf{T}(G))(x) = \inf\{g \in G; x \leq g\}$.

We have proved that *(i)* holds.

By *(i)* it follows easily that the set of all $\mathbf{C}(\mathbf{T}(G))$-closed elements includes G, contains e and the greatest lower bound of any set of its elements, i.e., includes $[G]$. On the other hand, any $\mathbf{C}(\mathbf{T}(G))$-closed element equals either e or a greatest lower bound of elements in G which implies that it is an element of $[G]$. Thus *(ii)* holds. □

Our considerations are directed to dependence spaces; their theory is incorporated in the theory of semilattices. We now present the definition of dependence space.

Let A be a finite nonempty set, K a congruence on the semilattice $(\mathbf{B}(A), \cup)$. Then the ordered pair (A, K) is said to be a *dependence space* (cf. [NP9]). In what follows we shall investigate dependence spaces and use the results in the theory of information systems. Particularly, we may define independent elements in $\mathbf{B}(A)$ and dependence between elements of $\mathbf{B}(A)$; this justifies the name "dependence space".

5 Rough Top Equality

We now present an example of a dependence space that is in a close connection with so called classifications.

Let A be a finite nonempty set, r an equivalence on A. Then the ordered pair (A, r) is said to be a *classification.*

Example 13. Let A be a set of pupils of a school; for two pupils $x \in A$, $y \in A$ let $(x, y) \in r$ mean that x and y are in the same class. Then (A, r) is a classification; the blocks of r coincide with school classes.

Let (A, r) be a classification. For any $X \in \mathbf{B}(A)$, we put

$$\mathbf{c}(r)(X) = \bigcup\{B \in A/r;\ B \cap X \neq \emptyset\};$$

this set is called the *upper approximation of the set X in r.*

Example 14. Let (A, r) be the same as in Example 13. Suppose that an infectious disease has appeared in the school and that $X \subseteq A$ is the set of all pupils suffering from this disease at a certain moment. Generally, the sick pupils and their class mates are supposed to spread the infectious disease. For this reason, they are ordered to be vaccinated. Thus, the set of all vaccinated pupils is $\mathbf{c}(r)(X)$.

Lemma 23. *Let (A, r) be a classification. Then $\mathbf{c}(r)$ is a closure operator on the semilattice $(\mathbf{B}(A), \cup)$.*

Proof. If $X \in \mathbf{B}(A)$ and $x \in X$, there exists $B \in A/r$ such that $x \in B$. Thus, $x \in B \cap X$ which implies that $x \in B \subseteq \mathbf{c}(r)(X)$. Hence, the mapping $\mathbf{c}(r)$ is extensive.

Suppose that X, Y are in $\mathbf{B}(A)$ and that $X \subseteq Y$ holds. If $x \in \mathbf{c}(r)(X)$, there exists $B \in A/r$ such that $x \in B$, $B \cap X \neq \emptyset$ which implies that $B \cap Y \neq \emptyset$. Thus, $x \in B \subseteq \mathbf{c}(r)(Y)$. Hence, $\mathbf{c}(r)(X) \subseteq \mathbf{c}(r)(Y)$ and the mapping $\mathbf{c}(r)$ is monotone.

If $X \in \mathbf{B}(A)$, the extensivity and monotony of $\mathbf{c}(r)$ imply that $\mathbf{c}(r)(X) \subseteq \mathbf{c}(r)(\mathbf{c}(r)(X))$. — Suppose $x \in \mathbf{c}(r)(\mathbf{c}(r)(X))$. Then there exists $B \in A/r$ such that $x \in B$, $B \cap \mathbf{c}(r)(X) \neq \emptyset$. Hence, there exists $y \in B \cap \mathbf{c}(r)(X)$. Thus, there exists $B' \in A/r$ such that $y \in B'$, $B' \cap X \neq \emptyset$. Since $y \in B$, we obtain that $B = B'$ and, therefore, $x \in B = B' \subseteq \mathbf{c}(r)(X)$. We have proved that $\mathbf{c}(r)(\mathbf{c}(r)(X)) \subseteq \mathbf{c}(r)(X)$. It follows that $\mathbf{c}(r)(\mathbf{c}(r)(X)) = \mathbf{c}(r)(X)$ and the mapping $\mathbf{c}(r)$ is idempotent. □

By Theorem 18, $\mathbf{K}(\mathbf{c}(r))$ is a congruence on the semilattice $(\mathbf{B}(A), \cup)$ which means that $(A, \mathbf{K}(\mathbf{c}(r)))$ is a dependence space. The congruence $\mathbf{K}(\mathbf{c}(r))$ is said to be the *rough top equality defined by* (A, r). Two sets $X \in \mathbf{B}(A)$, $Y \in \mathbf{B}(A)$ are called *roughly top equal* if $(X, Y) \in \mathbf{K}(\mathbf{c}(r))$ which means that $\mathbf{c}(r)(X) = \mathbf{c}(r)(Y)$.

Let A be a finite nonempty set, $\mathbf{K}$ a congruence on the semilattice $(\mathbf{B}(A), \cup)$. The congruence $\mathbf{K}$ is referred to as a *rough top equality* if there exists an equivalence r on A such that $\mathbf{K} = \mathbf{K}(\mathbf{c}(r))$.

Example 15. We continue Example 14. If one knows only the set of all vaccinated pupils, one cannot reconstruct the set of pupils suffering from the disease. All sets roughly top equal to the set of sick pupils would produce the same set of vaccinated pupils.

We know that the rough top equality $\mathbf{K}(\mathbf{c}(r))$ is a congruence on the semilattice $(\mathbf{B}(A), \cup)$. It is natural to ask how to recognize rough top equalities among congruences on $(\mathbf{B}(A), \cup)$. More exactly, we have

Problem 24. Let A be a finite nonempty set. Characterize rough top equalities among congruences on the semilattice $(\mathbf{B}(A), \cup)$.

Cf. [NP2], [NP9], [Pa3], [Pa4], [Pa7].

Some definitions are necessary for the formulation of a solution of our problem. Let A be a finite nonempty set. A subset $\mathbf{X}$ of $\mathbf{B}(A)$ is said to be *closed* in the Boolean algebra $(\mathbf{B}(A), \cup, \cap, Co, \emptyset, A)$ if $(\mathbf{X}, \cup, \cap, Co, \emptyset, A)$ is a Boolean algebra. We mention that an element $X \in \mathbf{B}(A)$ is said to be $\mathbf{c}(r)$-closed if $\mathbf{c}(r)(X) = X$, by definition presented in Section 4.

Lemma 25. *Let (A, r) be a classification. Then the set of all $\mathbf{c}(r)$-closed sets is closed in the Boolean algebra $(\mathbf{B}(A), \cup, \cap, Co, \emptyset, A)$.*

Proof. It is easy to see that a set $X \in \mathbf{B}(A)$ is $\mathbf{c}(r)$-closed if and only if it is the union of some blocks of r. Let $\mathbf{X}$ be the system of all sets $X \in \mathbf{B}(A)$ such that any of them can be expressed as a union of some blocks of r. Clearly, $\mathbf{X}$ is closed in the Boolean algebra $(\mathbf{B}(A), \cup, \cap, Co, \emptyset, A)$. □

Lemma 26. *Let A be a finite nonempty set. If $\mathbf{X}$ is a subset of $\mathbf{B}(A)$ that is closed in the Boolean algebra $(\mathbf{B}(A), \cup, \cap, Co, \emptyset, A)$, then there exists an equivalence r on A such that $\mathbf{X}$ is the set of all $\mathbf{c}(r)$-closed sets in $\mathbf{B}(A)$.*

Proof. By hypothesis, $(\mathbf{X}, \cup, \cap, Co, \emptyset, A)$ is a finite Boolean algebra. Thus $(\mathbf{X}, \cup)$ is a finite semilattice with a least element $\emptyset$. By Theorem 5, any element in $\mathbf{X}$ is a union of totally irreducible elements of $(\mathbf{X}, \cup)$.

Let X, Y, $X \neq Y$, be two totally irreducible elements. Since the least element $\emptyset$ is not totally irreducible, we have $X \neq \emptyset \neq Y$. Suppose $X \cap Y \neq \emptyset$. Since $X \neq Y$, either $X - Y$ or $Y - X$ is nonempty; without loss of generality, we may suppose $X - Y \neq \emptyset$. Then $X = (X \cap Y) \cup (X - Y)$ where $X \cap Y \neq X \neq X - Y$ which means that X is not totally irreducible. Thus, $X \cap Y = \emptyset$.

Since A is the union of totally irreducible elements, these elements form a decomposition of A. For x, $y \in A$ put $(x, y) \in r$ if and only if x, y are in the same block of the constructed decomposition. Then an element in $\mathbf{B}(A)$ is $\mathbf{c}(r)$-closed if and only if it is the union of some blocks of the decomposition which means that it is an element of $\mathbf{X}$ as we have seen. □

Theorem 27. *Let (A, K) be a dependence space. The following assertions are equivalent.*

(i) K is a rough top equality.

(ii) The set of all $\mathbf{C}(K)$-closed sets in $\mathbf{B}(A)$ is closed in the Boolean algebra $(\mathbf{B}(A), \cup, \cap, Co, \emptyset, A)$.

Proof. If *(i)* holds, then $K = \mathbf{K}(\mathbf{c}(r))$ for some equivalence r on A. Then $\mathbf{C}(K) = \mathbf{C}(\mathbf{K}(\mathbf{c}(r))) = \mathbf{c}(r)$ by Theorem 19. By Lemma 25, the set of all $\mathbf{C}(K)$-closed sets in $\mathbf{B}(A)$ is closed in the Boolean algebra $(\mathbf{B}(A), \cup, \cap, Co, \emptyset, A)$ and *(ii)* holds.

If *(ii)* holds, there exists an equivalence r on A such that the set of $\mathbf{C}(K)$-closed sets coincides with the set of all $\mathbf{c}(r)$-closed sets by Lemma 26; let $\mathbf{G}$ denote this set. By Theorem 19 and 21, we obtain $K = \mathbf{K}(\mathbf{C}(K)) = \mathbf{T}(\mathbf{G}) = \mathbf{K}(\mathbf{c}(r))$ and *(i)* holds. □

Theorem 27 solves our Problem 24. An algorithm recognizing rough top equalities may be deduced from the theorem. We describe it only informally.

Algorithm 28. (Algorithm for recognizing rough top equalities) *Let (A, K) be a dependence space.*

(1) *Construct $\mathbf{C}(K)(X)$ for any $X \in \mathbf{B}(A)$, let $\mathbf{M}$ be the system of all constructed sets.*

(2) *Test whether $\emptyset \in \mathbf{M}$, $A \in \mathbf{M}$, whether $CoX \in \mathbf{M}$ for any $X \in \mathbf{M}$, whether $X \cup Y \in \mathbf{M}, X \cap Y \in \mathbf{M}$ for any $X \in \mathbf{M}$, $Y \in \mathbf{M}$.*

If all these conditions are satisfied, K is a rough top equality, if one of these conditions is violated, K is no rough top equality.

Clearly, (2) is equivalent to

(2') Test whether $A \in \mathbf{M}$, whether $CoX \in \mathbf{M}$ for any $X \in \mathbf{M}$, and whether $X \cup Y \in \mathbf{M}$ for any $X \in \mathbf{M}$ and $Y \in \mathbf{M}$.

If $\mathbf{K}$ is a rough top equality, (2') will be more advantageous or as advantageous as (2) because (2) requires more tests than (2'). On the other hand, (2) will be more advantageous or as advantageous as (2') if $\mathbf{K}$ is not a rough top equality because the greater number of tests in (2) may reveal more quickly that one of the conditions is violated.

Example 16. Let $(\mathbf{B}(A), \cup)$ be the semilattice described in Section 2. Let K be the equivalence on $\mathbf{B}(A)$ whose blocks are $\{0\}$, $\{1\}$, $\{2\}$, $\{3\}$, $\{12, 13, 23, 123\}$. It is easy to see that K is a congruence on the semilattice $(\mathbf{B}(A), \cup)$. Using

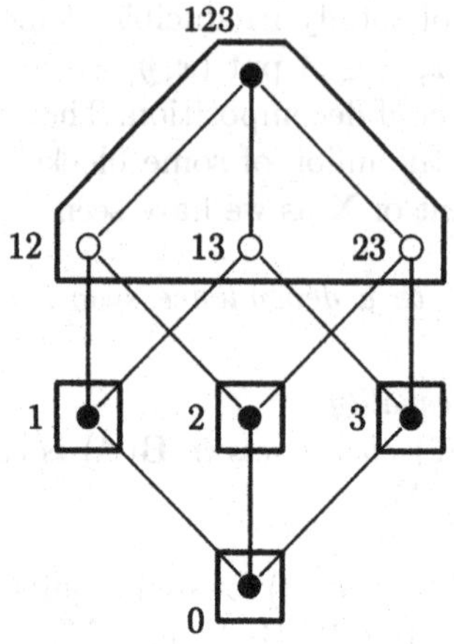

Figure 4

our algorithm, we construct $\mathbf{M} = \{0,1,2,3,123\}$. Clearly, $1 \in \mathbf{M}$, $2 \in \mathbf{M}$, $1 \cup 2 = 12 \notin \mathbf{M}$. Thus K is no rough top equality. Cf. Fig. 4.

A congruence on the semilattice $(\mathbf{B}(A), \cup)$ can be defined by means of the operator $\mathbf{T}$ starting with a nonempty subset of $\mathbf{B}(A)$. We give a necessary and sufficient condition for the so defined congruence to be a rough top equality. We remind that for a nonempty subset $\mathbf{G}$ of $\mathbf{B}(A)$, $[\mathbf{G}]$ is the least subset of $\mathbf{B}(A)$ with the following properties (cf. Section 4).

(a) $\mathbf{G} \subseteq [\mathbf{G}]$.
(b) $A \in [\mathbf{G}]$.
(c) If $X \in [\mathbf{G}], Y \in [\mathbf{G}]$, then $X \cap Y \in [\mathbf{G}]$.

A characterization of rough top equality is given by the following

Theorem 29. *Let A be a finite nonempty set, $\mathbf{G}$ a nonempty subset of $\mathbf{B}(A)$. Then the following assertions are equivalent.*

(i) $\mathbf{T}(\mathbf{G})$ is a rough top equality.
(ii) The set $[\mathbf{G}]$ is closed in the Boolean algebra $(\mathbf{B}(A), \cup, \cap, Co, \emptyset, A)$.

Proof. By Theorem 27, *(i)* is equivalent to the following condition.
(iii) The set of all $\mathbf{C}(\mathbf{T}(\mathbf{G}))$-closed sets in $\mathbf{B}(A)$ is closed in the Boolean algebra $(\mathbf{B}(A), \cup, \cap, Co, \emptyset, A)$.

By Lemma 22, the set of all $\mathbf{C}(\mathbf{T}(\mathbf{G}))$-closed sets coincides with $[\mathbf{G}]$; therefore, *(ii)* is equivalent to *(iii)* and the proof is finished. □

Example 17. Let $(\mathbf{B}(A), \cup)$ be the semilattice described in Section 2. Put $\mathbf{G} = \{1, 23\}$. Then $\mathbf{T}(\mathbf{G})$ has the following blocks: $\{0\}$, $\{1\}$, $\{2,3,23\}$, $\{12,13,123\}$. Furthermore, we obtain $[\mathbf{G}] = \{0,1,23,123\}$ which is closed in the Boolean algebra $(\mathbf{B}(A), \cup, \cap, Co, \emptyset, A)$. Thus $\mathbf{T}(\mathbf{G})$ is a rough top equality.

In Example 17, we would like to know the equivalence r on A such that $K = \mathbf{K}(\mathbf{c}(r))$. Thus, we have

Problem 30. Let A be a finite nonempty set, K a rough top equality on the set $\mathbf{B}(A)$. Construct the equivalence r on A such that $K = \mathbf{K}(\mathbf{c}(r))$.

This problem is solved by the following.

Theorem 31. *Let A be a finite nonempty set, K an equivalence on the set $\mathbf{B}(A)$. Put $r = \{(x,y) \in A \times A;\ (\{x\},\{y\}) \in K\}$. Then the following assertions are equivalent.*

(i) $K = \mathbf{K}(\mathbf{c}(r))$.

(ii) *For any $(X,Y) \in \mathbf{B}(A) \times \mathbf{B}(A)$ the condition $(X,Y) \in K$ is satisfied if and only if either $X \cap B = \emptyset$, $Y \cap B = \emptyset$ or $X \cap B \neq \emptyset$, $Y \cap B \neq \emptyset$ hold for any block B in A/r.*

Proof. Clearly, *(ii)* is equivalent to the following.

(iii) For any $(X,Y) \in \mathbf{B}(A) \times \mathbf{B}(A)$ the condition $(X,Y) \in K$ is satisfied if and only if $\mathbf{c}(r)(X) = \mathbf{c}(r)(Y)$.

It is easy to see that *(i)*, *(iii)* are equivalent. □

Example 18. We continue Example 17. Clearly, r has the following blocks: 1, 23. It is easy to see that $\mathbf{K}(\mathbf{c}(r)) = K$. Cf. Fig. 5.

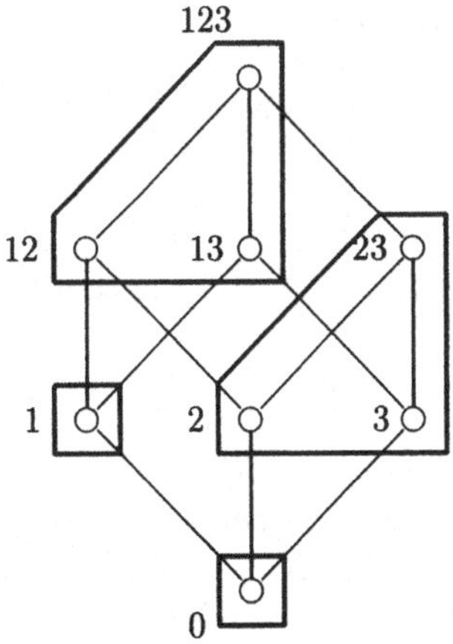

Figure 5

Corollary 32. *Let A be a finite nonempty set, K a rough top equality on the set $\mathbf{B}(A)$. Put $r = \{(x,y) \in A \times A;\ (\{x\},\{y\}) \in K\}$. Let $X \in \mathbf{B}(A)$, $X' \in \mathbf{B}(A)$ be arbitrary sets such that $X' \subseteq X$. Then the following assertions are equivalent.*

(i) X' *is minimal with respect to inclusion among all sets* Z *such that* $Z \subseteq X$, $(Z, X) \in K$.
(ii) *For any block* $B \in A/r$ *either* $X \cap B = \emptyset$, $X' \cap B = \emptyset$ *or* $X \cap B \neq \emptyset$ *and* $X' \cap B$ *has exactly one element.*

6 Rough Bottom Equality

The results of Section 5 can be dualized in the framework of semilattice theory. This will be done now.

Let (A, r) be a classification. For any $X \in \mathbf{B}(A)$, we put

$$\mathbf{d}(r)(X) = \bigcup\{B \in A/r;\ B \subseteq X\};$$

this set is said to be the *lower approximation of the set* X *in* r.

Example 19. We continue Example 14 where A is the set of all pupils of a school, r an equivalence on A whose blocks are school classes, and $X \subseteq A$ is the set of all pupils suffering from an infectious disease. The classes where all pupils are sick are closed. Clearly, the set of all pupils with stopped education equals $\mathbf{d}(r)(X)$.

There is a relationship between the operators **d** and **c**.

Lemma 33. *Let* (A, r) *be a classification and* $X \in \mathbf{B}(A)$. *Then the following assertions hold.*

(i) $\mathbf{d}(r)(X) = Co\ \mathbf{c}(r)(CoX)$.
(ii) $\mathbf{d}(r)(\mathbf{c}(r)(X)) = \mathbf{c}(r)(X)$.

Proof. Any two consecutive conditions in the following sequence are equivalent.

(1) $x \in \mathbf{d}(r)(X)$.
(2) There exists $B \in A/r$ such that $x \in B,\ B \subseteq X$.
(3) For any $B \in A/r$ with $B \cap CoX \neq \emptyset$ the condition $x \notin B$ holds.
(4) $x \notin \mathbf{c}(r)(CoX)$.
(5) $x \in Co\ \mathbf{c}(r)(CoX)$.

The equivalence of (1) and (5) is *(i)*.

By Lemma 23, $\mathbf{c}(r)$ is a closure operator on the semilattice $(\mathbf{B}(A), \cup)$. Thus, for any $X \in \mathbf{B}(A)$, we have $CoX \subseteq \mathbf{c}(r)(CoX)$ and, therefore, $\mathbf{d}(r)(X) = Co\ \mathbf{c}(r)(CoX) \subseteq X$. It follows that $\mathbf{d}(r)(\mathbf{c}(r)(X)) \subseteq \mathbf{c}(r)(X)$. On the other hand, if $x \in \mathbf{c}(r)(X)$, there exists $B \in A/r$ such that $x \in B$ and $B \subseteq \mathbf{c}(r)(X)$. We obtain $x \in B \subseteq \mathbf{d}(r)(\mathbf{c}(r)(X))$ and, therefore, $\mathbf{c}(r)(X) \subseteq \mathbf{d}(r)(\mathbf{c}(r))(X)$. Thus *(ii)* holds. □

We know, by Example 4, that $(\mathbf{B}(A), \cap)$ is a semilattice where the derived ordering is the relation $\supseteq$ and where the least element with respect to $\supseteq$ is A.

Lemma 34. *Let* (A, r) *be a classification. Then* $\mathbf{d}(r)$ *is a closure operator on the semilattice* $(\mathbf{B}(A), \cap)$.

Proof. By Lemma 23, $\mathbf{c}(r)$ is a closure operator on the semilattice $(\mathbf{B}(A), \cup)$. Furthermore, we use Lemma 33.

Let X, $Y \in \mathbf{B}(A)$ be arbitrary.

Since $CoX \subseteq \mathbf{c}(r)(CoX)$, we obtain $\mathbf{d}(r)(X) = Co(\mathbf{c}(r)(CoX)) \subseteq X$ which is the extensivity of $\mathbf{d}(r)$ with respect to $\supseteq$. If $X \supseteq Y$, then $CoX \subseteq CoY$ and $\mathbf{c}(r)(CoX) \subseteq \mathbf{c}(r)(CoY)$ which implies that $\mathbf{d}(r)(Y) = Co(\mathbf{c}(r)(CoY)) \subseteq Co(\mathbf{c}(r)(CoX)) = \mathbf{d}(r)(X)$ which is the monotony of $\mathbf{d}(r)$ with respect to $\supseteq$. Finally, $\mathbf{d}(r)(\mathbf{d}(r)(X)) = Co(\mathbf{c}(r)(Co(\mathbf{d}(r)(X)))) = Co(\mathbf{c}(r)(\mathbf{c}(r)(CoX))) = Co(\mathbf{c}(r)(CoX)) = \mathbf{d}(r)(X)$ which is the idempotence of the operator $\mathbf{d}(r)$. □

By Theorem 18, $\mathbf{K}(\mathbf{d}(r))$ is a congruence on the semilattice $(\mathbf{B}(A), \cap)$; it is said to be the *rough bottom equality defined by* (A, r). Two sets $X \in \mathbf{B}(A)$, $Y \in \mathbf{B}(A)$ are called *roughly bottom equal* if $(X, Y) \in \mathbf{K}(\mathbf{d}(r))$ which means that $\mathbf{d}(r)(X) = \mathbf{d}(r)(Y)$.

Let A be a finite nonempty set, $\mathbf{K}$ a congruence on the semilattice $(\mathbf{B}(A), \cap)$. The congruence $\mathbf{K}$ is referred to as a *rough bottom equality* if there exists an equivalence r on A such that $\mathbf{K} = \mathbf{K}(\mathbf{d}(r))$.

Formally, the properties of the operator $\mathbf{d}(r)$ are similar to the properties of interior if the inclusion is accepted as ordering.

Example 20. We continue Example 19. If we know only the set of all pupils with stopped education, we cannot reconstruct the set of all pupils suffering from the disease. All sets roughly bottom equal to the set of sick pupils would produce the same set of pupils with stopped education.

Analogously as in Section 5, we have the following problem.

Problem 35. Let A be a finite nonempty set. Characterize rough bottom equalities among congruences on the semilattice $(\mathbf{B}(A), \cap)$.

Cf. [NP2], [NP9], [Pa3], [Pa4], [Pa7].

Lemma 36. *Let (A, r) be a classification, $X \in \mathbf{B}(A)$ a set. Then X is $\mathbf{d}(r)$-closed if and only if it is $\mathbf{c}(r)$-closed.*

Proof. Let $X \in \mathbf{B}(A)$ be arbitrary. Then $\mathbf{d}(r)(X) = X$ means $\mathbf{c}(r)(CoX) = CoX$ by Lemma 33, i.e., X is $\mathbf{d}(r)$-closed if and only if CoX is $\mathbf{c}(r)$-closed. By Lemma 25, CoX is $\mathbf{c}(r)$-closed if and only if X is $\mathbf{c}(r)$-closed. This implies our assertion. □

Corollary 37. *Let (A, r) be a classification. Then the set of all $\mathbf{d}(r)$-closed sets is closed in the Boolean algebra $(\mathbf{B}(A), \cup, \cap, Co, \emptyset, A)$.*

Corollary 38. *Let A be a finite nonempty set. If $\mathbf{X}$ is a subset of $\mathbf{B}(A)$ that is closed in the Boolean algebra $(\mathbf{B}(A), \cup, \cap, Co, \emptyset, A)$, then there exists an equivalence r on A such that $\mathbf{X}$ is the set of all $\mathbf{d}(r)$-closed sets in $\mathbf{B}(A)$.*

Proof. By Lemma 26 there exists an equivalence r on A such that $\mathbf{X}$ is the set of all $\mathbf{c}(r)$-closed sets in $\mathbf{B}(A)$; by Lemma 36, we obtain the assertion. □

Theorem 39. *Let A be a finite nonempty set, K a congruence on the semilattice $(\mathbf{B}(A), \cap)$. Then the following assertions are equivalent.*

(i) K is a rough bottom equality.

(ii) The set of all $\mathbf{C}(K)$-closed sets in $\mathbf{B}(A)$ is closed in the Boolean algebra $(\mathbf{B}(A), \cup, \cap, Co, \emptyset, A)$.

Proof. If *(i)* holds, then $K = \mathbf{K}(\mathbf{d}(r))$ for some equivalence r on A. Then $\mathbf{C}(K) = \mathbf{C}(\mathbf{K}(\mathbf{d}(r))) = \mathbf{d}(r)$ by Theorem 19. By Corollary 37 we obtain *(ii)*.

Let *(ii)* hold, denote by $\mathbf{G}$ the set of all $\mathbf{C}(K)$-closed sets in $\mathbf{B}(A)$. By Corollary 38, there exists an equivalence r on the set A such that $\mathbf{G}$ is the set of all $\mathbf{d}(r)$-closed sets. By Theorem 19 and 21, we obtain $K = \mathbf{K}(\mathbf{C}(K)) = \mathbf{T}(\mathbf{G}) = \mathbf{K}(\mathbf{d}(r))$ and *(i)* holds. □

Theorem 39 solves our Problem 35. Similarly as in Section 5, an algorithm recognizing rough bottom equalities may be deduced from the theorem. It is similar to the algorithm described there, only the construction of $\mathbf{C}(K)(X)$ is different: We must take into account that the ordering derived from the operation $\cap$ in the semilattice $(\mathbf{B}(A), \cap)$ is the dual $\supseteq$ of inclusion; hence elements of any block of K that are maximal with respect to $\supseteq$ are minimal with respect to $\subseteq$. The rest of the algorithm is the same as in Section 5.

Example 21. Let $\mathbf{B}(A)$ be the same as in Section 2. Suppose that K is an equivalence on the set $\mathbf{B}(A)$ whose blocks are $\{0, 2, 3\}$, $\{1, 12, 13\}$, $\{23\}$, $\{123\}$. It is easy to see that K is a congruence on the semilattice $(\mathbf{B}(A), \cap)$. The set $\mathbf{M}$ of all sets of the form $\mathbf{C}(K)(X)$ where $X \in \mathbf{B}(A)$ is $\{0, 1, 23, 123\}$. Clearly $\mathbf{M}$ is closed in the Boolean algebra $(\mathbf{B}(A), \cup, \cap, Co, \emptyset, A)$. It follows that K is a rough bottom equality, $K = \mathbf{K}(\mathbf{d}(r))$ where r is an equivalence on A whose blocks are 1, 23. Cf. Fig. 6.

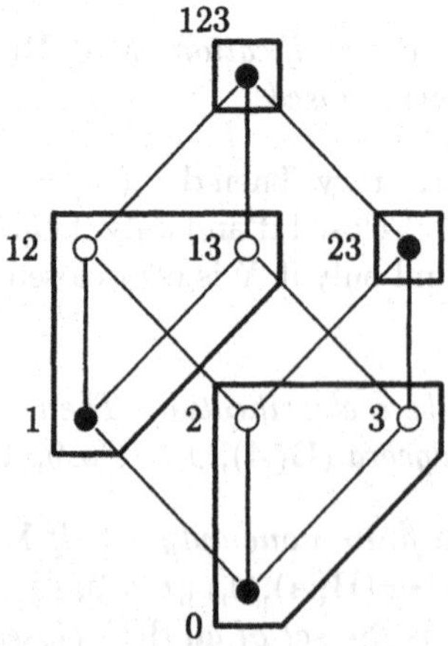

Figure 6

We now prove a theorem analogous to Theorem 29. It relates to the semilattice $(\mathbf{B}(A), \cap)$ and a nonempty subset $\mathbf{G}$ of $\mathbf{B}(A)$. Since the definitions of $[\mathbf{G}]$ and $\mathbf{T}(\mathbf{G})$ were transferred from Section 4 to Section 5 where we had supposed tacitly that the semilattice $(S, \bullet)$ from Section 4 is interpreted as $(\mathbf{B}(A), \cup)$, we need new symbols for $[\ ]$ and $\mathbf{T}$ in this new interpretation.

Let A be a finite nonempty set, $\mathbf{G}$ a nonempty subset of $\mathbf{B}(A)$. We denote by $]\mathbf{G}[$ the least subset of $\mathbf{B}(A)$ with the following properties.

(a) $\mathbf{G} \subseteq]\mathbf{G}[$.
(b) $\emptyset \in]\mathbf{G}[$.
(c) If X, $Y \in]\mathbf{G}[$, then $X \cup Y \in]\mathbf{G}[$.

Furthermore, we put
$\mathbf{R}(\mathbf{G}) = \{(X, Y) \in \mathbf{B}(A) \times \mathbf{B}(A);$ for any $G \in \mathbf{G}$ the conditions $G \subseteq X$ and $G \subseteq Y$ are equivalent$\}$.

Theorem 40. *Let A be a finite nonempty set $\mathbf{G}$ a nonempty subset of $\mathbf{B}(A)$. Then the following assertions are equivalent.*

(i) $\mathbf{R}(\mathbf{G})$ is a rough bottom equality.
(ii) The set $]\mathbf{G}[$ is closed in the Boolean algebra $(\mathbf{B}(A), \cup, \cap, Co, \emptyset, A)$.

Proof. By Theorem 39, *(i)* is equivalent to the following condition.

(iii) The set of all $\mathbf{C}(\mathbf{R}(\mathbf{G}))$-closed sets in $\mathbf{B}(A)$ is closed in the Boolean algebra $(\mathbf{B}(A), \cup, \cap, Co, \emptyset, A)$.

By Lemma 22, the set of all $\mathbf{C}(\mathbf{R}(\mathbf{G}))$-closed sets coincides with $]\mathbf{G}[$ and, therefore, *(ii)*, *(iii)* are equivalent. Thus, *(i)*, *(ii)* are equivalent, too. □

Example 22. Let $\mathbf{B}(A)$ be the same as in Section 2, put $\mathbf{G} = \{1, 13\}$. Then $]\mathbf{G}[= \{0, 1, 13\}$ which is not closed in the Boolean algebra $(\mathbf{B}(A), \cup, \cap, Co, \emptyset, A)$. Thus, $\mathbf{R}(\mathbf{G})$ is not a rough bottom equality. Cf. Fig. 7.

7 Rough Equality

Starting with the operators $\mathbf{c}(r)$, $\mathbf{d}(r)$ introduced in Sections 5 and 6, we define rough equality of sets to any classification (A, r).

Let (A, r) be a classification. We put
$\mathbf{E}(r) = \{(X, Y) \in \mathbf{B}(A) \times \mathbf{B}(A);\ \mathbf{c}(r)(X) = \mathbf{c}(r)(Y),\ \mathbf{d}(r)(X) = \mathbf{d}(r)(Y)\}$.

Clearly, $\mathbf{E}(r)$ is an equivalence on the set $\mathbf{B}(A)$ and is said to be the *rough equality defined by* (A, r). It is easy to see that $\mathbf{E}(r) = \mathbf{K}(\mathbf{c}(r)) \cap \mathbf{K}(\mathbf{d}(r))$. Two sets $X \in \mathbf{B}(A)$, $Y \in \mathbf{B}(A)$ are said to be *roughly equal* if $(X, Y) \in \mathbf{E}(r)$.

Let A be a finite nonempty set, E an equivalence on the set $\mathbf{B}(A)$. The equivalence E is said to be a *rough equality* if there exists an equivalence r on A such that $E = \mathbf{E}(r)$.

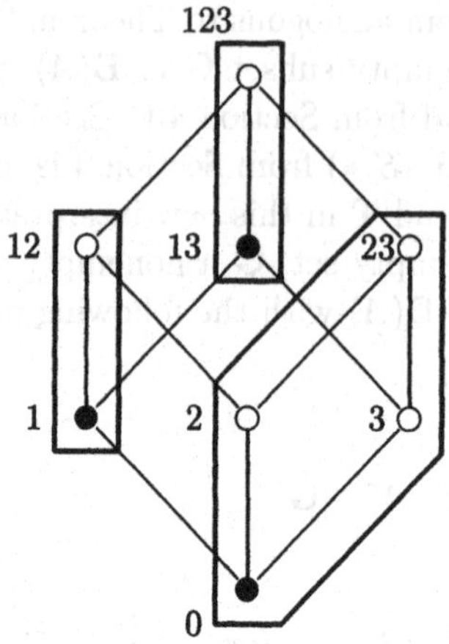

Figure 7

Example 23. We continue Example 15 and 20. Two sets X, Y of pupils are roughly equal if both produce the same set of vaccinated pupils and the same set of pupils with stopped education.

Rough equality is an intersection of two congruences but these congruences relate to different semilattices. Similarly as in Sections 5, 6, we are interested in the following problem.

Problem 41. Let A be a finite nonempty set. Characterize rough equalities among equivalences on the set $\mathbf{B}(A)$.

Cf. [NP3], [NP9], [Pa3], [Pa4], [Pa7].

Let A be a finite nonempty set, E an equivalence on the set $\mathbf{B}(A)$. We put

$$\mathbf{S}(E) = \{X \in \mathbf{B}(A);\ \{X\} \in \mathbf{B}(A)/E\},$$

i.e., $\mathbf{S}(E)$ consists of all subsets X of A such that $\{X\}$ is a block of E.

Lemma 42. *Let (A, r) be a classification. Then $\mathbf{S}(\mathbf{E}(r))$ coincides with the set of all $\mathbf{c}(r)$-closed sets in $\mathbf{B}(A)$.*

Proof. Let $X \in \mathbf{B}(A)$ be $\mathbf{c}(r)$-closed. Then $\mathbf{c}(r)(X) = X$ and, therefore, $\mathbf{d}(r)(X) = X$ by Lemma 36. Thus, $(X, Y) \in \mathbf{E}(r)$ implies that $X = \mathbf{d}(r)(X) = \mathbf{d}(r)(Y) \subseteq Y \subseteq \mathbf{c}(r)(Y) = \mathbf{c}(r)(X) = X$ by Lemma 34 and Lemma 23. It follows that $X = Y$ and, therefore, $X \in \mathbf{S}(\mathbf{E}(r))$.

Suppose that $X \in \mathbf{B}(A)$ is not $\mathbf{c}(r)$-closed. Thus, $X \neq \mathbf{c}(r)(X)$ which implies the existence of a block $B \in A/r$ and of elements $x \in B \cap X$, $y \in B - X$. We put $Y = (X - B) \cup ((B \cap X) - \{x\}) \cup \{y\}$. Then $X \neq Y$ and $\mathbf{c}(r)(X) = \mathbf{c}(r)(Y)$, $\mathbf{d}(r)(X) = \mathbf{d}(r)(Y)$. Thus, $(X, Y) \in \mathbf{E}(r)$ and $X \notin \mathbf{S}(\mathbf{E}(r))$. □

Let A be a finite nonempty set, $\mathbf{G}$ a nonempty subset of $\mathbf{B}(A)$, E an equivalence on $\mathbf{B}(A)$. The equivalence E is said to be *induced* by $\mathbf{G}$ if $E = \mathbf{T}(\mathbf{G}) \cap \mathbf{R}(\mathbf{G})$.

Lemma 43. *Let (A, r) be a classification. Then the rough equality $\mathbf{E}(r)$ is induced by the set $\mathbf{S}(\mathbf{E}(r))$.*

Proof. By Lemma 42, the set $\mathbf{S}(\mathbf{E}(r))$ coincides with the set of all $\mathbf{c}(r)$-closed sets in $\mathbf{B}(A)$ that is closed in the Boolean algebra $(\mathbf{B}(A), \cup, \cap, Co, \emptyset, A)$ by Lemma 25. It follows, particularly, $[\mathbf{S}(\mathbf{E}(r))] = \mathbf{S}(\mathbf{E}(r))$. By Theorem 29 the relation $\mathbf{T}(\mathbf{S}(\mathbf{E}(r)))$ is a rough top equality. By Theorem 21 it follows that $\mathbf{T}(\mathbf{S}(\mathbf{E}(r))) = \mathbf{K}(\mathbf{c}(r))$.

By Lemma 36 the set $\mathbf{S}(\mathbf{E}(r))$ coincides with the set of all $\mathbf{d}(r)$-closed sets in $\mathbf{B}(A)$ that is closed in the Boolean algebra $(\mathbf{B}(A), \cup, \cap, Co, \emptyset, A)$ by Corollary 37. It follows, particularly, $]\mathbf{S}(\mathbf{E}(r))[= \mathbf{S}(\mathbf{E}(r))$. By Theorem 40 the relation $\mathbf{R}(\mathbf{S}(\mathbf{E}(r)))$ is a rough bottom equality. By Theorem 21 it follows that $\mathbf{R}(\mathbf{S}(\mathbf{E}(r))) = \mathbf{K}(\mathbf{d}(r))$.

Hence $\mathbf{E}(r) = \mathbf{K}(\mathbf{c}(r)) \cap \mathbf{K}(\mathbf{d}(r)) = \mathbf{T}(\mathbf{S}(\mathbf{E}(r))) \cap \mathbf{R}(\mathbf{S}(\mathbf{E}(r)))$ and the equivalence $\mathbf{E}(r)$ is induced by the set $\mathbf{S}(\mathbf{E}(r))$. □

Lemma 44. *Let A be a finite nonempty set, E an equivalence on the set $\mathbf{B}(A)$ having the following properties.*

(i) The set $\mathbf{S}(E)$ is closed in the Boolean algebra $(\mathbf{B}(A), \cup, \cap, Co, \emptyset, A)$.
(ii) The equivalence E is induced by the set $\mathbf{S}(E)$.

Then the equivalence E is a rough equality on $\mathbf{B}(A)$.

Proof. Since the set $\mathbf{S}(E)$ is closed in the Boolean algebra $(\mathbf{B}(A), \cup, \cap, Co, \emptyset, A)$, we have $[\mathbf{S}(E)] = \mathbf{S}(E)$ which implies that the relation $\mathbf{T}(\mathbf{S}(E))$ is a rough top equality by Theorem 29. Thus, there exists an equivalence r on the set A such that $\mathbf{K}(\mathbf{c}(r)) = \mathbf{T}(\mathbf{S}(E))$. By Lemma 22, the set of all $\mathbf{C}(\mathbf{T}(\mathbf{S}(E)))$-closed sets coincides with $\mathbf{S}(E)$; but it coincides also with the set of $\mathbf{C}(\mathbf{K}(\mathbf{c}(r)))$-closed sets which equals the set of all $\mathbf{c}(r)$-closed sets by Theorem 19.

Similarly, we obtain $]\mathbf{S}(E)[= \mathbf{S}(E)$ which implies that the relation $\mathbf{R}(\mathbf{S}(E))$ is a rough bottom equality by Theorem 40. It follows the existence of an equivalence r' on the set A such that $\mathbf{K}(\mathbf{d}(r')) = \mathbf{R}(\mathbf{S}(E))$. By Lemma 22, the set of all $\mathbf{C}(\mathbf{R}(\mathbf{S}(E)))$-closed sets coincides with $\mathbf{S}(E)$; but it coincides also with the set of all $\mathbf{C}(\mathbf{K}(\mathbf{d}(r')))$-closed sets which equals the set of all $\mathbf{d}(r')$-closed sets by Theorem 19 and the set of all $\mathbf{c}(r')$-closed sets by Lemma 36.

Thus, $\mathbf{S}(E)$ coincides with the set of all $\mathbf{c}(r)$-closed sets and, simultaneously, with the set of all $\mathbf{c}(r')$-closed sets where r, r' are equivalences on A. It is easy to see that any $\mathbf{c}(r)$-closed set is the union of some blocks of r (cf. the proof of Lemma 26). Thus, any block of r is a union of some blocks of r' and vice versa. Hence r, r' have the same blocks which implies that $r = r'$.

We have proved that $E = \mathbf{T}(\mathbf{S}(E)) \cap \mathbf{R}(\mathbf{S}(E)) = \mathbf{K}(\mathbf{c}(r)) \cap \mathbf{K}(\mathbf{d}(r)) = \mathbf{E}(r)$; hence, E is a rough equality. □

Theorem 45. *Let A be a finite nonempty set, E an equivalence on the set $\mathbf{B}(A)$. Then the following assertions are equivalent.*

(i) E is a rough equality.
(ii) E has the following properties.
(a) The set $\mathbf{S}(E)$ *is closed in the Boolean algebra* $(\mathbf{B}(A), \cup, \cap, Co, \emptyset, A)$.
(b) The equivalence E is induced by the set $\mathbf{S}(E)$.

This is a consequence of Lemmas 42, 43, 44.

Theorem 45 solves our Problem 41. The algorithm for recognizing rough equalities is described below.

Algorithm 46. (Algorithm for recognizing rough equalities)
Let A be a finite nonempty set, E an equivalence on the set $\mathbf{B}(A)$.

(1) *Find all sets* $X \in \mathbf{B}(A)$ *such that* $\{X\}$ *is a block of E.*
(2) *Test whether the system* $\mathbf{S}(E)$ *of these sets is closed in the Boolean algebra* $(\mathbf{B}(A), \cup, \cap, Co, \emptyset, A)$, *i.e., test whether* $\emptyset \in \mathbf{S}(E), A \in \mathbf{S}(E)$, *whether* $CoX \in \mathbf{S}(E)$ *for any* $X \in \mathbf{S}(E)$ *and whether* $X \cup Y \in \mathbf{S}(E), X \cap Y \in \mathbf{S}(E)$ *for any* $X \in \mathbf{S}(E), Y \in \mathbf{S}(E)$. *If some of these conditions is violated, E is not a rough equality; if all are satisfied, go to the next step.*
(3) *Construct the relations* $\mathbf{T}(\mathbf{S}(E)), \mathbf{R}(\mathbf{S}(E))$ *and test whether* $\mathbf{T}(\mathbf{S}(E)) \cap \mathbf{R}(\mathbf{S}(E)) = E$ *holds or not. If this condition is satisfied, E is a rough equality, if it is violated, E is no rough equality.*

Example 24. Let us have A, $\mathbf{B}(A)$ as in Section 2. Suppose that E is the equivalence whose blocks are $\{0\}$, $\{1\}$, $\{2,3\}$, $\{12,13\}$, $\{23\}$, $\{123\}$. Then $\mathbf{S}(E) = \{0,1,23,123\}$ which is closed in the Boolean algebra $(\mathbf{B}(A), \cup, \cap, Co, \emptyset, A)$. The rough top equality $\mathbf{T}(\mathbf{S}(E))$ has the following blocks: $\{0\}$, $\{1\}$, $\{2,3,23\}$, $\{12,13,123\}$. Furthermore, the rough bottom equality $\mathbf{R}(\mathbf{S}(E))$ has the following blocks: $\{0,2,3\}$, $\{1,12,13\}$, $\{23\}$, $\{123\}$. Clearly, $\mathbf{T}(\mathbf{S}(E)) \cap \mathbf{R}(\mathbf{S}(E)) = E$ and E is a rough equality. See Fig. 8.

8 Independence

After having presented an important example of dependence space in Section 5 we continue the investigation of dependence spaces.

Let (A, K) be a dependence space. An element $X \in \mathbf{B}(A)$ is said to be K-*independent* if it is minimal with respect to inclusion in the block $\mathbf{B} \in \mathbf{B}(A)/K$ such that $X \in \mathbf{B}$. We denote by $\mathbf{I}(K)$ the set of all K-independent elements in $\mathbf{B}(A)$. Cf. [NP7].

The property of K-independence is hereditary in the following sense.

Lemma 47. *Let* (A, K) *be a dependence space,* $X \in \mathbf{I}(K)$. *If* $Y \subseteq X$, *then* $Y \in \mathbf{I}(K)$.

Proof. Suppose $Y \subseteq X$, $Y \neq X$ and $Y \notin \mathbf{I}(K)$. There exists a block $\mathbf{B} \in \mathbf{B}(A)/K$ such that $Y \in \mathbf{B}$; clearly, Y is not minimal in $\mathbf{B}$. Hence, there exists $Y_0 \subseteq Y$, $Y_0 \neq Y$ such that Y_0 is minimal in $\mathbf{B}$. Furthermore, $(Y_0, Y) \in K$ which implies that $(Y_0 \cup (X - Y), X) \in K$, $Y_0 \cup (X - Y) \subseteq X$, $Y_0 \cup (X - Y) \neq X$. Thus, X is not minimal in its block of K. Hence $X \notin \mathbf{I}(K)$ which is a contradiction. □

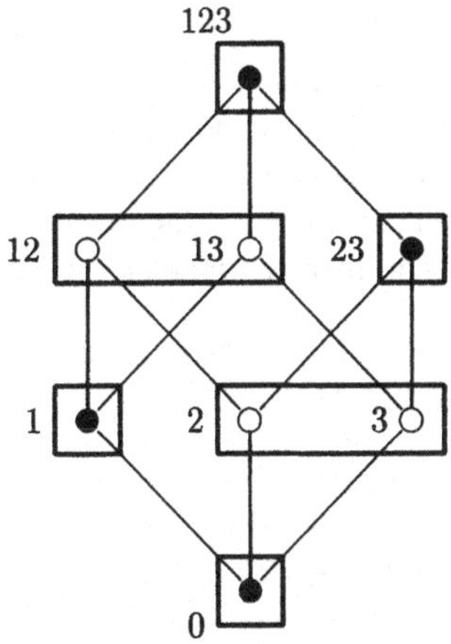

Figure 8

Lemma 48. *If* (A, K) *is a dependence space and* $X \in \mathbf{B}(A)$ *holds, then the following assertions are equivalent.*

(i) $X \in \mathbf{I}(K)$.

(ii) $(X, X - \{x\}) \notin K$ *for any* $x \in X$.

Proof. Clearly, *(i)* implies *(ii)*. Suppose that *(ii)* holds and that $X \notin \mathbf{I}(K)$. Thus, there exists $Y \in \mathbf{B}(A)$ such that $Y \subseteq X$, $Y \neq X$, and $(Y, X) \in K$. Let $x \in X - Y$ be arbitrary. Then $Y \subseteq X - \{x\} \subseteq X$ and, hence, $(X - \{x\}, X) \in K$ by Theorem 15 which is a contradiction. □

Let (A, K) be a dependence space, $X \in \mathbf{B}(A)$ a set. A set $Y \in \mathbf{B}(A)$ is said to be a *K-reduct of* X if $Y \in \mathbf{I}(K)$, $Y \subseteq X$, $(X, Y) \in K$ hold. The set of all K-reducts of X will be denoted by $\mathbf{RED}(K, X)$.

Example 25. Let (A, r) be a classification where $A = \{a, b, c\} = 123$ and the blocks of r are 1, 23 (see Section 2 for the notation). Then the blocks of $\mathbf{K}(\mathbf{c}(r))$ are $\{0\}$, $\{1\}$, $\{2, 3, 23\}$, $\{12, 13, 123\}$. The set 23 has two reducts: 2, 3; the set 123 has also two reducts 12, 13. Furthermore, 0 is the only reduct of 0, 1 is the only reduct of 1. See Fig. 5.

More generally, if (A, r) is a classification, then, for any $X \in \mathbf{B}(A)$ the construction of $\mathbf{K}(\mathbf{c}(r))$-reducts is described in Corollary 32.

Lemma 49. *Let* (A, K) *be a dependence space,* $X \in \mathbf{B}(A)$ *an arbitrary set. Then the set* $\mathbf{RED}(K, X)$ *is nonempty.*

This is a consequence of the fact that the set $\{Y \in \mathbf{B}(A); Y \subseteq X, (Y, X) \in K\}$ is finite and nonempty. Thus, the set of its minimal elements with respect to inclusion is nonempty.

We now analyze some of the concepts introduced above.

Let (A, K) be a dependence space, $X \in \mathbf{B}(A)$ a set, and $x \in X$ an element. The element x is said to be *K-dispensable in X* if $(X, X - \{x\}) \in K$. An element $x \in X$ is said to be *K-indispensable in X* if it is not K-dispensable in X, i.e., if $(X, X - \{x\}) \notin K$. The set of all K-indispensable elements in X is said to be the *K-core of X* and is denoted by $\mathbf{CORE}(K, X)$.

Theorem 50. *If (A, K) is a dependence space and $X \in \mathbf{B}(A)$ a set, then $\mathbf{CORE}(K, X) = \bigcap\{Y; Y \in \mathbf{RED}(K, X)\}$.*

Proof. If $Y \in \mathbf{RED}(K, X)$ and $x \in X - Y$, then $(Y, X) \in K$, $Y \subseteq X - \{x\} \subseteq X$ which implies that $(X - \{x\}, X) \in K$ by Theorem 15. Thus $x \notin \mathbf{CORE}(K, X)$ and, therefore, we have $\mathbf{CORE}(K, X) \subseteq \bigcap\{Y;\ Y \in \mathbf{RED}(K, X)\}$.

On the other hand, if $x \in Y$ for every $Y \in \mathbf{RED}(K, X)$ and $(X, X - \{x\}) \in K$, there exists a minimal set Y_0 in the set $\{Y \in \mathbf{B}(A);\ Y \subseteq X - \{x\},\ (Y, X) \in K\}$. Then $Y_0 \in \mathbf{RED}(K, X)$. Furthermore, $x \notin Y_0$ which is a contradiction. Thus $\bigcap\{Y;\ Y \in \mathbf{RED}(K, X)\} \subseteq \mathbf{CORE}(K, X)$.

It follows that the assertion holds. □

If (A, K) is a dependence space and $X \in \mathbf{B}(A)$ is a set, we put $\mathbf{I}(K, X) = \{Y \in \mathbf{I}(K);\ Y \subseteq X\}$. Let $\mathbf{SRED}(K, X)$ be the set of all elements of $\mathbf{I}(K, X)$ that are maximal with respect to inclusion; any element in $\mathbf{SRED}(K, X)$ is said to be a *K-subreduct of X*.

Lemma 51. *If (A, K) is a dependence space and $X \in \mathbf{B}(A)$ a set, then $\mathbf{RED}(K, X) \subseteq \mathbf{SRED}(K, X)$ holds.*

This is clear because a K-reduct Y of X is its K-subreduct satisfying $(Y, X) \in K$, by definitions.

Example 26. Let A, $\mathbf{B}(A)$ be the same as in Section 2. Suppose that K is a congruence on the semilattice $(\mathbf{B}(A), \cup)$ whose blocks are $\{0\}$, $\{2\}$, $\{3\}$, $\{1, 12, 13, 23, 123\}$. Then $\mathbf{RED}(K, 13) = \{1\}$, $\mathbf{SRED}(K, 13) = \{1, 3\}$. Clearly, 3 is a K-subreduct of 13 that is no K-reduct of this set. Cf. Fig. 9.

By Theorem 50, the intersection of all reducts of a set has a natural meaning. We prove that also the union of all subreducts of a set may be expressed in a simple way.

If (A, K) is a dependence space, then an element $X \in \mathbf{B}(A)$ is said to be an *almost K-zero* element if $(X, \emptyset) \in K$. Furthermore, an element $X \in \mathbf{B}(A)$ is called *K-accessible* if there exists a set $\mathbf{Z} \subseteq \mathbf{I}(K)$ and an almost K-zero element Y such that $X = Y \cup \bigcup\{Z;\ Z \in \mathbf{Z}\}$. Clearly

Lemma 52. *If (A, K) is a dependence space, then any almost K-zero element is K-accessible.*

Lemma 53. *If (A, K) is a dependence space and $X \in \mathbf{B}(A)$ is not an almost K-zero element, then there exists an element $Y \in \mathbf{B}(A)$ such that $X = Y \cup \bigcup\{Z;\ Z \in \mathbf{RED}(K, X)\}$, $Y \subseteq X$, $(Y, X) \notin K$.*

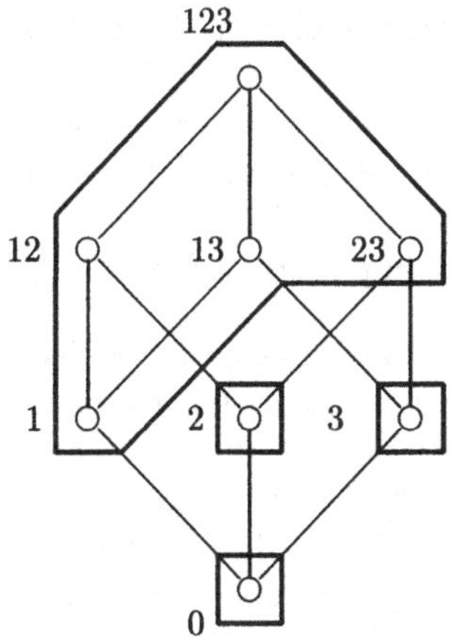

Figure 9

Proof. Since $\mathbf{RED}(K,X) \neq \emptyset$ by Lemma 49 and $(Z,X) \in K$ for any $Z \in \mathbf{RED}(K,X)$, we have $(\bigcup\{Z;\ Z \in \mathbf{RED}(K,X)\}, X) \in K$.

If $\bigcup\{Z;\ Z \in \mathbf{RED}(K,X)\} = X$, we put $Y = \emptyset$ and the assertion holds.

Suppose $\bigcup\{Z;\ Z \in \mathbf{RED}(K,X)\} \neq X$. Since $(\bigcup\{Z;\ Z \in \mathbf{RED}(K,X)\}, X) \in K$ and X is not an almost K-zero element, we have $\bigcup\{Z;\ Z \in \mathbf{RED}(K,X)\} \neq \emptyset$. Thus, $\emptyset \neq X - \bigcup\{Z;\ Z \in \mathbf{RED}(K,X)\} \neq X$. We put $Y = X - \bigcup\{Z;\ Z \in \mathbf{RED}(K,X)\}$. If $(X,Y) \in K$, there exists a set $Y_0 \in \mathbf{RED}(K,Y)$ by Lemma 49. Thus, $Y_0 \in \mathbf{I}(K)$ and $(Y_0,X) \in K$, $Y_0 \subseteq Y \subseteq X$. This implies that $Y_0 \in \mathbf{RED}(K,X)$ and, therefore, $Y_0 \subseteq \bigcup\{Z;\ Z \in \mathbf{RED}(K,X)\}$. Furthermore, $Y_0 \subseteq Y \subseteq X - \bigcup\{Z;\ Z \in \mathbf{RED}(K,X)\}$ which entails that $Y_0 = \emptyset$ and, consequently, X is an almost K-zero element contrary to our hypothesis. Thus, $(X,Y) \notin K$, $Y \subseteq X$, and $X = Y \cup \bigcup\{Z;\ Z \in \mathbf{RED}(K,X)\}$. □

Lemma 54. *Let (A,K) be a dependence space. If $X \in \mathbf{B}(A)$ is such that any $Z \in \mathbf{B}(A)$ with $Z \subseteq X$, $Z \neq X$ is K-accessible, then X is K-accessible.*

Proof. If X is an almost K-zero element, then it is K-accessible by Lemma 52. If X is not an almost K-zero element, there exists $Y \in \mathbf{B}(A)$ such that $X = Y \cup \bigcup\{Z;\ Z \in \mathbf{RED}(K,X)\}$, $Y \subseteq X$, $Y \neq X$, $(Y,X) \notin K$ by Lemma 53. By hypothesis, Y is K-accessible, i.e., there exists a set $\mathbf{M} \subseteq \mathbf{I}(K)$ and an almost K-zero element U such that $Y = U \cup \bigcup\{Z;\ Z \in \mathbf{M}\}$. It follows that $X = U \cup \bigcup\{Z;\ Z \in \mathbf{M} \cup \mathbf{RED}(K,X)\}$. Clearly, $\mathbf{M} \cup \mathbf{RED}(K,X) \subseteq \mathbf{I}(K)$. □

Corollary 55. *If (A,K) is a dependence space, then any element in $\mathbf{B}(A)$ is K-accessible.*

Proof. This is a direct consequence of Lemma 54. □

Theorem 56. *Let (A,K) be a dependence space. Then for any $X \in \mathbf{B}(A)$ there exists an almost K-zero element Y such that $X = Y \cup \bigcup\{Z;\ Z \in \mathbf{SRED}(K,X)\}$.*

Proof. By Corollary 55, there exists a set $\mathbf{Z} \subseteq \mathbf{I}(K)$ and an almost K-zero element Y such that $X = Y \cup \bigcup\{Z;\ Z \in \mathbf{Z}\}$. Clearly, $\mathbf{Z} \subseteq \mathbf{I}(K, X)$ which implies that $X \subseteq Y \cup \bigcup\{Z; Z \in \mathbf{I}(K, X)\}$. Since $\mathbf{SRED}(K, X)$ is the set of all maximal elements in $\mathbf{I}(K, X)$, for any $Z \in \mathbf{I}(K, X)$ there exists $V \in \mathbf{SRED}(K, X)$ such that $Z \subseteq V$; it follows that $X \subseteq Y \cup \bigcup\{Z;\ Z \in \mathbf{I}(K, X)\} \subseteq Y \cup \bigcup\{Z; Z \in \mathbf{SRED}(K, X)\} \subseteq X$ which implies that $X = Y \cup \bigcup\{Z;\ Z \in \mathbf{SRED}(K, X)\}$. □

Example 27. Let A, $\mathbf{B}(A)$ be the same as in Section 2, suppose that K is a congruence on the semilattice $(\mathbf{B}(A), \cup)$ whose blocks are $\{0\}$, $\{1\}$, $\{2\}$, $\{3\}$, $\{12, 13, 23, 123\}$; see Fig. 4 and Example 16. Then $\mathbf{I}(K) = \{0, 1, 2, 3, 12, 13, 23\}$. Clearly, $\mathbf{RED}(K, A) = \{12, 13, 23\} = \mathbf{SRED}(K, A)$, $\mathbf{RED}(K, X) = \{X\} = \mathbf{SRED}(K, X)$ for any $X \in \mathbf{B}(A) - \{A\}$. Furthermore, 0 is the only almost K-zero element. In Example 16, we have demonstrated that K is no rough top equality.

Rough top equality is a congruence on the semilattice $(\mathbf{B}(A), \cup)$ that is very important for the study of information systems. For this reason, we are interested to know the relationship of reducts and subreducts and the set of almost zero elements for rough top equalities. The answer is contained in the following.

Theorem 57. *Let (A, K) be a dependence space where K is a rough top equality. Then $\emptyset$ is the only almost K-zero element and $\mathbf{RED}(K, X) = \mathbf{SRED}(K, X)$ holds for any $X \in \mathbf{B}(A)$.*

Proof. There exists an equivalence r on A such that $K = \mathbf{K}(\mathbf{c}(r))$. By Theorem 31, we have $X \in \mathbf{I}(K)$ if and only if $X \cap B$ has at most one element for any block $B \in A/r$. If $X \in \mathbf{B}(A)$ is arbitrary, then $Y \in \mathbf{B}(A)$ is a K-subreduct of X if and only if Y contains exactly one element from any nonempty intersection $X \cap B$ where $B \in A/r$; but such a set Y is a K-reduct of X, too. Thus, $\mathbf{RED}(K, X) = \mathbf{SRED}(K, X)$ for any $X \in \mathbf{B}(A)$. Clearly, $(X, \emptyset) \in K$ implies $X = \emptyset$. □

Example 27 and Theorem 57 lead us to the following

Problem 58. Let A be a finite nonempty set. Characterize all dependence spaces (A, K) such that $\emptyset$ is the only almost K-zero element and that $\mathbf{RED}(K, X) = \mathbf{SRED}(K, X)$ for any $X \in \mathbf{B}(A)$.

The author does not know the solution of this problem.

9 Superreducts

Let (A, K) be a dependence space, $X \in \mathbf{B}(A)$ an arbitrary set. As we know (cf. Section 8), a set $Y \in \mathbf{B}(A)$ is said to be a K-reduct of X if Y is minimal with respect to inclusion among all sets $Z \in \mathbf{B}(A)$ such that $Z \subseteq X$, $(X, Z) \in K$. K-reducts have natural interpretation in information systems. The notion of K-reduct may be changed in such a way that the new version can be naturally interpreted, too.

Let (A, K) be a dependence space. We put $\mathbf{SPR}(K) = \{(X, Y) \in \mathbf{B}(A) \times \mathbf{B}(A)$; for any $Z \in \mathbf{B}(X)$ there exists $U \in \mathbf{B}(Y)$ such that $(Z, U) \in K$ and for any $V \in \mathbf{B}(Y)$ there exists $W \in \mathbf{B}(X)$ such that $(V, W) \in K\}$.

Theorem 59. *Let (A, K) be a dependence space. Then $\mathbf{SPR}(K)$ is a congruence on the semilattice $(\mathbf{B}(A), \cup)$.*

Proof. Clearly, $\mathbf{SPR}(K)$ is an equivalence on the set $\mathbf{B}(A)$.

Let us have $(X, Y) \in \mathbf{SPR}(K)$, let $Z \in \mathbf{B}(A)$ be arbitrary. Suppose $U \in \mathbf{B}(X \cup Z)$. Put $U_1 = X \cap U$, $U_2 = U - U_1$. Then $U_1 \in \mathbf{B}(X)$, $U_2 \in \mathbf{B}(Z)$. The first condition implies the existence of $V_1 \in \mathbf{B}(Y)$ such that $(U_1, V_1) \in K$. This entails $(U_1 \cup U_2, V_1 \cup U_2) \in K$. Put $V = V_1 \cup U_2$; clearly $V \in \mathbf{B}(Y \cup Z)$ while $U_1 \cup U_2 = U$. Hence, for any $U \in \mathbf{B}(X \cup Z)$, there exists $V \in \mathbf{B}(Y \cup Z)$ such that $(U, V) \in K$. — Similarly, for any $T \in \mathbf{B}(Y \cup Z)$, we find $W \in \mathbf{B}(X \cup Z)$ such that $(T, W) \in K$. It follows that $(X \cup Z, Y \cup Z) \in \mathbf{SPR}(K)$.

By Theorem 12, $\mathbf{SPR}(K)$ is a congruence on the semilattice $(\mathbf{B}(A), \cup)$. □

Corollary 60. *If (A, K) is a dependence space, then $(A, \mathbf{SPR}(K))$ is a dependence space.*

Lemma 61. *If (A, K) is a dependence space, then $\mathbf{SPR}(K) \subseteq K$.*

Proof. If $(X, Y) \in \mathbf{SPR}(K)$, there exist $X' \in \mathbf{B}(Y)$ and $Y' \in \mathbf{B}(X)$ such that $(X, X') \in K$, $(Y, Y') \in K$. Then $(X, Y) = (X \cup Y', X' \cup Y) \in K$. □

Let (A, K) be a dependence space, $X \in \mathbf{B}(A)$ a set. A set $Y \in \mathbf{B}(A)$ is said to be a *K-superreduct of X* if it is minimal with respect to inclusion among all sets $Z \in \mathbf{B}(A)$ having the following properties (i) and (ii).

(i) $Z \subseteq X$.

(ii) For any $X' \subseteq X$ there exists $Z' \subseteq Z$ such that $(Z', X') \in K$.

As a consequence of definitions we obtain

Theorem 62. *Let (A, K) be a dependence space, X, Y sets in $\mathbf{B}(A)$. Then the following conditions are equivalent.*

(i) Y is a K-superreduct of X.

(ii) Y is a $\mathbf{SPR}(K)$-reduct of X.

By Lemma 61 it follows that a K-superreduct of X must be looked for among all sets $Z \in \mathbf{B}(A)$ such that $Z \subseteq X$ and $(Z, X) \in K$. The condition $(Z, X) \notin \mathbf{SPR}(K)$ is satisfied if and only if there exists $X_0 \subseteq X$ such that $(X_0, Z') \notin K$ for every $Z' \in \mathbf{B}(Z)$.

Example 28. Let A, $\mathbf{B}(A)$ be the same as in Section 2. Suppose that K is a congruence on the semilattice $(\mathbf{B}(A), \cup)$ whose blocks are $\{0\}$, $\{1\}$, $\{3\}$, $\{2, 12, 13, 23, 123\}$. By Lemma 61, the sets $\{0\}$, $\{1\}$, $\{3\}$ are blocks of $\mathbf{SPR}(K)$. Suppose that $X \in \{12, 13, 23, 123\}$ and $(2, X) \in \mathbf{SPR}(K)$. Then either $1 \subseteq X$ or $3 \subseteq X$ which implies that there exists $Y \subseteq 2$ such that $(Y, 1) \in K$ in the first case and $(Y,3) \in K$ in the second; this is a contradiction because $Y = 1$ in the first and $Y = 3$ in the second case. Thus, $\{2\}$ is a block of $\mathbf{SPR}(K)$. Consider $X \in \{13, 23, 123\}$ and suppose that $(12, X) \in \mathbf{SPR}(K)$. Then $3 \subseteq X$ and there exists $Y \subseteq 12$ such that $(Y, 3) \in K$. This implies that $Y = 3$ and $3 \subseteq 12$ which is a contradiction. Thus, $\{12\}$ is a block of $\mathbf{SPR}(K)$. Similarly, $\{23\}$ is a block of $\mathbf{SPR}(K)$.

We now consider the possibility $(13, 123) \in \mathbf{SPR}(K)$. Suppose $X \subseteq 123$; if $X \subseteq 13$, then $(X, X) \in K$. Let us have $X \subseteq 123$, $X \not\subseteq 13$. Thus, $X \in \{2, 12, 23, 123\}$. In all possible cases, we have $(X, 13) \in K$. Therefore, $(13, 123) \in \mathbf{SPR}(K)$ and 13 is a K-superreduct of 123. Cf. Fig. 10.

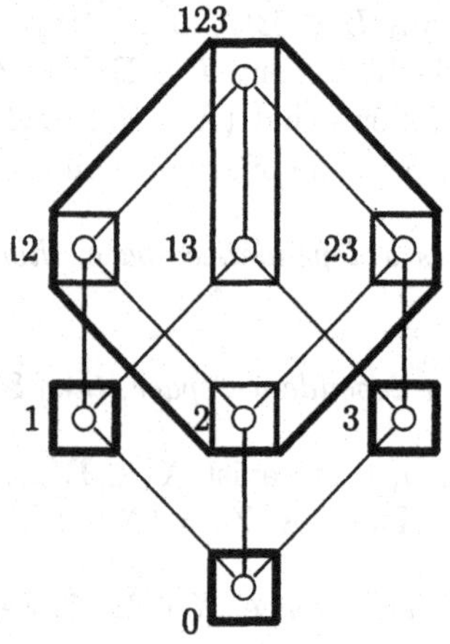

Figure 10

If (A, K) is a dependence space and $X \in \mathbf{B}(A)$ a set, then finding K-superreducts of X by means of Theorem 62 supposes that we have constructed the congruence $\mathbf{SPR}(K)$ which can be very laborious. Therefore, we present another method for construction of K-superreducts.

Lemma 63. *Let (A, K) be a dependence space, $X \in \mathbf{B}(A)$ a nonempty set. Then the following assertions hold.*

(i) $K \cap (\mathbf{B}(X) \times \mathbf{B}(X))$ is a congruence on the semilattice $(\mathbf{B}(X), \cup)$.

(ii) The K-superreducts of X coincide with $K \cap (\mathbf{B}(X) \times \mathbf{B}(X))$-superreducts of X.

Proof. Assertions *(i), (ii)* follow easily from the fact that for $Y \in \mathbf{B}(X)$, $Y' \in \mathbf{B}(X)$ the conditions $(Y, Y') \in K$ and $(Y, Y') \in K \cap (\mathbf{B}(X) \times \mathbf{B}(X))$ are equivalent. □

Hence, without loss of generality, it is sufficient to describe the construction of K-superreducts of the set A for the dependence space (A, K).

Lemma 64. *Let (A, K) be a dependence space, $X \in \mathbf{B}(A)$ a set. Then the following assertions are equivalent.*

(i) $(A, X) \in \mathbf{SPR}(K)$.

(ii) $\mathbf{B}(X)$ *has a nonempty intersection with any block of* K.

Proof. Suppose that *(i)* holds; if $\mathbf{B} \in \mathbf{B}(A)/K$ is a block of K and $Z \in \mathbf{B}$ holds, then $Z \in \mathbf{B}(A)$. By definition of $\mathbf{SPR}(K)$, there exists $Z' \in \mathbf{B}(X)$ such that $(Z, Z') \in K$. Then $Z' \in \mathbf{B}$ and, therefore, $Z' \in \mathbf{B} \cap \mathbf{B}(X)$. Hence *(ii)* holds.

If *(ii)* holds and $Z \in \mathbf{B}(A)$ is arbitrary, there exists a block $\mathbf{B} \in \mathbf{B}(A)/K$ such that $Z \in \mathbf{B}$. Furthermore, $\mathbf{B} \cap \mathbf{B}(X) \neq \emptyset$, i.e., there exists $Z' \in \mathbf{B} \cap \mathbf{B}(X)$. The fact $Z' \in \mathbf{B}$ implies that $(Z, Z') \in K$. It follows that $(A, X) \in \mathbf{SPR}(K)$ and *(i)* holds. □

Condition *(ii)* of Lemma 64 is equivalent to a formally weaker condition as it follows from the following.

Lemma 65. *Let (A, K) be a dependence space, $X \in \mathbf{B}(A)$ a set. Then the following assertions are equivalent.*

(i) $\mathbf{B}(X)$ *has a nonempty intersection with any block of* K *that is totally irreducible in the semilattice* $(\mathbf{B}(A), \cup)/K$.

(ii) $\mathbf{B}(X)$ *has a nonempty intersection with any block of* K.

Proof. Clearly *(ii)* implies *(i)*.

Let *(i)* hold. We prove that $\mathbf{B}(X)$ has a nonempty intersection with any block $\mathbf{B}$ of K that is not totally irreducible in $(\mathbf{B}(A), \cup)/K$.

If $\mathbf{B}$ is the least element in $(\mathbf{B}(A), \cup)/K$, then $\emptyset \in \mathbf{B} \cap \mathbf{B}(X)$.

Suppose that $\mathbf{B}$ is not the least element in $(\mathbf{B}(A), \cup)/K$. By Theorem 5 there exists an integer $p \geq 2$ and totally irreducible elements $\mathbf{B}_1, \dots, \mathbf{B}_p$ in $(\mathbf{B}(A), \cup)/K$ such that $\mathbf{B} = \sup\{\mathbf{B}_i;\ 1 \leq i \leq p\}$. By hypothesis $\mathbf{B}_i \cap \mathbf{B}(X) \neq \emptyset$ and, therefore, there exists $Z_i \in \mathbf{B}_i \cap \mathbf{B}(X)$ for any $i \in \{1, \dots, p\}$. Put $Z = \bigcup\{Z_i;\ 1 \leq i \leq p\} = \sup\{Z_i;\ 1 \leq i \leq p\}$ and denote by h the natural surjection of $\mathbf{B}(A)$ onto $\mathbf{B}(A)/K$; by Theorem 7 and 13, h is a surjective homomorphism of the semilattice $(\mathbf{B}(A), \cup)$ onto $(\mathbf{B}(A), \cup)/K$. By Lemma 8, we have $h(Z) = h(\sup\{Z_i;\ 1 \leq i \leq p\}) = \sup\{h(Z_i);\ 1 \leq i \leq p\} = \sup\{\mathbf{B}_i;\ 1 \leq i \leq p\} = \mathbf{B}$ and, hence, $Z \in \mathbf{B}$. Since $Z \in \mathbf{B}(X)$, we obtain $Z \in \mathbf{B} \cap \mathbf{B}(X)$. Thus, *(i)* implies *(ii)*. □

Lemma 66. *Let (A, K) be a dependence space, $X \in \mathbf{B}(A)$ a set, $\mathbf{B} \in \mathbf{B}(A)/K$ a block of K, h the natural surjection of $\mathbf{B}(A)$ onto $\mathbf{B}(A)/K$. Then the following assertions are equivalent.*

(i) $\mathbf{B} \cap \mathbf{B}(X) \neq \emptyset$.

(ii) There exists $Y \in \mathbf{B}(A)$ *such that* $Y \subseteq X$ *and* $\mathbf{B} = \sup\{h(\{y\});\ y \in Y\}$.

Proof. If *(i)* holds, then $Y \in \mathbf{B} \cap \mathbf{B}(X)$ for some Y. It follows that $Y \subseteq X$ and $\mathbf{B} = h(Y) = h(\bigcup\{\{y\};\ y \in Y\}) = \sup\{h(\{y\});\ y \in Y\}$ and *(ii)* holds.

If *(ii)* is satisfied, then $Y \subseteq X$ and $\mathbf{B} = \sup\{h(\{y\});\ y \in Y\} = h(\bigcup\{\{y\};\ y \in Y\}) = h(Y)$ and, hence, $Y \in \mathbf{B}$. Thus, $Y \in \mathbf{B} \cap \mathbf{B}(X)$ which implies *(i)*. □

If $\mathbf{B} \in \mathbf{B}(A)/K$ is totally irreducible in the semilattice $(\mathbf{B}(A), \cup)/K$, then there exists $a \in A$ such that $\mathbf{B} = h(\{a\})$, by Corollary 14 and Example 5, where h is the natural surjection of $\mathbf{B}(A)$ onto $\mathbf{B}(A)/K$.

Corollary 67. *Let (A, K) be a dependence space, $X \in \mathbf{B}(A)$ a set, h the natural surjection of $\mathbf{B}(A)$ onto $\mathbf{B}(A)/K$. Then the following assertions are equivalent.*

(i) $\mathbf{B}(X)$ has nonempty intersection with any totally irreducible block of K.

(ii) For any $a \in A$ such that $h(\{a\})$ is totally irreducible in $(\mathbf{B}(A), \cup)/K$ there exists $a' \in X$ such that $(\{a\}, \{a'\}) \in K$.

Proof. If *(i)* holds and $h(\{a\})$ is totally irreducible in $(\mathbf{B}(A), \cup)/K$, then, by Lemma 66, there exists $Y \subseteq X$ such that $h(\{a\}) = \sup\{h(\{y\});\ y \in Y\}$. Total irreducibility of $h(\{a\})$ implies the existence of $a' \in Y$ such that $h(\{a\}) = h(\{a'\})$, i.e., $(\{a\}, \{a'\}) \in K$. Thus *(ii)* holds.

If *(ii)* holds, then for any $a \in A$ such that $h(\{a\})$ is totally irreducible there exists $a' \in X$ such that $h(\{a\}) = h(\{a'\})$. Thus, $\{a'\} \in \mathbf{B}(X) \cap h(\{a\})$ and *(i)* is satisfied. □

Theorem 68. *Let (A, K) be a dependence space, $X \in \mathbf{B}(A)$ a set, h the natural surjection of $\mathbf{B}(A)$ onto $\mathbf{B}(A)/K$. Then the following assertions are equivalent.*

(i) X is a K-superreduct of A.

(ii) For any $a \in A$ such that $h(\{a\})$ is totally irreducible in the semilattice $(\mathbf{B}(A), \cup)/K$, there exists exactly one element $a' \in X$ with the property $(\{a\}, \{a'\}) \in K$.

Proof. By definition, *(i)* is equivalent to the following assertion.

(iii) X is minimal with respect to inclusion among all sets $Z \in \mathbf{B}(A)$ such that $(A, Z) \in \mathbf{SPR}(K)$.

By Lemma 64 and Lemma 65, *(iii)* is equivalent to the following.

(iv) X is minimal with respect to inclusion among all sets $Z \in \mathbf{B}(A)$ such that $\mathbf{B}(Z)$ has nonempty intersection with any block of K that is totally irreducible in $(\mathbf{B}(A), \cup)/K$.

By Corollary 67, *(iv)* is equivalent to *(ii)*. □

By Theorem 68 it is necessary to know which of blocks of K of the form $h(\{a\})$ are totally irreducible.

Theorem 69. *Let (A, K) be a dependence space, h the natural surjection of $\mathbf{B}(A)$ onto $\mathbf{B}(A)/K$, $a \in A$ an element. Then the following assertions are equivalent.*

(i) $h(\{a\})$ is totally irreducible in the semilattice $(\mathbf{B}(A), \cup)/K$.

(ii) If $Y(a) = \{y \in \mathbf{C}(K)(\{a\});\ (\{y\}, \{a\}) \notin K\}$, then $(Y(a), \{a\}) \notin K$.

Proof. Suppose that *(i)* holds. Since $(\{y\}, \{a\}) \notin K$, we have $h(\{y\}) \neq h(\{a\})$ for any $y \in Y(a)$. The fact $Y(a) = \bigcup\{\{y\};\ y \in Y(a)\} = \sup\{\{y\};\ y \in Y(a)\}$ implies that $h(Y(a)) = \sup\{h(\{y\});\ y \in Y(a)\}$ by Lemma 8. The total irreducibility of

$h(\{a\})$ together with the fact $h(\{y\}) \neq h(\{a\})$ for any $y \in Y(a)$ imply that $h(Y(a)) \neq h(\{a\})$, i.e., $(Y(a), \{a\}) \notin K$. Thus, *(i)* implies *(ii)*.

Suppose now that *(ii)* holds and that *(i)* is not satisfied. Thus, $h(\{a\})$ is not totally irreducible; by Theorem 5, there exists a set of totally irreducible elements such that $h(\{a\})$ is its least upper bound. Hence there exists a set $X \subseteq A$ such that $h(\{a\}) = \sup\{h(\{x\});\ x \in X\}$; since $h(\{x\})$ is totally irreducible while $h(\{a\})$ is not, we have $h(\{x\}) \neq h(\{a\})$ for any $x \in X$, which means $(\{x\}, \{a\}) \notin K$. Furthermore, we have $h(\{a\}) = h(\sup\{\{x\};\ x \in X\}) = h(\bigcup\{\{x\};\ x \in X\}) = h(X)$ which means that $(\{a\}, X) \in K$ and, thus, $\mathbf{C}(K)(\{a\}) = \mathbf{C}(K)(X)$. For any $x \in X$, we have $x \in X \subseteq \mathbf{C}(K)(X) = \mathbf{C}(K)(\{a\})$, $(\{x\}, \{a\}) \notin K$, i.e., $x \in Y(a)$. Thus, $X \subseteq Y(a)$ and, therefore, $\mathbf{C}(K)(\{a\}) = \mathbf{C}(K)(X) \subseteq \mathbf{C}(K)(Y(a)) \subseteq \mathbf{C}(K)(\{a\})$. It follows that $\mathbf{C}(K)(\{a\}) = \mathbf{C}(K)(Y(a))$ and, hence, $(Y(a), \{a\}) \in K$ which is a contradiction.

Thus *(ii)* implies *(i)*. □

If resuming constructions included in Theorem 68 and 69, we obtain (cf. [NP8])

Algorithm 70. (Algorithm for finding K-superreducts)
Let (A, K) be a dependence space.

(1) *For any $x \in A$ construct the set $\mathbf{C}(K)(\{x\})$ that is the union of all sets $X \in \mathbf{B}(A)$ with the property $(X, \{x\}) \in K$.*
(2) *Construct the relation $r = \{(x, y) \in A \times A;\ (\{x\}, \{y\}) \in K\}$.*
(3) *Construct a set Z having exactly one element in common with any block of r. (There may be several possibilities for the choice of Z.)*
(4) *For any $x \in Z$ construct the set $Y(x) = \{y \in \mathbf{C}(K)(\{x\});\ (y, x) \notin r\}$.*
(5) *Construct the set M that consists of all elements $x \in Z$ such that $(Y(x), \{x\}) \notin K$.*

The set M is a K-superreduct of the set A and any K-superreduct of A may be constructed in this way.

Example 29. Let (A, K) be the dependence space from Example 28. Then the blocks of r are 1, 2, 3. By Section 2, we have $1 = \{a\}$. Thus $\mathbf{C}(K)(\{a\}) = \{a\} = 1$ and $Y(a) = \emptyset = 0$. Since $(0, 1) \notin K$, we have $a \in M$. Similarly, $c \in M$. Finally, $\mathbf{C}(K)(\{b\}) = \mathbf{C}(K)(2) = 123$, $Y(b) = \{a, c\} = 13$. Since $(Y(b), \{b\}) = (13, 2) \in K$, we obtain $b \notin M$. Hence $M = \{a, c\} = 13$ is a K-superreduct of the set 123. Our K-superreduct 13 is, simultaneously, a K-reduct of the set 123. Clearly, 2 is a K-reduct of 123 that is not a K-superreduct of this set.

Example 30. Let us consider the dependence space (A, K) from Example 16. Clearly, the blocks of r are the sets 1, 2, 3. Similarly as in Example 29, we prove that a, b, $c \in M$, i.e., $M = 123$. Hence, 123 is the only K-superreduct of the set 123; but it is not a K-reduct of this set: K-reducts of 123 are: 12, 13, 23.

10 Reducts

Construction of K-reducts solves some important problems concerning information systems. K-reducts were introduced in Section 8; the definition can be paraphrazed as follows.

Let (A, K) be a dependence space, $X \in \mathbf{B}(A)$ a set. A set $Y \in \mathbf{B}(A)$ is said to be a K-reduct of X if it is minimal with respect to inclusion among all sets $Z \in \mathbf{B}(A)$ that have the following properties.

(i) $Z \subseteq X$.

(ii) $(X, Z) \in K$.

Natural interpretations of K-reducts will be found in Chapter 8 concerning applications of our theory to information systems. We now describe an algorithm for finding a K-reduct of a set and — using this algorithm — an algorithm for finding all K-reducts of a set.

Let (A, K) be a dependence space, Z, W elements of the set $\mathbf{B}(A)$ such that $W \subseteq Z$, o a linear ordering on Z. If z_1 and z_2 are in Z, then $(z_1, z_2) \in o$ means that z_1 is less or equal to z_2 with respect to o. We now define the *successor* $\mathbf{SC}(Z, K, W, o)$, the *set of bad elements* $\mathbf{BD}(Z, K, W, o)$, and the *free space* $\mathbf{FS}(Z, K, W, o)$ of Z with respect to K, W, o as follows.

$$\mathbf{SC}(Z,K,W,o) = \begin{cases} Z \text{ if } (Z, Z - \{z\}) \notin K \text{ for any } z \in W; \\ Z - \{a\} \text{ if } a \text{ is the least element in } W \text{ with respect to} \\ o \text{ such that } (Z, Z - \{a\}) \in K; \end{cases}$$

$$\mathbf{BD}(Z,K,W,o) = \begin{cases} \emptyset \text{ if } (Z, Z - \{z\}) \notin K \text{ for any } z \in W; \\ \{Z - \{z\};\ z \in W,\ (z,a) \in o,\ z \neq a\} \text{ if } a \text{ is the least} \\ \text{element in } W \text{ with respect to } o \text{ such that } (Z, Z - \\ \{a\}) \in K; \end{cases}$$

$$\mathbf{FS}(Z,K,W,o) = \begin{cases} \emptyset \text{ if } (Z, Z - \{z\}) \notin K \text{ for any } z \in W; \\ \{z \in W;\ (a,z) \in o,\ a \neq z\} \text{ if } a \text{ is the least element in} \\ W \text{ with respect to } o \text{ such that } (Z, Z - \{a\}) \in K. \end{cases}$$

The sense of these definitions is as follows: **SC** cancels in Z the first element a (with respect to o) in W such that $(Z, Z - \{a\}) \in K$; **BD** collects sets of the form $Z - \{z\}$ that have been tested and rejected during the construction of **SC**, i.e., sets of the form $Z - \{z\}$ where $z < a$ if we write $\leq$ for o. Finally, **FS** limits the space for construction to the set of elements $z \in W$ such that $a < z$. As in Section 2, the symbol o denotes an ordering on Z and, simultaneously, its restrictions to subsets of Z. We use the symbol o for the more usual $\leq$ because we shall deal with more orderings in the same situation; then, it is easier to distinguish them using different letters than different symbols for ordering. We mention that the condition

$$(Z, Z - \{z\}) \notin K \text{ for any } z \in W$$

appearing in these definitions is satisfied, particularly, if $W = \emptyset$. Conditions of a similar structure that appear in what follows must be understood analogously.

We now present two algorithms. Some of their steps require properties of the above defined objects that must be proved. The corresponding proofs are put into square brackets [ ] which are inserted into the description of algorithms. Algorithm 71 provides the sets $\mathbf{RD}(Z,K,o)$, $\mathbf{PD}(Z,K,o)$. Their meaning is given by Theorem 72.

Algorithm 71. (Algorithm for finding one reduct)

Let (A,K) be a dependence space, $Z \subseteq X \subseteq A$ sets such that $(Z,X) \in K$. Suppose that o is a linear ordering on Z. We put

$$\mathbf{SC}^{(0)}(Z,K,o) = Z,\ \mathbf{BD}^{(0)}(Z,K,o) = \emptyset,\ \mathbf{FS}^{(0)}(Z,K,o) = Z$$

and proceed by induction:

$$\mathbf{SC}^{(i+1)}(Z,K,o) = \mathbf{SC}(\mathbf{SC}^{(i)}(Z,K,o),K,\mathbf{FS}^{(i)}(Z,K,o),o),$$

$$\mathbf{BD}^{(i+1)}(Z,K,o) = \mathbf{BD}^{(i)}(Z,K,o) \cup \mathbf{BD}(\mathbf{SC}^{(i)}(Z,K,o),K,\mathbf{FS}^{(i)}(Z,K,o),o),$$

$$\mathbf{FS}^{(i+1)}(Z,K,o) = \mathbf{FS}(\mathbf{SC}^{(i)}(Z,K,o),K,\mathbf{FS}^{(i)}(Z,K,o),o)$$

for any integer $i \geq 0$.

[Clearly, $\mathbf{SC}^{(i+1)}(Z,K,o) \subseteq \mathbf{SC}^{(i)}(Z,K,o)$.]

There exists a least integer $q \geq 0$ such that $\mathbf{SC}^{(q+1)}(Z,K,o) = \mathbf{SC}^{(q)}(Z,K,o)$. We put

$$\mathbf{RD}(Z,K,o) = \mathbf{SC}^{(q)}(Z,K,o),\ \mathbf{PD}(Z,K,o) = \mathbf{BD}^{(q)}(Z,K,o).$$

Theorem 72. *Let (A,K) be a dependence space, $Z \subseteq X \subseteq A$ sets such that $(Z,X) \in K$. Suppose that o is a linear ordering on Z. Then the following assertions hold.*

(i) $\mathbf{RD}(Z,K,o)$ is a K-reduct of X.

(ii) $(X,Y) \notin K$ holds for any $Y \in \mathbf{PD}(Z,K,o)$.

Proof. (1) By an easy induction we obtain $\mathbf{SC}^{(i)}(Z,K,o) \subseteq Z$, $(\mathbf{SC}^{(i)}(Z,K,o), Z) \in K$ and, therefore, $(\mathbf{SC}^{(i)}(Z,K,o),X) \in K$ for any $i \geq 0$. Furthermore, $Y \in \mathbf{BD}(\mathbf{SC}^{(i)}(Z,K,o),K,\mathbf{FS}^{(i)}(Z,K,o),o)$ implies that $(\mathbf{SC}^{(i)}(Z,K,o),Y) \notin K$ and, therefore, $(Y,Z) \notin K$, $(Y,X) \notin K$ for any $i \geq 0$. It follows that $(Y,X) \notin K$ for any $Y \in \mathbf{BD}^{(q)}(Z,K,o) = \mathbf{PD}(Z,K,o)$ which is *(ii)*.

(2) For the sake of brevity, we shall omit the arguments Z,K,o in this part of the proof and write $\mathbf{RD}$, $\mathbf{SC}^{(j)}, \mathbf{FS}^{(j)}$ for $\mathbf{RD}(Z,K,o), \mathbf{SC}^{(j)}(Z,K,o)$, $\mathbf{FS}^{(j)}(Z,K,o)$, respectively.

We have $\mathbf{RD} = \mathbf{SC}^{(q)}$ for some $q \geq 0$ and, by (1), we obtain $\mathbf{SC}^{(q)} \subseteq Z \subseteq X$, $(\mathbf{SC}^{(q)},X) \in K$. We prove that $(\mathbf{SC}^{(q)}, \mathbf{SC}^{(q)} - \{z\}) \notin K$ for any $z \in \mathbf{SC}^{(q)}$.

This is clear if $z \in \mathbf{FS}^{(q)}$ because the condition $\mathbf{SC}^{(q)} = \mathbf{SC}^{(q+1)} = \mathbf{SC}(\mathbf{SC}^{(q)},K,\mathbf{FS}^{(q)},o)$ means $(\mathbf{SC}^{(q)}, \mathbf{SC}^{(q)} - \{z\}) \notin K$ for any $z \in \mathbf{FS}^{(q)}$.

Let us have $z_0 \in \mathbf{SC}^{(q)} - \mathbf{FS}^{(q)}$. Since $z_0 \in Z = \mathbf{FS}^{(0)}$, there exists a least integer i such that $z_0 \in \mathbf{FS}^{(i)} - \mathbf{FS}^{(i+1)}$. Two cases may occur.

(a) $(\mathbf{SC}^{(i)}, \mathbf{SC}^{(i)} - \{z\}) \notin K$ for any $z \in \mathbf{FS}^{(i)}$. Thus, $(\mathbf{SC}^{(i)}, \mathbf{SC}^{(i)} - \{z_0\}) \notin K$.

(b) There exists a least element a in $\mathbf{FS}^{(i)}$ with respect to o such that $(\mathbf{SC}^{(i)}, \mathbf{SC}^{(i)} - \{a\}) \in K$. Since all elements in $\mathbf{FS}^{(i)}$ that are different from a and follow a in o form the set $\mathbf{FS}^{(i+1)}$, we obtain $(z_0, a) \in o$. If $z_0 = a$, then $\mathbf{SC}^{(q)} \subseteq \mathbf{SC}^{(i+1)} = \mathbf{SC}(\mathbf{SC}^{(i)}, K, \mathbf{FS}^{(i)}, o) = \mathbf{SC}^{(i)} - \{z_0\}$ and, hence, $z_0 \notin \mathbf{SC}^{(q)}$ which is a contradiction. Thus, $(z_0, a) \in o$, $z_0 \neq a$. Since a is the least element in $\mathbf{FS}^{(i)}$ with $(\mathbf{SC}^{(i)}, \mathbf{SC}^{(i)} - \{a\}) \in K$ and z_0 precedes a in o, we obtain $(\mathbf{SC}^{(i)}, \mathbf{SC}^{(i)} - \{z_0\}) \notin K$.

Thus, $z_0 \in \mathbf{SC}^{(q)} - \mathbf{FS}^{(q)}$ implies $(\mathbf{SC}^{(i)}, \mathbf{SC}^{(i)} - \{z_0\}) \notin K$ for some i.

Suppose now $(\mathbf{SC}^{(q)}, \mathbf{SC}^{(q)} - \{z_0\}) \in K$. Since $(\mathbf{SC}^{(q)}, X) \in K$, we obtain $(\mathbf{SC}^{(q)} - \{z_0\}, X) \in K$. Clearly, $\mathbf{SC}^{(q)} \subseteq \mathbf{SC}^{(i)}$ and, therefore, $\mathbf{SC}^{(q)} - \{z_0\} \subseteq \mathbf{SC}^{(i)} - \{z_0\} \subseteq X$. By Theorem 15, we obtain $(\mathbf{SC}^{(i)} - \{z_0\}, X) \in K$, by (1) we have $(\mathbf{SC}^{(i)}, X) \in K$ and, thus, $(\mathbf{SC}^{(i)}, \mathbf{SC}^{(i)} - \{z_0\}) \in K$ which is a contradiction. Hence $(\mathbf{SC}^{(q)}, \mathbf{SC}^{(q)} - \{z_0\}) \notin K$ holds.

(3) We have proved that $(\mathbf{SC}^{(q)}, \mathbf{SC}^{(q)} - \{z\}) \notin K$ holds for any $z \in \mathbf{SC}^{(q)}$. By Lemma 48, the set $\mathbf{SC}^{(q)}$ is a K-reduct of X. Therefore, *(i)* holds. □

Thus, $\mathbf{RD}(Z, K, o)$ is a reduct and $\mathbf{PD}(Z, K, o)$ is a set of bad elements that have been found while constructing the reduct.

The described algorithm is a little more complicated than the algorithm described in [NP9]. Its basic idea is very simple: The given set X is linearly ordered, the elements are taken in the given order, and any of them is cancelled if the set obtained by cancelling is still in the relation K with the set X; this must be tested and $|X|$ tests suffice according to our algorithm while the version published in the above quoted paper requires some superfluous tests.

Example 31. Let A, $\mathbf{B}(A)$ be the same as in Section 2, suppose that the congruence K on the semilattice $(\mathbf{B}(A), \cup)$ has the following blocks: $\{0, 1\}$, $\{2, 12\}$, $\{3, 13\}$, $\{23, 123\}$. We look for a K-reduct of the set 123. Let o be a linear ordering of the set $123 = A = \{a, b, c\}$ where the order is: a, b, c (i.e., $(a, b) \in o$, $(a, c) \in o$, $(b, c) \in o$, and, naturally, $(x, x) \in o$ for any $x \in A$). Then

$\mathbf{SC}^{(0)} = 123$, $\mathbf{BD}^{(0)} = \emptyset$, $\mathbf{FS}^{(0)} = 123$;

$\mathbf{SC}^{(1)} = \mathbf{SC}(\mathbf{SC}^{(0)}, K, \mathbf{FS}^{(0)}, o) = \mathbf{SC}(123, K, 123, o) = 123 - 1 = 23$, $\mathbf{BD}^{(1)} = \emptyset$, $\mathbf{FS}^{(1)} = 23$;

$\mathbf{SC}^{(2)} = \mathbf{SC}(\mathbf{SC}^{(1)}, K, \mathbf{FS}^{(1)}, o) = \mathbf{SC}(23, K, 23, o) = 23$, $\mathbf{BD}^{(2)} = \emptyset$, $\mathbf{FS}^{(2)} = \emptyset$,

$$\mathbf{RD}(123, K, o) = 23, \ \mathbf{PD}(123, K, o) = \emptyset$$

where we have used similar abbreviations to those which have appeared in the proof of Theorem 72. See Fig. 11.

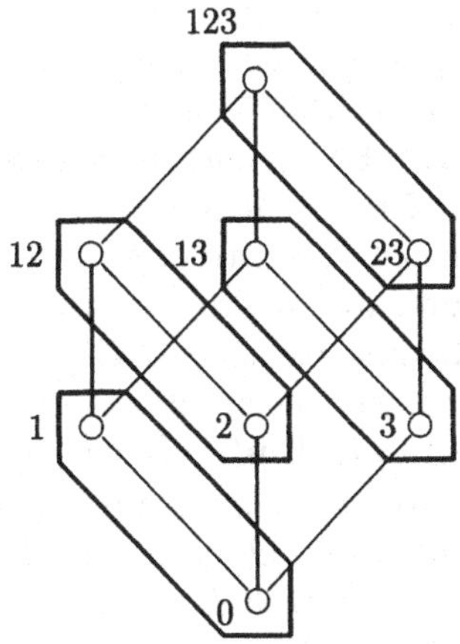

Figure 11

One parameter appearing in the construction of the set $\mathbf{RD}(Z,K,o)$ is the linear ordering o. Let $\mathbf{LO}(X)$ denote the set of all linear orderings on the set X. By Theorem 72, we obtain

Corollary 73. *Let (A,K) be a dependence space, $X \in \mathbf{B}(A)$ a set. Then $\mathbf{RED}(K,X) = \{\mathbf{RD}(X,K,o);\ o \in \mathbf{LO}(X)\}$.*

Proof. By Theorem 72, any $\mathbf{RD}(X,K,o)$ with $o \in \mathbf{LO}(X)$ is a member of $\mathbf{RED}(K,X)$. Conversely, if $X' \in \mathbf{RED}(K,X)$, we define a linear ordering o on X in such a way that elements of the set $X - X'$ precede elements of X' in o. It is easy to see that $X' = \mathbf{RD}(X,K,o)$. □

By Corollary 73, a K-reduct of X corresponds to a linear ordering on X and any linear ordering on X defines a K-reduct of X. But the construction of all K-reducts of X on the base of all linear orderings on X is difficult in practice and requires many elementary steps that can be excluded. The construction of all K-reducts of X may be simplified using the following

Theorem 74. *Let (A,K) be a dependence space, $X \in \mathbf{B}(A)$ a set, X' its K-reduct. Then the following assertions hold.*

- *(i) If Z is such that $X' \subseteq Z \subseteq X$, $X' \neq Z$, then Z is not a K-reduct of X.*
- *(ii) If Z is such that $Z \subseteq X'$, $X' \neq Z$, then Z is not a K-reduct of X.*
- *(iii) If Y, Z are such that $Z \subseteq Y \subseteq X$, $(X,Y) \notin K$, then Z is not a K-reduct of X.*

Proof. *(i)* and *(ii)* follow directly from the definition of a K-reduct, *(iii)* is a consequence of Theorem 15. □

This theorem characterizes some subsets of X that can be excluded from the construction of K-reducts if some K-reducts have been constructed.

We now present an algorithm for finding all K-reducts of a set (cf. [NP10]). We construct objects $\mathbf{z}(i)$, $\mathbf{Rd}(i)$, $\mathbf{Ex}(i)$, $\mathbf{Cn}(i)$, $\mathbf{Ma}(i)$, $\mathbf{t}(i)$, $\mathbf{Ns}(i)$, $\mathbf{Nc}(i)$, $\mathbf{Em}(i)$ by induction using Algorithm 71 as a step of this construction. The objects $\mathbf{z}(i)$, $\mathbf{t}(i)$ are elements in $\mathbf{B}(X)$, and $\mathbf{Rd}(i)$, $\mathbf{Ex}(i)$, $\mathbf{Cn}(i)$, $\mathbf{Ma}(i)$, $\mathbf{Ns}(i)$, $\mathbf{Nc}(i)$, $\mathbf{Em}(i)$ are subsets of $\mathbf{B}(X)$: $\mathbf{Rd}(i)$ consists of K-**R**e**d**ucts, $\mathbf{Ex}(i)$ of elements that can be **Ex**cluded if constructing new K-reducts, $\mathbf{Cn}(i)$ consists of elements that are **C**a**n**didates where constructions of new K-reducts can start, $\mathbf{Ma}(i)$ consists of **Ma**ximal elements in $\mathbf{Cn}(i)$, $\mathbf{Ns}(i)$ of elements in $\mathbf{Ma}(i)$ that are **N**ot **s**uitable for further construction, $\mathbf{Nc}(i)$ of elements that are **N**ot **c**ongruent to X with respect to K, $\mathbf{Em}(i)$ of elements that have been **E**xa**m**ined.

An important role is played by a linear ordering o on X. Furthermore, O is a linear ordering on $\mathbf{B}(X)$; $(Y,Z) \in O$ means that Y precedes Z in O or equals Z. Algorithm 75 provides the set $\mathbf{Red}(K,X)$ whose sense is given by Theorem 76.

Algorithm 75. (Algorithm for finding all reducts)

Let (A,K) be a dependence space, $X \in \mathbf{B}(A)$ a set, o a linear ordering on X, O a linear ordering on $\mathbf{B}(X)$. We put

$\mathbf{z}(0) = X$;

$\mathbf{Rd}(0) = \{\mathbf{RD}(\mathbf{z}(0),K,o)\}$;

$\mathbf{Ex}(0) = \{Y \in \mathbf{B}(X);\ Y \subseteq \mathbf{RD}(\mathbf{z}(0),K,o)\} \cup \{Y \in \mathbf{B}(X);\ \mathbf{RD}(\mathbf{z}(0),K,o) \subseteq Y\} \cup \{Y \in \mathbf{B}(X);$ there exists $W \in \mathbf{PD}(\mathbf{z}(0),K,o)$ with $Y \subseteq W\}$;

$\mathbf{Cn}(0) = \mathbf{B}(X) - \mathbf{Ex}(0)$;

$\mathbf{Ma}(0) = \{Y \in \mathbf{Cn}(0); Y$ is maximal in $\mathbf{Cn}(0)$ with respect to inclusion$\}$;

$$\mathbf{t}(0) = \begin{cases} X \text{ if } (Y,X) \notin K \text{ for any } Y \in \mathbf{Ma}(0), \\[1em] T \text{ where } T \text{ is the least element in } \mathbf{Ma}(0) \text{ with respect} \\ \text{to } O \text{ such that } (T,X) \in K; \end{cases}$$

$$\mathbf{Ns}(0) = \begin{cases} \mathbf{Ma}(0) \text{ if } (Y,X) \notin K \text{ for any } Y \in \mathbf{Ma}(0), \\[1em] \{Z \in \mathbf{Ma}(0);\ (Z,\mathbf{t}(0)) \in O,\ Z \neq \mathbf{t}(0)\} \text{ if there exists} \\ \text{at least one element } Y \in \mathbf{Ma}(0) \text{ such that } (Y,X) \in K; \end{cases}$$

$\mathbf{Nc}(0) = \{Y \in \mathbf{B}(X);$ there exists $W \in \mathbf{Ns}(0)$ with $Y \subseteq W\}$;

$\mathbf{Em}(0) = \mathbf{Ex}(0) \cup \mathbf{Nc}(0)$.

Let $i \geq 0$ and suppose that $\mathbf{z}(i)$, $\mathbf{Rd}(i)$, $\mathbf{Ex}(i)$, $\mathbf{Cn}(i)$, $\mathbf{Ma}(i)$, $\mathbf{t}(i)$, $\mathbf{Ns}(i)$, $\mathbf{Nc}(i)$, $\mathbf{Em}(i)$ have been constructed. Furthermore, suppose that $\mathbf{Em}(i) \neq \mathbf{B}(X)$. Then put

$\mathbf{z}(i+1) = \mathbf{t}(i)$;

$\mathbf{Rd}(i+1) = \mathbf{Rd}(i) \cup \{\mathbf{RD}(\mathbf{z}(i+1),K,o)\}$;

$\mathbf{Ex}(i+1) = \mathbf{Ex}(i) \cup \{Y \in \mathbf{B}(X);\ Y \subseteq \mathbf{RD}(\mathbf{z}(i+1),K,o)\} \cup \{Y \in \mathbf{B}(X);\ \mathbf{RD}(\mathbf{z}(i+1),K,o) \subseteq Y\} \cup \{Y \in \mathbf{B}(X);$ there exists $W \in \mathbf{PD}(\mathbf{z}(i+1),K,o)$ with $Y \subseteq W\}$;

$\mathbf{Cn}(i+1) = \mathbf{B}(X) - \mathbf{Ex}(i+1)$;

$\mathbf{Ma}(i+1) = \{Y \in \mathbf{Cn}(i+1); Y$ is maximal in $\mathbf{Cn}(i+1)$ with respect to inclusion $\}$;

$$\mathbf{t}(i+1) = \begin{cases} X \text{ if } (Y,X) \notin K \text{ for any } Y \in \mathbf{Ma}(i+1), \\ \\ T \text{ where } T \text{ is the least element in } \mathbf{Ma}(i+1) \text{ with respect to } O \text{ such that } (T,X) \in K; \end{cases}$$

$$\mathbf{Ns}(i+1) = \begin{cases} \mathbf{Ma}(i+1) \text{ if } (Y,X) \notin K \text{ for any } Y \in \mathbf{Ma}(i+1), \\ \\ \{Z \in \mathbf{Ma}(i+1);\ (Z, \mathbf{t}(i+1)) \in O,\ Z \neq \mathbf{t}(i+1)\} \text{ if there exists at least one element } Y \in \mathbf{Ma}(i+1) \text{ with } (Y,X) \in K; \end{cases}$$

$\mathbf{Nc}(i+1) = \{Y \in \mathbf{B}(X);$ there exists $W \in \mathbf{Ns}(i+1)$ with $Y \subseteq W\}$;
$\mathbf{Em}(i+1) = \mathbf{Em}(i) \cup \mathbf{Ex}(i+1) \cup \mathbf{Nc}(i+1)$.

[We now prove some properties of constructed objects.

(A) If $\mathbf{t}(i) = X$, then $\mathbf{Em}(i) = \mathbf{B}(X)$ holds.

Indeed, if $Z \in \mathbf{B}(X)$, then either $Z \in \mathbf{Ex}(i)$ or $Z \in \mathbf{Cn}(i)$. In the first case, we obtain $Z \in \mathbf{Em}(i)$ because $\mathbf{Ex}(i) \subseteq \mathbf{Em}(i)$. In the second case, there exists $Y \in \mathbf{Ma}(i)$ such that $Z \subseteq Y$. Using the fact $\mathbf{t}(i) = X$, we obtain $\mathbf{Ns}(i) = \mathbf{Ma}(i)$ which implies that $Z \in \mathbf{Nc}(i) \subseteq \mathbf{Em}(i)$.

(B) If $\mathbf{Em}(i) \neq \mathbf{B}(X)$, then $\mathbf{z}(i+1) \in \mathbf{Em}(i+1) - \mathbf{Em}(i)$.

Indeed, $\mathbf{z}(i+1) \supseteq \mathbf{RD}(\mathbf{z}(i+1), K, o)$ implies that $\mathbf{z}(i+1) \in \mathbf{Ex}(i+1) \subseteq \mathbf{Em}(i+1)$. Furthermore, $\mathbf{z}(i+1) = \mathbf{t}(i)$ and $\mathbf{t}(i) \neq X$ holds by (A). We have $\mathbf{Em}(i) = \mathbf{Ex}(0) \cup \mathbf{Nc}(0) \cup \ldots \cup \mathbf{Ex}(i) \cup \mathbf{Nc}(i) = \mathbf{Ex}(i) \cup \mathbf{Nc}(0) \cup \ldots \cup \mathbf{Nc}(i)$. Since $\mathbf{t}(i) \in \mathbf{Ma}(i) \subseteq \mathbf{Cn}(i)$ and $(\mathbf{t}(i), X) \in K$, we obtain $\mathbf{t}(i) \notin \mathbf{Ex}(i)$ and $\mathbf{t}(i) \notin \mathbf{Nc}(j)$ for any j with $0 \leq j \leq i$ by Theorem 15 which means that $\mathbf{z}(i+1) \notin \mathbf{Em}(i)$.]

There exists a least integer $r \geq 0$ *such that* $\mathbf{Em}(r) = \mathbf{B}(X)$. *Then we put* $\mathbf{Red}(K,X) = \mathbf{Rd}(r)$.

Theorem 76. *Let* (A,K) *be a dependence space and* $X \in \mathbf{B}(A)$ *a set. Then*

$$\mathbf{Red}(K,X) = \mathbf{RED}(K,X).$$

Proof. By definition, $(\mathbf{t}(i), X) \in K$ for any i with $0 \leq i \leq r$ which implies that $\mathbf{RD}(\mathbf{t}(i), K, o)$ is a K-reduct of X by Theorem 72. By definition of $\mathbf{Rd}(i)$, we have $\mathbf{Rd}(i) \subseteq \mathbf{RED}(K,X)$ for any i with $0 \leq i \leq r$. Thus, $\mathbf{Red}(K,X) = \mathbf{Rd}(r) \subseteq \mathbf{RED}(K,X)$.

Suppose $Y \in \mathbf{RED}(K,X)$. Thus, $Y \in \mathbf{B}(X) = \mathbf{Em}(r)$ for some $r \geq 0$. Let j be the least integer with $0 \leq j \leq r$, $Y \in \mathbf{Em}(j)$. Then either $Y \in \mathbf{Nc}(j)$ or $Y \in \mathbf{Ex}(j)$ holds.

If $Y \in \mathbf{Nc}(j)$, there exists $W \in \mathbf{Ns}(j)$ such that $Y \subseteq W$. By definition of $\mathbf{Ns}(j)$, we have $(W,X) \notin K$ and $(Y,X) \notin K$ by Theorem 15 which is a contradiction to the condition $Y \in \mathbf{RED}(K,X)$. It follows that $Y \in \mathbf{Ex}(j)$. Let h be the least integer with $0 \leq h \leq j$, $Y \in \mathbf{Ex}(h)$.

The case $Y \subseteq W$ for some $W \in \mathbf{PD}(\mathbf{z}(h), K, o)$ is excluded because $(\mathbf{z}(h), X) \in K$ holds by definition of $\mathbf{z}(h)$, $(W, \mathbf{z}(h)) \notin K$ holds by Theorem 72 which implies that $(W,X) \notin K$ by transitivity of K. Since $Y \in \mathbf{RED}(K,X)$, we have $(Y,X) \in K$ and $Y \subseteq W \subseteq X$ implies that $(W,X) \in K$ by Theorem 15 which contradicts Theorem 72.

Thus, we have either $Y \subseteq \mathbf{RD}(\mathbf{z}(h), K, o)$ or $\mathbf{RD}(\mathbf{z}(h), K, o) \subseteq Y$ by definition of $\mathbf{Ex}(h)$. Since $Y \in \mathbf{RED}(K, X)$, we obtain $Y = \mathbf{RD}(\mathbf{z}(h), K, o)$ by Theorem 74. Thus, $Y \in \mathbf{Rd}(h) \subseteq \mathbf{Rd}(r) = \mathbf{Red}(K, X)$. We have proved $\mathbf{RED}(K, X) \subseteq \mathbf{Red}(K, X)$. □

Example 32. Consider the dependence space (A, K) introduced in Example 26. We find all K-reducts of the set 123.

Let o prescribes the order c, b, a on A, suppose that O prescribes the order for elements in $\mathbf{B}(A)$ as follows: 0, 3, 2, 23, 1, 13, 12, 123. We obtain $\mathbf{z}(0) = 123$, $\mathbf{Rd}(0) = \{\mathbf{RD}(123, K, o)\}$. Now $\mathbf{RD}(123, K, o)$ must be calculated by means of Algorithm 71. We obtain (if using abbreviations as in Example 1): $\mathbf{SC}^{(0)} = 123$, $\mathbf{BD}^{(0)} = \emptyset$, $\mathbf{FS}^{(0)} = 123$; $\mathbf{SC}^{(1)} = \mathbf{SC}(\mathbf{SC}^{(0)}, K, \mathbf{FS}^{(0)}, o) = \mathbf{SC}(123, K, 123, o) = 123 - 3 = 12$, $\mathbf{BD}^{(1)} = \emptyset$, $\mathbf{FS}^{(1)} = 12$; $\mathbf{SC}^{(2)} = \mathbf{SC}(\mathbf{SC}^{(1)}, K, \mathbf{FS}^{(1)}, o) = \mathbf{SC}(12, K, 12, o) = 12 - 2 = 1$, $\mathbf{BD}^{(2)} = \emptyset$, $\mathbf{FS}^{(2)} = 1$; $\mathbf{SC}^{(3)} = \mathbf{SC}(\mathbf{SC}^{(2)}, K, \mathbf{FS}^{(2)}, o) = \mathbf{SC}(1, K, 1, o) = 1 = \mathbf{SC}^{(2)}$, $\mathbf{BD}^{(3)} = \emptyset$, $\mathbf{FS}^{(3)} = \emptyset$. Hence $\mathbf{RD}(123, K, o) = 1$.

Thus, $\mathbf{Rd}(0) = \{1\}$, $\mathbf{Ex}(0) = \{0, 1, 12, 13, 123\}$, $\mathbf{Cn}(0) = \{2, 3, 23\}$, $\mathbf{Ma}(0) = \{23\}$, $\mathbf{t}(0) = 23$, $\mathbf{Ns}(0) = \emptyset = \mathbf{Nc}(0)$, $\mathbf{Em}(0) = \{0, 1, 12, 13, 123\}$.

It follows that $\mathbf{z}(1) = 23$, $\mathbf{Rd}(1) = \mathbf{Rd}(0) \cup \{\mathbf{RD}(23, K, o)\}$ where $\mathbf{RD}(23, K, o)$ will be calculated by means of Algorithm 71. We obtain

$\mathbf{SC}^{(0)} = 23$, $\mathbf{BD}^{(0)} = \emptyset$, $\mathbf{FS}^{(0)} = 23$; $\mathbf{SC}^{(1)} = \mathbf{SC}(23, K, 23, o) = 23$, $\mathbf{BD}^{(1)} = \emptyset$, $\mathbf{FS}^{(1)} = \emptyset$. Thus, $\mathbf{RD}(23, K, o) = 23$. We obtain $\mathbf{Rd}(1) = \{1, 23\}$, $\mathbf{Ex}(1) = \mathbf{B}(123)$, $\mathbf{Cn}(1) = \mathbf{Ma}(1) = \mathbf{Ns}(1) = \mathbf{Nc}(1) = \emptyset$, $\mathbf{t}(1) = X$, $\mathbf{Em}(1) = \mathbf{B}(123)$. It follows that $r = 1$, $\mathbf{Red}(K, X) = \mathbf{Rd}(1) = \{1, 23\}$.

11 Dependence Relations

Dependence plays an important role in information systems. For this reason dependence relations in dependence spaces are investigated.

Let (A, K) be a dependence space and X, Y elements in $\mathbf{B}(A)$. Then Y is said to be *dependent on* X *in* (A, K), which will be denoted by $X \to Y\ (A, K)$, if $\mathbf{C}(K)(Y) \subseteq \mathbf{C}(K)(X)$ holds. The relation $\to\ (A, K)$ will be called the *dependence relation of the dependence space* (A, K). We mention that $\mathbf{C}(K)$ is a closure operator by Theorem 17; we use this fact without any reference. Cf. [NN1].

Example 33. If (A, K) is a dependence space, then $(X, Y) \in K$ means $\mathbf{C}(K)(X) = \mathbf{C}(K)(Y)$ which implies both $X \to Y\ (A, K)$, $Y \to X\ (A, K)$. Suppose now that (A, K) is the dependence space from Example 31. Then $\mathbf{C}(K)(13) = 13 \subseteq 123 = \mathbf{C}(K)(23)$. Thus, $23 \to 13\ (A, K)$.

Lemma 77. *Let* (A, K) *be a dependence space and* X, Y *be sets in* $\mathbf{B}(A)$. *Then* $X \to Y\ (A, K)$ *holds if and only if* $\mathbf{C}(K)(X \cup Y) = \mathbf{C}(K)(X)$.

Proof. Clearly, $\mathbf{C}(K)(Y) \subseteq \mathbf{C}(K)(X)$ implies that $X \cup Y \subseteq \mathbf{C}(K)(X) \cup \mathbf{C}(K)(Y) \subseteq \mathbf{C}(K)(X)$ which entails $\mathbf{C}(K)(X \cup Y) \subseteq \mathbf{C}(K)(X)$; this means $\mathbf{C}(K)(X \cup Y) = \mathbf{C}(K)(X)$ regarding the monotony of the operator $\mathbf{C}(K)$.

On the other hand, if $\mathbf{C}(K)(X \cup Y) = \mathbf{C}(K)(X)$, then we obtain $\mathbf{C}(K)(Y) \subseteq \mathbf{C}(K)(X \cup Y) = \mathbf{C}(K)(X)$. □

K-reducts may be expressed by means of dependence relations as follows.

Theorem 78. *Let (A, K) be a dependence space and X, Y be elements in $\mathbf{B}(A)$. Then the following assertions are equivalent.*

(i) Y is a K-reduct of X.

(ii) Y is minimal with respect to inclusion among all sets Z such that $Z \subseteq X$, $Z \to X$ (A, K).

Proof. Condition *(ii)* is equivalent to the following condition.
(iii) Y is minimal with respect to inclusion among all sets Z such that $Z \subseteq X$, $\mathbf{C}(K)(X) \subseteq \mathbf{C}(K)(Z)$.
Regarding that $Z \subseteq X$ implies $\mathbf{C}(K)(Z) \subseteq \mathbf{C}(K)(X)$, condition *(iii)* is equivalent to *(i)*. □

Important properties of the dependence relation are described in the following.

Theorem 79. *If (A, K) is a dependence space and X, X', Y, Y' are elements in $\mathbf{B}(A)$, then the following assertions hold.*

(i) If $X \to Y$ (A, K) and $X' \supseteq X$, then $X' \to Y$ (A, K).

(ii) If $X \to Y$ (A, K) and $Y' \subseteq Y$, then $X \to Y'$ (A, K).

Proof. Clearly, $X \to Y$ (A, K), $X' \supseteq X$ imply $\mathbf{C}(K)(Y) \subseteq \mathbf{C}(K)(X) \subseteq \mathbf{C}(K)(X')$ which is $X' \to Y$ (A, K). Similarly, $X \to Y$ (A, K) and $Y' \subseteq Y$ imply $\mathbf{C}(K)(Y') \subseteq \mathbf{C}(K)(Y) \subseteq \mathbf{C}(K)(X)$ which means $X \to Y'$ (A, K). □

A relation r on the set $\mathbf{B}(A)$ is said to be *compatible* with the operation $\cup$ in the semilattice $(\mathbf{B}(A), \cup)$ if for any X, X', Y, Y' in $\mathbf{B}(A)$ the conditions $(X, X') \in r$, $(Y, Y') \in r$ imply $(X \cup Y, X' \cup Y') \in r$.

Theorem 80. *Let (A, K) be a dependence space. Then the relation $\to$ (A, K) is a preordering compatible with the operation $\cup$ in $(\mathbf{B}(A), \cup)$.*

Proof. If X, Y, Z are in $\mathbf{B}(A)$ and $X \to Y$ (A, K), $Y \to Z$ (A, K) hold, then $\mathbf{C}(K)(Y) \subseteq \mathbf{C}(K)(X)$, $\mathbf{C}(K)(Z) \subseteq \mathbf{C}(K)(Y)$ which implies that $\mathbf{C}(K)(Z) \subseteq \mathbf{C}(K)(X)$ and, thus $X \to Z$ (A, K). Hence $\to$ (A, K) is a transitive relation; the reflexivity of $\to$ (A, K) being clear, $\to$ (A, K) is a preordering.

Let us have X, X', Y, Y' in $\mathbf{B}(A)$ such that $X \to X'$ (A, K), $Y \to Y'$ (A, K). Then $\mathbf{C}(K)(X') \subseteq \mathbf{C}(K)(X)$, $\mathbf{C}(K)(Y') \subseteq \mathbf{C}(K)(Y)$ and, therefore, $X' \subseteq \mathbf{C}(K)(X') \subseteq \mathbf{C}(K)(X) \subseteq \mathbf{C}(K)(X \cup Y)$ and, similarly, $Y' \subseteq \mathbf{C}(K)(X \cup Y)$. Thus, $X' \cup Y' \subseteq \mathbf{C}(K)(X \cup Y)$ and, therefore, $\mathbf{C}(K)(X' \cup Y') \subseteq \mathbf{C}(K)(\mathbf{C}(K)(X \cup Y)) = \mathbf{C}(K)(X \cup Y)$ which means $X \cup Y \to X' \cup Y'$ (A, K). □

Corollary 81. *Let (A, K) be a dependence space, X, Y, Z elements in $\mathbf{B}(A)$. Then the following assertions hold.*

(i) $X \to Z\ (A,K)$, $Y \to Z\ (A,K)$ *imply* $X \cup Y \to Z\ (A,K)$.

(ii) $X \to Y\ (A,K)$, $X \to Z\ (A,K)$ *imply* $X \to Y \cup Z\ (A,K)$.

Theorem 82. *Let A be a finite nonempty set and r be a preordering on $\mathbf{B}(A)$ that is compatible with the operation $\cup$ in $(\mathbf{B}(A), \cup)$ and that satisfies the following condition:*

$$(\star)\quad (X,Y) \in r,\ X' \supseteq X \textit{ imply } (X',Y) \in r.$$

Then there exists a dependence space (A, K) such that r is its dependence relation.

Proof. Let us put $K = r \cap r^{-1}$. Then K is an equivalence. If $(X, X') \in r^{-1}$, $(Y,Y') \in r^{-1}$, then $(X',X) \in r$, $(Y',Y) \in r$ hold and hence $(X' \cup Y', X \cup Y) \in r$, i.e., $(X \cup Y, X' \cup Y') \in r^{-1}$; thus, r^{-1} is also compatible with $\cup$ in $(\mathbf{B}(A), \cup)$. From this it follows that K is an equivalence compatible with $\cup$ in $(\mathbf{B}(A), \cup)$, i.e., a congruence.

For any $X \in \mathbf{B}(A)$, the set $\mathbf{C}(K)(X)$ is the greatest $Y \in \mathbf{B}(A)$ such that $(X,Y) \in K$. We should prove that $(X,Y) \in r$ if and only if $\mathbf{C}(K)(Y) \subseteq \mathbf{C}(K)(X)$.

Suppose $\mathbf{C}(K)(Y) \subseteq \mathbf{C}(K)(X)$. Then $(\mathbf{C}(K)(Y), \mathbf{C}(K)(Y)) \in r$ implies that $(\mathbf{C}(K)(X), \mathbf{C}(K)(Y)) \in r$ by $(\star)$. Furthermore, we have $(X, \mathbf{C}(K)(X)) \in K \subseteq r$, $(\mathbf{C}(K)(Y), Y) \in K \subseteq r$. Thus, we obtain $(X,Y) \in r$ according to the transitivity of r.

On the other hand, suppose $(X,Y) \in r$. Since $(\mathbf{C}(K)(X), X) \in K \subseteq r$ and $(Y, \mathbf{C}(K)(Y)) \in K \subseteq r$, we have $(\mathbf{C}(K)(X), \mathbf{C}(K)(Y)) \in r$ by transitivity of r. The compatibility of r implies that $(\mathbf{C}(K)(X), \mathbf{C}(K)(X) \cup \mathbf{C}(K)(Y)) \in r$. Furthermore, $(\mathbf{C}(K)(X), \mathbf{C}(K)(X)) \in r$ by reflexivity of r; thus, property $(\star)$ implies that $(\mathbf{C}(K)(X) \cup \mathbf{C}(K)(Y), \mathbf{C}(K)(X)) \in r$; hence, $(\mathbf{C}(K)(X), \mathbf{C}(K)(X) \cup \mathbf{C}(K)(Y)) \in r^{-1}$, thus, $(\mathbf{C}(K)(X), \mathbf{C}(K)(X) \cup \mathbf{C}(K)(Y)) \in K$. From the maximality of $\mathbf{C}(K)(X)$ in the corresponding block of K it follows that $\mathbf{C}(K)(Y) \subseteq \mathbf{C}(K)(X) \cup \mathbf{C}(K)(Y) \subseteq \mathbf{C}(K)(X)$. □

Example 34. Let A be an arbitrary finite nonempty set, consider the relation $r = \supseteq$ on $\mathbf{B}(A)$. Clearly, r is a preordering on $\mathbf{B}(A)$ that is compatible with the operation $\cup$ in the semilattice $(\mathbf{B}(A), \cup)$. Condition $(\star)$ is satisfied trivially. Thus, r is a dependence relation of the dependence space (A, K) where $K = \supseteq \cap (\supseteq)^{-1} = \supseteq \cap \subseteq = \mathrm{id}_{\mathbf{B}(A)} = \{(X,X);\ X \in \mathbf{B}(A)\}$.

We now give complete characterization of dependence relations.

Theorem 83. *Let A be a finite nonempty set, r a relation on the set $\mathbf{B}(A)$. Then the following assertions are equivalent.*

(i) *There exists a dependence space (A, K) such that r is its dependence relation.*

(ii) *The relation r is a preordering on $\mathbf{B}(A)$ that is compatible with the operation $\cup$ in the semilattice $(\mathbf{B}(A), \cup)$ and that satisfies condition $(\star)$.*

Proof. This is a consequence of Theorems 80, 79, and 82. □

We prove that dependence relations coincide with relations considered in [GJ1], p. 232.

Theorem 84. *Let A be a finite nonempty set, r a relation on the set $\mathbf{B}(A)$. Then the following assertions are equivalent.*

(i) *There exists a dependence space (A, K) such that r is its dependence relation.*
(ii) *For any sets X, Y, Z in $\mathbf{B}(A)$ the following conditions are satisfied.*
(1) *If $X \subseteq Y$, then $(Y, X) \in r$.*
(2) *If $(X, Y) \in r$, $(Y, Z) \in r$, then $(X, Z) \in r$.*
(3) *If $(X, Y) \in r$, $(X, Z) \in r$, then $(X, Y \cup Z) \in r$.*

Proof. We prove that condition *(ii)* of Theorem 83 and condition *(ii)* of Theorem 84 are equivalent.

Let *(ii)* of Theorem 83 be satisfied. If $X \subseteq Y \subseteq A$ holds, then $(X, X) \in r$ follows from the reflexivity of r and $(Y, X) \in r$ is a consequence of $(\star)$. Thus (1) holds. Since r is transitive, (2) holds as well. The compatibility of r with $\cup$ in $(\mathbf{B}(A), \cup)$ implies that $(X, Y) \in r$, $(X, Z) \in r$ entail $(X, Y \cup Z) = (X \cup X, Y \cup Z) \in r$ and (3) holds. Thus, *(ii)* of Theorem 84 is satisfied.

Suppose that *(ii)* of Theorem 84 holds. Then (1) implies the reflexivity of r and (2) means its transitivity; hence, r is a preordering on $\mathbf{B}(A)$. If $(X, X') \in r$, then $(X \cup Y, X) \in r$ by (1) and $(X \cup Y, X') \in r$ by (2). Similarly, $(Y, Y') \in r$ implies $(X \cup Y, Y') \in r$. By (3), we obtain $(X \cup Y, X' \cup Y') \in r$ which is the compatibility of r with $\cup$ in $(\mathbf{B}(A), \cup)$. Finally, $(X, Y) \in r$ and $X \subseteq X'$ imply that $(X', X) \in r$ by (1) and $(X', Y) \in r$ by (2) and, therefore, $(\star)$ is satisfied. Thus, *(ii)* of Theorem 83 holds.

The assertion follows by Theorem 83. □

Let A be a finite nonempty set, r a relation on $\mathbf{B}(A)$. The relation r is said to be a *dependence relation on* $\mathbf{B}(A)$ if there exists a dependence space (A, K) such that r is its dependence relation. As a consequence of Theorems 83, 84, we obtain

Theorem 85. (Characterization of dependence relations)

Let A be a finite nonempty set, r a relation on the set $\mathbf{B}(A)$. Then the following assertions are equivalent.

(i) *r is a dependence relation on $\mathbf{B}(A)$.*
(ii) *r is a preordering on $\mathbf{B}(A)$ compatible with the operation $\cup$ in the semilattice $(\mathbf{B}(A), \cup)$ satisfying condition $(\star)$.*
(iii) *r satisfies conditions (1), (2), (3) of Theorem 84.*

Example 35. If A is a finite nonempty set, the relation $\supseteq$ is the least dependence relation on $\mathbf{B}(A)$. — Indeed, $\supseteq$ is a dependence relation on $\mathbf{B}(A)$ by Example 34. If r is a dependence relation on $\mathbf{B}(A)$ then it satifies condition (1) of Theorem 84 which means that $\supseteq$ is a subset of r.

Clearly, if $r_1, \ldots, r_n$ are relations on $\mathbf{B}(A)$ satisfying (1), (2), (3) of Theorem 84, then $r_1 \cap \ldots \cap r_n$ satisfies the same conditions. Thus, we obtain

Theorem 86. *Let A be a finite nonempty set, $n \geq 1$ an integer, and $r_1, \ldots, r_n$ dependence relations on the set $\mathbf{B}(A)$. Then $r_1 \cap \ldots \cap r_n$ is a dependence relation on $\mathbf{B}(A)$.*

Corollary 87. *If A is a finite nonempty set and p a relation on the set $\mathbf{B}(A)$, then there exists a least dependence relation on $\mathbf{B}(A)$ including p.*

Proof. This is a consequence of the fact that $\mathbf{B}(A) \times \mathbf{B}(A)$ is a dependence relation on $\mathbf{B}(A)$ and, therefore, the set of all dependence relations including p has at least one element. The intersection of these relations is the least dependence relation on $\mathbf{B}(A)$ including p. □

Let A be a finite nonempty set, and p a relation on $\mathbf{B}(A)$. We denote by $\mathbf{CL}(p)$ the least dependence relation on $\mathbf{B}(A)$ including p.

Example 36. Let A be a finite nonempty set. Put $p = \{(X, Y) \in \mathbf{B}(A) \times \mathbf{B}(A);\ |X| \geq |Y|\}$. We calculate $\mathbf{CL}(p)$.

Let X, $Y \in \mathbf{B}(A)$ be arbitrary. If $|X| \geq |Y|$, then $(X, Y) \in p \subseteq \mathbf{CL}(p)$. Suppose $0 < |X| < |Y|$. Then we take a set $Y_0 \subseteq Y$ such that $|X| = |Y_0|$ and an element $y_0 \in Y - Y_0$. It follows that $(X, Y_0) \in p \subseteq \mathbf{CL}(p)$, $(X, \{y_0\}) \in p \subseteq \mathbf{CL}(p)$ which implies that $(X, Y_0 \cup \{y_0\}) \in \mathbf{CL}(p)$ by (3) of condition *(ii)* in Theorem 84. We put $Y_1 = Y_0 \cup \{y_0\}$ and take $y_1 \in Y - Y_1$ if there is any. We have $(X, Y_1) \in \mathbf{CL}(p)$, $(X, \{y_1\}) \in p \subseteq \mathbf{CL}(p)$. Similarly as above we obtain $(X, Y_1 \cup \{y_1\}) \in \mathbf{CL}(p)$. Repeating this construction, we obtain $(X, Y) \in \mathbf{CL}(p)$. It follows that $((\mathbf{B}(A) - \{\emptyset\}) \times \mathbf{B}(A)) \cup \{(\emptyset, \emptyset)\} \subseteq \mathbf{CL}(p)$. It is easy to see that $p \subseteq ((\mathbf{B}(A) - \{\emptyset\}) \times \mathbf{B}(A)) \cup \{(\emptyset, \emptyset)\}$ and that the last set satisfies (1), (2), (3) of condition *(ii)* in Theorem 84. It follows that $\mathbf{CL}(p) = ((\mathbf{B}(A) - \{\emptyset\}) \times \mathbf{B}(A)) \cup \{(\emptyset, \emptyset)\}$.

Let A be a finite nonempty set and p a relation on the set $\mathbf{B}(A)$. Then the ordered pair $(\mathbf{B}(A), p)$ may be considered to be a relational system; cf. Section 2 of Chapter 8. A set X that is minimal with respect to inclusion among all sets $Z \in \mathbf{B}(A)$ with $(Z, A) \in \mathbf{CL}(p)$ is said to be a *key for the relational system* $(\mathbf{B}(A), p)$ (cf. [GJ1], [Li1], [LO1], [Ra1]). Let m be a positive integer. The problem of deciding whether there exists a key of cardinality $\leq m$ for $(\mathbf{B}(A), p)$ is NP-complete.

It follows from the definition that for any dependence relation r on $\mathbf{B}(A)$ there exists a dependence space (A, K) such that $r = \rightarrow (A, K)$. Thus, a set $Y \in \mathbf{B}(A)$ is a key for $(\mathbf{B}(A), p)$ if and only if it is minimal among all sets $Z \in \mathbf{B}(A)$ with $Z \rightarrow A\ (A, K)$ where $\mathbf{CL}(p) = \rightarrow (A, K)$, i.e., if and only if it is a K-reduct of A, by Theorem 78. Hence, we obtain

Theorem 88. *Let A be a finite nonempty set, p a relation on the set $\mathbf{B}(A)$, K a congruence on the semilattice $(\mathbf{B}(A), \cup)$ such that $\mathbf{CL}(p)$ is its dependence relation, $Y \in \mathbf{B}(A)$ a set. Then the following assertions are equivalent.*

(i) Y is a key for $(\mathbf{B}(A), p)$.
(ii) Y is a K-reduct of A.

For applications the following problem is important.

Problem 89. Let (A, K) be a dependence space, X, Y sets in $\mathbf{B}(A)$ such that $X \to Y$ (A, K). Find a set X' that is minimal with respect to inclusion among all sets Z having the following properties:

(i) $Z \subseteq X$.
(ii) $Z \to Y$ (K).

Problem 89 may be solved by means of following results.

Theorem 90. *Let (A, K) be a dependence space, $Y \in \mathbf{B}(A)$ a set. For any $X \in \mathbf{B}(A)$, $X' \in \mathbf{B}(A)$ put $(X, X') \in \mathbf{D}(K, Y)$ if and only if one of the following conditions (i), (ii) is satisfied.*

(i) $\mathbf{C}(K)(Y) \subseteq \mathbf{C}(K)(X)$, $\mathbf{C}(K)(Y) \subseteq \mathbf{C}(K)(X')$.
(ii) $\mathbf{C}(K)(Y) \nsubseteq \mathbf{C}(K)(X) = \mathbf{C}(K)(X')$.

Then $\mathbf{D}(K, Y)$ is a congruence on the semilattice $(\mathbf{B}(A), \cup)$.

Proof. (1) Clearly, $\mathbf{D}(K, Y)$ is reflexive and symmetric. Suppose $(X, X') \in \mathbf{D}(K, Y)$, $(X', X'') \in \mathbf{D}(K, Y)$. Then the following cases may occur.

1. $\mathbf{C}(K)(Y) \subseteq \mathbf{C}(K)(X)$. Then $(X, X') \in \mathbf{D}(K, Y)$ implies that $\mathbf{C}(K)(Y) \subseteq \mathbf{C}(K)(X')$ by *(i)*; since $(X', X'') \in \mathbf{D}(K, Y)$, we obtain $\mathbf{C}(K)(Y) \subseteq \mathbf{C}(K)(X'')$ by *(i)* and, therefore, $(X, X'') \in \mathbf{D}(K, Y)$ by *(i)*.
2. $\mathbf{C}(K)(Y) \nsubseteq \mathbf{C}(K)(X)$. Then $(X, X') \in \mathbf{D}(K, Y)$ implies that $\mathbf{C}(K)(X) = \mathbf{C}(K)(X')$ by *(ii)* and, therefore, $\mathbf{C}(K)(Y) \nsubseteq \mathbf{C}(K)(X')$. Then $(X', X'') \in \mathbf{D}(K, Y)$ entails $\mathbf{C}(K)(X') = \mathbf{C}(K)(X'')$ by *(ii)*. Thus $\mathbf{C}(K)(Y) \nsubseteq \mathbf{C}(K)(X) = \mathbf{C}(K)(X'')$ and we obtain $(X, X'') \in \mathbf{D}(K, Y)$ by *(ii)*.

We have proved that $\mathbf{D}(K, Y)$ is transitive and, hence, an equivalence on $\mathbf{B}(A)$.

(2) Suppose $(X, X') \in \mathbf{D}(K, Y)$, $Z \in \mathbf{B}(A)$. Then the following cases may occur.

3. $\mathbf{C}(K)(Y) \subseteq \mathbf{C}(K)(X)$; then $\mathbf{C}(K)(Y) \subseteq \mathbf{C}(K)(X')$ by *(i)*. This implies that $\mathbf{C}(K)(Y) \subseteq \mathbf{C}(K)(X \cup Z)$, $\mathbf{C}(K)(Y) \subseteq \mathbf{C}(K)(X' \cup Z)$ and, thus, $(X \cup Z, X' \cup Z) \in \mathbf{D}(K, Y)$ by *(i)*.
4. $\mathbf{C}(K)(Y) \subseteq \mathbf{C}(K)(X')$. Interchanging X and X' in 3. we obtain $(X \cup Z, X' \cup Z) \in \mathbf{D}(K, Y)$.

5. $\mathbf{C}(K)(Y) \not\subseteq \mathbf{C}(K)(X)$, $\mathbf{C}(K)(Y) \not\subseteq \mathbf{C}(K)(X')$. By *(ii)*, we obtain $\mathbf{C}(K)(X) = \mathbf{C}(K)(X')$ which implies that $X \subseteq \mathbf{C}(K)(X) \subseteq \mathbf{C}(K)(X' \cup Z)$. Since $Z \subseteq X' \cup Z \subseteq \mathbf{C}(K)(X' \cup Z)$, we obtain $X \cup Z \subseteq \mathbf{C}(K)(X' \cup Z)$ which entails that $\mathbf{C}(K)(X \cup Z) \subseteq \mathbf{C}(K)(X' \cup Z)$. Similarly, we prove $\mathbf{C}(K)(X' \cup Z) \subseteq \mathbf{C}(K)(X \cup Z)$. Thus, $\mathbf{C}(X \cup Z) = \mathbf{C}(K)(X' \cup Z)$. Hence, either $\mathbf{C}(K)(Y) \subseteq \mathbf{C}(K)(X \cup Z) = \mathbf{C}(K)(X' \cup Z)$ and we obtain $(X \cup Z, X' \cup Z) \in \mathbf{D}(K,Y)$ by *(i)* or $\mathbf{C}(K)(Y) \not\subseteq \mathbf{C}(K)(X \cup Z) = \mathbf{C}(X' \cup Z)$ and we have $(X \cup Z, X' \cup Z) \in \mathbf{D}(K,Y)$ by *(ii)*.

By Theorem 12, $\mathbf{D}(K,Y)$ is a congruence on the semilattice $(\mathbf{B}(A), \cup)$. □

Corollary 91. *If (A,K) is a dependence space and $Y \in \mathbf{B}(A)$ a set, then $(A, \mathbf{D}(K,Y))$ is a dependence space.*

Lemma 92. *If (A,K) is a dependence space and $Y \in \mathbf{B}(A)$ a set, then $K \subseteq \mathbf{D}(K,Y)$.*

Proof. Indeed, if $(X,X') \in K$, then $\mathbf{C}(K)(X) = \mathbf{C}(K)(X')$ and either $\mathbf{C}(K)(Y) \subseteq \mathbf{C}(K)(X) = \mathbf{C}(K)(X')$ which is $(X,X') \in \mathbf{D}(K,Y)$ by *(i)* of Theorem 90, or $\mathbf{C}(K)(Y) \not\subseteq \mathbf{C}(K)(X) = \mathbf{C}(K)(X')$ which means $(X,X') \in \mathbf{D}(K,Y)$ by *(ii)* of Theorem 90. □

Thus, blocks of $\mathbf{D}(K,Y)$ are unions of blocks of K.

We prove that the solution of Problem 89 means finding a reduct in the new dependence space. More exactly

Theorem 93. *Let (A,K) be a dependence space and $X \in \mathbf{B}(A)$, $Y \in \mathbf{B}(A)$ be sets such that $X \to Y\ (A,K)$. Then for any $X' \in \mathbf{B}(A)$ the following assertions are equivalent.*

(i) X' is minimal with respect to inclusion among all sets Z such that $Z \subseteq X$, $Z \to Y\ (A,K)$.

(ii) X' is a $\mathbf{D}(K,Y)$-reduct of X.

Proof. By hypothesis, $\mathbf{C}(K)(Y) \subseteq \mathbf{C}(K)(X)$ holds. We prove that for any $Z \subseteq X$ the conditions $Z \to Y\ (A,K)$ and $(Z,X) \in \mathbf{D}(K,Y)$ are equivalent.

Indeed, $Z \to Y\ (A,K)$ means $\mathbf{C}(K)(Y) \subseteq \mathbf{C}(K)(Z)$ which is equivalent to $(Z,X) \in \mathbf{D}(K,Y)$ by *(i)* of Theorem 90 regarding that $\mathbf{C}(K)(Y) \subseteq \mathbf{C}(K)(X)$ holds.

If $(Z,X) \in \mathbf{D}(K,Y)$, then $\mathbf{C}(K)(Y) \subseteq \mathbf{C}(K)(X)$ implies that $\mathbf{C}(K)(Y) \subseteq \mathbf{C}(K)(Z)$ holds by *(i)* of Theorem 90 which means $Z \to Y\ (A,K)$.

The assertion of our Theorem is an immediate consequence of the just proved equivalence. □

Example 37. Consider the dependence space of Example 31 (cf. Fig. 11). We see that $\mathbf{C}(K)(1) \subseteq \mathbf{C}(K)(X)$ holds for any $X \in \mathbf{B}(A)$ which means that $X \to 1\ (A,K)$ for any $X \in \mathbf{B}(A)$. It follows that $(X,X') \in \mathbf{D}(K,1)$ for any $(X,X') \in \mathbf{B}(A) \times \mathbf{B}(A)$, i.e., $\mathbf{B}(A)$ is one block of $\mathbf{D}(K,1)$ and 0 is the only $\mathbf{D}(K,1)$-reduct of X.

By Theorem 93, a solution of Problem 89 may be found using Algorithm 71. Thus, we have a dependence space (A, K), two sets X, Y in $\mathbf{B}(A)$ with $X \to Y\ (A, K)$ and we are looking for $\mathbf{D}(K, Y)$-reducts of X. We start, in every step of the algorithm, with a set $Z \in \mathbf{B}(A)$ such that $Z \subseteq X$ and $(Z, X) \in \mathbf{D}(K, Y)$; we consider a subset $Z' \subseteq Z$ and test whether $(Z, Z') \in \mathbf{D}(K, Y)$ holds or not. This can be decided on the basis of the following.

Theorem 94. *Let (A, K) be a dependence space, X, Y sets in $\mathbf{B}(A)$ such that $X \to Y\ (A, K)$, Z a set such that $Z \subseteq X$, $(Z, X) \in \mathbf{D}(K, Y)$, Z' a set such that $Z' \subseteq Z$. Then the following assertions are equivalent.*

(i) $(Z, Z') \notin \mathbf{D}(K, Y)$.
(ii) $\mathbf{C}(K)(Y) \not\subseteq \mathbf{C}(K)(Z')$.
(iii) There exists $a \in A$ such that $(Y, Y \cup \{a\}) \in K$, $(Z', Z' \cup \{a\}) \notin K$.

Proof. Conditions $X \to Y\ (A, K)$, $(Z, X) \in \mathbf{D}(K, Y)$ mean $\mathbf{C}(K)(Y) \subseteq \mathbf{C}(K)(X)$, $\mathbf{C}(K)(Y) \subseteq \mathbf{C}(K)(Z)$.

Hence, *(i)* is equivalent to $\mathbf{C}(K)(Y) \not\subseteq \mathbf{C}(K)(Z')$ by Theorem 90 which is *(ii)*.

If *(ii)* holds, there exists $a \in \mathbf{C}(K)(Y) - \mathbf{C}(K)(Z')$. Then $Y \subseteq Y \cup \{a\} \subseteq \mathbf{C}(K)(Y)$ and, hence, $(Y, Y \cup \{a\}) \in K$ by Theorem 15. On the other hand, $(Z', Z' \cup \{a\}) \in K$ would imply $a \in Z' \cup \{a\} \subseteq \mathbf{C}(K)(Z')$ which is a contradiction; thus, $(Z', Z' \cup \{a\}) \notin K$. We have proved that *(ii)* implies *(iii)*.

If *(iii)* is satisfied, then $a \in Y \cup \{a\} \subseteq \mathbf{C}(K)(Y)$. The hypothesis $a \in \mathbf{C}(K)(Z')$ would imply that $Z' \subseteq Z' \cup \{a\} \subseteq \mathbf{C}(K)(Z')$ and, hence, $(Z', Z' \cup \{a\}) \in K$ by Theorem 15, contrary to the hypothesis. Thus, $a \in \mathbf{C}(K)(Y) - \mathbf{C}(K)(Z')$ and *(ii)* holds. □

Example 38. Consider the dependence space of Example 37. We have $\mathbf{C}(K)(12) \subseteq 123 = \mathbf{C}(K)(23)$, i.e. $23 \to 12\ (A, K)$. We shall look for $\mathbf{D}(K, 12)$-reducts of 23; abbreviations will be used omitting the arguments $\mathbf{D}(K, 12)$, 23, o where o is the ordering on 23 such that b precedes c. We obtain

$\mathbf{SC}^{(0)} = 23$, $\mathbf{BD}^{(0)} = \emptyset$, $\mathbf{FS}^{(0)} = 23$; $\mathbf{SC}^{(1)} = \mathbf{SC}(\mathbf{SC}^{(0)}, \mathbf{D}(K, 12), \mathbf{FS}^{(0)}, o) = \mathbf{SC}(23, \mathbf{D}(K, 12), 23, o) = 2$, $\mathbf{BD}^{(1)} = \mathbf{BD}(\mathbf{SC}^{(0)}, \mathbf{D}(K, 12), \mathbf{FS}^{(0)}, o) = \mathbf{BD}(23, \mathbf{D}(K, 12), 23, o) = \{3\}$, $\mathbf{FS}^{(1)} = \mathbf{FS}(\mathbf{SC}^{(0)}, \mathbf{D}(K, 12), \mathbf{FS}^{(0)}, o) = \mathbf{FS}(23, \mathbf{D}(K, 12), 23, o) = \emptyset$. We have used the fact that $\mathbf{C}(K)(12) \not\subseteq \mathbf{C}(K)(23 - 2) = \mathbf{C}(K)(3)$ to deduce that $(23, 3) \notin \mathbf{D}(K, 12)$. Finally, we have $\mathbf{SC}^{(2)} = \mathbf{SC}(\mathbf{SC}^{(1)}, \mathbf{D}(K, 12), \mathbf{FS}^{(1)}, o) = \mathbf{SC}(2, \mathbf{D}(K, 12), \emptyset, o) = 2$, $\mathbf{BD}^{(2)} = \emptyset$, $\mathbf{FS}^{(2)} = \emptyset$.

Thus, $\mathbf{RD}(23, \mathbf{D}(K, 12), o) = 2$, $\mathbf{PD}(23, \mathbf{D}(K, 12), o) = \{3\}$.

12 Sequents

We continue the study of dependence relations on the set $\mathbf{B}(A)$ where A is a finite nonempty set. The set $\mathbf{B}(A)$ is the carrier of the Boolean algebra $(\mathbf{B}(A), \cup, \cap, Co, \emptyset, A)$; a dependence relation is a relation defined on the carrier of this algebra.

We try to transfer this relation to the free Boolean algebra $(\mathbf{FR}(P), \vee, \wedge, ^{-}, 0, 1)$ where P is a finite nonempty set. The resulting relation is called the *sequent relation*. The notion of sequent goes back to Gentzen (cf. [Ge1]). In our considerations, there are three types of these relations as we shall see below. Cf. [NoM1], [NoM2], [NN1].

Let A, P be finite nonempty sets. An arbitrary homomorphism w of the free Boolean algebra $(\mathbf{FR}(P), \vee, \wedge, ^{-}, 0, 1)$ into the Boolean algebra $(\mathbf{B}(A), \cup, \cap, Co, \emptyset, A)$ is said to be a *valuation of* $\mathbf{FR}(P)$ *into* $\mathbf{B}(A)$; these concepts have been explained in Section 2. Such a valuation w is defined if the values $w(p)$ for any $p \in P$ are given. A Boolean expression $\alpha \in \mathbf{FR}(P)$ is formed from variables $p \in P$ and constants 0, 1 by means of operations $\vee$, $\wedge$, and $^{-}$. If we replace any p in such an expression by $w(p)$, 0 by $\emptyset$, 1 by A, $\vee$ by $\cup$, $\wedge$ by $\cap$, and $^{-}$ by Co, we obtain the value $w(\alpha)$ of the valuation w for the expression α.

We shall define three types of sequents.

(1) Let (A, K) be a dependence space, P a finite nonempty set, w a valuation of $\mathbf{FR}(P)$ into $\mathbf{B}(A)$. For any Boolean expressions $\alpha \in \mathbf{FR}(P)$, $\beta \in \mathbf{FR}(P)$ we put $\alpha \Rightarrow \beta\ ((A, K), w)$ if and only if $\mathbf{C}(K)(w(\beta)) \subseteq \mathbf{C}(K)(w(\alpha))$, i.e., if and only if $w(\alpha) \rightarrow w(\beta)\ (A, K)$. Then the expression β is said to be a *sequent* of the expression α *with respect to* (A, K) *and* w.

(2) Let (A, K) be a dependence space, P a finite nonempty set. For any Boolean expressions $\alpha \in \mathbf{FR}(P)$, $\beta \in \mathbf{FR}(P)$, we put $\alpha \Rightarrow \beta\ (A, K)$ if and only if $\alpha \Rightarrow \beta\ ((A, K), w)$ for any valuation w of $\mathbf{FR}(P)$ into $\mathbf{B}(A)$. In this case the expression β is said to be a *sequent* of the expression α *with respect to* (A, K).

(3) Let P be a finite nonempty set. For any expressions $\alpha \in \mathbf{FR}(P)$, $\beta \in \mathbf{FR}(P)$, we put $\alpha \Rightarrow \beta$ if and only if $\alpha \Rightarrow \beta\ (A, K)$ for any dependence space (A, K). In this case the expression β is said to be a *sequent* of the expression α.

The reader must be warned: $\Rightarrow$ is no implication!

The following assertion holds.

Theorem 95. *Let P be a finite nonempty set. For any dependence space (A, K), for any valuation w of the set $\mathbf{FR}(P)$ into $\mathbf{B}(A)$, and for any Boolean expressions $\alpha \in \mathbf{FR}(P)$, $\beta \in \mathbf{FR}(P)$, the condition $\alpha \Rightarrow \beta\ ((A, K), w)$ is satisfied if and only if $(w(\alpha), w(\alpha \vee \beta)) \in K$.*

Proof. The condition $\mathbf{C}(K)(w(\beta)) \subseteq \mathbf{C}(K)(w(\alpha))$ is equivalent to the condition $\mathbf{C}(K)(w(\alpha \vee \beta)) = \mathbf{C}(K)(w(\alpha) \cup w(\beta)) = \mathbf{C}(K)(w(\alpha))$ by Lemma 77 which means $(w(\alpha), w(\alpha \vee \beta)) \in K$. □

A dependence space (A, K) is said to be *trivial* if the congruence K on the semilattice $(\mathbf{B}(A), \cup)$ has exactly one block; it is called *nontrivial* if it is not trivial.

Theorem 96. *Let P, A be finite nonempty sets, (A, K) a trivial dependence space, and $\alpha \in \mathbf{FR}(P)$, $\beta \in \mathbf{FR}(P)$ arbitrary Boolean expressions. Then $\alpha \Rightarrow \beta\ (A, K)$ holds.*

Proof. Since the congruence K has exactly one block, the condition $(w(\alpha), w(\alpha \vee \beta)) \in K$ is satisfied for any valuation of $\mathbf{FR}(P)$ into $\mathbf{B}(A)$. The assertion follows by Theorem 95. □

Theorem 97. *Let P, A be finite nonempty sets, (A, K) a nontrivial dependence space, and $\alpha \in \mathbf{FR}(P)$, $\beta \in \mathbf{FR}(P)$ arbitrary Boolean expressions. Then $\alpha \Rightarrow \beta$ (A, K) holds if and only if $\alpha \vee \beta = \alpha$.*

Proof. Suppose $P = \{p_1, \ldots, p_n\}$ where $n \geq 1$. Put $At = \{q_1 \wedge \ldots \wedge q_n;$ either $q_i = p_i$ or $q_i = \bar{p_i}$ for any i with $1 \leq i \leq n\}$. Then for any element α in $\mathbf{FR}(P)$ there exists exactly one set $At(\alpha) \subseteq At$ such that $\alpha = \sup\{a;\ a \in At(\alpha)\}$ (disjunctive normal form of α, see, e.g., [BB1], Theorem 9 of Section 5.9). We mention that $(\mathbf{FR}(P), \vee)$ is a semilattice and that $\sup\{\alpha_i;\ i \in \{1, \ldots, p\}\} = \alpha_1 \vee \ldots \vee \alpha_p$ for any Boolean expressions $\alpha_1, \ldots, \alpha_p$ in $\mathbf{FR}(P)$.

Let us have $\alpha \in \mathbf{FR}(P)$, $\gamma \in \mathbf{FR}(P)$ such that $\alpha \neq \gamma, \alpha \vee \gamma = \gamma$. Then there exists $a_0 \in At(\gamma) - At(\alpha)$. For any $\xi \in \mathbf{FR}(P)$ put

$$w(\xi) = \begin{cases} A \text{ if } a_0 \in At(\xi), \\ \\ \emptyset \text{ if } a_0 \notin At(\xi). \end{cases}$$

Then w is a homomorphism of $(\mathbf{FR}(P), \vee, \wedge, {}^-, 0, 1)$ into $(\mathbf{B}(A), \cup, \cap, Co, \emptyset, A)$ such that $w(\alpha) = \emptyset$, $w(\gamma) = A$. It follows that $\mathbf{C}(K)(w(\gamma)) = A$, $\mathbf{C}(K)(w(\alpha)) = \mathbf{C}(K)(\emptyset) \neq A$ because (A, K) is nontrivial. Thus, w is a valuation of $\mathbf{FR}(P)$ into $\mathbf{B}(A)$ with the property $\mathbf{C}(K)(w(\alpha)) \neq \mathbf{C}(K)(w(\gamma))$.

Hence, if $\alpha \in \mathbf{FR}(P)$, $\beta \in \mathbf{FR}(P)$ are such that $\alpha \vee \beta \neq \alpha$, then — taking $\alpha \vee \beta$ for γ — we obtain the existence of a valuation w of $\mathbf{FR}(P)$ into $\mathbf{B}(A)$ with $\mathbf{C}(K)(w(\alpha)) \neq \mathbf{C}(K)(w(\alpha \vee \beta))$, i.e., with $(w(\alpha), w(\alpha \vee \beta)) \notin K$ which means that $\alpha \Rightarrow \beta$ $((A, K), w)$ does not hold by Theorem 95. Thus, $\alpha \Rightarrow \beta$ (A, K) is not satisfied.

On the other hand, if α, β are in $\mathbf{FR}(P)$ and $\alpha \vee \beta = \alpha$ holds, then $w(\alpha \vee \beta) = w(\alpha)$ and, thus, $(w(\alpha), w(\alpha \vee \beta)) \in K$ for any valuation w of $\mathbf{FR}(P)$ into $\mathbf{B}(A)$. Thus, $\alpha \vee \beta = \alpha$ implies $\alpha \Rightarrow \beta$ (A, K) by Theorem 95. □

Theorem 98. *Let P be a finite nonempty set and $\alpha \in \mathbf{FR}(P)$, $\beta \in \mathbf{FR}(P)$ be arbitrary Boolean expressions. Then $\alpha \Rightarrow \beta$ holds if and only if $\alpha \vee \beta = \alpha$.*

Proof. If $\alpha \Rightarrow \beta$ holds, then, particularly, $\alpha \Rightarrow \beta$ (A, K) for some nontrivial dependence space (A, K). By Theorem 97, we have $\alpha \vee \beta = \alpha$. On the other hand, $\alpha \vee \beta = \alpha$ implies $\alpha \Rightarrow \beta$ (A, K) for any dependence space (A, K) by Theorems 96 and 97. □

Thus, we have obtained a complete and simple characterization of sequent relation. There is a question whether this has some useful consequences for dependence spaces. We know that $\alpha \Rightarrow \beta$ means, particularly, $w(\alpha) \to w(\beta)$ (A, K) for any dependence space (A, K) and for any valuation w of $\mathbf{FR}(P)$ into $\mathbf{B}(A)$. But the condition $\alpha \Rightarrow \beta$, and the condition $\alpha \Rightarrow \beta$ (A, K) as well, is too strong as it follows from the next

Corollary 99. *Let (A,K) be a nontrivial dependence space, P a finite nonempty set, $\alpha \in \mathbf{FR}(P)$, $\beta \in \mathbf{FR}(P)$ Boolean expressions such that $\alpha \Rightarrow \beta$ (A,K), w a valuation of $\mathbf{FR}(P)$ into $\mathbf{B}(A)$. Then $w(\beta) \subseteq w(\alpha)$.*

Proof. By Theorem 97, we have $\alpha \vee \beta = \alpha$ which implies that $w(\alpha) = w(\alpha \vee \beta) = w(\alpha) \cup w(\beta)$ and, hence $w(\beta) \subseteq w(\alpha)$. □

Thus, using this method, we recognize only the least dependence relation $\supseteq$ (cf. Example 35).

Inspite of this result the method of sequents can simplify the recognition of dependence.

Example 39. Let (A,K) be a dependence space, Z_1, Z_2, Z_3, Z_4 elements in $\mathbf{B}(A)$. Put

$X_1 = ((Z_1 \cup Z_2) \cup Co(Z_3 \cap Z_4)) \cap (Co(Z_1 \cup Z_2) \cup (Z_3 \cap Z_4))$,
$X_2 = ((Z_1 \cup Z_3) \cup Co(Z_2 \cap Z_4)) \cap (Co(Z_1 \cup Z_3) \cup (Z_2 \cap Z_4))$,
$Y_1 = (Z_1 \cap Z_3 \cap Z_4) \cup (Z_2 \cap Z_3 \cap Z_4)$,
$Y_2 = (Z_1 \cap Z_2 \cap Z_4) \cup (Z_2 \cap Z_3 \cap Z_4)$.

Do the conditions $X_1 \to Y_1$ (A,K), $X_2 \to Y_2$ (A,K) hold ?

Clearly, $Y_1 = (Z_1 \cup Z_2) \cap (Z_3 \cap Z_4)$, $Y_2 = (Z_1 \cup Z_3) \cap (Z_2 \cap Z_4)$. Put $P = \{p_1, p_2\}$, $\alpha = (p_1 \vee \bar{p_2}) \wedge (\bar{p_1} \vee p_2)$, $\beta = p_1 \wedge p_2$. Then $\alpha = (p_1 \wedge \bar{p_1}) \vee (p_1 \wedge p_2) \vee (\bar{p_2} \wedge \bar{p_1}) \vee (\bar{p_2} \wedge p_2) = (p_1 \wedge p_2) \vee (\bar{p_1} \wedge \bar{p_2})$. Hence $\alpha \vee \beta = \alpha$.

If putting $w(p_1) = Z_1 \cup Z_2$, $w(p_2) = Z_3 \cap Z_4$, we obtain $w(\alpha) = (w(p_1) \cup Co(w(p_2))) \cap (Co(w(p_1)) \cup w(p_2)) = ((Z_1 \cup Z_2) \cup Co(Z_3 \cap Z_4)) \cap (Co(Z_1 \cup Z_2) \cup (Z_3 \cap Z_4)) = X_1$, $w(\beta) = w(p_1) \cap w(p_2) = (Z_1 \cup Z_2) \cap (Z_3 \cap Z_4) = Y_1$. Hence $X_1 \to Y_1$ (A,K) holds.

Similarly, if we set $w(p_1) = Z_1 \cup Z_3$, $w(p_2) = Z_2 \cap Z_4$, we obtain $w(\alpha) = X_2$, $w(\beta) = Y_2$. Thus $X_2 \to Y_2$ (A,K) holds.

References

[Bi1] Birkhoff, G.: Lattice Theory. Third edition, American Math. Society, Providence, (1984)

[BB1] Birkhoff, G., Bartee, T.C.: Modern Applied Algebra. McGraw Hill, New York, (1970)

[Bo1] Boruvka, O.: Grundlagen der Gruppoid- und Gruppentheorie. VEB Deutscher Verlag der Wissenschaften, Berlin, (1960)

[Ce1] Cendrowska, J.: PRISM: An algorithm for inducing modular rules. Int. J. Man-Machine Studies, **27**, (1987), 349–370

[Du1] Duda, J.: Boolean concept lattices and good contexts. Čas. Pěst. Mat. **114**, (1989), 165–175

[GJ1] Garey, M.R., Johnson, D.S.: Computers and intractability. A guide to the theory of NP-completeness. W.H. Freeman and Co., San Francisco, (1979)

[Ge1] Gentzen, G.: Untersuchungen über das logische Schließen. Mathematische Zeitschrift, **39**, (1935), 176–210

[Gl1] Głazek, K.: Some old and new problems of the independence in mathematics. Colloquium Math., **17**, (1979), 127–189

[HNP1] Haupt, O., Nöbeling, G., Pauc, C.: Über Abhängigkeitsräume. J. Reine Angew. Math., **181**, (1940), 193–217

[Li1] Lipski, W., Jr.: Two NP-complete problems related to information retrieval. Fundamentals of Computation Theory. Lecture Notes in Computer Science, **56**, Springer, Berlin, (1977), 452–458

[LO1] Lucchesi, C.L., Osborn, S.L.: Candidate keys for relations. J. Comput. System Sci., **17**, (1978), 270–279

[Ma1] Marczewski, E.: A general scheme of independence in mathematics. Bull. Acad. Polon. Sci. Sér. Math. Astronom. Phys., **6**, (1958), 731–736

[MP1] Marek, W., Pawlak, Z.: Mathematical foundations of information storage and retrieval I, II, III. CC PAS Reports, **135, 136, 137**, Warszawa, (1973)

[MP2] Marek, W., Pawlak, Z.: Information storage and retrieval system — mathematical foundations. CC PAS Reports, **149**, Warszawa, (1974). Also in: Theoretical Computer Science, **1**, (1976), 331–354

[Mr1] Mrózek, A.: Rough sets and some aspects of expert system realization. 7th International Workshop on Expert Systems and their Applications, Avignon, (1987), 597–611

[Mr2] Mrózek, A.: Rough sets and dependency analysis among attributes in computer implementation of expert's inference models. Int. J. Man-Machine Studies, **30**, (1989), 457–473

[NoJ1] Novotný, J.: Application of information systems to evaluation of pedagogical research. (Czech). To appear in Sborník prací pedagogické fakulty Masarykovy Univerzity (Publications of the Pedagogical Faculty, Masaryk University, Brno, (1993))

[NN1] Novotný, J., Novotný, M.: Notes on the algebraic approach to dependence in information systems. Fundamenta Informaticae, **16**, (1992), 263–273

[NN2] Novotný, J., Novotný, M.: On dependence in Wille's contexts. Fundamenta Informaticae, **19**, (1993), 343–353

[NoM1] Novotný, M.: On sequents defined by means of information systems. Fundamenta Informaticae, **4**, (1981), 1041–1048

[NoM2] Novotný, M.: Remarks on sequents defined by means of information systems. Fundamenta Informaticae, **6**, (1983), 71–79

[NP1] Novotný, M., Pawlak, Z.: On a representation of rough sets by means of information systems. Fundamenta Informaticae, **6**, (1983), 289–296

[NP2] Novotný, M., Pawlak, Z.: Characterization of rough top equalities and rough bottom equalities. Bull. Polish Acad. Sci. Math., **33**, (1985), 91–97

[NP3] Novotný, M., Pawlak, Z.: On rough equalities. Bull. Polish Acad. Sci. Math., **33**, (1985), 99–104

[NP4] Novotný, M., Pawlak, Z.: Black box analysis and rough top equality. Bull. Acad. Sci. Math., **33**, (1985), 105–113

[NP5] Novotný, M., Pawlak, Z.: Concept forming and black boxes. Bull. Polish Acad. Sci. Math., **35**, (1987), 133–141

[NP6] Novotný, M., Pawlak, Z.: Partial dependency of attributes. Bull. Polish Acad. Sci. Math., **36**, (1988), 453–458

[NP7] Novotný, M., Pawlak, Z.: Independence of attributes. Bull. Polish Acad. Sci. Math., **36**, (1988), 459–465

[NP8] Novotný, M., Pawlak, Z.: On superreducts. Bull. Polish Acad. Sci. Tech. Sci., **38**, (1990), 101–112

[NP9] Novotný, M., Pawlak, Z.: Algebraic theory of independence in information systems. Fundamenta Informaticae, **14**, (1991), 454–476

[NP10] Novotný, M., Pawlak, Z.: On a problem concerning dependence spaces. Fundamenta Informaticae, **16**, (1992), 275–287

[Pa1] Pawlak, Z.: Mathematical foundations of information retrieval. CC PAS Reports, **101**, (1973), Warszawa

[Pa2] Pawlak, Z.: Information systems. ICS PAS Reports, **338**, Warszawa, (1978)

[Pa3] Pawlak, Z.: Rough sets. ICS PAS Reports, **431**, Warszawa, (1981)

[Pa4] Pawlak, Z.: Rough sets. Algebraic and topological approach. Intern. Journ. of Computer and Information Sciences, **11**, (1982), 341–366

[Pa5] Pawlak, Z.: Systemy informacyjne, podstawy teoretyczne (Information systems, theoretical foundations). Wydawnictwa Naukowo-Techniczne, Warszawa, (1983)

[Pa6] Pawlak, Z.: Learning from examples – the case of an imperfect teacher. Bull. Polish Acad. Sci. Tech., **35**, (1987), 259–264

[Pa7] Pawlak, Z.: Rough Sets. Theoretical Aspects of Reasoning about Data. Kluwer, Dordrecht – Boston – London, (1991)

[Ra1] Rauszer, C.M.: Reducts in information systems. Fundamenta Informaticae, **15**, (1991), 1–12

[Sz1] Szász, G.: Introduction to Lattice Theory. Academic Press, Budapest, (1963)

[Wi1] Wille, R.: Restructuring lattice theory. In: Ordered Sets (Ed. I. Rival), Reidel, Dordrecht – Boston, (1982), 445–470

Chapter 8

Applications of Dependence Spaces

Miroslav Novotný

Masaryk University,
Botanická 68a, Brno, Czech Republic

Abstract: The dependence space models are applied to representation and investigation of domains with incomplete information. It is shown that various models of these domains can be uniformly treated within the framework of the theory of dependence spaces. In particular, dependence spaces are constructed for contexts ([Wil]), information systems ([Pa7]), decision tables. The problems are studied that arise in connection with discovery of knowledge from indiscernibility-type incomplete information. The algorithms are given for realisation of various relevant tasks. Among others, an algorithm for finding reducts of sets of attributes in an information system and an algorithm for reduction of a set of conditions in a decision table are presented.

1 Contexts

Practical problems inspired R. Wille to analyze concepts, their extent and intent (cf. [Wil], [NN2]). Some contributions of dependence spaces to this analysis are presented in this section.

A *context* is an ordered triple $T = (G, A, r)$ where G, A are finite nonempty sets and $r \subseteq G \times A$ is a correspondence from G to A. The elements in G are interpreted to be *objects*, elements in A are said to be *features*; if $(g, a) \in G \times A$ is such that $(g, a) \in r$, then the object g is said to have the feature a. The correspondence r can be naturally represented by an incidence table: the rows of the table are labelled by objects, columns by features; if $(g, a) \in r$, the intersection of the row labelled by g and the column labelled by a contains 1; otherwise it contains 0.

Example 1. Let $G = \{g_i;\ 1 \leq i \leq 4\}$ where g_i are persons and $A = \{a_j;\ 1 \leq j \leq 5\}$ where a_1 = man, a_2 = person wearing moustache, a_3 = person with blue eyes, a_4 = person wearing long hair, a_5 = old person. Let the incidence table of r be given by Table 1.

Then $T = (G, A, r)$ is a context. E.g., g_1 is an old man wearing moustache who has neither blue eyes nor long hair, g_4 is a long haired person with blue eyes who is not a man, is not old, and does not wear moustache.

Table 1.

	a_1	a_2	a_3	a_4	a_5
g_1	1	1	0	0	1
g_2	0	0	1	1	1
g_3	1	1	0	0	0
g_4	0	0	1	1	0

Let $T = (G, A, r)$ be a context. For any $X \in \mathbf{B}(G)$ and any $Y \in \mathbf{B}(A)$ we put

$\mathbf{s}^T(X) = \{y \in A;\ (x, y) \in r \text{ for any } x \in X\}$,
$\mathbf{t}^T(Y) = \{x \in G;\ (x, y) \in r \text{ for any } y \in Y\}$,
$\mathbf{p}^T(X) = \mathbf{t}^T(\mathbf{s}^T(X))$, $\mathbf{q}^T(Y) = \mathbf{s}^T(\mathbf{t}^T(Y))$.

It is well-known that the mappings $\mathbf{s}^T$, $\mathbf{t}^T$ establish a Galois connection (cf. [Bi1], Chapter V, Section 7, [Sz1], Sections 27, 28), i.e., that

(i) $X_1 \subseteq X_2$ implies $\mathbf{s}^T(X_2) \subseteq \mathbf{s}^T(X_1)$ for any $X_1,\ X_2 \in \mathbf{B}(G)$;
(ii) $X \subseteq \mathbf{t}^T(\mathbf{s}^T(X))$ for any $X \in \mathbf{B}(G)$

and, similarly,

(i') $Y_1 \subseteq Y_2$ implies $\mathbf{t}^T(Y_2) \subseteq \mathbf{t}^T(Y_1)$ for any $Y_1,\ Y_2 \in \mathbf{B}(A)$;
(ii') $Y \subseteq \mathbf{s}^T(\mathbf{t}^T(Y))$ for any $Y \in \mathbf{B}(A)$.

If X_1 and X_2 are in $\mathbf{B}(G)$, then $\mathbf{s}^T(X_1 \cup X_2) = \mathbf{s}^T(X_1) \cap \mathbf{s}^T(X_2)$. Similarly $t^T(Y_1 \cup Y_2) = t^T(Y_1) \cap t^T(Y_2)$ holds for any Y_1 and Y_2 in $\mathbf{B}(A)$. These Galois connections were studied by several authors (cf. [Du1]).

It follows easily that $\mathbf{p}^T$ is a closure operator on the set $\mathbf{B}(G)$ and that $\mathbf{q}^T$ is a closure operator on the set $\mathbf{B}(A)$.

If $X \subseteq G$, $Y \subseteq A$ are such that $\mathbf{s}^T(X) = Y$, $\mathbf{t}^T(Y) = X$, then the ordered pair (X, Y) is said to be a *concept*, the set X is called its *extent*, the set Y its *intent*. Particularly, if $Y \subseteq A$, then $(\mathbf{t}^T(Y), \mathbf{q}^T(Y))$ is a concept; it is said to be *generated by the set Y of features.*

Example 2. If we continue Example 1, we find that for $E = \{g_1, g_2\}$, $I = \{a_5\}$ the ordered pair (E, I) establishes a concept with the extent E and the intent I.

Now, let us choose $Y = \{a_2, a_3\}$. Then $\mathbf{t}^T(Y) = \emptyset$ and, thus, $\mathbf{q}^T(Y) = \mathbf{s}^T(\emptyset) = A$ and the set Y generates the concept $(\emptyset, A)$ with empty extent.

Let $T = (G, A, r)$ be a context. We define

$$\mathbf{K}^T = \{(Y_1, Y_2) \in \mathbf{B}(A) \times \mathbf{B}(A);\ \mathbf{t}^T(Y_1) = \mathbf{t}^T(Y_2)\}\ .$$

Theorem 1. *Let $T = (G, A, r)$ be a context. Then $\mathbf{K}^T$ is a congruence on the semilattice* $(\mathbf{B}(A), \cup)$.

Proof. Clearly, $\mathbf{K}^T$ is an equivalence. Let us have Y_1, Y_2, Z in $\mathbf{B}(A)$ such that $(Y_1, Y_2) \in \mathbf{K}^T$. Then $\mathbf{t}^T(Y_1) = \mathbf{t}^T(Y_2)$. It follows that $\mathbf{t}^T(Y_1 \cup Z) = \mathbf{t}^T(Y_1) \cap \mathbf{t}^T(Z) = \mathbf{t}^T(Y_2) \cap \mathbf{t}^T(Z) = \mathbf{t}^T(Y_2 \cup Z)$ which implies that $(Y_1 \cup Z, Y_2 \cup Z) \in \mathbf{K}^T$. By Theorem 12 of Chapter 7, the equivalence $\mathbf{K}^T$ is a congruence on $(\mathbf{B}(A), \cup)$. □

Corollary 2. *If $T = (G, A, r)$ is a context, then $(A, \mathbf{K}^T)$ is a dependence space.*

The dependence space $(A, \mathbf{K}^T)$ defined to the context $T = (G, A, r)$ will be said to be the *dependence space of the context T.*

Lemma 3. *Let $T = (G, A, r)$ be a context. Then $\mathbf{C}(\mathbf{K}^T)(Y) = \mathbf{q}^T(Y)$ for any $Y \in \mathbf{B}(A)$.*

Proof. It is easy to see that $\mathbf{t}^T(Y) = \mathbf{t}^T(\mathbf{s}^T(\mathbf{t}^T(Y)))$ which is a well-known fact concerning Galois connections. It follows that $\mathbf{t}^T(Y) = \mathbf{t}^T(\mathbf{q}^T(Y))$, thus $(Y, \mathbf{q}^T(Y)) \in \mathbf{K}^T$. Let $(Y, Z) \in \mathbf{K}^T$; then $\mathbf{t}^T(Y) = \mathbf{t}^T(Z)$ and, therefore, $Z \subseteq \mathbf{q}^T(Z) = \mathbf{s}^T(\mathbf{t}^T(Z)) = \mathbf{s}^T(\mathbf{t}^T(Y)) = \mathbf{q}^T(Y)$. It follows that $\mathbf{q}^T(Y)$ is the greatest element in the block of $\mathbf{K}^T$ that contains Y; thus $\mathbf{C}(\mathbf{K}^T) = \mathbf{q}^T(Y)$. □

Corollary 4. *Let $T = (G, A, r)$ be a context, X, Y elements in $\mathbf{B}(A)$. Then $X \to Y$ $(A, \mathbf{K}^T)$ holds if and only if $\mathbf{t}^T(X) \subseteq \mathbf{t}^T(Y)$.*

Proof. Indeed, $X \to Y$ $(A, \mathbf{K}^T)$ means $\mathbf{q}^T(Y) \subseteq \mathbf{q}^T(X)$ by Lemma 3 which is equivalent to $\mathbf{t}^T(X) \subseteq \mathbf{t}^T(Y)$ as it is easy to see. □

Corollary 5. *Let $T = (G, A, r)$ be a context and Y a set in $\mathbf{B}(A)$. Then for any X, $X' \in \mathbf{B}(A)$ the condition $(X, X') \in \mathbf{D}(\mathbf{K}^T, Y)$ holds if and only if one of the following conditions (i), (ii) is satisfied.*

(i) $\mathbf{t}^T(X) \subseteq \mathbf{t}^T(Y)$, $\mathbf{t}^T(X') \subseteq \mathbf{t}^T(Y)$;
(ii) $\mathbf{t}^T(X') = \mathbf{t}^T(X) \nsubseteq \mathbf{t}^T(Y)$.

Proof. From the fundamental properties of Galois connections it follows that conditions *(i)*, *(ii)* may be reformulated as follows.

(i') $\mathbf{q}^T(Y) \subseteq \mathbf{q}^T(X)$, $\mathbf{q}^T(Y) \subseteq \mathbf{q}^T(X')$;
(ii') $\mathbf{q}^T(Y) \nsubseteq \mathbf{q}^T(X) = \mathbf{q}^T(X')$.

Using Lemma 3, we see that $(X, X') \in \mathbf{D}(\mathbf{K}^T, Y)$ holds if and only if *(i')* or *(ii')* is satisfied (cf. Theorem 90 of Chapter 7). □

We have seen that a concept can be generated by a set of features. Several sets of features may generate the same concept. Thus, the following problem seems to be natural and important.

Problem 6. Let $T = (G, A, r)$ be a context, $Y \in \mathbf{B}(A)$ a set of features. Find a minimal subset with respect to inclusion among all sets Z such that $Z \subseteq Y$ and Z, Y generate the same concept.

Example 3. Let G be the set of all patients of a clinic, A the set of symptoms that are tested during introductory examinations of patients; for $(g, a) \in G \times A$ put $(g, a) \in r$ if and only if the patient g has the symptom a. Then $T = (G, A, r)$ is a context. It can happen that a set $Y \subseteq A$ of symptoms is characteristic for a disease, i.e., $\mathbf{t}^T(Y)$ is the set of all patients suffering from the disease and $\mathbf{q}^T(Y)$ is the set of all symptoms that are common to patients of the set $\mathbf{t}^T(Y)$. It is possible that a subset Y' of Y generates the same concept $(\mathbf{t}^T(Y), \mathbf{q}^T(Y))$. Then it is more advantageous to test only the set Y' and to cancel superfluous tests of symptoms in the set $Y - Y'$.

Theorem 7. *Let $T = (G, A, r)$ be a context, Y, Y' subsets of A. Then the following assertions are equivalent.*

(i) The set Y' is a $\mathbf{K}^T$-reduct of Y.

(ii) The set Y' is minimal with respect to inclusion among all sets Z such that $Z \subseteq Y$ and that Z, Y generate the same concept.

Proof. Clearly, *(i)* is equivalent to the following assertion:
(iii) The set Y' is minimal with respect to inclusion among all sets Z such that $Z \subseteq Y$ and $(Z, Y) \in \mathbf{K}^T$.

By definition of $\mathbf{K}^T$, the condition $(Z, Y) \in \mathbf{K}^T$ means $\mathbf{t}^T(Y) = \mathbf{t}^T(Z)$. Furthermore, $(Z, Y) \in \mathbf{K}^T$ is equivalent to $\mathbf{q}^T(Y) = \mathbf{C}(\mathbf{K}^T)(Y) = \mathbf{C}(\mathbf{K}^T)(Z) = \mathbf{q}^T(Y)$ by Lemma 3. Hence, $(Z, Y) \in \mathbf{K}^T$ means that Z, Y generate the same concept and *(iii)* is equivalent to *(ii)*. □

Example 4. Let $T = (G, A, r)$ be the same as in Example 1; consider $Y = \{a_1, a_2, a_5\}$. Then $\mathbf{t}^T(Y) = \{g_1\} = \mathbf{t}^T(\{a_2, a_5\})$, $\mathbf{t}^T(\{a_2\}) = \{g_1, g_3\}$, $\mathbf{t}^T(\{a_5\}) = \{g_1, g_2\}$. It follows that $(Y, \{a_2, a_5\}) \in \mathbf{K}^T$ while $(Y, \{a_2\}) \notin \mathbf{K}^T$, $(Y, \{a_5\}) \notin \mathbf{K}^T$. Thus, the set $\{a_2, a_5\}$ is a $\mathbf{K}^T$-reduct of Y and, therefore, is minimal among all sets Z such that $Z \subseteq Y$ and that Z, Y generate the same concept. Clearly, another possibility is $\{a_1, a_5\}$.

We now investigate the following problem.

Problem 8. Let (A, K) be a dependence space. Construct all contexts $T = (G, A, r)$ whose dependence spaces coincide with (A, K).

Lemma 9. *Let $T = (G, A, r)$ be a context. Put $h(g) = \{a \in A;\ (g, a) \in r\}$ for any $g \in G$, $\mathbf{G} = \{h(g);\ g \in G\}$. Then the following assertions hold.*

(i) $\mathbf{t}^T(Y) = \{g \in G;\ Y \subseteq h(g)\}$ for any $Y \in \mathbf{B}(A)$.

(ii) $\mathbf{K}^T = \mathbf{T}(\mathbf{G})$.

Proof. For any $Y \in \mathbf{B}(A)$, we have $\mathbf{t}^T(Y) = \{g \in G;\ (g, a) \in r$ for any $a \in Y\} = \{g \in G;\ a \in h(g)$ for any $a \in Y\} = \{g \in G;\ Y \subseteq h(g)\}$ which is *(i)*.

Let $(Y_1, Y_2) \in \mathbf{B}(A) \times \mathbf{B}(A)$ be arbitrary. By *(i)*, the condition $(Y_1, Y_2) \in \mathbf{K}^T$ is equivalent to $\{g \in G;\ Y_1 \subseteq h(g)\} = \{g \in G;\ Y_2 \subseteq h(g)\}$. By definition of $\mathbf{G}$ this means that for any $\mathbf{g} \in \mathbf{G}$ the conditions $Y_1 \subseteq \mathbf{g}$, $Y_2 \subseteq \mathbf{g}$ are equivalent which is $(Y_1, Y_2) \in \mathbf{T}(\mathbf{G})$; for the definition of $\mathbf{T}(\mathbf{G})$ cf. Theorem 16 of Chapter 7. □

Let (A, K) be a dependence space, $\mathbf{G} \neq \emptyset$ a subset of $\mathbf{B}(A)$. Then $\mathbf{G}$ is said to be *dense in* (A, K) if $\mathbf{T}(\mathbf{G}) = K$.

Lemma 10. *Let* (A, K) *be a dependence space and* $\mathbf{G}$ *a set that is dense in* (A, K). *Then* $(\mathbf{g}_1, \mathbf{g}_2) \notin K$ *holds for any* $\mathbf{g}_1 \in \mathbf{G}$, $\mathbf{g}_2 \in \mathbf{G}$ *with the property* $\mathbf{g}_1 \neq \mathbf{g}_2$.

Proof. If $\mathbf{g}_1 \neq \mathbf{g}_2$, then either $\mathbf{g}_1 \not\subseteq \mathbf{g}_2$ or $\mathbf{g}_2 \not\subseteq \mathbf{g}_1$; without loss of generality, we may suppose $\mathbf{g}_1 \not\subseteq \mathbf{g}_2$. Since $\mathbf{g}_2 \subseteq \mathbf{g}_2$, we obtain $(\mathbf{g}_1, \mathbf{g}_2) \notin \mathbf{T}(\mathbf{G})$ by definition of $\mathbf{T}(\mathbf{G})$. □

Corollary 11. *If* (A, K) *is a dependence space and* $\mathbf{G}$ *is a set that is dense in* (A, K), *then* $|\mathbf{G}| \leq |\mathbf{B}(A)/K|$.

Proof. By Lemma 10, any block of K contains at most one element of $\mathbf{G}$ which implies the assertion immediately. □

We now describe a construction of a context starting with a dependence space.

Construction 12. (Construction $\mathbf{C}_1$).

Let $P = (A, K)$ *be a dependence space.*

We take a finite nonempty set G, *a subset* $\mathbf{G}$ *of* $\mathbf{B}(A)$ *that is dense in* (A, K), *and a surjection* h *of* G *onto* $\mathbf{G}$. *We put*

$r = \{(g, a) \in G \times A;\ a \in h(g)\}$,

$T = (G, A, r)$,

$\mathbf{C}_1(P; G, \mathbf{G}, r) = T$.

The context T is said to be *constructed by* $\mathbf{C}_1$ *from* P *be means of parameters* G, $\mathbf{G}$, h.

Theorem 13. *The following assertions hold.*

(i) If P *is a dependence space and* $T = \mathbf{C}_1(P; G, \mathbf{G}, h)$ *where the parameters* G, $\mathbf{G}$, h *are arbitrary, then the dependence space of* T *coincides with* P.

(ii) If $T = (G, A, r)$ *is a context and* P *its dependence space, then there exist parameters* $\mathbf{G}$, h *such that* $T = \mathbf{C}_1(P; G, \mathbf{G}, h)$.

Proof. (1) If $P = (A, K)$ is a dependence space and $T = \mathbf{C}_1(P; G, \mathbf{G}, h)$ with arbitrary parameters, then $(g, a) \in r$ is equivalent to $a \in h(g)$ for any $(g, a) \in G \times A$ by definition of $\mathbf{C}_1$. It follows that $h(g) = \{a \in A;\ (g, a) \in r\}$ for any $g \in G$ and $\mathbf{G} = \{h(g);\ g \in G\}$ according to the definition of $\mathbf{C}_1$. By Lemma 9, we obtain $\mathbf{K}^T = \mathbf{T}(\mathbf{G}) = K$ because $\mathbf{G}$ is dense in (A, K). Thus, $(A, \mathbf{K}^T) = (A, K) = P$ and *(i)* holds.

(2) If $T = (G, A, r)$ is a context and $P = (A, K)$ its dependence space, put $h(g) = \{a \in A;\ (g, a) \in r\}$ for any $g \in G$. Furthermore, set $\mathbf{G} = \{h(g); g \in G\}$. By Lemma 9, we obtain $K = \mathbf{K}^T = \mathbf{T}(\mathbf{G})$ and, hence, $\mathbf{G}$ is dense in P. By definition, h is a surjection of G onto $\mathbf{G}$. Finally, $(g, a) \in r$ if and only if $a \in h(g)$ for any $(g, a) \in G \times A$ and, therefore, $r = \{(g, a) \in G \times A;\ a \in h(g)\}$. Clearly, $T = \mathbf{C}_1(P; G, \mathbf{G}, r)$. □

Example 5. Let $P = (A, K)$ be the dependence space of Example 16 in Chapter 7. Put $\mathbf{G} = \{1, 2, 3\}$; this set is dense in (A, K). We take $G = \{g_1, g_2, g_3, g_4\}$, $h(g_1) = h(g_2) = 1$, $h(g_3) = 2$, $h(g_4) = 3$. We obtain Table 2 for r.

Table 2.

	a	b	c
g_1	1	0	0
g_2	1	0	0
g_3	0	1	0
g_4	0	0	1

Put $T = (G, A, r)$. Then $T = \mathbf{C}_1(P; G, \mathbf{G}, h)$.

We construct the dependence space of the just constructed context. Using the table, we obtain $\mathbf{t}^T(0) = G$, $\mathbf{t}^T(1) = \{g_1, g_2\}$, $\mathbf{t}^T(2) = \{g_3\}$, $\mathbf{t}^T(3) = \{g_4\}$, $\mathbf{t}^T(Y) = \emptyset$ for the remaining subsets of A. It follows that $\mathbf{K}^T$ has the following blocks: $\{0\}$, $\{1\}$, $\{2\}$, $\{3\}$, $\{12, 13, 23, 123\}$; clearly, $\mathbf{K}^T = K$.

Corollary 14. *Let $T = (G, A, r)$ be a context and $P = (A, K)$ its dependence space. Put*

$h(g) = \{a \in A;\ (g, a) \in r\}$ for any $g \in G$,

$\mathbf{G} = \{h(g);\ g \in G\}$.

Then the parameters $\mathbf{G}$, h are such that $T = \mathbf{C}_1(P; G, \mathbf{G}, h)$.

Proof. This follows from the proof of Theorem 13. □

A context $T = (G, A, r)$ is said to be *row-reduced* if for any $g_1,\ g_2 \in G$ with $g_1 \neq g_2$ there exists $a \in A$ such that either $(g_1, a) \in r$, $(g_2, a) \notin r$ or $(g_1, a) \notin r$, $(g_2, a) \in r$. Thus, if T is a row-reduced context, then the rows of its table that are labelled by different objects are different.

Lemma 15. *Let $T = (G, A, r)$ be a context. Define*

$$s = \{(g, g') \in G \times G;\ (g, a) \in r \text{ and } (g', a) \in r \text{ are equivalent for any } a \in A\}\ .$$

Let G' be a set having exactly one element in any block of s, put

$r' = r \cap (G' \times A)$,

$T' = (G', A, r')$

Then T' is a row-reduced context whose dependence space coincides with the dependence space of T.

Proof. T' is evidently a row-reduced context.

Let $Y \in \mathbf{B}(A)$ be arbitrary. Then $\mathbf{t}^{T'}(Y) = \{g' \in G';\ (g', a) \in r' \text{ for any } a \in Y\} = G' \cap \{g \in G;\ (g, a) \in r \text{ for any } a \in Y\} = G' \cap \mathbf{t}^T(Y)$. On the other hand, $\mathbf{t}^T(Y)$ is obtained from $\mathbf{t}^{T'}(Y)$ by adding, to any $g' \in \mathbf{t}^{T'}(Y)$ all objects $g \in G$

such that $(g, g') \in s$, i.e., by constructing $\mathbf{c}(s)(\mathbf{t}^{T'}(Y))$ where $\mathbf{c}$ is the operator defined in Section 5 of Chapter 7.

If $Y_1 \in \mathbf{B}(A)$, $Y_2 \in \mathbf{B}(A)$, then $\mathbf{t}^T(Y_1) = \mathbf{t}^T(Y_2)$ implies that $\mathbf{t}^{T'}(Y_1) = G' \cap \mathbf{t}^T(Y_1) = G' \cap \mathbf{t}^T(Y_2) = \mathbf{t}^{T'}(Y_2)$. On the other hand, if $\mathbf{t}^{T'}(Y_1) = \mathbf{t}^{T'}(Y_2)$, then $\mathbf{t}^T(Y_1) = \mathbf{c}(s)(\mathbf{t}^{T'}(Y_1)) = \mathbf{c}(s)(\mathbf{t}^{T'}(Y_2)) = \mathbf{t}^T(Y_2)$. It follows that $\mathbf{K}^T = \mathbf{K}^{T'}$. □

Row reduced contexts may be obtained by Construction $\mathbf{C}_1$ when choosing parameters in a particular way.

Lemma 16. *Let $P = (A, K)$ be a context and $T = \mathbf{C}_1(P; G, \mathbf{G}, h)$ where the parameters are arbitrary. Then the following assertions are equivalent.*

(i) h is a bijection of G onto $\mathbf{G}$.

(ii) T is row-reduced.

Proof. If *(i)* holds and $g_1,\ g_2 \in G,\ g_1 \neq g_2$ is satisfied, then $h(g_1) \neq h(g_2)$ and there exists $a \in A$ such that either $a \in h(g_1) - h(g_2)$ or $a \in h(g_2) - h(g_1)$. In the first case, we obtain $(g_1, a) \in r,\ (g_2, a) \notin r$, in the second $(g_2, a) \in r,\ (g_1, a) \notin r$ which is *(ii)*.

If $g_1,\ g_2 \in G,\ g_1 \neq g_2$ and *(ii)* is satisfied, there exists $a \in A$ such that either $(g_1, a) \in r,\ (g_2, a) \notin r$ or $(g_1, a) \notin r,\ (g_2, a) \in r$ hold. Thus, either $a \in h(g_1) - h(g_2)$ or $a \in h(g_2) - h(g_1)$ and, hence, h is injective. Since h is surjective by definition, *(i)* holds. □

Construction 17. Construction $\mathbf{K}_1$ (of all contexts with a prescribed dependence space)

Let $P = (A, K)$ be a dependence space.

(1) *We find all subsets $\mathbf{G}$ of $\mathbf{B}(A)$ that are dense in (A, K) by testing all subsets $\mathbf{Y} \subseteq \mathbf{B}(A)$ such that any $\mathbf{Y}$ contains at most one element from any block of K. The test consists in constructing $\mathbf{T}(\mathbf{Y})$ and verifying whether $\mathbf{T}(\mathbf{Y}) = K$ or not.*

(2) *For any $\mathbf{G}$ that is dense in (A, K) we take an arbitrary set G' equipotent to $\mathbf{G}$ and a bijection h of G' onto $\mathbf{G}$. Put $T' = \mathbf{C}_1(P; G', \mathbf{G}, h)$. This construction provides exactly all row-reduced contexts whose dependence space is P.*

(3) *We take a context $T' = (G', A, r')$ constructed in (2), a finite set H disjoint to G' and a mapping i of H into G'. We put $T = (G, A, r)$ where $G = G' \cup H$ and r is an extension of r' such that for any $(g, a) \in H \times A$ we put $(g, a) \in r$ if and only if $(i(g), a) \in r'$.*

Theorem 18. *Let $P = (A, K)$ be a dependence space. Then the following assertions hold.*

(i) Any context obtained by means of the construction $\mathbf{K}_1$ has a dependence space coinciding with P.

(ii) Any context whose dependence space is P may be obtained by the construction $\mathbf{K}_1$.

Proof. Subsets $\mathbf{G}$ of $\mathbf{B}(A)$ that are dense in (A, K) constructed in (1) are chosen on the basis of Lemma 10. The context T' obtained in (2) has the dependence space P by Theorem 13 and is row-reduced by Lemma 16. If taking the context T constructed in (3), then the construction presented in Lemma 15 provides T'; by this lemma the dependence space of T is P. Thus *(i)* holds.

If T is an arbitrary context whose dependence space is P, we construct a row-reduced context $T' = (G', A, r')$ with the dependence space P on the basis of Lemma 15; T is obtained from T' by construction (3). By Theorem 13 and Lemma 16, there exist parameters $\mathbf{G}$, h such that $T' = \mathbf{C}_1(P; G', \mathbf{G}, h)$, i.e., T' is constructed by (2) where $\mathbf{G}$ is constructed by (1) using Lemma 10. Thus, *(ii)* holds. □

Example 6. We start with the dependence space of Example 5. Since $\mathbf{G} = \{1, 2, 3\}$, we take $G' = \{g_1, g_2, g_3\}$, $h(g_1) = 1$, $h(g_2) = 2$, $h(g_3) = 3$. The table of r' is as follows.

Table 3.

	a	b	c
g_1	1	0	0
g_2	0	1	0
g_3	0	0	1

We put $T' = (G', A, r')$. Clearly, T' is a row-reduced context whose dependence space is $P = (A, K)$ from Example 5. If taking $H = \{g'_1\}$, $i(g'_1) = g_1$, $G = G' \cup H$ and if r is the extension of r' described in (3), we obtain the table

Table 4.

	a	b	c
g_1	1	0	0
g'_1	1	0	0
g_2	0	1	0
g_3	0	0	1

Then $T = (G, A, r)$ is the same context as in Example 5, only the elements of G are denoted in a different way.

Relationship between contexts and the so called black boxes may be found in [NP4], [NP5].

2 Relational Systems

We now intend to investigate the relationship of dependence spaces to information systems. It is advantageous to deal with information systems as relational systems having particular properties.

By a *relational system* we mean a finite nonempty set U with a family $(r_i)_{i\in A}$ of (binary) relations on U where A is a finite nonempty set. A relational system will be denoted by $R = (U, (r_i)_{i\in A})$.

A relational system defines a context in a natural way.

Construction 19. (Construction H)
Let $R = (U, (r_i)_{i\in A})$ *be a relational system. Put*
$r = \{((u_1, u_2), i) \in (U \times U) \times A;\ (u_1, u_2) \in r_i\}$,
$T = (U \times U, A, r)$,
$\mathbf{H}(R) = T$.
The context $\mathbf{H}(R)$ *is said to be constructed by* $\mathbf{H}$ *from* R.

Let $R = (U, (r_i)_{i\in A})$ be a relational system. Then the dependence space $(A, \mathbf{K}^{\mathbf{H}(R)})$ is said to be the *dependence space of the relational system* R.

Relational systems may be assigned to contexts of a particular form in a natural way.

Construction 20. (Construction $\mathbf{H}^{-1}$)
Let $T = (U \times U, A, r)$ *be a context. Put*
$r_i = \{(u_1, u_2) \in U \times U;\ ((u_1, u_2), i) \in r\}$ *for any* $i \in A$,
$R = (U, (r_i)_{i\in A})$,
$\mathbf{H}^{-1}(T) = R$.

The relational system $\mathbf{H}^{-1}(T)$ is said to be *constructed by* $\mathbf{H}^{-1}$ *from* T.

Example 7. Let $U = \{1, 2, 3\}$, $A = \{a, b\}$, let r_a be the natural ordering on U, r_b its dual. We construct $\mathbf{H}(R) = (U \times U, A, r)$ where $R = (U, (r_i)_{i\in A})$. The relation r is presented in Table 5.

We calculate $\mathbf{K}^{\mathbf{H}(R)}$: $\mathbf{t}^{\mathbf{H}(R)}(\emptyset) = U \times U$, $\mathbf{t}^{\mathbf{H}(R)}(\{a\}) = \{(1,1), (1,2), (1,3), (2,2), (2,3), (3,3)\}$, $\mathbf{t}^{\mathbf{H}(R)}(\{b\}) = \{(1,1), (2,1), (2,2), (3,1), (3,2), (3,3)\}$, $\mathbf{t}^{\mathbf{H}(R)}(\{a, b\}) = \{(1,1), (2,2), (3,3)\}$. It follows that $\mathbf{K}^{\mathbf{H}(R)}$ has the following blocks: $\{\emptyset\}$, $\{\{a\}\}$, $\{\{b\}\}$, $\{\{a, b\}\}$.

Example 8. Suppose that $U = \{1, 2, 3\}$, $A = \{a, b, c\}$ and that r is given by Table 6. Then $T = (U \times U, A, r)$ is a context; we construct $\mathbf{H}^{-1}(T) = R$. It follows that
$r_a = \{(1,1), (1,2), (2,1), (2,2), (3,3)\}$,
$r_b = \{(1,1), (1,3), (2,2), (3,1), (3,3)\}$,
$r_c = \{(1,1), (2,2), (2,3), (3,2), (3,3)\}$.
We obtain $\mathbf{H}^{-1}(T) = (U, (r_i)_{i\in A})$ where r_i is an equivalence on U for any $i \in A$.

Table 5.

	a	b
(1, 1)	1	1
(1, 2)	1	0
(1, 3)	1	0
(2, 1)	0	1
(2, 2)	1	1
(2, 3)	1	0
(3, 1)	0	1
(3, 2)	0	1
(3, 3)	1	1

Table 6.

	a	b	c
(1, 1)	1	1	1
(1, 2)	1	0	0
(1, 3)	0	1	0
(2, 1)	1	0	0
(2, 2)	1	1	1
(2, 3)	0	0	1
(3, 1)	0	1	0
(3, 2)	0	0	1
(3, 3)	1	1	1

Theorem 21. *The following assertions hold.*

(i) $\mathbf{H}(\mathbf{H}^{-1}(T)) = T$ *holds for any context* $T = (U \times U, A, r)$.

(ii) $\mathbf{H}^{-1}(\mathbf{H}(R)) = R$ *holds for any relational system* R.

Proof. (1) Let $T = (U \times U, A, r)$ be a context. Then $\mathbf{H}^{-1}(T) = R = (U, (r_i)_{i \in A})$ where $r_i = \{(u_1, u_2) \in U \times U;\ ((u_1, u_2), i) \in r\}$. Furthermore, $\mathbf{H}(\mathbf{H}^{-1}(T)) = \mathbf{H}(R) = (U \times U, A, r')$ where $r' = \{((u_1, u_2), i) \in (U \times U) \times A; (u_1, u_2) \in r_i\}$. It is easy to see that $r' = r$. It follows that $\mathbf{H}(\mathbf{H}^{-1}(T)) = T$.

(2) Let $R = (U, (r_i)_{i \in A})$ be a relational system. Then $\mathbf{H}(R) = T = (U \times U, A, r)$ where $r = \{((u_1, u_2), i) \in (U \times U) \times A;\ (u_1, u_2) \in r_i\}$. Furthermore, $\mathbf{H}^{-1}(T) = (U, (r'_i)_{i \in A})$ where $r'_i = \{(u_1, u_2) \in U \times U;\ ((u_1, u_2), i) \in r\}$ for any $i \in A$. It is easy to see that $r'_i = r_i$ for any $i \in A$. It follows that $\mathbf{H}^{-1}(\mathbf{H}(R)) = \mathbf{H}^{-1}(T) = R$. □

We now solve the following

Problem 22. Construct all relational systems with a prescribed dependence space.

Construction 23. (Construction C_2)

Let $P = (A, K)$ be a dependence space.

We take a finite nonempty set U, a subset $\mathbf{G}$ of $\mathbf{B}(A)$ that is dense in P and a surjection h of $U \times U$ onto $\mathbf{G}$. We put

$r_i = \{(u_1, u_2) \in U \times U;\ i \in h(u_1, u_2)\}$ *for any* $i \in A$,

$R = (U, (r_i)_{i \in A})$,

$\mathbf{C}_2(P; U, \mathbf{G}, h) = R$.

The relational system $\mathbf{C}_2(P; U, \mathbf{G}, h)$ is said to be *constructed by* $\mathbf{C}_2$ *from* P *by means of parameters* U, $\mathbf{G}$, h.

Theorem 24. *Let $P = (A, K)$ be a dependence space, U a finite nonempty set, $\mathbf{G}$ a set dense in P, h a surjection of $U \times U$ onto $\mathbf{G}$. Then the following assertions hold.*

$\mathbf{H}(\mathbf{C}_2(P; U, \mathbf{G}, h)) = \mathbf{C}_1(P; U \times U, \mathbf{G}, h)$,

$\mathbf{H}^{-1}(\mathbf{C}_1(P; U \times U, \mathbf{G}, h) = \mathbf{C}_2(P; U, \mathbf{G}, h)$.

Proof. We have $\mathbf{C}_1(P; U \times U, \mathbf{G}, h) = (U \times U, A, r)$ where $r = \{((u_1, u_2), i) \in (U \times U) \times A;\ i \in h(u_1, u_2)\}$. Furthermore, $\mathbf{C}_2(P; U, \mathbf{G}, h) = (U, (r_i)_{i \in A}) = R$ where $r_i = \{(u_i, u_2) \in U \times U;\ i \in h(u_1, u_2)\}$ for any $i \in A$. It follows that $\mathbf{H}(\mathbf{C}_2(P; U, \mathbf{G}, h)) = \mathbf{H}(R) = (U \times U, A, r')$ where $((u_1, u_2), i) \in r'$ if and only if $(u_1, u_2) \in r_i$ for any $((u_1, u_2), i) \in (U \times U) \times A$. Since $(u_1, u_2) \in r_i$ is equivalent to $i \in h(u_1, u_2)$ for any $((u_1, u_2), i) \in (U \times U) \times A$, we obtain $r' = r$ and, hence, $\mathbf{H}(\mathbf{C}_2(P; U, \mathbf{G}, h)) = \mathbf{C}_1(P; U \times U, \mathbf{G}, h)$. By Theorem 21, we obtain $\mathbf{C}_2(P; U, \mathbf{G}, h) = \mathbf{H}^{-1}(\mathbf{H}(\mathbf{C}_2(P; U, \mathbf{G}, h))) = \mathbf{H}^{-1}(\mathbf{C}_1(P; U \times U, \mathbf{G}, h))$. □

Theorem 25. *The following assertions hold.*

(i) *If P is a dependence space and $R = \mathbf{C}_2(P; U, \mathbf{G}, h)$, where the parameters U, $\mathbf{G}$, h are arbitrary, then the dependence space of R coincides with P.*

(ii) *If $R = (U, (r_i)_{i \in A})$ is a relational system and P its dependence space, then there exist parameters $\mathbf{G}$, h such that $R = \mathbf{C}_2(P; U, \mathbf{G}, h)$.*

Proof. (1) The dependence space of $R = \mathbf{C}_2(P; U, \mathbf{G}, h)$ coincides with the dependence space of $\mathbf{H}(R)$ by definition. By Theorem 24, we obtain that $\mathbf{H}(R) = \mathbf{H}(\mathbf{C}_2(P; U, \mathbf{G}, h)) = \mathbf{C}_1(P; U \times U, \mathbf{G}, h)$. By Theorem 13, the dependence space of $\mathbf{H}(R)$ coincides with P which is *(i)*.

(2) If $R = (U, (r_i)_{i \in A})$ is a relational system and P its dependence space, then the dependence space of $\mathbf{H}(R) = (U \times U, A, r)$ coincides with P. By Theorem 13 there exist parameters $\mathbf{G}$, h such that $\mathbf{H}(R) = \mathbf{C}_1(P; U \times U, \mathbf{G}, h)$. By Theorems 21 and 24 we obtain $R = \mathbf{H}^{-1}(\mathbf{H}(R)) = \mathbf{H}^{-1}(\mathbf{C}_1(P; U \times U, \mathbf{G}, h)) = \mathbf{C}_2(P; U, \mathbf{G}, h)$ which is *(ii)*. □

Lemma 26. *Let $R = (U, (r_i)_{i \in A})$ be a relational system and $P = (A, K)$ its dependence space. Put*

$h(u_1, u_2) = \{i \in A;\ (u_1, u_2) \in r_i\}$ *for any* $(u_1, u_2) \in U \times U$,

$\mathbf{G} = \{h(u_1, u_2);\ (u_1, u_2) \in U \times U\}$.

Then the parameters $\mathbf{G}$, h are such that $R = \mathbf{C}_2(P; U, \mathbf{G}, h)$.

Proof. Put $T = \mathbf{H}(R) = (U \times U, A, r)$ where $r = \{((u_1, u_2), i) \in (U \times U) \times A;\ (u_1, u_2) \in r_i\}$. By Corollary 14, we have $\mathbf{H}(R) = \mathbf{C}_1(P; U \times U, \mathbf{G}, h)$ which implies that $R = \mathbf{H}^{-1}(\mathbf{H}(R)) = \mathbf{C}_2(P; U, \mathbf{G}, h)$ by Theorems 21 and 24. □

Construction 27. (Construction $\mathbf{K}_2$ of all relational systems with a prescribed dependence space)

Let $P = (A, K)$ be a dependence space.

(1) *We find all subsets $\mathbf{G}$ of $\mathbf{B}(A)$ that are dense in (A, K) in the same way as in Construction $\mathbf{K}_1$.*

(2) *For any $\mathbf{G}$ that is dense in P we take an arbitrary finite nonempty set U and a surjection h of $U \times U$ onto $\mathbf{G}$ and put $R = \mathbf{C}_2(P; U, \mathbf{G}, h)$.*

This construction provides exactly all relational systems whose dependence space is P.

In fact, by Theorem 25, the dependence space of the relational system constructed by $\mathbf{K}_2$ coincides with P. If $R = (U, (r_i)_{i \in A})$ is a relational system with the dependence space P, by Lemma 26 and Theorem 25 there exist parameters $\mathbf{G}$, h such that $R = \mathbf{C}_2(P; U, \mathbf{G}, h)$, i.e., R is constructed by $\mathbf{K}_2$.

Example 9. Let $A = \{a, b\}$, suppose that K has the following blocks: $\{\emptyset, \{a\}\}$, $\{\{b\}, \{a, b\}\}$. Then $\mathbf{G} = \{\{a\}, \{a, b\}\}$ is dense in $P = (A, K)$. Let $U = \{1, 2, 3\}$, $h(1,1) = h(1,3) = h(3,2) = \{a\}$, $h(u_1, u_2) = \{a, b\}$ for all remaining elements $(u_1, u_2) \in U \times U$. Then $r_a = U \times U$, $r_b = \{(1,2), (2,1), (2,2), (2,3), (3,1), (3,3)\}$, $R = (U, (r_i)_{i \in A}) = \mathbf{C}_2(P; U, \mathbf{G}, h)$ is constructed by $\mathbf{K}_2$.

Example 10. Let $R = (U, (r_i)_{i \in A})$ be the same as in Example 8. Then $\mathbf{H}(R) = \mathbf{H}(\mathbf{H}^{-1}(T)) = T = (U \times U, A, r)$ where r is given by Table 6. Therefore $\mathbf{t}^{\mathbf{H}(R)}(\emptyset) = U \times U$, $\mathbf{t}^{\mathbf{H}(R)}(\{a\}) = r_a$, $\mathbf{t}^{\mathbf{H}(R)}(\{b\}) = r_b$, $\mathbf{t}^{\mathbf{H}(R)}(\{c\}) = r_c$, $\mathbf{t}^{\mathbf{H}(R)}(Y) = \{(1,1), (2,2), (3,3)\}$ for any remaining $Y \in \mathbf{B}(A)$. Hence, $\mathbf{K}^{\mathbf{H}(R)}$ has the following blocks: $\{\emptyset\}$, $\{\{a\}\}$, $\{\{b\}\}$, $\{\{c\}\}$, $\{\{a,b\}, \{a,c\}, \{b,c\}, \{a,b,c\}\}$. Put $P = (A, \mathbf{K}^{\mathbf{H}(R)})$; P is the dependence space of R.

We now give the parameters $\mathbf{G}$, h such that $R = \mathbf{C}_2(P; U, \mathbf{G}, h)$. By Lemma 26, we put $h(1,1) = h(2,2) = h(3,3) = \{a, b, c\}$, $h(1,2) = h(2,1) = \{a\}$, $h(1,3) = h(3,1) = \{b\}$, $h(2,3) = h(3,2) = \{c\}$, $\mathbf{G} = \{\{a\}, \{b\}, \{c\}, \{a,b,c\}\}$. If constructing $\mathbf{C}_2(P; U, \mathbf{G}, h)$, we obtain R.

We have illustrated that any relational system may be constructed from its dependence space by means of $\mathbf{K}_2$.

A *classificatory system* is a relational system $R = (U, (r_i)_{i \in A})$ where r_i is an equivalence on U for any $i \in A$.

Let P be a dependence space and U, $\mathbf{G}$, h parameters such that $\mathbf{C}_2(P; U, \mathbf{G}, h)$ is a classificatory system. Then the parameters U, $\mathbf{G}$, h are said to be *classification-forming*.

Theorem 28. *The following assertions hold.*

(i) *If P is a dependence space and $R = \mathbf{C}_2(P; U, \mathbf{G}, h)$ where the parameters U, $\mathbf{G}$, h are classification-forming, then R is a classificatory system and its dependence space coincides with P.*

(ii) *If $R = (U, (r_i)_{i \in A})$ is a classificatory system and P its dependence space, then there exist parameters $\mathbf{G}$, h such that U, $\mathbf{G}$, h are classification-forming and $R = \mathbf{C}_2(P; U, \mathbf{G}, h)$.*

Proof. *(i)* is a special case of *(i)* in Theorem 25; the fact that U, $\mathbf{G}$, h are classification-forming implies that R is a classificatory system.

If $R = (U, (r_i)_{i \in A})$ is a classificatory system and P its dependence space, then there exist parameters $\mathbf{G}$, h such that $R = \mathbf{C}_2(P; U, \mathbf{G}, h)$ by *(ii)* of Theorem 25. Since $\mathbf{C}_2(P; U, \mathbf{G}, h)$ is a classificatory system, the parameters U, $\mathbf{G}$, h are classification-forming which is *(ii)*. □

Example 11. The relational system $R = (U, (r_i)_{i \in A})$ from Example 8 is a classificatory one. In Example 10, we have constructed parameters $\mathbf{G}$, h such that $R = \mathbf{C}_2(P; U, \mathbf{G}, h)$; thus U, $\mathbf{G}$, h are classification-forming parameters.

3 Information Systems

In Section 2, classificatory systems have been introduced. We now prove that the difference between information systems and classificatory systems is not essential and may be neglected in some investigations.

Let U, A, V be finite nonempty sets and f a mapping of the set $U \times A$ into V. Then the ordered quadruple $S = (U, A, V, f)$ is said to be an *information system* (cf. [Pa1] Section 5.3, [Pa2], [Pa3], [Pa4], [Pa5], [Pa6], [MP1], [MP2], [NP9]). Elements in U are interpreted as *objects*, elements in A as *attributes*, elements in V as *values of attributes*; if $f(u, a) = v$ for some $(u, a) \in U \times A$, then the attribute a is supposed to assume the value v for the object u.

An information system can be represented by its table. The rows of the table are labelled by objects, the columns by attributes. In the intersection of the row labelled by the object u and the column labelled by the attribute a, there is the value $f(u, a)$. From this point of view, contexts are particular cases of information systems where any attribute assumes only the values 0 or 1. We shall see later that, conversely, any information system may be regarded as a special case of a context; this point of view will be useful.

Example 12. Let $U = \{u_1, \ldots, u_5\}$, $A = \{a_1, \ldots, a_7\}$, $V = \{v_1, v_2, v_3\}$, let f be given by the following table.

Then $S = (U, A, V, f)$ is an information system.

A possible interpretation of this information system is that the objects $u_1, \ldots,$ u_5 are persons, and the attributes a_j represent various physical quantities as follows: a_1 = physical strength, a_2 = weight, a_3 = sprint speed, a_4 = run speed, a_5 = reaction speed, a_6 = gymnastic abilities, a_7 = adaptability. Furthermore, v_1, v_2, v_3 may be interpreted as great, average, and small, respectively. Then the table shows the values of every quality assigned to each person.

Table 7.

	a_1	a_2	a_3	a_4	a_5	a_6	a_7
u_1	v_1	v_1	v_2	v_1	v_1	v_1	v_2
u_2	v_1	v_1	v_2	v_1	v_1	v_2	v_1
u_3	v_1	v_2	v_1	v_1	v_2	v_2	v_2
u_4	v_1	v_2	v_1	v_2	v_3	v_1	v_1
u_5	v_1	v_2	v_1	v_2	v_3	v_1	v_2

First we investigate relationship of information systems to classificatory systems. We describe two constructions that enable to assign an information system to any classificatory one and vice versa.

Construction 29. (Construction F)
Let $R = (U, (r_i)_{i\in A})$ *be a classificatory system. We put*
$V = \bigcup\{U/r_i;\ i \in A\}$,
$f(u,i) = B$ *where* $B \in U/r_i$ *is such that* $u \in B$, *for any* $(u,i) \in U \times A$,
$S = (U, A, V, f)$,
$\mathbf{F}(R) = S$.

Construction 30. (Construction $\mathbf{F}^{-1}$)
Let $S = (U, A, V, f)$ *be an information system. Put*
$r_i = \{(u_1, u_2) \in U \times U;\ f(u_1, i) = f(u_2, i)\}$ *for any* $i \in A$,
$R = (U, (r_i)_{i\in A})$,
$\mathbf{F}^{-1}(S) = R$.

Theorem 31. *If* R *is a classificatory system, then* $\mathbf{F}^{-1}(\mathbf{F}(R)) = R$.

Proof. Suppose $R = (U, (r_i)_{i\in A})$. Then $\mathbf{F}(R) = S = (U, A, V, f)$ where $V = \bigcup\{U/r_i;\ i \in A\}$ and $f(u,i)$ is the block of r_i containing u for any $(u,i) \in U \times A$. Thus, $\mathbf{F}^{-1}(\mathbf{F}(R)) = \mathbf{F}^{-1}(S) = (U, (r_i')_{i\in A})$ where $r_i' = \{(u_1, u_2) \in U\times U;\ f(u_1, i) = f(u_2, i)\} = \{(u_1, u_2) \in U\times U;\ u_1,\ u_2$ are in the same block of $r_i\} = r_i$ for any $i \in A$. Thus $\mathbf{F}^{-1}(\mathbf{F}(R)) = R$. □

Thus, information systems and classificatory systems are almost identical; if constructing $\mathbf{F}^{-1}(S)$ to an information system S, we have forgotten the values of attributes but we have preserved the information whether the values of an attribute for two objects are the same or not; for the problems we are going to study this information is satisfactory.

Let $S = (U, A, V, f)$ be an information system. We define the *dependence space* of S to be the dependence space of $\mathbf{F}^{-1}(S)$. By Section 2, the dependence space of $\mathbf{F}^{-1}(S)$ is $(A, \mathbf{K}^{\mathbf{H}(\mathbf{F}^{-1}(S))})$. Clearly, $T = \mathbf{H}(\mathbf{F}^{-1}(S))$ is a context and $\mathbf{H}^{-1}(T) = \mathbf{F}^{-1}(S)$ holds by Theorem 21. In this sense, an information system may be regarded as a context.

Let $S = (U, A, V, f)$ be an information system. For any $Y \in \mathbf{B}(A)$, we put

$$\mathbf{IND}_S(Y) = \{(u_1, u_2) \in U \times U;\ f(u_1, i) = f(u_2, i) \text{ for any } i \in Y\}.$$

Clearly, $\mathbf{IND}_S(Y)$ is an equivalence on U.

Lemma 32. *If $S = (U, A, V, f)$ is an information system and $Y_1 \in \mathbf{B}(A)$, $Y_2 \in \mathbf{B}(A)$ are sets of attributes, then $\mathbf{IND}_S(Y_1 \cup Y_2) = \mathbf{IND}_S(Y_1) \cap \mathbf{IND}_S(Y_2)$.*

Proof. $\mathbf{IND}_S(Y_1 \cup Y_2) = \{(u_1, u_2) \in U \times U;\ f(u_1, i) = f(u_2, i) \text{ for any } i \in Y_1 \cup Y_2\} = \{(u_1, u_2) \in U \times U;\ f(u_1, i) = f(u_2, i) \text{ for any } i \in Y_1\} \cap \{(u_1, u_2) \in U \times U;\ f(u_1, i) = f(u_2, i) \text{ for any } i \in Y_2\} = \mathbf{IND}_S(Y_1) \cap \mathbf{IND}_S(Y_2)$. □

The assertion of Lemma 32 can be extended to an arbitrary finite sequence of elements $Y_1, \ldots, Y_n$ $(n \geq 1)$ in $\mathbf{B}(A)$ by an easy induction.

Clearly the following holds.

Lemma 33. *Let $S = (U, A, V, f)$ be an information system, $Y \in \mathbf{B}(A)$ a set of attributes, u, $u' \in U$ objects. Then u, u' are in different blocks of $\mathbf{IND}_S(Y)$ if and only if there exists $a \in Y$ such that $f(u, a) \neq f(u', a)$.*

If $S = (U, A, V, f)$ is an information system and $Y \in \mathbf{B}(A)$ is a set of attributes, then Y may be regarded as a *test*, the *result of* this *test* is the equivalence $\mathbf{IND}_S(Y)$; if $(u_1, u_2) \in \mathbf{IND}_S(Y)$, then u_1, u_2 are *indiscernible* by the test Y. If $Y' \subseteq Y \subseteq A$, the test Y' is said to be a *subtest* of Y.

Hence, Lemma 33 solves the following

Problem 34. If $S = (U, A, V, f)$ is an information system, $Y \in \mathbf{B}(A)$ is a test, and u_1, $u_2 \in U$ objects, decide whether u_1, u_2 are indiscernible by Y or not.

The following problem is very natural.

Problem 35. If $S = (U, A, V, f)$ is an information system and $Y_1 \in \mathbf{B}(A)$, $Y_2 \in \mathbf{B}(A)$ are tests, decide, whether the results of Y_1, Y_2 are the same or not.

If one of the sets Y_1, Y_2 is empty, it is sufficient to investigate whether the equivalence defined by the other set is $U \times U$; this can be done on the basis of Lemma 33.

The general case is solved by the following

Theorem 36. *Let $S = (U, A, V, f)$ be an information system and $Y_1 \in \mathbf{B}(A)$, $Y_2 \in \mathbf{B}(A)$ be nonempty sets. Then the following assertions are equivalent.*

(i) $\mathbf{IND}_S(Y_1) \not\subseteq \mathbf{IND}_S(Y_2)$.

(ii) There exist $u \in U$, $u' \in U$ and $a_0 \in Y_2$ such that $f(u, a_0) \neq f(u', a_0)$ and $f(u, a) = f(u', a)$ for any $a \in Y_1$.

Proof. If *(i)* holds, there exist $u \in U$, $u' \in U$ such that $(u, u') \in \mathbf{IND}_S(Y_1)$, $(u, u') \notin \mathbf{IND}_S(Y_2)$. By Lemma 33, there exists $a_0 \in Y_2$ such that $f(u, a_0) \neq f(u', a_0)$ while $f(u, a) = f(u', a)$ for any $a \in Y_1$ which is *(ii)*.

Clearly, *(ii)* means $(u, u') \notin \mathbf{IND}_S(Y_2)$, $(u, u') \in \mathbf{IND}(Y_1)$ by Lemma 33 which is *(i)*. □

Example 13. We continue Example 12. Put $Y_1 = \{a_1, \dots, a_5\}$, $Y_2 = \{a_2, a_3, a_6\}$, $Y_3 = \{a_4, a_5\}$.

Then $f(u_1, a_6) = v_1 \neq v_2 = f(u_2, a_6)$, $f(u_1, a) = f(u_2, a)$ for any $a \in Y_1$. Thus, the results of tests Y_1 and Y_2 are different by Theorem 36.

Furthermore, $Y_3 \subseteq Y_1$ which implies, by definition of $\mathbf{IND}_S$, that $\mathbf{IND}_S(Y_1) \subseteq \mathbf{IND}_S(Y_3)$. The equivalence $\mathbf{IND}_S(Y_3)$ has the following blocks: $\{u_1, u_2\}$, $\{u_3\}$, $\{u_4, u_5\}$. For any $a \in Y_1$ and any u, u' from one block, it follows from the table that $f(u, a) = f(u', a)$. Thus, $\mathbf{IND}_S(Y_3) \subseteq \mathbf{IND}_S(Y_1)$ by Theorem 36. Hence, $\mathbf{IND}_S(Y_1) = \mathbf{IND}_S(Y_3)$ and the tests Y_1, Y_3 provide the same results.

It follows that in the situation described in Example 12, the test Y_1 is too large; a smaller test Y_3 may render the same service.

Problem 35 inspires the following definition.

Let $S = (U, A, V, f)$ be an information system. We put

$$\mathbf{K}_S = \{(Y_1, Y_2) \in \mathbf{B}(A) \times \mathbf{B}(A);\ \mathbf{IND}_S(Y_1) = \mathbf{IND}_S(Y_2)\}.$$

Clearly, $\mathbf{K}_S$ is an equivalence on the set $\mathbf{B}(A)$.

Theorem 37. *If $S = (U, A, V, f)$ is an information system, then $\mathbf{K}_S$ is a congruence on the semilattice $(\mathbf{B}(A), \cup)$.*

Proof. Let Y_1, Y_1', Y_2, Y_2' be subsets of A such that $(Y_1, Y_1') \in \mathbf{K}_S$, $(Y_2, Y_2') \in \mathbf{K}_S$. Then $\mathbf{IND}_S(Y_1) = \mathbf{IND}_S(Y_1')$, $\mathbf{IND}_S(Y_2) = \mathbf{IND}_S(Y_2')$ which implies that $\mathbf{IND}_S(Y_1 \cup Y_2) = \mathbf{IND}_S(Y_1) \cap \mathbf{IND}_S(Y_2) = \mathbf{IND}_S(Y_1') \cap \mathbf{IND}_S(Y_2') = \mathbf{IND}_S(Y_1' \cup Y_2')$ by Lemma 32. Hence $(Y_1 \cup Y_2, Y_1' \cup Y_2') \in \mathbf{K}_S$ and the assertion holds. □

Corollary 38. *If $S = (U, A, V, f)$ is an information system, then $(A, \mathbf{K}_S)$ is a dependence space.*

Theorem 39. *The dependence space of an arbitrary information system $S = (U, A, V, f)$ coincides with $(A, \mathbf{K}_S)$.*

Proof. By Section 2, $\mathbf{F}^{-1}(S) = (U, (r_i)_{i \in A})$ where $r_i = \{(u_1, u_2) \in U \times U;\ f(u_1, i) = f(u_2, i)\}$ for any $i \in A$; we see that $r_i = \mathbf{IND}_S(\{i\})$. Furthermore $\mathbf{H}(\mathbf{F}^{-1}(S)) = (U \times U, A, r)$ where $r = \{((u_1, u_2), i) \in (U \times U) \times A;\ (u_1, u_2) \in r_i\} = \{((u_1, u_2), i) \in (U \times U) \times A;\ (u_1, u_2) \in \mathbf{IND}_S(\{i\})\}$. Thus for any $Y \in \mathbf{B}(A)$, we obtain $\mathbf{t}^{\mathbf{H}(\mathbf{F}^{-1}(S))}(Y) = \{(u_1, u_2) \in U \times U;\ ((u_1, u_2), i) \in r \text{ for any } i \in Y\} = \{(u_1, u_2) \in U \times U;\ (u_1, u_2) \in \mathbf{IND}_S(\{i\}) \text{ for any } i \in Y\} = \{(u_1, u_2) \in U \times U;\ (u_1, u_2) \in \bigcap\{\mathbf{IND}_S(\{i\}) \text{ for any } i \in Y\}\} = \mathbf{IND}_S(Y)$ by Lemma 32.

It follows that for any Y_1, $Y_2 \in \mathbf{B}(A)$ the following holds: $(Y_1, Y_2) \in \mathbf{K}^{\mathbf{H}(\mathbf{F}^{-1}(S))}$ is equivalent to $\mathbf{t}^{\mathbf{H}(\mathbf{F}^{-1}(S))}(Y_1) = \mathbf{t}^{\mathbf{H}(\mathbf{F}^{-1}(S))}(Y_2)$ which means $\mathbf{IND}_S(Y_1) = \mathbf{IND}_S(Y_2)$; this is equivalent to $(Y_1, Y_2) \in \mathbf{K}_S$.

We have proved that $\mathbf{K}^{\mathbf{H}(\mathbf{F}^{-1}(S))} = \mathbf{K}_S$. □

This enables to solve the following

Problem 40. If $S = (U, A, V, f)$ is an information system and $Y \in \mathbf{B}(A)$ a test, find its minimal subtest Y' such that the results of Y, Y' are the same.

The solution is presented in the following

Theorem 41. *Let $S = (U, A, V, f)$ be an information system, Y, Y' tests. Then the following assertions are equivalent.*

(i) *Y' is a $\mathbf{K}_S$-reduct of Y.*

(ii) *Y' is minimal with respect to inclusion among all sets Z such that $Z \subseteq Y$, $\mathbf{IND}_S(Z) = \mathbf{IND}_S(Y)$.*

Proof. This is only a paraphrase of the definition of a $\mathbf{K}_S$-reduct; cf. Section 10 of Chapter 7. □

This result enables to look for subtests using Algorithms 71 and 75 of Chapter 7; conditions of the form $(Y_1, Y_2) \in \mathbf{K}_S$ appearing in Algorithm 71 may be verified on the basis of Theorem 36.

Example 14. We continue Example 13. We have found that $Y_3 \subseteq Y_1$, $\mathbf{IND}_S(Y_3) = \mathbf{IND}_S(Y_1)$, i.e., $(Y_1, Y_3) \in \mathbf{K}_S$. Clearly, $(Y_3, \{a_5\}) \in \mathbf{K}_S$, $(Y_3, \{a_4\}) \notin \mathbf{K}_S$, $(\{a_5\}, \emptyset) \notin \mathbf{K}_S$. Thus, $\{a_5\}$ is minimal among all sets $Y \in \mathbf{B}(A)$ with the property $(Y_1, Y) \in \mathbf{K}_S$. Hence $\{a_5\}$ is a $\mathbf{K}_S$-reduct of Y_1.

Example 15. In our previous examples only small information systems appear and, owing to this fact, they are not too convincing. However, an information system may consist of many objects and several attributes on which tests are based. For example, U could be a set of products of a factory that are manufactured in the same way. They should be equal but they differ a little from each other. Thus, they are tested and classified by measuring certain characteristics, i.e., by stating the values of certain attributes. If Y is the set of these attributes and Y' is its subset that provides the same result, it is clear that it is more convenient to operate only with the set Y'.

One can object that the situation found for the information system $S = (U, A, V, f)$ need not take place for the information system $S' = (U', A, V, f')$ where U' is another set of products of the same type as above. But we may assume that the first information system S was large enough to provide objective knowledge valid in all information systems of the described type, namely, that the set of attributes Y and Y' provide the same results if they are regarded as tests. From this point of view the problem of finding reducts is important.

Let $S = (U, A, V, f)$ be an information system, $Y \in \mathbf{B}(A)$ a set of attributes. Any subset of Y may be regarded as a test, i.e., $\mathbf{B}(Y)$ is a set of tests. It is natural to ask whether Y may be reduced to some subset Y' such that the results of tests in $\mathbf{B}(Y)$ are the same as the results of tests in $\mathbf{B}(Y')$. More exactly, we have

Problem 42. If $S = (U, A, V, f)$ is an information system and $Y \in \mathbf{B}(A)$ a test, find its minimal subtest Y' such that for any test in $\mathbf{B}(Y)$ there exists a test in $\mathbf{B}(Y')$ providing the same result.

The solution is presented in the following

Theorem 43. *Let $S = (U, A, V, f)$ be an information system, Y, Y' sets of attributes. Then the following assertions are equivalent.*

(i) *Y' is a $\mathbf{K}_S$-superreduct of Y.*

(ii) *Y' is minimal with respect to inclusion among all sets Z with the following properties.*

(a) *$Z \subseteq Y$.*

(b) *For any subtest of Y there exists a subtest of Z providing the same result.*

Proof. This follows immediately from the definition of K-superreducts presented in Section 9 of Chapter 7 if we take $\mathbf{K}_S$ for K. □

Example 16. Consider the information system $S = (U, A, V, f)$ from Example 12, put $Y = \{a_1, \ldots, a_5\}$. We shall find its $\mathbf{K}_S$-superreducts. Thus, in the table of S we cancel the last two columns. Then we use Algorithm 70 of Section 9 in Chapter 7. We obtain $\mathbf{C}(\mathbf{K}_S)(\{a_1\}) = \{a_1\}$, $\mathbf{C}(\mathbf{K}_S)(\{a_2\}) = \mathbf{C}(\mathbf{K}_S)(\{a_3\}) = \{a_1, a_2, a_3\}$, $\mathbf{C}(\mathbf{K}_S)(\{a_4\}) = \{a_1, a_4\}$, $\mathbf{C}(\mathbf{K}_S)(\{a_5\}) = \{a_1, a_2, a_3, a_4, a_5\}$ which can be read from the table. Furthermore, r has the following blocks: $\{a_1\}$, $\{a_2, a_3\}$, $\{a_4\}$, $\{a_5\}$. Thus, the set Z may be chosen as follows: $Z = \{a_1, a_2, a_4, a_5\}$. Furthermore, $Y(a_1) = \emptyset$, $Y(a_2) = \{a_1\}$, $Y(a_4) = \{a_1\}$, $Y(a_5) = \{a_1, a_2, a_4\}$. It follows that $(Y(a_1), \{a_1\}) = (\emptyset, \{a_1\}) \in \mathbf{K}_S$, $(Y(a_2), \{a_2\}) = (\{a_1\}, \{a_2\}) \notin \mathbf{K}_S$, $(Y(a_4), \{a_4\}) = (\{a_1\}, \{a_4\}) \notin \mathbf{K}_S$, $(Y(a_5), \{a_5\}) = (\{a_1, a_2, a_4\}, \{a_5\}) \in \mathbf{K}_S$ which can be obtained by Theorem 36. It follows that $M = \{a_2, a_4\}$ is a $\mathbf{K}_S$-superreduct of Y. Clearly, M provides 2^2 tests while the number of tests provided by Y is 2^5. Another $\mathbf{K}_S$-superreduct of Y is $\{a_3, a_4\}$.

Example 17. Let $S = (U, A, V, f)$ be an information system. Then any object $u \in U$ is described by means of values of attributes in A. Two objects u, u' in U are indiscernible if and only if $f(u, a) = f(u', a)$ for any $a \in A$, i.e., if and only if $(u, u') \in \mathbf{IND}_S(A)$.

If a set $X \in \mathbf{B}(A)$ of objects is given, the information system has, generally, no instruments for an exact description of X; it can only present two approximations of X as follows.

(1) All objects in U are found such that for any of them there exists an object in X with the same values of attributes. Hence, the constructed set is $\{u' \in U;$ there exists $u \in X$ with $f(u, a) = f(u', a)$ for any $a \in A\} = \{u' \in U;$ there exists $u \in X$ with $(u, u') \in \mathbf{IND}_S(A)\} = \bigcup\{B \in U/\mathbf{IND}_S(A);\ B \cap X \neq \emptyset\} = \mathbf{c}(\mathbf{IND}_S(A))(X)$.

(2) All objects in U are found such that for any of them all objects with the same values of attributes are in X. Hence, the constructed set is $\{u' \in U;\ u \in U$, $f(u', a) = f(u, a)$ for any $a \in A$ imply that $u \in X\} = \{u' \in U;\ u \in U$, $(u, u') \in \mathbf{IND}_S(A)$ imply that $u \in X\} = \bigcup\{B \in U/\mathbf{IND}_S(A);\ B \subseteq X\} = \mathbf{d}(\mathbf{IND}_S(A))(X)$.

Thus, the upper approximations and lower approximations studied in Sections 5 and 6 of Chapter 7 play an important role.

4 Dependence in Information Systems

As we have seen, any information system $S = (U, A, V, f)$ has a dependence space $(A, \mathbf{K}_S)$ where the dependence relation between subsets of A is defined. The next theorem expresses its meaning in terms of information systems.

Theorem 44. *Let $S = (U, A, V, f)$ be an information system, X, Y elements in $\mathbf{B}(A)$. Then $X \to Y$ $(A, \mathbf{K}_S)$ holds if and only if $\mathbf{IND}_S(X) \subseteq \mathbf{IND}_S(Y)$.*

Proof. (1) If $\mathbf{IND}_S(X) \subseteq \mathbf{IND}_S(Y)$, then $\mathbf{IND}_S(X \cup Y) = \mathbf{IND}_S(X) \cap \mathbf{IND}_S(Y) = \mathbf{IND}_S(X)$ by Lemma 32. Thus, $(X \cup Y, X) \in \mathbf{K}_S$ which implies that $\mathbf{C}(\mathbf{K}_S)(Y) \subseteq \mathbf{C}(\mathbf{K}_S)(X \cup Y) = \mathbf{C}(\mathbf{K}_S)(X)$ using the fact that $\mathbf{C}(\mathbf{K}_S)$ is a closure operator (Theorem 17 of Chapter 7). Thus $X \to Y$ $(A, \mathbf{K}_S)$ holds.

(2) If $X \to Y$ $(A, \mathbf{K}_S)$, then $\mathbf{C}(\mathbf{K}_S)(Y) \subseteq \mathbf{C}(\mathbf{K}_S)(X)$. Hence we obtain $\mathbf{IND}_S(\mathbf{C}(\mathbf{K}_S)(X)) = \mathbf{IND}_S(\mathbf{C}(\mathbf{K}_S)(X) \cup \mathbf{C}(\mathbf{K}_S)(Y)) = \mathbf{IND}_S(\mathbf{C}(\mathbf{K}_S)(X)) \cap \mathbf{IND}_S(\mathbf{C}(\mathbf{K}_S)(Y))$ and, therefore, $\mathbf{IND}_S(\mathbf{C}(\mathbf{K}_S)(X)) \subseteq \mathbf{IND}_S(\mathbf{C}(\mathbf{K}_S)(Y))$. Clearly, $(X, \mathbf{C}(\mathbf{K}_S)(X)) \in \mathbf{K}_S$ by definition of $\mathbf{C}(\mathbf{K}_S)$; it follows that $\mathbf{IND}_S(X) = \mathbf{IND}_S(\mathbf{C}(\mathbf{K}_S)(X))$. Similarly, $\mathbf{IND}_S(Y) = \mathbf{IND}_S(\mathbf{C}(\mathbf{K}_S)(Y))$. Thus, we obtain that $\mathbf{IND}_S(X) \subseteq \mathbf{IND}_S(Y)$. □

Example 18. If $S = (U, A, V, f)$ is an information system and X, $Y \in \mathbf{B}(A)$ are tests, then $X \to Y$ $(A, \mathbf{K}_S)$ means that the result of the test X is finer or as fine as the result of the test Y. Thus, if we agree that a test with a finer result is better, then $X \to Y$ $(A, \mathbf{K}_S)$ expresses the fact that the test X is better or as good as Y. This means that it is superfluous to apply the test Y after the test X.

We come back to Example 15 where products of a factory that are manufactured in the same way are considered. They are tested by stating values of some attributes. We may imagine that fixed sets of attributes, so called compound attributes (cf. [Pa7], p. 55), are evaluated. To be more concrete, suppose that compound attributes Z_1, Z_2, Z_3, Z_4 are defined and evaluated for any product. Then new compound attributes X_1, X_2, Y_1, Y_2 are defined similarly as in Example 39 of Chapter 7. It is useful to know whether $X_1 \to Y_1$ $(A, \mathbf{K}_S)$ holds or not; in the positive case the test Y_1 is superfluous. Similarly for the condition $X_2 \to Y_2$ $(A, \mathbf{K}_S)$.

In Example 39 of Chapter 7 we have proved by means of sequent methods that both conditions are satisfied. Cf. also [NoM1], [NoM2].

Obviously, the fact $X \to Y$ $(A, \mathbf{K}_S)$ implies that if u, $u' \in U$ have the same values for all attributes in X, then they have the same values of all attributes in Y. In this sense, the values of attributes in X determine the values of attributes in Y. More exactly, let $S = (U, A, V, f)$ be an information system, X, Y sets of attributes. We say that the *values of attributes in Y are determined by the values of attributes in X* if the following holds: if u, u' are arbitrary objects and the values of attributes in X are the same for u and u', then also the values of attributes in Y are the same for u and u'. Clearly, the values of attributes in Y are determined by the values of attributes in X if and only if $\mathbf{IND}_S(X) \subseteq \mathbf{IND}_S(Y)$, i.e., if and only if $X \to Y\ (A, \mathbf{K}_S)$.

Thus, these facts give rise to a natural problem.

Problem 45. Let $S = (U, A, V, f)$ be an information system, X, Y elements in $\mathbf{B}(A)$. Recognize whether $X \to Y\ (A, \mathbf{K}_S)$ holds or not.

This problem is solved by Theorem 44 and Theorem 36.

Another natural problem is the following

Problem 46. Let $S = (U, A, V, f)$ be an information system, X, Y elements in $\mathbf{B}(A)$ such that $X \to Y\ (A, \mathbf{K}_S)$. Find a minimal subset X' of X such that $X' \to Y\ (A, \mathbf{K}_S)$.

This means also: Find a minimal subtest of the test X that is better or as good as the test Y.

Another formulation: Find a minimal subset X' of the set X such that the values of attributes in X' determine the values of attributes in Y.

This problem is solved by the following theorem.

Theorem 47. *Let $S = (U, A, V, f)$ be an information system, X, Y elements in $\mathbf{B}(A)$ such that $X \to Y\ (A, \mathbf{K}_S)$, X' an element in $\mathbf{B}(A)$. Then the following assertions are equivalent.*

(i) *X' is minimal with respect to inclusion among all sets Z with the properties $Z \subseteq X$, $Z \to Y\ (A, \mathbf{K}_S)$.*
(ii) *X' is a $\mathbf{D}(\mathbf{K}_S, Y)$-reduct of X.*

Proof. This is a particular case of Theorem 93 of Chapter 7. □

We complete these investigations by presenting the explicit definition of the congruence $\mathbf{D}(\mathbf{K}_S, Y)$.

Theorem 48. *Let $S = (U, A, V, f)$ be an information system, $Y \in \mathbf{B}(A)$ a set. For any $X \in \mathbf{B}(A)$ and any $X' \in \mathbf{B}(A)$ the condition $(X, X') \in \mathbf{D}(\mathbf{K}_S, Y)$ is satisfied if and only if one of the following conditions (i), (ii) holds.*

(i) $\mathbf{IND}_S(X) \subseteq \mathbf{IND}_S(Y)$, $\mathbf{IND}_S(X') \subseteq \mathbf{IND}_S(Y)$.
(ii) $\mathbf{IND}_S(X') = \mathbf{IND}_S(X) \not\subseteq \mathbf{IND}_S(Y)$.

Proof. This result is obtained from the definition of $\mathbf{D}(\mathbf{K}_S, Y)$ if it is expressed by means of the relation $\to\ (A, \mathbf{K}_S)$ and then by means of $\mathbf{IND}_S$ on the basis of Theorem 44. □

Example 19. Let $S = (U, A, V, f)$ be an information system where $U = \{1, 2, 3, 4\}$, $A = \{a, b, c, d, e\}$, $V = \{0, 1, 2\}$ and f is given by Table 8.
(cf. [Pa7] p. 70). Put $X = \{a, b, c\}$, $Y = \{d, e\}$. Then $\mathbf{IND}_S(X) = \mathrm{id}_U$ while $\mathbf{IND}_S(Y)$ has the following blocks: $\{1, 3\}$, $\{2\}$, $\{4\}$. Thus, $\mathbf{IND}_S(X) \subseteq \mathbf{IND}_S(Y)$ and, therefore, $X \to Y\ (A, \mathbf{K}_S)$.

Table 8.

	a	b	c	d	e
1	2	0	0	1	1
2	1	1	0	2	2
3	2	2	0	1	1
4	2	1	1	1	2

We shall look for $\mathbf{D}(\mathbf{K}_S, Y)$-reducts of X; suppose that o is the linear ordering of X where the order of elements is a, b, c. Put $\mathbf{SC}^{(0)} = X$. Using Algorithm 71 of Chapter 7, we state that $\mathbf{IND}_S(\{b, c\}) = \mathrm{id}_U$, which implies $\mathbf{IND}_S(X - \{a\}) \subseteq \mathbf{IND}_S(Y)$ and, therefore, $(X, X - \{a\}) \in \mathbf{D}(\mathbf{K}_S, Y)$. Thus $\mathbf{SC}^{(1)} = \mathbf{SC}(X, \mathbf{D}(\mathbf{K}_S, Y), X, o) = \{b, c\}$. Furthermore, $\mathbf{IND}_S(\{c\})$ has the blocks $\{1, 2, 3\}$, $\{4\}$, $\mathbf{IND}_S(\{b\})$ has the blocks $\{1\}$, $\{2, 4\}$, $\{3\}$. It follows that $\mathbf{IND}_S(\{c\}) \nsubseteq \mathbf{IND}_S(Y)$, $\mathbf{IND}_S(\{b\}) \nsubseteq \mathbf{IND}_S(Y)$; therefore $(\{b, c\}, \{b, c\} - \{z\}) \notin \mathbf{D}(\mathbf{K}_S, Y)$ for any $z \in \{b, c\}$. This implies that $\mathbf{SC}^{(2)} = \mathbf{SC}^{(1)}$ and $\{b, c\}$ is a $\mathbf{D}(\mathbf{K}_S, Y)$-reduct of X. Similarly, we find further $\mathbf{D}(\mathbf{K}_S, Y)$-reducts $\{a, c\}$, $\{a, b\}$. We have used abbreviated symbols similarly as in examples of Section 11 of Chapter 7.

In this example the values of attributes in Y are determined by the values of attributes in X and some attributes in X are superfluous. For example, the values of attributes b, c determine the values in Y, i.e., the attribute a is superfluous. But not only attributes may be superfluous, also some values of attributes can have this property. In order to express this property formally, we formulate some definitions.

Let $S = (U, A, V, f)$ be an information system. Elements in the set $A \times V$ are said to be *descriptors*. If $u \in U$, $(a, v) \in A \times V$ and $f(u, a) = v$, then (a, v) is said to be a *descriptor of the object* u. Put

$$r_S = \{(u, (a, v)) \in U \times (A \times V));\ f(u, a) = v\}\ .$$

Then r_S is a correspondence from U to $A \times V$; we set $T(S) = (U, A \times V, r_S)$. Clearly, $T(S)$ is a context. In accord with Section 1, we define the Galois connection to this context.

Let $S = (U, A, V, f)$ be an information system, $X \in \mathbf{B}(U)$, $Y \in \mathbf{B}(A \times V)$ sets. We put

$\mathbf{s}^{T(S)}(X) = \{(a, v) \in A \times V;\ (u, (a, v)) \in r_S$ for any $u \in X\} = \{(a, v) \in A \times V;\ f(u, a) = v$ for any $u \in X\}$,

$\mathbf{t}^{T(S)}(Y) = \{u \in U;\ (u, (a, v)) \in r_S$ for any $(a, v) \in Y\} = \{u \in U;\ f(u, a) = v$ for any $(a, v) \in Y\}$,

$\mathbf{p}^{T(S)}(X) = \mathbf{t}^{T(S)}(\mathbf{s}^{T(S)}(X))$,

$\mathbf{q}^{T(S)}(Y) = \mathbf{s}^{T(S)}(\mathbf{t}^{T(S)}(Y))$.

On the basis of Section 1, we define

$$\mathbf{K}^{T(S)} = \{(Z_1, Z_2) \in \mathbf{B}(A \times V) \times \mathbf{B}(A \times V);\ \mathbf{t}^{T(S)}(Z_1) = \mathbf{t}^{T(S)}(Z_2)\}.$$

By Theorem 1, $\mathbf{K}^{T(S)}$ is a congruence on the semilattice $(\mathbf{B}(A \times V), \cup)$ and, hence, $(A \times V, \mathbf{K}^{T(S)})$ is a dependence space.

By Lemma 3, we obtain immediately

Lemma 49. *Let $S = (U, A, V, f)$ be an information system and $Y \in \mathbf{B}(A \times V)$ a set of descriptors. Then $\mathbf{C}(\mathbf{K}^{T(S)})(Y) = \mathbf{q}^{T(S)}(Y)$.*

Similarly, by Corollary 4, we have

Theorem 50. *Let $S = (U, A, V, f)$ be an information system and X, Y sets in $\mathbf{B}(A \times V)$. Then $X \to Y$ $(A \times V, \mathbf{K}^{T(S)})$ holds if and only if $\mathbf{t}^{T(S)}(X) \subseteq \mathbf{t}^{T(S)}(Y)$.*

We know that the dependence relation $X \to Y$ $(A \times V, \mathbf{K}^{T(S)})$ is in a close connection with the congruence $\mathbf{D}(\mathbf{K}^{T(S)}, Y)$. By Corollary 5, we obtain

Theorem 51. *Let $S = (U, A, V, f)$ be an information system and Y a set in $\mathbf{B}(A \times V)$. Then for any X, $X' \in \mathbf{B}(A \times V)$ the condition $(X, X') \in \mathbf{D}(\mathbf{K}^{T(S)}, Y)$ is satisfied if and only if one of the following conditions (i), (ii) is satisfied.*

(i) $\mathbf{t}^{T(S)}(X) \subseteq \mathbf{t}^{T(S)}(Y)$, $\mathbf{t}^{T(S)}(X') \subseteq \mathbf{t}^{T(S)}(Y)$,
(ii) $\mathbf{t}^{T(S)}(X') = \mathbf{t}^{T(S)}(X) \not\subseteq \mathbf{t}^{T(S)}(Y)$.

Theorem 93 of Chapter 7 may be reformulated as follows.

Theorem 52. *Let $S = (U, A, V, f)$ be an information system and X, $Y \in \mathbf{B}(A \times V)$ sets of descriptors such that $X \to Y$ $(A \times V, \mathbf{K}^{T(S)})$. Then for any $X' \in \mathbf{B}(A \times V)$ the following conditions are equivalent.*

(i) X' is minimal with respect to inclusion among all sets Z such that $Z \subseteq X$, $Z \to Y$ $(A \times V, \mathbf{K}^{T(S)})$.
(ii) X' is a $\mathbf{D}(\mathbf{K}^{T(S)}, Y)$-reduct of X.

Example 20. We continue Example 19. Put $X = \{(a,2), (b,0), (b,2), (c,0)\}$, $Y = \{(d,1), (e,1)\}$. Then $\mathbf{t}^{T(S)}(X) = \emptyset \subseteq \{1,3\} = \mathbf{t}^{T(S)}(Y)$. Thus, $X \to Y$ $(A \times V, \mathbf{K}^{T(S)})$. We find a $\mathbf{D}(\mathbf{K}^{T(S)}, Y)$-reduct of X.

Put $X' = \{(a,2), (b,2), (c,0)\}$. Then $\mathbf{t}^{T(S)}(X') = \{3\} \subseteq \mathbf{t}^{T(S)}(Y)$. Thus, $(X', X) \in \mathbf{D}(\mathbf{K}^{T(S)}, Y)$. Set $X'' = \{(a,2), (b,2)\}$. Then $\mathbf{t}^{T(S)}(X'') = \{3\} \subseteq \mathbf{t}^{T(S)}(Y)$ which implies that $(X'', X') \in \mathbf{D}(\mathbf{K}^{T(S)}, Y)$. We now put $X''' = \{(b,2)\}$. Then $\mathbf{t}^{T(S)}(X''') = \{3\} \subseteq \mathbf{t}^{T(S)}(Y)$ and, hence, $(X''', X'') \in \mathbf{D}(\mathbf{K}^{T(S)}, Y)$. If $X^{(iv)} = \emptyset$, then $\mathbf{t}^{T(S)}(X^{(iv)}) = \{1,2,3,4\} \not\subseteq \mathbf{t}^{T(S)}(Y)$. Thus, X''' is a $\mathbf{D}(\mathbf{K}^{T(S)}, Y)$-reduct of X.

We now limit our considerations to sets of descriptors that belong to one row of the table. More exactly, let $S = (U, A, V, f)$ be an information system. For any $X \in \mathbf{B}(A \times V)$ we put $\mathbf{Pr}(X) = \{a \in A;$ there exists $v \in V$ such that $(a, v) \in X\}$. If $u_0 \in U$, we denote by $\mathbf{Bl}(S, u_0, X)$ the block of the equivalence $\mathbf{IND}_S(\mathbf{Pr}(X))$ containing u_0.

Lemma 53. *Let $S = (U, A, V, f)$ be an information system, $u_0 \in U$ an arbitrary object. If $X \subseteq \mathbf{s}^{T(S)}(\{u_0\})$, then $\mathbf{t}^{T(S)}(X) = \mathbf{Bl}(S, u_0, X)$.*

Proof. In the following sequence of conditions any two consecutive ones are equivalent.

(i) $u \in \mathbf{t}^{T(S)}(X)$;
(ii) $f(u, a) = v$ for any $(a, v) \in X$;
(iii) $f(u, a) = f(u_0, a)$ for any $a \in \mathbf{Pr}(X)$;
(iv) $(u, u_0) \in \mathbf{IND}_S(\mathbf{Pr}(X))$;
(v) $u \in \mathbf{Bl}(S, u_0, X)$.

□

Using this lemma, we may transcribe Theorem 50 as follows.

Theorem 54. *Let $S = (U, A, V, f)$ be an information system, $u_0 \in U$ an arbitrary object, X, Y sets of descriptors that are subsets of $\mathbf{s}^{T(S)}(\{u_0\})$. Then the condition $X \to Y$ $(A \times V, \mathbf{K}^{T(S)})$ holds if and only if $\mathbf{Bl}(S, u_0, X) \subseteq \mathbf{Bl}(S, u_0, Y)$.*

Hence, under the hypothesis of Theorem 54, the block of $\mathbf{IND}_S(\mathbf{Pr}(X))$ containing u_0 is a subset of the block of $\mathbf{IND}_S(\mathbf{Pr}(Y))$ that contains u_0. This means that objects whose descriptors are in X form a subset of the set of objects whose descriptors are in Y, i.e., descriptors in Y are determined by descriptors in X. More exactly, let $S = (U, A, V, f)$ be an information system, u_0 an object, X, Y sets of its descriptors. The *set Y of descriptors is said to be determined by the set X* if the following holds: If $u \in U$ is an arbitrary object such that all descriptors from X belong to u, then also all descriptors from Y belong to u. Clearly, the set Y of descriptors is determined by the set X if and only if $\mathbf{Bl}(S, u_0, X) \subseteq \mathbf{Bl}(S, u_0, Y)$, i.e., if and only if $X \to Y$ $(A \times V, \mathbf{K}^{T(S)})$.Thus, the following problem is natural.

Problem 55. Let $S = (U, A, V, f)$ be an information system, $u_0 \in U$ an arbitrary object, X, Y sets of descriptors that are subsets of $\mathbf{s}^{T(S)}(\{u_0\})$ such that $X \to Y$ $(A \times V, \mathbf{K}^{T(S)})$. Find a minimal subset X' of X such that $X' \to Y$ $(A \times V, \mathbf{K}^{T(S)})$.

This problem is solved by Theorem 52 where the relation $\mathbf{D}(\mathbf{K}^{T(S)}, Y)$ between two sets of descriptors may be recognized by means of the following

Theorem 56. *Let $S = (U, A, V, f)$ be an information system, $u_0 \in U$ an arbitrary object. If X, X', Y are subsets of $\mathbf{s}^{T(S)}(\{u_0\})$, then $(X, X') \in \mathbf{D}(\mathbf{K}^{T(S)}, Y)$ holds if and only if one of the following conditions (i), (ii) is satisfied.*

(i) $\mathbf{Bl}(S, u_0, X) \subseteq \mathbf{Bl}(S, u_0, Y)$, $\mathbf{Bl}(S, u_0, X') \subseteq \mathbf{Bl}(S, u_0, Y)$;
(ii) $\mathbf{Bl}(S, u_0, X') = \mathbf{Bl}(S, u_0, X) \nsubseteq \mathbf{Bl}(S, u_0, Y)$.

Proof. This is a transcription of Theorem 51 using Lemma 53. □

Example 21. We continue Example 20. We start with sets $X' = \{(a,2),(b,2),(c,0)\} \subseteq \mathbf{s}^{T(S)}(\{3\})$, $Y = \{(d,1),(e,1)\} \subseteq \mathbf{s}^{T(S)}(\{3\})$. We have found that $X''' = \{(b,2)\}$ is a $\mathbf{D}(\mathbf{K}^{T(S)}, Y)$-reduct of X'. It is easy to see from the table that the descriptor $(b,2)$ determines the descriptors $(d,1)$, $(e,1)$. Thus, the descriptors $(a,2)$, $(c,0)$ may be left out, i.e., the values 2 of the attribute a and the value 0 of the attribute c can be cancelled; the value 2 of the attribute b implies that d, e have the values 1, 1, respectively.

5 Consistent Decision Tables

The results of Section 4 can be used to simplify the so called consistent decision tables.

A *decision table* is an information system (U, A, V, f) such that $A = C \cup D$, $C \cap D = \emptyset$ where C and D are nonempty sets. Elements in C are said to be *conditions*, elements in D are called *decisions*, elements in U may be interpreted to be *states*.

A decision table (U, A, V, f) where C, D are sets of conditions and decisions, respectively, is said to be *consistent* if $C \to D\ (A, \mathbf{K}_S)$ holds. Cf [Pa7] p. 68, [NP10], [NN2].

In this Section, we study consistent decision tables.

By definition, $C \to D\ (A, \mathbf{K}_S)$ means that the values of decisions are determined by the values of conditions in the sense of Section 4. Therefore, two states with the same values of conditions have the same values of decisions. Hence, the values of decisions are defined by the values of conditions in a unique way as follows. We choose a state with the given values of conditions. Then the values of decisions of this state define the values of decisions that are determined by the given values of conditions. Thus, if $(c_1, v_1), \ldots, (c_p, v_p)$, $(d_1, w_1), \ldots, (d_q, w_q)$ are all descriptors of the state u_0 where $c_1, \ldots, c_p$ are conditions, $v_1, \ldots, v_p$ their values, and $d_1, \ldots, d_q$ are decisions, $w_1, \ldots, w_q$ their values, then we write

$$(\times) \quad (c_1, v_1) \wedge \ldots \wedge (c_p, v_p) \to (d_1, w_1) \wedge \ldots \wedge (d_q, w_q)$$

to express the fact that the descriptors $(c_1, v_1), \ldots, (c_p, v_p)$ determine the descriptors $(d_1, w_1), \ldots, (d_q, w_q)$ in a unique way. The expression $(\times)$ is called a *rule*, the symbols $\wedge$, $\to$ have their usual logical meaning: $\wedge$ is a symbol for conjunction, $\to$ symbol for implication: In the situation decribed by the consistent decision table the following holds. If the state is such that the condition c_1 has the value $v_1, \ldots$, the condition c_p has the value v_p, then the decision d_1 has the value $w_1, \ldots$, the decision d_q has the value w_q.

Typical examples of consistent decision tables may be found in Pawlak's book.

Example 22. An optician who wants to decide whether contact lenses are suitable for the patient examines the values of the following conditions: a (= age), b (= spectacle), c (= astigmatic), d (= tear production rate) where the values of these conditions are as follows.

a: 1 (= young), 2 (= pre-presbyopic), 3 (= presbyopic);
b: 1 (= myope), 2 (= hypermetrope);
c: 1 (= no), 2 (= yes);
d: 1 (= reduced), 2 (= normal).

Opticians decision is e with the values 1 (= hard contact lenses), 2 (= soft contact lenses), 3 (= no contact lenses).

The corresponding information system is $S = (U, A, V, f)$ where $U = \{1, \ldots, 24\}$. Any $i \in U$ corresponds to an ordered quadruple (v_1, v_2, v_3, v_4) where $v_1 \in \{1, 2, 3\}$, $v_i \in \{1, 2\}$ for $2 \leq i \leq 4$, i.e., any element in $\{1, 2, 3\} \times \{1, 2\} \times \{1, 2\} \times \{1, 2\}$ is admitted as a possible state in U. The function f is given by a table that will not be reproduced here, cf. [Pa7] p. 117. Since any element in $\{1, 2, 3\} \times \{1, 2\} \times \{1, 2\} \times \{1, 2\}$ appears in exactly one row of the table, we have $\mathbf{IND}_S(\{a, b, c, d\}) = \mathrm{id}_U$ and, therefore, $\mathbf{IND}_S(C) \subseteq \mathbf{IND}_S(D)$; hence $C \to D\ (A, \mathbf{K}_S)$ and this table is consistent. For the details see [Ce1].

Example 23. Similarly, from the protocol concerning the stoker's decisions while controlling the clinker kiln, instructions may be deduced in the form of a decision table. Conditions are as follows: a (= burning zone temperature) with 4 values, b (= burning zone color) with 5 values, c (= clinker granulation) with 4 values, d (= kiln inside color) with 3 values. The decisions are e (= kiln revolutions) with 2 values and f (= coal worm revolutions) with 4 values. The corresponding information system is $S = (U, A, V, f)$ where $U = \{1, \ldots, 13\}$ and f is given by a table that will not be reproduced here. For greater detail see [Pa7] p. 133, [Mr1], [Mr2]. The constructed information system is a consistent decision table.

Example 24. A pedagogical research on some Czech schools led to consistent decision tables. The aim was to find the dependence of ecological activity and attitude of pupils on their family situation, interests, etc. The pupils of a class had to answer some questions. Two of them played the role of decisions: ecological activity with the values active or passive and ecological attitude with the values engaged or not engaged. We present only some examples of the conditions: mother's (father's) education with the values primary, secondary, university; private interests with the values science, technics, aesthetic, sports, something else. The results of the research were presented in the form of consistent decision tables. Cf. [NoJ1].

It is clear that simplifications of decision tables are advantageous. Hence we have the following

Problem 57. Reduce the set of conditions in a consistent decision table.

More exactly, if (U, A, V, f) is a consistent decision table with the set C of conditions and the set D of decisions where $C \cup D = A$, $C \cap D = \emptyset$ and $C \to D\ (A, \mathbf{K}_S)$, find a minimal set C' such that $C' \subseteq C$ and $C' \to D\ (A, \mathbf{K}_S)$.

This is a particular case of Problem 46 that is solved by Theorem 47. Hence, we look for a $\mathbf{D}(\mathbf{K}_S, D)$-reduct of C. Since we start with the set C satisfying $\mathbf{IND}_S(C) \subseteq \mathbf{IND}_S(D)$, our $\mathbf{D}(\mathbf{K}_S, D)$-reduct of C is a minimal subset C' of C

such that $\mathbf{IND}_S(C') \subseteq \mathbf{IND}_S(D)$ by Theorem 48. For finding one reduct, we may use Algorithm 71 of Chapter 7, for finding all, Algorithm 75 of Chapter 7 is applicable. Algorithm 71 consists – roughly speaking – in successive cancelling of elements in C; if a set $X \subseteq C$ with $\mathbf{IND}_S(X) \subseteq \mathbf{IND}_S(D)$ has been found and $c \in X$ is to be cancelled, we must test whether $\mathbf{IND}_S(X - \{c\}) \subseteq \mathbf{IND}_S(D)$ holds or not; it is permitted to cancel c only if this condition is satisfied. Practically, we start with X where $\mathbf{IND}_S(X) \subseteq \mathbf{IND}_S(D)$ means that the values of attributes in X determine the values of attributes in D; condition $\mathbf{IND}_S(X - \{c\}) \subseteq \mathbf{IND}_S(D)$ has the meaning that the information system obtained by cancelling the attribute c and all its values has the same property, namely that the values of conditions determine the values of decisions.

Example 25. Consider Example 19 where $X = \{a, b, c\}$ is the set of conditions and $Y = \{d, e\}$ is the set of decisions. It was proved that this information system is a consistent decision table. Furthermore we have proved that the sets $\{b, c\}$, $\{a, c\}$, and $\{a, b\}$ are $\mathbf{D}(\mathbf{K}_S, Y)$-reducts of X. Thus, one of the conditions a, b, c may be cancelled.

The second possibility of how to simplify a consistent decision table consists in solving the following

Problem 58. Reduce the set of descriptors of an object where the descriptors correspond to conditions in a consistent decision table.

In a consistent decision table, we have dependence between sets of attributes and dependence between sets of descriptors. There is a close connection between these types of dependence (cf. [NN2]).

Theorem 59. *Let $S = (U, A, V, f)$ be a consistent decision table where $A = C \cup D$ and C, D are sets of conditions and decisions, respectively. If $u_0 \in U$ and $Z = \{(a, v) \in C \times V;\ f(u_0, a) = v\}$, $W = \{(a, v) \in D \times V;\ f(u_0, a) = v\}$, then $Z \rightarrow W\ (A \times V, \mathbf{K}^{T(S)})$.*

Proof. Condition $C \rightarrow D\ (A, \mathbf{K}_S)$ implies that $\mathbf{IND}_S(C) \subseteq \mathbf{IND}_S(D)$ by definition which entails that any block of $\mathbf{IND}_S(C)$ is included in a block of $\mathbf{IND}_S(D)$. By Lemma 53, $\mathbf{t}^{T(S)}(Z) = \mathbf{Bl}(S, u_0, Z)$ which is the block of $\mathbf{IND}_S(C)$ containing u_0; similarly, $\mathbf{t}^{T(S)}(W)$ is the block of $\mathbf{IND}_S(D)$ containing u_0. Thus, $\mathbf{t}^{T(S)}(Z) \subseteq \mathbf{t}^{T(S)}(W)$ which means $Z \rightarrow W\ (A \times V, \mathbf{K}^{T(S)})$ by Theorem 50. □

Thus, if the symbols have the same meaning as in Theorem 59, we are looking for a minimal set Z' such that $Z' \subseteq Z$, $Z' \rightarrow W\ (A \times V, \mathbf{K}^{T(S)})$. This problem is solved using Theorem 52, the $\mathbf{D}(\mathbf{K}^{T(S)}, W)$-reduct Z' of Z is a minimal subset of Z such that $\mathbf{Bl}(S, u_0, Z') \subseteq \mathbf{Bl}(S, u_0, W)$ by Theorem 54. We may apply Algorithms 71 and 75 of Chapter 7 as above. Algorithm 71 consists in successive cancelling of elements in Z; if a set $T \subseteq Z$ with $\mathbf{Bl}(S, u_0, T) \subseteq \mathbf{Bl}(S, u_0, W)$ has been found and a descriptor $d \in T$ is to be cancelled then the condition $\mathbf{Bl}(S, u_0, T - \{d\}) \subseteq \mathbf{Bl}(S, u_0, W)$ must be tested; it is permitted to cancel d

only if this condition is satisfied, by Theorem 56. The meaning of conditions of the type $\mathbf{Bl}(S, u_0, T) \subseteq \mathbf{Bl}(S, u_0, W)$ was explained in Section 4; this means that the set W of descriptors is determined by the set T in the sense presented there.

Example 26. We continue Example 25. In Examples 20 and 21 it was found that for $Z = \{(a,2),(b,2),(c,0)\}$, $W = \{(d,1),(e,1)\}$ the set $Z' = \{(b,2)\}$ is a $\mathbf{D}(\mathbf{K}^{T(S)}, W)$-reduct of Z, i.e., that the values 2 of the attribute a and 0 for the attribute c in the third row of the table may be left out.

Cancelling superfluous descriptors can be registered in the table of the information system by replacing the values of attributes in superfluous descriptors by - . Naturally, one row of the table can have more than one simplifications, but there could exist none.

The third type of simplifications in consistent decision tables allows to leave out a row where all values of attributes coincide with values of attributes of another row. If we interprete elements in U of a consistent decision table $S = (U, A, V, f)$ as states then two states with the same descriptors can be identified.

Thus simplification of a consistent decision table proceeds as follows.

(1) The system of conditions is simplified by cancelling superfluous conditions. This procedure can produce either the original table (no conditions have been superfluous) or a nonempty set of simplified tables.

(2) If two or more rows with the same values of attributes appear in a table simplified by (1), then only one of them is left in the table and the others are cancelled.

(3) If we have a table simplified by (1) and (2) (starting table), then we simplify any row by cancelling superfluous values of conditions in this starting table. This procedure can produce either the original row (no values of conditions in this row are superfluous) or a nonempty set of simplified rows. New simplified tables are constructed in such a way that any row of the starting table is replaced by one row obtained on the basis of the just described procedure.

(4) If two or more rows with the same values of attributes appear where also - is regarded as a value, then only one of them is left in the table and the others are cancelled.

Example 27. Suppose $U = \{1,2,3,4,5,6\}$, $A = C \cup D$ where $C = \{a,b,c\}$, $D = \{d\}$, $V = \{0,1,2,3\}$. Let f be given by Table 9.

Put $S = (U, A, V, f)$. Since $\mathbf{IND}_S(C) = \mathrm{id}_U$, we have $C \to D\ (A, \mathbf{K}_S)$ and S is a consistent decision table. Furthermore C is the only $\mathbf{D}(\mathbf{K}_S, D)$-reduct of C which implies that there are no superfluous conditions in C. Hence, the simplification of the table by (1) and (2) has no positive effect, the table does not change if (1) and (2) are applied. If simplifying the table by (3), we obtain $\mathbf{Bl}(S, 1, \{(a,0),(b,0)\}) = \{1,2,3\} \not\subseteq \{1,2,5\}$, $\mathbf{Bl}(S, 1, \{(a,0),(c,1)\}) = \{1,5\} \subseteq \{1,2,5\}$, $\mathbf{Bl}(S, 1, \{(b,0),(c,1)\}) = \{1,6\} \not\subseteq \{1,2,5\}$ where $\{1,2,5\} = \mathbf{Bl}(S, 1, \{(d,0)\})$. This implies that the set $\{(a,0),(c,1)\}$ is the only $\mathbf{D}(\mathbf{K}^{T(S)}$, $\{(d,0)\})$-reduct of the set $\{(a,0),(b,0),(c,1)\}$. Hence, in the first row of the table the value 0 for the condition b will be replaced by - . If we proceed like this for all rows of the table, we obtain one of the tables 10, 11.

Table 9.

	a	b	c	d
1	0	0	1	0
2	0	0	2	0
3	0	0	3	2
4	0	1	2	2
5	0	2	1	0
6	1	0	1	1

Table 10.

	a	b	c	d
1	0	–	1	0
2	–	0	2	0
3	–	–	3	2
4	–	1	–	2
5	–	2	–	0
6	1	–	–	1

These tables differ in the fifth row. Clearly, $\mathbf{Bl}(S,5,\{(b,2)\}) = \{5\} \subseteq \{1,2,5\}$, $\mathbf{Bl}(S,5,\emptyset) = \{1,2,3,4,5,6\} \not\subseteq \{1,2,5\}$, $\mathbf{Bl}(S,5,\{(a,0),(c,1)\}) = \{1,5\} \subseteq \{1,2,5\}$, $\mathbf{Bl}(S,5,\{(a,0)\}) = \{1,2,3,4,5\} \not\subseteq \{1,2,5\}$, $\mathbf{Bl}(S,5,\{(c,1)\}) = \{1,5,6\} \not\subseteq \{1,2,5\}$ where $\{1,2,5\} = \mathbf{Bl}(S,5,\{(d,0)\})$.

It follows that $\{(b,2)\}$, $\{(a,0),(c,1)\}$ are exactly all $\mathbf{D}(\mathbf{K}^{T(S)},\{(d,0)\})$-reducts of the set $\{(a,0),(b,2),(c,1)\}$.

In the second table, the first and fifth row have the same values of attributes. Thus, the table may be simplified by cancelling the fifth row.

The table of our example is simplified by (3) and (4) of the above mentioned procedure and is formed to this aim without any concrete interpretation of states, attributes, and values of attributes. The simplification of concrete decision tables that are derived from real situations may be relatively long. The reader is advised

Table 11.

	a	b	c	d
1	0	–	1	0
2	–	0	2	0
3	–	–	3	2
4	–	1	–	2
5	0	–	1	0
6	1	–	–	1

to look for more details in original papers, e.g., [Pa7] or [NoJ1].

6 Construction of All Classificatory Systems with a Prescribed Dependence Space

Any information system defines its dependence space as we have seen in Section 3. Thus, there is a natural problem whether to any dependence space there exists an information system whose dependence space coincides with the given one. This problem has a positive solution, cf. [NoM2], [NP1]. We shall study a more difficult problem.

Problem 60. For any dependence space P construct all classificatory systems whose dependence spaces coincide with P.

Using the operators $\mathbf{F}$, $\mathbf{F}^{-1}$, we may replace classificatory systems by information systems and vice versa without changing the corresponding dependence space; thus, the solution of Problem 60 provides also a solution of an analogous problem for information systems.

Let (U, r) be a classification (cf. Section 5 of Chapter 7), W a subset of U. We put $r(W) = r \cap (W \times W)$. Clearly, $r(W)$ is an equivalence on the set W that will be called the *restriction of r to W*. The following is obvious.

Lemma 61. *If $R = (U, (r_i)_{i \in A})$ is a classificatory system and $\emptyset \neq W \subseteq U$, then $(W, (r_i(W))_{i \in A})$ is a classificatory system.*

Let $R = (U, (r_i)_{i \in A})$ be a classificatory system. For any $Y \in \mathbf{B}(A)$ put

$$r_Y = \begin{cases} U \times U \text{ if } Y = \emptyset, \\ \\ \bigcap\{r_i;\ i \in Y\} \text{ if } Y \neq \emptyset. \end{cases}$$

Clearly, r_Y is an equivalence on the set U.

Theorem 62. *Let $R = (U, (r_i)_{i \in A})$ be a classificatory system, (A, K) its dependence space. Then for any $(Y_1, Y_2) \in \mathbf{B}(A) \times \mathbf{B}(A)$ the condition $(Y_1, Y_2) \in K$ is satisfied if and only if $r_{Y_1} = r_{Y_2}$.*

Proof. We have $\mathbf{H}(R) = T = (U \times U, A, r)$ where $r = \{((u_1, u_2), i) \in (U \times U) \times A;\ (u_1, u_2) \in r_i\}$ and, therefore, $\mathbf{t}^T(Y) = \{(u_1, u_2) \in U \times U;\ ((u_1, u_2), i) \in r \text{ for any } i \in Y\} = \bigcap\{r_i;\ i \in Y\} = r_Y$ for any nonempty $Y \in \mathbf{B}(A)$. For $Y = \emptyset$ the equality $\mathbf{t}^T(Y) = r_Y$ holds trivially. Hence, for any $(Y_1, Y_2) \in \mathbf{B}(A) \times \mathbf{B}(A)$ we have $(Y_1, Y_2) \in \mathbf{K}^T$ if and only if $\mathbf{t}^T(Y_1) = \mathbf{t}^T(Y_2)$ which is equivalent to $r_{Y_1} = r_{Y_2}$. By definition $K = \mathbf{K}^T$ and, hence, $(Y_1, Y_2) \in K$ holds if and only if $r_{Y_1} = r_{Y2}$. □

Let $R = (U, (r_i)_{i \in A})$ be a classificatory system. A nonempty subset W of U is said to be *distinguishing in R* if for any Y_1, Y_2 in $\mathbf{B}(A)$ with the property $r_{Y_1} \neq r_{Y_2}$ there exist u_1, $u_2 \in W$ such that $(u_1, u_2) \in (r_{Y_1} - r_{Y_2}) \cup (r_{Y_2} - r_{Y_1})$.

Theorem 63. *Let $R = (U, (r_i)_{i\in A})$ be a classificatory system, W a nonempty subset of U. Then the following assertions are equivalent.*

(i) *For any Y_1, Y_2 in $\mathbf{B}(A)$ the condition $r_{Y_1} = r_{Y_2}$ is equivalent to $r_{Y_1}(W) = r_{Y_2}(W)$.*

(ii) *W is a distinguishing subset in R.*

Proof. (1) Let *(i)* hold. Suppose Y_1, $Y_2 \in \mathbf{B}(A)$, $r_{Y_1} \neq r_{Y_2}$. Thus, $r_{Y_1}(W) \neq r_{Y_2}(W)$ and there exist u_1, $u_2 \in W$ such that $(u_1, u_2) \in (r_{Y_1}(W) - r_{Y_2}(W)) \cup (r_{Y_2}(W) - r_{Y_1}(W))$. Without loss of generality, we may suppose that $(u_1, u_2) \in r_{Y_1}(W) - r_{Y_2}(W)$. Since $r_{Y_1}(W) \subseteq r_{Y_1}$, we have $(u_1, u_2) \in r_{Y_1}$. If $(u_1, u_2) \in r_{Y_2}$ held, we should obtain $(u_1, u_2) \in r_{Y_2}(W)$ which is a contradiction. Thus, $(u_1, u_2) \in r_{Y_1} - r_{Y_2}$. Hence *(ii)* holds.

(2) Suppose that *(ii)* is satisfied. For any $Y \in \mathbf{B}(A)$, $Y \neq \emptyset$, we have $r_Y(W) = \bigcap\{r_i(W);\ i \in Y\} = \bigcap\{r_i \cap (W \times W);\ i \in Y\} = \bigcap\{r_i;\ i \in Y\} \cap (W \times W) = r_Y \cap (W \times W)$; the equality $r_Y(W) = r_Y \cap (W \times W)$ holds for $Y = \emptyset$, too. Thus, if Y_1, $Y_2 \in \mathbf{B}(A)$ and $r_{Y_1} = r_{Y_2}$, we obtain $r_{Y_1}(W) = r_{Y_1} \cap (W \times W) = r_{Y_2} \cap (W \times W) = r_{Y_2}(W)$. If Y_1, $Y_2 \in \mathbf{B}(A)$ and $r_{Y_1} \neq r_{Y_2}$, there exists $(u_1, u_2) \in W \times W$ such that $(u_1, u_2) \in (r_{y_1} - r_{Y_2}) \cup (r_{Y_2} - r_{Y_1})$. If $(u_1, u_2) \in r_{Y_1} - r_{Y_2}$, then $(u_1, u_2) \in r_{Y_1} \cap (W \times W) - r_{Y_2} \cap (W \times W) = r_{Y_1}(W) - r_{Y_2}(W)$. Similarly, $(u_1, u_2) \in r_{Y_2} - r_{Y_1}$ implies that $(u_1, u_2) \in r_{Y_2}(W) - r_{Y_1}(W)$. Therefore, $r_{Y_1} \neq r_{Y_2}$ entails $r_{Y_1}(W) \neq r_{Y_2}(W)$. Thus, *(i)* holds. □

Theorem 64. *Let $R = (U, (r_i)_{i\in A})$ be a classificatory system, W a nonempty subset of U. Then the following assertions are equivalent.*

(i) *The dependence space of $(W, (r_i(W))_{i\in A})$ coincides with the dependence space of R.*

(ii) *W is a distinguishing subset in R.*

Proof. Let (A, K), (A, K') be dependence spaces of R and $(W, (r_i(W))_{i\in A})$ respectively. Condition *(ii)* is equivalent to condition *(i)* of Theorem 63 that can be reformulated, using Theorem 62, as follows.

(iii) For any $(Y_1, Y_2) \in \mathbf{B}(A) \times \mathbf{B}(A)$ the condition $(Y_1, Y_2) \in K$ is equivalent to $(Y_1, Y_2) \in K'$.

Clearly, *(iii)* means $K = K'$. □

A classificatory system is said to be *nontrivial* if its dependence space is nontrivial (cf. Section 12 of Chapter 7).

Lemma 65. *Let $R = (U, (r_i)_{i\in A})$ be a nontrivial classificatory system, (A, K) its dependence space. Suppose that $|U| > 2|\mathbf{B}(A)/K|^2$. Then there exists a distinguishing subset W in R such that $|W| \leq 2|\mathbf{B}(A)/K|^2$.*

Proof. Let $\mathbf{R} \subseteq \mathbf{B}(A)$ be a set having with any block of K exactly one element in common. For any $(Y_1, Y_2) \in \mathbf{R} \times \mathbf{R}$ with $Y_1 \neq Y_2$, we have $(Y_1, Y_2) \notin K$ and, therefore, $r_{Y_1} \neq r_{Y_2}$ by Theorem 62. Thus, there exists $(u_1(Y_1, Y_2), u_2(Y_1, Y_2)) \in U \times U$ such that $(u_1(Y_1, Y_2), u_2(Y_1, Y_2)) \in (r_{Y_1} - r_{Y_2}) \cup (r_{Y_2} - r_{Y_1})$. We put

$W = \{u_1(Y_1,Y_2); (Y_1,Y_2) \in \mathbf{R} \times \mathbf{R},\ Y_1 \neq Y_2\} \cup \{u_2(Y_1,Y_2);\ (Y_1,Y_2) \in \mathbf{R} \times \mathbf{R},\ Y_1 \neq Y_2\}$. Clearly, $|W| \leq 2|\mathbf{R} \times \mathbf{R}| = 2|\mathbf{R}|^2 = 2|\mathbf{B}(A)/K|^2$; $W \neq \emptyset$ follows from the fact that R is nontrivial.

If $Z_1,\ Z_2 \in \mathbf{B}(A)$ are such that $r_{Z_1} \neq r_{Z_2}$, there exist $Y_1,\ Y_2 \in \mathbf{R}$ such that $(Z_1,Y_1) \in K,\ (Z_2,Y_2) \in K$. By Theorem 62, we obtain $r_{Z_1} = r_{Y_1},\ r_{Z_2} = r_{Y_2}$. Then $(u_1(Y_1,Y_2), u_2(Y_1,Y_2)) \in (r_{Y_1} - r_{Y_2}) \cup (r_{Y_2} - r_{Y_1}) = (r_{Z_1} - r_{Z_2}) \cup (r_{Z_2} - r_{Z_1}),\ u_1(Y_1,Y_2) \in W,\ u_2(Y_1,Y_2) \in W$. It follows that W is distinguishing in R. □

Let $P = (A,K)$ be a dependence space. Put $q = |\mathbf{B}(A)/K|,\ p = 2q^2$. Let U be an arbitrary nonempty set such that $|U| \leq p$, $\mathbf{G}$ a subset of $\mathbf{B}(A)$ that is dense in (A,K); by Corollary 11, we have $|\mathbf{G}| \leq q$. Take a surjection h of the set $U \times U$ onto $\mathbf{G}$ and test whether $U,\ \mathbf{G},\ h$ are classification-forming parameters (see Section 2). In the positive case, the triple $(U,\mathbf{G},h)$ is said to be a *basic classification-forming triple of parameters corresponding to* P.

As a consequence of Theorem 28 we obtain immediately

Corollary 66. *If* $(U,\mathbf{G},h)$ *is a basic classification-forming triple of parameters corresponding to a dependence space* $P = (A,K)$*, then* $\mathbf{C}_2(P;U,\mathbf{G},h)$ *is a classificatory system whose dependence space coincides with* P.

Let $R = (U,(r_i)_{i\in A}),\ R^+ = (U^+,(r_i^+)_{i\in A})$ be classificatory systems. The system R^+ is called a *successor* of R if it has the following properties.

(1) $U \subseteq U^+,\ |U^+ - U| = 1$.
(2) The equivalence r_i is a restriction of r_i^+ to U for any $i \in A$.
(3) The dependence spaces of R and R^+ coincide.

A successor of a classificatory system $R = (U,(r_i)_{i\in A})$ can be constructed by choosing an element $u_0 \notin U$, by putting $U^+ = U \cup \{u_0\}$, by extending the equivalences r_i; the extended equivalence r_i^+ on U^+ is chosen in such a way that its restriction to U is r_i for any $i \in A$. Then the dependence spaces $R,\ R^+$ must be tested; only such systems R^+ are admitted whose dependence spaces coincide with the dependence space of R.

Construction 67. (Construction $\mathbf{K}_3$ of all classificatory systems with a prescribed dependence space)

Let $P = (A,K)$ *be a dependence space.*

(1) *We find all subsets* $\mathbf{G}$ *of* $\mathbf{B}(A)$ *that are dense in* (A,K) *by testing all subsets* $\mathbf{Y} \subseteq \mathbf{B}(A)$ *such that any* $\mathbf{Y}$ *contains at most one element from any block of* K*. The test consists in constructing* $\mathbf{T}(\mathbf{Y})$ *and verifying whether* $\mathbf{T}(\mathbf{Y}) = K$ *or not. Only subsets* $\mathbf{Y}$ *satsfying this condition are admitted.*

(2) *Put* $q = |\mathbf{B}(A)/K|,\ p = 2q^2$*. For a* $\mathbf{G}$ *that is dense in* (A,K) *choose an arbitrary nonempty set* U *such that* $|U| \leq p$ *and a surjection* h *of the set* $U \times U$ *onto* $\mathbf{G}$ *and test whether* $U,\ \mathbf{G},\ h$ *are classification-forming parameters. The test consists in constructing the relational system* $\mathbf{C}_2(P;U,\mathbf{G},h)$ *and verifying whether it is a classificatory system or not. In the positive case,* $(U,\mathbf{G},h)$ *is a basic classification-forming triple of parameters corresponding to* P.

(3) *Put* $R_0 = \mathbf{C}_2(P; U, \mathbf{G}, h)$ *where* $(U, \mathbf{G}, h)$ *is a basic classification-forming triple of parameters corresponding to* P. *Take an arbitrary integer* $n \geq 0$ *and define* R_{j+1} *to be a successor of* R_j *for any* j *with* $0 \leq j \leq n-1$.

The classificatory system $R = R_n$ *is said to be constructed by* $\mathbf{K}_3$ *starting with* P.

We must prove that $\mathbf{K}_3$ provides exactly all classificatory systems whose dependence space is prescribed.

Lemma 68. *If* P *is a dependence space and* R *is constructed by* $\mathbf{K}_3$ *starting with* P, *then* R *is a classificatory system whose dependence space coincides with* P.

Proof. By definition of a basic classification-forming triple of parameters, R_0 is a classificatory system and its dependence space coincides with P by Theorem 25. By definition of successor, any R_i is a classificatory system and its dependence space is P for any j with $0 \leq j \leq n$. □

In order to prove that any classificatory system with a prescribed dependence space is constructed by $\mathbf{K}_3$ we proceed as follows.

Let $R = (U, (r_i)_{i \in A})$ be a classificatory system. For any nonempty $X \in \mathbf{B}(U)$ put $R(X) = (X, r_i(X))_{i \in A}$); we denote by $(A, \mathbf{L}(X))$ its dependence space. For $X = \emptyset$ put $\mathbf{L}(X) = A \times A$.

Lemma 69. *Let* $R = (U, (r_i)_{i \in A})$ *be a classificatory system. If* $X_1 \subseteq X_2 \subseteq U$ *then* $\mathbf{L}(X_2) \subseteq \mathbf{L}(X_1)$.

Proof. The assertion holds if $X_1 = \emptyset$.

Suppose that X_1, X_2 are nonempty sets. Let us have $(Y_1, Y_2) \in \mathbf{B}(A) \times \mathbf{B}(A)$ such that $(Y_1, Y_2) \in \mathbf{L}(X_2)$. By Theorem 62 it follows that $r_{Y_1} \cap (X_2 \times X_2) = r_{Y_1}(X_2) = r_{Y_2}(X_2) = r_{Y_2} \cap (X_2 \times X_2)$. Since $X_1 \subseteq X_2$, we obtain $r_{Y_1}(X_1) = r_{Y_1} \cap (X_1 \times X_1) = r_{Y_1} \cap (X_2 \times X_2) \cap (X_1 \times X_1) = r_{Y_2} \cap (X_2 \times X_2) \cap (X_1 \times X_1) = r_{Y_2} \cap (X_1 \times X_1) = r_{Y_2}(X_1)$ and, thus, $(Y_1, Y_2) \in \mathbf{L}(X_1)$ by Theorem 62. □

Let $R = (U, (r_i)_{i \in A})$ be a classificatory system. We define an equivalence $\mathbf{M}$ on the set $\mathbf{B}(U)$ as follows. For $(X, X') \in \mathbf{B}(U) \times \mathbf{B}(U)$ we put $(X, X') \in \mathbf{M}$ if and only if one of the following conditions (i), (ii) is satisfied.

(i) $\mathbf{L}(X) = \mathbf{L}(U) = \mathbf{L}(X')$.

(ii) $X = X'$, $\mathbf{L}(X) \neq \mathbf{L}(U)$.

Theorem 70. *Let* $R = (U, (r_i)_{i \in A})$ *be a classificatory system and* $\mathbf{M}$ *be defined as above. Then* $\mathbf{M}$ *is a congruence on the semilattice* $(\mathbf{B}(U), \cup)$.

Proof. Let X, X', Y be elements in $\mathbf{B}(U)$, suppose $(X, X') \in \mathbf{M}$.

If $\mathbf{L}(X) \neq \mathbf{L}(U)$, then $X = X'$ and, therefore, $X \cup Y = X' \cup Y$. Thus, either $\mathbf{L}(X \cup Y) = \mathbf{L}(U) = \mathbf{L}(X' \cup Y)$ and (i) holds or $\mathbf{L}(X \cup Y) \neq \mathbf{L}(U)$ and (ii) is satisfied.

If $\mathbf{L}(X) = \mathbf{L}(U)$, we have $\mathbf{L}(U) = \mathbf{L}(X')$. Since $X \subseteq X \cup Y \subseteq U$, we obtain $\mathbf{L}(X) = \mathbf{L}(U) \subseteq \mathbf{L}(X \cup Y) \subseteq \mathbf{L}(X)$ by Lemma 69 and, similarly, $\mathbf{L}(X') =$

$\mathbf{L}(U) \subseteq \mathbf{L}(X' \cup Y) \subseteq \mathbf{L}(X')$ which implies that $\mathbf{L}(X \cup Y) = \mathbf{L}(U) = \mathbf{L}(X' \cup Y)$ and (i) is satisfied.

Thus, $(X, X') \in \mathbf{M}$ entails $(X \cup Y, X' \cup Y) \in \mathbf{M}$ and $\mathbf{M}$ is a congruence on the semilattice $(\mathbf{B}(U), \cup)$ by Theorem 12 of Chapter 7. □

Corollary 71. *If* $R = (U, (r_i)_{i \in A})$ *is a classificatory system and* $\mathbf{M}$ *is defined as above, then* $(U, \mathbf{M})$ *is a dependence space.*

Theorem 72. *Let* $R = (U, (r_i)_{i \in A})$ *be a nontrivial classificatory system and* $\mathbf{M}$ *be defined as above. Let* W *be a subset of* U. *Then the following assertions are equivalent.*

(i) W *is a minimal distinguishing subset in* R.
(ii) W *is a* $\mathbf{M}$*-reduct of* U.

Proof. Any two consecutive conditions in the following sequence are equivalent.

(1) W is distiguishing in R.
(2) Dependence spaces of R, $R(W)$ coincide and $W \neq \emptyset$.
(3) $(W, U) \in \mathbf{M}$, $W \neq \emptyset$.
(4) $(W, U) \in \mathbf{M}$.

Indeed, the equivalence of (1) and (2) is a consequence of Theorem 64; condition $W \neq \emptyset$ in (2) is a part of the definition of a distinguishing subset. The equivalence of (2) and (3) is a consequence of the definition of $\mathbf{M}$. The equivalence of (3) and (4) follows from the fact that R is nontrivial which means $\mathbf{L}(U) \neq A \times A$ and the fact $\mathbf{L}(\emptyset) = A \times A$.

Thus, a set is minimal among all sets satisfying (1) if and only if it is minimal among all sets satisfying (4), i.e., *(i)* and *(ii)* are equivalent. □

Lemma 73. *If* R *is a nontrivial classificatory system and* P *its dependence space, then* R *can be constructed by* $\mathbf{K}_3$ *starting with* P.

Proof. (1) Put $R = (U, (r_i)_{i \in A})$. By Corollary 71, we define the dependence space $(U, \mathbf{M})$ and find a $\mathbf{M}$-reduct W of U by Algorithm 71 of Chapter 7. Using abbreviated notation, we have $U = U_0 = \mathbf{SC}^0$ and construct $U_j = \mathbf{SC}^{(j)}$ for $0 \leq j \leq p$, $U_p = \mathbf{SC}^{(p)} = W$ where $p \geq 0$ is an integer. The symbol $\mathbf{SC}^{(j)}$ means $\mathbf{SC}^{(j)}(U, \mathbf{M}, o)$ where o is a linear ordering on U. Put $W_j = U_{p-j}$ for any j with the property $0 \leq j \leq p$. By definition of $\mathbf{SC}^{(j)}$, we obtain $(W_j, W_{j+1}) \in \mathbf{M}$ and $|W_{j+1} - W_j| = 1$ for any j with $0 \leq j \leq p - 1$.

(2) By Theorem 72, $W_0 = W$ is a minimal distinguishing subset in R. Then $|W| \leq 2|\mathbf{B}(A)/K|^2$ holds.

Indeed, if $|W| > 2|\mathbf{B}(A)/K|^2$, then, by Lemma 65, there exists $W' \subseteq W$ with $|W'| \leq 2|\mathbf{B}(A)/K|^2$ such that W' is distinguishing in $R(W)$. By Theorem 64, $R(W')$, $R(W)$, R have the same dependence spaces and, therefore, W' is a distinguishing subset in R. Hence, W is not minimal contrary to our hypothesis.

By Theorem 64, the dependence spaces of R and $R(W)$ coincide. By Theorem 25, there exist parameters $\mathbf{G}$, h such that $R(W) = \mathbf{C}_2(P; W, \mathbf{G}, h)$. Thus,

$(W, \mathbf{G}, h)$ is a basic classification-forming triple of parameters corresponding to P.

(3) Furthermore, $R(W_{j+1})$ is a successor of $R(W_j)$ for any j with $0 \leq j \leq p-1$.

Indeed, condition (1) and (3) of the definition is satisfied as we have seen in the first part of this proof. Condition (2) is satisfied, too, because $r_i(W_j)$ is a restriction of r_i to W_j for any j with $0 \leq j \leq p$ and any $i \in A$.

Thus $W_p = U_0 = U$ and $R = (W_p, (r_i(W_p))_{i \in A})$ is the result of the construction $\mathbf{K}_3$ starting with P. □

By Lemmas 68, 73, we obtain

Theorem 74. *Let $P = (A, K)$ be a nontrivial dependence space. Then the following assertions hold.*

(i) *If R is a relational system constructed by $\mathbf{K}_3$ starting with P, then R is a classificatory system whose dependence space coincides with P.*
(ii) *If R is a classificatory system whose dependence space is P, then R can be constructed by $\mathbf{K}_3$ starting with P.*

Example 28. We start with the dependence space (A, K) of Example 9: $A = \{a, b\}$, K has the following blocks: $\{\emptyset, \{a\}\}$, $\{\{b\}, \{a, b\}\}$. Then $\mathbf{G} = \{\{a\}, \{a, b\}\}$ is dense in $P = (A, K)$. Put $U = \{1, 2, 3\}$. In the above mentioned example, a relational system was constructed by $\mathbf{C}_2$; it was no classificatory system. We now put $h(1, 2) = h(1, 3) = h(2, 1) = h(3, 1) = \{a\}$, $h(u_1, u_2) = \{a, b\}$ for all remaining elements $(u_1, u_2) \in U \times U$. Then $r_a = U \times U$, $r_b = \{(1, 1), (2, 2), (2, 3), (3, 2), (3, 3)\}$, $R = (U, (r_i)_{i \in A}) = \mathbf{C}_2(P; U, \mathbf{G}, h)$. Clearly, r_a, r_b are equivalences on U and, therefore, U, $\mathbf{G}$, h are classification-forming parameters. Since $|U| = 3 \leq 8 = 2.2^2 = 2|\mathbf{B}(A)/K|^2$, $(U, \mathbf{G}, h)$ is a basic triple of parameters corresponding to P.

We now construct a successor $R^+ = (U^+, (r_i^+)_{i \in A})$ of R. Put $U^+ = U \cup \{4\}$, $r_a^+ = U^+ \times U^+$, $r_b^+ = r_b \cup \{(4, 4)\}$. We construct the information system $\mathbf{F}(R^+) = (U^+, A, V, f) = S$ where $V = \{0, 0', 1', 2'\}$, elements in V are blocks of the decompositions U^+/r_i^+, $i \in A$, and f is given by Table 12.

Table 12.

	a	b
1	0	0′
2	0	1′
3	0	1′
4	0	2′

Clearly, $\mathbf{IND}_S(\emptyset) = U^+ \times U^+ = \mathbf{IND}_S(\{a\})$; the blocks of $\mathbf{IND}_S(\{b\}) = \mathbf{IND}_S(\{a, b\})$ are $\{1\}$, $\{2, 3\}$, $\{4\}$. It follows that $\mathbf{K}_S$ has the following blocks:

$\{\emptyset, \{a\}\}$, $\{\{b\}, \{a,b\}\}$. By definition, the dependence space of $\mathbf{F}(R^+)$ coincides with the dependence space of R^+. Thus, R, R^+ have the same dependence space and R^+ is a successor of R.

Thus, R^+ is constructed by $\mathbf{K}_3$ starting with P; its dependence space is P.

Example 29. Let $U = \{u_1, \ldots, u_5\}$, $A = \{a_1, \ldots, a_5\}$, $V = \{v_1, v_2, v_3\}$, let f be given by the following table

Table 13.

	a_1	a_2	a_3	a_4	a_5
u_1	v_1	v_1	v_2	v_1	v_1
u_2	v_1	v_1	v_2	v_1	v_1
u_3	v_1	v_2	v_1	v_1	v_2
u_4	v_1	v_2	v_1	v_2	v_3
u_5	v_1	v_2	v_1	v_2	v_3

Then $S = (U, A, V, f)$ is an information system. Clearly, $\mathbf{IND}_S(\{a_1\}) = U \times U$, $\mathbf{IND}_S(\{a_2\}) = \mathbf{IND}_S(\{a_3\})$ has the blocks $\{u_1, u_2\}$, $\{u_3, u_4, u_5\}$. Furthermore the blocks of $\mathbf{IND}_S(\{a_4\})$ are $\{u_1, u_2, u_3\}$, $\{u_4, u_5\}$. Finally, the blocks of $\mathbf{IND}_S(\{a_5\})$ are $\{u_1, u_2\}$, $\{u_3\}$, $\{u_4, u_5\}$. It follows that $\mathbf{K}_S$ has the following blocks: $\{\emptyset, \{a_1\}\}$, $\{\{a_2\}, \{a_3\}, \{a_1, a_2\}, \{a_1, a_3\}, \{a_2, a_3\}, \{a_1, a_2, a_3\}\}$, $\{\{a_4\}, \{a_1, a_4\}\}$, B, where B contains all remaining elements of $\mathbf{B}(A)$.

Thus $|\mathbf{B}(A)/K| = 4$. Since $|U| = 5 \leq 32 = 2|\mathbf{B}(A)/K|^2$, we have $\mathbf{F}^{-1}(S) = \mathbf{C}_2(P; U, \mathbf{G}, h)$ for some basic triple $(U, \mathbf{G}, h)$ of parameters corresponding to P.

It is easy to see that the information system S may be reduced: If putting $W = \{u_2, u_3, u_5\}$, $f'(u,i) = f(u,i)$ for any $(u,i) \in W \times A$, we obtain an information system $S' = (W, A, V, f')$ with the same dependence space. This corresponds to the fact that W is a minimal distinguishing subset in $R = \mathbf{F}^{-1}(S)$.

Example 30. It is easy to see that there is no problem to construct all classificatory systems to a trivial dependence space (A, K). We take an arbitrary nonempty set U and put $r_i = U \times U$ for any $i \in A$. Then, clearly, $r_Y = U \times U$ for any $Y \in \mathbf{B}(A)$. On the other hand, if $R = (U, (r_i)_{i \in A})$ is a classificatory system where $r_i \neq U \times U$ for some $i \in A$, then it is easy to see that the dependence space of R is not trivial.

7 Partial Dependence

Using the results of Section 6 we may construct, to any dependence space $P = (A, K)$, all information systems $S = (U, A, V, f)$ whose dependence spaces coincide with P. We now prove that any information system with this property defines a distance function on the set $\mathbf{B}(A)/K$, i.e., for any dependence space (A, K) there exists a family of naturally defined distance functions on $\mathbf{B}(A)/K$.

First, we remind some definitions of Example 2 in Chapter 7.

Let U be a finite nonempty set. We denote by $\mathbf{DI}(U)$ the set whose elements are all disjoint systems of nonempty subsets of the set U. Let $\mathbf{DE}(U)$ be the set whose elements are all decompositions of the set U. Clearly, $\mathbf{DE}(U) \subseteq \mathbf{DI}(U)$.

We define an operation $*$ on the set $\mathbf{DI}(U)$ as follows: for any P, $Q \in \mathbf{DI}(U)$, we put $P * Q = \{p \in P;\ \text{there exists } q \in Q \text{ such that } p \subseteq q\}$.

Clearly, $(\mathbf{DI}(U), *)$ is a groupoid.

For any P, $Q \in \mathbf{DI}(U)$, we put $P \leq Q$ if and only if $P * Q = P$.

Lemma 75. *For any P, $Q \in \mathbf{DI}(U)$, the conditions $P \leq Q$ and $P \subseteq P * Q$ are equivalent.*

Proof. If $P \leq Q$, then $P = P * Q$ holds. If $P \subseteq P * Q$ then $P = P * Q$ because $P * Q \subseteq P$ follows from the definition of the operation $*$. Hence, $P \subseteq P * Q$ implies that $P \leq Q$. □

Lemma 76. *If P, Q, $R \in \mathbf{DI}(U)$ and $Q \leq R$ holds, then $P * Q \subseteq P * R$.*

Proof. If $t \in P * Q$, then $t \in P$ and there exists $q \in Q$ such that $t \subseteq q$. Since $Q = Q * R$, there exists $r \in R$ such that $q \subseteq r$ and, hence, $t \subseteq r$. Thus $t \in P * R$. □

We introduce another operation on the set $\mathbf{DI}(U)$. For any P, $Q \in \mathbf{DI}(U)$ we set $P \wedge Q = \{p \cap q :\ p \in P,\ q \in Q,\ p \cap q \neq \emptyset\}$. Clearly, $P \wedge Q \in \mathbf{DI}(U)$.

Theorem 77. *Relation $\leq$ is an ordering on the set $\mathbf{DI}(U)$ and $\inf\{P, Q\} = P \wedge Q$ holds for any P, $Q \in \mathbf{DI}(U)$.*

Proof. Since $P * P = P$, the relation $\leq$ is reflexive. If P, Q, R are in $\mathbf{DI}(U)$ and $P \leq Q$, $Q \leq R$ hold, then $P = P * Q \subseteq P * R$ by Lemma 76 which implies that $P \leq R$ by Lemma 75. Thus, the relation $\leq$ is transitive.

If $P \leq Q$, $Q \leq P$ hold, then $P \subseteq P * Q$, $Q \subseteq Q * P$ by Lemma 75. Hence, to any $p \in P$, there exists $q \in Q$ such that $p \subseteq q$ and to $q \in Q$ there exists $p' \in P$ such that $q \subseteq p'$. Thus, $p \subseteq q \subseteq p'$. Since p, q, p' are nonempty and $P \in \mathbf{DI}(U)$, we obtain $p = p'$ which implies $p = q$. We have proved $P \subseteq Q$. Similarly, we prove $Q \subseteq P$ which entails $P = Q$. Therefore, $\leq$ is an antisymmetric relation.

Hence $\leq$ is an ordering on $\mathbf{DI}(U)$.

For any $P \in \mathbf{DI}(U)$ and any $Q \in \mathbf{DI}(U)$, we have $P \wedge Q \subseteq (P \wedge Q) * P$ because $p \cap q \subseteq p$ for any $p \in P$ and any $q \in Q$. Thus, $P \wedge Q \leq P$ by Lemma 75. Similarly $P \wedge Q \leq Q$ holds and, hence, $P \wedge Q$ is a lower bound of the set $\{P, Q\}$. If $R \leq P$ and $R \leq Q$ hold, then $R \subseteq R * P$, $R \subseteq R * Q$ by Lemma 75. Thus, for any $r \in R$, there are $p \in P$ and $q \in Q$ such that $r \subseteq p$, $r \subseteq q$ which implies that $r \subseteq p \cap q \in P \wedge Q$. Thus, $R \subseteq R * (P \wedge Q)$ which entails that $R \leq P \wedge Q$ by Lemma 75. It follows that $P \wedge Q$ is the greatest lower bound of the set $\{P, Q\}$. □

It is easy to see that $P \wedge Q \in \mathbf{DE}(U)$ for any $P \in \mathbf{DE}(U)$ and any $Q \in \mathbf{DE}(U)$. If the relation $\leq$ and the operation $\wedge$ are restricted to $\mathbf{DE}(U)$, we obtain the usual ordering of decompositions and the well-known meet-operation for decompositions as they appear in the so called partition lattice.

Corollary 78. *If* P, Q, R *are in* $\mathbf{DI}(U)$, *then the following assertions hold.*

(i) $P * (Q \wedge R) \subseteq P * Q$,

(ii) $Q \wedge (R * P) \subseteq (Q \wedge R) * P$.

Proof. By Theorem 77 we have $Q \wedge R \leq Q$ and *(i)* follows by Lemma 76.

If $t \in Q \wedge (R * P)$, there exist $q \in Q$ and $r \in R * P$ such that $t = q \cap r$. Furthermore, $r \in R$ and there exists $p \in P$ such that $r \subseteq p$. It follows that $t \in Q \wedge R$ and $t \subseteq r \subseteq p$ which means $t \in (Q \wedge R) * P$ and *(ii)* holds. □

If P is a system of sets we put $\bigcup P = \bigcup\{p;\ p \in P\}$.

Lemma 79. *If* $Q \in \mathbf{DE}(U)$ *and* $P \in \mathbf{DI}(U)$, *then* $\bigcup(Q \wedge P) = \bigcup P$.

Proof. For any $x \in U$ the condition $x \in \bigcup(Q \wedge P)$ is equivalent with the existence of $p \in P$ such that $x \in p$ because a $q \in Q$ with $x \in q$ always exists. Thus, $x \in \bigcup(Q \wedge P)$ is equivalent to $x \in \bigcup P$ which is our assertion. □

Lemma 80. *If* P, Q, R *are in* $\mathbf{DI}(U)$, *then* $\bigcup(P * Q) \cap \bigcup(Q * R) \subseteq \bigcup(P * R)$.

Proof. If $x \in \bigcup(P * Q) \cap \bigcup(Q * R)$, there are $p \in P$, $q \in Q$, $q' \in Q$, $r \in R$ such that $x \in p \subseteq q$, $x \in q' \subseteq r$. It follows that $q = q'$ and, thus, $x \in p \subseteq q \subseteq r$ which implies that $x \in \bigcup(P * R)$. □

If α, β are equivalences on the set U, then $\alpha \cap \beta$ is an equivalence on U as well. It follows that U/α, U/β, $U/\alpha \cap \beta$ are in $\mathbf{DE}(U)$. Then the following is obvious.

Lemma 81. *If* α, β *are equivalences on the set* U, *then* $U/\alpha \cap \beta = (U/\alpha) \wedge (U/\beta)$.

Let $S = (U, A, V, f)$ be an information system. For the sake of brevity we write $\mathbf{i}$ for $\mathbf{IND}_S$.

Theorem 82. *Let* $S = (U, A, V, f)$ *be an information system,* X, Y, Z *elements in* $\mathbf{B}(A)$. *Then the following assertions hold.*

(i) $(U/\mathbf{i}(X)) * (U/\mathbf{i}(Y \cup Z)) \subseteq (U/\mathbf{i}(X)) * (U/\mathbf{i}(Y))$,

(ii) $(U/\mathbf{i}(Y)) \wedge ((U/\mathbf{i}(Z)) * (U/\mathbf{i}(X))) \subseteq (U/\mathbf{i}(Y \cup Z)) * (U/\mathbf{i}(X))$.

Proof. We have $(U/\mathbf{i}(X)) * (U/\mathbf{i}(Y \cup Z)) = (U/\mathbf{i}(X)) * (U/(\mathbf{i}(Y) \cap \mathbf{i}(Z))) = (U/\mathbf{i}(X)) * ((U/\mathbf{i}(Y)) \wedge (U/\mathbf{i}(Z))) \subseteq (U/\mathbf{i}(X)) * (U/\mathbf{i}(Y))$ by Lemma 32, Lemma 81, and Corollary 78, which is *(i)*.

Furthermore, $(U/\mathbf{i}(Y)) \wedge ((U/\mathbf{i}(Z)) * (U/\mathbf{i}(X))) \subseteq ((U/\mathbf{i}(Y)) \wedge (U/\mathbf{i}(Z))) * (U/\mathbf{i}(X)) = (U/(\mathbf{i}(Y) \cap \mathbf{i}(Z))) * (U/\mathbf{i}(X)) = (U/\mathbf{i}(Y \cup Z)) * (U/\mathbf{i}(X))$ by Corollary 78, Lemma 81, and Lemma 32, which is *(ii)*. □

These definitions and results are destined to the study of the so called partial dependence of two sets of attributes in an information system. Cf. [NP6].

Let $S = (U, A, V, f)$ be an information system, $X \in \mathbf{B}(A)$, $Y \in \mathbf{B}(A)$ sets of attributes. We put

$$k_S(X,Y) = |U|^{-1} |\bigcup((U/\mathbf{i}(X)) * (U/\mathbf{i}(Y)))| \ .$$

If $k_S(X,Y) = k$, the set Y is said to *depend* on X *in degree* k *with respect to* S which is written as $X \to_S^k Y$. Clearly, for any $X \in \mathbf{B}(A)$ and any $Y \in \mathbf{B}(A)$ there exists exactly one number k such that $0 \leq k \leq 1$, $X \to_S^k Y$.

Let $S = (U, A, V, f)$ be an information system, X, Y elements in $\mathbf{B}(A)$, $u \in U$ an arbitrary object. The set X is said to *respect* the set Y *in* u if the block of $\mathbf{i}(X)$ containing u is included in the block of $\mathbf{i}(Y)$ that contains u. Regarding this definition, we find out that $\bigcup((U/\mathbf{i}(X)) * (U/\mathbf{i}(Y)))$ is the set of all elements $u \in U$ where X respects Y. It follows immediately

Theorem 83. *Let $S = (U, A, V, f)$ be an information system, X, Y arbitrary elements in $\mathbf{B}(A)$. Then $k_S(X,Y)$ is the probability that the set X respects Y in an arbitrarily chosen $u \in U$.*

Example 31. Let $S = (U, A, V, f)$ be an information system, X, Y elements in $\mathbf{B}(A)$. Then $X \to_S^1 Y$ holds if and only if $\mathbf{i}(X) \subseteq \mathbf{i}(Y)$. Indeed, $X \to_S^1 Y$ holds if and only if $U = \bigcup((U/\mathbf{i}(X) * (U/\mathbf{i}(Y)))$ which means that for any $x \in U/\mathbf{i}(X)$ there exists $y \in U/\mathbf{i}(Y)$ such that $x \subseteq y$ which is equivalent to $\mathbf{i}(X) \subseteq \mathbf{i}(Y)$; this means $X \to Y$ $(A, \mathbf{K}_S)$ by Theorem 44. Hence, X respects Y in any element of U.

Furthermore, $X \to_S^0 Y$ holds if and only if $(U/\mathbf{i}(X)) * (U/\mathbf{i}(Y)) = \emptyset$ which means that for no $x \in U/\mathbf{i}(X)$ there exists any $y \in U/\mathbf{i}(Y)$ with $x \subseteq y$, i.e., for any $x \in U/\mathbf{i}(X)$ and any $y \in U/\mathbf{i}(Y)$ the condition $x \cap y \neq x$ holds. This means that $((U/\mathbf{i}(X)) \wedge (U/\mathbf{i}(Y))) \cap (U/\mathbf{i}(X)) = \emptyset$. The last condition can be expressed in the form $(U/(\mathbf{i}(X) \cap \mathbf{i}(Y))) \cap (U/\mathbf{i}(X)) = \emptyset$ by Lemma 81 and in the form $(U/\mathbf{i}(X \cup Y)) \cap (U/\mathbf{i}(X)) = \emptyset$ by Lemma 32.

Theorem 84. *Let $S = (U, A, V, f)$ be an information system, X, Y, Z elements in $\mathbf{B}(A)$, let k, l, m be numbers in the interval $[0,1]$. Then the following assertions hold.*

(i) If $X \to_S^k Y$, $X \to_S^l Z$, $X \to_S^m Y \cup Z$, then $m \leq \min\{k, l\}$.
(ii) If $Y \to_S^k X$, $Z \to_S^l X$, $Y \cup Z \to_S^m X$, then $m \geq \max\{k, l\}$.
(iii) If $X \to_S^k Y$, $Y \to_S^l Z$, $X \to_S^m Z$, then $m \geq k + l - 1$.

Proof. By *(i)* of Theorem 82, we have $|\bigcup((U/\mathbf{i}(X)) * (U/\mathbf{i}(Y \cup Z)))| \leq |\bigcup((U/\mathbf{i}(X)) * (U/\mathbf{i}(Y)))|$ which implies that $m \leq k$. Similarly, we obtain $m \leq l$ which entails *(i)*.

By Lemma 79 and *(ii)* of Theorem 82, we have $|\bigcup((U/\mathbf{i}(Z)) * (U/\mathbf{i}(X)))| = |\bigcup((U/\mathbf{i}(Y) \wedge ((U/\mathbf{i}(Z)) * (U/\mathbf{i}(X))))| \leq |\bigcup((U/\mathbf{i}(Y \cup Z)) * (U/\mathbf{i}(X)))|$ which implies that $l \leq m$. Similarly, we obtain $k \leq m$ which entails *(ii)*.

If B, C are arbitrary sets, then $|B| + |C| = |B \cup C| + |B \cap C|$. We put $B = \bigcup((U/\mathbf{i}(X)) * (U/\mathbf{i}(Y)))$, $C = \bigcup((U/\mathbf{i}(Y)) * (U/\mathbf{i}(Z)))$. By Lemma 80, we obtain $B \cap C \subseteq \bigcup((U/\mathbf{i}(X)) * (U/\mathbf{i}(Z)))$. Thus, we obtain that $k + l \leq 1 + m$ because $B \cup C \subseteq U$. Thus *(iii)* holds. □

If $S = (U, A, V, f)$ is an information system, then k_S is a real function defined on the set $\mathbf{B}(A) \times \mathbf{B}(A)$. Starting with k_S we define two further functions on the set $\mathbf{B}(A) \times \mathbf{B}(A)$. For any $(X, Y) \in \mathbf{B}(A) \times \mathbf{B}(A)$ we put

$$\sigma_S(X, Y) = 1 - k_S(X, Y),$$

$$\rho_S = \frac{1}{2}(\sigma_S(X, Y) + \sigma_S(Y, X)).$$

The function ρ_S has some important properties.

Theorem 85. *If $S = (U, A, V, f)$ is an information system and X, X', Y, Y', Z are sets of attributes, then the following assertions hold.*

(i) $0 \leq \rho_S(X, Y) \leq 1$.
(ii) $\rho_S(X, X) = 0$.
(iii) $\rho_S(X, Y) = 0$ *if and only if* $\mathbf{i}(X) = \mathbf{i}(Y)$.
(iv) $\rho_S(X, Y) = \rho_S(Y, X)$.
(v) $\rho_S(X, Z) \leq \rho_S(X, Y) + \rho_S(Y, Z)$.
(vi) If $\mathbf{i}(X) = \mathbf{i}(X')$ *and* $\mathbf{i}(Y) = \mathbf{i}(Y')$, *then* $\rho_S(X, Y) = \rho_S(X', Y')$.

Proof. Since $X \rightarrow_S^k Y$ implies $0 \leq k \leq 1$, we have $0 \leq \sigma_S(X, Y) \leq 1$; similarly, we obtain $0 \leq \sigma_S(Y, X) \leq 1$ which implies *(i)*. Furthermore, *(ii)* follows from the fact that $X \rightarrow_S^1 X$ holds. If $\rho_S(X, Y) = 0$, then $\sigma_S(X, Y) = 0$, $\sigma_S(Y, X) = 0$ which implies that $X \rightarrow_S^1 Y$, $Y \rightarrow_S^1 X$; this means $\mathbf{i}(X) = \mathbf{i}(Y)$ by Example 31. On the other hand, $\mathbf{i}(X) = \mathbf{i}(Y)$ is equivalent to $X \rightarrow_S^1 Y$, $Y \rightarrow_S^1 X$ by Example 31 which implies that $\rho_S(X, Y) = 0$. Thus *(iii)* holds. Property *(iv)* follows from the definition of ρ_S. Furthermore, if $\sigma_S(X, Y) = 1 - k$, $\sigma_S(Y, Z) = 1 - l$, $\sigma_S(X, Z) = 1 - m$, then $m \geq k + l - 1$ by *(iii)* of Theorem 84. It follows that $1 - m \leq 2 - k - l$ which implies that $\sigma_S(X, Z) \leq \sigma_S(X, Y) + \sigma_S(Y, Z)$. Similarly, $\sigma_S(Z, X) \leq \sigma_S(Z, Y) + \sigma_S(Y, X)$; these inequalities imply *(v)*. Finally, if $\mathbf{i}(X) = \mathbf{i}(X')$, $\mathbf{i}(Y) = \mathbf{i}(Y')$, then $\rho_S(X, X') = 0$, $\rho_S(Y, Y') = 0$ by *(iii)* and $\rho_S(X', Y') \leq \rho_S(X', X) + \rho_S(X, Y') \leq \rho_S(X, X') + \rho_S(X, Y) + \rho_S(Y, Y') = \rho_S(X, Y)$ by *(iv)* and *(v)*. Similarly, we obtain $\rho_S(X, Y) \leq \rho_S(X', Y')$ and we have *(vi)*. □

As a consequence of Theorem 85, we obtain

Theorem 86. *Let $S = (U, A, V, f)$ be an information system, $(A, \mathbf{K}_S)$ its dependence space. For any $\mathbf{X} \in \mathbf{B}(A)/\mathbf{K}_S$, $\mathbf{Y} \in \mathbf{B}(A)/\mathbf{K}_S$ put $d_S(\mathbf{X}, \mathbf{Y}) = \rho_S(X, Y)$ where $X \in \mathbf{X}$, $Y \in \mathbf{Y}$ are arbitrary. Then d_S is a distance function on the set $\mathbf{B}(A)/\mathbf{K}_S$.*

Proof. Indeed, if X, $X' \in \mathbf{X}$, then $(X, X') \in \mathbf{K}_S$ which means $\mathbf{i}(X) = \mathbf{i}(X')$. By *(vi)* of Theorem 85 the definition of $d_S(\mathbf{X}, \mathbf{Y})$ is correct because it does not depend of the choice of representatives $X \in \mathbf{X}$, $Y \in \mathbf{Y}$ of blocks $\mathbf{X}$, $\mathbf{Y}$. □

Example 32. Let $S = (U, A, V, f)$ be a decision table, C its set of conditions, and D its set of decisions. There exists exactly one number k such that $0 \leq k \leq 1$ and $C \to_S^k D$. By definition of k we obtain $k = |U|^{-1}|\bigcup((U/\mathbf{i}(C)) * (U/\mathbf{i}(D)))|$. Put $U' = \bigcup((U/\mathbf{i}(C)) * (U/\mathbf{i}(D)))$, $f' = f \cap (U' \times A)$, $S' = (U', A, V, f')$ and suppose $U' \neq \emptyset$. Then U' is the union of all blocks of $\mathbf{i}(C)$ such that any of them is included in a block of $\mathbf{i}(D)$ which means that $\mathbf{IND}_{S'}(C) \subseteq \mathbf{IND}_{S'}(D)$ and, therefore, $C \to D\ (A, \mathbf{K}_{S'})$. It follows that S' is a consistent decision table. Thus, the values of decisions are determined by the values of conditions in S'. Hence, the number k indicates the percentage of elements in U such that the values of decisions are defined by the values of conditions in the sense described in Section 5.

Let us have $U = \{u_1, \ldots, u_5\}$, $A = \{a, b, c, d\}$, $V = \{p, w, n, h, o, t\}$. Suppose that $S = (U, A, V, f)$ is an information system with the following table.

Table 14.

	a	b	c	d
u_1	p	h	h	o
u_2	p	h	h	o
u_3	w	n	h	o
u_4	w	n	h	t
u_5	p	n	n	t

This may be interpreted as follows. Elements in U are patients of a surgery clinic, a, b, c are medical examinations and d is a decision. The examination a will be interpreted as patient's state with values p (= pains) and w (= without pains); b and c are blood coagulation and temperature, respectively, with values n (= normal) and h (= high). The decision d may have values o (= operation) and t (= treatment without operation).

For the patients the table gives values of all examinations and decisions. We try to find to which extent the values of decisions are destined by the results of examinations. Put $C = \{a, b, c\}$, $D = \{d\}$. Hence S is a decision table. By Theorem 83, $k_S(C, D)$ is the probability that in an arbitrarily chosen $u \in U$, the set C respects D, i.e., the percentage of patients whose block of $\mathbf{i}(C)$ is included in a block of $\mathbf{i}(D)$. This means that for these patients the values of attributes in D are destined by the values of attributes in C.

Clearly, $U/\mathbf{i}(C) = \{\{u_1, u_2\}, \{u_3, u_4\}, \{u_5\}\}$, $U/\mathbf{i}(D) = \{\{u_1, u_2, u_3\}, \{u_4, u_5\}\}$. It follows that $(U/\mathbf{i}(C)) * (U/\mathbf{i}(D)) = \{\{u_1, u_2\}, \{u_5\}\}$, and, therefore, $\bigcup((U/\mathbf{i}(C)) * (U/\mathbf{i}(D))) = \{u_1, u_2, u_5\}$. Hence $k_S(C, D) = 0.6$. Thus, the percentage of patients for which the correct decision can be made on the basis of results of examinations a, b, c only is 60; these patients are u_1, u_2, u_5. Clearly, $f(u, a) = p$, $f(u, b) = h$, $f(u, c) = h$ lead to the decision o while $f(u, a) = p$, $f(u, b) = n$, $f(u, c) = n$ lead to decision t. The cases u_3, u_4 where $f(u, a) = w$, $f(u, b) = n$, $f(u, c) = n$ cannot be decided on the basis of results of a, b, c only, because in this set of patients the same values of conditions lead to different values of decisions.

Put $U' = \{u_1, u_2, u_5\}$, let f' be defined by the following table.

Table 15.

	a	b	c	d
u_1	p	h	h	o
u_2	p	h	h	o
u_5	p	n	n	t

Then $S' = (U', A, V, f')$ is a consistent decision table. Clearly, $\{b\}$ and $\{c\}$ are $\mathbf{D}(\mathbf{K}_{S'}, D)$-reducts of the set C, i.e., S' may be simplified by cancelling either a, c or a, b.

The results of Sections 6 and 7 enable to construct, to any dependence space (A, K) any information system S whose dependence space coincides with (A, K) and to define a distance function ρ_S on the set $\mathbf{B}(A)/K$. Clearly, the values of ρ_S are rational. This correspondence of information systems and distance functions provokes the following problems.

Problem 87. Let (A, K) be a dependence space and d a distance function on the set $\mathbf{B}(A)/K$ having rational values. Does there exist an information system $S = (U, A, V, f)$ such that $d_S = d$?

Let $S = (U, A, V, f)$, $S' = (U', A, V, f')$ be information systems. They are said to be *isomorphic* if there exists a bijection b of U onto U' such that $f'(b(u), a) = f(u, a)$ for any $(u, a) \in U \times A$.

Problem 88. Let $S = (U, A, V, f)$, $S' = (U', A, V, f')$ be information systems whose dependence spaces coincide and $d_S = d_{S'}$ holds. Are they isomorphic ?

The author does not know the solutions of these problems.

References

[Bi1] Birkhoff, G.: Lattice Theory. Third edition, American Math. Society, Providence, (1984)

[BB1] Birkhoff, G., Bartee, T.C.: Modern Applied Algebra. McGraw Hill, New York, (1970)

[Bo1] Boruvka, O.: Grundlagen der Gruppoid- und Gruppentheorie. VEB Deutscher Verlag der Wissenschaften, Berlin, (1960)

[Ce1] Cendrowska, J.: PRISM: An algorithm for inducing modular rules. Int. J. Man-Machine Studies, **27**, (1987), 349–370

[Du1] Duda, J.: Boolean concept lattices and good contexts. Čas. Pěst. Mat. **114**, (1989), 165–175

[GJ1] Garey, M.R., Johnson, D.S.: Computers and intractability. A guide to the theory of NP-completeness. W.H. Freeman and Co., San Francisco, (1979)

[Ge1] Gentzen, G.: Untersuchungen über das logische Schließen. Mathematische Zeitschrift, **39**, (1935), 176–210

[Gl1] Głazek, K.: Some old and new problems of the independence in mathematics. Colloquium Math., **17**, (1979), 127–189

[HNP1] Haupt, O., Nöbeling, G., Pauc, C.: Über Abhängigkeitsräume. J. Reine Angew. Math., **181**, (1940), 193–217

[Li1] Lipski, W., Jr.: Two NP-complete problems related to information retrieval. Fundamentals of Computation Theory. Lecture Notes in Computer Science, **56**, Springer, Berlin, (1977), 452–458

[LO1] Lucchesi, C.L., Osborn, S.L.: Candidate keys for relations. J. Comput. System Sci., **17**, (1978), 270–279

[Ma1] Marczewski, E.: A general scheme of independence in mathematics. Bull. Acad. Polon. Sci. Sér. Math. Astronom. Phys., **6**, (1958), 731–736

[MP1] Marek, W., Pawlak, Z.: Mathematical foundations of information storage and retrieval I, II, III. CC PAS Reports, **135, 136, 137**, Warszawa, (1973)

[MP2] Marek, W., Pawlak, Z.: Information storage and retrieval system — mathematical foundations. CC PAS Reports, **149**, Warszawa, (1974). Also in: Theoretical Computer Science, **1**, (1976), 331–354

[Mr1] Mrózek, A.: Rough sets and some aspects of expert system realization. 7th International Workshop on Expert Systems and their Applications, Avignon, (1987), 597–611

[Mr2] Mrózek, A.: Rough sets and dependency analysis among attributes in computer implementation of expert's inference models. Int. J. Man-Machine Studies, **30**, (1989), 457–473

[NoJ1] Novotný, J.: Application of information systems to evaluation of pedagogical research. (Czech). To appear in Sborník prací pedagogické fakulty Masarykovy Univerzity (Publications of the Pedagogical Faculty, Masaryk University, Brno, (1993))

[NN1] Novotný, J., Novotný, M.: Notes on the algebraic approach to dependence in information systems. Fundamenta Informaticae, **16**, (1992), 263–273

[NN2] Novotný, J., Novotný, M.: On dependence in Wille's contexts. Fundamenta Informaticae, **19**, (1993), 343–353

[NoM1] Novotný, M.: On sequents defined by means of information systems. Fundamenta Informaticae, **4**, (1981), 1041–1048

[NoM2] Novotný, M.: Remarks on sequents defined by means of information systems. Fundamenta Informaticae, **6**, (1983), 71–79

[NP1] Novotný, M., Pawlak, Z.: On a representation of rough sets by means of information systems. Fundamenta Informaticae, **6**, (1983), 289–296

[NP2] Novotný, M., Pawlak, Z.: Characterization of rough top equalities and rough bottom equalities. Bull. Polish Acad. Sci. Math., **33**, (1985), 91–97

[NP3] Novotný, M., Pawlak, Z.: On rough equalities. Bull. Polish Acad. Sci. Math., **33**, (1985), 99–104

[NP4] Novotný, M., Pawlak, Z.: Black box analysis and rough top equality. Bull. Acad. Sci. Math., **33**, (1985), 105–113

[NP5] Novotný, M., Pawlak, Z.: Concept forming and black boxes. Bull. Polish Acad. Sci. Math., **35**, (1987), 133–141

[NP6] Novotný, M., Pawlak, Z.: Partial dependency of attributes. Bull. Polish Acad. Sci. Math., **36**, (1988), 453–458

[NP7] Novotný, M., Pawlak, Z.: Independence of attributes. Bull. Polish Acad. Sci. Math., **36**, (1988), 459–465

[NP8] Novotný, M., Pawlak, Z.: On superreducts. Bull. Polish Acad. Sci. Tech. Sci., **38**, (1990), 101–112

[NP9] Novotný, M., Pawlak, Z.: Algebraic theory of independence in information systems. Fundamenta Informaticae, **14**, (1991), 454–476

[NP10] Novotný, M., Pawlak, Z.: On a problem concerning dependence spaces. Fundamenta Informaticae, **16**, (1992), 275–287

[Pa1] Pawlak, Z.: Mathematical foundations of information retrieval. CC PAS Reports, **101**, (1973), Warszawa

[Pa2] Pawlak, Z.: Information systems. ICS PAS Reports, **338**, Warszawa, (1978)

[Pa3] Pawlak, Z.: Rough sets. ICS PAS Reports, **431**, Warszawa, (1981)

[Pa4] Pawlak, Z.: Rough sets. Algebraic and topological approach. Intern. Journ. of Computer and Information Sciences, **11**, (1982), 341–366

[Pa5] Pawlak, Z.: Systemy informacyjne, podstawy teoretyczne (Information systems, theoretical foundations). Wydawnictwa Naukowo-Techniczne, Warszawa, (1983)

[Pa6] Pawlak, Z.: Learning from examples – the case of an imperfect teacher. Bull. Polish Acad. Sci. Tech., **35**, (1987), 259–264

[Pa7] Pawlak, Z.: Rough Sets. Theoretical Aspects of Reasoning about Data. Kluwer, Dordrecht – Boston – London, (1991)

[Ra1] Rauszer, C.M.: Reducts in information systems. Fundamenta Informaticae, **15**, (1991), 1–12

[Sz1] Szász, G.: Introduction to Lattice Theory. Academic Press, Budapest, (1963)

[Wi1] Wille, R.: Restructuring lattice theory. In: Ordered Sets (Ed. I. Rival), Reidel, Dordrecht – Boston, (1982), 445–470

IV

REASONING ABOUT CONSTRAINTS

Chapter 9

Indiscernibility-Based Formalization of Dependencies in Information Systems

Wojciech Buszkowski[1] *and Ewa Orlowska*[2]

1 Institute of Mathematics, Adam Mickiewicz University, Poznan,
e-mail: buszko@math.amu.edu.pl

2 Institute of Telecommunications, Warsaw, Poland,
e–mail: orlowska@itl.waw.pl

Abstract: Various classes of data constraints in information systems are modelled by means of indiscernibility relations induced by sets of attributes. A relational logic is presented that enables us to express these constraints. A proof system for the logic is given and its completeness is proved with respect to a class of algebras of relations generated by indiscernibility relations. Some other classes of models for the logic are defined that correspond to typical kinds of constraints in information systems. Decidability of the validity problem with respect to these classes of models is discussed and some classes of formulas with the decidable validity problem are given.

1 Introduction and Preliminaries

Dependencies between information items play an important role in knowledge representation. Their crucial role in databases, decision tables, knowledge bases is commonly recognized. The important issue in all these fields is specification of constraints that the data must satisfy. Intuitively, the meaning of a dependency is that if some information items exist in a knowledge base, then either they are somehow related to each other, or some other information items must exist in the knowledge base. Various classes of dependencies have been extensively studied in the literature. The study of dependency theory began with the introduction of the notion of functional dependency in relational databases (Codd 1972). This opened up the possibility of specifying data in the form of facts and constraints. In this connection the problem arose of development of formal systems for proving implications of dependencies. In those systems any set of dependencies is identified with a set of sentences of a formal language, and a proof system for the language serves as an inference tool for proving dependencies and various relationships between them. The first formal system for dependencies was given in Armstrong (1974); a survey of dependency theory can be found in Fagin and Vardi (1986).

In this paper we develop a relational formalism for representation of and reasoning about data dependencies. The formalism is a fragment of the classical relational calculus RC (Tarski 1941). The paper is organized as follows.

In section 2 we provide representation of various kinds of dependencies in terms of indiscernibility relations, i.e. binary relations that are associated with any collection of data and reflect a certain type of incompleteness of those data.

In section 3 we present a formal logical system for proving dependencies and relationships between them. The system is referred to as the Restricted Relational Calculus (RRC). While in RC the relation variables range over arbitrary binary relations, RRC limits their range to equivalence relations. It is sufficient since indiscernibility relations are equivalence relations. We present a natural semantics for the language of RRC, next we develop a Rasiowa–Sikorski style axiomatization of RRC and prove its completeness.

Section 4 is concerned with decidability problems. First, we show that RRC is undecidable. The proof employs a reduction of the word problem for semigroups to the validity problem for RRC. The reduction appears to need essentially more sophistication than in the case of RC. Second, we distinguish some decidable fragments of RRC by showing that they possess the finite model property.

In section 5 our relational formalization of dependencies is compared with the formalization within the classical logic. We show how the propositional formulas that represent functional and multivalued dependencies can be derived from the respective relational formulas.

Algebras of binary relations generated by equivalence relations, and RRC as their logical counterpart, appear to be a natural framework for dealing with many theoretical problems concerning data dependencies. Within this framework we can formulate much more types of useful dependencies, than in e.g. propositional logic. On the other hand, compared with first order logic, RRC is more compatible with the actual needs of knowledge representation. It exibits just that fragment of logic that is needed to reason about dependencies. In particular, the decidable subclasses of RRC provide useful and interesting classes of dependencies. The basic ideas of the relational approach to data dependencies have been presented in Orlowska (1983, 1987). The main results of this paper have been announced in Buszkowski and Orlowska (1985, 1986).

Below we recall basic notions relevant to dependency theory. We motivate our approach with applications to database dependencies, however its scope is broader and refers to data dependencies in general. Given a finite set AT of attributes, and a set VAL of values of attributes, by a tuple we mean a mapping $t: AT \rightarrow VAL$. For $X \subseteq AT$, $t[X]$ denotes the restriction of tuple t to set X. Any set of tuples with a common domain is called a (database) relation. The variables M,N (resp. t,u; A,B,C; X,Y,Z) will range over database relations (resp. tuples, attributes, sets of attributes). Given a relation M, by AT_M we denote the set of attributes that is the domain of the tuples from M.

For $X \subseteq AT_M$, by the projection of relation M onto set X we mean the relation:

$$pr_X(M)=\{t[X]: t \in M\}.$$

By the join M#N of relations M an N we mean the following relation:

$$M\#N=\{t: \text{domain of } t \text{ is } AT_M \cup AT_N,\ t[AT_M]\in M,\ t[AT_N]\in N\}$$

Let M be a database relation, and let $X\subseteq AT_M$. Tuples $t,u\in M$ are said to be indiscernible in M with respect to X whenever their restrictions to X are equal. We define the respective indiscernibility relation as follows:

$$(t,u)\in ind_M(X) \text{ iff } t[X]=u[X].$$

Clearly, for any X the relation ind(X) is an equivalence relation on M. In the sequel we often omit the subscript, and write ind(X) when a database relation in question is clear from the context or immaterial.

Example 1.1. Consider relation M defined as follows:

	attributes		
tuples	A	B	C
t_1	a	b	c
t_2	a'	b	c
t_3	a'	b'	c
t_4	a	b'	c'

Indiscernibility relation ind(A) determined by attribute A consists of the following pairs of tuples:

$$ind(A)=\{(t_1,t_1), (t_2,t_2), (t_3,t_3), (t_4,t_4), (t_1,t_4), (t_4,t_1), (t_2,t_3), (t_3,t_2)\}.$$

Indiscernibility relation ind(BC) determined by attributes B and C consists of the following tuples:

$$ind(BC)=\{(t_1,t_1), (t_2,t_2), (t_3,t_3), (t_4,t_4), (t_1,t_2), (t_2,t_1)\}.$$

The term 'relation' has been used in the two meanings: as referring to a set of tuples or to a binary relation in a set of tuples. To avoid confusion throughout the paper we write, if necessary, 'database relation' when referring to a set of tuples and 'relation' when referring to a binary relation on a set. Binary relations are denoted by R,S,T.

Given binary relations R and S, the operations of product and conversion are defined as usual:

$$R;S=\{(x,y): \text{for some } z, (x,z)\in R \text{ and } (z,y)\in S\}$$

$$R^c=\{(x,y): (y,x)\in R\}.$$

By I_W we denote the identity relation on set W:

$$I_W=\{(x,x): x\in W\}.$$

The following lemma provides some elementary properties of indiscernibility relations.

Lemma 1.1. For any database relation M and for any $X,Y\subseteq AT_M$ the following conditions are satisfied:

(a) $ind(AT_M)=I_M$, $ind(\emptyset)=M\times M$

(b) $ind(X\cup Y)=ind(X)\cap ind(Y)$

(c) $(ind(X)\cup ind(Y))^*\subseteq ind(X\cap Y)$, where * is the operation of the reflexive and transitive closure

(d) $ind(X)\cup ind(Y)\subseteq ind(X);ind(Y)$

(e) If $X\subseteq Y$, then $ind(Y)\subseteq ind(X)$

(f) $ind(X)=\bigcap\{ind(A): A\in X\}$.

2 Relational Formulation of Dependencies

Let a database relation M be given. Various attribute dependencies in M can be defined in terms of indiscernibility relations. We recall the standard definitions of those dependencies and we give their relational representation developed in Orlowska (1987). Let X,Y,Z be subsets of AT_M.

Functional dependency:

$X\rightarrow Y$ holds in M iff for all tuples $t,u\in M$ if $t[X]=u[X]$, then $t[Y]=u[Y]$.

Fact 2.1. The following conditions are equivalent:

(a) Functional dependency $X\rightarrow Y$ holds in M

(b) $ind(X)\subseteq ind(Y)$.

Example 2.1. Consider relation M defined as follows:

	A	B	C
t_1	0	0	0
t_2	1	1	1
t_3	2	1	0
t_4	2	2	1

Equivalence classes of indiscernibility relations determined by attributes A,B,and C are as follows.

ind(A): $\{t_1\}$ $\{t_2\}$ $\{t_3,t_4\}$

ind(B): $\{t_1\}$ $\{t_2,t_3\}$ $\{t_4\}$

ind(C): $\{t_1,t_3\}$ $\{t_2,t_4\}$.

Relations ind(AB), ind(BC), ind(AC) are identity relations on set $\{t_1,t_2,t_3,t_4\}$. The following functional dependencies hold in M:

$AB\rightarrow C$ $BC\rightarrow A$ $AC\rightarrow B$

Multivalued dependency:

$X\rightarrow\rightarrow Y$ holds in M iff for all tuples $t,u\in M$ if $t[X]=u[X]$, then there is $t'\in M$ such that $t'[X\cup Y]=t[X\cup Y]$ and $t'[AT_M-(X\cup Y)]=u[AT_M-(X\cup Y)]$.

Fact 2.2. The following conditions are equivalent:

(a) Multivalued dependency $X\rightarrow\rightarrow Y$ holds in M

(b) $ind(X)\subseteq ind(X\cup Y);ind(AT_M-(X\cup Y))$.

Example 2.2. Let database relation M be defined as follows:

	A	B	C
t_1	a	b	c
t_2	a	b	c'
t_3	a'	b	c
t_4	a'	b	c'

It is easy to see that multivalued dependency $B\rightarrow\rightarrow A$ holds in M.

Embedded multivalued dependency:
$X\rightarrow\rightarrow Y|Z$ holds in M iff $X\rightarrow\rightarrow Y$ holds in $pr_{X\cup Y\cup Z}(M)$.

Fact 2.3. The following conditions are equivalent:
(a) Embedded multivalued dependency $X\rightarrow\rightarrow Y|Z$ holds in M
(b) $ind(X)\subseteq ind(X\cup Y);ind(Z-(X\cup Y))$.

Decomposition:
(X,Y) holds in M iff $X\cup Y=AT_M$ and for all $t,u\in M$ if $t[X\cap Y]=u[X\cap Y]$, then there exists a $t'\in M$ such that $t'[X]=t[X]$ and $t'[Y]=u[Y]$.

Fact 2.4.
(a) Decomposition (X,Y) holds in M
(b) $X\cup Y=AT_M$ and $ind(X\cap Y)\subseteq ind(X);ind(Y)$.

Example 2.3. Consider the following database relation M:

	A	B	C
t_1	0	0	0
t_2	0	0	1
t_3	1	0	1
t_4	1	1	1
t_5	1	0	0

Decomposition $(\{A,B\},\{B,C\})$ holds in M.

Join dependency:
$*(X_1,...,X_n)$ holds in M iff $X_1\cup...\cup X_n=AT_M$ and M is the join of relations $pr_{Xi}(M)$, $i=1,...,n$.

Fact 2.5.
(a) Join dependency $*(X_1,...X_n)$ holds in M implies
(b) $ind(X_1\cap...\cap X_n)\subseteq ind(X_1);...;ind(X_n)$.

A dependency defined by condition (b) above for $X_1,...,X_n$ such that $X_1\cup...\cup X_n=AT_M$ will be called a generalized join dependency and denoted by $\#(X_1,...,X_n)$.

In the next section we show that also Boolean dependencies (Sagiv et al. 1981) admit a straightforward formulation in terms of indiscernibility relations. A similar approach can be applied to many other kinds of dependencies. However, equality–generating or tuple–generating dependencies (Beeri and Vardi 1984) seem to be not expressible in that form, since they require relations between more than two tuples.

Below we give two examples of application of the above framework to proving equivalences of dependencies. Two dependencies are said to be equivalent in a database relation M iff either they both hold in M or both do not hold in M. First, we state a useful lemma.

Lemma 2.6. If binary relations R,S,T are symmetric and transitive, then the following conditions are equivalent:
(a) $R \subseteq (R \cap S);T$
(b) $R \subseteq (R \cap S);(R \cap T)$.

Proof: Assume (a). We have $R = R \cap ((R \cap S);T) = R \cap ((R \cap S);((R \cap T) \cup (-R \cap T))) = (R \cap ((R \cap S);(R \cap T))) \cup (R \cap ((R \cap S);(-R \cap T)))$. From symmetry and transitivity of R it follows that $R;-R \subseteq -R$, and hence $R \cap ((R \cap S);(-R \cap T)) \subseteq R \cap -R = \emptyset$, which yields (b). Implication from (b) to (a) is obvious.

Example 2.4. We show that in any database relation M the following holds:
(a) Dependencies $X \to\to Y$ and $(X \cup Y, X \cup Z)$ are equivalent, where $Z = AT_M - Y$.

Let $Z' = AT_M - (X \cup Y)$. By lemma 2.2, $X \to\to Y$ holds in M iff

(i) $ind(X) \subseteq ind(X \cup Y);ind(Z')$.

By lemma 1.1(b) and lemma 2.6 condition (i) is equivalent to:

(ii) $ind(X) \subseteq ind(X \cup Y);ind(X \cup Z')$.

Since $X \cup Z' = X \cup Z$ and $X = (X \cup Y) \cap (X \cup Z)$, we conclude from (ii) that decomposition $(X \cup Y, X \cup Z)$ holds in M.

Example 2.5. We show that in any database relation M the following holds:
(a) If $X \cup Y \cup Z = AT_M$ and $Y \cap Z \subseteq X$, then dependencies $X \to\to Y$ and $X \to\to Z$ are equivalent in M.

By lemma 2.2 these multivalued dependencies hold in M iff the following conditions are satisfied:

(i) $ind(X) \subseteq ind(X \cup Y);ind(AT_M - (X \cup Y))$ and

(i') $ind(X) \subseteq ind(X \cup Z);ind(AT_M - (X \cup Z))$.

By the first assumption conditions (i) and (i') are equivalent to the following (ii) and (ii'), respectively:

(ii) $ind(X) \subseteq ind(X \cup Y);ind(Z - (X \cup Y))$

(ii') $ind(X) \subseteq ind(X \cup Z);ind(Y - (X \cup Z))$

Using lemma 2.6 and equalities $X \cup (Z - (X \cup Y) = X \cup (Z - Y)$ and $X \cup (Y - (X \cup Z)) = X \cup (Y - Z)$ we transform (ii) and (ii') into (iii) and (iii'), respectively:

(iii) $ind(X) \subseteq ind(X \cup Y);ind(X \cup (Z - Y))$

(iii') $ind(X) \subseteq ind(X \cup Z);ind(X \cup (Y - Z))$

From the second assumption and lemma 1.1(e) we obtain $ind(X) \subseteq ind(Y \cap Z)$, and hence we have:

(iv) $ind(X\cup Y)=ind(X)\cap ind(Y)=ind(X)\cap ind(Y\cap Z)\cap ind(Y-Z)=ind(X)\cap ind(Y-Z)=ind(X\cup(Y-Z))$

(v) $ind(X\cup Z)=ind(X\cup(Z-Y))$.

Accordingly, (iii) and (iii') are of the forms (vi) and (vi'), respectively::

(vi) $R\subseteq S;T$

(vi') $R\subseteq T;S$.

If R,S,T are symmetric relations, then (vi) and (vi') are equivalent, since $R\subseteq S;T$ entails $R=R^c\subseteq(S;T)^c=T^c;S^c=T;S$, and conversely. This completes the proof of condition (a).

Arguments of that kind can easily be formalized within a two–sorted formal system, employing variables for sets of attributes, the operator ind, and Boolean operations, as well as relational operations on the resulting relations between tuples. In the present paper we suggest another approach. The equality from lemma 1.1(f) enables us to eliminate application of ind to sets of cardinality greater than one. Next, by identifying syntactically ind(A) with A we can abandon ind altogether in the syntax of the underlying expressions. The simple formalism obtained in this way enables us to carry out proofs of the above form, and it has an advantage of being compatible with the standard relational calculus. In the following sections we present these ideas in detail.

3 Restricted Relational Calculus

In this section we present a formal system that will be referred to as Restricted Relational calculus (RRC). The language of the system enables us to express relational definitions of dependencies, and deduction apparatus of the system provides a means for proving dependencies as well as various relationships between them. The alphabet of RRC consists of the following pairwise disjoint sets of symbols:

AT an infinite denumerable set of attribute variables (for the sake of simplicity we denote them in the same way as attributes that is A,B, etc., and finite sets of attribute variables are denoted by X,Y,Z),

CON={1} the set consisting of the relational constant 1 interpreted as the universal relation,

$\{-,\cup,\cap,;\}$ the set of relational operations,

{(,)} the set of parentheses.

The set FOR of formulas of RRC is defined inductively:

$AT\subseteq FOR$, $1\in FOR$,

If $P,Q\in FOR$, then $-P$, $P\cup Q$, $P\cap Q$, $P;Q\in FOR$.

A natural database semantics of RRC is defined as follows. By a model we mean a pair (M,m) such that M is a database relation, and a function m is a mapping from AT into AT_M that assigns attributes of M to attribute variables. For a set X of variables we define $m(X)=\{m(A): A\in X\}$. Given a model (M,m), we define a family of relations $r(P)\subseteq M\times M$, for $P\in FOR$. Relation r(P) is referred to as the meaning of formula P in model (M,m).

(m1) $r(A)=ind_M(m(A))$ for every attribute variable A,
(m2) $r(1)= M \times M$,
(m3) $r(-P)=M \times M-r(P)$,
(m4) $r(P \# Q)=r(P) \# r(Q)$ for $\# = \cup, \cap, ;$.

Accordingly, attribute variables are interpreted as indiscernibility relations determined by the respective attributes, constant 1 is interpreted as the universal relation in the underlying set of tuples, and relational operations are interpreted in the standard way. Each formula of RRC represents a binary relation in a set of tuples, however, its meaning is not necessarily an equivalence relation.

A formula P is said to be true in model (M,m) iff $r(P)=M \times M$. P is valid iff it is true in all models. We say that a set F of formulas implies a formula P iff for any model (M,m), P is true in (M,m) whenever all the formulas form F are true in (M,m). By True(M,m), Val, Cn(F) we denote the set of all formulas true in (M,m), the set of all valid formulas, and all the formulas implied by the formulas from F, respectively. Clearly, $Val=Cn(\emptyset)$.

It is easy to see that all the relational definitions of dependencies given in section 2 can be represented as formulas of RRC. For a finite set F of formulas, formula con(F) is defined as follows:

$$con(F)=1 \text{ if } F=\emptyset,\ con(F)=P_1 \cap \ldots \cap P_n \text{ if } F=\{P_1,\ldots,P_n\}.$$

Consider formulas of the form:

(FD) $-con(X) \cup con(Y)$
(EMVD) $-con(X) \cup (con(X \cup Y);con(Z-(X \cup Y)))$
(GJD) $-con(X_1 \cap \ldots \cap X_n) \cup (con(X_1);\ldots;con(X_n))$
(GDC) $-con(X \cap Y) \cup (con(X);con(Y))$

They are referred to as functional dependency formulas (FD–formulas), embedded multivalued dependency formulas (EMVD–formulas), generalized join dependency formulas (GJD–formulas), and generalized decomposition formulas (GDC–formulas), respectively.

Let a database relation M be given, and let $f:AT_M \rightarrow AT$ be a mapping such that if $A \neq B$, then $f(A) \neq f(B)$. We define a database model (M,m_f) determined by f as follows:

(m5) $m_f(A)=f^{-1}(A)$ if $A \in f(AT_M)$ and otherwise $m_f(A)=B$

where B is a fixed attribute from AT_M, $f^{-1}(A)$ is the inverse image of A under f, and for any $X \subseteq AT_M$ the image of X under f is defined as $f(X)=\{f(A): A \in X\}$.
Clearly, if for some $X \subseteq AT$ we have $X=f(AT_M)$, then $m_f(X)=AT_M$. It is easy to verify that the above formulas represent dependencies in the following natural way.

Theorem 3.1. For every M and f as above the following conditions hold:
(a) (FD) is true in (M,m_f) iff functional dependency $f^{-1}(X) \rightarrow f^{-1}(Y)$ holds in M
(b) (EMVD) formula such that $Z=f(AT_M)$ is true in (M,m_f) iff multivalued dependency $f^{-1}(X) \rightarrow\rightarrow f^{-1}(Y)$ holds in M
(c) (EMVD) is true in (M,m_f) iff embedded multivalued dependency $f^{-1}(X) \rightarrow\rightarrow f^{-1}(Y) | f^{-1}(Z)$ holds in M

(d) (GDC) formula such that $X \cup Y = f(AT_M)$ is true in (M, m_f) iff decomposition $(f^{-1}(X), f^{-1}(Y))$ holds in M

(e) (GJD) formula such that $X_1 \cup ... \cup X_n = f(AT_M)$ is true in (M, m_f) iff generalized join dependency $\#(f^{-1}(X_1), ..., f^{-1}(X)_n)$ holds in M

Any formula of RRC can be treated as a generalized dependency. Such a dependency P is said to hold in M iff P is true in (M, m_f) for some f.

We distinguish some particular classes of generalized dependencies. A formula P of RRC is said to be positive (resp. negative) iff every occurrence of product operation ; in P falls into the scope of an even (resp. odd) number of complementation symbols –. A formula that is both positive and negative, that is it contains no product symbol at all, is said to be Boolean. Observe, that FD–formulas, EMVD–formulas, GJD–formulas, and GDC–formulas are positive. Moreover, FD–formulas are Boolean. Boolean formulas are counterparts of Boolean dependencies considered in Sagiv et al. (1981).

In the following we introduce a relational semantics for the language of RRC. Let U be nonemty set, by REL(U) and EQ(U) we denote the set of all binary relations on U and the set of all equivalence relations on U, respectively. By an r–model (resp. e–model) for RRC we mean any pair (U,m) such that

(m6) m is a mapping of AT into REL(U) (resp. EQ(U)).

We extend the mapping m to all the formulas be setting:

(m7) $m(1) = U \times U$

(m8) $m(-P) = U \times U - m(P)$

(m9) $m(P \# Q) = m(P) \# m(Q)$ for $\# = \cup, \cap, ;$.

A formula P is said to be true in an r–model (e–model) (U,m) iff $m(P) = U \times U$. It is r–valid (e–valid) iff it is true in all r–models (e–models). In a natural way we define entailments of the form: a set F of formulas r–implies (e–implies) a formula P.

We show that database semantics of RRC is equivalent to semantics of e–models.

Theorem 3.2.

(a) For every database model (M,m) there is an e–model (U,m') with m'(AT) finite such that the models verify the same formulas

(b) For every e–model (U,m) with m(AT) finite, there is a database model (M,m') such that the models verify the same formulas.

Proof: Given a database model (M,m), we define e–model (U,m') as follows. We put U=M, and define $m': AT \rightarrow EQ(U)$ by setting $m'(A) = ind_M(A)$. Clearly, the formulas that are true in (M,m) are precisely those that are true in (U,m').

Conversely, given an e–model (U,m), with m(AT) finte, we define M and m' as follows. Take $AT_M = m(AT)$. For $u \in U$ define tuple t_u by setting $t_u(m(A)) = u/m(A)$, where u/m(A) is the equivalence class of m(A) generated by u. Next, define $M = \{t_u : u \in U\}$. It is easy to see that for $u, w \in U$ we have $(t_u, t_w) \in ind_M(m(A))$ iff $(u, w) \in m(A)$.

Define m'(A)=m(A). It is easy to check that the formulas true in (U,m) coincide with those true in (M,m').

As a consequence we obtain the following theorem.

Theorem 3.3. For any finite set F of formulas and for any formula P the following conditions are satisfied:
(a) F implies P iff F e–implies P
(b) P is valid iff P is e–valid.

A similar logical system RC can be defined for the standard relational calculus investigated in Tarski (1941). The language of RC is an extension of the language of RRC obtained by adjoining the operation symbol of converse and a constant for the identity relation. The semantics of RC is that of r–models. We have abandoned converse and identity in RRC, since they do not enter the definitions of dependencies, but this limitation is inessential, all the forthcoming results can easily be modified to cover RC. RRC can be viewed as a fragment of RC, since we can translate RRC formulas into RC formulas applying the well known definition of equivalence relation that is expressible in RC.

RRC is expressive enough to admit an internal definition of entailment. For any formula P define a formula neg(P) as follows:

$$neg(P)=1;-P;1.$$

It is easy to check that for any database model (M,m) we have:

(m10) $r(neg(P))=\varnothing$ if $r(P)=M\times M$, otherwise $r(neg(P))=M\times M$.

As a consequence we have:

(m11) $neg(P)\in True(M,m)$ iff $P\notin True(M,m)$.

We recall that for any formulas P and Q we have $con(P,Q)=P\cap Q$.

It is easy to see that:

(m12) $con(P,Q)\in True(M,m)$ iff both $P\in True(M,m)$ and $Q\in True(M,m)$.

Now, we define implication from P to Q as follows:

$$imp(P,Q)=neg(P)\cup Q.$$

Clearly, we have:

(m13) $imp(P,Q)\in True(M,m)$ iff either $P\notin True(M,m)$ or $Q\in True(M,m)$.

Accordingly, the following form of deduction theorem holds for RRC.

Theorem 3.4. For any finite set F of formulas and for any formula P the following conditions are equivalent:
(a) $P\in Cn(F)$
(b) $imp(con(F),P)\in Val$.

The above theorem shows that the implication problem for generalized dependencies reduces to the validity problem for them. The possibility of such a reduction strongly motivates the need for development of proof theory for RRC. Having a proof system for RRC we would be able not only to derive universally valid dependencies, which are of no particular interst, but also to establish valid implications. Below we present a Rasiowa–Sikorski–style (Rasiowa and Sikorski

1963) axiomatization of RRC. Our proof system processes expressions of the form xPy, where P is a formula of RRC and x,y are tuple variables. To be more formal, we define system GRRC whose formulas xPy are built from variables taken from an infinite denumerable set VAR and from formulas of RRC. By a G–model we mean a triple (U,m,v) where (U,m) is an e–model and v is a mapping, referred to as valuation, that assigns elements from U to variables from VAR. A formula xPy is said to be true in a G–model iff $(v(x),v(y))\in m(P)$. It is true in e–model (U,m) iff it is true in (U,m,v) for all valuations $v:VAR\rightarrow U$. It is said to be valid iff it is true in all e–models. We clearly have the following semantic relationship between RRC and GRRC.

Lemma 3.5. The following conditions are equivalent:
(a) Formula P of RRC is true in an e–model (U,m)
(b) For any variables x,y, formula xPy of GRRC is true in (U,m).

The deduction rules for GRRC are of the following two forms: K/H or $K/H_1,H_2$, where K,H,H_1,H_2 are finite sequences of formulas. There are two groups of rules: decomposition rules and specific rules. Decomposition rules enable us to decompose formulas in a sequence into some simpler formulas. Decomposition depends on relational operations occurring in a formula. The specific rules enable us to modify a sequence to which they are applied, they have a status of structural rules. The role of axioms is played by what is called fundamental sequences. In what follows K and H denote finite, possibly empty, sequences of formulas of GRRC. A variable is said to be restricted in a rule whenever it does not appear in any formula of the upper sequence in that rule.

(DEC) Decomposition rules

$$(\cup)\quad \frac{K,\ xP\cup Qy,\ H}{K,\ xPy,\ xQy,\ H} \qquad (-\cup)\quad \frac{K,\ x-(P\cup Q)y,\ H}{K,\ x-Py,\ H \quad K,\ x-Qy,\ H}$$

$$(\cap)\quad \frac{K,\ xP\cap Qy,\ H}{K,\ xPy,\ H \quad K,\ xQy,\ H} \qquad (-\cap)\quad \frac{K,\ x-(P\cap Q)y,\ H}{K,\ x-Py,\ x-Qy,\ H}$$

$$(--)\quad \frac{K,\ x--Py,\ H}{K,\ xPy,\ H}$$

$$(;)\quad \frac{K,\ xP;Qy,\ H}{K,\ xPz,\ H,\ xP;Qy \quad K,\ zQy,\ H,\ xP;Qy} \quad z \text{ is a variable}$$

$$(-;)\quad \frac{K,\ x-(P;Q)y,\ H}{K,\ x-Pz,\ z-Qy,\ H} \quad z \text{ is a restricted variable}$$

(SPE) Specific rules:

(tran) $\dfrac{K, xAy, H}{K, xAz, xAy, H \quad K, zAy, xAy, H}$ z is a variable, A∈AT

(sym) $\dfrac{K, xAy, H}{K, yAx, H, xAy}$ A∈AT

A sequence of formulas is said to be fundamental whenever it contains formulas of the following form.

(FND) Fundamental sequences:

(f1) xPy, x–Py for any formula P of RRC

(f2) xAx for any A∈AT

(f3) x1y

A sequence K of formulas is true in a G–model (U,m,v) iff there is a formula in K that is true in this G–model. The truth of a sequence in e–model (U,m) and the validity of a sequence are defined in the way analogous to the respective definitions for formulas. It follows that sequences of formulas are interpreted as disjunctions of their elements. A rule of the form K/H is admissible whenever sequence K is valid iff sequence H is valid. A rule of the form $K/H_1,H_2$ is admissible whenever sequence K is valid iff both H_1 and H_2 are valid. It is easy to see that the fundamental sequences are valid and all the rules given above are admissible.

Lemma 3.6.

(a) All the rules in (DEC) and (SPE) are admissible

(b) All the sequences in (FND) are valid.

Proof: Admissibility of the decomposition rules and validity of (f1) follow from definitions of the respective relational operations. Admissibility of specific rules and validity of (f2) follow from symmetry, transitivity and reflexivity, respectively, of relations assigned in G–models to attribute variables. Validity of (f3) follows from the definition of the universal relation.

Proofs in GRRC have the form of trees. Given a formula xPy, where P might be a compound formula of RRC, we successively apply decomposition or specific rules. In this way we form a tree whose root consists of xPy and whose nodes consist of finite sequences of formulas. We stop applying rules to formulas in a node after obtaining a fundamental sequence, or when none of the rules is applicable to the formulas in this node. A branch of a proof tree is said to be closed whenever it contains a node with a fundamental sequence of formulas. A tree is closed iff all of its branches are closed.

In the following a completeness theorem for GRRC is given.

Theorem 3.7. The following conditions are equivalent:

(a) A formula xPy is valid

(b) There is a closed proof tree with formula xPy in the root.

Proof: (→) Suppose that there is no closed proof tree for xPy and consider a tree satisfying the following conditions for every non–closed branch b. We write G∈b whenever formula G is a member of a sequence of formulas in a certain node of b.

(b1) xPy∈b

(b2) If x(Q∪R)y (x–(Q∩R)y)∈b then both xQy (x–Qy)∈b and xRy (x–Ry)∈b obtained by application of rule (∪) (resp. (–∩))

(b3) If x–(Q∪R)y (x(Q∩R)y)∈b then either x–Qy (xQy)∈b or x–Ry (xRy)∈b obtained by application of rule (–∪) (resp. (∩))

(b4) If x(Q;R)y∈b then for every z∈VAR either xQz∈b or zRy∈b obtained by application of rule (;)

(b5) If x–(Q;R)y∈b then for some z∈VAR both x–Qz∈b and z–Ry∈b obtained by application of rule (–;)

(b6) If x– –Qy∈b then xQy∈b obtained by application of rule (– –)

(b7) If xAy∈b with A∈AT, then for every z∈VAR either xAz∈b or zAy∈b obtained by application of rule (tran)

(b8) If xAy∈b with A∈AT, then yAx∈b obtained by application of rule (sym).

Any tree satisfying conditions (b1),...,(b8) is referred to as a complete proof tree. The standard proof–theoretic construction shows that for every formula there is a complete proof tree with this formula in the root.

Let b be a non–closed branch of a complete proof tree. We define the system:

$$M^b=(U^b,m^b) \text{ such that}$$
$$U^b=VAR$$
$$m^b(A)=\{(x,y)\in U^b\times U^b\text{: } xAy\notin b\} \text{ for } A\in AT\cup\{1\}$$

We extend m^b in a homomorphic way to all the formulas, according to (m8), (m9). Observe that:

(i) For every A∈AT, $m^b(A)$ is an equivalence relation in set U^b.

For suppose that for some x we have $(x,x)\notin m^b(A)$. It follows that xAx∈b, and then branch b would be closed, a contradiction. Now let $(x,y)\in m^b(A)$, and hence xAy ∉b. If $(y,x)\notin m^b(A)$, then yAx∈b, and by (b8) we have xAy∈b, a contradiction. Similarly, (b7) enables us to prove transitivity of $m^b(A)$.

(ii) $m^b(1)$ is the universal relation on U^b

For otherwise x1y∈b for some x,y which would make branch b closed.

We conclude that (U^b,m^b) is an e–model. Let v^b be a valuation such that $v^b(x)=x$ for every variable x. We say that formula xQy is indecomposable whenever Q ∈AT∪{1}. Let IND^b be the set of all the indecomposable formulas occurring in the nodes of branch b. From definition of m^b we have:

(iii) Any formula from IND^b is not true in (U^b,m^b,v^b)

We define an order of a formula of RRC:

If A is an attribute variable then ord(A)=ord(1)=1,

If ord(Q)=n then we define ord(–Q)=n+1,

If ord(Q)≤n and ord(R)≤n and at least one of the inequalities is =, then for every binary relational operation # we define ord(B#C)=n+1.

We will show that:

(iv) xPy is not true in (U^b,m^b,v^b)

For suppose conversely, and let F^b be the set of formulas on b that are true in (U^b,m^b,v^b). F^b is nonempty since xPy is its member. Let Q be a formula of a minimal order such that uQw is in F^b for some variables u,w. We show that Q must be either an attribute variable or 1. Q cannot be of the form u–Aw for an attribute variable A, for otherwise we would have u–Aw∈b and is true in (U^b,m^b,v^b), and from definition of m^b the latter is equivalent to uAw∈b. The similar argument shows that Q is not of the form –1. Suppose that Q is of the form Q1;Q2. Hence conditions (a1) uQ1;Q2w∈ b and (a2) uQ1;Q2w is true in (U^b,m^b,v^b) hold. From (a1) and (b4) we conclude that for all z either uQ1z∈b or zQ2w∈b. From (a2) we obtain that there is t such that uQ1t is true in (U^b,m^b,v^b) and tQ2w is true in (U^b,m^b,v^b). Hence either uQ1t∈F^b or tQ2w∈F^b, and Q1,Q2 have the smaller value of ord than Q, a contradiction. In a similar way we show that Q is neither a formula built with any other relational operator nor a complemented compound formula.

In view of the above uQw∈IND^b, and hence by (iii) uQw is not true in (U^b,m^b,v^b), a contradiction that completes the proof of (iv) and the proof of (→) part of the theorem. The proof of part (←) of the theorem can be easily obtained using lemma 3.6

Example 3.1. We show that dependency –(P;(Q∩S))∪P;Q is valid.

x–(P;(Q∩S))∪P;Qy
(∪)
x–(P;(Q∩S))y, xP;Qy
(–;) new variable:=z
x–Pz, z–(Q∩S)y, xP;Qy
(–∩)
x–Pz, z–Qy, z–Sy, xP;Qy
(;) variable:=z

x–Pz, z–Qy, z–Sy, xPz, xP;Qy	x–Pz, z–Qy, z–Sy, zQy, xP;Qy
fundamental	fundamental

4 Decidability Problems

In this section we prove that the validity problem for RRC is undecidable, and hence there is no decision procedure for verifying the validity of dependencies and validity of implication of dependencies. One can only get a proof procedure, as for example the procedure provided by GRRC in section 3. Next, we establish some decidable cases of the validity problem for RRC.

Given a finite alphabet V, by V^+ we denote the set of all the nonempty words over V. Any pair (a,b) such that a,b∈V^+ is referred to as an equality over V. By E(V) we denote the set of all equalities over V. By an assignment we mean any mapping f:V→G, where G is a semigroup. Clearly, any assignment f can be treated as a homomorphism of V^+ into G. An equality (a,b)∈E(V) is said to be satisfied by an assignment f if f(a)=f(b). We say that an equality (a,b) is a consequence of a set $E\subseteq E(V)$ ($E|-(a,b)$) if (a,b) is satisfied by every assignment that satisfies all the equalities from E.

Fact 4.1. (Davis 1958) There exists a finite set $E\subseteq E(\{0,1\})$ such that the problem of whether $E|-(a,b)$, for $a,b\in\{0,1\}^+$, is undecidable.

The above theorem states undecidability of the word problem for semigroups. Since each semigroup is isomorphic to a semigroup of relations with the operation of relational product, the validity problem for RC is at least as complex as the latter problem, and hence it is undecidable. The situation with RRC is more complicated, because not every semigroup is isomorphic to a semigroup of relations, generated by equivalence relations. We shall nonetheless show that the word problem for semigroups can also be reduced to the validity problem for RRC.

By a function on a set U we mean a relation $R\subseteq U\times U$ such that for all $x\in U$ there is exactly one $y\in U$ such that $(y,x)\in R$. By FUN(U) we denote the set of all functions on U. For any relation $R\in FUN(U)$ we define sets Ker(R) and Rng(R) as follows:

$$Ker(R)=\{(x,y)\in U\times U\text{: for all } z, (z,x)\in R \text{ iff } (z,y)\in R\}$$
$$Rng(R)=\{y\in U\text{: for some } x, (y,x)\in R\}.$$

A function R is said to be idempotent iff R;R=R. It is said to be non–constant iff Rng(R) contains at least two elements.

We show that every non–constant and idempotent function on U admits a uniform representation as a combination of equivalence relations on U built with relational operations admitted in RRC. First, observe that:

Fact 4.2. If $R\in FUN(U)$ is idempotent, then $R=I_{Rng(R)};Ker(R)$.

The above formula does not yield the required representation, because $I_{Rng(R)}$ might not belong to EQ(U). However, we have the following:

Fact 4.3.
(a) If $W\subseteq U$ has at least two elements, then $I_W=I_U\cap((W\times W-I_W);(W\times W-I_W))$
(b) For all $W\subseteq U$, $W\times W-I_W=-I_U\cap E_{U,W}$, where $E_{U,W}=W\times W\cup I_{U-W}$.

As a straightforward consequence of 4.2 and 4.3 we obtain the following lemma.

Lemma 4.4. If $R\in FUN(U)$ is a non–constant and idempotent function, then:
(a) $R=(I_U\cap((-I_U\cap E_{U,Rng(R)});(-I_U\cap E_{U,Rng(R)})));Ker(R)$.

Clearly, the above formula provides representation of R in terms of equivalence relations on U.

In what follows we recall the Thue process representation of the word problem (Davis 1958). Given a set $K \subseteq E(W)$ of equalities over a set W, and $a,b \in W^+$, we write $a|\!\rightarrow_K b$ whenever there exists $(c,d) \in K$ such that $a=a_1ca_2$ and $b=a_1da_2$ for some (possibly empty) words a_1, a_2. By $\rightarrow_K$ we denote the reflexive, symmetric and transitive closure of relation $|\!\rightarrow_K$. The following fact is well known:

Fact 4.5. For all $a,b \in W^+$ and $K \subseteq E(W)$, the following conditions are equivalent:
(a) $K|\!-(a,b)$
(b) $a \rightarrow_K b$.

We fix a finite set $E \subseteq \{0,1\}^+$ such that entailment $E|\!-(a,b)$, for $a,b \in \{0,1\}^+$ is undecidable. Let $V=\{v_0,v_0',v_1,v_1'\}$ be a four–element alphabet such that $0,1 \notin V$. We define a homomorphism $h:\{0,1\}^+ \rightarrow V^+$ by setting:

$$h(0)=v_0v_0', \quad h(1)=v_1v_1'.$$

We define two finite sets of equalities over V:

$$E'=\{(h(a),h(b)): (a,b) \in E\}$$
$$E''=E' \cup \{(vv,v): v \in V\}.$$

Lemma 4.6. For all $a,b \in \{0,1\}^+$ the following conditions are equivalent:
(a) $E|\!-(a,b)$
(b) $E'|\!-(h(a),h(b))$
(c) $E''|\!-(h(a),h(b))$.

Proof. The implications (a)→(b) and (b)→(c) are obvious.

To prove (b)→(a) assume that $E'|\!-(h(a),h(b))$, where $a,b \in \{0,1\}^+$. It follows from 4.5 that $h(a) \rightarrow_K h(b)$. This means that there exist $c_0,\ldots,c_n \in V^+$ such that $c_0=h(a)$, $c_n=h(b)$ and for all $0 \leq i < n$, either $c_i|\!\rightarrow_{E'} c_{i+1}$ or $c_{i+1}|\!\rightarrow_{E'} c_i$. By induction on n one can easily prove that $c_i=h(a_i)$ for some $a_i \in \{0,1\}^+$, $0 \leq i < n$, and furthermore, $a_0=a$, $a_n=b$, and for all $0 \leq i < n$, either $a_i|\!\rightarrow_E a_{i+1}$ or $a_{i+1}|\!\rightarrow_E a_i$. Consequently, $a \rightarrow_E b$, and hence $E|\!-(a,b)$.

To prove (c)→(b), let $L \subseteq V^+$ consists of those words that contain no subword of the form vv, for $v \in V$. Clearly, for every $a \in V^+$ there is exactly one $b \in L$ such that $a \rightarrow_{E''-E'} b$. This unique b will be denoted by g(a). It is easy to show by induction that for all $a,b \in V^+$, $a \rightarrow_{E''} b$ iff $g(a) \rightarrow_{E'} g(b)$. Now assume that $E''|\!-(h(a),h(b))$. Then by 4.5 we have $h(a) \rightarrow_{E''} h(b)$, and hence using the above equivalence we obtain $h(a)=g(h(a)) \rightarrow_{E'} g(h(b))=h(b)$, which completes the proof.

As a corollary we obtain:

Lemma 4.7. The problem of whether $E''|\!-(a,b)$ for $a,b \in V^+$ is undecidable.

To any $a \in V^+$ we assign a formula P(a) of RRC in the following way. We choose nine distinct attribute variables $A,B_0,C_0,B_1,C_1,B_0',C_0',B_1',C_1'$. Then for $v \in V$, P(v) is defined as follows:

$$P(v_i)=(A \cap ((-A \cap B_i);(-A \cap B_i)));C_i$$

$P(v_{i'})=(A\cap((-A\cap B_i');(-A\cap B_i')));C_i'$ where i=0,1.

Next, for words over V we set:

$$P(v_{j1},\ldots,v_{jn})=P(v_{j1});\ldots;P(v_{jn}).$$

For any formulas P and Q of RRC we define a formula denoted by P=Q:

$$(P=Q)=(-P\cup Q)\cap(-Q\cup P).$$

We clearly have:

Fact 4.8. P=Q is true in an r–model (e–model) (U,m) iff m(P)=m(Q).

With any equality $(a,b)\in E(V)$ we associate a formula of RRC in the following way:

$$P(a,b)=(P(a)=P(b)).$$

We also define:

$$P(E'')=\{P(a,b): (a,b)\in E''\}.$$

Lemma 4.9. For all $a,b\in V^+$ the following conditions are equivalent:
(a) $E''\vdash(a,b)$
(b) $P(a,b)\in Cn(P(E''))$

Proof: Assume (a), and let (U,m) be an e–model such that every formula from P(E'') is true in (U,m). Consider the semigroup (REL(U),;). We define an assignment $f:V\to REL(U)$ by setting f(v)=m(P(v)) for $v\in V$. We clearly have f(a)=m(P(a)) for all $a\in V^+$, and consequently for all $a,b\in V^+$ we have:

(i) f(a)=f(b) iff P(a,b) is true in (U,m).

Accordingly, f satisfies every equality from E'', and hence by the assumption we obtain f(a)=f(b) which yields the truth of P(a,b) in (U,m). We have proved that P(E'') e–implies P(a,b), and hence by proposition 3.3 we obtain $P(a,b)\in Cn(P(E''))$.

Conversely, assume that (a) does not hold. Then there exists a semigroup G' and an assignment $f:V\to G'$ such that every equality from E'' is satisfied by f but $f(a)\neq f(b)$. We may extend G' to semigroup $G=G'\cup\{e,o\}$ such that e is the unit in G and $o\neq e$ is an anihilator in G, that is ox=xo=o for all $x\in G$ (Clifford and Preston 1964). To each $x\in G$ we assign a function $R\in FUN(U)$ by setting:

(ii) yR_xz iff y=xz.

Clearly, the mapping $x\to R_x$ establishes a monomorphism of G into the semigroup (FUN(U),;), and hence we can identify G with a subalgebra of (FUN(U),;). Observe that $G-\{R_o\}$ consists of non–constant functions, since for all R_x if $x\neq o$, then $o,x\in Rng(R_x)$. Moreover, R_o is not in the range of the assignment f, and for any $v\in V$ f(v) is idempotent, since we have f(v);f(v)=f(vv), and f(vv)=f(v) because $(vv,v)\in E''$. By lemma 4.4 we obtain for all v:

(iii) $f(v)=(I_G\cap((-I_G\cap E_{G,Rng(f(v))});(-I_G\cap E_{G,Rng(f(v))})));Ker(f(v))$.

We define an e–model (U,m) by setting for i=0,1:

(iv) $U=G$, $m(A)=I_G$,
$m(B_i)=E_{G,Rng(f(vi))}$, $m(C_i)=Ker(f(v_i)$,
$m(B_i')=E_{G,Rng(f(vi))}$, $m(C_i')=Ker(F(v_i'))$.

We clearly have m(P(v))=f(v), for all v, and consequently m(P(a))=f(a) for all a $\in V^+$. In particular (i) holds for our model. As a consequence, every formula from P(E") is true in (U,m) but P(a,b) is not. It follows that P(a,b)$\notin$Cn(P(E")), which completes the proof.

From lemmas 3.4, 4.7 and 4.9 we obtain the main result of this section:

Theorem 4.10. The validity problem for RRC is undecidable.

A database model (M,m) (resp. an e–model (U,m)) is said to be finite iff the relation M (resp. the set U) is finite. A formula P of RRC is said to be finitely valid (f –valid) iff it is true in all finite models (resp. e–models). A set F of formulas possesses a finite model property (fmp) iff for every formula P$\in$F, P is valid iff P is f–valid. It is well known that:

Fact 4.11. If a set F of formulas is recursive and possesses fmp, then the valid formulas from F form a recursive class.

In view of theorem 4.10, we obtain:

Lemma 4.12. The set of formulas of RRC does not possess fmp.

In what follows we distinguish some effectively defined classes of formulas of RRC that possess fmp, and in view of fact 4.11 they admit a decision procedure for checking validity.

With any e–model (U,m) we associate a first order structure (U, {m(A): A$\in$ AT}), where U is a universe and m(A)'s are binary predicates. Furthermore, with any P$\in$FOR we associate a first order formula P(x,y) obtained by a natural translation of expression '(x,y)$\in$m(P)'. Clearly, for any e–model (U,m) and for all x,y$\in$U, (x,y)$\in$ m(P) iff P(x,y) is true in (U,{m(A): A$\in$AT}).

A first order formula is said to be $\forall$–formula (resp. $\exists$–formula) iff it is of the form Qα, where Q is a prefix of universal (resp. existential) quantifiers and α is a quantifier–free formula. A formula is said to be $\forall\exists$–formula if it is of the form Q_1Q_2 α, where Q_1 is a string of universal quantifiers, Q_2 is a string of existential quantifiers, and α is a quantifier–free formula. It is well known that the class of $\forall\exists$–formulas possesses fmp with respect to the standard semantics of first order languages. We recall that a formula P$\in$FOR is positive (negative) iff every occurrence of the sign ; of product falls into the scope of an even (odd) number of complementation symbol –.

By an easy structural induction we obtain:

Lemma 4.13. If a formula P of RRC is positive (negative), then P(x,y) is $\exists$–formula ($\forall$–formula).

As a corollary we obtain:

Lemma 4.14. If a formula P of RRC is positive (negative), then the sentence '$P\in Val(M,m)$' can be expressed as $\forall\exists$–sentence ($\forall$–sentence).

Theorem 4.15. The class of positive formulas of RRC and the class of negative formulas of RRC possess fmp.

Observe that if $P\in FOR$ is negative, then neg(P) is positive. It follows that if $F\subseteq FOR$ is a finite set of negative formulas and $P\in FOR$ is positive, then imp(con(F),P) is positive as well. Moreover, a positive combination of $\forall\exists$–formulas is equivalent to an $\forall\exists$–formula. Hence we have the following theorem:

Theorem 4.16.
(a) The problem of whether a finite set of negative formulas implies a positive formula is decidable
(b) The implication problem for negative formulas is decidable.

We are especially interested in the relation $P\in Cn(F)$ in the case when F contains positive formulas, because many formulas that express database dependencies, e.g. EMVD–formulas, are positive. Below we prove a result in this direction.

Lemma 4.17. Let $P\in Val(M,m)$, where P is an EMVD–formula. Then for every finite $N\subseteq M$ there exists a finite $N'\subseteq M$ such that $N\subseteq N'$ and $P\in Val(N',m)$.

Proof: Let P be equal to (EMVD) from section 3, then $P\in Val(M,m)$ amounts to:
(i) $ind_M(X)\subseteq(ind_M(X)\cap ind_M(Y));(ind_M(X)\cap ind_M(Z'))$
where, for the sake of simplicity, X,Y,Z denote sets af attributes of M assigned by m to the respective variables, and $Z'=Z-(X\cup Y)$.

For a tuple $t\in M$ and $X\subseteq AT_M$, by $t_M(X)$ we denote the equivalence class of $ind_M(X)$ which contains t. Clearly, condition (i) can be expressed as follows:
(ii) For all $t,u,v\in M$, if $t,u\in v_M(X)$, then $t_M(Y)\cap u_M(Z')\cap v_M(X)\neq\emptyset$.

Fix a finite $N\subseteq M$. If $P\in Val(N,m)$, then take $N'=N$. Otherwise, let $M_1,\ldots,M_k$ be all the classes of $v_M(X)$, for $v\in N$, and let $N_i=M_i\cap N$, $1\leq i\leq k$. Observe that $N\neq\emptyset$ and hence $k\geq1$. We shall construct firnite sets N_i', $1\leq i\leq k$, such that $N_i\subseteq N_i'\subseteq M_i$ and $P\in Val(N_i',m)$. Then, clearly, for $N'=N_1'\cup\ldots\cup N_k'$ we obtain $N\subseteq N'\subseteq M$, N' is finite, and $P\in Val(N',m)$.

We fix an i such that $1\leq i\leq k$. We define a mapping $f:N_i\times N_i\rightarrow M_i$ as follows:
(iii) $f(t,u)=t$ if $t=u$, $f(t,u)$=an element from $t_M(Y)\cap u_M(Z')\cap N_i$ if $t_M(Y)\cap u_M(Z')\cap N_i\neq\emptyset$, otherwise $f(t,u)$=an element of $t_M(Y)\cap u_M(Z')\cap M_i$.

Put $N_i'=f(N_i\times N_i)$. Clearly, N_i' is finite and $N_i\subseteq N_i'\subseteq M_i$. We show that $P\in Val(N_i',m)$. Since all the tuples from N_i' belong to the same equivalence class of $ind_{N'i}(X)$, we have that $P\in Val(N_i',m)$ is equivalent to:
(iv) For all $t,u\in N_i'$, $t_{N'i}(Y)\cap u_{N'i}(Z')\neq\emptyset$.

Now we prove that (iv) holds. Let $t,u \in N_i'$. Then $t=f(v_1,v_2)$ and $u=f(v_1',v_2')$ for some $v_1,v_1',v_2,v_2' \in N_i$. We have:

(v) $t_{N'i}(Y)=(v_1)_{N'i}(Y)$ and $u_{N'i}(Z')=(v_2')_{N'i}(Z')$.

It follows that:

(vi) $t_{N'i}(Y) \cap u_{N'i}(Z')=(v_1)_{N'i}(Y) \cap (v_2')_{N'i}(Z')=(v_1)_M(Y) \cap (v_2')_M(Z') \cap N_i'$.

By the construction of N_i' we know that $f(v_1,v_2')$ belongs to the latter set of (vi), which completes the proof.

Lemma 4.18. The class of formulas of the form imp(con(F),P), where F contains at most one EMVD–formula, the remaining formulas in F are negative, and P is a positive formula possesses fmp.

Proof: Clearly, validity implies f–validity. Assume that $Q \in F$ is an EMVD–formula, the remaining formulas in F are negative, and P is a positive formula. Suppose that $P \notin Cn(F)$, or equivalently imp(con(F),P)$\notin$Val. Take a model (M,m) such that imp(con(F),P)$\notin$True(M,m). If M is finite, then the formula in question is not f–valid. So assume that M is not finite. Let the first order formula that expresses '$P \in$ True(M,m)' be of the form $\forall x_1 \ldots \forall x_k \exists y_1 \ldots \exists y_l \alpha$, where α is a quantifier–free formula. Since the latter does not hold in (M,{$ind_M(A)$: $A \in AT$}), there are $t_1,\ldots,t_k \in$ M such that the formula $\forall y_1 \ldots \forall y_l \neg \alpha(x_1/t_1,\ldots,x_k/t_k)$ holds in this structure. Take $N=\{t_1,\ldots,t_k\}$. By lemma 4.17 there is a finite $N' \subseteq M$ such that $N \subseteq N'$ and $Q \in$ True(N,m). Obviously, the remaining formulas in F are also true in (N',m), but P is not. Hence, imp(con(F),P)$\notin$True(N',m). Therefore this formula fails to be f–valid.

Some other decidable cases of the validity problem in RRC will be given the following section.

5 From Relational to Propositional Calculus

In the present section we show that relational formalization of the implication problem for functional and multivalued dependencies can be reduced to a formalization within the framework of the classical propositional calculus. This result is analogous to the result presented in Sagiv et al. (1981).

Let BFOR be the set of Boolean formulas of RRC, and let B_2 be the least Boolean algebra, that is the algebra of classical truth–values {0,1}. Each valuation $w: AT \to B_2$ uniquely extends to a homomorphism $w: BFOR \to B_2$. For $F \subseteq BFOR$, $P \in$ BFOR, we say that P is a propositional consequence of F iff for every valuation w, $w(P)=1$ whenever $w(Q)=1$for all $Q \in F$.

Lemma 5.1. (Sagiv et al. 1981) Let F be a finite set of FD and/or MVD–formulas, and let P be such a formula. Let (M,m) be a model such that every formula from F is true in (M,m) but P is not. Then there exist tuples $t,u \in M$, $t \neq u$, such that in the model ({t,u},m) every formula from F is true and P is not true.

We define a 2–consequence relation Cn_2 in RRC as follows:

$P \in Cn_2(F)$ iff for every model (M,m) such that M contains exactly two tuples, P is true in (M,m) whenever each formula from F is true in (M,m).

As a straightforward corollary from lemma 5.1 we obtain:

Lemma 5.2. Let F be a finite set of FD and/or MVD–formulas, and let P be such a formula. Then the following conditions are equivalent:
(a) $P \in Cn(F)$
(b) $P \in Cn_2(F)$.

By a reflexive model (ref–model) we mean a model (M,m) such that the meaning function r_{ref} is defined by means of conditions (m1), (m2), (m4) from section 3, and the following:
(m15) $r_{ref}(-P)=(M \times M - r_{ref}(P)) \cup I_M$.

Observe, that for any P, relation $r_{ref}(P)$ determined by a ref–model is a reflexive relation.

Let the unary relational operation $-_{ref}$ be defined as follows:

$$-_{ref}P=-P \cup I.$$

Lemma 5.3. The algebra REF(U) of all the reflexive relations on a set U with operations $\cup, \cap, -_{ref}$ is a Boolean algebra, where I_U is the zero element.

Lemma 5.4. If U is a two–element set, then:
(a) $EQ(U)=\{I_U, U \times U\}$ is a subalgebra of REF(U) isomorphic to B_2
(b) For any $R,S \in EQ(U)$, $R;S=R \cup S$.

We define a 2,ref–consequence relation $Cn_{2,ref}$ in RRC as follows:

$P \in Cn_{2,ref}(F)$ iff for every ref–model (M,m) such that M consists of exactly two elements, P is true in (M,m) whenever all the formulas from F are true in (M,m).

For a formula P of RRC by Bool(P) we denote a formula obtained from P through replacement of every occurrence of the sign ; of product by $\cup$. Similarly, for a set F of formulas we define $Bool(F)=\{Bool(P): P \in F\}$.

Lemma 5.5. For every set F of formulas and for every formula P the following conditions are equivalent:
(a) $P \in Cn_{2,ref}(F)$
(b) Bool(P) is a propositional consequence of Bool(F).

Proof: In view of lemmas 5.3 and 5.4 we have $P \in Cn_{2,ref}(F)$ iff $Bool(P) \in Cn_{2,ref}(Bool(F))$ iff Bool(P) is a propositional consequence of Bool(F).

A formula $P \in FOR$ is said to be invariant iff for every model (M,m) we have $r(P)=M\times M$ iff $r_{ref}(P)=M\times M$.

Lemma 5.6. If F is a set of invariant formulas and P is an invariant formula, then the following conditions are equivalent:
(a) $P \in Cn_2(F)$
(b) $P \in Cn_{2,ref}(F)$.

Lemma 5.7.
(a) If formulas P and Q do not contain the complement sign –, then $-P \cup Q$ is an invariant formula
(b) Every FD–formula is invariant
(c) Every MVD–formula is invariant.
Proof: To show (a) observe that by the assumption in every model we have $r(P)=r_{ref}(P)$ and $r(Q)=r_{ref}(Q)$. Moreover, $I_M \subseteq r(Q)$. Hence $r(-P \cup Q)=r_{ref}(-P \cup Q)$. Conditions (b) and (c) follow from (a).

Lemmas 5.2, 5.5, 5.6, and 5.7 yield the following theorem.

Theorem 5.8. Let F be a finite set of FD and/or MVD–fomulas, and let P be such a formula. Then the following conditions are equivalent:
(a) $P \in Cn(F)$
(b) Bool(P) is a propositional consequence of Bool(F).

This theorem can be strengthened in different ways. For instance, we may admit in F arbitrary invariant negative formulas besides FD–formulas, or if P is an FD–formula, instead of MVD–formulas we may admit in F arbitrary EMVD–formulas whose sets of attributes form a chain and contain all the attributes that occur in P. However, as shown in Sagiv et al. (1981), the equivalence fails if one allows for arbitrary EMVD–formulas both in F and P.

References

[1] Armstrong, W. W.: (1974) Dependency structures of database relationships. Proceedings IFIP'74, 580–583

[2] Beeri, C. and Vardi, M. Y.: (1984) A proof procedure for data dependencies. Journal of the ACM 31, 718–741

[3] Buszkowski, W. and Orłowska, E.: (1985) On the logic of database dependencies. Proceedings of the Fourth Hungarian Computer Science Conference, 373–383

[4] Buszkowski, W. and Orłowska, E.: (1986) Relational calculus and data dependencies. ICS PAS Report 583, Warsaw

[5] Clifford, A. H. and Preston, G. B.: (1964) The Algebraic Theory of Semigroups. Vol. I, American Mathematical Society, Providence

[6] Codd, E. F.: (1970) A relational model for large shared data banks. Communications of ACM 13, 377–387

[7] Codd, E. F.: (1972) Further normalization of the data base relational model. In: Rustin, R. (ed) Data Base Systems. Prentice–Hall, Englewood Cliffs, NJ, 33–64

[8] Davis, M.: (1958) Computability and Unsolvability. McGraw–Hill, New York

[9] Fagin, R. and Vardi, M. Y.: (1986) The theory of data dependencies: a survey. In: Anshel, M. and Gewirtz, W.: (eds) Mathematics of Information Processing. Symposia in Applied Mathematics, Vol 34, 19–72

[10] Kanellakis, P. C.: (1990) Elements of relational database theory. In: Van Leeuwen, J. (ed) Handbook of Theoretical Computer Science. Elsevier Science Publishers, 1075–1156

[11] Orlowska, E.: (1987) Algebraic approach to database constraints. Fundamenta Informaticae 10, 57–68. See also: Report 182, Langages et Systemes Informatiques, Toulouse, 1983

[12] Orlowska, E.: (1988) Relational interpretation of modal logics. In: Andreka, H., Monk, D. and Nemeti, I. Algebraic Logic. Colloquia Mathematica Societatis Janos Bolyai 54, North Holland, Amsterdam, 443–471

[13] Rasiowa, H. and Sikorski, R.: (1963) The Mathematics of Metamathematics. Polish Science Publishers, Warsaw

[14] Sagiv, Y., Delobel, C., Parker, D. S. and Fagin, R.: (1981) An equivalence between relational database dependencies and a fragment of propositional logic. Journal of ACM 28, 435–453

[15] Tarski, A.: (1941) On the calculus of relations. Journal of Symbolic Logic 6, 73–89

[16] Ullman, J.: (1988) Principles of Database and Knowledge Base Systems. Vol. I. Computer Science Press, Rockville

Chapter 10

Dependencies between Many-Valued Attributes

Michael Luxenburger

Fachbereich Mathematik, Technische Hochschule Darmstadt
Schloßgartenstraße 7, 64289 Darmstadt, Germany

Abstract: A variety of forms of dependencies in empirical data is studied. It is shown how the existing models can be extended in order to capture the revelant features of data. In particular, scaling of data in the context–style models is investigated and an algebraic framework is proposed for processing scales. A deduction system for providing data dependencies in scaled context is given.

1 Introduction

Dependencies between attributes are of great interest in data analysis if the connection between objects and attributes shall be clarified. Formal concept analysis provides a unifying tool for introducing and analysing dependencies between many–valued attributes. This approach covers quite different types of dependencies as for instance functional, ordinal, or interordinal dependency, and linear dependency in vector spaces [GW2, Wi4]. In conceptual measurement, the so–called scaling of data contexts is used to derive conceptual hierarchies for the data which lead to a general notion of dependency.

First we recall basic notions and some results and show certain limits for a further generalization of this attempt (Section 2). Then we will study the influence of the so–called composition operator involved in a scaling. Moreover, we will investigate the interrelationships between Armstrong–axioms and their validity for the derived dependencies (Section 3).

Section 4 deals with the problem of representing dependencies as implications of a suitable one–valued context. With the results of Section 3 it is shown that such a representation cannot be obtained in general. Moreover, not all representations which can be constructed are efficient ones.

The last section introduces accuracies of partial dependencies. These are dependencies valid for a subset of the underlying objects. Several notions of accuracy are developped and a comparision with the theory of rough sets [Pa1, Pa2, Pa3] is drawn. Finally, this approach is illustrated by an example from [FR1] to compare our results with those of certain other methods as factor analysis and analysis of principal components.

2 Contexts, Many–Valued Contexts and Scaling

An often used method to represent data consists of giving the correspondences between the considered objects and attributes. This representation can be formalized in set–theoretical language. Let us recall that a *context* is a triple (G, M, I) where G and M are sets and I a binary relation between G and M, i.e., $I \subseteq G \times M$. The elements of G (resp. M) are called *objects* (resp. *attributes*) and gIm can be read as "the object g has the attribute m". For every $A \subseteq G$ and $B \subseteq M$ we define

$$A^{\uparrow} := \{m \in M : \ gIm \quad \text{for all } g \in A\}$$
$$B^{\downarrow} := \{g \in G : \ gIm \quad \text{for all } m \in B\}$$

The mappings $^{\uparrow} : \ \mathcal{P}(G) \rightarrow \mathcal{P}(M)$ and $^{\downarrow} : \ \mathcal{P}(M) \rightarrow \mathcal{P}(G)$ form a Galois connection between G and M and the mappings $^{\uparrow\downarrow} : \ \mathcal{P}(G) \rightarrow \mathcal{P}(G)$ with $A \mapsto A^{\uparrow} \mapsto A^{\uparrow\downarrow}$ and $^{\downarrow\uparrow} : \ \mathcal{P}(M) \rightarrow \mathcal{P}(M)$ with $B \mapsto B^{\uparrow} \mapsto B^{\downarrow\uparrow}$ are closure operators on $\mathcal{P}(G)$ and $\mathcal{P}(M)$ (resp.). In the following, we will use the symbol ^{I} for both mappings $^{\uparrow}$ and $^{\downarrow}$, and ^{II} instead of $^{\uparrow\downarrow}$ and $^{\downarrow\uparrow}$.

We call a pair (A, B) *concept* of the context (G, M, I) if $A^I = B$ and $B^I = A$ (for $A \subseteq G$ and $B \subseteq M$). A (resp. B) can be understood as the *extent* (resp. the *intent*) of the concept (A, B). Thus, the extents and the intents are closed sets of $\mathcal{P}(G)$ and $\mathcal{P}(M)$ with respect to the closure operators ^{II} (resp.). Finally, an order relation between the concepts is given by the subconcept–superconcept relation

$$(A_1, B_1) \leq (A_2, B_2) :\Leftrightarrow A_1 \subseteq A_2 \quad (\Leftrightarrow B_1 \supseteq B_2) \ .$$

The order $\leq$ constitutes a complete lattice on the set $\mathfrak{B}(G, M, I)$ of all concepts of the context (G, M, I). It will be denoted by $\underline{\mathfrak{B}}(G, M, I)$ and called the *concept lattice* of (G, M, I) [Wil]. The infima and suprema can be calculated as follows:

$$\bigwedge_{i \in I}(A_i, B_i) = \left(\bigcap_{i \in I} A_i, \left(\bigcup_{i \in I} B_i \right)^{II} \right)$$
$$\bigvee_{i \in I}(A_i, \ B_i) = \left(\left(\bigcup_{i \in I} A_i \right)^{II}, \bigcap_{i \in I} B_i \right) \ .$$

An *implication* is a pair (B, D) of subsets of attributes of M and is denoted by $B \rightarrow D$. We say that an implication $B \rightarrow D$ is *valid* in the context $\mathbb{K} := (G, M, I)$ (or that B implies D in $\mathbb{K}$) if and only if $B^I \subseteq D^I$ ($\Leftrightarrow D \subseteq B^{II}$) [Dul, GW1]. For $g \in G$ ($m \in M$ resp.) we will write g^I (m^I resp.) rather that $\{g\}^I$ ($\{m\}^I$ resp.).

Scaling is the development of formal patterns and their use for analyzing empirical data. In conceptual scaling these formal patterns consist of formal contexts and their concept lattices which have a clear structure and which reflect some meaning. Such a context is called a *scale*. Empirical contexts are connected with scales by scale measures: a *scale measure* or, more precisely, an (H, N, J)–measure of context (G, M, I) is defined to be a mapping σ from G into H such that, for every extent A of (H, N, J), the preimage $\sigma^{-1}A$ is an extent of (G, M, I). That reflects the idea of a continuous map between topological spaces and that each projection has to be continuous relative to the product topology [GW1, GW2].

Very common are scales of ordinal type. We list some standarized scales with their basic meaning: The ordinal scale $(P, P, \leq)$ (hierarchy), the nominal scale $(\{1, \ldots, n\}, \{1, \ldots, n\}, =)$ (partition), the complementary nominal scale $(\{1, \ldots, n\}, \{1, \ldots, n\}, \neq)$ (partition and independence), and the n–dimensional boolean scale $(\mathcal{P}(\{1, \ldots, n\}), \mathcal{P}(\{1, \ldots, n\}), \subseteq)$ (attribute dependency).

Empirical data models often arise in a form which does not a priori fall under the data type of a context. It is natural to generalize this definition to that of a many–valued context. We say that a quadruple (G, M, W, I) is a *many–valued context* if G, M, and W are sets and I is a ternary relation between G, M, and W (i.e., $I \subseteq G \times M \times W$) such that $(g, m, w_1) \in I$ and $(g, m, w_2) \in I$ always imply $w_1 = w_2$. Note that the term "many–valued" is used in a different sense in the literature on database systems and information systems but this should not give rise to confusion. The elements of G, M, and W are called *objects, (many–valued) attributes*, and *attribute values*, respectively. (G, M, W, I) is called n–valued context if the cardinality of W is n. An attribute m of a many–valued context may be considered as a partial map from G to W which suggests to write $m(g) = w$ rather that $(g, m, w) \in I$, and to define the domain of m by $\text{dom}(m) := \{g \in G : (g, m, w) \in I \text{ for some } w \in W\}$. An attribute $m \in M$ is said to be *complete* if $\text{dom}(m) = G$, and the many–valued context (G, M, W, I) is called *complete* if all its attributes are.

To define notions of dependencies between attributes in a many–valued context, our basic view is that this requires a scaling of the context. In the frame of formal concept analysis, a scaling of the many–valued context (G, M, W, I) is carried out in two steps: First, we assign to each attribute $m \in M$ a scale $\$_m := (G_m, M_m, I_m)$ with $G_m \supseteq m(G)$ and where the structure of the concept lattice $\underline{\mathfrak{B}}(\$_m)$ is significant for the values taken by attribute m (in practice, there values are often implicitely structured); then we apply an operator $\prod$ to compose these scales to a common scale $\$:= \prod_{m \in M} \$_m := (\times_{m \in M} G_m, N, J)$ where N and J depend on the operator $\prod$ [Wi4, GW2]. The only restrictions on the operator $\prod$ are that the set of objects of $\$$ is the direct product of the objects in the scales and that every projection $\prod_i : \times_{m \in M} G_m \to G_i$ defined by $\prod_i \left((g_m)_{m \in M}\right) = g_i$ is a $\$_i$–measure of $\$$, i.e., the preimage of an extent of $\$_i$ has to be an extent of $\$$ under each projection. This connection ensures a certain influence of the structure of the scales $\$_m$ on the structure of $\$$. The many–valued context $\mathbb{K}$ together with the scale $\prod_{m \in M} \$_m$ is called the *scaled context* and is denoted by $\left(\mathbb{K}; \prod_{m \in M} \$_m\right)$ [GW2, Wi4].

As common and important composition operators we introduce the following examples:

(i) *Semi-product:*

$$\otimes(\$_m : m \in M) := \left(\times_{m\in M} G_m, \bigcup_{m\in M} M_m, \nabla \right)$$

where $(g_m)_{m\in M} \nabla n$ iff $g_m I_m n$ for some $m \in M$.

(ii) *Direct product* (let $\$_m$ contain no object g with $g^{I_m} = M_m$):

$$\times(\$_m : m \in M) := (\times_{m\in M} G_m, \times_{m\in M} M_m, \nabla)$$

where $(g_m)_{m\in M} \nabla (n_m)_{m\in M}$ iff $g_m I_m n_m$ for some $m \in M$.

(iii) *Algebraic product:* If W is the subset of a field K one can choose the linear scale $(K, K, \perp)$ for each $\$_m$ where $h \perp k$ iff $h \cdot k = 0$, and compose these scales by the algebraic product operator $\perp$:

$$\perp(\$_m : m \in M) := \left(K^{|M|}, K^{|M|}, \perp \right)$$

where $(a_m)_{m\in M} \perp (b_m)_{m\in M}$ iff $\sum_{m\in M} a_m \cdot b_m = 0$.

We have to show that the projections are measured as desired:

(i)

$$\begin{aligned} \prod\nolimits_i^{-1}(U)^{\nabla\nabla} = \{\mathbf{g} \in \times_{m\in M} G_m : g_i \in U\}^{\nabla\nabla} = \\ \left(U^{I_i} \cup \{l_m : l_m^{I_m} = G_m, m \in M\}\right)^{\nabla} = \\ \{\mathbf{g} \in \times_{m\in M} G_m : g_i \in U^{I_i I_i}\} \ . \end{aligned}$$

Thus, if U is an extent of $\$_i$ then $\prod_i^{-1}(U)$ is an extent of $\$$.

(ii)

$$\begin{aligned} \prod\nolimits_i^{-1}(U)^{\nabla\nabla} &= \{\mathbf{g} \in \times_{m\in M} G_m : g_i \in A\}^{\nabla\nabla} \\ &\overset{(*)}{=} \{\mathbf{n} \in \times_{m\in M} M_m : n_i \in A^{I_i} \text{ or } n_m^{I_m} = G_m \\ &\qquad \text{for some } m \in M \setminus \{i\}\}^{\nabla} \\ &\overset{(**)}{=} \{\mathbf{g} \in \times_{m\in M} G_m : g_i \in A^{I_i I_i} \text{ or } g_m^{I_m} = M_m \\ &\qquad \text{for some } m \in M \setminus \{i\}\} \ . \end{aligned}$$

We only show $(**)$, since the proof for $(*)$ is similar: It obvious that the right–hand side is contained in the left–hand side. For a proof of the reverse inclusion let $g_i \notin A^{I_i I_i}$ and $g_m^{I_m} \subset M_m$ for all $m \in M \setminus \{i\}$, i.e., for all $m \in M \setminus \{i\}$ there exist $n_m \in M_m$ such that not $g_m I_m n_m$ and a $n_i \in A^{I_i}$ such that not $g_i I_i n_i$, thus $\mathbf{g}$ is not contained in the left–hand side.
Thus, if any scale contains an object g_m such that $g_m^{I_m} = M_m$ then projections are no measures (except the case where $I_m = G_m \times M_m$ for all $m \in M$). To guarantee that the direct product is applicable for all families of scales, we equip each scale with an additional attribute 0_m such that $0_m^{I_m} = \emptyset$ (if there is not already such an attribute).

(iii)

$$\begin{aligned}
\mathcal{U}(K,K,\perp) &= \{\{0\},K\},\\
\textstyle\prod_i^{-1}(\{0\})^{\perp\perp} &= \{\mathbf{k}\in K^{|M|}:\ k_i=0\}^{\perp\perp}\\
&= \{(l_m)_{m\in M}:\ l_m=0 \quad \text{for all } m\in M\setminus\{i\}\}^{\perp}\\
&= \{\mathbf{k}\in K^{|M|}:\ k_i=0\}
\end{aligned}$$

and $\prod_i^{-1}(K)=K^{|M|}$ are extents.

To define dependencies between many-valued attributes we need to know how one may restrict a composition operator $\prod$ to a subfamily of scales. Let $\prod(\$_m\ :\ m\in M)=(\times_{m\in M}G_m,N,J)$. For $R\subseteq M$, define an equivalence relation Θ_R on $\times_{m\in M}G_m$ by

$$\Theta_R := \{((g_m)_{m\in M},(h_m)_{m\in M})\in \times_{m\in M}G_m\times \times_{m\in M}G_m:\ g_r=h_r \\ \text{for all } r\in R\}$$

and the subset N_R of N by

$$N_r := \{n\in N:\ gJn \Leftrightarrow hJn \quad \text{for all } (g,h)\in\Theta_R\}\ .$$

This allows us to restrict the incidence J in the following way to $(\times_{r\in R}G_r)\times N_R$: $(g_r)_{r\in R}J_Rn$ for $n\in N_R$ iff $(h_m)_{m\in M}Jn$ for all $(h_m)_{m\in M}\in\times_{m\in M}G_m$ with $h_m=g_m$ for all $m\in R$ (iff $(h_m)_{m\in M}Jn$ for one $(h_m)_{m\in M}\in\times_{m\in M}G_m$ with $h_m=g_m$ for all $m\in R$). Then the restricted operator $\prod_R$ is defined by $\prod_R(\$_m\ :\ m\in M):=(\times_{r\in R}G_r,N_R,J_R)$. Note that $A\subseteq B$ implies $\Theta_A\supseteq\Theta_B$ and $N_A\subseteq N_B$.

Examples (continued):

(i) Semi-product: $N_\emptyset=\{n\in N\ :\ n^{I_k}=\emptyset$ or $n^{I_k}=G_k$ for some $k\in M\}$ and $N_R=N_\emptyset\cup\bigcup\{M_r\ :\ r\in R\}$. It is obvious that the right-hand side is contained in the left-hand side. For a proof of the reverse inclusion let m not be contained in the right-hand side. Thus $m\in M_k$ for some $k\in M\setminus R$ and $\emptyset\neq m^{I_j}\neq G_j$ for all $j\in M$. Then there exist $g_k,h_k\in G_k$ such that g_kI_km but not h_kI_km. For $j\in M\setminus\{k\}$ we choose $g_j=h_j\in G_j$ arbitrary. Then $((g_k)_{k\in M},(h_k)_{k\in M})\in\Theta_R$ and $(g_k)_{k\in M}\nabla m$ but not $(h_k)_{k\in M}\nabla m$. Thus $m\notin N_R$.

(ii) Direct product: $N_\emptyset=\{(n_k)_{k\in M}\in N:\ n^{I_k}=G_k$ for some $k\in M\}$ and $N_R=N_\emptyset\cup\{(n_k)_{k\in M}\in N:\ n^{I_k}=\emptyset$ for all $k\in M\setminus R\}$.
It is obvious that the right-hand side is contained in the left-hand side. For a proof of the reverse inclusion let m not be contained in the right-hand side. Thus $m_k^{I_k}\subset G_k$ for all $k\in M$ and $m_r^{I_r}\neq\emptyset$ for some $r\in M\setminus R$. Hence, for all $k\in M$ there exist $h_k\in G_k$ such that not $h_kI_km_k$ and a $g_r\in G_r$ with $g_rI_rm_r$. For $j\in M\setminus\{r\}$ let $g_j=h_j$. Then $((g_k)_{k\in M},(h_k)_{k\in M})\in\Theta_R$ and $(g_k)_{k\in M}\nabla m$ but not $(h_k)_{k\in M}\nabla m$. Thus $m\notin N_r$.

Thus if, for some $k \in M \setminus R$, M_k does not contain an attribute m such that $m^{I_k} = \emptyset$ then $N_R = N_\emptyset$. Therefore it is advantageous to equip each scale $\$_m$with an additional attribute 0_m, if necessary.

(iii) Algebraic product: $N_R = \{(k_m)_{m\in M} : \ k_r = 0 \text{ for all } r \in M \setminus R\}$.
It is obvious that the right–hand side is contained in the left–hand side. For a proof of the reverse inclusion let $k_r \neq 0$ for some $r \in M \setminus R$. Let $g_r = 1$ and $g_m = 0$ for all $m \in M \setminus \{r\}$ and $h_m = 0$ for all $m \in M$. Then $((g_m)_{m\in M}, (h_m)_{m\in M}) \in \Theta_R$ and $\sum_{m\in M} g_m \cdot k_m = k_r \neq 0$ but $\sum_{m\in M} h_m \cdot k_m = 0$. Thus $m \notin N_R$.

To obtain the conceptual structure of a scaled context $\left(\mathbb{K};\ \prod_{m\in M} \$_m\right)$, we define a one–valued context $\tilde{\mathbb{K}} := (G, N, \tilde{J})$ as its *derived context* where the relation $\tilde{J}$ is defined as follows: For $R(g) := \{m \in M :\ \ g \in \text{dom}(m)\}$, $g\tilde{J}n$ iff $n \in N_{R(g)}$ and $(r(g)_{r\in R(g)} J_{R(g)} n$. (if $\mathbb{K}$ is complete then $g\tilde{J}n$ iff $(m(g))_{m\in N} Jn$ in $\$$). As concepts of $\left(\mathbb{K};\ \prod_{m\in M} \$_m\right)$ we take the concepts of the derived context $(G, N, \tilde{J})$ [Wi4]. For the restricted operator $\prod_R$, as concepts of $(\mathbb{K};\ \prod_R(\$_m : m \in M))$ we take the concepts of $\tilde{\mathbb{K}}_R := (G, N_R, \tilde{J}_R)$ with $\tilde{J}_R := \tilde{J} \cap (G \times N_R)$.

In general, we may say that an attribute depends on other attributes if it can be expressed by them or, more explicit, if its conceptual contribution can be already furnished by the other attributes. Thus, a general definition of dependency has to reflect the scaling of the values. Let $\mathcal{U}\left(\mathbb{K};\ \prod_{m\in M} \$_m\right)$ denote the extents of all concepts of the scaled context $\left(\mathbb{K};\ \prod_{m\in M} \$_m\right)$, i.e., the extents of $(G, N, \tilde{J})$, and, for $X \subseteq M$, $\mathcal{U}(\mathbb{K};\ \prod_X(\$_m :\ m \in M)) := \mathcal{U}\left(G, N_X, \tilde{J}_X\right)$ the extents of the derived context of the restriction. If no confusion has to be expected, we will use the short notation $\mathcal{U}_X$ for $\mathcal{U}(G, N_X, \tilde{J}_X)$.

We say that a set Y of attributes *depends* on a set X of attributes in $(\mathbb{K}; \prod_{m\in M} \$_m)$ iff $\mathcal{U}_X = \mathcal{U}_{X\cup Y}$, and this dependency will be denoted by $X \to Y$.

Furthermore, we say that a set Y of attributes *weakly depends* on a set X of attributes in $(\mathbb{K};\ \prod_{m\in M} \$_m)$ iff $\mathcal{U}_X \supseteq \mathcal{U}_Y$, and this weak dependency will be denoted by $X \overset{w}{\to} Y$.

Dependency and weak dependency coincide when applying the semi–product operator, but not in general for the direct and algebraic product operator.

Note that the following statements are equivalent:

- $X \to Y$
- iff $\mathcal{U}_X = \mathcal{U}_{X\cup Y}$
- if $\mathcal{U}(G, N_X, \tilde{J}_X) = \mathcal{U}(G, N_{X\cup Y}, \tilde{J}_{X\cup Y})$
- iff $m^{\tilde{J}} = \bigcap\left\{n^{\tilde{J}} :\ n \in N_X,\ n^{\tilde{J}} \supseteq m^{\tilde{J}}\right\}$ for all $m \in N_{X\cup Y}$
- iff all attributes in $N_{X\cup Y} \setminus N_X$ are reducible relative to N_X.

For the semi–product as composition–operator we have $N_{X\cup Y} = N_X \cup N_Y$ and therefore $\mathcal{U}_X = \left\{\bigcap_{m\in X} U_m :\ U_m \in \mathcal{U}_{\{m\}}\right\}$. In general, a connection between the scaled context $(\mathbb{K}; \$)$ and the scale $\$$ is given by the supremum–preserving surjective mapping $\epsilon: \underline{\mathfrak{B}}(\mathbb{K};\$) \to \underline{\mathfrak{B}}(\$)$ defined by $\epsilon(A,B) := (B^{I_\$}, B)$. Therefore $\underline{\mathfrak{B}}(\mathbb{K};\$)$ can be regarded as a subsemilattice of $\underline{\mathfrak{B}}(\$)$.

Let us introduce some usefull abbreviations. We define for a (one–valued) context $\mathbb{K} := (G,M,I)$ the *complementary context* K^c by $\mathbb{K}^c := (G,M,(G\times M)\setminus I)$ and the *dual context* K^d by $\mathbb{K}^d := (M,G,I^{-1})$. Furthermore, let $K^{\overline{0}} := (G, M\dot{\cup}\{0\}, I)$ and $K^{\overline{1}} := (G, M\dot{\cup}\{1\}, I \cup (G\times\{1\}))$ and, if $\mathbb{K}_1 := (G, M_1, I_1)$ and $\mathbb{K}_2 := (G, M_2, I_2)$ are two contexts with the same set of objects, $K_1|K_2 := (G, M_1\dot{\cup}M_2, I_1\dot{\cup}I_2)$ denotes the *apposition* of both (assume the two sets of attributes to be disjoint).

2.1 Functional Dependencies

Functional dependencies are introduced in the theory of relational databases and read in the language of formal concept analysis as follows: In a complete many–valued context a set Y of attributes *functionally depends* on a set X of attributes if, for all $g,h\in G$, $x(g)=x(h)$ for all $x\in X$ implies $y(g)=y(h)$ for all $y\in Y$, i.e., if there exists a mapping $f:\ W^{|X|}\to W^{|Y|}$ such that $f((x(g))_{x\in X}) = (y(g)_{y\in Y})$ for all $g\in G$.

Proposition 1. *[Wi4] Let $\mathbb{K} := (G,M,W,I)$ be a complete many–valued context and $X,Y\subseteq M$. Then Y functionally depends on X in $\mathbb{K}$ iff Y depends on X in* $\left(\mathbb{K};\ \times_{m\in M}(\{m(g):\ g\in G\},\{m(g):\ g\in G\},\neq)^{\overline{0_m}}\right)$.

We assume the many–valued context to be complete, since for the partial (i.e., not necessarily complete) case several definitions for functional dependencies are possible: In [Mal], Y functionality depends on X in a partial many–valued context $\mathbb{K}$ iff Y functionality depends on X in some completion of $\mathbb{K}$, whereas in [GW1], Y functionally depends on X in a partial many–valued context $\mathbb{K}$ iff $\mathrm{dom}(y)\subseteq\bigcap\{\mathrm{dom}(x):\ x\in X\}$ for all $y\in Y$ and $y(g)\neq y(h)$ for some $y\in Y$ implies the existence of an $x\in X$ such that $x(g)\neq x(h)$.

2.2 Ordinal Dependencies

For a generalization of functional dependencies to ordinal dependencies we need the values of every attribute m of $\mathbb{K}$ to be ordered by the ordered set $(P_m,\leq_m)$. We say that a set Y of attributes *ordinally depends* on a set X of attributes in a complete many–valued context $\mathbb{K}$ if, for all $g,h\in G$, $x(g)\leq_x x(h)$ for all $x\in X$ implies $y(g)\leq_y y(h)$ for all $y\in Y$, i.e., if there exists an order preserving mapping $f:\ W^{|X|}\to W^{|Y|}$ such that $f((x(g))_{x\in X}) = (y(g)_{y\in Y})$ for all $g\in G$.

Lemma 2. *Let $\mathbb{K} := (G,M,W,I)$ be a complete many–valued context and $X,Y\subseteq M$. Then Y ordinally depends on X in $\mathbb{K}$ if and only if Y depends on X in* $\left(\mathbb{K};\ \times_{m\in M}(P_m,P_m,\not\geq_m)^{\overline{0_m}}\right)$.

Note that a proof for this lemma for complete many–valued contexts with a finite set of objects is already given in [Wi4], but it does not become clear how the transitivity and reflexivity of the relations $\leq_m$ contribute. Our proof is for arbitrary G and the reflexivity and transitivity are explicitely used.

Proof. For $R \subseteq M$, let $g \leq_R h :\Leftrightarrow r(g) \leq r(h)$ for all $r \in R$. Let $\mathcal{J}(G, \leq_R)$ denote the order ideals of the ordered set $(G, \leq_R)$, and let $\mathcal{U}(G, M, I)$ denote the extents of a (one–valued) context (G, M, I). Furthermore, define $\nabla_R \subseteq G \times \times_{r \in R} P_r$ by $g \nabla_R (p_r)_{r \in R} :\Leftrightarrow r(g) \not\geq_r p_r$ for some $r \in R$. Then

$$\begin{aligned} \mathcal{J}(G, \leq_R) &= \mathcal{U}(G, G, \not\geq_R) \quad \text{[Wi3]} \\ &= \mathcal{U}(G, \{(m(g))_{m \in R} : g \in G\}, \nabla_R \cap (G \times \{(m(g))_{m \in R} : g \in G\})) \\ &\overset{(*)}{=} \mathcal{U}(G, \times_{m \in R} P_m, \nabla_R) \\ &\overset{(**)}{=} \mathcal{U}\left(\mathbb{K}; \times_{m \in R} (P_m, P_m, \not\geq_m)^{\bar{0}_m}\right) \\ &= \mathcal{U}(G, N_R, \tilde{J}_R) \end{aligned}$$

Thus, Y depends on X in $\left(\mathbb{K}; \times_{m \in R}(P_m, Pm, \not\geq_m)^{\bar{0}_m}\right)$ iff $\mathcal{J}(G, \leq_X) = \mathcal{J}(G, \leq_{X \cup Y})$ iff Y ordinally depends on X in $\mathbb{K}$.

(*) "$\subseteq$" is valid for every extension of the set of attributes.
"$\supseteq$": We have to show that the "new" attributes are reducible. Note that $g \tilde{J} (p_r)_{r \in R} \Leftrightarrow (r(g))_{r \in R} J_R (p_r)_{r \in R} \Leftrightarrow r(g) \not\geq_r p_r$ for some $r \in R \Leftrightarrow g \nabla_R (p_r)_{r \in R}$. Let $\mathbf{n} = (p_r)_{r \in R} \in \times_{r \in R} P_r$. Then

$$\mathbf{n}^{\tilde{J}} = \bigcap \left\{ (r(g))_{r \in R}^{\tilde{J}} : g \in G, g \notin \mathbf{n}^{\tilde{J}} \right\} \quad :$$

Reflexivity of $\leq_R$ implies $\supseteq$:
Let $h \notin \mathbf{n}^{\tilde{J}}$, then $h \notin (r(h))_{r \in R}^{\tilde{J}} \supseteq \bigcap \left\{ (r(g))_{r \in R}^{\tilde{J}} : g \in G, g \notin \mathbf{n}^{\tilde{J}} \right\}$.
Transitivity of $\leq_R$ implies $\subseteq$:
Let $h \notin \bigcap \left\{ (r(g))_{r \in R}^{\tilde{J}} : g \in G, g \notin \mathbf{n}^{\tilde{J}} \right\}$. Hence there is some $g \in G$ such that $g \notin \mathbf{n}^{\tilde{J}}$ and $h \notin (r(g))_{r \in R}^{\tilde{J}}$. Thus $r(g) \geq p_r$ (note that $\mathbf{n} = (p_r)_{r \in R}$) and $r(h) \geq r(g)$ for all $r \in R$, hence $r(h) \geq p_r$ for all $r \in R$, and finally $h \notin \mathbf{n}^{\tilde{J}}$.

(**) The additional attributes 0_m, $m \in M$, do not generate additional extents since the attributes $\times_{m \in M}(P_m \cup \{0_m\})$ are reducible relative to $\times_{m \in M} P_m$: For any $(p_m)_{m \in M} \in \times_{m \in M}(P_m \cup \{0_m\})$ we have the equality $(p_m)_{m \in M}^{\nabla} = \bigcap \{(q_m)_{m \in M}^{\nabla} : (q_m)_{m \in M} \in \times_{m \in M} P_m$ such that $q_m = p_m$ for all m with $p_m \neq 0_m\}$. It is obvious that the right–hand side is contained in the left–hand side. For a proof of the reverse inclusion, let $(s_m)_{m \in M}$ be an object not contained in the left–hand side. Then $s_m \geq p_m$ for all $m \in M$. Now, let $\tilde{p}_m = p_m$ for $m \in M$ with $p_m \neq 0_m$ and $\tilde{p}_m = s_m$ for $m \in M$ with $p_m = 0_m$. Thus $(s_m)_{m \in M} \notin (\tilde{p}_m)_{m \in M}^{\nabla}$ and therefore $(s_m)_{m \in M}$ is not contained in the right–hand side.

□

2.3 Interordinal Dependencies

For the definition of interordinal dependencies, let again the values of every attribute m of $\mathbb{K}$ be ordered by the ordered set $(P_m, \leq_m)$. For every $m \in M$, we introduce the ternary relation "betweeness" $[.,.,.]_m \subseteq G^3$ by $[f,g,h]_m :\Leftrightarrow (m(f) \leq_m m(g) \leq_m m(h)$ or $m(f) \geq_m m(g) \geq_m m(h)$. Then a set Y of attributes *interordinally depends* on a set X of attributes in a complete many–valued context $\mathbb{K}$ if, for all $f,g,h \in G$, $[f,g,h]_x$ for all $x \in X$ implies $[f,g,h]_y$ for all $y \in Y$, i.e., if there exists an betweeness preserving mapping $f: W^{|X|} \to W^{|Y|}$ such that $f((x(g))_{x\in X}) = (y(g)_{y\in Y})$ for all $g \in G$.

Proposition 3. *[GW2] Let $\mathbb{K} := (G, M, W, I)$ be a complete many-valued context and let $X, Y \subseteq M$. Then Y interordinally depends on X in $\mathbb{K}$ if and only if Y depends on X in $\left(\mathbb{K};\ \times_{m\in M} O_{P_m}^{\mathrm{cd}\bar{0}_m} \mid \times_{m\in M} O_{P_m}^{\mathrm{c}\bar{1}_m}\right)$.*

Note that, in all of the above cases, dependencies and weak dependencies coincide.

We would like to generalize nominal, ordinal, and interordinal dependencies to "relational" dependencies: Let R be an n_R-ary relation on the set W of values of a complete many–valued context $\mathbb{K} := (G, M, W, I)$, and let $X, Y \subseteq M$. Then we define $X \overset{R}{\to} Y :\Leftrightarrow$ for all $g_1, \ldots, g_{nR} \in G:\ [(x(g_1), \ldots, x(g_{n_R})) \in R$ for all $x \in X$ implies $(y(g_1), \ldots, y(g_{nR})) \in R$ for all $y \in Y]$. Note that we can define an *assigned context* K_R by $\mathbb{K}_R := (G^{n_R}, M, I_R)$ where $(g_1, \ldots, g_{n_R}) I_R m :\Leftrightarrow (m(g_1), \ldots, m(g_{n_R})) \in R$. Then $X \overset{R}{\to} Y$ in $\mathbb{K}$

- iff, for all $\mathbf{g} \in G^{n_R}$, $x(g) \in R$ for all $x \in X$ implies $y(g) \in R$ for all $y \in Y$
- iff, for all $\mathbf{g} \in G^{n_R}$, gI_Rx for all $x \in X$ implies gI_Ry for all $y \in Y$
- iff $X \to Y$ is an implication in $\mathbb{K}_R$.

Which scaling (i.e., which scales $\$_m$ and which operator $\prod$) yield $X \overset{R}{\to} Y$ in $\mathbb{K}$ if and only if $\mathcal{U}_X = \mathcal{U}_{X\cup Y}$ (or $\mathcal{U}_Y \subseteq \mathcal{U}_X$) in $(\mathbb{K}; \prod(\$_M : m \in M))$? Unfortunately, such relational dependencies cannot be expressed in general with the introduced theory. This will be shown by the following example for binary relations:

$\mathbb{K}$	a	b	c	d
1	1	2	3	2
2	2	3	2	1

$\mathbb{K}_R$	a	b	c	d
(1,1)		×	×	×
(1,2)	×		×	×
(2,1)	×	×		×
(2,2)	×	×	×	

Fig. 1.

Let $R \subseteq \{1,2,3\} \times \{1,2,3\}$ be a binary relation with $(1,2)$, $(2,1)$, $(2,2)$, $(3,2)$, $(3,3) \in R$, but $(1,1)$, $(2,3) \notin R$ (the pairs $(1,3)$ and $(3,1)$ may be in relation R or not), and let $\mathbb{K}$ be the complete many–valued context given in Fig. 1. Then there is no non–trivial relational dependency since the concept lattice of the assigned context $\mathbb{K}_R$ (see Fig. 1) is isomorphic to the 16–element Boolean lattice. But every scaling of a many–valued context with 3 objects and 4 attributes yields at least one non–trivial dependency:

Let $G := \{1, 2\}$ and $M := \{a, b, c, d\}$. Let us assume that no non–trivial dependency holds in (G, M, W, I). Thus in particular $\mathcal{U}_\emptyset \subset \mathcal{U}_{\{a\}} \subset \mathcal{U}_{\{a,b,c\}} \subset \mathcal{U}_M$. Since G is an extent for every context with set G of objects, there have to exist at least four extents all different from G to distinguish the above given sets of extents. This leads to a contradiction since $|\mathcal{P}(G) \setminus \{G\}| = 3$.

2.4 Linear Dependency

Proposition 4. *[Wi4] Let* $\mathbb{K} := (G, M, W, I)$ *be a complete many–valued context and* $X, Y \subseteq M$. *Then* $(y(g))_{g \in G}$ *is linear dependent from* $\{(x(g))_{g \in G} : x \in X\}$ *for all* $y \in Y$ *iff* Y *depends on* X *in* $(\mathbb{K};\ \bot_{m \in M}(K, K, \bot))$.

In the model of relational databases, multivalued dependencies as a generalization of functional dependencies are introduced as an attempt to detect and discover lossless decompositions [Ma1]. In the language of formal concept analysis, we can describe a *multivalued dependency* $X \rightarrow\!\!\rightarrow Y|Z$ for $Z \subseteq M \backslash (X \cup Y)$ by $[(x(g))_{x \in X} = (x(h))_{x \in X}$ for some $g, h \in G$ imply the existence of $i, j, \in G$ such that $(x(g))_{x \in X} = (x(h))_{x \in X} = (x(i))_{x \in X} = (x(j))_{x \in X}$, $(y(g))_{y \in Y} = (y(i))_{y \in Y}$, $(y(h))_{y \in Y} = (y(j))_{y \in Y}$, $(z(i))_{z \in Z} = (z(h))_{z \in Z}$ and $(z(j))_{z \in Z} = (z(g))_{z \in Z}]$ (note that $i, j \in \{g, h\}$ is possible) and say that Y and Z are independent relative to X (for each X–value, the set of all Y–values is repeated for every Z–value) [Ma1].

Note that, in relational databases, the multivalued dependencies are not necessarily determined by the relations, but by the underlying semantical data–model. Therefore, the significance of multivalued dependencies in formal concept analysis and relational databases is different.

Multivalued dependencies cannot be represented as dependencies of a many–valued context: Multivalued dependencies may be valid in a many–valued context (G, M, W, I) but not in a subcontext $(H, M, W, I \cap (H \times M \times W))$ where the set of objects G is restricted to $H \subseteq G$. Dependencies of many–valued contexts remain valid in such a subcontext. But one can define the join of two two–valued contexts like in relational databases as a certain generalization of the above defined semi–product. This yieds a generalization of functional dependencies to multivalued dependencies [Lo1].

3 Properties of Dependencies

For a general investigation of the properties of dependencies we will consider the following Armstrong–axioms:

(R1) $\quad X \rightarrow X \quad$ (reflexitivity)

$$\text{(R1')} \quad \frac{Y \subseteq X}{X \to Y} \quad \text{(generalized reflexitivity)}$$
$$\text{(R2)} \quad \frac{X \to Y}{X \cup Z \to Y} \quad \text{(augmentation)}$$
$$\text{(R2')} \quad \frac{X \to Y}{X \cup Z \to Y \cup Z} \quad \text{(extension)}$$
$$\text{(R3)} \quad \frac{X \to Y,\ X \to Z}{X \to Y \cup Z} \quad \text{(additivity)}$$
$$\text{(R4)} \quad \frac{X \to Y \cup Z}{X \to Y} \quad \text{(projectivity)}$$
$$\text{(R5)} \quad \frac{X \to Y,\ V \cup Y \to Z}{V \cup X \to Z} \quad \text{(pseudotransitivity)}$$
$$\text{(R6)} \quad \frac{X \to Y,\ Y \to Z}{X \to Z} \quad \text{(transitivity)}$$
$$\text{(R7)} \quad \frac{X \to Y \cup Z,\ Z \to W}{X \to Y \cup Z \cup W} \quad \text{(accumulation)}$$
$$\text{(R8)} \quad \frac{X \to Y,\ Z \to W}{X \cup Z \to Y \cup W} \quad \text{(generalized additivity)}$$

Let us remark that for dependencies and weak dependencied (R1), (R1'), and (R4) are valid (note that if $Z \subseteq Y$ then $\mathcal{U}_{X \cup Z} \subseteq \mathcal{U}_{X \cup Y}$ for any $X \subseteq M$):

- $Y \subseteq X \Rightarrow \mathcal{U}_X = \mathcal{U}_{X \cup Y} \Leftrightarrow: X \to Y$ thus (R1) and (R1') are valid for dependencies.
- $X \to Y \cup Z :\Leftrightarrow \mathcal{U}_X = \mathcal{U}_{X \cup Y \cup Z}$ together with $\mathcal{U}_X \subseteq \mathcal{U}_{X \cup Z} \subseteq \mathcal{U}_{X \cup Y \cup Z}$ implies $\mathcal{U}_X = \mathcal{U}_{X \cup Z}$, hence $X \to Z$, thus (R4) is valid for dependencies.
- $Y \subseteq X \Rightarrow \mathcal{U}_Y \subseteq \mathcal{U}_X \Leftrightarrow: X \overset{w}{\to} Y$ thus (R1) and (R1') are valid for weak dependencies.
- $X \overset{w}{\to} Y \cup Z :\Leftrightarrow \mathcal{U}_{Y \cup Z} \subseteq \mathcal{U}_X$ together with $\mathcal{U}_Z \subseteq \mathcal{U}_{Y \cup Z}$ implies $\mathcal{U}_Z \subseteq \mathcal{U}_X$, hence $X \overset{w}{\to} Z$, thus (R4) is valid for weak dependencies.

For further considerations we will treat only the case where the rules (R1), (R1'), and (R4) are valid.

Lemma 5. *Under the assumptions (R1), (R1'), and (R4) the following implications between the deduction rules are valid and this list is a complete basis:*

(i) ⇒ (R1), (R1'), (R4)
(ii) (R2') ⇒ (R2)
(iii) (R8) ⇒ (R2'), (R3)
(iv) (R2), (R3) ⇒ (R8)
(v) (R3), (R6) ⇒ (R7)
(vi) (R2'), (R6) ⇒ (R7)
(vii) (R5) ⇒ (R2'), (R6)
(viii) (R7) ⇒ (R2'), (R3), (R5), (R6)
(ix) (R6) ⇒ (R2)

Proof. (i) is valid by assumption.
(ii) follows by an application of (R4).

$$\text{(iii)} \quad \dfrac{X \to Y, \overline{Z \to Z}\ \text{(R1)}}{X \cup Z \to Y \cup Z}\ \text{(R8)}$$

and (R3) is the special case where $X = Z$

$$\text{(iv)}\quad \cfrac{\cfrac{X\to Y,\ Z\to U}{X\cup Z\to Y,\ X\cup Z\to U}\ \text{(R2)}}{X\cup Z\to Y\cup U}\ \text{(R3)}$$

$$\text{(v)}\quad \cfrac{\cfrac{\cfrac{X\to Y\cup Z}{X\to Z,\ Z\to W}\ \text{(R4)}}{X\to W,\ X\to X\cup Z}\ \text{(R6)}}{X\to W\cup X\cup Z}\ \text{(R3)}$$

$$\text{(vi)}\quad \cfrac{\cfrac{Z\to W}{Y\cup Z\to Y\cup W\cup Z,\ X\to Y\cup Z}\ \text{(R2')}}{X\to W\cup Y\cup Z}\ \text{(R6)}$$

(vii) $V=\emptyset$ yields (R6)

$$\cfrac{X\to Y,\overline{V\cup Y\to V\cup Y}\ \text{(R1)}}{X\cup V\to V\cup Y}\ \text{(R5)}$$

$$\text{(viii)}\quad \cfrac{\cfrac{\overline{X\cup Y\to X\cup Y}\ \text{(R1)},Y\to Z}{X\cup Y\to X\cup Y\cup Z}\ \text{(R7)}}{X\cup Y\to X\cup Z}\ \text{(R4)}$$

$Y=Z$ and an application of (R4) yields (R6).

$$\cfrac{\cfrac{\cfrac{X\to Y}{X\to X\cup Y,\ X\to Z}\ \text{(R2')}}{X\to X\cup Y\cup Z}\ \text{(R7)}}{X\to Y\cup Z}\ \text{(R4)}$$

$$\cfrac{\cfrac{X\to Y}{X\cup V\to Y\cup V,\ V\cup Y\to Z}\ \text{(R2')}}{X\cup V\to Z}\ \text{(R6)}$$

$$\text{(ix)}\quad \cfrac{\overline{X\cup Z\to X}\ \text{(R1')},X\to Y}{X\cup Z\to Y}\ \text{(R6)}$$

The given list is complete: Every implication that is not a consequence of the above implications $(i),\ldots,(ix)$ is not valid in at least one of the (counter)examples 1-5 introduced later (but whose deduction rules are indicated in the context $\mathbb{K}$ of Fig. 2). □

Note that the concept lattice $\underline{\mathfrak{B}}(\mathbb{K})$ (see Fig. 2) yields an excellent survey of the valid implications since a complete basis of implications of a (one–valued) context is not uniquely determined. The implications between attributes of a (one–valued) context can be read from its concept lattice and they are uniquely determined by its concept lattice. Furthermore, for each set $\{X\to Y:\ X\subseteq Y\subseteq M\}$ of implications a context can be found such that its concept lattice is already determined by $\{X\to Y:\ X\subseteq Y\subseteq M\}$ [GW2].

The list of implications given in Lemma 5 has been found with the aid of an interactive computer program [Bu1]. This program is based on a description of a basis of a set of implications in a context via the pseudoclosed sets of the corresponding closure operator [Du1] and an algorithm who generates

	(R1)	(R1')	(R2)	(R2')	(R3)	(R4)	(R5)	(R6)	(R7)	(R8)
Ex.1	X	X			X	X				
Ex.2	X	X				X				
Ex.3	X	X	X			X		X		
Ex.4	X	X	X	X	X	X				X
Ex.5	X	X	X	X		X				

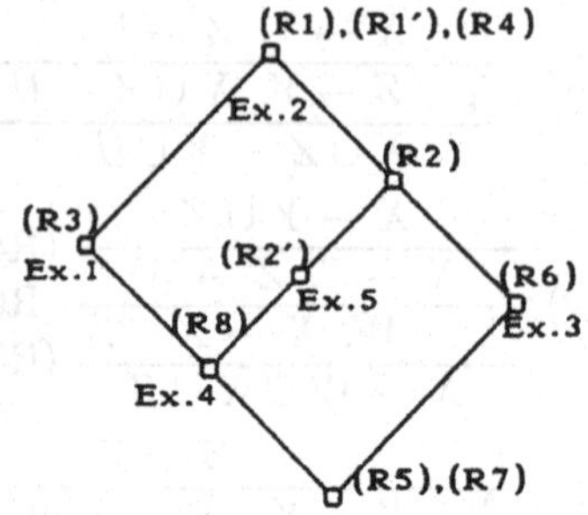

Fig. 2.

these pseudoclosed sets [Ga1]: The computer asks in a certain order all not yet concludable implications in such a way that no superfluous question is asked.

Lemma 6. *For the dependencies of a many–valued context the following connections between the deduction rules are valid and this list is complete:*

(i) Equivalent are all the rules (R2), (R2'), (R5), (R6), (R7), (R8)
(ii) Equivalent are all the rules (R1), (R1'), (R4)
(iii) (R2) implies (R3) implies (R1) but not vice versa.

Proof. As additional implications (relative to Lemma 5) we have:

(R2') $\Rightarrow$ (R3): $X \to Y$ and $Y \to Z$ yield $Y \cup X \to Z \cup X$ (R2'), thus $\mathcal{U}_X = \mathcal{U}_{X\cup Y}$ and $\mathcal{U}_{X\cup Y} = \mathcal{U}_{X\cup Y\cup Z}$ which implies $\mathcal{U}_X = \mathcal{U}_{X\cup Y\cup Z}$, hence $X \to Y \cup Z$.
(R2') $\Rightarrow$ (R6): Like the preceding case, $X \to Y$ and $Y \to Z$ yield $\mathcal{U}_X = \mathcal{U}_{X\cup Y\cup Z}$. Together with $\mathcal{U}_{X\cup Y\cup Z} \supseteq \mathcal{U}_{X\cup Y} \supseteq \mathcal{U}_X$ this implies $\mathcal{U}_X = \mathcal{U}_{X\cup Z}$, thus $X \to Z$.
(R2) $\Rightarrow$ (R2'): $X \to Y$ yields $X \cup Z \to Y$ (R2), thus $\mathcal{U}_{X\cup Y\cup Z} = \mathcal{U}_{X\cup Z}$, hence $X \cup Z \to Y \cup Z$.

The Examples 1 and 2 show that neither (R3) $\to$ (R2) nor (R1) $\to$ (R3) hold in general for dependencies of many–valued contexts. □

Lemma 7. *For the weak dependencies of a many–valued context the following connections between the deduction rules are valid and this list is complete:*

(i) Equivalent are all the rules (R2'), (R3), (R5), (R7), (R8)
(ii) Equivalent are all the rules (R1), (R1'), (R2), (R4), (R6)
(iii) (R2') implies (R2) but not vice versa.

Proof. As additional implications (relative to Lemma 5) we have:

$\Rightarrow$ (R2), (R6): $X \overset{w}{\to} Y$ yields $\mathcal{U}_Y \subseteq \mathcal{U}_X$. Together with $\mathcal{U}_X \subseteq \mathcal{U}_{X\cup Z}$ we conclude that $X \cup Z \overset{w}{\to} Y$. $X \overset{w}{\to} Y$ and $Y \overset{w}{\to} Z$ yield $\mathcal{U}_Z \subseteq \mathcal{U}_Y \subseteq \mathcal{U}_X$, hence $X \overset{w}{\to} Z$.

(R3) ⇒ (R7): $X \overset{w}{\to} Y \cup Z$ and $Z \overset{w}{\to} W$ yield $\mathcal{U}_{Y\cup Z} \subseteq \mathcal{U}_X$ and $\mathcal{U}_W \subseteq \mathcal{U}_Z$. Together with $\mathcal{U}_Z \subseteq \mathcal{U}_{Y\cup Z}$ we conclude that $\mathcal{U}_W \subseteq \mathcal{U}_X$, hence $X \overset{w}{\to} W$ and $X \overset{w}{\to} Y \cup Z$. An application of (R3) yields $X \overset{w}{\to} W \cup Y \cup Z$.

(R2') ⇒ (R7): $Z \overset{w}{\to} W$ yields $Z \cup Y \overset{w}{\to} W \cup Y \cup Z$ (R2'). Together with $X \overset{w}{\to} Y \cup Z$ we conclude that $\mathcal{U}_{W\cup Y\cup Z} \subseteq \mathcal{U}_{Z\cup Y} \subseteq \mathcal{U}_X$, thus $X \overset{w}{\to} W \cup Y \cup Z$.

The Example 3 shows that (R2) → (R2') does not hold in general for weak dependencies of a many–valued context. □

3.1 The Counterexamples

For a many–valued context $\mathbb{K} := (G, M, \mathbb{N}, I)$ and $\$_m := (\mathbb{N}, \emptyset, \emptyset)$ define an operator $\sum$ by $\sum_{m\in M} \$_m := (\times_{m\in M}\mathbb{N}, \mathcal{P}(M), \sum)$ with $(G_m)_{m\in M} \sum N :\Leftrightarrow \sum_{n\in N} g_n \geq 2|N|$.

It is evident that the projections are measures. Furthermore, $N_X = \mathcal{P}(X)$: $N_X \supseteq \mathcal{P}(X)$ is obvious. For the proof of $N_X \subseteq \mathcal{P}(X)$, let $K \nsubseteq X$ and $n \in K \setminus X$; define $g_x = 1$ for all $x \in M$, $h_X = 1$ for all $x \in M \setminus \{n\}$, and $h_n = 2|K|$. Then $(h_m)_{m\in M} \sum K$ and $g_x = h_x$ for all $x \in X$ but not $(g_m)_{m\in M} \sum K$. Thus $K \notin N_X$.

$\mathbb{K}$	a	b
1	2	2
2	2	1
3	3	1

$\tilde{\mathbb{K}}$	$\emptyset$	$\{a\}$	$\{b\}$	$\{a,b\}$
1	×	×	×	×
2	×	×		
3	×	×		×

Fig. 3.

Example 1. Let $\mathbb{K}$ be the many–valued context in Fig. 3 scaled by $\sum(\$_m : m \in M)$. Then, in the derived context $\tilde{\mathbb{K}}$ (also shown in Fig. 3), we have the following inclusions of the sets of extents: $\mathcal{U}_\emptyset = \mathcal{U}_{\{a\}} \subset \mathcal{U}_{\{b\}} \subset \mathcal{U}_{\{a,b\}}$. Thus, $\emptyset \to \{a\}$ is the only non–trivial dependency (beside $\{a\} \to \emptyset$, $\{b\} \to \emptyset$, $\{a,b\} \to \emptyset$, $\emptyset \to \emptyset$). Thus, (R2) is not valid since $\emptyset \to \{a\}$, $\{b\} \to \emptyset$ are dependencies but $\{b\} \to \{a\}$ is not. (R3) is valid since $\emptyset$ is the only premise that occurs twice. Lemma 6 implies the validity of (R1), (R1'), (R4) and that (R2), (R2'), (R5), (R6), (R7), (R8) do not hold.

Example 2. Let $\mathbb{K}$ be the many–valued context in Fig. 4 scaled by $\sum(\$_m : m \in M)$. For the derived context $\tilde{\mathbb{K}}$ (also shown in Fig. 4) we have the following inclusions of the sets of extents: $\mathcal{U}_\emptyset = \mathcal{U}_{\{b\}} = \mathcal{U}_{\{c\}} = \mathcal{U}_{\{b,c\}} \subset \mathcal{U}_{\{a\}} = \mathcal{U}_{\{a,b\}} = \mathcal{U}_{\{a,c\}} \subset \mathcal{U}_{\{a,b,c\}}$. Thus $\{b\} \to \{c\}$, $\{c\} \to \{b\}$, $\{a\} \to \{c\}$, $\{a\} \to \{b\}$ and $X \to Y$ for $Y \subseteq X$ are the only dependencies. (R3) is not valid since $\{a\} \to \{c\}$ and $\{a\} \to \{b\}$ are dependencies but $\{a\} \to \{b,c\}$ is not. (R2') is not valid since

$\mathbb{K}$	a	b	c
1	2	2	2
2	0	3	3
3	1	2	2

$\tilde{\mathbb{K}}$	$\emptyset$	$\{a\}$	$\{b\}$	$\{c\}$	$\{a,b\}$	$\{a,c\}$	$\{b,c\}$	$\{a,b,c\}$
1	×	×	×	×	×	×	×	×
2	×		×	×			×	×
3	×		×	×			×	

Fig. 4.

$\{a\} \to \{c\}$ is a dependency but $\{a,b\} \to \{b,c\}$ is not. (R2) is not valid since $\{a\} \to \{c\}$ is a dependency but $\{a,b\} \to \{c\}$ is not.

Lemma 6 shows that (R1), (R1') and (R4) are the only valid deduction rules.

$\mathbb{K}$	a	b	c
1	1	1	1
2	2	2	2
3	3	3	3

$\$_a$	a	0
1	×	
2		
3		

$\$_b$	b	0
1		
2	×	
3		

$\$_c$	c	d	0
1	×		
2		×	
3			

Fig. 5.

$\tilde{\mathbb{K}}$	$(0,0,0)$	$(a,0,0)$	$(0,b,0)$	$(0,0,c)$	$(0,0,d)$	$(a,b,0)$	$(a,0,c)$	$(a,0,d)$	$(0,b,c)$	$(0,b,d)$	(a,b,c)	(a,b,d)
1		×		×		×	×	×	×		×	×
2			×		×	×		×	×	×	×	×
3												

Fig. 6.

Example 3. (weak dependencies of a direct product). Let $\mathbb{K}$ be the many–valued context and $\$_a$, $\$_b$, and $\$_c$ be the scales given in Fig. 5. The scaled context $(\mathbb{K}; \times_{m \in M} \$_m)$ yields the derived context $\tilde{\mathbb{K}}$ indicated in Fig. 6 with the following connections between the sets of extents (remeber that $N_R = \{(k_m)_{m \in M} : k_m = 0_m \text{ for all } m \in M \backslash R\}$): $\mathcal{U}_\emptyset \subset \mathcal{U}_{\{a\}}, \mathcal{U}_\emptyset \subseteq \mathcal{U}_{\{b\}}$, but neither $\mathcal{U}_{\{a\}} \subseteq \mathcal{U}_{\{b\}}$ nor $\mathcal{U}_{\{a\}} \supseteq \mathcal{U}_{\{b\}}$, and $\mathcal{U}_{\{a\}}$, $\mathcal{U}_{\{b\}} \subset \mathcal{U}_{\{c\}} \subset \mathcal{U}_{\{a,b\}} = \mathcal{U}_{\{a,c\}} = \mathcal{U}_{\{b,c\}} = \mathcal{U}_{\{a,b,c\}}$. Thus $\{c\} \to \{a\}$, $\{c\} \to \{b\}$, $\{a,b\} \to \{a,b,c\}$, $\{a,c\} \to \{a,b,c\}$, $\{b,c\} \to \{a,b,c\}$ and $X \to Y$ for $Y \subseteq X$ are the only dependencies. (R3) is not valid since $\{c\} \to \{a\}$ and $\{c\} \to \{c\}$ are dependencies but $\{c\} \to \{a,c\}$ is not. (R2') is not valid since $\{c\} \to \{a\}$ is a dependency but $\{c\} \to \{a,c\}$ is not. Hence (R5), (R7), (R8) are not valid. But (R1), (R1'), (R2), (R4), (R6) are valid by Lemma 7.

Therefore, the weak dependencies of a many–valued context scaled by a direct product of scales cannot be represented as implications of a suitable one–valued context in general.

Example 4. Let $\mathcal{J}$ be the closure of $\{a\} \to \{b\}$, $\{b\} \to \{c\}$ under (R1), (R1'), (R4), (R8). By Lemma 5, J is also closed under (R2), (R2'), (R3). This closure does not contain $\{a\} \to \{c\}$ since $\{a\} \to \{b\}$, $\{a\} \to \{a\}$, and $\{a\} \to \emptyset$ are the only dependencies with premise $\{a\}$ in this closure. Thus (R6) is not valid and therefore neither (R5) nor (R7) are valid by Lemma 5.

Example 5. Let $\mathcal{J} := \{\{a\} \to \{b\}, \{a\} \to \{c\}, \{a\} \to \{a,b\}, \{a\} \to \{a,c\}, \{a,c\} \to \{b,c\}, \{a,c\} \to \{b\}, \{a,c\} \to \{a,b\}, \{a,b\} \to \{b,c\}, \{a,b\} \to \{c\}, \{a,b\} \to \{a,c\}, \{a,c\} \to \{a,b,c\}, \{a,b\} \to \{a,b,c\}\}$. One can easily check that $\mathcal{J}$ is closed under (R1), (R1'), (R2), (R2'), and (R4). Since $\{a\} \to \{b\}, \{a\} \to \{c\} \in \mathcal{J}$ but $\{a\} \to \{b,c\} \notin \mathcal{J}$, (R3) fails (and therefore also (R5), (R7), (R8) by Lemma 5). Since $\{a,b\} \to \{b,c\}, \{a\} \to \{a,b\} \in \mathcal{J}$, but $\{a\} \to \{b,c\} \notin \mathcal{J}$, (R6) fails.

Corollary 8. *For the dependencies of a many–valued context* $\mathbb{K}$ *scaled by the semi–product, the direct product, or the algebraic product of scales all deduction rules are valid.*

Proof. (i) For the semi–product we have $N_{X\cup Y} = N_X \cup N_Y$. Thus, (R7) is valid which implies all others rules by Lemma 6: $\mathcal{U}_X = \mathcal{U}_{X\cup Y\cup Z}$ and $\mathcal{U}_Z = \mathcal{U}_{Z\cup W}$ are valid iff $N_{X\cup Y\cup Z} = N_X \cup N_Y \cup N_Z$ is reducible relative to N_X and $N_{Z\cup W} = N_Z \cup N_W$ is reducible relative to N_Z. Hence $N_X \cup N_Y \cup N_Z \cup N_W = N_{X\cup Y\cup Z\cup W}$ is reducible relative to N_X, thus $\mathcal{U}_X = \mathcal{U}_{X\cup Y\cup Z\cup W}$.

(ii) Direct product: Let $0_r \in M_r$ be the (uniquely determined) attribute in $\$_r$ such that $0_r^{I_r} = \emptyset$. For $n \in \times_{m\in M} M_m$ and $A \subseteq M$, we define $n_A \in \times_{m\in M} M_m$ by $(n_A)_r := n_r$ if $r \in A$ and $(n_A)_r := 0_r$ if $r \in M \setminus A$. Lemma 6 shows that it is sufficient to check the validity of (R2') since (R2') implies all other rules. So let $m \in N_{X\cup Y\cup Z}$.

$$\begin{aligned} m^J &= (m_{X\cup Y})^J \cup (m_{Z\setminus X})^J \\ &\overset{X\to Y}{=} \bigcap\{n^J : n^J \supseteq (m_{X\cup Y})^J,\ n \in N_X\} \cup (m_{Z\setminus X})^J \\ &= \bigcap\{n^J \cup (m_{Z\setminus X})^J : n^J \supseteq (m_{X\cup Y})^J,\ n \in N_X\} \\ &= \bigcap\{c_{X,Z}(n,m)^J : n^J \supseteq (m_{X\cup Y})^J,\ n \in N_X\} \end{aligned}$$

with $(c_{X,Z}(n,m))_x := \begin{cases} n_x & x \in X \\ m_x & x \in Z \setminus X \\ 0_x & x \in M \setminus (X \cup Z) \end{cases}$

Since $c_{X,Z}(n,m) \in N_{X\cup Z}$ we have $\mathcal{U}_{X\cup Y\cup Z} = \mathcal{U}_{X\cup Z}$ and therefore $X \cup Z \to Y \cup Z$.

(iii) Algebraic product: The dependencies obtained for the algebraic product can be represented as implications of a suitable (one–valued) context (see [Wi4] or next section). But for implications (R1), (R2), (R2'), (R4) and (R6) are valid which implies all other deduction rules for dependencies by Lemma 5.

□

Note that, for complementary nominal scales or contrary ordinal scales [GW2] and the direct product as composition operator, the above result is a consequence of the possibility to represent the derived dependencies as implications of a suitable one–valued context.

4 Determination and Representation of Dependencies

In several cases it is possible to determine and represent the dependencies of a scaled context as the implications of a suitable one–valued context. In the case where $\mathbb{K}$ is a complete many–valued context this leads us to the following assigned contexts [GW2]:

(I) Functional dependencies as implications of the context $\mathbb{K}_n$:
$\mathbb{K}_n := (\mathcal{P}_2(G), M, I_n)$ with $\mathcal{P}_2(G) := \{A \subseteq G : |A| = 2\}$ and $(g,h)I_n m :\Leftrightarrow m(g) = m(h)$.
(II) Ordinal dependencies as implications of the context $\mathbb{K}_o$:
$\mathbb{K}_o := (G^2, M, I_o)$ with $(g,h)I_o m :\Leftrightarrow m(g) \leq_m m(h)$.
(III) Interordinal dependencies as implications of the context $\mathbb{K}_{io}$:
$\mathbb{K}_{io} := (G^3, M, I_{io})$ with $(g,h,f)I_{io} m :\Leftrightarrow m(g) \leq m(h) \leq m(f)$ or $m(g) \geq m(h) \geq m(f)$.
(IV) Linear dependencies as implications of the context $\mathbb{K}_\perp$:
$\mathbb{K}_\perp := (K^{|G|}, M, \perp)$ with $(k_g)_{g\in G} \perp m :\Leftrightarrow \sum_{g\in G} k_g \cdot m(g) = 0$.

For the non–complete case the notation becomes a little bit more difficult. If we refer to the definition of functional dependencies for non–complete many–valued contexts given in [GW1] we receive the context $\mathbb{K}_N := (\mathcal{P}_2(G), M \dot{\cup} \hat{M}, I_n)$ where $\hat{M} := \{\hat{m} : m \in M \text{ and } \operatorname{dom}(m) \neq G\}$ and $(g,h)I_n m :\Leftrightarrow m(g) = m(h)$, $(g,h)I_n \hat{m} :\Leftrightarrow (g,h) \in \operatorname{dom}(m)^2$. Then m functionality depends on A in $\mathbb{K}$ iff $A \to m$ or $A \cup \{\hat{m}\} \to m$ is an implication in $\mathbb{K}_n$.

Since the last paragraph made clear that the dependencies of a many–valued context need not to fulfill all the mentioned deduction rules but implications do, there are depedencies of many–valued contexts that cannot be represented by implications of a suitable (one–valued) context. But if all of the mentioned deduction rules are fulfilled by the set of dependencies of a complete many–valued context (e.g. if we take the direct product as compositon operator) it is an elementary result that such a representation can be given:

Proposition 9. *(A posteriori representation of the dependencies of a many–valued context). Let* $(\mathbb{K}; \prod(\$_m : m \in M))$ *be a scaled context whose dependencies fulfill all the deduction rules mentioned in Lemma 5. Let* $\hat{\mathbb{K}} := (\mathcal{P}(M).M, \hat{I})$ *be a one–valued context with* $K\hat{I}m$ *iff* $K \to \{m\}$ *is a dependency in* $(\mathbb{K}; \prod(\$_m : m \in M))$*, and* $A, B \subseteq M$*. Then* $A \to B$ *is a dependency in* $(\mathbb{K}; \prod(\$_m : m \in M))$ *if and only if* $A \to B$ *is an implication in* $\hat{\mathbb{K}}$*.*

Proof. Since implications of a one–valued context and the dependencies of the scaled context fulfill additivity (R3) and projectivity (R4) it suffices to show that $A \to \{m\}$ is a dependency iff $A \to \{m\}$ is an implication in $\hat{\mathbb{K}}$ (for $A \subseteq M$, $m \in M$).

$A \to \{m\}$ in $\hat{\mathbb{K}}$

- iff, for all $K \subseteq M$, $K\hat{I}a$ for all $a \in A$ implies $K\hat{I}m$
- iff, for all $K \subseteq M$, $\mathcal{U}_K = \mathcal{U}_{K\cup\{a\}}$ for all $a \in A$ implies $\mathcal{U}_K = \mathcal{U}_{K\cup\{m\}}$
- iff, for all $K \subseteq M$, $\mathcal{U}_K = \mathcal{U}_{K\cup A}$ implies $\mathcal{U}_K = \mathcal{U}_{K\cup\{m\}}$ (since the dependencies fulfill (R3)).

Now, $K := A$ yields $\mathcal{U}_A = \mathcal{U}_{A\cup\{m\}}$.

For the converse, $\mathcal{U}_A = \mathcal{U}_{A\cup\{m\}}$ implies $\mathcal{U}_{K\cup A} = \mathcal{U}_{K\cup A\cup\{m\}}$ for all $K \subseteq M$ (since the dependencies fulfill (R2')). Using the above equivalences, it is sufficient to show that, for all $K \subseteq M$, $\mathcal{U}_K = \mathcal{U}_{K\cup A}$ implies $\mathcal{U}_K = \mathcal{U}_{K\cup\{m\}}$. Combining $\mathcal{U}_{K\cup A} = \mathcal{U}_{K\cup A\cup\{m\}}$ with $\mathcal{U}_K = \mathcal{U}_{K\cup A}$ for all $K \subseteq M$, this yields $\mathcal{U}_K \subseteq \mathcal{U}_{K\cup\{m\}} \subseteq \mathcal{U}_{K\cup A\cup\{m\}} = \mathcal{U}_{K\cup A} = \mathcal{U}_K$, hence $\mathcal{U}_K = \mathcal{U}_{K\cup\{m\}}$ for all $K \subseteq M$ and therefore $A \to \{m\}$ in $\hat{\mathbb{K}}$. □

But in general, the set of objects of the constructed context $\hat{\mathbb{K}}$ is far too big and all dependencies have to be determined first. The dependencies in the above mentioned cases can be determined via the implications of the assigned one–valued contexts which seems not to be possible in general.

The following Lemma gives a necessary condition for the dependencies of many–valued contexts scaled by direct products of scales, i.e., we construct a one–valued context whose implications contain the dependencies of the original many–valued context. But in general not every implication gives rise to a dependency in the original many–valued context.

Lemma 10. *Let* $\mathbb{K} := (G, M, W, I)$ *be a complete many–valued context, let* $\$_m := (G_m, M_m, I_m)$ $(m \in M)$ *be a suitable family of scales, and let* $(G, \times_{m\in M} M_m, J)$ *be the derived context of the scaled context* $(\mathbb{K};\ \times(\$_m : m \in M))$. *Let* $\hat{\mathbb{K}} := (G \times G, M \hat{I})$ *where* $(g,h)\hat{I}m :\Leftrightarrow \bigcap\{\mathbf{n}^J : \mathbf{n} \in \times_{m\in M} M_m,\ n_m \in m(g)^{I_m}\} \supseteq \bigcap\{\mathbf{n}^J : \mathbf{n} \in \times_{m\in M} M_m,\ n_m \in m(h)^{I_m}\}$. *If* $A \to B$ *is a dependency of* $(\mathbb{K};\ \times(\$_m : m \in M))$ *then* $A \to B$ *is an implication in* $\hat{\mathbb{K}}$.

Proof. Again, we can restrict ourself to the case $|B| = 1$. Let $K \to \{m\}$ not be valid in $\hat{\mathbb{K}}$, i.e, there exist $g, h \in G$ such that

$$(*) \quad \bigcap\{\mathbf{n}^J : n_k \in k(g)^{I_k}\} \supseteq \bigcap\{\mathbf{n}^J : n_k \in k(h)^{I_k}\} \quad \text{for all } k \in K\ ,$$

but $\bigcap\{\mathbf{n}^J : n_m \in m(g)^{I_m}\} \not\supseteq \bigcap\{\mathbf{n}^J : n_m \in m(h)^{I_m}\}$. Then there exists a $z \in M_m$ with $m(g)I_m z$ but not $m(h)I_m z$. Now we choose $n_m = z$ and $n_l = 0_l$ for all $l \in M\backslash\{m\}$. Then $g \in \mathbf{n}^J$ but $h \notin \mathbf{n}^J$ since the direct product is the composition operator. From (*) it follows that $g \in \mathbf{k}^J$ implies $h \in \mathbf{k}^J$ for all $\mathbf{k} \in N_K$ with $\mathbf{k}^J \supseteq \mathbf{n}^J$. We conclude that $h \in \bigcap\{\mathbf{k}^J : \mathbf{k} \in N_K \text{ and } \mathbf{k}^J \supseteq \mathbf{n}^J\}$ and therefore $\mathbf{n}^J \supset \bigcap\{\mathbf{k}^J : \mathbf{k} \in N_K \text{ and } \mathbf{k}^J \supseteq \mathbf{n}^J\}$. Thus $\mathcal{U}_K \subset \mathcal{U}_{K\cap\{m\}}$, hence $K \to \{m\}$ is no dependency in $(\mathbb{K};\ \times(\$_m : m \in M))$. □

5 Accuracies of Partial Dependencies

For a one–valued context (G, M, I), $A, B \subseteq M$, and $p \in \mathbb{Q} \cap [0,1]$, a partial implication $A \xrightarrow{p} B$ is said to be *valid* in (G, M, I) iff $p = |(A \cup B)^I| \setminus |A^I|$ [Lu2]. A *partial dependency* in a many–valued context is defined as a triple (A, B, p) where A and B are sets of attributes and $p \in \mathbb{Q} \cap [0,1]$ and is also denoted by $A \xrightarrow{p} B$. But there is no such meaningful and unique way to define the validity of a partial dependency in a many–valued context as for partial implications in the one–valued case. For a many–valued context $K := (G, M, W, I)$ we call a mapping

$$\beta_{\mathbb{K}} : \mathcal{P}(M) \times \mathcal{P}(M) \to \mathbb{Q} \cap [0,1]$$

an *accuracy* of the many–valued context $\mathbb{K}$ if $B \subseteq A \subseteq M$ implies $\beta(A, B) = 1$ and $\beta(A, C) \geq \beta(B, C)$, $\beta(C, A) \leq \beta(C, B)$ for any $C \subseteq M$. Note that we drop the subscript $\mathbb{K}$ if it is clear that we refer to $\mathbb{K}$. We say that a partial dependency $A \xrightarrow{p} B$ is *valid* in $\mathbb{K}$ relative to $\beta_{\mathbb{K}}$ iff $p = \beta_{\mathbb{K}}(A, B)$.

In the sequel, we will introduce several different notions for an accuracy of a partial dependency. These accuracies are established as criteria by which one can judge the correctness of a dependency and the relative number of objects for which a dependency is not valid. First we will consider the case of partial functional dependencies whereas ordinal, interordinal, and other relational dependencies will be discussed in Section 5.2. The idea behind the subsequent definitions is that one wants to conclude the values taken by some attributes from the values taken by other attributes. For instance one wants to conclude the weigth of a person by its tallness and girth. First let us consider the case where the many–valued context $\mathbb{K} := (G, M, W, I)$ is complete. The non–complete case will be treated later. If the values of $\mathbb{K}$ have a nominal structure it makes sense to define for all $A \subseteq M$ an equivalence relation $E(A)$ on G by

$$E(A) := \{(g, h) \in G \times G : \ n(g) = n(h) \quad \text{for all } n \in A\} \ .$$

Let $[g]_{E(A)} := \{h \in G : \ (g, h) \in E(A)\}$ denote the equivalence class represented by g. For $A, B \subseteq M$, we define

$$\gamma(A, B) := \frac{1}{|G|} \left|\{g \in G : \ [g]_{E(A)} \subseteq [g]_{E(B)}\}\right| \ .$$

In this case we "count" only those objects whose values taken by the attributes $b \in B$ can be concluded by the values taken by the attributes $a \in A$. Let $G/E(A) := \{[g]_{E(A)} : \ g \in G\}$ denote the set of equivalence classes of $E(A)$. Now, we introduce

$$\overline{\alpha}(A, B) := \frac{1}{|G|} \sum_{C \in G/E(A)} \max\{|C \cap D| : \ D \in G/E(B)\} \ .$$

In this case we want to evaluate the attributes B for every equivalence class C of the reltion $E(A)$. For a more detailed explanation of the meaning of these accuracies we refer to the example given in Section 5.5. The normalization

$$\alpha(A,B) := \begin{cases} \frac{|G/E(B)|\overline{\alpha}(A,B)-1}{|G/E(B)|-1} & \text{if } |G/E(B)| \neq 1 \\ 1 & \text{otherwise} \end{cases}$$

yields $0 \leq \gamma(A,B) \leq \alpha(A,B) \leq 1$ and the limits are sharp [Lu1].

One should use both accuracies α and γ, since they give different information (see the example at the end of this paragraph). Unfortunately, the normalization of $\overline{\alpha}$ yields a distorsion with an awkward property: Let $\mathbb{K} := (G,M,W,I)$ be any many-valued context and $\tilde{\mathbb{K}} := (G \times \{1,2\}, M, W \times \{1,2\}, \tilde{I})$ where $((g,l),m,(w,k)) \in \tilde{I} :\Leftrightarrow l = k$ and $(g,m,w) \in I$. Then $\overline{\alpha}_{\mathbb{K}} = \overline{\alpha}_{\tilde{\mathbb{K}}}$, but the normalization yields $\alpha_{\mathbb{K}} \leq \alpha_{\tilde{\mathbb{K}}}$ and $\alpha_{\mathbb{K}}(A,B) = \alpha_{\tilde{\mathbb{K}}}(A,B)$ iff $\overline{\alpha}_{\mathbb{K}}(A,B) \in \{0,1\}$, since $|G/E(B)_{\tilde{\mathbb{K}}}| = 2|G/E(B)_{\mathbb{K}}|$. Thus, α will increase if we "double" each object in the described way.

5.1 Rough Sets and Partial Dependencies

In his theory of *rough sets*, Z. Pawlak calls a 4-tuple $S := (U,A,V,f)$ an *information systems* if U, A, and V are finite sets (the universe, the set of attributes, and the set of values), and if $f: U \times A \to V$ is a total function (information function) [Pa1, Pa2, Pa3]. Obviously, information systems and finite complete many-valued contexts are equivalent. Contrary to the theory of formal concept analysis, any subset $X \subseteq U$ is called a concept and any subset $B \subseteq A$ is called an extent of the information systems S. The *indiscernability relation* $\tilde{B} \subseteq U \times U$ is introduced for all $B \subseteq A$ by

$$(x,y) \in \tilde{B} :\Leftrightarrow f(x,a) = f(y,a) \quad \text{for all } a \in B\ .$$

Hence $\tilde{B} = E(B)$ for the corresponding many-valued context $(U,A,V,\{(u,a,f(u,a)) : u \in U,\ a \in A\})$.

Furthermore, for $X \subseteq A$, the sets

$$\underline{B}(X) := \{x \in U : [x]_{\tilde{B}} \subseteq X\}$$

($= \{g \in G = U : [g]_{E(B)} \subseteq X\}$ for the corresponding many-valued context) and

$$\overline{B}(X) := \{x \in U : [x]_{\tilde{B}} \cap X \neq \emptyset\}$$

($= \{g \in G = U : [g]_{E(B)} \cap X \neq \emptyset\}$ for the corresponding many-valued context) are established. $\underline{B}(X)$ ($\overline{B}(X)$ resp.) is called the *B-lower* (*B-upper* resp.) *approximation* of X in S with respect to B. The value

$$\mu_B(X) := \frac{|\underline{B}(X)|}{|\overline{B}(X)|}$$

is called the *accuracy* of X with respect to B and is a measure for the quality of the approximation of X by the sets $\underline{B}(X)$ and $\overline{B}(X)$. X is called *B-definable* iff $\mu_B(X) = 1$ and X is called *B-rough* iff $\mu_B(X) < 1$. Note that X is B-definable iff X is the union of equivalence–classes of $\tilde{B}$ iff X is an extent of the context $(\{[u]_{E(B)}\}, \{[u]_{E(B)}\}, \neq)$. The equivalence–classes of $\tilde{B}$ are called *B-elementary sets*. The accuracy of a partition F of U (with respect to B) is defined by

$$\gamma_B(F) := \frac{1}{|U|}\left|\bigcup_{X\in F} \underline{B}(X)\right|$$

Note that $F := G/E(A)$ yields $\gamma_B(F) = \gamma(A, B)$.

In the theory of rough sets a set B of attributes is called *independent* if $\tilde{C} \supset \tilde{B}$ for every $C \subset B$, otherwise B is called *dependent.* A set B is called *reduct* of the set C if B is an independent subset of C such that $\tilde{B} = \tilde{C}$. One of the important problems treated in rough set theory is to find all reducts of a set C of attributes. Thus, finding all reducts of a set C is equivalent to find all sets B who are minimal with the property $\gamma(B, C) = 1$, or to find all sets B who are minimal with the property that $B \to C$ is a functional dependency. Since the functional dependencies of an information system or a many–valued context $\mathbb{K}$ are exactly the implications of the derived (one–valued) context $\mathbb{K}_n$ (see the first part of Section 4), we can profit from the theory of implications developped in [Du1, Ga1]. Thus, for $B \subset C$, B is a reduct of C in the many–valued context $\mathbb{K}$ (or in the information system S) iff B is a pseudoclosed set with $B^{I_nI_n} = C$ in the derived one–valued context $\mathbb{K}_n$. In this case of "crisp" functional dependencies, the representation of dependencies as implications of a context is advantageous. But the theory of rough sets is developped especially for non-crisp dependencies and provides a lot of investigation in the field of decision rules, decision tables and decomposition of decision tables as well as in automatical learning. With the above introduced transformation, we can express an essential part of the rough set theory in the language of formal concept analysis. In the following, we will develop a generalization of partial functional dependencies. Let us remark that Z. Pawlak treats only complete information systems and that a structure on the set of values is not considered. In the next section, we discuss the case where the set of values is equipped with a relation.

5.2 Relations on the Set W of Values

If R is an n_R–ary relation on W, we can define an n_R–ary relation R_N on G for all $N \subseteq M$ in the following way: For $g_1, \ldots, g_{n_R} \in G$, $R_N(g_1, \ldots, g_{n_R})$ iff, for all $m \in N$, $R(m(g_1), \ldots, m(g_{n_R}))$. In the sequel we do not want to consider those tupels which are trivially in relation R_M. Therefore, let $R_{\text{triv}} := \{\mathbf{g} \in G^{n_R} : R_m(g) \text{ for all } m \in W^G\}$ denote the set of those tupels $\mathbf{g} \in G^{n_R}$ which are in relation R_m for every possible attribute m (recall that an attribute m can be understood as a mapping from G to W). Then we define for $A, B \subseteq M$

$$\rho_R(A, B) := \begin{cases} \frac{|R_{A\cup B} - R_{\text{triv}}|}{|R_A - R_{\text{triv}}|} & \text{if } R_A \neq R_{\text{triv}} \\ 1 & \text{otherwise} \end{cases}$$

Examples:

(i) If W is partially ordered by $\leq$, then

$$\rho_{\leq}(A,B) = \begin{cases} \frac{|\leq_{A\cup B} - \{(g,g):\ g\in G\}|}{|\leq_A - \{(g,g):\ g\in G\}|} & \text{if } \leq_A \neq \{(g,g):\ g \in G\} \\ 1 & \text{otherwise} \end{cases}$$

(ii) Again, let W be partially ordered by $\leq$, and let $[.,.,.]$ be the betweeness relation defined by $[a,b,c] :\Leftrightarrow a \leq b \leq c$ or $a \geq b \geq c$. Then:

$$\rho_{[.,.,.]}(A,B) = \begin{cases} \frac{|[.,.,.]_{A\cup B} - \{(g,g,g):\ g\in G\}|}{|[.,.,.]_A - \{(g,g,g):\ g\in G\}|} & \text{if } [.,.,.]_A \neq \{(g,g,g):\ g \in G\} \\ 1 & \text{otherwise} \end{cases}$$

(iii) If the order relation $\leq$ in (i) leads to an antichain we obtain the nominal case:

$$\rho_{=}(A,B) = \begin{cases} \frac{|=_{A\cup B} - \{(g,g):\ g\in G\}|}{|=_A - \{(g,g):\ g\in G\}|} & \text{if } =_A \neq \{(g,g):\ g \in G\} \\ 1 & \text{otherwise} \end{cases}$$

Note that in general neither $\alpha = \rho_=$ nor $\gamma = \rho_=$ are valid.

5.3 Missing Information

In the non–complete case we suggest to consider all possibilities how to complete a non–complete many–valued context. Let β be any accuracy. For a many–valued context $\mathbb{K} := (G, M, W, I)$ and $X \subseteq M$ we say that the many–valued context $\tilde{\mathbb{K}} := (G, M, W, \tilde{I})$ is a X*-completion* of $\mathbb{K}$ iff $\tilde{I} \supseteq I$, $(G, X, W, \tilde{I} \cap (G \times X \times W))$ is complete, and $(G, M\backslash X, W, \tilde{I} \cap (G \times M\backslash X \times W)) = (G, M\backslash X, W, I \cap (G \times M\backslash X \times W))$. The set of X–completions of a many–valued context will be denoted by $\mathrm{Comp}_X(K)$. Let $P(\tilde{\mathbb{K}}|\mathbb{K})$ denote the relative frequency of the completion $\tilde{\mathbb{K}}$ of $\mathbb{K}$. Then we define

$$\beta_{\mathbb{K}}(A,B) := \sum_{\tilde{\mathbb{K}} \in \mathrm{Comp}_{A\cup B(\mathbb{K})}} P(\tilde{\mathbb{K}}|\mathbb{K}) \cdot \beta_{\tilde{\mathbb{K}}}(A,B)$$

Often, all completions $\tilde{\mathbb{K}}$ of $\mathbb{K}$ occur with the same frequency (assume that $|W| < \infty$), thus $P(\tilde{\mathbb{K}}|\mathbb{K})$ will have the value $1/\prod_{m\in A\cup B} |W|^{|G-\mathrm{def}(m)|}$.

A less convincing possibility is to interpret the missing information as a value itself.

5.4 Partial Dependencies as Partial Implications of a Suitable One–Valued Context

In Section 4 we intorduced a method to determine the dependencies of a scaled context $(\mathbb{K}; \$)$ as implications of a suitable one–valued context $(\hat{G}, M, \hat{I})$ with the same set of attributes as $\mathbb{K}$. For partial dependencies we construct such a context as follows (for an intorduction to partial implications of a context see [Lu2]):

Lemma 11. *Let* $\mathbb{K} := (G, M, W, I)$ *be a complete many-valued context. For an* n_R*-ary relation* R *on* W*, let* $G_R := G^{n_R} - R_{triv}$ *and, for* $\mathbf{g} \in G_R$*, let* $\mathbf{g} I_R m :\Leftrightarrow R_{\{m\}}(\mathbf{g})$*. Then* $\rho_R(A, B) = p$ *in* $\mathbb{K}$ *iff* $A \xrightarrow{p} B$ *is a partial implication in* $\mathbb{K}_R := (G_R, M, I_R)$*.*

Proof. This is a consequence of $(A \cup B)^{I_R} = \{\mathbf{g} \in G^{n_R} : R_{\{m\}}(g)$ for all $m \in A \cup B\} - R_{\text{triv}}$. □

Often, a many-valued context $\mathbb{K} := (G, D\dot{\cup}E, W, I)$ is given where the set of attributes is the disjoint union of two sets D and E: The attributes $d \in D$ can be measured, whereas the attributes $e \in E$ can only be determined by experts. In this case, one wants to determine the values taken by an attribute $e \in E$ from the values taken by the attributes of D (assuming that W has a nominal structure). In general, the dependency $D \to E$ is not valid in $\mathbb{K}$. If we can choose the order in which we can evaluate the attributes, the values $\beta(N, E)$ may support our decision. We can evaluate those attributes $d \in C \subseteq D$ first, where $\beta(C, E)$ is "big" (and such that we can conclude the values taken by the attributes $e \in E$ for a large part of objects).

Or, one determines only the values taken by the attributes $d \in C$ (with $\beta(C, E) \approx \beta(D, E)$ where the relation $\approx$ has to be made precise by an expert): The evaluation of attributes $d \in D \setminus C$ does not give more information and their determination is difficult or expensive. We say that a subset $N \subseteq D$ is *reducible* relative to β and E if $\beta(N, E) = \beta(D, E)$ (note that this equality is implied by $\beta(N, D \setminus N) = 1$ but not vice versa!). So in the above case, we are looking for reducible attributes.

Furthermore, the values $\beta(N, E)$ $(N \subseteq D)$ give us some hints how to seperate the set of attributes for a subdirect–decomposition with which we obtain for example a nested line diagram [Wi2].

5.5 An Application of Partial Dependencies and Accuracies of Decision Rules

In [FR1] one has measured some sizes of 100 genuine bank–notes and of 100 counterfeit bank–notes to compare the methods of factor–analysis, variance–analysis, the analysis of principal components, and some statistical methods. The variables are:

X_1: Lenght of the bank–note;
X_2: Width of the bank–note on the left side;
X_3: Width of the bank–note on the right side;
X_4: Width of the margin at the bottom;
X_5: Width of the margin at the top;
X_6: Length of the diagonal of the image area;

To illustarte the method of partial dependencies we introduce the seven following many–valued attributes:

$$m_1(g) := \begin{cases} 1 \text{ if } x_1 < 214,25 \\ 2 \text{ if } 214,25 \leq x_1 < 214,85 \\ 3 \text{ if } 214,85 \leq x_1 < 215,55 \\ 4 \text{ if } 215,55 \leq x_1 \end{cases},$$

$$m_2(g) := \begin{cases} 1 \text{ if } x_2 < 129,55 \\ 2 \text{ if } 129,55 \leq x_2 < 130,15 \\ 3 \text{ if } 130,15 \leq x_2 < 130,75 \\ 4 \text{ if } 130,75 \leq x_2 \end{cases},$$

$$m_3(g) := \begin{cases} 1 \text{ if } x_3 < 129,25 \\ 2 \text{ if } 129,25 \leq x_3 < 129,95 \\ 3 \text{ if } 129,95 \leq x_3 < 130,65 \\ 4 \text{ if } 130,65 \leq x_3 \end{cases},$$

$$m_4(g) := \begin{cases} 1 \text{ if } x_4 < 7,05 \\ 2 \text{ if } 7,05 \leq x_4 < 9,45 \\ 3 \text{ if } 9,45 \leq x_4 < 11,75 \\ 4 \text{ if } 11,75 \leq x_4 \end{cases},$$

$$m_5(g) := \begin{cases} 1 \text{ if } x_5 < 9,35 \\ 2 \text{ if } 9,35 \leq x_5 < 10,65 \\ 3 \text{ if } 10,65 \leq x_5 < 11,95 \\ 4 \text{ if } 11,95 \leq x_5 \end{cases},$$

$$m_6(g) := \begin{cases} 1 \text{ if } x_6 < 138,55 \\ 2 \text{ if } 138,55 \leq x_6 < 140,45 \\ 3 \text{ if } 140,45 \leq x_6 < 142,35 \\ 4 \text{ if } 142,35 \leq x_6 \end{cases},$$

$$m_7(g) := \begin{cases} g \text{ if the bank–note is genuine} \\ c \text{ if the bank–note is counterfeit} \end{cases}$$

The used limits are the 0.05, 0.5, and 0.95 quantiles of a normal distribution with mean value equal to the empirical mean value and a variance equal to the empirical variance. Of course, the variables X_i can be regarded as many–valued attributes themselves, but for the reason of a short description we introduced the m_i.

Then $\mathbb{K} := (\{1,2,\ldots,200\}, \{m_1, m_2, \ldots, m_6, m_7\}, \{1,2,3,4,b,f\}, I)$ with $gI(m,w) :\Leftrightarrow m(g) = w$ is a complete many–valued context (see Fig 7).

$\mathbb{K}$	m_1	m_2	m_3	m_4	m_5	m_6	m_7
1	2	4	4	2	2	3	g
2	2	2	2	2	2	3	g
3	2	2	2	2	2	3	g
⋮	⋮	⋮	⋮	⋮	⋮	⋮	⋮
100	2	2	2	2	2	3	g
101	2	2	3	3	3	2	c
⋮	⋮	⋮	⋮	⋮	⋮	⋮	⋮
199	2	3	4	3	3	2	c
200	2	2	2	3	3	2	c

Fig. 7. Part of $\mathbb{K} := (\{1,2,\ldots,200\}, \{m_1, m_2, \ldots, m_6, m_7\}, \{1,2,3,4,b,f\}, I)$

Let $M := \{m_1, m_2, \ldots, m_6\}$ and $E := \{m_7\}$. For some subsets $N \subseteq M$ the values $\alpha(N, E)$ and $\gamma(N, E)$ are:

$$\gamma(M,E) = \tfrac{97}{100} \qquad \alpha(M \setminus \{m_4\}, E) = \tfrac{99}{100}$$
$$\alpha(M,E) = \tfrac{99}{100} \qquad \gamma(M \setminus \{m_4, m_6\}, E) = \tfrac{44}{100}$$
$$\gamma(M \setminus \{m_6\}, E) = \tfrac{183}{200} \qquad \alpha(M \setminus \{m_4, m_6\}, E) = \tfrac{73}{100}$$
$$\alpha(M \setminus \{m_6\}, E) = \tfrac{92}{100} \qquad \gamma(\{m_4, m_6\}, E) = \tfrac{94}{100}$$
$$\gamma(M \setminus \{m_4\}, E) = \tfrac{181}{200} \qquad \alpha(\{m_4, m_6\}, E) = \tfrac{98}{100}$$

Let us recall the meaning of α and γ with this example. These two accuracies correspond to two different ways of concluding the values taken by the expert–attributes E. The first way is that only a decision is made if it is correct for the underlying data. E.g. if $m_4 = 2$ and $m_6 = 1$ then we conclude that the bank–note is counterfeit. In case of $m_4 = 2$ and $m_6 = 2$ we make no decision, since there are genuine and counterfeit bank–notes with these values (see Fig. 8). The accuracy γ counts the percentage of cases where a decision is made.

The second way is to make a decision each time, even if the concluded value is wrong for an object of the underlying data. E.g. in the case of $m_4 = 2$ and $m_6 = 2$ we conclude that the bank–note is counterfeit, although there is a genuine one with these values. $\overline{\alpha}$ counts the percentage of correct decisions and the normalization yields the accuracy α.

We see that in 94% of all cases we can determine the values taken by attribut m_7 from the values taken by the attributes m_4, m_6 since $\gamma(\{m_4, m_6\}, E) = \frac{94}{100}$. The consideration of all attributes M would increase this value to 97%. Thus, we will consider the many–valued context $(G, \{m_4, m_6\}, W, I \cap (G \times \{m_4, m_6\} \times W))$ scaled by the semiproduct $\otimes_{m \in \{m_4, m_6\}} (\{1,2,3,4\}, \{1,2,3,4\}, =)$ of nominal scales (see Fig. 8).

Only in the cases $m_4 = 2$, $m_6 = 2$ and $m_4 = 3$, $m_6 = 3$ we do not know yet if a bank–note is genuine or counterfeit. We have to consider the other attributes

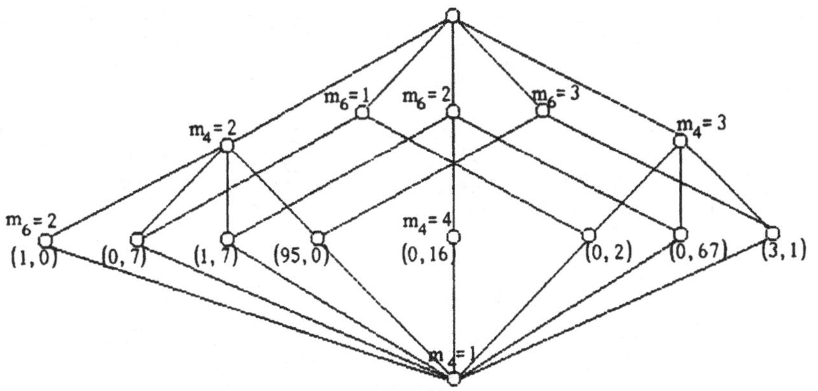

Fig. 8. $\underline{\mathfrak{B}}\left((G,\{m_4,m_6\},W,I\cap(G\times\{m_4,m_6\}\times W)); \otimes_{m\in\{m_4,m_6\}}(\{1,2,3,4\},\{1,2,3,4\},=)\right)$. The first number of the tuple indicates the number of genuine bank–notes with the corresponding attributes and the second number indicates the number of counterfeit bank–notes.

in addition.

	m_1	m_2	m_3	m_4	m_5	m_6	m_7
1	3	3	3	2	3	2	g
5	3	3	3	2	3	2	c
1	3	3	3	2	4	2	c
1	2	3	3	2	3	2	c

	m_1	m_2	m_3	m_4	m_5	m_6	m_7
2	3	3	3	3	2	3	g
1	3	3	4	3	3	3	c
1	3	2	2	3	1	3	g

Fig. 9.

The contexts (H,M,J_1) and (F,M,J_2) for $H := \{g\in G: m_3(g)=3=m_2(g), m_4(g)=2=m_6(g)\}$, $J_1 := I\cap(H\times M\times W)$, and $F := \{g\in G: m_1(g)=3=m_4(g)=m_6(g)\}$, $J_2 := I\cap(F\times M\times W)$. Note that the numeral in the first row of the contexts indicates the number of bank–notes having the respective evaluation.

Our method yields the same classification an in [FR1]: Using all attributes, only one genuine bank–note cannot be classified correctly. We are not interested to classify the bank–notes with which we constructed our decision rules, but we want to classify others. The four additional not yet mentioned counterfeit bank–notes in Fig. 11 can be classified in a correct way. At the most the assignment of no.204 could be critical: From the seven bank–notes with the same values as no.204, one is genuine (note that in [FR1] the assigment of no.203 is critical).

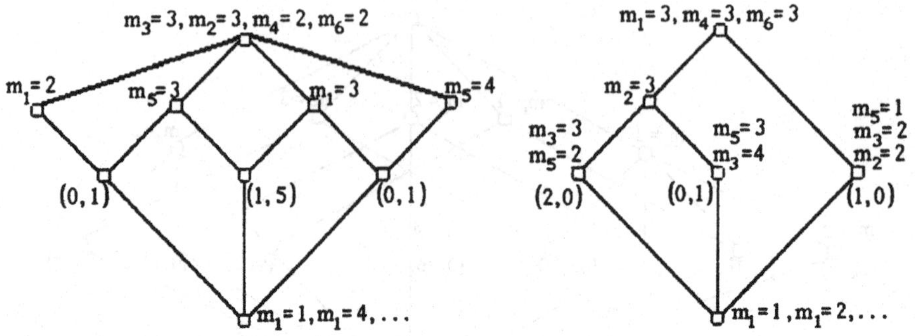

Fig. 10. $\underline{\mathfrak{B}}((H, M, J); \otimes_{m \in M} (\{1,2,3,4\}, \{1,2,3,4\}, =))$, $\underline{\mathfrak{B}}((F, M, J); \otimes_{m \in M} (\{1,2,3,4\}, \{1,2,3,4\}, =))$.

	m_1	m_2	m_3	m_4	m_5	m_6	m_7
201	3	3	3	3	3	2	c
202	3	3	3	3	3	2	c
203	3	3	3	2	4	2	c
204	3	3	3	2	3	2	c

Fig. 11. Four additional bank-notes.

References

[Bu1] Burmeister, P.: Programm zur formalen Begriffsanalyse einwertiger Kontexte. TH Darmstadt (1987)

[Du1] Duquenne, V.: Contextual implications between attributes and some properties of finite lattices. In: Ganter, B., Wille, R., Wolff, K.E. (eds.): Beiträge zur Begriffsanalyse, BI Wissenschaftsverlag, Mannheim, (1987), 213–239

[FR1] Flury, B. and Riedwyl, H.: Angewandte multivariate Statistik. Fischer, Stuttgart, New York, (1983)

[Ga1] Gänter, B.: Algorithmen zur formalen Begriffsanalyse. In: Ganter, B., Wille, R., Wolff, K.E. (eds.): Beiträge zur Begriffsanalyse, BI Wissenschaftsverlag, Mannheim, (1987), 241–254

[GW1] Gänter, B. and Wille, R.: Implikationen und Abhängigkeiten zwischen Merkmalen. In: Degens, P.O., Hermes, H.J., Opitz, O. (eds.): Die Klassifikation und ihr Umfeld, **17**, INDEKS–Verlag, Frankfurt, (1986), 171–185

[GW2] Gänter, B. and Wille, R.: Conceptual scaling. In: Roberts, F. (ed.): Applications of Combinatorics and Graph Theory to the Biological and Social Sciences, Springer Verlag, New York, (1989), 139–167

[GWS1] Gänter, B., Stahl, J. and Wille, R.: Conceptual measurement and many valued contexts. In: Gaul, W., Schader, M. (eds.): Classification as a Tool of Research, North–Holland, Amsterdam, (1986), 169–176

[Lo1] Lotzer, J.: Zerlegung von Begriffsverbänden mit Ansätzen aus der Theorie relationaler Datenbanken. Diplomarbeit, TH Darmstadt, (1991)

[Lu1] Luxenburger, M.: Partielle Implikationen und partielle Abhängigkeiten zwischen Merkmalen. Diplomarbeit, TH Darmstadt, (1988)

[Lu2] Luxenburger, M.: Implications partielles dans un contexte. Math., Inf. Sc. Hum. **113**, (1991), 35–55

[Ma1] Maier, D.: The Theory of Relational Databases. Computer Science Press, Rockville (1983)

[Pa1] Pawlak, Z.: Rough concept analysis. Bulletin of the Polish Academy of Sciences. Technics, **33**, 9–10, (1985), 495–498

[Pa2] Pawlak, Z.: On rough dependency of attributes in information systems. Bulletin of the Polish Academy of Sciences. Technics, **33**, 9–10, (1985), 551–559

[Pa3] Pawlak, Z.: Rough sets and multiexpert systems. Bulletin of the Polish Academy of Sciences. Technics, **33**, 9–10, (1985), 499–504

[Wi1] Wille, R.: Restructuring lattice theory: an approach based on hierarchies of concepts. In: Ivan Rival (ed.): Ordered Sets, Reidel, Dordrecht, Boston, (1982), 445-470

[Wi2] Wille, R.: Line diagrams of hierarchical concept systems. International Classification **11**, (1984), 77-86

[Wi3] Wille, R.: Finite distributive lattices as concept lattices. Atti inc. Logica Mathematica **2**, (1985), 635–648

[Wi4] Wille, R.: Dependencies of many–valued attributes. In: Bock, H.H. (ed.): Classification and Related Methods of Data Analysis, North–Holland, Amsterdam, (1988), 581–586

V

INDISCERNIBILITY-BASED REASONING

Chapter 11

Logical Analysis of Indiscernibility

Stéphane Demri[1] and Ewa Orlowska[2]

1 Laboratoire LEIBNIZ - C.N.R.S.
Grenoble, France
2 Institute of Telecommunications
Warsaw, Poland

Abstract: In this paper we explain the role of indiscernibility in the analysis of vagueness of concepts and in concept learning. We develop deduction methods that enable us making inferences from incomplete information in the presence of indiscernibility.

1 Introduction

The major goal of this paper is to study the structure of indiscernibility-type incomplete information and to present logical formalisms which provide methods of reasoning that are capable of making inferences from such an information. In particular, we analyse the problem of learning concepts from incomplete information.

Indiscernibility is one of the manifestations of incompleteness: if in a collection of data information about some objects is the same, then these objects are indistinguishable with respect to the given data. The typical form of data is a collection of (names of) objects and properties meaningful for these objects. One of the important problems in data analysis is to find regularities and to introduce patterns in a set of data items. These patterns lead to formation or invention of concepts. In a literary sense concept is an abstract entity which is formed in one's mind as a result of a mental process of our consciousness. Concepts are units of thought not given in experience but sought by analysis of data.

In the philosophy of science concepts are classified into four groups (Bunge 1967):

(a) Individual concepts (e.g. Newton) which apply to individuals. What is regarded as an individual depends on the level of analysis, an individual on a given level may be an agregate of lower level individuals,

(b) Class concepts (e.g. living) which apply to sets of individuals,

(c) Relation concepts (e.g. ordering relation) which apply to relations among objects of some kind (e.g. individuals or sets),

(d) Function concepts (e.g. length) which apply to functions of one or more arguments.

The two central questions in research on knowledge representation and acquisition in AI systems concern how knowledge is organized and how it can be increased. Construction of AI systems has involved the development of procedures that allow not only accumulation of facts but also enable us to make intelligent synthesis, that is to agregate primitive components of knowledge into complex ones.

Although concepts themselves are unobservable, we can articulate, express or represent them by defining their extension or denotation and intension or connotation. The extension of a concept is the set of objects which are instances of the concept, that is the objects to which the concept applies. Extensions consist of individuals, of subsets, of tuples, and so on, depending on the kind of concept. The intension of a concept is the set of properties that characterize the objects to which the concept applies. In general the determination of a concept is made jointly by the intension and by the extension of the concept. For example, to define the concept 'organism' we should list the earmarks of organisms and typical species of organism. In the present paper we give a formal formulation and discussion of the following facts:

(a) A set of properties characterizes completely and exhaustively a given set of instances of a concept.

(b) Some objects are representative instances of a given concept.

(c) A set of objects is an extension of a concept whose intension is given.

(d) A family of sets of objects provides approximate extensions of a concept whose approximate intension is given.

In this paper we analyse the problem of how extension and intension should be acquired from indiscernibility-type incomplete information in order to represent a concept properly. Fact (a) tells that the properties under consideration are the intension of the concept. Fact (b) tells that the extension of the concept is completely determined by the given objects. (c) and (d) refer to acquisition of an extension or a family of approximate extensions of a concept.

In the analysis of the acquisition of concepts we take into account unavailability of total information about objects which are supposed to be instances of concepts. Lack of information is a source of indiscernibility and leads to the existence of borderline instances of concepts. As a consequence we are not able to grasp concepts as the crisp wholes, and we perceive them as vague concepts. Both extension and intension of a vague concept can be determined with a tolerance. A process of learning concepts should be organized in a way enabling us to find a set of entities that are as close as possible to the extension of the concept and to find a set of properties characterizing instances of the concept as adequately as possible.

The approach to learning concepts presented in this paper is based on the rough set theory (Pawlak 1982, 1991). The paper provides an elaborated version of learning tasks formulated in Orlowska (1988a). Several ideas included in Orlowska (1984, 1988b) and Pawlak (1985) are an inspiration for the developments of the present paper. Some other formal approach to concept analysis can be found in Wille (1984). An application of rough set theory to learning was originated in Konrad et al. (1982), and next it was considered in a number of papers, among others in Ras and Zemankova (1984), Wong et al. (1986), Pawlak (1987), Grzymala-Busse (1988), and in chapter 3 and 4 of this volume.

2 Indiscernibility

Following the theory of relational databases (Codd 1970) and the theory of information systems (Pawlak 1981) we split properties of objects into pairs of the form (attribute, value). For example, the property of 'being green' is transformed into the pair (colour, green), the counterpart of the property of ' being large' is the pair (size, large). In these examples 'colour' and 'size' are attributes of objects, and 'green', 'large' are values of these attributes, respectively. Any green object possesses the property (colour, green), and any small object does not possess the property (size, large). Consequently, intensions of concepts consist of properties formed from pairs (attribute, value) by means of propositional operations 'not', 'and', 'or', for some attributes which are meaningful for the objects to which the concepts apply.

We consider the universes of discourse of the following form (see Pawlak 1981).

Definition 2.1. By a universe we mean a system $U=(OB,AT,\{VAL_a: a \in AT\},f)$ where OB is a non-empty set of objects, AT is a non-empty set of attributes, for any $a \in AT$ the set VAL_a consists of values of attribute a, and $f:OB\times AT\rightarrow VAL=\bigcup\{VAL_a:a \in AT\}$ is an information function which assigns values of attributes to objects. We require that for $(o,a) \in OB \times AT$, $f(o,a) \in VAL_a$.

Given an object x, an attribute a, and a value v of a, if $f(x,a)=v$, then we say that the object x possesses the property (a,v).

Attributes of objects serve as discriminative resources in the universe of discourse. Objects may be distinguishable with respect to some attributes but indistinguishable with respect to others.

Definition 2.2. Let a universe $U=(OB,AT,\{VAL_a: a \in AT\},f)$ be given, and let $A\subseteq AT$. By an indiscernibility relation determined by A we mean the relation ind(A) in set OB of objects such that $(x,y)\in ind(A)$ iff $f(x,a)=f(y,a)$ for all $a \in A$.

For the sake of simplicity of notation we sometime omit brackets if it is clear from the context which set we use. The following properties of indiscernibility relations are easily obtained from the definition.

Proposition 2.1. (a) ind(A) is reflexive, symmetric, and transitive
(b) $ind(A\cup B)=ind(A)\cap ind(B)$
(c) $A\subseteq B$ implies $ind(B)\subseteq ind(A)$
(d) $ind(\emptyset)=OB x OB$.

Condition (a) says that indiscernibility relations are equivalence relations. Condition (b) shows that discrimination power of the union of sets of attributes is possibly better than that of the parts of the union.

Let $R(x)=\{y \in OB:(x,y) \in R\}$ be the equivalence class of an indiscernibility relation R generated by an object x. Every equivalence class of the form ind(a)(x) for $a \in AT$ corresponds to an atomic property of objects, namely to property (a,v) such that f(x,a)=v. For a set $A \subseteq AT$ the class ind(A)(x) corresponds to the conjunction of all properties (a,v) such that $a \in A$ and f(x,a)=v.

We clearly have $ind(A \cup B)(x)=ind(A)(x) \cap ind(B)(x)$, and for any binary relation R and S, $R \subseteq S$ implies $R(x) \subseteq S(x)$. Hence, making intersection of indiscernibility relations we form new properties from some given properties. Properties obtained by means of conjunction from some other properties provide a finer partition of the set of objects than the properties which are the components of the conjunction.

Example 2.1. This example is a modification of an example presented in Wille (1982). Let OB be the set of planets OB={Mercury (Me), Venus (V), Earth (E), Mars (Ma), Jupiter (J), Saturn (Sa), Uranus (U), Neptune (N), Pluto (P)}. Let AT consist of three attributes: D='distance from the Sun', S='size', and M='possession of a moon'. The values of attribute D are 'near' and 'far', the values of attribute S are 'small', 'medium', 'large', and the values of attribute M are 'yes', 'no'. Information function is given in the following table.

	S	D	M
Me	small	near	no
V	small	near	no
E	small	near	yes
Ma	small	near	yes
J	large	far	yes
Sa	large	far	yes
U	medium	far	yes
N	medium	far	yes
P	small	far	yes

Equivalence classes determined by indiscernibility relations corresponding to the given attributes are as follows:

ind(S):	X_1={Me,V,E,Ma,P} X_2={J,Sa} X_3={U,N}
ind(D):	Y_1={Me,V,E,Ma} Y_2={J,Sa,U,N,P}
ind(M):	Z_1={Me,V} Z_2={E,Ma,J,Sa,U,N,P}
ind(M,D):	T_1={Me,V} T_2={E,Ma} T_3={J,Sa,U,N,P}
ind(S,D):	W_1={Me,V,E,Ma) W_2={J,Sa} W_3={U,N} W_4={P}
ind(S,D,M):	{Me,V} {E,Ma} {J,Sa} {U,N} {P}

Equivalence classes of indiscernibility relations correspond to properties:

X_1:	being small	(S, small)
X_2:	being large	(S, large)
X_3:	being medium	(S, medium)
Y_1:	being near to Sun	(D, near)
Y_2:	being far from Sun	(D, far)
Z_1:	having no moon	(M, no)

Z_2: having at least one moon (M, yes)

$T_2=Y_1 \cap Z_2$: being near to Sun and having a moon (D, near) and (M, yes)

$W_4=X_1 \cap Y_2$: being small and being far from Sun (S, small) and (D, far)

In what follows we explain how to obtain new properties by forming the transitive closure of the union of indiscernibility relations. We recall that for a binary relation R in a set OB, $R^*=\bigcup\{R^j: j\in\omega\}$, where R^0=identity on OB, $R^{j+1}=R;R^j$, and ; denotes the composition of relations. Throughout the paper we write $R \cup^* S$ instead of $(R\cup S)^*$.

Since the relation $ind(A)\cup^* ind(B)$ cannot be obtained from ind(A) and ind(B) by means of the standard set–theoretical operations, the properties corresponding to its equivalence classes are not expressible as propositional combinations of properties represented by ind(A) and ind(B). Moreover, in general, $ind(A)\cup^* ind(B)$ is not of the form ind(C) for some $C\subseteq AT$.

Example 2.2. Assume, that we are given seven objects consisting of circles and crosses. We have $OB=\{o_1,o_2,o_3,o_4,o_5,o_6,o_7\}$, and AT={number of circles (o), number of crosses (+)}. The information function is given in the following table:

	o	+
o_1	1	1
o_2	1	2
o_3	2	1
o_4	2	2
o_5	3	3
o_6	3	4
o_7	3	4

Equivalence classes of indiscernibility relations ind(o) and ind(+) are as follows:

ind(o): $\{o_1,o_2\}$ $\{o_3,o_4\}$ $\{o_5,o_6,o_7\}$

ind(+): $\{o_1,o_3\}$ $\{o_2,o_4\}$ $\{o_5\}$ $\{o_6,o_7\}$.

The transitive closure of the union of these relations provides the following equivalence classes:

$ind(o)\cup^* ind(+)$: $X_1=\{o_1,o_2,o_3,o_4\}$ $X_2=\{o_5,o_6,o_7\}$.

Observe that the names of properties corresponding to these equivalence classes cannot be obtained as a propositional combination of names of properties represented by the equivalence classes of ind(o) and ind(+), since there is no Boolean relationship between $ind(A)\cup^* ind(B)$ and its components. However, we observe that X_1 corresponds to a new property that might be expressed as 'number of circles and number of crosses less than 3'.

We conclude that performing operations on indiscernibility relations we form new properties from the primitive properties given in the universe under consideration. Formally, we can extend a given system U by assuming that the new relation becomes an attribute, say R, its equivalence classes become the values of this attribute, and information function f is extended to f(x,R)=R(x) for every object x from U.

3 Relative Definability of Sets of Objects

Let a universe U=(OB, AT, $\{VAL_a: a \in AT\}$, f) be given. Indiscernibility relations induced by attributes influence definability of sets of objects in terms of properties determined by these relations. Given a set $A \subseteq AT$, in general sets of objects cannot be defined uniquely in terms of the properties determined by ind(A). For any subset X of the set OB we define its approximations with respect to an indiscernibility relation R as follows.

Definition 3.1. A lower R-approximation L(R)X of X is the union of those equivalence classes of R which are included in X.
An upper R-approximation U(R)X of X is the union of those equivalence classes of R which have an element in common with X.

Definition 3.2. A set X is R–definable iff L(R)X=X=U(R)X or X=∅.
A set X is strongly R–definable iff X is an equivalence class of R.

In what follows, if in the name of an indiscernibility relation a respective set of attributes is indicated explicitly e.g. ind(A), then in the corresponding approximation operations we shall write L(A) and U(A), instead of L(ind(A)) and U(ind(A)).

Proposition 3.1. The following conditions are equivalent:
(a) A set X is R-definable
(b) $X=\bigcup\{R(x): x \in X\}$

In view of the above fact, every R-definable set X can be covered with some of the equivalence classes of relation R. As a consequence, the property that defines set X is formed as a disjunction of properties corresponding to the equivalence classes R(x) of R for objects x from X. We say that two properties are equivalent in a system U whenever the sets of objects that they define are equal. If ind(A)(x)=ind(B)(x) and $A \subseteq B$, then in view of Proposition 2.1(b) the property corresponding to ind(A)(x) is possibly simpler, than that corresponding to ind(B)(x), because it might consist of less conjuncts. Hence, in that situation we can simplify any property that defines an ind(B)-definable set by replacing a disjunct corresponding to ind(B)(x) by property corresponding to ind(A)(x). The following example illustrates this idea.

Example 3.1. Consider the universe from Example 2.1 and the set X={Me,V,J,Sa,P}. Its approximations with respect to ind(S) are as follows.

L(S)X={J,Sa}=X–{Me,V,P}
U(S)X=X∪{E,Ma}.

Hence, the set X is not definable by means of the attribute S. It is easy to see that X is not definable by any proper subset of {S,D,M}. It is definable by means of all the attributes in our system, namely X={Me,V}∪{J,Sa}∪{P}. However, {Me,V} is a class of ind(M) and {J,Sa} and {P} are classes of ind(S,D). Hence, to form a definition of X we can use the respective properties formulated in terms of attribute M alone for the part {Me,V} of X and in terms of attributes S, D for the part {J,Sa,P} of X. In other words property '(M, no) and (D, near) and (S, small)' is equivalent in our system to (M,no), and similarly property '((S, large) and (D, far) and (M, yes)) or ((S, small) and (D, far) and (M, yes))' is equivalent to '((S, large) and (D, far)) or ((S, small) and (D, far))'. As a consequence a definition of X is:

x∈X iff x possesses the following property: '(M, no) or ((S, large) and (D, far)) or ((S, small) and (D, far))'.

Example 3.2. Consider the universe from Example 2.2 and set $X=\{o_1,o_2,o_3,o_4\}$. It is ind(o)–definable. To obtain strong definability we have to construct a compound property. It is easy to see that X is strongly definable with respect to $ind(o)\cup^{*}ind(+)$.

Let us observe that approximations satisfy the following conditions.

Proposition 3.2. If R⊆S then for any X⊆OB the following conditions hold:
(a) L(S)X⊆L(R)X, U(R)X⊆U(S)X
(b) If X is S–definable then it is R–definable.

In terms of approximations we define sets of positive, negative, and borderline instances of sets of objects (Orlowska 1983).

Definition 3.3. Let R be an indiscernibility relation in a set OB, and let X⊆OB.
A set of R-positive instances of X is POS(R)X=L(R)X.
A set of R-negative instances of X is NEG(R)X=OB–U(R)X.
A set of R-borderline instances of X is BOR(R)X=U(R)X–L(R)X.

The elements of POS(R)X definitely, relative to the properties corresponding to R, belong to X. The elements of NEG(R)X definitely, up to R, do not belong to X. BOR(R)X is a doubtful region, its elements possibly belong to X, but we cannot decide it for certain considering only the properties corresponding to R. In other words, as far as indiscernibility R is concerned, nothing can be said about membership to X of the elements from BOR(R)X.

The following lemmas state basic properties of operators POS(R), NEG(R), and BOR(R).

Proposition 3.3. (a) POS(R)X, NEG(R)X, BOR(R)X are pairwise disjoint
(b) POS(R)X∪NEG(R)X∪BOR(R)X=OB
(c) POS(R)X, NEG(R)X, BOR(R)X are R–definable.

Proposition 3.4. (a) If $A \subseteq B$ then $POS(ind(A))X \subseteq POS(ind(B))X$, $NEG(ind(A))X \subseteq NEG(ind(B))X$, $BOR(ind(B))X \subseteq BOR(ind(A))X$
(b) If $R \subseteq S$ then $POS(S)X \subseteq POS(R)X$, $NEG(S)X \subseteq NEG(R)X$, $BOR(R)X \subseteq BOR(S)X$.

Proposition 3.5. (a) $POS(R)X \subseteq X$, $NEG(R)X \subseteq -X$
(b) $POS(R)\varnothing=\varnothing$, $NEG(R)OB=\varnothing$
(c) $POS(ind(\varnothing))X=\varnothing$ for $X \neq OB$, $POS(ind(\varnothing))OB=OB$
(d) $NEG(ind(\varnothing))X=\varnothing$ for $X \neq \varnothing$, $NEG(ind(\varnothing))\varnothing=OB$
(e) If $X \subseteq Y$ then $POS(R)X \subseteq POS(R)Y$ and $NEG(R)Y \subseteq NEG(R)X$.

Proposition 3.6. (a) $POS(R)X \cup POS(R)Y \subseteq POS(R)(X \cup Y)$
(b) $POS(R)(X \cap Y)=POS(R)X \cap POS(R)Y$
(c) $POS(R)(-X)=NEG(R)X$.

Proposition 3.7. (a) $NEG(R)(X \cup Y)=NEG(R)X \cap NEG(R)Y$
(b) $NEG(R)X \cup NEG(R)Y \subseteq NEG(R)(X \cap Y)$
(c) $NEG(R)(-X)=POS(R)X$.

Proposition 3.8. (a) $BOR(R)(X \cup Y) \subseteq BOR(R)X \cup BOR(R)Y$
(b) If $X \cap Y=\varnothing$ then $BOR(X \cup Y)=BOR(R)X \cup BOR(R)Y$
(c) $BOR(R)(X \cap Y) \subseteq BOR(R)X \cap BOR(R)Y$
(d) $BOR(R)(-X)=BOR(R)X$.

Proposition 3.9. (a) $POS(ind(A))X \cup POS(ind(B))X \subseteq POS(ind(A \cup B))X$
(b) $POS(ind(A \cap B))X \subseteq POS(ind(A))X \cap POS(ind(B))X$
(c) $NEG(ind(A))X \cup NEG(ind(B))X \subseteq NEG(ind(A \cup B))X$
(d) $NEG(ind(A \cap B))X \subseteq NEG(ind(A))X \cap NEG(ind(B))X$.

Proposition 3.10. The following conditions are equivalent:
(a) A set X is R–definable
(b) $BOR(R)X=\varnothing$
(c) $POS(R)X=-NEG(R)X$.

We conclude that subsets of a set OB, corresponding to the extensions of concepts, might not be uniquely definable in terms of properties belonging to the intensions of these concepts. The unique correspondence between the extension and the intension of a concept is reflected by definability of the extension with respect to the indiscernibility relation that corresponds to the properties from its intension. If the extension is definable, then all the objects can be classified into positive or negative instances of the respective concept. If the extension is not definable with respect to the underlying indiscernibility relation, then the corresponding set of borderline instances is non-empty, and consequently some of the objects can be classified neither as the positive instances nor as the negative instances of the respective concept. In the following two sections we shall discuss the problem of acquisition of concepts. We split the problem into two tasks: the task of learning intensions, and the task of learning extensions. The fact that extensions are defined up to indiscernibility determined by intensions plays the crucial role in these investigations.

4 Learning Intensions of Concepts

Let a universe $U=(OB,AT,\{VAL_a: a \in AT\},f)$ be given. Let us assume that a set $X \subseteq OB$ is the extension of a certain concept. The task of learning the intension of this concept can be formulated as follows:

Given: A set $X \subseteq OB$ representing the extension of a concept,

Find: A minimal set A of attributes such that X is ind(A)–definable, or if X is not ind(AT)–definable find a minimal set $A \subseteq AT$ such that for every $B \subseteq AT$ $L(B)X \subseteq L(A)X$ and $U(A)X \subseteq U(B)X$.

Thus the intension of the concept whose extension is X consists of those properties which are determined by a relation ind(A) such that A provides either definability of X or, if it is not possible to obtain its definability in the given universe, A provides the approximations of X which are as close as possible (with respect to inclusion) to X.

Example 4.1. We give an example which is a slight modification of an example from Hunt et al. (1966). The set OB consists of seven animals $x_1,x_2,x_3,x_4,x_5,x_6,x_7$ which are characterized by means of attributes 'size'(S), 'animality'(A), and 'colour'(C). Values of attribute 'size' are VAL_S={small, medium, large}, values of attribute 'animality' are VAL_A={bear, dog, cat, horse}, and values of attribute 'colour' are VAL_C={black, brown}. The following table shows what are the values of attributes for the given objects.

	S	A	C
x_1	small	bear	black
x_2	medium	bear	black
x_3	large	dog	brown
x_4	small	cat	black
x_5	medium	horse	black
x_6	large	horse	black
x_7	large	horse	brown

Assume that we are given the extension $X=\{x_1,x_2,x_3,x_6,x_7\}$ of concept 'dangerous animal', and we are looking for its intension. Consider the indiscernibility relation ind(S,A). Its equivalence classes are as follows:

ind(S,A): $\{x_1\}$ $\{x_2\}$ $\{x_3\}$ $\{x_4\}$ $\{x_5\}$ $\{x_6,x_7\}$.

It is easy to see that X is ind(S,A)–definable and it is not definable by means of any single attribute. Observe that property '((animality, bear) and (size, small)) or ((animality, bear) and (size, medium))' is equivalent in our universe to property '(animality, bear)'. Similarly, property '((animality, dog) and (size, large)) or ((animality, horse) and (size, large))' is equivalent to '(size, large)'. We conclude that the intension of the given concept consists of the property '(animality, bear) or (size, large)'.

Example 4.2. Let $OB=\{o_1,o_2,o_3,o_4,o_5,o_6,o_7\}$ and $AT=\{a,b\}$. Assume that the attributes provide the following equivalence classes:

ind(a): $\{o_1,o_2,o_3\}$ $\{o_4,o_5\}$ $\{o_6,o_7\}$

ind(b): $\{o_1,o_4,o_5\}$ $\{o_2,o_3\}$ $\{o_6,o_7\}$

ind(a,b): $\{o_1\}$ $\{o_2,o_3\}$ $\{o_4,o_5\}$ $\{o_6,o_7\}$

Let $X=\{o_5,o_6,o_7\}$ be the extension of a certain concept. The approximations of set X are as follows:

$L(a)X=\{o_6,o_7\}$ $\quad$ $U(a)X=\{o_4,o_5,o_6,o_7\}$

$L(b)X=\{o_6,o_7\}$ $\quad$ $U(b)X=\{o_1,o_4,o_5,o_6,o_7\}$

$L(a,b)X=\{o_6,o_7\}$ $\quad$ $U(a,b)X=\{o_4,o_5,o_6,o_7\}$.

The set X is not ind(a,b)–definable. The set $\{a\}$ is a minimal set of attributes providing the best approximations of X.

A set of attributes obtained as a result of learning the intension determines the properties which enable us to discern, as precisely as possible, the objects which are the positive instances of the given concept from the objects which are its negative instances. If the extension is definable with respect to the indiscernibility relation that determines the properties from its intension, then the distinguishability is perfect, and if definability cannot be obtained, then distinguishability is the optimal possible in the given universe. Hence, the obtained properties are really the characteristic properties of instances of the concept. Moreover, the number of those properties is as small as possible.

5 Learning Extensions of Concepts

Let a universe $U=(OB,AT,\{VAL_a: a\in AT\},f)$ be given. Assume that we are given the intension of a concept, that is a set of properties expressed as propositional combinations of some pairs (a,v) for $a \in AT$ and $v \in VAL_a$. In order to define the extension of the concept we have to find all the objects that possess all the properties from the intension.

Given: A set P of properties,

Find: A maximal set X such that $x\in X$ iff x possesses all the properties from P.

Example 5.1. Let the set of objects consist of eight patients of a certain hospital, $OB=\{x_1,x_2,x_3,x_4,x_5,x_6,x_7,x_8\}$, and let $AT=\{s_1,s_2\}$ be a set of parameters whose values can confirm the occurrence of a certain illness. For example, we can have the parameters 'blood pressure' and 'occurrence of myeloblasts'. Let VAL_{s1}={normal, low, high} and $VAL_{s2}=\{+,-\}$. Assume that the respective indiscernibility relations provide the following equivalence classes and properties:

$ind(s_1)$:	$\{x_1,x_2,x_3\}$	$(s_1$, normal)
	$\{x_4,x_5\}$	$(s_1$, low)
	$\{x_6,x_7,x_8\}$	$(s_1$, high)
$ind(s_2)$:	$\{x_1,x_2,x_3,x_8\}$	$(s_2, -)$
	$\{x_4,x_5,x_6,x_7\}$	$(s_2, +)$.

Assume that the intension of concept 'leukemia' consists of the two following properties:

$p_1=(s_1$, low) or $(s_1$, high)

$p_2=(s_2, +)$.

It is easy to see that every object from the set $X=\{x_4,x_5,x_6,x_7\}$ possesses these properties, and X is the greatest such a set.

In some applications it is useful to have a set of representative instances of a concept, instead of the extension itself. These representative instances should be typical instances of this concept such that membership of any other object to its extension can be established by comparing this object with those typical instances. To be more formal, the task of learning representative instances can be formulated as follows.

Given: A set P of properties expressed in terms of attributes from a set $A \subseteq AT$,

Find: A minimal set $X \subseteq OB$ such that for all $x \in OB$ $x \in U(A)X$ iff x possesses all the properties from set P.

Example 5.2. Consider the universe defined in Example 5.1 and the intension $\{p_1,p_2\}$ of concept 'leukemia' given there.

To get the representative instances of the extension $X=\{x_4,x_5,x_6,x_7\}$ of this concept we should pick up exactly one element from equivalence classes $\{x_4,x_5\}$ and $\{x_6,x_7\}$ of relation $ind(s_1,s_2)$. It is easy to see that the sets $Y_1=\{x_4,x_6\}$, $Y_2=\{x_4,x_7\}$, $Y_3=\{x_5,x_6\}$, and $Y_4=\{x_5,x_7\}$ satisfy the condition $U(s_1,s_2)Y_i=X$, $i=1,2,3,4$.

The set of objects obtained as a result of learning representative elements of the extension provides the pattern of any other instance of the concept. Moreover, the set of these typical examples is exactly as big as it is necessary to represent properly all the other instances.

Now we consider the task of learning extension in the situation when we do not have an exact information about the intension of a concept and we are only given a range of properties that the instances of the concept are supposed to satisfy. Given a universe $U=(OB,AT,\{VAL_a\colon a \in AT\},f)$, the task of learning an approximate extension of a concept can be formulated as follows.

Given: two sets P_1 and P_2 of properties expressed in terms of attributes from a set $A \subseteq AT$ and such that for any object x from OB, if x possesses every property from P_1, then x possesses every property from P_2,

Find: a set of objects such that its lower ind(A)-approximation is defined by the properties from P_1 and its upper ind(A)-approximation is defined by the properties from P_2.

Example 5.3. Consider the universe defined in Example 5.1 and sets P_1={(s_1, high), (s_2, -)} and P_2={(s_1, high) or (s_1, normal), (s_2, -)}. Let X={x_8}, Y={x_1,x_2,x_3,x_8}. Object x_8 possesses every property from P_1 and each object from Y possesses every property from P_2. Moreover, these are the only sets whose elements possess the respective properties. Each of the sets of the form X∪Z, where Z is a subset of {x_1,x_2,x_3} satisfies the required conditions, that is L(ind(s_1,s_2))(X∪Z)=X and U(ind(s_1,s_2))(X∪Z)=Y. Hence, the sets of the form X∪Z are approximate extensions of a concept whose approximate intension is determined by sets P_1 and P_2 of properties.

The tasks of learning extensions and learning intensions are defined for a fixed universe. In case of a dynamic change in the object population the analysis should be remade. A discussion of dynamic learning can be found in Pawlak (1986).

In the following sections we introduce and study logical formalisms that enable us to represent extensions and intensions of concepts and to reason about their compatibility. In the language of these formalisms we admit operators that enable us to perform Boolean transformations of sets of objects as well as to represent their approximations determined by indiscernibility relations. We explicitly allow for applying operations of intersection and transitive closure of union to indiscernibility relations, thus providing for property-forming mechanism directly in the language. The language has been introduced in Fariñas del Cerro and Orlowska (1985). It evolved from earlier investigations of logical systems for reasoning about indiscernibility-type incompleteness (Orlowska 1983, 1984, Konikowska 1987). In the present paper we investigate several classes of models for the language and we give complete axiom systems for sets of formulas that are true in all the models from these classes, respectively. We also recall the class of models introduced in Gargov (1986).

6 Logic DAL

The language of the logic DAL is determined by four sets which are assumed to be pairwise disjoint:

(i) a set VARPROP of propositional variables,

(ii) a set CONAC of relational constants, representing accessibility relations,

(iii) a set OPAC of relational operators,

(iv) a set OPPROP of propositional operators.

The set EAC of accessibility relation expressions is the smallest set that satisfies the following conditions:

(i) CONAC $\subseteq$ EAC

(ii) if ϕ is any n-ary relational operator and $a_1, \ldots, a_n \in$ EAC then $\phi(a_1, \ldots, a_n) \in$ EAC

Elements of EAC are interpreted as indiscernibility relations and are denoted by a,b,c with indices if necessary. We assume throughout the chapter that the fixed language of DAL satisfies the following conditions:

(i) the set VARPROP is an infinite denumerable set,

(ii) the set of relational constants is finite or infinite denumerable,

(iii) the propositional operators are the unary $\neg$ (negation), [a], <a> for a $\in$ EAC (modal operators) and the binary $\Leftrightarrow$ (equivalence), $\Rightarrow$ (implication), $\wedge$ (conjuction), $\vee$ (disjunction),

(iv) the only relational operators are the binary operators $\cap$ of intersection and $\cup^*$ of the transitive closure of the union of relations.

The set FOR of formulae is the smallest set that satisfies the following conditions:

(i) VARPROP $\cup$ {true,false} $\subseteq$ FOR,

(ii) if ϕ is a n-ary propositional operator and $A_1, \ldots, A_n \in$ FOR then $\phi(A_1, \ldots, A_n) \in$ FOR,

(iii) if a $\in$ EAC and A $\in$ FOR then [a]A $\in$ FOR and <a>A $\in$ FOR.

We denote by FOR_c the set of formulae in FOR that do not contain relational operators, that is modal operators can only be indexed by relational constants. We write $[a]^kA$ ($k \geq 0$) to denote the formula A prefixed by the sequence composed of k modal operators [a].

Definition 6.1. By a frame we understand a pair (OB, $\{r_a$: a $\in$ EAC}) such that OB is a non-empty set of objects and for a $\in$ EAC, r_a is a binary relation on the set OB. A frame of DAL is a frame such that the following conditions are satisfied:

(i) for every a $\in$ CONAC, r_a is an equivalence relation,

(ii) $r_{a1 \cap a2} = r_{a1} \cap r_{a2}$ $(a_1, a_2 \in \text{EAC})$

(iii) $r_{a1 \cup^* a2} = r_{a1} \cup^* r_{a2}$

Definition 6.2. By a model we understand a triple (OB, $\{r_a$: a $\in$ EAC}, m) such that (OB, $\{r_a$: a $\in$ EAC}) is a frame and m is a meaning function, that is we have,

(i) m(p) $\subseteq$ OB for p $\in$ VARPROP

(ii) m(a) = r_a for a $\in$ EAC

We say that the model (OB, $\{r_a$: a $\in$ EAC}, m) is based on the frame (OB, $\{r_a$: a $\in$ EAC}). A model of DAL is a model (OB, $\{r_a$: a $\in$ EAC}, m) based on a frame of DAL.

Since both intersections and transitive closures of union of equivalence relations are equivalence relations as well, we conclude that for each model of DAL, m(a) is an equivalence relation for any a $\in$ EAC. Given a model M, let E(M)={m(a):

$a \in EAC\}$ be a family of relations assigned in the model to the accessibility relation expressions.

Proposition 6.1. For every model $M = (OB, \{r_a: a \in EAC\}, m)$ of DAL, the algebra $(E(M), \cap, \cup^*)$ is a lattice of equivalence relations, generated by $\{r_a: a \in CONAC\}$.

Let $M = (OB, \{r_a: a \in EAC\}, m)$ be a model (not necessarily a model of DAL). The concept of satisfiability of a formula by an object in M is recursively defined as follows. Let $x \in OB$,

(i) M, x sat p iff $x \in m(p)$ for $p \in VARPROP$,

(ii) M, x sat $\neg$ A iff not M, x sat A,

(iii) M, x sat $A \Rightarrow B$ iff M, x sat A only if M, x sat B,

(iv) M, x sat $A \wedge B$ iff M, x sat A and M, x sat B,

(v) M, x sat $A \vee B$ iff either M, x sat A or M, x sat B,

(vi) M, x sat [a] A iff, for all $y \in OB$, if $(x,y) \in r_a$ then M, y sat A.

A formula A is true in a model M (written $M \models A$) iff for all $x \in OB$, M, x sat A. A formula A is true in a frame F (written $F \models A$) iff A is true in every model based on F. A formula is satisfiable in M (M sat A) iff there is $x \in OB$ such that M, x sat A. Formulae A, B are equivalent (equivalent in DAL), denoted by $A \equiv B$ ($A \equiv B$ in DAL, respectively) iff $A \Leftrightarrow B$ is valid (valid in DAL). A is valid (valid in DAL) iff A is true in all the frames (in all the frames of DAL). A complete axiomatization of the logic DAL is presented in (Archangelsky and Taitslin 1989) – see also chapter 17. In what follows we will also consider some other classes of frames and models, and then the notions of validity and equivalence will be modified accordingly, as referring to a logic determined by a given class of frames.

Elements of universes of models are referred to as objects rather than states, because applications of logic DAL are concerned with concepts and their instances. We recall that the extension of formulae in a model M is defined as follows: $ext_M A=\{x \in OB: M, x \text{ sat } A\}$.

Proposition 6.2. Let $M = (OB, \{r_a: a \in EAC\}, m)$ be a model of DAL, $a \in EAC$ and $A \in FOR$.

(a) $ext_M[a]A=L(m(a))ext_M A$.

(b) $ext_M\langle a\rangle A=U(m(a))ext_M A$.

A proof can easily be obtained from the respective definitions. Proposition 6.2 says that modal operations of necessity and possibility correspond to operations of lower and upper approximation, respectively.

Below some facts about concepts that are expressible in the given language are listed.

Proposition 6.3. Let $M = (OB, \{r_a: a \in EAC\}, m)$ be a model of DAL, $a \in EAC$ and $A \in FOR$.

(a) $M \models A \Rightarrow [a]A$ iff $ext_M A$ is m(a)–definable

(b) $M \models [a]A$ iff $POS(m(a))ext_M A = OB$ iff $ext_M A = OB$ iff $M \models A$

(c) $M \models \neg[a]A$ iff $POS(m(a))ext_M A = \emptyset$

(d) $M \models \neg\langle a\rangle A$ iff $NEG(m(a))ext_M A = OB$

(e) $M \models \langle a\rangle A$ iff $NEG(m(a))ext_M A = \emptyset$

(f) $M \models \langle a\rangle A \wedge \langle a\rangle \neg A$ iff $BOR(m(a))ext_M A = OB$

(g) $M \models [a]A \vee [a]\neg A$ iff $BOR(m(a))ext_M A = \emptyset$.

Proposition 6.4.

(a) M sat $[a]A$ iff $POS(m(a))ext_M A \neq \emptyset$

(b) M sat $\neg\langle a\rangle A$ iff $NEG(m(a))ext_M A \neq \emptyset$

(c) M sat $\langle a\rangle A \wedge \langle a\rangle \neg A$ iff $BOR(m(a))ext_M A \neq \emptyset$

(d) M sat $\neg[a]A$ iff $POS(m(a))ext_M A \neq OB$

(e) M sat $\langle a\rangle A$ iff $NEG(m(a))ext_M A \neq OB$

(f) M sat $[a]A \vee [a]\neg A$ iff $BOR(m(a))ext_M A \neq OB$.

Since indiscernibility relations, their intersections and transitive closures of their unions are equivalence relations, the operations [a] and $\langle a\rangle$ are S5 modalities (Chellas 1980). Hence, all the formulae which are substitutions of theorems of logic S5 are valid in the given logic.

7 Bounded Chain Conditions

The accessibility relations in a frame of DAL may satisfy additional conditions that reflect relationships between objects.

Definition 7.1. Let R be a binary relation on a set OB. A R-chain of length N is defined as a sequence of objects $(x_1, \ldots, x_N)$ such that for all $1 \leq i \leq (N-1)$, $(x_i, x_{i+1}) \in R$.

Let $(o_1,\ldots,o_N)$ be a $(R \cup S)$-chain of objects where R and S are indiscernibility relations. The condition C_i presented in Definition 7.2 states the existence of a $(R \cup S)$-chain $(o'_1,\ldots,o'_j)$ such that $o'_1=o_1$ and $o'_j = o_N$ with $1 \leq j \leq i$. In that sense any two objects indistinguishable with respect to the indiscernibility relation $(R \cup^* S)$ are also indistinguishable with respect to the indiscernibility relation $\bigcup\{(R \cup S)^j, 0 \leq j \leq i-$

1} which provides a condition of proximity between indistinguishable objects with respect to $(R \cup^* S)$.

Definition 7.2. Let R and S be two binary relations on a set OB. For all $i \in \omega \backslash \{0,1\}$ we say that R and S satisfy the condition C_i iff for every $(R \cup S)$-chain $(x_1,...,x_N)$ of length $N>i$ there exists a $(R \cup S)$-chain $(y_1,...,y_j)$ of length $1 \leq j \leq i$ such that $y_1=x_1$ and $y_j = x_N$.

Proposition 7.1. Let R and S be two binary relations. R and S satisfy C_i for some $i \in \omega \backslash \{0,1\}$ iff $(R \cup^* S) = \bigcup\{(R \cup S)^j, 0 \leq j \leq i-1\}$.

Proof: By way of example only the implication '→' is proved. Assume $(x, y) \in (R \cup S)^k$ with $k \geq i$. It follows from Definition 7.2 that there exists a $(R \cup S)$-chain of length $1 \leq j \leq i$ $(y_1,...,y_j)$ such that $y_1 = x$ and $y_j = y$. So $(x,y) \in (R \cup S)^{j-1}$. We conclude that for $k \geq i$ $(R \cup S)^k \subseteq \bigcup\{(R \cup S)^j ,0 \leq j \leq i-1\}$. Since $(R \cup^* S) = \bigcup\{(R \cup S)^j : j \in \omega\}$ we naturally get that $(R \cup^* S) = \bigcup\{(R \cup S)^j : 0 \leq j \leq i-1\}$.

Q.E.D.

Proposition 7.2. Let R and S be two binary relations on a set OB. For all $i \in \omega \backslash \{0,1\}$, if R and S satisfy C_i then R and S satisfy C_{i+1}.

The proof of Proposition 7.2 is by an easy verification. Proposition 7.3 below states a necessary and sufficient condition for checking whether the binary relations R and S satisfy C_i: only the chains of length at most i+1 have to be considered.

Proposition 7.3. Let R and S be two binary relations on a set OB. For all $i \in \omega \backslash \{0,1\}$, R and S satisfy C_i iff for every $(R \cup S)$-chain $(x_1,..., x_{i+1})$ of length i+1 there exists a $(R \cup S)$-chain $(y_1,\dots,y_j)$ of length $1 \leq j \leq i$ such that $y_1 = x_1$ and $y_j = x_{i+1}$.

Proof: The proof of '→' is immediate. Now assume the second condition holds and $(x_1,\dots, x_N)$ is a $(R \cup S)$-chain of length $N > i$. The proof is by induction on N. For $N = i+1$ it is immediate by the assumption.

Induction hypothesis: for every $(R \cup S)$-chain $(x_1, \dots,x_K)$ of length at most $K \geq i+1$ there exists a $(R \cup S)$-chain $(y_1,\dots,y_j)$ of length $1 \leq j \leq i$ such that $y_1 = x_1$ and $y_j = x_K$.

Let $(x_1, \dots,x_{K+1})$ be a $(R \cup S)$-chain. By the induction hypothesis there exists a $(R \cup S)$-chain $(y_1,\dots,y_j)$ of length $1 \leq j \leq i$ such that $y_1=x_1$ and $y_j = x_K$. So $(x_1, y_2,..., y_j,$

x_{K+1}) is a ($R \cup S$)-chain of length at most i+1. By the assumption, there exists a ($R \cup S$)-chain $(y'_1,\ldots,y'_j)$ of length $1 \le j \le i$ such that $y'_1 = x_1$ and $y'_j = x_{K+1}$.
Q.E.D.

For any relations R and S, when R and S satisfy C_i for some $i \geq 2$, $R \cup^* S$ has a particular form as stated in Proposition 7.1. This leads to a characterization of the lower and the upper ($R \cup^* S$)-approximations (see Corollary 7.6). Some preliminary definitions and propositions are needed.

Definition 7.3. Let R be a binary relation on the set OB and $X \subseteq OB$. We denote by LL(R)(X) the set $LL(R)(X) = \bigcup\{R(x); x \in X\} \setminus \bigcup\{R(x); x \notin X\}$.

In case R is an equivalence relation it can be easily shown that LL(R)(X) = L(R)X (lower R-approximation of X). Proposition 7.4 below relates $LL(\bigcup\{R_i: 1 \le i \le N\})(X)$ (for a given set X) with the sets $LL(R_i)(X)$ for $1 \le i \le N$.

Proposition 7.4. Let R be a binary relation on a set OB and $X \subseteq OB$. Let $\{R_i: 1 \le i \le N\}$ be a family of binary relations on OB. Then $LL(\bigcup\{R_i: 1 \le i \le N\})(X) = \bigcup\{LL(R_i)(X) \setminus \bigcup\{R_j(x): j \neq i,\ 1 \le j \le N, x \notin X\}: 1 \le i \le N\}$.

Proof: By induction on N.
Base case: N = 2

$LL(R_1 \cup R_2)(X) = \bigcup\{(R_1 \cup R_2)(x): x \in X\} \setminus \bigcup\{(R_1 \cup R_2)(x): x \notin X\}$. It follows that $LL(R_1 \cup R_2)(x) = (\bigcup\{R_1(x): x \in X\} \cup \bigcup\{R_2(x): x \in X\}) \setminus (\bigcup\{R_1(x): x \notin X\} \cup \bigcup\{R_2(x): x \notin X\})$. Knowing that for any sets S_1, S_2, S_3, we have $(S_1 \cup S_2) \setminus S_3 = (S_1 \setminus S_3) \cup (S_2 \setminus S_3)$ and $S_1 \setminus (S_3 \cup S_2) = (S_1 \setminus S_3) \setminus S_2 = (S_1 \setminus S_2) \setminus S_3$, we get $LL(R_1 \cup R_2)(x) = ((\bigcup\{R_1(x): x \in X\} \setminus \bigcup\{R_1(x): x \notin X\}) \setminus \bigcup\{R_2(x): x \notin X\}) \cup ((\bigcup\{R_2(x): x \in X\} \setminus \bigcup\{R_2(x): x \notin X\}) \setminus \bigcup\{R_1(x): x \notin X\})$. Hence $LL(R_1 \cup R_2)(X) = (LL(R_1)(X) \setminus \bigcup\{R_2(x): x \notin X\}) \cup (LL(R_2)(X) \setminus \bigcup\{R_1(x): x \notin X\})$.

Induction step: We write LL to denote the set $LL(\bigcup\{R_i: 1 \le i \le N+1\})(X)$. By induction hypothesis, $LL = [LL(\bigcup\{R_i: 1 \le i \le N\})(X) \setminus \bigcup\{R_{N+1}(x): x \notin X\}] \cup [LL(R_{N+1})(X) \setminus \bigcup\{R_i(x): 1 \le i \le N, x \notin X\}] = [\bigcup\{LL(R_i)(X) \setminus \bigcup\{R_j(x): j \neq i,\ 1 \le j \le N, x \notin X\}: 1 \le i \le N\} \setminus \bigcup\{R_{N+1}(x): x \notin X\}] \cup [LL(R_{N+1})(X) \setminus \bigcup\{R_i(x): 1 \le i \le N, x \notin X\}]$. Since $(S_1 \setminus S_3) \setminus S_2 = (S_1 \setminus S_2) \setminus S_3 = S_1 \setminus (S_2 \cup S_3)$, $LL = [\bigcup\{LL(R_i)(X) \setminus \bigcup\{R_j(x): j \neq i,\ 1 \le j \le N+1, x \notin X\}, 1 \le i \le N\}] \cup [LL(R_{N+1})(X) \setminus \bigcup\{R_i(x): 1 \le i \le N, x \notin X\}]$.

So $LL = \bigcup\{LL(R_i)(X) \setminus \bigcup\{R_j(x): j \neq i,\ 1 \leq j \leq N+1, x \notin X\}: 1 \leq i \leq N+1\}$.
Q.E.D.

Corollary 7.5. Let R and S be two binary relations on a set OB satisfying the condition C_i for some $i > 1$. Then $LL(R \cup^* S)(X) = \bigcup\{LL((R \cup S)^j)(X) \setminus \bigcup\{(R \cup S)^k(x): k \neq j,\ 0 \leq k \leq i\text{-}1, x \notin X\}: 0 \leq j \leq i\text{-}1\}$.

Proof: From Proposition 7.1, $R \cup^* S = \bigcup\{(R \cup S)^j: 0 \leq j \leq i\text{-}1\}$ and from Proposition 7.4, $LL(R \cup^* S)(X) = \bigcup\{LL((R \cup S)^j)(X) \setminus \bigcup\{(R \cup S)^k(x): k \neq j,\ 0 \leq k \leq i\text{-}1, x \notin X\}, 0 \leq j \leq i\text{-}1\}$.
Q.E.D.

Corollary 7.6. Let R and S be two binary relations on a set OB satisfying the condition C_i for some $i > 1$. We have $L(R \cup^* S)X = \bigcup\{L((R \cup S)^j)X \setminus \bigcup\{(R \cup S)^k(x): k \neq j,\ 0 \leq k \leq i\text{-}1, x \notin X\}: 0 \leq j \leq i\text{-}1\}$.

Moreover, knowing that $U(R)X = -L(R)\text{-}X$, the set $U(R \cup^* S)X$ can be straightforwardly characterized.

It can be shown that there are some relations {Q, R, S} that pairwise satisfy C_i and such that $(R \cup^* S)$ and Q do not satisfy C_i for some $i > 1$. That is why a restricted set of models is considered in Section 8. Consider the set OB = {1, 2, 3, 4, 5} and equivalence relations R, S, Q on OB defined as follows:

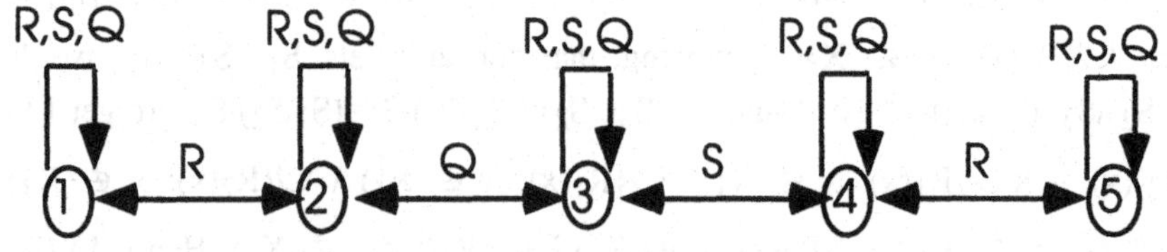

The relations in {Q, R, S} pairwise satisfy C_3. We write T to denote the equivalence relation $(R \cup^* S)$. Although (1,2,3,4) is a $(T \cup Q)$-chain of length 4 there is no $n \in$ OB such that (1,n,4) is a $(T \cup Q)$-chain. So $(R \cup^* S)$ and Q do not satisfy C_3.

The conditions C_i can be generalized in such a way that the chains may involve more than two binary relations, which is done with the conditions $D^{i'}_i$.

Definition 7.4. Let $(R_j)_{j \in J}$ be a family of binary relations on a set OB, $i \in \omega \setminus \{0,1\}$ and $i' \in \omega \setminus \{0,1\}$. We say that $(R_j)_{j \in J}$ satisfies the condition $D^{i'}_i$ iff for all $J' \subseteq J$ such that $card(J') \leq i'$, for every $(\bigcup\{R_j: j \in J'\})$-chain $(x_1,...,x_N)$ of length $N>i$ there exists a $(\bigcup\{R_j: j \in J'\})$-chain $(y_1,...,y_k)$ of length $1 \leq k \leq i$ such that $y_1=x_1$ and $y_k = x_N$.

Proposition 7.7 below states a necessary and sufficient condition for checking whether the family $(R_j)_{j\in J}$ satisfies the condition $D^{i'}{}_i$: only the chains of length at most i+1 are considered.

Proposition 7.7. Let $(R_j)_{j\in J}$ be a family of binary relations on a set OB, $i \in \omega\backslash\{0,1\}$ and $i' \in \omega\backslash\{0,1\}$. $(R_j)_{j\in J}$ satisfies the condition $D^{i'}{}_i$ iff for all $J' \subseteq J$ such that card(J') $\leq i'$, for every $(\bigcup\{R_j: j \in J'\})$-chain $(x_1,...,x_{i+1})$ of length i+1 there exists a $(\bigcup\{R_j: j \in J'\})$-chain $(y_1,...,y_k)$ of length $1 \leq k \leq i$ such that $y_1=x_1$ and $y_k = x_{i+1}$.

The proof of Proposition 7.7 is similar to the proof of Proposition 7.3. Moreover, relationships between the conditions C_i and $D^{i'}{}_i$ are also presented in Proposition 7.8 below.

Proposition 7.8. Let $(R_j)_{j\in J}$ be a family of binary relations on a set OB and $i \in \omega\backslash\{0,1\}$.

(a) $(R_j)_{j\in J}$ satisfies $D^2{}_i$ iff the relations from $(R_j)_{j\in J}$ pairwise satisfy C_i.

(b) If card(J) = 2 then for all $i' \in \omega\backslash\{0,1\}$, $(R_j)_{j\in J}$ satisfies $D^2{}_i$ iff $(R_j)_{j\in J}$ satisfies $D^{i'}{}_i$.

(c) For $i' \in \omega\backslash\{0,1\}$, if $(R_j)_{j\in J}$ satisfies $D^{i'}{}_i$ then $(R_j)_{j\in J}$ satisfies $D^{i'}{}_{i+1}$.

(d) For $i' \in \omega\backslash\{0,1\}$, if $(R_j)_{j\in J}$ satisfies $D^{i'+1}{}_i$ then $(R_j)_{j\in J}$ satisfies $D^{i'}{}_i$.

(e) For $i' \geq i$, $(R_j)_{j\in J}$ satisfies $D^{i'}{}_i$ iff $(R_j)_{j\in J}$ satisfies $D^{i}{}_i$.

Proof: Proof of (a), (b), (c) and (d) follows from the definitions of C_i and $D^{i'}{}_i$. Proof of (e) follows from Proposition 7.7 and the fact that a chain of length i+1 does not involve more than i relations.
Q.E.D.

The condition $D^2{}_2$ appears to be of special importance, since for $i \in \omega\backslash\{0,1\}$ and $i' \in \omega\backslash\{0,1\}$, if $(R_j)_{j\in J}$ satisfies $D^2{}_2$ then $(R_j)_{j\in J}$ satisfies $D^{i'}{}_i$. Moreover, from Proposition 7.8(e) it follows that we can confine ourselves to the conditions $D^{i'}{}_i$ for $i \in \omega\backslash\{0,1\}$ and $2 \leq i' \leq i$. In the sequel we shall show that the condition $D^2{}_2$ for equivalence relations corresponds to the condition of local agreement defined in (Gargov 86).

8 Logics $DALC_i$ and $DALD^{i'}_i$

Two families of logics are defined, namely $(DALC_i)_{i>1}$ and $(DALD^{i'}_i)_{i>1,i'>1}$ sharing the common language FOR_c (restriction of FOR obtained by deleting the relational operators). Each logic in $(DALD^{i'}_i)_{i>1,i'>1}$ (resp. in $(DALC_i)_{i>1}$) is characterized by a class of models such that the relations satisfy $D^{i'}_i$ for some $i>1, i'>1$ (resp. C_i for some $i>1$). Considering the relations between the conditions $D^{i'}_i$'s and the conditions C_i's (see Proposition 7.8) $(DALC_i)_{i>1}$ can be seen as a particular subfamily of $(DALD^{i'}_i)_{i>1,i'>1}$.

Definition 8.1. By a reduced frame we understand a pair $(OB, \{r_a: a \in CONAC\})$ such that OB is a non-empty set of objects and for every $a \in CONAC$, r_a is an equivalence relation in set OB. By a frame of $DALD^{i'}_i$, $i>1$, $i'>1$- (resp. $DALC_i$, $i > 1$) we understand a reduced frame $(OB, \{r_a: a \in CONAC\})$ such that $\{r_a: a \in CONAC\}$ satisfy $D^{i'}_i$ (resp. the relations in $\{r_a: a \in CONAC\}$ pairwise satisfy C_i). By a reduced model we understand a triple $(OB, \{r_a: a \in CONAC\}, m)$ such that $(OB, \{r_a: a \in CONAC\})$ is a reduced frame and m is a meaning function, that is we have:

(i) $m(p) \subseteq OB$ for $p \in VARPROP$

(ii) $m(a) = r_a$ for $a \in CONAC$

A model of $DALD^{i'}_i$, $i>1$, $i'>1$- (resp. $DALC_i$, $i > 1$) is a reduced model based on a frame of $DALD^{i'}_i$ (resp. $DALC_i$).

Let $MOD(D^{i'}_i)$, $i>1$, $i'>1$- (resp. $MOD(C_i)$, $i > 1$) denote the set of models of $DALD^{i'}_i$ (resp. $DALC_i$). As a consequence of Proposition 7.2, we have $MOD(C_i) \subseteq MOD(C_{i+1})$ for $i > 1$. Observe that $MOD(D^2_i) = MOD(C_i)$ and $MOD(D^2_i) \supseteq MOD(D^3_i) \supseteq \ldots \supseteq MOD(D^{i-1}_i) \supseteq MOD(D^i_i) = MOD(D^{i+1}_i)$. Considering Proposition 7.8(e) we can confine ourselves to the logics $DALD^{i'}_i$ such that $i>1$ and $1< i' \leq i$.

Definition 8.2. Let $a_1, a_2 \in CONAC$, $A \in FOR_c$ and $i > 1$. Let $\alpha(i, a_1, a_2, A)$ and $\beta(i, a_1, a_2, A)$ be the following formulae:

$$\alpha(i, a_1, a_2, A): [c_0]\ldots[c_{i-1}]A \wedge [b_0]\ldots[b_{i-1}]A \Leftrightarrow [c_1]\ldots[c_{i-1}]A \wedge [b_1]\ldots[b_{i-1}]A,$$

$$\beta(i, a_1, a_2, A): [c_0]\ldots[c_{i-1}]A \wedge [b_0]\ldots[b_{i-1}]A,$$

with $c_0 = a_1$, for all $1 \leq j \leq i-1$ $\{c_j\} = \{a_1,a_2\} \setminus \{c_{j-1}\}$ and with $b_0 = a_2$, for all $1 \leq j \leq i-1$ $\{b_j\} = \{a_1,a_2\} \setminus \{b_{j-1}\}$.

Moreover $\beta(1, a_1, a_2, A)$ is defined as the formula $[a_1]A \wedge [a_2]A$.

The definition of $\alpha(i, a_1, a_2, A)$ is generalized in Definition 8.3.

Definition 8.3. Let i be in $\omega\backslash\{0\}$ and S be a non-empty finite subset of CONAC. We denote by $T_i(S)$ the subset of S^i such that $(c_1,...,c_i) \in T_i(S)$ iff $(c_1,...,c_i) \in S^i$ and for all $j \in \{1,...,i-1\}$, $c_j \neq c_{j+1}$. Let $A \in FOR_c$, $i \geq 2$. $\alpha'(i, S, A)$ denotes the following formula.

$$\bigwedge\{[b_1]\ldots[b_i]A : (b_1,\ldots,b_i) \in T_i(S)\} \Leftrightarrow \bigwedge\{[c_1]\ldots[c_{i-1}]A : (c_1,\ldots,c_{i-1}) \in T_{i-1}(S)\}$$

Observe the similarities between $\alpha(i, a_1, a_2, A)$ and $\alpha'(i, \{a_1,a_2\}, A)$.

Proposition 8.1. Let $M = (OB, \{r_a: a \in CONAC\}, m)$ be a reduced model and $x \in OB$. Let $a_1,a_2 \in CONAC$, S be a non-empty finite subset of CONAC, $A \in FOR_c$ and $i \geq 1$. The two following conditions are equivalent:

(a) M, x sat $\beta(i, a_1, a_2, A)$

(b) For all $y \in OB$ such that $(x,y) \in \cup\{(r_{a1} \cup r_{a2})^j, 0 \leq j \leq i\}$, M, y sat A.

Moreover the two following conditions are equivalent:

(c) M, x sat $\bigwedge\{[b_1]\ldots[b_i]A : (b_1,\ldots,b_i) \in T_i(S)\}$

(d) For $y \in OB$ such that $(x,y) \in \bigcup\{(\bigcup\{r_a : a \in S\})^k, 0 \leq k \leq i\}$, M, y sat A.

Proof: By way of example the first equivalence shall be proved. The proof is by induction on i. The base case (i = 1) is immediate.

Induction hypothesis: for $1 \leq k \leq i-1$, for $x \in OB$, the two following conditions are equivalent:

(i) M, x sat $\beta(k, a_1, a_2, A)$

(ii) For $y \in OB$ such that $(x,y) \in \bigcup\{(r_{a1} \cup r_{a2})^j, 0 \leq j \leq k\}$, M, y sat A.

($\rightarrow$) Let $(x,y) \in (r_{a1} \cup r_{a2})^i$ and J_0 be the minimal element of the set $\{j : (x,y) \in (r_{a1} \cup r_{a2})^j\} \cap \{0, \ldots, i\}$. If $J_0 \neq i$ then by the induction hypothesis, M, y sat A (since M, x sat $\beta(i, a_1, a_2, A) \Rightarrow \beta(i-1, a_1, a_2, A)$). Now assume $J_0 = i$. There is a $(r_{a1} \cup r_{a2})$-chain $(x_1, \ldots, x_{i+1})$ such that $x_1 = x$ and $x_{i+1} = y$. Assume $(x_1, x_2) \in r_{a1}$ (the case $(x_1, x_2) \in r_{a2}$ is similar). So M, x_2 sat $[c_1]\ldots[c_{i-1}]A$. By the construction for $2 \leq k \leq i$, $(x_k, x_{k+1}) \in r_{c_{k-1}}$. Hence M, y sat A.

($\leftarrow$) Suppose not M, x sat $[c_0]\ldots[c_{i-1}]A$ (the case not M, x sat $[b_0]\ldots[b_{i-1}]A$ is similar). It follows that M, x sat $\langle c_0\rangle \ldots \langle c_{i-1}\rangle \neg A$. There exists $y \in OB$ such that $(x,y) \in r_{c_0}; \ldots ; r_{c_{i-1}}$ and not M, y sat A. However $r_{c_0}; \ldots ; r_{c_{i-1}} \subseteq \bigcup\{(r_{a1} \cup r_{a2})^j, 0 \leq j \leq i\}$ which leads to a contradiction.

Q.E.D.

The reduced frames such that the indiscernibility relations satisfy $D^{i'}_i$ can be characterized by formulae of FOR_c, giving the following correspondence result.

Proposition 8.2. Let $p \in$ VARPROP, S be a non-empty finite subset of CONAC and $i > 1$. $\alpha'(i, S, p)$ is true in a reduced frame (OB, $\{r_a: a \in$ CONAC$\}$) iff for every $(\bigcup\{r_a: a \in S\})$-chain $(x_1,..., x_{i+1})$ of length i+1 there exists a $(\bigcup\{r_a: a \in S\})$-chain $(y_1,...,y_k)$ of length $1 \leq k \leq i$ such that $y_1=x_1$ and $y_k = x_{i+1}$.

Proof: ($\rightarrow$) Suppose there exists a $(\bigcup\{r_a: a \in S\})$-chain $(x_1,\ldots, x_{i+1})$ such that there is no $(\bigcup\{r_a:a \in S\})$-chain $(y_1, \ldots, y_j)$ such that $1 \leq j \leq i$, $y_1 = x_1$ and $y_j = x_{i+1}$. Observe that for $1 \leq k \leq i-1$ if $(x_k, x_{k+1}) \in r_a$ for some $a \in S$ then $(x_{k+1},x_{k+2}) \notin r_a$. This is due to the transitivity of the relations. Assume that $(x_1,x_{i+1}) \in r_{a1}; \ldots ;r_{ai}$ for $1 \leq j \leq (i-1)$, $a_j \neq a_{j+1}$.
Consider the reduced model M_0 = (OB, $\{r_a: a \in$ CONAC$\}$, m_0) such that $m_0(p) = \{u: (x_1, u) \in \bigcup\{(\bigcup\{r_a: a \in S\})^j: 0 \leq j \leq i-1\}\}$. By hypothesis M_0, x_1 sat $\bigwedge\{[b_1]\ldots[b_i]p : (b_1,\ldots,b_i) \in T_i(S)\} \Leftrightarrow \bigwedge\{[c_1]\ldots[c_{i-1}]p : (c_1,\ldots,c_{i-1}) \in T_{i-1}(S)\}$. By construction of m_0, M_0, x_1 sat $\bigwedge\{[c_1]\ldots[c_{i-1}]p : (c_1,\ldots,c_{i-1}) \in T_{i-1}(S)\}$ (see Proposition 8.1) and therefore M_0, x_1 sat $\bigwedge\{[b_1]\ldots[b_i]p : (b_1,\ldots,b_i) \in T_i(S)\}$. By construction of x_{i+1}, we have M_0, x_{i+1} sat p since, in particular, M_0, x_1 sat $[a_1]\ldots[a_i]p$. By hypothesis, $(x_1,x_{i+1}) \notin \bigcup\{(\bigcup\{r_a: a \in S\})^j: 0 \leq j \leq i-1\}$ and therefore not M_0, x_{i+1} sat p which leads to a contradiction.

($\leftarrow$) Assume for every $(\bigcup\{r_a: a \in S\})$-chain $(x_1,..., x_{i+1})$ of length i+1 there exists a $(\bigcup\{r_a: a \in S\})$-chain $(y_1,...,y_k)$ of length $1 \leq k \leq i$ such that $y_1=x_1$ and $y_k = x_{i+1}$. Let M = (OB, $\{r_a: a \in$ CONAC$\}$, m) be a reduced model and $x \in$ OB. By reflexivity we naturally get that M, x sat $\bigwedge\{[b_1]\ldots[b_i]p : (b_1,\ldots,b_i) \in T_i(S)\} \Rightarrow \bigwedge\{[c_1]\ldots[c_{i-1}]p : (c_1,\ldots,c_{i-1}) \in T_{i-1}(S)\}$. Moreover, from the satisfaction of the condition, $\bigcup\{(\bigcup\{r_a:a \in S\})^j: 0 \leq j \leq i\} = \bigcup\{(\bigcup\{r_a:a \in S\})^j: 0 \leq j \leq i-1\}$, it follows that M, x sat $\bigwedge\{[c_1]\ldots[c_{i-1}]p : (c_1,\ldots,c_{i-1}) \in T_{i-1}(S)\} \Rightarrow \bigwedge\{[b_1]\ldots[b_i]p : (b_1,\ldots,b_i) \in T_i(S)\}$.
Q.E.D.

As $\alpha'(i, S, p)$, $\alpha(i, a_1, a_2, p)$ characterizes reduced frames such that the indiscernibility relations satisfy C_i.

Proposition 8.3. Let a_1 and $a_2 \in$ CONAC, $p \in$ VARPROP and $i > 1$. $\alpha(i, a_1, a_2, p)$ is true in a reduced frame (OB, $\{r_a$: $a \in$ CONAC$\}$) iff r_{a1} and r_{a2} satisfy C_i.

Proof: The proof can be obtained by easy modification of the proof of Proposition 8.2.
Q.E.D.

We admit the following axioms for each logic $DALD^{i'}_i$ $(i > 1, i' > 1)$:
A1C_i. All formulae having the form of a tautology of the classical propositional calculus
A2C_i. $[a](A \Rightarrow B) \Rightarrow ([a]A \Rightarrow [a]B)$
A3C_i. $[a]A \Rightarrow A$
A4C_i. $<a>A \Rightarrow [a]<a>A$
A5$D^{i'}_i$. $\alpha'(i, S, A)$ for $S \subseteq$ CONAC and $2 \leq card(S) \leq i'$.
The rules of inference are modus ponens and necessitation for all operations [a]. Axioms A1C_i,..., A4C_i are substitutions of the axioms of logic S5. It follows that all the theorems of logic S5 are theorems of $DALD^{i'}_i$. Axiom A5$D^{i'}_i$ is related to the satisfaction of the bounded chain condition $D^{i'}_i$.

Each logic $DALC_i$ $(i > 1)$ is axiomatized as D^{i}_i except that A5D^{i}_i is replaced by A5C_i : $\alpha(i,a_1,a_2, A)$. Similarly the theorems of logic S5 are theorems of $DALC_i$. Axiom A5C_i is related to the satisfaction of bounded chain condition C_i. Observe that by Definition 8.2 we have $\alpha(i, a_1, a_2, A) \equiv (\beta(i, a_1, a_2, A) \Leftrightarrow \beta(i\text{-}1, a_2, a_1, A))$ in $DALC_i$.

Proposition 8.4. (a) Axiomatization of $DALD^{i'}_i$, $i>1$, $i'>1$, is sound with respect to the models from the class MOD($D^{i'}_i$), that is every theorem of $DALD^{i'}_i$ is true in every reduced model in MOD($D^{i'}_i$).
(b) Axiomatization of $DALC_i$, $i>1$, is sound with respect to the models from the class MOD(C_i), that is every theorem of $DALC_i$ is true in every reduced model in MOD(C_i).

Proof: See Proposition 8.2 and Proposition 8.3.
Q.E.D.

By a theory we mean any set of formulae which includes all the theorems of logic $DALD^{i'}_i$, $i>1$, $i'>1$, (resp. $DALC_i$, $i>1$) and is closed with respect to modus ponens rule. Let T be a theory, we denote by [a]T the set $\{A$: $[a]A \in T\}$. In a standard way, we use the notions of consistent set and maximal consistent sets. The set of all the maximal consistent theories is denoted by MTH.

Proposition 8.5. Let L be an element in $(DALD^{i'}_i)_{i>1,i'>1}$ (resp. in $(DALC_i)_{i>1}$). For any theory T (with respect to L) the following conditions are satisfied:
(a) Set [a]T is a theory
(b) T consistent implies [a]T consistent

Proof: First, we show that [a]T includes all the theorems of L. If a formula A is a theorem, then the formula [a]A obtained from A by application of necessitation rule is a theorem as well. Since T is a theory, we have $[a]A \in T$. Hence $A \in [a]T$. Now we show that [a]T is closed with respect to modus ponens rule. Assume that $A \in [a]T$ and $A \Rightarrow B \in [a]T$. It follows that (i) $[a]A \in T$ and (ii)$[a](A \Rightarrow B) \in T$. Since the set T is a theory, from $A2C_i$ and (ii) we have $[a]A \Rightarrow [a]B \in T$. By modus ponens $[a]B \in T$, which completes the proof of (a).
To prove (b) assume that T is consistent and suppose that [a]T is not, that is $A \wedge \neg A \in [a]T$.
It follows that there are $A_1,...,A_n \in [a]T$ such that $A_1 \Rightarrow (A_2 \Rightarrow ...(A_n \Rightarrow A \wedge \neg A)...) \in [a]T$. From $A2C_i$ we obtain $[a]A_1 \Rightarrow ([a]A_2 \Rightarrow ...([a]A_n \Rightarrow [a](A \wedge \neg A))...) \in T$. Since for all $i = 1,...,n$ $[a]A_i \in T$, we have $[a](A \wedge \neg A) \in T$. From $A3C_i$ by modus ponens we obtain $A \wedge \neg A \in T$, a contradiction.
Q.E.D.

Now we define a canonical model for each logic $DALD^{i'}_i$, $i>1$, $i'>1$ (resp. $DALC_i$, $i>1$) and we show that for each logic $DALD^{i'}_i$ (resp. $DALC_i$) the canonical model is a member of $MOD(D^{i'}_i)$ (resp. $MOD(C_i)$).

Definition 8.4. Let L be an element in $(DALD^{i'}_i)_{i>1,i'>1}$ (resp. in $(DALC_i)_{i>1}$). We define the canonical structure for L:

$M^c=(MTH,\{r^c_a: a \in CONAC\},m^c)$,

where MTH is the set of maximal consistent theories related to L

$r^c_a=\{(x,y) \in MTHxMTH: [a]x \subseteq y\}$,

$m^c(p)=\{x \in MTH: p \in x\}$ for any $p \in VARPROP$,

$m^c(a)=r^c_a$ for any $a \in CONAC$.

Proposition 8.6. Let L be an element in $(DALD^{i'}_i)_{i>1,i'>1}$ (resp. in $(DALC_i)_{i>1}$). Let $\{a_1, \ldots, a_k\}$ be a finite subset of CONAC. For $x, y \in MTH$,
(a) $(x,y) \in r^c_{a1}$ iff $\{A : [a_1]^i A \in x, i > 0\} \subseteq y$
(b) $(x,y) \in r^c_{a1} ;\ldots ; r^c_{ak}$ iff $\{A : [a_1] \ldots [a_k] A \in x\} \subseteq y$.

Proof: (a) Since for $A \in FOR_c$, $[a]A \Rightarrow A$ is a theorem of L, $[a]A \in x$ iff for some $j > 1$ $[a]^j A \in x$. So $\{A : [a_1]^i A \in x, i > 0\} = \{A : [a_1]A \in x\}$.

(b) Similar to the proof of Theorem 2.8 in Hughes and Cresswell (1984).
Q.E.D.

Proposition 8.7 below states various properties of the relations in the canonical models.

Proposition 8.7. Let L be an element in $(DALD^{i'}_{i})_{i>1,i'>1}$ (resp. in $(DALC_i)_{i>1}$).
(a) Every relation in $\{r^c_a : a \in CONAC\}$ is an equivalence relation.
(b) The set $\{r^c_a : a \in CONAC\}$ satisfies the condition $D^{i'}_{i}$ (resp. the relations in $\{r^c_a : a \in CONAC\}$ pairwise satisfy the condition C_i).

Proof: (a) To prove reflexivity we have to show that $[a]x \subseteq x$. Let $A \in [a]x$, that is $[a]A \in x$. Suppose that $A \notin x$. Since x is maximal, we have $\neg A \in x$. From A3C_i we have $\neg A \Rightarrow \neg[a]A \in x$. Since x is closed on modus ponens, we have $\neg[a]A \in x$, a contradiction, because x is consistent.
To prove symmetry assume that $[a]x \subseteq y$, which means that (i) for any formula A if $[a]A \in x$, then $A \in y$. Suppose that $[a]y$ is not included in x. Hence, there is a formula B such that $B \in [a]y$ and $B \notin x$. It follows that (ii) $[a]B \in y$ and (iii) $\neg B \in x$. From A3C_i and A4C_i we have (iv) $\neg B \Rightarrow [a]\langle a\rangle\neg B \in x$. Applying modus ponens to formulae in (iii) and (iv) we obtain $[a]\langle a\rangle\neg B \in x$. From (i) we obtain $\langle a\rangle\neg B \in y$, or equivalently $\neg[a]B \in y$, which contradicts (ii).
To prove transitivity assume that (i) for any formula A if $[a]A \in x$, then $A \in y$, and (ii) for any formula B if $[a]B \in y$, then $B \in z$. Suppose that there is a formula C such that (iii) $[a]C \in x$ and (iv) $C \notin z$. From (iii), it is easy to show that $[a][a]C \in x$. Then from (i) $[a]C \in y$ and from (ii) we have $C \in z$, which contradicts (iv).
(b) By way of example, only the first part of the statement is proved. Suppose that there exist $x, y \in MTH$ such that there is $S \subseteq CONAC$ with $2 \leq card(S) \leq i'$ and there is a $(\bigcup\{r^c_a : a \in S\})$-chain $(x_1,\ldots,x_{i+1})$ such that $x_1 = x$ and $x_{i+1} = y$ and for all $(\bigcup\{r^c_a : a \in S\})$-chain of length $1 \leq j \leq i$ $(y_1,\ldots, y_j)$ either $y_1 \neq x_1$ or $y_j \neq y$. It follows that i is the minimal element of the set $\{j : (x,y) \in (\bigcup\{r^c_a : a \in S\})^j\}$. We have $(x,y) \in r^c_{c1} ; \ldots ; r^c_{ci}$ with for $1 \leq j \leq (i-1)$, $c_j \neq c_{j+1}$ $(c_j, c_{j+1} \in S)$.
From Proposition 8.6(b) it follows that $\{A : [c_1] \ldots [c_i] A \in x\} \subseteq y$.
Since $(x,y) \notin (\bigcup\{r^c_a : a \in S\})^{i-1}$, for all $s = (b_1,\ldots, b_{i-1}) \in T_{i-1}(S)$ there is a formula A^s such that $[b_1]\ldots[b_{i-1}]A^s \in x$ and $A^s \notin y$. It follows that for all $s = (b_1,\ldots, b_{i-1}) \in T_{i-1}(S)$, $[b_1]\ldots[b_{i-1}] (\bigvee\{A^{s'} : s' \in T_{i-1}(S)\}) \in x$.
By using $\alpha'(i, S, (\bigvee\{A^{s'} : s' \in T_{i-1}(S)\}))$ we get that for all $s = (b_1,\ldots, b_i) \in T_i(S)$, $[b_1]\ldots[b_i] (\bigvee\{A^{s'} : s' \in T_{i-1}(S)\}) \in x$.

Since $[c_1] \ldots [c_i](\vee\{A^{s'}: s' \in T_{i-1}(S)\}) \in x$ it follows that $(\vee\{A^{s'}: s' \in T_{i-1}(S)\}) \in y$ which leads to a contradiction, since by construction for all $s' \in T_{i-1}(S)$, $A^{s'} \notin y$.
Q.E.D.

Proposition 8.8. Let L be an element in $(DALD^{i'}_i)_{i>1,i'>1}$ (resp. in $(DALC_i)_{i>1}$). For all $x \in MTH$, $A \in FOR_c$, (a) $A \in x$ iff (b) M^c, x sat A.

Proof: The proof is by induction on the complexity of the formula A. If A is a propositional variable, then the proposition holds by definition of meaning function m^c. If A is of the form $\neg B$ then, since x is a maximal set, we have $B \notin x$ iff $\neg B \in x$. Hence M^c, x sat $\neg B$ iff $\neg B \in x$. For A of the form $B \vee C$ we can show that a maximal set x satisfies $G \vee H \in x$ iff $G \in x$ or $H \in x$.
Now consider a formula of the form [a]B. Assume that $[a]B \in x$. By definition of r^c_a we have $B \in y$ for every y such that $[a]x \subseteq y$. Since the theorem is assumed to hold for B, we have M^c, x sat [a]B. Now suppose that $[a]B \notin x$. It follows that $\neg[a]B \in x$ and there is $y \in MTH$ such that $[a]x \cup \{\neg B\} \subseteq y$ ($[a]x \cup \{\neg B\}$ is consistent). Since $(x,y) \in r^c_a$ and since by the induction hypothesis not M^c, y sat B, then not M^c, x sat [a]B.
For the remaining types of formulae the proof is similar.
Q.E.D.

Proposition 8.9. (Completeness) Let L be an element in $(DALD^{i'}_i)_{i>1,i'>1}$ (resp. in $(DALC_i)_{i>1}$).
Axiomatization of logic L is complete: if A is true in all models of L then A is a theorem of L.

The standard proof is based on Proposition 8.8. The relationship between the conditions C_i and the conditions $D^{i'}_{i+1}$ entails that the notions of theoremhood in the different logics are not independent.

Corollary 8.10. For all $i,i' > 1$,
(a) If A is a theorem of $DALC_{i+1}$ then A is a theorem of $DALC_i$ as well.
(b) If A is a theorem of $DALD^{i'}_{i+1}$ then A is a theorem of $DALD^{i'}_i$ as well.
(c) If A is a theorem of $DALD^{i'}_i$ then A is a theorem of $DALD^{i'+1}_i$ as well.

9 Local Agreement of Relations

The condition of local agreement defined in Gargov (1986) corresponds to the condition C_2 as shown in Proposition 9.2.

Definition 9.1. Equivalence relations R and S in a set OB are said to be in local agreement (Gargov 1986) iff the following holds:

LA: for every $x \in OB$ either $R(x) \subseteq S(x)$ or $S(x) \subseteq R(x)$.

Proposition 9.1. If equivalence relations R and S in a set OB are in local agreement, then for any $x \in OB$ it holds:
(a) $(R \cap S)(x) = R(x)$ whenever $R(x) \subseteq S(x)$ and $(R \cap S)(x) = S(x)$ whenever $S(x) \subseteq R(x)$
(b) $(R \cup^* S)(x) = R(x)$ whenever $S(x) \subseteq R(x)$ and $(R \cup^* S)(x) = S(x)$ whenever $R(x) \subseteq S(x)$.

Proof: Condition (a) follows easily from Definition 9.1. To prove (b) assume that $R(x) \subseteq S(x)$. Then $\bigcup\{S(t): t \in R(x)\} = S(x)$. We also have $\bigcup\{R(t): t \in S(x)\} \subseteq S(x)$. For let $z \in R(t)$ and $t \in S(x)$ for some t. Then we have the two cases. If $R(t) \subseteq S(t)$, then $z \in S(t)$, and by transitivity $z \in S(x)$. If $S(t) \subseteq R(t)$, then since, by symmetry, $x \in S(t)$, we have $t \in R(x)$. By transitivity $z \in R(x)$, and hence $z \in S(x)$. We conclude that the second part of (b) holds. The proof of the first part is similar.
Q.E.D.

It follows that if $(R_i)_{i \in I}$ is a family of equivalence relations that are pairwise in local agreement, then the family generated from $(R_i)_{i \in I}$ with $\cap$ and $\cup^*$ is again a family of equivalence relations that are pairwise in local agreement.

Proposition 9.2. Let R and S be two equivalence relations in a set OB. The following conditions are equivalent:
(a) R and S are in local agreement.
(b) $(R \cap S)(x) = R(x)$ or $(R \cap S)(x) = S(x)$ for every $x \in OB$.
(c) R and S satisfy C_2.
(d) $R \cup^* S = R \cup S$.
(e) $R \cup S$ is transitive.

Proof: By way of example only the conditions (a), (c) and (e) are considered.
(a) → (c). Let (x_1, x_2, x_3) be a $(R \cup S)$-chain. If $(x_1, x_2) \in R$ (resp. S) and $(x_2, x_3) \in R$ (resp. S), then by transitivity of R (resp. S), we have $(x_1, x_3) \in R$ (resp. S). Now assume $(x_1, x_2) \in R$ and $(x_2, x_3) \in S$. If $R(x_1) \subseteq S(x_1)$, then by transitivity of S we have $(x_1, x_3) \in S$. Now assume $S(x_1) \subseteq R(x_1)$. If $S(x_2) \subseteq R(x_2)$, then by transitivity of R we have $(x_1, x_3) \in R$. Now assume $R(x_2) \subseteq S(x_2)$. Since R and S are equivalence relations, $R(x_1) = R(x_2)$ and $S(x_3) = S(x_2)$. Hence $S(x_1) \subseteq S(x_2)$. Since $x_1 \in S(x_1)$ and by symmetry $(x_1, x_2) \in S$. By transitivity of S, we have $(x_1, x_3) \in S$. The other case $(x_1, x_2) \in S$ and $(x_2, x_3) \in R$ is similar.

$\neg$ (a) $\rightarrow \neg$ (c). Assume that there exists x, y_1, y_2 such that $(x,y_1) \in R$, $(x,y_1) \notin S$, $(x,y_2) \in S$, and $(x,y_2) \notin R$. Suppose $(y_1,y_2) \in R$. By transitivity of R, $(x, y_2) \in R$ which leads to a contradiction. Now suppose $(y_1,y_2) \in S$. By symmetry and transitivity of S we have $(x, y_1) \in S$ which leads to a contradiction. So (y_1, x, y_2) is a $(R \cup S)$-chain and (y_1,y_2) is not a $(R \cup S)$-chain which implies that R and S do not satisfy C_2.

(c) $\rightarrow$ (e). Let $(x_1,x_2) \in R \cup S$ and $(x_2,x_3) \in R \cup S$. So (x_1,x_2,x_3) is a $(R \cup S)$-chain. By (c) it follows that $(x_1,x_3) \in R \cup S$. So $R \cup S$ is transitive.

(e) $\rightarrow$ (c). Let (x_1,x_2,x_3) be a $(R \cup S)$-chain. It follows that $(x_1,x_2) \in R \cup S$ and $(x_2,x_3) \in R \cup S$. By transitivity of the relation $(R \cup S)$, we obtain $(x_1, x_3) \in R \cup S$. So R and S satisfy C_2.

Q.E.D.

In Proposition 7.2, we have shown that if R and S satisfy C_i, then R and S satisfy C_{i+1}. However, even if R and S are equivalence relations the converse does not necessarily hold.

Proposition 9.3. There exist equivalence relations R and S such that R and S satisfy C_3 and R and S do not satisfy C_2.

Proof: We present two equivalence relations satisfying C_3 but not C_2. Consider R = {(x,x), (y,y), (z,z), (t,t), (v,v), (x,y), (y,x), (z,t), (t,z), (v,t),(v,t), (v,z), (z,v)} and S = {(x,x), (y,y), (z,z), (t,t), (v,v), (y,z), (z,y), (x,v), (v,x)}. R and S satisfy C_3. However $(x,y) \in R$, $(y, z) \in S$ and $(y,z) \notin R \cup S$.

Q.E.D.

Proposition 9.3 can be extended to any C_i, i.e., there exist equivalence relations R and S such that R and S satisfy C_i and R and S do not satisfy C_{i+1}.

Proposition 9.4. Let $(R_i)_{i \in I}$ be a family of equivalence relations (on a set OB) that are pairwise in local agreement. For all X, Y $\in \{R_i(x): i \in I, x \in OB\}$ either $X \subseteq Y$ or $Y \subseteq X$ or $X \cap Y = \emptyset$.

Proof: Assume $X = R_i(x)$ and $Y = R_j(y)$ for some $i, j \in I$ and $x, y \in OB$. Suppose that not $X \subseteq Y$, not $Y \subseteq X$ and $X \cap Y \neq \emptyset$. Hence there exist $x_1, x_2, x_3 \in OB$ such that $(x,x_1) \in R_i$, $(y,x_1) \notin R_j$, $(x,x_2) \notin R_i$, $(y,x_2) \in R_j$, $(x,x_3) \in R_i$ and $(y,x_3) \in R_j$. By transitivity and symmetry of the relations R_i and R_j, we get $(x_1,x_3) \in R_i$ and $(x_3,x_2) \in R_j$. By LA either $(x_1,x_2) \in R_i$ or $(x_1,x_2) \in R_j$. Suppose $(x_1,x_2) \in R_i$ (resp.

$(x_1,x_2) \in R_j$). By transitivity and symmetry, $(x,x_2) \in R_i$ (resp. $(x_1,y) \in R_j$) which leads to a contradiction.
Q.E.D.

10 Logic DALLA

The local agreement property between two relations in a frame of DAL can be characterized by a formula of FOR, giving the following correspondence result.

Proposition 10.1. Let $a_1, a_2 \in EAC$, $p \in VARPROP$ and $i > 1$. $[a_1 \cap a_2]p \Leftrightarrow [a_1]p \vee [a_2]p$ is true in the frame of DAL $(OB, \{r_a: a \in EAC\})$ iff r_{a1} and r_{a2} are in local agreement.

Proof: ($\rightarrow$) Suppose there exist x, y_1 and $y_2 \in OB$ such that $(x,y_1) \in r_{a1}$, $(x,y_1) \notin r_{a2}$, $(x,y_2) \notin r_{a1}$ and $(x,y_2) \in r_{a2}$. Consider the model $M_0 = (OB, \{r_a: a \in EAC\}, m_0)$ such that $m_0(p) = \{u \in OB : (x,u) \in r_{a1} \cap r_{a2}\}$. By the assumption, M_0, x sat $[a_1 \cap a_2]p \Leftrightarrow [a_1]p \vee [a_2]p$. By the construction of m_0 we have M_0, x sat $[a_1 \cap a_2]p$. Hence M_0, x sat $[a_1]p \vee [a_2]p$. Since $y_1 \notin (r_{a1} \cap r_{a2})(x)$ and $y_2 \notin (r_{a1} \cap r_{a2})(x)$ we have M_0, y_1 sat $\neg p$ and M_0, y_2 sat $\neg p$. However, either M_0, x sat $[a_1]p$ or M_0, x sat $[a_2]p$. In both cases it leads to a contradiction since $(x,y_1) \in r_{a1}$ and $(x, y_2) \in r_{a2}$.
($\leftarrow$) Assume r_{a1} and r_{a2} are in local agreement in the model of DAL $M = (OB, \{r_a: a \in EAC\}, m)$. Let $x \in OB$ and assume M, x sat $[a_1 \cap a_2]p$. For all $x' \in OB$ such that $(x,x') \in r_{a1 \cap a2} = r_{a1} \cap r_{a2}$ we have M, x' sat p. Since either $r_{a1 \cap a2}(x) = r_{a1}(x)$ or $r_{a1 \cap a2}(x) = r_{a2}(x)$ we get M, x sat $[a_1]p \vee [a_2]p$. Now assume M, x sat $[a_1]p \vee [a_2]p$. Since $r_{a1 \cap a2}(x) \subseteq r_{a1}(x)$ and $r_{a1 \cap a2}(x) \subseteq r_{a2}(x)$ then M, x sat $[a_1 \cap a_2]p$.
Q.E.D

Definition 10.1. A model $M=(OB,\{r_a: a \in EAC\},m)$ is a model with local agreement of indiscernibility relations (Gargov 1986) if all relations from $\{r_a: a \in EAC\}$ are pairwise in local agreement.

The extension of DAL obtained by restricting the class of models to the models satisfying condition LA given in Definition 9.1 is denoted by DALLA (DAL with Local Agreement). From Proposition 6.1 we obtain the following fact:

Proposition 10.2. For every model M of DALLA any two relations from E(M) are in local agreement.

We admit the following axioms for logic DALLA ($a, a_1, a_2 \in EAC$):

A1LA. All formulae having the form of a tautology of the classical propositional calculus

A2LA. $[a](A \Rightarrow B) \Rightarrow ([a]A \Rightarrow [a]B)$

A3LA. $[a]A \Rightarrow A$

A4LA. $\langle a \rangle A \Rightarrow [a]\langle a \rangle A$

A5LA. $[a_1 \cup^* a_2]A \Leftrightarrow [a_1]A \wedge [a_2]A$

A6LA. $[a_1 \cap a_2]A \Leftrightarrow [a_1]A \vee [a_2]A$.

The rules of inference are modus ponens and necessitation for all operations [a]. Axiom A5LA provides the definition of operation $\cup^*$, axiom A6LA gives the definition of $\cap$ under the assumption LA.

Proposition 10.3. Axiomatization of DALLA is sound, that is every theorem of DALLA is true in all the models of DALLA.

Proof: We use condition LA to prove that axioms A5LA and A6LA are tautologies (see Proposition 10.1). For the remaining axioms and rules the proof is standard.

In what follows, by a theory we mean any set of formulae which includes all the theorems of logic DALLA and is closed with respect to modus ponens rule -see Section 8.

Proposition 10.4. For any theory T the following conditions are satisfied:

(a) Set $[a]T$ is a theory

(b) T consistent implies $[a]T$ consistent

(c) $[a_1 \cup^* a_2]T = [a_1]T \cap [a_2]T$

(d) $[a_1 \cap a_2]T = [a_1]T \cup [a_2]T$.

Proof: For (a) and (b) see the proof of Proposition 8.5.

To prove (c) let (i) $[a_1 \cup^* a_2]A \in T$. From the axiom scheme A5LA part ($\rightarrow$) we have $[a_1]A \wedge [a_2]A \in T$. So we have $[a_1]A \in T$ and $[a_2]A \in T$. It follows that $A \in [a_1]T$ and $A \in [a_2]T$, which yields $A \in [a_1]T \cap [a_2]T$. Now assume that $[a_1]A \in T$ and $[a_2]A \in T$ and hence $[a_1]A \wedge [a_2]A \in T$. From the axiom scheme A5LA part ($\leftarrow$) we obtain $[a_1 \cup^* a_2]A \in T$. Similarly, condition (d) follows from the axiom scheme A6LA.

Q.E.D.

Proposition 10.5. If T_1 and T_2 are consistent theories, and D is a maximal extension of $T_1 \cap T_2$, then $T_1 \subseteq D$ or $T_2 \subseteq D$.

Proof: Assume that $T_1 \cap T_2 \subseteq D$ and suppose that there are formulae A and B such that (i) $A \in T_1$, (ii) $A \notin D$, (iii) $B \in T_2$ and (iv) $B \notin D$. Since T_1 is a theory, we conclude from (i) that $A \vee B \in T_1$, and similarly by (iii) $A \vee B \in T_2$. Hence $A \vee B \in T_1 \cap T_2$, and as a consequence $A \vee B \in D$. Since D is a maximal set, from (ii) and (iv) we have $\neg A \in D$ and $\neg B \in D$, which yields $\neg(A \vee B) \in D$, a contradiction.
Q.E.D.

Definition 10.2. We define the canonical structure for DALLA:
(i) $M^c=(MTH, \{r^c{}_a: a \in EAC\}, m^c)$,
(ii) $m^c(p)=\{x \in MTH: p \in x\}$ for any $p \in VARPROP$,
(iii) $m^c(a)=\{(x,y) \in MTH \times MTH: [a]x \subseteq y\}$ for all $a \in CONAC$,
(iv) $m^c(a_1 \cup^* a_2)=m^c(a_1) \cup m^c(a_2)$
(v) $m^c(a_1 \cap a_2)=m^c(a_1) \cap m^c(a_2)$
(vi) $r^c{}_a=m^c(a)$ for all $a \in EAC$

Proposition 10.6. For all $a_1, a_2 \in CONAC$,
(a) $r^c{}_{a1}$ is an equivalence relation.
(b) $r^c{}_{a1}$ and $r^c{}_{a2}$ are in local agreement.

Proof: (a) The proof is analogous to the proof of Proposition 8.7(a).
(b) To show that in M^c the local agreement condition is satisfied suppose conversely, and let for some $x, y, z \in MTH$ have (i) $[a_1]\, x \subseteq y$, (ii) not $[a_2]x \subseteq y$, (iii) $[a_2]x \subseteq z$ and (iv) not $[a_1]x \subseteq z$. It follows from (ii) and (iv) that there are formulae A and B such that $[a_2]A \in x$, $A \notin y$, $[a_1]B \in x$ and $B \notin z$. From 10.4(d) we have $[a_1 \cap a_2]A \in x$ and $[a_1 \cap a_2]B \in x$. Hence, we obtain $[a_1 \cap a_2](A \wedge B) \in x$. According to 10.4(d) we have to consider the two cases. If $[a_1](A \wedge B) \in x$, then by (i) we have $A \wedge B \in y$, and hence $A \in y$, a contradiction. If $[a_2](A \wedge B) \in x$, then by (iii) we obtain $A \wedge B \in z$, and hence $B \in z$, a contradiction.
Q.E.D.

Proposition 10.7. For all $a, a_1, a_2 \in EAC$,
(a) $r^c{}_{a1}$ is an equivalence relation.
(b) $r^c{}_{a1}$ and $r^c{}_{a2}$ are in local agreement.
(c) $m^c(a)=\{(x,y) \in MTH \times MTH: [a]\, x \subseteq y\}$.

Proof: The conditions (a) and (b) follows from Proposition 10.6 and Proposition 9.1. The proof of (c) is by induction with respect to the complexity of expression a. Let a be of the form $a_1 \cap a_2$. We have to show that (i) $[a_1]x \subseteq y$ and $[a_2]x \subseteq y$ iff $[a_1 \cap a_2]x \subseteq y$. In view of Proposition 10.1 and (b) of the present proposition, condition (i) is

satisfied. Now let a be of the form $a_1 \cup^* a_2$. In view of 10.4(c), condition (b) of the present theorem, and 9.2(d), (c) is equivalent to (ii) $[a_1]x \subseteq y$ or $[a_2]x \subseteq y$ iff $[a_1]x \cap [a_2]x \subseteq y$, which clearly holds.
Q.E.D.

We conclude, that M^c is a model of DALLA.

Proposition 10.8. For all $x \in$ MTH, $A \in$ FOR, (a) $A \in x$ iff (b) M^c, x sat A.

Proof: The proof is analogous to the proof of Proposition 8.8.
Q.E.D.

Proposition 10.9. (Completeness of DALLA) Axiomatization of logic DALLA is complete: if A is true in all the models of DALLA, then A is a theorem of DALLA.

Proof: Suppose that a formula A is not a theorem of DALLA. Hence the set $\{\neg A\}$ is consistent. There is a maximal consistent set D such that $A \notin D$. By Proposition 10.8 not M^c,D sat A, and hence A is not true in all the models of DALLA, a contradiction.
Q.E.D.

Proposition 10.10. The logic DALLA is an extension of $DALC_2$, that is every theorem of $DALC_2$ is a theorem of DALLA.

Proof: It sufficient to show that $\alpha(2,a_1,a_2,p)$ is a theorem of DALLA. We recall that $\alpha(2,a_1,a_2,p) \equiv ([a_1]p \wedge [a_2]p \Leftrightarrow [a_1][a_2]p \wedge [a_2][a_1]p)$. The formula $[a_1][a_2]p \wedge [a_2][a_1]p \Rightarrow [a_1]p \wedge [a_2]p$ is a theorem of DALLA which can be shown by using A3LA. Using the axiom scheme A5LA, we obtain that $[a_1]p \wedge [a_2]p \Rightarrow [a_1 \cup^* a_2]p$ is a theorem of DALLA. Moreover, $[a_1 \cup^* a_2]p \Rightarrow [a_1 \cup^* a_2][a_1 \cup^* a_2]p$ is also a theorem of DALLA. Using the axiom scheme A5LA and the fact that for all A, B $\in$ FOR, a $\in$ EAC, $[a](A \wedge B) \Leftrightarrow [a]A \wedge [a]B$ is a theorem of DALLA, it can be easily shown that $[a_1 \cup^* a_2][a_1 \cup^* a_2]p \Rightarrow [a_1][a_2]p \wedge [a_2][a_1]p$. Using modus ponens, $\alpha(2,a_1,a_2, p)$ is a theorem of DALLA.
Q.E.D.

A semantical proof of Proposition 10.10 is also possible.

Proposition 10.11. The formulae of the form $[a_1]...[a_n]A \Leftrightarrow [a_1] A \wedge ... \wedge [a_n]A$ and $<a_1>...<a_n>A \Leftrightarrow <a_1> A \vee ... \vee <a_n>A$ are theorems in DALLA with $\{a_1,...,a_n\} \subseteq$ EAC.

The decidability of the satisfiability problem for the logics $DALC_i$ and $DALD^{i'}{}_i$ is an open problem. The usual filtration constructions do not preserve the satisfaction of

$D^{i'}_i$. In that sense these logics are examples of multimodal logics with relationships between the accessibility relations in the frames for which the classical techniques of proving the finite model property cannot be straightforwardly used. However, the satisfiability problem for DALLA can be shown to be decidable (see (Demri 1996a)) by using a suitable filtration technique (see also (Demri 1996b)).

11 Conclusion

In this paper we have presented a rough set-style modelling of vague concepts. We developed logical formalism that enabled us to represent extensions and intensions of the concepts and to reason about them. The logics elaborated in the paper are multimodal logics such that the accessibilty relations that determine modal operators are mutually dependent. We introduced and discussed several relationships among these relations and we presented the respective modal correspondence results. Axiom systems for the logics were given and completeness theorems were proved.

References

[AT1] Archangelsky, D. A. and Taitslin, M. A. (1989). A logic for data description. In A. R. Meyer and M.A. Taitslin, editors, Symposium on Logic Foundations of Computer Science, Pereslavl-Zalessky, pages 2-11. Springer-Verlag, LNCS 363, July 1989

[Bu1] Bunge, M. (1967) Scientific research I. The search for system. Springer

[Co1] Codd, E.F. (1970) A relational model for large shared data banks. Communications of ACM 13, 377–387

[Ch1] Chellas, B. (1980) Modal Logic. An Introduction. Cambridge University Press, Cambridge

[De1] Demri, S. (1996a) The validity problem for the logic DALLA is decidable. Bulletin of the Polish Academy of Sciences, Math. Section, 44(1):79-86, 1996

[De2] Demri, S. (1996b) A class of information logics with a decidable validity problem. In W. Penczek and A. Szalas, editors, Symposium on Mathematical Foundations of Computer Sciences (MFCS'96), pages 291-302, LNCS 1113, Springer-Verlag, 1996

[FO1] Fariñas del Cerro, L., Orlowska, E. (1985) DAL – a logic for data analysis. Theoretical Computer Science 36, 251–264. Corrigendum: Theoretical Computer Science 47 (1986) 345

[Ga1] Gargov, G. (1986) Two completeness theorems in the logic for data analysis. ICS PAS Reports 581

[Gr1] Grzymala-Busse, J. (1988) Knowledge acquisition under uncertainty: a rough set approach. Journal of Intelligent and Robotic Systems 1, 3-16

[HMS1] Hunt, E.B., Marin, J., Stone, P.J. (1966) Experiments in Induction. Academic Press, New York–London

[HC1] Hughes, G., Cresswell, M. (1984) A Companion to Modal Logic. Methuen, London and New-York

[Ko1] Konikowska, B. (1987) A formal language for reasoning about indiscernibility. Bulletin of the PAS 35, Ser. Math., 239-249

[KOP1] Konrad, E., Orlowska, E. and Pawlak, Z. (1982) On approximate concept learning. Proceedings of the European Conference on AI, Orsay, France

[Or1] Orlowska, E. (1983) Semantics of vague concepts. In: Dorn, G.,Weingartner, P.(eds) Foundations of Logic and Linguistics. Problems and Solutions. Selected contributions to the 7th International Congress of Logic, Methodology and Philosophy of Science, Salzburg 1983. Plenum Press, 465–482

[Or2] Orlowska, E. (1984) Logic of indiscernibility relations. Proceedings of the Conference on Computation Theory, Zaborow, Poland. Lecture Notes in Computer Science 208, Springer-Verlag,177–186

[Or3] Orlowska, E. (1988a) Representation of vague information. Information Systems 13, 167–174

[OR4] Orlowska, E. (1988b) Logical aspects of learning concepts. International Journal of Approximate Reasoning 2, 349–364

[Pa1] Pawlak, Z. (1981) Information systems–theoretical foundations. Information Systems 6, 205–218

[Pa2] Pawlak, Z. (1982) Rough sets. International Journal of Computer and Information Sciences 11, 341–356

[Pa3] Pawlak, Z. (1985) Rough concept analysis. Bulletin of the PAS 33, Ser. Math., 495–498

[Pa4] Pawlak, Z. (1986) On learning–a rough set approach. Proceedings of the Conference on Computation Theory, Zaborow, Poland. Lecture Notes in Computer Science 208, Springer-Verlag, 197–227

[Pa5] Pawlak, Z. (1987) Learning from examples–the case of an imperfect teacher. Bulletin of the PAS 35, Ser.Tech., 259–264

[Pa6] Pawlak, Z. (1991). Rough Sets. Kluwer, Dordrecht

[RZ1] Ras, Z. and Zemankova, M. (1984) Rough set based learning systems. Proceedings of the Conference on Computation Theory, Zaborow, Poland. Lecture Notes in Computer Science 208, Springer-Verlag, 265–276

[Wi1] Wille, R. (1982) Restructuring lattice theory: An approach based on hierachies of concepts. In: I. Rival (ed) Oredered Sets. Reidel, Dordrecht, 445-470

[Wi2] Wille, R. (1984) Liniendiagramme hierarhischer Begrieffssysteme. Preprint 812, Technische Hochschule Darmstadt

[WLZ1] Wong, S.K.M., Ye Li and Ziarko, W. (1986) Comparision of rough set and statistical methods in inductive learning. International Journal of Man–Machine Studies 24, 53–72

Chapter 12

Some Philosophical Aspects of Indiscernibility

Anna Lissowska-Wójtowicz

Institute of Philosophy and Sociology,
University of Warsaw

Abstract: In this article the relationship between the identity relation and the indiscernibility relation is discussed. A generalization of the standard definition of the indiscernibility relation considered in the theory of rough sets is given, and some basic theorems about it are formulated and proved.

1 Introduction

Information systems and the theory of rough sets connected to them find broad applications in problems of information retrieval and information classification. In order to present philosophical assumptions which underlie this theory, it is necessary in our opinion to examine the problem of interdependence between the identity relation and one of the basic concepts of the rough sets theory, the indiscernibility relation.

The problem of identity relation has frequently been addressed by philosophers (e.g. [No1], [Kr1]). What is the sense of the expression '$a = b$' and when is it true – these are the questions to be answered. From antiquity comes the problem of identity of spatio – temporal objects (extended in time and space) that undergo gradual changes (cf. the classical problem of Theseus' ship). We also consider the problem of personal identity – we ask about the criteria of deciding whether we are still dealing with the same person; about the criteria of calling people by the same proper name at different times. It seems that with the further development in health science and genetic engineering this problem will play an increasingly important role in ethics and law.

In this article we consider two questions: to what degree does the language structure alone allow to resolve the identity problem of objects from the universe of its models and what are the conditions for the relations that could play the role of identity relation in a language? We will compare some definitions of the identity relation (which seems to be essentially an ontological notion) and the indiscernibility relation (which seems to be more of an epistemological notion) and then we will present theories in which these relations are discerned and theories in which they are identified. (We think that should bring out different meanings of the expression "to be identical"). In conclusion we will present some generalizations of the theory of information systems assuming that the indiscernibility relation is defined in terms of binary predicates and it is not an equivalence relation. Such a definition of the indiscernibility relation is philosophically and practically justified.

2 Identity and Indiscernibility

Generally speaking we will understand the *indiscernibility relation* (*ind*) for a given language L as a relation which holds between any two objects x and y if and only if these objects share all the characteristic features expressed in that language. The assumption concerning the identity relation (*eq*) is that every object is identical with itself and that the identity relation is symmetrical. For this reason the strongest definition of *numerical identity* is as follows:

Definition 1. Every object is identical only with itself.

Both relations *ind* and *eq* are (at least) reflexive and symmetrical so they make it possible to distinguish in the universe of every model of the considered language, some classes of objects. (We do not claim that in the case of indiscernibility relation they are equivalence classes).

Two cases can be distinguished:

(1) Identity is not equivalent to indiscernibility (the classes set by *eq* are not the same as the classes set by *ind*).
(2) Identity is equivalent to indiscernibility (the classes set by *eq* are the same as the classes set by *ind*).

In the case (1), we can deny either the fact (1a) that if the identity relation holds, then the indiscernibility relation holds, or (1b) the fact that the indiscernibility relation implies the identity relation. Let us consider each case separately.

(1a) According to the principle of extensionality identical objects are indiscernible in every respect. In the language of second order logic it is expressed by the formula:

$$\text{if } x \text{ } eq \text{ } y \text{ then } \forall\phi[\phi(a_1,\ldots,x,\ldots,a_n) \Leftrightarrow \phi(a_1,\ldots,y,\ldots,a_n)] \ ,$$

for each formula ϕ of language L and for each valuation of variables $a_1,\ldots,a_n$.

In short we will denote it by *In.Id* (indiscernibility of identical). Sometimes (eg. in the theory of rough sets) this principle is simplified to

$$\text{if } x \text{ } eq \text{ } y \text{ then } \forall P[P(x) \Leftrightarrow P(y)] \ .$$

The consequent of implication represents here a particular case of a more general definition of the indiscernibility relation mentioned above because in this case we consider only non-relational properties of objects (indiscernibility is limited only to unary predicates). We will return to this problem later.

When can this principle be denied? That seems to be the case with the identification of objects in different possible worlds and – which can be treated as a particular case of this first one (admitting different world's time periods as other possible worlds) – with the identification of objects extended in time and space. In general, the following questions are asked: Is object x in a world W the same as object y in world V? Can x and y be given by the same proper name? A. Kenny [Ke1] writes about that:

> A proper name is being used correctly, only if it is used on each occasion of its use to refer to the same object. If I yesterday named an object "Charles" and I today call an object which I see "Charles", then I am using the name "Charles" correctly only if the object which I see today is the same object which I named yesterday.

Different authors had different opinions regarding this question. According to Kripke [Kri1] the question about the identity of objects in different possible worlds (or in different periods of time in the same world) is wrong. It should be – what worlds are possible so that a person called by proper name e.g. "Nixon" in one possible world will exist as Nixon in another world? According to Hintikka [Hi1], in order to determine such an identity it is necessary to solve a differential equation which permits to observe a continuity of changes when the object goes from one of its states to another. According to other authors, we have to check if x and y have the same essential features (although there is the problem of how to differentiate such features). But invariably we ask if this is one and the same object or only a very similar one. From the assumption that they exist in other possible worlds or in different time periods of the same world, it follows that they differ at least in relational properties. Thus, in this case the identity predicate is assigned a special meaning which can be expressed by the following:

Definition 2. Two objects x and y are identical (x *eq* y) if and only if

$$\forall P \in I[P(a_1, \ldots, x, \ldots a_n) \Leftrightarrow P(a_1, \ldots, y, \ldots a_n)]$$

where I is a distinguished set of essential properties.

Such identity of objects can be determined as *the identity of the essence* of objects.

(1b) According to some authors (e.g. Geach [Ge1]) the identity relation existing in a given language is always relative to means of expression in this language. Two objects are always identical in respect to some (or all) features expressible in this language and there is no such thing as *an absolute* (independent of language) identity relation. We will characterize this thesis as *identity of indiscernible* (*Id.In*). It expresses the verifiability of predicate *ind* towards *eq* :

$$\text{if } x \textit{ ind } y \text{ then } x \textit{ eq } y \ .$$

This is a principle which treats indiscernible objects as identical objects giving the same meaning to qualitative identity and numerical identity. In order to deny that principle we can ask if it is possible that there are two different objects all of whose features (expressible in a given language) are the same. This is a question about the existence in a language of an identity predicate stronger (or at least not weaker) than the indiscernibility predicate, thus a question if it is possible in the language to formulate, in a sensible way, sentences about the cardinality of indiscernibility classes of objects (classes of objects which cannot be discerned from a given object). One possible representation of these sentences are formulas of the type:

$$\exists x \exists y\, (x \; ind \; y \wedge \neg (x \; eq \; y)) \;\; ,$$

which say that the class determined by x consists of at least two elements. If we contradict this statement we will question the sense of predicate *eq* in the language. Observe that in the inductive definition of satisfaction admitted in the predicate calculus with equality, an atomic formula of the type $t_i = t_j$ plays an essential role and it is true in the model M if and only if the denotation of t_i is identical to the denotation of t_j. Thus, we refer in fact to some other metalanguage identity and its conditions of satisfaction. Let us consider the consequences of rejecting the principle $Id.In$. If we do that we assume that there is another outer-linguistic access to the objects, which permits to determine that the same description denotes different objects. There is a situation where one (extensional) language L refers to a given domain of objects and in this language we can speak about at least some features of these objects. Moreover, there is the predicate of absolute identity, the identity which allows to determine that two given objects – although they cannot be discerned in the given language L (but maybe they can be in a richer one) – are different objects.

It is assumed that regardless of the expressive power of the language, there is a predicate which discerns all the objects belonging to any domain of this language. There is no reason, in this case, to maintain that one language is more precise or richer than another. In all languages with the same domain the atomic sentences built with identity predicate alone would have the same truth-value.

It seems that without an additional assumption concerning the domain of a given language this foundation is contrary to intuition. The problem of reduction of identity to indiscernibility can be approached in a different way. Let us assume after Geach [Ge1], [Kr1] that it is possible to give a definition of several different binary identity predicates (I-predicates). These predicates divide the universe of models of a given language into equivalence classes. Thus, I-predicate has formal properties of identity relation – reflexivity, symmetry and transitivity. An exemplary definition of this predicate in a language L is as follows:

$$\langle x, y \rangle \in I \text{ if and only if } [S(x) \Leftrightarrow S(y)] \wedge [R(x) \Leftrightarrow R(y)]$$

for S and R belonging to a given language L. (*Definiens* is built exclusively with predicates of L).

This corresponds to Geach's intuition that when speaking about the identity of two objects we must always determine their features which are identical, e.g. x and y are the same (identical) in respect of R and S. The set of I-predicates defined in that way can be partially ordered by relation defined as:

$$I' \geq I'' \text{ if and only if } \forall x, y \langle x, y \rangle \in I' \Rightarrow \langle x, y \rangle \in I'' \;\; .$$

In other words the predicate I' is stronger than the predicate I'' when it devides the universe of models of language L into smaller equivalence classes. It is easy to show (e.g. from Zorn-Kuratowski lemma) that in each predicate set there is a maximal element, and moreover, this element is unique (which means the biggest). Such an element is identified precisely with the indiscernibility relation. If we reject the $Id.In$ principle, we will have to define an additional identity predicate *eq*. We have shown that definiens of such a definition cannot be a function of predicates which already exist in the language – in this case the identity relation would be equivalent to the indiscernibility relation. This relation must be defined in another outer-verbal way. This brings us to the next definition of indentity relation.

Definition 3. Two objects x and y are identical (x *eq* y) if and only if

$$Os(x, y)$$

where Os is a metalanguage predicate (nondefinable in a given language) which is reflexive, symmetrical and transitive.

Very often in a natural language identical objects are defined that way – the predicate Os is taken by the ostention [Qu1].

Such identity can be called *ontological identity* because it expresses information about objects independently of our conceptual access to them.

3 Theory of Rough Sets

One example of a formal theory where the principle $Id.In.$ is refuted is the theory of rough sets.

In this theory we assume that a given set of individuals is described in a language which contains the set of unary predicates $P = \{P_1, \dots P_n\}$ as the only nonlogical constants. Then we define the relation *ind*(A) which holds between the objects verifying exactly the same sentences built of predicates from the set A. In Geach's terminology these would be the objects identical in respect to A. In the extreme case $A = P$. We then have the frame $\langle D, q\rangle$, where $q = ind(P)$ is an equivalence relation which holds between indiscernible objects. This structure is often called "*approximation space*". For each set $X \subseteq D$ we define the upper approximation of this set $ind'(P)X$ and the lower approximation $ind(P)X$:

$$x \in \; ind'(P)X \text{ if and only if } \exists y[\langle x, y\rangle \in q \wedge y \in X] \; ;$$
$$x \in \; ind(P)X \text{ if and only if } \forall y[\langle x, y\rangle \in q \Rightarrow y \in X] \; .$$

To speak about the approximation of a given set by classes of indiscernible objects is sensible only if we assume that q is a stronger relation than *ind*. The fact the set D is fixed at the beginning (e.g. by enumeration) does away with the problem of discrimination of its elements. We immediately know the elements of set D between which the relation Os holds. Simultaneously the definition of relation q on this set says how this set is described with the language (which objects are indiscernible with this language). Equivalence classes of relation q are the smallest definable classes in these structures (the smallest set which can be named in the language of this structure). The sets included in these classes can only be described by their upper approximation. On this ground we can resolve two kinds of problems. First, given set K, we can consider how by means of concepts of language L we can describe this set (how it can be approximated by equivalence classes of relation q). This problem is connected with artificial intelligence, with logic of induction and analysis of hypotheses. We are making efforts to construct such a precise language (a machine using this language) so that we can describe the elements of a given set with the greatest precision. In other words, we are trying to construct an artificial language through whose spectacles (applying a famous Dummett [Du1] comparison) we can see all features of objects.

Second, if we have a given concept from language L we can search for the set which corresponds to this concept. This is one of the problems in the theory of information systems [Pa1]. Among given objects we look for the one which suits the present description most. This theory applies in many ways. We can mention at least the approximate classification of objects, the description of nondeterministic information, the classification of scientific theories, the construction of epistemic logic system, etc [Pa1], [OP1], [OP2]]. Rough quantifiers defined in this theory are also interesting from the logical point of view (c.f. e.g. [Kry1], [Sz1]).

In general this structure gives us a model of viewing a given reality – the world – through "the spectacles" of our language. Due to the conceptual discernibility of this language we are not always able to describe a given object univocally – actually we very often describe a whole class of them. Introducing new concepts to the language we try to decrease the size of these classes. In particular, we can try to describe science development in this way – each new scientific theory has a more precise language at its disposal (cf. classification of scientific theories [Or1]).

A common feature of all the theories where the predicate *eq* is really stronger than the predicate *ind* is the fact that we assume in these theories an outer verbal access to the objects of the universe. In the theory of rough sets, the individuals of the set D are presented at the outset. In the communication systems to which a natural language belongs we have the possibility of using ostention. So, we are faced with the situation where the universe (e.g. set D or real world) is primary and the language describing this universe (the language of information system theory, natural language) is secondary.

Now, consider the case (2). The principles *Id.In.* and *In.Id.* lead to the identification of the predicate *eq* with *ind.* As a result we get very strong dependence between the language and the structure of the universe of its models. Let us assume, for example, that in the language there are only n unary predicates. According to the definition, the relation *ind* divides the universe of models of this language in 2^n equivalence classes of indiscernible objects. (When we have multi-place predicates in the language the situation becomes more complicated).

If we now agree with the normal definition of satisfaction for the sentences built by means of identity (t_j *eq* t_i), we will get information about the universes of models – the universes consist of not more than 2^n objects. Such identification of relations *ind* and *eq* exists wherever the universe of language models is created of abstract objects which can be approached through the notions. There is no sense, in this case, to talk about identity defined by means of a mysterious predicate Os. Mathematics is a good example here – if two mathematical objects, e.g. two numbers, have all features the same, they are undoubtedly one and the same object (*Id.In* principle). Of course there is also the opposite dependence – identical objects have all features the same (*In.Id.* principle). We thus get the following definition of the identity relation:

Definition 4. Two objects x and y are identical (x *eq* y) if and only if

$$x \ ind \ y \ .$$

This definition is related to the language in which the relation *ind* is determined.

4 Possibilities of Generalizing the Theory of Rough Sets

Let us get back to the *Id.In.* principle and to the identity which is defined by this principle in terms of nonrelational features. Many philosophers maintain that such features do not exist. In other words, if we want to talk about properties of an object we should use (at least) binary predicates. The fact that the property P is *relational* can be defined in the following way:

The property P is relational if and only if

- $\forall x\{P(x) \Leftrightarrow \exists y R(x,y)\}$, for some relation R
  or if and only if
- $\forall x\{P(x) \Leftrightarrow \forall y R(x,y)\}$, for some relation R
  or if and only if
- $\forall x[P(x) \Leftrightarrow R(x,a)]$, for some relation R and some constant a.

This definition evidently embraces such relational features as (1) being father (for x to be a father there must exist a relation of being a father to somebody, and there must be a y to whom x is father); (2) being the oldest (for x to be the oldest in a given set of people there must exist a relation of being older determined in this set for each person y who belongs to this set, x must be older than y); (3) being God's creature (for x to be God's creature there must exist a relation of creation and a distinguished object – God – who created x). However, in case the relation R stays unlimited every feature (according to the definition) is a relation feature. E.g., being red is a relation feature because we can point out the relation R – being of the same color – as a fact that x is red if and only if it has the same color as a paradigm red object. So, we must agree (as many philosophers do) that all features are relation features or demand that the relation R, which appears in the definition of the relation feature, is not an equivalence relation. Even though we impose these limits, many properties remain relational properties and if we want to determine that the object x has one of them we must determine beforehand the existence of the relation between x and the other objects.

All these reflections are very general, but they boil down to the conlusion that if we want to solve some problems connected with the determination of the set of essential features of objects or with the method of their classification, relational features play an important role and must not be ignored. This objection can also be raised with respect to the theory of rough sets. Given indiscernibility criteria, this theory takes into consideration only unary predicates.

Quine [Qu2] suggested two general notions of indiscernibility – partial and strong indiscernibility.

Two objects a and b are *partially indiscernible* in language L if and only if language L does not contain any sentence about objects a and b which is true only if the names of these objects are appearing in a determined order in every predicate occurring in this sentence.

Two objects a and b are *strongly indiscernible* in language L if and only if there is no sentence in L which is true about the object a and not true about the object b.

This is the strongest meaning of the indiscernibility concept. In the language of second order calculus (for simplicity we confine ourselves to unary and binary predicates) these definitions can be written as, respectively:

$$x\ ind_p y \text{ if and only if}$$

$$\forall P^1[P^1(x) \Leftrightarrow P^1(y)] \wedge \forall P^2[P^2(x,y) \Leftrightarrow P^2(y,x)] \vee (x = y)$$

(partial indiscernibility);

$$x\ ind_s y \text{ if and only if } \forall P^1[P^1(x) \Leftrightarrow P^1(y)] \wedge$$

$$\forall P^2[\forall z P^2(x,z) \Leftrightarrow P^2(y,z)] \wedge [\forall v P^2(v,x) \Leftrightarrow P^2(v,y)] \vee (x = y)$$

(strong indiscernibility);
(P^1 and P^2 mean unary and binary predicates, respectively).

However, the abovementioned definition of partial indiscernibility has a defect; namely, if the relations P^2 were symmetrical (and this is the only type of relation used in examining indiscernibility of objects), any two objects would be indiscernible. Let P be the relation of being a friend. Intuitively, only those people are indiscernible who are in the relation of friendship. So, the definition of partial indiscernibility can be modified as follows:

$$x\ ind_p y \text{ if and only if } \forall P^1[P^1(x) \Leftrightarrow P^1(y)] \wedge \forall P^2[(\forall v,z[P^2(v,z) \Leftrightarrow P^2(z,v)]) \Rightarrow P^2(x,y)\} \wedge \{\neg\forall v,z[P^2(v,z) \Leftrightarrow P^2(z,v)]\} \Rightarrow (P^2(x,y) \Leftrightarrow P^2(y,x))] \vee (x = y),$$

Of course if $x\ ind_s y$ then $x\ ind_p y$. Practically and from the natural language point of view it seems that the notion of partial indiscernibility is more "realistic". It determines that if, in our language, no (nonsymmetrical) relation discerns the first element within the pair of elements x and y, these elements are indiscernible.

Strong indiscernibility requires that x and y are related exactly to the same objects. In other words, they have all relational features the same. In case the universe of considered objects is infinite, the definition is non-effective; in order to determine indiscernibility of two objects one must make an infinite number of comparisons [Mo1]. Let us assume, however, that we have in the language a nontransitive relation, e.g. of being heavier by three units (and there is no more precise relation which compares weights). This relation is established in a physical object set. It corresponds to the inaccuracy of our measurements. We would intuitively say that the objects whose weight differs by two units are indiscernible in this language. Our language is not precise enough for this purpose. But this intuition is consistent with the definition of partial indiscernibility and not with strong indiscernibility. It seems that if we compare two objects in respect to their relational features, we examine first of all whether there is such a relation where the first object is related to the second, but not conversely.

Let us note that the relation ind_p defined in this way does not have to be an equivalence relation. If we accept the abovementioned assumptions, we can define the next two versions of the identity relation which specify definition 4:

Definition 5. Two objects x and y are identical (x eq y) if and only if x $ind_p y$.

Definition 6. Two objects x and y are identical (x eq y) if and only if x $ind_s y$.

Just as before these definitions are relative to the language in which the relations ind_p and ind_s are determined. Identity in definition D5 does not have to be an equivalence relation.

5 Conclusions

Different definitions of the identity relation can be partially put in order (in a fixed language) in respect of their decreasing strength or, in other words, in respect to the inclusion of classes of objects considered identical (they do not always have to be equivalence classes). This order is as follows:

$$D1 \subseteq D6 \subseteq D5 \ ;$$
$$D1 \subseteq D4 \subseteq D2 \ ;$$
$$D1 \subseteq D3 \ .$$

Definitions D5 and D2 are independent (of each other), although definition D6 is stronger than both of them. Definition D5 and D6 are modifications of D4. They are definitions of the qualitative (or epistemological) identity relation. Definition D3 is independent of this family of definitions, it defines the *ontological* identity relation. Objects actually identical in the universe can very often be recognized as different (e.g. happy John today and sad John yesterday can be seen as two different men). Similarly, objects, which posses the same features expressible in a given language, do not always have to be identical in the universe of models for this language. When we use a language in which there is only one unary predicate as an outer logical predicate, only two objects can be recognized as different.

Definition D1 creates a common basis for both kinds of these definitions – qualitative and ontological, and it is the only statement on identity issue to which we can assert in every theory.

6 The Construction of a Generalized Rough Sets Theory

If we accept the suggested definition of the identity relation (partial indiscernibility enriched with the assumption of symmetry of relations) determined on a set of objects U, we can talk about lower and upper approximations of the sets included in U, about set-theoretical properties of such approximations and about the definability of a given set expressed in terms of approximation operation – so, about all notions characteristic of the theory of rough sets. Similarly to the standard theory of rough sets, these notions correspond to quite natural intuitions. In order to define them let us start by considering the following example.

6.1 Example

Let us consider a set O of agents with a list of properties (e.g. a blood group, a list of their illnesses etc.) which will be denoted by unary predicates $P_1^1, \ldots, P_n^1$. A binary relation between the agents (e.g. to be a sexual partner) will be denoted by binary predicate P_1^2. We assume (maybe a little bit artificially) that this relation is reflexive. Some members of this group suffer from a disease A which can be discovered by blood test. This set will be denoted by X. The question arises whether suffering from A can be stated in terms of properties $P_1^1, \ldots, P_n^1, P_1^2$.

Let $O = \langle o_1, \ldots, o_{25}\rangle$ and $X = \langle o_1, o_2, o_3, o_5, o_7, o_8, o_9, o_{16}, o_{21}\rangle$. According to the general definition of the indiscernibility relation and taking into account that relation P_1^2 is symmetrical, relation *ind* on the set O is defined as follows:

$$\forall x, y \in O \; x \; ind \; y \text{ if and only if}$$

$$\forall i = 1, \ldots, n \; (P_i^1(x) \Leftrightarrow P_i^1(y)) \wedge P_1^2(x, y) \;\; ,$$

We assume that $ind = B \cup B' \cup B''$ where $B = \{\langle o_2, o_3\rangle, \langle o_3, o_4\rangle, \langle o_5, o_6\rangle, \langle o_6, o_{20}\rangle,$ $\langle o_7, o_8\rangle, \langle o_8, o_9\rangle, \langle o_9, o_{10}\rangle, \langle o_{10}, o_{11}\rangle, \langle o_{10}, o_{12}\rangle, \langle o_8, o_{13}\rangle, \langle o_{13}, o_{14}\rangle, \langle o_{14}, o_{15}\rangle,$ $\langle o_{15}, o_{19}\rangle, \langle o_{19}, o_{18}\rangle, \langle o_{18}, o_{16}\rangle, \langle o_{16}, o_{17}\rangle, \langle o_{21}, o_{22}\rangle, \langle o_{23}, o_{24}\rangle, \langle o_{24}, o_{25}\rangle, \langle o_7, o_{16}\rangle,$ $\langle o_{17}, o_{18}\rangle\}$, $B' = \{\langle o_i, o_i\rangle : 1 \leq i, j \leq 25\}$, $B'' = \{\langle o_i, o_j\rangle : \langle o_j, o_i\rangle \in B\}$ as ilustrated in figure 1.

The agents who have the same nonrelational properties and who are sexual partners for each other are precisely indiscernible.

We would like to approximate the set X from below and from above using classes of indiscernibility. Generally speaking, *lower approximation* of the set

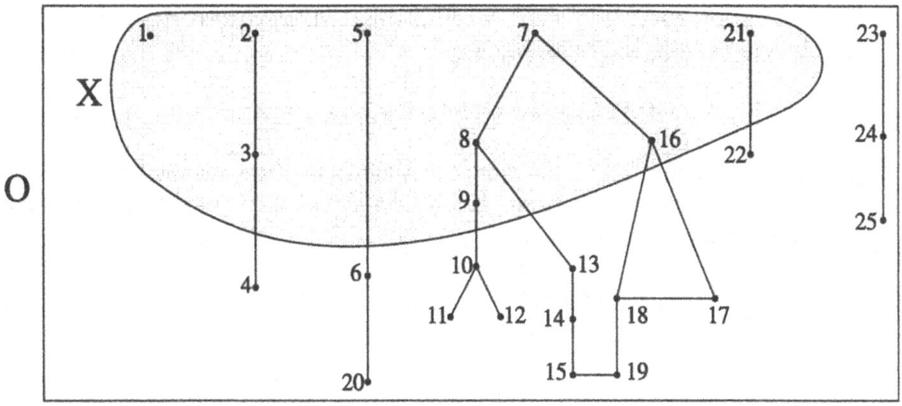

Fig. 1.

$X \subseteq O$ is an operation $F : 2^O \to 2^O$, such that $F(X) \subseteq X$ and F is definable by means of $P_1^1, \dots, P_n^1, P_1^2$. An *upper approximation* of the set $X \subseteq O$ is an operation $F' : 2^O \to 2^O$ such that $X \subseteq F'(X)$ and F' is definable by means $P_1^1, \dots, P_n^1, P_1^2$. The definitions of the approximations considered below can also be found in [Po2], [Po1], but they are expressed in a different language and require the use of a more complicated terminology.

6.2 Lower Approximation

The following observations about the set X are quite natural.

1. There are agents in the set X whose all the partners are ill and they probably infected all of their partners. We call them "ill pattern agents". Agents o_1, o_2, o_7 in our example are ill pattern agents.
2. There are agents in the set X who were probably infected by ill pattern agents because they had contact with them. They are agents o_1, o_2, o_7, o_3, o_8, o_{16} in our example.
3. There are agents in the set X who had contact with some other ill agents in the set X (and either they infected those agents or were infected by them). They are agents o_1, o_2, o_7, o_3, o_8, o_{16}, o_9 in our example.
4. There are agents in the set X who can be at least indirectly discerned from a healthy agent, i.e. there is at least one partner who is not a partner of both of them. They are agents o_1, o_2, o_7, o_3, o_8, o_{16}, o_9, o_5 in our example.

From these observations it results, in particular, that there are other ways of infection (different from a sexual contact) and it is also possible to be a carrier of the infection but not being ill. Several definitions of different lower approximations of the set X correspond to these observations.

1. The operation PAT: $2^O \to 2^O$ which distinguishes pattern elements of the set X is defined in the following way:

$$PAT(X) = \{x : \forall y(y \; ind \; x \Rightarrow y \in X)\} \; .$$

2. The operation $F_1 : 2^O \to 2^O$ which distinguishes those elements of the set X which are indiscernible from the pattern elements of the set X is defined in the following way:

$$F_1(X) = \{x : \exists y(y \in PAT(X) \wedge x \; ind \; y)\} = PAT(X) \cup \\ \{x : x \notin PAT(X) \wedge \exists y(y \in PAT(X) \wedge x \; ind \; y)\} \; .$$

3. The operation $F_2 : 2^O \to 2^O$ which distinguishes those elements of the set X which are either completely isolated (i.e which are discernible from all other objects and indiscernible only from themselves) or indiscernible from some other objects in the set X is defined in the following way:

$$F_2(X) = \{x \in X : x \in PAT(X) \vee \exists y(y \in X \wedge y \neq x \wedge x \; ind \; y)\} = \\ F_1(X) \cup \{x \in X : \exists y(y \in X - PAT(X) \wedge y \neq x \wedge x \; ind \; y)\}$$

4. The operation $F_3 : 2^O \to 2^O$ which distinguishes those elements of the set X which are at least indirectly discernible from the elements of the complement of the set X is defined in the following way:

$$F_3(X) = \{x \in X : \forall y[(y \notin X \wedge y \; ind \; x) \Rightarrow \exists z \neg(x \; ind \; z \Leftrightarrow y \; ind \; z)]\} \\ = F_2(X) \cup \{x \in X : \forall y[(y \notin X \wedge y \; ind \; x) \Rightarrow \\ \exists z[z \notin X \wedge z \neq y \wedge \neg z \; ind \; x]\} \; .$$

6.3 Properties of the Lower Approximations

The operation $PAT(X)$ can be iterated.

$$PAT^1(X) = PAT(X); \\ PAT^{n+1}(X) = PAT(PAT^n(X)),$$

that agrees with the idea of considering the pattern elements in increasingly stronger sense.

The operation PAT is monotonic: $\forall X, Y, [X \subseteq Y \Rightarrow PAT(X) \subseteq PAT(Y)]$. It can easily be seen that if for certain k $PAT^k(X) = PAT^{k+1}(X)$, then for every $j \geq k$, $PAT^k(X) = PAT^j(X)$. Two cases are possible – $PAT^k(X) = \emptyset$ or $PAT^k(X) \neq \emptyset$. If $PAT^k(X) \neq \emptyset$, it means that in the set X "isolated" classes of indiscernible objects must exist. In our example it means, that these agents have had sexual relationships only with an ill agent similar to them. It confirms the conclusion that one can get infected with the disease A also in other ways than a sexual contact. Similarly, different lower approximations F_1, F_2 and F_3 can be iterated. The following facts can be easily proved:

Fact 7. $\forall X,Y\ [X \subseteq Y \Rightarrow F_j(X) \subseteq F_j(Y)]$, *i.e. the operations* F_1, F_2 *and* F_3 *are monotonic.*

Fact 8. $\forall i\ F_j^i(X) = F_j(X)$, *for* $j = 1,2,3$, *i.e. the operations* F_1, F_2 *and* F_3 *are idempotent.*

Fact 9.

$$PAT^{n+1}(X) \subseteq PAT^n(X) \subseteq \ldots \subseteq PAT(X) \subseteq F_1(X) \subseteq F_2(X) \subseteq F_3(X) \subseteq X\ .$$

6.4 Upper Approximations

Similar consideration also apply to the set $-X$.

1. There are agents in the set $-X$ who are not health pattern and had no contact with the agents who are health pattern (in the sense defined above). They are agents o_4, o_{22}, o_{17} in our example.
2. There are agents in the set $-X$ who had contact only with the ill agents. They are agents o_4, o_{22} in our example.
3. There are agents in the set $-X$ who are not discerned from the ill agents even in the indirect (defined above) way. This is agent o_{22} in our example.
4. There are agents in the set $-X$ who had contact with at least one ill agent. They are agents o_4, o_6, o_{10}, o_{13}, o_{17}, o_{18}, o_{22} in our example.

Several definitions of different upper approximations of the set $-X$ correspond to these observations.

1. The operation $G_1(X) : 2^O \to 2^O$, which distinguishes those elements of the set $-X$, which are neither pattern elements of the set $-X$ nor are indiscernible from such elements, is defined in the following way:

$$G_1(X) = \{x : x \notin PAT(-X) \land \neg\exists y(y \in PAT(-X) \land x\ ind\ y)\}\ .$$

2. The operation $G_2 : 2^O \to 2^O$ which distinguishes those elements of the set $-X$ which are indiscernible only from the elements of the set X, is defined in the following way:

$$G_2(X) = \{x : \forall y[(y \neq x \land y\ ind\ x) \Rightarrow y \in X]\}\ .$$

3. The operation $G_3 : 2^O \to 2^O$ which distinguishes those elements of the set $-X$ which are not even indirectly discernible from the elements of the set X, is defined in the following way:

$$G_3(X) = \{x : \exists z(z \in X \land z\ ind\ x \land \neg\exists y[(y\ ind\ x \Leftrightarrow y\ ind\ z) \land y \neq x \land y \neq z])\}\ .$$

4. The operation $IND(X) : 2^O \to 2^O$, which distinguishes those elements of the set $-X$ which are indiscernible from at least one element of the set X, is defined in the following way:

$$IND(X) = \{x : \exists z(z \in X \land z\ ind\ x)\}\ .$$

6.5 Properties of the Upper Approximations

Let us notice that the operations of lower approximation defined above are in a certain sense reverse to the upper approximations. The following facts tell us about it.

Fact 10. $F_i(X) = -G_i(-X)$, *for* $i = 1, 2, 3$.

Fact 11. $PAT(X) = -IND(-X)$.

The operation IND can be viewed as a closure of the set with respect to indiscernible elements. It can be iterated just like operation PAT:

$$IND^1(X) = IND(X) \ ;$$
$$IND^{n+1}(X) = IND(IND^n(X)) \ ,$$

which corresponds to the idea of taking elements which are indiscernible from the elements of the set X in weaker and weaker sense.

The operation IND is monotonic and just like the operation PAT it has the property that if for a certain k $IND^k(X) = IND^{k+1}(X)$, then $IND^j(X) = IND^k(X)$ for any $j \geq k$.

The upper approximation operations G_1, G_2 and G_3 can also be iterated. The following facts can be easily proved:

Fact 12. $\forall X, Y[X \subseteq Y \Rightarrow G_j(X) \subseteq G_j(Y)]$, *for* $j = 1, 2, 3$, *i.e. the operations* G_1, G_2 *and* G_3 *are monotonic.*

Fact 13. $\forall i \ G_j^i(X) = G_j(X)$, *for* $j = 1, 2, 3$, *i.e the operations* G_1, G_2 *and* G_3 *are idempotent.*

Fact 14.

$$X \subseteq G_3(X) \subseteq G_2(X) \subseteq G_1(X) \subseteq IND^1(X) \subseteq \ldots \subseteq IND^n(X) \subseteq O \ .$$

6.6 Set-theoretical Properties of Approximations

The following theorems are true:

Theorem 15. *(i) Let T be an approximation operation belonging to the set $\{PAT, F_1, F_3\}$. Then $T(X \cap Y) = T(X) \cap T(Y)$, for any sets X, Y.*
(ii) Let T be an approximation operation belonging to the set $\{IND, G_1, G_3\}$. Then $T(X \cup Y) = T(X) \cup T(Y)$, for any sets X, Y.

Proof. The proof will be given for the operations PAT, F_1, F_3:

(i') From the monotonicity of the operation PAT $PAT(X \cap Y) \subseteq PAT(X) \cap PAT(Y)$.
We want to show that $PAT(X \cap Y) \supseteq PAT(X) \cap PAT(Y)$.
Assume the contrary: $\exists z(z \in PAT(X) \wedge z \in PAT(Y) \wedge z \notin PAT(X \cap Y))$.
$z \notin PAT(X \cap Y) \Leftrightarrow \exists x(z \ ind \ x \wedge x \notin X \cap Y) \Leftrightarrow \exists x(z \ ind \ x \wedge (x \notin X \vee x \notin Y)) \Leftrightarrow \exists x(z \ ind \ x \wedge x \notin Y) \vee \exists x(z \ ind \ x \wedge x \notin Y)$, which contradicts the assumption that $z \in PAT(X) \wedge z \in PAT(Y)$.

(ii") From the monotonicity of the operation F_1 $F_1(X \cap Y) \subseteq F_1(X) \cap F_1(Y)$.
We want to show that $F_1(X \cap Y) \supseteq F_1(X) \cap F_2(Y)$.
Assume the contrary: $\exists z(z \in F_1(X) \wedge z \in F_1(Y) \wedge z \notin F_1(X \cap Y))$.
$z \in F_1(X) \Leftrightarrow z \in PAT(X) \vee z \in \{x : x \notin PAT(X) \wedge \exists y(y \in PAT(X) \wedge x\ ind\ y)\}$;
$z \in F_1(Y) \Leftrightarrow z \in PAT(Y) \vee z \in \{x : x \notin PAT(Y) \wedge \exists y(y \in PAT(Y) \wedge x\ ind\ y)\}$;
$z \notin F_1(X \cap Y) \Leftrightarrow z \notin \{(PAT(X \cap Y) \cup \{x : x \notin PAT(X \cap Y) \wedge \exists y(y \in PAT(X \cap Y) \wedge x\ ind\ y)\}\} \Leftrightarrow z \notin PAT(X \cap Y) \wedge z \notin \{x : x \notin PAT(X \cap Y) \wedge \exists y(y \in PAT(X \cap Y) \wedge x\ ind\ y)\} \Leftrightarrow z \notin PAT(X) \wedge z \notin PAT(Y) \wedge z \notin \{x : x \notin PAT(X) \wedge z \notin PAT(Y) \wedge \exists y(y \in PAT(X) \wedge y \in PAT(Y) \wedge x\ ind\ y)\} \Leftrightarrow z \notin PAT(X) \wedge z \notin PAT(Y) \wedge [z \notin \{x : x \notin PAT(X) \wedge \exists y(y \in PAT(X) \wedge x\ ind\ y)\} \vee z \notin \{x : x \notin PAT(Y) \wedge \exists y(y \in PAT(Y) \wedge x\ ind\ y)\}]$, which contradicts with first and second assumption.

(iii"') From the monotonicity of the operation F_3 $F_3(X \cap Y) \subseteq F_3(X) \cap F_3(Y)$.
We want to show that $F_3(X \cap Y) \supseteq F_3(X) \cap F_3(Y)$.
Assume the contrary: $\exists z(z \in F_3(X) \wedge z \in F_3(Y) \wedge z \notin F_3(X \cap Y))$.
$z \in F_3(X) \Leftrightarrow z \in X \wedge \forall v[(v \notin X \wedge v\ ind\ z) \Rightarrow \exists y \neg(z\ ind\ y \Leftrightarrow v\ ind\ y)]$.
$z \in F_3(Y) \Leftrightarrow z \in Y \wedge \forall v[(v \notin Y \wedge v\ ind\ z) \Rightarrow \exists y \neg(z\ ind\ y \Leftrightarrow v\ ind\ y)]$.
$z \notin F_3(X \cap Y) \Leftrightarrow z \notin (X \cap Y) \vee \neg\{\forall v[(v \notin Y \cap X \wedge v\ ind\ z) \Rightarrow \exists y \neg(z\ ind\ y \Leftrightarrow v\ ind\ y)]\} \Leftrightarrow (z \notin X \vee z \notin Y) \vee \neg\{\forall v[(v \notin X \wedge v\ ind\ z) \Rightarrow \exists y \neg(z\ ind\ y \Leftrightarrow v\ ind\ y)] \vee [(v \notin Y \wedge v\ ind\ z) \Rightarrow \exists y \neg(z\ ind\ y \Leftrightarrow v\ ind\ y)]\}$, which contradicts with first and second assumption.

Condition (ii) for IND, G_1 and G_3 follows directly from cases (i'), (i"), (i"'), Fact 10 and Fact 11. □

7 Superposition of Approximations

The question arises whether the superposition of approximations of the same kind (e.g. lower) gives us new approximations. The answer is given by the following theorems.

Theorem 16. *$PAT(F_i(X)) = PAT(X)$, for $i = 1, 2, 3$.*

Proof. The proof will be given, first, for $i = 1$.

We want to show that $PAT(F_1(X)) = PAT(X)$.

From the monotonicity of the operation PAT and from the fact that F_1 is the lower approximation we have $PAT(F_i(X)) \subseteq PAT(X)$.

We want to show that $PAT(F_i(X)) \supseteq PAT(X)$.

Assume the contrary. It means that $\exists x(x \in PAT(X) \wedge x \notin PAT(F_1(X)))$.

$x \notin PAT(F_1(X)) \Leftrightarrow \exists z(x\ ind\ z \wedge z \notin F_1(X)) \Leftrightarrow \exists z[x\ ind\ z \wedge z \notin PAT(X) \wedge \neg\exists y(y \in PAT(X) \wedge z\ ind\ y)]$, which contradicts the assumption $x \in PAT(X) \wedge x\ ind\ z$.

We know (Fact 9) that $F_1(X) \subseteq F_2(X) \subseteq F_3(X)$, so from the monotonicity of PAT it follows that

$PAT(F_1(X)) \subseteq PAT(F_2(X)) \subseteq PAT(F_3(X)) \subseteq PAT(X)$,
and hence from the case $i = 1$
$PAT(F_1(X)) = PAT(F_2(X)) = PAT(F_3(X)) = PAT(X)$. □

Theorem 17. *If $PAT^2(X) = F_j(PAT(X))$ for $j = 1,2,3$, then $\forall n \geq 2$ $PAT^n(X) = PAT^2(X)$ (i.e the set $PAT^2(X)$ is the least set of pattern elements in the set X).*

Proof. Assume that $PAT^2(X) = F_j(PAT(X))$. It means that
$PAT(PAT^2(X)) = PAT(F_j(PAT(X)))$.
From Theorem 16 $PAT(F_j(PAT(X))) = PAT(PAT(X))$ hence $PAT^3(X) = PAT^2(X)$ and from the properties of the operation PAT
$\forall n \geq 2$ $PAT^n(X) = PAT^2(X)$. □

Theorem 18. $F_1(F_i(X)) = F_1(X)$ *for* $i = 1,2,3$.

Proof. For $i = 1$ – see properties of the operation F_1.
Let us consider the case $i > 1$.
From the monotonicity of the operation $F_1 : F_1(F_2(X)) \subseteq F_1(X)$.
From the definition of the operation F_2 we have
$F_1(F_2(X)) = F_1(F_1(X) \cup \{x : \exists y(y \in X - PAT(X) \wedge y \neq x \wedge x \; ind \; y)\})$.
From Fact 10 and Fact 11 we obtain
$F_1(F_1(X) \cup \{x : \exists y(y \in X - PAT(X) \wedge y \neq x \wedge x \; ind \; y)\}) = F_1(F_1(X)) \cup F_1(\{x : \exists y(y \in X - PAT(X) \wedge y \neq x \wedge x \; ind \; y)\} = F_1(X) \cup F_1(\{x : \exists y(y \in X - PAT(X) \wedge y \neq x \wedge x \; ind \; y)\})$, hence $F_1(F_2(X)) \supseteq F_1(X)$.
For $i = 3$ the proof is similar. □

Theorem 19. $F_i(F_1(X)) = F_1(X)$, *for* $i = 1,2,3$.

Proof. Let us consider $i = 2$.
Since F_2 is the lower approximation, we have:
$F_2(F_1(X)) \subseteq F_1(X)$.
From the definition of F_2,
$F_2(F_1(X)) = F_1(F_1(X)) \cup \{x : \exists y(y \in F_1(X) - PAT(X) \wedge y \neq x \wedge x \; ind \; y)\}$.
From Fact 10 and Fact 11 we obtain
$F_1(F_1(X)) \cup \{x : \exists y(y \in F_1(X) - PAT(X) \wedge y \neq x \wedge x \; ind \; y)\} = F_1(X) \cup \{x : \exists y(y \in F_1(X) - PAT(X) \wedge y \neq x \wedge x \; ind \; y)\}$, hence $F_2(F_1(X)) \supseteq F_1(X)$.
For $i = 3$ the proof is similar. □

Theorem 20. $F_2(F_3(X)) = F_2(X)$.

Proof. From the monotonicity of the operation $F_2 : F_2(F_3(X)) \subseteq F_2(X)$.
From the definition of F_3 we have
$F_2(F_3(X)) = F_2(F_2(X) \cup \{x : \forall y[(y \notin X \wedge y \; ind \; x) \Rightarrow \exists z(z \notin X \wedge z \neq y \wedge \neg z \; ind \; x]\})$.
From Fact 10 and Fact 11
$F_2(F_2(X) \cup \{x : \forall y[(y \notin X \wedge y \; ind \; x) \Rightarrow \exists z(z \notin X \wedge z \neq y \wedge \neg z \; ind \; x)]\}) = F_2(X) \cup F_2(\{x : \forall y[(y \notin X \wedge y \; ind \; x) \Rightarrow \exists z(z \notin X \wedge z \neq y \wedge \neg z \; ind \; x)]\})$, hence $F_2(X) \subseteq F_2(F_3(X))$. □

Theorem 21. $F_3(F_2(X)) = F_2(X)$.

Proof. Since F_3 is a lower approximation operation we have:
$F_3(F_2(X)) \subseteq F_2(X)$.
From the definition of F_3 we obtain
$F_3(F_2(X)) = F_2(F_2(X)) \cup \{x : \forall y[(y \notin F_2(X) \wedge y \text{ } ind \text{ } x) \Rightarrow \exists z(z \notin F_2(X) \wedge z \neq y \wedge \neg z \text{ } ind \text{ } x)]\} = F_2(X) \cup \{x : \forall y[(y \notin F_2(X) \wedge y \text{ } ind \text{ } x) \Rightarrow \exists z(z \notin F_2(X) \wedge z \neq y \wedge \neg z \text{ } ind \text{ } x)]\}$, hence $F_3(F_2(X)) \supseteq F_2(X)$. □

Intuitions which underline the definitions and the fact that superpositions of lower and upper approximations do not give us anything new suggest that the approximations defined above are the only reasonable ones.

7.1 Definability

In the last section let us consider the idea of definability which is one of the basic concepts of the theory of information systems. It makes possible the determination of how precise the language of an information system is. Broadly speaking, the set X is definable in a given information system if it can be "described precisely" in this system, i.e. when it is equal to its approximations (lower, upper or both). Taking into account the way lower and upper approximations are defined and the resulting relationship between these notions, this property can be defined formally:

X is definable in $\langle U, \text{ } ind\rangle$ in the sense of approximation F_i if and only if $F_i(X) = X$.

From the Fact 9 the following facts follow immediately:

1. $PAT(X) = X \Leftrightarrow IND(X) = X$;
2. $F_i(X) = X \Leftrightarrow G_i(X) = X$, for $i = 1, 2, 3$;
3. $PAT(X) = X \Rightarrow \forall F_i F_i(X) = X$, for $i = 1, 2, 3$;
4. $F_i(X) = X \Rightarrow F_j(X) = X$, for $i, j = 1, 2, 3; i \leq j$.

A simple example of a set which is not definable in any sense is the set X of ill agents from our example. The following problem is interesting from this point of view: which relation selected from a given class of "natural" relations should be added to the language of a given information system $\langle U, \text{ } ind\rangle$ to make an undefinable set $X \subseteq U$ definable. (We require that this relation is minimal in the sense of inclusion). In our example it should be the relation which determines how one can get infected.

References

[Du1] Dummett, M.: Frege: Philosophy of Language. London, Duckworth, (1973)
[Fr1] Frege, W.: Sinn und Bedeutung. Ztschr. f. Philos. u. philos. Kritik, NF, **100**, (1892)
[Ge1] Geach, P.T.: Identity. In: Logic Matters, Oxford, (1972)

[Hi1] Hintikka, J.: Towards a General Theory of Individuation and Identification. In: Language and Ontology. Proccedings of the Sixth International Wittgenstein Symposiumm 23th to 30th August 1981, W. Leinfellner, E. Kraemer, J. Schank (ed.), (1981)

[Ke1] Kenny, A.: Oratio Obliqua. Aris. Soc. Sup., **XXXVI**, (1963), 139

[Kr1] Kraut, P.: Indniscernibility and Ontology. Synthese, **44**, (1980)

[Kri1] Kripke, S.: Naming and Necessity. Oxford, (1980)

[Kry1] Krynicki, M.: A note on rough concepts logic. Fund. Inf., **XIII**, (1990)

[Mo1] Mostowski, M.: Similarities and Topology. Studies in Logic, Grammar and Rhetoric, **III**, (1983)

[No1] Nooann, W.: Object and Identity. Martinus Nijhoff Puglishers, (1980)

[Or1] Orłowska, E.: Verisimilitude based on concept analysis. Studia Logica, **3**, (1990)

[OP1] Orłowska, E., Pawlak, Z.: Representation of nondeterministic information. Theoretical Computer Science, **29**, (1984)

[OP2] Orłowska, E., Pawlak, Z.: Measurment and indiscernibility. Bulletin of the Polish Academy of Science, **32**, 9-10, (1984)

[Pa1] Pawlak, Z.: Information systems, theoretical foundation. Information Systems, **3**, (1981)

[Po1] Pomykała, J.A.: On definability in the nondeterministic information system. Bulletin of the Polish Academy of Science, **36**, 3-4, (1988)

[Po2] Pomykała, J.A.: Approximation operations in approximation space. Bulletin of the Polish Academy of Science, **35**, 9-10 (1987)

[Qu1] Quine, W.V.: Identity, ostention and hypostasis. In: From a Logical Point of View, N. Y.: Harper and Row, (1961)

[Qu2] Quine, W.V.: Grades of discriminability. Journal of Philosophy, **73**, (1976)

[Sz1] Szczerba, L.W.: Rough quantifiers. Bulletin of the Polish Academy of Science, **35**, (1987)

Chapter 13

Rough Mereology and Analytical Morphology

Andrzej Skowron[1] *and Lech Polkowski*[2]

1 Institute of Mathematics, Warsaw University,
Banacha 2, 02-097 Warszawa, Poland
2 Institute of Mathematics, Warsaw University of Technology,
Pl.Politechniki 1, 00-650 Warszawa, Poland

Abstract: We present two theories that emerge in connection with rough set-based methods for classifying dynamic populations of objects. The first theory, referred to as rough mereology aims at the analysis of complex objects in terms of properties of their parts. The second theory – analytical morphology of rough sets is a generalization of mathematical morphology obtained by imposing a geometrical structure on the attributes in information systems.

1 Introduction

In the rough set theory the synthesis of adaptive decision algorithms of satisfactory capabilities for classifying new unseen objects sets serious demands on the tools to be used [SP94]. In particular, one has to take into account the chaotic nature of data e.g. the fact that reducts [P91], [SR92] of a given decision table are not stable with respect to randomly chosen subtables and therefore, the decision rules generated from them may not be satisfactory when new data arrive. The upshot of the situation is the emergence of new ideas aimed at data filtration [SP94], generation of dynamic reducts and rules [BSS94a,b] and investigation of relationships among a complex object and its parts [PoSk94a,b] by means of a hierarchy of relations of being a part to a certain degree between 0 and 1, where being a part in degree 1 means being a full part.

In this paper we present some of these new ideas; we concentrate on two theories that link rough set theory with the mereology of Lesniewski [Le16] and mathematical morphology [GD88] respectively. We outline some possible applications of the resulting theories: rough mereology [PoSk94b] and analytical morphology [SP94].

The paper is structured as follows. In Section 2 we present some basic facts from rough set theory. Then in Section 3 we discuss rough mereology as an extension of mereology in the sense that the mereological relation of being a (proper) part is replaced with the rough mereological relation of being a part in a degree. Section 4 brings a discussion of analytical morphology along with some basic parts of mathematical morphology of rough sets.

2 Basic Rough Set Theory

2.1 Information Systems

Information systems [P82,P91] (sometimes called data tables, attribute-value systems, condition-action tables, knowledge representation systems etc.) are used for representing knowledge. Rough sets have been introduced [P91] as a tool to deal with inexact, uncertain or vague knowledge in artificial intelligence applications. In this section we recall some basic notions related to information systems and rough sets.

An *information system* is a pair $\mathbf{A} = (U, A)$, where U is a non-empty, finite set called the *universe* and A is a non-empty, finite set of *attributes*, i.e. $a: U \rightarrow V_a$ for $a \in A$, where V_a is called the *value set* of a. Elements of U are called *objects* and interpreted as, e.g. cases, states, processes, patients, observations. Attributes are interpreted as features, variables, characteristic conditions etc.

Every information system $\mathbf{A} = (U, A)$ and non-empty set $B \subseteq A$ determine a *B-information function*

$$Inf_B : U \rightarrow \mathbf{P}(B \times \bigcup_{a \in B} V_a)$$

defined by $Inf_B(x)=\{(a,a(x)):\ a \in B\}$. The set $\{Inf_A(x):\ x \in U\}$ is called the *A-information set* and it is denoted by INF($\mathbf{A}$). With every subset of attributes $B \subseteq A$, an equivalence relation, denoted by $IND_A(B)$ (or $IND(B)$) called the *B-indiscernibility relation*, is associated and defined by

$$IND(B)=\{(s,s') \in U^2: \text{for every } a \in B,\ a(s)=a(s')\}$$

Objects s,s' satisfying relation $IND(B)$ are *indiscernible* by attributes from B.

Hence $xIND(A)y$ iff $Inf_A(x)=Inf_A(y)$.

We consider a special case of information systems called *decision tables.* A decision table [P91] is any information system of the form $\mathbf{A}=(U, A \cup \{d\})$, where $d \notin A$ is a distinguished attribute called the *decision*. The elements of A are called *conditions.*

One can interpret a decision attribute as a kind of classification of the universe of objects given by an expert, decision-maker, operator, physician, etc. Decision tables are called *training sets of examples* in machine learning [KM90]. The cardinality of the image $d(U)=\{k: d(s)=k$ for some $s \in U\}$ is called the *rank* of d and is denoted by $r(d)$. We assume that the set V_d of values of the decision d is equal to $\{1,...,r(d)\}$. Let us observe that the decision d determines the partition $CLASS_A(d)=\{X_1, ..., X_{r(d)}\}$ of the universe U, where $X_k = \{x \in U: d(x)=k\}$ for $1 \leq k \leq r(d)$. $CLASS_{\mathcal{A}}(d)$ will be called *the classification of objects in* $\mathcal{A}$ *determined by the decision d*. The set X_i is called the *i-th decision class of* $\mathcal{A}$.

2.2 Reducts

Any minimal subset $B \subseteq A$ such that $IND(A)=IND(B)$ is called *a reduct in the information system* $\mathcal{A}$. The set of all reducts in $\mathcal{A}$ is denoted by $RED(\mathcal{A})$.

Let $\mathcal{A}$ be an information system with n objects. By $M(\mathcal{A})$ [SR92] we denote an $n \times n$ matrix (c_{ij}) called the *discernibility matrix* of $\mathcal{A}$ such that

$$c_{ij} = \{a \in A: a(x_i) \neq a(x_j)\} \text{ for } i,j=1,\ldots,n.$$

A *discernibility function* $f_{\mathcal{A}}$ for an information system $\mathcal{A}$ is a boolean function of m boolean variables $\bar{a}_1,\ldots,\bar{a}_m$ corresponding to the attributes $a_1,\ldots,a_m$ respectively, and defined by

$$f_{\mathcal{A}}(\bar{a}_1,\ldots,\bar{a}_m) = \wedge\{\vee \bar{c}_{ij} : 1 \leq j < i \leq n,\ c_{ij} \neq \emptyset\}$$

where $\bar{c}_{ij} = \{\bar{a} : a \in c_{ij}\}$.

It can be shown [SR92] that the set of all prime implicants of $f_{\mathcal{A}}$ determines the set $RED(\mathcal{A})$ of all reducts of $\mathcal{A}$ i.e.

$$a_{i_1} \wedge \ldots \wedge a_{i_k} \text{ is a prime implicant of } f_{\mathcal{A}}.$$

iff

$$\{a_{i_1},\ldots, a_{i_k}\} \in RED(\mathcal{A}).$$

One can show that the problem of finding a minimal (with respect to the cardinality) reduct is NP-hard [SR92]. In general the number of reducts of a given information system can be exponential with respect to the number of attributes. Nevertheless, existing procedures for reduct computation are efficient in many practical applications and for more complex cases one can apply some efficient heuristics (see e.g. [BSS94a,b]).

2.3 Set Approximations

If $\mathcal{A} = (U, A)$ is an information system, $B \in A$ is a set of attributes and $X \subseteq U$ is a set of objects then the sets $\{s \in U: [s]_B \subseteq X\}$ and $\{s \in U: [s]_B \cap X \neq \emptyset\}$ are called *B-lower and B-upper approximation* of X in $\mathcal{A}$, and they are denoted by $\underline{B}X$ and $\overline{B}X$, respectively.

The set $BN_B(X) = \underline{B}X - \overline{B}X$, will be called the *B-boundary* of X. When $B=A$ we write also $BN_{\mathcal{A}}(X)$ instead of $BN(X)$.

Sets which are unions of some classes of the indiscernibility relation *IND*(*B*) are called definable by *B*. The set *X* is *B-definable* iff $\underline{B}X=\overline{B}X$. Some subsets (categories) of objects in an information system cannot be expressed exactly by employing available attributes but they can be roughly defined.

The set $\underline{B}X$ is the set of all elements of *U* which can be with certainty classified as elements of *X*, given the knowledge represented by attributes from *B*; $\overline{B}X$ is the set of elements of *U* which can be possibly classified as elements of *X*, employing the knowledge represented by attributes from *B*; set $BN_B(X)$ is the set of elements which can be classified neither to *X* nor to -*X*, given knowledge *B*.

If $X_1,...,X_{r(d)}$ are decision classes of **A** then the set

$$\underline{B}X_1\cup...\cup\underline{B}X_{r(d)}$$

is called the *B-positive region* of **A** and is denoted by $POS_B(d)$.

If $C\subseteq A$ then the set $POS_B(C)$ is defined as $POS_B(d)$ where $d(x)=\{a(x):a\in C\}$ for $x\in U$ is an attribute representing the set *C* of attributes.

If $B,C\in A$, then $B\rightarrow_{A,k} C$ where $k=\frac{|POS_B(C)|}{|U|}$ denotes the *partial dependence* of *C* on *B* [P91].

One can measure the importance of an attribute *a* with respect to the decision *d* [P91] in a given decision table as $|POS_a(d)| / |U|$.

Vagueness of a set (category) is due to the existence of a boundary region. The following qualities of the lower approximation of *X* by *B* in **A** and upper approximation of *X* by *B* in **A** were introduced in [P82]:

$$\underline{\gamma}_B(X)=\frac{|\underline{B}X|}{|U|} \quad \text{and} \quad \overline{\gamma}_B(X)=\frac{|\overline{B}X|}{|U|}$$

Thus, the quality of lower approximation of *X* by *B* in **A** is the ratio of the number of all certainly classified objects by attributes from *B* as being in *X* to the number of all objects in the system. $\underline{\gamma}_B(X)$ is intended to capture the degree of completeness of our knowledge about the set *X*. It is a kind of a relative frequency. The quality of upper approximation of *X* by *B* in A is the ratio of the number of all possibly classified objects by attributes from *B* as being in *X* to the number of all objects in the system. It is also a kind of a relative frequency.

One can also consider another measure of the set vagueness [P94] with respect to a given set *B* of attributes:

$$\alpha_B(X)=\frac{|\underline{B}X|}{|\overline{B}X|}$$

If $\mathbf{A}=(U,A\cup\{d\})$ is a decision table then we define a function $\delta_A(x):U\rightarrow\mathbf{P}(\{1,...,r(d)\})$, called the generalized decision in **A**, by

$$\delta_A(x) = \{i: \exists x' \in U\ x'\ IND(A)\ x \text{ and } d(x)=i\}.$$

A decision table $\mathbf{A}$ is called *consistent* (*deterministic*) if $|\delta_A(x)=1|$ for any $x \in U$, otherwise $\mathbf{A}$ is *inconsistent* (*non-deterministic*). It is easy to see that a decision table $\mathbf{A}$ is consistent iff $POS_A(d)=U$. Moreover, if $\delta_B = \delta_{B'}$ then $POS_B(d)=POS_{B'}(d)$ for any non-empty sets $B,B' \subseteq A$.

A subset B of the set A of attributes of decision table $\mathbf{A} = (U, A \cup \{d\})$ is a relative reduct of $\mathbf{A}$ iff B is a minimal set with the following property: $\delta_B = \delta_A$. The set of all relative reducts in $\mathbf{A}$ is denoted by $RED(\mathbf{A},d)$.

2.4 Rough Membership Functions

Let $\mathbf{A}= (U, A)$ be an information system and let $\emptyset \neq X \in U$. The rough $\mathbf{A}$-*membership function of the set X* [PS93], [PS94] (or *rm-function*, for short) denoted by $\mu_X^{\mathbf{A}}$ is defined as follows :

$$\mu_X^{\mathbf{A}}(x) = \frac{|[x]_A \cap X|}{|[x]_A|} \quad \text{for } x \in U$$

where $[x]_A$ denotes the equivalence class of $IND(A)$ containing x.

2.5 Decision Rules

Now we recall the definition of decision rules. Let $\mathbf{A} = (U,A \cup \{d\})$ be a decision table and let

$$V = \bigcup_{a \in A} V_a \cup V_d$$

The atomic formulas over $B \subseteq A \cup \{d\}$ and V are expressions of the form $a=v$, called *descriptors* over B and V, where $a \in B$ and $v \in V_a$.

The *set* $\mathbf{F}(B,V)$ *of formulas* over B and V is the least set containing all atomic formulas over B and V and closed with respect to the classical propositional connectives $\vee$ (disjunction) and $\wedge$ (conjunction).

Let $\tau \in \mathbf{F}(B,V)$. Then by $\tau_{\mathbf{A}}$ we denote the *meaning* of τ in the decision table $\mathbf{A}$, i.e. the set of all objects in U with property τ, defined inductively as follows:

1. if τ is of the form $a = v$ then $\tau_{\mathbf{A}} = \{x \in U: a(x)=v\}$;
2. $(\tau \wedge \tau')_{\mathbf{A}} = \tau_{\mathbf{A}} \cap \tau'_{\mathbf{A}}$; $(\tau \vee \tau')_{\mathbf{A}} = \tau_{\mathbf{A}} \cup \tau'_{\mathbf{A}}$.

We do not use the negation connective because in the case of information systems the complement of any definable set is expressible in terms of union and intersection.

The set $\mathbf{F}(A,V)$ is called the set of *conditional formulas* of $\mathbf{A}$ and is denoted by $\mathbf{C}(A,V)$.

A *decision rule* of A is any expression of the form

$$\tau \rightarrow d=v \text{ where } \tau \in \mathbf{C}(A,V) \text{ and } v \in V_d .$$

The decision rule $\tau \rightarrow d=v$ for $\mathbf{A}$ is *true* in $\mathbf{A}$ iff $\tau_{\mathbf{A}} \subseteq (d=v)_{\mathbf{A}}$; if $\tau_{\mathbf{A}} = (d=v)_{\mathbf{A}}$ then we say that the rule is $\mathbf{A}$-*exact*. The problems concerning decision rules are discussed in [PS93b], [Sk93a,b,c].

3 Rough Mereology

Rough mereology offers, in a sense, a semantics for a higher level language built for reasoning about complex structures when it is sufficient to deal only with objects and relations of being a part to some degree. In this case we are "free" from the implementation details of this language in a lower level language which is more specific and can be based on set theory. This higher level language is more natural for applications concerning e.g. assembling of complex objects from parts or the specifying and analysing of complex structures.

There are various approaches to measure a degree to which elements belong to a given set. Among them are fuzzy set theory [Z65], rough set theory [P91] and mathematical morphology [GD88]. In many applications we have only a partial information about objects and, as a consequence, we can point only collections of objects rather than separate objects. This is the starting point for rough set theory. In this case for any object x an information Inf(x) is defined as the attribute value vector on x. Inf(x) permits us to define only the class [x] of all objects indiscernible from x by means of the given information Inf(x).

The degree to which x belongs to a given set X is measured by the rough membership function [PS94]. The rough membership function is constant on [x]. This suggests a more natural approach, viz. to take as a primitive notion a function measuring the degree of inclusion of one set in another rather than the degree of a membership of an element in a set. We extract from our definition of the rough membership function some basic properties which seem to characterize such rough inclusion. The rough inclusion can be treated as a family of partial inclusion relations (indexed by degree of inclusion which is the value of the rough inclusion function).

The main goal of this chapter is to extend Lesniewski's mereology [Le16] to rough mereology. The basic primitive notion in mereology is the relation of being a part. We present an approach by which it is possible to work with a family of relations of being a part to some degree. Among them are the relations of being a (full) part in the sense of mereology. An analogy to properties of rough inclusion allows us to specify some natural connections between the relations of being a part in different degrees. This leads to a very natural interpretation of rough mereology and in particular of mereology itself. We outline the basic facts of rough mereology .

Our point of departure is the rough membership function (see Section 2).

We observe that the rough membership function can be lifted to the powerset of the universe U and that this extended function $\mu(X,Y)$ defined as above with the additional proviso that $\mu(\emptyset,\emptyset)=1$ satisfies the following conditions:

(A) $\mu(X,Y) \in [0,1]$

(B) $\mu(X,X)=1$
(C1) $\mu(X,Y)=1 \Rightarrow \mu(Z,Y)\geq\mu(Z,X)$ (monotonicity of μ with respect to the second argument),
(C2) $\mu(X,Y)=1=\mu(Y,X) \Rightarrow \mu(Z,Y) = \mu(Z,X)$ (μ - identity of objects)
(D) there exists X such that: $\forall Y\ \mu(X,Y)=1$ (the existence of null object; cf. Comment 2, below)
(E) for any pair X,Y of objects, the condition:
$\forall Z\neq\emptyset\ [\mu(Z,Y)=1 \Rightarrow \exists T\neq\emptyset\ (\mu(T,Z)=1=\mu(T,X))]$
implies that $\mu(Y,X)=1$ (inference condition for being a part from being a sub-part)
(F) for each collection $\mathcal{U}$ of concepts (i.e. subsets of the universe) there exists X such that:

(i) $\forall Z\neq\emptyset\ [\mu(Z,X)=1 \Rightarrow \exists W\neq\emptyset\ \exists T\in\mathcal{U}\ \mu(W,Z)=\mu(W,T)=\mu(T,X)$

(ii) $\forall Z\ \mu(Z,X)=1$

(iii) $\forall Y\ \mu(X,Y)<1 \Rightarrow$ *non*(Y satisfies (i)-(ii) with X replaced by Y) (existence of an object class for any collection).

Any function $\mu(X,Y)$ satisfying (A)-(F) will be called *rough inclusion*.

Observe also that instead of the above function μ we could use a variant of its variable precision modification [Zi93] $\mu(f, \beta)$ defined as the composition $f_\beta \circ\mu$ where f_β is an increasing function from [0,1] onto [0,1] with $f_\beta(t)=0$ for $t<\beta$ and $f_\beta^{-1}(1)=1$.

In Lesniewski approach the treatment of the part - whole relationship is founded on the notion of a relation of being a part[Le16], [Le27-Le31]. The formal treatment of mereology by Lesniewski underwent some changes in the subsequent revisions, however, the core of the theory exposed in [Le16] may be taken as its fair representation and we adopt it for our purposes. Other formalizations can be found in [Ta29], [Ta35], [Ta37], [Cl81], [Cl85]. A parallel approach, based on the converse relation of 'extending over' was advocated by Whitehead [Wh19] (cf.also [Cl85]). We intend to give an outline of the development of mereology attempted by us for the purpose of working out a metalanguage for describing relationships among representations of objects not accessible to our direct scrutiny and therefore not liable for describetion in the standard language of point set theory.

The starting point is a function $\mu(X,Y)$ on a collection of objects, satisfying postulates (A), (B) and (C). In this way we introduce a family of relations **part**$_\alpha$ of being a part in degree α for any $\alpha\in[0,1]$ defined by X**part**$_\alpha$Y iff $\mu(X,Y)=\alpha$. Hence, we obtain a generalization of Lesniewski's mereology to rough mereology.

We show how to define mereology inside rough mereology. We introduce relations **part** and **ingr** by means of μ satisfying (A)-(C) and we show that these relations satisfy the axioms A1, A2 of the Lesniewski mereology [Le16].

We begin with properties of μ immediate from (A)-(C1) and useful in the sequel.

Lemma 1. $\mu(X,Y)=1$ and $\mu(Y,Z)=1$ imply $\mu(X,Z)=1$.

Lemma 2. $\mu(Y,Z)=1$ and $\mu(Y,X)<1$ imply $\mu(Z,X)<1$.

Lemma 3. $\mu(X,Y)=1$ and $\mu(Z,Y)<1$ imply $\mu(Z,X)<1$.

To begin with, we define the relation **part** (read: is a (proper) part of') by means of the following

Definition 1. We define a relation **part** (cf.[Le16;par.1]) of being a (proper) part of an object by means of:

$$X\,\mathbf{part}\,Y \text{ iff } \mu(X,Y)=1 \wedge \mu(Y,X)<1.$$

Then we have

Proposition 4.

(i) if $X\,\mathbf{part}\,Y$ and $Y\,\mathbf{part}\,Z$, then $X\,\mathbf{part}\,Z$,
(ii) $X\,\mathbf{part}\,X$ for no X.

Proposition 4 shows that our relation **part** satisfies the axioms A1 and A2 of [Le16].

The relation $=_\mu$ of μ-identity defined via

$$X=_\mu Y \text{ iff } \mu(X,Y)=1=\mu(Y,X)$$

turns out to be a **part-congruence** i.e.

Proposition 5.

(i) if $X\,\mathbf{part}\,Y$ and $Y=_\mu Z$, then $X\,\mathbf{part}\,Z$
(ii) if $X=_\mu Y$ and $Y\,\mathbf{part}\,Z$, then $X\,\mathbf{part}\,Z$
(iii) $=_\mu$ is an equivalence relation.

We now are able to define the relation **ingr** of being an *ingredient of an object* (cf. [Le16;par.2]). We let to this end

Definition 2. $X\,\mathbf{ingr}\,Y$ iff either $X\,\mathbf{part}\,Y$ or $X=_\mu Y$.

Then we can prove the following

Proposition 6.
(i) **ingr** is a partial order on objects
(ii) $X\,\mathbf{ingr}\,Y$ iff $\mu(X,Y)=1$.

We will give some comments here.

Comment 1. The principal characteristics of the Lesniewski mereology is its collapsing the set-theoretic hierarchy of set, power set etc. by successive applications of the operation taking as a new object a collection of objects. We show that this can be done by means of the function μ satisfying in addition postulates (E), (F).

Comment 2. Yet another characteristic of the Lesniewski mereology is the absence of the 'null' object i.e. the object which would be an ingredient of every object (cf.[Ta35; p.333, footnote 1]; the existence of such an object would imply the equality of all objects). However, our setting providing us with the reals via the function μ makes it possible to introduce such a null object L by means of a postulate (D) in which as well as in (E), (F) L replaces the empty set $\emptyset$.

By adding this element we can express the existence of empty approximations of objects. Without this element we obtain a pure generalization of Lesniewski's mereology. This is the reason that in conditions (E) and (F) we assume that considered objects are non-null.

The null object L defined by means of (D) has then the following properties.

Proposition 7.

(i) L**ingr**X for every X

(ii) if *non*($X=_{\mu} L$), then *non*(X**ingr**L).

Introducing (D) causes analogous modifications in definitions of a set and a class given by Lesniewski (cf. [Le16; par.4]).

Accordingly, we restrict some of the objects appearing in these definitions to non-null objects. It turns out that this modification permits to obtain all the results proved in [Le16] with proofs that are more concise and transparent.

Let ***m*** be any property of objects. We will write X object ***m*** in case X has the property ***m***.

Definition 3. An object X is a *set of objects* ***m***, X**set*m*** in short, if X satisfies the following condition:

$\forall Z\ (non(Z=_{\mu} L) \wedge \mu(Z,X)=1) \Rightarrow$

$\exists T,W\ (non(T=_{\mu}L) \wedge \mu(T,Z)=1 \wedge \mu(T,W)=1 \wedge \mu(W,X)=1 \wedge W$ object***m***).

Definition 4. An object X is a *class of objects* ***m***, X**class*m*** in short, if *X* satisfies the following:

(i) X**set*m***

(ii) $\mu(Y,X)=1$ for any Y object ***m***

(iii) if $\mu(X,Y)<1$, then Y doesn't satisfy (i)-(ii) with X replaced by Y.

Then we have the following propositions.

Proposition 8. Xclass$\mathfrak{m} \Rightarrow$ **Xset**$\mathfrak{m}$.

Proposition 9. Xclass(ingrX).

Proposition 10. Lset$\mathfrak{m}$.

Proposition 11. Xclass(X).

Proposition 12. X object $\mathfrak{m} \Rightarrow$**Xset**$\mathfrak{m}$.

Proposition 13. **Xset**$\mathfrak{m} \wedge \mathfrak{m} \Rightarrow \mathfrak{n} \Rightarrow$**Xset**$\mathfrak{n}$

Proposition 14. **Xclass(set**$\mathfrak{m}$**)** $\Rightarrow$**Xclass**$\mathfrak{m}$.

Proposition 15. **Xset(set**$\mathfrak{m}$**)**$\Rightarrow$**Xset**$\mathfrak{m}$.

Proposition 16.

(i) **Xclass**$\mathfrak{m} \Leftrightarrow$ **Xclass(set**$\mathfrak{m}$**)**

(ii) **Xset**$\mathfrak{m} \Leftrightarrow$**Xset(set**$\mathfrak{m}$**)**.

The notions of an element and a subset are introduced in a standard way viz.

Definition 5. An object X is *an element* of an object Y if there exists $\mathfrak{m}$ such that (i) X object $\mathfrak{m}$ and (ii) Y**class**$\mathfrak{m}$.

Definition 6. An object X is *a subset* of an object Y if the following condition holds: for any Z, if **ZingrX**, then **ZingrY**.
We will write XelY in case X is an element of Y and **Xsub**Y in case X is a subset of Y.

Proposition 17. XelY $\Leftrightarrow$ **Xingr**Y.

Proposition 18. **Xsub**Y $\Leftrightarrow$**Xingr**Y.

Proposition 19. XelY $\Leftrightarrow$**Xsub**Y.

Proposition 20.
(i) **Xclass(elX)**

(ii) X**class**(**sub**X).

The notion of a proper subset is introduced via

Definition 7. An object X is *a proper subset* of an object Y if X**sub**Y and *non*(X=Y). We will write X**psub**Y in case X is a proper subset of Y.

Proposition 21. X**psub**Y ⇔ X**part**Y.

The disjointness of objects is expressed by means of the notion of *an object exterior* to an object. Let objects X, Y be given.

Definition 8. X is *exterior* to Y if the following condition holds:
non(∃Z *non*($Z=_{\mu}L$) ∧ Z**ingr**X ∧Z**ingr**Y).

We will write X**ext**Y in case X is exterior to Y.

Proposition 22. L**ext**X for any X.

Proposition 23. X**ingr**Y ∧ X**ext**Y ⇒$X=_{\mu}$ L.

Proposition 24. *non*($X=_{\mu}L$) ⇒ *non*(X**ext**X).

Proposition 25. X**ext**Y⇒Y**ext**X.

Proposition 26. Z**ingr**Y ∧ Y**ext**X⇒Z**ext**X.

Assume that X**sub**Y. We define an object $\mathbf{com}_Y$ X, the complement of X relative to Y as follows.

Definition 9. An object Z is the *complement* of an object X relative to an object Y if the following conditions hold:
(i) X**sub**Y
(ii) Z**class**m where m is satisfied by an object T if and only if T**sub**Y ∧ T**ext**X.

Observe that $Z=_{\mu}\mathbf{com}_Y X$ is defined uniquely.

Proposition 27. $L=_{\mu}\mathbf{com}_X$ X.

Proposition 28. X**part**Y⇒ *non*($\mathbf{com}_Y X=_{\mu}L$).

Proposition 29. **com**$_Y$X**ingr**Y.

Proposition 30. **com**$_Y$X**ext**X.

The notions of an element and a subset in mereology turn out to be redundant since they are equivalent to the notion of an ingredient (cf. [Le16; par.6, par.10]).

It was noticed (cf. [Ta29, l.c.]) that classical mereology of Lesniewski and complete Boolean algebras are such that removing the null element from a model of complete Boolean algebra produces a model for mereology while adding the null element to a model of mereology results in a model of complete Boolean algebra. Our modified approach permits us to introduce the structure of a Boolean algebra into the collection of objects on which our μ is acting. We define Boolean operations of complement (.) , the join **add**, and the meet **int** in a standard way (cf. [Cl81]) going back to Tarski [Ta37] .

Definition 10. $X^c =_\mu$ **class**$\mathcal{m}$ where $\mathcal{m}$ is the property which is satisfied by an object T if and only if: *non*(∃Z *non*($Z=_\mu L$) ∧ Z**ingr**T ∧ Z**ingr**X).

Proposition 31. $X =_\mu X^{cc}$.

Definition 11. For objects X, Y we let: X**add**Y$=_\mu$ **class**$\mathcal{m}$ where $\mathcal{m}$ is the property that is satisfied by an object T if and only if: either T**ingr**X or T**ingr**Y.

Proposition 32. X**add**Y$=_\mu$Y**add**X.

Proposition 33. (X**add**Y)**add**Z$=_\mu$ X**add**(Y**add**Z).

Proposition 34. X**add**X$=_\mu$X.

Proposition 35. X**add**L$=_\mu$X.

We introduce a new object Ω (the universe).

Definition 12. $\Omega =_\mu L^c$.

Proposition 36. X**add**$X^c =_\mu \Omega$.

Yet another binary operation is **int** introduced as follows.

Definition 13. For objects X, Y , we let: X**int**Y= **class**$\mathcal{m}_\wedge$ where $\mathcal{m}_\wedge$ is the property that is satisfied by an object T if and only if: T**ingr**X and T**ingr**Y.

Proposition 37. $X\mathbf{int}Y =_{\mu} Y\mathbf{int}X$.

Proposition 38. $(X\mathbf{int}Y)\mathbf{int}Z =_{\mu} X\mathbf{int}(Y\mathbf{int}Z)$.

Proposition 39. $X\mathbf{int}X =_{\mu} X$.

Proposition 40. $X\mathbf{int}X^{c} =_{\mu} L$.

Proposition 41. $X\mathbf{int}\Omega =_{\mu} X$.

Proposition 42. $(X\mathbf{add}Y)^{c} =_{\mu} X^{c}\,\mathbf{int}Y^{c}$.

Proposition 43. $(X\mathbf{int}Y)^{c} =_{\mu} X^{c}\mathbf{add}Y^{c}$.

We conclude with further properties that relate **add** and **int.**

Proposition 44. $X\mathbf{int}(Y\mathbf{add}Z) =_{\mu} (X\mathbf{int}Y)\mathbf{add}(X\mathbf{int}Z)$.

Proposition 45. $X\mathbf{add}(Y\mathbf{int}Z) =_{\mu} (X\mathbf{add}Y)\mathbf{int}(X\mathbf{add}Z)$.

Proposition 46. $X\mathbf{int}(X\mathbf{add}Y) =_{\mu} X$.

Proposition 47. $X\mathbf{add}(X\mathbf{int}Y) =_{\mu} X$.

Operations $(.)^{c}$, **add**, **int** introduce into collection of all objects a structure of a Boolean algebra. (see Propositions 31-47).

Let us register the following properties of **add** and **int**.

Proposition 48.
(i) $X\mathbf{ingr}X\mathbf{add}Y$
(ii) $X\mathbf{int}Y\mathbf{ingr}X$.

The function μ has the following properties with respect to **add** and **int**.

Proposition 49.
(i) $\mu(Z, X\mathbf{add}Y) \geq \max[\mu(Z,X), \mu(Z,Y)]$
(ii) $\mu(Z, X\mathbf{int}Y) \leq \min[\mu(Z,X), \mu(Z,Y)]$.

Let us comment briefly on Proposition 49: the results (i) and (ii) show that the function μ is bounded on Boolean joins and meets by functionals *min* and *max* as it is the case with triangular norms and co-norms used in the fuzzy set theory

The propositions listed above show that rough mereology includes Lesniewski's mereology in the following sense: any model of rough mereology contains a model of Lesniewski's mereology (obtained by removing the null object and restricting the rough mereological hierarchy of relations of being a part in some degree to the relation of being a (proper) part).

Our current work in this field is directed towards a theory of relations of being a part in degree < 1.

3.1 Rough Mereological Controllers

The main application of rough mereology that is presented here is the principle of a rough mereological controller. An example where a rough mereological controller serves the purpose of quality control is given in [PoSk94a], [SkPo94].

We will call a *rough mereological connective* any mapping $\mathcal{F}:[0,1]^2 \to [0,1]$ such that

(i) $\mathcal{F}(x,y) = \mathcal{F}(y,x)$;

(ii) $\mathcal{F}$ is increasing with respect to both coordinates, i.e. $x \le x' \Rightarrow F(x,y) \le F(x',y)$ and $y \le y' \Rightarrow F(x,y) \le F(x,y')$.

Given a rough mereological connective $\mathcal{F}(x,y)$, and a rough inclusion μ, we define the function E(X,Y) of *rough mereological closeness* by

$$E(X,Y) = \mathcal{F}(\mu(X,Y), \mu(Y,X)).$$

For any $\alpha \in (0,1)$, the relation τ_α : $X\tau_\alpha Y$ iff $E(X,Y) > \alpha$ is a tolerance relation; choosing τ_α amounts to considering objects which are their mutual parts in some satisfactory degree.

The synthesis of complex objects falls into the province of cooperative product development [SLF91]. The basic aspects are: the spatial aspect (organizing process steps into a hierarchy), the communication aspect (negotiation among nodes, conflict resolution, sending assemblies and information about assemblies), the quality aspect i.e. assigning the quality value to final assemblies which will agree with quality value determined by a posteriori testing.

We will apply rough mereological tools to the problem of quality control.

To this end we define a system of cooperating intelligent agents acting as a *rough mereological controller.* It transforms an input (a semantic constraint (specification) which may be expressed in a natural language) into an output being the final assembly and its quality value.

By a *rough mereological controller* we mean a system of intelligent cooperating agents organized according to the following principles.

1. The agents are attached to the nodes of a tree which is a scheme of the assembly process organization. Any agent is provided by the designer with an information system. Indiscernibility classes of the system are represented by pattern assemblies. The root agent is provided with a decision system whose decision attribute **Q** represents the quality. The leaf agents have an access to the inventory subsets and are given a strategy for computing values of the so called *initial rough inclusion* μ^0 from their information systems. Any non-leaf agent a is given a set S_a of *assembling procedures*, a set C_a of rough mereological connectives and a mapping $\Phi_a : S_a \to C_a$.

2. The *root agent* receives an input which is a semantic constraint (specification) on the final assembly expressed as a formula in the variables representing conditional attributes of the root agent (or in natural language descriptors of these attributes). The root agent decomposes this input into a constraint sent to its children.
3. *The top-down communication* consists in decomposing the input constraint at each agent into constraints for its children nodes.
4. Any *leaf agent a* satisfies its constraint by selecting a part X from the inventory satisfying the constraint. The agent a applies rough mereology by covering the space of information vectors $INF(X)$ of inputs by information vectors of its patterns i.e. by vectors of the form $INF(Y_i)$ for pattern objects Y_i . Choosing a part X it calculates from the initial rough inclusion μ^0 the vector $[E(X,Y_1),..,E(X,Y_k)]$ of rough mereological distances from X to its pattern parts

$$Y_1,...,Y_k.$$

5. The *horizontal communication* consists of children nodes of a given parent node *negotiating* their constraints by means of some strategy and finding a *conflict resolution* i.e. an assignment of a constraint to any of them.
6. The *bottom-up communication* consists in any child a sending to the parental node the object X assembled at a along with the vector $[E(X,Y_1)..,E(X,Y_k)]$ of rough mereological distances from the assembly X to the pattern assemblies at a..
7. Any *parent agent a* selects a procedure $\circ$ from S_a, applies $\circ$ to objects $X_1, X_2, ..., X_n$ sent by its children to assembly $X=\circ(X_1,X_2,...,X_n)$ and applies $\Phi_a(\circ)$ to vectors $[E(X_i, Y_1^i),...,E(X_i, Y_{k_i}^i)]$ sent by children to calculate the vector $[E(X,Y_1),...,E(X,Y_k)]$ where Y_i are pattern assemblies at a.
8. The *root agent* performs Step 7 assembling a final product X and calculating the vector $[E(X,Y_1),...,E(X,Y_k)]$ and applies some best-fit strategy to this vector in order to to find a pattern Y_i^* best-fitting X. Then it outputs the pair $(X, \mathbf{Q}(Y_i^*))$.

Let us stress the main points of this approach.

a) The rule structure of a rough controller is twofold:
   i) the *deep structure* of the controller is expressed in terms of semantic relations among information systems of an agent and its children: it may be expressed either as natural language expressions relating conditional attributes of the agent to conditional attributes of its children or as true formulae in variables of conditional attributes of the agent and its children
   ii) the *surface structure* of the controller is expressed by rules of selecting $\Phi_a(\circ)$ and of propagating rough mereological closeness E from the children of an agent to the agent.

b) *Quantization of fuzzy variables* in a fuzzy controller into a number of points corresponding to elements of universe of discourse has its counterpart in rough controller by covering the space of information vectors of primitive inputs at each leaf agent by a family of information vector patterns. Choosing a strategy for μ^0 permits to calculate the relative mereological distance of the given input from pattern inputs and gives a numerical characteristic of the input.

c) The *fuzzification process* known for fuzzy controllers [MA75] is realized here as a sequence of steps providing the decomposition of the input into primitive inputs for leaf agents in terms of their primitive attributes and assignment of values of initial rough inclusion μ^0.

d) *Local deep control rules* of a rough controller are of the form:

(ρ_{oa}) **if** *a semantic specification (constraint)* χ *is received by an agent a* **then** *a list* $[\chi_1\chi_2 \ldots \chi_k]$ *of semantic specifications (constraints) for children of a is issued;*

e) *Local surface control rules* of a rough controller are of the form:

(σ_{oa}) **if** (Y, τ_α) **then** *a list* $[\chi_1\chi_2 \ldots \chi_k]$ *of semantic specifications (constraints) for children of a is issued;*

f) *Global deep structure control rules* of a rough controller are of the form:

(γ) **if** *a semantic specification (constraint)* χ *is received at the root agent a* **then** *a issues the output* $(X, \mathbf{Q}(Y_i^*))$;

g) *Global surface structure control rules* of a rough controller are of the form:

(η) **if** (Y, τ_α) **then** $(X, \mathbf{Q}(Y_i^*))$;

h) *The defuzzification process* is realized by *propagation of rough mereological closeness* by algorithms based on functions Φ_a. These algorithms are the rough counterpart of defuzzification in fuzzy controllers.

We can apply rough mereological controllers [PoSk94a], [SkPo94] to the task of quality control: the main problem of quality control is to assign the quality value to a final assembly issued by the root agent which is determined by a posteriori testing of the final assembly. When the initial rough inclusions are properly learned and the process of propagation of rough mereological closeness is properly learned we can hope that the quality assigned a priori and the quality determined a posteriori are in agreement.

4 Analytic Morphology

4.1 Mathematical Morphology

In this section we present some basic ideas of mathematical morphology and its higher-level abstraction called analytical morphology [SP94] which serves the purpose of data filtration in decision tables e.g. as a preprocessing stage [PoSk94b].

Mathematical morphology was motivated by practical purposes: it originated in the works of Matheron on predicting permeability of porous media from their geometric properties and of Serra on petrography of iron ores in the context of their milling properties. In this early stages basic mathematical theory of morphology was developed and summed up in monographs [Ma75], [Se82].

The ideas of mathematical morphology have been assimilated and further developed by image and signal processing communities (see [St86], [GD88]). As a result the mathematical morphology has been extended to grayscale objects and signals. Mathematical morphology is an actively developing discipline with main stream of research directed towards new efficient algorithms [Bl92a,b], analysis of complex filters [SoD90], and analysis of theoretical foundations of morphology [HR90], [RH91].

Mathematical morphology concerns the problems of geometrical filtering of objects. It describes the unknown structure of an object in terms of an algebra $\mathbf{R}$ of relations among objects (considered as sets of elements or points) and their elements generated by two primitive relations of set inclusion and set intersection. A verification whether a given relation from $\mathbf{R}$ is fulfilled is achieved by means of a model pattern called a structuring object. Moving a structuring object about an object X generates the object $\phi(X)$ of elements satisfying this relation with respect to X. The operation ϕ is a *morphological operation*. The aim of ϕ is to reveal a certain texture of X that permits us to characterize X in terms of some qualitative attributes (area, perimeter, number of connected components etc...).

4.2 The Binary Case

We begin with the binary case, i.e. our objects will be subsets of either a Euclidean or a digital space $\mathcal{E}$.

Let us assume that B is a given subset of $\mathcal{E}$ called a *structuring object*. We denote the vector addition in $\mathcal{E}$ by +. Morphological operations are defined by means of two set operations on subsets of $\mathcal{E}$ called the *Minkowski sum* and the *Minkowski difference*. For the sake of simplicity, in presenting morphological operations we assume from now on that the set B is symmetric i.e. B= -B.

The Minkowski sum $\oplus$ is defined for subsets A, $B \subseteq \mathcal{E}$ by

$$A \oplus B = \{x + y: x \in A \text{ and } y \in B\}$$

and the Minkowski difference Θ is defined for A, $B \subseteq \mathcal{E}$ by

$$A \Theta B = \{x \in \mathcal{E}: \{x\} \oplus B \subseteq A\}.$$

The Minkowski sum and the Minkowski difference operations are employed in the definitions of two basic morphological operations viz. the dilation by B and the erosion by B.

The *dilation of* $X \subseteq \mathcal{E}$ by B, denoted by $d_B(X)$ is defined by

$$d_B(X) = X \oplus B$$

the *erosion* of X by B, denoted by $e_B(X)$ is defined by

$$e_B(X) = X \Theta B.$$

Morphological operations can be composed and new operations can be generated by means of set-theoretical operations (see [Se82]). The body of operations produced from erosions and dilations is the *morphological algebra of operations*.

In particular, the composition: the erosion by B followed by the dilation by B is *the opening by* B, denoted by o_B, and the composition: the dilation by B followed by the erosion by B is *the closing by* B, denoted by c_B.

Formally

$$o_B(X) = d_B {}^\circ e_B(X)$$

and

$$c_B(X) = e_B {}^\circ d_B(X) \text{ for any } X \subseteq \mathcal{E}.$$

The meaning of the opening by B and the closing by B can be best understood from the following characterizations (see [Ma75] or [Se82]).

Proposition 1.

(i) $o_B(X) = \{x\in\mathcal{E}: \exists y(x\in\{y\}\oplus B\subseteq X)\}$

(ii) $c_B(X) = \{x\in E: \forall y(x\in\{y\}\oplus B\Rightarrow(\{y\}\oplus B)\cap X\neq\emptyset)\}$.

Let us observe the parallelism between the description of X provided by the opening of *X* by B and the closing of *X* by B and the description of X provided by the B-lower and the B-upper approximations of X in the rough set theory (see Section 2).

The operations in the binary case based on the additive structure of $\mathcal{E}$ and set theoretical notions of inclusion and intersection have been extended for needs of image and signal processing to grayscale and signal morphology, respectively (see [St86], [Ha87], [GD88]). In what follows we present the most essential points of grayscale morphology.

4.3 The Grayscale Case

The objects of grayscale morphology are functions, representing, e.g. grayscale visual objects or signals.

An object F is a function $F: A\rightarrow\mathcal{E}$ where $A\subseteq E^n$ for some *n*. The operations of mathematical morphology are performed indirectly on functions by means of associated objects called *umbrae*.

A subset $X\subseteq E^n\times E$ is called an *umbra* if the following holds:

$$(x,y)\in X \wedge z\leq y \Rightarrow (x,z)\in X.$$

For a function $F:A\rightarrow\mathcal{E}$, the *umbra of* F, denoted by U[F] is the set

$$\{(x,y)\in A\times\mathcal{E}: y\leq F(x)\}.$$

The objects are recovered from operations on umbrae by means of the envelope operation. Suppose that X is an umbra. The *envelope of* X, denoted by E(X), is defined as follows

$$E(X)(x) = \sup\{y\in\mathcal{E}:(x,y)\in X\} \text{ for } x\in\mathcal{E}^n.$$

Let $F:A\rightarrow\mathcal{E}$ be an object and $K:C\rightarrow\mathcal{E}$ be a fixed object called a *structuring object*. We denote by $\oplus$, Θ, the Minkowski sum and the Minkowski difference operators, respectively, induced by the vector addition + in the space $\mathcal{E}^{n+1}$. The operations of *dilation by* K, denoted by d_K and of *erosion by* K, denoted by e_K, are defined on F by

$$d_K(F) = E(U[F]\oplus U[K])$$

$$e_K(F) = E(U[F]\Theta U[K])$$

The morphological algebra is defined in the grayscale case in the manner analogous to the case of binary morphology. In particular, the *opening by* K, denoted by o_K, and the *closing by* K, denoted by c_K are defined as

$$c_K(F) = E(c_{U[K]}(U[F]))$$

$$o_K(F) = E(o_{U[K]}(U[F]))$$

It will be convenient for our purposes to present the above operations in binary as well as grayscale case in an analytical form.

We will represent morphological operations in an analytical form, i.e. as operations on vector representations of objects.

4.4 Analytical Formulae - the Binary Case

We will represent binary objects $X \subseteq \mathcal{E}$ as binary vectors of the form

$$v = \langle v_x : x \in \mathcal{E} \rangle \text{ (where } v_x = 1 \text{ iff } x \in X \text{ i.e. } X = \{x: v_x = 1\}).$$

The functions $\mathcal{D}$, $\mathcal{E}$, O and C on $Z_2^{\mathcal{E}}$ into $Z_2^{\mathcal{E}}$ which represent the dilation by B, the erosion by B, the opening by B, and the closing by B, respectively, for any symmetric structuring object B are defined as follows

(i) $\mathcal{D}(v) = v'$ where $v'_x = \max\{v_y : x \in \{y\} \oplus B\}$

(ii) $\mathcal{E}(v) = v'$ where $v'_x = \min\ \{v_y : y \in \{x\} \oplus B\}$

(iii) $O(v) = v'$ where $v'_x = \max\{\min\{v_z : z \in \{y\} \oplus B\} : x \in \{y\} \oplus B\}$

(iv) $C(v) = v'$ where $v'_x = \min\ \{\max\{v_z : y \in \{z\} \oplus B\} : y \in \{x\} \oplus B\}$.

For a subset $X \in \mathcal{E}$, let $v^X \in Z_2^{\mathcal{E}}$ denote the binary vector defined by setting

$$\left(v^X\right)_x = \begin{cases} 1 & \text{if } x \in X \\ 0 & \text{otherwise} \end{cases}$$

and given a binary vector $v \in Z_2^{\mathcal{E}}$, we denote by supp(v), and call the *support of* v, the subset $\{x \in \mathcal{E}: v_X = 1\} \subseteq \mathcal{E}$. Then we have

Proposition 2. (**[SP94]**) The functions $\mathcal{D}$, $\mathcal{E}$ defined by (i), (ii) above represent binary morphological operations of dilation and erosion, respectively, viz.

(i) $\text{supp}(\mathcal{D}(v)) = d_B(X)$

(ii) $\text{supp}(\mathcal{E}(v)) = e_B(X)$ for any subset $X \subseteq \mathcal{E}$.

We call x a *centre* of $\{x\} \oplus B$ and we call the set $\{x\} \oplus B$ the *influence set of* x. Let us observe the following:

a. The operations $\mathcal{D}$ and $\mathcal{E}$ can be regarded as analytical representations of some strategies for negotiating among conflicting influences on x of centers of influence sets containing x and among conflicting influences on x of elements of the influence set of x, respectively.

b. Similarly, the operations O and C can be regarded as analytical representations of some strategies for expressing a common influence on an element x of influence sets containing x (first we erode $\{y\} \oplus B$ to y for $x \in \{y\} \oplus B$ next we dilate these y's to x) and of influence sets intersecting the influence set of x, respectively (first we dilate centers of influence sets $\{z\} \oplus B$ containing y to y for $y \in \{x\} \oplus B$ next we erode $\{x\} \oplus B$ to x).

4.5 Analytical Formulae - the Grayscale Case

Given $x \in \mathcal{E}^n$, we let $V_x = E \cup \{-\infty\}$. Selecting $v_x \in V_x$ for each x defines a function $F: A \to \mathcal{E}$ where $A = \{x \in E^n: v_x \neq -\infty\}$ and $F(x) = v_x$ for $x \in A$. Therefore, we can represent morphological grayscale objects by means of vectors $v = \langle v_x: x \in \mathcal{E}^n \rangle$.

Let $K: C \to \mathcal{E}$ be a fixed structuring object. The vector representation of K will be denoted by $v^* = \langle v_x^*: x \in \mathcal{E}^n \rangle$.

Analytical operations $\mathcal{D}$, $\mathcal{E}$, O and C which represent grayscale morphological operations of the dilation by K, the erosion by K, the opening by K, and the closing by K, respectively, are functions on $(\mathcal{E} \cup \{-\infty\})^{\mathcal{E}^n}$ into $(\mathcal{E} \cup \{-\infty\})^{\mathcal{E}^n}$ given by the following

(i) $\mathcal{D}(v) = v'$ where $v'_x = sup\{v_{x-z} + v_z^*: z \in C\}$

(ii) $\mathcal{E}(v) = v'$ where $v'_x = inf\{v_{x+z} - v_z^*: z \in C\}$

(iii) $O(v) = v'$ where $v' = sup\{inf\{v_{x-z'+z} - v_z^* : z \in C\} + v_z^* : z' \in C\}$

(iv) $C(v) = v'$ where $v' = inf\{sup\{v_{x-z+z'} + v_z^*: z \in C\} - v_z^* : z' \in C\}$.

Given a grayscale object $F: A \to \mathcal{E}$ where $A \subseteq \mathcal{E}^n$, we denote by v^F the vector in $(\mathcal{E} \cup \{-\infty\})^{\mathcal{E}^n}$ defined by setting

$$(v^X)_x = \begin{cases} 1 & if\ x \in X \\ 0 & otherwise \end{cases}$$

and given a vector $v \in (\mathcal{E} \cup \{-\infty\})^{\mathcal{E}^n}$, we denote by supp(v), and call the *support of* v, the subset $F \subseteq \mathcal{E}^n * \mathcal{E}$ defined by

$$(x,y) \in F \text{ if and only if } v_x \neq -\infty \text{ and } y = v_x.$$

Then we have

Proposition 3. (**[SP94]**) The functions $\mathcal{D}$, $\mathcal{E}$ defined by (i), (ii) above represent the grayscale morphological operations of dilation, respectively, erosion, by the structuring element $K: C \to \mathcal{E}$ viz.

(i) $supp(\mathcal{D}(v^F)) = d_K(F)$

(ii) $supp(\mathcal{E}(v^F)) = e_K(F)$.

Let us recall the remarks above and observe that the formulas (i) - (iv) can be regarded as analytical representations of strategies for negotiating among conflicting influences at a point of distinct translates of K.

Let us conclude the last two subsections with the observation that morphological operations regarded as strategies of conflict negotiations among disagreeing influences of elements as well as sets of objects, fall into one of the two following categories:

a. strategies which negotiate among conflicting influences of elements (dilations, erosions...);

b. strategies which delineate the area of influence (openings, closings ...).

In the following Section, we will formulate an abstract version of morphology called *analytical morphology* and apply it to some problems related to data filtration in decision tables

4.6 Analytical Morphology

Let k be a real number from the interval (0,1]. Let $\mathbf{A}=(U, A\cup\{d\})$ be a decision table and let τ be a formula over A and V. If $\alpha=\{(a_1,v_1),\dots,(a_m,v_m)\}$ then $\wedge\alpha$ denotes the formula $a_1 =v_1\wedge\dots\wedge a_m=v_m$. If τ is a formula over $\mathbf{A}$ and V then by $\mathbf{A}_\tau$ we denote the restriction of $\mathbf{A}$ to the set of all objects from U satisfying τ, i.e. $\mathbf{A}_\tau = (\tau_A, A\cup\{d\})$. By $T(\mathbf{A},\tau,k)$ we denote the conjunction of the following conditions:

(i) $\tau_A\neq\emptyset$

(ii) for any $\alpha\in INF(A_\tau)$:

(*) $\max_i \mu_i(\mathbf{A}, \wedge\alpha\wedge\tau)>k$

and

(**) there exists exactly one i_o with the following property:

$\mu_{i_0}(\mathbf{A}, \wedge\alpha\wedge\tau)= \max_i \mu_i(\mathbf{A}, \wedge\alpha\wedge\tau)$.

Conditions (*) and (**) say that exactly one of distribution coefficients $\mu_i(\mathbf{A},\tau)$ $(i\in\theta)$ exceeds the threshold k .

For any decision table $\mathbf{A}=(U, A\cup\{d\})$, formula τ over A and V, and a threshold k satisfying the condition $T(\mathbf{A},\tau,k)$ one can define *a τ-approximation function in $\mathbf{A}$ with threshold k*

$$F(\mathbf{A},\tau,k) : INF(A\ )\,|\,B \rightarrow INF(\{d\},\tau_A,V)$$

by $F(\mathbf{A},\tau,k)(\alpha)=\{(u,i_0): u\in\tau_A\}$ for any $\alpha\in INF(\mathbf{A}_\tau)\,|\,B$, where

$$\mu_{i_0}(\mathbf{A}, \wedge\alpha\wedge\tau) = \max \{ \mu_i(\mathbf{A}, \wedge\alpha\wedge\tau): i\in\theta_\tau \}$$

and B is the set of conditions occurring in τ.

In the sequel we consider $F(\mathbf{A},\tau,k)$ as a function from $INF(\mathbf{A}_\tau)\,|\,B$ into $INF(\{d\},V)$ assuming additionally that if $F(\mathbf{A},\tau,k) =f$ then $f(\alpha)(u)=d(u)$ if $u\notin\tau_A$.

We apply the above construction to decision tables derived from a given decision table $\mathbf{A}=(U, A\cup\{d\})$. These decision tables are of the form $\mathbf{B}=(U, B \cup\{c\})$ and they are constructed from information systems $\mathbf{B}=(U, B\cup C)$, where B, $C\subseteq A$ and $B\cap C=\emptyset$ by representing C by means of one decision attribute c. By $code_C$ (or, $code$, in short) we denote a fixed coding function for information vectors restricted to C in V_c and we define c by $c(u)=code_C$ $(\{(a, a(u)): a\in C\})$ for any $u\in U$. For a given threshold k we consider decision tables of the form $\mathbf{B}=(U, B \cup\{c\})$ with the property that there exists a formula τ over B and V such that $T(\mathbf{B},\tau,k)$ holds. These tables correspond to near-to-functional relations of data represented in $\mathbf{A}$ which means that only one decision is pointed out with the strength exceeding the threshold k. Let us observe that by assumption we have $INF(\mathbf{B}_\tau)\,|\,B = INF(\mathbf{A}_\tau)\,|\,B$.

Let l be a positive integer called the *critical level of examples*. We denote by

F($\mathbf{A}$,k,l) the family of all functions of the form $F(\mathbf{B},\tau,k)$ such that T($\mathbf{B}$,τ,k) holds and $\max_i n(\mathbf{B},\tau,i) > l$. By F($\mathbf{A}$,$l$) (or, F($\mathbf{A}$), in short) we denote the union of the family $\{F(\mathbf{A},k,l): 0<k\leq l\}$.

Let us observe that, given the decision table $\mathbf{A}=(U,A\cup\{d\})$ with $A=\{a_1,...,a_m\}$, the function $F(\mathbf{B},\tau,k)$ produces a new decision table $\mathbf{A}'=(U,A'\cup\{d\})$ with $\mathbf{A}'=\{a_1',...,a_m'\}$ defined by $\{(c, code_C\{(a_i', a_i'(u)): a_i \in C\})\} = F(\mathbf{B},\tau,k)(INF_B^{\mathbf{A}}(u))$ and $a_i'(u)=a_i(u)$ when $a\notin C$, for any $u\in\tau_B$; if $u\in U - \tau_B$ then $a_i'(u)=a_i(u)$ for any i.

The definition of an approximation function presented here can be treated as one of the possible formalizations of near-to-functional relations between data. Such an approximation function could choose the mean value from the set of values exceeding a given threshold. We plan to test the properties of different notions of approximation functions on various data tables from the point of view of application to data filtering.

4.7 Analytical Morphology for Decision Tables

Let $\mathbf{A}=(U, A\cup\{d\})$ be a decision table. *An object of analytical morphology for* $\mathbf{A}$ is any non-empty subset x of $INF(C, U_0, V)$ where $C\subseteq A$, $\emptyset \neq U_0 \in U$ such that if f_C, $f_C' \in x$ for some $c\in C$ then $f_C(u)=f_C'(u)$ for any $u\in U$. The sets C, U_0 are called the *attribute domain* and the *object domain* of x.

A structuring object $S_{\mathcal{F}}$ is defined by a given family $\mathcal{F}$ of approximation functions in the following way:

$$S_{\mathcal{F}} = \{S_{F(\mathbf{B},\tau,k)} : F(\mathbf{B},\tau,k)\in\mathcal{F}\} \text{ where } S_{F(\mathbf{B},\tau,k)}=\{\alpha\cup\{(d,i_0)\}: \alpha\in INF(\mathbf{A}_\tau)\,|\,B \text{ and } F(\mathbf{B},\tau,k)(\alpha) \text{ is a constant function on } \tau_A \text{ taking the value } i_0\}.$$

The influence set S(x) for a given $x\subseteq INF(C, U_0, V)$ is equal to

$$\{S_{F(\mathbf{B},\tau,k)}: F(\mathbf{B},\tau,k):INF(\mathbf{A}_\tau)\,|\,B \rightarrow INF(C',V) \text{ where } C\cap C'\neq\emptyset \text{ and } U_0\cap\tau_A\neq\emptyset\}$$

One can consider any approximation function

$$F(\mathbf{B},\tau,k):INF(\mathbf{A}_\tau)\,|\,B \rightarrow INF(C,V)$$

as a partial function from $INF(B,V)$ into $INF(C,V)$ with the domain $INF(\mathbf{A}_\tau)\,|\,B$ on which the partial function equals to $F(\mathbf{B},\tau,k)$. We assume that $V_x=INF(C,V)$ if $x\subseteq INF(C, U_0, V)$.

For the family $\mathcal{F}$ we define the sets $\mathcal{N}(x)$ and $\mathcal{M}(x)$ where

$$\mathcal{N}(x)=\{B\subseteq A : \exists F(\mathbf{A},\tau,k)\in\mathcal{F}\ \ (F(\mathbf{A},\tau,k):INF(\mathbf{A}_\tau)\,|\,B \rightarrow INF(C',V), C\cap C'\neq\emptyset \text{ and } U_0\cap\tau_A'\neq\emptyset\}$$

$$\mathcal{M}(x)=\{B\subseteq A: \exists F(\mathbf{A},\tau,k)\in\mathcal{F}\ (F(\mathbf{A},\tau,k):INF(\mathbf{A}_\tau)\,|\,B'\rightarrow INF(C',V), B\cap C'\neq\emptyset \text{ and } C=B'\cup C'\}$$

If F: $INF(\mathbf{A}_\tau)\,|\,B\rightarrow INF(C',V)$ then (B,C') is treated as a component of the influence set S(x) of x if $C\cap C'\neq\emptyset$. The set $\mathcal{N}(x)$ corresponds to all the first elements of such components. The set $\mathcal{N}(x)$ contains all subsets of attributes which can influence x.

$\mathcal{M}$(x) corresponds to all the objects influenced by some approximation functions generated within C.

For each $x \in \mathcal{Ob}_A$ the erosion at x, denoted by e_x is a mapping

$$e_x: Z \rightarrow V_X$$

where

$$Z = \{(\alpha_B) \in \Pi \{ INF(\mathbf{A}) | B: B \in \mathcal{N}(x)\}: \exists \alpha' \in INF(\mathbf{A} | U_0) \cup \{\alpha_B: B \in \mathcal{N}(x)\} \subseteq \alpha'\}.$$

One can observe that, given the decision table $\mathbf{A}$, any erosion at $x \in \mathcal{Ob}_A$ produces a new decision table $\mathbf{A}'$ obtained by replacing x in $\mathbf{A}$ by the result of e_x on corresponding information vectors. We say that the erosion e_x is *$\mathbf{A}$-correct* if $\mathbf{A}'$ is a δ-filtration of A for some $\delta<1$. The erosion is defined by choosing a strategy for conflict resolving among different influences of approximation functions on x. In practical applications we are searching for strategies to synthesize correct erosions.

The *dilation at* $x \in \mathcal{Ob}_A$ denoted by d_x, is a mapping

$$d_x : Z \rightarrow V_X$$

where

$$Z = \{(\alpha_B) \in \Pi \{ INF(\mathbf{A}) | B: B \in \mathcal{M}(x)\}: \exists \alpha' \in INF(\mathbf{A} | U_0) \cup \{\alpha_B: B \in \mathcal{M}(x)\} \subseteq \alpha'\}.$$

One can observe that, given the decision table $\mathbf{A}$, any dilation at $x \in \mathcal{Ob}_A$ produces a new decision table $\mathbf{A}'$ obtained by replacing x in $\mathbf{A}$ by the result of d_x on corresponding information vectors. We say that the dilation e_x is *$\mathbf{A}$-correct* if $\mathbf{A}'$ is δ-filtration of $\mathbf{A}$ for some $\delta<1$. The dilation is defined by choosing a strategy for conflict resolving among influences on x from all objects influenced by some approximation functions generated within C.

Let us present some exemplary ideas about the nature of erosions and dilations. Due to the amorphous structure of data one should not expect that morphological operations will be as regular as in the ordinary binary or grayscale morphology.

Consider $x \in \mathcal{Ob}_A$ and let C and U_0 be the attribute and object domains of x, respectively. We say that $c \in INF(C, U_0, V)$ is *x-stable* in case

$$c \in C' \wedge c \in C'' \Rightarrow F'(Inf_{B'}(u)) = c(u) = F''(Inf_{B''}(u))$$

for any $u \in U_0$ and any pair F', F'' of approximation functions

$$F': INF(\mathbf{A})|B' \rightarrow C',\ F'': INF(\mathbf{A})|B'' \rightarrow C''$$

with $S_{F'}$ and $S_{F''}$ being elements of S(x).

Then we let $s(x) = \{c \in x: c \text{ is x-stable}\}$. The set s(x) is called the *stable region* of x.

Proposition 4. The operation s is

(i) invariant with respect to erosions, i.e. $e_{s(x)}(s(x)) = s(x)$

(ii) anti-extensive, i.e. $s(x) \subseteq x$

(iii) increasing, i.e. $x \subseteq x' \Rightarrow s(x) \subseteq s(x')$.

The operation s is similar to the classical binary morphological erosion [Se82] (see properties (ii), (iii) in Proposition 4). The property (i) in Proposition 4 says that objects which are stable regions are invariant with respect to the higher level analytical erosion.

Consider $x \in \mathcal{O}b_{\mathbf{A}}$ and let C and U_0 be the attribute and object domain of x. We say that $c \in INF(C, U_0, V)$ is x-*co-stable* in case

$$c \in C' \wedge c \in C'' \Rightarrow F'(Inf_{B'}(u)) = c(u) = F''(Inf_{B''}(u))$$

for any $u \in U_0$ and any pair F', F" of approximation functions

$$F': INF(\mathbf{A})|B' \rightarrow C',\ F'': INF(\mathbf{A})|B'' \rightarrow C'' \text{ with } B', B'' \in \mathcal{M}(x).$$

Consider the set $t(x) = \{y \subseteq x\colon y \text{ is x-co-stable}\}$. The set t(x) is called the *co-stable region of* x.

Proposition 5. The operation t is anti-extensive, i.e. $t(x) \subseteq x$.
In general, t is neither invariant with respect to dilations nor increasing.

The compositions $t \circ s$ and $s \circ t$ are analogous to the classical morphological opening and closing operations, receptively. We have

Proposition 6. The operations t and s have the following properties:
(i) $s \circ s = s$
(ii) $t \circ s = s$
(iii) $t \circ s \circ t \circ s = t \circ s$.

In general, $s \circ t$ need not be idempotent. Moreover, the operations d and e generate a dynamical system $(INF(A,V), d, e)$. Strategies searching for correct compositions of d and e will therefore depend on the ergodic properties of the decision table.

In classical mathematical morphology mappings of erosion and dilation may be regarded as negotiation strategies among conflicting influences of points from a neighborhood on its center (erosion) or influences on a point of centers of neighborhoods containing this point (dilation). In analytical morphology this mappings negotiate among conflicting influences of sets of conditions expressed by approximation functions from F. In analytical morphology one can also define opening and closing operations as respective composition of dilations and erosions according to the general scheme of Section 4.1.

It may be convenient to have also some forms of masks for preventing some attributes from being modified when their values are already satisfactory.
Analytical morphology of decision table $\mathbf{A}$ is a system:

$$(S, H, \mathcal{F}, \{\mathcal{N}(x)\}_{x \in Ob_{\mathbf{A}}}, \{\mathcal{M}(x)\}_{x \in Ob_{\mathbf{A}}}, \{e_x\}_{x \in Ob_{\mathbf{A}}}, \{d_x\}_{x \in Ob_{\mathbf{A}}})$$

where, given a decision table $\mathbf{A}$, the strategy S produces a sequence of decision rules from which the set $\mathcal{F}$ is defined by the strategy H. In the case of analytical morphology the strategy H defines $\mathcal{F}$ and sequences of functions from $\mathcal{F}$ applied to decision table $\mathbf{A}$ by means of specific choices of erosions, dilations and their compositions.

The strategy for defining erosion and dilation can be based on distributions μ and coefficients n discussed in Section 4.6 or on algorithms for decision rules synthesis [Sk93b]. In the first case the strategy calculates the global distribution from the local μ's and n 's. In the second case the global decision rule is synthesized taking into account all conditions occurring on the left hand sides of local decision rules.

4.8 Morphology of Rough Sets

In its theoretical studies mathematical morphology has been concerned with the problem of stability of morphological operations. The solution to this problem has been worked out in terms of appropriate topology. We will outline the underlying ideas.

As a rule, the structuring element B - in studies concerning the local structure of e.g. planar objects - can be taken as an open disc of small diameter. The relations of an object B to the studied compact (i.e. bounded) object X can be expressed in terms of the basic relations of inclusion and intersection by a topology in which any basic open set is determined by a finite family $\mathcal{G}$ of open sets containing X and a finite family $\mathcal{F}$ of open sets intersecting X.

Topology of this kind has been introduced into mathematics in [Vie21]. It has been extensively studied both within topology (as *finite* or *Vietoris topology*) [Mi51] as well as in applications to analysis [Ch48], stochastic geometry [Ke73] (as the *trap topology*) and last but not least in mathematical morphology [Ma75]. It has been proved [Ma75] (see also [Se82]) that a natural stability condition of a morphological operation ϕ expressed as the requirement that

$$\phi\,(\lim_n BdX_n) = \lim_n \phi\,(BdX_n)$$

is equivalent to the requirement that ϕ be semicontinuous in the finite topology [Ma75].

Mathematical Morphology can be regarded as sharing a common stock of basic methodological assumptions with rough set theory i.e.

(a) it describes the structure of an object in terms of a Boolean algebra of relations generated by the primitive relations of set inclusion and set-theoretic non-empty intersection;

(b) verifying whether a given relation is fulfilled is achieved by means of some model objects: structuring elements in morphology and indiscernibility classes in rough set theory;

(c) it represents the uncertain structure of an object X by some objects of certain structure obtain by performing on X morphological filtering operations: in the simplest case it approximates X by the opening of X as well as by the closing of X by a given structuring element.

A morphological action on an object results in a geometrical filtering of the object which extracts some features permiting to characterize the object in qualitative terms (like area, perimeter, number of connected components etc.). Moving a structural object B about X generates the object $\alpha(X)$ of elements at which the relations represented by B are fulfilled.

Morphological operations may be regarded as attributes: an operation α induces the attribute $[\alpha]$ whose value on the object X is α (X). The advantage of this abstract view of morphological operations is that, while morphological operations act directly in the plane of an object, the attribute [α] works on collections of objects.

These analogies on the and the necessity of having a dynamical theory of rough sets for the purposes of further studies of data filtration and dynamic phenomena in data tables, prompt us to develop a topological theory of rough sets. Therefore we present a study of topological aspects of rough sets which we regard as introducing morphological tools into rough set theory by creating a rough set-theoretical counterpart of morphological topological theory. The underlying parallelism is that of

$$\text{structuring element } B \leftrightarrow \text{attribute set } B.$$

As a result, in the corresponding morphology of rough sets upper semi-continuous mappings will preserve upper approximations and lower semi-continuous mappings will preserve lower approximations.

Morphological study of rough sets can be carried out, as it is the case here, in the framework of knowledge bases in the sense of [P91] i.e. collections of equivalence relations on a given universe. In case of a single equivalence relation on a set, the partition topology generated by this relation was studied in [Ton64], [Ma61], [Ma83] in the context of Graph Theory and Algebraic Linguistics, respectively: the connection between the partition topology and rough sets has been pointed out and investigated in [MP84], [Sk82] and [Wi88]. These papers are among the antecedents of our work. Another source of motivation has been provided by papers [MP84] and [MR86] on convergence and rough sets in knowledge bases consisting of countable descending sequences of equivalence relations. The attempt to introduce a metric (metrics) in this context underlies the results presented here.

Our context is more complex; we prefer to discuss knowledge bases (or equivalently, information systems) where the collection of equivalence relations is linearly ordered under set-theoretic inclusion. It suffices in the context of rough sets to restrict ourselves to cofinal well-ordered subcollections and the reader will be aware that our results concerning rough sets do not depend on any particular choice of such a cofinal subcollection.

The term "mathematical morphology" is used here in the sense of Serra [Se82], meaning essentially a study of rough sets and their transformations by set-theoretical, algebraic and topological tools. All proofs may be found in [Po94].

4.9 Taxonomy of Rough Sets

For an information system $\mathbf{A}=(U, A)$ with $R_a = IND(\{a\})$ for each $a \in A$, we will say that A is well-ordered whenever the set $(R_a \mid a \in A)$ is well-ordered by the relation $\prec$ of inverse inclusion defined via

$$R_a \prec R_b \text{ if and only if } R_b \subseteq R_a .$$

By T($\mathbf{A}$) we denote the ordinal type of $((R_a \mid a \in A), \prec)$. The reader will check easily that all our reasonings below are valid under simplifying assumption that T($\mathbf{A}$) is a regular cardinal.

Let $\mathbf{A} = (U, A) = (U, (R_a \mid a\in A))$ be a well-ordered information system ordered into type $T(\mathbf{A}) = \kappa$, where κ is a regular cardinal. We assume that $T(\mathbf{A})=\kappa$.

The topological interpretation of a rough set gives rise to the notion of a topological rough set (see [Wi88]; cf also an early attempt in [Ma75]; 1.3) viz. given a topological space (T, π), one calls a subset $X\subseteq T$ a *topological pre-rough set* (or, *π-pre-rough set*, for short) whenever $Int_\pi X \neq Cl_\pi X$ (Int_π, resp. Cl_π , denoting the interior, resp. the closure, operator in the topology π); the set R_π of *topological rough sets* (or, *π-rough sets*) is then defined as the quotient $R_\pi'/\sim$ where R_π' is the set of topological π-pre-rough sets and $\sim$ is the equivalence relation defined via

$$X \sim Y \text{ if and only if } Int_\pi X = Int_\pi Y \text{ and } Cl_\pi X = Cl_\pi Y.$$

By π_A we denote the topology generated by the family $(R_a \mid a\in A)$ of partitions i.e. equivalence classes $[x]_a$ of R_a, $a\in A$, constitute an open basis for π_a.

By R_A we denote the set of π_A-rough sets. We will say that a subset $X\subseteq U$ is *pre-rough in small cardinality* (or, *pre - r.s.c.*) in case when X is *B*-rough for each $B\subseteq A$ of cardinality less than cardinality of *A*. Clearly, for the well-ordered information system $\mathbf{A}$, a subset X is pre-r.s.c. if and only if X is R_a-rough for each $a\in A$.

By S_A we denote the set of sets rough in small cardinality (or, r.s.c. sets) defined as the quotient set $S_A'/\approx$ where S_A' is the collection of pre-r.s.c. sets and the equivalence relation $\approx$ is defined via

$$X \approx Y \text{ if and only if } Int_{\pi_a} X = Int_{\pi_a} Y \text{ and } Cl_{\pi_a} X = Cl_{\pi_a} Y$$

for each $a\in A$, where π_a is the partition topology introduced by the relation R_a.

Finally, we take into account those subsets of *U* that may become exact at some sufficiently fine partition R_a viz. for $a < \kappa$, we let

$$E_a' = \{X\subseteq U \mid X \text{ is } \pi_b\text{-rough for each } b < a \text{ and } X \text{ is } \pi_a\text{-definable}\}$$

and

$$E' = \cup\{E_a' \mid a < \kappa\}.$$

We denote by E_a, resp. E, the quotient $E_a'/\approx$, resp . the quotient $E'/\approx$.

We will be concerned in the sequel with plausible topologies on the sets R_A , S_A and E and with their applications.

Our aim here is to give characterizations of π_a -rough sets as well as r.s.c.-sets. These characterizations will enable us to introduce in the following sections some plausible topologies into R_A, S_A and E.

We begin with the characterization of π_A -rough sets. For a subset $X\subseteq U$ with $Int_{\pi_A} \neq Cl_{\pi_A} X\subseteq U$, we denote by $[X]$ the corresponding element of R_A i.e.

$$[X]=\{Y\subseteq U \mid Int_{\pi_A} X= Int_{\pi_A} Y \;\&\; Cl_{\pi_A} X= Int_{\pi_A} Y\}.$$

Letting $Q=Cl_{\pi_A} X$, $P=Int_{\pi_A} X$, and $T=U\text{-}P$, we can represent $[X]$ as the ordered pair (Q, T) of π_A-closed sets. The question which pairs (Q, T) do represent π_A-rough sets is answered by the following proposition.

Proposition 7. A pair (Q, T) of π_A-closed sets represents a π_A-rough set [X] with $Q=Cl_{\pi_A} X$ and $T=U\text{-}Int_{\pi_A} X$ if and only if

(i) $U=Q\cup T$

(ii) $Q\cap T=\varnothing$

(iii) $Q\cap T$ does not contains any π_A-isolated point of U.

Proposition 7 settles the matter of characterizing elements of R_A and we proceed with the case of S_A.

Clearly, for $[X]\in S_A$, the κ-sequence $(Q_a, T_a)_{a<\kappa}$, where $Q=Cl\pi_a X$ and $T=U\text{-}Int\pi_a X$ for $a<\kappa$, with (Q_a, T_a) satisfying (i)-(iii) of Proposition 7 with π_a in place of π_A, represents the fact that X is π_a-rough for each $a<\kappa$. As with Proposition 7, we have to single out those sequences of the form $(Q_a, T_a)_{a<\kappa}$ with (i)-(iii) satisfied for each $a<\kappa$, that do represent elements of S_A.

First, we denote by **T** the collection of all descending κ- sequences $([x_a]_a)_{a<\kappa}$ of equivalence classes i.e.

$$([x_a]_a)_{a<\kappa}\in \mathbf{T} \text{ if and only if } ([x_{a'}]_{a'})\subseteq([x_a]_a) \text{ whenever } a'>a.$$

We let **T**(Q) and **T**(T), respectively, to be the subsets of **T** specified by the following

$$\mathbf{T}(Q)=\{\ ([x_a]_a)_{a<\kappa}\in \mathbf{T}|([x_a]_a)\cap Q_a\neq\varnothing \text{ for each } a<\kappa\ \}$$

and

$$\mathbf{T}(T)=\{\ ([x_a]_a)_{a<\kappa}\in \mathbf{T}|([x_a]_a)\cap T_a\neq\varnothing \text{ for each } a<\kappa\ \}$$

For $y\in U$ and $a'<\kappa$, we let

$$\mathbf{T}(Q)(y, a')=\{([x_a]_a)_{a<\kappa}\in\mathbf{T}(Q)\mid [x_{a'}]_{a'}=[y]_{a'}\}$$

and

$$\mathbf{T}(T)(y, a')=\{([x_a]_a)_{a<\kappa}\in\mathbf{T}(T)\mid [x_{a'}]_{a'}=[y]_{a'}\}$$

For a limit ordinal $a<\kappa$, we let $R^{-}_a=\cap\{R_{a'}| a'<a\}$; π^{-}_a will denote the partition topology generated by R^{-}_a, and Cl^{-}_a, Int^{-}_a will denote the closure and the interior operator with respect to the topology π^{-}_a, respectively.

Our characterization of elements of S_A reads as follows .

Proposition 8. A κ- sequence $(Q_a, T_a)_{a<\kappa}$ does represent an element of S_A if and only if

(i) $U=Q_a\cup T_a$ for each $a<\kappa$

(ii) $Q_a\cap T_a\neq\varnothing$ for each $a<\kappa$

(iii) $Q_a\cap T_a$ does not contain any π_a-isolated point for each $a<\kappa$.

(iv) $Cl_b Q_a=Q_b$ and $Cl_b T_a=T_a$ for $b<a<\kappa$

(v) $\mathbf{T}(Q)(y,a')\neq\varnothing$, respectively $\mathbf{T}(T)(y, a')\neq\varnothing$, implies that there exist $([x_a]_a)_{a<\kappa}\in\mathbf{T}(Q)(y,a')$ and $([x_a]_a)_{a<\kappa}\in\mathbf{T}(T)(y,a')$, respectively, with $\cap\{[x_a]_a| a<\kappa\}\neq\varnothing$ for each $y\in U$ and each $a'<\kappa$

(vi) $Cl^{-}_a Q_a=\cap\{Q_{a'}\mid a'<a\}$ and $Cl^{-}_a T_a=\cap\{T_{a'} |a'<a\}$ for each limit $a<\kappa$.

The characterization of elements of S_A provided by Proposition 8 can be easily modified to yield the corresponding characterization for elements of E_a, $a < \kappa$, as well as of E viz. one may check that the following holds.

Proposition 9. (a) An element of E_a is represented by a κ- sequence $(Q_a, T_a)_{a<\kappa}$ such that

(i) $Q_a \cap T_a = \emptyset$, $U = Q_a \cup T_a$, Q_a, $T_a \in \pi_a$

(ii) $Cl_{a'} Q_a = Q_{a'}$, $Cl_{a'} T_a = T_{a'}$ for $a' < a$

(iii) $(Q_{a'}, T_{a'})$ is a $\pi_{a'}$-rough set for $a' < a$.

Proposition 9 immediately yields a characterization of elements of $E = \cup(E_a \mid a < \kappa)$.

4.10 Proper Topologies on R_A and S_A

We will say that a topology π on R_A (a topology π on S_A) is *proper* whenever given $(Q, T) \in R_A$ and a neighborhood $V \in \pi$ of (Q, T) (given $(Q_a, T_a)_{a<\kappa} \in S_A$ and a neighborhood $V \in \pi$ of $(Q_a, T_a)_{a<\kappa}$), there exists $b < \kappa$ with the property that $Cl_b Q = Cl_b Q'$ and $Cl_b T = Cl_b T'$ imply that $(Q', T') \in V$ for each $(Q', T') \in R_A$ ($Q_b = Q_{b'}$ and $T_b = T_{b'}$ imply that $(Q_a', T_a')_{a<\kappa} \in V$ for each $(Q_a, T_a)_{a<\kappa} \in S_A$).

Proper topologies are therefore invariants of relational systems associated with the considered information systems; in particular, they are invariant under passing to a cofinal subsystem.

Now we will introduce two proper topologies π and π^* on R_A and a proper topology π' on S_A. These topologies will be some appropriate variations on the theme of the Vietoris or finite topology (see [Vie21]) studied extensively, among others, by [Mi51] and [Ch48] and being a basic tool of mathematical morphology (see [Ma75], [Se82], and [Ke73]). Our modifications will take into account the context of general information systems; due to this they will loose finitistic character of topologies of Vietoris type mentioned above.

To define π, we denote by $((W, V, \mathcal{U}, \mathcal{V}, a_1, a_2, a_3, a_4))$ the collection of elements of R_A defined via

$$(Q, T) \in ((W, V, \mathcal{U}, \mathcal{V}, a_1, a_2, a_3, a_4)) \text{ if and only if}$$

a. there exists $b_1 \geq a_1$ with $Cl_{b_1} Q \subseteq W \in \pi_A$

b. there exists $b_2 \geq a_2$ with $Cl_{b_2} T \subseteq V \in \pi_A$

c. $Q \cap H \neq \emptyset$ for each $H \in \mathcal{U} \subseteq \bigcup(\pi_a \mid a < a_3)$

d. $T \cap H \neq \emptyset$ for each $H \in \mathcal{V} \subseteq \bigcup(\pi_a \mid a < a_4)$

Then π is the topology on R_A obtained by taking sets of the form $((W, V, \mathcal{U}, \mathcal{V}, a_1, a_2, a_3, a_4))$, where $W, V \in \pi_A$, $\mathcal{U} \subseteq \bigcup \{\pi_a \mid a < a_3\}$, $\mathcal{V} \subseteq \bigcup \{\pi_a \mid a < a_4\}$ and $a_1, a_2, a_3, a_4 < \kappa$, as an open subbase.

Similarly, $((W, V, \mathcal{U}, \mathcal{V}, a_1, a_2, a_3, a_4, a_5, a_6))$ will stand for the collection of elements of R_A defined via

$$(Q, T) \in ((W, V, \mathcal{U}, \mathcal{V}, a_1, a_2, a_3, a_4, a_5, a_6)) \text{ if and only if}$$

e. there exists $b_3 \geq a_5$ with $Cl_b(Q \cap T) \subseteq G \in \pi_A$ and

f. $Q \cap T \cap H \neq \emptyset$ for each $H \in W \subseteq \bigcup \{\pi_a \mid a < a_4\}$

Then π^* is the topology on S_A obtained by taking sets of the form $((W, V, \mathcal{U}, \mathcal{V}, a_1, a_2, a_3, a_4, a_5, a_6))$, where $W, V, G \in \pi_A$, $\mathcal{U} \subseteq \bigcup \{\pi_a \mid a < a_3\}$, $\mathcal{V} \subseteq \bigcup \{\pi_a \mid a < a_4\}$, $W \subseteq \bigcup \{\pi_a \mid a < a_6\}$, and $a_1, a_2, a_3, a_4, a_5, a_6 < \kappa$, as an open subbase.

The topology π' on S_A is defined in a similar vein; we let $((W, V, \mathcal{U}, \mathcal{V}, a_1, a_2, a_3, a_4))$ to denote the collection of elements of S_A defined via

$$(Q_a, T_a)_{a<\kappa} \in ((W, V, \mathcal{U}, \mathcal{V}, a_1, a_2, a_3, a_4)) \text{ if and only if}$$

g. there exists $b_1 \leq a_1$ with $Q_{b_1} \subseteq W \in \pi_A$

h. there exists $b_2 \leq a_2$ with $T_{b_2} \subseteq V \in \pi_A$

i. $Q_{a_3} \cap H \neq \emptyset$ for each $H \in \mathcal{U} \subseteq \bigcup \{\pi_a \mid a < a_3\}$

j. $T_{a_4} \cap H \neq \emptyset$ for each $H \in \mathcal{V} \subseteq \bigcup \{\pi_a \mid a < a_4\}$

Then the topology π' on S_A is obtained by taking the collection of all the sets of the form $((W, V, \mathcal{U}, \mathcal{V}, a_1, a_2, a_3, a_4))$, where $W, V \in \pi_A$, $\mathcal{U} \subseteq \bigcup \{\pi_a \mid a < a_3\}$, $\mathcal{V} \subseteq \bigcup \{\pi_a \mid a < a_4\}$, and $a_1, a_2, a_3, a_4 < \kappa$ as an open subbase.

One easily checks that both π and π^* are proper on R_A and that π' is proper on S_A.

In the sequel we will be concerned with the problem of finding metrics on R_A and on S_A, respectively, that correspond to π, π^* and π', respectively, under plausible conditions. Our next section will be therefore devoted to the special case when π, π^*, and π' are metrizable.

4.11 R_A and S_A Metric

We say that a well-ordered information system $\mathbf{A} = (U, (R_a : a < \kappa))$ is *countable generated* whenever there exists a countable $\kappa' \subseteq \kappa$ such that $(R_a : a < \kappa')$ is $\prec$-cofinal in $(R_a: a<\kappa)$. We let $A_0 = (U, (R_a : a<\kappa'))$ to denote the corresponding subsystem; clearly, we may assume that $\kappa'=\omega$. We denote by π_0, π_0^*, resp. π_0' topologies on R_{A_0}, resp. S_{A_0} generated by $(R_a : a<\kappa'=\omega)$.

It turns out that the spaces (R_{A_0}, π_0), (R_{A_0}, π_0^*) and (S_{A_0}, π_0') may be endowed with compatible metrics.

A metric for dealing with closed sets was first proposed by [Pom05] and then in a modified form by [Hau14]. Although both are topologically equivalent, it is the Hausdorff metric that has been applied successively in various contexts (see [Ma75], [Se82]) of mathematical morphology. We will apply the Hausdorff metric here to impose some metrics on rough sets.

It will be sufficient to consider a countable information system $\mathbf{A}_0=(U, (R_n: n<\omega))$ well-ordered into type ω of natural numbers.

To begin with, we define a function d_n for $n<\omega$ by letting

$$d_n(x,y)=1 \text{ if } [x]_n=[y]_n \text{ and } d_n(x,y)=0, \text{ otherwise.}$$

Then the function

$$d(x, y)=\sum_n 10^{-n} d_n(x, y)$$

is a pseudometric on U compatible with π_0. We recall that, given $x\in U$ and a π_0-closed set $A\subseteq U$, the *d-distance d-dist*(x, A) is given via

$$d\text{-}dist(x, A)=min\{d(x, y)|y\in A\}.$$

For π_0-closed sets A, $B \subseteq U$ the *Hausdorff distance* $d_H(A, B)$ of A and B is given via

$$d_H(A, B)=max\{max\{d\text{-}dist(x, B)|x\in A\}, max\{d\text{-}dist(y, A)|y\in B\}\}$$

One checks easily that d is a metric on π_0-closed subsets of U.

We will apply d_H to define two functions, D and D*, on pairs of π_0-rough sets, viz., we let

(i) $D((Q, T), (Q', T'))=max\{d_H(Q, Q'), d_H(T, T')\}$

(ii) $D^*((Q, T), (Q',T'))=max\{D((Q,T),(Q',T')), d_H(Q\cap T,Q'\cap T')\}$.

One checks easily that both D and D* are metrics on R_{A_0}.

The following procedure P calculates values of D, resp. D*

Procedure P.

Inputs: $(Q, T), (Q', T')\in R_{A_0}$

Outputs: a. $D((Q, T),(Q', T'))$
b. $D^*((Q, T), (Q', T'))$.

a. Check whether $Cl_nQ=Cl_nQ'$ and $Cl_nT=Cl_nT'$ for each n. If so, the output is 0. Otherwise, find the first n that fails at least one of these identities. The output is $10^{-n+1} \cdot 1/9$.

b. Check whether $Cl_n Q = Cl_n Q'$, $Cl_n T = Cl_n T'$ and $Cl_n(Q \cap T) = Cl_n(Q' \cap T')$ for each n. If so, the output is 0. Otherwise the output is $10^{-n+1} \cdot 1/9$ with the first n that fails at least one of these identities.

We have the following

Proposition 10.
(i) The metric topology on R_{A_0} generated by D coincides with π
(ii) The metric topology on R_{A_0} generated by D* coincides with π*.

In case of S_{A_0}, we begin with $d_n(x, y)=1$ if $[x]_n \neq [y]_n$ and 0, otherwise. We define then the Hausdorff distance $d_{H,n}$ via

$$d_{H,n}(A, B)=max\{max\{d_n\text{-}dist(x, B)|x \in A\}, max\{d_n\text{-}dist(y, A)|y \in B\}\}$$

for each pair A, B of π_n-closed subsets of U. Then the formula

$D'_n((Q_n, T_n), (Q'_n, T'_n))=max\{d_{H,n}(Q_n, Q'_n), d_{H,n}(T_n, T'_n)\}$ defines a metric on the set of π_n- rough sets.

Letting

$D'((Q_n, T_n)_{n<\omega}, (Q'_n, T'_n)_{n<\omega})=\Sigma_n 10^{-n} D'_n((Q_n, T_n), (Q'_n, T'_n))$

for each pair $(Q_n, T_n)_{n<\omega}, (Q'_n, T'_n)_{n<\omega} \in S_{A_0}$, we define a metric D' on S_{A_0}.

The following procedure establishes a correct way of calculating D'.

Procedure P'.

Input: $(Q_n, T_n)_{n<\omega}, (Q'_n, T'_n)_{n<\omega} \in S_{A_0}$

Output: $D'((Q_n, T_n)_{n<\omega}, (Q'_n, T'_n)_{n<\omega})$.

Check for each n whether $Q_n=Q_n'$ and $T_n=T_n'$; if so the output is 0. Otherwise, find the first $n = n_0$ such that it fails either of the above identities. The output is $10^{-n_0+1} \cdot 1/9$.

The relationship between π' and D' is similar to these established in Proposition 7, above, with π, D and π*, D*. The proof of the following Proposition parallels that of Proposition 7.

Proposition 11. The metric topology on S_{A_0} generated by D' coincides with π'.

We will finally settle the problem of introducing into R_{A_0} and S_{A_0}, respectively, metrics compatible with π, π^* and π', respectively, by checking that this is possible, up to trivial cases in the countable generated case only.

Proposition 12. For an information system $\mathbf{A}=(U, (R_a \mid a<\kappa))$ the topology π, respectively π^*, on R_{A_0} can be introduced via a compatible metric if and only if either $\mathbf{A}$ is countable generated or the topology π_A is discrete (in which case $R_{A_0}=\varnothing$).

The parallel question for π' on S_A is answered as follows.

Proposition 13. For an information system $\mathbf{A}=(U, (R_a \mid a<\kappa))$, the topology π' on S_{A_0} can be introduced via a compatible metric if and only if either $\mathbf{A}$ is countable generated or $S_A=\varnothing$.

4.12 Embedding R_A into S_A. Completeness

It is easy to see that each π_A-rough set is a set rough in small cardinality. We formally express this statement by defining a mapping j_A: $R_A \to S_A$ via

$$j_A((Q, T))=(Cl_a Q, Cl_a T)_{a<\kappa}.$$

Clearly, j_A: $(R_A,\pi)\to(S_A,\pi')$ is a homeomorphic embedding.

In the countable generated case, Procedures P and P' imply the following

Proposition 14. $j_{A_0}: (R_{A_0}, D)\to(S_{A_0}, D')$ is an isometric embedding.

We devote the remainder of the section to the completeness properties of spaces (R_{A_0}, D), (R_{A_0}, D^*), (S_{A_0}, D'). We will impose on U an additional and necessary in the context condition

(C) each descending sequence $([x_n]_n)_n$ has a non - empty intersection

We begin with the case of (S_{A_0}, D').

Proposition 15. Under (C), each D'-fundamental sequence $((Q_m^n, T_m^n)_m)_n \subseteq S_{A_0}$ D'-converges in S_{A_0}.

The case of (R_{A_0}, D), and (R_{A_0}, D^*) is more complex. We begin with a positive result, viz., that R_{A_0} is (D^*, D)-complete meaning.

Proposition 16. Each D^*-fundamental sequence $((Q_n,T_n))_n \subseteq R_{A_0}$ D-converges in R_{A_0}.

These results open up a promising field of research concerning stable operations on rough sets.

4.13 Some Natural Transformations

We will examine here in terms of our topologies some natural transformations of mathematical morphology (cf.[Ma75], Ch.1, or [Se82], Ch. I - II).

First, we examine the notion of a complement of a rough set. We begin with elements of R_A ; for $(Q,T)\in R_A$, we define the complement of (Q,T) which we denote by $(Q,T)^C$ via

$$(Q,T)^C=(T,Q).$$

Clearly, $(Q,T)^C\in R_A$. The following proposition sums up the behavior of complement with respect to topologies π and π^*.

Proposition 17.
(i) $(*)^C$ is a homeomorphism from (R_A, π) onto (R_A, π)
(ii) $(*)^C$ is a homeomorphism from (R_A, π^*) onto (R_A, π^*).

The operator $(*)^C$ of complement may be defined as well on S_A via

$$((Q_a, T_a)_{a<k})^C=(T_a, Q_a)_{a<k};$$

again we have

Proposition 18. $(*)^C$ is a homeomorphism from (S_A, π') onto (S_A, π')

Next we consider the boundary mapping B. To define B, we first denote by R_A' the set of reduced π_A-rough sets and then we define $B: R_A \rightarrow R_A'$ via $B((Q,T))=[[Q,T]]$.

Our proposition below establishes relations between B and topologies π^* and π, respectively.

A mapping $f: (R_A,\pi)\rightarrow(R_A,\pi)$ is *upper semicontinuous* (*u.s.c.*) at $(Q,T)\in R_A$ if given $W,V\in\pi_A$ and $a<k$ with $b\leq a$ such that $Cl_b Q_1 \subseteq V$ and $Cl_b T_1\subseteq W$, there exists a π-open $H \ni (Q,T)$ with :

$$(Q',T')\in H \Rightarrow \exists b' \geq a .(Cl_{b'} Q'\subseteq V \text{ and } Cl_{b'} T'\subseteq W).$$

Proposition 19.
(i) B is continuous as a mapping from (R_A ,π^*) into $(R_A ',\pi|R_A ')$
(ii) B is u.s.c. as a mapping from (R_A,π) into $(R_A',\pi|R_A')$ at each $(Q,T)\in R_A$ such that $\{Q\cap[x]_a, T\cap[x]_a\}$ is not a partition of any $[x]_a$.

We will discuss some algebraic operations on rough sets.

Consider the set

$$A=\{((Q_1,T_1),(Q_2,T_2))\in R^2_A : (Q_1\cup Q_2)\cap T_1\cap T_2\neq\emptyset\};$$

it is not difficult to check that A is a closed subset of $(R_A, \pi)^2$. Given a pair $((Q_1,T_1),(Q_2,T_2))\in A$, we define the rough union of (Q_1,T_1) and (Q_2,T_2) via

$$(Q_1,T_1)\cup_R(Q_2,T_2)=(Q_1\cup Q_2,\ T_1\cap T_2).$$

Then clearly $(Q_1,T_1)\cup_R(Q_2,T_2)\in R_A$. We have

Proposition 20. The rough union $\cup_R$ from $(A, \pi^2|A)$ into (R_A, π) is a u.s.c. mapping at each pair $((Q_1,T_1),(Q_2,T_2))$ such that $\{T_1\cap[x]_a, T_2\cap[x]_a\}$ is not a partition of any $[x]_a$.

Dually, consider the set

$$B=\{((Q_1,T_1),(Q_2,T_2))\in R^2_A : (Q_1\cup Q_2)\cap T_1\cup T_2\neq\emptyset\};$$

again, B is a closed subset of $(R_A,\pi)^2$. Given $((Q_1,T_1),(Q_2,T_2))\in B$, we define the rough intersection $(Q_1,T_1)\cap_R(Q_2,T_2)$ as $(Q_1\cap Q_2, T_1\cap T_2)\in R_A$.

The following relation establishes the connection of $\cup_R$, $\cap_R$, and $(*)^C$:

$$(*)\ X\cap_R Y=(X^C\cup_R Y^C)^C.$$

It implies immediately the counterpart of Proposition 20.

Proposition 21. The rough intersection $\cap_R$ from $(B,\pi^2|B)$ into (R_A,π) is a u.s.c. mapping at each pair such that $\{Q_1\cap[x]_a, Q_2\cap[x]_a\}$ is not a partition of any $[x]_a$.

Before we embark upon further investigations we will unify collections D_A of definable sets and S_A of **A**. r. s. c. sets into the collection $F_A=D_A\cup S_A$. We will impose on F_A the topology π'.

Then we have

Proposition 22.

(i) In case **A** is countable generated the topology π' on F_A is generated by the metric D' extended over F_A

(ii) The space (F_A,D') is complete.

Extending $\cup_R$ and $\cap_R$ to F_A-valued operations we get

Proposition 23. $\cup_R$, respectively, $\cap_R$ are u.s.c. mappings from (R_A^2, π^2) into (F_A, π') at each pair $((Q_1,T_1),(Q_2,T_2))$ with $\{T_1 \cap [x]_a, T_2 \cap [x]_a\}$, respectively, $\{Q_1 \cap [x]_a, Q_2 \cap [x]_a\}$ not a partition of any $[x]_a$.

We now will introduce and discuss two more operations viz. the B-erosion and the B-increment which serve as rough sets counterparts of the operations of opening and closing studied in Mathematical Morphology (of. [Ma75]; 1.5 or [Se82] ; Ch.III).

Let $B=[x]_a$, for some $x \in U$ and an $a < \kappa$, contain no π_A-open singletons. We define the map e_B, the B-erosion, on R_A via

$$e_B((Q, T))=(Q \cup B, T \cup B).$$

Then

Proposition 24.

(i) $e_B : (R_A, \pi) \to (R_A, \pi)$ is continuous

(ii) $e_B : (R_A, \pi^*) \to (R_A, \pi^*)$ is continuous.

The B-erosion in case of S_A is defined in a similar way viz. given $B=[x]_{a_0}$ for some $x \in U$, $a_0 < \kappa$, containing no π_{a_0}-open singleton, we let

$$e_B((Q_a, T_a)_{a<\kappa})=(Q_a', T_a')_{a<\kappa}$$

where

a. $Q_a'=Q_a \cup Cl_a B$, $T_a'=T_a \cup Cl_a B$ for $a<a_0$

b. $Q_a'=Q_a \cup B$, $T_a'=T_a \cup B$ for $a \geq a_0$.

We have then

Proposition 25. e_B is a continuous mapping from (S_A, π') into (S_A, π').

The dual operation of B-increment defined on R_A via

$$i_B((Q,T))=(Q \cup B, T-B)$$

may lead to a π_A-definable set in case $Q \cap T=B$.

We will then consider i_B as a map from R_A into F_A which leads to

Proposition 26. i_B: $(R_A, \pi) \to (F_A, \pi')$ is a continuous mapping.

The above results demonstrate that we are now in possession of a morphological theory of rough sets by means of which we plan to study dynamic aspects of the process of decision rules generation.

This work has been partially supported by grant # 8-T11C 01011 from the State Commitee for Scientific Research (Komitet Badan Naukowych).

References

[Bl92a] Bleau A., deGuise J., LeBlanc R.: A new set of fast algorithms for mathematical morphology I; Idempotent geodesic transforms, Computer Vision Graphics and Image Processing: Image Understanding 56(2) (1992), 178 -209

[Bl92b] Bleau A., deGuise J., LeBlanc R.:A new set of fast algorithms for mathematical morphology II; Identification of topographic features on grayscale images, Computer Vision Graphics and Image Processing: Image Understanding 56(2) (1992), 210-229

[BSS94a] Bazan J., Skowron A., Synak P.:Dynamic reducts as a tool for extracting laws from decision tables, (ISMIS'94), Proc. of the Symp. on Methodologies for Intelligent Systems}, Charlotte, NC, October 16-19, 1994, Lecture Notes in Artificial Intelligence Vol. 869, Springer-Verlag 1994 , 346-355.

[BSS94b] Bazan J., Skowron A., Synak P.: Market data analysis: A rough set approach, ICS Research Report 6/94 Warsaw University of Technology 1994

[BSTSS94b] Bazan J., Son H.N., Trung T.N., Skowron A., Synak P.: Some logic and rough set applications for classifying objects, ICS Research Report 38/94, Warsaw University of Technology 1994.

[Ch48] Choquet G.: Converqences, Ann. Univ. Grenoble, 23 (1948), 55-112

[Cl81] Clarke B.L.: A calculus of individuals based on "Connection", Notre Dame Journal of Formal Logic, 22(1981),204-218

[Cl85] Clarke B.L.: Individuals and points, Notre Dame Journal of Formal Logic, 26 (1985), 61-75

[GD88] Giardina C.R., Dougherty E.R.: Morphological Methods in Image and Signal Processing, Prentice Hall, Englewood Cliffs, 1988

[Ha87] Haralick R.M., Sternberg S., Zhuong X.: Image analysis using mathematical morphology, IEEE Trans. Pattern Anal. Mach. Intelligence PAMI-9(1987), 532-550

[Hau14] Hausdorff F.: Grundzuge der Mengenlehre, Leipzig (Wien), 1914

[HR90] Heijmans H.J.A.M., Ronse C.: The algebraic basis of mathematical morphology I. Dilations and erosions, Computer Vision Graphics and Image Processing 50 (1990), 245-295

[Ke73] Kendall D.G.: Foundations of the theory of random sets, in: Stochastic Geometry (E.F. Harding and D.G. Kendall, eds.), Wiley, 1973, pp. 322-376

[KM90] Kodratoff Y., Michalski R.: Machine learning: An Artificial Intelligence approach, Vol.3. San Mateo: Morgan Kaufmann 1990

[Le16] Lesniewski, S.: Foundations of the general theory of sets (in Polish), Moscow, 1916; engl. transl. in:Surma, Srzednicki, Barnett, Rickey (eds.), Stanislaw Lesniewski, Collected Works, Kluwer, Dordrecht 1992, 128-173

[Le27] Lesniewski S.: On the foundations of Mathematics. Ch.I-III (in Polish), Przeglad Filozoficzny, 30 (1927), 164-206; Eng. transl. in [SSBR; 175-226]

[Le28] Lesniewski S.: On the foundations of Mathematics. Ch.IV (in Polish), Przeglad Filozoficzny 31 (1928), 261-291; Eng. transl. in [SSBR; 227-263]

[Le29] Lesniewski S.: On the foundations of Mathematics. Ch.V (in Polish), Przeglad Filozoficzny,32(1929), 60-101; Eng. transl. in [SSBR; 264 - 314]

[Le30] Lesniewski S.: On the foundations of Mathematics. Ch.VI-Ch.IX (in Polish), Przeglad Filozoficzny, 33 (1930), 77-105; Eng. transl. in [SSBR; 315-349]

[Le31] Lesniewski S.: On the foundations of Mathematics. Ch.X, Ch.XI (in Polish), Przeglad Filozoficzny 34 (1931), 142-170; Eng. transl. in [SSBR; 350-382]

[Ma61] Marcus S.: Structures linguistiques et structures topologiques, Rev. Math. Pures Appl. 6 (30), (1961), 501-506

[MA75] Mamdani E.H., Assilian S.: An experiment in linguistic synthesis with a fuzzy logic controller, International Journal of Man-Machine Studies, 7, 1975, 1-13

[Ma75] Matheron G.: Random Sets and Integral Geometry, Wiley, 1975

[Ma83] Marcus S.: Modeles mathematiques pour la categorie grammaticale du cas, Rev. Math. Pures Appl. 8 (4) (1963), 585-610

[Mi51] Michael E., Topologies on spaces of subsets, Trans. Amer. Math. Soc. 71 (1951), 152-183

[MP84] Marek W., Pawlak Z.: Information systems and rough sets, Fund. Inform. VIII (1984), 105-115

[MR86] Marek W., Rasiowa H.: Approximating sets with equivalence relations, Theoretical Computer Sc. 48 (1986), 145-152

[P82] Pawlak, Z.: Rough sets, International Journal of Information and Computer Science 11 (1982),344-356

[P91] Pawlak Z.: Rough sets: Theoretical aspects of reasoning about data. Dordrecht: Kluwer 1991

[P94] Pawlak Z.: Vagueness and Uncertainty a Rough Set Perspective, ICS ICS Research Report 19/94, Warsaw University of Technology 1994

[Po94] Polkowski L.T.: Mathematical morphology of rough sets, Bull. Acad. Polon. Sci., Ser. Sci. Math. 41(3) (1993), 241-273

[Pom05] Pompeiu D.: Ann. de Toulouse (2), 7, (1905)

[PoSk94a] Polkowski L., Skowron A.: Rough mereology, Proc. of the Symp. On Methodologies for Intelligent Systems, Charlotte, NC, October 16-19, 1994, Lecture Notes in Artificial Intelligence Vol. 869, Springer Verlag, Berlin 1994, 85-94.

[PoSk94b] Polkowski L., Skowron A.: Decision Support Systems, Rough Set Approach, Warszawa, 1994.

[PS93a] Pawlak Z., Skowron A.: Rough membership functions: A tool for reasoning with uncertainty, Algebraic Methods in Logic and their Computer Science, Banach Center Publications Vol.28., Polish Academy of Sciences, Warszawa 1993, 135-150

[PS93b] Pawlak Z., Skowron A.: A rough set approach for decision rules generation. ICS Research Report 23/93, Warsaw University of Technology 1993, Proc. of the IJCAI'93 Workshop: The Management of Uncertainty in AI, France 1993

[PS94] Pawlak Z., Skowron A.: Rough membership functions, In: M.Fedrizzi, J. Kacprzyk and R.R. Yager (eds.): Advances in the Dempster-Shafer Theory of Evidence. New York: John Wiley and Sons 1994, 251-271

[RH91] Ronse C., Heijmans H.J.A.M.: The algebraic basis of mathematical morphology II. Openings and closings, Computer Vision Graphics and Image Processing: Image Understanding 54(1) (1991), 74 - 97

[Se82] Serra J.: Image Analysis and Mathematical Morphology, Academic Press, New York 1982

[Sk82] Skowron A.: On topology in information systems, Bull. Acad. Polon. Sci. Math., 36 (1988)

[Sk91] Skowron A.: The rough set theory as a basis for the evidence theory, ICS Research Report 2/91, Warsaw University of Technology 1991, 1-53

[Sk93] Skowron A.: Boolean reasoning for decision rules generation. Proceedings of the 7-th International Symposium ISMIS'93, Trondheim, Norway 1993, In: J.Komorowski and Z.Ras (eds.): Lecture Notes in Artificial Intelligence, Vol.689. Springer-Verlag 1993, 295-305

[Sk93a] Skowron A.: A synthesis of decision rules: Applications of discernibility matrices, Proc. of the Conf. Intelligent Information Systems, Augustow, June 7-11, 1993, 30-46

[Sk93b] Skowron A.: Extracting laws from decision tables - a rough set approach, Proc. of the International Workshop on Rough Sets and Knowledge Discovery RSKD'93, Banff, Canada 1993, 101-104

[Sk93c] Skowron, A.: Management of uncertainty: A rough set approach, ICS Research Report 46/93, Warsaw University of Technology 1994, also in: Proc. Int. Workshop Incompleteness and ncertainty in Information Systems, Montreal, October 8-9, 1993, 36-61, Springer Verlag, in print.

[SkPo94] Skowron,A., Polkowski,L.: Introducing rough mereological controllers: rough quality control, In: T.Y. Lin, and A.M. Wildberger (eds.), Soft Computing, Simulation Councils, Inc., San Diego 1995, 240-243

[SP94] Skowron A., Polkowski L.: Analytical Morphology: Mathematical Morphology of Decision Tables, Fundamenta Informaticae 27(2-3) (1996), 255-272.

[SR92] Skowron, A. and Rauszer C.: The Discernibility Matrices and Functions in Information Systems. In: R. Slowinski (ed.): Intelligent Decision Support. Handbook of Applications and Advances of the Rough Sets Theory. Dordrecht: Kluwer 1992, 331-362

[SoD90] Song J., Delp E. J.: The analysis of morphological filters with multiple structuring elements, Computer Vision Graphics and Image Processing 50 (1990), 308-328

[SLF91] Sriram D., Logcher R., Fukuda S.: Computer - Aided Cooperative Product Development, LNCS 492, Springer-Verlag, Berlin Heidelberg, 1991

[SSBR] Surma S.J., Srzednicki J.T., Barnett D.I., Rickey V.F. (eds.): Stanislaw Lesniewski, Collected Works, Kluwer - Polish Scientific Publishers, Dordrecht-Warsaw, 1992

[St86] Sternberg R. S.: Grayscale morphology, Computer Vision Graphics and Image Processing 35(3) (1986), 333-355

[Ta29] Tarski A.: Les fondements de la geometrie des corps, Annales de la Societe Polonaise de Mathematique (Supplement), Krakow, 1929, 29-33; Eng. transl. in: [Wo; 24-29]

[Ta35] Tarski A.: Zur Grundlegung der Booleschen Algebra.I, Fundamenta Mathematicae, 24 (1935), 177-198; Eng. transl. in [Wo; 320-341]

[Ta37] Tarski A.: Appendix E in: Woodger, J.H., The Axiomatic Method in Biology, Cambridge University Press, Cambridge 1937

[Ton64] Tondeur: Ein Beispiel zur Allgemeinen Topologie: die Topologie einer Aequivalenz-relation, Annales Academiae Scientiarum Fennicae, ser. A, I. Math., No.344, Helsinki, 1964

[Vie21] Vietoris L.: Monat. Math. Ph., 31 (1921), 173-204

[Wh19] Whitehead A.N.: An Enquiry Concerning the Principles of Natural Knowledge,Cambridge U.Press, Cambridge, 1919

[Wi88] Wiweger A.: On topological rough sets, Bull. Acad. Polon. Sci. Math., 37 (1988), 89-93

[Wo56] Woodger J.H.,transl.:Logic, Semantics, Metamathematics. Papers from 1923 to 1938 by Alfred Tarski, Clarendon, Oxford, 1956

[Z65] Zadeh L.A.: Fuzzy sets, Information and Control 8, (1965) 338-353

[Zi93] Ziarko W.: Variable precision rough set model, Journal of Computer and System Sciences, 46(1993), 39-59

VI

SIMILARITY-BASED REASONING

Chapter 14

Similarity versus Preference in Fuzzy Set-Based Logics*

Didier Dubois and Henri Prade

Institut de Recherche en Informatique de Toulouse (I.R.I.T.) -C.N.R.S.,
Université Paul Sabatier, 118 route de Narbonne,
31062 TOULOUSE Cedex - FRANCE

Abstract: There are presently two kinds of fuzzy set-based theories of approximate reasoning: possibilistic logic, and similarity-based logic. This paper is devoted to a comparison between the two lines of research, both at the formal and interpretation level. Similarity calculus, initiated by Ruspini, exploits the idea that interpretations of a formal classical propositional language are more or less close to each other. This is done by equipping this set of interpretations with a metric-like structure, under the form of a fuzzy similarity relation. Then "p approximately implies q" means that p is "not far" from implying q, where "not far" is evaluated by the amount of stretching applied to the models of q so as to make the conditional statement true. On the contrary, in possibilistic logic, the set of interpretations is equipped with a preference relation encoded as a possibility distribution. This possibility distribution expresses that some worlds are more plausible than others. Then "p approximately implies q" means that q is true in the most plausible worlds where p is true. Similarity-based reasoning is also compared with rough set theory, and it is pointed out that while the two approaches are strongly connected at the formal level, the former is devoted to casting interpolation in a logical setting while the latter focuses on incomplete information systems where objects cannot be distinguished.

1 Introduction

Approximate or plausible reasoning, as referring to attempts to overcome limitations of classical logic-based reasoning, may apply to different kinds of situations. This can be easily seen if, for instance, we consider possible desirable extensions

* This paper reformulates and expands the contents of two previous papers, namely i) an extended abstract entitled "Graded indiscernibility, fuzzy rough sets and modal logics" presented at the 5th International Fuzzy Systems Association Congress (IFSA'93) (Seoul, Korea, July 4-9, 1993; proceedings pp. 85-88), and ii) a conference paper entitled "Comparison of two fuzzy set-based logics: Similarity logic and possibilistic logic" presented at the 4th IEEE International Conference on Fuzzy Systems (FUZZ-IEEE'95) (Yokohama, Japan, March 20-24, 1995; proceedings pp. 1219-1226).

of the modus ponens rule of inference in classical logic. Modus ponens allows to deduce 'q' from 'p' and 'p implies q' (in the sense of the material implication $p \to q \equiv \neg p \vee q$). Notwithstanding the problem of extending modus ponens to vague propositions which no longer satisfy all the properties of Boolean algebra (e.g., the excluded-middle law), we can think of extensions of modus ponens, still working with Boolean propositions, by introducing modalities expressing uncertainty (caused by the incompleteness of the available information), or expressing similarity (due to the indiscernibility or closeness of interpretations).

In case of uncertainty, we are looking for a pattern of reasoning of the form "from 'p somewhat certain' and 'if p then q is somewhat certain', deduce 'q is somewhat certain"'. Using the idea of similarity (when the set of possible worlds is equipped with some metrics) leads to a pattern of the form "from 'p is close to being true', and 'if p, then q is close to being true', deduce 'q is close to being true' " (where 'p is close to being true' means that the current state of the world corresponds to an interpretation which is close to an interpretation which makes p true). Clearly, the two patterns refer to different kinds of reasoning. With the first one we are interested in concluding that "q is likely to be true" (but it might exist exceptional situations where q is false while p is true). With the second pattern we are completely certain that, even if q is false, it is at least not far from being true in the sense of the metrics equipping the set of interpretations. The first pattern provides plausible conclusions while the second one performs some kind of extrapolation.

Moreover, it might be desirable to distinguish between various degrees of certainty, and various degrees of closeness in these two patterns, respectively (in order to acknowledge that a conclusion cannot be more certain than the premises, or to take into account the possible degradation of the closeness in the second pattern).

As we can see from this informal discussion, different kinds of approximate reasoning, which require a step beyond classical logic, make sense. Moreover, in each case the use of an ordering among interpretations seems appealing. In the next section, we reformulate Ruspini [Ru3] similarity-based semantics of fuzzy logic. Section 3 points out relations between Ruspini's approach and the idea of a fuzzy rough set (where the equivalence relation giving birth to the rough set construction (Pawlak [Pa2]) is replaced by a fuzzy similarity relation). Possibilistic logic treatment of uncertainty is recalled in Section 4. Possibilistic logic's preference-based semantics is compared with the similarity-based semantics in Section 5. Instead of stressing that a possibility distribution is mathematically subsumed by a similarity relation on the set of interpretations (as done by Esteva et al. [EGG1]), we emphasize their complementarity as capturing strikingly distinct types of commonsense reasoning.

2 Similarity-Based Semantics

In a series of papers, Ruspini [Ru1], [Ru2], [Ru3], [Ru4] has proposed a view of fuzzy logic where fuzziness comes from closeness between possible worlds. We shall denote classical Boolean propositions (belonging to a finite language) by letters p, q, r and $m(p)$ will denote the set of models of p, i.e., $m(p) = \{\omega \in \Omega, \omega \models p\}$ where Ω is the set of interpretations. Ruspini understands the fact that "a proposition p implies the proposition q to degree α", denoted in the following by $p \models_S^\alpha q$, as

$$p \models_S^\alpha q \text{ iff } \forall\omega \in m(p),\ \exists\omega' \in m(q) \text{ and } \mu_S(\omega,\omega') \geq \alpha \tag{1}$$

where S is a fuzzy relation which is assumed to be reflexive ($\mu_S(\omega,\omega) = 1,\ \forall\omega$), symmetrical ($\mu_S(\omega,\omega') = \mu_S(\omega',\omega),\ \forall\omega,\omega'$), and $*$-transitive. $*$-transitivity means that $\mu_S(\omega,\omega'') \geq \mu_S(\omega,\omega') * \mu_S(\omega',\omega''), \forall\omega,\omega',\omega''$, where $*$ is a continuous triangular norm operation[2] (i.e., $*$ is associative, commutative, monotonically increasing in both places and such that $0 * 0 = 0$, $a * 1 = a$, $\forall a \in [0,1]$). Such a fuzzy relation is also called an indistinguishability relation, see Valverde [Val]. In other words, a degree of entailment of q by p based on S, denoted by $I_S(q|p)$ is computed by Ruspini's as

$$I_S(q|p) = \ \inf_{\omega\models p} \sup_{\omega'\models q} \mu_S(\omega,\omega')\ . \tag{2}$$

This degree of entailment is obtained by "stretching" $m(q)$ into $m(q) \circ S$, where $\mu_{m(q)\circ S}(\omega) = \sup_{\omega' \in m(q)} \mu_S(\omega,\omega') \geq \mu_{m(q)}(\omega), i.e., m(q) \circ S \supseteq m(q)$. We shall also denote $\mu_{m(q)\circ S}(\omega)$ as $I_S(q|\omega)$ in agreement with (2), denoting by ω both the interpretation and the proposition which has ω as a unique model. The inequality $I_S(q|p) \geq \alpha$ can be equivalently written $m(p) \subseteq m(q) \circ S_\alpha$ where S_α is the ordinary relation defined by $S_\alpha = \{(\omega,\omega'), \mu_S(\omega,\omega') \geq \alpha\}$ and $\circ$ is the classical composition $A \circ R = \{\omega', \exists\omega \in A \text{ and } (\omega,\omega') \in R\}$. Based on index $I_S(q|p)$, the parameterized entailment relation in agreement with (1) reads

$$p \models_S^\alpha q \Leftrightarrow I_S(q|p) \geq \alpha\ .$$

The degree of entailment plays in similarity logic the same role as the confirmation index in Carnap's inductive logic (e.g., Dubucs [Du1]). Denoting $S_\alpha(q)$ the classical proposition whose set of models is $m(q) \circ S_\alpha$, $p \models_S^\alpha q$ is still equivalent to $\models p \to S_\alpha(q)$ where $\to$ is the "material implication" of classical logic. When S is the strict equality (i.e., $\mu_S(\omega,\omega') = 1$ if $\omega = \omega'$ and $\mu_S(\omega,\omega') = 0$ otherwise), $\models_S^\alpha$ coincides with the classical semantic entailment $\models$ when $\alpha > 0$. The degree of entailment $I_S(q|p)$ satisfies the following noticeable properties (Ruspini, [Ru3])

[2] A thorough study of triangular norms can be found in Schweizer and Sklar [SS1]. Representatives of the three main families of continuous triangular norms are $\alpha * \beta = \min(\alpha,\beta)$, $\alpha * \beta = \alpha \cdot \beta$ and $\alpha * \beta = \max(0, \alpha + \beta - 1)$. Any triangular norm $*$ is such that $\alpha * \beta \leq \min(\alpha,\beta)$. A dual operation $\perp$, called triangular co-norm, is associated to each triangular norm $*$, by $\alpha \perp \beta = 1 - (1-\alpha) * (1-\beta)$. The main co-norms are thus $\alpha \perp \beta = \max(\alpha,\beta)$, $\alpha \perp \beta = \alpha + \beta - \alpha \cdot \beta$ and $\alpha \perp \beta = \min(1, \alpha + \beta)$.

The $*$-transitivity of the fuzzy relation S can be equivalently written, introducing $d(\omega,\omega') = 1 - \mu_S(\omega,\omega')$, $d(\omega,\omega'') \leq d(\omega,\omega') \perp d(\omega',\omega'')$. Thus, min-transitive (resp. $\max(0, \cdot + \cdot - 1)$-transitive) fuzzy similarity relations are closely related to distances (resp. ultrametrics).

- $I_S(p|p) = 1$, i.e., $\forall\alpha > 0$, $p \models_S^\alpha p$ (Reflexivity)
- if $q \models r$ then $I_S(q|p) \leq I_S(r|p)$, i.e., if $p \models_S^\alpha q$ then $p \models_S^\alpha r$ (Right weakening)
- if $p \models r$ then $I_S(q|p) \geq I_S(q|r)$, i.e., if $r \models_S^\alpha q$ then $p \models_S^\alpha q$ (Left strengthening)
- $I_S(q|p) \geq I_S(q|r) * I_S(r|p)$, i.e., if $p \models_S^\alpha r$ and $r \models_S^\beta q$ then $p \models_S^{\alpha*\beta} q$ (Transitivity).

Left strenghtening is also called monotonicity (if $p \models_S^\alpha q$ then $p \wedge r \models_S^\alpha q$). Transitivity subsumes both right weakening and left strengthening. A particular case of the above transitivity property, obtained when p focuses on a unique interpretation ω, can be written

$$\text{if } \omega \models S_\alpha(r), \models r \rightarrow S_\alpha(q) \text{ then } \omega \models S_{\alpha*\alpha}(q)$$

since $I_S(r|\omega) \geq \alpha$ means $\omega \models S_\alpha(r)$. Indeed, $m(r) \subseteq m(q) \circ S_\alpha \Rightarrow m(r) \circ S_\alpha \subseteq m(q) \circ S_\alpha \circ S_\alpha \subseteq m(q) \circ S_{\alpha*\alpha}$ since $S_\alpha \circ S_\alpha \subseteq S_{\alpha*\alpha}$. Thus, it corresponds to the extended modus ponens pattern informally discussed in the introduction, which expresses that from "r is close to being true in the current state of the world ω" and "if r, then q is close to being true" we can deduce that "q is (somewhat) close to being true (in the state ω)". Usually, there is some deterioration of the closeness, except if $* = \min$ since then $S_{\alpha*\alpha} = S_\alpha$.

Ruspini [Ru3] also pointed out the following properties of $I_S(\cdot|p)$ with respect to conjunction and disjunction. We have

- $I_S(q \wedge r|p) \leq min(I_S(q|p), I_S(r|p))$,
  i.e., if $p \models_S^\alpha q \wedge r$ then $p \models_S^\alpha q$ and $p \models_S^\alpha r$
- $I_S(q \vee r|p) \geq \max(I_S(q|p), I_S(r|p))$,
  i.e., if $p \models_S^\alpha q$ and $p \models_S^\alpha r$ then $p \models_S^\alpha q \vee r$.

The above inequalities are direct consequences of the Right weakening property. In fact it is easy to see that if p has a single model then $I_S(q \vee r|p) = \max(I_S(q|p), I_S(r|p))$ so that in this particular case $p \models_S^\alpha q \vee r$ if and only if $p \models_S^\alpha q$ or $p \models_S^\alpha r$ (Dubois et al. [DEGGP1]).

It is worth-noticing that the reverse inequality does not hold for the above conjunction pattern; namely $\models_S^\alpha$ does not satisfy the Right AND property, i.e.,

we do not have if $p \models_S^\alpha q$ and $p \models_S^\alpha r$ then $p \models_S^\alpha q \wedge r$

due to the fact that we only have $(m(q) \cap m(r)) \circ S \subseteq (m(q) \circ S) \cap (m(r) \circ S)$; in particular $(m(q) \cap m(r)) \circ S$ may be empty while the other set of interpretations is not empty. The failure of the Right AND property implies that the set of consequences in the sense of $\models_S^\alpha$ cannot be closed under classical inference, since it would require both the Right weakening and the Right AND properties. Nevertheless, concerning the disjunctive connective, $\models_S^\alpha$ satisfies the OR property

- $p \models_S^\alpha r$ and $q \models_S^\alpha r$ if and only if $p \vee q \models_S^\alpha r$

since

$$I_S(r|p \vee q) = \min(I_S(r|p), I_S(r|q))$$

as it can be easily checked.

Ruspini [Ru3] proposes another degree of entailment where the current state of the world ω is known to belong to a subset $E = m(p) \subseteq \Omega$ of possible worlds (one of which being the true one) representing the background knowledge. In order to do that, he modifies the degree of inclusion $I_S(q|r)$ in the following way

$$I_{S,p}(q|r) = \inf_{\omega \models p} I_S(r|\omega) * \rightarrow I_S(q|\omega) \tag{3}$$

where $* \rightarrow$ is the residuated implication associated to the triangular norm $*$ (i.e., $\alpha * \rightarrow \beta = sup\{x \in [0,1], \alpha * x \leq \beta\}$). It generalizes the classical notion of deducing q from r, given evidence p, since letting S be the equality relation, we have

$$\begin{aligned} I_{S,p}(q|r) = 1 \ &\text{if and only if } m(p) \subseteq m(\neg r \vee q) \\ &\text{if and only if } m(p) \cap m(r) \subseteq m(q). \end{aligned}$$

Note that $I_{S,r}(q|r) = I_S(q|r)$ since $I_S(r|\omega) = 1$, $\forall \omega, \omega \models r$ (due to the reflexivity of S) and $1* \rightarrow \beta = \beta$. Then Ruspini [Ru3] shows that the following noticeable property holds

$$I_S(q|p) \geq I_{S,p}(q|r) * I_S(r|p) \ . \tag{4}$$

Indeed, noticing that $I_S(r|p) \leq I_S(r|\omega)$, $\forall \omega, \omega \models p$ and that $\alpha * \rightarrow \beta$ increases when α decreases,

$$\begin{aligned} I_S(r|p) * I_{S,p}(q|r) &\leq I_S(r|p) * [\inf_{\omega \models p} I_S(r|p) * \rightarrow I_S(q|\omega)] \\ &= \inf_{\omega \models p}[I_S(r|p) * (I_S(r|p) * \rightarrow I_S(q|\omega))] \\ &\leq \inf_{\omega \models p} I_S(q|\omega) = I_S(q|p), \end{aligned}$$

using the property $\alpha * (\alpha * \rightarrow \beta) \leq \beta$ that characterizes residuated implications. Ruspini's idea in introducing $I_{S,p}(q|r)$ is to "conditionalize" $I_S(q|r)$ on p. However, the result $I_{S,p}(q|r)$ is not exactly of the same nature as $I_S(q|r)$ and corresponds to another notion of consequence relation between propositions; see [DEGGP2] for more developments. Moreover, we do not have that $I_{S,p}(q|r) = I_S(q|r)$ when p is a tautology T. In fact the statement $I_{S,T}(q|r) \geq \alpha$ corresponds to a consequence relation distinct from $r \models_S^\alpha q$, and actually stronger. $I_{S,T}(q|r) = 1$ means that "the closer to true is r, the closer to true is q" and involves models in the neighborhood of r as well as models in the neighborhood of q, while $r \models_S^\alpha q$ only involves the latter. See Dubois et al. [DEGGP2] for a comparative study of $I_S(q|r) \geq \alpha$ and $I_{S,T}(q|r) \geq \alpha$.

Note that $I_S(q|r) = I_{S,r}(q|r)$, since $I_S(r|\omega) = 1$ for $\omega \models r$ in (3). It suggests that in $I_{S,p}(q|r)$, p should not be interpreted as characterizing an "evidential set" as Ruspini [Ru2] suggests, but represents the background knowledge.

We might think of a simpler, more natural, way of "conditioning" on p by considering the degree of inclusion $I_S(q|p \wedge r)$. First, observe that

$$I_S(q|p) \leq I_{S,p}(q|r) \leq I_S(q|p \wedge r) \ . \tag{5}$$

Indeed

$$\begin{aligned} I_{S,p}(q|r) &= \inf_{\omega \models p} I_S(r|\omega) * \to I_S(q|\omega) \\ &\leq \inf_{\omega \models p} \mu_{m(r)}(\omega) * \to I_S(q|\omega) \\ &= \inf_{\omega \models p \wedge r} I_S(q|\omega) = I_S(q|p \wedge r) \end{aligned}$$

where $\mu_{m(r)}$ denotes the characteristic function of the set of models of r, and $\mu_{m(r)}(\omega) \leq \mu_{m(r) \circ S}(\omega)$. The left inequality is easily obtained observing that $a * \to b \geq 1 * \to b = b$. When S is the equality, $I_{S,p}(q|r)$ is equal to $I_S(q|p \wedge r)$.

But $I_S(q|p \wedge r)$ does not satisfy the counterpart of property (4); namely

$$\textit{we do not have } I_S(q|p) \geq I_S(q|p \wedge r) * I_S(r|p) \ .$$

Indeed, consider the case where $m(p) \cap m(r) = \emptyset$, then $I_S(q|p \wedge r) = 1$. In general there exists q such that $I_S(q|p) = 0$ while there exist p and r such that $I_S(q|p \wedge r) * I_S(r|p) = 1 * I_S(r|p) > 0$, i.e., $\exists \alpha, m(p) \subseteq m(r) \circ S_\alpha$ (with $m(p) \cap m(r) = \emptyset$). Indeed $I_S(r|p) > \alpha$ only expresses the inclusion of the set of models of p into the set of neighbours of the models of q, but not necessarily into the subset of the models of q. Thus we have the *failure* of a property, sometimes named "Cut", which holds for classical semantical entailment, namely

$$p \models_S^\alpha r \text{ and } p \wedge r \models_S^\beta q \not\Rightarrow p \models_S^{f(\alpha,\beta)} q$$

with $\alpha > 0$ and $\beta > 0 \Rightarrow f(\alpha, \beta) > 0$. Only the weaker version expressed by (4) holds, where $I_S(q|p \wedge r)$ is replaced by $I_{S,p}(q|r)$. See Dubois et al. [DEGGP1] for a comparative study of $I_S(q|p \wedge r)$ and $I_{S,p}(q|r)$ in terms of induced consequence relations.

Although $I_{S,p}(q|r)$ cannot be written as an instance of the relation $\models_S^\alpha$, it can be easily understood in terms of extensions. Namely, $I_{S,p}(q|r) \geq \beta \Leftrightarrow \forall \omega \in m(p), I_S(r|\omega) * \to I_S(q|\omega) \geq \beta$. It entails $I_S(q|\omega) \geq \alpha * \beta$ if we know that $I_S(r|\omega) \geq \alpha$, since $a * \to b \geq \beta$ and $a \geq \alpha$ lead to $b \geq \alpha * \beta$ by virtue of residuated implications. Thus, $I_S(r|p) \geq \alpha$ is equivalent to $m(p) \subseteq m(r) \circ S_\alpha$ as already said, and $I_{S,p}(q|r) \geq \beta$ means

$$\forall \gamma, m(p) \cap (m(r) \circ S_\gamma) \subseteq m(q) \circ S_{\gamma * \beta} \ ,$$

since $I_S(r|\omega) \geq \alpha \Leftrightarrow \omega \in m(r) \circ S_\alpha$ and $I_S(q|\omega) \geq \gamma * \beta \Leftrightarrow \omega \in m(q) \circ S_{\gamma * \beta}$. Since $m(p) \subseteq m(r) \circ S_\alpha$, it leads as expected to $m(p) \subseteq m(q) \circ S_{\alpha * \beta}$, which is equivalent to $I_S(q|p) \geq \alpha * \beta$. Notice that using $I_S(q|p \wedge r) \geq \beta$ in place of $I_{S,p}(q|p) \geq \beta$ would lead to $(m(p) \cap m(r)) \circ S_\alpha \subseteq m(q) \circ S_{\alpha * \beta}$ which is not sufficient for concluding that $I_S(q|p) \geq \alpha * \beta$ when $I_S(r|p) \geq \alpha$.

Besides, in parallel with the degree of inclusion $I_S(q|p)$ (of $m(p)$ into $m(q) \circ S$) Ruspini [Ru3] also introduces a companion degree of consistency $C_S(q|p)$ of $m(p)$ with $m(q) \circ S$, i.e.,

$$C_S(q|p) = \sup_{\omega \models p} \sup_{\omega' \models q} \mu_S(\omega, \omega') = \sup_{\omega \models p} I_S(q|\omega) \ . \tag{6}$$

Clearly, $C(q|p) = C(p|q)$, and $C(\cdot|\cdot)$ is monotonically increasing, i.e.,

$$q \models r \Rightarrow C_S(r|p) \geq C_S(q|p) \ .$$

Moreover

$$C_S(q \vee r|p) = \max(C_S(q|p), C_S(r|p)) \ . \tag{7}$$

It can be also shown (Ruspini [Ru3]) that

$$C_S(q|p) \geq I_{S,p}(q|r) * C_S(r|p) \ . \tag{8}$$

Indeed

$$\begin{aligned} C_S(r|p) * I_{S,p}(q|r) &= [\sup_{\omega \models p} I_S(r|\omega)] * [\inf_{\omega \models p} I_S(r|\omega) * \to I_S(q|\omega)] \\ &\leq \sup_{\omega \models p} [I_S(r|\omega) * (I_S(r|\omega) * \to I_S(q|\omega))] \\ &\leq \sup_{\omega \models p} I_S(q|\omega) = C_S(q|p) \ . \end{aligned}$$

The inequality (8) expresses that if $C_S(r|p) \geq \alpha$, i.e., $m(p) \cap (m(r) \circ S_\alpha) \neq \emptyset$, and if $I_{S,p}(q|r) \geq \beta$, i.e., as said before, $\forall \alpha, m(p) \cap (m(r) \circ S_\alpha) \subseteq m(q) \circ S_{\alpha * \beta}$, we have indeed $m(p) \cap (m(q) \circ S_{\alpha * \beta}) \neq \emptyset$, i.e., $C_S(q|p) \geq \alpha * \beta$.

This completes the presentation of the similarity-based semantics proposed and developed by Ruspini. Investigations into fully-fledged logic for similarity reasoning have been recently proposed by Dubois et al. [DEGGP1], [DEGGP2] and Esteva et al. [EGGR1]. These investigations suggest that Ruspini's approach to fuzzy logic comes close to attempts at devising modal logics of rough sets by Orlowska and to extensions as done by Nakamura, although Ruspini does not try to propose a modal logic system per se.

3 Similarity Semantics and Rough Sets

Let A be a subset of a referential Ω. The main question addressed by rough sets (Pawlak [Pa1], [Pa2]) is: how to represent A by means of the quotient set Ω/S where S is an equivalence relation on Ω. Denoting $[\omega]_S$ the equivalence class of $\omega \in \Omega$, a *rough set* is a pair of subsets $S^*(A)$ and $S_*(A)$ of Ω/S that approach as close as possible A from outside and inside, respectively:

$$\begin{aligned} S^*(A) &= \{[\omega]_S | \ [\omega]_S \cap A \neq \emptyset, \omega \in \Omega\} \\ S_*(A) &= \{[\omega]_S | \ [\omega]_S \subseteq A, \omega \in \Omega\} \end{aligned}$$

$S^*(A)$ (resp.: $S_*(A)$) is called the upper (resp.: lower) approximation of A by S.

There have been several works by Orlowska [Or1], Fariñas del Cerro and Orlowska [FO1] that relate rough sets to modal logic. The basic idea is to interpret a rough set in terms of the two modalities L (necessary) and M (possible). Namely, if p is a proposition whose meaning is defined via the subset $A \subseteq \Omega$, Lp and Mp then correspond to $S_*(A)$ and $S^*(A)$, respectively. S plays the role of the accessibility relation on Ω in order to equip modal logic with the usual semantics (Chellas [Ch1]). A modal logic in the usual sense is thus defined at the syntactic level. At the semantic level, a model is viewed as a triple (Ω, S, m)

where Ω is a set of interpretations, S an equivalence relation on Ω and m is the meaning function. m defines, for each formula p, the set of interpretations $m(p)$ for which p is true. Satisfiability is defined in the usual sense, especially for Lp and Mp:

$$\begin{aligned}
&\omega \text{ satisfies } p && \text{if and only if } \omega \in m(p)\\
&\omega \text{ satisfies } Lp && \text{if and only if } \forall\omega' \in [\omega]_S, \omega' \in m(p),\\
& && \qquad \text{i.e., } [\omega]_S \subseteq m(p).\\
&\omega \text{ satisfies } Mp && \text{if and only if } \exists\omega' \in [\omega]_S, \omega' \in m(p),\\
& && \qquad \text{i.e., } [\omega]_S \cap m(p) \neq \emptyset.
\end{aligned}$$

Clearly, this can be written $m(Lp) = S_*(m(p))$, $m(Mp) = S^*(m(p))$. Since S is an equivalence relation the corresponding modal logic is the S5 system (Orlowska [Or1], [Or2]; Nakamura [Na2]). The axioms of this system reflect the properties of rough sets with respect to set-theoretic operations and to iteration of lower and upper approximation operations.

Fuzzy rough sets (Dubois and Prade [DP3], [DP6]) are defined through membership functions *on* Ω, as

$$\mu_{S^*(A)}(\omega) = \sup_{\omega' \in A} \mu_S(\omega, \omega')$$
$$\mu_{S_*(A)}(\omega) = \inf_{\omega' \notin A} 1 - \mu_S(\omega, \omega').$$

When S is a fuzzy relation, the extent to which $\omega \in S^*(m(q)) = m(q) \circ S$ is true is a matter of degree although q is a classical proposition. It reflects the distance between ω and the worlds in which q is true (the complement $\bar{S}$ of a similarity relation S, with $\mu_{\bar{S}} = 1 - \mu_S$, corresponds to a distance on Ω). We are not far from Weston [We1] approximate truth, but no longer very close to Zadeh's notion of fuzzy logic. Indeed, viewed as degrees of truth the quantities $I_S(q|\omega) = \sup_{\omega' \models q} \mu_S(\omega, \omega')$, no longer satisfy truth functionality for all connectives, namely $I_S(q \wedge q'|\omega) \leq \min(I_S(q|\omega), I_S(q'|\omega))$, even if S is not fuzzy, i.e., even if $I_S(\cdot|\omega)$ is 2-valued. Then S is an equivalence relation and Ruspini's calculus is then formally related to rough set theory where only the inclusion $S^*(m(q \wedge q')) \subseteq S^*(m(q)) \cap S^*(m(q'))$ holds. So one may have $I_S(q|\omega) = 1, I_S(q'|\omega) = 1$ but $I_S(q \wedge q'|\omega) = 0$. This lack of truth-functionality suggests that modal logic is a natural setting for capturing Ruspini's concepts [EGGR1].

Fuzzy rough sets offer a nice opportunity for developing a meaningful modal-like logic involving fuzzy modalities (induced by a fuzzy accessibility relation) acting on fuzzy propositions (whose meanings are fuzzy sets of Ω). Some attempts have been made in the past along this line. Nakamura and Gao [NG1] have pointed out that since fuzzy rough sets (viewed as an indexed family of rough sets) satisfy all properties of rough sets, it is possible to develop a S5-like modal fuzzy logic; this logic has been proposed by Nakamura [Na2]; see also Nakamura and Kuniyoshi [NK1]. The same author considers the case when the fuzzy relation is only symmetric and reflexive in (Nakamura [Na1]). He basically focuses on indexed modalities, L_α denoting the necessity modality associated with the level-cut relation S_α (see also Nakamura [Na3]).

Namely, let us assume that $m(p)$ is not attainable, and that only fuzzy upper and lower approximations $S^*(m(p))$ and $S_*(m(p))$ make sense. S is defined as a $\perp$-transitive similarity relation, and (Lp, Mp) correspond again to the fuzzy rough sets $S_*(m(p))$ and $S^*(m(p))$. Ruspini's entailment can be understood in terms of rough deduction; namely, when a proposition p implies the proposition q to degree α, it means that $\forall\omega \in m(p), \exists\omega' \in m(q)$ which is α-similar to ω, i.e., such that $\mu_S(\omega, \omega') \geq \alpha$. In other words, the degree of entailment of q by p can be written

$$I_S(q|p) = \inf_{\omega \in m(p)} \mu_{S^*(m(q))}(\omega) \ .$$

This degree is a degree of inclusion of $m(p)$ in the upper approximation of $m(q)$ obtained by "stretching" the set of interpretations ω satisfying q in a suitable way. The companion degree of consistency is defined by

$$C_S(q|p) = \sup_{\omega \in m(p)} \mu_{S^*(m(q))}(\omega) \ .$$

The quantity $I_S(q|\omega)$ is the degree of membership of interpretation ω to the upper approximation of $m(q)$. Ruspini [Ru3] restricted entailment degree, here denoted $I_{S,p}(q|r)$ is a degree of inclusion into $S^*(m(q))$ of the restriction to $m(p)$ of the upper approximation $S^*(m(r))$.

Ruspini's view of fuzzy logic considers fuzziness as a by-product of the presence of a metric or a similarity relation on the set of interpretations. Namely, any subset A of a set Ω of possible worlds is perceived as a fuzzy set $S^*(A)$ of elements close to A due to the similarity relation S on Ω. This is not exactly in accordance with Orlowska and Pawlak's intuitions. For instance, Ruspini never considers the lower approximation $S_*(A)$ which is another fuzzy set included in $S^*(A)$. It is the pair $(S_*(A), S^*(A))$ that should be regarded as the result of blurring A by means of S. This fuzzy rough set involves both fuzziness (grades of membership) and imprecision (interval-valued membership grades). Particularly, there are three companion entailment degrees to $I_{S,p}(q|r)$, changing upper approximations into lower approximations, as done in (Dubois and Prade [DP6]), corresponding to so-called "rough implications".

In the rough set concept the indistinguishability notion is basic, while in Ruspini's fuzzy logic, it is the idea of closeness. In particular Ruspini's similarity logic is most efficient when the considered similarity are fuzzy equality relations, such that $S(\omega, \omega') = 1$ implies $\omega = \omega'$. Then any interpretation can be distinguished from another. By contrast, in fuzzy rough sets, the similarity relation is generally not required to satisfy this property. Rough set theory is a method for handling incomplete information, while Ruspini's intent is to devise a logic of interpolation. To conclude, rough set theory and Ruspini's similarity-based reasoning are tightly connected at the formal level but the intended purposes of each work differ noticeably.

We now give a synthetic presentation of possibilistic logic and of its preference-based semantics.

4 Preference-Based Semantics and Possibilistic Logic

Let us assume that the set of possible worlds Ω is equipped with a complete ordering structure $\sqsubseteq$ encoded by a so-called possibility distribution π from Ω to

[0,1], under the form

$$\omega \sqsubseteq \omega' \Leftrightarrow \pi(\omega) \le \pi(\omega') \ . \tag{9}$$

Clearly, $\sqsubseteq$ is a reflexive, transitive and complete relation. The possibility distribution π is supposed to express the respective levels of plausibility of each world according to the available information; namely $\omega \sqsubseteq \omega'$ means that ω' is at least as plausible as ω. When $\omega \sqsubset \omega' \Leftrightarrow \pi(\omega) < \pi(\omega'), \omega'$ is also said to be preferred to ω. We shall see later how such a possibility distribution can be derived from a possibilistic logic knowledge base. A possibility measure Π (Zadeh [Za1]) is associated with π, namely

$$\Pi(p) = \sup_{\omega \models p} \pi(\omega) \ . \tag{10}$$

The possibility distribution is said to be normalized if $\sup_{\omega \in \Omega} \pi(\omega) = 1$. In the following, we assume that we work with a finite language, in order to ensure that $\exists \omega \models p$, $\pi(\omega) = \Pi(p)$ (i.e., the supremum is reached in (10)). By duality a necessity measure N is also defined by

$$N(p) = 1 - \Pi(\neg p) \ . \tag{11}$$

Possibility theory offers a nice framework for expressing a preference relation-based semantics in the sense of Shoham [Sh1]. We restate the main results of Dubois and Prade [DP4]. An interpretation ω is said to be a π-preferential model of p, which is denoted $\omega \models_\pi p$, iff

$$\begin{aligned} \omega \models_\pi p &\Leftrightarrow \omega \models p,\ \Pi(p) > 0 \text{ and } \not\exists \omega', \omega' \models p, \pi(\omega') > \pi(\omega) \\ &\Leftrightarrow \Pi(p) = \pi(\omega) > 0 \ . \end{aligned} \tag{12}$$

Note that the extra-condition $\Pi(p) > 0$ excludes the case when p is a contradiction. The π-preferential entailment $p \models_\pi q$ is then defined by

$$p \models_\pi q \Leftrightarrow \exists \omega, \omega \models_\pi p, \text{ and } \forall \omega, \omega \models_\pi p \Rightarrow \omega \models q \ . \tag{13}$$

It can be easily seen that if $\Pi(p) > 0$,

$$\begin{aligned} p \models_\pi q &\Leftrightarrow \{\omega, \omega \models p, \Pi(p) = \pi(\omega) > 0\} \subseteq \{\omega, \omega \models q\} \\ &\Leftrightarrow \Pi(p) = \Pi(p \wedge q) > \Pi(p \wedge \neg q) \end{aligned}$$

because no preferential model of p is a model of $\neg q$, and $\Pi(p) = \max(\Pi(p \wedge q), \Pi(p \wedge \neg q))$. Since a preferential model of $p \wedge r$ is not necessarily a preferential model of p, $\models_\pi$ cannot be monotonic, i.e.,

$$\textit{we do not have } p \models_\pi q \Rightarrow p \wedge r \models_\pi q \ .$$

Besides, the conditional possibility measure $\Pi(\cdot|p)$ is defined as the maximal solution of the equation, first proposed by Hisdal [Hi1]:

$$\forall q \neq \bot, \Pi(p \wedge q) = \min(\Pi(q|p), \Pi(p)) \tag{14}$$

and $\Pi(\perp|p) = 0$. This solution has been first suggested in (Dubois and Prade [DP2]) and reads:

$$\Pi(q|p) = 1 \text{ if } \Pi(p) = \Pi(p \wedge q); \qquad (15)$$
$$\Pi(q|p) = \Pi(p \wedge q) < 1 \text{ if } \Pi(p) > \Pi(p \wedge q) \ .$$

Thus, we have the equivalence

$$p \models_\pi q \Leftrightarrow N(q|p) > 0 \qquad (16)$$

using $N(q|p) = 1 - \Pi(\neg q|p)$. Note that $N(q|p) = N(\neg p \vee q)$ as soon as $N(q|p) \neq 0$, since $\Pi(q|p) = \Pi(p \wedge q)$ if $\Pi(p \wedge q) \neq 1$. The preferential possibilistic entailment satisfies the following properties (Dubois and Prade [DP4], [DP5])

- if $p \neq \perp$ then $p \models_\pi p$ (Restricted reflexivity)
  where $\perp$ denotes contradiction, due to $N(p|p) = 1$ if $p \neq \perp$
- if $q \models r$ then $p \models_\pi q \Rightarrow p \models_\pi r$ (Right weakening)
  due to $N(q|p) \leq N(r|p)$
- if $p \models\mid p'$ then $p \models_\pi q \Leftrightarrow p' \models_\pi q$ (Left equivalence)
- if $p \models_\pi q$ and $p \models_\pi r$ then $p \models_\pi q \wedge r$ (Right AND)
  due to $N(q \wedge r|p) = \min(N(q|p), N(r|p))$
- if $p \models_\pi q$ and $p \wedge q \models_\pi r$ then $p \models_\pi r$ (Cut)
  due to $N(r|p) \geq \min(N(q|p), N(r|p \wedge q))$
- if $p \models_\pi q$ and $p \models_\pi r$ then $p \wedge q \models_\pi r$ (Restricted monotonicity)
  since $N(r|p \wedge q) \geq \min(N(q|p), N(r|p))$ (see Dubois and Prade [DP4]).

  In fact, a stronger property holds, namely
- if $p \models_\pi r$ and $\neg(p \models_\pi \neg q)$ then $p \wedge q \models_\pi r$ (Rational monotony)
  due to $N(r|p \wedge q) > N(r|p)$ when $N(\neg q|p) = 0$ (see Benferhat et al. [BDP1])
- if $p \models_\pi r$ and $q \models_\pi r$ then $p \vee q \models_\pi r$ (OR)
  due to $N(r|p \vee q) = \min(N(r|p), N(r|q))$ when $N(r|p) > 0$, $N(r|q) > 0$.

A noticeable particular case of the Cut rule is

$$T \models_\pi p \text{ and } p \models_\pi q \Rightarrow T \models_\pi q$$

since

$$N(q|T) \geq \min(N(q|p), N(p|T))$$

where T denotes the tautology. It expresses that if p is accepted as true (i.e., p is somewhat certain) according to the available information represented by π, and if in the context of this information when p is true q is accepted as true (i.e., q is somewhat certain when p is true), we can conclude that q is accepted as true (i.e., q is somewhat certain) taking into account the available information. The statement "p is accepted as true", which corresponds to $N(p) > 0$ (and entails $N(\neg p) = 0$) should be understood in a provisional way, since it may be defeated when new information is added to $\mathcal{K}$. This is a restricted form of transitivity that does not hold when the tautology is changed into some other proposition. Indeed

$$\textit{we do not have } p \models_\pi q \text{ and } q \models_\pi r \Rightarrow p \models_\pi r \ .$$

This is due to the fact that it may happen that the preferred models of p (in the sense of π) are included in the models of q, and that the preferred models of q are included in the models of r, while the preferred models of p are *not* among the preferred models of q. Note that the Cut property together with the Monotonicity (which does not hold for $\models_\pi$) would entail the Transitivity property.

It is has been shown (Benferhat et al. [BDP1]) that any nonmonotonic consequence relation obeying to the following properties: Restricted reflexivity, Right weakening, Left logical equivalence, Right AND, Rational monotony, OR, and a "Nihil ex absurdo" condition, i.e., $\neg(\bot \models_\pi p)$, can be represented in terms of a possibilistic entailment $\models_\pi$ (the Cut property is a consequence of the other properties). See also Gärdenfors and Makinson [GM1] for a similar result.

A possibility distribution π is naturally obtained from a necessity-valued knowledge base. A necessity-valued knowledge base $\mathcal{K}$ in possibilistic logic is a collection of pairs (p_i, α_i), $i = 1, n$, where p_i is a classical logic formula, here a proposition for the sake of simplicity, and α_i is a number belonging to $(0,1]$ interpreted as a lower bound of the value of a necessity measure N for p_i, i.e., $N(p_i) \geq \alpha_i$, $i = 1, n$. This necessity measure N is associated with a possibility distribution π on the set of interpretations Ω, which represents the semantics of $\mathcal{K}$ and which can be built in the following way (Dubois, Lang and Prade [DLP2]). To (p_i, α_i) is associated the fuzzy set of interpretations defined by the membership function μ_i

$$\mu_i(\omega) = 1 \text{ if } \omega \models p_i; \ \mu_i(\omega) = 1 - \alpha_i \text{ if } \omega \models \neg p_i$$

in agreement with the duality $N(p_i) \geq \alpha_i \Leftrightarrow \Pi(\neg p_i) \leq 1 - \alpha_i$. Then π is obtained by intersection of these fuzzy sets (since $\mathcal{K}$ is viewed as the conjunction of the pairs (p_i, α_i)), i.e.,

$$\pi(\omega) = \min_{i=1,n} \mu_i(\omega) \ .$$

It can be checked that the necessity measure N defined from π, namely

$$N(p) = \inf_{\omega \models \neg p}(1 - \pi(\omega))$$

is such that $\forall i = 1, n, N(p_i) = \alpha_i$. In other words, in agreement with the principle of minimum specificity, the least restrictive, i.e., the largest, possibility distribution π on Ω, which saturates the constraints $N(p_i) \geq \alpha_i$, is associated with $\mathcal{K}$ in accordance with the semantics. Indeed, the principle of minimum specificity stipulates that each interpretation should receive the greatest possibility degree allowed by the constraints. Note that here the possibility distribution π on the set of interpretations is built from the weights given in $\mathcal{K}$ and is not given a priori.

The degree of inconsistency of $\mathcal{K}$, $\mathrm{Inc}(\mathcal{K})$ is defined from π, by $Inc(\mathcal{K}) = 1 - \sup_{\omega\in\Omega}\pi(\omega)$. In other words, $\mathcal{K}$ is all the more inconsistent as π is subnormalized. When $\mathrm{Inc}(\mathcal{K}) = 0$, $\mathcal{K}$ is said to be consistent. It can be shown (Dubois, Lang and Prade [DLP2]) that the three following statements are equivalent:

i) $\mathrm{Inc}(\mathcal{K}) = 0$;
ii) K is consistent in the usual sense, where K is the set of propositions obtained from $\mathcal{K}$ by ignoring the weights α_i;
iii) the assignment of the α_i's is such that $\forall p, \min(N(p), N(\neg p)) = 0$.

When $1 > Inc(K) = \alpha > 0$, $\mathcal{K}$ is said to be α-inconsistent and we have $\forall p, \min(N(p), N(\neg p)) = \mathrm{Inc}(\mathcal{K})$ (indeed $\max(\Pi(p), \Pi(\neg p)) = \sup_{\omega\in\Omega}\pi(\omega) = 1 - \mathrm{Inc}(\mathcal{K})$).

Semantic entailment from such a partially inconsistent possibilistic knowledge base $\mathcal{K}$ is defined by

$$\exists\beta > \mathrm{Inc}(\mathcal{K}), \mathcal{K} \models (p,\beta) \Leftrightarrow N(p) > N(\neg p) \tag{17}$$

where N is defined from the possibility distribution π associated with $\mathcal{K}$. Then $N(\neg p) = \mathrm{Inc}(\mathcal{K}) = 1 - \Pi(p)$ since $\min(N(p), N(\neg p)) = \mathrm{Inc}(\mathcal{K})$, and $\exists\beta, N(p) \geq \beta > \mathrm{Inc}(\mathcal{K})$.

The following equivalence which relates, in the possibilistic framework, nonmonotonicity and belief revision can be established (Dubois and Prade [DP4]):

$$N(q|p) > 0 \Leftrightarrow \exists\beta > \mathrm{Inc}(\mathcal{K} \cap \{(p,1)\}), (\mathcal{K} \cap \{(p,1)\}) \models (q,\beta) \tag{18}$$

where N is the necessity measure defined from the possibility distribution associated with $\mathcal{K}$. The above equivalence illustrates, in the possibilistic framework, the translation in the sense of Makinson and Gärdenfors [MG1] of a nonmonotonic consequence relation $p \mid\!\sim_K q$ (where K is a belief set representing our background beliefs), into a belief revision statement $q \in K_p^*$, where K_p^* denotes the result of the revision of K when adding p. Namely, $N(q|p) > 0$ plays the role of the nonmonotonic consequence relation $p \mid\!\sim_K q$, and $q \in K_p^*$ is expressed in our framework by $(\mathcal{K} \cap \{(p,1)\}) \models (q,\alpha)$. Moreover, note that it is also equivalent to preferential entailment in the sense of Shoham (up to the trivial entailment from contradictory propositions), here denoted $p \models_\pi q$. Here, instead of a belief set K, closed under deduction and without explicit ordering, we use any *weighted* set $\mathcal{K}$ of propositions, and we derive a preference relation on interpretations.

A machinery described elsewhere (Dubois, Lang and Prade [DLP1], [DLP2]), based on extended resolution and refutation implements this non-monotonic/belief revision mechanism. Let us briefly restate the main points. The necessity-valued possibilistic knowledge base $\mathcal{K}$ with which we start is supposed to be put in clausal form. This is not restrictive since if a formula p is the conjunction of n formulas $p_1, \ldots, p_n$, then $N(p) \geq \alpha \Leftrightarrow N(p_1 \wedge \ldots \wedge p_n) = \min(N(p_1), \ldots, N(p_n)) \geq \alpha \Leftrightarrow \forall i = 1, n, N(p_i) \geq \alpha$. Extended resolution corresponds to the following pattern

$$\frac{(c,\alpha) \quad (c',\beta)}{(\mathrm{Res}(c,c'), \min(\alpha,\beta))} \tag{19}$$

where $\text{Res}(c, c')$ is the classical resolvent of clauses c and c'. Classical resolution is recovered for $\alpha = \beta = 1$.

Refutation consists in adding to $\mathcal{K}$ the set of clauses generated by the negation $(\neg p, 1)$ of the proposition p of interest, with the weight 1 (total certainty). Then it can be shown that any weight obtained with the empty clause by the repeated application of the resolution pattern on $\mathcal{K} \cap \{(\neg p, 1)\}$ is indeed a lower bound of the value of the necessity measure (associated with $\mathcal{K}$) for the event "p is true". So we are interested in obtaining the empty clause with the greatest possible lower bound. A procedure yielding such a refutation with the best possible weight first has been implemented using an ordered search method. Let us denote by $\mathcal{K} \mapsto (p, \alpha)$ the fact that $(\bot, \alpha)$ can be obtained by a refutation from $\mathcal{K} \cap \{(\neg p, 1)\}$ (here α does not necessarily correspond to the best lower bound). Then the following soundness and completeness results hold, whether $\mathcal{K}$ is totally consistent (Dubois, Lang and Prade [DLP2]) or partially inconsistent (Lang et al. [LDP1]):

$$\mathcal{K} \mapsto (p, \alpha) \Leftrightarrow \mathcal{K} \models (p, \alpha), \text{ for } \alpha > \text{Inc}(\mathcal{K})$$

which guarantees the perfect agreement of the extended refutation machinery with the semantics presented above. See Dubois et al. [DP8], [DP9] for more details on possibilistic logic.

Different connections between possibilistic logic and modal logic can be searched for. In an information system perspective, Dubois, Prade and Testemale [DPT1] have built graded accessibility relations between incomplete states of information s and s' which account for the fact that the statements which are sufficiently certain in s are at least as certain in s' in the sense of possibility theory. More recently, Fariñas del Cerro and Herzig [FH1] have shown an equivalence between (qualitative) possibilistic logic and a conditional logic studied by Lewis [Le1]. Briefly, a model in this conditional logic consists of a set of classical interpretations Ω and an ***absolute sphere system*** S, which is a set of nested subsets of Ω, closed for union and intersection (S corresponds to the set of α-level cuts induced by the qualitative possibility distribution attached to a qualitative necessity measure). In the finite propositional case, it has been shown that a qualitative necessity relation is equivalent to such a model. Then, satisfiability and validity in qualitative possibilistic logic are equivalent to satisfiability and validity in the conditional logic. See also Fariñas del Cerro et al. [FHL1].

5 Comparison Between Preference and Similarity-Based Inferences

It should be now clear that the preference and the similarity semantics serve different inference purposes. This can be seen by the comparative inspection of the properties fulfilled by $\models_S^\alpha$ and $\models_\pi$, respectively. Namely, $\models_S^\alpha$ is monotonic, while $\models_\pi$ is not. Moreover, $\models_S^\alpha$ satisfies a Transitivity property (with a weakening effect if $* \neq \min$) closely related to the max $-*$ transitivity property of S, while $\models_\pi$, as any nonmonotonic consequence relation, does not satisfy the transitivity property in general. Besides, $\models_\pi$ satisfies a Cut property, which fails to hold for $\models_S^\alpha$ as explained in Section 2.

This clash between characteristic inferential properties should not be surprising if we remember that S and π are aimed to represent very different things. The possibility distribution π reflects the incomplete and uncertain information from which we want to draw inferences, by providing a ranking between more or less plausible states of the world. Note that the type of incomplete information modelled by π differs from the one modelled by a rough set, since the latter deals within distinguishability due to a coarse granularity, while the former expresses that some situations are more plausible than others. The fuzzy similarity relation S is aimed at modelling the fact that there are states of the world, or interpretations of propositions which are close to one another. Then $\models_\pi$ captures the idea of deriving the most plausible conclusions in a given state of knowledge. By contrast, $\models_S^\alpha$ expresses that if we are close to an interpretation which makes p true, and if we are close to having q true when p is known to be true, then we are close to an interpretation which makes q true (with the underlying idea of interpreting 'we are close to an interpretation that makes p true' as 'p is somewhat true'). Note also that π is obtained from the levels of certainty of the statements stored in the knowledge base, while S, which models the closeness of interpretations, is supposed to be given independently from the contents of the knowledge base, once the logical language is defined.

Esteva, Garcia-Calves and Godo [EGG1] have pointed out that a proposition p together with a similarity relation S gives birth to a possibility distribution

$$\pi_{p,S}(\omega) = \mu_{m(p)\circ S}(\omega) = \sup_{\omega' \models p} \mu_S(\omega, \omega') \ . \tag{20}$$

Conversely, it is possible to associate with a possibility distribution π a proposition p_π such that $m(p_\pi) = \{\omega, \pi(\omega) = 1\}$ and a similarity relation S_π defined by

$$\mu_{S_\pi}(\omega, \omega') = \min(\pi(\omega) * \rightarrow \pi(\omega'), \pi(\omega') * \rightarrow \pi(\omega)) \ . \tag{21}$$

The fuzzy relation S_π is reflexive, symmetrical and max $-*$ transitive (Valverde, [Val]). It provides a systematic way for relating the encodings of preferences and similarities; see Ruspini [Ru5], [Ru6], [Ru7] for a general discussion. Moreover, Esteva et al. [EGG1] have shown that

$$\pi_{p_\pi, S_\pi} = \pi \tag{22}$$

i.e., starting with a possibility distribution π, and defining an associated proposition p_π and an associated similarity relation S_π using (21), it is possible to recover π from p_π, and S_π using (20). This formally expresses that a possibility distribution π, representing the contents of a possibilistic knowledge base $\mathcal{K}$, can always be interpreted as the set of *preferred* models of the proposition obtained as the conjunction of the formulas in $\mathcal{K}$, enlarged (in the sense of (20)) by a similarity relation induced by the levels of plausibility of the different interpretations (the greater the plausibility, the closer the interpretation to the preferred models). However, this does not mean that the types of inference embedded in $\models_\pi$ and in $\models_S^\alpha$ are the same, nor can they be translated into each other. In other words, $N(q)$ and $I_S(q|p)$ are not exchanged in the transformation expressed by (20)-(21).

Indeed $I_S(q|p)$ can be viewed as the necessity measure of a *fuzzy* proposition $\tilde{q}$ whose fuzzy set of models is $m(q) \circ S$, based on the possibility distribution $\pi = \mu_{m(p)}$, and $C_S(q|p)$ as the possibility measure of $\tilde{q}$ based on the same possibility distribution. So the situation is completely reversed with respect to the one encountered in possibilistic logic where $N(q)$ is defined from a possibility distribution π which is not $\{0,1\}$-valued generally, as $\mu_{m(p)}$ is, and where q is a classical (i.e., non-fuzzy) proposition. The same remark holds when comparing $N(q|r)$ and $I_{S,r}(q|p)$.

As logics of similarity and preference respectively, Ruspini's fuzzy logic and possibilistic logic are complementary. It would be fruitful to put them together by keeping the similarity relation, but allowing for fuzzy evidence under the form of a possibility distribution ranking the possible worlds in terms of preference. Then the inclusion index could be generalized, when $m(p)$ is a fuzzy set with $\pi = \mu_{m(p)}$, into

$$I_S(q|\pi) = \inf_\omega \pi(\omega) * \Rightarrow \mu_{S^*(m(q))}(\omega)$$

using an implication $* \Rightarrow$ of the form $a* \Rightarrow b = 1 - (a * (1-b))$ where $*$ is a triangular norm. $* \Rightarrow$ is an implication of the form $\neg p \vee q = \neg(p \wedge \neg q)$ using fuzzy logic connectives. This implication lets $I_S(q|\pi) = 1$ if and only if all the interpretations that are whatsoever possible ($\pi(\omega) > 0$) belong to the core of the upper approximation of q. Similarly, $I_S(q|\pi) > 0$ if and only if the most plausible interpretations ($\pi(\omega) = 1$) are in the vicinity of $q(\mu_{S^*(m(q))}(\omega) > 0)$. Clearly, when S is the equality on Ω, $I_S(q|\pi)$ reduces to the degree of necessity of possibilistic logic. And if $\pi(\omega) = 1$, $\pi(\omega') = 0$ for $\omega' \neq \omega$, $I_S(q|\pi) = I_S(q|\omega)$. Similarly,

$$C_S(q|\pi) = \sup_\omega \pi(\omega) * \mu_{S^*(m(q))}(\omega)$$

generalizes both the consistency index and the possibility measure. When $m(p)$ is fuzzy, the following extension of $I_{S,p}$ can be proposed where $\pi = \mu_{m(p)}$

$$I_{S,\pi}(q|r) = \inf_\omega \pi(\omega) * \Rightarrow (I_S(r|\omega) * \rightarrow I_S(q|\omega)) \ .$$

Note that we cannot use implication $* \rightarrow$ to combine π with the other expression in order to encompass $N(\neg r \vee q)$ as a particular case of the above expression, when S is an equality. Indeed, $N(\neg r \vee q) = \inf_{\omega \notin m(\neg r \vee q)} 1 - \pi(\omega) \neq \inf_\omega \pi(\omega) * \rightarrow \mu_{m(\neg r \vee q)}(\omega)$, generally. Instead of implication $* \Rightarrow$, we could use the contra position of $* \rightarrow$ (which differs from $* \rightarrow$, generally). Indeed, we do have that

$$N(\neg r \vee q) = \inf_\omega (1 - \mu_{m(\neg r \vee q)}(\omega) * \rightarrow 1 - \pi(\omega))$$

when S is an equality relation. Then it means that we accept $I_S(q|\pi) = 1$ as soon as $\pi \leq \mu_{S^*(m(q))}$. What is the most natural choice is a matter of further investigation.

6 Concluding Remarks

This paper has provided a parallel presentation of the similarity-based semantics of Ruspini's view of fuzzy logic, and of the preferential semantics of possibilistic logic. It has been shown that their inferential behaviors are completely different and that they serve different approximate reasoning purposes. Possibilistic logic enables us to infer plausible but defeasible conclusions on the basis of the available information which is incomplete and pervaded with uncertainty. Ruspini's semantics takes advantage of a notion of closeness between interpretations for defining a kind of graded truth. See (Dubois and Prade [DP8]) for a more general overview of similarity-based approximate reasoning in the fuzzy set setting including qualitative reasoning (in order to deal with the approximate equality of numerical values which are close to each other), interpolative reasoning (by computing intermediate conclusions as weighted combinations of conclusions which can be inferred in situations which are close to the current one), and case-based reasoning (where already-known cases similar to the current one are looked for in order to suggest possible conclusions or actions).

Ruspini's proposal for introducing similarity notions in logic and reasoning is appealing. However, the reasonableness of the choices made for defining $I_S(p|\omega)$, $I_S(q|p)$ and $I_{S,p}(q|r)$ may still be discussed: why using only upper approximations and not lower approximations (in the sense of rough sets)? Why defining $I_{S,p}(q|r)$ as the degree of inclusion of $m(p) \cap (m(r) \circ S)$ into $m(q) \circ S$ rather than, for instance, $m(p) \cap m(r)$ into $m(q) \circ S$? These questions are more precisely studied by Dubois et al. [DEGGP1], [DEGGP2]. This may have some impact on the failure or not of desirable properties (Right AND, Cut). Moreover, as done in possibilistic logic, when building a possibility distribution from a possibilistic knowledge base, it would be interesting to start in similarity logic with a set of weighted conditional propositions in the sense of some $I_S(q|r)$-like index, and to associate them with a piece of evidence p and a similarity relation S. Results in Dubois et al. [DEGGP1], [DEGGP2] suggest that it is a promising alley of research.

It is obvious that fuzzy rough sets offer a good opportunity to formally relate and/or put together fuzzy sets, especially similarity semantics, and modal logic, a task that has been considered in the past from various perspectives. Fuzzy rough sets offer a tool for graded extensions of the S5 system as pointed out by Nakamura [Na2], [Na3]. Rather than looking for a graded versions of S5, another worth investigating direction might be to view the rough set semantics (or Ruspini's similarity semantics as well) in terms of systems of spheres in the sense of Lewis. Indeed, a (fuzzy) similarity relation turns to be a natural way of representing a system of spheres. In such a framework, possibilistic logic (whose semantics is equivalent to a unique sphere system) might then appear as a particular case of a similarity logic just as revision might be *formally* viewed as a particular case of updating; see (Dubois and Prade [DP9]). Indeed, possibilistic logic has been shown to encode revision in the sense of Gärdenfors [Ga1] in a natural way (Dubois and Prade [DP7]), while updating in the sense of Katsuno and Mendelzon [KM1] can be expressed in terms of closeness relations at the semantic level. These considerations are further developed by Rodriguez et al. [RGG1], [EGGR1].

Acknowledgements

This work has been partially supported by the European ESPRIT Basic Research Action no 6156 entitled "Defeasible Reasoning and Uncertainty Management Systems (DRUMS-II)".

References

[BDP1] Benferhat, S., Dubois, D., Prade, H.: Representing default rules in possibilistic logic. Proc. of the 3rd Inter. Conf. on Principles of Knowledge Representation and Reasoning (KR'92) (Nebel, B., Rich, C., Swartout, W. eds.), Cambridge, MA, Oct. 25-29, (1992), 673-684

[Ch1] Chellas, B.F.: Modal Logic: An Introduction. Cambridge University Press, Cambridge, UK, (1980)

[DEGGP1] Dubois, D., Esteva, F., Garcia, P., Godo, L., Prade, H.: Similarity-based consequence relations. In: Symbolic and Quantitative Approaches to Reasoning and Uncertainty (Proc. of the Europ. Conf. On ECSQARU'95, Fribourg, Switzerland, July 1995) (Froidevaux, C., Kohlas, J. eds.), Lecture Notes in Artificial Intelligence, Vol. 946, Springer Verlag, Berlin, (1995), 171-179

[DEGGP2] Dubois, D., Esteva, F., Garcia, P., Godo, L., Prade, H.: A logical approach to interpolation based on similarity relations. To appear in Int. J. of Approximate Reasoning, (1997)

[DLP1] Dubois, D., Lang, J., Prade, H.: Theorem proving under uncertainty - A possibility theory-based approach. Proc. the Inter. Joint Conf. on Artificial Intelligence (IJCAI'87), Milan, Italy, (1987), 984-986

[DLP2] Dubois, D., Lang, J., Prade, H.: Automated reasoning using possibilistic logic: semantics, belief revision and variable certainty weights. IEEE Trans. on Data and Knowledge Engineering, 6(1), (1994), 64-71

[DLP3] Dubois, D., Lang, J., Prade, H.: Possibilistic logic. In: Handbook of Logic in Artificial Intelligence and Logic Programming, Vol. 3: Nonmonotonic Reasoning and Uncertain Reasoning (Gabbay, D.M., Hogger, C.J., Robinson, J.A., Nute, D. eds.), Oxford University Press, (1994), 439-513

[DP1] Dubois, D., Prade, H.: Fuzzy Sets and Systems: Theory and Applications. Academic Press, New York, (1980)

[DP2] Dubois, D., Prade, H.: Possibilistic inference under matrix form. In: Fuzzy Logic in Knowledge Engineering (Prade, H., Negoita, C.V. eds.), Verlag TÜV Rheinland, (1986), 112-126

[DP3] Dubois, D., Prade, H.: Rough sets and fuzzy rough sets. Int. J. of General Systems, 17, (1990), 191-209

[DP4] Dubois, D., Prade, H.: Possibilistic logic, preferential models, nonmonotonicity and related issues. Proc. of the 12th Inter. Joint Conf. on Artificial Intelligence (IJCAI'91), Sydney, Australia, Aug. 24-30, (1991), 419-424

[DP5] Dubois, D., Prade, H.: Conditional objects and non-monotonic reasoning. Proc. of the 2nd Inter. Conf. on Principles of Knowledge Representation and Reasoning (KR'91) (Allen, J., Fikes, R., Sandewall, E. eds.), Cambridge, MA, April 22-25, (1991), 175-185

[DP6] Dubois, D., Prade, H.: Putting rough sets and fuzzy sets together. In: Intelligent Decision Support – Handbook of Applications and Advances of the Rough Sets Theory (Slowinski, R. ed.), Kluwer Academic Publ., (1992), 203-232

[DP7] Dubois, D., Prade, H.: Belief change and possibility theory. In: Belief Revision (Gärdenfors, P. ed.), Cambridge University Press, Cambridge, UK, (1992), 142-182

[DP8] Dubois, D., Prade, H.: Similarity-based approximate reasoning. In: Computational Intelligence Imitating Life (Proc. of the IEEE Symp., Orlando, FL, June 27-July 1st, 1994) (Zurada, J.M., Marks II, R.J., Robinson, X.C.J. eds.), IEEE Press, (1994), 69-80

[DP9] Dubois, D., Prade, H.: A survey of belief revision and updating rules in various uncertainty models. Int. J. of Intelligent Systems, 9, (1994), 61-100

[DPT1] Dubois, D., Prade, H., Testemale, C.: In search of a modal system for possibility theory. Proc. of the Conf. on Artificial Intelligence, Munich, Germany, Aug. 1-5, (1988), 501-506

[Du1] Dubucs, J.P.: Inductive logic revisited. In: Philosophy of Probability (Dubucs, J.P. ed.), Kluwer Academic Publ., Dordrecht, (1993), 79-108

[EGG1] Esteva, F., Garcia-Calves, P., Godo, L.: On the relationship between preference and similarity-based approaches to possibilistic reasoning. Proc. of the 2nd IEEE Inter. Conf. on Fuzzy Systems (FUZZ-IEEE'93), San Francisco, CA, March 28-April 1st, (1993), 918-923

[EGGR1] Esteva, F., Garcia-Calves, P., Godo, L., Rodriguez, R.: A modal account of similarity-based reasoning. International Journal of Approximate Reasoning, 16, (1997), 235-260

[FH1] Fariñas del Cerro, L., Herzig, A.: A modal analysis of possibility theory. Proc. of the Inter. Workshop on Fundamentals of Artificial Intelligence (FAIR'91) (Jorrand, Ph., Kelemen, J. eds.), Smolenice Castle, Czechoslovakia, Sept. 8-12, 1991, SpringerVerlag, Berlin, (1991), 11-18

[FHL1] Fariñas del Cerro, L., Herzig, A., Lang, J.: From ordering-based nonmonotonic reasoning to conditional logics. Proc. of the 10th Europ. Conf. On Artificial Intelligence (ECAI'92) (Neumann, B. ed.), Vienna, Austria, Aug. 3-7, (1992), 38-42

[FO1] Fariñas del Cerro, L., Orlowska, E.: DAL - A logic for data analysis. Theoretical Computer Science, 36, (1985), 251-264

[Ga1] Gärdenfors, P.: Knowledge in Flux - Modeling the Dynamics of Epistemic States. The MIT Press, Cambridge, MA, (1988)

[GM1] Gärdenfors, P., Makinson, D.: Non-monotonic inference based on expectations. Artificial Intelligence, 65, (1994), 197-245

[Hi1] Hisdal, E.: Conditional possibilities - Independence and non-interactivity. Fuzzy Sets and Systems, 1, (1978), 283-297

[KM1] Katsuno, H., Mendelzon, A.O.: On the difference between updating a knowledge base and revising it. Proc. of the 2nd Inter. Conf. on Principles of Knowledge Representation and Reasoning (KR'91) (Allen, J., Fikes, R., Sandewall, E. eds.), Cambridge, MA, April 22-25, 387-394. Revised version in: Belief Revision (Gärdenfors, P. ed.), Cambridge University Press,

Cambridge, UK, 1992, (1991), 301-311

[LDP1] Lang, J., Dubois, D., Prade, H.: A logic of graded possibility and certainty coping with partial inconsistency. Proc. of the 7th Conf. On Uncertainty in Artificial Intelligence (D'Ambrosio, B.D., Smets, P., Bonissone, P.P. eds.), Los Angeles, CA, July 13-15, 1991, Morgan & Kaufmann, San Mateo, CA, (1991), 188-196

[Le1] Lewis, D.: Counterfactuals. Blackwell, Oxford, (1973)

[MG1] Makinson, D., Gärdenfors, P.: Relations between the logic of theory change and nonmonotonic logic. In: The Logic of Theory Change (Proc. of the Workshop, Konstanz, Germany, Oct. 1989) (Fuhrmann, A., Morreau, M. eds.), Lecture Notes in Artificial Intelligence, Vol. 465, Springer Verlag, Berlin, (1991), 185-205

[Na1] Nakamura, A.: On a KTB-modal fuzzy logic. Tech. Report no C-31, Dept. of Applied Mathematics, Hiroshima University, Japan, (1989)

[Na2] Nakamura, A.: Topological soft algebra for the S5 modal fuzzy logic. Proc. of the 21st Inter. Symp. on Multiple-Valued Logic, Victoria, BC, (1991), 80-84

[Na3] Nakamura, A.: On a logic based on fuzzy modalities. Report MCS-10, Dept. of Computer Science, Meiji University, Japan, (1991)

[NG1] Nakamura, A., Gao, J.M.: A logic for fuzzy data analysis. Fuzzy Sets and Systems, 39, (1991), 127-132

[NK1] Nakamura, A., Kuniyoshi, M.: Graded rough-modal logic. Tech. Report TRCSN-2, Dept. of Computer Science, Meiji University, Kawasaki 214, Japan, (1993)

[Or1] Orlowska, E.: Modal logics in the theory of information systems. Zeitschrift für Mathematische Logik und Grundlagen der Mathematik, 30(3), (1984), 213-222

[Or2] Orlowska, E.: A logic of indiscernibility relations. In: Lecture Notes in Computer Sciences, Vol. 208, Springer Verlag, Berlin, (1985), 177-186

[Pa1] Pawlak, Z.: Rough sets. Int. J. of Information and Computer Sciences, 11, (1982), 341-356

[Pa2] Pawlak, Z.: Rough Sets -Theoretical Aspects of Reasoning about Data. Kluwer Academic Publ., Dordrecht, (1991)

[RGG1] Rodriguez, R.O., Garcia, P., Godo, L.: Similarity-based models, counterfactuals and belief change. Research Report IIIA-95/5, IIIA-CSIC, University of Barcelona, Bellaterra, Spain, (1995)

[Ru1] Ruspini, E.H.: The semantics of vague knowledge. Revue Inter. de Systémique (Dunod, Paris), 3(4), (1989), 387-420

[Ru2] Ruspini, E.H.: Similarity-based interpretations of fuzzy-logic concepts. Proc. of the 2nd Inter. Conf. On Fuzzy Logic & Neural Networks (IIZUKA'90), Iizuka, Japan, July 20-24,Vol. 2, (1990), 735-738

[Ru3] Ruspini, E.H.: On the semantics of fuzzy logic. Int. J. of Approximate Reasoning, 5, (1991), 45-88

[Ru4] Ruspini, E.H.: Approximate reasoning: Past, present, future. Information Sciences, 57/58, (1991), 297-327

[Ru5] Ruspini, E.H.: Truth as utility: A conceptual synthesis. Proc. of the 7th Conf. on Uncertainty in Artificial Intelligence (D'Ambrosio, B.D., Smets, Ph., Bonissone, P.P. eds.), Los Angeles CA, July 13-15, Morgan & Kaufmann, San Mateo, CA, (1991), 316-322

[Ru6] Ruspini, E.H.: On truth and utility. In: Symbolic and Quantitative Approaches to Uncertainty (Proc. Of the Europ. Conf. ECSQAU, Marseille, Oct. 1991) (Kruse, R., Siegel, P. eds.), Lecture Notes in Computer Science, Vol. 548, Springer Verlag, Berlin, (1991), 297-304

[Ru7] Ruspini, E.H.: On truth, utility and similarity. Proc. of the Inter. Fuzzy Engineering Symp. (IFES'91), Yokohama, Japan, Nov. 13-15, Vol. 1: Fuzzy Engineering toward Human Friendly Systems, (1991), 42-50

[SS1] Schweizer, B., Sklar, A.: Probabilistic Metric Spaces. North-Holland, New York, (1983)

[Sh1] Shoham, Y.: Reasoning About Change – Time and Causation from the Standpoint of Artificial Intelligence. The MIT Press, Cambridge, MA, (1988)

[Va1] Valverde, L.: On the structure of F-indistinguishability operators. Fuzzy Sets and Systems, 17, (1985), 313-328

[We1] Weston, T.: Approximate truth. J. of Philos. Logic, 16, (1987), 203-227

[Za1] Zadeh, L.A.: Fuzzy sets as a basis for a theory of possibility. Fuzzy Sets and Systems, 1, (1978), 3-28

Chapter 15

A Logic for Reasoning about Similarity

Beata Konikowska

Institute of Computer Science, Polish Academy of Sciences, 01-237 Warsaw, Ordona 21[1]

Abstract: A similarity relation is a reflexive and symmetric, but in general not transitive binary relation between objects. Similarity can be regarded as a relative notion parametrised by the set of classification attributes used as a basis for determining similarity or dissimilairty of objects. In the paper we present a polymodal formal language for reasoning about such a relative notion of similarity. For each subset of a given set of attributes, we have two modalities, corresponding semantically to so-called upper and lower approximations of a set of objects with respect to that set of attributes; intuitively, the latter approximations could be described as the interior and completion of a set of objects with respect to the similarity relation generated by the considered set of attributes, respectively. Formulae of the language evaluate to sets of objects, and a formula is said to be true if it evaluates to the whole universe of the model. The language is given a sound and complete deduction system in Rasiowa-Sikorski style: it consists of fundamental sequences of formulae which represent axioms of the system, and decomposition rules for sequences of formulae which represent inference rules.

1 Introduction

An informal notion of similarity is widely used in everyday life. We say that somebody is just like his brother - that is, similar to him in looks and/or character. We talk about similarity of two cars, two houses, two countries... Even from such unformal examples it is clearly evident that the notion of similarity is a relative one - two object can be quite similar in one aspect, but completely dissimilar in another one. For example, Mary can look just like her mother, but at the same time have a very different temper: then we say that Mary is similar to her mother in looks, but quite dissimilar in temper. Thus the notion of similarity is parametrised by a set of attributes on which we base our comparison of two objects.

Further, a similarity relation is clearly reflexive - since any object is always similar to itself - and symmetric: if A is similar to B, then B is also similar to A. However, one can easily see that similarity is not in general transitive: the fact that A is similar to B and B is similar to C need not imply that A is also similar to C. This can be illustrated by the following simple example. Assume that we consider a set of

[1]An initial version of the paper was sponsored by the Ministry of Education grant RPBP III/24.B, and the present one – by the State Committee for Scientific Research grant No 2 P 301 007 04.

possible locations for a new school in a given town. We may say that two location are similar if they distance between them is less than two miles. Such a similarity relation is perfectly sensible, but obviously not transitive. Indeed: if three locations A, B, C are situated along one street, in that order, and the distances between A and B and between B and C are 1.5 miles each, then locations A and B are obviously similar. However, A and C are not similar, because the distance between A and C is 3 miles. Similarity of locations defined as above is an example of a similarity relation relation based on a threshold value: two objects are considered to be similar if the the values of a given attribute of these objects differ by at most the threshold value (in our case, 5 years). One can encounter a multitude of such "threshold" similarity relations in almost all areas.

Similarity relations are used extensively (though often informally) not only in everyday life, but also in many fields of science, including the traditional ones, like biology, linguistics, archeology, as well as in many modern branches of science connected with computer applications, like expert systems, knowledge bases and image recognition. This justifies the widely recognized need to formally describe similarity relations. Some of the attempts in this direction can be found in [10,11].

In the paper we propose a formal logical system for reasoning about similarity understood in the way, described above: that is, as a reflexive and symmetric relation parametrised by a set of properties with respect to which the considered objects are judged as either similar or dissimilar. To capture the relative character of similarity, in our language we talk about a whole family of similarity relations corresponding to different subsets of a given set of properties of objects. The logical language discussed here is similar to that proposed by E. Orłowska in [3] for the logic of indiscernibility relations. Indiscernibility is in fact a special case of similarity, for an indiscernibility relation is a similarity relation which has the additional property of transitivity (so any indiscernibility relation is an equivalence relation). In the literature on the subject, similarity is sometimes referred to as "weak indiscernibility". The approach to similarity we present here stems (like the approach to indiscernibility in [3]) from the rough set methodology ([5]). The semantic aspect of such an approach to smilarity has been extensively discussed by J. Pomykała in [6, 7].

2 Universe of Discourse

Throughout the paper, we consider a given set ENT of entities (objects) and a given set PROP of their properties. The sets ENT and PROP are assumed to be nonempty. The entities are both described and discerned in terms of these properties. In this framework we examine the notion of similarity of entities relative to an arbitrary subset P of properties from PROP. Thus in fact we have to do with a whole family of similarity relations, corresponding to all possible choices of the subset $P \subseteq$ PROP. Hence, for a given ENT and PROP, we consider a family $\{sim(\mathrm{P})\}_{P \subseteq \mathrm{PROP}}$ such that, for any $P, Q \subseteq$PROP, the following conditions are satisfied:

(C1) $sim(P)$ is reflexive and symmetric,

(C2) $sim(P \cup Q) = sim(\mathrm{P}) \cap sim(Q)$,

(C3) $sim(\emptyset) = \text{ENT} \times \text{ENT}$.

Condition (C1) expresses the general properties of similarity discussed in the introduction. Let us stress once more that in contrast to discernibility relations a similarity relation need not be transitive and hence in general it is not an equivalence relation. Condition (C2) says that a pair of entities is similar relative to properties in $P \cup Q$ iff it is similar relative to properties in P as well as relative to the properties in Q. Obviously, this condition is perfectly justifiable from the intuitional point of view. A simple consequence of (C2) is the condition

(C4) $P \subseteq Q$ implies $sim(Q) \subseteq sim(P)$,

which says that the bigger the considered set of properties, the smaller the similarity relation corresponding to this set.

Finally, condition (C3) says that any two entities are similar with respect to an empty set of properties.

Throughout the paper, by a universe of discourse we understand any ordered triple of the form

$$U = <\text{ENT, PROP}, \{sim(P)\}_{P \subseteq \text{PROP}}> \tag{2.1}$$

Within any universe U of the above form, for any set of properties $P \subseteq \text{PROP}$ we define the operations of a lower approximation $\underline{sim}(P)$ and of an upper approximation $\overline{sim}(P)$ relative to the set P on sets of entities. Namely, for any $E \subseteq$ ENT we put

$$\underline{sim}(P)E = \{e' \in ENT\text{: } (\forall\, e \in ENT)((e,e') \in sim(P) \Rightarrow e \in E)\},$$

$$\overline{sim}(P)E = \{e' \in ENT\text{: } (\exists\, e \in E)((e',e) \in sim(P))\}$$

One can easily see that $\underline{sim}(P)E$ consists of all entities belonging to E which are not similar relative to P to any entity outside E; in other words, $\underline{sim}(P)E$ could be referred to as the interior of E with respect to the similarity relation $sim(P)$. On the other hand, $\overline{sim}(P)E$ consists of all entites in ENT which are similar relative to P to some entity in E. Thus, obviously, $\overline{sim}(P)E$ contains E, and in fact the upper approximation of E could be interpreted as the completion of E with respect to to the similarity relation $sim(P)$.

The above notions of approximations correspond to those examined in the rough set theory - a detailed discussion of their properties can be found in [4,5]. For the purposes of this paper, a reader should only know the following properties of lower and upper approximation:

$$\underline{sim}(P)E \subseteq E \subseteq \overline{sim}(P)E, \tag{2.2}$$

$$\underline{sim}(P)E = \text{ENT} - \overline{sim}(P)(\text{ENT} - E), \tag{2.3}$$

$$\underline{sim}(P \cup Q)E \subseteq \underline{sim}(P)E \cap \underline{sim}(Q)E, \tag{2.4}$$

$$\overline{sim}(P \cup Q)\{e\} = \overline{sim}(P)\{e\} \cap \overline{sim}(Q)\{e\}, \tag{2.5}$$

$$\overline{sim}(P)(E \cup F) = \overline{sim}(P)E \cup \overline{sim}(P)F, \tag{2.6}$$

$$\overline{sim}(P)(E \cap F) \subseteq \overline{sim}(P)E \cap \overline{sim}(P)F. \tag{2.7}$$

3 Syntax of the Language

As we have already defined the framework we are going to work in, now we can pass to our main objective: the definition of a formal language for reasoning about similarity. The language in question is parametrised by the set of properties PROP. In other words, given the set PROP, we develop a language to talk about all universes of type (2.1), where ENT is an arbitrary set of entities, and $\{sim(P)\}_{P \subseteq PROP}$ is a family of similarity relations satisfying conditions (C1) to (C3).

Assume that PROP is an arbitrary set of properties, to be fixed throughout the paper (except of some examples). The expressions of our language are built of symbols belonging to the following pairwise disjoint sets:

CONP = $\{\underline{p}: p \in PROP\}$ - a set of constants representing individual properties in PROP,
VARSP - a set of variables representing sets of properties, i.e. subsets of PROP,
VARE - a set of variables representing individual entities,
VARSE - a set of variables representing sets of entities,
$\underline{0}$ - a constant representing the empty subset of PROP,
$-, \cup, \cap$ - symbols for set-theoretical operations on sets of properties,
$\neg, \vee, \wedge$ - symbols for set-theoretical operations on sets of entities,
$\underline{sim}, \overline{sim}$ - symbols for lower and upper approximation, respectively,
(,) - brackets.

The *terms* of our language are intended to represent sets of properties; they are constructed from the elements of CONP, VARSP and $\underline{0}$ by means of the operation symbols $-, \cup, \cap$. Thus the set TERM of terms is the least set satisfying the following properties:

(i) VARSP $\cup$ CONP $\cup$ $\{\underline{0}\} \subseteq$ TERM,
(ii) if $A, B \in$ TERM, then $-A, A \cup B, A \cap B \in$ TERM.

The *formulas* of our language are intended to represent sets of entities; they are constructed from terms included in brackets and symbols in VARE $\cup$ VARSE by means of the operation symbols $\neg, \vee, \wedge$ and $\underline{sim}, \overline{sim}$. Formally, the set FORM of formulas is the least set satisfying the following conditions:

(i) VARE $\cup$ VARSE $\subseteq$ FORM,
(ii) if $F, G \in$ FORM, then $\neg F, F \vee G, F \wedge G \in$ FORM,
(iii) if $A \in$ TERM and $F \in$ FORM, then $\underline{sim}(A)F, \overline{sim}(A)F \in$ FORM.

Besides the basic operations on formulas introduced in the above definitions, we shall also make use of the following derived operations:

$$F \rightarrow G \equiv \neg F \vee G, \quad F \leftrightarrow G \equiv F \rightarrow G \wedge G \rightarrow F, \tag{3.8}$$

where F, G are arbitrary formulas in FORM and $\equiv$ is the identity on FORM. In other words, the expressions appearing on the left hand sides of the identites (3.8) should be understood as notational abbreviations for the formulas on the right hand side of these identities.

In the sequel, the elements of VARSP will be usually denoted by *P, Q*,..., the elements of VARE - by *x, y*,..., the elements of VARSE - by *D, E*,... Terms will be denoted by *A, B, C*,..., and formulas - by *F, G*,...

4 Semantics of the Language

As we have already said, our language is tailored to describe the similarity relationships between entities in an universe of type (2.1) with the set PROP being the parameter of the language. Thus by a *model* in which the language is to be interpreted we mean any system of the form

$$M = \langle U, v \rangle,$$

where

$$U = \langle \text{ENT}, \text{PROP}, \{sim(P)\}_{P \subseteq \text{PROP}} \rangle$$

is a universe defined as in Section 2 and v is a valuation function such that

$v(\underline{p}) = p$ for $\underline{p} \in$ CONP (recall that $\underline{p}$ was the constant corresponding to the property $p \in$ PROP),

$v(P) \subseteq$ PROP for $P \in$ VARSP, $v(\underline{0}) = \varnothing$,

$v(x) \in$ ENT for $x \in$ VARE, $v(E) \subseteq$ ENT for $E \in$ VARSE.

The *interpretation of terms in a model M* is a function τ_M: TERM $\rightarrow 2^{\text{PROP}}$ defined inductively as follows:

(i) $\tau_M(\underline{p}) = \{v(\underline{p})\}$ for $\underline{p} \in$ CONP,

(ii) $\tau_M(P) = v(P)$ for $P \in$ VARSP $\cup \{\underline{0}\}$,

(iii) $\tau_M(-A) =$ PROP $- \tau_M(A)$, $\tau_M(A \cup B) = \tau_M(A) \cup \tau_M(B)$, $\tau_M(A \cap B) = \tau_M(A) \cap \tau_M(B)$ for any $A, B \in$ TERM.

The *interpretation of formulas in a model M* is a function φ_M: FORM $\rightarrow 2^{\text{ENT}}$ defined inductively as follows:

(i) $\varphi M(x) = \{v(x)\}$ for $x \in$ VARE,

(ii) $\varphi_M(E) = v(E)$ for $E \in$ VARSE,

(iii) $\varphi_M(\neg F) =$ ENT $- \varphi_M(F)$, $\varphi_M(F \vee G) = \varphi_M(F) \cup \varphi_M(G)$, $\varphi_M(F \wedge G) = \varphi_M(F) \cap \varphi_M(G)$ for any $F, G \in$ FORM,

(iv) $\varphi_M(\underline{sim}(A)F) = \underline{sim}(\tau_M(A))\varphi_M(F)$, $\varphi_M(\overline{sim}(A)F) = \overline{sim}(\tau_M(A))\varphi_M(F)$ for any $A \in$ TERM and any $F \in$ FORM (where $\underline{sim}$ and $\overline{sim}$ are the operations of lower and upper approximation, respectively, defined as in Section 2).

In view of (3.8), the derived operations on formulas $\rightarrow$, $\leftrightarrow$ are interepreted as follows:

(v) $\varphi_M(F \rightarrow G) = (\text{ENT} - \varphi_M(F)) \cup \varphi_M(G)$, $\varphi_M(F \leftrightarrow G) = ((\text{ENT} - \varphi_M(F)) \cup \varphi_M(G)) \cap ((\text{ENT} - \varphi_M(G)) \cup \varphi_M(F))$.

We say that a formula $F \in$ FORM *is true in model M*, and write $\models_M F$, whenever $\varphi_M(F) =$ ENT. We say that F is valid, and write $\models F$, whenever F is true in every model M.

5 Normalization of Formulas

As it was stated in the introduction, the similarity language we develop in this paper is styled on the indiscernibility language discussed in [3]. However, we introduce a certain rather important modification: namely, we use individual variables representing entities in place of the constants employed in [3]. Such a solution is certainly justified in view of the existing practical applications. Indeed, in most of them, like e.g. data bases, expert systems or knowledge representation systems, the set of properties under consideration is fixed (either permanently or over long periods of time), whereas the set of entities we deal with usually varies over time - in many cases quite quickly. Hence in a formal language tailored to such applications it is natural to use constants representing individual properties - but there seems to be rather little sense in using constants representing entities. For this reason, we have decided to introduce in the language variables representing entities in place of constants. In the sequel of the paper we will see that such a decision brings important benefits: namely, it is just those variables that allow us to develop a set of decomposition rules for sentences of formulas providing a complete axiomatization for our logic in a Gentzen-type natural deduction style. This is a considerable feat, since the indiscernibility language introduced in [3] does not possess a complete axiomatization up to this day. It should be noted that after replacing similarity by indiscernibility in formulation of the language and augmenting the above mentioned system with certain rules expresing transitivity of indescernibility relations we obtain a completely axiomatized formal language for reasoning about indiscernibility.

A crucial part in developing the aforementioned decomposition rules is played by special formulas containing individual variables representing entities, defined as follows:

$$x \in F \equiv x \rightarrow F, \quad x \notin F \equiv x \in \neg F, \tag{5.1}$$

$$x\, sim(A)\, y \equiv x \in \overline{sim}\,(A)\, y, \quad x\, dis(A)\, y \equiv x \notin \overline{sim}\,(A)\, y, \tag{5.2}$$

where x, $y \in$ VARE, $A \in$ TERM and $\equiv$ is the identity on FORM. Note that the "newly introduced" formulas are only notational abbreviations to be used instead of the formulas appearing on the right-hand sides of the respective identities.

Just what makes these formulas so important for developing the proof systems for our logic is evident from the following lemma:

Lemma 5.1. For any model M = <U, V>, the following conditions are satisfied:

(i) $|=_M x \in F$ *iff* $v(x) \in \varphi_M(F)$, $|=_M x \notin F$ *iff* $v(x) \notin \varphi_M(F)$,

(ii) $|=_M x\, sim(A)\, y$ *iff* $(v(x), v(y)) \in sim(\tau_M(A))$,

$|=_M x\, dis(A)\, y$ *iff* $(v(x), v(y)) \notin sim(\tau_M(A))$.

Proof: The proof follows directly from (5.1) - (5.2) and the definition of interpretation. In case of (i) , we have $\varphi_M(x \in F) = \varphi_M(x \rightarrow F) = \varphi_M(\neg x \vee F) =$ (ENT $- \varphi_M(x)) \cup \varphi_M(F) =$. (ENT $- v(x)) \cup \varphi_M(F)$. Thus $|=_M x \in F$ (i.e. $\varphi_M(x \in F)$ = ENT) iff $v(x) \in \varphi_M(F)$. As $x \notin F \equiv x \in \neg F$, then from the above we conclude that $|=_M x \notin F$ iff $v(x) \in \varphi_M(\neg F)$. Since $\varphi_M(\neg F) =$ ENT $- \varphi_M(F)$, this condition is tantamount to $v(x) \notin \varphi_M(F)$. Obviously, (ii) follows directly from (i) and (5.2).

Hence using such formulas we have at our disposal the powerful mechanism of the membership relation. Moreover, each formula in FORM is semantically equivalent to a certain formula of type (5.1). Namely, (i) of Lemma 5.1 directly implies the following:

Lemma 5.2. *For any* $F \in$ FORM, $\models F$ *iff* $\models x \in F$, *where* x *is any variable in* VARE *which does not occur in* F.

Making use of the above fact, we shall tailor our decomposition rules to the formulas of type $x \in F$. This trick - together with decomposition of sets of properties into components that we shall discuss below - is in fact the main technical idea allowing us to develop a complete proof system for our language. In order to keep the set of decomposition rules as small as possible, we shall assume that those rules are applying only to formulas "preprocessed" , or normalized, in the way described below.

Let us begin with defining components. Assume that for any set X we denote by X^ the set of all the finite sequences of elements of X containing no repetitions. Given $\underline{P} = \underline{p}_1, \underline{p}_2, \ldots, \underline{p}_n \in$ CONP^ and $\mathbf{Q} = Q_1, Q_2, \ldots, Q_m \in$ VARSP^, we define for any $\mathbf{i}: \{1,2,\ldots, m\} \to \{-, +\}$ the following terms:

$$C(\mathbf{i}, \mathbf{Q}) \equiv Q_1^{i(1)} \cap Q_2^{i(2)} \cap Q_m^{i(m)}, \tag{5.3}$$

$$C(-\underline{P}, \mathbf{i}, \mathbf{Q}) \equiv -\underline{p}_1 \cap -\underline{p}_2 \cap \ldots \cap -\underline{p}_n \cap C(\mathbf{i}, \mathbf{Q}) \tag{5.4}$$

$$C(\underline{p}_j, \mathbf{i}, \mathbf{Q}) \equiv \underline{p}_j \cap C(\mathbf{i}, \mathbf{Q}), \tag{5.5}$$

where $Q^+ \equiv Q$ and $Q^- \equiv -Q$.

Terms of the form (5.3) are called *components* for **Q**, whereas terms of the form (5.4)-(5.5) are called *components* for $\underline{P}$ and **Q**. The set of all components for **Q** is denoted by COMP(Q), and the set of all components for $\underline{P}$ and **Q** by COMP($\underline{P}$, **Q**).

A well known fact of the set theory is that in any model the components corresponding to a given family of set variables evaluate to mutually disjoint sets which consititute a cover of the universe. Thus in our case we have the following

Lemma 5.3. *Let* $\underline{P} = \underline{p}_1, \underline{p}_2, \ldots, \underline{p}_n \in$ CONP^ *and* $\mathbf{Q} = Q_1, Q_2, \ldots, Q_m \in$ VARSP^. *Then, for every model M, the following conditions are satisfied*:

(i) *for any two different components C, C' in* COMP(**Q**), *we have* $\tau_M(C) \cap \tau_M(C') = \varnothing$,

(ii) $\bigcup_{C \in COMP(Q)} \tau_M(C) =$ PROP,

(iii) *for any two different components C, C' in* COMP($\underline{P}$, **Q**), *we have* $\tau_M(C) \cap \tau_M(C') = \varnothing$,

(iv) $\bigcup_{C \in COMP(\underline{P}, Q)} \tau_M(C) =$ PROP.

A formula $F \in$ FORM is said to be *nondegenerate* if F contains at least one constant $\underline{p} \in$ CONP (remember that $\underline{0} \notin$ CONP) or at least one variable in VARSP. With every nondegenerate formula we associate a set of components COMP(F) defined as follows. For an arbitrary nondegenerate formula $F \in$ FORM, we define:

$$\text{CONP}(F) = \{\underline{p} \in \text{CONP}: \underline{p} \text{ occurs in } F\}, \tag{5.6}$$

$$\text{VARSP}(F) = \{P \in \text{VARSP}: P \text{ occurs in } F\}, \tag{5.7}$$

$$\text{COMP}(F) = \text{COMP}(\text{CONP}(F),\ \text{VARSP}(F)). \tag{5.8}$$

The elements of COMP(F) will be called *F-components*.

The above definition poses a slight technical problem. Namely, note that for CONP(F) = ∅ we get $n = 0$ in (5.3)-(5.5), and for VARSP(F) = ∅ we get $m = 0$ (but n and m cannot be simultaneously 0, since F is nondegenerate). Hence the definition of COMP(F) requires extending definitions (5.4)-(5.5) to the cases when either m or n (but not both) is equal to zero. If $m = 0$ (but $n \neq 0$), then $C(\mathbf{i}, Q)$ is simply deleted form (5.4) and (5.5); on the other hand, if $n = 0$ (but $m \neq 0$), then the left hand sides of (5.4) and (5.5) are identified with $C(\mathbf{i}, Q)$. It can be easily checked that Lemma 5.3 is preserved under such an extension.

The properties of components, including those given in Lemma 5.3, which of course apply also to the F-components, allow us to replace any term appearing in F by the union of some F-components. As we know, components evaluate to disjoint sets of properties in any model - and just this property, simplifying many issues, will considerably help us to develop a complete proof system for our logic. Thus we prove the following

Lemma 5.4. *Let F be any nondegenerate formula in* FORM, *and let $A \in$* TERM *be any term occuring in F. Then there exist a unique subset $\boldsymbol{C} = \{C_1, C_2, \ldots, C_n\} \subseteq$* COMP($F$) *such that for the expression*

$$N(A) \equiv C_1 \cup C_2 \cup \ldots \cup C_n \tag{5.9}$$

we have

$$\tau_M(N(A)) = \tau_M(A) \tag{5.10}$$

for every model M.

Remark: If $n = 0$, i.e. $\boldsymbol{C} = \varnothing$, then the vacuous union (5.9) is identified with $\underline{0}$. An analogous convention is adopted throughout the paper for any union over an empty set of indices.

Proof: We have the two following cases:

CASE A: Let $\underline{P} = \underline{p}_1, \underline{p}_2, \ldots, \underline{p}_n \in \text{CONP}^\wedge$ and $\boldsymbol{Q} = Q_1, Q_2, \ldots, Q_m \in \text{VARSP}^\wedge$ be such that

$$\text{CONP}(F) = \{\underline{p}_1, \underline{p}_2, \ldots, \underline{p}_n\}, \quad \text{VARSP}(F) = \{Q_1, Q_2, \ldots, Q_m\},$$

i.e. let $\underline{P}$ and $\boldsymbol{Q}$ be sequences consisting of all the elements of CONP(F) and of all the elements of VARSP(F), respectively. Since F is nondegenerate, we have either $n \neq 0$ or $m \neq 0$, and COMP(F) consists of all the components of the form either

$$\text{C}(-\underline{P}, \mathbf{i}, \mathbf{Q}) \equiv -\underline{p}_1 \cap -\underline{p}_2 \cap \ldots \cap -\underline{p}_n \cap \text{C}(\mathbf{i}, \mathbf{Q}) \tag{5.11}$$

or

$$C(\underline{p}_j, \mathbf{i}, \mathbf{Q}) \equiv \underline{p}_j \cap \mathrm{C}(\mathbf{i}, \mathbf{Q}), \tag{5.12}$$

where

$$\mathrm{C}(\mathbf{i}, \mathbf{Q}) \equiv Q_1^{i(1)} \cap Q_2^{i(2)} \cap Q_m^{i(m)},$$

$Q^+ \equiv Q$ and $Q^- \equiv -Q$ (recall the convention about interpreting (5.10) and (5.11) in the cases when either n or m (but not both) equals 0). Evidently, the term A is a Boolean expression over $\underline{p}_1, \underline{p}_2, \ldots, \underline{p}_n$, $Q_1, Q_2, \ldots, Q_m$, and (eventually) $\underline{0}$. Hence employing a universally known, standard procedure (see e.g. [2]), we can transform A into complete disjunctive normal form

$$\mathrm{DN}(A) = \bigcup_{(l,i,j) \in L} (\underline{p}_1^{l(1)} \cap \ldots \cap \underline{p}_n^{l(n)} \cap Q_1^{i(1)} \cap \ldots \cap Q_m^{i(m)} \cap \underline{0}^j), \tag{5.13}$$

where $\mathbf{L} \subseteq \{-, +\}^{n+m+1}$. Since in our semantics $-$, $\cup$ and $\cap$ are interpreted as normal set-theoretical operations, we obviously have

$$\tau_M(DN(A)) = \tau_M(A) \tag{5.14}$$

for every model M.

It is easy to see that for any $i, j \in \{1, 2, \ldots, n\}$ with $i \neq j$ we have

$$\tau_M(\underline{p}_i \cap \underline{p}_j) = \varnothing, \quad \tau_M(\underline{p}_i) \subseteq \tau_M(-\underline{p}_j),$$

whence

$$\tau_M(\underline{p}_i) \cap \tau_M(-\underline{p}_j) = \tau_M(\underline{p}_i).$$

Further, as

$$\tau_M(\underline{0}) = \varnothing, \quad \tau_M(-\underline{0}) = \mathrm{PROP},$$

then

$$\tau_M(C \cap \underline{0}) = \varnothing, \; \tau_M(C \cap -\underline{0}) = \tau_M(C)$$

for any term C. Hence without changing the interpretation of $DN(A)$ in any model M we can:

(i) delete from $DN(A)$ all the summands given in (5.13) which contain either $\underline{0}$ (i.e. $\underline{0}^+$) or both $\underline{p}_i$ and $\underline{p}_j$ (i.e. $\underline{p}_i^+$ and $\underline{p}_j^+$) for some i, j with $i \neq j$ (since they evaluate to $\varnothing$ in every model),

(ii) replace each summand of the form $C \cap \underline{0}^-$ by C,

(iii) replace each summand of the form

$$-\underline{p}_1 \cap \ldots \cap -\underline{p}_{k-1} \cap \underline{p}_k \cap -\underline{p}_{k+1} \cap \ldots \cap -\underline{p}_n \cap C(\mathbf{i}, \mathbf{Q})$$

appearing in (5.12) by the term $\underline{p}_k \cap C(\mathbf{i}, \mathbf{Q})$, i.e. the component $C(\underline{p}_k, \mathbf{i}, \mathbf{Q})$.

Let us denote by $N(A)$ the expression obtained by modifying $DN(A)$ according to the rules (i), (ii), (iii). Then, obviously, $N(A)$ is the union (possibly, vacuous) of some components of the form $C(\underline{p}_j, \mathbf{i}, \mathbf{Q})$ and of some terms of the form (5.13) containing only negative occurences of the $\underline{p}_j$'s. As the latter obviously coincide with $C(-\underline{P}, \mathbf{i}, \mathbf{Q})$, then $N(A)$ is the union of some components in COMP(F). Denoting the set of these components by $\mathbf{C}$ ($\mathbf{C} \subseteq$ COMP(F)) we see that $N(A)$ is of the desired form (5.9). The uniqueness of $\mathbf{C}$ (which is a quite standard property) follows from the fact that any two components evaluate to disjoint sets in any model, so the unions of two different sets of components could not have evaluated to the same set $\tau_M(N(A))$. Note that we get $\mathbf{C} = \varnothing$ (i.e. $N(A) = \underline{0}$ in view of our notational convention) if A is either $\underline{0}$, or if A's semantical equivalence to $\underline{0}$ can be deduced using rules (i)-(iii).

Moreover, as rules (i), (ii) preserve the interpretation of the term to which they are applied in any model, then we have $\tau_M(N(A)) = \tau_M(DN(A))$ for any model M. Hence from (5.14) it follows that $\tau_M(N(A)) = \tau_M(A)$ for any model M, QED.

The term $N(A)$ discussed in the above lemma is determined uniquely up to the order of the summands in the union (5.9). If we assume that the sets of constants and variables of our language are ordered, then we can take as $N(A)$ the union of lexicographically ordered F-components in the uniquely determined set C. Hence from now on we shall assume that $N(A)$ is unique.

Thus, for any nondegenerate formula F and any term A occuring in F, the unique (in the sense described above) term $N(A)$ satisfying the conditions of Lemma 5.4 will be called *the normal form of A (with respect to F)*. It should be noted that $N(A)$ can be obtained form A in an effective way. Indeed, to get an algorithm generating $N(A)$, it suffices to augment the standard algorithm generating the (complete) disjunctive normal form by rules (i)-(iii).

For convenience, the notion of the normal form will also be extended to degenerate formulas, containing at most $\underline{0}$ and no other symbol in CONP or VARSP. If F is such a formula, and A is an expression occuring in F, then F is a Boolean expression over the single constant $\underline{0}$ - in other words, it consists of some occurences of $\underline{0}$ bound together by the set-theoretical operators. Then, obviously, using a standard procedure like that described in the proof of Lemma 5.4, we can effectively transform A into a degenerate disjunctive normal form, which will coincide with one of the following terms: $\underline{0}$, $-\underline{0}$, $\underline{0} \cup -\underline{0}$. As the latter two terms are semantically equivalent, then as the "normal form" $N(A)$ of A we can take either $\underline{0}$ or $-\underline{0}$. From now on, the meaning of this notion will be extended also to terms in degenerate formulas in the way defined above.

By the *normal form of F*, in symbols $N(F)$, we mean the formula obtained by replacing each expression A occuring in F by its normal form $N(A)$. In view of lemma 5.4, we obviously have

$$\varphi_M(N(F)) = \varphi_M(F)$$

for any model F. Of course, also $N(F)$ can be obtained from F in an effective way. We should bear it in mind later on, since this constitutes the justfication for the fact that we tailor our deduction system to formulas in normal form rather than to arbitrary formulas.

6 The Proof Mechanism

The deduction mechanism we propose for our language consists of a set of decomposition rules for sequences of formulas. They follow the style of the rules for classical logic given by Rasiowa and Sikorski in [8], and are in fact a variant of Gentzen's natural deduction rules. The rules are applied to construct a decomposition tree for a formula by breaking it down into sequences of more and more elementary formulas, until all "atomic" elements of the original formula have been extracted. It will be shown that the shape of these trees (i.e. the fact whether they are finite and have only "fundamental" sequences of formulas at their leaves) predetermines the validity of a formula. Using the terminology of more orthodox proof systems, we can say that in our deduction system fundamental sequences play the part of axioms, and the decomposition rules - that of inference rules. The actual form of the rules we are going to give her relies heavily on the fact that the procedure of constructing the decomposition tree will be applied only to formulas of the form

$$x \in N(F)$$

where F is a formula in FORM, $N(F)$ is the normal form of F defined as in the preceding section, and x is a variable in VARE which does not occur in F. Thus to verify the validity of a formula F we first transform it to normal form $N(F)$, and then construct the decomposition tree for the formula $x \in N(F)$. This is justified by the following two facts:

- first, $N(F)$ is semantically equivalent to F, and $N(F)$ can be effectively obtained from F;
- second, $x \in N(F)$ is valid iff F is (since the validity of $x \in N(F)$ is equivalent to the validity of $N(F)$ by Lemma 5.2, and $N(F)$ is valid iff F is valid, for they are semantically equivalent).

Of course, replacing F by $N(F)$ before the proper decomposition process begins is slightly inelegant. In fact, we do could do without it - but at the price of incorporating all the rules for transforming terms (i.e. substitution of the Boolean algebra rules for terms) into our deduction system. However, we decided against it, for the rules are quite standard, so their introduction would be of little interest, and it would at the same time unnecessarily enlarge the deduction system and needlessly complicate the completeness proof.

Let us begin with introducing the necessary notions and notation. The letter Γ (possibly with indices) will always denote a finite (or empty) sequence of formulas in FORM. A sequence $\Gamma = (F_1, \ldots, F_k)$ is said to be *true in a model M*, in symbols $\models_M \Gamma$, iff $\models_M F_i$ for some i. The sequence Γ is said to be *valid*, in symbols $\models \Gamma$, if $\models_M \Gamma$ for every model M of the language.

By a *decomposition rule* we understand either a pair (Γ, Γ_1) or a triple $(\Gamma, \Gamma_1, \Gamma_2)$ of non-empty sequences of formulas written usually in the form

$$\frac{\Gamma}{\Gamma_1} \tag{6.1}$$

and

$$\frac{\Gamma}{\Gamma_1 \mid \Gamma_2}, \tag{6.2}$$

respectively. Here Γ is called the *conclusion* of the rule, and Γ_1 (or Γ_1, Γ_2, resp.) - its *premise* (*premises*). A decomposition rule is said to be *sound* provided that its conclusion Γ is valid iff all its premises are valid (that is, a single premise Γ_1 in case of rule (6.1), or both the premises Γ_1, Γ_2 in case of rule (6.2)).

A sequence of formulas is said to be *fundamental* iff it contains either one of the following formulas:

(i) $x \in x$,

(ii) $x\ sim(\underline{0})\ y$,

(iii) $x\ sim(A)\ x$,

or one of the following pairs of formulas:

(iv) $x \in F, x \notin F$,

(v) $x\ sim(A)\ y, x\ dis(A)\ y$,

(vi) $x\ sim(C(\underline{p}_j, \mathbf{i}, \underline{Q}))\ y, x'\ sim(C(\underline{p}_j, \mathbf{i}', \underline{Q}))\ y'$ $(\mathbf{i} \neq \mathbf{i}')$,

where $x, y, x', y' \in$ VARE, $F \in$ FORM, $A \in$ EXPR and the $C(\underline{p}_j, \mathbf{i}, \underline{Q})$'s are components in COMP($\underline{P}$, $\underline{Q}$) for some $\underline{P} = \underline{p}_1, ..., \underline{p}_n \in$ CONP^ and some $\underline{Q} = Q_1, ..., Q_m \in$ VARSP^ defined by (5.5), with $\mathbf{i}$: $\{1,2,..., m\} \rightarrow \{-, +\}$ (recall that by X^ we denote the set of all finite sequences without repetitions consisting of the elements of X).

Lemma 6.1. *Every fundamental sequence Γ is valid.*

Proof. Evidently, what we have to prove is that the formulas (i)-(iii) as well as the pairs (iv)-(vi) (considered as two-element sequences of formulas) are valid - because then and only then every sequence containing either one of the formulas (i)-(iii) or one of the pairs (iv)-(vi) will be valid.

Let us consider any model $M = \langle U, v \rangle$, where $U = \langle$ENT, PROP, $\{sim(P)\}_{P \subseteq \text{PROP}}\rangle$ is a universe defined as in section 2. Since $v(x) \in \{v(x)\} = \varphi_M(x)$, then by Lemma 5.1 $\models_M x \in x$. As $v(\underline{0}) = \varnothing$ and $sim(\varnothing) =$ ENT × ENT by property (C3) of similarity relations (see Section 2), then $(v(x), v(y)) \in sim(\tau_M(\underline{0}))$, whence $\models_M x\ sim(\underline{0})\ y$ by Lemma 5.1. Analogously, as $sim(v(A))$ is reflexive by property (C1) of similarity relations (see again section 2), we have $(v(x), v(x)) \in sim(\tau_M(A))$, whence $\models_M x\ sim(A)\ x$ by Lemma 5.1. Thus the formulas (i)-(iii) are true in M.

Consider now the pairs (iv)-(vi). From (5.1), (5.2) it follows that both (iv) and (v) are of the form $x \in G, x \notin G$, where $G \in$ FORM. Obviously, we have either $v(x) \in \varphi_M(G)$ or $v(x) \in$ ENT $- \varphi_M(G) = \varphi_M(\neg G)$. In view of lemma 5.1, this means that either $\models_M x \in G$ or $\models_M x \notin G$, i.e. $\models_M (x \in G, x \notin G)$ by the definition of $\models_M \Gamma$ for a sequence Γ of formulas. As to (vi), by (5.5) we have $C(\underline{p}_j, \mathbf{i}, \underline{Q}) = \underline{p}_j \cap C(\mathbf{i}, \underline{Q})$, $C(\underline{p}_j, \mathbf{i}', \underline{Q}) = \underline{p}_j \cap C(\mathbf{i}', \underline{Q})$, where $C(\mathbf{i}, \underline{Q})$, $C(\mathbf{i}', \underline{Q})$ are defined by (5.3). Since $\tau_M(\underline{p}_j) = \{p_j\}$ by the definition of interpretation and $\tau_M(C(\mathbf{i}, \underline{Q})) \cap \tau_M(C(\mathbf{i}', \underline{Q})) = \varnothing$ for $\mathbf{i} \neq \mathbf{i}'$ by Lemma 5.3, then we have either $\tau_M(\underline{p}_j) \cap \tau_M(C(\mathbf{i}, \underline{Q})) = \varnothing$ or $\tau_M(\underline{p}_j) \cap \tau_M(C(\mathbf{i}', \underline{Q})) = \varnothing$, i.e. either $\tau_M(C(\underline{p}_j, \mathbf{i}, \underline{Q})) = \tau_M(\underline{p}_j \cap C(\mathbf{i}, \underline{Q})) = \varnothing$ or $\tau_M(C(\underline{p}_j, \mathbf{i}', \underline{Q})) = \tau_M(\underline{p}_j \cap C(\mathbf{i}', \underline{Q})) = \varnothing$. As $sim(\varnothing) =$ ENT × ENT, this implies that for $\mathbf{i} \neq \mathbf{i}'$ we have either $\models_M x\ sim(C(\underline{p}_j, \mathbf{i}, \underline{Q}))\ y$ or $\models_M x'\ sim(C(\underline{p}_j, \mathbf{i}', \underline{Q}))\ y'$ for any x, x', y, y' in VARE. Hence $\models_M (x\ sim(C(\underline{p}_j, \mathbf{i}, \underline{Q}))\ y,\ x'\ sim(C(\underline{p}_j, \mathbf{i}', \underline{Q}))\ y')$ for $\mathbf{i} \neq \mathbf{i}'$.

Considering the fact that M was an arbitrary model, we have obviously shown that the formulas (i)-(iii) as well as the pairs (iv)-(vi) are valid, QED.

6.1 Decomposition Rules

After these preliminaries, we can finally formulate the decomposition rules for our language. For the reasons we have already discussed, all rules are tailored to formulas of the form $x \in F$ (note that $x \notin F$, $x\ sim(C)\ y$ and $x\ dis(C)\ y$ are only a special case of such formulas - see (5.1), (5.2)). For any constructor of formulas C

that can occur in F, there are two decomposition rules: one for C itself, and one for its negation (but for the sake of brevity there are no rules for the derived constructors $\rightarrow$ and $\leftrightarrow$). There are also additional rules expressing the fact that our derived "membership" constructor $\in$ applied to variables is transitive and symmetric (since variables evaluate to singleton sets, and the interpretation of $\in$ on such sets coincides with identity of their single elements), and that all the relative similarity and "dissimilarity" relation are also symmetric. (note that the reflexivity of "membership" and similarity is expressed in the definition of fundamental sequences, i.e. the "axioms" of our language). Finally, there is a special rule connecting membership with similarity.

In all the rules given below, Γ' denotes an indecomposable sequence of formulas, and Γ'' is an arbitrary sequence of formulas.

The decomposition rules for formulas (DR)

$(\in\neg)$
$$\frac{\Gamma', x \in \neg F, \Gamma''}{\Gamma', x \notin F, \Gamma''}$$

$(\notin\neg)$
$$\frac{\Gamma', x \notin \neg F, \Gamma''}{\Gamma', x \in F, \Gamma''}$$

$(\in\wedge)$
$$\frac{\Gamma', x \in F \wedge G, \Gamma''}{\Gamma', x \in F, \Gamma'' \mid \Gamma', x \in G, \Gamma''}$$

$(\notin\wedge)$
$$\frac{\Gamma', x \notin F \wedge G, \Gamma}{\Gamma', x \notin F, x \notin G, \Gamma''}$$

$(\in\vee)$
$$\frac{\Gamma', x \in F \vee G, \Gamma''}{\Gamma', x \in F, x \in G, \Gamma''}$$

$(\notin\vee)$
$$\frac{\Gamma', x \notin F \vee G, \Gamma''}{\Gamma', x \notin F, \Gamma'' \mid \Gamma', x \notin G, \Gamma''}$$

$(\in \overline{sim})$
$$\frac{\Gamma', x \in \overline{sim}(A)F, \Gamma''}{\Gamma', y \in F, \Gamma'', x \in \overline{sim}(A)F \mid \Gamma', x\, sim(A)\, y, \Gamma'', x \in \overline{sim}(A)F},$$
where y is an arbitrary variable in VARE,

$(\notin \overline{sim})$
$$\frac{\Gamma', x \notin \overline{sim}(A)F, \Gamma''}{\Gamma', x \in \underline{sim}(A)\neg F, \Gamma''} \qquad (*)$$

$(\in \underline{sim})$
$$\frac{\Gamma', x \in \underline{sim}(A)F, \Gamma''}{\Gamma', x\, dis(A)\, y, y \in F, \Gamma''},$$
where $y \in$VARE and y does not occur above the double line,

$(\notin \underline{sim})$
$$\frac{\Gamma', x \notin \underline{sim}(A)F, \Gamma''}{\Gamma', x \in \overline{sim}(A)\neg(F), \Gamma''}$$

$(sim \cup)$
$$\frac{\Gamma', x\, sim(A \cup B)\, y, \Gamma''}{\Gamma', x\, sim(A)\, y, \Gamma'' \mid \Gamma', x\, sim(B)\, y, \Gamma''}$$

$$(dis\ \cup)\quad \frac{\Gamma', x\ dis(A \cup B) y, \Gamma''}{\Gamma', x\ dis(A) y, x\ dis(B) y, \Gamma''}$$

$$(\text{sym} \in)\quad \frac{\Gamma', x \notin y, \Gamma''}{\Gamma', \Gamma'', x \notin y, y \notin x} \qquad (*)$$

$$(\text{tran} \in)\quad \frac{\Gamma', x \notin y, \Gamma'', y \notin F, \Gamma'''}{\Gamma', \Gamma'', \Gamma''', x \notin y, y \notin F, x \notin F} \qquad (*)$$

$$(\text{sym}\ sim)\quad \frac{\Gamma', x\ sim(C) y, \Gamma''}{\Gamma', \Gamma'', x\ sim(C) y, y\ sim(C) x} \qquad (*)$$

$$(\text{sym}\ dis)\quad \frac{\Gamma', x\ dis(C) y, \Gamma''}{\Gamma', \Gamma'', x\ dis(C) y, y\ dis(C) x} \qquad (*)$$

$$(\text{tran} \in sim)\quad \frac{\Gamma', x \notin y, \Gamma'', y\ sim(C) z, \Gamma'''}{\Gamma', \Gamma'', \Gamma''', x \notin y, y\ sim(C) z, x\ sim(C) z} \qquad (*)$$

If PROP is finite, then we augment our deduction system (DR) by two additional rules, which allow us to replace the "negative" components by a sum of some "positive" ones:

$$(sim\ -\underline{P})\quad \frac{\Gamma', x\ sim(C(-\underline{P}, \mathbf{i}, \mathbf{Q})) y, \Gamma''}{\Gamma', x\ sim(\bigcup_{\underline{p}' \in CONP - \underline{P}} C(\underline{p}', \mathbf{i}, \mathbf{Q})) y, \Gamma''},$$

$$(\text{dis}\ -\underline{P})\quad \frac{\Gamma', x\ dis(C(-\underline{P}, \mathbf{i}, \mathbf{Q})) y, \Gamma''}{\Gamma' x\ dis(\bigcup_{\underline{p}' \in CONP - \underline{P}} C(\underline{p}', \mathbf{i}, \mathbf{Q})) y, \Gamma''},$$

where $C(-\underline{P}, \mathbf{i}, Q)$ is a component of the form (5.4) for some $\underline{P} = \underline{p}_1, \underline{p}_2, \ldots, \underline{p}_n \in$ CONP^ , $\mathbf{Q} = Q_1, Q_2, \ldots, Q_m \in$ VARSP^, and $\mathbf{i}$: $\{1,2,\ldots, m\} \to \{-, +\}$ (recall that X^ is the set of all finite sequences of elements of X without repetitions). For $\underline{p} \notin \underline{P}$, $C(\underline{p}, \mathbf{i}, Q)$ is a component in COMP(CONP, Q) which has the form (5.5) with $\underline{p}_j$ replaced by $\underline{p}$. The union of the $C(\underline{p}, \mathbf{i}, Q)$'s over $\underline{p}$ in CONP − $\underline{P}$ is understood as $C(\underline{q}_1, \mathbf{i}, Q) \cup C(\underline{q}_2, \mathbf{i}, Q) \cup \ldots \cup C(\underline{q}_k, \mathbf{i}, Q)$ with $\{q_1, \ldots, q_k\}$ = CONP − $\underline{P}$. Note that CONP = $\{\underline{p}: p \in$ PROP$\}$.

In all the rules listed above we assume that $x, y \in$ VARE, $F, G \in$ FORM, $A, B \in$ TERM and C is a component of either the $C(-\underline{P}, \mathbf{i}, Q)$ type or the $C(\underline{p}_j, \mathbf{i}, Q)$ type (see (5.4), (5,5)) for some $\underline{P}$, Q and $\mathbf{i}$ as described above.

In the sequel, the six rules marked by (*) will be called *expansion rules*; all other rules will be called *replacement rules*. The expansion rules differ from the others in that they do not replace the formula they are applied to by some new formulas, eliminating the original formula from the sequence. Instead of this, they only add some new formulas to the sequence, leaving the original formula unchanged.

A formula G is said to be *indecomposable* if it has one of the following forms:

(i) $x \in F, x \notin F$, where $x \in$ VARE, $F \in$ VARSE $\cup$ VARE,

(ii) $x\ sim(C)\ y$, $x\ dis(C)\ y$, where $x, y \in$ VARE and C is either $\underline{0}$, or $-\underline{0}$, or a component in COMP(F) of the form

(a) either $C(-\underline{P}, \mathbf{i}, Q)$ or $C(\underline{p}_j, \mathbf{i}, Q)$, if PROP is infinite,

(b) $C(\underline{p}_j, \mathbf{i}, Q)$, if PROP is finite.

Otherwise, the formula is said to be *decomposable*.

Intuitively, a formula F is said to be indecomposable iff using the decomposition rules given above we cannot "extract" from it some simpler formulas - in other words, if neither any replacement rule nor the expansion rule ($\in \overline{sim}$) rule is applicable to F (note that the latter rule is a certain "borderline" case - though it does not replace the original formula by some simple ones, yet it introduces some simpler formulas into the sequence).

Point (iii) above requires some explanation. The decomposition process starts with the formula $x \in N(F)$, so every term we encounter is either a sum of components in COMP(F) (or, eventually, COMP'(F) = COMP(CONP, VARSP(F), if PROP is finite) or $\underline{0}$ or $-\underline{0}$. When decomposing the formulas, we split the sums of components into individual components (see rules ($sim \cup$) and ($dis \cup$)) which are considered as indecomposable. Obviously, $\underline{0}$ is also indecomposable. But why do we treat $-\underline{0}$. in the same way? The answer is simple: $-\underline{0}$ can occur only in the case when the source of the decomposition process was a degenerate formula, containing only $\underline{0}$ and no other constants or variables representing properties or sets of properties. In this case there are no components of F, so we cannot break down $-\underline{0}$ into anything smaller.

A sequence of formulas is said to be *indecomposable* iff all its elements are indecomposable.

It is easy to see that, consistently with our intutions regarding decomposability,

replacement rules can be only applied to decomposable sequences (6.3)

Moreover, as the in any decomposition rule the initial sequence Γ' in the conclusion is to be indecomposable, then it is easy to see that

To any decomposable sequence of formulas we can apply at most one replacement rule: namely, the unique rule applicable to the leftmost decomposable formula in this sequence which is not of the form $x \in \overline{sim}(A)F$. (6.4)

Note that if a decomposable sequence contains no decomposable formulas other than those of the form $x \in \overline{sim}(A)F$, then we cannot apply to it any "true" replacement rule, but only the "borderline" expansion rule ($\in \overline{sim}$).

The fact that a sequence is indecomposable need not terminate the decomposition process. Namely, one can easily see that

expansion rules can be also applied to indecomposable sequences. (6.5)

However, in case of expansion rules the "uniqueness" principle is not preserved: in many cases, we can apply several rules to a given sequence of formulas. The above properties are important, for they will be needed to define in a correct way the decomposition tree of a formula.

For the reasons discussed at the begining of Section 6, all the rules rules given above are expressed in terms of formulas of the form $x \in F$, $x \notin F$, $x\ sim(C)\ y$, $x\ dis(C)\ y$, with the three latter formulas being in fact a special case of the first. A formal justification for this fact will be provided in Section 6.3, in connection with the definition of the decomposition tree.

Lemma 6.2. *The decomposition rules (DR) given above are sound.*

Proof. Considering Lemma 5.1 and the definition of interpretation, the rules ($\in \neg$) up to ($\notin \vee$) are evidently sound. Of the next four rules concerning *sim*(*A*), the crucial ones are ($\in \overline{sim}$) and ($\in \underline{sim}$), since the two others are obviously sound in view of the duality principle for lower and upper aproximation (see (2.3)). In fact, the former two rules are a cornerstone of our proof theory for the similarity logic. For that reason, we shall now give a detailed proof of their soundness.

Let us begin with the ($\in \overline{sim}$) rule, i.e.

$$\frac{\Gamma', x \in \overline{sim}(A)F, \Gamma''}{\Gamma', y \in F, \Gamma'', x \in \overline{sim}(A)F \mid \Gamma', x\ sim(A)\,y, \Gamma'', x \in \overline{sim}(A)F},$$

We have to show that its conclusion is valid iff both its premises are valid. As the conclusion is contained in each of the premises, then the forward (or rather "downward") implication obviously holds, so it remains to prove the backward ("upward") one. We argue by contradiction. Thus let us assume that the premises are valid, and suppose that the conclusion is not valid. Then there exists a model $M = \langle U, v\rangle$, where U is of the form

$$U = \langle \text{ENT}, \text{PROP}, \{sim(P)\}_{P \subseteq \text{PROP}}\rangle, \tag{6.6}$$

such that neither Γ', nor Γ'', nor $x \in \overline{sim}(A)F$ is true in M. However, both the premises are true in M. As neither Γ', nor Γ'' nor $x \in \overline{sim}(A)F$ is true in M, this implies $\models_M y \in F$ and $\models_M x\ sim(A)\ y$. In view of Lemma 5.1, this yields $v(y) \in \varphi_M(F)$ and $(v(x), v(y)) \in sim(\tau_M(A))$, i.e. $v(x) \in \overline{sim}(\tau_M(A))\varphi_M(F) = \varphi_M(\overline{sim}(A)F)$, which contradicts the fact that non $\models_M x \in \overline{sim}(A)F$. Hence the conclusion must be also valid, which ends the proof of the "upward" implication.

Now let us consider the ($\in \underline{sim}$) rule, i.e.

$$\frac{\Gamma', x \in \underline{sim}(A)F, \Gamma''}{\Gamma', x\ dis(A)\,y, y \in F, \Gamma''},$$

where y does not occur above the double line. We start with proving the downward implication. Assume that the conclusion is valid. To prove that the premise is also valid, we again argue by contradiction. Suppose that it is not so. Then there exists a model $M = \langle U, v\rangle$, with U being of the form (6.6), such that non $\models_M \Gamma'$, non $\models_M \Gamma''$, non $\models_M x\ dis(A)\ y$ and non $\models_M y \in F$. By Lemma 5.1, this implies $(v(x), v(y)) \in sim(\tau_M(A))$ and $v(y) \notin \varphi_M(F)$, whence non $\models_M x \in \underline{sim}(A)F$ by the definition of interpretation. Hence the conclusion cannot be true in M, which contradicts our assumption about its validity. Thus the downward implication holds.

Now let us turn to the upward implication. Assume that the premise is valid. We will prove that the conclusion must be valid, too, arguing once more by contradiction. Suppose that the conclusion is not valid. Then there exists a model $M = \langle U, v\rangle$ with U given by (6.6) such that non $\models_M \Gamma'$, non $\models_M \Gamma''$ and non $\models_M x \in \underline{sim}(A)F$. In consequence, $v(x) \notin \varphi_M(\underline{sim}(A)F)$, i.e. by the definitions of interpretation and lower approximation there exists an $e \in \text{ENT}$ such that $(v(x), e) \in$

$sim(\tau_M(A))$ and $e \notin \varphi_M(F)$. Let us take $M' = <U, v'>$, where v' agrees with v on all arguments except y, and $v'(y) = e$. Then $(v'(x), v'(y)) = (v(x), e) \in sim(\tau_M(A)) = sim(\tau_{M'}(A))$, whence non $\models_{M'} x\ dis(A)\ y$. Further, since y does not occur in F, we have also $\varphi_{M'}(F) = \varphi_M(F)$, whence $v'(y) = e \notin \varphi_{M'}(F)$, which implies non $\models_{M'} y \in F$. Finally, since y does not occur in Γ' or Γ'' either, the interpretations of the elements of these sequences in M' are identical as in M, whence obviously non $\models_{M'} \Gamma'$ and non $\models_{M'} \Gamma''$. Thus the premise is not true in M', which contradicts our assumption about its validity. Hence the upward implication must hold, too.

Soundness of the ($sim \cup$) rule folows immediately from the (C2) property of the similarity relations given in Section 2 and from lemma 5.1. The ($dis \cup$) rule is simply a dual of the former one, and its soundness follows from (C2), Lemma 5.1 and the properties of negation. The (sym $\in$) rule is obviously sound, since the "$\in$" operator applied to a pair of individual variables coincides semantically with the identity relation on the values of these variables - and identity is symmetric. The fact that this property is expressed in trems of $\notin$ rather than in terms of $\in$ is justified by purely technical reasons. Analogously, soundness of the (sym *sim*) and (sym *dis*) rules is a consequence of the symmetry of similarity relations (the C1 property in Section 2). In turn, the (trans $\in$) and (trans $\in$ *sim*) rules are again sound because $\in$ applied to a pair of individual variables corresponds semantically to identity.

Finally, we are left with the (sim $-\underline{P}$) and (dis $-\underline{P}$) rules, i.e.

$$\frac{\Gamma', x\ sim(C(-\underline{P},\mathbf{i},Q))\,y, \Gamma''}{\Gamma', x\ sim(\bigcup_{\underline{p'}\in CONP-\underline{P}} C(\underline{p'},\mathbf{i},Q))\,y, \Gamma''}$$

and

$$\frac{\Gamma', x\ dis(C(-\underline{P},\mathbf{i},Q))\,y, \Gamma''}{\Gamma' x\ dis(\bigcup_{\underline{p'}\in CONP-\underline{P}} C(\underline{p'},\mathbf{i},Q))\,y, \Gamma''},$$

which are added to the proof system if PROP is finite. Without any loss of generality, we can assume that PROP = $\{p_1, p_2, \ldots, p_N\}$ and $\underline{P} = \underline{p}_1, \underline{p}_2, \ldots, \underline{p}_n$, where $n \le$ N. In this case for any model M we obviously have

$$\tau_M(-\underline{p}_1 \cap -\underline{p}_2 \cap \ldots \cap -\underline{p}_N) = \text{PROP} - \{p_1, p_2, \ldots, p_n\} = \{p_{n+1}, p_{n+2}, \ldots, p_N\}$$

$$= \tau_M(\bigcup_{p'\in PROP-\underline{P}} \underline{p'}) = \tau_M(\bigcup_{\underline{p'}\in CONP-\underline{P}} \underline{p'}).$$

Considering that $C(-\underline{P}, \mathbf{i}, Q) = -\underline{p}_1 \cap -\underline{p}_2 \cap \ldots \cap -\underline{p}_n \cap C(\mathbf{i}, Q)$ and $C(\underline{p'}, \mathbf{i}, Q) = \underline{p'} \cap C(\mathbf{i}, Q)$, where $C(\mathbf{i}, Q)$ is defined by (5.3), this implies

$$\tau_M(C(-\underline{P}, \mathbf{i}, Q)) = \tau_M(-\underline{p}_1 \cap -\underline{p}_2 \cap \ldots \cap -\underline{p}_N \cap C(\mathbf{i}, Q)) =$$

$$\tau_M(-\underline{p}_1 \cap -\underline{p}_2 \cap \ldots \cap -\underline{p}_N) \cap \tau_M(C(\mathbf{i}, Q)) = \tau_M(\bigcup_{\underline{p'}\in CONP-\underline{P}} \underline{p'}) \cap \tau_M(C(\mathbf{i}, Q)) =$$

$$\tau_M((\bigcup_{\underline{p}' \in CONP-\underline{P}} \underline{p}') \cap C(\mathbf{i}, \underline{Q})) = \tau_M(\bigcup_{\underline{p}' \in CONP-\underline{P}} \underline{p}' \cap C(\mathbf{i}, \underline{Q})) = \bigcup_{\underline{p}' \in CONP-\underline{P}} \tau_M(\underline{p}' \cap C(\mathbf{i}, \underline{\mathbf{Q}}))$$

$$= \bigcup_{\underline{p}' \in CONP-\underline{P}} \tau_M(C(\underline{p}', \mathbf{i}, \underline{\mathbf{Q}})).$$

Hence both the considered rules are obviously sound.

6.2 Decomposition Trees

Now we can describe the final stage of our proof system - namely, the decomposition tree of a formula, which is the main tool for proving or disproving validity of the formula. As we have mentioned at the beginning of Section 6, the tree for a formula F will in fact start with the formula $x \in N(F)$, where x is any individual variable in VARE which does not occur in F (and hence also in $N(F)$), and $N(F)$ is the normal form of F defined in Section 5.

Before we give the formal definition of a decomposition tree, we must introduce one additional notion. Let Γ be any sequence of formulas. By *the rule applicable to* Γ we mean a decomposition rule R in DR such that one of the following conditions is satisfied:

(i) R is a replacement rule applicable to Γ,

(ii) only expansion rules are applicable to Γ, and R is an expansion rule such that:

  (1) the application of R yields some new formula which does not occur in Γ,

  (2) there is no expansion rule with the above property which can be applied to a formula or a pair of formulas in Γ lying to the left of the formula or formulas to which R can be applied.

The terms *replacement rule* and *expansion rule* were defined in the preceding subsection, following the statement of decomposition rules (see properties (6.3)-(6.5)). As by (6.4) at most one replacement rule is applicable to any given sequence Γ of formulas, and (ii)(2) uniquely defines the expansion rule which is correctly applicable to Γ in the case when no replacement rule can be applied to Γ, then

At most one decomposition rule is correctly applicable to any given sequence Γ. (6.7)

Hence we can talk about *the unique* rule R correctly applicable to a given sequence Γ - which is of a crucial importance for the definition of a decomposition tree.

For the sequel of this paper, we assume that VARE is a well-ordered set - such an assumption is necessary to ensure a unique choice of variables in the decomposition process.

The decomposition tree of a formula $F \in$ FOR, denoted by DT(F), is a binary tree with vertices labeled by sequences of formulas. DT(F) is defined inductively as follows:

(i) The root of DT(F) is labeled by $x \in N(F)$, where x is the first variable in VARE which does not occur in F, and $N(F)$ is the normal form of F,

(ii) Let w be an end vertex of the part of DT(F) constructed up to now, and suppose that w lies on a branch B of this tree. Let Γ be the sequence of formulas constituting the label of w. Then:

(a) **we terminate the branch B at the vertex w** if one of the following conditions is satisfied:

(a1) Γ is a fundamental sequence of formulas,

(a2) Γ is an indecomposable sequence of formulas* , and no expansion rule is applicable to Γ,

(a3) Γ is an indecomposable sequence of formulas, and each expansion rule applicable to Γ adds no new formula to Γ**,

(b) **otherwise we expand the branch B beyond the vertex w** by attaching to the latter:

(b1) a single son labeled by Γ_1, if the unique rule correctly applicable to Γ is of the form $\dfrac{\Gamma}{\Gamma_1}$,

(b2) two sons labeled by Γ_1 and Γ_2, respectively, if the unique rule correctly applicable to Γ is of the form $\dfrac{\Gamma}{\Gamma_1 \mid \Gamma_2}$.

(iii) DT(F) is the maximal tree that can be constructed according to the above rules.

* And hence by (6.5) no replacement rule is applicable to Γ.

** And thus we cannot augment Γ by a new formula using any expansion rule.

Obviously, in case (a) there is no possibility of expanding the branch B beyond the vertex w. As we have already stated in (6.7), at most one decomposition rule is correctly applicable to any sequence Γ - so in case (b) the rule which can be used to extend B beyond w is defined uniquely. Thus if we assume that the variables y appaearing in the rules ($\in \overline{sim}$) and ($\in \underline{sim}$) are chosen one after another, according to the order in VARE, (the details in question can be found in [8]), then DT(F) is uniquely determined by F. Hence from now on we shall assume that it is so.

The definition of DT(F) requires some futher comment. First, the fact that we can start building DT(F) from the formula $x \in N(F)$ rather than from the original formula F is justified by lemmas 5.1, 5.2, in the force of which F is valid iff $x \in N(F)$ is. Second, as we have already said, the normal form $N(F)$ can be effectively obtained from F. Third, since DT(F) starts with a formula of the form $x \in G$, then all decomposition rules can be tailored to such formulas - and indeed they are: they are applicable to formulas of this form, and yield only formulas of this form (recall that $x \notin G$, $x\ sim(A)\ y$ and $x\ dis(A)\ y$ are only special cases of formulas of the form $x \in G$ - see (5.1), (5.2)). Fourth, as $N(F)$ contains either only terms being the union of some components in COMP(F) (with the empty union interpreted as $\underline{0}$) - or solely the terms $\underline{0}$ and $-\underline{0}$ (in the case when F contains $\underline{0}$, but no other constant in CONP or variable in VARSP), then the rules ($\cup$ sim), ($\cup$ dis) are sufficient to break up all formulas of the form $x\ sim(A)\ y$, $x\ dis(A)\ y$ appearing in DT(F) into formulas of the form $x\ sim(C)\ y$, $x\ dis(C)\ y$, where C is either a component in COMP(F) or $\underline{0}$ or $-\underline{0}$. If F were not "preprocessed" to normal form before the actual construction of decomposition tree for F starts, then in order to achieve the above result we would have to augment the proof system by a full set of decomposition rules corresponding to the Boolean algebra rules for terms. Of course, this would have needlessly complicated both the proof system itself and the proof of its completeness - so we have decided against it.

It is easy to see that DT(F) may be inifinte - due to the rules ($\in \overline{sim}$) and ($\in \underline{sim}$). Moreover, it is easy to see that

a vertex w of DT(F) labeled by Γ is a terminal vertex (a leaf) iff Γ is either fundamental, or indecomposable and closed under all the expansion rules. (6.8)

(Naturally enough, we say that Γ is closed under an expansion rule R if R is either not applicable to Γ, or its application to Γ cannot yield a sequence or sequences which contain some formulas not occuring in Γ).

The notion of *provability* in our deduction system is defined as follows:
A formula F in FORM is said to be *provable,* in symbols $\vdash F$, iff DT(F) is finite and all its terminal sequences are fundamental.
(By a terminal sequence of DT(F) we mean a sequence labeling one of the leaves of this tree.)

It is quite evident that our deduction system is sound. Namely, we have the following

Lemma 6.3. *Every provable formula F is valid.*

Proof. Suppose F is provable. Then DT(F) is a finite tree, with the formula $x \in N(F)$ at its root (where x does not occur in F), and only fundamental sequences at its leaves. Hence, by the definition of DT(F), the formula $x \in N(F)$ can be obtained from a finite set of fundamental sequences by applying the decomposition rules "backwards" finitely many times. By Lemma 6.1, every fundamental sequence is valid. Hence the fact that each decomposition rule is sound by lemma 6.2 implies that the formula $x \in N(F)$ is valid, too. As we already know, the validity of $x \in N(F)$ implies validity of F, QED.

7 Completeness of the Axiom System

Now we are going to prove the main result of this paper: namely, that our deduction system for the similarity logic is complete in the sense that every valid formula is provable. To this end we need the following lemma:

Lemma 7.1. *A terminal sequence Γ of* DT(F) *is valid iff it is fundamental.*

Proof. The backward implication obviously holds, since every fundamental sequence is valid. Thus we are left with the forward implication - we must show that Γ must be fundamental in order to be valid.

Suppose Γ is not fundamental. Then from (6.8) it follows that Γ must be indecomposable and closed under all expansion rules. Hence, considering the remarks following the definition of DT(F), the definition of an idecomposable sequence given in Section 6.1 implies that each element of Γ must have one of the following forms:

$$x \in E, x \notin E, \ x\ sim(C)\ y, x\ dis(C)\ y, \tag{7.1}$$

where $x, y \in$ VARE, $E \in$ VARSE $\cup$ VARE, and C is either $\underline{0}$ or $-\underline{0}$ or a component in COMP(F).

Let CONP(F) = $\{\underline{p}_1,..., \underline{p}_n\}$ be the set of all constants in CONP occuring in F($n \geq 0$), and VARSP (F) = $\{Q_1,..., Q_m\}$ - the set of all variables in VARSP occuring in F ($m \geq 0$). Then the following is true with respect to the terms C appearing in (7.1):

(i) C can be $-\underline{0}$ only if F is a degenerate formula which contains $\underline{0}$, but no element of CONP $\cup$ VARSP;

(ii) If PROP is infinite, then C may be of the form either $C(\underline{p}_j, \mathbf{i}, Q)$ or $C(-\underline{P}, \mathbf{i}, Q)$ for some j, $1 \leq j \leq n$, $\mathbf{i}$: $\{1,2,..., m\} \rightarrow \{-, +\}$,

(iii) If PROP is finite, then C may be only of the form $C(\underline{p}_k, \mathbf{i}, Q)$, where $\underline{p}_k$ is in CONP (for in this case the $C(-\underline{P}, \mathbf{i}, Q)$'s are eliminated with help of the additional (*sim* $-\underline{P}$) and (*dis* $-\underline{P}$) rules).

Here $C(\underline{p}_j, \mathbf{i}, Q)$ and $C(-\underline{P}, \mathbf{i}, Q)$ are defined as in Section 5, i.e.

$$C(\underline{p}_j, \mathbf{i}, Q) = \underline{p}_j \cap C(\mathbf{i}, Q) \tag{7.2}$$

and

$$C(-\underline{P}, \mathbf{i}, Q) = -\underline{p}_1 \cap -\underline{p}_2 \cap ... \cap -\underline{p}_n \cap C(\mathbf{i}, Q), \tag{7.3}$$

where

$$C(\mathbf{i}, Q) = Q_1^{\mathbf{i}(1)} \cap Q_2^{\mathbf{i}(2)} \cap \quad \cap Q_m^{\mathbf{i}(m)} \tag{7.4}$$

and $Q^+ \equiv Q$, $Q^- = -Q$.

Moreover, the sequence Γ must be closed under all the expansion rules understood as transformations of sequences of formulas.

We are going to construct a counter-example to Γ, i.e. a model in which Γ is not true.

First, let us define a relation $S \subset$ VARE $\times$ VARE as follows:

$$S(x, y) \text{ iff the formula } x \notin y \text{ belongs to } \Gamma.$$

Since Γ is closed under the rules (sym $\in$) and (tran $\in$), S is obviously symmetric and transitive. Hence the relation

$$S^* = S \cup \{(x, x): x \in \text{VARE}\}$$

is an equivalence relation on VARE. Let us denote by VARE$_{/S^*}$ the set of all equivalence classes of S^*.

As our counter-example we shall take a modified Herbrand type of a model - namely,

$$H = \langle U, v\rangle,$$

where U = <VARE$_{/S^*}$, PROP, $\{sim(P)\}_{P \subseteq \text{PROP}}$>. In the sequel, VARE$_{/S^*}$ shall be often denoted by ENT$_H$ to stress the fact that we are talking about the set of entities for our model H.

The valuation v for individual variables in VARE is defined as follows:

$$v(x) = [x]_{S^*}, \tag{7.5}$$

where $[x]_{S^*}$ is the unique equivalence class of S^* which contains x. Obviously, the above definition is corect and, for any $x, y \in$ VARE such that $x \neq y$ we have

$$v(x) = v(y) \text{ iff the formula } x \notin y \text{ is in } \Gamma. \tag{7.6}$$

The valuation of the set variables in VARSE is defined by

$$v(E) = \{v(x): x \notin E \text{ belongs to } \Gamma\}. \tag{7.7}$$

The valuation of the constants in CONP is, of course, standard, i.e. $v(\underline{p}) = p$ for any $\underline{p}$ in CONP, where $\underline{p}$ is the constant representing the element p of PROP, and $v(\underline{0}) = \varnothing$.

The last - and the most intricate - thing is the valuation of the set variables in VARSP. Recall that $\underline{p}_1,..., \underline{p}_n$ are all the distinct elements of CONP occuring in F, and $Q_1,..., Q_m$ are all the distinct elements of VARSP occuring in F. Obviously, Γ cannot contain any other elements of CONP or VARSP. If F (and hence Γ, too) contains no variables in VARSP, i.e. $m = 0$, then we simply take $v(Q) = \varnothing$ for any Q in VARSP. Suppose now that it is not so, i.e. $m \geq 1$. We have to consider the following two cases:

(i) PROP is infinite,

(ii) PROP is finite.

Case (i). In this case the set $P' = \text{PROP} - \{p_1,..., p_n\}$ is inifinite. Denote by $\{-, +\}^m$ the set of all functions $\mathbf{i}:\{1,2,..., m\} \to \{-, +\}$, and let Φ be any one-to-one mapping of $\{-, +\}^m$ into P'. Then

$$\Phi(\mathbf{i}) \neq \underline{p}_j \text{ for any } \mathbf{i} \text{ in } \{-, +\}^m \text{ and any } j \text{ in } \{1, 2,..., n\}. \tag{7.8}$$

Since Γ is not a fundamental sequence, then, for any $j \in \{1,..., n\}$, there exists at most one $\mathbf{i}$ in $\{-, +\}^m$ such that for some x, y in VARE the formula $x\ sim(C(\underline{p}_j, \mathbf{i}, Q))\ y$ belongs to Γ (for any sequence containing both $x\ sim(C(\underline{p}_j, \mathbf{i}, Q))\ y$ and $x'\ sim(C(\underline{p}_j, \mathbf{i}', Q))\ y'$ with $\mathbf{i} \neq \mathbf{i}'$ is fundamental). If such an $\mathbf{i}$ exist for a given j, then we denote it by $\mathbf{i}_j$ and say that *j is positive in* Γ.

We define $v(Q) = \varnothing$ for any Q in VARSP such that $Q \notin \{Q_1,..., Q_m\}$, and

$$v(Q_k) = \{\Phi(\mathbf{i}): \mathbf{i} \in \{-, +\}^m \text{ and } \mathbf{i}(k) = +\} \cup \{p_j: j \text{ is positive in } \Gamma \text{ and } \mathbf{i}_j(k) = +\}. \tag{7.9}$$

As we see, the definition of $v\,|_{\text{VARSP}}$ we have given earlier for the trivial case of $m = 0$ can be considered as a special case of the above definition, and hence in the sequel we shall not distinguish the case of $m = 0$. All the properties of the interpretation we give below are valid for this special case, too (the reader should only recall our covention about interpreting the components in this special case, adopted in Section 5).

One can easily verify that the interpretation τ_H of terms induced by valuation of the variables in VARSP defined as above has the following properties:

$$\tau_H(C(\underline{p}_j, \mathbf{i}, Q)) = \begin{cases} \{p_j\}, & \textit{if } j \textit{ is positive in } \Gamma \textit{ and } \mathbf{i}_j = \mathbf{i}, \\ \varnothing & \textit{in the opposite case.} \end{cases} \tag{7.10}$$

$$\tau_H(C(-\underline{P}, \mathbf{i}, Q)) = \{\Phi(\mathbf{i})\} \neq \underline{p}_j \text{ for any } j \text{ in } \{1, 2,..., n\} \tag{7.11}$$

(recall the definitions (7.2)-(7.4) of the components $C(\underline{p}_j, \mathbf{i}, Q)$ and $C(-\underline{P}, \mathbf{i}, Q))$, as well as (7.8)).

Case (ii). Assume that PROP is finite and card(PROP) = N. As CONP(F) = $\{\underline{p}_1,..., \underline{p}_n\}$, then PROP $\supseteq \{p_1,..., p_n\}$, whence $N \geq n$ and without any loss of generality we can assume that PROP = $\{p_1,...,p_n, p_{n+1},..., p_N\}$. In this case the only components which can occur in Γ are those in COMP'(F) of the form $C(\underline{p}_j, \mathbf{i}, Q)$, but this time for $1 \leq j \leq N$. As before, for any given j there is at most one $\mathbf{i} \in \{-, +\}^m$ such that Γ contains a formula of the form $x\ sim(C(\underline{p}_j, \mathbf{i}, Q))\ y$ for some x, y in VARE. If such an $\mathbf{i}$ exists, then it is denoted by $\mathbf{i}_j$ and j is again said to be positive in Γ. Considering this, we define

$$v(Q_k) = \{p_j : j \text{ is positive in } \Gamma \text{ and } \mathbf{i}_j(k) = +\} \tag{7.12}$$

for $k = 1,..., m$, and $v(Q) = \varnothing$ for $Q \in$ VARSP $- \{Q_1,..., Q_m\}$. As we see, the first summand from (7.10) is now eliminated , for (as it will turn out in the sequel) it is superfluous if Γ contains no components of the form $C(-\underline{P}, \mathbf{i}, Q)$. Obviously, also in this case the interpretation τ_H of terms in our model H induced by v retains the property (7.10).

In order to complete the definition of the model H, we have to do one more thing: namely, define the family $\{sim(P)\}_{P \subseteq \text{PROP}}$ of similarity relations on ENT$_H$ $\times$ ENT$_H$. First we shall define a family of auxiliary relations $\{R(p)\}_{p \in \text{PROP}}$ on ENT$_H \times$ ENT$_H$. We have to consider the following four cases:

CASE 1. Γ contains no formulas of the form $x\ sim(C)\ y$ or $x\ dis(C)\ y$. In this case we simply put $R(p) = \varnothing$ for $p \in$ PROP.
CASE 2. Γ contains a formula of the form $x\ sim(-\underline{0})\ y$ or $x\ dis(-\underline{0})\ y$ for some x, y in VARE. As we recall, this is only possible in the case when F is a degenerate formula containing $\underline{0}$, but no other constants in CONP or variables in VARSP. Hence in this case for any formula of the form either $x\ sim(C)\ y$ or $x\ dis(C)\ y$ occuring in Γ we have $C = \underline{0}$ or $C = -\underline{0}$. We put

$$R(p) = \{(v(x), v(y)) : \text{the formula } x\ sim(-\underline{0})\ y \text{ is in } \Gamma\} \tag{7.13}$$

for every p in PROP.
CASE 3. Γ contains some formulas of the form $x\ sim(C)\ y$ or $x\ dis(C)\ y$, but no C occuring in such a formula is $-\underline{0}$ (hence any such C is either $\underline{0}$ or a component).

Again, we have to consider the two subcases corresponding to inifinite and finite PROP, respectively:

(i) **PROP is infinite.** Then, for any p in PROP, we define

$$R(p) = \begin{cases} \{(v(x), v(y)) : x\ sim(C(\underline{p}_j, \mathbf{i}_j, \mathbf{Q}))y \textit{ is in } \Gamma\} & \textit{if } p = p_j, \textit{ where } 1 \leq j \leq n \\ \qquad \textit{and } j \textit{ is positive in } \Gamma, & \\ \{(v(x), v(y)) : x\ sim(C(-\underline{P}, \mathbf{i}, \mathbf{Q}))y \textit{ is in } \Gamma\} & \textit{if } p = \Phi(i), \\ \varnothing \quad \textit{in the remaining cases.} & \end{cases} \tag{7.14}$$

The definition is correct, since by (7.8) we have $\Phi(\mathbf{i}) \neq \underline{p}_j$ for any $\mathbf{i}$ in $\{-, +\}^m$ and any j in $\{1, 2,..., n\}$, and Φ is a one-to-one mapping, so for any p there can be at most one $\mathbf{i}$ such that $p = \Phi(\mathbf{i})$.

(i) **PROP is finite,** PROP $= \{p_1,...,p_n, p_{n+1},..., p_N\}$. Then, for $j = 1,2,...N$, we define

$$R(p_j) = \begin{cases} \{(v(x), v(y)) : x\ sim(C(\underline{p}_j, \mathbf{i}_j, \mathbf{Q}))y \ \textit{ is in } \Gamma\} & \textit{if } j \textit{ is positive in } \Gamma, \\ \varnothing \quad \textit{in the opposite case.} & \end{cases} \tag{7.15}$$

In all the above cases (1)-(3), we define

$$sim(p) = \mathrm{ENT}_H \times \mathrm{ENT}_H - R(p) \tag{7.16}$$

for every p in PROP, $sim(\varnothing) = \mathrm{ENT}_H \times \mathrm{ENT}_H$ and

$$sim(P) = \bigcap_{p \in P} sim(p) \tag{7.17}$$

for any $P \subseteq$ PROP.

Obviously, the above definition implies that the family of relations $\{sim(P)\}_{P \subseteq \mathrm{PROP}}$ satisfies conditions (C2) and (C3) for similarity relations given in Section 2, i.e. $sim(\varnothing) = \mathrm{ENT}_H \times \mathrm{ENT}_H$ and $sim(P \cup Q) = sim(P) \cap sim(Q)$ for any $P, Q \subseteq$ PROP. We will show that condition (C1) is also satisfied.

First we prove that $sim(P)$ is reflexive for every $P \subseteq$ PROP, i.e. for any e in ENT_H we have $(e, e) \in sim(P)$. Considering (7.16), (7.17) and the fact that $\mathrm{ENT}_H = \mathrm{VARE}_{/S*}$, all we have to show that $([x]_{S*}, [x]_{S*})$ does not belong to $R(p)$ for any x in VARE and any p in PROP. Consider any p in PROP. If $([x]_{S*}, [x]_{S*})$ were in $R(p)$ for some x in VARE, then by the definition of $R(p)$ (all the cases of it) there would be an y in VARE such that $v(y) = v(x) = [x]_{S*}$ and $x\ sim(C)\ y$ is in Γ. As $(x, y) \in S^*$, then by the definition of S^* either $x = y$ or the formula $x \notin y$ would be in Γ. However, as Γ is closed under the rules (tran $\notin$ *sim*) and (sym *sim*), the latter as well as the first would imply that the formula $x\ sim(C)\ x$ is in Γ - which is a contradiction, since Γ is not fundamental. In this way we have proved by contradiction that for every p in PROP we have $([x]_{S*}, [x]_{S*}) \in sim(p)$ for any x in VARE, whence $sim(P)$ is indeed reflexive for any $P \subseteq$ PROP.

Further, as Γ is closed under the (sym *sim*) rule, then for every p in PROP the relation $R(p)$ is symmetric, whence the relation $sim(p)$ is also symmetric. Thus, in view of (7.16) for any $P \subseteq$ PROP, the relation $sim(P)$ is also symmetric, and hence it satisfies condition (C1).

In consequence, $U = \langle \mathrm{VARE}_{/S*}, \mathrm{PROP}, \{sim(P)\}_{P \subseteq \mathrm{PROP}} \rangle$ is a correctly defined universe, and $H = \langle U, v \rangle$ is a correctly defined model for our similarity language.

The last - but not least - step is to show that non $\models_H \Gamma$. We will do it considering - one by one - all types of fomulas that can occur in Γ. The discussion refers to all the cases 1-4 considered in connection with the definition of similarity relations, unless stated otherwise.

(a) **A formula of the form $x \notin y$** ($x, y \in$ VARE). Then by (7. 6) we have $v(x) = v(y)$, whence $v(x) \in \{v(y)\}$ and non $\models_H x \notin y$ by Lemma 5.1;

(b) **A formula of the form $x \in y$** ($x, y \in$ VARE). We will show that $v(x) \neq v(y)$. First, we have $x \neq y$, since Γ is not fundamental. Supose now that $v(x) = v(y)$. Then in view of (7.6) $x \notin y$ is also in Γ, which contradicts the assumption that Γ is not fundamental. Thus $v(x) \neq v(y)$, whence we have non $\models_H x \in y$ by Lemma 5.1;

(c) **A formula of the form $x \notin E$** ($x \in$ VARE, $E \in$ VARSE). Then $v(x) \in v(E)$ by (7.7), whence non $\models_H x \notin E$ by Lemma 5.1;

(d) **A formula of the form $x \in E$** ($x \in$ VARE, $E \in$ VARSE). Suppose that $v(x) \in v(E)$. Then by (7.7) there is an $y \in$ VARE such that the formula $y \notin E$

belongs to Γ and $v(x) = v(y)$. We cannot have $x = y$, for Γ is not fundamental. Hence $x \neq y$, whence in view of (7.6) the equality $v(x) = v(y)$ implies that $x \notin y$ is in Γ. As Γ is closed under the (tran $\in$) rule, the fact that the pair $(x \notin y, y \notin E)$ is contained in Γ implies that $x \notin E$ is also in Γ. Considering that $x \in E$ is in Γ, this contradicts our assumption that Γ is not fundamental. Hence $v(x) \notin v(E)$, i.e. non $\models_H x \in E$ by Lemma 5.1;

(e) **A formula of the form x *sim*(C) y,** where $x, y \in$ VARE and C is either a component in COMP(F) (eventually COMP'(F) for finite PROP) or the constant $-\underline{0}$ (note that C cannot be $\underline{0}$, for Γ is not a fundamental sequence). We have the following three cases:

(e1) $C \equiv -\underline{0}$. Then we have $\tau_H(C)$ = PROP $- \tau_H(\underline{0})$ = PROP $- \varnothing$ = PROP. Moreover, since x *sim*$(-\underline{0})$ y is in Γ, by (7.13) we have $(v(x), v(y)) \in R(p)$ for every p in PROP, whence by (7.16) $(v(x), v(y)) \notin sim(p)$ for every p in PROP. Thus by (7.17) $(v(x), v(y)) \notin sim$(PROP). As PROP = $\tau_H(C)$, then by Lemma 5.1 we have non $\models_H x$ *sim*(C) y;

(e2) $C \equiv C(\underline{p}_j, \mathbf{i}, \underline{Q})$ for some j, and some $\mathbf{i} \in \{-, +\}^m$. Then, obviously, j is positive in Γ and $\mathbf{i} = \mathbf{i}_j$, whence by (7.10) we have $\tau_H(C) = \{p_j\}$. Considering both (7.14) and (7.15), $(v(x), v(y)) \in R(p_j)$, so $(v(x), v(y)) \notin sim(p_j)$ by (7.16). Thus we have $(v(x), v(y)) \notin sim(\tau_H(C))$, i.e. non $\models_H x$ *sim*(C) y by Lemma 5.1;

(e3) PROP is infinite and $C \equiv C(-\underline{P}, \mathbf{i}, \underline{Q})$ for some $\mathbf{i} \in \{-, +\}^m$. Then by (7.11) we have $\tau_H(C) = \{\Phi(\mathbf{i})\}$. Moreover, since (7.14) implies that $(v(x), v(y)) \in R_{\Phi(\mathbf{i})}$, in this case we also have $(v(x), v(y)) \notin sim(\{\Phi(\mathbf{i})\}) = sim(\tau_H(C))$, and in consequence non $\models_H x$ *sim*(C) y by Lemma 5.1;

(f) **A formula of the form x *dis*(C) y,** where C is a component in COMP(F), $\underline{0}$ or $-\underline{0}$, and $x, y \in$ VARE. In view of (7.10), (7.11), we have to consider the three following cases:

(f1) $\tau_H(C) = \varnothing$ (this includes the case when C is $\underline{0}$). Then $sim(\tau_H(C))$ = ENT $\times$ ENT, whence $(v(x), v(y)) \in sim(\tau_H(C))$ and non $\models_H x$ *dis*(C) y by Lemma 5.1;

(f2) $\tau_H(C) = \{p\} \neq \varnothing$, where $p \in$ PROP. Suppose that $(v(x), v(y)) \notin sim(p)$. In view of (7.14)-(7.16), this means that there exist $x', y' \in$ VARE such that x' *sim*(C) y' is in Γ and $v(x) = v(x')$, $v(y) = v(y')$. The following cases are possible:

(1) $x = x', y \neq y'$; (2) $x \neq x', y = y'$; (3) $x \neq x', y \neq y'$ (the case of $x \neq x'$ and $y = y'$ is obviously ruled out, since x *dis*(C) y is in Γ, and Γ is not fundamental).

Clearly, it suffices to consider the third case as the most general one. In that case the formulas $x \notin x'$ and $y \notin y'$ are in Γ by (7.6). As Γ is closed under the (tran $\in$ *sim*) rule, then the fact that the pair $(x \notin x', x'$ *sim*(C) $y')$ is included in Γ implies that also x *sim*(C) y' is in Γ. Since Γ is also closed under the rule (sym *sim*), then y' *sim*(C) x is in Γ, too. This together with the fact that $y \notin y'$ is in Γ implies that y *sim*(C) x is in Γ, because Γ is closed under (tran $\in$ *sim*). As Γ is also closed under

under (sym *sim*), we conclude that $x\ sim(C)\ y$ is in Γ, which in view of the fact that $x\ dis(C)\ y$ is in Γ contradicts our assumption that Γ is not fundamental.

Thus we have proved by contradiction that $(v(x), v(y)) \in sim(p)$. As $\tau_H(C) = \{p\}$, this yields non $\models_H x\ dis(C)\ y$ by Lemma 5.1.

(f3) $\tau_H(C)$ = PROP, i.e. $C \equiv -\underline{0}$. Then, considering (7.13), we can prove in exactly the same way as in (f2) that $(v(x), v(y)) \in sim(p)$ for every p in PROP. Hence $(v(x), v(y)) \in sim(\mathrm{PROP}) = \bigcap_{p \in PROP} sim(p)$ and again we have non $\models_H x\ dis(C)\ y$ by Lemma 5.1.

By considering the cases (a)-(f), which exhaust the whole range of possibilities, we have indeed shown that no formula in Γ can be true in the model H. This contradicts our assumption about the validity of Γ. Hence we have proved by contradiction that Γ must be fundamental, which ends the proof of Lemma 7. 1.

Now we can prove the completeness theorem:

Theorem 7.1. *Every valid formula* $F \in$ FORM *is provable, i.e. has a finite decomposition tree with only fundamental sequences at its leaves.*

Proof. Suppose that F is valid. If DT(F) is finite, then from the definition of DT(F) and from the soundness of the decomposition rules of our system (see Section 6.1) it follows that F is valid iff all the terminal sequences of DT(F) are valid. However, by Lemma 7.1 we have just proved the latter holds iff all the terminal sequences of DT(F) are fundamental. Thus if F is valid and DT(F) is finite, then all the terminal sequences of DT(F) are fundamental.

Thus to complete the proof of the theorem we have to prove that if DT(F) is inifinite, then F is not valid. We shall do it by modifying the standard proof method used in [8] to suit the structure of our language. For the sake of simplicity, we shall omit some more cumbersome details.

Suppose that DT(F) is inifinite. Then by Koenig's lemma it posesses an infinite branch B starting from the root. Let us denote by Δ the set of all indecomposable formulas labeling the vertices of B. It is quite obvious that Δ cannot contain a fundamental seuqence Γ'. Indeed, as every vertex in DT(F) inherits all the indecomposable formulas from the labels of its ancestors, then all elements of a hypothetical fundamental sequence Γ' included in Δ would belong to a label Γ'' of some vertex v of B; in consequence, Γ'' would be also fundamental, which would make w a terminal vertex - and this is a contradiction, since w lies on B, and B is infinite. Thus for the Herbrand-type model H defined just like that in the proof of Lemma 7.1, but basing on Δ instead of Γ, we have

$$\text{non} \models_H G \quad \text{for every } G \text{ in } \Delta. \tag{7.18}$$

In fact, the only difference between our set Δ and the sequence Γ from the proof of Lemma 7.1 is that Δ is infinite, whereas Γ was finite; however, in the proof of the discussed lemma we have never made use of the fact that Γ was finite, and hence all the definitions and subsequent arguments can be repeated almost word for word.

As we know, the root of DT(F) is labeled by the formula $z \in F$, where z is the first variable in VARE which not occur in F (we denote it here by z rather than by x to avoid collision with the common notation of decomposition rules). Basing on (7.18), we shall now prove by induction on the *order* of a formula that $x \in F$ cannot be true in H.

We begin with defining the order of a formula G, denoted by o(G). For the sake of brevity, we limit the definition to formulas containing only terms of the form

$$A \equiv C_1 \cup ... \cup C_k,$$

where $C_i \in$ COMP(F) $\cup$ {$\underline{0}$, $-\underline{0}$} - since only such formulas may be encountered in the labels of DT(F). We define the *rank* r(A) of such a term A as k, i.e. the number of the component-like summands constituting A. Basing on such an assumption, we put:

$$o(E) = o(x) = 1 \text{ for } x \in \text{VARE, E} \in \text{VARSE},$$

$$o(\neg G) = 1 + o(G), \quad o(G' \vee G'') = o(G' \wedge G'') = 1 + \max(o(G''), o(G'')),$$

$$o(\overline{sim}(A)G) = o(\underline{sim}(A)G) = 1 + r(A) + o(G).$$

In consequence, by the definition of our special formulas (see (5.1) and (5.2) in Section 5) we have

$$o(x \in G) = 1 + \max(2, o(G)), \quad o(x \notin G) = 2 + o(G),$$

$$o(x\ sim(A)\ y) = 3 + r(A), \quad o(x\ dis(A)\ y) = 4 + r(A).$$

For any vertex w of DT(F), denote by $l(w)$ the sequence Γ of formulas which is the label of w, and let

$$\Lambda = \{G\colon G \text{ is in } l(w) \text{ for some vertex } w \text{ of the branch } B\}.$$

Suppose that $\models_H z \in F$. Then the set

$$\Sigma = \{G\colon G \in \Lambda \text{ and } \models_H G\}$$

is non-empty, since $z \in F$ is in Λ as the label of the root of DT(F). Let G_o be a formula in Σ such that $o(G_o) \le o(G)$ for every formula G in Σ. Then there exists a vertex w_o on B such that $l(w_o) = (\Gamma', G_o, \Gamma'')$, where Γ' is indecomposable.

We may suppose that G_o is not of the form

(1) $x \in \neg G$ or (2) $x \notin \overline{sim}(A)G$ or (3) $x \notin \underline{sim}(A)G$,

since then the formula

(1') $x \notin G$ or (2') $x \in \underline{sim}(A) \neg G$ or (3') $x \in \overline{sim}(A) \neg G$

would also be in Σ, and the orders of the two formulas are equal.

One can show that the formula G_o cannot be of one of the forms

$$x \notin \neg G, \quad x \notin G' \vee G'', \quad x \notin G' \wedge G'', \quad x\ sim(A \cup B)\ y, \quad x\ dis(A \cup B)\ y.$$

Indeed: if G_o were in in one of those forms, then the vertex w_o would have a son w' on B such that either $l(w') = (\Gamma', F', \Gamma'')$ or $l(w') = (\Gamma', F', F'', \Gamma'')$, where $F' \in \Sigma$ in the former case, and either $F' \in \Sigma$ or $F'' \in \Sigma$ in the latter case, and $o(F') < o(G_o)$, $o(F'') < o(G_o)$.

For the same reasons, G_o cannot be of the form

(a) $x \in G' \vee G''$ or (b) $x \in G' \wedge G''$,

where $\max(o(G'), o(G'')) > 1$. However, G_o cannot be of one of those forms also for G', G'' with $o(G') = o(G'') = 1$. Indeed: in this case $G', G'' \in$ VARE $\cup$ VARSE, and hence the formulas $x \in G'$, $x \in G''$ are indecomposable. As G_o is true in H, then - by virtue of the soundness of rules ($\in \vee$) and ($\in \wedge$) - at least one of them must be true in H in case (a), and both in case (b). However, in case (a) both of them, and in case (b) at least one occur in the label of a son w' of w_o which belongs to B - whence in case (a) they both are in Δ, and in case (b) at least one of them is in Δ. Clearly, this is a contradiction, because by (7.18) no formula in Δ can be true in H.

G_o cannot be of the form $x \in \underline{sim}(A)G$ with $o(G) \geq 2$, for then w_o would have a son w' on B such that $l(w') = (\Gamma', G', G'', \Gamma'')$, where $G' = x\ dis(A)\ y$, $G'' = y \in G$, $o(G') < o(G_o)$, $o(G'') < o(G_o)$, and either G' or G'' is in Σ by the soundness of the ($\in$ $\underline{sim}$) rule. Suppose that G_o is of the form $x \in \underline{sim}(A)G$, where $o(G) = 1$. As in this case $y \in G$ is indecomposable, and $y \in G$ is in $l(w')$ for the son w' of w_o discussed above, then $y \in G$ is in Δ, and hence cannot be true in H. Thus the formula $G' =$ $x\ dis(A)\ y$ must be true in H. Suppose $A \equiv C_1 \cup \ldots \cup C_k$, where each C_i is in COMP(F) $\cup \{\underline{0}, -\underline{0}\}$. Then, by the soundness of the ($dis \cup$) rule, $x\ dis(C_i)\ y$ must be true in H for some i. However, this is a contradiction, for the latter formula is indecomposable and occurs in the label of some vertex on B (the k-th descendant of w_o), and hence it belongs to Δ.

Finally, G_o cannot be of the form $x \in \overline{sim}(A)G$. Indeed: suppose G_o is of this form. Then $x \in \overline{sim}(A)G$ is true in H, whence $v(x) \in \overline{sim}(\tau_H(A))\varphi_H(G)$. Thus by the definition of H (see the proof of Lemma 7.1) there exists an $y \in$ VARE such that $[y_{S*}] \in \varphi_H(G)$ and $([x_{S*}], [y_{S*}]) \in sim(\tau_H(A))$ But then for such an y we have $v(y)$ $\in \varphi_H(G)$ and $(v(x), v(y)) \in sim(\tau_H(A))$, i.e. $\models_H\ y \in G$ and $\models_H\ x\ sim(A)\ y$. Moreover, there is a vertex w' on B such that $l(w')$ contains either $y \in G$ or $x\ sim(A)\ y$. In the former case $o(G) \geq 2$, for otherwise $y \in G$ would be an element of Δ and as such could not be true in H. Consider the latter case. If $o(G) \geq 2$, then $o(x\ sim(A)\ y) <$ $o(G_o)$ and $x\ sim(A)\ y$ is in Σ. If $o(G) = 1$, then $r(A) > 1$, for otherwise $x\ sim(A)\ y$ would be in Δ, which is a contradiction. Suppose $A \equiv C_1 \cup \ldots \cup C_k$, where $k > 1$. Then, by the soundness of the ($sim \cup$) rule, $x\ sim(C_i)\ y$ must be true in H for some i. However, this is a contradiction, for the latter formula is indecomposable and occurs in the label of some vertex on B (the k-th descendant of w'), and hence it belongs to Δ.

Thus the only forms of G_o we are left with are $x \in G$, $x \notin$ G for G in VARE $\cup$ VARSE and $x\ sim(C)\ y$, $x\ dis(C)\ y$, where C is in COMP(F) $\cup \{\underline{0}, -\underline{0}\}$. However, in this case G_o is in Δ, which contradicts (7.18).

Hence we have proved by contradiction that the set Σ is empty. In consequence, the formula $z \in F$ cannot be true in H, which implies that non $\models_H F$. This completes the proof of our theorem.

8 Conclusions and Final Remarks

The deduction system presented here is not minimal; as it was aimed rather at a clear presentation of the properties of the logic than at brevity. For this reason, we have used both the connectives AND and OR, though one of them is definable in terms of the other and NOT. Analogously, the (sym dis) rule could have been deleted without making the system incomplete, since it has not been used in the completeness proof.

Since our attention has been focused at the completeness proof and the technical complexities connected with this proof have taken up quite a lot of place here, we have refrained from treating other issues, like the expressive possibilities of the language. For a detailed discussion of the latter subject, the reader is referred to the paper [3] on indiscernibility logic, containing a wide range of examples; the ones which are not based on transitivity of indiscernibility relations remain true also in our case. However, there is one aspect of the expresiveness of the similarity language we have introduced here which should be highlighted: namely, due to the introduction of individual variables representing entities, the membership connective of the set theory is expressible within our logic. This fact is of a paramount importance, as the whole proof mechanism we have developed here is based on that connective - and on the use of components, which are a well-known tool of the set theory.

The main result of this paper is the completeness proof for the logic of relative similarity, which is in fact a polymodal logic, with two modalities - the operations of lower and upper approximation - corresponding to every subset of a given set of properties. Up to now, the full indiscernibility logic discussed in [3] has not been equipped with a complete deduction systems - despite many attempts in this direction (see e.g [1, 9]). Evidently, the method employed here can be used to develop a complete deduction system for the logic of relative indiscernibility. In fact, it suffices to augment the proof system given here by two rules expressing the transitivity of indiscernibility relations.

A different approach to a similarity logic was presented in [10, 11]. However, the logics discussed there do not allow for relative similarity. Instead of discussing a whole family of similarity relations parametrised by sets of properties, they are aimed at describing either a single similarity relation, or some of its variants, like negative similarity in [11].

Finally, let us note that we can introduce into our language a family $\{\mathrm{ind}(P)\}_{P \subseteq \mathrm{PROP}}$ of derived indiscernibility relations, which can be defined in any universe U as follows:

$$(e, f) \in \mathrm{ind}(P) \text{ iff, for every } e \text{ in ENT, } (e, g) \in sim(P) \text{ iff } (f, g) \in sim(P).$$

It is possible to augment our proof systems with some rules for the lower and upper approximation modalities corresponding to the above notion of relative indiscernibility in such a way that the resulting proof system will also be complete. In such a way one can get a hybrid similarity- indiscernibility logic, which will be discussed in a separate paper.

The method of employing individual variables to develop decomposition rules for a formal language used in this paper was inspired by [4].

References

[1] B. Konikowska, *A formal language for reasoning about indiscernibility*, Bull. Pol. Acad. Sci., **35** (1987), No. 3-4, 230-249

[2] C. Lyndon, *Notes on Logic*, D. Van Nostrand, Princeton 1964

[3] E. Orłowska, *Logic of indiscernibility relations*, Bull. Pol. Acad. Sci., **33** (1985), No. 9-10, 476-485

[4] E. Orłowska, *Relational interpretation of modal logic*, in: H. Andreka, D. Monk, I. Nemeti (eds.), Algebraic Logic, Colloquia Mathematica Societatis Jano Bolyai, North Holland, 1988, 443-471

[5] Z. Pawlak, *Rough sets*, Intl. Journal of Computer and Information Sciences, **11** (1982), 341-356

[6] J. Pomykała, *Approximation operations in an approximation space*, Bull. Pol. Acad. Sci., **35** (1987), 653-662

[7] J. Pomykała, On definability in nondeterministic information systems, Bull. Pol. Acad. Sci., **36** (1988), 193-210

[8] H. Rasiowa, R. Sikorski, *The Mathematics of Metamathematics*, Warsaw, Polish Scientific Publishers 1963

[9] D. Vakarelov, *Modal logic for knowledge representation*, 6th Symposium on Computation Theory, Wedisch-Rietz (Germany), 1987

[10] D. Vakarelov, *Modal logics for similarity relations in Pawlak knowledge representation systems*, Fundamenta Informaticae **15** (1991), 61-79

[11] D. Vakarelov, *Logical analysis of positive and negative similarity relations in property systems*, Proceedings of the First World Conference on the Fundamentals of Artificial Intelligence, Paris, France, 1991, 491-500

Chapter 16

Information Systems, Similarity Relations and Modal Logics

Dimiter Vakarelov

Department of Mathematical Logic with Laboratory for Applied Logic,
Faculty of Mathematics and Computer Science,
Sofia University, blvd James Bouchier 5, 1126, Sofia, Bulgaria
e-mail: dvak@fmi.uni-sofia.bg

Abstract: In the paper we study two types of information systems: ontological and logical. Systems of ontological type are Property systems and Attribute systems, where the information is represented in terms of the ontological concepts of object, property and attribute. Systems of logical type are Consequence systems and Bi-consequence systems where the information is represented by a collection of sentences, equipped with some inference mechanism. We prove that each Consequence system can be embedded into a certain Property system. The similar results hold for Bi-consequence systems and Attribute systems. These representation theorems are used to give an abstract characterization (by means of a finite set of first-order sentences) of some information relations in Property systems and Attribute systems, including various kinds of similarity relations. Several modal logics with modalities corresponding to some collections of information relations are introduced and their "query meaning" is discussed. One of the main results of the paper are the completeness theorems for the introduced modal logics with respect to their standard semantics.

1 Introduction

This paper is devoted to a systematic study of similarity relations in some information systems and the corresponding modal logics. This is a continuation of the research line of applications of mathematical logic to some problems in Information Science and Artificial Intelligence started by Orlowska and Pawlak [OP1], [OP2] and then by Orlowska [Or1], [Or2], [Or3], [Or6], Farinas and Orlowska [FCO1], Vakarelov [Va1], [Va2], [Va4], [Va5], [Va6], [Va7], [Va8], Gargov [Gar1], Archangelski & Taitslin [AT1], Rasiowa [Ra1], Rasiowa & Skowron [RS1] and others.

The notion of similarity relation is important at least in two respects: theoretical – to make an inexact notion precise, and practical – how to use this notion in the AI systems. This paper deals with theoretical aspects of the problem. Similarity relations are special kinds of informational relations, so their study is a contribution to the general study of informational relations in information systems.

The modal logics for information systems, are poly-modal systems with Kripke semantics based on some informational relations. The aim of these logics is to provide a formal account for reasoning about objects in information systems in terms of some informational relations like indiscernibility, similarity, informational inclusion and so on. The informational relations in a given information system are concretely defined relations. So in order to axiomatize the corresponding modal logic we need to characterize these relations by a certain set of first-order sentences, i.e. to characterize them as an abstract first-order structure, and then to find the corresponding modal logic, complete in the class of all such structures. One of the main novelty in this paper is a systematic study of several methods of such abstract characterization theorems for several kinds of similarity relations. However, not all first order conditions possess a modal translation. So the second novelty is a method called "copying", designed to axiomatize structures with modally undefinable first-order conditions. The third new thing is a demonstration that the method of filtration from the classical modal logic may work to show the decidability of such complicated poly-modal logics as these, considered in the paper.

Special attention here needs the notion of information system. There is no a unique mathematical notion of information system, because in the practice work several different schemes for representing information. There are mainly two groups of information systems: systems of logical type in which the information is represented by a collection of sentences, equipped with some inference mechanism, and information systems of ontological type, based on the ontological concepts of object, property, attribute. In this paper we consider information systems of both types and establish a kind of duality between them, which provides a suitable framework for the abstract characterization theorems for the similarity relations.

The rest of the paper is divided into four sections. Section 2 is devoted to information systems, section 3 – to similarity relations in information systems, section 4 – to modal logics for similarity relations in information systems, and section 5 for some concluding remarks: generalizations and open problems. Each section has a short introduction and summary of its content.

For the reading of the paper some elementary knowledge of modal logic and Kripke semantics is supposed. One of the books [Se1], [HC1], may help the reader.

2 Information Systems

In this section we introduce four abstract notions of information systems: property systems, attribute systems, consequence systems and bi-consequence systems .

The information represented in property systems (P-systems) is given in terms of objects and properties, which they possess. In attribute systems (A-systems) the information is given in terms of objects, attributes and values of attributes. An example of an attribute is, for instance, "color" and the values of this attribute are concrete colors like "green", "red" etc. The information about some object with respect to some attribute is a subset of the values of this attribute, which this object possesses. The notion of an A-system was introduced by Pawlak ([Pa1, Pa3]) under the name of information system. Pawlak's information systems lay down in the so called "Rough sets approach", which now is one of the fundamentals of some directions in AI ([Pa2, Pa4, Sl1]). P-systems were introduced in [Va6] as a simplification of Pawlak's information systems. As can be seen later on in this paper, P-systems may help in understanding the theory of A-systems.

P-systems and A-systems are information systems of non-logical type and since they deal with some basic ontological concepts, such as "object", "property", "attribute" and "value of attribute", it is natural to classify them as "ontological information systems". The other kind of information systems are the systems of logical type. The information in an information system of logical type is represented by a set of sentences equipped with one or more consequence relations. In this paper we study two information systems of such a kind: consequence systems (C-systems) and bi-consequence systems (B-systems).

C-systems are pairs $(W, \vdash)$ where W is a non-empty set of sentences and $\vdash$ is a consequence relation between finite subsets of W satisfying the standard Scott's axioms. Similar systems were introduced by Scott [Sc1]. We present in [Va8] a simple duality between P-systems and C-systems. In a sense C-systems are the logical counterparts of P-systems, although they have completely different nature.

B-systems are like C-systems and they are equipped with two consequence relations – a strong one $\vdash$ and a weak one $\succ$. These systems are introduced as logical counterparts of A-systems.

The structure of the section 2 of the paper is the following. In sec. 2.1 and 2.2 we introduce P-systems and A-systems respectively. In sec. 2.4 we introduce C-systems. The main theorem here is the Characterization theorem for C-systems (Theorem 5) which can be considered as a kind of representation theorem of C-systems in P-systems, generalizing the Stone representation theorem for distributive lattices [St1]. In sec. 2.4 we introduce B-systems and prove analogous Characterization theorem for B-systems (Theorem 12), which also can be considered as a kind of representation theorem of B-systems in A-systems.

2.1 Property Systems

By a property system, P-system for short, we will mean any system of the form $S = (Ob, Pr, f)$ where:

- $Ob \neq \emptyset$ is a set, whose elements are called objects,
- Pr is a set, whose elements are called properties and
- f is a total function, called information function, which assigns to each object $x \in Ob$ a subset $f(x) \subseteq Pr$, called the information of x in S. By $\overline{f}(x)$ we denote the set $Pr \setminus f(x)$.

Very often the components of a given system S will be denoted by Ob_S, Pr_S and f_S. If $Pr_S = \emptyset$ then S is called trivial P-system, otherwise S is called non-trivial P-system. S is called total P-system if for any $x \in Ob_S$ we have $f(x) \neq \emptyset$.

The notion of a P-system follows the simple ontological idea that some things are objects, some other things are properties and that objects possess properties. The notions of an object and a property are taken as primitives and the possession of a property is formalized by the function f: "x has (possesses) the property A" can be expressed by "$A \in f(x)$".

In the natural language the sentence stating that certain object x possesses certain property A is expressed very often by the phrase "x is A", like "x is green". In this example the property is "being a green". There are many other ways, which express the situation of possession of a property. Examples:

- "x speaks English". This means "x has the property of speaking English". The property here is "to speak English".
- "x weights 2 kilo". The property here is: "to weight 2 kilo".
- "x drives a car". The property is "to drive a car".
- "x drives a bicycle". The property is "to drive a bicycle".
- "x is born on 18.4.1938". The property here is "to be born on 18.4.1938", etc.

We do not assume in general that in a given P-system S Pr_S is the set of all possible properties of the objects contained in Ob_S. Rather Pr_S is a set of some properties meaningful for the objects from Ob_S, which are interesting from a certain point of view. In trivial systems we have only objects and no properties. Also we do not assume, in general, that for every $x \in Ob_S$ we have $f(x) \neq \emptyset$ (totality). It is quite possible for some object $x \in Ob_S$ to have $f_S(x) = \emptyset$. This does not say that x has no properties at all, it says only that x does not have properties from the given set Pr_S.

The set-theoretical counterpart of properties are sets. Then $x \in A$ means that x has the property A. This motivates the following set-theoretical construction of P-systems.

Let (W, V) be a pair such that $W \neq \emptyset$ and $V \subseteq P(W)$ be a set of subsets of W. Define a system $S = P(W, V)$ as follows: $Ob_S = W$, $Pr_S = V$ and $f_S = \{A \in V | x \in A\}$. Then obviously $P(W, V)$ is a P-system, which we will call set-theoretical P-system over the pair (W, V).

Now we shall introduce the notion of a homomorphism between P- systems.

Let S and S' be two P-systems and let h be a function from $Ob_S \cup Pr_S$ into $Ob_{S'} \cup Pr_{S'}$. We say that h is a homomorphism from S into S' if it satisfies the following conditions:

- $x \in Ob_S$ iff $h(x) \in Ob_{S''}$,
- $A \in Pr_S$ iff $h(A) \in Pr_{S''}$,
- if $A \in f_S(x)$ then $h(A) \in f_{S'}(h(x))$.

The function h is called a strong homomorphism if it is a homomorphism, satisfying the condition:

– if $h(A) \in f_{S'}(h(x))$ then $A \in f_S(x)$.

S' is called a homomorphic image of S if there exists a homomorphism h which maps S onto S'.

Let S be a P-system. We shall define a P-system $|S|$, called set-theoretical P-system associated with S, which will be a strong homomorphic image of S. The construction is as follows: put $W = Ob_S$, for any $A \in Pr_S$ define $|A| = \{x \in Pr_S | A \in f_S(x)\}$, $V = \{|A| | A \in Pr_S\}$ and define $|S|$ to be the set-theoretical P-system $P(W, V)$ over the pair (W, V). The following lemma is true:

Lemma 1. *(i) Let S be a P-system. Then $|S|$ is a strong homomorphic image of S.*
(ii) If S is a set-theoretical P-system then $|S| = S$.

Proof. (i) Define h in the following way: for $x \in Ob_S$ $h(x) = x$, for $A \in Pr_S$ $h(A) = |A|$. Then by an easy calculation one can see that h is a strong homomorphism from S onto $|S|$.
(ii) If S is a set theoretical P-system then the construction of $|S|$ gives the same system S and h is the identity function.

□

The strong homomorphism h, defined in the above proof, is called the natural homomorphism from S onto $|S|$.

2.2 Attribute Systems

Let S be a concrete P-system such that in the set Pr_S we have the following concrete properties: E: "to speak English", F: "to speak French", G: "to speak German" and R: "to speak Russian". But $\{E, F, G, R\}$ are all official languages. So the above four properties form a general property "to speak an official language". Such a general property will be called an attribute and its concrete cases will be called values of this attribute. Thus the set of values of the attribute a = "to speak an official language" (shortly "official language") is the set $Val_S(a) = \{E, F, G, R\}$. Let $x \in Ob_S$ be a person and let $f_S(x, a) = f_S(x) \cap Val_S(a)$. Then $f_S(x, a)$ can be considered as the information about x with respect to the attribute a. Let for example $f_S(x, a) = \{E, R\}$. This is an information about x, which states that x speaks English and Russian but not French and German.

Other examples of attributes and their sets of values are the following:

- a = "to have a color...", shortly "color". The set $Val(a)$ is the set of all (or some) concrete colors: red, green, etc.
- a = "to weight ... kilo", shortly "weight". $Val(a)$ may be the set (or some subsets) of non-negative rational numbers.
- a = "to drive a ...", $Val(a) = \{\text{car, bicycle, motorcycle}\}$
- a = "to be born on ...", $Val(a)$ = any interval of possible dates.
- a = "age", $Val = \{1, 2, \ldots, 120\}$ or $Val(a) = \{\text{childhood, boyhood, adult}\}$.

These examples show that we can consider attributes as sets of similar properties, which are called values of the corresponding attribute.

Thus we arrive to the following formal definition.

By an attribute system, A-system for short, we mean any system of the form $S = (Ob, At, \{Val(a) | a \in At\}, f)$, where:

- $Ob \neq \emptyset$ is a set, whose elements are called objects,
- At is a set, whose elements are called attributes,
- for each $a \in At$, $Val(a)$ is a set, whose elements are called values of the attribute a,
- f is a two-argument total function, called information function, which assigns to each object $x \in Ob$ and attribute $a \in At$ a subset $f(x, a) \subseteq Val(a)$, called the information about x according to a.

Sometimes the components of a given A-system S will be written with subscript S: Ob_S, At_S, $Val_S(a)$ and f_S. S is called a total A-system if for every $x \in Ob_S$ and $a \in At_S$ $f_S(x, a) \neq \emptyset$. S is called a single-valued A-system if for any $x \in Ob_S$ and $a \in At_S$ the set $f_S(x, a)$ has at most one element, i.e. $Card(f_S(x, a)) \leq 1$. If $f_S(x, a) = \{A\}$ then we will write simply $f_S(x, a) = A$. S is called a finite system if all components of S are finite sets.

The notion of non-trivial single-valued and total finite A-system is introduced by Pawlak in [Pa1] under the name of information system. These systems are very simple and can be represented as a table, whose rows are labeled by objects and whose columns are labeled by attributes.

The notion of A-system given above is a slight generalization of the notion of many-valued information system, given by Pawlak in [Pa3], (Pawlak always assumes that S is non-trivial, total and finite), (see also [OP1], [Va1] and [Va4], where this notion is used under the name of knowledge representation system, and single-valued systems are under the name of deterministic knowledge representation systems).

Now we shall define some constructions of P-systems from A-systems.

Let S be an A-system. Then for each $a \in At_S$ we can define a P-system $S(a)$ with the following construction. Put $Ob_{S(a)} = Ob_{S'}$, $Pr_{S(a)} = Val_S(a)$, for $x \in Ob_{S(a)}$ define $f_{S(a)}(x) = f_S(x, a)$. The P-system $S(a)$ is called the restriction of S to the attribute a.

Let S be an A-system. Define a P-system $S' = Under(S)$ – the underlying P-system of S, putting $Ob_{S'} = Ob_S$, $Pr_{S'} = \bigcup\{Val(a) | a \in At_S\}$ and $f_{S'}(x) = \bigcup\{f_S(x, a) | a \in At_S\}$.

The following two constructions transform P-systems into A-systems.

Let S be a P-system. We can associate a single-valued A-system S' to S in the following way. Put $Ob_{S'} = Ob_S$, $At_{S'} = Pr_{S'}$, for each $a \in At_{S'}$ define $Val(a)_{S'} = \{a\}$ and for $x \in Ob_{S'}$ and $a \in At_{S'}$ define $f_{S'}(x, a) = f_S(x) \cap \{a\}$. Obviously S' is a single-valued A-system This construction shows that each property A can be considered as an attribute whose set of values is the one-element set $\{A\}$.

We can associate with S another A-system S'' having only one attribute, with the following construction. Put $Ob_{S''} = Ob_S$, $At_{S''} = \{p\} = \{\text{property}\} = Pr_S$, define $Val(p)_{S''} = Pr_S$ and for each $x \in Obs_{S''}$ put $f_{S''}(x,p) = f_S(x)$. Obviously S'' is not in general a single valued A-system. This construction shows that each set of properties Pr can be considered as one attribute, namely the attribute p: "to have a property", with the set of values $Val(p) = Pr$.

Now we shall give a set-theoretical construction of A-systems, following the intuition of set-theoretical P-systems. Since attributes can be considered as sets of properties and the set-theoretical analog of a property is a set of objects, then the set-theoretical analog of an attribute is a set of sets of objects. This leads to the following construction.

Let (W,V) be a pair with $W \neq \emptyset$ and $V \subseteq P(P(W))$, i.e. the elements of V are sets of subsets of W. Define an A-system $S = A(W,V)$ as follows: Put $Obs_S = W$, $At_S = V$, for each $a \in At_S$ define $Val_S(a) = a$, and for each $x \in Obs_S$ and $a \in At_S$ put $f_S(x,a) = \{A \in a | x \in A\}$. The system $S = A(W,V)$, will be called the set-theoretical A-system over the pair (W,V).

Let S and S' be two A-systems. A function h from the union of all components of S to the union of all components of S' will be called a homomorphism from S into S' if it satisfies the following conditions for any $x \in Obs_S$, $a \in At_S$, $A \in Val_S(a)$:

- $x \in Obs_S$ iff $h(x) \in Obs_{S'}$,
- $a \in At_S$ iff $h(a) \in At_{S'}$,
- $A \in Val_S(a)$ iff $h(A) \in Val_{S'}(h(a))$,
- if $A \in f_S(x,a)$ then $h(A) \in f_{S'}(h(x),h(a))$.

h is called a strong homomorphism if, in addition, it satisfies the condition

- if $h(A) \in f_{S'}(h(x),h(A))$ then $A \in f_S(x,a)$.

S' is a homomorphic image of S if there is a homomorphism h which maps S onto S'.

Let S be an A-system. We shall associate with S a set-theoretical A-system denoted by $|S|$, which will be a strong homomorphic image of S. The construction is as follows: put $W = Obs_S$, for $a \in At_S$ and $A \in Val_S(a)$ define $g_a(A) = \{x \in W | A \in f(x,a)\}$ and $|a| = \{g_a(A) | A \in Val_S(a)\}$, put $V = \{|a| | a \in At_S\}$. Then we let $|S|$ to be the set-theoretical A-system $S(W,V)$ over the pair (W,V). The following lemma is true:

Lemma 2. *Let S be an A-system. Then:*

(i) $|S|$ is a strong homomorphic image of S.
(ii) If S is a set-theoretical A-system then $|S| = S$.
(iii) If S is a set-theoretical A-system over some pair (W,V) then S is a single-valued iff the following condition is satisfied:

$$(Aa \in V)(\forall A, B \in a)(A \cap B \neq \emptyset \rightarrow A = B) .$$

Proof. (i). Let h be defined as follows: for $x \in Obs_S$ $h(x) = x$, for $a \in At_S$ $h(a) = |a|$ and for $A \in Val_S(a)$ let $h(A) = g_a(A)$. Then h is the required strong homomorphism from S onto $|S|$.

The proof of (ii) and (iii) is straightforward. □

The function h defined in the proof of lemma 2 will be called the natural strong homomorphism from S onto $|S|$.

2.3 Consequence Systems

In this section we will introduce a kind of logical information systems, called consequence systems, which in a sense can be considered as logical counterparts of property systems. Intuitively, each consequence system contains a set of sentences and a certain consequence relation. There are various kinds of consequence relations: intuitionistic, classical, non-monotonic and so on. We will take an abstract version of the so called Scott's consequence relation ([Gab1, Se2, Va8]) which is a binary relation $\vdash$ between finite sets of sentences, satisfying some axioms, coming from classical logic. The formal definition is as follows:

By a consequence information system, C-system for short, we will mean any system of the form $S = (Sen, \vdash)$, where

- $Sen \neq \emptyset$ is a set, whose elements are called sentences,
- $\vdash$ is a binary relation in the set $P_{fin}(Sen)$ of all finite subsets of Sen, called Scott's consequence relation, satisfying the following axioms: for any $A, B, A', B' \in P_{fin}(Sen)$ and $x \in Sen$:
  - (Refl) If $A \cap B \neq \emptyset$ then $A \vdash B$,
  - (Mono) If $A \vdash B$, $A \subseteq A'$ and $B \subseteq B'$ then $A' \vdash B'$,
  - (Cut) If $A \vdash B \cup \{x\}$ and $\{x\} \cup A \vdash B$ then $A \vdash B$.

S is called non-trivial C-system if $\emptyset \nvdash \emptyset$, otherwise S is called trivial.

If S is a C-system then the components of S sometimes will be denoted by Sen_S and $\vdash_S$.

As usual, instead of $\{a_1, \dots, a_n\} \vdash \{b_1, \dots, b_m\}$ and $A \cup \{x_1, \dots, x_m\} \vdash B \cup \{y_1, \dots y_n\}$ we will write $a_1, \dots, a_n \vdash b_1, \dots, b_m$ and $A, x_1, \dots, x_m \vdash B, y_1, \dots y_n$. We assume that for $n = 0$ $\{x_1, \dots, x_n\} = \emptyset$.

For a set $A \in P_{fin}(Sen_S)$ and $x, y \in Sen_S$ we say that:

- x implies y in S iff $x \vdash_S y$,
- A is inconsistent (contradictory) in S iff $A \vdash \emptyset$,
- A is consistent in S iff $A \nvdash_S \emptyset$,
- A is complete (tautological) in S iff $\emptyset \vdash A$,
- A is incomplete in S iff $\emptyset \nvdash_S A$.

The axioms (Refl), (Mono) and (Cut) are known under the names of Reflexivity, Monotonicity and Cut.

The following lemma states some easy consequences of the axioms of a C-system.

Lemma 3. *Let S be a C-system. Then for any $x, y, z \in Sen_S$, and A, B, C, D, A', $B' \in P_{fin}(Sen_S)$ we have:*

- *(Ref)* $x \vdash_S x$,

- (Trans) If $x \vdash_S y$, $y \vdash_S z$ then $x \vdash_S z$
- (Cut0) If $A \vdash_S B, x$ and $x, A' \vdash_S B'$ then $A, A' \vdash_S B, B'$,
- (Cut1) If $A \vdash_S B$ and $A, x \vdash_S C$ for any $x \in B$ then $A \vdash_S C$.
- (Cut2) If $A \vdash_S B$ and $A, x \vdash_S C$ for any $x \in B$ then $A \vdash_S C$.
- (Cut3) If $A \vdash_S B$ and for any $x \in A$ and $y \in B$ we have $C \vdash_S x, D$ and $C, y \vdash_S D$ then $C \vdash_S D$.

Proof. As an example we shall prove (Cut1). Suppose $A \vdash_S B$ and $A, x \vdash_S C$ for every $x \in B$. Let $B = \{b_1, \ldots, b_n\}$. Then we have $A \vdash_S b_1, \ldots, b_n$. We shall prove by backward induction that for any $0 \leq i \leq n$, $A \vdash_S b_1, \ldots, b_i, C$. Then taking $i = 0$ we get $A \vdash_S C$.

Basic step: $i = n$. From $A \vdash_S b_1, \ldots, b_n$ by (Mono) we obtain $A \vdash_S b_1, \ldots, b_n$, C.

Induction hypothesis: Suppose that the assertion is true for $i = k, 1 \leq k \leq n$. We shall show that the assertion is true for $i = k - 1$.

By assumption we have $A, b_k \vdash_S C$. Then by (Mono) we have $A, b_1, \ldots, b_{k-1}$, $b_k \vdash_S C$. By the induction hypothesis we have $A \vdash_S b_1, \ldots, b_{k-1}, b_k, C$. Then by (Cut) we obtain $A \vdash_S b_1, \ldots, b_{k-1}, C$. □

A typical example of a C-system is a logical theory L, based on the classical logic. In such an example the elements of Sen are real sentences and the relation $a_1, \ldots, a_n \vdash b_1, \ldots, b_m$ holds if the implication $(a_1 \wedge \ldots \wedge a_n) \Rightarrow (b_1 \vee \ldots \vee b_m)$ is true in L.

Another example, which is connected with the previous one, can be constructed as follows. Let $(D, \leq, \wedge, \vee)$ be a distributive lattice (for the relevant definitions see [RS2]) and for finite subsets $A = \{a_1, \ldots, a_m\}$, $B = \{b_1, \ldots, b_n\} \subseteq D$ define

$A \vdash B$ iff $a_1 \wedge \ldots \wedge a_m \leq b_1 \vee \ldots \vee b_n$.

Then $(D, \vdash)$ is a C-system.

The next example, which is connected with P-systems, will play a fundamental role in this paper.

Let S be a P-system. We shall construct a C-system $C(S)$, called the C-system over S, in the following way. Define $Sen_{C(S)} = Ob_S$ and for the finite subsets $A = \{a_1, \ldots, a_m\}$, $B = \{b_1, \ldots, b_n\} \subseteq Sen_{C(S)}$ put $A \vdash_{C(S)} B$ iff $f_S(a_1) \cap \ldots \cap f_S(a_m) \subseteq f_S(b_1) \cup \ldots \cup f_S(b_n)$.

We assume here that for $m = 0$ and $n = 0$ we have $A = \emptyset$, $B = \emptyset$, $f(a_1) \cap \ldots \cap f(a_m) = Pr_S$ and $f(b_1) \cup \ldots \cup f(b_n) = \emptyset$.

Lemma 4. *Let S be a P-system. Then:*

(i) The system $C(S)$ is a C-system.

(ii) Let $S = P(W, V)$ be set-theoretical P-system over the pair (W, V) and $A, B \subseteq P_{fin}(W)$. Then

$A \vdash_{C(S)} B$ iff $(\forall C \in V)(A \subseteq C \rightarrow B \cap C \neq \emptyset)$.

Let $|S|$ be the set-theoretical P-system associated with S. Then:

(iii) for any $A, B \subseteq P_{fin}(Ob_S)$ we have $A \vdash_S B$ iff $A \vdash_{|S|} B$,

(iv) $C(|S|) = C(S)$.

Proof. A long but easy routine check, which is left to the reader. □

The above example shows that the objects of a P-system, which may be of an arbitrary nature, may be considered as sentences of certain C-system. In an abstract sense this means that P-systems may be considered as a semantic base for C-systems. The next theorem shows that each C-system can be represented as a C-system over some P-system.

Theorem 5. (Characterization theorem for C-systems) *Let S be a C-system. Then there is a P-system $P(S)$ such that $S = C(P(S))$.*

Proof. The system $P(S)$, we are going to construct, will be of set-theoretical type over some pair (W, V). Since we want to have $S = C(P(S))$ then W should be equal to Sen_S. So it remains to show how to define the set V as a subset of $P(W)$. We shall do this by defining a suitable property of the elements of the set $P(W)$, which will be taken as characteristic property for the elements of V. Suppose for a moment that V is defined. Then by lemma 4(ii) we will have the following: for any $A, B \in P_{fin}(W)$:

$$A \vdash_S B \text{ iff } (\forall x \in V)(A \subseteq x \rightarrow B \cap x \neq \emptyset) \ .$$

Suppose now that x is an arbitrary element of V. Then we have: for any $A, B \in P_{fin}(W)$:

$$\text{If } A \vdash_S B \text{ and } A \subseteq x \text{ then } B \cap x \neq \emptyset \ . \quad (1)$$

We take (1) to be the needed characteristic property for the elements of V. This leads to the following formal definition.

Let S be a C-system. A subset $x \subseteq Sen_S$ is called a prime filter in S, if for any two finite subsets A, B of Sen_S the condition (1) is true. The set of all prime filters of S will be denoted by $PrFil(S)$.

The name "prime filter" comes from the example with distributive lattices, namely, all prime filters in distributive lattices are prime filters according to the definition given above.

Now we define $P(S)$ as follows. Put $W = Sen_S$, $V = PrFil(S)$ and let $P(S)$ be the set-theoretical P-system $P(W, V)$ over the pair (W, V).

We need the following lemma, which is a generalization of the separation lemma for distributive lattices (see [RS2]).

Lemma 6. (Separation Lemma for C-systems) *Let S be a C-system, $A, B \in P_{fin}(Sen_S)$ and $A \not\vdash_S B$. Then there exists a prime filter x in S such that $A \subseteq x$ and $x \cap B = \emptyset$.*

Proof. The proof is by an application of the Zorn's Lemma. Let M be the following set:

$$M = \{y \subseteq Sen_S | A \subseteq y \text{ and for any finite } C \subseteq y: \ C \not\vdash_S B\} \ .$$

We consider M as a partially-ordered set by the set-inclusion $\subseteq$. In order to apply the Zorn's Lemma we have to show the following:

(i) M is not empty,
(ii) Every non-empty chain N in M has an upper bound in M.

To prove (i) we shall show that $A \in M$. We have $A \subseteq A$. Let $C \subseteq A$. Then from $A \nvdash_S B$ and (Mono) we obtain contrapositively that $C \nvdash_S B$.

To prove (ii) suppose that N is a non-empty chain in M. This means that for any two members $u, v \in N$: either $u \subseteq v$ or $v \subseteq u$. This property of the chain can be generalized as follows: for any finite number $u_1, u_2 \ldots u_n$, $n \leq 1$, of elements of N there exists a permutation $i_1 i_2 \ldots i_n$ of the indices $1, 2, \ldots, n$ such that $u_{i_1} \subseteq u_{i_2} \subseteq \ldots \subseteq u_{i_n}$. Let $y = \bigcup\{u | u \in N\}$, y is an upper bound of N. We shall show that $y \in M$. Obviously $A \subseteq y$. Let $C = \{c_1, c_2 \ldots, c_n\}$ be a finite subset of y. We shall show that $C \nvdash_S B$.

Case 1: $C = \emptyset$. Then $C \subseteq A$ and by (Mono) and $A \nvdash_S B$ we get $C \nvdash_S B$.

Case 2: $C \neq \emptyset$. Then $n \neq 0$ and there exists $u_1, u_2, \ldots, u_n \in N$ such that $c_1 \in u_1$, $c_2 \in u_2, \ldots, c_n \in u_n$. Now we can find a permutation $i_1, i_2, \ldots, i_n$ such that $u_{i_1} \subseteq u_{i_2} \subseteq \ldots \subseteq u_{i_n} = v$. Obviously $C \subseteq v \in M$, which implies $C \nvdash_S B$. This shows that $y \in M$, which proves the assertion (ii).

Now we can apply the Zorn's Lemma which states that if in a non-empty partially ordered set M, every non-empty chain in M has an upper bound in M, then M has a maximal element, say x. We shall show that x is a prime filter in S.

Suppose, in order to get a contradiction, that x is not a prime filter in S. Then there exist finite sets P and $Q = \{q_1, \ldots, q_n\}$ such that $P \vdash_S Q$, $P \subseteq x$ and $x \cap Q = \emptyset$.

Case 1: $Q = \emptyset$. Then $Q \subseteq B$ and from $P \vdash_S Q$ we get $P \vdash_S B$. From $P \subseteq x$ and $x \in M$ we get $P \nvdash_S B$ – a contradiction.

Case 2: $Q \neq \emptyset$. Then $n \geq 1$ and for any $i = 1, \ldots, n$ $q_i \notin x$. Let $x_i = x \cup \{q_i\}$. Then by the maximality of x we have that for any $i = 1, \ldots, n$ $x_i \notin M$ and hence there exist finite sets $C_i \subseteq x_i$ such that $C_i \vdash_S B$, $i = 1, \ldots, n$.

Case 2.1: $q_i \notin C_i$ for some i. Then we have $C_i \subseteq x$ and thus $C \nvdash_S B$ – a contradiction.

Case 2.2: for any $i = 1, \ldots, n$ $q_i \in C_i$. Let $C_i \cap x = D_i$. Then $C_i = D_i \cup \{q_i\}$ and $D_i \subseteq x$. From $C \vdash_S B$ we get $D_i, q_i \vdash_S B$ for $i = 1, \ldots, n$. Let $D = P \cup D_i \cup \ldots \cup D_n$. From $P \subseteq x$ and $D_i \subseteq x$ we get $D \subseteq x$ and since $x \in M$ we obtain $D \nvdash_S B$. From $P \vdash_S Q$, $D_i, q_i \vdash_S B$, $P \subseteq D$ and $D_i \subseteq D$ we obtain by (Mono) $D \vdash_S Q$, $D, q_i \vdash_S B$ for any $q_i \in Q$. Then applying (Cut1) from lemma 3.1 we obtain $D \vdash_S B$ – a contradiction.

So we have proved that x is a prime filter in S. Since $x \in M$ we have $A \subseteq x$. It remains to show that $x \cap B = \emptyset$. Suppose that $x \cap B \neq \emptyset$. Then for some $a \in Sens$ $a \in x$ and $a \in B$ and hence $\{a\} \subseteq x$. Consequently $\{a\} \nvdash_S B$, which implies $\{a\} \cap B = \emptyset$. From here we get $a \notin B$ – a contradiction.

This completes the proof of the lemma. □

Corollary 7. *Let S be a C-system. then for every $A, B \in P_{fin}(Sens_S)$ we have: $A \vdash_S B$ iff $(\forall x \in PrFil(S))(A \subseteq x \rightarrow B \cap x \neq \emptyset)$.*

Proof. The impilication (→) follows from the definition of a prime filter and the implication (←) follows from the separation lemma. □

Now the proof of the theorem 5 follows directly from corollary 7 and lemma 4(ii). □

The P-system $P(S)$, constructed in the proof of theorem 5 will be called the canonical P-system over S.

Theorem 5 may be considered as an abstract form of "completeness theorem" for C-systems with respect to their "semantics" in the class of P-systems.

Theorem 5 shows a very close connection between C-systems and P-systems. We have two constructions – P and C. P maps a C-system S into a P-system $P(S)$, and C maps a P-system S into a C-system $C(S)$. Theorem 5 shows that starting from a C-system S and applying alternatively P and C we get a cycle $S \rightarrow P(S) \rightarrow C(P(S)) = S$. If we start from a P-system S, then the situation is not the same. Namely we have the following

Theorem 8. *Let S be a P-system and consider the P-system $P(C(S))$. Then $Ob_S = Ob_{P(C(S))}$ and there exists a strong homomorphism h from S into $P(C(S))$, which is the identity in Ob_S.*

Proof. The equality $Ob_S = Ob_{P(C(S))}$ is true by definition. Let h be the natural strong homomorphism from S onto $|S|$ (lemma 1(ii)). In Ob_S h is the identity by definition. We shall show that h is a strong homomorphism from S into $P(C(S))$.

By lemma 4(iv) $C(S) = C(|S|)$, so $P(C(S)) = P(C(|S|))$. We shall show that the identity is a strong homomorphism from $|S|$ into (not onto) $P(C(|S|))$, which will prove the theorem. This will follow from the following

Lemma 9. *Let $S = P(W, V)$ be a set-theoretical P-system over the pair (W, V) and let $C(S)$ be the C-system over S. Then:*

(i) All elements of V are prime filters in $C(S)$.
(ii) $Pr_S \subseteq Pr_{P(C(S))}$.
(iii) The identity function is a strong homomorphism from S into $P(C(S))$.

Proof. (i) follows directly from the definition of a prime filter and lemma 4(ii), (ii) is the same as (i) and (iii) follows from (ii) and the equality $Ob_S = Ob_{P(C(S))}$.

□

□

2.4 Bi-consequence Systems

We have seen that C-systems are adequate logical counterparts of P-systems. Now we will define a new kind of information systems, which may be considered as a logical counterpart of A-systems. There are several possibilities to do this. Since A-systems may be considered as P-systems with a family of property sets, then, following this analogy we may consider C-systems with a family of Scott's consequence relations. However, for the purposes of this paper we will prefer a simpler notion, admitting two consequence relations, called respectively strong and weak. That is why we will call such systems bi-consequence information systems. First we shall give the formal definition and then we will discuss the intuition connected with this kind of information system.

By a bi-consequence information system, B-system for short, we will mean a system S of the following form $S = (Sen, \vdash, \succ)$, where:

- $(Sen, \vdash)$ is a C-system and $\vdash$ is called here strong consequence relation
- $\succ$ is a binary relation in the set $P_{fin}(Sen)$, called weak consequence relation and satisfying the following axioms for any $A, B, A'B' \in P_{fin}(Sen)$:

(Refl $\succ$) If $A \cap B \neq \emptyset$ then $A \succ B$,
(Mono $\succ$) If $A \succ B$, $A \subseteq A'$ and $B \subseteq B'$ then $A' \succ B'$,
(Cut $\succ$ 1) If $A \vdash x, B$ and $A, x \succ B$ then $A \succ B$,
(Cut $\succ$ 2) If $A, x \vdash B$ and $A \succ x, B$ then $A \succ B$,
(Incl) If $A \vdash B$ then $A \succ B$.

Let us note that axiom (Incl) is equivalent (in the presence of the remaining axioms) to the following more simple axiom

(Incl $\succ$) If $\emptyset \vdash \emptyset$ then $\emptyset \succ \emptyset$.

The following example of a B-system will give the main intuition of this notion. Let $S_i = (Sen, \vdash_i)$ $i \in I$ be a non-empty class of C-systems with one and the same set of sentences Sen. Define the relations $\vdash$ and $\succ$ in $P_{fin}(Sen)$ as follows:

$$A \vdash B \text{ iff } \forall i \in I \; A \vdash_i B, \; A \succ B \text{ iff } \exists i \in I \; A \succ_i B \; .$$

Then it is easy to see that the system $(Sen, \vdash, \succ)$ is a B-system. It is now clear why $\vdash$ and $\succ$ are called strong and weak consequence relations, respectively.

Lemma 10. *Let S be a B-system. Then the following Cut condition is true in S for any $X, Y, A, B \in P_{fin}(Sen_S)$*

(Cut $\succ$) If $X \succ_S Y$ and for any $x \in X$ and $y \in Y$ we have $A \vdash_S x, B$ and $A, y \vdash_S B$ then $A \succ B$.

Proof. Let $X = \{x_1, \ldots, x_m\}$ and $Y = \{y_1, \ldots, y_n\}$. Then we prove by induction that for any i and j, $0 \leq i \leq m$, $0 \leq j \leq m$ the following is true: $x_1, \ldots, x_i, A \succ_S y, \ldots, y_j, B$. Then the assertion is obtained from $i = j = 0$. □

The next example of a B-system is connected with A-systems and will be of a great importance.

Let S be an A-system. We shall construct a system $B(S)$, called the B-system over S, in the following way. Put $Sen_{B(S)} = Ob_S$ and for any finite sets $A = \{x_1, \ldots, x_m\}$ and $B = \{y_1, \ldots, y_n\}$ of Ob_S define

$$A \vdash_{B(S)} B \text{ iff}$$
$$(\forall a \in At_S) f_S(x_1, a) \cap \ldots \cap f_S(x_m, a) \subseteq f_S(y_1, a) \cup \ldots \cup f_S(y_n, a),$$
$$A \succ_{B(S)} B \text{ iff}$$
$$(\exists a \in At_S) f_S(x_1, a) \cap \ldots \cap f_S(x_m, a) \subseteq f_S(y_1, a) \cup \ldots \cup f_S(y_n, a).$$

Lemma 11. *(i) Let S be an A-system. Then the system $B(S)$ defined as above is a B-system.*

(ii) Let $S = A(W,V)$ be set-theoretical A-system over the pair (W,V) and $A, B \subseteq P_{fin}(W)$. Then:

$A \vdash_{B(S)} B$ *iff* $(\forall a \in V)(\forall C \in a)(A \subseteq C \rightarrow B \cap C \neq \emptyset)$.

$A \succ_{B(S)} B$ *iff* $(\exists a \in V)(\forall C \in a)(A \subseteq C \rightarrow B \cap C \neq \emptyset)$.

Let $|S|$ be the set-theoretical P-system associated with S. Then:

(iii) for any $A, B \subseteq P_{fin}(Obs_S)$ we have

$A \vdash_S B$ *iff* $A \vdash_{|S|} B$, $A \succ_S B$ *iff* $A \succ_{|S|} B$,

(iv) $B(|S|) = B(S)$.

Proof. Straightforward, using the relevant definitions. □

Lemma 11 shows that in some abstract sense A-systems constitute a correct "semantics" for the B-systems. The next theorem shows that each B-system can be represented as a B-system over some A-system.

Theorem 12. (Characterization theorem for B-systems) *Let S be a B-system. Then there exists an A-system $S' = A(S)$ such that $S = B(A(S))$.*

Proof. The system S', which we are going to define will be a set theoretical A-system $A(W,V)$ over a pair (W,V). Since we want that $S = B(A(W,V))$, then we have to put $W = Sen_S$. It remains to show how to define the set V (recall that $V \subseteq P(P(W))$). We will do this by finding a characteristic property of the elements of V, which will separate it from the set $P(P(W))$. Suppose for the moment that the set V is defined. Then by the equality $S = B(A(W,V))$ and lemma 11(ii) we will have

$A \vdash_S B$ iff $(\forall a \in V)(\forall C \in a)(A \subseteq C \rightarrow B \cap C \neq \emptyset)$,

$A \succ_S B$ iff $(\exists a \in V)(\forall C \in a)(A \subseteq C \rightarrow B \cap C \neq \emptyset)$.

If a is an arbitrary element of V, then it will satisfy the following two conditions for any two sets $A, B \in P_{fin}(W)$:

$$A \vdash_S B \rightarrow (\forall C \in a)(A \subseteq C \rightarrow B \cap C \neq \emptyset) \ , \tag{2}$$

$$A \succ_S B \rightarrow (\exists C \in a)(A \subseteq C \text{ and } B \cap C = \emptyset) \ . \tag{3}$$

The required characteristic property for a will be to satisfy (2) and (3).

So we define: a set of subsets of Sen_S is called a good set in S if it satisfies (2) and (3). Note that condition (2) says that the elements of a good set are prime filters in $(Sen_S, \vdash_S)$.

Now we can start the proof of the theorem.

Put $W = Sen_S$ and let V be the set of all good sets in S. Since we have $V \subseteq P(P(W))$, put S' to be the set-theoretical A-system $A(W,V)$ over the pair (W,V), and denote S' by $A(S)$. $A(S)$ will be called the canonical A-system over S.

To prove the theorem we need some lemmas.

Lemma 13. *Let $A, B, X, Y \in P_{fin}(Sen_S)$. Then:*

(i) If $X \not\vdash_S Y$, then there exists $C \in PrFil(S)$, denoted by $C(X \not\vdash_S Y)$, such that $X \subseteq C$ and $Y \cap C = \emptyset$.
(ii) If $A \not\succ_S B$, then there exists $C \in PrFil(S)$, denoted by $C(A \not\succ_S B)$, such that $A \subseteq C$ and $B \cap C = \emptyset$.
(iii) If $X \succ_S Y$ and $A \not\succ_S B$, then there exists $C \in PrFil(S)$ denoted by $C(X \succ_S Y, A \not\succ_S B)$ such that:
1) either $X \not\subseteq C$ or $Y \cap C \neq \emptyset$,
2) $A \subseteq C$ and $B \cap C = \emptyset$.

Proof. (i) is exactly the Separation lemma for C-systems (lemma 6).
(ii) Let $A \not\succ_S B$. Then by (Incl) $A \not\vdash_S B$ and by (i) there exists a $C \in PrFil(S)$ such that $A \subseteq C$ and $B \cap C$. Put $C(A \not\succ_S B) = C$.
(iii) Suppose $X \succ_S Y$ and $A \not\succ_S B$. Then by lemma 10 either $\exists x \in X$ such that $A \not\vdash_S x, B$ or $\exists y \in Y$ such that $A, y \not\vdash_S B$.
Case 1: $\exists x \in X$ $A \not\vdash_S x, B$. Then by (i) there exists $C_1 \in PrFil(S)$ such that $A \subseteq X$ and $(\{x\} \cup B) \cap C_1 = \emptyset$, hence $x \notin C$, $B \cap C_1 = \emptyset$ and $X \not\subseteq C_1$. This yields the conditions 1) and 2) of the assertion. In this case put $C(X \succ_S Y, A \not\succ_S B) = C_1$.
Case 2: $\exists y \in Y$ $A, y \not\vdash_S B$. Then by (i) there exists $C_2 \in PrFil(S)$ such that $A \cup \{y\} \subseteq C_2$ and $B \cap C_2 = \emptyset$. Then $A \subseteq C_2$, $y \in C_2$ and consequently $Y \cap C_2 \neq \emptyset$. This yields the conditions 1) and 2) of the assertion. In this case put $C(X \succ_S Y, A \not\succ_S B) = C_2$.

□

Lemma 14. *For any $X, Y \in P_{fin}(W)$ the following holds:*

(i) $X \vdash_S Y$ iff $(\forall a \in V)(\forall C \in a)(X \subseteq C \rightarrow Y \cap C \neq \emptyset)$,
(ii) $X \succ_S Y$ iff $(\exists a \in V)(\forall C \in a)(X \subseteq C \rightarrow Y \cap C \neq \emptyset)$.

Proof. (i) ($\rightarrow$) Suppose $X \vdash_S Y$, $a \in V$. Then a satisfies (2) and consequently $(\forall C \in a)(\forall C \in a)(X \subseteq C \rightarrow Y \cap C \neq \emptyset)$.

($\leftarrow$) Suppose $X \not\vdash_S Y$. We shall define a good set $a \in V$ such that $(\exists C \in a)(X \subseteq C$ and $Y \cap C = \emptyset)$. Put $a = \{C(X \not\vdash_S Y)\} \cup \{C(A \not\succ_S B) | A, B \in P_{fin}(W)$ and $A \not\succ_S B\}$ and let $C = C(X \not\vdash_S Y)$. We have $C \in a$ and by lemma 13(i) that $X \subseteq C$ and $Y \cap C = \emptyset$. It remains to show that a is a good set. By lemma 13 all elements of a are prime filters of S so (2) is fulfilled. To prove (3) suppose $A \not\succ_S B$. Then by the construction of a $C = C(A \not\succ_S B) \in a$ and by lemma 13(ii) $A \subseteq C$ and $B \cap C \neq \emptyset$. So (3) is fulfilled and hence $a \in V$.

(ii) ($\rightarrow$) Suppose $X \succ_S Y$. We shall construct $a \in V$ such that $(\forall C \in a)(X \subseteq C \rightarrow Y \cap C \neq \emptyset)$. Put $a = \{C(X \succ_S Y, A \not\succ_S B) | A, B \in P(W)$ and $A \not\succ_S B\}$. Lemma 13(iii) guarantees that $a \in V$ and that it satisfies the assertion. This completes the proof of the lemma. □

Now the proof of theorem 12 follows immediately from lemma 14 and lemma 11 □

In some abstract sense theorem 12 may be considered as "completeness" theorem for B-systems with respect to their "semantics" in the class of A-systems.

Theorem 12 has also the following meaning. We have defined two operations – A and B, such that for any B-system S $A(S)$ is an A-system, and that for any A-system S $B(S)$ is a B-system. Then theorem 12 says that, starting from a given B-system S we may produce first $A(S)$, second $B(A(S)) = S$, coming again to the system S. The picture is not the same if we start with some A-system S and then produce $B(S)$ and $A(B(S))$. The connection between S and $A(B(S))$ is studied in the next theorem.

Theorem 15. *Let S be an A-system and consider the A-system $A(B(S))$. Then $Ob_S = Ob_{A(B(S))}$ and there exists a strong homomorphism h from S into $A(B(S))$, which is the identity function in Ob_S.*

Proof. The equality $Ob_S = Ob_{A(B(S))}$ is true by definition. Let h be the natural strong homomorphism from S onto $|S|$ (lemma 2). In Ob_S h is the identity by definition. We shall show that h is a strong homomorphism from S into $A(B(S))$.

By lemma 11(iv) $C(S) = C(|S|)$, so $A(B(S)) = A(B(|S|))$. We shall show that the identity is a strong homomorphism from $|S|$ into (not onto) $A(B(|S|))$, which will prove the theorem. This will follow from the following

Lemma 16. *Let $S = A(W, V)$ be a set-theoretical A-system over the pair (W, V) and let $B(S)$ be the B-system over S. Then:*

(i) Let a be any element of V. Then all elements of a are prime filters in $B(S)$.
(ii) All elements of V are good sets in S.
(iii) $At_S \subseteq At_{A(B(S))}$.
(iv) The identity function is a strong homomorphism from S into $A(B(S))$.

□

The proof is similar to the proof of lemma 9.

3 Similarity Relations in Information Systems

The main aim of this section is to give a formal analysis of sentences of the form "x is similar to y". Information systems provided a good basis for giving a precise meaning to various kinds of similarities. In P-systems we formalize the so called positive and negative similarities. Roughly speaking x and y are positively similar if they both possess a common property; x and y are negatively similar if there is a property, which is possessed neither by x nor by y. In A-systems, following Orlowska and Pawlak [OP1], [OP2] and Orlowska [Or1], [Or2], [Or3], we can give a more detailed classification introducing weak and strong versions of similarity relations.

The structure of the section is the following.

In section 3.1, following the paper [Va6] we introduce positive similarity, negative similarity and informational inclusion as binary relations between objects in P-systems and their counterparts in C-systems. The main result here is an abstract characterization of these relations by means of a finite set of first-order sentences (theorem 23). This characterization is obtained as a consequence of the duality between P-systems and C-systems, studied in section 2.

Similarity relations in P-systems are special cases of the notion of informational relations in P-systems. Informational relations in P-systems are studied in section 3.2. A first-order characterization of all informational relations, as well as a characterization of the two-place informational relations is given.

Section 3.3 is devoted to similarity relations in A-systems and their counterparts in B-systems. The main result is an abstract characterization by means of a finite set of first-order sentences (theorem 32).

In section 3.4 similarity relations in single-valued A-systems are studied. Several characterization theorems for some collections of similarity relations is given.

Section 3.5 is a short introduction to the more general notion of informational relations in A-systems.

3.1 Similarity Relations in Property Systems and their Counterparts in Consequence Systems

Very often, when we say that two objects are similar, we mean that they have a common property. For instance, the son is similar to his father if they both have blue eyes. This is a kind of a positive similarity. In this sense we say that two objects x and y are similar if there exists a property A from a given set of properties Pr, such that A is possessed both by x and y. We can say also that the son is similar to his father, because they both are not smokers. This is a kind of a negative similarity. We say that two objects x and y are negatively similar if there exists a property A from a given set of properties Pr, such that A is possessed neither by x nor by y. One can say that there is no difference between these two kinds of similarity, interpreting negative similarity "positively" as follows. The argument is that for each property A we can introduce a new property non A, the complement $\overline{A}$ of A, with the following meaning: x possesses $\overline{A}$ iff x does not possess A. For instance if A is "to be a smoker" then $\overline{A}$ is "to be a non-smoker". The difference appears when we are working with limited sets of properties, which are not closed under taking a complement.

Positive and negative similarity relations between objects can be easily formalized in P-systems. The formal definitions are the following:

Let S be a P-system. Positive similarity in S is a binary relation in Ob_S denoted by Σ_S and defined as follows: for any $x, y \in Ob_S$

$x\Sigma_S y$ iff $(\exists A \in Pr_S)(A \in f_S(x)$ and $A \in_S f(y))$ iff $f_S(x) \cap f_S(y) \neq \emptyset$.

Negative similarity in S is a binary relation in Ob_S denoted by N_S and defined as follows: for any $x, y \in Ob_S$

$xN_S y$ iff $(\exists A \in Pr_S)(A \notin f_S(x)$ and $A \notin f_S(y))$ iff $\overline{f}_S(x) \cap \overline{f}_S(y) \neq \emptyset$

The formal theory of these two relations can be better described if we add one more binary relation between objects in P-systems, called informational inclusion.

Let S be a P-system. Informational inclusion in S, or simply inclusion, is a binary relation in Obs denoted by $\leq_S$ and defined as follows: for any two objects $x, y \in Ob_S$:

$x \leq_S y$ iff $f_S(x) \subseteq f_S(y)$ iff $\overline{f}_S(x) \cap \overline{f}_S(y) = \emptyset$.

If for two objects x and y we have $x \leq_S y$ we say that x is (informationally) included in y, or, that y possesses all properties from Pr_S, which are possessed by x. Obviously $\leq_S$ is a quasi ordering relation in Ob_S, i.e. a reflexive and transitive relation in Ob_S.

By means of informational inclusion we can define another important relation between objects, called indiscernibility relation and denoted by $\equiv$:

$x \equiv y$ iff $x \leq y$ & $y \leq x$ iff $f(x) = f(y)$.

Lemma 17. *(i) Let S be a P-system. Then:*

- *S is a total P-system iff $(\forall x \in Ob_S) x \Sigma_S x$,*
- *S is a nontrivial P-system iff $(\forall x \in Ob_S) x \Sigma_S x$ or $x N_S x$.*

(ii) Let $W \neq \emptyset$, $V \subseteq P(W)$ and let $S = P(W, V)$ be the set-theoretical P-system over the pair (W, V). Then for any $x, y \in W$ we have:

- *$x \Sigma_S y$ iff $(\exists A \in V)(x \in A$ and $y \in A)$,*
- *$x N_S y$ iff $(\exists A \in V)(x \notin A$ and $y \notin A)$,*
- *$x \leq_S y$ iff $(\forall A \in V)(x \in A \rightarrow y \in A)$.*

(iii) Let S and S' be P-systems and let h be a strong homomorphism from S into S'. Then for any $x, y \in Ob_S$:

- *$x \Sigma_S y$ iff $h(x) \Sigma_{S'} h(y)$,*
- *$x N_S y$ iff $h(x) N_{S'} h(y)$,*
- *$x \leq_S y$ iff $h(x) \leq_{S'} h(y)$.*

(iv) Let S be a P-system and let $|S|$ be the set-theoretical P-system associated with S. Then for any $x, y \in S$ we have:

- *$x \Sigma_S y$ iff $x \Sigma_{|S|} y$,*
- *$x N_S y$ iff $x N_{|S|} y$,*
- *$x \leq_S y$ iff $x \leq_{|S|} y$.*

Proof. Straightforward. □

By lemma 17(i) we see that the relation Σ is not in general reflexive. This means that it is possible to have $x \overline{\Sigma} x$ for some object x. In a sense this is contrary to our intuition, because in this case x is not similar to itself. By the definition of Σ this yields $f(x) = \emptyset$. This says that x does not have any property from Pr.

Lemma 18. *Let S be a P-system and let $S' = C(S)$ be the C-system over S. Then the following conditions are true for any $x, y \in Ob_S$:*

(i) $x \leq_S y$ iff $x \vdash_{S'} y$,
(ii) $x \Sigma_S y$ iff $x, y \not\vdash_{S'} \emptyset$,
(iii) $x N_S y$ iff $\emptyset \not\vdash_{S'} x, y$.

Proof. Let $x, y \in Ob_S$. Then by the definition of a $C(S)$ we have:

(i) $x \vdash_{S'} y$ iff $f_S(x) \subseteq f_S(y)$ iff $x \leq_S y$,

(ii) $x, y \not\vdash_{S'} \emptyset$ iff $f_S(x) \cap f_S(y) \neq \emptyset$ iff $x \Sigma_S y$,
(iii) $\emptyset \not\vdash_{S'} x, y$ iff $Pr_S = f_S(x) \cup f_S(y)$ iff $x N_S y$.

□

Lemma 19. *Let S' be a C-system and let $S = P(S')$ be the canonical P-system over S Then for any $x, y \in Sen_S$ we have:*

(i) $x \leq_S y$ iff $x \not\vdash_{S'} y$,
(ii) $x \Sigma_S y$ iff $x, y \not\vdash_{S'} \emptyset$,
(iii) $x N_S y$ iff $\emptyset \not\vdash_{S'} x, y$.

Proof. By the definition of $P(S')$ $Ob_S = W = Sen_{S''}$, $Pr_S = V = PrFil(S')$, and for $x \in Ob_S$, $f_S(x) = \{A \in V | x \in A\}$. Let $x, y \in Sen_S$. Then:

(i) $x \vdash_{S'} y$ iff (Corollary 7) $(\forall A \in V)(\{x\} \subseteq A \to \{y\} \cap A \neq \emptyset)$ iff $(\forall A \in V)(x \in A \to y \in A)$ iff (lemma 17) $x \leq_S y$.
(ii) $x, y \not\vdash_{S'} \emptyset$ iff (Corollary 7) $(\exists A \in V)(\{x, y\} \subseteq A$ and $\emptyset \cap A = \emptyset)$ iff $(\exists A \in V)(x \in A$ and $y \in A)$ iff (lemma 17) $x \Sigma_S y$.
(iii) $\emptyset \not\vdash_{S'} x, y$ iff (Corollary 7) $(\exists A \in V)(\emptyset \subseteq A$ and $\{x, y\} \cap A = \emptyset)$ iff $(\exists A \in V)(x \notin A$ and $y \notin A)$ iff (lemma 17) $x N_S y$.

□

Lemma 18 and lemma 19 assign the following unexpected new logical meaning to the introduced three relations:

- $x \leq_S y$ iff $x \vdash_{S'} y$ iff "x implies y in S'",
- $x \Sigma_S y$ iff $x, y \not\vdash_{S'} \emptyset$, iff "the set $\{x, y\}$ is consistent in S'",
- $x N_S y$ iff $\emptyset \not\vdash_{S'} x, y$, iff "the set $\{x, y\}$ is incomplete in S'".

This suggests the following definition. Let S be a C-system. Then we define the relations $\leq$, Σ and N in S as follows:

- $x \leq_S y$ iff $x \vdash_S y$,
- $x \Sigma_S y$ iff $x, y \not\vdash_S \emptyset$,
- $x N_S y$ iff $\emptyset \not\vdash_S y$.

In the next lemma we list some abstract properties of the relations $\leq$, Σ and N.

Lemma 20. *Let S be a P-system (C-system). Then the following conditions are true for any $x, y, z \in Ob_S$ ($x, y, z \in Sen_S$) (the subscript S is omitted):*

S1 $x \leq x$,	$x \vdash x$,	*(Ref)*
S2 $x \leq y$ & $y \leq z \to x \leq z$,	$x \vdash y$ & $y \vdash z \to x \vdash z$,	*(Cut)*
S3 $x \Sigma_S y \to y \Sigma_S x$,	$y, x \vdash \emptyset \to x, y \vdash \emptyset$,	*(Permutation)*
S4 $x \Sigma_S y \to x \Sigma_S x$,	$x \vdash \emptyset \to x, y \vdash \emptyset$,	*(Mono)*
S5 $x \Sigma_S y$ & $y \leq z \to x \Sigma_S z$,	$x, z \vdash \emptyset$ & $y \vdash z$ *then* $x, y \vdash \emptyset$,	*(Cut)*
S6 $x \Sigma_S x$ *or* $x \leq y$,	$x \vdash \emptyset \to x \vdash y$,	*(Mono)*
S7 $x N y \to y N x$,	$\emptyset \vdash y, x \to \emptyset \vdash x, y$,	*(Permutation)*
S8 $x N y \to x N x$,	$\emptyset \vdash x \to \emptyset \vdash x, y$,	*(Mono)*
S9 $x \leq y$ & $y N z \to x N z$,	$x \vdash y$ & $\emptyset \vdash x, z \to \emptyset \vdash y, z$,	*(Cut)*
S10 $y N y$ *or* $x \leq y$,	$\emptyset \vdash y \to x \vdash y$,	*(Mono)*
S11 $x \Sigma_S z$ *or* $x N z$ *or* $x \leq y$,	$x, z \vdash \emptyset$ & $\emptyset \vdash z, x \to x \vdash y$,	*(Cut)*

Note. On the right hand side of the above list, the conditions S1-S11 for the C-system are written in order to indicate that they are special cases of the conditions (Ref), (Mono) and (Cut).

Proof. Straightforward verification. □

In order to give an abstract characterization of the relations $\leq$, Σ and N we introduce the following notion.

Let $\underline{W} = (W, \leq, \Sigma, N)$ be a relational system such that $W \neq \emptyset$ and $\leq, \Sigma$ and N are binary relations in W. We say that $\underline{W}$ is a similarity structure if it satisfies the conditions S1-S11 from lemma 20. If S is a P-system (C-system) then lemma 20 says that the system $Sim(S) = (Ob_S, \leq, \Sigma, N)$ (the system $Sim(S) = (Sen, \leq, \Sigma, N)$ is a similarity structure, called similarity structure over S).

In the following lemma some easy consequences of the axioms S1-S11 are stated.

Lemma 21. *Let $\underline{W} = (W, \leq, \Sigma, N)$ be a similarity structure. Then for any $x, y, u, v \in W$ the following is true:*

(Σ) If $u\Sigma v$ and $x, y \in \{u, v\}$ then $x\Sigma y$,
(N) If uNv and $x, y \in \{u, v\}$ then xNy,
S5' $x\Sigma y$ & $x \leq u$ & $y \leq v \rightarrow u\Sigma v$ - monotonicity of Σ,
S9' xNy & $u \leq x$ & $v \leq y \rightarrow uNv$ - antymonotonicity of N,
S11' ($x\overline{\Sigma}z$ or $z\overline{\Sigma}x$) & ($y\overline{N}z$ or $z\overline{N}y$) $\rightarrow x \leq y$,
($\Sigma N1$) $u\Sigma v$ & $u\overline{\Sigma}x$ & $v\overline{\Sigma}y \rightarrow xNy$,
($\Sigma N2$) uNv & $u\overline{N}x$ & $v\overline{N}y \rightarrow x\Sigma y$
(Triv) If $\exists a \in W$ $a\overline{\Sigma}a$ & $a\overline{N}a$ then $\forall x, y \in W$: $x \leq y$ & $x\overline{\Sigma}y$ & $x\overline{N}y$.

The following lemma is a simple consequence of lemma 18 and lemma 19.

Lemma 22. *(i) Let S be a P-system and $C(S)$ be the C-system over S. Then $Sim(S) = Sim(C(S))$.*
(ii) Let S be a C-system and $P(S)$ be the canonical P-system over S. Then $Sim(S) = Sim(P(S))$.

The main theorem of this section is the following.

Theorem 23. (Characterization theorem for similarity structures) *Let $\underline{W} = (W, \leq, \Sigma, N)$ be a similarity structure. Then:*

(i) There exists a C-system S such that $\underline{W} = Sim(S)$.
(ii) There exists a P-system S' such that $\underline{W} = Sim(S')$

Proof. (i) We define S as follows. Put $Sen_S = W$ and for $X, Y \in P_{fin}(W)$ define:
$X \vdash Y$ iff

(I) $\exists x \in X\ \exists y \in Y\ x \leq y$, or

(II) $\exists x, y \in X\ x\overline{\Sigma}y$, or
(III) $\exists x, y \in Y\ x\overline{N}y$, or
(IV) $\exists a \in W\ a\overline{\Sigma}a\ \&\ a\overline{N}a$.

Now we have to show that $\vdash$ satisfies the Scott's axioms (Ref), (Mono) and (Cut).

For (Ref) suppose that $X \cap Y \neq \emptyset$. Then $\exists x \in X, Y$. By S1 we have $x \leq x$ and by (I) we obtain $X \vdash Y$.

For (Mono) suppose $X \vdash Y$, $X \subseteq X'$ and $Y \subseteq Y'$. From $X \vdash Y$ we have that one of the cases (I)-(IV) holds. From the inclusions $X \subseteq X'$ and $Y \subseteq Y'$ the same case will be true for X' and Y', which implies $X' \vdash Y'$.

For (Cut) suppose

(1) $X, a \vdash Y$,
(2) $X \vdash a, Y$ and proceed to show
(3) $X \vdash Y$.

For (1) and (2) we have to consider several cases following the definition of $\vdash$. Then we shall combine each case for (1) with each case for (2).

(1I) $\exists x \in X \cup \{a\}\ \exists y \in Y x \leq y$. If $x \in X$ then by (I) we get (3), so we consider: $x = a:\ a \leq y:\ y \in Y$.
(1II) $\exists x, y \in X \cup \{a\}\ x\overline{\Sigma}y$. If $x, y \in X$ then by (II) we get (3). So we consider here three cases:
 (i) $x = a:\ a\overline{\Sigma}y,\ y \in X$,
 (ii) $y = a:\ x\overline{\Sigma}a,\ x \in X$.
 (iii) $x = y = a:\ a\overline{\Sigma}a$.
(1III) $\exists x, y \in Y\ x\overline{N}y$. Then directly by (III) we obtain (3). So this case will not be combined with any other case for (2).
(1IV) $\exists a\ a\overline{\Sigma}a\ \&\ a\overline{N}a$. By (IV) we get (3) so this case also will not be combined with any other case for (2).
(2I) $\exists u \in X\ \exists v \in \{a\} \cup Y\ u \leq v$. If $v \in Y$ then by (I) we get (3) so in this case we consider:
 $v = a:\ u \leq a$ and $u \in X$.
(2II) $\exists u, v \in X\ u\overline{\Sigma}v$. Then by (II) we obtain (3). This case will not be combined with any other case for (1).
(2III) $\exists u, v \in \{a\} \cup Y\ u\overline{N}v$. If $u, v \in V$ then we obtain (3) by (III), so we will consider here three cases:
 (j) $u = a:\ a\overline{N}v, v \in Y$,
 (jj) $v = a:\ u\overline{N}a, u \in Y$,
 (jjj) $u = v = a:\ a\overline{N}a$.
(2IV) $\exists a \in W\ a\overline{\Sigma}a\ \&\ a\overline{N}a$. Then by (IV) we get (3), so this case will not be combined with any other case of (1).

Now we start to combine the possible cases for (1) and (2).

Case (1I)(2I): $a \leq y$, $y \in Y$, $u \leq a$, $u \in X$. By S1 we get $u \leq v$ and by (I) we get (3).

Case (1I)(2III). Here we have three sub-cases:

(j) $a \leq y$, $y \in Y$, $a\overline{N}v$, $v \in Y$. By S9' we obtain $y\overline{N}y$ and by (III) we obtain (3).
(jj) $a \leq y$, $y \in Y$, $u\overline{N}a$, $u \in Y$ – similar to (j).
(jjj) $a \leq y$, $y \in Y$, $a\overline{N}a$. By S9 we obtain $y\overline{N}y$ and by (III) we obtain (3).

Case (1II)(2I) We have to consider three cases.

(i) $a\overline{\Sigma}y$, $y \in X$, $u \leq a$, $u \in X$. Then by S5' we get $u\overline{\Sigma}y$ and by (II) we obtain (3).
(ii) $x\overline{\Sigma}a$, $x \in X$, $u \leq a$, $u \in X$. Proceed as in (i).
(iii) $a\overline{\Sigma}a$, $u \leq a$, $u\overline{\Sigma}a$, $u \in X$. By S5' we obtain $u\overline{\Sigma}u$ and by (II) we obtain (3).

Case (1II)(2III). We have to combine the cases (i)-(iii) with the cases (j)-(jjj).

(i)(j) $a\overline{\Sigma}y$, $x \in X$, $a\overline{N}v$, $v \in Y$. Then by S11' we get $y \leq v$ and by (I) we obtain (3). The cases (i)(jj), (ii)(j) and (ii)(jj) can be treated similarly.
(iii)(jjj) $a\overline{\Sigma}a$, $a\overline{N}a$. By (IV) we obtain (3).

This completes the proof that the system $S = (W, \vdash)$ is a C-system. To complete the prove of the first part of the theorem we need the following

Assertion 24. *For any $u, v \in W$ the following is true:*

(a) $u \leq v$ iff $u \vdash v$,
(b) $u\Sigma v$ iff $u, v \not\vdash_S \emptyset$,
(c) uNv iff $\emptyset \not\vdash_S u, v$.

Proof. (a)($\rightarrow$) Suppose $u \leq v$. Then by (I) we have $u \vdash v$.
(a)($\leftarrow$) Suppose $u \vdash v$, i.e. $\{u\} \vdash \{v\}$. We have to show $u \leq v$. For that purpose we have to consider the possible cases of the definition of $\vdash$.
Case (I): $\exists x \in \{u\}\ \exists y \in \{v\}\ x \leq y$. Then $x = u$, $y = v$ and hence $u \leq v$.
Case (II): $\exists x, y \in \{u\}\ x\overline{\Sigma}y$. Then $x = y = u$ and $u\overline{\Sigma}u$. By S6 we obtain $u \leq v$.
Case (III): $\exists x, y \in \{v\}\ x\overline{N}y$. Then $x = y = v$ and $v\overline{N}v$. By S10 we obtain $u \leq v$.
Case (IV) $\exists a\ a\overline{\Sigma}a$ & $a\overline{N}a$. By Lemma 21(Triv) we obtain $u \leq v$.
(b)($\rightarrow$) Let $u\Sigma v$ and suppose that $u, v \vdash \emptyset$. There are only two possible cases for $\{u, v\} \vdash \emptyset$ – case (II) and case (IV).
Case (II): $\exists x, y \in \{u, v\}\ x\overline{\Sigma}y$. Then by ($\Sigma$) of lemma 21 we get $x\Sigma y$ – a contradiction.
Case (IV): $\exists a \in W\ a\overline{\Sigma}a$ & $a\overline{N}a$. By lemma 21(Triv) we obtain $u\overline{\Sigma}v$ – a contradiction.
(b)($\leftarrow$) Let $u, v \not\vdash \emptyset$ and suppose that $u\overline{\Sigma}v$. Then by (II) we obtain that $u, v \vdash \emptyset$ – a contradiction.
(c)($\rightarrow$) Let uNv and suppose that $\emptyset \vdash u, v$. There are only two possible cases for $\emptyset \vdash u, v$ – (III) and (IV).
Case (III): $\exists x, y \in \{u, v\}\ x\overline{N}y$. From uNv, $x, y \in \{u, v\}$ and by lemma 21 (N) we obtain xNy – a contradiction.
Case (IV): $\exists a \in W\ a\overline{\Sigma}a$ & $a\overline{N}a$. Then by (Triv) we get $u\overline{N}v$ — a contradiction.

(c)(←) Let $\emptyset \not\vdash_S u, v$ and suppose that $u\overline{N}v$. Then by (III) we get $\emptyset \vdash u, v$ – a contradiction.

□

This completes the proof of the assertion 24. From this assertion we obtain that $Sim(S) = \underline{W}$, which completes the proof of part (1) of the theorem.

Proof of part (2) of the theorem. We have to find a P-system S' such that $Sim(S') = \underline{W}$. For the constructed C-system S we have by (1) that $Sim(S) = \underline{W}$. Let S' be the canonical P-system over S. Then by lemma 22 we have $Sim(S) = Sim(P(S)) = Sim(S')$, hence $W = Sim(S')$. This completes the proof of the theorem. □

The notion of similarity structure provides an abstract characterization of the relations $\leq_S, \Sigma_S$ and N_S by means of first-order axioms. It is possible to give a similar characterization of any subset of these relations.

We say that (W, ρ) is a ρ-structure if $\rho \subseteq \{\leq, \Sigma, N\}$ and the relations from ρ satisfy those axioms from the list S1-S11, $\Sigma N1$ and $\Sigma N2$, which contain relations from ρ.

Below we list the relevant axioms and changes in the proof of the Characterization theorem for any concrete ρ.

$\leq$-structure – $(W, \leq)$. Axioms: S1 and S2. The definition of $\vdash$ in the proof of the Characterization theorem is the following:

$X \vdash Y$ iff (I) $\exists x \in X\ \exists y \in Y\ x \leq y$, or (IV′) for any $u, v:\ u \leq v$.

Σ-structure – (W, Σ). Axioms: S3 and S4.

$X \vdash Y$ iff (I′) $X \cap Y \neq \emptyset$, or (II) $\exists x, y \in X\ x\overline{\Sigma}y$, or (IV″) $\forall u, v \in W\ u\overline{\Sigma}v$.

N-structure – (W, N). Axioms: S7 and S8. The definition of $\vdash$:

$X \vdash Y$ iff (I′) or (III) $\exists x, y \in Y\ x\overline{N}y$, or (IV‴) $\forall u, v \in W\ u\overline{N}v$.

$\Sigma \leq$-structure – $(W, \leq, \Sigma)$. Axioms: S1, S2, S3, S4, S5, S6.

$X \vdash Y$ iff (I) or (II) or (IV′) or (IV″).

$N \leq$-structure – $(W, \leq, N)$. Axioms: S1, S2, S7, S8, S9, S10.

$X \vdash Y$ iff (I) or (III) or (IV′) or (IV‴).

ΣN-structure – (W, Σ, N). Axioms: S3, S4, S7, S8, $\Sigma N1$ and $\Sigma N2$ from lemma 21.

$X \vdash Y$ iff (I′) or (I″) $\exists x \in X\ \exists y \in Y\ \exists b \in W\ x\overline{\Sigma}b\ \&\ b\overline{N}y$, or (II), or (III), or (IV) $\exists a \in W\ a\overline{\Sigma}a\ \&\ a\overline{N}a$.

The proof of the characterization theorem for arbitrary ρ-structure can be obtained in a way similar to the proof of theorem 23. The next lemma shows that the characterization theorem for any ρ -structure can be derived directly from theorem 23.

Lemma 25. *(i) Let $\underline{W} = (W, \rho)$ be an ρ-structure with $\emptyset \neq \rho \neq \{\leq, \Sigma, N\}$. Then we can define the missing relations from $\{\leq, \Sigma, N\} \setminus \rho$ in such a way as to obtain similarity structure.*

(ii) Let us add to the axioms of similarity structure the conditions $\Sigma N1$ and $\Sigma N2$ from lemma 21. Then the first-order theory of similarity structures is a conservative extension of the first- order theory of any ρ-structure.

Proof. (i) First, we shall give the relevant definitions.
Case 1: $\rho = \{\leq\}$. Define $\Sigma = N = W \times W$.
Case 2: $\rho = \{\Sigma\}$. Define $N = W \times W$ and for $x, y \in W$:
$x \leq y$ iff $x\overline{\Sigma}x$ or $x = y$.
Case 3: $\rho = \{N\}$. Define $\Sigma = W \times W$ and for $x, y \in W$:
$x \leq y$ iff $y\overline{N}y$ or $x = y$.
Case 4: $\rho = \{\leq, \Sigma\}$. Define $N = W \times W$.
Case 5: $\rho = \{\leq, N\}$. Define $\Sigma = W \times W$.
Case 6: $\rho = \{\Sigma, N\}$. Define for $x, y \in W$:
$x \leq y$ iff $x\overline{\Sigma}x$ or $y\overline{N}y$ or $(\exists z)(x\overline{\Sigma}z \;\&\; z\overline{N}y)$ or $x = y$.
The proof that each of the above systems is a similarity structure is easy.
(ii) - follows from (i).

□

Theorem 26. (Characterization theorem for ρ-structures) *Each ρ-structure is a ρ-structure over some P-system.*

Proof. Let $\underline{W} = (W, \rho)$ be a ρ-structure. Then by lemma 5.8 we can extend ρ to the set $\{\leq, \Sigma, N\}$ such that $(W, \leq, \Sigma, N)$ is a similarity structure. Then by theorem 5.7.(ii) we conclude that $(W, \leq, \Sigma, N)$ is a similarity structure over some P-system S. Then, obviously, $W = (W, \rho)$ as a reduct of $(W, \leq, \Sigma, N)$ is a ρ-structure over S. □

Each $\leq$-structure is a quasi-ordered set, so we have the following

Corollary 27. *Each quasi-ordering can be represented as an informational inclusion.*

3.2 Informational Relations in Property Systems and their Counterparts in Consequence Systems

Now we shall analyze in more details the way of defining the relations $\leq, \Sigma$ and N (the subscript S is omitted) in P-systems in order to obtain the more general notion of informational relation. Similar attempt is sketched in Orlowska [Or7].

In the next table we repeat the definitions of $\leq, \Sigma$ and N and some obvious equivalents:
$x \leq y$ iff $f(x) \subseteq f(y)$ iff $f(x) \cap \overline{f}(y) = \emptyset$,
$x\Sigma y$ iff $f(x) \cap f(y) \neq \emptyset$,
xNy iff $\overline{f}(x) \cap \overline{f}(y) \neq \emptyset$.

The general form of the above three relations is the following: there exists a Boolean term $B(u, v)$ of two different variables u and v and the relation R is of one of the following two forms:

(1) xRy iff $B(f(x), f(y)) \neq \emptyset$,
(2) xRy iff $B(f(x), f(y)) = \emptyset$.

Obviously, if R is in the one of these forms then the complement of $R, \overline{R}$ will be in the other form.

The above observation leads to the following definition.

Let $B = B(u_1, \ldots, u_n)$ be a Boolean term of n different variables. Then in each P-system S the n-place relation $R_S(x_1, \ldots, x_n)$ is called a primitive informational relation of type B if one of the following conditions holds:

(1) $R_S(x_1, \ldots, x_n)$ iff $B(f_S(x_1), \ldots, f_S(x_n)) = \emptyset$
(2) $R_S(x_1, \ldots, x_n)$ iff $B(f_S(x_1), \ldots, f_S(x_n)) \neq \emptyset$.

Let $A = A(x_1, \ldots, x_n)$ be a first-order open formula built from primitive informational relations, considered as predicates, and let $x_1, \ldots, x_n$ be a list of individual variables containing all variables of A. Then the standard interpretation of A in any given P-system S will define an n-place relation in S, called informational relation of type A.

Since there are exactly 2^{2^n} non-equivalent Boolean terms of n arguments (including the constant terms 0 and 1), then there exist exactly 2^{2^n} types of primitive informational relations in the form (1) and 2^{2^n} in the form (2). Since 1 and 0 are in both types then the total sum is $2.2^{2^n} - 2$. For $n = 2$ there exist exactly 30 different types of primitive informational relations.

In the next table we list all primitive informational relations of two variables of the form (1). The relations of the form (2) are negations of some relations of the form (1). Instead of $f(x)$ and $f(y)$ we write x and y; instead of $x \cap y$ we write xy; instead of $\emptyset$ we write 0.

1. $xy = 0$ iff $x\overline{\Sigma}y$,
2. $x\overline{y} = 0$ iff $x \leq y$,
3. $\overline{x}y = 0$ iff $y \leq x$,
4. $\overline{x}\overline{y} = 0$ iff $x\overline{N}y$,
5. $1 \cup 2 = xy \cup x\overline{y} = x = xx = 0$ iff $x\overline{\Sigma}y$ and $x \leq y$ iff $x\overline{\Sigma}x$,
6. $1 \cup 3 = xy \cup \overline{x}y = y = 0$ iff $x\overline{\Sigma}y$ and $y \leq x$ iff $y\overline{\Sigma}y$,
7. $1 \cup 4 = xy \cup \overline{x}\overline{y} = 0$ iff $xy = 0$ and $\overline{x}\overline{y} = 0$ iff $x\overline{\Sigma}y$ and $x\overline{N}y$,
8. $2 \cup 3 = x\overline{y} \cup \overline{x}y = 0$ iff $x\overline{y} = 0$ and $\overline{x}y = 0$ iff $x \leq y$ and $y \leq x$ iff $x \equiv y$,
9. $2 \cup 4 = x\overline{y} \cup \overline{x}\overline{y} = \overline{y} = 0$ iff $\overline{y}\overline{y} = 0$ iff $x \leq y$ and $x\overline{N}y$ iff $y\overline{N}y$,
10. $3 \cup 4 = \overline{x}y \cup \overline{x}\overline{y} = \overline{x} = 0$ iff $y \leq x$ and $x\overline{N}y$ iff $x\overline{N}x$,
11. $1 \cup 2 \cup 3 = x \cup \overline{x}y = x \cup y = 0$ iff $x = 0$ and $y = 0$ iff $x\overline{\Sigma}x$ and $y\overline{\Sigma}y$,
12. $1 \cup 2 \cup 4 = x \cup \overline{x}\overline{y} = x \cup \overline{y} = 0$ iff $x = 0$ and $\overline{y} = 0$ iff $x\overline{\Sigma}x$ and $y\overline{N}y$,
13. $1 \cup 3 \cup 4 = y \cup \overline{x}\overline{y} = \overline{x} \cup y = 0$ iff $\overline{x} = 0$ and $y = 0$ iff $x\overline{N}x$ and $y\overline{\Sigma}y$,
14. $2 \cup 3 \cup 4 = x\overline{y} \cup \overline{x} = \overline{x} \cup \overline{y} = 0$ iff $\overline{x} = 0$ and $\overline{y} = 0$ iff $x\overline{N}x$ and $y\overline{N}y$,
15. $1 \cup 2 \cup 3 \cup 4 = x \cup \overline{x} = 1 = 0$ iff false iff $x\overline{\Sigma}y$ and $x\Sigma y$
16. truth iff $x\overline{\Sigma}y$ or $x\Sigma sy$

From the above table we can obtain the proof of the following

Theorem 28. *(i) There exist exactly 30 different types of primitive informational relations in P-systems of two variables.*

(ii) All informational relations of two variables are first- order definable by the relations $\leq, \Sigma$ and N.

(iii) *All informational relations of two variables x and y are Boolean combinations of the formulas $x \leq y, y \leq x, x\Sigma y$ and xNy.*
(iv) *There exists no more than $2^{2^4} = 256$ informational relations of two variables.*

Theorem 29. *The first-order theory of all two-place informational relations in P-systems coincides with the first-order theory of similarity structures.*

Proof. Direct consequence of theorem 28 and Characterization theorem for similarity structures (theorem 23). □

In the above list of two-place informational relations we see only two interesting new relations: the indiscernibility relation No8 and the relation No7: $x\overline{\Sigma}y$ and $x\overline{N}y$. The complement of this relation, denote it by S, means: xSy iff $x\Sigma y$ or xNy, x is either positively or negatively similar to y. So this is another kind of similarity relation. The complement $\overline{S}$ of S has the following interesting meaning: $x\overline{S}y$ iff $f(x) \cap f(y) = \emptyset$ and $\overline{f}(x) \cap \overline{f}(y) = \emptyset$ iff $f(x) = \overline{f}(y) - f(x)$ is the complement of $f(y)$. A possible reading of $x\overline{S}y$ is: "x complements y", or in other words, "x possesses those and only those properties (from the given set of properties Pr), which are not possessed by y". The corresponding relations of $\equiv$ and $\overline{S}$ in C-systems are these: $x \equiv y$ iff $x \vdash y$ and $y \vdash x$ iff "x is equivalent to y"; $x\overline{S}y$ iff $x, y \vdash \emptyset$ and $\emptyset \vdash x, y$ iff $x \vdash \neg y$ and $\neg y \vdash x$ iff "x is equivalent to $\neg y$" iff "x is the negation of y".

For n-place informational relations also there is a basis consisting of $n+1$ relations, such that all the other informational relations are first-order definable by the relations from the basis. One possible basis is in the following table (on the right hand side there are the corresponding relations in C-systems).

$I_0^n(x_1, \ldots, x_n)$ iff $\overline{f}(x_1) \cap \ldots \cap \overline{f}(x_n) = \emptyset$,	$\emptyset \vdash x_1, \ldots, x_n$
$I_1^n(x_1, x_2, \ldots, x_n)$ iff $f(x_1) \cap \overline{f}(x_2) \ldots \cap \overline{f}(x_n) = \emptyset$,	$x_1 \vdash x_2, \ldots, x_n$
$I_2^n(x_1, x_2, x_3, \ldots, x_n)$ iff $f(x_1) \cap f(x_2) \cap \overline{f}(x_3) \cap \ldots \cap \overline{f}(x_n) = \emptyset$,	$x_1, x_2 \vdash x_3, \ldots, x_n$
...	...
$I_n^n(x_1, \ldots, x_n)$ iff $f(x_1) \cap \ldots \cap f(x_n) = \emptyset$,	$x_1, \ldots, x_n \vdash \emptyset$

Theorem 30. *(i) There exist exactly $2.2^{2^n} - 2$ different types of primitive n-place informational relations in P-systems.*
(ii) All n-place informational relations in P-systems are first-order definable by the relations $I_0^n, \ldots, I_n^n$.

Proof. The proof of (i) is given above. To prove (ii) Let $f_1 = f$ and $f_0 = \overline{f}$. Then obviously all relations of the form $R_{i_1,\ldots,i_n}(x_1, \ldots, x_n)$ iff $f_{i_1}(x_1) \cap \ldots \cap f_{i_n}(x_n) = \emptyset$, $i_1, \ldots, i_n \in \{0, 1\}$ are definable by the relations $I_0^n, \ldots, I_n^{n^n}$ using only permutation of variables. Then all the informational relations of type (1) are some conjunctions of the relations $R_{i_1,\ldots,i_n}$. The relations of the type (2) are negations of the relations of type (1). □

The relations I_m^n can be used to reformulate the definition of a C-system in order to consider C-systems as first-order structures. Let $I_{mn} = I_m^{m+n}$, $m =$

$0, 1, 2, \ldots$, $n = 1, 2, \ldots$. Then the following set of axioms provides an equivalent definition of a C-system.

(Ref) $I_{12}(x, x)$

(Mono') $I_{mn}(x_1, \ldots, x_m; y_1, \ldots, y_m) \rightarrow I_{m+1n}(a, x_1, \ldots, x_m; y_1, \ldots, y_n)$,

(Mono") $I_{mn}(x_1, \ldots, x_m; y_1, \ldots, y_m) \rightarrow I_{mn+1}(x_1, \ldots, x_m; a, y_1, \ldots, y_n)$,

(Perm') $I_{mn}(x_1, \ldots, x_m; y_1, \ldots, y_m) \rightarrow I_{mn}(x_{i_1}, \ldots, x_{i_m}; y_{j_1}, \ldots, y_{j_n})$,

where $(i_1, \ldots, i_m)$ and $(j_1, \ldots, j_n)$ are permutations of $(1, \ldots, m)$ and $(1, \ldots, n)$ respectively.

(Weak')

$I_{m+1n}(x_1, x_1, x_2, \ldots, x_m; y_1, \ldots, y_n) \rightarrow I(x_1, x_2, \ldots, x_m; y_1, \ldots, y_n)$,

(Weak")

$I_{mn+1}(x_1, \ldots, x_m; y_1, y_1, y_2 \ldots, y_n) \rightarrow I_{mn}(x_1, \ldots, x_m; y_1, y_2, \ldots, y_n)$,

(Cut)

If $I_{m+1n}(x_1, \ldots, x_m, a; y_1, \ldots, y_n)$ and $I_{mn+1}(x_1, \ldots, x_m; a, y_1, \ldots, y_n)$ then $I(x_1, \ldots, x_m; y_1, \ldots, y_n)$.

Now it is clear that C-systems are first-order structures.

Theorem 31. *First-order theory of all the informational relations in P-systems coincides with the first-order theory of C-systems.*

Proof. A direct consequence of the above first-order reformulation of C-systems and the characterization theorem for C-systems (theorem 5). □

Let us note that the problem of characterization of the first- order theory of all n-place informational relations for $n \geq 3$ is an open problem.

This section is out of the scope of this paper, because we are mainly interested here in two-place relations in information systems. We include this material in order to show the place of similarity relations in the family of all informational relations, and also to formulate the open problem mentioned above.

3.3 Similarity Relations in Attribute Systems and their Counterparts in Bi-Consequence Systems

In A-systems we can easily extend the definitions of the similarity relations Σ, N and the inclusion relation $\leq$ in two different ways, obtaining weak and strong versions. The formal definitions are the following.

Let S be an A-system and $x, y \in Ob_S$. We introduce the following six relations in S defined in the following way:

- Weak positive similarity
  $x\Sigma_S y$ iff $(\exists a \in At_S) f_S(x, a) \cap f_S(y, a) \neq \emptyset$,
- Weak negative similarity
  $xN_S y$ iff $(\exists a \in At_S) \overline{f}_S(x, a) \cap \overline{f}_S(y, a) \neq \emptyset$,
- Weak informational inclusion
  $x <_S y$ iff $(\exists a \in At_S) f_S(x, a) \subseteq f_S(y, a)$,
- Strong positive similarity
  $x\sigma_S y$ iff $(\forall a \in At_S) f_S(x, a) \cap f_S(y, a) \neq \emptyset$,

- Strong negative similarity
  $x\nu_S y$ iff $(\forall a \in At_S)\overline{f}_S(x,a) \cap \overline{f}_S(y,a) \neq \emptyset$,
- Strong informational inclusion
  $x \leq_S y$ $(\forall a \in At) f_S(x,a) \subseteq f_S(y,a)$.

Lemma 32. *(i) Let $S = A(W,V)$ be a set-theoretical A-system over the pair (W,V). Then for any $x, y \in W$ the following is true:*
- $x\Sigma_S y$ *iff* $(\exists a \in V)(\exists A \in a)(x \in A \,\&\, y \in A)$,
- $xN_S y$ *iff* $(\exists a \in V)(\exists A \in a)(x \notin A \,\&\, y \notin A)$,
- $x <_S y$ *iff* $(\exists a \in V)(\forall A \in a)(x \in A \rightarrow y \in A)$,
- $x\sigma_S y$ *iff* $(\forall a \in V)(\exists A \in a)(x \in A \,\&\, y \in A)$,
- $x\nu_S y$ *iff* $(\forall a \in V)(\exists A \in a)(x \notin A \,\&\, y \notin A)$,
- $x \leq_S y$ *iff* $(\forall a \in V)(\forall A \in a)(x \in A \rightarrow y \in A)$.

(ii) Let S and S' be two A-systems and let h be a strong homomorphism from S into S'. Then for any $x, y \in Ob_S$ and $R \in \{\Sigma_S, N, <, \sigma, \nu, \leq\}$ the following is true: $xR_S y$ iff $h(x)R_{S'}h(y)$.

(iii) Let S be an A-system and let $|S|$ be the set-theoretical A-system associated with S. Then for any $x, y \in Ob_S$ and $R \in \{\Sigma_S, N, <, \sigma, \nu, \leq\}$ the following is true: $xR_S y$ iff $xR_{|S|}y$.

Proof. Straightforward. □

Lemma 33. *(i) Let S be an A-system and $S' = B(S)$ be the B-system over S. Then for any $x, y \in Ob_S$ the following is true:*
- $x\Sigma_S y$ *iff* $x, y \not\vdash_{S'} \emptyset$,
- $xN_S y$ *iff* $\emptyset \not\vdash_{S'} x, y$,
- $x <_S y$ *iff* $x \succ_{S'} y$,
- $x\sigma_S y$ *iff* $x, y \not\succ_{S'} \emptyset$,
- $x\nu_S y$ *iff* $\emptyset \not\succ_{S'} x, y$,
- $x \leq_S y$ *iff* $x \vdash_{S'} y$.

(ii) Let S' be a B-system and $S = A(S')$ be the canonical A-system over S'. Then for any $x, y \in Ob_S$ the following is true:
- $x\Sigma_S y$ *iff* $x, y \not\vdash_{S'} \emptyset$,
- $xN_S y$ *iff* $\emptyset \not\vdash_{S'} x, y$,
- $x <_S y$ *iff* $x \succ_{S'} y$,
- $x\sigma_S y$ *iff* $x, y \not\succ_{S'} \emptyset$,
- $x\nu_S y$ *iff* $\emptyset \not\succ_{S'} x, y$,
- $x \leq_S y$ *iff* $x \vdash_{S'} y$.

Proof. Straightforward, using the relevant definitions. □

Lemma 33 provides a new meaning for the relations $\Sigma, N, <, \sigma, \nu, \leq$ and suggests how to define them in B-systems. Namely, we have the following definition.

Let S be a B-system. Then for $x, y \in Sen_S$ we define:

- $x\Sigma_S y$ iff $x, y \not\vdash_S \emptyset$,
- $xN_S y$ iff $\emptyset \not\vdash_S x, y$,

- $x <_S y$ iff $x \succ_S y$,
- $x \sigma_S y$ iff $x, y \not\succ_S \emptyset$,
- $x \nu_S y$ iff $\emptyset \not\succ_S x, y$,
- $x \leq_S y$ iff $x \vdash_S y$.

Lemma 34. *Let S be an A-system (B-system). Then the following conditions are true for any $x, y, z \in Ob_S$ ($x, y, z \in Sen_S$): (the subscript S is omitted)*

S1 $x \leq x$,	$x \vdash x$,	*(Ref⊢)*
S2 $x \leq y \,\&\, y \leq z \rightarrow x \leq z$,	$x \vdash y \,\&\, y \vdash z \rightarrow x \vdash z$,	*(Cut⊢)*
S3 $x \Sigma y \rightarrow y \Sigma x$,	$y, xi \vdash \emptyset \rightarrow x, y \vdash \emptyset$,	*(Permutation⊢)*
S4 $x \Sigma y \rightarrow x \Sigma x$,	$x \vdash \emptyset \rightarrow x, y \vdash \emptyset$,	*(Mono⊢)*
S5 $x \Sigma y \,\&\, y \leq z \rightarrow x \Sigma z$,	$x, z \vdash \emptyset \,\&\, y \vdash z$ *then* $x, y \vdash \emptyset$,	*(Cut⊢)*
S6 $x \Sigma x$ *or* $x \leq y$,	$x \vdash \emptyset \rightarrow x \vdash y$,	*(Mono⊢)*
S7 $x N y \rightarrow y N x$,	$\emptyset \vdash y, x \rightarrow \emptyset \vdash x, y$,	*(Permutation ⊢)*
S8 $x N y \rightarrow x N x$,	$\emptyset \vdash x \rightarrow \emptyset \vdash x, y$,	*(Mono⊢)*
S9 $x \leq y \,\&\, y N z \rightarrow x N z$,	$x \vdash y \,\&\, \emptyset \vdash x, z \rightarrow \emptyset \vdash y, z$,	*(Cut⊢)*
S10 $y N y$ *or* $x \leq y$,	$\emptyset \vdash y \rightarrow x \vdash y$,	*(Mono⊢)*
S11 $x \Sigma z$ *or* $y N z$ *or* $x \leq y$,	$x, z \vdash \emptyset \,\&\, \emptyset \vdash z, x \rightarrow x \vdash y$,	*(Cut⊢)*
S12 $x < x$,	$x \succ x$,	*(Ref≻)*
S13 $x \leq y \,\&\, y < z \rightarrow x < z$,	$x \vdash y \,\&\, y \succ z \rightarrow x \succ z$,	*(Cut≻)*
S14 $x < y \,\&\, y \leq z \rightarrow x < z$,	$x \succ y \,\&\, y \vdash z \rightarrow x \succ z$,	*(Cut≻)*
S15 $x \sigma y \rightarrow y \sigma x$,	$x, y \succ \emptyset \rightarrow y, x \succ \emptyset$,	*(Permutation≻)*
S16 $x \sigma y \rightarrow x \sigma x$,	$x \succ \emptyset \rightarrow x, y \succ \emptyset$,	*(Mono≻)*
S17 $x \sigma y \,\&\, y \leq z \rightarrow x \sigma z$,	$x, z \succ \emptyset \,\&\, y \vdash z \rightarrow x, y \succ \emptyset$,	*(Cut≻)*
S18 $x \sigma x$ *or* $x < y$,	$x \succ \emptyset \rightarrow x \succ y$,	*(Mono≻)*
S19 $x \sigma y \,\&\, y < z \rightarrow x \Sigma z$,	$x, z \vdash \emptyset \,\&\, y \succ z \rightarrow x, y \succ \emptyset$,	*(Cut≻)*
S20 $x \sigma z$ *or* $y N z$ *or* $x < y$,	$x, z \succ \emptyset \,\&\, \emptyset \vdash y, z \rightarrow x \succ y$,	*(Cut≻)*
S21 $x \nu y \rightarrow y \nu x$,	$\emptyset \succ y, x \rightarrow \emptyset \succ x, y$,	*(Permutation≻)*
S22 $x \nu y \rightarrow x \nu x$,	$\emptyset \succ x \rightarrow \emptyset \succ x, y$,	*(Mono≻)*
S23 $x \leq y \,\&\, y \nu z \rightarrow x \nu z$,	$\emptyset \succ x, z \,\&\, x \vdash y \rightarrow \emptyset \succ y, z$,	*(Cut≻)*
S24 $y \nu y$ *or* $x < y$,	$\emptyset \succ y \rightarrow x \succ y$,	*(Mono≻)*
S25 $x < y \,\&\, y \nu z \rightarrow x N z$,	$\emptyset \vdash x, z \,\&\, x \succ y \rightarrow \emptyset \neq y, z$,	*(Cut≻)*
S26 $x \Sigma z$ *or* $y \nu z$ *or* $x < y$,	$x, z \vdash \emptyset \,\&\, \emptyset \succ y, z \rightarrow x \succ y$,	*(Cut≻).*

Proof. Straightforward verification. □

Lemma 34 suggests the following definition, which is the first step in the abstract characterization of the relations $\leq$, Σ, N, $<$, σ, ν.

Let $\underline{W} = (W, \leq, \Sigma, N, <, \sigma, \nu)$ be a relational system with $W \neq \emptyset$ and $\leq$, Σ, N, $<$, σ, ν be binary relations in W. We call $\underline{W}$ a bi- similarity structure if it satisfies the conditions S1-S26 from lemma 34.

Obviously each bi-similarity structure is a similarity structure with respect to $\leq, \Sigma, N$. This is the reason why we preserve the notations from similarity structures for these relations.

Now lemma 34 says that if S is an A-system (B-system) then the system $BiSim(S) = (W, \leq_S, \Sigma_S, N_S, <_S, \sigma_S, \nu_S)$ with $W = Ob_S$ ($W = Sen_S$) is a bi-similarity structure, called the bi-similarity structure over S.

The next lemma states some consequences of the axioms of a bi-similarity structure.

Lemma 35. *The following conditions hold in each bi-similarity structure*

(i) Let $S \in \{\Sigma, N, \sigma, \nu\}$. Then xSy and $u, v \in \{x, y\}$ imply uSv.
(ii) a. $xSy \;\&\; x \leq u \;\&\; y \leq v \rightarrow uSv,\ S \in \{\Sigma, \sigma\}$,
b. $xSy \;\&\; u \leq x \;\&\; v \leq y \rightarrow uSv,\ S \in \{N, \nu\}$,
c. $x\sigma y \;\&\; ((x \leq u \;\&\; y < v)$ or $(x < u \;\&\; y \leq v)) \rightarrow u\Sigma v$,
d. $x\nu y \;\&\; ((u \leq x \;\&\; v < y)$ or $(u < x \;\&\; v \leq y)) \rightarrow uNv$,
e. $x\sigma x \;\&\; x < y \rightarrow x\Sigma x$,
f. $y\nu y \;\&\; x < y \rightarrow xNx$.
(iii) a. $x\sigma y \rightarrow x\Sigma y$,
b. $x\nu y \rightarrow xNy$,
c. $x \underline{\leq} y \rightarrow x < y$.
(iv) a. $x\overline{\Sigma}x \;\&\; x\overline{N}x \rightarrow \forall u, v\ u \leq v, u < v, u\overline{\Sigma}v, u\overline{N}v, u\overline{\sigma}v, u\overline{\nu}v$,
b. $x\overline{\Sigma}x \;\&\; x\overline{N}y \rightarrow (y\overline{\Sigma}y \;\&\; \underline{y\overline{\nu}y}) \;\&\; (y\overline{\sigma}y \;\&\; y\overline{N}y)$.
c. $(x\overline{\Sigma}x \;\&\; x\overline{\nu}x)$ or $(x\overline{\sigma}x \;\&\; x\overline{N}x) \rightarrow \forall u, v\ u < v, u\overline{\sigma}v, u\overline{\nu}v$

Proof. Conditions (i) and (ii) are easy. Let us prove (iii). For (iiia) suppose $x\sigma y$. By S12 we have $y < y$ and by S19 we get $x\Sigma y$. In a similar way one can prove (iiib) and (iiic).

For (iva) suppose $x\overline{\Sigma}x \;\&\; x\overline{N}x$. Then by lemma 21 (Triv) we have $\forall u, v\ u \leq v, u\overline{\Sigma}v$ and $u\overline{N}v$. Then by (iii) and we get $u\overline{\sigma}v, u\overline{\nu}v$ and $u < v$.

For (ivb) suppose, first, $x\overline{\Sigma}x$ and $x\overline{\nu}x$. From $x\overline{\Sigma}x$ we obtain $x \leq v$. From $x\overline{\nu}x$ we obtain $u < x$, and then by S14 we get $u < v$. For $u\overline{\sigma}v$ we proceed as follows. From $x\overline{\Sigma}x$ we get by S16 $x\overline{\Sigma}v$. From $x\overline{\nu}x$ we obtain by S24 $u < x$. Then by (iic) we obtain $u\overline{\sigma}v$. For $u\overline{\nu}v$ we proceed in a similar way: $x\overline{\Sigma}x$ gives $x \leq u$ (by S6), $x\overline{\nu}x$ gives $x\overline{\nu}v$ (by S22), and from here we obtain (by (iib)) $u\overline{\nu}v$. In a similar way we proceed with the assumption $(x\overline{\sigma}x \;\&\; x\overline{N}x)$. □

Lemma 36. *(i) Let S be an A-system and $B(S)$ be the B-system over S. Then $BiSim(S) = BiSim(B(S))$.*
(ii) Let S be a B-system and $A(S)$ be the canonical A-system over S. Then $BiSim(S) = BiSim(A(S))$.

Proof. Direct consequence of lemma 34 and lemma 35. □

Theorem 37. (Characterization theorem for bi-similarity structures) *Let $\underline{W} = (W, \leq, \Sigma, N, <, \sigma, \nu)$ be a bi-similarity structure. Then:*

(i) There exists a B-system S such that $\underline{W} = BiSim(S)$.
(ii) There exists an A-system S' such that $\underline{W} = BiSim(S')$.

Proof. (i) Since we want to have $\underline{W} = BiSim(S)$ then we have to put $Sen_S = W$. For the relation $\vdash$ we adopt the definition from theorem 23. Namely for $X, Y \in P_{fin}(W)$ define:
$X \vdash Y$ iff

(I) $\exists x \in X\ \exists y \in Y\ x \leq y$, or
(II) $\exists x, y \in X\ x\overline{\Sigma}y$, or
(III) $\exists x, y \in Y\ x\overline{N}y$, or
(IV) $\exists a \in W\ a\overline{\Sigma}a\ \&\ a\overline{N}a$.
For the relation $\succ$ we take the following definition: for $X, Y \in P_{fin}(W)$ we define:
$X \succ Y$ iff
(J) $\exists x \in X\ \exists y \in Y\ x < y$, or
(JJ) $\exists x, y \in X\ x\overline{\sigma}y$, or
(JJJ) $\exists x, y \in Y\ x\overline{\nu}y$, or
(JV) $\exists x((x\overline{\Sigma}x\ \&\ x\overline{\nu}x)$ or $(x\overline{\sigma}x\ \&\ x\overline{N}x))$.
The proof of (i) will follow from the following two assertions.

Assertion 38. *$(W, \vdash, \succ)$ is a B-system.*

Assertion 39. *For any $x, y \in W$ the following holds:*
(a) $u \leq v$ iff $u \vdash_{S'} v$,
(b) $u\Sigma v$ iff $u, v \not\vdash_{S'} \emptyset$,
(c) uNv iff $\emptyset \not\vdash_{S'} u, v$,
(d) $u < v$ iff $u \succ v$,
(e) $u\sigma v$ iff $u, v \not\succ_{S'} \emptyset$,
(f) $u\nu v$ iff $\emptyset \not\succ_{S'} u, v$.

Proof. Assertion 38. Since $\underline{W}$ is also a similarity structure with respect to $\leq, \Sigma$ and N, then by theorem 23 $(W, \vdash)$ is a C-system. So we have only to show that $\succ$ satisfies the remaining axioms of a B-system.
For (Refl $\succ$) suppose $X \cap Y \neq \emptyset$, then $\exists x \in X$ such that $x \in Y$. By S12 we have $x < x$ and by (J) of the definition of $\succ$ we obtain $X \succ Y$. Axiom (Mono $\succ$) does not present any difficulties and (Incl) follows from lemma 36(iiiabc)-(ivb).
For (Cut $\succ$ 1) suppose
(1) $X \vdash a, Y$,
(2) $X, a \succ Y$ and proceed to show
(3) $X \succ Y$.
We have to consider the possible cases for (1) and (2) and then to combine all the cases of (1) with all the cases of (2).
For (1) $X \vdash a, Y$ we have the following cases.

(1I) $\exists x \in X, \exists y \in \{a\} \cup Y\ x \leq y$. Then we have (by lemma 35(iiic)) $x < y$. If $y \in Y$ then by (J) we obtain (3). So for the combination with the other cases of (2) we consider only one subcase:
(i) $y = a:\ x \in X,\ x \leq a$ and $x < a$.

(1II) $\exists x, y \in X\ x\overline{\Sigma}y$. Then by lemma 35(iiia) we obtain $x\overline{\sigma}y$ and by (JJ) we get (3). So this case will not be combined with the other cases of (2).

(1III) $\exists x, y \in \{a\} \cup Y\ x\overline{N}y$. By lemma 35(iiib) we obtain $x\overline{\nu}y$. If $x, y \in Y$ then by (JJJ) we get (3). So, for the combination with the other cases we consider only the following sub cases:

(i) $x = a : \; y \in Y,\; a\overline{N}y,\; a\overline{N}y,$
(ii) $y = a : \; x \in Y,\; x\overline{N}a,\; x\overline{\nu}a,$
(iii) $x = y = a : \; a\overline{N}a,\; a\overline{\nu}a.$

(1IV) $\exists x\; x\overline{\Sigma}x \;\&\; x\overline{N}x$. Then by lemma 35(ivb) and (IJ) we get (3). So this case will not be combined with the other cases of (2).

For (2) $X, a \succ Y$ we have the following cases.

(2J) $\exists u \in X \cup \{a\}\; \exists v \in Y\; u < v$. If $u \in X$ then by (J) we get (3), so for the combination with the other cases of (1) we consider only one sub case:
(j) $u = a : \; a < v,\; v \in Y$.

(2JJ) $\exists u, v \in X \cup \{a\}\; u\overline{\sigma}v$. If $u, v \in X$ then by (JJ) we obtain (3) so for the combinations with the other cases of (1) we will consider only the following:
(j) $u = a : \; a\overline{\sigma}v,\; v \in X,$
(jj) $v = a : \; u\overline{\sigma}a,\; u \in X,$
(jjj) $u = v = a : \; a\overline{\sigma}a.$

(2JJJ) $\exists u, v \in Y\; u\overline{\nu}v$. By (JJJ) we directly obtain (3), so this case will not be combined with the other cases of (1).

(2JV) $\exists x\; ((x\overline{\Sigma}x \;\&\; x\overline{\nu}x)$ or $(x\overline{N}x \;\&\; x\overline{\sigma}x))$. By (JV) we directly obtain (3), so this case will not be combined with the other cases for (1).

Now we start with the combination of the possible case for (1)and (2).
Case (1I)(2J), (i)(j): $x \in X,\; x \leq a;\; a < v,\; v \in Y$. Then by S13 we obtain $x < v$ and by (J) - (3).
Case (1I)(2JJ). We have to combine (i) with (j), (jj) and (jjj).

(i)(j) $x \in X,\; x \leq a;\; a\overline{\sigma}v,\; v \in X$. By lemma 35(iia) we get $x\overline{\sigma}v$ and by (JJ) we obtain (3).
(i)(jj) $x \in X,\; x \leq a;\; u\sigma a,\; u \in X$. We treat this case as above.
(i)(jjj) $x \in X,\; x \leq a;\; a\overline{\sigma}a$. By lemma 35(iia) we obtain $x\overline{\sigma}x$ and by (JJJ) we get (3).

Case (1III)(2J). We have to combine (i), (ii) and (iii) with (j).

(i)(j) $a\overline{N}y,\; y \in Y;\; a < v,\; v \in Y$. By S25 we obtain $v\overline{\nu}y$ and by (JJJ) we obtain (3).
(ii)(j) $x \in Y,\; x\overline{N}a;\; a < v,\; v \in Y$. The proof is as above.
(iii)(j) $a\overline{N}a;\; a < v,\; v \in Y$. By lemma 35(iif) we get $v\overline{\nu}v$ and by (JJJ) we obtain (3).

Case (1III)(2JJ) We have to combine (i)-(iii) with (j)-(jjj).

(i)(j) $y \in Y,\; a\overline{N}y;\; a\overline{\sigma}v,\; v \in X$. By S20, S15 and S7 we get $v < y$ and by (J) we obtain (3).

The other combinations except for (iii)(jjj) are similar to the above one.

(iii)(jjj) $a\overline{N}a;\; a\overline{\sigma}a$. By (JV) we get (3).

Thus we have completed the combinations of the possible cases for (1) and (2) and hence (Cut$\succ$ 1) is verified.

The proof of (Cut$\succ$ 2) can be given in the same manner. This completes the proof of assertion 38. □

Assertion 39. The proofs of (a), (b) and (c) are the same as the corresponding proofs in theorem 23.

(d)($\rightarrow$) Suppose $u < v$. Then by (J) we obtain $u \succ v$.

(d)($\leftarrow$) Suppose $u \succ v$. To show $u < v$ we will inspect the cases (J)-(JV) of the definition of $\succ$.

Case (J): $\exists x \in \{u\}\ \exists y \in \{v\}\ x < y$. Then obviously we have $u < v$.

Case (JJ): $\exists x, y \in \{u\}\ x\overline{\sigma}y$. Then we obtain $u\overline{\sigma}u$ and by S18 we get $u < v$.

Case (JJJ): $\exists x, y \in \{v\}\ x\overline{\nu}y$. Then we obtain $v\overline{\nu}v$ and by S24 we get $u < v$.

Case (JV): $\exists x\ ((x\Sigma x\ \&\ x\nu x)$ or $(x\sigma x\ \&\ xNx))$. By lemma 35(ivc) we obtain $u < v$.

(e) We shall prove $u\overline{\sigma}v$ iff $u, v \succ \emptyset$.

($\rightarrow$) Suppose $u\overline{\sigma}v$. Then by (JJ) we get $u, v \succ \emptyset$.

($\leftarrow$) Suppose $u, v \succ \emptyset$. We shall prove $u\overline{\sigma}v$ inspecting the possible cases (J)-(JV) of the definition of $\succ$. The cases (J) and (JJJ) are impossible.

Case (JJ): $\exists x, y \in \{u, v\}\ x\overline{\sigma}y$. Then by lemma 35(i) we obtain $u\overline{\sigma}v$.

Case (JV): $\exists x((x\overline{\Sigma}x\ \&\ x\overline{\nu}x)$ or $(x\overline{\sigma}x\ \&\ x\overline{N}x))$. Then by lemma 35(ivc) we obtain $u\overline{\sigma}v$.

(f) We shall prove $u\overline{\nu}v$ iff $\emptyset \succ u, v$.

($\rightarrow$) Suppose $u\overline{\nu}v$. Then by (JJJ) we have $\emptyset \succ u, v$.

($\leftarrow$) Suppose $\emptyset \succ u, v$. The cases (J) and (JJ) are impossible, so we have to inspect only the cases (JJJ) and (JV).

Case (JJJ): $\exists x, y \in \{u, v\}\ x\overline{\nu}y$. By lemma 35(i) we obtain $u\overline{\sigma}v$.

Case (JV): $\exists x((x\overline{\Sigma}x\ \&\ x\overline{\nu}x)$ or $(x\overline{\sigma}x\ \&\ x\overline{N}x))$. Then by lemma 35(ivc) we obtain $u\overline{\nu}v$.

This completes the proof of assertion 39 and the part (i) of the theorem 37. □

(ii) Put $S' = A(S)$. Then S' is an A-system. By lemma 36 $BiSim(S) = BiSim(A(S))$. By (i) we have $\underline{W} = BiSim(S)$, hence $\underline{W} = BiSim(S')$. This ends the proof of the theorem.

□

As we have done for similarity structures, we can give an abstract characterization of any subfamily of the relations $\leq, \Sigma, N, <, \sigma, \nu$ formulating an independent set of axioms and a theorem similar to theorem 37. We left this work to the reader.

3.4 Similarity Relations in Single-Valued Attribute Systems

Recall that an A-system S is a single-valued if for all $x \in Ob_S$ and $a \in At_S$ the cardinality of the set $f_S(x, a)$ is less or equal to 1. The main aim of this section is to give an abstract characterization theorem for the relations from the set $Re = \{\leq, \Sigma, N, <, \sigma, \nu\}$ in single-valued A-systems. However, such a characterization for all relations together is an open problem. We shall give characterization theorems only for some concrete subsets of the set Re. A pair (W, R) with $R \subseteq Re$, satisfying some relevant axioms, is called an R-structure. The notion of a ρ-structure ($\rho \subseteq \{\leq, \Sigma, N\}$) introduced in sec. 3.1 is an R-structure with $R = \rho$. If a relational system $\underline{W}$ can be obtained from a bi-similarity structure $\underline{W}'$ by omitting some of the relations of $\underline{W}'$ we will say that $\underline{W}$ is a reduct of $\underline{W}'$. Consequently, each R-structure is a reduct of some bi-similarity structure.

Let $\mathcal{A}$ be the class of all bi-similarity structures over A-systems and $\mathcal{A}_{sv}$ be the class of all bi-similarity structures over single-valued A-systems. Let α be a first-order sentence build from some relations from Re considered as binary predicates. We say that α separates $\mathcal{A}$ from $\mathcal{A}_{sv}$ if α is true in $\mathcal{A}_{sv}$ but not in $\mathcal{A}$. The conditions S27-S35 from the next lemma are examples of such sentences.

Lemma 40. *Let S be a single-valued A-system. Then the following conditions are satisfied for any $x, y, z, u, v \in Ob_S$:*

(i)
- *S27.* $x\sigma_S y \rightarrow x \leq_S y$,
- *S28.* $x\Sigma_S y \rightarrow x <_S y$,
- *S29.* $x\nu_S u \;\&\; u\sigma_S v \;\&\; v\nu_S y \rightarrow x\nu_S y$,
- *S30.* $x\nu_S y \;\&\; x\sigma_S z \rightarrow u\nu_S u$,
- *S31.* $x\sigma_S u \;\&\; u\nu_S v \;\&\; v\sigma_S y \rightarrow x\nu_S y$,
- *S32.* $x\sigma_S y \;\&\; y\sigma_S z \rightarrow x\sigma_S z$,
- *S33.* $x >_S y \rightarrow y >_S x$ *or* $x >_S z$,
- *S34.* $x\sigma_S y \;\&\; y\Sigma_S z \rightarrow x\Sigma_S z$,
- *S35.* $x\Sigma_S y \;\&\; y\nu_S z \rightarrow xN_S z$.

(ii) On the ground of S1-S26:
- *S31 follows from S27,*
- *S32 follows from S27,*
- *S33 follows from S28,*
- *S34 follows from S27 or S28,*
- *S35 follows from S28.*

Proof. (i) follows directly from the definition of a single valued A-system.
(ii) By way of example we shall show how S33 follows from S28. Suppose $x <_S y$ and not $x <_S z$ and proceed to show $y <_S x$. Then by S18 we obtain $x\sigma_S x$ and applying S19 we get $x\Sigma_S y$. Then by S3 we have $y\Sigma_S x$ and finally by S28 we conclude that $y <_S x$.

□

Looking at the sentences S27-S35 we can see that in each of them at least one of the relations $<, \sigma$ and ν is used. We shall show that there is no a first-order formula, built with $\leq, \Sigma$ and N, which separates $\mathcal{A}$ from $\mathcal{A}_{sv}$. First, we shall prove the following theorem.

Theorem 41. (Characterization theorem for similarity structures in single-valued *A*-systems) *Each similarity structure is a reduct of some bi-similarity structure over some single-valued A-system.*

Proof. By theorem 23 (the characterization theorem for similarity structures) there exists a *P*-system $S' = (Ob_{S'}, Pr_{S'}, f_{S'})$ such that $\underline{W}$ coincides with the similarity structure over S'. This means that $W = Ob_S$ and the relations $\leq, \Sigma$ and N coincide with the relations $\leq_S, \Sigma_S$ and N_S respectively, that is, for any $x, y \in W$ $x \leq y$ iff $f_{S'}(x) \subseteq f_{S'}(y)$, $x\Sigma y$ iff $f_{S'}(x) \cap f_{S'}(y) \neq \emptyset$, xNy iff $\overline{f}_S(x) \cap \overline{f}_S(y) \neq \emptyset$. We define a single-valued *A*-system S in the following way. Put $Ob_S = Ob_{S'} = W$, $At_S = Pr_{S'}$, for each $a \in Pr_S$ put $Val_S(a) = \{a\}$ and for each $x \in Ob_S = Ob_{S'}$ and $a \in At_S = Pr_{S'}$ define $f_S(x, a) = f_{S'}(x) \cap \{a\}$. Obviously S is a single valued *A*-system. It is a routine check to see that for any $x, y \in Ob_{S'}$ we have: $x \leq_{S'} y$ iff $x \leq_S y$, $x\Sigma_S y$ iff $x\Sigma_S y$ and $xN_{S'}y$ iff $xN_S y$, which proves the theorem. □

Corollary 42. *There is no a first-order formula built with the relations $\leq, \Sigma$ and N, considered as predicates, which separates $\mathcal{A}$ and $\mathcal{A}_{sv}$.*

Proof. Suppose that such a formula exists and let it be α. Then α is true in $\mathcal{A}_{sv}$ but not in $\mathcal{A}$. So there exists a bi-similarity structure $\underline{W} = (W, \leq, \Sigma, N, <, \sigma, \nu)$ in which α is not true. Since α is built with the relations $\leq, \Sigma$ and N, then α will not be true in the similarity structure $(W, \leq, \Sigma, N)$, which is a reduct of $\underline{W}$. By theorem 41 there exists a single valued *A*-system S such that $Ob_S = W$ and the relations $\leq, \Sigma$ and N coincide with the relations $\leq_S, \Sigma_S$, and N_S respectively. So α will not be true in the bi-similarity structure $Sim(S)$ over S. Since S is a single-valued *A*-system then $Sim(S) \in \mathcal{A}_{sv}$. By the assumption α is true in $\mathcal{A}_{sv}$, so α is true in $Sim(S)$ – a contradiction. This completes the proof. □

Theorem 43. (Characterization theorem for ρ-structures in single-valued *A*-systems) *Each ρ-structure $\underline{W} = (W, \rho)$ $(\rho \subseteq \{\leq, \Sigma, N\})$ is a reduct of some bi-similarity structure over some single-valued A-system.*

Proof. Let $\underline{W} = (W, \rho)$ be a ρ-structure. By theorem 25 ρ can be extended to the set $\{\leq, \Sigma, N\}$ so that the system $(W, \leq, \Sigma, N)$ becomes a similarity structure. Then by theorem 41 $(W, \leq, \Sigma, N)$ is a reduct of some bi-similarity structure over some single-valued *A*-system S, which proves the theorem. □

Corollary 44. *Each quasi-ordered set $(W, \leq)$ can be represented as a $\leq$-structure over some single-valued A-system S with $Ob_S = W$.*

By a positive bi-similarity structure we mean any system $\underline{W} = (W, \leq, \Sigma, <, \sigma)$ satisfying the conditions S1-S6, S12-S19. If $\underline{W}$ satisfies also S27 and S28 it will be called a strong positive bi-similarity structure.

Let us note that in positive bi-similarity structures we consider only positive similarities. The following theorem is one of the main results in this section.

Theorem 45. (Characterization theorem for strong positive bi-similarity structures in single-valued A-systems) *Let $\underline{W} = (W, \leq, \Sigma, <, \sigma)$ be a strong bi-similarity structure. Then $\underline{W}$ is a reduct of some bi-similarity structure over a single-valued A-system.*

Proof. The proof of this theorem will be given using a method that is different from those in the proof of the characterization theorems for similarity structures and bi-similarity structures. It was applied for the first time in [Va1] and later in [Va2], [Va3], [Va4], [Va5].

First, we shall introduce some notions and prove some lemmas.

Let $\underline{W} = (W, \leq)$ be a $\leq$-structure. A subset $A \subseteq W$ is called a $\leq$-filter in W if it satisfies the following condition

$$(\forall x, y \in W)(x \in A \;\&\; x \leq y \rightarrow y \in A) \;.$$

For $x \in W$ define $[x) = \{y \in W | x \leq y\}$.

Lemma 46. *(i) $[x)$ is the smallest $\leq$-filter in W containing x.*
(ii) A union and intersection of any number of $\leq$-filters is a $\leq$-filter.

Proof. Straightforward. □

Let $S \in \{\Sigma, \sigma\}$ and $\underline{W} = (W, \leq, S)$ be $\leq$ S-structure. A subset $A \subseteq W$ is called an S-filter in W if it is a $\leq$-filter and for any $x, y \in A$ we have xSy.

Lemma 47. *(i) If xSy then $[x) \cup [y)$ is the smallest S-filter containing x and y.*
(ii) Each σ-filter is a Σ-filter.
(iii) Let $\underline{W} = (W, \leq, \Sigma, <, \sigma)$ be a strong positive bi-similarity structure, and A and B be σ-filters in W. Then $A \cap B \neq \emptyset$ implies $A = B$.

Proof. The proof of (i) and (ii) is straightforward. To prove (iii) suppose that A and B are σ-filters and that $A \cap B \neq \emptyset$. Then for some x we have $x \in A$ and $x \in B$. To prove $A = B$ suppose that $y \in A$. Then we have $x\sigma y$ and by S27 $x \leq y$. Since $x \in B$, we obtain that $y \in B$. This shows that $A \subseteq B$. In the same manner we show that $B \subseteq A$. □

Let $\underline{W}$ be a strong positive bi-similarity structure. A set a of subsets of W is called a good set in $\underline{W}$ if the following conditions are satisfied for any $x, y \in W$:

(g1) $x \leq y \rightarrow (\forall A \in a)(x \in A \rightarrow y \in A)$,
(g2) $x\overline{\Sigma}y \rightarrow (\forall A \in a)(x \notin A \;\&\; y \notin A)$,
(g3) not $x < y \rightarrow (\exists A \in a)(x \in A \;\&\; y \notin A)$,
(g4) $x\sigma y \rightarrow (\exists A \in a)(x \in A \;\&\; y \in A)$,
(g5) $(\forall A, B \in a)(A \cap B \neq \emptyset \rightarrow A = B)$.

The set of all good sets in $\underline{W}$ is denoted by V. Note that conditions (g1) and (g2) say that all the elements of a are Σ-filters. The following lemma is important for the proof of theorem 45.

Lemma 48. *(i)* $x \leq y \leftrightarrow (\forall a \in V)(\forall A \in a)(x \in A \rightarrow y \in A)$,
(ii) $x\Sigma y \leftrightarrow (\exists a \in V)(\exists A \in a)(x \in A \,\&\, y \in A)$,
(iii) $x < y \leftrightarrow (\exists a \in V)(\forall A \in a)(x \in A \rightarrow y \in A)$,
(iv) $x\sigma y \leftrightarrow (\forall a \in V)(\exists A \in a)(x \in A \,\&\, y \in A)$.

Proof. (i)($\rightarrow$) Suppose $x \leq y$, $a \in V$, $A \in a$ and $x \in A$. Then by (g1) we obtain that $y \in A$.

($\rightarrow$) Suppose $x \not\leq y$. We shall show that $(\exists a \in V)(\exists A \in a)(x \in A \,\&\, y \notin A)$. We put $A = [x)$ $a_1 = \{A\}, a_2 = \{[u)|u\sigma u \,\&\, u \notin A\}$ and $a = a_1 \cup a_2$. Since we have not $x \leq y$, we get $x \in A$ and $y \notin A$, so there exists $A \in a$ such that $x \in A$ and $y \notin A$. By $x \not\leq y$ and S6 we have $x\Sigma x$. Then by lemma 47(i) A is a Σ-filter. By lemma 47(i) all the elements of a are σ-filters and by lemma 8.8.(ii) they are Σ-filters. Consequently, conditions (g1) and (g2) of good sets are fulfilled for a.

For (g3) suppose $u \not< v$ and proceed to show that there exists $B \in a$ such that $u \in B$ and $v \notin B$. From $u \not< v$ by S18 we get $u\sigma u$ and by lemma 47(i) and (ii) that $[u)$ is a Σ filter. We have to consider two cases.

Case 1: $u \notin A$. Then $[u) \in a$ and $u \in [u)$. We shall show that $v \notin [u)$. Suppose that $v \in [u)$. Since $[u)$ is a Σ-filter, then we get $u\Sigma v$ and by S28 $u < v$, contrary to the assumption $u \not< v$. So in this case $B = [u)$.

Case 2: $u \in A$. Suppose $v \in A$. Since A is a Σ-filter, we have $u\Sigma v$ and by S28 we get $u < v$ – a contradiction with the assumption. So $u \notin A$. In this case $B = A$.

For the condition (g4) suppose $u\sigma v$ and proceed to show that there exists $B \in a$ such that $u, v \in B$. From $u\sigma v$ we obtain by S16 $u\sigma u$ and by S27 $u \leq v$. So $u, v \in [u)$. We have to consider two cases.

Case 1: $u \notin A$. Then $[u) \in a_2$. In this case $B = [u)$.

Case 2: $u \in A$. Then by $u \leq v$ we obtain that $v \in A$. In this case $B = A$.

For (g5) suppose $B, C \in a$, $B \cap C \neq \emptyset$ and proceed to show that $B = C$. We shall consider several cases.

Case 1: $B, C \in a_2$. Since all the elements of a are σ-filters, the assertion follows from lemma 47(iii).

Case 2: $B, C \in a_1$. Then obviously $B = C$.

Case 3: $B \in a_1$, $C \in a_2$. Then $B = [x)$ and $C = [u)$ with $u\sigma u$ and $x \not\leq u$. From $B \cap C \neq \emptyset$ we obtain that for some y: $y \in [x)$ and $y \in [u)$. Since $[u)$ is a σ-filter, we get $y\sigma u$ and by S27 $y \leq u$. Then we obtain $u \in [x)$, so $x \leq u$ – a contradiction. This contradiction shows that the case is impossible. This completes the proof that $a \in V$ and the proof of (i).

(ii)($\rightarrow$) Suppose $x\Sigma y$ and proceed to show that $(\exists a \in V)(\exists A \in a)(x \in A \,\&\, y \in A)$. We put $A = [x) \cup [y)$, $a_1 = \{A\}$, $a_2 = \{[u)|u\sigma u \,\&\, u \notin A\}$ and $a = a_1 \cup a_2$. Hence there exists $A \in a$ such that $x, y \in A$. As in the above case we can show that all the elements of a are Σ-filters, so conditions (g1) and (g2) of a good set are fulfilled.

To verify (g3) suppose $u \not< v$ and proceed to show that there exists $B \in a$ such that $u \in B$ and $v \notin B$. From $u \not< v$ we get by S18 $u\sigma u$, so $[u)$ is a σ-filter. We have to consider two cases.

Case 1: $u \notin A$. Then $[u) \in a_2$. We shall show that $v \notin [u)$. Suppose that $v \in [u)$, then we get $u \leq v$ and hence $u < v$ – a contradiction with the assumption. So $v \notin [u)$. In this case $B = [u)$.

Case 2: $u \in A$. We shall show that $v \notin A$. Suppose that $v \in A$. Since A is a Σ-filter, we obtain $u\Sigma v$ and by S28 we get $u < v$ – a contradiction with the assumption. So $v \notin A$. In this case $B = A$.

For (g4) suppose $u\sigma v$ and proceed to show that there exists $B \in a$ such that $u, v \in B$. From $u\sigma v$ we obtain by S16 $u\sigma u$, so $[u)$ is a σ-filter. We have to consider two cases.

Case 1: $u \notin A$. Then $[u) \in a_2$. By S27 we have $u \leq v$ and from here we get $u, v \in [u)$. In this case $B = [u)$.

Case 2: $u \in A$. By $u \leq v$ we obtain that $v \in A$. In this case $B = A$.

For (g5) suppose $B, C \in a$ and $B \cap C \neq \emptyset$. As in (i)($\leftarrow$) we can conclude that $B = C$. This completes the proof that $a \in V$.

($\leftarrow$) We have to show that $x\Sigma y \rightarrow (\forall a \in V)(\forall A \in a)(x \notin A$ or $y \notin A)$. This follows directly from (g2). This completes the proof of (ii).

(iii)($\rightarrow$) Suppose $x < y$ and proceed to show that $(\exists a \in V)(\forall A \in a)(x \in A \rightarrow y \in A)$. We shall consider two cases.

Case 1: $x\Sigma y$. In this case we put $a_1 = \{[x) \cup [y)\}$, $a_2 = \{[u) | u\sigma u \ \&\ u \notin [x) \cup [y)\}$ and $a = a_1 \cup a_2$. We shall show that $(\forall A \in a)(x \notin A$ or $y \in A)$. For $A \in a_1$ this is obvious. Suppose $A \in a_2$, $x \in A$ and $y \notin A$. Then $A = [u)$ for some $u\sigma u$ and $u \notin [x) \cup [y)$, $x \in [u)$ and $y \notin [u)$. From $u\sigma u$ we obtain that $[u)$ is a σ-filter, containing u. From $x, u \in [u)$ we obtain $x\sigma u$ and by S27 $x \leq u$, so $u \in [x) \cup [y)$ – a contradiction. As in (ii) we can show that $a \in V$.

Case 2: $x\overline{\Sigma}y$. We shall show that for any $u \in W$: if $u\sigma u$ then $u \not\leq x$. Suppose that for some $u \in W$ we have $u\sigma u$ and $u \leq x$. From here we obtain $x\sigma x$. Since we have $x < y$ then by S19 we get $x\Sigma y$, contrary to the assumption $x\overline{\Sigma}y$. In this case we put $a = \{[u) | u\sigma u\}$ and by the above property we have that for any $A \in a$ we have that $x \notin A$. The proof that $a \in V$ is easy.

($\leftarrow$) Suppose $x \not< y$. Then by (g3) $(\forall a \in V)(\exists A \in a)(x \in A \ \&\ y \notin A)$ which have to be proved.

(iv)($\rightarrow$) Suppose $x\sigma y$, $a \in V$. Then by (g4) $(\exists A \in a)(x \in A \ \&\ y \in A)$.

($\leftarrow$) Let $x\overline{\sigma}y$ and proceed to show that $(\exists a \in V)(\forall A \in a)(x \notin A$ or $y \notin A)$. Put $a = \{[x) | x\sigma x\}$. Then all the elements of a are σ-filters, so if $x, y \in A \in a$ then $x\sigma y$, contrary to the assumption. Thus, for any $A \in a$, either $x \notin A$ or $y \notin A$. The proof that $a \in V$ can be given as in the above statements. This completes the proof of the lemma.

□

Proof of theorem 45. Let $\underline{W} = (W, \leq, \Sigma, <, \sigma)$ be a strong positive bi-similarity structure. Let V be the set of all good sets of $\underline{W}$ and let S be the A-system over the pair (W, V). By lemma 2(iii) S is a single-valued A-system and by theorem 32 and lemma 48 we have $x \leq y$ iff $x \leq_S y$, $x\Sigma y$ iff $x\Sigma_S y$, $x < y$ iff $x <_S y$, $x\sigma y$ iff $x\sigma_S y$, which completes the proof. □

3.5 Informational Relations in Attribute Systems

In this section we will generalize the definitions of the similarity relations in A-systems in order to obtain a more general notion of informational relations in A-systems.

Let S be an A-system. Then for each attribute $a \in At_S$ the system $S_a = (Ob_S, Val_S(a), f_S^a)$ is a P-system, where f_S^a is a function from Ob_S to the set $P(Val_S(a))$ defined as $f_S^a(x) = f_S(x, a)$. Then the relation Σ_a in S_a has the following definition:

$x\Sigma_a y$ iff $f_S^a(x) \cap f_S^a(y) \neq \emptyset$ iff $f_S(x,a) \cap f_S(y,a) \neq \emptyset$.

Now the relations Σ_S and σ_S can be defined as follows: $x\Sigma_S y$ iff $(\exists a \in At_S) f_S(x,a) \cap f_S(y,a) \neq \emptyset$ iff $(\exists a \in At_S) x\Sigma_a y$, so $\Sigma_S = \bigcup\{\Sigma_a | a \in At_S\}$ $x\sigma_S y$ iff $(\forall a \in At_S) f_S(x,a) \cap f_S(y,a) \neq \emptyset$ iff $(\forall a \in At_S) x\Sigma_S y$, so $\Sigma_S = \bigcap\{\Sigma_a | a \in At_S\}$

This analysis suggests the following definition. Let R be a type of informational relation in P-systems (like Σ) and let S be an A-system. Denote by R_a the informational relation in each P-system S_a for $a \in At_S$. Then the relations $\bigcup\{R_a | a \in At_S\}$ and $\bigcap\{R_a | a \in At_S\}$ are called weak informational relation in S of type R and strong informational relation S of type R, respectively.

The general study of informational relations in A-systems is an open area, which is out of the scope of this paper. Let us note that the theory developed in the paper is suitable for studying only the similarity relations in A systems. We include this material to show the role of the similarity relations in the family of all informational relations in A-systems.

4 Modal Logics for Similarity Relations in Information Systems

In this section we introduce modal logics for similarity relations in P-systems and A-systems. The aim of these logics is to provide a formal account for reasoning about objects in an information system, including different modalities corresponding to some similarity relations and other kinds of informational relations. The first systems of this type have been introduced by Orlowska and Pawlak in [OP1] and [OP2]. Later this line of investigations was continued by Orlowska [Or1], [Or2], [Or3], [Or6], Farinas and Orlowska [FCO1], Vakarelov [Va1], [Va2], [Va4], [Va5] and [Va6].

The main results in the section 4 are some completeness theorems for the introduced modal logics with respect to their standard semantics. The proofs of these completeness theorems are essentially based on the characterization theorems proved in section 3. Another kind of results are the completeness theorems with respect to the finite models of the considered systems, which yield their decidability. Let us mention also the discussion in sec. 4.1 of the possibility to give a "query" meaning of the considered modal languages, in which atomic formulas can be considered as simple queries and compound formulas as compound queries. Then modal formulas form a special kind of queries, which can be named as "modal queries".

The structure of section 4 is the following. In sec. 4.1 we introduce the logic SIM-1 and some related subsystems, connected with P-systems. Section 4.2 is devoted to the logic SIM-2, connected with A-systems. In sec. 4.3 we consider some logics interpreted in single-valued A-systems. In sec. 4.4 we briefly discuss some results about modal logics for information systems, containing some new modalities as for instance the modalities $[\equiv]$ and $[\cong]$ for the strong and weak indiscernibility relations in A-systems, studied by the author in some previous papers. Let us note here that the joint axiomatization of the modalities $[\leq]$ and $[\equiv]$ presents some difficulties, due to the fact that the equivalence $x \equiv y$ iff $x \leq y$ & $y \leq x$ is not modally definable. To overcome this difficulty, a new technics has been developed, called a "copying method", applied since then in many other similar situations ([Va2, Va3, Va4, Va7]).

4.1 SIM-1 – a Modal Logic for Similarity Relations in Property Systems

In this section we will introduce a modal logic, called SIM-1, with standard interpretation in similarity structures. This logic is a slight generalization of the logic Sim, introduced in [Va6]. The main difference is that Sim is interpreted in similarity structures over non-trivial P-systems, while SIM-1 is interpreted in similarity structures over arbitrary P-systems. The logic SIM-1 can be used to reason about similarity relations between data determined in terms of properties. The language of SIM-1 with a given interpretation can be used also as a query language in which special modal queries can be expressed. We shall discuss this in more details after giving the semantics of SIM-1.

Syntax of SIM-1 The language of SIM-1 contains the following primitive symbols:

- VAR - an infinite set, whose elements are called propositional variables,
- $\wedge, \vee, \neg$ – the classical Boolean connectives,
- $[\leq], [\geq][\Sigma], [N], [U]$ – modal operations,
- () - parentheses.

The notion of formula is the usual one, namely:

- all propositional variables are formulas,
- if A and B are formulas then $\neg A$, $(A \wedge B)$ and $(A \vee B)$ are formulas,
- if A is a formula then $[R]A$ is a formula, $R \in \{\leq, \geq, \Sigma, N, U\}$.
- Abbreviations: $A \Rightarrow B = \neg A \vee B$, $1 = \neg A \vee A$, $0 = \neg 1$, $\langle R \rangle = \neg[R]\neg$, $R \in \{\leq, \geq, \Sigma, N, U\}$.

Semantics of SIM-1 We interpret the language of SIM-1 in a similarity structures as in the usual Kripke semantics. Let $\underline{W} = (W, \Sigma, N, \leq)$ be a similarity structure, for $x, y \in W$ we put $x \geq y$ iff $y \leq x$. A function $v : VAR \rightarrow P(W)$ is called a valuation if it assigns to each variable A a subset $V(A) \subseteq W$. Then the pair $M = (\underline{W}, v)$ is called a model over $\underline{W}$. The satisfiability relation $x \| \!-_v A$ (the formula A is true in a point $x \in W$ at the valuation v) is defined inductively:

- $x\|\!-_v A$ iff $x \in v(A)$ for $a \in VAR$,
- $x\|\!-_v \neg A$ iff $xN\|\!\not-_v A$,
- $x\|\!-_v A \wedge B$ iff $x\|\!-_v A$ and $x\|\!-_v B$,
- $x\|\!-_v A \vee B$ iff $x\|\!-_v A$ or $x\|\!-_v B$,
- $x\|\!-_v [R]A$ iff $(\forall y \in W)(xRy \rightarrow y\|\!-_v A)$ for $R \in \{\Sigma, N, \leq, \geq\}$,
- $x\|\!-_v [U]A$ iff $(\forall y \in W)y\|\!-_v A$.

Using the definition of $\langle R\rangle$ we obtain the following interpretation of $\langle R\rangle A$ and $\langle U\rangle A$:

- $x\|\!-_v \langle R\rangle A$ iff $(\exists y \in W)(xRy$ and $y\|\!-_v A)$,
- $x\|\!-_v \langle U\rangle A$ iff $(\exists y \in A)(y\|\!-_v A)$.

We say that a formula A is true in a similarity structure $\underline{W}$ if for any valuation v and $x \in W$ we have $x\|\!-_v A$.

Let S be a P-system, $\underline{W}$ be the similarity structure over S and $M = (\underline{W}, v)$ be a model over $\underline{W}$. For any formula A we put $v(A) = \{x \in W | x\|\!-_v A\}$. The set $v(A)$ may have different meanings. One of them is that it is the set of all the objects from $W = Ob_S$ for which A is true (at v). Another meaning is that $v(A)$ may be considered also as a query to S: "give the set of these objects $x \in Ob_S$, for which A is true". This meaning leads to an interpretation of propositional variables in a given model as simple queries and formulas as compound queries. Consequently, modal formulas will be "modal queries". Let us consider the following example. Suppose that in the above model M A is a propositional variable such that $v(A) = \{x_0\}$. Then for $v(\langle\Sigma\rangle A)$ we can compute: $v(\langle\Sigma\rangle A) = \{x \in Ob_0 | (\exists y \in Ob_S)(x\Sigma y$ and $y \in \{x_0\}) = \{x \in Ob_S | x\Sigma x_0\}$. This is the following query to S: "give those objects of S which are positively similar to x_0".

This informational meaning of models of SIM-1 can be given to the models of all logics considered in the paper, so we will not discuss it any more.

Axiomatization of SIM-1

Axiom schemes:

(Bool) All Boolean tautologies,
(K) $[R](A \Rightarrow B) \Rightarrow ([R]A \Rightarrow [R]B)$, for $R \in \{\Sigma, N, \leq, \geq, U\}$
A0 $\langle\leq\rangle[\geq]A \Rightarrow A, \langle\geq\rangle[\leq]A \Rightarrow A, [U]A \Rightarrow A, \langle U\rangle[U]A \Rightarrow A, [U]A \Rightarrow [U][U]A,$
$[U]A \Rightarrow [R]A$, for $R \in \{\leq, \geq, \Sigma, N\}$,
A1 $[\leq]A \Rightarrow A$,
A2 $[\leq]A \Rightarrow [\leq][\leq]A$,
A3 $\langle\Sigma\rangle[\Sigma]A \Rightarrow A$,
A4 $\langle\Sigma\rangle 1 \Rightarrow ([\Sigma]A \Rightarrow A)$,
A5 $[\Sigma]A \Rightarrow [\Sigma][\leq]A$,
A6 $[\leq]A \Rightarrow ([U]B \vee ([\Sigma_S]B \Rightarrow B))$,

A7 $\langle N\rangle[N]A \Rightarrow A$,
A8 $\langle N\rangle 1 \Rightarrow ([N]A \Rightarrow A)$,
A9 $[N]A \Rightarrow [N][\geq]A$,
A10 $[\geq]A \Rightarrow ([U]A \vee ([N]B \Rightarrow B))$,
A11 $[\leq]A \wedge [\Sigma]B \Rightarrow ([U]B \vee [U]([N]B \Rightarrow A))$,

Rules of inference:

- modus ponens (MP) $A, A \Rightarrow B/B$,
- necessitation (N) $A/[R]A$, for $R \in \{\Sigma, N, \leq, \geq, U\}$

The logic SIM-1 is the smallest set of formulas, containing all the axiom schemes and closed under the rules of inference. A formula A is a theorem of SIM-1 if there exists a finite sequence of formulas $A_1, \ldots, A_n = A$ such that for each $i = 1, \ldots, n$ the formula A_i is either an axiom of SIM-1, or can be obtained from one or two formulas with smaller indices by one of the rules of inference.

Let us note that using the standard modal definability theory (see [Be1]) the axioms in $A0$ say that $\geq$ is the converse relation of $\leq$ and that U is an equivalence relation, containing the relations $\Sigma, N, \leq$ and $\geq$. In our semantics we have taken U to be the universal relation $W \times W$, which gives the names of $[U]$ and $\langle U\rangle$ as universal modalities. The axioms A1-A11 are modal translations of the conditions S1-S11. Let us note that we need to introduce the universal modality to be able to find modal translations of S6, S10 and S11. We introduce the modality $[\geq]$ in order to obtain the following duality: $[\Sigma] - [N]$, $[\leq] - [\geq]$ and $[U] - [U]$.

Theorem 49. (Completeness theorem for SIM-1) *For any formula A of SIM-1 the following conditions are equivalent:*

(i) A is a theorem of SIM-1,
(ii) A is true in all similarity structures,
(iii) A is true in all similarity structures over P-systems.

Proof. (i)$\rightarrow$(ii) in a standard way by showing the validity of all the axioms and that the rules preserve validity.

(ii)$\leftrightarrow$(iii) – by theorem 23.

(ii)$\rightarrow$(i) The proof can be obtained by the standard canonical model construction (for the relevant definitions and facts see [HC1] or [Se1]).

Let W be the set of all the maximal consistent sets of SIM-1. Define for $x, y \in W$ and $R \in \{\Sigma, N, \leq, \geq, U\}$, $[R]x = \{A \in FOR | [R]A \in x\}$, xRy iff $[R]x \subseteq y$. It is easy to show by $A0$ that U is an equivalence relation containing $\Sigma, N, \leq, \geq$. For $a \in W$ let $W_a = \{x | aUx\}$ and $\Sigma_a, N_a, \leq_a, \geq_a$ and U_a be the restrictions of $\Sigma, N, \leq$ and $\geq$ in the set W_a. Since U is an equivalence relation, U_a is the universal relation in W_a. Then, using the axioms of SIM-1, one can prove in a standard way the following

Lemma 50. *For any $a \in W$ the system $\underline{W_a} = (W_a, \Sigma_a, N_a, \leq_a, \geq_a)$ is a similarity structure.*

Now, suppose that A is not a theorem of SIM-1. Then there exists a maximal consistent set $a \in W$ such that $A \notin a$. Take the canonical valuation $v(p) = \{x \in W_a | p \in x\}$, $p \in VAR$. Then in a standard way one can prove by induction on the construction of B that for any $x \in W_a : x \Vdash_v B$ iff $B \in x$. From here we get $a \not\Vdash_v A$, so A is not true in the similarity structure W_a, which completes the proof of the theorem.

□

Now we shall prove by means of the filtration method (see [Sel]) that SIM-1 possesses finite model property in a sense that each non-theorem of SIM-1 can be falsified in a finite model. First, we shall formulate some basic definitions and facts about filtration, adapted to the logic SIM-1.

Let Γ be a finite set of formulas, closed under subformulas and $M = ((W, \leq, \Sigma, N)v)$ be a model over some similarity structure $\underline{W}$. Define an equivalence relation $\sim$ in W in the following way:

$$x \sim y \text{ iff } (\forall A \in \Gamma)(x \Vdash_v A \leftrightarrow y \Vdash_v A) \ .$$

Let for $x \in W$ $|x| = \{y \in W | x \sim y\}$, $|W| = \{|x| | x \in W\}$ and

$$v'(p) = \{|x| | x \in v(p)\} \text{ for } p \in VAR \ .$$

We say that the model $M' = ((|W|, \leq', \Sigma', N'), v')$ is a filtration of M through Γ if M' is a model over similarity structure and the following conditions are satisfied for any $x, y \in W$ and $R \in \{\Sigma, N, \leq, \geq, U\}$:

(FR1) If xRy then $|x|R'|y|$,
(FR2) If $|x|R'|y|$ then $(A[R]A \in \Gamma)(x \Vdash_v A \to y \Vdash_v A)$.

Lemma 51. (Filtration lemma)

(i) The following is true for any formula $A \in \Gamma$ and $x \in W$: $x \Vdash_v A$ iff $|x| \Vdash_{v'} A$.
(ii) The set $|W|$ has at most 2^n elements, where n is the number of the elements of Γ.

Proof. The proof of (i) is the same as in the standard modal logic (see [Sel]) and can be done by induction on the complexity of A. Conditions (FR1) and (FR2) are used when A is of the form $[R]B$.

For (ii) let f be a function from $|W|$ to the set $P(\Gamma)$ of all subsets of Γ defined as follows: $f(|x|) = \{B \in \Gamma | x \Vdash_v B\}$. It is easy to see that f is 1-1-function from $|W|$ into $P(\Gamma)$. Since $P(\Gamma)$ has 2^n elements then $|W|$ has no more than 2^n elements. □

Theorem 52. (Filtration of SIM-1) *For any model $M = ((W, \leq, \Sigma, N), v)$ over a similarity structure $\underline{W}$ and formula A' there exist a finite set Γ of formulas, containing A' and closed under subformulas and a filtration $M' = ((|W|, \leq', \Sigma', N'), v')$ of M through Γ.*

Proof. Let A' be a given formula and define Γ to be the smallest set of formulas, containing A', $\langle\Sigma\rangle 1$, $\langle N\rangle 1$, closed under subformulas and satisfying the following closure condition

(γ) For any formula A, if one of the formulas $[\Sigma]A$, $[N]A$, $[\leq]A$, $[\geq]A$ is in Γ, then the others are also in Γ.

Obviously Γ is a finite set of formulas. Define $|W|$ and v' as in the definition of filtration and the relations $\Sigma', N', \leq'$ and $\geq'$ as follows:

(1) $|x| \leq' |y|$ iff $(\forall[\leq]A \in \Gamma)$
$(x\|\!-_v [\leq]A \to y\|\!-_v [\leq]A)$ & $(y\|\!-_v [\geq]A \to x\|\!-_v [\geq]A)$ &
$(y\|\!-_v [\Sigma]A \to x\|\!-_v [\Sigma]A)$ & $(x\|\!-_v [N]A \to y\|\!-_v [N]A)$ &
$(x\|\!-_v \langle\Sigma\rangle 1 \to y\|\!-_v \langle\Sigma\rangle 1)$ & $(y\|\!-_v \langle N\rangle 1 \to x\|\!-_v \langle N\rangle 1)$,

(2) $|x| \geq' |y|$ iff $|y| \leq' |x|$,

(3) $|x|\Sigma'|y|$ iff $(\forall[\Sigma]A \in \Gamma)$
$(x\|\!-_v [\Sigma]A \to y\|\!-_v [\leq]A)$ & $(y\|\!-_v [\Sigma]A \to x\|\!-_v [\leq]A)$ &
$x\|\!-_v \langle\Sigma\rangle 1$ & $y\|\!-_v \langle\Sigma\rangle 1$,

(4) $|x|N'|y|$ iff $(\forall[N]A \in \Gamma)$
$(x\|\!-_v [N]A \to y\|\!-_v [\geq]A)$ & $(y\|\!-_v [N]A \to x\|\!-_v [\geq]A)$ &
$x\|\!-_v \langle N\rangle 1$ & $y\|\!-_v \langle N\rangle 1$.

□

The proof that the model $M' = (|W|, \Sigma', N', \leq', \geq', v')$ is a filtration of M through Γ follows from the following lemmas.

Lemma 53. *(i) If $x \leq y$ then $|x| \leq' |y|$,*
(ii) If $|x| \leq' |y|$ then $(\forall[\leq]A \in \Gamma)(x\|\!-_v [\leq]A \to y\|\!-_v A)$,
(iii) S1 and S2 are satisfied.

Proof. (i) The proof follows from the following implications:
- $x \leq y$ & $x\|\!-_v [\leq]A$ & $y \leq z \to z\|\!-_v A$,
- $x \leq y$ & $y\|\!-_v [\geq]A$ & $x \geq z \to z\|\!-_v A$,
- $x \leq y$ & $x\|\!-_v [N]A$ & $yNz \to z\|\!-_v A$,
- $x \leq y$ & $y\|\!-_v [\Sigma]A$ & $x\Sigma z \to z\|\!-_v A$,
- $x \leq y$ & $x\|\!-_v \langle\Sigma\rangle 1 \to y\|\!-_v \langle\Sigma\rangle 1$,
- $x \leq y$ & $y\|\!-_v \langle N\rangle 1 \to x\|\!-_v \langle N\rangle 1$.

(ii) Suppose $|x| \leq' |y|$, $[\leq]A \in \Gamma$ and $x\|\!-_v [\leq]A$. Then by (1) we get $y\|\!-_v [\leq]A$ and since $y \leq y$ we obtain $y\|\!-_v A$.

(iii) Conditions S1 and S2 follow directly from (1).

□

Lemma 54. *(i) If $x \geq y$ then $|x| \geq' |y|$,*
(ii) If $|x| \geq' |y|$ then $(\forall[\geq]A \in \Gamma)(x\|\!-_v [\geq]A \to y\|\!-_v A)$.

Proof. (i) Suppose $x \geq y$. Then we have $y \leq x$ and by lemma 53(i) we obtain $|y| \leq' |x|$. By (2) we have $|x| \geq' |y|$.

(ii) Suppose $|x| \geq' |y|$, $[\geq]A \in \Gamma$ and $x \Vdash_v [\geq]A$. Then by (γ) we have $[\leq]A \in \Gamma$ and by (2) $|y| \leq' |x|$. Thus by (1) we get $y \Vdash_v [\geq]A$ and by $y \geq y$ we obtained $y \Vdash_v A$.

□

Lemma 55. *(i) If $x\Sigma y$ then $|x|\Sigma'|y|$,*
(ii) If $|x|\Sigma'|y|$ then $(\forall[\Sigma]A \in \Gamma)(x \Vdash_v [\Sigma]A \to y \Vdash_v A)$,
(iii) Conditions S3-S6 are satisfied.

Proof. (i) The proof follows from the following implications:

- $x\Sigma y \;\&\; y \leq z \;\&\; x \Vdash_v [\Sigma]A \to z \Vdash_v A$,
- $x\Sigma y \;\&\; x \leq z \;\&\; y \Vdash_v [\Sigma]A \to z \Vdash_v A$,
- $x\Sigma y \to x \Vdash_v \langle\Sigma\rangle 1 \;\&\; y \Vdash_v \langle\Sigma\rangle 1$.

(ii) Suppose $|x|\Sigma'|y|$, $[\Sigma]A \in \Gamma$ and $x \Vdash_v [\Sigma]A$. By (3) we get $y \Vdash_v [\leq]A$ and by $y \leq y$ we obtain $y \Vdash_v A$.

(iii) To prove S3 suppose $|x|\Sigma'|y|$. Then by (3) we obviously have $|y|\Sigma'|x|$.
For S4 suppose $|x|\Sigma'|y|$ and proceed to show $|x|\Sigma'|x|$. By (3) this means that: $(\forall[\Sigma]A \in \Gamma)(x \Vdash_v [\Sigma]A \to x \Vdash_v [\leq]A) \;\&\; x \Vdash_v \langle\Sigma\rangle 1$.
First, from $|x|\Sigma'|y|$ we get $x \Vdash_v \langle\Sigma\rangle 1$, so $\exists z$ such that $x\Sigma z$ and by S3 – $x\Sigma x$.
Suppose $[\Sigma]A \in \Gamma, x \Vdash_v [\Sigma]A$ and $x \leq z$. Then by $x\Sigma x$ and S5 we obtain $x\Sigma z$ and, consequently, $x \Vdash_v A$, which has to be proved.
In a similar way we can verify S5.
For S6 suppose $|x|\Sigma'|x|$ and proceed to show $|x| \leq' |y|$. We shall consider two cases.
Case 1: $x \leq y$. Then by lemma 53(i) we obtain $|x| \leq' |y|$.
Case 2: $x \not\leq y$. Then by S6 we get $x\Sigma x$ and by lemma 53(i) we obtain $|x|\Sigma'|x|$ – a contradiction. This completes the proof of the lemma.

□

Lemma 56. *(i) If xNy then $|x|N'|y|$,*
(ii) If $|x|N'|y|$ then $(\forall[N]A \in \Gamma)(x \Vdash_v [N]A \to y \Vdash_v A)$,
(iii) Conditions S7-S11 are true.

The proof of this lemma is similar to the proof of lemma 55.

Theorem 57. (Finite completeness theorem for SIM-1) *The following conditions are equivalent for any formula A of SIM-1:*

(i) A is a theorem of SIM-1,
(ii) A is true in all finite similarity structures.

Proof. (i)→(ii) is obvious.
(ii)→(i) . Suppose A is not a theorem of *Sim*. Then by the completeness theorem of *Sim* there exist a similarity structure $\underline{W}$, a valuation v in $\underline{W}$ and $x \in W$ such that $x \not\Vdash_v A$. By theorem 52 there exist a finite set Γ, containing A and closed under sub formulas, and a filtration $M' = ((|W|, \leq', \Sigma', N'), v')$ of the model $M = (\underline{W}, v)$ through Γ. Then by the filtration lemma $|W|$ is

a finite set and $|x|||\not\vDash_v A$. So A is not true in the finite similarity structure $(|W|, \leq', \Sigma', N')$. This completes the proof of theorem.

□

Corollary 58. *The logic SIM-1 possesses the finite model property and is decidable.*

In section 3.1 we introduced the notion of ρ-structure for $\rho \subseteq \{\leq, \Sigma, N\}$. Let ρ be given. We can axiomatize the modal logic SIM-1(ρ) of ρ-structures in the following way. The language $L\rho$ of this logic is a restriction of the language of SIM-1 obtained by deleting the modal operations which do not correspond to the relations of ρ. The axioms of SIM-1(ρ) can be obtained as follows. First, add to the axioms of SIM-1 the following two axioms which correspond to the conditions $\Sigma N1$ and $\Sigma N2$ from lemma 5.5:

- $(A\Sigma N1)([\Sigma]A \Rightarrow [\Sigma]\neg[\Sigma]B) \vee [U]B \vee [U]([N]B \Rightarrow A)$,
- $(A\Sigma N2)([N]A \Rightarrow [N]\neg[N]B) \vee [U]B \vee [U]([\Sigma]B \Rightarrow A)$.

Then take from the axioms of SIM-1 only those axioms and rules of inference which contain modalities from $L\rho$. Then we can prove the following theorem.

Theorem 59. (Completeness theorem for SIM-1(ρ)) *Let $\rho \subseteq \{\leq, \Sigma, N\}$ be given. Then the following conditions are true for any formula A of $L\rho$:*

(i) A is a theorem of SIM-1(ρ),
(ii) A is true in any ρ-structure,
(iii) A is true in any ρ structure over a P-system,
(iv) A is true in any finite ρ-structure.

Proof. The proof of this theorem is similar to the proof of theorem 49 with combination with theorem 52. The equivalence (ii)↔(iii) follows from lemma 25. We left the details to the reader. □

Let us note that the logic SIM-1($\leq$) is the well-known logic S4. So we have the following

Corollary 60. *The modal logic S4 is complete in the class of all $\leq$-structures over P-systems.*

This corollary presents an informational semantics for S4.
As a corollary of lemma 25 we have

Corollary 61. *Let us add to the logic SIM-1 the formulas $(A\Sigma N1)$ and $(A\Sigma N2)$ as new axioms. Then the logic SIM-1 is a conservative extension of the logic SIM-1(ρ) for any $\rho \subseteq \{\leq, \Sigma, N\}$.*

4.2 SIM-2 – a Modal Logic for Similarity Relations in Attribute Systems

In this section we shall introduce a new modal logic, denoted by SIM-2, connected with A-systems.

The language of SIM-2 is an extension of the language of SIM-1 by new modalities, denoted by $[<]$, $[>]$, $[\sigma]$, $[\nu]$. These modalities correspond to the relations $<, >$ – the converse of $<, \sigma$ and ν in A-systems.

The standard semantics of SIM-2 is a Kripke semantics of the language of SIM-2 in the class of bi-similarity structures.

Now we shall give an axiomatic system of SIM-2.

Axiomatization of SIM-2

Axiom schemes:

(Bool) All Boolean tautologies,
(K) $[R](A \Rightarrow B) \Rightarrow ([R]A \Rightarrow [R]B)$, for $R \in \{\leq, \geq, \Sigma, N, <, >, \sigma, \nu, U\}$
A0-A11 of SIM-1,
A0' $\langle<\rangle[>]A \Rightarrow A$, $\langle>\rangle[<]A \Rightarrow A$, $[U]A \Rightarrow [R]A$, for $R \in \{<, >, \sigma, \nu\}$
A12 $[<]A \Rightarrow A$,
A13 $[<]A \Rightarrow [\leq][<]A$,
A14 $[<]A \Rightarrow [<][\leq]$,
A15 $\langle\sigma\rangle[\sigma]A \Rightarrow A$,
A16 $\langle\sigma\rangle 1 \Rightarrow ([\sigma]A \Rightarrow A)$,
A17 $[\sigma]A \Rightarrow [\sigma][\leq]A$,
A18 $[<]A \Rightarrow ([U]A \vee ([\sigma]B \Rightarrow B))$,
A19 $[\sigma]A \Rightarrow [\sigma][<]A$,
A20 $[<]A \wedge [\sigma]B \Rightarrow ([U]B \vee [U]([N]B \Rightarrow A))$,
A21 $\langle\nu\rangle[\nu]A \Rightarrow A$,
A22 $\langle\nu\rangle 1 \Rightarrow ([\nu]A \Rightarrow A)$,
A23 $[\nu]A \Rightarrow [\nu][\geq]A$,
A24 $[>]A \Rightarrow ([U]A \vee ([\nu]B \Rightarrow B))$,
A25 $[N]A \Rightarrow [\nu][>]A$,
A26 $[<]A \wedge [\Sigma]B \Rightarrow ([U]B \vee [U]([\nu]B \Rightarrow A))]$.

Rules of inference:

- (MP) $A, A \Rightarrow B/B$,
- (N) $A/[R]A$, for $R \in \{\leq, \geq, \Sigma, N, <, >, \sigma, \nu, U\}$.

The logic SIM-2 is the smallest set of formulas, containing all the axiom schemes and closed under the rules of inference.

Let us note that the axioms A1-A26 are modal translations of the conditions S1-S26. Obviously SIM-2 is an extension of SIM-1.

Theorem 62. (Completeness theorem for SIM-2) *For any formula A of SIM-2 the following conditions are equivalent:*

(i) A is a theorem of SIM-2,
(ii) A is true in all bi-similarity structures,
(iii) A is true in all bi-similarity structures over A-systems.

Proof. (i)→(ii) in the standard way by showing the validity of the axioms and that the rules preserve validity.
(ii)↔(iii) – by theorem 37.
(ii)→(i) The proof can be obtained by the standard canonical model construction as in theorem 49.

□

Theorem 63. *The logic SIM-2 is a conservative extension of SIM-1.*

Proof. We have to prove the following: for any formula A in the language of SIM-1, if A is a theorem of SIM-2 then A is a theorem of SIM-1.

Let A be a formula in the language of SIM-1. Suppose that A is a theorem of SIM-2 but not of SIM-1. Then, by the completeness theorem for SIM-1, there exists a similarity structure $\underline{W} = (W, \leq, \Sigma, N)$ in which A is not true. Define in W $<=\leq, \sigma = \Sigma$ and $\nu = N$. It can be easily verified that the system $\underline{W}' = (W, \leq, \Sigma, N, <, \sigma, \nu)$ is a bi-similarity structure. Hence, since A does not contain $<, \sigma$ and ν, then A is not true in $\underline{W}'$. But by the assumption A is true in $\underline{W}'$ – a contradiction. This completes the theorem. □

Now we shall prove, using the filtration method, that the logic SIM-2 possesses finite model property and that it is decidable.

Theorem 64. (Filtration theorem for SIM-2) *For any model $M = ((W, \leq, \Sigma_S, N, <, \sigma, \nu), v)$ over a similarity structure $\underline{W}$ and formula A' there exist a finite set Γ of formulas, containing A' and closed under subformulas and a filtration $M' = ((|W|, \leq', \Sigma', N', <', \sigma', \nu'), v')$ of M through Γ.*

Proof. Let the model M and the formula A' be given. Let Γ be the smallest set of formulas containing $A', \langle\Sigma\rangle 1, \langle N\rangle 1, \langle\sigma\rangle 1, \langle\nu\rangle 1$, closed under subformulas and satisfying the following closure condition

(γ) For any formula A, if one of the formulas $[\Sigma]A$, $[N]A$, $[\leq]A$, $[\geq]A$, $[\sigma]A$, $[\nu]A$, $[<]A$, $[>]A$ is in Γ, then the remaining formulas are also in Γ.

Obviously, Γ is a finite set of formulas. Define $|W|$ and v' as in the definition of filtration. For $|x|, |y| \in |W|$ define:

(1) $|x| \leq' |y|$ iff $(\forall [\leq]A \in \Gamma)$
$(x||\!-_v [\leq]A \to y||\!-_v [\leq]A)$ & $(y||\!-_v [\geq]A \to x||\!-_v [\geq]A)$ &
$(y||\!-_v [\Sigma]A \to x||\!-_v [\Sigma]A)$ & $(x||\!-_v [N]A \to y||\!-_v [N]A)$ &
$(x||\!-_v [<]A \to y||\!-_v [<]A)$ & $(y||\!-_v [>]A \to x||\!-_v [>]A)$ &
$(y||\!-_v [\sigma]A \to x||\!-_v [\sigma]A)$ & $(x||\!-_v [\nu]A \to y||\!-_v [\nu]A)$ &
$(x||\!-_v \langle\Sigma\rangle 1 \to y||\!-_v \langle\Sigma\rangle 1)$ & $(y||\!-_v \langle N\rangle 1 \to x||\!-_v \langle N\rangle 1)$ &
$(x||\!-_v \langle\sigma\rangle 1 \to y||\!-_v \langle\sigma\rangle 1)$ & $(y||\!-_v \langle\nu\rangle 1 \to y||\!-_v \langle\nu\rangle 1)$,

(2) $|x| \geq' |y|$ iff $|y| \leq' |x|$,

(3) $|x|\Sigma'|y|$ iff $(\forall[\Sigma]A \in \Gamma)$
$(x\|\!-_v [\Sigma]A \to y\|\!-_v [\leq]A)$ & $(y\|\!-_v [\Sigma]A \to x\|\!-_v [\leq]A)$ &
$x\|\!-_v \langle\Sigma\rangle 1$ & $y\|\!-_v \langle\Sigma\rangle 1$,
(4) $|x|N'|y|$ iff $(\forall[N]A \in \Gamma)$
$(x\|\!-_v [N]A \to y\|\!-_v [\geq]A)$ & $(y\|\!-_v [N]A \to x\|\!-_v [\geq]A)$ &
$x\|\!-_v \langle N\rangle 1$ & $y\|\!-_v \langle N\rangle 1$,
(5) $|x| <' |y|$ iff $(\forall[<]A \in \Gamma)$
$(x\|\!-_v [<]A \to y\|\!-_v [\leq]A)$ & $(y\|\!-_v [>]A \to y\|\!-_v [\geq]A)$ &
$(y\|\!-_v [\Sigma]A \to x\|\!-_v [\sigma]A)$ & $(x\|\!-_v [N]A \to y\|\!-_v [\nu]A)$ &
$(x\|\!-_v \langle\sigma\rangle 1 \to y\|\!-_v \langle\Sigma\rangle 1)$ & $(y\|\!-_v \langle\nu\rangle 1 \to x\|\!-_v \langle N\rangle 1)$ &,
(6) $|x| >' |y|$ iff $|y| <' |x|$,
(7) $|x|\sigma'|y|$ iff $(\forall[\sigma]A \in \Gamma)$
$(x\|\!-_v [\sigma]A \to y\|\!-_v [\leq]A)$ & $(y\|\!-_v [\sigma]A \to x\|\!-_v [\leq]A)$ &
$(x\|\!-_v [\Sigma]A \to y\|\!-_v [<]A)$ & $(y\|\!-_v [\Sigma]A \to x\|\!-_v [<]A)$ &
$x\|\!-_v \langle\sigma\rangle 1$ & $y\|\!-_v \langle\sigma\rangle 1$,
(8) $|x|\nu'|y|$ iff $(A[\nu]A \in \Gamma)$
$(x\|\!-_v [\nu]A \to y\|\!-_v [\geq]A)$ & $(y\|\!-_v [\nu]A \to x\|\!-_v [\geq]A)$ &
$(x\|\!-_v [N]A \to y\|\!-_v [>]A)$ & $(y\|\!-_v [N]A \to x\|\!-_v [>]A)$ &
$x\|\!-_v \langle\nu\rangle 1$ & $x\|\!-_v \langle\nu\rangle 1$,

The required model is $M' = ((|W|, \leq', \Sigma', N', <', \sigma', \nu'), v')$. The proof that M' is a filtration of the model M through Γ is similar to the corresponding proof for SIM-1 and therefore is left to the reader. Let us note that the above filtration is an extension of the filtration of SIM-1. □

Let us mention that the filtration theorem of SIM-1 can be obtained as a corollary of theorem 63 and theorem 64.

4.3 Modal Logics for Similarity Relations in Single-Valued Attribute Systems

In this section we shall consider several modal logics that are complete in single-valued A-systems.

The first system is SIM-1. Since the language of SIM-1 is a part of the language of SIM-2 we can interpret SIM-1 also in bi- similarity structures using only the relations $\leq, \Sigma$ and N. We have the following completeness theorem for SIM-1.

Theorem 65. (Completeness theorem of SIM-1 in bi-similarity structures over single-valued A-structures) *The following conditions are equivalent for any formula A of SIM-1:*

(i) A is a theorem of SIM-1,
(ii) A is true in all bi-similarity structures over single-valued A-systems.

Proof. The implication (i)→(ii) is trivial because bi-similarity structures satisfy the conditions S1-S11, which are needed to verify the axioms of SIM-1.

For the converse implication (ii)→(i) we shall proceed by contraposition: supposing that A is not a theorem of SIM-1 we shall show that A is falsified in some bi-similarity structure over a single-valued A system. Now, let A be a non-theorem of SIM-1. By the completeness theorem of SIM-1 A is falsified in some similarity structure $\underline{W} = (W, \leq, \Sigma, N)$. Then by theorem 41 there exists a single-valued A-system S such that $\underline{W}$ is a reduct of the bi-similarity structure over S, which proves the theorem. □

Corollary 66. *Let* $\rho \subseteq \{\leq, \Sigma, N\}$. *Then the following conditions are equivalent for any formula A of the logic SIM-1(*ρ*):*

(i) A is a theorem of SIM-1(ρ*),*
(ii) A is true in all bi-similarity structures over a single-valued A-systems.

Corollary 67. (A completeness theorem for the modal logic S4 in single valued *A*-systems) *The modal logic S4 is complete in the class of all bi-similarity structures over a single-valued A-systems.*

Let $L+$ be a modal language containing only the positive modal operations $[\leq], [\geq], [\Sigma], [<], [>], [\sigma]$ and $[U]$. The standard interpretation of this language will be in the class of all strong positive bi-similarity structures and in the class of all bi-similarity structures over single-valued A-systems. The corresponding logic will be denoted by SIM-2+. The axioms and rules of SIM-2+ are the following:

Axiomatization of SIM-2+

Axioms schemes:

(Bool), (K) and (A0), for $R \in \{\leq, \geq, \Sigma, <, >, \sigma, U\}$,
(A1)-(A6) and (A12)-(A19) from the axioms of SIM-2,
(A27) $[\leq]A \Rightarrow [\sigma]A$,
(A28) $[<]A \Rightarrow [\Sigma]A$.

Rules of inference:

- (MP) $A, A \Rightarrow B/B$,
- (N) $A/[R]A$, for $R \in \{\leq, \geq, \Sigma, <, >, \sigma, U\}$.

Theorem 68. (Completeness theorem for SIM-2+) *The following conditions are equivalent for any formula A of SIM-2+:*

(i) A is a theorem of SIM-2+,
(ii) A is true in all strong positive bi-similarity structures,
(iii) A is true in all bi-similarity structures over single- valued A-systems.

Proof. The equivalence (i)↔(ii) can be proved by the canonical construction as in the corresponding proof of the completeness theorem for SIM-1 (theorem 49). The equivalence (ii)↔(iii) follows from the characterization theorem for strong positive bi-similarity structures (theorem 45). □

Theorem 69. (Filtration theorem for SIM-2+) *For any model* $M = ((W, \leq, \Sigma_S, <, \sigma), v)$ *over a strong bi- similarity structure* $\underline{W}$ *and formula* A' *there exist a finite set* Γ *of formulas, containing* A' *and closed under subformulas and a filtration* $M' = ((|W|, \leq', \Sigma', <', \sigma'), v')$ *of* M *through* Γ.

Proof. Let A' and M be given. Define Γ as in theorem 67. Define $|W|$ and v' as in the definition of filtration. Then for any $|x|, |y| \in |W|$ define:

(1) $|x| \leq' |y|$ iff $(\forall[\leq]A \in \Gamma)$
$(x \Vdash_v [\leq]A \rightarrow y \Vdash_v [\leq]A)$ & $(y \Vdash_v [\geq]A \rightarrow x \Vdash_v [\geq]A)$ &
$(y \Vdash_v [\Sigma]A \rightarrow x \Vdash_v [\Sigma]A)$ & $(x \Vdash_v [<]A \rightarrow y \Vdash_v [<]A)$ &
$(y \Vdash_v [>]A \rightarrow x \Vdash_v [>]A)$ & $(y \Vdash_v [\sigma]A \rightarrow x \Vdash_v [\sigma]A)$ &
$(x \Vdash_v \langle\Sigma\rangle 1 \rightarrow y \Vdash_v \langle\Sigma\rangle 1)$ & $(x \Vdash_v \langle\sigma\rangle 1 \rightarrow y \Vdash_v \langle\sigma\rangle 1)$,
(2) $|x| \geq' |y|$ iff $|y| \leq' |x|$,
(3) $|x| <' |y|$ iff $(\forall[<]A \in \Gamma)$
$(x \Vdash_v [<]A \rightarrow y \Vdash_v [\leq]A)$ & $(y \Vdash_v [>]A \rightarrow y \Vdash_v [\geq]A)$ &
$(y \Vdash_v [\Sigma]A \rightarrow x \Vdash_v [\sigma]A)$ & $(x \Vdash_v \langle\sigma\rangle 1 \rightarrow y \Vdash_v \langle\Sigma\rangle 1)$,
(4) $|x| >' |y|$ iff $|y| <' |x|$,
(5) $|x|\Sigma'|y|$ iff $|x| <' |y|$ & $|x| >' |y|$ & $(\forall[\Sigma]A \in \Gamma)$
$(x \Vdash_v [\Sigma]A \rightarrow y \Vdash_v [\leq]A)$ & $(y \Vdash_v [\Sigma]A \rightarrow x \Vdash_v [\leq]A)$ &
$x \Vdash_v \langle\Sigma\rangle 1$ & $y \Vdash_v \langle\Sigma\rangle 1$,
(6) $|x|\sigma'|y|$ iff $|x| \leq' |y|$ & $|x| \geq' |y|$ & $(\forall[\sigma]A \in \Gamma)$
$(x \Vdash_v [\sigma]A \rightarrow y \Vdash_v [\leq]A)$ & $(y \Vdash_v [\sigma]A \rightarrow x \Vdash_v [\leq]A)$ &
$(x \Vdash_v [\Sigma]A \rightarrow y \Vdash_v [<]A)$ & $(y \Vdash_v [\Sigma]A \rightarrow x \Vdash_v [<]A)$ &
$x \Vdash_v \langle\sigma\rangle 1$ & $y \Vdash_v \langle\sigma\rangle 1$,

The required model is $M' = ((|W|, \leq', \Sigma', <', \sigma'), v')$. The verification that M' is a filtration of the model M through Γ and that $(|W|, \leq', \Sigma', <', \sigma')$ is a strong positive bi-similarity structure is similar to the corresponding proof for SIM-1 (theorem 52). The details are left to the reader. □

4.4 Other Modal Logics for Attribute Systems

In this section we shall briefly describe some other modal logics for A-systems, containing new modalities.

The modal logic S4+5 The modal logic S4+5 was introduced in [Va2]. The logic S4+5 contains two modalities – $[\leq]$ and $[\equiv]$, the latter being interpreted by the indiscernibility relation $\equiv$ in A-systems, which is defined as follows:

$$x \equiv y \text{ iff } x \leq y \text{ and } y \leq x \text{ iff } (\forall a \in At) f(x, a) = f(y, a) \ . \tag{4}$$

The name S4+5 comes from the fact that $[\leq]$ is an S4 modality and $[\equiv]$ is an S5 modality and they are connected by the above condition (4). The main difficulty in the axiomatization of S4+5 is that (4) is not modally definable condition, so it cannot be characterized by any formula in the language of S4+5. Since the informational inclusion $\leq$ is characterized by the first-order conditions of reflexivity and transitivity, the standard structures of S4+5 are relational systems $(W, \leq, \equiv)$, satisfying the following conditions, modally definable with the modal formulas on the right hand side:

C1 $x \leq x$	Ax1 $[\leq]A \Rightarrow A$
C2 $x \leq y \;\&\; y \leq z \rightarrow x \leq z$	Ax2 $[\leq]A \Rightarrow [\leq][\leq]A$
C3 $x \equiv x$	Ax3 $[\equiv]A \Rightarrow A$
C4 $x \equiv y \rightarrow y \equiv x$	Ax4 $\langle\equiv\rangle[\equiv]A \Rightarrow A$
C5 $x \equiv y \;\&\; y \equiv z \rightarrow x \equiv z$	Ax5 $[\equiv]A \Rightarrow [\equiv][\equiv]A$
C6 $x \equiv y \rightarrow x \leq y$	Ax6 $[\leq]A \Rightarrow [\equiv]A$
C7 $x \leq y \;\&\; y \leq x \rightarrow x \equiv y$.	

Let us note that the conditions C3-C7 are equivalent to the condition (4) and that C7 is not modally definable. So, to axiomatize the logic S4+5 we consider two kinds of models: the standard ones, defined above, and the non-standard models satisfying C1-C6. Using the standard canonical method ([Se1, HC1]) one can axiomatize the logic based on the non-standard models by the following axioms and rules of inference (see [Va2] and [Va3]).

Axiomatization of S4+5

Axiom schemes:

(Bool) All (or enough) Boolean tautologies,
(K[R]) $[R](A \Rightarrow B) \Rightarrow ([R]A \Rightarrow [R]B)$, for $R = \leq, \equiv$,
Ax1-Ax6 (see above).

Rules of inference:

- (MP) $A, A \Rightarrow B/B$,
- (N) $A/[R]A$, for $R = \leq, \equiv$.

However, to prove that S4+5 is complete in the class of all the standard structures we apply a special construction, called copying, transforming non-standard models into the standard ones. We shall sketch the proof given in [Va4] and [Va3] using the abstract definition of copying given, for instance, in [Va4] and [Va6].

The definition of copying for structures with binary relations is the following. Let $\underline{W} = (W, \{R_j | j \in J\})$ and $\underline{W}' = (W', \{R'_j | j \in J\})$ be two relational structures, $M = (\underline{W}, v)$ and $M' = (\underline{W}', v')$ be models over $\underline{W}$ and $\underline{W}'$ and I be a non-empty set of mappings from $\underline{W}$ into $\underline{W}'$. We say that I is a copying from $\underline{W}$ to $\underline{W}'$ if the following conditions are satisfied:

(CI1) For any $y' \in W'$ there exist $x \in W$ and $f \in I$ such that $f(x) = y'$,
(CI2) For any $x, y \in W$: if for some $f, g \in I$ $f(x) = g(y)$ then $x = y$,
(CR1) For any $x, y \in W$: if xR_jy then $(\forall f \in I)(\exists g \in I) f(x)R'_j g(y), j \in J$,
(CR2) For any $x, y \in W$ and $f, g \in I$: if $f(x)R'_j g(y)$ then $xR_jy, j \in J$.

We say that I is a copying from the model M to the model M' if I is a copying from $\underline{W}$ to $\underline{W}'$ satisfying the condition

(Cv) For any $x \in W$, $f \in I$ and propositional variable p:

$$x \in v(p) \text{ iff } f(x) \in v'(p).$$

The importance of the copying construction is in the following

Lemma 70. (Copying lemma)

(i) Let I be a copying from $\underline{W}$ to $\underline{W}'$ and $M = (\underline{W}, v)$ be a model over $\underline{W}$. Then there exists a valuation v' in W' such that I is a copying from the model M to the model $M' = (\underline{W}', v')$.

(ii) For any $x \in W$, $f \in I$ and a formula A in the modal language with modalities $\{[R_j] | j \in J\}$, interpreted in this kind of structures, the following equivalence holds:

$$x \Vdash_v A \text{ iff } f(x) \Vdash_{v'} A \ .$$

Proof. (i) Define for any propositional variable p:

$$v'(p) = \{y' \in W' | (\exists x' \in v(p) \exists g \in I)(g(x') = y'\} \ .$$

Now let $x \in W$, $f \in I$ and suppose that $x \in f(p)$. Then by the above definition $f(x) \in v'(p)$. For the converse implication suppose that $f(x) \in v'(p)$. Then there exist $x' \in v(p)$ and $g \in I$ such that $f(x) = g(x')$. By (CI2) we obtain that $x = x'$, so $x \in v(p)$. Combining the two cases we get: $x \in v(p)$ iff $f(x) \in v'(p)$, $x \in W$, $f \in I$, $p \in VAR$.

The proof of (ii) is by induction on the construction of A (see [Va4]). Let us note that the conditions (CR1) and (CR2) are used when A has the form $[R]B$. □

Theorem 71. *Let $\underline{W} = (W, \leq, \equiv)$ be a nonstandard structure (satisfying C1-C6). Then there exist a standard structure $\underline{W}' = (W', \leq', \equiv)$ and a copying I from $\underline{W}$ to $\underline{W}'$.*

Proof. Let $I = N = \{0, 1, \ldots\}$ be the set of natural numbers. Define $W' = W \times N$ and for $i \in I$ and $x \in W$ let $i(x) = (x, i)$. Instead of $i(x)$ we will write x_i. To define the relation $\leq'$ we, first, define the following relation, called a defect of the pair (x, y):

$$xDy \text{ iff } x \leq y \ \&\ y \leq x \ \&\ x \not\equiv y$$

Then for x_i and $y_j \in W'$ we define:

- $x_i \leq_0 y_j$ iff $x \leq y$ & $((j = i$ & not $xDy)$ or $j = i + 1$ & $xDy))$
- $\leq'$ is the transitive closure of $\leq_0$,
- $x_i \equiv' x_j$ iff $x \equiv y$ & $i = j$.

It is easy to see that $\underline{W}' = (W', \leq', \equiv')$ is a nonstandard structure for S4+5 (S1-S6 are fulfilled) and that I is a copying from $\underline{W}$ to $\underline{W}'$. It remains to show that the condition S7 is satisfied. For, suppose that $x_i \leq' y_j$ and $y_j \leq' x_i$. Then by the definition of $\leq'$ we conclude: there exists n and $x^0_{k_0}, x^1_{k_1}, \ldots, x^n_{k_n}$ such that $i = k_0$, $j = k_n$ and $x_i = x^0_{k_0} \leq_0 x^1_{k_1} \leq_0 \ldots \leq_0 x^n_{k_n} = y_j$. Then by the definition of $\leq_0$ we obtain: $x = x^0 \leq x^1 \leq \ldots \leq x^n = y$ and $i = k_0 \leq k_1 \leq \ldots \leq k_n = j$, so, by transitivity of $\leq$ we get $x \leq y$ and $i \leq j$. In a similar way we obtain $y \leq x$ and $j \leq i$, which yields $i = j$. Hence, by the definition of $\leq_0$ we have not xDy and by $x \leq y$ and $y \leq x$ we obtain $x \equiv y$. Then together with $i = j$ this implies $x_i \equiv' y_j$, which proves the condition C7 and shows that $\underline{W}'$ is a standard structure for S4+5. This completes the proof of the theorem. □

Let us note that the structure W' in the above proof is infinite and this is not a defect of the proof as we shall see.

Theorem 72. (Completeness theorem for S4+5) *The following conditions are equivalent for any formula A of S4+5:*

(i) A is a theorem of S4+5,
(ii) A is a true in all nonstandard structures of S4+5,
(iii) A is true in all infinite standard structure of S4+5 (infinite quasi-ordered sets with ≡ defined by (4) at the begining of section 4.4),
(iv) A is true in all bi-similarity structures over single-valued A-systems with ≡ defined by (4).

Proof. [Va2], [Va3]. The equivalence (i)↔(ii) is obtained by the standard canonical construction; (ii)↔(iii) follows from theorem 71 and (iii)↔(iv) follows from corollary 45. □

Let us note that the word "infinite" in (iii) can not be replaced by "finite". It is proved in [Va3] that adding to the logic S4+5 the following formula, called generalized Grzegorczyk axiom, makes the logic complete in the class of finite quasi-ordered sets.

$$gGrz \quad [\leq]([\leq]([\equiv]A \Rightarrow [\leq]A) \Rightarrow A) \Rightarrow A$$

The information logic Il The information logic Il is introduced in [Va4] as an extension of the logic S4+5 with the modality of strong similarity $[\sigma]$ and a propositional constant D, which is interpreted in A-systems S with the following set: $D_S = \{x \in Ob | \forall a \in At\ Card\ f(x,a) \leq 1\}$. In other words, $x \in D_S$ iff for any attribute $a \in At_S$ the set $f_S(x,a)$ is either empty or a singleton (one-element set). Obviously, S is a single-valued A system iff $D_S = Ob_S$. This makes possible to consider the single-valued case and the general case in one system.

Axiomatization of IL

Axiom schemes:

(Bool) All or enough Boolean tautologies,
(K) $[R](A \Rightarrow B) \Rightarrow ([R]A \Rightarrow [R]B)$, for $R \in \{\equiv, \leq, \sigma\}$,
Ax1-Ax6 of S4+5,
Ax7 $A \vee [\sigma]\neg[\sigma]A$,
Ax8 $\langle\sigma\rangle 1 \wedge [\sigma]A \Rightarrow A$,

Ax9 $\langle\leq\rangle[\sigma]A \Rightarrow [\sigma]A$,
Ax10 $\langle\leq\rangle D \Rightarrow D$,
Ax11 $D \wedge [\leq]A \Rightarrow [\sigma]A$,
Ax12 $D \wedge [\equiv]A \Rightarrow [\sigma](D \Rightarrow A)$.

Rules of inference:

- (MP) $A, A \Rightarrow B/B$,
- (N) $A/[R]A$, for $R \in \{\equiv, \leq, \sigma\}$.

The semantics for Il is determined by A-systems. The interpretation of D in a system S is the following:

$$x \|\!-_v D \text{ iff } x \in D_S \ .$$

The completeness theorem for Il is given in [Va4] and goes trough an abstract characterization theorem (by a method similar to that applied in the proof of theorem 45), canonical construction and copying. It is proved that Il, like S4+5, does not possess finite model property with respect to its finite standard models, but possesses this property with respect to its non-standard models, which yields its decidability.

The modal logic MLSim The logic MLSim is introduced in [Va5]. It contains the modalities of weak similarity $[\Sigma]$, strong similarity $[\sigma]$, weak indiscernibility $[\cong]$ and strong indiscernibility $[\equiv]$. While the strong indiscernibility relation is definable by the informational inclusion $\leq$, the relation of weak indiscernibility relation is a new informational relation defined in A-systems as follows:

$$x \cong_S y \text{ iff } (\exists a \in At) f(x, a) = f(y, a) \ .$$

Let us note that this relation cannot be defined in bi-consequence systems, so the theory developed in this paper is not suitable for studying this relation.

Axiomatization of MLSim
Axiom schemes:

(Bool) All or enough Boolean tautologies,
(K) $[R](A \Rightarrow B) \Rightarrow ([R]A \Rightarrow [R]B)$, for $R \in \{\equiv, \cong, \sigma, \Sigma, U\}$,
Ax3, Ax4, Ax5 of S4+5,
Ax7, Ax8 of IL,
The formulas obtained from Ax3, Ax4, Ax5 through replacement of $\equiv$ by U,
Ax13 $[\cong]A \Rightarrow A$,
Ax14 $A \vee [\cong]\neg[\cong]A$,
Ax15 $[\cong]A \Rightarrow [\equiv][\cong]A$,
Ax16 $[\sigma]A \Rightarrow [\equiv][\sigma]A$,
Ax17 $A \vee [\Sigma]\neg[\Sigma]A$,
Ax18 $\langle\Sigma\rangle 1 \wedge [\Sigma]A \Rightarrow A$,
Ax19 $[\sigma]A \Rightarrow [\equiv][\Sigma]A$,

Ax20 $[\Sigma]A \Rightarrow [\cong][\Sigma]A$,
Ax21 $([\Sigma]A \Rightarrow A) \vee [U]([\equiv]A \Rightarrow ([\Sigma]B \Rightarrow B))$,
Ax22 $([\Sigma]A \Rightarrow A) \vee [U]([\cong]A \Rightarrow ([\Sigma]B \Rightarrow [\cong]B))$
Ax23 $([\Sigma]A \Rightarrow A) \vee [U]([\cong]A \Rightarrow ([\sigma]B \Rightarrow B))$,
Ax24 $[U]A = [R]A$, for $R \in \{\equiv, \cong, \sigma, \Sigma\}$.

Rules of inference:

- (MP) $A, A \Rightarrow B/B$,
- (N) $A/[R]A$, for $R \in \{\equiv, \cong, \sigma, \Sigma_S, U\}$.

The completeness theorem for MLSim is given in [Va5] and goes trough an abstract characterization theorem for the standard structures of MLSim by a method similar to that applied in the proof of theorem 45. It is proved that MLSim possesses finite model property with respect to its standard models, which yields its decidability.

5 Concluding Remarks

5.1 Some Possible Generalizations of Property Systems and Attribute Systems

The notions of P-system and A-system seem to be special cases of a more general notion of information system. One possible generalization is the following.

First, we shall unify in some sense the definitions of P-systems and A-systems.

Let $S = (Ob, Pr, f)$ be a P-system. Consider the set Ob in S as consisting of objects of level 0 and denote it by Ob_0. Consider the set Pr in S as consisting of objects of level 1 and denote it by Ob_1. Instead of the information function f let us postulate a binary relation $Is \subseteq Ob_0 \times Ob_1$ with the following meaning: for $x \in Ob_0$ and $A \in Ob_1$ "$xIsA$" means "x is A" or "x possesses the property A". The function f is now easily definable: $f(x) = \{A \in Ob_1 | xIsA\}$. Now instead of the notion of a P-system we introduce the notion of an information system of level 1 (1-system for short) as a triple $S = (Ob_0, Ob_1, Is)$ where $Ob \neq \emptyset$, $Ob_0 \cap Ob_1 = \emptyset$ and $Is \subseteq Ob_0 \times Ob_1$.

Now the generalization to arbitrary n is the following. By information system of level n, or n-hierarchial system (n-system for short) we mean any system of the form $S = (Ob_0, Ob_1, \ldots Ob_n, Is)$, where $Ob_0 \neq \emptyset$, for each $i \neq j$ $Ob_i \cap Ob_j = \emptyset$ and Is is a binary relation in the the set $Ob_0 \cup Ob_1 \cup \ldots \cup Ob_n$ with the following property; for $i < n$: if $xIsY$ and $x \in Ob_i$ then $Y \in Ob_{i+1}$. The elements of Ob_i are called objects of level i. The case $n = 2$ will correspond to the notion of an A-system as follows. Let (Ob_0, Ob_1, Ob_2, Is) be a 2-system. We shall define an A-system S in the following way. Put $Ob_S = Ob_0$, $At_S = Ob_2$ and for each $a \in Ob_2$ put $Val_S(a) = \{A \in Ob_1 | AIsa\}$. Let for $x \in Ob_0$ define $f(x) = \{A \in Ob_1 | xIsA\}$. Now for $x \in Ob_0$ and $a \in Ob_2 = At_S$ put $f(x, a) = f(x) \cap Val_S(a)$. Obviously, S is an A-system. Conversely, each A-system determines a 2-system in the following way. Let $S = (Ob, AT, \{Val(a) | a \in At\}, f)$ be an A-system. Then we construct a 2-system $S' = (Ob_0, Ob_1, Ob_2, Is)$ as follows. Put $Ob_0 = Ob$,

$Ob_1 = \bigcup\{Val(a)|a \in At\}$, $Ob_2 = At$. For $x \in Ob_0$ define $f(x) = \mathcal{U}\{f(x,a)|a \in At\}$. Then define for $x \in Ob_0$, $A \in Ob_1$ and $a \in Ob_2$: $xIsA$ iff $A \in f(x)$, $AIsa$ iff $A \in Val(a)$. This shows that the notion of 2-system is just another (almost equivalent) formulation of A-system. In this new terminology the objects of level 1 are properties, the objects of level 2 are attributes. The general name of the objects of level i are i-level attributes or i-level categories. The case $n = 0$ corresponds simply to the notion of a set.

Open Problems Some open problems are formulated in the text. We shall list some new ones.

- Open problems related to P-systems.
  - Develop the theory of information relations in P-systems.
  - Characterize the n-place informational relations in P-systems, at least for $n \leq 3$, or some interesting concrete examples and the corresponding polyadic modal logics (for the definition of polyadic modal logic see [Va7]). Examples:
    Complement: xCy iff $f(x) = \overline{f}(y)$, Intersection: $x \cap y \subseteq z$ iff $f(x) \cap f(y) \subseteq f(z)$, Union: $z \subseteq x \cup y$ iff $f(z) \subseteq f(x) \cup f(y)$.
  - Axiomatize the polymodal logic of all two-place informational relations in P-systems. This logic may be considered as Dynamic Logic over SIM-1 with program constants $\leq, \Sigma$ and N and as a program operations take the Booleans $\cup, \cap$ and $-$.
- Open problems related to A-systems.
  - Characterize the bi-similarity structures over single-valued A-systems.
  - Develop the theory of information relations in A-systems. Find more convenient logical counterpart of A-systems (bi-consequence systems are not convenient to study all the informational relations in A-systems).
  - Describe the 2-place (3-place, n-place) relations in A-systems, at least some concrete interesting new examples, for instance the weak and strong versions of the informational relations in P-systems introduced above.
  - Axiomatize some new modal logics with modalities corresponding to informational relations in A-systems.
- Open problems related to generalizations of information systems.
  - Develop the theory of n-systems for arbitrary n, or at least for $n = 3$. Find a suitable logical counterpart (like consequence systems) of n-systems.
  - Characterize the informational relations in n-systems for an arbitrary n or $n = 3$.

Acknowledgments

The author wishes to thank Z. Pawlak and especially E. Orlowska for many stimulating discussions over the years, which encourage the investigations in this field and writing of this paper.

References

[AT1] Archangelsky, D. and Taitslin, M.: A logic for data description. LNCS, **363**, (1989), 2-12

[Be1] Benthem, J.F.A.K.: Modal Logic and Classical Logic. Bibliopolis, Napoly, (1986)

[Gab1] Gabbay, D.: Semantical Considerations in Heyting's Intuitionistic Logic. Synthese Library, **148**, D. Reidel Publishing Company, Holland, (1981)

[Gar1] Gargov, G.: Two completeness theorems in the logic for data analysis. ICS PAS Reports, **581**, Warsaw, (1986)

[HC1] Hughes, G. & Cresswell, M.J.: A Companion to Modal Logic. Methuen, London, (1984)

[Or1] Orłowska, E.: Modal logics in the theory of information systems. Zeitschrift für Mathematishe Logik und Grundlagen Der Mathematik, **30**, (1984), 213–222

[Or2] Orłowska, E.: Logic of nondeterministic information. Studia Logica, **XLIV**, (1985), 93–102.

[Or3] Orłowska, E.: Logic of indiscernibility relations. ICS PAS Reports, **546**, (1984); LNCS, **208**, 1985, 177–186

[Or4] Orłowska, E.: Kripke models with relative accessibility relations and their applications to inferences from incomplete information. In: Mirkowska, G. and Rasiowa, H. (eds.) Mathematical Problems in Computation Theory. Banach Center Publications, **21**, Polish Scientific Publishers, Warsaw, (1987), 327–337

[Or5] Orłowska, E.: Logic approach to information systems. Fundamenta Informaticae, **8**, (1988), 359–378

[Or6] Orłowska, E.: Kripke semantics for knowledge representation logics. Studia Logica, **XLIX**, 2, (1990), 255–272

[Or7] Orłowska, E.: Rough set semantics for nonclassical logics. Manuscript, (1993)

[OP1] Orłowska, E. and Pawlak, Z.: Logical foundations of knowledge representation systems. ICS PAS Reports, **573**, (1984)

[OP2] Orłowska, E. and Pawlak, Z.: Representation of nondeterministic information. Theoretical Computer Science, **29**, (1984), 27–39

[FCO1] Fariñas, L., del Cerro and Orłowska, E.: DAL – a logic for data analysis. Theoretical Computer Science, **36**, (1985), 251–264

[Pa1] Pawlak, Z.: Information systems – theoretical foundations. Information Systems, **6**, (1981), 205–218

[Pa2] Pawlak, Z.: Rough sets. International Journal of Information and Computer Science, **11**, 5, (1982), 341–356

[Pa3] Pawlak, Z.: Systemy Informacyjne. WNT, Warszawa, (1983), In Polish

[Pa4] Pawlak, Z.: Rough Sets. Theoretical Aspects of Reasoning about Data. Kluwer Academic Publishers, Dordrecht/Boston/London, (1991)

[Ra1] Rasiowa, H.: Logic of approximating sequences of sets. Invited lecture, Proc. Advanced International School and Symposium of Mathematical Logic and Applications, Drushba, Bulgaria, (1986), 167–186

[RS1] Rasiowa, H. and Skowron, A.: Rough concepts logic. In: Computation Theory, **88**, (ed.) Skowron, A., LNCS, **208**, (1985), 288–297

[RS2] Rasiowa, H. and Sikorski, R.: The Mathematics of Metamathematics. PWN, Warsaw, (1963)

[Sc1] Scott, D.: Domains for denotational Semantics. A corrected and expanded version of a paper prepared for ICALP'82, Aarhus, Denmark, (1982)

[Se1] Segerberg, K.: Essay in Classical Modal Logic. Uppsala, (1971)

[Se2] Segerberg, K.: Classical Propositional Operators. Clarendon Press, Oxford, (1982)

[Sl1] Slowinski, R. (ed.): Intelligent Decision Support, Handbook of Applications and Advances of Rough Sets Theory. Kluver Academic Publishers, (1992)

[St1] Stone, M.: Topological Representation of Distributive Lattices and Brouwerian Logics. Cas. Mat. Fys., **67**, (1937), 1–25

[Va1] Vakarelov, D.: Abstract characterization of some knowledge representation systems and the logic NIL of nondeterministic information. In: Jorrand, Ph. and Sgurev, V. (ed.), Artificial Intelligence II, Methodology, Systems, Applications. North-Holland, (1987)

[Va2] Vakarelov, D.: S4 and S5 together – S4+5. In: 8th International Congress of Logic, Methodology and Philosophy of Science, LMPS'87, Moscow, USSR, 17-22 August 1987, Abstracts, **5**, 3, (1987), 271–274

[Va3] Vakarelov, D.: Modal characterization of the classes of finite and infinite quasi-ordered sets. SU/LAL/preprint, **1**, (1988), Proc. Summer School and Conference on Mathematical Logic, Heyting'88, Chajka near Varna, Bulgaria, (1988)

[Va4] Vakarelov, D.: Modal logics for knowledge representation systems. LNCS, **363**, (1989), 257–277, Theoretical Computer Science, **90**, (1991), 433–456

[Va5] Vakarelov, D.: A modal logic for similarity relations in Pawlak knowledge representation systems. Fundamenta Informaticae, **XV**, (1991), 61–79

[Va6] Vakarelov, D.: Logical analysis of positive and negative similarity relations in property systems. In: WOCFAI'91, First World Conference on the Fundamentals of Artificial Intelligence, 1-5 July 1991, Paris, France, Proceedings (ed.) Michel De Glas and Dov Gabbay, (1991), 491–499

[Va7] Vakarelov, D.: Rough polyadic modal logics. Journal of Applied Non-Classical Logics, **1**, 1, (1991), 9–35

[Va8] Vakarelov, D.: Consequence relations and information systems. In: [Sl1].

VII

EXTENDED ROUGH SET-BASED DEDUCTION METHODS

Chapter 17

Axiomatization of Logics Based on Kripke Models with Relative Accessibility Relations

Philippe Balbiani

Philippe Balbiani, balbiani@lipn.univ-paris13.fr,
Laboratoire d'informatique de Paris-Nord,
Institut Galilée, Université Paris-Nord,
Avenue Jean-Baptiste Clément, F-93430 Villetaneuse

Abstract: This paper presents a systematic study of the logics based on Kripke models with relative accessibility relations as well as a general method for proving their completeness. The Kripke models with relative accessibility relations come out in the context of the analysis of indiscernability in the information systems.

1 Introduction

The semantics of the modal logics usually consists of Kripke models which are relational structures of the form $\mathcal{F} = (W, R)$, where W is a nonempty set of possible worlds and R is a binary relation on W. However, there are several multimodal logics whose Kripke models are relational structures of the form $\mathcal{F} = (W, R)$, where W is a nonempty set of possible worlds but, R is a mapping on $\mathcal{P}(PAR)$ to the set of the binary relations on W; for PAR being a nonempty set of parameters. For example the propositional dynamic logic [Hal] where PAR is a set of atomic programs, the modal logic in the theory of information systems [Or1] where PAR is a set of attributes, the deontic logic with individuals [Bal] where PAR is a set of agents in a hierarchical universe, the epistemic logic with common knowledge and distributed knowledge [FHMV1] where PAR is a set of agents in a distributed environment.

Let PAR be a nonempty set of parameters. In the context of the modal logic in the theory of information systems, Orłowska [Or2] considers relational structures of the form $\mathcal{F} = (W, R)$ where W is a nonempty set of possible worlds and R is a mapping on $\mathcal{P}(PAR)$ to the set of the binary relations on W such that $R(\emptyset) = W \times W$ and, for every subset $P, Q \in \mathcal{P}(PAR)$, $R(P \cup Q) = R(P) \cap R(Q)$. According to Orłowska [Or3]:

> The first condition says that the empty set of parameters does not enable us to distinguish any states. The second condition says that if we have more parameters, then the relation is smaller, less states will be glue together.

What's more, she adds:

> Relative accessibility relations provide two kinds of information. First, they tell us which states are associated one with the other, and second, with respect to which of their characteristic features they are associated.

She finally concludes that:

> Axiomatization of logics based on Kripke models with relative accessibility relations is an open problem.

As a matter of fact, many researchers come up against this problem. Harel [Ha1] writes that the validity problem for $IPDL$ – the propositional dynamic logic with the intersection operator on programs – is not known to be undecidable. Fariñas del Cerro and Orłowska [FO1] as well as their followers never prove the completeness of DAL – the logic for data analysis – in the general setting. Bailhache [Ba1] only conjectures the completeness of his deontic logic with individuals. Fagin, Halpern and Vardi [FHV1] and van der Hoek and Meyer [HM1] succeed in proving the completeness of their epistemic logic with distributed knowledge with respect to the class of all knowledge models[1].

This paper presents a systematic study of the logics based on Kripke models with relative accessibility relations as well as a general method for proving their completeness. This method uses the technics of the copying introduced by Vakarelov [Va1] in the context of the modal logic for knowledge representation systems. The logics based on Kripke models with relative accessibility relations are divided up into two categories:

- the growing modal logics,
- the decreasing modal logics.

The growing modal logics are presented in sections 3 and 5. They are based on relational structures of the form $\mathcal{F} = (W, R)$ where R is such that $R(P \cap Q) = R(P) \cap R(Q)$. Among them one can find: DAL – the logic for data analysis introduced by Fariñas del Cerro and Orłowska [FO1] – a proof of its completeness is presented in section 7, BML – the Boolean modal logic introduced by Gargov and Passy [GP1] – and $DALLA$ – the logic for data analysis with local agreement introduced by Gargov and further studied by Demri and Orłowska [De1] [DO1] – a proof of its completeness is presented in section 5.4. The decreasing modal logics are presented in sections 4 and 6. They are based on relational structures of the form $\mathcal{F} = (W, R)$ where R is such that $R(P \cup Q) = R(P) \cap R(Q)$. Among them, one can find $IPDL$ – the propositional dynamic logic with the intersection operator on programs [Ha1] –, KR – the modal logic in the theory of information systems introduced by Orłowska [Or3] – a proof of its completeness is presented in section 4.4, the modal logics for reasoning about indiscernability and relative similarity introduced by Konikowska [Ko1] [Ko2], $DABXY$ – the deontic logic of action introduced by Bailhache [Ba1] – a proof of it completeness is presented

[1] However, the proof presented by these researchers – who use the technics of the unravelling introduced by Sahlqvist [Sa1] – is extremely complicated. The proof presented in section 9 is more simple.

in section 8, and $S5_n^D$ – the epistemic logic of distributed knowledge introduced by Fagin, Halpern and Vardi [FHV1] – a proof of its completeness is presented in section 9.

From now on, PAR is a nonempty set of parameters and $\mathcal{P}(PAR)$ ($\mathcal{P}(PAR)^\bullet$, $\mathcal{P}(PAR)^\circ$, $\mathcal{P}(PAR)^*$) is the set of its subsets (finite subsets, cofinite subsets, nonempty and finite subsets, respectively). For every parameter $a \in PAR$, let $\overline{a} = \{a\}$ and $\underline{a} = PAR \setminus \{a\}$. For every subset $P \in \mathcal{P}(PAR)$, let $\underline{P} = PAR \setminus P$.

2 Relative Modal Logics

Among the logics based on Kripke models with relative accessibility relations, the relative modal logics are the most elementary.

2.1 Language

The linguistic basis of the relative modal logics is the propositional calculus. Let VAR be a nonempty set of *atomic formulas*. For every subset $P \in \mathcal{P}(PAR)$, the modal operator $[P]$ is added to the standard propositional formalism.

2.2 Semantics

The semantics of the relative modal logics is defined in terms of the notions of relative frame, relative model, and the satisfiability of the formulas of the language.

Relative frames A *relative frame* is a pair $\mathcal{F} = (W, R)$ where W is a nonempty set of *possible worlds* and R is a mapping on $\mathcal{P}(PAR)$ to the set of the binary relations on W.

Relative models Let $\mathcal{F} = (W, R)$ be a relative frame. A mapping m on VAR to the set of the subsets of W is called *assignment* on $\mathcal{F}$. A pair $\mathcal{M} = (\mathcal{F}, m)$ where $\mathcal{F}$ is a relative frame and m is an assignment on $\mathcal{F}$ is called *relative model on* $\mathcal{F}$.

Satisfiability Let $\mathcal{F} = (W, R)$ be a frame and m be an assignment on $\mathcal{F}$. The *satisfiability relation* in the model $\mathcal{M} = (\mathcal{F}, m)$ between a possible world $x \in W$ and a formula A is defined in the following way:

- for every atomic formula A, $x \models_{\mathcal{M}} A$ iff $x \in m(A)$,
- $x \models_{\mathcal{M}} \neg A$ iff $x \not\models_{\mathcal{M}} A$,
- $x \models_{\mathcal{M}} A \wedge B$ iff $x \models_{\mathcal{M}} A$ and $x \models_{\mathcal{M}} B$,
- for every subset $P \in \mathcal{P}(PAR)$, $x \models_{\mathcal{M}} [P]A$ iff, for every possible world $y \in W$, $x\ R(P)\ y$ only if $y \models_{\mathcal{M}} A$.

A formula is *valid* in a model when it is satisfied in every possible world of this model. A schema is *valid* in a frame when every instance of the schema is valid in every model of the frame.

Copying Let $\mathcal{F} = (W, R)$ be a frame. Let $\mathcal{F}' = (W', R')$ be a frame and I be a set of mappings on W to W'. I is a *copying from $\mathcal{F}$ into $\mathcal{F}'$* when:

- for every mapping $f, g \in I$ and for every possible world $x, y \in W$, $f(x) = g(y)$ only if $x = y$,
- for every possible world $x' \in W'$, there exists a mapping $f \in I$ and a possible world $x \in W$ such that $f(x) = x'$,
- for every subset $P \in \mathcal{P}(PAR)$, for every mapping $f \in I$ and for every possible world $x, y \in W$, $x\ R(P)\ y$ only if there exists a mapping $g \in I$ such that $f(x)\ R'(P)\ g(y)$,
- for every subset $P \in \mathcal{P}(PAR)$, for every mapping $f, g \in I$ and for every possible world $x, y \in W$, $f(x)\ R'(P)\ g(y)$ only if $x\ R(P)\ y$.

Copying preserves the satisfiability of a formula according to the following lemma:

Lemma 1. *Let $\mathcal{F} = (W, R)$ be a frame. Let $\mathcal{F}' = (W', R')$ be a frame and I be a copying from $\mathcal{F}$ into $\mathcal{F}'$. Let m be an assignment on $\mathcal{F}$ and m' be the assignment on $\mathcal{F}'$ defined in the following way:*

- *for every atomic formula A, $m'(A) = \{f(x) \colon f \in I \text{ and } x \in m(A)\}$.*

Let $\mathcal{M} = (\mathcal{F}, m)$, $\mathcal{M}' = (\mathcal{F}', m')$. Then, for every formula A, for every mapping $f \in I$ and for every possible world $x \in W$, $x \models_{\mathcal{M}} A$ iff $f(x) \models_{\mathcal{M}'} A$.

The proof can be done by induction on the complexity of A.

The technics of the copying have been introduced by Vakarelov [Va1] in the context of the modal logic for knowledge representation systems. They are mainly used for proving that a modal logic which is characterized by a certain class of frames is also characterized by another class.

2.3 Logic K

Together with the classical tautologies, all the instances of the following schema are axioms of logic K:

- $[P](A \rightarrow B) \rightarrow ([P]A \rightarrow [P]B)$.

Together with the modus ponens, the instances of the following schema are rules of K:

- if $\vdash_K A$ then $\vdash_K [P]A$.

Direct calculations would lead to the conclusion that:

Theorem 2. *The theorems of logic K are valid in every model.*

Let $\mathcal{M} = (W, R, m)$ be the *canonical model of K*, that is:

- $W = \{x \colon x \text{ is a maximal consistent set of formulas}\}$,

- for every subset $P \in \mathcal{P}(PAR)$ and for every possible world $x, y \in W$, $x\ R(P)\ y$ iff, for every formula $[P]A \in x$, $A \in y$,
- for every atomic formula A, $m(A) = \{x\colon x \in W \text{ and } A \in x\}$.

Direct calculations would lead to the conclusion that, for every possible world $x \in W$ and for every formula A, $x \models_{\mathcal{M}} A$ iff $A \in x$. Consequently:

Theorem 3. *Logic K is complete with respect to the class of all models, that is every formula valid in every model is a theorem of K.*

The technics of the canonical model are mainly used for proving that a modal logic is complete for a certain class of models, that is for proving that the formulas valid in every model of a certain class are exactly the theorems of a modal logic [Ch1] [HC1].

2.4 Extensions of Logic *K*

K is the most elementary relative modal logic. The extensions of K are obtained by means of additional axioms:

D The axioms and rules of D are those of K plus all the instances of the schema $[P]A \rightarrow \neg[P]\neg A$. Since the canonical model of D is serial, then D is complete with respect to the class of all serial models.

T The axioms and rules of T are those of K plus all the instances of the schema $[P]A \rightarrow A$. Since the canonical model of T is reflexive, then T is complete with respect to the class of all reflexive models.

B The axioms and rules of B are those of K plus all the instances of the schema $A \rightarrow [P]\neg[P]\neg A$. Since the canonical model of B is symmetrical, then B is complete with respect to the class of all symmetrical models.

S The axioms and rules of S are those of K plus all the instances of the schemata $[P]A \rightarrow A$ and $A \rightarrow [P]\neg[P]\neg A$. Since the canonical model of S is a model of similarity[2], then S is complete with respect to the class of all models of similarity.

I The axioms and rules of I are those of K plus all the instances of the schemata $[P]A \rightarrow A$, $A \rightarrow [P]\neg[P]\neg A$ and $[P]A \rightarrow [P][P]A$. Since the canonical model of I is a model of indiscernability[3], then I is complete with respect to the class of all models of indiscernability.

3 Growing Modal Logics

The language and the semantics of the growing modal logics are those of the relative modal logics where tha class of reltives frames is restricted to growing frames.

[2] A frame of similarity is a reflexive and symmetrical frame.

[3] A frame of indiscernability is a reflexive, symmetrical and transitive frame.

3.1 Growing frames

The reletive frame $\mathcal{F} = (W, R)$ is *growing* if for every subset $P, Q \in \mathcal{P}(PAR)$:

- $R(P \cap Q) \subseteq R(P) \cap R(Q)$.

The frame $\mathcal{F} = (W, R)$ is *strongly growing* if for every subset $P, Q \in \mathcal{P}(PAR)$:

- $R(P \cap Q) = R(P) \cap R(Q)$.

Example 1. DAL – the logic for data analysis introduced by Fariñas del Cerro and Orłowska [FO1] – is a logic based on growing Kripke models with relative accessibility relations. The proof of its completeness is presented in section 7.

3.2 Logic GK

The axioms and rules of GK are those of K plus all the instances of the following schema:

- $[P]A \vee [Q]A \rightarrow [P \cap Q]A$.

Direct calculations would lead to the conclusion that:

Theorem 4. *The theorems of GK are valid in every growing model.*

Since the canonical model of GK is growing, then:

Theorem 5. *GK is complete with respect to the class of all growing models.*

However, the canonical model of GK is not strongly growing. The following section presents the proof of the completeness of GK with respect to the class of all strongly growing models.

3.3 Standard completeness

Let $\mathcal{F} = (W, R)$ be a growing frame. Let $\mathcal{B} = \mathcal{P}(W)$ be a Boolean ring where:

- $0_{\mathcal{B}} = \emptyset$,
- $1_{\mathcal{B}} = W$,
- $A +_{\mathcal{B}} B = (A \setminus B) \cup (B \setminus A)$,
- $A \times_{\mathcal{B}} B = A \cap B$.

Let I be the set of the mappings f on $\mathcal{P}(PAR) \times PAR$ to $\mathcal{P}(W)$ such that for every subset $P \in \mathcal{P}(PAR)$, the set $\{\alpha\colon \alpha \in \underline{P} \text{ and } f(P, \alpha) \neq \emptyset\}$ is finite. Let $W' = W \times I$.

For every subset $P \in \mathcal{P}(PAR)$, let $\pi(P)$ be a mapping on $W \times W$ to $\mathcal{P}(W)$ such that, for every possible world $x, y \in W$, $\pi(P)(x, y) = \emptyset$ iff $x\ R(P)\ y$. For every subset $P \in \mathcal{P}(PAR)$, let $R'(P)$ be the binary relation on W' defined by: $(x, f)\ R'(P)\ (y, g)$ iff

- $x\ R(P)\ y$ and

- for every parameter $\alpha \in \underline{P}$ and for every subset $Q \in \mathcal{P}(PAR)$, if $\alpha \in \underline{Q}$ then $f(Q,\alpha) + g(Q,\alpha) = \emptyset$ and
- for every subset $Q \in \mathcal{P}(PAR)$, $\Sigma_{\alpha \in \underline{Q}} f(Q,\alpha) + g(Q,\alpha) = \pi(Q)(x,y)$.

Direct calculations would lead to the conclusion that $\mathcal{F}' = (W', R')$ is growing.

Let ϕ be a mapping on $\mathcal{P}(PAR) \times \mathcal{P}(PAR)$ to PAR such that for every subset $P, Q \in \mathcal{P}(PAR)$, if $\underline{Q} \not\subseteq \underline{P}$ then $\phi(P,Q) \in \underline{Q}$ and $\phi(P,Q) \notin \underline{P}$. For every subset $P \in \mathcal{P}(PAR)$, for every mapping $f \in I$ and for every possible world $x, y \in W$, if $x\ R(P)\ y$ then, for every subset $Q \in \mathcal{P}(PAR)$ and for every parameter $\alpha \in PAR$, let $g(Q,\alpha)$ be the subset of W defined in the following way:

- If $\alpha \notin \underline{Q}$ then $g(Q,\alpha) = \emptyset$.
- If $\alpha \in \underline{Q}$ and $\alpha \in \underline{P}$ then $g(Q,\alpha) = f(Q,\alpha)$.
- If $\alpha \in \underline{Q}$ and $\alpha \notin \underline{P}$ then either $\alpha = \phi(P,Q)$ — in this case $g(Q,\alpha) = \Sigma_{\beta \in \underline{Q} \setminus \underline{P}} f(Q,\beta) + \pi(Q)(x,y)$ — or $\alpha \neq \phi(P,Q)$ — in this case $g(Q,\alpha) = \emptyset$.

Direct calculations would lead to the conclusion that $g \in I$ and $(x,f)\ R'(P)\ (y,g)$. Consequently, for every subset $P \in \mathcal{P}(PAR)$, for every mapping $f \in I$ and for every possible world $x, y \in W$, $x\ R(P)\ y$ only if there exists a mapping $g \in I$ such that $(x,f)\ R'(P)\ (y,g)$.

Every mapping $f \in I$ can be considered as the mapping on W to W' defined in the following way:

- $f(x) = (x, f)$.

Hence, I is a copying from $\mathcal{F}$ into $\mathcal{F}'$.

For every subset $P, Q \in \mathcal{P}(PAR)$, for every mapping $f, g \in I$ and for every possible world $x, y \in W$, if $(x,f)\ R'(P)\ (y,g)$ and $(x,f)\ R'(Q)\ (y,g)$ then, for every parameter $\alpha \in \underline{P \cap Q}$, either $\alpha \in \underline{P}$ or $\alpha \in \underline{Q}$ and, for every subset $O \in \mathcal{P}(PAR)$, if $\alpha \in \underline{O}$ then $f(O,\alpha) + g(O,\alpha) = \emptyset$. Moreover, for every subset $O \in \mathcal{P}(PAR)$, $\Sigma_{\alpha \in \underline{O}} f(O,\alpha) + g(O,\alpha) = \pi(O)(x,y)$. Since, for every parameter $\alpha \in \underline{P \cap Q}$, $f(P \cap Q, \alpha) + g(P \cap Q, \alpha) = \emptyset$, then $\pi(P \cap Q)(x,y) = \emptyset$ and $x\ R(P \cap Q)\ y$. Consequently, $(x,f)\ R'(P \cap Q)\ (y,g)$. Therefore, for every subset $P, Q \in \mathcal{P}(PAR)$, $R'(P) \cap R'(Q) \subseteq R'(P \cap Q)$.

We conlude that $\mathcal{F}'$ is strongly growing. Consequently:

Lemma 6. *For every growing frame $\mathcal{F}$, there exists a strongly growing frame $\mathcal{F}'$ and a copying from $\mathcal{F}$ into $\mathcal{F}'$.*

Hence, we obtain:

Theorem 7. *Logic GK is complete with respect to the class of all strongly growing models.*

3.4 Extensions of Logic GK

GK is the most elementary growing modal logic. Similarly as the extensions of K, the extensions of GK are obtained by means of additional axioms:

GD The axioms and rules of GD are those of GK plus all the instances of the schema $[P]A \rightarrow \neg[P]\neg A$. Since the canonical model of GD is serial and growing, then GD is complete with respect to the class of all serial and growing models. Let $\mathcal{F}$ be a serial and growing frame. Direct calculations would lead to the conclusion that the frame $\mathcal{F}'$ of lemma 6 is serial and strongly growing. Therefore, GD is complete with respect to the class of all serial and strongly growing models.

GT The axioms and rules of GT are those of GK plus all the instances of the schema $[P]A \rightarrow A$. Since the canonical model of GT is reflexive and growing, then GT is complete with respect to the class of all reflexive and growing models. Let $\mathcal{F}$ be a reflexive and growing frame. Direct calculations would lead to the conclusion that the frame $\mathcal{F}'$ of lemma 6 is reflexive and strongly growing. Therefore, GT is complete with respect to the class of all reflexive and strongly growing models.

GB The axioms and rules of GB are those of GK plus all the instances of the schema $A \rightarrow [P]\neg[P]\neg A$. Since the canonical model of GB is symmetrical and growing, then GB is complete with respect to the class of all symmetrical and growing models. Let $\mathcal{F} = (W, R)$ be a symmetrical and growing frame. For every subset $P \in \mathcal{P}(PAR)$, let $\pi(P)$ be a mapping on $W \times W$ to $\mathcal{P}(W)$ such that for every possible world $x, y \in W$, $\pi(P)(x, y) = \emptyset$ iff $x\ R(P)\ y$ and $\pi(P)(x, y) = \pi(P)(y, x)$. Direct calculations would lead to the conclusion that the frame $\mathcal{F}'$ of lemma 6 is symmetrical and strongly growing. Therefore, GB is complete with respect to the class of all symmetrical and strongly growing models.

GS The axioms and rules of GS are those of GK plus all the instances of the schemata $[P]A \rightarrow A$ and $A \rightarrow [P]\neg[P]\neg A$. Since the canonical model of GS is a growing model of similarity, then GS is complete with respect to the class of all growing models of similarity. Let $\mathcal{F} = (W, R)$ be a growing frame of similarity. For every subset $P \in \mathcal{P}(PAR)$, let $\pi(P)$ be a mapping on $W \times W$ to $\mathcal{P}(W)$ such that, for every possible world $x, y \in W$, on one hand, $\pi(P)(x, y) = \emptyset$ iff $x\ R(P)\ y$ and, on the other hand, $\pi(P)(x, y) = \pi(P)(y, x)$. Direct calculations would lead to the conclusion that the frame $\mathcal{F}'$ of lemma 6 is a strongly growing frame of similarity. Therefore, GS is complete with respect to the class of all strongly growing models of similarity.

GI The axioms and rules of GI are those of GK plus all the instances of the schemata $[P]A \rightarrow A$, $A \rightarrow [P]\neg[P]\neg A$ and $[P]A \rightarrow [P][P]A$. Since the canonical model of GI is a growing model of indiscernability, then GI is complete with respect to the class of all growing models of indiscernability. Let $\mathcal{F} = (W, R)$ be a growing frame of indiscernability. For every subset $P \in \mathcal{P}(PAR)$, let $\pi(P)$ be the mapping on $W \times W$ to $\mathcal{P}(W)$ defined by: for every possible world $x, y \in W$, $\pi(P)(x, y) = R(P)(x) + R(P)(y)$. Direct calculations would lead to the conclusion that the frame $\mathcal{F}'$ of lemma 6 is a strongly growing frame of indiscernability. Therefore, GI is complete with respect to the class of all strongly growing models of indiscernability.

Since the canonical model of GK plus $[P]A \to [P][P]A$ is transitive and growing, then GK plus $[P]A \to [P][P]A$ is complete with respect to the class of all transitive and growing models. Let $\mathcal{F} = (W, R)$ be a transitive and growing frame. For every subset $P \in \mathcal{P}(PAR)$, let $\pi(P)$ be a mapping on $W \times W$ to $\mathcal{P}(W)$ such that:

C_a for every $x, y \in W$, $\pi(P)(x, y) = \emptyset$ iff $x\ R(P)\ y$,
C_b for every $x, y, z \in W$, $\pi(P)(x, y) + \pi(P)(y, z) = \pi(P)(x, z)$.

Direct calculations would lead to the conclusion that the frame $\mathcal{F}'$ of lemma 6 is transitive and strongly growing. Therefore, GK plus $[P]A \to [P][P]A$ is complete with respect to the class of all transitive and strongly growing models provided that for every transitive and growing frame $\mathcal{F} = (W, R)$ and for every subset $P \in \mathcal{P}(PAR)$, there exists a mapping $\pi(P)$ on $W \times W$ to $\mathcal{P}(W)$ satisfying the conditions C_a and C_b mentioned above.

Since the canonical model of GK plus $[P]A \to A$ and $[P]A \to [P][P]A$ is reflexive, transitive and growing, then GK plus $[P]A \to A$ and $[P]A \to [P][P]A$ is complete with respect to the class of all reflexive, transitive and growing models. Let $\mathcal{F} = (W, R)$ be a reflexive, transitive and growing frame. For every subset $P \in \mathcal{P}(PAR)$, let $\pi(P)$ be a mapping on $W \times W$ to $\mathcal{P}(W)$ satisfying the conditions C_a and C_b mentioned above. Direct calculations would lead to the conclusion that the frame $\mathcal{F}'$ of lemma 6 is reflexive, transitive and strongly growing. Therefore, GK plus $[P]A \to A$ and $[P]A \to [P][P]A$ is complete with respect to the class of all reflexive, transitive and strongly growing models provided that for every reflexive, transitive and growing frame $\mathcal{F} = (W, R)$ and for every subset $P \in \mathcal{P}(PAR)$, there exists a mapping $\pi(P)$ on $W \times W$ to $\mathcal{P}(W)$ satisfying the conditions C_a and C_b mentioned above.

Hence, the method of the copying developed so far does not apply to the proof of the standard completeness of the logics based on transitive and growing models or based on reflexive, transitive and growing models.

4 Decreasing Modal Logics

The language and the semantics of the decreasing modal logics are those of the relative modal logics where the class of the relatives frames is restricted to decreasing frames.

4.1 Decreasing frames

The relative frame $\mathcal{F} = (W, R)$ is *decreasing* if for every subset $P, Q \in \mathcal{P}(PAR)$:

- $R(P \cup Q) \subseteq R(P) \cap R(Q)$.

The frame $\mathcal{F} = (W, R)$ is *strongly decreasing* if for every subset $P, Q \in \mathcal{P}(PAR)$:

- $R(P \cup Q) = R(P) \cap R(Q)$.

Example 2. $IPDL$ – the propositional dynamic logic with the intersection operator on programs [Ha1] – is a logic based on decreasing Kripke models with relative accessibility relations.

Example 3. KR – the modal logic in the theory of information systems introduced by Orłowska [Or3] – is a logic based on decreasing Kripke models with relative accessibility relations. A proof of its completeness is presented in section 4.4.

Example 4. The modal logics for reasoning about indiscernability and relative similarity introduced by Konikowska are logics based on decreasing Kripke models with relative accessibility relations. A proof of their completeness in the context of finite models is presented in [Ko1] and [Ko2].

Example 5. $DABXY$ – the deontic logic of action introduced by Bailhache [Ba1] – is a logic based on decreasing Kripke models with relative accessibility relations. A proof of its completeness is presented in section 8.

Example 6. $S5_n^D$ – the epistemic logic of distributed knowledge introduced by Fagin, Halpern and Vardi [FHV1] – is a logic based on decreasing Kripke models with relative accessibility relations. A proof of its completeness is presented in section 9.

4.2 Logic DK

The axioms and rules of DK are those of K plus all the instances of the following schema:

- $[P]A \vee [Q]A \rightarrow [P \cup Q]A$.

Direct calculations would lead to the conclusion that:

Theorem 8. *The theorems of DK are valid in every decreasing model.*

Since the canonical model of DK is decreasing, then:

Theorem 9. *DK is complete with respect to the class of all decreasing models.*

However, the canonical model of DK is not strongly decreasing. The following section presents the proof of the completeness of DK with respect to the class of all strongly decreasing models.

4.3 Standard completeness

Let $\mathcal{F} = (W, R)$ be a decreasing frame. Let I be the set of the mappings f on $\mathcal{P}(PAR) \times PAR$ to $\mathcal{P}(W)$ such that, for every subset $P \in \mathcal{P}(PAR)$, the set $\{\alpha$: $\alpha \in P$ and $f(P, \alpha) \neq \emptyset\}$ is finite. Let $W' = W \times I$.

For every subset $P \in \mathcal{P}(PAR)$, let $\pi(P)$ be a mapping on $W \times W$ to $\mathcal{P}(W)$ such that, for every possible world $x, y \in W$, $\pi(P)(x, y) = \emptyset$ iff $x\ R(P)\ y$. For every subset $P \in \mathcal{P}(PAR)$, let $R'(P)$ be the binary relation on W' defined by: $(x, f)\ R'(P)\ (y, g)$ iff

- $x\ R(P)\ y$ and
- for every parameter $\alpha \in P$ and for every subset $Q \in \mathcal{P}(PAR)$, if $\alpha \in Q$ then $f(Q, \alpha) + g(Q, \alpha) = \emptyset$ and
- for every subset $Q \in \mathcal{P}(PAR)$, $\Sigma_{\alpha \in Q} f(Q, \alpha) + g(Q, \alpha) = \pi(Q)(x, y)$.

Direct calculations would lead to the conclusion that $\mathcal{F}' = (W', R')$ is decreasing.

Let ϕ be a mapping on $\mathcal{P}(PAR) \times \mathcal{P}(PAR)$ to PAR such that, for every subset $P, Q \in \mathcal{P}(PAR)$, if $Q \not\subseteq P$ then $\phi(P, Q) \in Q$ and $\phi(P, Q) \notin P$. For every subset $P \in \mathcal{P}(PAR)$, for every mapping $f \in I$ and for every possible world $x, y \in W$, if $x\ R(P)\ y$ then, for every subset $Q \in \mathcal{P}(PAR)$ and for every parameter $\alpha \in PAR$, let $g(Q, \alpha)$ be the subset of W defined in the following way:

- If $\alpha \notin Q$ then $g(Q, \alpha) = \emptyset$.
- If $\alpha \in Q$ and $\alpha \in P$ then $g(Q, \alpha) = f(Q, \alpha)$.
- If $\alpha \in Q$ and $\alpha \notin P$ then either $\alpha = \phi(P, Q)$ — in this case $g(Q, \alpha) = \Sigma_{\beta \in Q \setminus P} f(Q, \beta) + \pi(Q)(x, y)$ — or $\alpha \neq \phi(P, Q)$ — in this case $g(Q, \alpha) = \emptyset$.

Direct calculations would lead to the conclusion that $g \in I$ and $(x, f)\ R'(P)\ (y, g)$. Consequently, for every subset $P \in \mathcal{P}(PAR)$, for every mapping $f \in I$ and for every possible world $x, y \in W$, $x\ R(P)\ y$ only if there exists a mapping $g \in I$ such that $(x, f)\ R'(P)\ (y, g)$.

Every mapping $f \in I$ can equally be considered as the mapping on W to W' defined in the following way:

- $f(x) = (x, f)$.

Hence, I is a copying from $\mathcal{F}$ into $\mathcal{F}'$.

For every subset $P, Q \in \mathcal{P}(PAR)$, for every mapping $f, g \in I$ and for every possible world $x, y \in W$, if $(x, f)\ R'(P)\ (y, g)$ and $(x, f)\ R'(Q)\ (y, g)$ then, for every parameter $\alpha \in P \cup Q$, either $\alpha \in P$ or $\alpha \in Q$ and, for every subset $O \in \mathcal{P}(PAR)$, if $\alpha \in O$ then $f(O, \alpha) + g(O, \alpha) = \emptyset$. Moreover, for every subset $O \in \mathcal{P}(PAR)$, $\Sigma_{\alpha \in O} f(O, \alpha) + g(O, \alpha) = \pi(O)(x, y)$. Since, for every parameter $\alpha \in P \cup Q$, $f(P \cup Q, \alpha) + g(P \cup Q, \alpha) = \emptyset$, then $\pi(P \cup Q)(x, y) = \emptyset$ and $x\ R(P \cup Q)\ y$. Consequently, $(x, f)\ R'(P \cup Q)\ (y, g)$. Therefore, for every subset $P, Q \in \mathcal{P}(PAR)$, $R'(P) \cap R'(Q) \subseteq R'(P \cup Q)$.

Therefore, $\mathcal{F}'$ is strongly decreasing. Consequently:

Lemma 10. *For every decreasing frame $\mathcal{F}$, there exists a strongly decreasing frame $\mathcal{F}'$ and a copying from $\mathcal{F}$ into $\mathcal{F}'$.*

Therefore:

Theorem 11. *DK is complete with respect to the class of all strongly decreasing models.*

4.4 Extensions of *DK*

DK is the most elementary decreasing modal logic. As for the extensions of *GK*, direct calculations would lead to the conclusion that:

- $DD = DK$ plus $[P]A \to \neg[P]\neg A$ is complete with respect to the class of all serial and strongly decreasing models.
- $DT = DK$ plus $[P]A \to A$ is complete with respect to the class of all reflexive and strongly decreasing models.
- $DB = DK$ plus $A \to [P]\neg[P]\neg A$ is complete with respect to the class of all symmetrical and strongly decreasing models.
- $DS = DK$ plus $[P]A \to A$ and $A \to [P]\neg[P]\neg A$ is complete with respect to the class of all strongly decreasing models of similarity.
- $KR = DI = DK$ plus $[P]A \to A$, $A \to [P]\neg[P]\neg A$ and $[P]A \to [P][P]A$ is complete with respect to the class of all strongly decreasing models of indiscernability[4].

As for the transitive or the reflexive and transitive extensions of *GK*, the method of the copying developed so far does not apply to the proof of the standard completeness of the logics based on transitive and decreasing models or based on reflexive, transitive and decreasing models.

5 Cosy Growing Modal Logics

The language and the semantics of the cosy growing modal logics are those of the relative modal logics. The only modifications are that the set $\mathcal{P}(PAR)$ of the subsets of PAR should be replaced by the set $\mathcal{P}(PAR)^\bullet$ of the finite subsets of PAR, and moreover, the class of relatives frames should be restricted to cosy growing frames.

5.1 Cosy growing frames

The frame $\mathcal{F} = (W, R)$ is *cosy growing* if for every subset $P, Q \in \mathcal{P}(PAR)^\bullet$:

- $R(P \cap Q) \subseteq R(P) \cap R(Q)$ and
- $R(P \cup Q) = R(P) \cup R(Q)$.

[4] *KR* is the modal logic in the theory of information systems introduced by Orłowska [Or3].

Since, for every subset $P \in \mathcal{P}(PAR)^\bullet$, if $|P| \geq 2$ then $P = \bigcup_{a \in P} \overline{a}$, then[5]:

Lemma 12. *Let $\mathcal{F} = (W, R)$ be a cosy growing frame. Then, for every subset $P \in \mathcal{P}(PAR)^\bullet$, if $|P| \geq 2$ then $R(P) = \bigcup_{a \in P} R(\overline{a})$.*

The frame $\mathcal{F} = (W, R)$ is *strongly cosy growing* if for every subset $P, Q \in \mathcal{P}(PAR)^\bullet$:

- $R(P \cap Q) = R(P) \cap R(Q)$ and
- $R(P \cup Q) = R(P) \cup R(Q)$.

Example 7. BML – the Boolean modal logic introduced by Gargov and Passy [GP1] – is a logic based on cosy growing Kripke models with relative accessibility relations.

Example 8. $DALLA$ – the logic for data analysis with local agreement introduced by Gargov and further studied by Demri and Orłowska [De1] [DO1] – is a logic based on cosy growing Kripke models with relative accessibility relations. A proof of its completeness is presented in section 5.4.

5.2 Logic *CGK*

The axiomatic basis of the cosy growing modal logics is that of the relative modal logics. The only modification if that the set $\mathcal{P}(PAR)$ should be replaced by the set $\mathcal{P}(PAR)^\bullet$ of the finite subsets of PAR. The axioms and rules of CGK are those of K plus all the instances of the following schemata:

- $[P]A \vee [Q]A \rightarrow [P \cap Q]A$,
- $[P]A \wedge [Q]A \rightarrow [P \cup Q]A$.

Direct calculations would lead to the conclusion that:

Theorem 13. *The theorems of CGK are valid in every cosy growing model.*

Since the canonical model of CGK is cosy growing, then:

Theorem 14. *CGK is complete with respect to the class of all cosy growing models.*

However, the canonical model of CGK is not strongly cosy growing. The following section presents the proof of the completeness of CGK with respect to the class of all strongly cosy growing models.

[5] The main part of the proof of lemma 12 uses the fact that the elements of $\mathcal{P}(PAR)^\bullet$ are finite subsets of PAR.

5.3 Standard completeness

Let $\mathcal{F} = (W, R)$ be a cosy growing frame. Let I be the set of the mappings f on $\mathcal{P}(PAR)^{\bullet} \times PAR$ to $\mathcal{P}(W)$ such that, for every subset $P \in \mathcal{P}(PAR)^{\bullet}$, the set $\{\alpha: \alpha \in \underline{P}$ and $f(P,\alpha) \neq \emptyset\}$ is finite. Let $W' = W \times I$.

For every subset $P \in \mathcal{P}(PAR)^{\bullet}$, let $\pi(P)$ be a mapping on $W \times W$ to $\mathcal{P}(W)$ such that, for every possible world $x, y \in W$, $\pi(P)(x,y) = \emptyset$ iff $x\ R(P)\ y$. Let $R'(\emptyset)$ be the binary relation on W' defined by:

$(x, f)\ R'(\emptyset)\ (y, g)$ iff

- $x\ R(\emptyset)\ y$ and
- for every parameter $\alpha \in PAR$ and for every subset $P \in \mathcal{P}(PAR)^{\bullet}$, if $\alpha \in \underline{P}$ then $f(P,\alpha) + g(P,\alpha) = \emptyset$.

For every parameter $a \in PAR$, let $R'(\overline{a})$ be the binary relation on W' defined by:

$(x, f)\ R'(\overline{a})\ (y, g)$ iff

- $x\ R(\overline{a})\ y$ and
- for every parameter $\alpha \in \underline{a}$ and for every subset $P \in \mathcal{P}(PAR)^{\bullet}$, if $\alpha \in \underline{P}$ then $f(P,\alpha) + g(P,\alpha) = \emptyset$ and
- for every subset $P \in \mathcal{P}(PAR)^{\bullet}$, $\Sigma_{\alpha \in \underline{P}} f(P,\alpha) + g(P,\alpha) = \pi(P)(x,y)$.

For every subset $P \in \mathcal{P}(PAR)^{\bullet}$, if $|P| \geq 2$ then let $R'(P) = \bigcup_{a \in P} R'(\overline{a})$. Direct calculations would lead to the conclusion that $\mathcal{F}' = (W', R')$ is cosy growing and I is a copying from $\mathcal{F}$ into $\mathcal{F}'$.

For every parameter $a, b \in PAR$, if $a \neq b$ then, for every mapping $f, g \in I$ and for every possible world $x, y \in W$, if $(x, f)\ R'(\overline{a})\ (y, g)$ and $(x, f)\ R'(\overline{b})\ (y, g)$ then, for every parameter $\alpha \in PAR$, either $\alpha \in \underline{a}$ or $\alpha \in \underline{b}$ and, for every subset $P \in \mathcal{P}(PAR)^{\bullet}$, if $\alpha \in \underline{P}$ then $f(P,\alpha) + g(P,\alpha) = \emptyset$. Moreover, $\Sigma_{\alpha \in \underline{\emptyset}} f(\emptyset,\alpha) + g(\emptyset,\alpha) = \pi(\emptyset)(x,y)$. Since, for every parameter $\alpha \in \underline{\emptyset}$, $f(\emptyset,\alpha) + g(\emptyset,\alpha) = \emptyset$, then $\pi(\emptyset)(x,y) = \emptyset$ and $x\ R(\emptyset)\ y$. Consequently, $(x, f)\ R'(\emptyset)\ (y, g)$. Therefore, for every parameter $a, b \in PAR$, if $a \neq b$ then $R'(\overline{a}) \cap R'(\overline{b}) \subseteq R'(\emptyset)$. Consequently, for every subset $P, Q \in \mathcal{P}(PAR)^{\bullet}$, $R'(P) \cap R'(Q) \subseteq R'(P \cap Q)$.

Therefore, $\mathcal{F}'$ is strongly cosy growing. Consequently:

Lemma 15. *For every cosy growing frame $\mathcal{F}$, there exists a strongly cosy growing frame $\mathcal{F}'$ and a copying from $\mathcal{F}$ into $\mathcal{F}'$.*

Therefore:

Theorem 16. *CGK is complete with respect to the class of all strongly cosy growing models.*

5.4 Extensions of Logic *CGK*

CGK is the most elementary cosy growing modal logic. As for the extensions of *GK*, direct calculations would lead to the conclusion that:

- $CGD = CGK$ plus $[P]A \to \neg[P]\neg A$ is complete with respect to the class of all serial and strongly cosy growing models.
- $CGT = CGK$ plus $[P]A \to A$ is complete with respect to the class of all reflexive and strongly cosy growing models.
- $CGB = CGK$ plus $A \to [P]\neg[P]\neg A$ is complete with respect to the class of all symmetrical and strongly cosy growing models.
- $CGS = CGK$ plus $[P]A \to A$ and $A \to [P]\neg[P]\neg A$ is complete with respect to the class of all strongly cosy growing models of similarity.

As for the class of all strongly cosy growing models of indiscernability, direct calculations would lead to the conclusion that:

Lemma 17. *Let $\mathcal{F} = (W, R)$ be a cosy growing frame of indiscernability. Then, $\mathcal{F}$ is strongly cosy growing iff the schema $[P \cap Q]A \to [P]A \vee [Q]A$ is valid in $\mathcal{F}$.*

Consequently, $DALLA = CGI = CGK$ plus $[P]A \to A$, $A \to [P]\neg[P]\neg A$, $[P]A \to [P][P]A$ and $[P \cap Q]A \to [P]A \vee [Q]A$ is complete with respect to the class of all strongly cosy growing models of indiscernability[6].

As for the transitive or the reflexive and transitive extensions of GK, the method of the copying developed so far does not apply to the proof of the standard completeness of the logics based on transitive and cosy growing models or based on reflexive, transitive and cosy growing models.

6 Cosy Decreasing Modal Logics

The language and the semantics of the cosy decreasing modal logics are those of the relative modal logics with the following modifications: the set $\mathcal{P}(PAR)$ of the subsets of PAR should be replaced by the set $\mathcal{P}(PAR)^\circ$ of the cofinite subsets of PAR, and moreover, the class of relative frames should be restricted to cosy decreasing frames.

6.1 Cosy decreasing frames

The frame $\mathcal{F} = (W, R)$ is *cosy decreasing* if for every subset $P, Q \in \mathcal{P}(PAR)^\circ$:

- $R(P \cup Q) \subseteq R(P) \cap R(Q)$ and
- $R(P \cap Q) = R(P) \cup R(Q)$.

Since, for every subset $P \in \mathcal{P}(PAR)^\circ$, if $|\underline{P}| \geq 2$ then $P = \bigcap_{a \in \underline{P}} \underline{a}$, then[7]:

Lemma 18. *Let $\mathcal{F} = (W, R)$ be a cosy decreasing frame. Then, for every subset $P \in \mathcal{P}(PAR)^\circ$, if $|\underline{P}| \geq 2$ then $R(P) = \bigcup_{a \in \underline{P}} R(\underline{a})$.*

---

[6] $DALLA$ is the logic for data analysis with local agreement introduced by Gargov and further studied by Demri and Orłowska [De1] [DO1].

[7] The main part of the proof of lemma 18 uses the fact that the elements of $\mathcal{P}(PAR)^\circ$ are cofinite subsets of PAR.

The frame $\mathcal{F} = (W, R)$ is *strongly cosy decreasing* when, for every subset $P, Q \in \mathcal{P}(PAR)^{\circ}$:

- $R(P \cup Q) = R(P) \cap R(Q)$ and
- $R(P \cap Q) = R(P) \cup R(Q)$.

6.2 Logic CDK

The axiomatic basis of the cosy decreasing modal logics is that of the relative modal logics. The only modification is that the set $\mathcal{P}(PAR)$ should be replaced by the set $\mathcal{P}(PAR)^{\circ}$. The axioms and rules of CDK are those of K plus all the instances of the following schemata:

- $[P]A \vee [Q]A \rightarrow [P \cup Q]A$,
- $[P]A \wedge [Q]A \rightarrow [P \cap Q]A$.

Direct calculations would lead to the conclusion that:

Theorem 19. *The theorems of CDK are valid in every cosy decreasing model.*

Since the canonical model of CDK is cosy decreasing, then:

Theorem 20. *CDK is complete with respect to the class of all cosy decreasing models.*

However, the canonical model of CDK is not strongly cosy decreasing. The following section presents the proof of the completeness of CDK with respect to the class of all strongly cosy decreasing models.

6.3 Standard completeness

Let $\mathcal{F} = (W, R)$ be a cosy decreasing frame. Let I be the set of the mappings f on $\mathcal{P}(PAR)^{\circ} \times PAR$ to $\mathcal{P}(W)$ such that, for every subset $P \in \mathcal{P}(PAR)^{\circ}$, the set $\{\alpha \colon \alpha \in P \text{ and } f(P, \alpha) \neq \emptyset\}$ is finite. Let $W' = W \times I$.

For every subset $P \in \mathcal{P}(PAR)^{\circ}$, let $\pi(P)$ be a mapping on $W \times W$ to $\mathcal{P}(W)$ such that, for every possible world $x, y \in W$, $\pi(P)(x, y) = \emptyset$ iff $x\ R(P)\ y$. Let $R'(PAR)$ be the binary relation on W' defined by:

$(x, f)\ R'(PAR)\ (y, g)$ iff

- $x\ R(PAR)\ y$ and
- for every parameter $\alpha \in PAR$ and for every subset $P \in \mathcal{P}(PAR)^{\circ}$, if $\alpha \in P$ then $f(P, \alpha) + g(P, \alpha) = \emptyset$.

For every parameter $a \in PAR$, let $R'(\underline{a})$ be the binary relation on W' defined by:

$(x, f)\ R'(\underline{a})\ (y, g)$ iff

- $x\ R(\underline{a})\ y$ and

- for every parameter $\alpha \in \underline{a}$ and for every subset $P \in \mathcal{P}(PAR)^\circ$, if $\alpha \in P$ then $f(P, \alpha) + g(P, \alpha) = \emptyset$ and
- for every subset $P \in \mathcal{P}(PAR)^\circ$, $\Sigma_{\alpha \in P} f(P, \alpha) + g(P, \alpha) = \pi(P)(x, y)$.

For every subset $P \in \mathcal{P}(PAR)^\circ$, if $|\underline{P}| \geq 2$ then let $R'(P) = \bigcup_{a \in \underline{P}} R'(\underline{a})$. Direct calculations would lead to the conclusion that $\mathcal{F}' = (W', R')$ is cosy decreasing and I is a copying from $\mathcal{F}$ into $\mathcal{F}'$.

For every parameter $a, b \in PAR$, if $a \neq b$ then, for every mapping $f, g \in I$ and for every possible world $x, y \in W$, if $(x, f)\ R'(\underline{a})\ (y, g)$ and $(x, f)\ R'(\underline{b})\ (y, g)$ then, for every parameter $\alpha \in PAR$, either $\alpha \in \underline{a}$ or $\alpha \in \underline{b}$ and, for every subset $P \in \mathcal{P}(PAR)^\circ$, if $\alpha \in P$ then $f(P, \alpha) + g(P, \alpha) = \emptyset$. Moreover, $\Sigma_{\alpha \in PAR} f(PAR, \alpha) + g(PAR, \alpha) = \pi(PAR)(x, y)$. Since, for every parameter $\alpha \in PAR$, $f(PAR, \alpha) + g(PAR, \alpha) = \emptyset$, then $\pi(PAR)(x, y) = \emptyset$ and $x\ R(PAR)\ y$. Consequently, $(x, f)\ R'(PAR)\ (y, g)$. Therefore, for every parameter $a, b \in PAR$, if $a \neq b$ then $R'(\underline{a}) \cap R'(\underline{b}) \subseteq R'(PAR)$. Consequently, for every subset $P, Q \in \mathcal{P}(PAR)^\circ$, $R'(P) \cap R'(Q) \subseteq R'(P \cup Q)$.

Therefore, $\mathcal{F}'$ is strongly cosy decreasing. Consequently:

Lemma 21. *For every cosy decreasing frame $\mathcal{F}$, there exists a strongly cosy decreasing frame $\mathcal{F}'$ and a copying from $\mathcal{F}$ into $\mathcal{F}'$.*

Therefore:

Theorem 22. *CDK is complete with respect to the class of all strongly cosy decreasing models.*

6.4 Extensions of Logic CDK

CDK is the most elementary cosy decreasing modal logic. As for the extensions of GK, direct calculations would lead to the conclusion that:

- $CDD = CDK$ plus $[P]A \rightarrow \neg[P]\neg A$ is complete with respect to the class of all serial and strongly cosy decreasing models.
- $CDT = CDK$ plus $[P]A \rightarrow A$ is complete with respect to the class of all reflexive and strongly cosy decreasing models.
- $CDB = CDK$ plus $A \rightarrow [P]\neg[P]\neg A$ is complete with respect to the class of all symmetrical and strongly cosy decreasing models.
- $CDS = CDK$ plus $[P]A \rightarrow A$ and $A \rightarrow [P]\neg[P]\neg A$ is complete with respect to the class of all strongly cosy decreasing models of similarity.

As for the class of all strongly cosy decreasing models of indiscernability, direct calculations would lead to the conclusion that:

Lemma 23. *Let $\mathcal{F} = (W, R)$ be a cosy decreasing frame of indiscernability. Then, $\mathcal{F}$ is strongly cosy decreasing iff the schema $[P \cup Q]A \rightarrow [P]A \vee [Q]A$ is valid in $\mathcal{F}$.*

Consequently, $CDI = CDK$ plus $[P]A \rightarrow A$, $A \rightarrow [P]\neg[P]\neg A$, $[P]A \rightarrow [P][P]A$ and $[P \cup Q]A \rightarrow [P]A \vee [Q]A$ is complete with respect to the class of all strongly cosy decreasing models of indiscernability.

As for the transitive or the reflexive and transitive extensions of GK, the method of the copying developed so far does not apply to the proof of the standard completeness of the logics based on transitive and cosy decreasing models or based on reflexive, transitive and cosy decreasing models.

7 *DAL* – a Logic for Data Analysis

This section presents a logic DAL (a logic for date analysis) which is based on growing Kripke models with relative accessibility relations. The proof of its completeness partly solves an open problem brought up by Fariñas del Cerro and Orłowska [FO1].

The objective of DAL is the formalization of reasoning with incomplete information about objects given in terms of attributes. Fariñas del Cerro and Orłowska [FO1] consider the objects of a system of information and suggest that the language of DAL should included, for every subset, $P \in \mathcal{P}(PAR)^{\bullet}$, the modal operator $[P]$.

7.1 Language

The linguistic basis of the modal logic for data analysis is the propositional calculus. Let VAR be a nonempty set of *atomic formulas.* For every subset $P \in \mathcal{P}(PAR)^{\bullet}$, the modal operator $[P]$ is added to the standard propositional formalism.

7.2 Semantics

Frames for data analysis A *frame for data analysis* is a relational structure of the form $\mathcal{F} = (W, R)$ where W is a nonempty set of *possible worlds* and R is a mapping on $\mathcal{P}(PAR)^{\bullet}$ to the set of the equivalence relations on W such that, for every subset $P, Q \in \mathcal{P}(PAR)^{\bullet}$:

- $R(P \cap Q) \subseteq R(P) \cap R(Q)$ and
- if $|P| \geq 2$ then $R(P) = \bigcup^{*}_{a \in P} R(\overline{a})^{8}$.

The data frame $\mathcal{F} = (W, R)$ is *standard* if for every subset $P, Q \in \mathcal{P}(PAR)^{\bullet}$:

- if $P \cap Q = \emptyset$ then $R(P \cap Q) = R(P) \cap R(Q)$.

The data frame $\mathcal{F} = (W, R)$ is *strictly standard* if for every subset $P, Q \in \mathcal{P}(PAR)^{\bullet}$:

- $R(P \cap Q) = R(P) \cap R(Q)$.

[8] For every subset $P \in \mathcal{P}(PAR)^{\bullet}$, if $|P| \geq 2$ then the relation $\bigcup^{*}_{a \in P} R(\overline{a})$ is the transitive closure of the relation $\bigcup_{a \in P} R(\overline{a})$.

Satisfiability Let $\mathcal{F} = (W, R)$ be a data frame and m be an assignment on $\mathcal{F}$. The *satisfiability relation* in the model $\mathcal{M} = (\mathcal{F}, m)$ between a possible world $x \in W$ and a formula A is defined in the following way:

- for every subset $P \in \mathcal{P}(PAR)^\bullet$, $x \models_\mathcal{M} [P]A$ iff, for every possible world $y \in W$, $x\ R(P)\ y$ only if $y \models_\mathcal{M} A$.

7.3 Logic *DAL*

Together with the classical tautologies, all the instances of the following schemata are axioms of DAL:

- $[P](A \rightarrow B) \rightarrow ([P]A \rightarrow [P]B)$,
- $[P]A \rightarrow A$,
- $A \rightarrow [P]\neg[P]\neg A$,
- $[P]A \rightarrow [P][P]A$,
- $[P]A \vee [Q]A \rightarrow [P \cap Q]A$,
- if $|P| \geq 2$ then $[P]A \rightarrow \bigwedge_{a \in P}[\overline{a}][P]A$,
- if $|P| \geq 2$ then $[P](A \rightarrow \bigwedge_{a \in P}[\overline{a}]A) \rightarrow (A \rightarrow [P]A)$.

Together with the modus ponens, the instances of the following schema is a rule of DAL:

- if $\vdash_{DAL} A$ then $\vdash_{DAL} [P]A$.

Direct calculations would lead to the conclusion that:

Theorem 24. *The theorems of DAL are valid in every data model.*

Since the canonical model of DAL can be filtered into a data model[9], then:

Theorem 25. *DAL is complete with respect to the class of all data models.*

However, the canonical model of DAL cannot be filtered into a standard data model. The following section presents the proof of the completeness of DAL with respect to the class of all standard data models.

7.4 Standard completeness

Let $\mathcal{F} = (W, R)$ be a data frame. Let I be the set of the mappings f on $\mathcal{P}(PAR)^\bullet \times PAR$ to $\mathcal{P}(W)$ such that, for every subset $P \in \mathcal{P}(PAR)^\bullet$, the set $\{\alpha\colon \alpha \in \underline{P}$ and $f(P, \alpha) \neq \emptyset\}$ is finite. Let $W' = W \times I$.

For every subset $P \in \mathcal{P}(PAR)^\bullet$, let $\pi(P)$ be the mapping on $W \times W$ to $\mathcal{P}(W)$ defined by: for every possible world $x, y \in W$, $\pi(P)(x, y) = R(P)(x) + R(P)(y)$. Let $R'(\emptyset)$ be the binary relation on W' defined by:

$(x, f)\ R'(\emptyset)\ (y, g)$ iff

[9] See Goldblatt [Gol] for a similar use of the technics of the filtration in the context of the propositional dynamic logic.

- $x\ R(\emptyset)\ y$ and
- for every parameter $\alpha \in PAR$ and for every subset $P \in \mathcal{P}(PAR)^{\bullet}$, if $\alpha \in \underline{P}$ then $f(P,\alpha) + g(P,\alpha) = \emptyset$.

For every parameter $a \in PAR$, let $R'(\overline{a})$ be the binary relation on W' defined by:

$(x, f)\ R'(\overline{a})\ (y, g)$ iff

- $x\ R(\overline{a})\ y$ and
- for every parameter $\alpha \in \underline{a}$ and for every subset $P \in \mathcal{P}(PAR)^{\bullet}$, if $\alpha \in \underline{P}$ then $f(P,\alpha) + g(P,\alpha) = \emptyset$ and
- for every subset $P \in \mathcal{P}(PAR)^{\bullet}$, $\Sigma_{\alpha \in \underline{P}} f(P,\alpha) + g(P,\alpha) = \pi(P)(x,y)$.

For every subset $P \in \mathcal{P}(PAR)^{\bullet}$, if $|P| \geq 2$ then let $R'(P) = \bigcup^{*}_{a \in P} R'(\overline{a})$. Direct calculations would lead to the conclusion that the data frame $\mathcal{F}' = (W', R')$ is standard and I is a copying from $\mathcal{F}$ into $\mathcal{F}'$. Consequently:

Theorem 26. *DAL is complete with respect to the class of all standard data models.*

8 *DABXY*: a Deontic Logic of Action

This section presents a logic *DABXY* (a deontic logic of action) based on decreasing Kripke models with relative accessibility relations. The proof of its completeness solves an open problem brought up by Bailhache [Ba1].

The objective of deontic logic is the formalization of reasoning about the concepts of obligation and permission [Wr1]. Bailhache [Ba1] considers the agents of a hierarchical universe, like the servicemen of an army or the civil servants of an administration, and suggests that the language of deontic logic should be based on the modal operator $\bigcirc$ ("it is obligatory that") and, for every subset $P \in \mathcal{P}(PAR)^{*}$ (the sets of nonempty finite subsets of PAR), the modal operators $[P]$ ("every nonempty subset of P makes it necessary that") and $[P]'$ ("some nonempty subset of P makes it necessary that").

8.1 Language

The linguistic basis of the deontic logic of action is the propositional calculus. Let VAR be a nonempty set of *atomic formulas*. The modal operator $\bigcirc$ and, for every subset $P \in \mathcal{P}(PAR)^{*}$, the modal operators $[P]$ and $[P]'$ are added to the standard propositional formalism.

8.2 Semantics

Deontic frames of action A *deontic frame of action* is a relational structure of the form $\mathcal{F} = (W, S, R, R')$ where W is a nonempty set of *possible worlds*, S

is a serial[10] and post-reflexive[11] relation on W and R and R' are mappings on $\mathcal{P}(PAR)^*$ to the set of the reflexive relations on W such that, for every subset $P, Q \in \mathcal{P}(PAR)^*$ and for every parameter $a \in PAR$ the following conditions are satisfied:

- $R(P \cup Q) \subseteq R(P) \cap R(Q)$,
- $R'(P \cup Q) = R'(P) \cup R'(Q)$,
- $R(\overline{a}) = R'(\overline{a})$.

The deontic frame $\mathcal{F} = (W, S, R, R')$ is *standard* if for every subset $P, Q \in \mathcal{P}(PAR)^*$:

- $R(P \cup Q) = R(P) \cap R(Q)$.

Satisfiability Let $\mathcal{F} = (W, S, R, R')$ be a deontic frame and m be an assignment on $\mathcal{F}$. The *satisfiability relation* in the model $\mathcal{M} = (\mathcal{F}, m)$ between a possible world $x \in W$ and a formula A is defined in the following way:

- $x \models_{\mathcal{M}} \bigcirc A$ iff, for every possible world $y \in W$, $x\ S\ y$ only if $y \models_{\mathcal{M}} A$,
- for every subset $P \in \mathcal{P}(PAR)^*$, $x \models_{\mathcal{M}} [P]A$ iff, for every possible world $y \in W$, $x\ R(P)\ y$ only if $y \models_{\mathcal{M}} A$,
- for every subset $P \in \mathcal{P}(PAR)^*$, $x \models_{\mathcal{M}} [P]'A$ iff, for every possible world $y \in W$, $x\ R'(P)\ y$ only if $y \models_{\mathcal{M}} A$.

8.3 Logic *DABXY*

Together with the classical tautologies, all the instances of the following schemata are axioms of $DABXY$:

- $\bigcirc(A \to B) \to (\bigcirc A \to \bigcirc B)$,
- $\bigcirc A \to \neg \bigcirc \neg A$,
- $\bigcirc(\bigcirc A \to A)$,
- $[P](A \to B) \to ([P]A \to [P]B)$,
- $[P]A \to A$,
- $[P]A \vee [Q]A \to [P \cup Q]A$,
- $[P]'(A \to B) \to ([P]'A \to [P]'B)$,
- $[P]'A \to A$,
- $[P]'A \wedge [Q]'A \leftrightarrow [P \cup Q]'A$,
- $[\overline{a}]A \leftrightarrow [\overline{a}]'A$.

Together with the modus ponens, the instances of the following schemata are rules of $DABXY$:

- if $\vdash_{DABXY} A$ then $\vdash_{DABXY} \bigcirc A$,
- if $\vdash_{DABXY} A$ then $\vdash_{DABXY} [P]A$,

[10] A relation R is serial if for every x there is an y such that xRy.

[11] A relation R is post-reflexive if for any x, y if xRy then yRy.

- if $\vdash_{DABXY} A$ then $\vdash_{DABXY} [P]'A$.

Direct calculations would lead to the conclusion that:

Theorem 27. *The theorems of $DABXY$ are valid in every deontic model.*

Sin‹e the canonical model of $DABXY$ is a deontic model, then:

Theorem 28. *$DABXY$ is complete with respect to the class of all deontic models.*

However, the canonical model of $DABXY$ is not standard. The following section presents the proof of the completeness of $DABXY$ with respect to the class of all standard deontic models.

8.4 Standard completeness

Let $\mathcal{F} = (W, S, R, R')$ be a deontic frame. Let I be the set of the mappings f on $\mathcal{P}(PAR)^* \times PAR$ to $\mathcal{P}(W)$ such that, for every subset $P \in \mathcal{P}(PAR)^*$, the set $\{\alpha\colon \alpha \in P$ and $f(P,\alpha) \neq \emptyset\}$ is finite. Let $\omega = W \times I$.

Let σ be the binary relation on ω defined by $(x, f)\ \sigma\ (y, g)$ iff $x\ S\ y$. For every subset $P \in \mathcal{P}(PAR)^*$, let $\pi(P)$ be a mapping on $W \times W$ to $\mathcal{P}(W)$ such that, for every possible world $x, y \in W$, $\pi(P)(x, y) = \emptyset$ iff $x\ R(P)\ y$. For every subset $P \in \mathcal{P}(PAR)^*$, let $\rho(P)$ be the binary relation on ω defined by (x, f) $\rho(P)\ (y, g)$ iff:

- $x\ R(P)\ y$,
- for every parameter $\alpha \in P$ and for every subset $Q \in \mathcal{P}(PAR)^*$, if $\alpha \in Q$ then $f(Q,\alpha) + g(Q,\alpha) = \emptyset$,
- for every subset $Q \in \mathcal{P}(PAR)^*$, $\Sigma_{\alpha \in Q} f(Q,\alpha) + g(Q,\alpha) = \pi(Q)(x,y)$.

For every subset $P \in \mathcal{P}(PAR)^*$, if $|P| \geq 2$ then let $\rho'(P) = \bigcup_{a \in P} \rho(\overline{a})$. For every parameter $a \in PAR$, let $\rho'(\overline{a}) = \rho(\overline{a})$. Direct calculations would lead to the conclusion that the deontic frame $\Phi = (\omega, \sigma, \rho, \rho')$ is standard and I is a copying from $\mathcal{F}$ into Φ. Consequently:

Theorem 29. *$DABXY$ is complete with respect to the class of all standard deontic models.*

9 $S5_n^D$: an Epistemic Logic of Distributed Knowledge

This section presents a logic $S5_n^D$ (an epistemic logic of distributed knowledge) based on decreasing Kripke models with relative accessibility relations. The proof of its completeness – based on an idea by Vakarelov [Va2] – greatly simplifies the proof given by Fagin, Halpern and Vardi [FHV1] as well as the proof given by van der Hoek and Meyer [HM1].

The objective of epistemic logic is the formalization of reasoning about the concept of knowledge [Hil]. Fagin, Halpern and Vardi [FHV1] consider the machines of a distributed environment and suggests that the language of epistemic logic should be based on the modal operator D ("sharing their resources, the machines know that") and, for every $i \in (n) = \{1, \ldots, n\}$ where n is a natural number, the modal operator K_i ("the machine i knows that").

9.1 Language

The linguistic basis of the epistemic logic of distributed knowledge is the propositional calculus. Let VAR be a nonempty set of *atomic formulas*. The modal operator D and, for every $i \in (n)$, the modal operator K_i are added to the standard propositional formalism.

9.2 Semantics

Frames of distributed knowledge A *frame of distributed knowledge* is a relational structure of the form $\mathcal{F} = (W, R, R_1, \ldots, R_n)$ where W is a nonempty set of *possible worlds*, R is an equivalence relation on W and, for every $i \in (n)$, R_i is a equivalence relation on W such that:

- $R \subseteq R_1 \cap \ldots \cap R_n$.

The knowledge frame $\mathcal{F} = (W, R, R_1, \ldots, R_n)$ is *standard* if:

- $R = R_1 \cap \ldots \cap R_n$.

Satisfiability Let $\mathcal{F} = (W, R, R_1, \ldots, R_n)$ be a knowledge frame and m be an assignment on $\mathcal{F}$. The *satisfiability relation* in the model $\mathcal{M} = (\mathcal{F}, m)$ between a possible world $x \in W$ and a formula A is defined in the following way:

- $x \models_{\mathcal{M}} DA$ iff, for every possible world $y \in W$, $x\ R\ y$ only if $y \models_{\mathcal{M}} A$,
- for every $i \in (n)$, $x \models_{\mathcal{M}} K_iA$ iff, for every possible world $y \in W$, $x\ R_i\ y$ only if $y \models_{\mathcal{M}} A$.

9.3 Logic $S5_n^D$

Together with the classical tautologies, all the instances of the following schemata are axioms of $S5_n^D$:

- $D(A \to B) \to (DA \to DB)$,
- $DA \to A$,
- $A \to D\neg D\neg A$,
- $DA \to DDA$,
- $K_i(A \to B) \to (K_iA \to K_iB)$,
- $K_iA \to A$,
- $A \to K_i\neg K_i\neg A$,

- $K_iA \to K_iK_iA$,
- $K_1A \vee \ldots \vee K_nA \to DA$.

Together with the modus ponens, the instances of the following schema are rules of $S5_n^D$:

- if $\vdash_{S5_n^D} A$ then $\vdash_{S5_n^D} DA$,
- if $\vdash_{S5_n^D} A$ then $\vdash_{S5_n^D} K_iA$.

Direct calculations would lead to the conclusion that:

Theorem 30. *The theorems of $S5_n^D$ are valid in every knowledge model.*

Since the canonical model of $S5_n^D$ is a knowledge model, then:

Theorem 31. *$S5_n^D$ is complete with respect to the class of all knowledge models.*

However, the canonical model of $S5_n^D$ is not standard. The following section presents the proof of the completeness of $S5_n^D$ with respect to the class of all standard knowledge models.

9.4 Standard completeness

Let $\mathcal{F} = (W, R, R_1, \ldots, R_n)$ be a knowledge frame. Let I be the set of the mappings f on (n) to $\mathcal{P}(W)$. Let $W' = W \times I$.

Let π be the mapping on $W \times W$ to $\mathcal{P}(W)$ defined by, for every possible world $x, y \in W$, $\pi(x, y) = R(x) + R(y)$. Let R' be the binary relation on W' defined by $(x, f)\ R'\ (y, g)$ iff:

- $x\ R\ y$,
- for every $i \in (n)$, $f(i) + g(i) = \emptyset$.

For every $i \in (n)$, let R'_i be the binary relation on W' defined by $(x, f)\ R'_i\ (y, g)$ iff:

- $x\ R_i\ y$,
- $f(i) + g(i) = \emptyset$,
- $\Sigma_{j \in (n)} f(j) + g(j) = \pi(x, y)$.

Direct calculations would lead to the conclusion that the knowledge frame $\mathcal{F}' = (W', R', R'_1, \ldots, R'_n)$ is standard and I is a copying from $\mathcal{F}$ into $\mathcal{F}'$. Consequently:

Theorem 32. *$S5_n^D$ is complete with respect to the class of all standard knowledge models.*

10 Conclusion

The general method presented above succeeds in proving the completeness of several logics based on Kripke models with relative accessibility relations whose axiomatizability was open for many years. However, one should not intend to apply it as it stands to every open problem of completeness in the context of the relative modal logics. As a matter of fact, it adapts with difficulty to the proof of the completeness of DAL with respect to the class of all strictly standard data models. Similarly it adapts with difficulty to the proof of the completeness of $IPDL$. One might observe a parallel between this difficulty and the difficulty met with the proof of the standard completeness of the logics based on transitive and growing models or those based on reflexive, transitive and growing models.

However, there are several questions that this paper does not tackle:

- Decidability of the relative modal logics. In this respect, the technics of the filtration [Ch1] [Go1] [HC1] should be of some help.
- Mechanization of the relative modal logics. In this respect, the technics of the resolution [FH1] should be of some help.
- Systematic study of the logics based on Kripke models with relative neighborhood functions. A Kripke model with relative neighborhood functions is a functional structure of the form $\mathcal{F} = (W, N)$ where W is even a nonempty set of possible worlds but, N is a mapping on $\mathcal{P}(PAR)$ to the set of the subsets of $W \times \mathcal{P}(W)$ for PAR being a nonempty set of parameters. In this respect, the parameter structures for parametrized modal operators of Ohlbach and Herzig [OH1] constitute a good introduction to this question.

Acknowledgement

The author wishes to express his thanks and his gratitude to Dimiter Vakarelov as well as to his former colleagues of the *Institut de recherche en informatique de Toulouse* for their valuable comments about the preliminary draft of this paper.

References

[Ba1] Bailhache, P.: Essai de logique déontique. Vrin, (1991)

[Ch1] Chellas, B.: Modal Logic: an Introduction. Cambridge University Press, (1980)

[De1] Demri, S.: The validity problem for the logic *DALLA* is decidable. Bulletin of the Polish Academy of Sciences, **4**, (1996), 79-86

[DO1] Demri, S. and Orłowska, E.: Logical analysis of indiscernability. ICS Research Report 11/96, (1996), Warsaw University of Technology. See also chapter 11.

[FHMV1] Fagin, R., Halpern, J., Moses, Y. and Vardi, M.: Reasoning About Knowledge. MIT Press, (1995)

[FHV1] Fagin, R., Halpern, J. and Vardi, M.: What can machines know? On the properties of knowledge in distributed systems. Journal of the ACM, **39**, (1992), 328-376

[FH1] Fariñas del Cerro, L. and Herzig, A.: Modal deduction with applications in epistemic and temporal logics. D. Gabbay, C. Hogger and J. Robinson (editors), Handbook of Logic in Artificial Intelligence and Logic Programming, **4**, Epistemic and Temporal Reasoning, Oxford University Press, (1995), 499-594

[FO1] Fariñas del Cerro, L. and Orłowska, E.: *DAL* - a logic for data analysis. Theoretical Computer Science, **36**, (1985), 251-264

[GP1] Gargov, G. and Passy, S.: A note on Boolean modal logic. P. Petkov (editor), Mathematical Logic. Plenum Press, (1990), 299-309

[Go1] Goldblatt, R.: Logics of Time and Computation. Center for the Study of Language and Computation, Lecture Notes Number, **7**, (1987)

[Ha1] Harel, D.: Dynamic logic. D. Gabbay and F. Guenthner (editors), Handbook of Philosophical Logic, **2**, Extensions of Classical Logic. Reidel, (1984), 497-604

[Hi1] Hintikka, J.: Knowledge and Belief: an Introduction to the Logic of the two Notions. Cornell University Press, (1962)

[HM1] van der Hoek, W. and Meyer, J.-J.: Making some issues of implicit knowledge explicit. Foundations of Computer Science, **3**, (1992), 193-223

[HC1] Hughes, G. and Cresswell, M.: A Companion to Modal Logic. Methuen, (1984)

[Ko1] Konikowska, B.: A formal language for reasoning about indiscernability. Bulletin of the Polish Academy of Sciences, **35**, (1987), 239-249

[Ko2] Konikowska, B.: A logic for reasoning about relative similarity. E. Orłowska and H. Rasiowa (editors), Reasoning with Incomplete Information. Special issue of Studia Logica 58, (1997), 185-226

[OH1] Ohlbach, H.-J. and Herzig, A.: Parameter structures for parametrized modal operators. J. Mylopoulos and R. Reiter (editors), IJCAI-91, Proceedings of the Twelfth International Conference on Artificial Intelligence, **1**, Darling Harbour, Sydney, Australia, 24-30 August 1991, Morgan Kaufmann, (1991), 512-517

[Or1] Orłowska, E.: Modal logics in the theory of information systems. Zeitschr. f. math. Logik und Grundlagen d. Math., **30**, (1984), 213-222

[Or2] Orłowska, E.: Kripke models with relative accessibility relations and their applications to inferences with incomplete information. G. Mirkowska and H. Rasiowa (editors), Mathematical Problems in Computation Theory. Banach Center Publications, **21**, Polish Scientific Publishers, (1988), 327-337

[Or3] Orłowska, E.: Kripke semantics for knowledge representation logics. Studia Logica, **49**, (1990), 255-272

[Sa1] Sahlqvist, H.: Completeness and correspondence in the first and second order semantics for modal logic. S. Kanger (editor), Proceedings of the Third Scandinavian Logic Symposium. North-Holland, (1975), 110-143

[Va1] Vakarelov, D.: Modal logics for knowledge representation systems. Theoretical Computer Science, **90**, (1991), 433-456

[Va2] Vakarelov, D.: A modal theory of arrows. Arrow logics I. D. Pearce and G. Wagner (editors), Logics in AI, European Workshop JELIA '92, Berlin, Germany, September 1992, Proceedings. Lecture Notes in Artificial Intelligence **633**, Springer-Verlag, (1992), 1-24

[Wr1] von Wright, G.: Deontic logic. Mind, **60**, (1951), 1-15

Chapter 18

Rough Logics: A Survey with Further Directions*

Mohua Banerjee[1] *and Mihir K. Chakraborty*[2]

[1] Machine Intelligence Unit, Indian Statistical Institute, 203, B.T. Road, Calcutta 700 035, India, miux9503@isical.ernet.in

[2] Department of Pure Mathematics, University of Calcutta, 35, Ballygunge Circular Road, Calcutta 700 019, India, itbpc@gems.vsnl.net.in

Abstract: This article surveys syntactic and semantic formalizations of various notions that have arisen in the course of development of rough set theory. To be more specific, the first order theories proposed so far in this connection have been brought into discussion. In the process, comparisons of these systems are made. Some new ideas in this regard have been offered at the end.

1 Introduction

Since the publication of the first work on the theory of rough sets (Pawlak, 1982 [Pa1]), there have been quite a few attempts to accommodate its basic features in formal theories, or, in other words, towards the formulation of what could be termed "rough logic". Needless to say, there are both similarities and divergences among these attempts. As the title of this article indicates, a number of formal systems are now present in the literature on this theory, each of which captures some aspects of the theory. So it seems to be the proper time for introspection, that is a comparative study of the systems proposed so far. This research aims partially at such a study, although it is indeed a hard task. There may be various angles of comparison, of which only one or two can be taken up. Apart from the comparison in which shortcomings of the existing systems will be pointed out, we shall propose some further improvements and express our criticism about these proposals too.

The theory of rough sets considers as its universe of discourse a non-empty set A together with an equivalence relation $\sim$ defined on it. The pair $\langle A, \sim \rangle$ is called an 'approximation space'. As the name suggests, for members x and y of A, it may be said that "x approximates y" or "x approximately equals y" if $x \sim y$ holds. This is a kind of identification at the object level and is crucial in that it is the fundamental indiscernibility relation at the root of a rough set structure.

* Research supported by the Council of Scientific and Industrial Research, Government of India.

This indiscernibility may be induced by a set of attributes, relative to which an object in the universe A is described or understood. Another identification at the higher level, amongst concepts, i.e. subsets of A, also takes place very naturally. Two subsets S, T of A are considered identical, called 'S roughly equals T', if they have the same lower and upper approximations [Pa1]. The lower approximation of a subset S of A is the union of all $\sim$-equivalence classes contained in S, and its upper approximation is the union of all $\sim$-equivalence classes that properly intersect S. Hence, for a logic for rough sets which intends to carry out discourses within an approximation space, it is imperative that its language possesses the capacity for expressing both the above kinds of identifications and its derivation procedure is able to discover facts about them.

It has been observed from the beginning that the lower and upper approximations of a set render modalities in any discourse on rough sets. In fact, not only one but more pairs of mutually dual modalities seem to be relevant, and so multi-modal systems are proposed. Besides, a pair of rough quantifiers, viz. $\mathbb{V}$ (roughly all) and $\exists$ (roughly some) has appeared [Sz1]. In the semantics, notions of 'rough truth' and "rough validity" were proposed by Pawlak himself [Pa2] and in [BC3, CB1] respectively. It will be noticed that most of the formal theories to be discussed have incorporated some or other of the afore-mentioned notions.

From the very inception it was clear that the propositional aspect of rough set theory is well-captured by the modal system S_5. By this we mean that if the well-formed formulae (formulae) of S_5 are interpreted as subsets in an approximation space $\langle A, \sim \rangle$, the operators $\neg, \wedge, \vee, L, M$ can tell the stories related with complementation, intersection, union, lower approximation and upper approximation respectively, of the subsets of A. In essence, this rough set-theoretic interpretation of the modal system S_5 is equivalent to the Kripke semantics. Various authors have contributed to investigations in this direction [BC2, Na1, NG1, Or1, Or2, Or3, Or4, Va1]. In fact, as mentioned before, multi-modal systems have appeared to be more significant in this context, or, to be more precise, in the context of an information system. This is so because any subcollection of attributes in an information system gives rise to an equivalence relation in the set of objects and consideration of various subcollections of attributes plays a crucial role in rough set theory.

It is not our intention to discuss rough propositional logics in this paper. We shall be rather concerned with rough predicate logics. It may be mentioned that a notion called "rough consequence" was introduced by the present authors in [CB1]. Through this notion it was possible to formalize the semantic notions like rough truth and rough validity. Inclusion of rough consequence in the predicate logic is presented at the end of this paper. Secondly, if the calculus of sets in a rough set-up (i.e. in an approximation space) is defined in such a way that the operations (i.e. newly defined union, intersection etc.) are to be compatible with rough equality (and which is quite a natural expectation), the logical system S_5 does not serve the purpose. In a recent work [BC4], the present authors have been able to address this issue satisfactorily, although it was first raised in [BC3]. In this work, a hierarchy of algebras, viz. topological quasi-Boolean algebra, pre-rough algebra and rough algebra has been presented. Their logical counterparts leading to rough (propositional) logic have been proposed. Incidentally, the algebraic system called topological quasi-Boolean algebra was obtained by abstracting some features observed in the so–called "Rough algebra" introduced in [BC1]. The formal definition of the system came up during discussions between the second author and A. Wasilewska in 1993. It was further considered in [WB1, WV1].

While discussing various systems proposed for rough logic, we shall raise the following questions:

(i) does the system allow names for objects?
(ii) does the system require that ordinary identity in A be named?
(iii) are the modal operators definable?
(iv) are the modal operators definable in terms of rough quantifiers only?
(v) is there "roughness" in the semantics too?

These questions, obviously, are related with the semantics that one should like to associate with the corresponding syntax. It will gradually be clear why we would like to attach so much importance to them, particularly to the first two. All the systems, quite naturally, seek interpretations in or using a domain A with an equivalence relation $\sim$, i.e. in an approximation space $\langle A, \sim \rangle$ or in A with more than one equivalence relation. Some of the systems have names for $\sim$ in their languages and some do not.

In the following section, the systems under discussion shall be presented in some detail.

2 Rough Logics

It should be mentioned at the very beginning that the systems proposed by Lin and Liu [LL1] and Nakamura [Na1] have only been presented (we have access to the unpublished rough versions of these texts), while all other systems have been critically appreciated.

$\boldsymbol{L_{RS}}$:

The first proposal was in 1986, by Rasiowa and Skowron [RSk1]. Let this system be denoted by L_{RS}. The syntax of L_{RS} has a countable first order predicate language. The significant features are that the alphabet contains one additional one-place propositional connective L, a special binary predicate π and no constant symbols.

The axioms are such that L may play the role of necessity operator of the modal system S_5 and π turns out to be the name of an equivalence relation in all interpretations. The following axioms, however, need mentioning.

$L_{RS}1.$ $\pi(x,y) \rightarrow (L\alpha(x) \rightarrow L\alpha(y))$,

$\alpha(y)$ is obtained from $\alpha(x)$ by substituting all free occurrences of x in $\alpha(x)$ by y.

$L_{RS}2.$

$$\forall y_1 \ldots \forall y_n((\pi(x_1, y_1) \wedge \ldots \wedge \pi(x_n, y_n)) \rightarrow \alpha(y_1, \ldots, y_n)) \rightarrow L\alpha(x_1, \ldots, x_n) \ ,$$

where $\{x_1, \ldots, x_n\}$ is the set of free variables in $\alpha, \alpha(y_1, \ldots, y_n)$ is the formula obtained by substituting y_i for x_i in $\alpha, i = 1, \ldots, n$.

$L_{RS}3.$ $\alpha \rightarrow L\alpha$
if α contains no free variable.

The rules are:

- $\dfrac{\alpha, \alpha \rightarrow \beta}{\beta}$ (Modus ponens),
- $\dfrac{\alpha}{L\alpha}$ (Necessitation),
- $\dfrac{\alpha(x_1, \ldots, x_n)}{\alpha(\tau_1, \ldots, \tau_n)}$ (Rule of substitution of free individual variables),

where $\alpha(\tau_1, \ldots, \tau_n)$ is obtained from α by substitution of some terms $\tau_1, \ldots, \tau_n$ for free individual variables $x_1, \ldots, x_n$ respectively, and the introduction and elimination of quantifiers $\exists$ and $\forall$, the latter three rules being formulated, we presume, as in [RSi1].

The semantic part consists in a relational structure $\mathcal{U} \equiv \langle A, \sim; \mathcal{P} \rangle$, where $\sim$ is, as before, an equivalence relation and $\mathcal{P}$ a sequence of relations. Because of the axioms for π, π is always interpreted as an equivalence relation denoted by $\sim$. Interpretations of all other symbols are usual ones except that of L. The satisfaction of $L\alpha(x_1, \ldots, x_n)$ by a valuation $\bar{a}$ for the variables is defined thus:

$\mathcal{U}, \bar{a} \models L\alpha(x_1, \ldots, x_n), \{x_1, \ldots, x_n\}$ being the set of free variables in α, if and only if for all $u_1, \ldots, u_n \in A$, if $\bar{a}(x_j) \sim u_j$ for $j = 1, \ldots, n$, then $\mathcal{U}, \bar{a}(u_j/\bar{a}(x_j)) \models \alpha(x_1, \ldots, x_n)$.

Semantic consequence relation $\models$ is defined by:

$\Gamma \models \alpha$ holds if and only if for every structure $\mathcal{U}$, if all the elements in Γ are true then α is also true.

Generalized soundness and completeness theorems, viz. $\Gamma \vdash \alpha$ implies $\Gamma \models \alpha$ and conversely, have been established for any set Γ of formulae and a single formula α.

L_S :

In 1987, Szczerba [Sz1] introduced the notion of rough quantifiers in rough logic. The syntax, in this case, consists of a language that includes, with other usual symbols of first order predicate logic, two more quantifiers viz. $\mathbb{V}$, the rough universal quantifier and $\mathbb{E}$, the rough existential quantifier. It does not contain function symbols (which, Szczerba states, may be included "at the expense of some complications"), neither does it include the equality predicate in general. No axiomatization of this system, which we denote by L_S, was given in [Sz1]. Strictly speaking, therefore, it cannot be called a system. The semantics requires interpretation in a relational structure $\mathcal{U} \equiv \langle A, \sim; \mathcal{P} \rangle$, called the "rough structure", where $\sim$ is an equivalence relation over A and $\mathcal{P}$ a collection of relations to which the predicates of the system correspond. In L_S there is no name for $\sim$. Satisfiability for rough-quantified formulae has been defined thus:

- $\mathcal{U}, \bar{a} \models \boldsymbol{\forall} x\alpha$ if and only if for every a there is a' such that $a \sim a'$ and $\mathcal{U}, \bar{a}(a'/\bar{a}(x)) \models \alpha$.
- $\mathcal{U}, \bar{a} \models \boldsymbol{\exists} x\alpha$ if and only if there is a such that for each a' if $a \sim a'$ then $\mathcal{U}, \bar{a}(a'/\bar{a}(x)) \models \alpha$.

Rough tautologies are those formulae of L_S which are true in every rough structure. Some instances:

1. $\forall x\alpha(x) \rightarrow \boldsymbol{\forall} x\alpha(x)$,
2. $\boldsymbol{\exists} x\alpha(x) \rightarrow \exists x\alpha(x)$,
3. $\forall x(\alpha(x) \rightarrow \beta(x)) \rightarrow (\boldsymbol{\forall} x\alpha(x) \rightarrow \boldsymbol{\forall} x\beta(x))$,
4. $\boldsymbol{\forall} x(\boldsymbol{\forall} x\alpha(x) \rightarrow \alpha(x))$,
5. $\boldsymbol{\forall} x\forall y\alpha(x,y) \rightarrow \forall y\boldsymbol{\forall} x\alpha(x,y)$,
6. $\boldsymbol{\forall} x\forall y\alpha(x,y) \rightarrow \boldsymbol{\forall} x\alpha(x,x)$,
7. $\forall x(\alpha(x) \rightarrow \beta(x)) \rightarrow \boldsymbol{\exists} x\alpha(x) \rightarrow \boldsymbol{\exists} x\beta(x))$,
8. $\exists x\boldsymbol{\exists} y\alpha(x,y) \rightarrow \boldsymbol{\exists} y\exists x\alpha(x,y)$,
9. $\neg\, \boldsymbol{\forall} x\alpha(x) \rightarrow \boldsymbol{\exists} x\neg\alpha(x)$,
10. $\neg\, \boldsymbol{\exists} x\alpha(x) \rightarrow \boldsymbol{\forall} x\neg\alpha(x)$.

L_S is essentially undecidable and compact [Sz1].

$\boldsymbol{L_{KT}}$:

An axiomatization for the rough quantifiers, however, has been proposed by Krynicki and Tuschik [KT1] in 1991. The language of their system is a countable first order language with constants and with an additional quantifier, the rough existential quantifier $\boldsymbol{\exists}$. Rough universal quantifier $\boldsymbol{\forall}$ is taken as the dual of $\boldsymbol{\exists}$. They also have not included any name for the equivalence relation in their language, but need referring to the identity $(=)$ in the domain A of the approximation space $\langle A, \sim\rangle$. It may be recalled that L_S neither requires nor excludes identity within its syntax. The set of axioms is proved to be complete relative to rough tautologies given by Szczerba [Sz1]. This system shall be called L_{KT}.

Some relevant axioms of L_{KT}:

$L_{KT}1$. $\forall x(\alpha(x) \rightarrow \beta(x)) \rightarrow (\boldsymbol{\exists} x\alpha(x) \rightarrow \boldsymbol{\exists} x\beta(x))$,

$L_{KT}2a$. $\boldsymbol{\exists} x(x = x)$,

$L_{KT}2b$. $\boldsymbol{\forall} x(x = x)$,

$L_{KT}3$. $(\boldsymbol{\exists}! x\alpha \wedge \boldsymbol{\exists}! x\beta \wedge \exists x(\alpha \wedge \beta)) \rightarrow \forall x(\alpha \leftrightarrow \beta)$,

$L_{KT}4$. for every natural number $n \geq 1$,

$$\boldsymbol{\exists}^{=n} x(x = x) \rightarrow \exists y_1 \ldots \exists y_n \ \Big(\bigwedge_{i,j=1(i \neq j)}^{n} y_i \neq y_j \wedge \bigwedge_{i=1}^{n} \boldsymbol{\exists}! x(x \sim_n y_i) \wedge \forall x(\bigvee_{i=1}^{n} x \sim_n y_i)\Big) \ ,$$

$L_{KT}5$. for every natural number $n \geq 1$,

$$\exists^{=n} x\alpha(x) \rightarrow \exists y_1 \ldots \exists y_n \; (\bigwedge_{i,j=1 (i \neq j)}^{n} y_i \neq y_j \wedge \bigwedge_{i=1}^{n} \exists ! x (x \sim_n y_i \mathrm{mod}\alpha) \wedge \bigwedge_{i=1}^{n} \forall x((x \sim_n y_i \mathrm{mod}\alpha) \rightarrow \alpha(x))) \;,$$

$L_{KT}6$. for every natural number $n \geq 1$,

$$[\exists^{\geq n+1} x\alpha(x) \wedge \bigwedge_{j=1}^{m} \forall x \beta_j(x) \wedge \bigwedge_{i=1}^{k} Cx(\chi_i(x, \bar{y}_i) \not\subset \alpha(x))] \rightarrow \exists x_1 \ldots \exists x_m$$

$$\bigwedge_{j=1}^{m} [\alpha(x_j) \wedge \beta_j(x_j) \wedge \bigwedge_{i=1}^{n} x_j \neq z_i \wedge \bigwedge_{i=1}^{k} \forall \bar{y}_i (\exists ! x \chi_i(x, \bar{y}_i) \rightarrow \neg \chi_i(x_j, \bar{y}_i))] \;,$$

where we have the following.

For every formula $\alpha(x, \bar{y})$, $\exists ! x\alpha(x, \bar{y})$ denotes the formula

$$\exists x\alpha(x, \bar{y}) \wedge \forall z(\alpha(z, \bar{y}) \rightarrow \neg \exists x(\alpha(x, \bar{y}) \wedge x \neq z)) \;,$$

where z is a variable not occurring in α.

For every formula $\alpha(x)$ and natural number $n \geq 1$, $\exists^{\leq n} x\alpha(x)$ formally denotes the formula

$$\exists x_1 \ldots \exists x_n \forall x(\alpha(x) \rightarrow \bigvee_{i=1}^{n} x = x_i) \;,$$

$x_1, \ldots, x_n$ being pairwise distinct variables not occurring in α. For convenience, $\exists^{\leq 0} x\alpha$ is included, which abbreviates the formula $\neg \exists x\alpha$. Similarly, $\exists^{\geq n} x\alpha$ and $\exists^{=n} x\alpha$ are abbreviations of the formulae $\neg \exists^{\leq n-1} x\alpha$ and $\exists^{\geq n} x\alpha \wedge \exists^{\leq n} x\alpha$, respectively.

For every formula α and any natural number $n \geq 1$, the formula $y \sim_n z \ \mathrm{mod}\alpha$ is short for

$$\exists y_1 \ldots \exists y_{n-1} \; (\forall x(\alpha(x) \rightarrow \bigvee_{i=1}^{n-1} x = y_i \vee x = y) \wedge \forall x(\alpha(x) \rightarrow \bigvee_{i=1}^{n-1} x = y_i \vee x = z)) \;,$$

where the pairwise different variables $y_1, \ldots, y_{n-1}, y$ and z do not occur in α. In case α is the formula $x = x$, $y \sim_n z$ is written instead of $y \sim_n z \ \mathrm{mod}(x = x)$.

The expression $Cx(\chi(x, \bar{y}) \not\subset \alpha(x))$ denotes the formula

$$\forall \bar{y}(\exists ! x\chi(x, \bar{y}) \rightarrow \exists x(\chi(x, \bar{y}) \wedge \neg \alpha(x))) \;.$$

Rules are Modus ponens and Generalization.

L_K :

Another system was proposed by Krynicki [Kr1] earlier in 1990. Its language is that of an elementary first order theory with equality, including an additional type of strings as formulae, viz. $[\tau]x\alpha$, where τ is any term, x is a variable and α is any formula. The system, called L_K, say, does not have any name for the equivalence relation $\sim$. The axioms taken are the standard first order ones along with the following:

L_K1. $[\tau]x\alpha(x) \to \alpha(\tau)$,
L_K2. $\forall x(\alpha \to \beta) \to ([\tau]x\alpha \to [\tau]x\beta)$,
L_K3. $[\tau]x(x \neq \tau') \to [\tau']x(x \neq \tau)$,
L_K4. $[\tau]x(x \neq \tau'') \to [\tau]x(x \neq \tau') \vee [\tau']x(x \neq \tau'')$,
L_K5. $\forall y(\alpha(y) \to [\tau]x(x \neq y)) \to [\tau]x\neg\alpha$.

The rules of inference of L_K are Modus ponens and Generalization. The set of free variables of $[\tau]x\alpha$ is taken as $Fr([\tau]x\alpha) \equiv (Fr(\alpha) \setminus \{x\}) \cup Fr(\tau)$.

Some theorems of L_K:

1. $\forall x\alpha \to [\tau]x\alpha$,
2. $[\tau]x\alpha \to \exists x\alpha$,
3. $\neg[\tau]x(x \neq \tau)$,
4. $\forall x(\alpha \leftrightarrow \beta) \to ([\tau]x\alpha \to [\tau]x\beta)$,
5. $[\tau]x\alpha \vee [\tau]x\beta \to [\tau]x(\alpha \vee \beta)$,
6. $[\tau]x\alpha \to \forall y(\neg\alpha(y) \to [\tau]x(x \neq y))$,
7. $[\tau]x\alpha \wedge [\tau]x\beta \to [\tau]x(\alpha \wedge \beta)$,
8. $[\tau]x\alpha \wedge \neg[\tau]x(\alpha \wedge x \neq \tau') \to [\tau']x\alpha$,
9. $[\tau]x(\alpha \to \beta) \to ([\tau]x\alpha \to [\tau]x\beta)$,
10. $[\tau]x(x = \tau') \to (([\tau]x\alpha(x)) \leftrightarrow \alpha(\tau'))$.

Semantics for L_K is sought in a rough structure $\mathcal{U} \equiv \langle A, \sim; \mathcal{P}\rangle$. The rules for satisfaction are as usual with the addition that $[\tau]x$ plays the role of a restricted quantifier meaning "for all x such that x is equivalent to the object named τ". Formally, a formula $[\tau]x\alpha(x)$ is satisfied by a valuation $\bar{a}$, i.e.
$\mathcal{U}, \bar{a} \models [\tau]x\alpha(x)$ if and only if for all b such that $b \sim \bar{a}(\tau)$, $\mathcal{U}, \bar{a}(b/\bar{a}(x)) \models \alpha(x)$.

It has been proved that a set T of sentences (closed formulae) of L_K has a model if and only if T is consistent.

Skolem-Löwenheim and compactness theorems for L_K are also established, viz.

if a countable set of sentences of L_K has a model then it has a countable model,

a set of sentences of L_K has a model if and only if each of its finite subsets has a model.

L_{CB} :

A further addition is the system (let it be called L_{CB}) presented in [CB2] in 1993. The language and axioms of L_{CB} are essentially the same as L_{RS}, but the rules differ a little. For making the comparison transparent, we restate the system here.

Axiom schemes:

Axiom schemes of the propositional modal system S_5,

$L_{CB}1$. $\forall x(\alpha \to \beta) \to (\forall x\alpha \to \forall x\beta)$,

$L_{CB}2$. $\forall x\alpha \to \alpha(y/x), y$ is free for x in α,

$L_{CB}3$. $\alpha \to \forall x\alpha, x$ is not free in α,

$L_{CB}4$. $\pi(x,x)$,

$L_{CB}5$. $\pi(x,y) \to \pi(y,x)$,

$L_{CB}6$. $\pi(x,y) \wedge \pi(y,z) \to \pi(x,z)$,

$L_{CB}7$. $\pi(x,y) \wedge L\alpha(x) \to L\alpha(y/x)$,

$L_{CB}8$.

$$\forall y_1 \ldots \forall y_n((\pi(x_1,y_1) \wedge \ldots \wedge \pi(x_n,y_n)) \to \alpha(y_1/x_1,\ldots,y_n/x_n)) \to L(x_1,\ldots,x_n) \ ,$$

$\{x_1,\ldots,x_n\}$ is the set of free variables in α ,

$L_{CB}9$. $\alpha \to L\alpha$, for any closed formula α,

$L_{CB}10$. If α is an axiom and x is free in α then $\forall x\alpha$ is an axiom.

The rules of inference are Modus ponens and Necessitation.

The axioms are designed following Margaris [Ma1]. The distinguishing feature of L_{CB} is that it includes rough quantifiers too as defined symbols and that it does not require identity.

Formally,

$$\mathbb{V}x\alpha \text{ stands for } \forall x\exists y(\pi(x,y) \wedge \alpha(y/x)), \text{ and}$$

$$\mathbb{E}x\alpha \text{ stands for } \exists x\forall y(\pi(x,y) \to \alpha(y/x)) \ ,$$

where y is a variable not occurring in α.

An important aspect of its semantics is that it establishes a direct, natural link between the formulae of the system and rough sets relative to some appropriate approximation space $\langle A^\infty, R_\infty\rangle$ corresponding to each relational structure $\langle A, \sim; \mathcal{P}\rangle$ in which the interpretation is sought. A^∞ is the set of all infinite sequences $\bar{a}$ over A and R_∞ an equivalence relation given by:

$$\bar{a}R_\infty\bar{b} \text{ if and only if } a_i \sim b_i, i = 1,2,\ldots, \bar{a},\bar{b} \in A^\infty \ .$$

A formula α is interpreted as the rough set $\langle A^\infty, R_\infty, v(\alpha)\rangle$ by the map v defined as follows.

$$v(\pi(x,y)) \equiv \{\bar{a} : \bar{a}(x) \sim \bar{a}(y)\} \ ,$$

$v(p_j x_{i_1} \ldots x_{i_k}) \equiv \{\bar{a} : \langle \bar{a}(x_{i_1}),\ldots,\bar{a}(x_{i_k})\rangle \in P_j\}$, where $P_j \in \mathcal{P}$ and is the relation corresponding to the predicate symbol p_j.

$\bar{a}$ is said to satisfy an atomic formula α if and only if $\bar{a} \in v(\alpha)$.

For non-atomic formulae, the notion of satisfaction is extended thus:

- $\bar{a}$ satisfies $\neg\alpha$ if and only if $\bar{a}$ does not satisfy α.
- $\bar{a}$ satisfies $\alpha \to \beta$ if and only if either $\bar{a}$ does not satisfy α or $\bar{a}$ satisfies β.
- $\bar{a}$ satisfies $L\alpha$ if and only if for every $\bar{b}$ with $\bar{a}R_\infty\bar{b}, \bar{b}$ satisfies α.
- $\bar{a}$ satisfies $\forall x\alpha$ if and only if for all $d \in A, \bar{a}(d/\bar{a}(x))$ satisfies α.

As a consequence of the above definitions, the following are also obtained.

- $\bar{a}$ satisfies $M\alpha$ if and only if there exists $\bar{b}$ such that $\bar{a}R_{\infty}\bar{b}$, and $\bar{b}$ satisfies α.
- $\bar{a}$ satisfies $\forall\!\!\!\forall x\alpha$ if and only if for all $d \in A$, there exists $d' \in A$ such that $d \sim d'$ and $\bar{a}(d'/j)$ satisfies $\alpha(y/x)$, where y is the first variable not occurring in α.
- $\bar{a}$ satisfies $\exists\!\!\!\exists x\alpha$ if and only if there exists $d \in A$ such that for all $d' \in A$, if $d \sim d'$ holds then $\bar{a}(d'/j)$ satisfies $\alpha(y/x)$, where y is, as before, the first variable not occurring in α.

The function v is then extended by

$$v(\alpha) \equiv \{\bar{a} : \bar{a} \text{ satisfies } \alpha\} \ .$$

For any formulae α, β,

- $v(\neg\alpha) \equiv A^{\infty} \setminus v(\alpha)$,
- $v(L\alpha) \equiv \underline{v(\alpha)}$ (lower approximation),
- $v(M\alpha) \equiv \overline{v(\alpha)}$ (upper approximation),
- $v(\alpha \wedge \beta) \equiv v(\alpha) \cap v(\beta)$,
- $v(\alpha \vee \beta) \equiv v(\alpha) \cup v(\beta)$.

The semantics also incorporates notions like rough truth and rough validity. More explicitly, α is true, roughly true, false, roughly false in $\langle A^{\infty}, R_{\infty}\rangle$ according as $v(\alpha) = A^{\infty}$, the upper approximation of $v(\alpha)$ in $\langle A^{\infty}, R_{\infty}\rangle$ is A^{∞}, $v(\alpha) = \emptyset$ and the lower approximation of $v(\alpha)$ in $\langle A^{\infty}, R_{\infty}\rangle$ is the null set $\emptyset$. α is valid if and only if α is true in all $\langle A^{\infty}, R_{\infty}\rangle$ and roughly valid if and only if α is roughly true in all $\langle A^{\infty}, R_{\infty}\rangle$.

Some theorems of L_{CB}:

1. $\pi(x,y) \wedge M\alpha(x) \rightarrow M\alpha(y/x)$, y is not free in $\alpha(x)$,
2. $M\alpha(x) \rightarrow \exists y(\pi(x,y) \wedge \alpha(y/x)), x$ is the only free variable in α,
3. $L\alpha(x) \rightarrow \forall y(\pi(x,y) \rightarrow \alpha(y/x)), y$ is not free in $\alpha(x)$,
4. $\pi(x,y) \wedge \alpha(x) \rightarrow M\alpha(y/x), y$ is not free in $\alpha(x)$,
5. $M\alpha \rightarrow \alpha, \alpha$ is any closed formula,
6. $\forall x(L\alpha(x) \rightarrow \beta(x) \wedge L\beta(x) \rightarrow \alpha(x)) \leftrightarrow \forall x(L\alpha(x) \leftrightarrow L\beta(x))$, x is the only free variable in α and β.
7. $\forall x\alpha(x) \rightarrow \forall\!\!\!\forall x\alpha(x)$,
8. $\forall\!\!\!\forall x\alpha(x) \rightarrow \exists x\alpha(x)$,
9. $\forall\!\!\!\forall xL\alpha(x) \rightarrow \forall x\alpha(x)$,
10. $\forall x(\alpha(x) \rightarrow \beta(x)) \rightarrow (\forall\!\!\!\forall x\alpha(x) \rightarrow \forall\!\!\!\forall x\beta(x))$,
11. $\forall\!\!\!\forall x(\alpha(x) \prec \beta(x)) \rightarrow (\forall\!\!\!\forall x\alpha(x) \rightarrow \forall\!\!\!\forall x\beta(x))$,
12. $\forall\!\!\!\forall x(\alpha(x) \wedge \beta(x)) \rightarrow (\forall\!\!\!\forall x\alpha(x) \wedge \forall\!\!\!\forall x\beta(x))$,
13. $\forall\!\!\!\forall x(\alpha(x) \succ\!\!\prec \beta(x)) \rightarrow (\forall\!\!\!\forall x\alpha(x) \leftrightarrow \forall\!\!\!\forall x\beta(x))$,
14. $\exists\!\!\!\exists x\alpha(x) \leftrightarrow \neg\forall\!\!\!\forall x\neg\alpha(x)$,
15. $\forall\!\!\!\forall x\alpha(x) \leftrightarrow \neg\exists\!\!\!\exists x\neg\alpha(x)$,
16. $\exists\!\!\!\exists x\alpha(x) \rightarrow \exists x\alpha(x)$,
17. $\forall x\alpha(x) \rightarrow \exists\!\!\!\exists x\alpha(x)$,

18. $\boldsymbol{\forall} x L\alpha(x) \rightarrow \boldsymbol{\exists} x\alpha(x)$,
19. $\forall x(\alpha(x) \rightarrow \beta(x)) \rightarrow (\boldsymbol{\exists} x\alpha(x) \rightarrow \boldsymbol{\exists} x\beta(x))$,
20. $\boldsymbol{\forall} x(\alpha(x){-\!\!\prec}\beta(x)) \rightarrow (\ \boldsymbol{\exists} x\alpha(x) \rightarrow \boldsymbol{\exists} x\beta(x))$,
21. $\boldsymbol{\forall} x(\alpha(x) \approx \beta(x)) \rightarrow (\alpha(x) \approx \beta(x))$,
22. $\forall x\exists y(\pi(x,y) \wedge \alpha(y/x)) \leftrightarrow \forall y\exists x(\pi(x,y) \wedge \alpha(x))$,

where $\alpha{-\!\!\prec}\beta, \alpha{\succ\!\!-\!\!\prec}\beta$ and $\alpha \approx \beta$ respectively stand for $L(\alpha \rightarrow \beta), (\alpha{-\!\!\prec}\beta) \wedge (\beta{-\!\!\prec}\alpha)$ and $(L\alpha \leftrightarrow L\beta) \wedge (M\alpha \leftrightarrow M\beta)$.

A few non-theorems of L_{CB}:

1. $\boldsymbol{\forall} x\alpha(x) \rightarrow \alpha(x)$,
2. $\boldsymbol{\forall} x(\alpha \rightarrow \beta) \rightarrow (\alpha \rightarrow \beta)$,
3. $\boldsymbol{\forall} x(\alpha(x) \rightarrow \beta(x)) \rightarrow (\ \boldsymbol{\forall} x\alpha(x) \rightarrow \boldsymbol{\forall} x\beta(x))$,
4. $\boldsymbol{\forall} x\alpha(x) \rightarrow \boldsymbol{\exists} x\alpha(x)$.

The system is sound, but its completeness is not yet settled.

2.1 The System of Lin and Liu

Lin and Liu [LL1] have proposed the first order rough logic as equivalent to the modal predicate logic S_5. But they have given a new semantics which "enriches the intuitive meaning of rough sets".

The semantics is proposed in terms of rough frames, defined as follows.

A "relational structure" $\mathcal{U}$ is $\langle U, N, R, F\rangle$, where U is a non-empty set, N a subset of distinguished objects, R a set of relations on U and F a set of partial functions.

A "rough structure" W is $\langle W, \mathcal{U}, \sim\rangle$, where $\mathcal{U}$ is a relational structure and $\sim$ is a partition on U. W is a collection of observable worlds $\{W^h\}$, where each $W^h \equiv \langle W^h, N^h, R^h, F^h\rangle$ such that

- W^h consists of one representative from each equivalence class of U,
- $U = \cup W^h$,
- $N^h =$ (Upper approximation of N) $\cap W^h$,
- $R^h = R$ restricted to W^h,
- $F^h = F$ restricted to W^h.

Any assignment function γ from the language to the set U, assigning objects to constants, relations to predicates and partial functions to function symbols, gives rise to a relational structure. And relative to some partitioning $\sim, \gamma$ induces an assignment function γ^h in each observable world W^h in the following way. $[a]$ denotes the upper approximation of $\{a\}$.

$$\begin{aligned}
\gamma^h(c) &= \gamma(c), \text{ if } \gamma(c) \text{ is in } N^h \ , \\
&= [\gamma(c)] \cap W^h, \text{ if } \gamma(c) \text{ is not in } N^h \ . \\
\gamma^h(p) &= R^h, \text{ where } \gamma(p) = R, \text{ if } R \text{ is different from } = \text{(the identity)} \ , \\
\gamma^h(f) &= F^h, \text{ where } \gamma(f) = F \ .
\end{aligned}$$

Now, if $\bar{a}$ is an assignment to the variables in U, there is an induced valuation $\bar{a}^h$ in each W^h, given by

$$\bar{a}^h(x) = \bar{a}(x), \text{ if } \bar{a}(x) \text{ is in } W^h \ ,$$
$$\bar{a}^h(x) = [\bar{a}(x)] \cap W^h, \text{ if } \bar{a}(x) \text{ is not in } W^h \ .$$

Thus satisfaction in $\langle W^h, \gamma^h, \bar{a}^h \rangle$ can be defined in the usual way with the following modification for the modal formulae:

$$\langle W^h, \gamma^h, \bar{a}^h \rangle \models L\alpha \text{ if and only if for every } k, \langle W^k, \gamma^k, \bar{a}^k \rangle \models \alpha \ ,$$
$$\langle W^h, \gamma^h, \bar{a}^h \rangle \models M\alpha \text{ if and only if for some } k, \langle W^k, \gamma^k, \bar{a}^k \rangle \models \alpha \ .$$

A "rough model" is the triple $\langle W, \gamma, \bar{a} \rangle$, where W is a rough structure, $\gamma, \bar{a}$ are assignments.

A formula α is true in a rough model if it is satisfied in $\langle W^h, \gamma^h, \bar{a}^h \rangle$, for every h.

A formula α is valid if it is true in every rough model.

Lin and Liu have established the soundness theorem relative to this semantics.

2.2 The System of Nakamura

The novelty of Nakamura's system [Na1] lies in introducing so-called graded modalities Δ^i, ∇^j at the object level and graded quantifiers $\exists^i, \forall^j$, for $i, j \in [0,1]$. These grades, however, should not be confused with fuzziness, i, j are simply indices taken from $[0,1]$.

Formally, the language of the syntax consists of object names, object variables, predicate symbols, logical connectives, a set $\{\Delta^i, \nabla^i\}$ for each i in $[0,1]$, a set $\{\exists^i, \forall^i\}$ of quantifiers for each i in $[0,1]$, the modal operators $\{L, M\}$ and the parentheses. $\exists^1$ and $\forall^1$ are the usual quantifiers $\exists$ and $\forall$ respectively.

Terms consist of the object names, variables and $\Delta^i x, \nabla^i x$, where x is a variable.

Formulae are usual, including $\exists^i x\alpha$ and $\forall^i x\alpha$, when α is a formula.

A model $M = \langle U, W, \{\pi^i\}_{i \in [0,1]}, R, \rho, \sigma \rangle$, where

- U is a non-empty set of objects,
- W is a non-empty set of worlds,

for each $i \in [0,1], \pi^i$ is an equivalence relation on U such that

- if $j \leq i$ then $\pi^i \subseteq \pi^j, \pi^1$ is the identity $(=)$,
- R is an equivalence relation on W,
- ρ is a mapping from the set of object names to U,
- σ is an assignment of a relation on U for each $w \in W$.

Let $\bar{a}$ be an assignment to the variables.

Satisfaction for a closed formula α is defined in the usual way relative to $M, \bar{a}$ and $w \in W$ with the following specialities.

- $M, \bar{a}, w \models \alpha(\Delta^i x)$ if and only if for all $a \in U$ such that $\pi^i(a, \bar{a}(x))$, $M, \bar{a}(a/x)$, $w \models \alpha(x)$.
- $M, \bar{a}, w \models \alpha(\nabla^i x)$ if and only if for some $a \in U$ such that $\pi^i(a, \bar{a}(x))$, $M, \bar{a}(a/x)$, $w \models \alpha(x)$.
- $M, \bar{a}, w \models \exists^i x\alpha$ if and only if for some $a \in U$, $\pi^i(a, b)$ implies $M, \bar{a}(b/x), w \models \alpha$.
- $M, \bar{a}, w \models \forall^i x\alpha$ if and only if for every $a \in U$, there is b such that $\pi^i(a, b)$ and $M, \bar{a}(b/x), w \models \alpha$.
- $M, \bar{a}, w \models L\alpha$ if and only if for every w' such that wRw' holds, $M, \bar{a}, w' \models \alpha$.
- $M, \bar{a}, w \models M\alpha$ if and only if for some w' such that wRw' holds, $M, \bar{a}, w' \models \alpha$.

Interestingly, Δ^i plays a role somewhat similar to $[\tau]x$ in L_K and $\forall^i, \exists^i$ are rough quantifiers relative to the i-th partitioning of the space.

A closed formula is true in a model if it is satisfied at every world w in that model.

A closed formula is valid if it is true in every model.

Nakamura has presented a deductive apparatus (tableaux method), which is claimed to be sound and complete with respect to the above semantics.

Krynicki in his paper [Kr1] initiated a kind of comparison among the systems available till then with respect to the power of expressibility. He observed that

(a) $L_S < L_{RS}$, (b) $L_S \leq L_K$ and (c) $L_{RS} \equiv L_K$.

Of course, from (a) and (c) it follows that $L_S < L_K$. The relations $<, \leq$ and $\equiv$ need some clarification. We have seen that the languages of all the systems $L_{RS}, L_S, L_{KT}, L_K, L_{CB}$, are interpreted in an arbitrary approximation space $\langle A, \sim \rangle$, the predicate symbols, constants (if any) and function symbols (if any) having the standard meanings.

Now $L \leq L'$, where L, L' are any two systems, if and only if for every formula α of L there corresponds a formula α^* of L' such that α is true in $\langle A, \sim \rangle$ relative to the semantics of L if and only if α^* is true in $\langle A, \sim \rangle$ relative to the semantics of L'.

$L < L'$ if and only if $L \leq L'$ and $L' \not\leq L$.
$L \equiv L'$ if and only if $L \leq L'$ and $L' \leq L$.

For (a) the following transformation is required.

- $(\exists x\alpha)^*$ is $\exists y \forall x(\pi(x, y) \to \alpha^*)$. ... I

That $L_{RS} \not\leq L_S$ has been proved by addressing to the fact that in L_{RS} one can speak about the equivalence $\sim$ with the help of its linguistic name π, whereas such a reference cannot be made in L_S.

For (b) the required transformation is as follows.

- $(\exists x\alpha)^*$ is $\exists y([y]x\alpha^*)$. ... II

For (c) two transformations III and III' are needed.

- $([\tau]x\alpha)^*$ is $\forall x(\pi(x, t) \to \alpha^*)$. ... III

This gives $L_K \leq L_{RS}$. III' consists of the following.

- $(\pi(\tau, \tau'))^*$ is $\neg[\tau]x(x \neq \tau')$,
- $(L\alpha(\tau_1, \ldots, \tau_n))^*$ is $\forall z_1 \ldots \forall z_n(\bigwedge_{i=1}^{n} \pi(\tau_i, z_i) \to \alpha^*(z_1, \ldots, z_n))$ and
- $(L\alpha)^*$ is α^*, if α is a sentence.

III' establishes that $L_{RS} \leq L_K$.

Two remarks can be made at this point. Firstly, the above comparisons are valid only in a restricted sense. Taking into consideration the facts that while L_K can admit constant symbols L_{RS} cannot (this is an important point and will be discussed later), we see that only those formulae of the form $[\tau]x\alpha$ that have a variable in place of τ and no constants in α have their counterparts in L_{RS}. Applicability of the transformation III' is to be restricted accordingly. Secondly, formulae like $x = y$, more generally, any formula involving the equality predicate has no counterpart in L_{RS} if the latter does not contain equality. That is, $L_K \equiv L_{RS}$ only when L_K does not contain constants and L_{RS} contains equality. Similarly while asserting that $L_S < L_{RS}$, it should be mentioned that L_S does not include constants in its alphabet.

3 A Critique

Limitations of each of the systems $L_{RS}, L_S, L_{KT}, L_K, L_{CB}$ mentioned in the previous section shall be discussed now. In the process, the systems will be subjected to comparisons too.

As stated earlier, one cannot refer to the indiscernibility relation $\sim$ within the language of L_S, i.e. there is no name for $\sim$ in the language. Neither can it express all statements involving the lower (upper) approximations of a rough set in $\langle A, \sim\rangle$. This latter, because the language does not have any operator like L. For example, if formulae α and β represent sets in the approximation space $\langle A, \sim\rangle$, there is, in general, no formula which represents the sentence "α and β are roughly equal". This is not accomplished even if the language has equality, as is taken in L_{KT}. However, in L_{RS}, L_K (using III') and L_{CB}, one can represent this sentence by the formula $(L\alpha \leftrightarrow L\beta) \wedge (M\alpha \leftrightarrow M\beta)$.

Interestingly, notions like "roughly definable", "internally undefinable", "externally undefinable" and "totally undefinable" can be expressed in L_S (without equality) [Kr1].

- α is roughly definable if and only if $\exists x \neg\alpha \wedge \exists x\alpha$ is true.
- α is internally undefinable if and only if $\neg\exists x\alpha \wedge \exists x\neg\alpha$ is true.
- α is externally undefinable if and only if $\exists x\alpha \wedge \neg \exists x\neg\alpha$ is true.
- α is totally undefinable if and only if $\neg\exists x\alpha \wedge \neg \exists x\neg\alpha$ is true.

The dependence on identity (featured in L_K also) is a serious drawback in our view, to any formalization of rough sets and rough concepts as this violates the starting premise of rough set theory that the elements of discourse are indiscernible relative to some class of attributes and thus an identification at the object level creeps in. This results in one's inability to discern an object a from b when $a \sim b$ holds.

The system L_K too suffers from the drawback just mentioned – it banks on taking equality in its language. It is, though, an elegant formalization. The idea of taking $[\tau]x\alpha$ as a formula and its down-to-earth meaning may lead to interesting developments in formal theories in future. There is another point to be made. The transformation III' translates $L\alpha$ in L_K. As L_K allows constants, we may obtain the following:

$$(Lpc)^* \text{ is } \forall z(\neg[c]x(x \neq z) \to pz) \ ,$$

where c is a constant and p a unary predicate. This means that Lpc is true if and only if the object called c occurs in the lower approximation of the interpretation of p. This interpretation (let it be called $\mathcal{I}$) of Lpc is also taken in one of the systems proposed in the concluding section of this paper, but we are not sure if the rough-theorists will agree to it. For example, the system L_{RS} would not allow this interpretation if constants could be taken within it (discussion follows).

The main difficulty with the system L_{RS} is that it cannot include names of individuals within its language because then the following derivation would be possible in it.

$$\alpha(x,y): \ \pi(x,y) \to (Lpx \to Lpy) \text{ (Axiom } L_{RS}1).$$

So

$$\alpha(c,y): \ \pi(c,y) \to (Lpc \to Lpy) \text{ (Rule } \tfrac{\alpha(x,y)}{\alpha(c,y)}).$$

In order to make the above formula true in an interpretation, Lpc should be interpreted as $\mathcal{I}$ and the difficulty with the Necessitation rule arises. The rule derives Lpc from pc but truth of pc does not imply truth of Lpc as interpreted by $\mathcal{I}$. Thus the rule fails to be sound. Any restriction on the applicability of the rule (as adopted in the system $L_{\pi(N)}$ proposed later) does not save the situation, as still then, $pc \to Lpc$ is to be valid because of the axiom $L_{RS}3$, and the interpretation does not yield this. We are not sure if restrictions on both the rule and the axiom would help. It is, however, a reality that in the present form, L_{RS} does not admit constants.

The criticism just made applies to L_{CB} also. The derivation takes the following form in this system.

$$\alpha(x,y): \pi(x,y) \wedge Lpx \to Lpy \text{ (Axiom } L_{CB}7).$$
$$\forall x \forall y(\pi(x,y) \wedge Lpx \to Lpy) \text{ (Generalization Rule)}.$$

So

$$\alpha(c,y): \pi(c,y) \wedge Lpc \to Lpy \text{ (Specialization Rule)}.$$

By the same argument, validity of this formula and soundness of the Necessitation rule are not acceptable together. So constants cannot be admitted in L_{CB} either. As far as the power of expressibility is concerned, $L_{CB} \equiv L_{RS}$ (without equality). The semantics of L_{CB} and L_{RS} are not the same although they are equivalent in the sense that

(a) a sequence $\bar{a}$ satisfies a formula α in L_{CB} if and only if $\bar{a}$ satisfies α in L_{RS} and

(b) the notions of logical consequence $\models$ in both the systems are the same.

The deductive apparatus of L_{CB} is however weaker than that of L_{RS}. It seems therefore that though L_{RS} is complete, i.e. $\Gamma \models \alpha$ implies $\Gamma \vdash \alpha$, where Γ is any set of formulae and α is a formula, such completeness cannot be proved in L_{CB}. Gödel-Henkin method for proving completeness cannot be adopted for L_{CB} due to its non-admittance of constants.

4 New Systems

Three new systems $L_\pi, L_{\pi(N)}$ and $L_{\pi(R)}$ are presented in this section. The former two were first discussed in [Ba1], while a version of the latter was presented in [Ba2]. $L_\pi, L_{\pi(N)}$ are systems that may be considered as developments over the earlier systems, while $L_{\pi(R)}$ is capable of capturing the notions of rough truth and validity.

L_π is an elementary first order theory without equality. The alphabet consists of variables: $x_1, x_2, \ldots$; constants: $c_1, c_2, \ldots$; predicate symbols: $p_1, p_2, \ldots$; one special binary predicate symbol π; the usual logical symbols, quantifiers and brackets. Some defined symbols are: $\mathbb{V}$, $\mathbb{E}$, L, M, given as follows.

$$\mathbb{V} x\alpha \text{ is } \forall x \exists y(\pi(x,y) \wedge \alpha(y/x)) \ ,$$

$$\mathbb{E} x\alpha \text{ is } \exists x \forall y(\pi(x,y) \rightarrow \alpha(y/x)) \ ,$$

where y is the first variable not occurring in α; if $\{c_1, \ldots, c_m\}, \{x_1, \ldots, x_n\}$ are the sets of constants and free variables respectively in α,

$$L\alpha(c_1, \ldots, c_m, x_1, \ldots, x_n) \text{ is}$$

$$\forall y_1 \ldots \forall y_m \forall z_1 \ldots \forall z_n (\pi(c_1, y_1) \wedge \ldots \wedge \pi(c_m, y_m) \wedge \pi(x_1, z_1) \wedge \ldots \wedge \pi(x_n, z_n) \rightarrow$$
$$\alpha(y_1/c_1, \ldots, y_m/c_m, z_1/x_1, \ldots, z_n/x_n)) \ ,$$

where $\alpha(y_1/c_1, \ldots, y_m/c_m, z_1/x_1, \ldots, z_n/x_n))$ is obtained from α by replacing each occurrence of c_i by $y_i, i = 1, \ldots, m$ and each free occurrence of x_j by z_j, $j = 1, \ldots, n$, such that $y_1, \ldots, y_m, z_1, \ldots, z_n$ are the first variables not present in α;

$$M\alpha \text{ is } \neg L \neg \alpha \ .$$

Note. $L\alpha$ and $M\alpha$ are not defined when α is a sentence without constants.

The axiom set comprises $L_{CB}1, L_{CB}3, L_{CB}4-6, L_{CB}10$ and $L_{CB}2$ in the modified form: $\forall x\alpha \rightarrow \alpha(\tau/x)$, where τ is a term free for x in α.

The only rule of inference is Modus ponens.

The interpretation is sought in a relational structure $\mathcal{U} \equiv \langle A, \sim, P_1, P_2, \ldots, c_1, c_2, \ldots \rangle$, where $\sim$ is an equivalence relation so that $\langle A, \sim \rangle$ is an approximation space. π is interpreted as $\sim$, P_i's correspond to the predicate symbols p_i's and

c_j's to the constants c_j's (same symbol being used for objects and their names). The notions of satisfaction and truth are the usual ones.

Lemmas 1 and 2 that follow are obtained by extending results of standard first order theory. Lemma 3, which will be used in the sequel, can be proved easily.

Lemma 1. *Let $\{x_1, \ldots, x_n\}$ be the set of free variables in α. Let $\bar{a}, \bar{b}$ be such that $\bar{a}(x_i) = \bar{b}(x_i), i = 1, \ldots, n$. Then $\mathcal{U}, \bar{a} \models \alpha$ if and only if $\mathcal{U}, \bar{b} \models \alpha$.*

Lemma 2. *$\mathcal{U}, \bar{a} \models \alpha(\tau/x)$ if and only if $\mathcal{U}, \bar{a}(\bar{a}(\tau)/\bar{a}(x)) \models \alpha(x)$.*

Lemma 3. *Let α be a formula without constants and with the set $\{x_1, \ldots, x_n\}$ of free variables. $\mathcal{U}, \bar{a} \models L\alpha(x_1, \ldots, x_n)$ if and only if for all $u_1, \ldots, u_n$ in A, if $\bar{a}(x_j) \sim u_j, j = 1, \ldots, n$ then $\mathcal{U}, \bar{a}(u_1/\bar{a}(x_1), \ldots, u_n/\bar{a}(x_n)) \models \alpha(x_1, \ldots, x_n)$.*

Let $\Gamma \models_s \alpha$ hold if and only if for every structure $\mathcal{U}$, if a valuation $\bar{a}$ satisfies all the elements of Γ then $\bar{a}$ satisfies α. With the help of the preceding lemmas, the soundness theorem can be established, viz.

Theorem 4. (Soundness theorem) *If $\Gamma \vdash \alpha$ then $\Gamma \models_s \alpha$.*

The logical consequence relation $\models$ is defined as in the other systems, viz. for every structure $\mathcal{U}$, if all the elements of Γ are true then α is true. Then $\Gamma \models_s \alpha$ implies $\Gamma \models \alpha$. So if $\Gamma \vdash \alpha$ then $\Gamma \models \alpha$. Also $\models_s \alpha$ if and only if $\models \alpha$.

Theorem 5. (Completeness theorem I) *If $\Gamma \models_s \alpha$ then $\Gamma \vdash \alpha$.*

Proof. The proof follows standard methods (Enderton [En1]) adopting necessary modifications. □

Remark It follows that $\vdash \alpha$ if and only if $\models_s \alpha$, so that $\vdash \alpha$ if and only if $\models \alpha$ also.

The following completeness theorem is also provable.

Theorem 6. (Completeness theorem II) *Every consistent set Γ of sentences has a countable model.*

We give next a few theorems of L_π.

1. $L\alpha \rightarrow \alpha$.
2. $L(\alpha \rightarrow \beta) \rightarrow (L\alpha \rightarrow L\beta)$.
3. $L\alpha \rightarrow LL\alpha$.
4. $M\alpha \rightarrow LM\alpha$.
5. $\pi(\tau_1, \tau_2) \wedge L\alpha(\tau_1) \rightarrow L\alpha(\tau_2/\tau_1)$.
6. $\forall x_1 \ldots \forall x_k(\pi(\tau_1, x_1) \wedge \ldots \wedge \pi(\tau_k, x_k) \rightarrow \alpha(x_1/\tau_1, \ldots, x_k/\tau_k)) \rightarrow L\alpha(\tau_1, \ldots, \tau_k)$.

Thus L_π meets almost all the demands put forward to any theory for rough sets. The operator L (a defined symbol), wherever defined, satisfies the modal principles of S_5, constants can be taken in, identity is replaced by equivalence. As regards expressibility, $L_{RS} \equiv L_\pi$ (without constants). Though $L\alpha$ is undefined when α is a sentence without constants, the equivalence holds good. This is because in L_{RS}-semantics, for such α, $L\alpha$ is true if and only if α is true.

Yet, L_π has a shortcoming. In this system, from $\alpha(x_1, \ldots, x_n)$, $L\alpha(x_1, \ldots, x_n)$ cannot be derived, where α contains no constant symbols and $Fr(\alpha) \equiv \{x_1, \ldots, x_n\}$. But truth (not satisfaction) of $\alpha(x_1, \ldots, x_n)$ in any approximation space should entail truth of $L\alpha(x_1, \ldots, x_n)$. And the semantics for L_π admits that too. It is to be noted that deriving $L\alpha$ from α is not expected generally. For example, if α contains a constant, such a derivation would not be sound, and if α is a sentence without constants, $L\alpha$ is not defined at all. This observation leads to another system $L_{\pi(N)}$.

$L_{\pi(N)}$ is L_π with an additional rule, viz.

$$\frac{\alpha(x_1, \ldots, x_n)}{L\alpha(x_1, \ldots, x_n)},$$

provided α contains no constants.

To ensure soundness (i.e. if $\Gamma \vdash \alpha$ then $\Gamma \models \alpha, \Gamma$ being any set of formulae), the semantic entailment taken is $\models$ defined previously. The following completeness theorem can then be established.

Theorem 7. (Completeness theorem) *Any consistent set Γ of sentences has a model.*

The system $L_{\pi(N)}$ is not any of the standard modal predicate logics, it admits constants, does not refer to ordinary equality and includes modal operators L, M, rough quantifiers and rough equality as definable notions.

However, a more general completeness theorem for any set Γ of formulae, viz. if $\Gamma \models \alpha$ then $\Gamma \vdash \alpha$, is yet to be explored.

In a later work [Ba2], the system L_π has been enhanced by incorporating the notion of rough consequence, which was originally proposed in the context of rough propositional logic [CB1]. By this inclusion, the notions of rough satisfaction, rough truth, rough validity and rough consistency can be meaningfully defined. We present now a developed form of this system, and call it $L_{\pi(R)}$.

$L_{\pi(R)}$ is obtained by introducing additionally in L_π the three following rules of inference, viz.

RMP1

$$\frac{\begin{array}{c}\alpha \\ \vdash \alpha' \rightarrow \beta\end{array}}{\beta},$$

where $\vdash M\alpha \rightarrow M\alpha'$,

RMP2

$$\frac{\begin{array}{c}\vdash \alpha \\ \alpha' \to \beta\end{array}}{\beta},$$

where $\vdash L\alpha \to L\alpha'$,

RMP3

$$\frac{\begin{array}{c}\alpha \\ \vdash \alpha \to \beta\end{array}}{\beta},$$

where $L\beta$ is defined in RMP1 and RMP2, while in RMP3, $L\alpha$ is undefined and there is no restriction on β.

Let Γ be any set of formulae and α any formula in L_π.

We write $\Gamma \mid\!\sim \alpha$ and say that α is a *rough consequence* of Γ if and only if there is a sequence $\alpha_1, \ldots, \alpha_n (\equiv \alpha)$ such that each $\alpha_i (i = 1, \ldots, n)$ is either (i) a theorem of L_π or (ii) a member of Γ or (iii) derived from some of $\alpha_1, \ldots, \alpha_{i-1}$ by RMP1, RMP2 or RMP3.

If Γ is empty, α is said to be a *rough theorem*, written $\mid\!\sim \alpha$.

Note. If α is a sentence without constants, $\mid\!\sim \alpha$ if and only if $\vdash \alpha$. In fact, in such a case, $\Gamma \mid\!\sim \alpha$ implies $\Gamma \vdash \alpha$, for any Γ.

The system is then strictly enhanced, in the sense that the set of rough theorems properly contains that of L_π-theorems (e.g. $\mid\!\sim \alpha \to L\alpha$, but $\nvdash \alpha \to L\alpha$).

The interpretation is again sought in a relational structure of the kind $\mathcal{U} \equiv \langle A, \sim, P_1, P_2, \ldots, c_1, c_2, \ldots \rangle$.

- A sequence $\bar{a}$ in $\mathcal{U}$ *roughly satisfies* a formula α if and only if $\bar{a}$ satisfies $M\alpha$ in $\mathcal{U}$, when $M\alpha$ is defined. Otherwise, $\bar{a}$ roughly satisfies α in $\mathcal{U}$ if and only if $\bar{a}$ satisfies α in $\mathcal{U}$.
- A formula α is *roughly true* in $\mathcal{U}$ if and only if α is roughly satisfied by every sequence in $\mathcal{U}$.
- α is *roughly false* in $\mathcal{U}$ if and only if $L\alpha$ is false in $\mathcal{U}$, when $L\alpha$ is defined. Otherwise, α is roughly false in $\mathcal{U}$ if and only if α is false in $\mathcal{U}$.
- α is *roughly valid* if and only if α is roughly true in every interpretation.

One can define semantic consequence relations $\mid\!\approx$ and $\mid\!\approx_s$ analogous to $\models$ and $\models_s$, introducing "roughness" in the notions of truth and satisfaction.

Note. For any α, $\mid\!\approx \alpha$ if and only if $\mid\!\approx_s \alpha$, and that is if and only if α is roughly valid.

The following propositions can then be established.

Theorem 8. *(i) Truth (falsity, validity) implies rough truth (falsity, validity), (ii) For any Γ, α, if $\Gamma \mid\!\approx_s \alpha$ then $\Gamma \mid\!\approx \alpha$.*

The converses of (i) and (ii) do not hold. To see this for (ii) let $\Gamma \equiv \{px\}$, where p is a unary predicate symbol, and $\alpha \equiv \forall x px$.

Theorem 9. (**Soundness Theorem**) *For any Γ, α, if $\Gamma \mathrel{|\!\!\sim} \alpha$ then $\Gamma \approx\!\!\!\!| \; \alpha$ and also $\Gamma \approx\!\!\!\!|_s \alpha$.*

It may be observed here that the standard rule of Modus ponens is not being taken in $L_{\pi(R)}$, the reason being that it fails to be sound with respect to the above semantics.

Theorem 10. *(i) $\mathrel{|\!\!\sim} \alpha$ if and only if $\vdash M\alpha$, when $M\alpha$ is defined.*
(ii) For any α, $\mathrel{|\!\!\sim} \alpha$ if and only if α is roughly valid.

Theorem 11. (**Deduction Theorem**) *For any Γ, α, β, if $\Gamma \cup \{\alpha\} \mathrel{|\!\!\sim} \beta$ then $\Gamma \mathrel{|\!\!\sim} \alpha \to \beta$.*

The converse of Deduction Theorem does not hold e.g. $\mathrel{|\!\!\sim} px \to Lpx$, but $\{px\} \not\mathrel{|\!\!\sim} Lp\,x$.

Let Γ be any set of formulae of L_π.

- Γ is *roughly consistent* if and only if $M\Gamma \equiv \{M\gamma, \gamma \in \Gamma : M\gamma \text{ is defined}\} \cup \{\gamma \in \Gamma : M\gamma \text{ is not defined}\}$ is consistent;
- Γ is *roughly inconsistent* if and only if $L\Gamma \equiv \{L\gamma, \gamma \in \Gamma : L\gamma \text{ is defined}\} \cup \{\gamma \in \Gamma : L\gamma \text{ is not defined}\}$ is inconsistent.

The following results are obtained in this context.

Theorem 12. *(i) Consistency (inconsistency) implies rough consistency (inconsistency).*
(ii) There is Γ that is both roughly consistent and roughly inconsistent.

The converse of (i) does not hold e.g. for any constant c, $\{pc, \neg pc\}$ is roughly consistent, but not consistent; $\{pc, M(\neg pc)\}$ is inconsistent, but not roughly inconsistent. To see (ii) take $\Gamma \equiv \{pc, \neg pc\}$.

Theorem 13. *If $\Gamma \mathrel{|\!\!\sim} \alpha$ then $\Gamma \cup \{\neg\alpha\}$ is roughly inconsistent.*

Proof. If $L\alpha$ is undefined, $\Gamma \mathrel{|\!\!\sim} \alpha$ implies $\Gamma \vdash \alpha$, whence $\Gamma \cup \{\neg\alpha\}$ is inconsistent, and therefore roughly so.

Let $L\alpha$ be defined. There are $\gamma_1, \dots \gamma_n \in \Gamma$ such that $\{\gamma_1, \dots \gamma_n\} \mathrel{|\!\!\sim} \alpha$. By deduction theorem, $\mathrel{|\!\!\sim} \gamma_1 \to (\gamma_2 \to \dots \to (\gamma_n \to \alpha)\dots)$, i.e. $\vdash M(\neg\gamma_1 \vee \dots \vee \neg\gamma_n \vee \alpha)$. So $\vdash \neg(\beta_1 \wedge \dots \wedge \beta_n \wedge L\neg\alpha)$, where β_i is $L\gamma_i$ or γ_i, according as $L\gamma_i$ is defined or undefined, $i = 1, \dots, n$. Then by definition, $\Gamma \cup \{\neg\alpha\}$ is roughly inconsistent. □

Observe that the converse of Theorem 13 does not hold (e.g. $\{px\} \cup \{\neg Lpx\}$ is roughly inconsistent, but $\{px\} \not\mathrel{|\!\!\sim} Lpx$).

Theorem 14. *If $\Gamma \mathrel{|\!\!\sim} \alpha$ for every formula α then Γ is roughly inconsistent.*

Proof. For every formala α, if $\Gamma \mid\!\sim \alpha$ then $\Gamma \cup \{\neg\alpha\}$ is roughly inconsistent, by Theorem 13. We take α such that $L\alpha$ is defined and $\vdash \neg\alpha$. There is a finite subset Γ' of $\Gamma \cup \{\neg\alpha\}$ which is roughly inconsistent.

If $\Gamma' \subseteq \Gamma$, then Γ is roughly inconsistent.

$\Gamma' \not\equiv \{\neg\alpha\}$, for in that case, $\vdash M\alpha$ and $\neg\alpha$ imply that in any interpretation $\mathcal{U}$, $M\alpha$ and $\neg\alpha$ are true together, which is not possible.

So $\Gamma' \equiv \{\gamma_1, \ldots, \gamma_n, \neg\alpha\}, \gamma_1, \ldots, \gamma_n \in \Gamma$. Then $\vdash \neg(\beta_1 \wedge \ldots \wedge \beta_n \wedge L\neg\alpha)$, where β_i is $L\gamma_i$ or γ_i, according as $L\gamma_i$ is defined or undefined, $i = 1, \ldots, n$.

Also $\vdash \neg\alpha$ implies $L\neg\alpha$. So in any interpretation $\mathcal{U}$, $\neg(\beta_1 \wedge \ldots \wedge \beta_n \wedge L\neg\alpha)$and $L\neg\alpha$ are both true, i.e. any valuation $\bar{a}$ satisfies $L\neg\alpha$, but does not satisfy $(\beta_1 \wedge \ldots \wedge \beta_n \wedge L\neg\alpha)$, i.e. it satisfies $\neg(\beta_1 \wedge \ldots \wedge \beta_n)$, so that $\neg(\beta_1 \wedge \ldots \wedge \beta_n)$ is true in $\mathcal{U}$. Thus $\vdash \neg(\beta_1 \wedge \ldots \wedge \beta_n)$, by completeness of L_π, whence Γ is roughly inconsistent. □

Theorem 15. *If Γ is finite and roughly consistent, there is an interpretation in which each member of Γ is roughly satisfiable.*

Proof. Let $\Gamma \equiv \{\gamma_1, \ldots, \gamma_n\}$. As Γ is roughly consistent, $\not\vdash \neg(\beta_1 \wedge \ldots \wedge \beta_n)$, where β_i is $M\gamma_i$ or γ_i, according as $M\gamma_i$ is defined or undefined, $i = 1, \ldots, n$.

So $\not\models \neg(\beta_1 \wedge \ldots \wedge \beta_n)$, by completeness of L_π. Then there is $\mathcal{U}$ and $\bar{a}$ such that $\bar{a}$ does not satisfy $\neg(\beta_1 \wedge \ldots \wedge \beta_n)$, i.e. $\bar{a}$ satisfies $\beta_1 \wedge \ldots \wedge \beta_n$, i.e. $\bar{a}$ satisfies each $\beta_i, i = 1, \ldots, n$ and hence roughly satisfies each $\gamma_i, i = 1, \ldots, n$. □

Theorem 16. *If $\Gamma \mid\!\sim L\alpha$ and $\Gamma \mid\!\sim L\neg\alpha$ for some α, Γ is roughly inconsistent.*

Proof. There is $\{\gamma_1, \ldots, \gamma_n, \mu_1, \ldots, \mu_m\} \subseteq \Gamma$ such that $\{\gamma_1, \ldots, \gamma_n\} \mid\!\sim L\alpha$ and $\{\mu_1, \ldots, \mu_m\} \mid\!\sim L\neg\alpha$. By deduction theorem,

$\mid\!\sim \gamma_1 \to (\gamma_2 \to \ldots \to (\gamma_n \to L\alpha)\ldots)$ and $\mid\!\sim \mu_1 \to (\mu_2 \to \ldots \to (\mu_m \to L\neg\alpha)\ldots)$.

Then $\vdash M(\gamma_1 \to (\gamma_2 \to \ldots \to (\gamma_n \to L\alpha)\ldots))$ and $\vdash M(\mu_1 \to (\mu_2 \to \ldots \to (\mu_m \to L\neg\alpha)\ldots))$.

So $\vdash M(\gamma_1 \wedge \ldots \wedge \gamma_n \to L\alpha)$ and $\vdash M(\mu_1 \wedge \ldots \wedge \mu_m \to L\neg\alpha)$. Then $\vdash \beta \to ML\alpha$ and $\vdash \delta \to ML\neg\alpha$, where β is $L(\gamma_1 \wedge \ldots \wedge \gamma_n)$ or $\gamma_1 \wedge \ldots \wedge \gamma_n$ according as $L(\gamma_1 \wedge \ldots \wedge \gamma_n)$ is defined or undefined, and δ is $L(\mu_1 \wedge \ldots \wedge \mu_m)$ or $\mu_1 \wedge \ldots \wedge \mu_m$ according as $L(\mu_1 \wedge \ldots \wedge \mu_m)$ is defined or undefined. So $\vdash \beta \wedge \delta \to (L\alpha \wedge L\neg\alpha)$, and then as $\vdash \neg(L\alpha \wedge L\neg\alpha)$, $\vdash \neg(\beta \wedge \delta)$. Thus $\vdash \neg(\beta_1 \wedge \ldots \wedge \beta_n \wedge \delta_1 \wedge \ldots \wedge \delta_m)$, where β_i is $L\gamma_i$ or γ_i, according as $L\gamma_i$ is defined or undefined, $i = 1, \ldots, n$ and δ_i is $L\mu_i$ or μ_i, according as $L\mu_i$ is defined or undefined, $i = 1, \ldots, m$ and so Γ is roughly inconsistent. □

The study of the system $L_{\pi(R)}$ is incomplete. Many relevant questions, e.g. about the converse of deduction theorem, general completeness, Craig interpolation or Beth definability theorems, are to be investigated in the future. Some of these problems were mentioned by M. Krynicki in a personal communication.

It is interesting that several proposals for rough predicate logic have been offered – this reflects on the various ways of understanding of and reasoning with incomplete information. Future years may see more interesting interpretations coming up and their formalizations looked into.

References

[Ba1] Banerjee, M.: A Categorial Approach to the Algebra and Logic of the Indiscernible. Ph.D. Thesis, University of Calcutta, India, (1995)

[Ba2] Banerjee, M.: Rough predicate logics and a new system. In: Soft Computing, Proc. Int. Workshop on Rough Sets and Soft Computing (RSSC'94), San José, U.S.A., (1994), (eds.), Lin, T.Y. and Wildberger, A.M., The Society for Computer Simulation, San Diego, U.S.A., (1995), 48-50

[BC1] Banerjee, M. and Chakraborty, M.K.: Rough algebra. Bull. Polish Acad. Sc. (Math.), **41**, 4, (1993), 293-297

[BC2] Banerjee, M. and Chakraborty, M.K.: Logic of rough sets. In: Incompleteness and Uncertainty in Information Systems, Proc. SOFTEKS Workshop on Incompleteness and Uncertainty in Information Systems, Concordia Univ., Montreal, Canada, (1993), (ed.) Alagar, V.S., et. al., Springer-Verlag, (1994), 223-233

[BC3] Banerjee, M. and Chakraborty, M.K.: Rough consequence and rough algebra. In: Rough Sets, Fuzzy Sets and Knowledge Discovery, Proc. Int. Workshop on Rough Sets and Knowledge Discovery (RSKD'93), Banff, Canada, (1993), (ed.), Ziarko, W.P., Springer-Verlag, 196-207

[BC4] Banerjee, M. and Chakraborty, M.K.: Rough sets through algebraic logic. Fund. Inf., **3**, 4, (1996), 211-221

[CB1] Chakraborty, M.K. and Banerjee, M.: Rough consequence. Bull. Polish Acad. Sc. (Math.), **41**, 4, (1993), 299-304

[CB2] Chakraborty, M.K. and Banerjee, M.: Rough logic with rough quantifiers. Bull. Polish Acad. Sc. (Math.), **41**, 4, (1993), 305-315

[En1] Enderton, H.B.: A Mathematical Introduction to Logic. Academic Press, (1972)

[Kr1] Krynicki, M.: A note on rough concepts logic. Fund. Inf., **XIII**, (1990), 227-235

[KT1] Krynicki, M. and Tuschik, H-P.: An axiomatization of the logic with the rough quantifier. J. Symb. Logic, **56**, 2, (1991), 608-617

[LL1] Lin, T.Y. and Liu, Qing: First-order rough logic I: approximate reasoning via rough sets. Preprint, (1994)

[Ma1] Margaris, A.: First Order Mathematical Logic. Blaisdell Pub. Co., (1967)

[Na1] Nakamura, A.: On a modal predicate logic based on rough concepts. Preprint, (1994)

[NG1] Nakamura, A. and Gao, J.M.: A modal logic for similarity based data analysis. Tech. Report, Hirosima Univ., (1988)

[Or1] Orlowska, E.: Semantics of vague concepts. In: Foundations of Logic and Linguistics. Problems and Solutions. Selected contributions to the 7th International Congress of Logic, Methodology and Philosophy of Science, Salzburg 1983. (eds.) Dorn, G. and Weingartner, P., Plenum Press, 465-482

[Or2] Orlowska, E.: Logic of indiscernibility relations. In: Computation Theory, (ed.), Skowron, A., LNCS, **208**, (1985), 177-186

[Or3] Orlowska, E.: Kripke semantics for knowledge representation logics. Studia Logica, **XLIX**, (1990), 255-272

[Or4] Orlowska, E., Reasoning with incomplete information, rough set based information logics. In: Incompleteness and Uncertainty in Information Systems, Proc. SOFTEKS Workshop on Incompleteness and Uncertainty in Information Systems, Concordia Univ., Montreal, Canada, (1993), (ed.), Alagar, V.S., et. al., Springer-Verlag, (1994), 16-33

[Pa1] Pawlak, Z.: Rough sets. Int. J. Comp. Inf. Sci., **11**, (1982), 341-356

[Pa2] Pawlak, Z.: Rough logic. Bull. Polish Acad. Sc. (Tech. Sc.), **35**, 5-6, (1987), 253-258

[RSi1] Rasiowa, H. and Sikorski, R.: The Mathematics of Metamathematics. Warsaw, (1963)

[RSk1] Rasiowa, H. and Skowron, A.: Rough concepts logic. In: Computation Theory, (ed.), Skowron, A., LNCS, **208**, (1985), 288-297

[Sz1] Szczerba, L.W.: Rough quantifiers, Bull. Polish Acad. Sc. (Math.), **35**, 3-4, (1987), 251-254

[Va1] Vakarelov, D.: A modal logic for similarity relations in Pawlak knowledge representation systems. Fund. Inf., **XV**, (1991), 61-79

[WB1] Wasilewska, A. and Banerjee, M.: Rough sets and topological quasi-Boolean algebras. In: Proc. 23rd Ann. ACM CSC'95 Rough Sets and Database Mining, San José State Univ., U.S.A., (1995), (ed.), Lin, T.Y., 121-128

[WV1] Wasilewska, A. and Vigneron, L.: Rough equality algebras. Proceedings of the Annual Joint Conference on Information Sciences, (1995), Wrightsville Beach, North Carolina, USA, 26-30

Chapter 19

On the Logic with Rough Quantifier

Michał Krynicki[1] *and Lesław W. Szczerba*[2]

[1] Institute of Mathematics, University of Warsaw,
[2] Siedlce University

Abstract: The main aim of this paper is to present a survey of results on the logic with rough quantifier. Besides, a classification of simplicity of formulas of the logic with rough quantifier is defined and a criterion for placing a formula on the exact simplicity level is given.

1 Introduction

The idea of rough quantifiers emerged from the study of rough logic. The cornerstone of rough logic is the notion of "indistinguishability". The relation of indistinguishability is assumed to be an equivalence relation. The rough universal quantifier is ment as formalisation of the notion of "almost everywhere": the elements satisfying the formula under quantifier are to be found in every equivalence class. The rough existential quantifier is just a dual quantifier to the rough universal one: there is an equivalence class whose all the elements satisfy the formula. It may be assumed that the main idea is that we have no access to the individual elements but only to the equivalence classes. With such an interpretation the rough existential quantifier means that we may choose an element satisfying the formula, it is sufficient to take it from a proper equivalence class.

The language of the logic with rough quantifier is a first order language[3] extended by two additional quantifier symbols $\mathbb{\exists}$, $\mathbb{\forall}$ called *existential* and *universal rough quantifier*. The rough quantifiers bind one variable in one formula each. Models have the form $(R, \mathfrak{A})$, (we denote this by $\mathfrak{A}^R$), where $\mathfrak{A}$ is a first order structure of a given signature and R is an equivalence relation on the universe

[3] The terminology "the first order language" is a little misleading. Language is a collection of finite sequences of symbols, or if somebody prefers, productions for such collections. It has nothing to do with first or higher order, except if it concerns some kind of type theory. In fact the problem concerns rather logic which may be elementary or nonelementary, depending whether all realisations (models) are allowed or some are excluded, giving weaker or stronger consequence.

Traditionally elementary logic is referred to as "first order logic". Hovewer the terminology "elementary" describes the situation better, we shall use the term "first order" for the sake of tradition.

of $\mathfrak{A}$. These models are called *rough models*. The definition of the satisfaction relation is the usual Tarski definition extended by the following clause:

$$\mathfrak{A}^R \models \exists x\varphi[\bar{a}] \textit{ iff there is } a \in |\mathfrak{A}| \textit{ s.t. for all } b \in |\mathfrak{A}| \textit{ if } a \underset{R}{\sim} b \textit{ then } \mathfrak{A}^R \models \varphi[\bar{a}(x/b)].$$

$$\mathfrak{A}^R \models \forall x\varphi[\bar{a}] \textit{ iff for all } a \in |\mathfrak{A}| \textit{ there is } b \textit{ such that } a \underset{R}{\sim} b \textit{ and } \mathfrak{A}^R \models \varphi[\bar{a}(x/b)].$$

As follows from the above definitions the meaning of the formula $\forall v\varphi$ is the same as the meaning of the formula $\neg\exists v\neg\varphi$ and the meaning of the formula $\exists v\varphi$ is the same as the meaning of the formula $\neg\forall v\neg\varphi$. This means that existential and universal rough quantifiers are mutually definable. This allows us to omit sometimes the universal rough quantifirer in our considerations. We denote the logic with rough quantifier by $\mathsf{L}(\exists)$.

The logic $\mathsf{L}(\exists)$ inspired consideration of classes of logics with quantifiers determined by some classes of binary relations. Such logics are defined in a similar manner as $\mathsf{L}(\exists)$ but with the following restriction: models have form $\mathfrak{A}^R$, where R is a binary relation from some fixed class. In this paper we omit detailed description of these logics and their properties. The reader interested in this problem is referred to [Kr2].

The logic $\mathsf{L}(\exists)$ is only one of numerous possible logics with rough concepts, *i.e.* so called rough logics (e.g. [RS1], [Kr1]). In our paper we omit a considerations about connections between $\mathsf{L}(\exists)$ and other rough logics since they are presented in the chapter 19 of this volume.

The aim of this paper is to present a survey of results on the $\mathsf{L}(\exists)$. This aim is realized in the second and third sections of this paper where the logical and model theoretical properties of $\mathsf{L}(\exists)$ are described. In the section four we define some classification of simplicity of formulas of $\mathsf{L}(\exists)$ and give a criterion to place the formula on the exact simplicity level. The simplicity classification is similar to that given in [KS1]. The criterion is based on a version of Ehrenfeucht–Fraïssé games introduced in [Ba1] and [Im1], called pebble–games. The pebble games for logics with additional quantifier were studied extensively in [KV1]. In the last (fifth) section we consider some simplicity problems for $\mathsf{L}(\exists)$.

We use standard model–theoretic notation (as for example in [CK1]). By $Dom(f)$ and $Rg(f)$ we denote domain and range of a function f respectively. A set of free variables of a formula φ is denoted by $Fr(\varphi)$.

2 Axiomatizability

A formula φ is called a *rough tautology* if it is satisfied in each rough model under arbitrary valuation. Now we can ask, if the set of rough tautologies is axiomatizable? The answer for this question is positive. Namely, we have:

Theorem 1. *The set of rough tautologies is recursively enumerable.*

Proof. The proof is by interpretating $\mathsf{L}(\exists\!\!\!\exists)$ in first order logic. To prove this interpretability we define a translation F from the set of formulas of $\mathsf{L}(\exists\!\!\!\exists)$ into the set of first order formulas of the language of the same signature extended by one symbol for binary relation P. The definition goes by induction. For atomic formula φ put $\mathsf{F}(\varphi) = \varphi$. The function F commutes with the connectives and the classical quantifiers. The inductive clause for rough quantifier is as follows:

$$\mathsf{F}(\exists\!\!\!\exists x\varphi) = \text{"}\exists y \forall x(P(y,x) \Rightarrow \mathsf{F}(\varphi))\text{"},$$

where y is not free in φ. It easy to verify that for an arbitrary rough structure $\mathfrak{A}^R$, a valuation $\overline{a}$ in $\mathfrak{A}^R$ and a formula φ, we have

$$\mathfrak{A}^R \models \varphi[\overline{a}] \quad if\ and\ only\ if \quad (\mathfrak{A}, R) \models \mathsf{F}(\varphi)[\overline{a}].$$

Therefore φ is a rough tautology if and only if $\mathsf{T}_{eq} \vdash \mathsf{F}(\varphi)$, where T_{eq} is the theory of one equivalence relation (i.e. $\mathsf{T}_{eq} = \{\text{"}P \text{ is an equivalence relation"}\}$). □

An explicit axiomatization of $\mathsf{L}(\exists\!\!\!\exists)$ is presented in [KT1]. It consists of nine axioms. The first five are following:

A0. Each substitution of the first order tautology,
A1. $\exists\!\!\!\exists x\varphi(x) \Rightarrow \exists\!\!\!\exists y\varphi(y)$ if y is not free in $\varphi(x)$ and x does not occur in the scope of the quantifier binding y,
A2. $\forall x(\varphi \Rightarrow \psi) \Rightarrow (\exists\!\!\!\exists x\varphi \Rightarrow \exists\!\!\!\exists x\psi)$,
A3. $\exists\!\!\!\exists x(x = x)$,
A4. $\forall\!\!\!\forall x(x = x)$.

The remaining axioms are rather complicated. To formulate them we need some abbrevations. By $\exists\!\!\!\exists! x\varphi$ we denote the formula $\exists\!\!\!\exists x\varphi \wedge \forall y(\varphi \Rightarrow \neg\exists\!\!\!\exists x(\varphi \wedge x \neq y)$), where y is not free variable in φ. Thus $\exists\!\!\!\exists! x\varphi$ means that φ defines one equivalence class.

The next axiom is the following:

A5. $(\exists\!\!\!\exists! x\varphi \wedge \exists\!\!\!\exists! x\psi \wedge \exists x(\varphi \wedge \psi)) \Rightarrow \forall x(\varphi \Leftrightarrow \psi)$.

This axiom says that if two formulas define equivalence classess having non-empty intersection, then these equivalence classes are the same, which means that these formulas are equivalent.

Let $\exists\!\!\!\exists^{\leq n} x\varphi$ denote the formula $\exists x_1 \ldots \exists x_n \forall\!\!\!\forall x(\varphi \Rightarrow (\bigvee_{i=1}^{n} x = x_i))$. Analogously, $\exists\!\!\!\exists^{\geq n} x\varphi$ and $\exists\!\!\!\exists^{=n} x\varphi$ are abbrevations of the formulas $\neg\exists\!\!\!\exists^{\leq n-1} x\varphi$ and $\exists\!\!\!\exists^{\geq n} x\varphi \wedge \exists\!\!\!\exists^{\leq n} x\varphi$, respectively. The meaning of the formula $\exists\!\!\!\exists^{\leq n} x\varphi$ ($\exists\!\!\!\exists^{\geq n} x\varphi$, $\exists\!\!\!\exists^{=n} x\varphi$) is the following: there exists at most (at least, exactly) n equivalence classes contained in the set of elements satisfying φ.

For a formula φ and natural number n, the formula $y \underset{n}{\approx} z\ mod(\varphi)$ is a shorthand for the following formula:

$$\exists y_1 \ldots \exists y_{n-1}(\forall\!\!\!\forall x(\varphi \Rightarrow (x = y \vee \bigvee_{i=1}^{n-1} x = y_i)) \wedge \forall\!\!\!\forall x(\varphi \Rightarrow (x = z \vee \bigvee_{i=1}^{n-1} x = y_i))$$

where the pairwaise different variables $y_1, \ldots, y_{n-1}, y$ and z do not occur in φ. We write $y \underset{n}{\approx} z$ instead of $y \underset{n}{\approx} z \ mod(x = x)$. If the set of elements satisfying a formula φ in a given model is a union of exactly n equivalence classes then the formula $y \underset{n}{\approx} z \ mod(\varphi)$ says that elements y and z satisfy φ and belong to the same equivalence class.

The next two axioms are the following:

A6. $\exists^{=n} x(x = x) \Rightarrow \exists y_1 \ldots \exists y_n (\bigwedge_{0<i<j\leq n} y_i \neq y_j \wedge$
$\bigwedge_{1\leq i\leq n} \exists! x(x \underset{n}{\approx} y_i) \wedge \forall x \bigvee_{1\leq i\leq n} x \underset{n}{\approx} y_i)$,

A7. $\exists^{=n} x\varphi \Rightarrow \exists y_1 .. \exists y_n (\bigwedge_{0<i<j\leq n} y_i \neq y_j \wedge$
$\bigwedge_{1\leq i\leq n} \exists! x(x \underset{n}{\approx} y_i \ mod(\varphi)) \wedge \bigwedge_{1\leq i\leq n} \forall x((x \underset{n}{\approx} y_i \ mod(\varphi)) \Rightarrow \varphi))$.

The axiom A6 says that if there exist exactly n equivalence classes, then we can find n elements from these classes representing them. The axiom A7 expresses exactly the same, but relatively to a given formula φ.

Finally, the expression $\not\subset x(\chi(x, y), \varphi(x))$ denotes the formula

$$\forall y(\exists! x\chi(x, y) \Rightarrow \exists x(\chi(x, y) \wedge \neg\varphi(x))).$$

This formula says that if χ parametrically defines an equivalence class then this class is not contained in the set of elements satisfying φ. The last axiom is the following:

A8. $[\exists^{\geq n+1} x\varphi(x) \wedge \bigwedge_{j=1}^{m} \forall x\psi_j(x) \wedge \bigwedge_{i=1}^{k} \not\subset x(\chi_i(x, y_i), \varphi)] \Rightarrow$
$\exists x_1 \ldots \exists x_m \bigwedge_{j=1}^{m} [\varphi(x_j) \wedge \psi_j(x_j) \wedge \bigwedge_{i=1}^{n} x_j \neq z_i \wedge$
$\bigwedge_{i=1}^{k} \forall y_i(\exists! x\chi_i(x, y_i) \Rightarrow \neg\chi_i(x_i, y_i))]$.

The content of the axiom A8 is following: assume that a set of elements satisfying φ contains at least $n + 1$ equivalence classes, for each $j = 1, \ldots, m$ a set of elements satisfying ψ_j intersects each equivalence class and for each $i = 1, \ldots, k$ there is no equivalence class parametrically definable by χ_i contained in the set of elements satisfying φ. Under these assumptions for arbitrary n elements there are m elements $a_1, \ldots, a_m$ satisfying φ different than given n elements and such that for each $j = 1, \ldots, m$ a_j satisfies ψ_j and does not belong to any class parametrically definable by χ_i for each $i = 1, \ldots, k$.

In [KT1] the following has been proved:

Theorem 2. *A0-A8 form a complete axiomatization of* $\mathsf{L}(\exists)$.

The main tool in the proof of this theorem is so called *weak model* introduced by Keisler in [Kel] as an appropriate structure for languages with additional quantifier $\mathsf{L}(Q)$. Weak models are structures of the form $(\mathfrak{A}, q)$ where $\mathfrak{A}$ is a usual first order model and q is a family of subsets of the universe of $\mathfrak{A}$. The definition of the satisfaction is enriched by the following clause:

$$(\mathfrak{A}, q) \models Qx\varphi[\bar{a}] \quad \textit{iff} \quad \{b : (\mathfrak{A}, q) \models \varphi[\bar{a}(x/b)]\} \in q.$$

It is known (see [Kel]) that the logic $\mathsf{L}(Q)$ with semantic based on the weak models has many nice properties analogous to classical first order logic. We can observe that each rough structure $\mathfrak{A}^R$ determines a weak model $(\mathfrak{A}, q_R)$, where $q_R = \{X \subseteq |\mathfrak{A}| : X \textit{ contains an equivalence class of } R\}$. For arbitrary formula φ of $\mathsf{L}(\exists)$ and a valuation $\bar{a}$ in $\mathfrak{A}^R$ we have: $\mathfrak{A}^R \models \varphi[\bar{a}]$ iff $(\mathfrak{A}, q_R) \models \varphi[\bar{a}]$. To prove the completeness theorem for the logic with rough quantifer we prove that each consistent set of sentences has a model. Thus at the first stage we take a weak model for this theory. Then we construct a chain of weak models satisfying some special conditions. These conditions allow us to classify all the elements into disjoint classes. Using this classification we define a union of the constructed chain of models in such a way that it has a form $(\mathfrak{A}, q_R)$ where R is an equivalence relation on the universe of $\mathfrak{A}$. Finally we show that $\mathfrak{A}^R$ is a rough model for the consistent theory under consideration.

As we can see the presented axiomatization contains rather complicated axioms. Similarly, several tautologies of $\mathsf{L}(\exists)$ are very complicated. However, in some cases for deciding if a given formula is a tautology, the following criterion observed in [Sz1] could be applied.

Theorem 3. *If a sentence φ of $\mathsf{L}(\exists)$ is a tautology then the first order sentence φ' obtained from φ by replacing each quantifier $\exists$ by $\exists$ and each quantifier $\forall$ by $\forall$ as well as the first order sentence φ'' obtained from φ by replacing each quantifier $\exists$ by $\forall$ and each quantifier $\forall$ by $\exists$ are first order tautologies.*

Proof. If φ' is false in $\mathfrak{A}$ then φ is false in $\mathfrak{A}^R$ where $R = Id_{|\mathfrak{A}|}$. If φ'' is false in $\mathfrak{A}$ then φ is false in $\mathfrak{A}^R$ where $R = |\mathfrak{A}|^2$. □

3 Further Properties

In the proof of the theorem 2.1 we proved the interpretability of $\mathsf{L}(\exists)$ in the first order logic. This interpretability has also some other consequences.

Theorem 4. (Compactness of $\mathsf{L}(\exists)$) *Let T be a set of sentences of $\mathsf{L}(\exists)$. Then T has a model if and only if each finite subset of T has a model.*

Proof. For a given set of sentences S of $\mathsf{L}(\exists)$ let us denote $\mathsf{F}(\mathsf{S}) = \{\mathsf{F}(\sigma) : \sigma \in \mathsf{S}\}$. Thus $\mathfrak{A}^R$ is a model for S if and only $(\mathfrak{A}, R)$ is a model for $\mathsf{T}_{eq} \cup \mathsf{F}(\mathsf{S})$, where T_{eq} is the theory of one equivalence relation. Now using this equivalence and the compactness property of the first order logic we can easily obtain in our theorem. □

We say that a structure $\mathfrak{A}^R$ is an *elementary substructure of* $\mathfrak{B}^S$, and denote this by $\mathfrak{A}^R \prec \mathfrak{B}^S$, if $(\mathfrak{A}, R)$ is a substructure of $(\mathfrak{B}, S)$ in the usual sense and for each formula φ of $\mathsf{L}(\exists)$ and valuation $\overline{a}$ in $\mathfrak{A}$, if $\mathfrak{A}^R \models \varphi[\overline{a}]$ then $\mathfrak{B}^S \models \varphi[\overline{a}]$.

Similarly as the compactness theorem we can prove the following downward and upward Skolem-Löwenheim theorem.

Theorem 5. *For each infinite model $\mathfrak{A}^R$ and a cardinal number $\kappa \geq card(\mathfrak{A})$ there is a model $\mathfrak{B}^S$ of the cardinality κ such that $\mathfrak{A}^R \prec \mathfrak{B}^S$.*

Theorem 6. *For each infinite model $\mathfrak{A}^R$ and a set X contained in the universe of $\mathfrak{A}^R$ and infinite cardinal number κ such that $card(X) \leq \kappa \leq card(\mathfrak{A})$ there is a model $\mathfrak{B}^S$ such that $card(\mathfrak{B}) = \kappa$, X is contained in the universe of $\mathfrak{B}^S$ and $\mathfrak{B}^S \prec \mathfrak{A}^R$.*

Let $\{\mathfrak{A}_i^{R_i}\}_{i \in I}$ be a family of structures and F an ultrafiltr on I. We define the *ultraproduct* of this family $\Pi_{i\in I}\mathfrak{A}_i^{R_i}/F$ as a structure $\mathfrak{B}^S$ such that $(\mathfrak{B}, S) = \Pi_{i \in I}(\mathfrak{A}_i, R_i)/F$. We have

Theorem 7. (Łoś theorem) *For each formula φ of $\mathsf{L}(\exists)$ and valuation $\overline{a}$ in $\Pi_{i\in I}\mathfrak{A}_i^{R_i}/F$ we have:*

$$\Pi_{i\in I}\mathfrak{A}_i^{R_i}/F \models \varphi[\overline{a}] \ \ iff \ \ \{\, i \in I\, ;\ \mathfrak{A}_i^{R_i} \models \varphi[\overline{a}(i)]\} \in F.$$

Using this theorem we can also prove the compactness theorem for $\mathsf{L}(\exists)$ as well as several other theorems for example, the characterization of elementary classes in $\mathsf{L}(\exists)$ or Frayne's and Scott's lemmas (see *e.g.* [BS1]).

A product of two structures $\mathfrak{A}^R$ and $\mathfrak{B}^S$ is a structure $\mathfrak{C}^T$ such that $(\mathfrak{C}, T)$ is a product of structures $(\mathfrak{A}, R)$ and $(\mathfrak{B}, S)$ in the usual sense (i.e. for first order logic). We denote such a product by $\mathfrak{A}^R \times \mathfrak{B}^S$.

We say that two structures $\mathfrak{A}^R$, $\mathfrak{B}^S$ of the same signature are *elementary equivalent*, what is denoted by $\mathfrak{A}^R \equiv \mathfrak{B}^S$, if each sentence true in $\mathfrak{A}^R$ is also true in $\mathfrak{B}^S$.

Theorem 8. *If $\mathfrak{A}^R \equiv \mathfrak{B}^S$ and $\mathfrak{C}^T \equiv \mathfrak{D}^U$ then $\mathfrak{A}^R \times \mathfrak{C}^T \equiv \mathfrak{B}^S \times \mathfrak{D}^U$.*

This result could be proved using the so called Ehrenfeucht-Fraïssé method (see [Eh1] and [Fr1]). The rough quantifier is a monotone quantifier thus we can define the corresponding game-theoretical characterization of elementary equivalence relation (see [KK1] or [MT1]). In case of the logic $\mathsf{L}(\exists)$ the appropriate characterization is the following: For two structures $\mathfrak{A}^R$ and $\mathfrak{B}^S$ and $n \in \omega$ we define the game $G_n(\mathfrak{A}^R, \mathfrak{B}^S)$ for two players. In this game there are moves of two sorts. One move is for the classical existential quantifier and the second is for the rough existential quantifier. The move for existential quantifier is as in the usual Ehrenfeucht game. It goes as follows: The first player chooses a model (say $\mathfrak{A}^R$) and an element a from it. Then the second player chooses an element b from the other model. At the end of the move the pair (a, b) is added to the set of pairs constructed in the game. The move for the rough existential quantifier is more complex. The first player chooses a model (say $\mathfrak{A}^R$) and an equivalence class A (with respect to R) in it. Next, the second player chooses an equivalence class B from the model $\mathfrak{B}^S$, then in turn the first player chooses an element b from B and finally the second player chooses an element a from A. The pair (a, b) is also added to the set of pairs constructed in the game. The second player wins the game if this set of pairs turns out to be a partial isomorphism from $\mathfrak{A}^R$ to $\mathfrak{B}^S$. Otherwise, the first player wins. We write $\mathfrak{A}^R \underset{n}{\sim} \mathfrak{B}^S$ if the second player has a winning strategy in the game $G_n(\mathfrak{A}^R, \mathfrak{B}^S)$. In a standard way (see *e.g.* [KK1]) we prove the following:

Theorem 9. *(i) If for all $n \in \omega$ $\mathfrak{A}^R \underset{n}{\sim} \mathfrak{B}^S$ then $\mathfrak{A}^R \equiv \mathfrak{B}^S$.*
(ii) If $\mathfrak{A}^R$, $\mathfrak{B}^S$ are structures of a finite signature and $\mathfrak{A}^R \equiv \mathfrak{B}^S$ then for all $n \in \omega$ $\mathfrak{A}^R \underset{n}{\sim} \mathfrak{B}^S$.

The above characterization could be formulated using the notion of partial isomorphism only (see [Fr1]). In this convention the fact $\mathfrak{A}^R \underset{n}{\sim} \mathfrak{B}^S$ means that the empty set can be extended n–times to a partial isomorphism. We will use this notation in the fourth part of our paper. The next section will be devoted to a refinement of the mentioned method. Using this characterization we can prove the theorem 8. In fact, to prove it we show that, for an arbitrary n, we have $\mathfrak{A}^R \times \mathfrak{C}^T \underset{n}{\sim} \mathfrak{B}^S \times \mathfrak{D}^U$. To do this we use the winning strategies for the second player in the games $G_n(\mathfrak{A}^R, \mathfrak{B}^S)$ and $G_n(\mathfrak{C}^T, \mathfrak{D}^U)$, existing by our assumption.

Let $\{\mathfrak{A}_n^{R_n}\}_{n\in\omega}$ be a sequence of structures such that $(\mathfrak{A}_n, R_n) \subseteq (\mathfrak{A}_{n+1}, R_{n+1})$ for every $n \in \omega$. We define the *union* $\bigcup_{n\in\omega} \mathfrak{A}_n^{R_n}$ of such a chain as a structure $\mathfrak{B}^S$ such that $(\mathfrak{B}, S)$ is the union of structures $(\mathfrak{A}_n, R_n)$. A sequence of structures $\{\mathfrak{A}_n^{R_n}\}_{n\in\omega}$ is called *elementary* if $\mathfrak{A}_n^{R_n} \prec \mathfrak{A}_{n+1}^{R_{n+1}}$ for every $n \in \omega$.

In the case of first order logic each union of first order sequence of structures is an elementary substructure of any element of this sequence. As it is proved in [Sz2] it does not hold in the case of $\mathsf{L}(\boxminus)$.

Theorem 10. *There is an elementary sequence of structures $\{\mathfrak{A}_n^{R_n}\}_{n\in\omega}$ such that $\mathfrak{A}_k^{R_k} \prec \bigcup_{n\in\omega} \mathfrak{A}_n^{R_n}$ does not hold for any k.*

Proof. We define a sequence of models of the empty signature $\{\mathfrak{A}_n^{R_n}\}_{n\in\omega}$ such that $|\mathfrak{A}_n| = \mathbb{N} \times \mathbb{N}$ for all $n \in \omega$, and $R_n((k,l),(p,q))$ holds if and only if $k = p$ or $k, p \leq n$. Thus an arbitrary formula with parameters φ of $\mathsf{L}(\boxminus)$ defines a finite or a cofinite set in $\mathfrak{A}_n^{R_n}$. Moreover, for all $n \in \omega$ this set is the same. This enables us to show that the rough quantifiers are eliminable and deduce that $\{\mathfrak{A}_n^{R_n}\}_{n\in\omega}$ is an elementary sequence. But $\mathfrak{A}_n^{R_n} \not\prec \bigcup_{n\in\omega} \mathfrak{A}_n^{R_n}$ because the sentence $\exists x \boxplus y\ x = y$ is true in $\bigcup_{n\in\omega} \mathfrak{A}_n^{R_n}$ and false in $\mathfrak{A}_n^{R_n}$. □

Finally we consider the definability problem for $\mathsf{L}(\boxminus)$.

Theorem 11. *Neither the Craig theorem nor the Beth theorem hold for $\mathsf{L}(\boxminus)$.*

Proof. The following sentence σ:*"P is an equivalence relation"* $\wedge \forall x \exists! y P(x,y)$ define implicitely P. In fact, for arbitrary rough structure $(\mathfrak{A}, P)^R$ we have $P = R$ provided that $(\mathfrak{A}, P)^R \models \sigma$. Thus, explicite, definability of P implies explicite definability of R. However, R is not definable in $(\mathfrak{A}, P)^R$ (cf. [Kr1]). Therefore $\mathsf{L}(\boxminus)$ does not have the Beth property. It is easy to see that from this it follows that $\mathsf{L}(\boxminus)$ does not hove the Craig property too. □

However, the logic $\mathsf{L}(\boxminus)$ is, in a sense, similar to the first order logic, althought some theorems concerning first order logic do not hold for it (cf. theorems 10 and 11). There are also some properties of first order logic that we do not know if they hold for $\mathsf{L}(\boldsymbol{\exists})$. Among these the following one seems to be especially interesting.

Open problem.

Preservation problem for $\mathsf{L}(\boldsymbol{\exists})$. Could we determine a class of formulas of $\mathsf{L}(\boldsymbol{\exists})$ preserved by substructures (product, union, homomorphism etc.)?

4 Simplicity of Formulas

Consider a language with a finite number of finitary predicate symbols and without function symbols. By a *type* of a formula we mean a pair (k, σ), where k is a natural number and σ is a finite sequence of $\exists$, $\forall$, $\boldsymbol{\exists}$ and $\boldsymbol{\forall}$. The intuitive meaning of the type (k, σ) is the following: k is the number of different variables occuring in a formula and σ is the sequence of quantifiers which we use constructing the formula. By σ^* we denote the sequence obtained from σ by replacing $\exists$ by $\forall$, and $\boldsymbol{\exists}$ by $\boldsymbol{\forall}$ (and conversly). A type (k, σ) is *simpler* than a type (l, τ) if $k \leq l$ and σ is a subsequence of τ. For instance types $(2, \exists\exists\boldsymbol{\exists}\exists\forall)$ and $(3, \exists\boldsymbol{\forall}\exists\forall)$ are simpler that $(3, \exists\exists\boldsymbol{\forall}\boldsymbol{\exists}\exists\forall)$, but types $(4, \exists)$ and $(1, \forall\exists)$ are not.

Definition 12. The relation "*σ is a type of a formula φ* or *φ has a type σ*" is a least relation such that

(i) if φ has a type (k, σ) and (k, σ) is simpler than (l, τ) then φ has the type (l, τ)

(ii) quantifier–free formula φ has type $(k, \emptyset)$ iff for any variable x_i occuring in φ, $i < k$ holds

(iii) if φ has a type (k, σ) and $i < k$ then
- $\neg\varphi$ has type (k, σ^*)
- $\exists x_i \varphi$ has type $(k, \exists\sigma)$
- $\forall x_i \varphi$ has type $(k, \forall\sigma)$
- $\boldsymbol{\exists} x_i \varphi$ has type $(k, \boldsymbol{\exists}\sigma)$
- $\boldsymbol{\forall} x_i \varphi$ has type $(k, \boldsymbol{\forall}\sigma)$

(iv) if φ and ψ have a type (k, σ) then $\varphi \vee \psi$ and $\varphi \wedge \psi$ have the type (k, σ).

For instance, the formula $(\exists x_0 \boldsymbol{\forall} x_1\, x_0 = x_1) \vee (\boldsymbol{\forall} x_0 \forall x_1\, x_0 \neq x_1)$ has the type $(2, \exists\boldsymbol{\forall}\exists)$ as well as $(2, \boldsymbol{\forall}\exists\boldsymbol{\forall})$ as well as any more complicated one. We denote the set of formulas of $\mathsf{L}(\boldsymbol{\exists})$ of type (k, σ) by $L^{(k,\sigma)}(\boldsymbol{\exists})$.

We say that a formula φ is *simpler* than ψ if each type of ψ is a type of φ. A formula φ is *(k, σ)-expressible* iff there is a formula of type (k, σ) equivalent to φ.

Let two structures $\mathfrak{A}^R$ and $\mathfrak{B}^S$ for $\mathsf{L}(\boldsymbol{\exists})$ be given. Suppose that they are similar *i.e.* have the same signature. Let A be the universe of $\mathfrak{A}$ and B the universe of $\mathfrak{B}$. By induction on the length of σ we define a set of partial functions from $\{1, \ldots, k\}$ into $A \times B$ which will be denoted by $Iso^{(k,\sigma)}(\mathfrak{A}^R, \mathfrak{B}^S)$. We put $f(i/(a, b)) = (f \setminus \{(i, f(i))\}) \cup \{(i, (a, b))\}$ provided that $i \in Dom(f)$, otherwise $f(i/(a, b)) = f \cup \{(i, (a, b))\}$.

$f \in Iso^{(k,\emptyset)}(\mathfrak{A}^R, \mathfrak{B}^S)$ iff $Rg(f)$ is a partial isomorphism from $\mathfrak{A}^R$ to $\mathfrak{B}^S$.

$f \in Iso^{(k,\exists\sigma)}(\mathfrak{A}^R, \mathfrak{B}^S)$ iff for all $i = 1, \ldots, k$ and $a \in A$ there is $b \in B$ such that $f(i/(a,b)) \in Iso^{(k,\sigma)}(\mathfrak{A}^R, \mathfrak{B}^S)$.

$f \in Iso^{(k,\forall\sigma)}(\mathfrak{A}^R, \mathfrak{B}^S)$ iff for all $i = 1, \ldots, k$ and $b \in B$ there is $a \in A$ such that $f(i/(a,b)) \in Iso^{(k,\sigma)}(\mathfrak{A}^R, \mathfrak{B}^S)$.

$f \in Iso^{(k,\exists\!\!\exists\sigma)}(\mathfrak{A}^R, \mathfrak{B}^S)$ iff for all $i = 1, \ldots, k$ and $a' \in A$ there is $b' \in B$ such that for all $b \in B$ if $b \underset{S}{\sim} b'$ then there exists $a \in A$ such that $a \underset{R}{\sim} a'$ and $f(i/(a,b)) \in Iso^{(k,\sigma)}(\mathfrak{A}^R, \mathfrak{B}^S)$.

$f \in Iso^{(k,\forall\!\!\forall\sigma)}(\mathfrak{A}^R, \mathfrak{B}^S)$ iff for all $i = 1, \ldots, k$ and $b' \in B$ there is $a' \in A$ such that for all $a \in A$ if $a \underset{R}{\sim} a'$ then there exists $b \in B$ such that $b \underset{S}{\sim} b'$ and $f(i/(a,b)) \in Iso^{(k,\sigma)}(\mathfrak{A}^R, \mathfrak{B}^S)$.

Definition 13. A formula φ is (k,σ)*-preserved* iff for arbitrary models $\mathfrak{A}^R$, $\mathfrak{B}^S$, $f \in Iso^{(k,\sigma)}(\mathfrak{A}^R, \mathfrak{B}^S)$ and sequence $\overline{a}$ of elements from $Dom(Rg(f))$ the following holds:

$$\mathfrak{A}^R \models \varphi[\overline{a}] \Rightarrow \mathfrak{B}^S \models \varphi[f(\overline{a})] \tag{1}$$

where $f(\overline{a})$ denotes the sequence of elements of $Rg(Rg(f))$ corresponding to $\overline{a}$.

Lemma 14. *If φ is of type (k,σ) then it is (k,σ)-preserved.*

Proof. By induction on the length of σ. For $\sigma = \emptyset$ the lemma follows directly from the respective definitions. The cases $\sigma = \exists\tau$ and $\sigma = \forall\tau$ are considered as in [KS1]. Let us consider the case $\sigma = \exists\!\!\exists\tau$. Let $\mathfrak{A}^R \models \varphi[\overline{a}]$ where φ has the type $(k, \exists\!\!\exists\tau)$ and $f \in Iso^{(k,\exists\!\!\exists\tau)}(\mathfrak{A}^R, \mathfrak{B}^S)$. We can assume that φ has the form $\exists\!\!\exists x_i\psi$ and only the variables $x_1, \ldots, x_k$ may occur in ψ. By definition of satisfaction relation there is $a' \in A$ such that $[a']_R \subseteq \{a : \mathfrak{A}^R \models \psi[\overline{a}(x_i/a)]\}$. Since $f \in Iso^{(k,\exists\!\!\exists\tau)}(\mathfrak{A}^R, \mathfrak{B}^S)$, there is $b' \in B$ such that for all $b \in B$, if $b \underset{S}{\sim} b'$ then there exists $a \in A$ such that $a \underset{R}{\sim} a'$ and $f(i/(a,b)) \in Iso^{(k,\tau)}(\mathfrak{A}^R, \mathfrak{B}^S)$. But for every a such that $a \underset{R}{\sim} a'$ holds, $\mathfrak{A}^R \models \psi[\overline{a}(x_i/a)]$. Thus, by the induction hypotesis, $[b]_S \subseteq \{B : \mathfrak{B}^S \models \psi[f(\overline{a}(x_i/b)]\}$. This means that $\mathfrak{B}^S \models \exists\!\!\exists x_i\psi[f(\overline{a})]$.

The case of $\sigma = \forall\!\!\forall\tau$ is similar. □

Lemma 15. *Let f be a partial function from $\{1, \ldots, k\}$ to $A \times B$. If the implication (1) holds for arbitrary φ of the type (k,σ) then $f \in Iso^{(k,\sigma)}(\mathfrak{A}^R, \mathfrak{B}^S)$.*

Proof. By induction on the length of σ. For $\sigma = \emptyset$ the lemma follows directly from the respective definitions.

Let us consider the case $\sigma = \exists\tau$. Let a natural number $i \leq k$ and $a \in A$ are given. We consider the set

$$F_f = \{\varphi \in L^{(k,\tau)}(\exists\!\!\exists) : \\ \text{for all } j \text{ if } x_j \in Fr(\varphi) \text{ then } j \in Dom(f) \text{ and } \mathfrak{A}^R \models \varphi[\overline{a}(j/a)]\},$$

where $\overline{a}$ is such that if $(j,(a',b)) \in f$ then $\overline{a}(j) = a'$. There is only finitely many nonequivalent formulas in F_f. Let ψ be their conjunction. Thus ψ has type (k,τ) and $\mathfrak{A}^R \models \exists x_i\psi[\overline{a}]$, where $\overline{a}$ is as above. By the assumption, $\mathfrak{B}^S \models$

$\exists x_i \psi[f(\overline{a})]$. Then there is $b \in B$ such that $\mathfrak{B}^S \models \psi[f(\overline{a})(i/b)]$. Hence $f' = f(i/(a,b))$ satisfies the assumptions of the lemma. By the induction hypothesis we have $f' \in Iso^{(k,\tau)}(\mathfrak{A}^R, \mathfrak{B}^S)$. This concludes the proof in case of $\sigma = \exists \tau$. The case $\sigma = \forall \tau$ is analogous.

Now, let us assume that $\sigma = \exists\tau$. Let us consider

$$F_f = \{\varphi \in L^{(k,\tau)}(\mathfrak{A}^R, \mathfrak{B}^S) : \textit{ if } x_j \in Fr(\varphi) \textit{ then } j \in Dom(f)\} \ .$$

There is only a finite number of logically nonequivalent formulas in F_f. Let $\varphi_0, \ldots, \varphi_s$ be all the minimal elements in F_f nonequivalent to an inconsistent formula. This means that each φ_j decides all formulas from F_f (*i.e.* for $\psi \in R_f$ the formula φ_j implies either ψ or $\neg\psi$). Let $i \in \{1, \ldots, k\}$ and $a' \in A$ are given. Let

$$I = \{j : \exists c \in [a']_R \textit{ such that } \mathfrak{A}^R \models \varphi_j[\overline{a}(i/c)]\} \ ,$$

where $\overline{a}$ is as before. Denote the disjunction of all φ_j, where $j \in I$, by χ. Thus

$$[a']_R \subseteq \{d : \mathfrak{A}^R \models \chi[\overline{a}(i/d)]\} \ .$$

Hence $\mathfrak{A}^R \models \exists x_i \chi[\overline{a}]$. But χ has type (k, τ), and hence by the induction hypothesis $\mathfrak{B}^S \models \exists x_j \chi[f(\overline{a})]$. Thus there is $b' \in B$ such that

$$[b']_S \subseteq \{d : \mathfrak{B}^S \models \chi[f(\overline{a})(i/d)]\} \ .$$

If now $b \in [b']_S$ then for some $j \in I$ holds $\mathfrak{B}^S \models \varphi_j[f(\overline{a})(i/b)]$. Let $a \in [a']_R$ be such that $\mathfrak{A}^R \models \varphi_j[\overline{a}(i/a)]$. But φ_j is minimal in F_f then the implication (1) holds for arbitrary $\varphi \in F_f$ and $f(i/(a,b))$. By the induction hypothesis $f(i/(a,b)) \in Iso^{k,\tau}(\mathfrak{A}^R, \mathfrak{B}^S)$. This concludes the case $\sigma = \exists\tau$. The case $\sigma = \forall\tau$ is similar. □

From the above lemmas we prove in the standard way (see *e.g.* [KS1]) the following

Theorem 16. *A formula φ is (k, σ)-expressible iff it is (k, σ)-preserved.*

Corollary 17. *A sentence φ is (k, σ)-expressible iff it is (k, σ)-preserved by empty mappings.*

Corollary 18. *A sentence φ is not (k, σ)-expressible iff there are two structures $\mathfrak{A}^R$ and $\mathfrak{B}^S$ such that φ is true in one of them but not in the other, and empty mapping is a (k, σ)-isomorphism from $\mathfrak{A}^R$ to $\mathfrak{B}^S$.*

5 The Number of Equivalence Classes

Any structure suitable for being a model of a theory based on rough logic consists of classical structure, say $\mathcal{A}$ with the universe A, and an equivalence relation R on the universe A. The equivalence relation partitions the universe into some number of equivalence classes. There is at least one equivalence class, but if $\eta_1 = (\exists x_0 \forall\!\!\forall x_1\ x_0 = x_1)$ is true in $\mathcal{A}^R$ then there is also at most one equivalence class. In general, if $\eta_k = (\exists x_0 \ldots \exists x_{k-1} \forall\!\!\forall x_k\ x_0 = x_k \vee \ldots \vee x_{k-1} = x_k)$ is true in $\mathcal{A}^R$ then the equivalence relation R partitions the universe A onto at most k equivalence classes. The sentence η_k is $(k+1, \exists^k \forall\!\!\forall)$–expressible in the language with equality as the only nonlogical symbol (or, if you prefer to consider equality as logical symbol, simply in logic). Is it expressible in simpler way?

Let $\mathcal{A}$ be any infinite structure of the empty signature with the universe A. Let, furthermore, R be an equivalence relation over the universe A, partitioning this universe into exactly k equivalence classes, each of which is infinite. Similarly, let $\mathcal{B}$ be any infinite structure of the empty signature with the universe B, and let S be an equivalence relation over the universe B, partitioning this universe into exactly $k+1$ equivalence classes, each of which is infinite.

Lemma 19. *If $m \leq k$ and $Iso^{(m,\emptyset)}((\mathcal{A},R)^R,(\mathcal{B},S)^S) \subseteq Iso^{(m,\sigma)}(\mathcal{A}^R,\mathcal{B}^S)$ then*

(i) $Iso^{(m,\emptyset)}((\mathcal{A},R)^R,(\mathcal{B},S)^S) \subseteq Iso^{(m,\exists\sigma)}(\mathcal{A}^R,\mathcal{B}^S)$,
(ii) $Iso^{(m,\emptyset)}((\mathcal{A},R)^R,(\mathcal{B},S)^S) \subseteq Iso^{(m,\forall\sigma)}(\mathcal{A}^R,\mathcal{B}^S)$,
(iii) $Iso^{(m,\emptyset)}((\mathcal{A},R)^R,(\mathcal{B},S)^S) \subseteq Iso^{(m,\exists\!\!\exists\sigma)}(\mathcal{A}^R,\mathcal{B}^S)$
(iv) $Iso^{(m,\emptyset)}((\mathcal{A},R)^R,(\mathcal{B},S)^S) \subseteq Iso^{(m,\forall\!\!\forall\sigma)}(\mathcal{A}^R,\mathcal{B}^S)$.

Proof. (i) and (ii) are obvious.

(iii) Let $f \in Iso^{(m,\emptyset)}((\mathcal{A},R)^R,(\mathcal{B},S)^S)$. Suppose that $i < m$ and $a' \in A$. There is b' satisfying the following condition: for arbitrary $j \in Dom(f) \setminus \{i\}$ if $f(j) = (c,d)$ then $R(a',c)$ holds if and only if $S(b',d)$ holds. Now for arbitrary element b from the equivalence class of b' we can easily find an element a from the equivalence class of a' such that $f(i/(a,b)) \in Iso^{(m,\emptyset)}((\mathcal{A},R)^R,(\mathcal{B},S)^S)$. Thus, by our assumption $f(i/(a,b)) \in Iso^{(m,\sigma)}(\mathcal{A}^R,\mathcal{B}^S)$ and therefore $f \in Iso^{(m,\exists\!\!\exists\sigma)}(\mathcal{A}^R,\mathcal{B}^S)$.

The proof of (iv) is analogous. □

The last lemma gives us the following

Corollary 20. *If $m \leq k$ then $Iso^{(m,\emptyset)}((\mathcal{A},R)^R,(\mathcal{B},S)^S) \subseteq Iso^{(m,\sigma)}(\mathcal{A}^R,\mathcal{B}^S)$.*

It is easy to see that the elements of $Iso^{(m,\emptyset)}((\mathcal{A},R)^R,(\mathcal{B},S)^S)$ correspond to partial isomorphisms between $(\mathcal{A},R)$ and $(\mathcal{B},S)$ having a domain with no more than m elements. Thus, this set is not empty. This means that the second player has a winning strategy in the game $G_m(\mathcal{A}^R,\mathcal{B}^S)$ (see the third section) for $m \leq k$. Therefore we have

Corollary 21. *If $m \leq k$ then η_k is not (m,σ)–expressible.*

Now we shall study expressibility of η_k with more than k variables. Let F_n be the set of all partial functions f from $\{1, \ldots, n\}$ into $A \times B$ such that $Rg(f)$ is a one–one function and there is no more than two elements $a, a' \in Dom(Rg(f))$ such that $R(a, a')$ holds and $S(Rg(f)(a), Rg(f)(a'))$ does not hold.

Analogously to the above, the following lemma can be proved

Lemma 22. *If* $F_n \subseteq Iso^{(n,\sigma)}(\mathcal{A}^R, \mathcal{B}^S)$ *then*

(i) $F_n \subseteq Iso^{(n,\boldsymbol{\forall}\sigma)}(\mathcal{A}^R, \mathcal{B}^S)$,
(ii) $F_n \subseteq Iso^{(n,\exists\sigma)}(\mathcal{A}^R, \mathcal{B}^S)$,
(iii) $F_n \subseteq Iso^{(n,\boldsymbol{\exists}\sigma)}(\mathcal{A}^R, \mathcal{B}^S)$.

Therefore we have

Corollary 23. *If* σ *does not contain* $\boldsymbol{\forall}$ *then* $F_n \subseteq Iso^{(n,\sigma)}(\mathcal{A}^R, \mathcal{B}^S)$.

Now let F_n^m be the set of mappings f such that $f \in F_n$ and the following conditions are satisfied:

1. if $a, a' \in Dom(Rg(f))$ then $R(a, a')$ holds if and only if $S(Rg(f)(a), Rg(f)(a'))$ holds.
2. $Dom(Rg(f))$ intersects at most m equivalence classes.

We can easily observe the following

Lemma 24. *If* $m > 1$ *and* $F_n^m \subseteq Iso^{(n,\sigma)}(\mathcal{A}^R, \mathcal{B}^S)$ *then*

(i) $F_n^{m-1} \subseteq Iso^{(n,\boldsymbol{\forall}\sigma)}(\mathcal{A}^R, \mathcal{B}^S)$,
(ii) $F_n^{m-1} \subseteq Iso^{(n,\exists\sigma)}(\mathcal{A}^R, \mathcal{B}^S)$,
(iii) $F_n^{m-1} \subseteq Iso^{(n,\boldsymbol{\exists}\sigma)}(\mathcal{A}^R, \mathcal{B}^S)$,
(iv) $F_n^{m-1} \subseteq Iso^{(n,\forall\!\!\forall\sigma)}(\mathcal{A}^R, \mathcal{B}^S)$.

Therefore finally we get

Theorem 25. η_k *is* (m, τ)*-expressible if and only if* $k < m$ *and* τ *contains symbol* $\boldsymbol{\forall}$ *preceded by* n *symbols from the set* $\{\exists, \boldsymbol{\exists}, \forall, \boldsymbol{\forall}\}$.

Proof. In fact the "if" part follows immediately from the above considerations. It remains to prove the "only if" part. Notice that each one of $\mathcal{A}^S \models \boldsymbol{\exists} x_0 \boldsymbol{\forall} x_1\; x_0 = x_1$, $\mathcal{A}^S \models \forall x_0 \boldsymbol{\forall} x_1\; x_0 = x_1$, and $\mathcal{A}^S \models \boldsymbol{\forall} x_0 \boldsymbol{\forall} x_1\; x_0 = x_1$ implies that the equivalence relation S has exactly one equivalence class. This observation can be easily generalised for more quantifiers. □

References

[Ba1] Barwise, J.: On Moskovakis closure ordinals. The Journal of Symbolic Logic, **42**, (1977), 292–296

[BS1] Bell, J.L. and Slomson, A.B.: Models and Ultraproducts. An Introduction. North–Holland Publ. Co., (1969)

[CK1] Chang, C.C. and Keisler, H.J.: Model Theory. North-Holland, Publ. Comp., (1973)

[Eh1] Ehrenfeucht, A.: An applications of games to the completeness problem for formalized theories. Fundamenta Mathematicae, **49**, (1961), 129-141

[Fr1] Fraïssé, R.J.: Sur quelques classifications des systémes des relations. Publ. Sci. Univ. Alger, **A 1**, (1954), 35-182

[Im1] Immerman, N.: Upper and lower bounds for first–order logic. Information and Control, **68**, (1982), 76–98

[Ke1] Keisler, H.J.: Logic with the quantifier "there exist uncountably many". Annals of Mathematical Logic, **1**, (1970), 1–93

[KV1] Kolaitis, P.G. and Väänänen, J.: Generalized quantifiers and pebble games on finite structures. Annals of Pure and Applied Logic, **74**, (1995), 23–75

[KK1] Krawczyk, A. and Krynicki, M.: Ehrenfeucht games for generalized quantifiers. In: Set Theory and Hierarchy Theory, Lecture Notes in Mathematics, **537**, Springer, (1976), 145-152

[Kr1] Krynicki, M.: A note on rough concepts logic. Fundamenta Informaticae, **13**, (1990), 227–235

[Kr2] Krynicki, M.: Relational Quantifiers. Dissertationes Mathematicae, **347**, (1995)

[KS1] Krynicki, M., Szczerba, L.W.: On simplicity of formulas. Studia Logica, **49**, (1990), 401–419

[KT1] Krynicki, M. and Tuschik, H-P.: An axiomatization of the logic with the rough quantifier. The Journal of Symbolic Logic, **56**, (1991), 608-617

[MT1] Makowsky, J.A. and Tulipani, S.: Some model theory for monotone quantifiers. Archive fur Math. Logik und Grundlagenforschung, **18**, (1977), 115-134

[RS1] Rasiowa, H. and Skowron, A.: Rough concepts logic. In: Computation Theory, A.Skowron (ed.), Lecture Notes in Computer Science, **208**, Springer, (1985), 288-297

[Sz1] Szczerba, L.W.: Rough Quantifiers. Bulletin of the Polish Academy of Science, Mathematics, **35**, (1987), 251-254

[Sz2] Szczerba, L.W.: Rough Quantifiers have no Tarski property. Bulletin of the Polish Academy of Science, Mathematics, **35**, (1987), 663-665

